2021 EDITION

The ELIAS BOOK of BASEBALL RECORDS

MAJOR LEAGUE BASEBALL RECORDS

WORLD SERIES RECORDS

CHAMPIONSHIP SERIES RECORDS

DIVISION SERIES RECORDS

ALL-STAR GAME RECORDS

HALL OF FAME RECORDS

ELIAS SPORTS BUREAU, INC., Editor and Publisher
500 Fifth Avenue, New York, NY 10110

A STATEMENT FROM THE PUBLISHER

THE ELIAS BOOK OF BASEBALL RECORDS is the most accurate baseball record book ever published. It is produced by the acknowledged authority for sports history, information and statistics.

THE ELIAS BOOK OF BASEBALL RECORDS contains five major sections

- REGULAR-SEASON RECORDS
- WORLD SERIES RECORDS
- CHAMPIONSHIP SERIES RECORDS
- DIVISION SERIES RECORDS
- ALL-STAR GAME RECORDS

Each section lists records in the following order:
- LIFETIME   • SEASON   • GAME   • INNING

If a single-game record was set in a game that extended into extra innings, the record for a nine-inning game is also listed.

The index, and various tables showing annual leaders in major categories, are located at the back of the book.

YEARS: Hyphenated items are inclusive and consecutive.
CLUB, LEAGUE & INDIVIDUAL RECORDS: Generally disregard the following seasons:
   1918 - abbreviated due to World War I
   1972, 1981, 1994, 1995 & 2020 - shortened seasons
   1994 - Division Series and League Championship Series not played
   1904 & 1994 - World Series not played

International Standard Book Number: 9780917050237

COMMISSIONERS

Kenesaw M. Landis	1920-1944
Albert B. Chandler	1945-1951
Ford C. Frick	1951-1965
William D. Eckert	1965-1968
Bowie K. Kuhn	1969-1984
Peter V. Ueberroth	1984-1989
A. Bartlett Giamatti	1989
Francis T. Vincent	1989-1992
Allan H. Selig	1998-2015
Robert D. Manfred Jr.	2015-

AMERICAN LEAGUE PRESIDENTS

B. Bancroft Johnson	1901-1927
Ernest S. Barnard	1927-1931
William Harridge	1931-1959
Joseph E. Cronin	1959-1973
Leland S. MacPhail Jr.	1974-1983
Robert W. Brown	1984-1994
Gene A. Budig	1994-1999

NATIONAL LEAGUE PRESIDENTS

Morgan G. Bulkeley	1876
William A. Hulbert	1877-1882
Arthur H. Soden	1882
Abraham G. Mills	1883-1884
Nicholas E. Young	1885-1902
Harry C. Pulliam	1903-1909
John A. Heydler	1909
Thomas J. Lynch	1910-1913
John K. Tener	1913-1918
John A. Heydler	1918-1934
Ford C. Frick	1934-1951
Warren C. Giles	1951-1969
Charles S. Feeney	1970-1986
A. Bartlett Giamatti	1987-1989
William D. White	1989-1994
Leonard S. Coleman Jr.	1994-1999

ABBREVIATIONS

LEAGUES

ML	Major leagues
AL	American League
NL	National League
AA	American Association
UA	Union Association
PL	Players League
FL	Federal League

CLUBS

Alt	Altoona
Ana	Anaheim
Ari	Arizona
Atl	Atlanta
Balt	Baltimore
Bos	Boston
Brk	Brooklyn
Buff	Buffalo
Cal	California
Chi	Chicago
Cin	Cincinnati
Clev	Cleveland
Col	Colorado
Colu	Columbus
Det	Detroit
Fla	Florida
Hart	Hartford
Hou	Houston
Ind	Indianapolis
KC	Kansas City
LA	Los Angeles
Lou	Louisville
Mia	Miami
Mil	Milwaukee
Minn	Minnesota
Mtl	Montreal
Nwk	Newark
NY	New York
Oak	Oakland

Phil	Philadelphia
Pitt	Pittsburgh
Prov	Providence
Rich	Richmond
Roch	Rochester
StL	St. Louis
StP	St. Paul
SD	San Diego
SF	San Francisco
Sea	Seattle
Syr	Syracuse
TB	Tampa Bay
Tex	Texas
Tol	Toledo
Tor	Toronto
Wash	Washington
Wil	Wilmington
Wor	Worcester

GENERAL

g	games
cons	consecutive
dec	decisions
dh	doubleheader
1g	first game
2g	second game
inn	inning
n	night game

BATTING

ab	at-bats
pa	plate appearances
r	runs
h	hits
tb	total bases
1b	singles
2b	doubles
3b	triples
hr	home runs
rbi	runs batted in

sh	sacrifice hits
sf	sacrifice flies
bb	walks
hp	hit by pitch
so	strikeouts
sb	stolen bases
cs	caught stealing
lob	left on base
ba	batting average
slg	slugging percentage
pct	percentage
avg	average
dh	designated hitter

FIELDING

tc	total chances
ca	chances accepted, errorless
po	putouts
a	assists
e	errors
dp	double plays
tp	triple plays
pb	passed balls

PITCHING

lhp	left-handed pitcher
rhp	right-handed pitcher
gs	games started
cg	complete games
gf	games finished
sv	saves
sho	shutouts
era	earned run average
ip	innings pitched
er	earned runs
bfp	batters faced
hb	hit batters
wp	wild pitches
bk	balks

NATIONAL LEAGUE CLUB HISTORY

NUMBER	CLUB	YEARS
# 1	Chicago	1876-
# 2	Boston	1876-1952 to Milwaukee #32
# 3	New York (Mutual Club)	1876
# 4	Philadelphia (Athletic Club)	1876
# 5	Hartford	1876-1877
# 6	St. Louis	1876-1877
# 7	Cincinnati	1876-1880
# 8	Louisville	1876-1877
# 9	Indianapolis	1878
#10	Milwaukee	1878
#11	Providence	1878-1885
#12	Buffalo	1879-1885
#13	Cleveland	1879-1884
#14	Syracuse	1879
#15	Troy	1879-1882
#16	Worcester	1880-1882
#17	Detroit	1881-1888
#18	New York	1883-1957 to San Francisco #33
#19	Philadelphia	1883-
#20	St. Louis	1885-1886
#21	Washington	1886-1889
#22	Kansas City	1886
#23	Pittsburgh	1887-
#24	Indianapolis	1887-1889
#25	Cleveland	1889-1899
#26	Brooklyn	1890-1957 to Los Angeles #34
#27	Cincinnati	1890-
#28	St. Louis	1892-
#29	Baltimore	1892-1899
#30	Louisville	1892-1899
#31	Washington	1892-1899
#32	Milwaukee	1953-1965 to Atlanta #37
#33	San Francisco	1958-
#34	Los Angeles	1958-
#35	Houston	1962-2012 to American League #24
#36	New York	1962-
#37	Atlanta	1966-
#38	Montreal	1969-2004 to Washington #44
#39	San Diego	1969-
#40	Colorado	1993-
#41	Miami	1993-
#42	Arizona	1998-
#43	Milwaukee	1998-
#44	Washington	2005-

AMERICAN LEAGUE CLUB HISTORY

NUMBER	CLUB	YEARS
# 1	Chicago	1901-
# 2	Milwaukee	1901 to St. Louis #9
# 3	Cleveland	1901-
# 4	Detroit	1901-
# 5	Washington	1901-1960 to Minnesota #13
# 6	Boston	1901-
# 7	Baltimore	1901-1902
# 8	Philadelphia	1901-1954 to Kansas City #12
# 9	St. Louis	1902-1953 to Baltimore #11
#10	New York	1903-
#11	Baltimore	1954-
#12	Kansas City	1955-1967 to Oakland #16
#13	Minnesota	1961-
#14	Washington	1961-1971 to Texas #20
#15	Los Angeles	1961-
#16	Oakland	1968-
#17	Kansas City	1969-
#18	Seattle	1969 to Milwaukee #19
#19	Milwaukee	1970-1997 to National League #43
#20	Texas	1972-
#21	Seattle	1977-
#22	Toronto	1977-
#23	Tampa Bay	1998-
#24	Houston	2013-

INDIVIDUAL BATTING RECORDS

SERVICE (See INDIVIDUAL PITCHING RECORDS for pitchers' service)

Most Seasons, Lifetime
26   Deacon McGuire, AA:Tol. 1884; Clev. 88; Roch. 90; Wash. 91
         NL:Det. 85, 88; Phil. 86-88; Wash. 92-99; Brk. 1899-1901
         AL:Det. 02-03, 12; NY 04-07; Bos. 07-08; Clev. 08, 10

Most Seasons, Consecutive, Lifetime
25   Bobby Wallace, NL:Clev. 1894-98; StL. 1899-1901, 17-18; AL:StL. 1902-16
         Eddie Collins, AL:Phil. 1906-14, 27-30; Chi. 15-26
         Rickey Henderson, AL:Oak. 1979-84, 89-95, 98; NY 85-89; Tor. 93; Ana. 97; Sea. 2000;
                 Bos. 02; NL:SD 96-97, 2001; NY 99-2000; LA 03

Most Seasons, League
25   Eddie Collins, AL:Phil. 1906-14, 27-30; Chi. 15-26
24   Pete Rose, NL:Cin. 1963-78, 84-86; Phil. 79-83; Mtl. 84

Most Seasons, Consecutive, League
25   Eddie Collins, AL:Phil. 1906-14, 27-30; Chi. 15-26
24   Pete Rose, NL:Cin. 1963-78, 84-86; Phil. 79-83; Mtl. 84

Most Leagues, Lifetime
4   By many; last:
         Lave Cross, AA 1887-89, 91; Lou. 1887-88; Phil. 1889, 91; PL:1980; Phil. 1890;
           NL 1892-1900; Phil. 1892-97; StL. 1898-1900; Clev. 1899; Brk. 1900;
           AL 1901-07; Phil. 1901-05; Wash. 1906-07

Most Clubs, Lifetime
12   Deacon McGuire, AA:Tol. 1884; Clev. 88; Roch. 90; Wash. 91; NL:Det. 85, 88; Phil. 86-88;
           Wash. 92-99; Brk. 1899-1901; AL:Det. 02-03, 12; NY 04-07; Bos. 07-08; Clev. 08, 10
         Matt Stairs, NL:Mtl./Wash.1992-93, 2011; Chi. 01; Mil. 02; Pitt. 03; Phil. 08-09; SD 10
           AL:Bos. 95; Oak. 96-2000; KC 04-06; Tex. 06; Det. 06; Tor. 07-08

Most Clubs, League
9   Dan Brouthers, NL:Troy 1879-80; Buff. 81-85; Det. 86-88; Bos. 89; Brk. 92-93;Balt. 94-95;
           Lou. 95; Phil. 96; NY 1904
         Since 1900:
8   Juan Beniquez, AL:Bos. 1971-72, 74-75; Tex. 76-78; NY 79; Sea. 80;
           Cal. 81-85; Balt. 86; KC 87; Tor. 87-88
         Ruben Sierra, AL:Tex. 1986-92, 2000-01, 03; Oak. 92-95; NY 95-96, 2003-05;
           Det. 96; Tor. 97; Chi. 98; Sea. 2002; Minn. 2006
         Chris Jones, NL:Cin. 1991; Hou. 92; Col. 93-94; NY 95-96; SD 97; Ari. 98; SF 98, Mil. 2000
         Todd Zeile, NL:StL.1989-95; Chi. 95; Phil. 96; LA 97-98; Fla. 98; NY 2000-01, 04; Col. 02; Mtl. 03
         Lenny Harris, NL:Cin. 1988-89, 95-98; LA 89-93; NY 98, 2000-01; Col. 99;
           Ari. 99-2000; Mil. 02, Chi. 03; Fla. 03-05
         Gary Bennett, NL:Phil. 1995-2001; NY 01; Col. 01-02; SD 03; Mil. 04; Wash. 05; StL. 06-07; LA 08
         Paul Bako, NL:Hou. 1999-2000; Fla. 00; Atl. 00-01; Mil. 02; Chi. 03-04; LA 05; Cin. 08; Phil. 09
         Henry Blanco, NL:LA 1997; Col. 99; Mil. 2000-01; Atl. 02-03; Chi. 05-08; SD 09; NY 10; Ari.11-12

Most Clubs, Season
4   By many; last:
         Oswaldo Arcia, AL:Minn.; TB; NL: Mia.; SD 2016

Most Clubs, League, Season
4   Tom Dowse, NL:Lou-Cin.-Phil.-Wash. 1892
         Frank Huelsman, AL:Chi.Det.-StL.-Wash. 1904
         Paul Lehner, AL:Phil.-Chi.-StL.-Clev. 1951

Most Clubs, One Day
2   Max Flack, NL:Chi.-StL. May 30, 1922
         Cliff Heathcote, NL:StL.-Chi. May 30, 1922
         Joel Youngblood, NL:NY-Mtl. Aug. 4, 1982

One Club, Most Seasons
23   Brooks Robinson, AL:Balt. 1955-77
         Carl Yastrzemski, AL:Bos. 1961-83
22   Cap Anson, NL:Chi. 1876-97
         Mel Ott, NL:NY 1926-47
         Stan Musial, NL:StL. 1941-63 (1945 Military Service)

One Club, Most Seasons, Consecutive
23   Brooks Robinson, AL:Balt. 1955-77
         Carl Yastrzemski, AL:Bos. 1961-83
22   Cap Anson, NL:Chi. 1876-97
         Mel Ott, NL:NY 1926-47
         Stan Musial, NL:StL. 1941-63 (1945 Military Service)

POSITIONS

Most Positions, Lifetime
9   By many

Most Positions, League
9   By many

Played Nine Positions, Season, Since 1900
9   Sam Mertes, AL:Chi. 1902
Jack Rothrock, AL:Bos. 1928
Bert Campaneris, AL:KC 1965
Cesar Tovar, AL:Minn. 1968
Shane Halter, AL:Det. 2000
Scott Sheldon, AL:Tex. 2000
Jake Elmore, AL:Hou 2013
Andrew Romine, AL:Det. 2017
Jimmy Walsh, NL:Phil. 1911
Gene Paulette, NL:StL. 1918
Jose Oquendo, NL:StL. 1988

Played Nine Positions, Game
9   Bert Campaneris, AL:KC Sept. 8, 1965 (13 inn)
Cesar Tovar, AL:Minn. Sept. 22, 1968
Scott Sheldon, AL:Tex. Sept. 6, 2000
Shane Halter, AL:Det. Oct. 1, 2000
Andrew Romine, AL:Det. Sept. 30, 2017

Most Games, One Day, One Position
3   Clyde Barnhart, NL:Pitt. Oct. 2, 1920 (3b)
Pat Duncan, NL:Cin. Oct. 2, 1920 (lf)

BATTING AVERAGE

Most Seasons Leading Major Leagues
11   Ty Cobb, AL:Det. 1907, 09-15, 17-19

Most Seasons, Consecutive, Leading Major Leagues
7   Ty Cobb, AL:Det. 1909-15

Most Seasons Leading League
12   Ty Cobb, AL:Det. 1907-15, 17-19
8   Honus Wagner, NL:Pitt. 1900, 03-04, 06-09, 11
Tony Gwynn, NL:SD 1984, 87-89, 94-97

Most Seasons, Consecutive, Leading League
9   Ty Cobb, AL:Det. 1907-15
6   Rogers Hornsby, NL:StL. 1920-25

Highest Batting Average, Lifetime, Since 1900 (Minimum: 5000 at-bats)
.367   Ty Cobb, AL:Det. 1905-26; Phil. 27-28
.359   Rogers Hornsby, NL:StL. 1915-26, 33; NY 27; Bos. 28; Chi. 29-32

Highest Batting Average, Season
.442   Tip O'Neill, AA:StL. 1887
.438   Hugh Duffy, NL:Bos. 1894
       Since 1900:
.424   Rogers Hornsby, NL:StL. 1924
.422   Napoleon Lajoie, AL:Phil. 1901

Most Seasons, .400 or higher Batting Average (Minimum: 400 at-bats or 500 plate appearances)
3   Jesse Burkett, NL:Clev. 1895-96; StL. 99
Rogers Hornsby, NL:StL. 1922, 24-25
Ty Cobb, AL:Det. 1911-12, 22

Most Seasons, Consecutive, .400 or higher Batting Average (Minimum: 400 at-bats or 500 plate appearances)
2   Jesse Burkett, NL:Clev. 1895-96
Rogers Hornsby, NL:StL. 1924-25
Ty Cobb, AL:Det. 1911-12

Most Seasons, .300 or higher Batting Average (Minimum: 400 at-bats or 500 plate appearances)
19   Ty Cobb, AL:Det. 1907-13, 15-25; Phil. 27
17   Stan Musial, NL:StL. 1942-44, 46-58, 62

Most Seasons, Consecutive, .300 or higher Batting Average (Minimum: 400 at-bats or 500 plate appearances)
16   Honus Wagner, NL:Lou. 1898-99; Pitt. 1900-13
Tony Gwynn, NL:SD 1984-99
12   Lou Gehrig, NL:NY 1926-37

Lowest Batting Average, Lifetime (Minimum: 5000 at-bats)
.218   George McBride, AL:Mil. 1901, Wash. 08-20, NL:Pitt. 1905; StL. 05-06

Lowest Batting Average, League (Minimum: 5000 at-bats)
.224   Ed Brinkman, AL:Wash. 1961-70; Det. 71-74; Tex.-NY 75
.232   Mickey Doolin, NL:Phil. 1905-13; Chi.-NY 16; Brk. 18

Lowest Batting Average, Season (Minimum: 400 at-bats or 500 plate appearances)
.159   Adam Dunn, AL:Chi. 2011 (415 at-bats)
.166   Jim Canavan, NL:Chi. 1892 (439 at-bats)
            NL Since 1900:
.179   Dan Uggla, NL:Atl. 2013 (448 at-bats)

SLUGGING PERCENTAGE

Most Seasons Leading Major Leagues
12   Babe Ruth, AL:Bos. 1918-19; NY 20-21, 23-24, 26-31

Most Seasons, Consecutive, Leading Major Leagues
6   Babe Ruth, AL:NY 1926-31

Most Seasons Leading League
13   Babe Ruth, AL:Bos. 1918-19; NY 20-24, 26-31
9   Rogers Hornsby, NL:StL. 1917, 20-25; Bos. 28; Chi. 29

Most Seasons, Consecutive, Leading League
7   Babe Ruth, AL:Bos. 1918-19; NY 20-24
6   Dan Brouthers, NL:Buff. 1881-85, Det. 86
         Rogers Hornsby, NL:StL. 1920-25

Highest Slugging Percentage, Lifetime (Minimum: 5000 at-bats)
.690   Babe Ruth, AL:Bos. 1914-19; NY 20-34 NL:Bos. 35

Highest Slugging Percentage, League (Minimum: 5000 at-bats)
.692   Babe Ruth, AL:Bos. 1914-19; NY 20-34
.617   Albert Pujols, NL:StL. 2001-11

Highest Slugging Percentage, Season (Minimum: 400 at-bats or 500 plate appearances)
.863   Barry Bonds, NL:SF 2001
.849   Babe Ruth, AL:NY 1920

Most Seasons, .700 or higher Slugging Percentage (Minimum: 400 at-bats or 500 plate appearances)
9   Babe Ruth, AL:NY 1920-21, 23-24, 26-28, 30-31
4   Barry Bonds, NL:SF 2001-04

Most Seasons, Consecutive, .700 or higher Slugging Percentage (Minimum: 400 at-bats or 500 plate appearances)
4   Barry Bonds, NL:SF 2001-04
3   Babe Ruth, AL:NY 1926-28

Most Seasons, .600 or higher Slugging Percentage (Minimum: 400 at-bats or 500 plate appearances)
13   Babe Ruth, AL:Bos. 1919; NY 20-24, 26-32
9   Barry Bonds, NL:Pitt. 1992; SF 1993, 96, 98, 2000-04

Most Seasons, Consecutive, .600 or higher Slugging Percentage (Minimum: 400 at-bats or 500 plate appearances)
7   Babe Ruth, AL:NY 1926-32
5   Rogers Hornsby, NL:StL. 1921-25
         Barry Bonds, NL:SF 2000-04

Lowest Slugging Percentage, Lifetime (Minimum: 5000 at-bats)
.264   George McBride, AL:Mil. 1901; Wash. 08-20; NL:Pitt.-StL. 05; StL. 06

Lowest Slugging Percentage, League (Minimum: 5000 at-bats)
.280   Mark Belanger, AL:Balt. 1965-81
.307   Mickey Doolin, NL:Phil. 1905-13; Chi.-NY 16; Brk. 18

Lowest Slugging Percentage, Season (Minimum: 400 at-bats or 500 plate appearances)
.197   Jim Lillie, NL:KC 1886
         Since 1900:
.206   Pete Childs, NL:Phil. 1902
.225   Charlie Moran, AL:Wash.-StL. 1904

PLATE APPEARANCES

Most Plate Appearances, Lifetime
15,890   Pete Rose, NL:Cin. 1963-78, 84-86; Phil. 79-83; Mtl. 84
13,992   Carl Yastrzemski, AL:Bos. 1961-83

Most Plate Appearances, Season
778   Jimmy Rollins, NL:Phil. 2007
762   Ichiro Suzuki, AL:Sea. 2004

Most Plate Appearances, Game
8 By many; last:
  Frank Catalanotto, AL:Tex. Aug. 22(1g), 2007
  Ian Kinsler, AL:Tex. Aug. 22(1g), 2007
  Mike Cameron, NL:Cin. May 19, 1999
  Extra-Inning Game:
12 Felix Millan, NL:NY Sept. 11, 1974 (25 inn)
  John Milner, NL:NY Sept. 11, 1974 (25 inn)
  Rudy Law, AL:Chi. May 8, 1984 (25 inn)
  Carlton Fisk, AL:Chi. May 8, 1984 (25 inn)
  Harold Baines, AL:Chi. May 8, 1984 (25 inn)

Most Plate Appearances, Inning
3 Larry Murphy, AA:Wash. June 17, 1891 (1st)
  Marty Callaghan, NL:Chi. Aug. 25, 1922 (4th)
  Billy Cox, NL:Brk. May 21, 1952 (1st)
  Pee Wee Reese, NL:Brk. May 21, 1952 (1st)
  Duke Snider, NL:Brk. May 21, 1952 (1st)
  Gil Hodges, NL:Brk. Aug. 8, 1954 (8th)
  Dusty Baker, NL:Atl. Sept. 20, 1972 (2nd)
  Luis Quinones, NL:Cin. Aug. 3, 1989 (1st)
  Mariano Duncan, NL:Cin. Aug. 3, 1989 (1st)
  Stan Javier, NL:SF July 15, 1997 (7th)
  Ted Williams, AL:Bos. July 4, 1948 (7th)
  Sammy White AL:Bos. June 18, 1953 (7th)
  Gene Stephens, AL:Bos. June 18, 1953 (7th)
  Tom Umphlett, AL:Bos. June 18, 1953 (7th)
  Johnny Lipon, AL:Bos. June 18, 1953 (7th)
  George Kell, AL:Bos. June 18, 1953 (7th)
  Darryl Hamilton, AL:Tex. Apr. 19, 1996 (8th)
  Johnny Damon, AL:Bos. June 27, 2003 (1st)

REACHING BASE SAFELY (via hit, walk or hit by pitch)

Most Times Reaching Base Safely, Lifetime
5929 Pete Rose, NL:Cin. 1963-78, 84-86; Phil. 79-83; Mtl. 84
5538 Ty Cobb, AL:Det. 1905-26; Phil. 27-28

Most Times Reaching Base Safely, Season
  Since 1900:
379 Babe Ruth, AL:NY 1923
376 Barry Bonds, NL:SF 2004

Most Times Reaching Base Safely, Game
8 Piggy Ward, NL:Cin. June 18, 1893
  Since 1900:
7 Joe Judge, AL:Wash. July 27(2g), 1920
  Ben Chapman, AL:NY May 24, 1936
  Cliff Heathcote, NL:Chi. Aug. 25, 1922
  Taylor Douthit, NL:StL. July 6, 1929
  Cookie Lavagetto, NL:Brk. Sept. 23(1g), 1939
  Harry Craft, NL:Cin. June 8, 1940
  Mel Ott, NL:NY Apr. 30, 1944
  Rennie Stennett, NL:Pitt. Sept. 16, 1975
  Sean Casey, NL:Cin. May 19, 1999
  Extra-Inning Game:
9 Max Carey, NL:Pitt. July 7, 1922 (18 inn)
  Stan Hack, NL:Chi. Aug. 9(1g), 1942 (18 inn)
  Johnny Burnett, AL:Clev. July 10, 1932 (18 inn)

Most Times Reaching Base Safely, Inning
3 Ned Williamson, NL:Chi. Sept. 6, 1883 (7th)
  Tommy Burns, NL:Chi. Sept. 6, 1883 (7th)
  Fred Pfeffer, NL:Chi. Sept. 6, 1883 (7th)
  Herman Long, NL:Bos. June 18(1g), 1894 (1st)
  Bobby Lowe, NL:Bos. June 18(1g), 1894 (1st)
  Hugh Duffy, NL:Bos. June 18(1g), 1894 (1st)
  Pee Wee Reese, NL:Brk. May 21, 1952 (1st)
  Sammy White, AL:Bos. June 18, 1953 (7th)
  Gene Stephens, AL:Bos. June 18, 1953 (7th)
  Tom Umphlett, AL:Bos. June 18, 1953 (7th)
  Johnny Damon, AL:Bos. June 27, 2003 (1st)

GAMES

Most Seasons Leading Major Leagues
8   Cal Ripken, AL:Balt. 1983-84, 87, 91-93, 96-97

Most Seasons, Consecutive, Leading Major Leagues
4   Juan Pierre, NL:Fla. 2004-05; Chi. 06; LA 07

Most Seasons Leading League
9   Cal Ripken, AL:Balt. 1983-84, 87, 89, 91-93, 96-97
6   Ernie Banks, NL:Chi. 1954-55, 57-60
           Steve Garvey, NL:LA 1977-78, 80-82; SD 85

Most Seasons, Consecutive, Leading League
5   Juan Pierre, NL:Fla. 2003-05; Chi. 06; LA 07
4   Del Pratt, AL:StL. 1913-16
           Brooks Robinson, AL:Balt. 1961-64

Most Games, Lifetime
3562   Pete Rose, NL:Cin. 1963-78, 84-86 Phil. 79-83; Mtl. 84
3308   Carl Yastrzemski, AL:Bos. 1961-83

Most Games, Consecutive, Lifetime
2632   Cal Ripken, AL:Balt. May 30, 1982-Sept. 19, 1998
1207   Steve Garvey, NL:LA-SD Sept. 3, 1975-July 29(1g), 1983

Most Games, One Club
3308   Carl Yastrzemski, AL:Bos. 1961-83
3076   Hank Aaron, NL:Mil./Atl. 1954-74

Most Games, Season
165   Maury Wills, NL:LA 1962
164   Cesar Tovar, AL:Minn. 1967

Most Seasons, 150 or more Games
17   Pete Rose, NL:Cin. 1963, 65-66, 69-78; Phil. 79-80, 82-83
15   Cal Ripken, AL:Balt. 1982-93, 96-98

Most Seasons, Consecutive, 150 or more Games
13   Bobby Abreu, NL:Phil. 1998-2005; NL:Phil.-AL:NY 06; AL:NY 07-08; LA 09-10
           Willie Mays, NL:NY/SF 1954-66
12   Cal Ripken, AL:Balt. 1982-93

Most Seasons, 100 or more Games, Lifetime
23   Pete Rose, NL:Cin. 1963-78, 84-85; Phil. 79-83; Mtl. 84
22   Carl Yastrzemski, AL:Bos. 1961-80, 82-83

Most Seasons, Consecutive. 100 or more Games
23   Pete Rose, NL:Cin. 1963-78, 84-85; Phil. 79-83; Mtl. 84
20   Carl Yastrzemski AL:Bos. 1961-80

Most Games, One Day, Since 1900
3   Clyde Barnhart, NL:Pitt. Oct. 2, 1920
           Pat Duncan, NL:Cin. Oct. 2, 1920
           Fred Nicholson, NL:Pitt. Oct. 2, 1920
           Morrie Rath, NL:Cin. Oct. 2, 1920
           Jim Tierney, NL:Pitt. Oct. 2, 1920

AT-BATS

Most Seasons Leading Major Leagues
6   Doc Cramer, AL:Phil. 1933-34; Bos. 38, 40; Wash. 41; Det. 42

Most Seasons, Consecutive, Leading Major Leagues
3   Doc Cramer, AL:Bos. 1940-Wash. 41-Det. 42
           Dave Cash, NL:Phil. 1974-76

Most Seasons Leading League
8   Ichiro Suzuki, AL:Sea. 2001, 04-08, 10-11
4   Abner Dalrymple, NL:Chi. 1880, 82, 84-85
           Pete Rose, NL:Cin. 1965, 72-73, 77
           Jimmy Rollins, NL:Phil. 2001-02, 07, 09

Most Seasons, Consecutive, Leading League
5   Ichiro Suzuki, AL:Sea. 2004-08
3   Sparky Adams, NL:Chi. 1925-27
           Dave Cash, NL:Phil. 1974-76
           Starlin Castro, NL:Chi. 2011-13

Most At-Bats, Lifetime
14,053   Pete Rose, NL:Cin. 1963-78, 84-86; Phil. 79-83; Mtl. 84
11,988   Carl Yastrzemski, AL:Bos. 1961-83

Most At-Bats, Season
716	Jimmy Rollins, NL:Phil. 2007
705	Willie Wilson, AL:KC 1980

Most Seasons, 600 or more At-Bats
17	Pete Rose, NL:Cin. 1963, 65-66, 68-78; Phil. 79-80, 82
13	Cal Ripken, AL:Balt. 1983-87, 89-93, 96-98

Most Seasons, Consecutive, 600 or more At-Bats
13	Pete Rose, NL:Cin. 1968-78; Phil. 79-80
12	Nellie Fox, AL:Chi. 1951-62
	Ichiro Suzuki, AL:Sea. 2001-11; Sea.-NY 12

Most At-Bats, Game
8	By many prior to 1900
7	By many since 1900

Extra-Inning Game:
11	Carson Bigbee, NL:Pitt. Aug. 22, 1917 (22 inn)
	Charlie Pick, NL:Bos. May 1, 1920 (26 inn)
	Tony Boeckel, NL:Bos. May 1, 1920 (26 inn)
	Ralph Garr, NL:Atl. May 4, 1973 (20 inn)
	Dave Schneck, NL:NY Sept. 11, 1974 (25 inn)
	Dave Cash, NL:Mtl. May 21, 1977 (21 inn)
	Johnny Burnett, AL:Clev. July 10, 1932 (18 inn)
	Ed Morgan, AL:Clev. July 10, 1932 (18 inn)
	Irv Hall, AL:Phil. July 21, 1945 (24 inn)
	Bobby Richardson, AL:NY June 24, 1962 (22 inn)
	Cecil Cooper, AL:Mil. May 8, 1984 (25 inn)
	Rudy Law, AL:Chi. May 8, 1984 (25 inn)
	Carlton Fisk, AL:Chi. May 8, 1984 (25 inn)
	Julio Cruz, AL:Chi. May 8, 1984 (25 inn)

Most At-Bats, Doubleheader
13	Rabbit Maranville, NL:Pitt. Aug. 8, 1922
	Billy Herman, NL:Chi. Aug. 21, 1935
	Lyn Lary, AL:Clev. July 5, 1937
	Red Rolfe, AL:NY June 28, 1939
	Dave Philley, AL:Chi. May 30, 1950

Extra Innings:
14	Joe Christopher, NL:NY May 31, 1964 (32 inn)
	Jim Hickman, NL:NY May 31, 1964 (32 inn)
	Ed Kranepool, NL:NY May 31, 1964 (32 inn)
	Roy McMillan, NL:NY May 31, 1964 (32 inn)
	Frank Thomas, NL:NY May 31, 1964 (32 inn)
	Jesus Alou, NL:SF May 31, 1964 (32 inn)
	John Jeter, NL:SD Sept. 24, 1971 (30 inn)
	Dave Cash, NL:Pitt. June 7, 1972 (27 inn)
	Al Oliver, NL:Pitt. June 7, 1972 (27 inn)
	Rick Monday, AL:KC June 17, 1967 (28 inn)
	Ramon Webster, AL:KC June 17, 1967 (28 inn)
	Dick Billings, AL:Wash. Sept. 14, 1971 (29 inn)
	Ted Uhlander AL:Clev. Sept. 14, 1971 (29 inn)

Most At-Bats, Inning
3	By many; last:
	Johnny Damon, AL:Bos. June 27, 2003 (1st)
	Luis Quinones, NL:Cin. Aug. 3, 1989 (1st)

RUNS

Most Seasons Leading Major Leagues
8	Babe Ruth, AL:Bos. 1919; NY 20-21, 23-24, 26-28

Most Seasons, Consecutive, Leading Major Leagues
3	Eddie Collins, AL:Phil. 1912-14
	Babe Ruth, AL:Bos. 1919; NY 20-21, 26-28
	Ted Williams, AL:Bos. 1940-42
	Mickey Mantle, AL:NY 1956-58
	Pete Rose, NL:Cin. 1974-76
	Albert Pujols, NL:StL. 2003-05

Most Seasons Leading League
8	Babe Ruth, AL:Bos. 1919; NY 20-21, 23-24, 26-28
5	George Burns, NL:NY 1914, 16-17, 19-20
	Rogers Hornsby, NL:StL. 1921-22, 24; NY 27; Chi. 29
	Stan Musial, NL:StL. 1946, 48, 51-52, 54
	Albert Pujols, NL:StL. 2003-05, 09-10

Most Seasons, Consecutive, Leading League
3	King Kelly, NL:Chi. 1884-86
	Chuck Klein, NL:Phil. 1930-32
	Duke Snider, NL:Brk. 1953-55
	Pete Rose, NL:Cin. 1974-76
	Albert Pujols, NL:StL. 2003-05
	Ty Cobb, AL:Det. 1909-11
	Eddie Collins, AL:Phil. 1912-14
	Babe Ruth, AL:Bos. 1919-NY 20-21; 26-28
	Ted Williams, AL:Bos. 1940-42
	Mickey Mantle, AL:NY 1956-58
	Mike Trout, AL:LA 2012-14

Most Runs Scored, Lifetime
2295	Rickey Henderson, AL:Oak. 1979-84, 89-95, 98; NY 85-89; Tor. 93; Ana. 97; Sea. 2000; Bos. 02; NL:SD 96-97, 2001; NY 99-2000; LA 03

Most Runs Scored, League
2245	Ty Cobb, AL:Det. 1905-26; Phil. 27-28
2227	Barry Bonds, NL:Pitt. 1986-92; SF 1993-2007

Most Runs Scored, Season
196	Billy Hamilton, NL:Phil. 1894
	Since 1900:
177	Babe Ruth, AL:NY 1921
158	Chuck Klein, NL:Phil. 1930

Most Seasons, 100 or more Runs Scored
15	Hank Aaron, NL:Mil./Atl. 1955-70
13	Lou Gehrig, AL:NY 1926-38
	Alex Rodriguez, AL:Sea. 1996-2000; Tex. 01-03; NY 04-08
	Derek Jeter, AL:NY 1996-2002, 04-07, 09-10

Most Seasons, Consecutive, 100 or more Runs Scored
13	Lou Gehrig, AL:NY 1926-38
	Alex Rodriguez, AL:Sea. 1996-2000; Tex. 01-03; NY 04-08
	Hank Aaron, NL:Mil./Atl. 1955-67

Most Runs Scored, Game
7	Guy Hecker, AA:Lou. Aug. 15(2g), 1886
6	Jim Whitney, NL:Bos. June 9, 1883
	Cap Anson, NL:Chi. Aug. 24, 1886
	Mike Tiernan, NL:NY June 15, 1887
	King Kelly, NL:Bos. Aug. 27, 1887
	Ezra Sutton, NL:Bos. Aug. 27, 1887
	Jimmy Ryan, NL:Chi. July 25, 1894
	Bobby Lowe, NL:Bos. May 3, 1895
	Ginger Beaumont, NL:Pitt. July 22, 1899
	Mel Ott, NL:NY Aug. 4(2g), 1934
	Mel Ott, NL:NY Apr. 30(1g), 1944
	Frank Torre, NL:Mil. Sept. 2(1g), 1957
	Edgardo Alfonzo, NL:NY Aug. 30, 1999
	Shawn Green, NL:LA May 23, 2002
	Johnny Pesky, AL:Bos. May 8, 1946
	Spike Owen, AL:Bos. Aug. 21, 1986
	Joe Randa, AL:KC Sept. 9(1g), 2004

Most Games, Consecutive, Runs Scored
24	Billy Hamilton, NL:Phil. July 6-Aug. 2, 1894 (35 runs)
	Since 1900:
18	Red Rolfe, AL:NY Aug. 9-25, 1939 (30 runs)
	Kenny Lofton, AL:Clev. Aug. 15-Sept. 3, 2000 (26 runs)
17	Rogers Hornsby, NL:StL. July 3-20, 1921 (21 runs)
	Ted Kluszewski, NL:Cin. Aug. 27-Sept. 13, 1954 (24 runs)
	Rickie Weeks, NL:Mil. Sept. 18, 2007-Apr. 4, 2008 (24 runs)

Most Runs Scored, Inning
3	Tommy Burns, NL:Chi. Sept. 6, 1883 (7th)
	Ned Williamson, NL:Chi. Sept. 6, 1883 (7th)
	Since 1900:
3	Sammy White, AL:Bos. June 18, 1953 (7th)
2	By many in NL

HITS

Most Seasons Leading Major Leagues
7	Ty Cobb, AL:Det. 1907, 09, 11-12, 15, 17, 19
	Pete Rose, NL:Cin. 1965, 68, 70, 72-73, 76; Phil. 81
	Ichiro Suzuki, AL:Sea. 2001, 04, 06-10

Most Seasons, Consecutive, Leading Major Leagues
5   Ichiro Suzuki, AL:Sea. 2006-10

Most Seasons Leading League
8   Ty Cobb, AL:Det. 1907-09, 11-12, 15, 17, 19
7   Pete Rose, NL:Cin. 1965, 68, 70, 72-73, 76; Phil. 81
     Tony Gwynn, NL:SD 1984, 86-87, 89, 94-95, 97

Most Seasons, Consecutive, Leading League
5   Ichiro Suzuki, AL:Sea. 2006-10
3   Ginger Beaumont, NL:Pitt. 1902-04
     Rogers Hornsby, NL:StL. 1920-22
     Frank McCormick, NL:Cin. 1938-40

Most Hits, Lifetime
4256   Pete Rose, NL:Cin. 1963-78, 84-86; Phil. 79-83; Mtl. 84
4191   Ty Cobb, AL:Det. 1905-26; Phil. 27-28

Most Hits, Season
262   Ichiro Suzuki, AL:Sea. 2004
254   Lefty O'Doul, NL:Phil. 1929
     Bill Terry, NL:NY 1930

Most Seasons, 200 or more Hits
10   Pete Rose, NL:Cin. 1965-66, 68-70, 73, 75-77; Phil. 79
     Ichiro Suzuki, AL:Sea. 2001-10

Most Seasons, Consecutive, 200 or more Hits
10   Ichiro Suzuki, AL:Sea. 2001-10
8   Willie Keeler, NL:Balt. 1894-98, Brk. 99-1901
     NL Since 1900:
5   Chuck Klein, NL:Phil. 1929-33

Most Hits, Consecutive, Season
12   Johnny Kling, NL:Chi. Aug. 24(2g)-28, 1902
     Pinky Higgins, AL:Bos. June 19-21, 1938 (2-bb)
     Walt Dropo, AL:Det. July 14-15, 1952

Most Hits, Game
7   Wilbert Robinson, NL:Balt. June 10(1g), 1892
     Rennie Stennett, NL:Pitt. Sept. 16, 1975
     Brandon Crawford, NL:SF Aug. 8, 2016 (14 inn)
6   By many in AL; last:
     George Springer, AL:Hou. May 7, 2018
     Extra-Inning Game:
9   Johnny Burnett, AL:Clev. July 10, 1932 (18 inn)

Most Hits, Consecutive, Game
7   Wilbert Robinson, NL:Balt. June 10(1g), 1892
     Rennie Stennett, NL:Pitt. Sept. 16, 1975
6   By many in AL
     Extra-Inning Game:
7   Cesar Gutierrez, AL:Det. June 21, 1970 (2g, 12 inn)

Most Hits, First Major League Game
5   Fred Clarke, NL:Lou. June 30, 1894 (1-3b)
     Since 1900:
4   Wid Conroy, AL:Mil. Apr. 25, 1901
     Tom Jones, AL:Balt. Aug. 25, 1902
     Ray Jansen, AL:StL. Sept. 30, 1910
     Art Shires, AL:Chi. Aug. 20, 1928 (1-3b)
     Russ Van Atta, AL:NY Apr. 25, 1933
     Spook Jacobs, AL:Phil. Apr. 13, 1954
     Ted Cox, AL:Bos. Sept. 18, 1977 (1-2b)
     Kirby Puckett, AL:Minn. May 8, 1984
     Billy Bean, AL:Det. Apr. 25, 1987 (2-2b)
     Wilson Ramos, AL:Minn. May 2, 2010 (1-2b)
     J.P. Arencibia, AL:Tor. Aug. 7, 2010 (1-2b, 2-hr)
     Mike Mitchell, NL:Cin. Apr. 11, 1907 (1-3b)
     Casey Stengel, NL:Brk. Sept. 17, 1912
     Ed Freed, NL:Phil. Sept. 11, 1942 (2-2b, 1-3b; 11 inn)
     Joe Burns, NL:Bos. Apr. 24, 1943
     Willie McCovey, NL:SF July 30, 1959 (2-3b)
     Mack Jones, NL:Mil. July 13, 1961 (1-2b)
     Delino DeShields, NL:Mtl. Apr. 9, 1990 (1-2b; 11 inn)
     Derrick Gibson, NL:Col. Sept. 8, 1998 (1-2b)
     Extra-Inning Game:
5   Cecil Travis, AL:Wash. May 16, 1933 (12 inn)

Most Games, 6 or more Hits, Lifetime
2   Cal McVey, NL:Chi. July 22-25, 1876 (cons)
     Ed Delahanty, PL:Clev. June 2, 1890; NL:Phil. June 16, 1894
     Jim Bottomley, NL:StL. Sept. 16, 1924, Aug. 5, 1931
     Jimmie Foxx, AL:Phil. May 30, 1930 (13 inn), July 10, 1932 (18 inn)
     Doc Cramer, AL:Phil. June 20, 1932, July 13(1g), 1935
     Kirby Puckett, AL:Minn. Aug. 30, 1987; May 23, 1991 (11 inn)

Most Games, 5 or more Hits, Lifetime
14	Ty Cobb, AL:Det. 1905-26; Phil. 27-28
10	Willie Keeler, NL:NY 1892-93, 1910; Brk. 93, 99-1902; Balt. 94-98
	Pete Rose, NL:Cin. 1963-78, 84-86; Phil. 79-83; Mtl. 84

Most Games, 5 or more Hits, Season
4	Willie Keeler, NL:Balt. July 17, Aug. 14, Sept. 3, 6, 1897
	Stan Musial, NL:StL. Apr. 30, May 19, June 22, Sept. 22, 1948
	Tony Gwynn, NL:SD Apr. 18, 30, July 27, Aug. 4, 1993
	Ty Cobb, AL:Det. May 7, July 7, 12, 17, 1922
	Ichiro Suzuki, AL:Sea. July 29, Aug. 3(1g), Sept. 4, 21, 2004

Most Games, 1 or more Hits, Season
135	Rogers Hornsby, NL:StL. 1922 (154 g)
	Chuck Klein, NL:Phil. 1930 (156 g)
	Wade Boggs, AL:Bos. 1985 (161 g)
	Derek Jeter, AL:NY 1999 (158 g)
	Ichiro Suzuki, AL:Sea. 2001 (157 g)

Most Games, Consecutive, 1 or more Hits, Lifetime
56	Joe DiMaggio, AL:NY May 15-July 16, 1941
45	Willie Keeler, NL:Balt. Sept. 26, 1896-June 18, 1897
	NL Since 1900:
44	Pete Rose, NL:Cin. June 14-July 31, 1978

Most Games, Consecutive, 1 or more Hits, Season
56	Joe DiMaggio, AL:NY May 15-July 16, 1941
44	Willie Keeler, NL:Balt. Apr. 22-June 18, 1897
	Pete Rose, NL:Cin. June 14-July 31, 1978

Most Games, Consecutive, 1 or more Hits, Start of Season
44	Willie Keeler, NL:Balt. Apr. 22-June 18, 1897
	Since 1900:
34	George Sisler, AL:StL. Apr. 14-May 19, 1925
25	Charlie Grimm, NL:Pitt. Apr. 17-May 16, 1923

Most Hits, 2 Consecutive Games
12	Cal McVey, NL:Chi. July 22-25, 1876
	Since 1900:
10	Hy Myers, NL:Brk. Aug. 21-22, 1917
	Lloyd Waner, NL:Pitt. June 15-16(1g), 1929
	Roberto Clemente, NL:Pitt. Aug. 22-23, 1970
	Rennie Stennett, NL:Pitt. Sept. 16-17, 1975
	Mike Benjamin, NL:SF June 13-14, 1995
	Johnny Burnett, AL:Clev. July 9(2g)-10; 10-11(1g), 1932
	Kirby Puckett, AL:Minn. Aug. 29-30, 1987

Most Hits, Doubleheader
9	Fred Carroll, AA:Pitt. July 5, 1886
	Wilbert Robinson, NL:Balt. June 10, 1892
	Joe Kelley, NL:Balt. Sept. 3, 1894 (cons)
	Fred Lindstrom, NL:NY June 25, 1928
	Bill Terry, NL:NY June 18, 1929
	Ray Morehart, AL:Chi. Aug. 31, 1926
	George Case, AL:Wash. July 4, 1940
	Pete Runnels, AL:Bos. Aug. 30, 1960 (25 inn)
	Lee Thomas, AL:LA Sept. 5, 1961

Most Hits, 3 Consecutive Games
14	Willie Keeler, NL:Balt. Sept. 3-6, 1897
	Mike Benjamin, NL:SF June 11-14, 1995
13	Joe Cronin, AL:Wash. June. 19-22, 1933
	Walt Dropo, AL:Det. July 14-15, 1952
	Tim Salmon, AL:Cal. May 10-13, 1994

Most Hits, Inning
3	Tommy Burns, NL:Chi. Sept. 6, 1883 (7th; hr, 2-2b)
	Fred Pfeffer, NL:Chi. Sept. 6, 1883 (7th; 2b, 2-1b)
	Ned Williamson, NL:Chi. Sept. 6, 1883 (7th; 2b, 2-1b)
	Gene Stephens, AL:Bos. June 18, 1953 (7th; 2b, 2-1b)
	Johnny Damon, AL:Bos. June 27, 2003 (1st; 3b, 2b, 1b)
	NL Since 1900:
2	By many in NL

Fewest Hits, Season (Most at-bats)
0	Bob Buhl, NL:Mil.-Chi. 1962 (70 at-bats)
	Bill Wight, AL:Chi. 1950 (61 at-bats)

Fewest Hits, Game (Most at-bats)
0	Charlie Pick, NL:Bos. May 1, 1920 (11 ab, 26 inn)
	George Kell, AL:Phil. July 21, 1945 (10 ab, 24 inn)
	Danny Thompson, AL:Minn. May 12, 1972 (10 ab, 22 inn)

EXTRA-BASE HITS

Most Seasons Leading Major Leagues
7   Stan Musial, NL:StL. 1943-44, 46, 48-50, 53

Most Seasons, Consecutive, Leading Major Leagues
4   Babe Ruth, AL:Bos. 1918-19; NY 20-21

Most Seasons Leading League
7   Honus Wagner, NL:Pitt. 1900, 02-04, 07-09
      Stan Musial, NL:StL. 1943-44, 46, 48-50, 53
      Babe Ruth, AL:Bos. 1918-19; NY 20-21, 23-24, 28

Most Seasons, Consecutive, Leading League
4   Babe Ruth, AL:Bos. 1918-19; NY 20-21
3   Dan Brouthers, NL:Buff. 1885; Det. 86-87
      Honus Wagner, NL:Pitt.1902-04
      Honus Wagner, NL:Pitt. 1907-09
      Rogers Hornsby, NL:StL. 1920-22
      Joe Medwick, NL:StL. 1935-37
      Johnny Mize, NL:StL. 1938-40
      Stan Musial, NL:StL. 1948-50
      Duke Snider, NL:Brk. 1954-56

Most Extra-Base Hits, Lifetime
1477   Hank Aaron, NL:Mil./Atl. 1954-74; AL:Mil. 75-76

Most Extra-Base Hits, League
1440   Barry Bonds, NL:Pitt. 1986-92; SF 93-2007
1350   Babe Ruth, AL:Bos. 1914-19; NY 20-34

Most Extra-Base Hits, Season
119   Babe Ruth, AL:NY 1921
107   Chuck Klein, NL:Phil. 1930
      Barry Bonds, NL:SF 2001

Most Games, 4 or more Extra-Base Hits, League
5   Lou Gehrig, AL:NY 1926, 28, 30, 32, 34
      Joe DiMaggio, AL:NY 1936-37, 41, 48, 50
4   Willie Stargell, NL:Pitt. 1965, 68, 70, 73

Most Games, 4 or more Extra-Base Hits, Season
2   Henry Larkin, AA:Phil. June 16, July 29, 1885
      George Burns, AL:Clev. June 19(1g), July 23, 1924
      Lou Fonseca, AL:Clev. May 19, 29, 1929
      Jimmie Foxx, AL:Phil. Apr. 24, July 2(2g), 1933
      Rafael Palmeiro, AL:Tex. July 15, Sept. 6, 1993
      Albert Belle, AL:Balt. Aug. 29, Sept. 23, 1999
      Shannon Stewart, AL:Tor. June 9, July 18, 2000
      Adrian Beltre, AL:Sea. May 28, July 6, 2007
      Francisco Lindor, AL:Clev. May 12, 31, 2018
      Joe Medwick, NL:StL. May 12, Aug. 4, 1937
      Billy Williams, NL:Chi. Apr. 9, Sept. 5, 1969
      Paul O'Neill, NL:Cin. May 11, Sept. 13, 1991
      Jim Edmonds, NL:StL. Apr. 4, June 28, 2003
      Alfonso Soriano, NL:Wash. Apr. 21, July 22, 2006
      Aaron Rowand, NL:Phil. July 14, 17, 2007
      Matt Carpenter, NL:StL. July 20, Aug. 26, 2018

Most Extra-Base Hits, Consecutive, Season
7   Elmer Smith, AL:Clev. Sept. 4-5, 1921 (4-hr, 3-2b)
      Earl Sheely, AL:Chi. May 20-21, 1926 (1-hr, 6-2b)
      Vic Wertz, AL:Det. July 28-30, 1950 (4-hr, 3-2b)
6   Larry Walker, NL:Col. May 21-22, 1996 (1-hr, 3-3b, 2-2b)
      Joc Pederson. NL:LA Sept. 1-4, 2019 (5-hr, 1-2b)

Most Extra-Base Hits, Game
5   George Strief, AA:Phil. June 25, 1885 (4-3b, 1-2b)
      George Gore, NL:Chi. July 9, 1885 (2-3b, 3-2b)
      Larry Twitchell, NL:Clev. Aug. 15, 1889 (1-hr, 3-3b, 1-2b)
      Joe Adcock, NL:Mil. July 31, 1954 (4-hr, 1-2b)
      Willie Stargell, NL:Pitt. Aug. 1, 1970 (2-hr, 3-2b)
      Steve Garvey, NL:LA Aug. 28, 1977 (2-hr, 3-2b)
      Shawn Green, NL:LA May 23, 2002 (4-hr, 1-2b)
      Kris Bryant, NL:Chi. June 27, 2016 (3-hr, 2-2b)
      Matt Carpenter, NL:StL. July 20, 2018 (3-hr, 2-2b)
      Alex Dickerson, NL:SF Sept. 1, 2020 (3-hr, 2-2b)
      Lou Boudreau, AL:Clev. July 14(1g), 1946 (1-hr, 4-2b)
      Kelly Shoppach, AL:Clev. July 30, 2008 (13 inn.; 2-hr, 3-2b)
      Josh Hamilton, AL:Tex. May 8, 2012 (4-hr, 1-2b)
      Jackie Bradley Jr., AL:Bos. Aug. 15, 2015 (2-hr, 3-2b)
      Jose Ramirez, AL:Clev. Sept. 3, 2017 (2-hr, 3-2b)

Most Extra-Base Hits, 2 Consecutive Games

7	Ed Delahanty, NL:Phil. July 13-14, 1896 (4-hr, 1-3b, 2-2b)
	Red Schoendienst, NL:StL. June 5-6, 1948 (1 hr, 6-2b)
	Joe Adcock, NL:Mil. July 30-31, 1954 (5-hr, 2-2b)
	Larry Walker, NL:Col. May 21-22, 1996 (2-hr, 3-3b, 2-2b)
	Jim Edmonds, NL:StL. Apr. 4-8, 2003 (3-hr, 4-2b)
	Christian Yelich, NL:Mia. July 25-26, 2017 (2-hr, 5-2b)
	Willson Contreras, NL:Chi. May 9-11, 2018 (2-hr, 2-3b, 3-2b)
	Earl Sheely, AL:Chi. May 20-21, 1926 (1-hr, 6-2b)
	Alex Bregman, AL:Hou. June 26-27, 2018 (2-hr, 5-2b)

Most Extra-Base Hits, Inning

3	Tommy Burns, NL:Chi. Sept. 6, 1883 (7th: 1-hr, 2-2b)
	Since 1900:
2	By many

TOTAL BASES

Most Seasons Leading Major Leagues

6	Babe Ruth, AL:Bos. 1919; NY 21, 23-24, 26, 28
	Stan Musial, NL:StL. 1943, 46, 48-49, 51-52

Most Seasons, Consecutive, Leading Major Leagues

2	Dan Brouthers, NL:Buff. 1882-83
	Jimmy Ryan, NL:Chi. 1888-89
	Babe Ruth, AL:NY 1923-24
	Jimmie Foxx, AL:Phil. 1932-33
	Stan Musial, NL:StL. 1948-49
	Stan Musial, NL:StL. 1951-52
	Duke Snider, NL:Brk. 1953-54
	Hank Aaron, NL:Mil. 1959-60
	Frank Howard, AL:Wash. 1968-69
	Jim Rice, AL:Bos. 1978-79
	Mike Schmidt, NL:Phil. 1980-81
	Don Mattingly, AL:NY 1985-86
	Sammy Sosa, NL:Chi. 1998-99
	Albert Pujols, NL:StL. 2003-04
	Albert Pujols, NL:StL. 2008-09

Most Seasons Leading League

8	Hank Aaron, NL:Mil./Atl. 1956-57, 59-61, 63,67, 69
6	Ty Cobb, AL:Det. 1907-09, 11, 15, 17
	Babe Ruth, AL:Bos. 1919; NY 21, 23-24, 26, 28
	Ted Williams, AL:Bos. 1939, 42, 46-47, 49, 51

Most Seasons, Consecutive, Leading League

4	Honus Wagner, NL:Pitt. 1906-09
	Chuck Klein, NL:Phil. 1930-33
3	Ty Cobb, AL:Det. 1907-09
	Jim Rice, AL:Bos. 1977-79

Most Total Bases, Lifetime

6856	Hank Aaron, NL:Mil./Atl. 1954-74; AL:Mil. 75-76

Most Total Bases, League

6591	Hank Aaron, NL:Mil./Atl. 1954-74
5862	Ty Cobb, AL:Det. 1905-26; Phil. 27-28

Most Total Bases, Season

457	Babe Ruth, AL:NY 1921
450	Rogers Hornsby, NL:StL. 1922

Most Seasons, 400 or more Total Bases

5	Lou Gehrig, AL:NY 1927, 30-31, 34, 36
3	Chuck Klein, NL:Phil. 1929-30, 32

Most Seasons, Consecutive, 400 or more Total Bases

2	Lou Gehrig, AL:NY 1930-31
	Jimmie Foxx, AL:Phil. 1932-33
	Chuck Klein, NL:Phil. 1929-30
	Todd Helton, NL:Col. 2000-01

Most Seasons, 300 or more Total Bases

15	Hank Aaron, NL:Mil./Atl. 1955-63, 69, 71
13	Lou Gehrig, AL:NY 1926-38

Most Seasons, Consecutive, 300 or more Total Bases

13	Lou Gehrig, AL:NY 1926-38
	Willie Mays, NL:NY/SF 1954-66

Most Total Bases, Game

19	Shawn Green, NL:LA May 23, 2002 (4-hr, 1-2b, 1-1b)
18	Josh Hamilton, AL:Tex. May 8, 2012 (4-hr, 1-2b)

Most Total Bases, 2 Consecutive Games
25   Ty Cobb, AL:Det. May 5-6, 1925
                Joe Adcock, NL:Mil. July 30-31, 1954
                Shawn Green, NL:LA May 23-24, 2002

Most Total Bases, Doubleheader
22   Nate Colbert, NL:SD Aug. 1, 1972
21   Jimmie Foxx, AL:Phil. July 2, 1933 (19 inn)
                Al Oliver, AL:Tex. Aug. 17, 1980

Most Total Bases, Inning
8   Tommy Burns, NL:Chi. Sept. 6, 1883 (7th)
                Also by many (2 home runs, inning; see page 24)

SINGLES

Most Seasons Leading Major Leagues
9   Ichiro Suzuki, AL:Sea. 2001-02, 04-10

Most Seasons, Consecutive, Leading Major Leagues
7   Ichiro Suzuki, AL:Sea. 2004-10

Most Seasons Leading League
10   Ichiro Suzuki, AL:Sea. 2001-10
7   Tony Gwynn, NL:SD 1984, 86-87, 89, 94-95, 97

Most Seasons, Consecutive, Leading League
10   Ichiro Suzuki, AL:Sea. 2001-10
4   Brett Butler, NL:SF 1990; LA 1991-93

Most Singles, Lifetime
3215   Pete Rose, NL:Cin. 1963-78, 84-86; Phil. 79-83; Mtl. 84
3052   Ty Cobb, AL:Det. 1905-26; Phil. 27-28

Most Singles, Season
225   Ichiro Suzuki, AL:Sea. 2004
201   Willie Keeler, NL:Balt. 1898
            NL Since 1900:
198   Lloyd Waner, NL:Pitt. 1927

Most Singles, Game
6   Hick Carpenter, AA:Cin. Sept. 12, 1883
            George Pinkney, AA:Brk. June 25, 1885
            By many since 1900; last:
            Jean Segura, NL:Mil. May 28, 2013 (14 inn)
            Raul Ibanez, AL:Sea. Sept. 22, 2004
            Extra-Inning Game:
7   Johnny Burnett, AL:Clev. July 10, 1932 (18 inn)

Most Singles, Inning
2   By many

DOUBLES

Most Seasons Leading Major Leagues
7   Tris Speaker, AL:Bos. 1912, 14; Clev. 18, 20-23

Most Seasons, Consecutive, Leading Major Leagues
4   Tris Speaker, AL:Clev. 1920-23

Most Seasons Leading League
8   Honus Wagner, NL:Pitt. 1900-02, 04, 06-09
            Stan Musial, NL:StL. 1943-44, 46, 48-49, 52-54
7   Tris Speaker, AL:Bos. 1912, 14; Clev. 18, 20-23

Most Seasons, Consecutive, Leading League
4   Honus Wagner, NL:Pitt. 1906-09
            Tris Speaker, AL:Clev. 1920-23

Most Doubles, Lifetime
793   Tris Speaker, AL:Bos. 1907-15; Clev. 16-26; Wash. 27; Phil. 28
746   Pete Rose, NL:Cin. 1963-78, 84-86; Phil. 79-83; Mtl. 84

Most Doubles, Season
67   Earl Webb, AL:Bos. 1931
64   Joe Medwick, NL:StL. 1936

Most Seasons, 50 or more Doubles
5   Tris Speaker, AL:Bos. 1912; Clev. 20-21, 23, 26
3   Paul Waner, NL:Pitt. 1928, 32, 36
            Stan Musial, NL:StL. 1944, 46, 53

Most Doubles, Game
4   By many; last:
Rafael Devers, AL:Bos. Aug. 13, 2019 (10 inn)
Adam Frazier, NL:Pitt. July 1, 2019

Most Doubles, Consecutive, Game
4   Frank Bonner, NL:Balt. Aug. 4, 1894
Joe Kelley, NL:Balt. Sept. 3, 1894
Dick Bartell, NL:Phil. Apr. 25, 1933
Ernie Lombardi, NL:Cin. May 8(1g), 1935
Bill Werber, NL:Cin. May 13, 1940
Willie Jones, NL:Phil. Apr. 20, 1949
Billy Williams, NL:Chi. Apr. 9, 1969
Marcus Giles, NL:Atl. July 27, 2003
Matt Murton, NL:Chi. Aug. 3(2g), 2006
Jeff Baker, NL:Col. May 30, 2008
Bill Werber, AL:Bos. July 17(1g), 1935
Mike Kreevich, AL:Chi. Sept. 4, 1937
Johnny Lindell, AL:NY Aug. 17, 1944
Lou Boudreau, AL:Clev. July 14(1g), 1946
Vic Wertz, AL:Clev. Sept. 26, 1956
Bill Bruton, AL:Det. May 19, 1963
Dave Duncan, AL:Balt. June 30(2g), 1975
Sandy Alomar Jr., AL:Clev. June 6, 1997
Albert Belle, AL:Balt. Aug. 29 & Sept. 23(2g), 1999
Victor Martinez, AL:Bos. June 1, 2010
Brock Holt, AL:Bos. June 1, 2014

Most Doubles, 2 Consecutive Games
6   Cap Anson, NL:Chi. July 3-4, 1883
Sam Thompson, NL:Phil. June 29-July 1, 1895
Paul Waner, NL:Pitt. May 19-20, 1932
Red Schoendienst, NL:StL. June 5-6, 1948
Joe Dugan, AL:Phil. Sept. 24-25, 1920
Earl Sheely, AL:Chi. May 20-21, 1926
Carl Reynolds, AL:Chi. July 3-4(1g), 1929
Hank Majeski, AL:Phil. Aug. 27-27, 1948
Kirby Puckett, AL:Minn. May 13-14, 1989

Most Doubles, 3 Consecutive Games
8   Red Schoendienst, NL:StL. June 5-6(dh), 1948
7   Joe Dugan, AL:Phil. Sept. 23-25, 1920
Earl Sheely, AL:Chi. May 20-22, 1926
Carl Reynolds, AL:Chi. July 2(2g)-4(1g), 1929
Lu Blue, AL:StL. Aug. 30-Sept. 1(1g), 1930

Most Doubles, Inning
2   By many

TRIPLES

Most Seasons Leading Major Leagues
5   Sam Crawford, NL:Cin. 1902; AL:Det. 03, 10, 13-14

Most Seasons, Consecutive, Leading Major Leagues
2   Dave Orr, AA:NY 1885-86
Sam Crawford, NL:Cin. 1902-AL:Det. 03 & Det. 13-14
Elmer Flick, AL:Clev. 1906-07
Earle Combs, AL:NY 1927-28
George Brett, AL:KC 1975-76
Lance Johnson, AL:Chi. 1993-94
Jose Offerman, AL:KC 1998-Bos. 99
Cristian Guzman, AL:Minn. 2000-01
Jose Reyes, NL:NY 2005-06

Most Seasons Leading League
6   Sam Crawford, NL:Cin. 1902; AL:Det. 1903, 10, 13-15
5   Sam Crawford, AL:Det. 1903, 10, 13-15
Willie Wilson, AL:KC 1980, 82, 85, 87-88
Stan Musial, NL:StL. 1943, 46, 48-49, 51

Most Seasons, Consecutive, Leading League
4   Lance Johnson, AL:Chi. 1991-94
3   Garry Templeton, NL:StL. 1977-79

Most Triples, Lifetime
312   Sam Crawford, NL:Cin. 1899-1902; AL:Det. 03-17

Most Triples, League
298   Ty Cobb, AL:Det. 1905-26; Phil. 27-28
252   Honus Wagner, NL:Lou. 1897-99; Pitt. 1900-17

Most Triples, Season
36	Owen Wilson, NL:Pitt. 1912
26	Joe Jackson, AL:Clev. 1912
	Sam Crawford, AL:Det. 1914

Most Seasons, 20 or more Triples, Lifetime
5	Sam Crawford, NL:Cin. 1902; AL:Det. 03, 12-14

Most Seasons, 20 or more Triples, League
4	Sam Crawford, AL:Det. 1903, 12-14
	Ty Cobb, AL:Det. 1908, 11-12, 17
3	Dan Brouthers, NL:Det. 1887; Brk. 92; Balt. 94
	Roger Connor, NL:NY 1886-87; NY-StL. 94
	Sam Thompson, NL:Det. 1887; Phil. 94-95
	NL Since 1900:
2	By many

Most Seasons, Consecutive, 20 or more Triples
3	Sam Crawford, AL:Det. 1912-14
2	Roger Connor, NL:NY 1886-87
	George Davis, NL:NY 1893-94
	Sam Thompson, NL:Phil. 1894-95

Most Triples, Game
4	George Strief, AA:Phil. June 25, 1885
	Bill Joyce, NL:NY May 18, 1897
	Since 1900:
3	By many; last:
	Yasiel Puig, NL:LA July 25, 2014
	Denard Span, AL:Minn. June 29, 2010

Most Triples, Consecutive, Game
3	By many

Most Triples, Inning
2	Harry Wheeler, AA:Cin. June 28, 1882(11th)
	Harry Stovey, AA:Phil. Aug. 18, 1884 (8th)
	Joe Hornung, NL:Bos. May 6, 1882 (8th)
	Heinie Peitz, NL:StL. July 2, 1895 (1st)
	Frank Shugart, NL:Lou. July 30, 1895 (5th)
	Buck Freeman, NL:Bos. July 25, 1900 (1st)
	Bill Dahlen, NL:Brk. Aug. 30, 1900 (8th)
	Curt Walker, NL:Cin. July 22, 1926 (2nd)
	Cory Sullivan, NL:Col. Apr. 9, 2006 (5th)
	Al Zarilla, AL:StL. July 13, 1946 (4th)
	Gil Coan, AL:Wash. Apr. 21, 1951 (6th)

Fewest Triples, Season (most at-bats)
0	Derek Jeter, AL:NY 2012 (683 at-bats)
	Sammy Sosa, NL:Chi. 1998 (643 at-bats)

HOME RUNS

Most Seasons Leading Major Leagues
11	Babe Ruth, AL:Bos. 1918-19; NY 20-21, 23-24, 26-29, 31

Most Seasons, Consecutive, Leading Major Leagues
6	Ralph Kiner, NL:Pitt. 1947-52

Most Seasons Leading League
12	Babe Ruth, AL:Bos. 1918-19; NY 20-21, 23-24, 26-31
8	Mike Schmidt, NL:Phil. 1974-76, 80-81, 83-84, 86

Most Seasons, Consecutive, Leading League
7	Ralph Kiner, NL:Pitt. 1946-52
6	Babe Ruth, AL:NY 1926-31

Most Home Runs, Lifetime
762	Barry Bonds, NL:Pitt. 1986-92; SF 93-2007
708	Babe Ruth, AL:Bos. 1914-19; NY 20-34

Most Home Runs, Season
73	Barry Bonds, NL:SF 2001
61	Roger Maris, AL:NY 1961

Most Seasons, 50 or more Home Runs
4	Babe Ruth, AL:NY 1920-21, 27-28
	Mark McGwire, AL:Oak. 1996; AL:Oak.-NL:StL. 97; NL:StL. 98-99
	Sammy Sosa, NL:Chi. 1998-2001

Most Seasons, Consecutive, 50 or more Home Runs
4	Mark McGwire, AL:Oak. 1996; AL:Oak.-NL:StL. 97, NL:StL. 98-99
	Sammy Sosa, NL:Chi. 1998-2001
2	Babe Ruth, AL:NY 1920-21; 27-28
	Ken Griffey Jr., AL:Sea. 1997-98
	Alex Rodriguez, AL:Tex. 2001-02

Most Seasons, 40 or more Home Runs
11	Babe Ruth, AL:NY 1920-21, 23-24, 26-32
8	Hank Aaron, NL:Mil./Atl. 1957, 60, 62-63, 66, 69, 71, 73
	Barry Bonds, NL:SF 1993, 96-97, 2000-04

Most Seasons, Consecutive, 40 or more Home Runs
7	Babe Ruth, AL:NY 1926-32
6	Sammy Sosa, NL:Chi. 1998-2003

Most Seasons, 30 or more Home Runs
15	Hank Aaron, NL:Mil./Atl. 1957-63, 65-67, 69-73
	Alex Rodriguez, AL:Sea. 1996, 98-2000; Tex. 01-03; NY 04-10, 15

Most Seasons, Consecutive, 30 or more Home Runs
13	Barry Bonds, NL:Pitt. 1992; SF 93-2004
	Alex Rodriguez, AL:Sea. 1998-2000; Tex. 01-03; NY 04-10

Most Seasons, 20 or more Home Runs
20	Hank Aaron, NL:Mil./Atl. 1955-74
16	Babe Ruth, AL:Bos. 1919; NY 20-34
	Ted Williams, AL:Bos. 1939-42, 46-51, 54-58, 60
	Reggie Jackson, AL:Oak. 1968-75; Balt. 76; NY 77-80; Cal. 82, 84-85
	Alex Rodriguez, AL:Sea. 1996-2000; Tex. 01-03; NY 04-10, 15

Most Seasons, Consecutive, 20 or more Home Runs
20	Hank Aaron, NL:Mil./Atl. 1955-74
16	Babe Ruth, AL:Bos. 1919; NY 20-34

Most Home Runs, Consecutive Seasons
135	Mark McGwire, NL:StL. 1998 (70)-99 (65)
114	Babe Ruth, AL:NY 1927 (60)-28 (54)

Most Home Runs, Season, Home
39	Hank Greenberg, AL:Det. 1938
38	Mark McGwire, NL:StL. 1998

Most Home Runs, Season, Road
36	Barry Bonds, NL:SF 2001
32	Babe Ruth, AL:NY 1927
	David Ortiz, AL:Bos. 2006

Most Home Runs, Season, vs. One Club
14	Lou Gehrig, AL:NY vs. Clev. 1936
13	Hank Sauer, NL:Chi. vs. Pitt. 1954
	Joe Adcock, NL:Mil. vs. Brk. 1956

Most Home Runs, Season, vs. One Club, Home
10	Gus Zernial, AL:Chi.-Phil. vs. StL. 1951
9	Stan Musial, NL:StL. vs. NY 1954

Most Home Runs, Season, vs. One Club, Road
10	Harry Heilmann, AL:Det. vs. Phil. 1922
9	Joe Adcock, NL:Mil. vs. Brk. 1954
	Willie Mays, NL:NY vs. Brk. 1955

Most Home Runs, One Month
20	Sammy Sosa, NL:Chi. June 1998
18	Rudy York, AL:Det. Aug. 1937

Most Home Runs, Game
4	Bobby Lowe, NL:Bos. May 30(2g), 1894 (cons)
	Ed Delahanty, NL:Phil. July 13, 1896
	Chuck Klein, NL:Phil. July 10, 1936 (10 inn)
	Gil Hodges, NL:Brk. Aug. 31, 1950
	Joe Adcock, NL:Mil. July 31, 1954
	Willie Mays, NL:SF Apr. 30, 1961
	Mike Schmidt, NL:Phil. Apr. 17, 1976 (10 inn; cons)
	Bob Horner, NL:Atl. July 6, 1986
	Mark Whiten, NL:StL. Sept. 7(2g), 1993
	Shawn Green, NL:LA May 23, 2002
	Scooter Gennett, NL: Cin. June 6, 2017 (cons)
	J.D. Martinez, NL:Ari. Sept. 4, 2017 (cons)
	Lou Gehrig, AL:NY June 3, 1932 (cons)
	Pat Seerey, AL:Chi. July 18(1g), 1948 (11 inn)
	Rocky Colavito, AL:Clev. June 10, 1959 (cons)
	Mike Cameron, AL:Sea. May 2, 2002 (cons)
	Carlos Delgado, AL:Tor. Sept. 25, 2003 (cons)
	Josh Hamilton, AL:Tex. May 8, 2012

Most Home Runs, Leadoff Batter, First Inning, Lifetime
81   Rickey Henderson, AL:Oak. 1979-84, 89-95, 98; NY 85-89; Tor. 93; Ana. 97; Sea. 2000;
          Bos. 02; NL:SD 96-97, 2001; NY 99-2000; LA 03

Most Home Runs, Leadoff Batter, First Inning, League
73   Rickey Henderson, AL:Oak. 1979-84, 89-95, 98; NY 85-89; Tor. 93; Ana. 97; Sea. 2000; Bos. 02
53   Craig Biggio, NL:Hou. 1992-94, 97-99, 2001-07

Most Home Runs, Leadoff Batter, First Inning, Season
13   Alfonso Soriano, AL:NY 2003
12   Alfonso Soriano, NL:Chi. 2007

Most Games, 3 or more Home Runs, Lifetime
6   Johnny Mize, NL:StL.-NY; AL:NY
     Mookie Betts, AL:Bos.-NL:LA
     Sammy Sosa, NL:Chi.
5   Joe Carter, AL:Clev.; Tor.
     Carlos Delgado, AL:Tor.
     Alex Rodriguez, AL:Sea.-Tex.-NY
     Mookie Betts, AL:Bos.

Most Games, 3 or more Home Runs, Season
3   Sammy Sosa, NL:Chi. 2001
2   Ted Williams, AL:Bos. 1957
     Doug DeCinces, AL:Balt. 1982
     Joe Carter, AL:Clev. 1989
     Cecil Fielder, AL:Det. 1990
     Geronimo Berroa, AL:Oak. 1996
     Carlos Delgado, AL:Tor. 2001
     Mookie Betts, AL:Bos. 2016
     Mookie Betts, AL:Bos. 2018
     Nelson Cruz, AL:Minn. 2019

Most Games, 2 or more Home Runs, Lifetime
72   Babe Ruth, AL:Bos. 1914-19; NY 20-34; NL:Bos. 35

Most Games, 2 or more Home Runs, League
71   Babe Ruth, AL:Bos. 1914-19; NY 20-34
     Barry Bonds, NL:Pitt. 1987-92, SF 93-2004, 06-07

Most Games, 2 or more Home Runs, Season
11   Hank Greenberg, AL:Det. 1938
     Sammy Sosa, NL:Chi. 1998

Most Games, Switch-Hitting Home Runs, Lifetime
14   Mark Teixeira, AL:Tex. 2004-06, NY 09-12, 15; NL:Atl. 08
     Nick Swisher, AL:Oak. 2005-07; Chi. 08; NY 09, 12; Clev. 13; NL:Atl. 15
13   Nick Swisher, AL:Oak. 2005-07; Chi. 08; NY 09, 12; Clev. 13
10   Ken Caminiti, NL:Hou. 1994, 99; SD 95-96, 98

Most Games, Switch-Hitting Home Runs, Season
4   Ken Caminiti, NL:SD 1996
3   Tony Clark, AL:Det. 1998
     Nick Swisher, AL:Oak. 2007
     Nick Swisher, AL:NY 2009
     Mark Teixeira, AL:NY 2009
     Jose Ramirez, AL:Clev. 2017

Most Times Switch-Hitting Home Runs, Inning, Lifetime
1   Carlos Baerga, AL:Clev. Apr. 8, 1993 (7th)
     Kendrys Morales, AL:LA July 30, 2012 (6th)
     Mark Bellhorn, NL:Chi. Aug. 29, 2002 (4th)

Most Consecutive Innings, Home Run, Game
3   George Kelly, NL:NY Sept. 17, 1923 (3rd, 4th, 5th)
     Larry Parrish, NL:Mtl. July 30, 1978 (3rd, 4th, 5th)
     Andres Galarraga, NL:Col. June 25, 1995 (6th, 7th, 8th)
     Sammy Sosa, NL:Chi. Aug. 10, 2002 (3rd, 4th, 5th)
     Shea Hillenbrand, NL:Ari. July 7, 2003 (4th, 5th, 6th)
     Nolan Arenado, NL:Col. July 19, 2017 (4th, 5th, 6th)
     J.D. Martinez, NL:Ari. Sept. 4, 2017 (7th, 8th, 9th)
     Kris Bryant, NL:Chi. May 17, 2019 (7th, 8th, 9th)
     Aristides Aquino, NL:Cin. Aug. 10, 2019 (2nd, 3rd, 4th)
     Carl Reynolds, AL:Chi. July 2(2g), 1930 (1st, 2nd, 3rd)
     Pat Seerey, AL:Chi. July 18(1g), 1948 (4th, 5th, 6th)
     Kevin Mench, AL:Tex. June 30, 2005 (5th, 6th, 7th)
     Manny Machado, AL:Balt. Aug. 7, 2016 (1st, 2nd, 3rd)

Most Home Runs, 2 Consecutive Innings, Game
3   Nomar Garciaparra, AL:Bos. July 23(1g), 2002 (3rd, 4th)
2   By many in NL

Most Home Runs, Doubleheader
5   Stan Musial, NL:StL. May 2, 1954
     Nate Colbert, NL:SD Aug. 1, 1972
4   Earl Averill, AL:Clev. Sept. 17, 1930
     Jimmie Foxx, AL:Phil. July 2, 1933
     Jim Tabor, AL:Bos. July 4, 1939
     Gus Zernial, AL:Chi. Oct. 1, 1950
     Charlie Maxwell, AL:Det. May 3, 1959
     Roger Maris, AL:NY July 25, 1961
     Rocky Colavito, AL:Det. Aug. 27, 1961
     Harmon Killebrew, AL:Minn. Sept. 21, 1963
     Bobby Murcer, AL:NY June 24, 1970
     Graig Nettles, AL:NY Apr. 14, 1974
     Otto Velez, AL:Tor. May 4, 1980
     Al Oliver, AL:Tex. Aug. 17, 1980

Most Home Runs, Consecutive At-Bats (*consecutive plate appearances)

4   Bobby Lowe, NL:Bos. May 30(2g), 1894*
     Bill Nicholson, NL:Chi. July 22-23, 1944
     Ralph Kiner, NL:Pitt. Aug. 15-16, 1947
     Ralph Kiner, NL:Pitt. Sept. 11-13, 1949*
     Stan Musial, NL:StL. July 7-8, 1962
     Art Shamsky, NL:Cin. Aug. 12-14, 1966*
     Deron Johnson, NL:Phil. July 10-11, 1971*
     Johnny Bench, NL:Cin. May 8-9, 1973
     Mike Schmidt, NL:Phil. Apr. 17, 1976*
     Mike Schmidt, NL:Phil. July 6-7, 1979*
     Tuffy Rhodes, NL:Chi. Oct. 3, 1993-Apr. 4, 1994
     Benito Santiago, NL:Phil. Sept. 14-15, 1996
     Barry Bonds, NL:SF May 19-20, 2001
     Shawn Green, NL:LA June 14-15, 2002*
     Andruw Jones, NL:Atl. Sept. 7-10, 2002
     Albert Pujols, NL:StL. Apr. 16-17, 2006*
     Carlos Gonzalez, NL:Col. May 30-31, 2012*
     Adrian Gonzalez, NL:LA Apr. 7-8, 2015*
     Giancarlo Stanton, NL:Mia. July 5-6, 2016
     Scooter Gennett, NL:Cin. June 6, 2017*
     J.D. Martinez, NL:Ari. Sept. 4, 2017*
     Tilly Walker, AL:Phil. July 1(2g)-2, 1922
     Lou Gehrig, AL:NY June 3, 1932*
     Jimmie Foxx, AL:Phil. June 7-8, 1933*
     Hank Greenberg, AL:Det. July 26-27, 1938*
     Ted Williams, AL:Bos. Sept. 17-20-21-22, 1957
     Charlie Maxwell, AL:Det. May 3(1g)-3(2g), 1959
     Rocky Colavito, AL:Clev. June 10, 1959*
     Willie Kirkland, AL:Clev. July 9(2g)-13, 1961
     Johnny Blanchard, AL:NY July 21-22-26, 1961*
     Mickey Mantle, AL:NY July 4-6, 1962*
     Bobby Murcer, AL:NY June 24(1g)-24(2g), 1970
     Mike Epstein, AL:Oak. June 15-16, 1971*
     Don Baylor, AL:Balt. July 1-2, 1975
     Larry Herndon, AL:Det. May 16-18, 1982*
     Bo Jackson, AL:KC July 17-Aug. 26, 1990*
     Jeff Manto, AL:Balt. June 8-10, 1995
     Bobby Higginson, AL:Det. June 30-July 1, 1997
     Manny Ramirez, AL:Clev. Sept. 15-16, 1998*
     Mike Cameron, AL:Sea. May 2, 2002*
     Troy Glaus, AL:Ana. Sept. 15-16, 2002*
     Carlos Delgado, AL:Tor. Sept. 25, 2003*
     Jose Abreu, AL:Chi. Aug. 22-23, 2020*

Most Games, Consecutive, 1 or more Home Runs

8   Dale Long, NL:Pitt. May 19-28, 1956
     Don Mattingly, AL:NY July 8-18, 1987
     Ken Griffey Jr., AL:Sea. July 20-28, 1993

Most Home Runs, 2 Consecutive Games

5   Cap Anson, NL:Chi. Aug. 5-6, 1884
     Ralph Kiner, NL:Pitt. Aug. 15-16, 1947
     Ralph Kiner, NL:Pitt. Sept. 11(2g)-12, 1947
     Don Mueller, NL:NY Sept. 1-2, 1951
     Stan Musial, NL:StL. May 2, 1954 (dh)
     Joe Adcock, NL:Mil. July 30-31, 1954
     Billy Williams, NL:Chi. Sept. 8-10, 1968
     Nate Colbert, NL:SD Aug. 1, 1972 (dh)
     Mike Schmidt, NL:Phil. Apr. 17-18, 1976
     Dave Kingman, NL:Chi. July 27-28, 1979
     Gary Carter, NL:NY Sept. 3-4, 1985
     Barry Larkin, NL:Cin. June 27-28, 1991
     Geoff Jenkins, NL:Mil. Apr. 28-29, 2001
     Barry Bonds, NL:SF May 19-20, 2001
     Shawn Green, NL:LA May 23-24, 2002
     Bryce Harper, NL:Wash. May 6-8, 2015
     J.D. Martinez, NL:Ari. Sept. 2-4, 2017
     Yasiel Puig, NL:LA Sept. 14-15, 2018
     Ty Cobb, AL:Det. May 5-6, 1925
     Tony Lazzeri, AL:NY May 23-24, 1936
     Carl Yastrzemski, AL:Bos. May 19-20, 1976
     Mark McGwire, AL:Oak. June 27-28, 1987
     Joe Carter, AL:Clev. July 18-19, 1989
     Mark McGwire, AL:Oak. June 10-11, 1995
     Albert Belle, AL:Clev. Sept. 18-19, 1995
     Matt Williams, AL:Clev. Apr. 25-26, 1997
     Manny Ramirez, AL:Clev. Sept. 15-16, 1998
     Edgar Martinez, AL:Sea. May 17-18, 1999
     Nomar Garciaparra, AL:Bos. July 21-23(1g), 2002
     Alex Rodriguez, AL:Tex. Aug. 17-18, 2002
     Travis Hafner, AL:Clev. July 19-20, 2004
     Josh Hamilton, AL:Tex. May 7-8, 2012
     Josh Reddick, AL:Oak. Aug. 9-10, 2013
     Mookie Betts, AL:Bos. May 31-June 1, 2016
     Jose Abreu, AL:Chi. Aug. 21-22, 2020

Most Home Runs, 3 Consecutive Games

7	Shawn Green, NL:LA May 23-25, 2002
6	Tony Lazzeri, AL:NY May 23(dh)-24, 1936
	Gus Zernial, AL:Phil. May 13-16, 1951
	Manny Ramirez, AL:Clev. Sept. 15-17, 1998
	Alex Rodriguez, AL:Tex. Aug. 16-18, 2002
	Jeff DaVanon, AL:Ana. June 1-4, 2003
	Jose Abreu, AL:Chi. Aug. 21-23, 2020

Most Home Runs, 4 Consecutive Games

8	Ralph Kiner, NL:Pitt. Sept. 10-12, 1947
7	Tony Lazzeri, AL:NY May 21-24, 1936
	Gus Zernial, AL:Phil. May 13-17, 1951
	Frank Howard, AL:Wash. May 12-16, 1968
	Josh Hamilton, AL:Tex. May 8-11, 2012

Most Home Runs, 5 Consecutive Games

9	Shawn Green, NL:LA May 21-25, 2002
8	Frank Howard, AL:Wash. May 12-17; 14-18, 1968
	Manny Ramirez, AL:Clev. Sept. 15-19, 1998
	Josh Hamilton, AL:Tex. May 7-11; 8-12, 2012

Most Home Runs, 6 Consecutive Games

10	Frank Howard, AL:Wash. May 12-18, 1968
9	Barry Bonds, NL:SF May 17-22, 2001
	Shawn Green, NL:LA May 19-25; 21-26, 2002

Most Home Runs, 7 Consecutive Games

10	Frank Howard, AL:Wash. May 11-18; 12-19, 1968
	Albert Belle, AL:Clev. Sept. 18-27, 1995
	Shawn Green, NL:LA May 21-27, 2002

Most Home Runs, 8 Consecutive Games

11	Frank Howard, AL:Wash. May 10-18, 1968
10	Willie Mays, NL:SF May 9-17, 1958
	Mike Schmidt, NL:Phil. Apr. 17-26, 1976
	Barry Bonds, NL:SF May 17-24, 2001
	Shawn Green, NL:LA May 19-27; 21-28, 2002

Most Home Runs, First Major League Game

2	Charlie Reilly, AA:Colu. Oct. 9, 1889
	Bob Nieman, AL:StL. Sept. 14, 1951
	Bert Campaneris, AL:KC July 23, 1964
	Mark Quinn, AL:KC Sept. 14(2g), 1999
	J.P. Arencibia, AL:Tor. Aug. 7, 2010
	Trevor Story, NL:Col. Apr. 4, 2016

Most Home Runs, First Two Major League Games

3	Charlie Reilly, AA:Colu. Oct. 9-10, 1889
	Joe Cunningham, NL:StL. June 30-July 1(2g), 1954
	Trevor Story, NL:Col. Apr. 4-5, 2016
2	Earl Averill, AL:Clev. Apr. 16-17, 1929
	Zeke Bonura, AL:Chi. Apr. 17-18, 1934
	Bob Nieman, AL:StL. Sept. 14-15, 1951
	Bert Campaneris, AL:KC July 23-24, 1964
	Curt Blefary, AL:Balt. Apr. 14-17, 1965
	Mike Ryan, AL:Bos. Oct. 3, 1964-May 2, 1965
	Dan Meyer, AL:Det. Sept. 14-20, 1974
	Joe Lefebvre, AL:NY May 22-23, 1980
	Dave Stapleton, AL:Bos. May 30-31, 1980
	Tim Laudner, AL:Minn. Aug. 28-29, 1981
	Alvin Davis, AL:Sea. Apr. 11-13, 1984
	Sam Horn, AL:Bos. July 25-26, 1987
	Manny Ramirez, AL:Clev. Sept. 2-3, 1993
	Gabe Alvarez, AL:Det. June 22-23, 1998
	Mark Quinn, AL:KC Sept. 14(2g)-15, 1999
	Josh Bard, AL:Clev. Aug. 23-24, 2002
	Kenji Johjima, AL:Sea. Apr. 3-4, 2006
	Kevin Kouzmanoff, AL:Clev. Sept. 2-3, 2006
	Elijah Dukes, AL:TB Apr. 2-5, 2007
	J.P. Arencibia, AL:Tor. Aug. 7-10, 2010
	Manny Machado, AL:Balt. Aug. 9-10, 2012
	Joey Gallo, AL:Tex. June 2-3, 2015
	Aaron Judge, AL:NY Aug. 13-14, 2016
	Francisco Arcia, AL:LA July 26-28, 2018
	Yordan Alvarez, AL:Hou. June 9-11, 2019
	Kyle Lewis, AL:Sea. Sept. 10-11, 2019

Most Home Runs, Inning

2	Lou Bierbauer, PL:Brk. July 12, 1890 (3rd)
	Ed Cartwright, AA:StL. Sept. 23, 1890 (3rd)
	Charley Jones, NL:Bos. June 10, 1880 (8th)
	Bobby Lowe, NL:Bos. May 30(2g), 1894 (3rd)
	Jake Stenzel, NL:Pitt. June 6, 1894 (3rd)
	Hack Wilson, NL:NY July 1(2g), 1925 (3rd)
	Hank Leiber, NL:NY Aug. 24, 1935 (2nd)
	Sid Gordon, NL:NY July 31(2g), 1949 (2nd)
	Andy Seminick, NL:Phil. June 2, 1949 (8th)
	Willie McCovey, NL:SF Apr. 12, 1973 (4th)
	John Boccabella, NL:Mtl. July 6, 1973 (6th)
	Lee May, NL:Hou. Apr. 29, 1974 (6th)
	Willie McCovey, NL:SF June 27, 1977 (6th)
	Andre Dawson, NL:Mtl. July 30, 1978 (3rd)
	Ray Knight, NL:Cin. May 13, 1980 (5th)
	Von Hayes, NL:Phil. June 11, 1985 (1st)
	Andre Dawson, NL:Mtl. Sept. 24, 1985 (5th)
	Dale Murphy, NL:Atl. July 27, 1989 (6th)
	Jeff Bagwell, NL:Hou. June 24, 1994 (6th)
	Jeff King, NL:Pitt. Aug. 8, 1995 (2nd)
	Jeff King, NL:Pitt. Apr. 30, 1996 (4th)
	Sammy Sosa, NL:Chi. May 16, 1996 (7th)
	Mike Lansing, NL:Mtl. May 7, 1997 (6th)
	Gary Sheffield, NL:Fla. July 13, 1997 (4th)
	Fernando Tatis, NL:StL. Apr. 23, 1999 (3rd)
	Eric Karros, NL:LA Aug. 22, 2000 (6th)
	Aaron Boone, NL:Cin. Aug. 9, 2002 (1st)
	Mark Bellhorn, NL:Chi. Aug. 29, 2002 (4th)
	Reggie Sanders, NL:Pitt. Aug. 20, 2003 (5th)
	Juan Rivera, NL:Mtl. June 19, 2004 (2nd)
	Bengie Molina, NL:SF May 7, 2007 (5th)
	Jim Edmonds, NL:Chi. June 21, 2008 (4th)
	Juan Uribe, NL:SF Sept. 23, 2010 (2nd)
	Pablo Sandoval, NL:SF Sept. 18, 2011 (4th)
	Ken Williams, AL:StL. Aug. 7, 1922 (6th)
	Bill Regan, AL:Bos. June 16, 1928 (4th)
	Joe DiMaggio, AL:NY June 24, 1936 (5th)
	Al Kaline, AL:Det. Apr. 17, 1955 (6th)
	Jim Lemon, AL:Wash. Sept. 5, 1959 (3rd)
	Joe Pepitone, AL:NY May 23, 1962 (8th)
	Rick Reichardt, AL:Cal. Apr. 30, 1966 (8th)
	Cliff Johnson, AL:NY June 30, 1977 (8th)
	Ellis Burks, AL:Bos. Aug. 27, 1990 (4th)
	Carlos Baerga, AL:Clev. Apr. 8, 1993 (7th)
	Joe Carter, AL:Tor. Oct. 3, 1993 (2nd)
	Dave Nilsson, AL:Mil. May 17, 1996 (6th)
	Mark McGwire, AL:Oak. Sept. 22, 1996 (5th)
	Bret Boone, AL:Sea. May 2, 2002 (1st)
	Mike Cameron, AL:Sea. May 2, 2002 (1st)
	Jared Sandberg, AL:TB June 11, 2002 (5th)
	Nomar Garciaparra, AL:Bos. July 23(1g), 2002 (3rd)
	Carl Everett, AL:Tex. July 26, 2002 (7th)
	Julio Lugo, AL:TB July 22, 2006 (5th)
	Magglio Ordonez, AL:Det. Aug. 12, 2007 (2nd)
	Alex Rodriguez, AL:NY Sept. 5, 2007 (7th)
	David Ortiz, AL:Bos. Aug. 12, 2008 (1st)
	Michael Cuddyer, AL:Minn. Aug. 23, 2009 (7th)
	Alex Rodriguez, AL:NY Oct. 4, 2009 (6th)
	Kendrys Morales, AL:LA July 30, 2012 (6th)
	Adrian Beltre, AL:Tex. Aug. 22, 2012 (4th)
	Edwin Encarnacion, AL:Tor. July 26, 2013 (7th)
	Mark Trumbo, AL:Balt. Apr. 15, 2016 (7th)
	Edwin Encarnacion, AL:Sea. Apr. 8, 2019 (6th)

Most At-Bats, No Home Runs, Season

671	Rabbit Maranville, NL:Pitt. 1922
658	Doc Cramer, AL:Bos. 1938

GRAND SLAM HOME RUNS

Most Grand Slam Home Runs, Lifetime

25	Alex Rodriguez, AL:Sea. 1994-2000; Tex. 01-03; NY 04-13, 15-16
18	Willie McCovey, NL:SF 1959-73, 77-80; SD 74-76

Most Grand Slam Home Runs, Season
6	Don Mattingly, AL:NY 1987
	Travis Hafner, AL:Clev. 2006
5	Ernie Banks, NL:Chi. 1955
	Albert Pujols, NL:StL. 2009

Most Grand Slam Home Runs, One Month
3	Rudy York, AL:Det. May 16, 22, 30, 1938
	Jim Northrup, AL:Det. June 24 (2), 29, 1968
	Larry Parrish, AL:Tex. July 4, 7, 10, 1982
	Mike Blowers, AL:Sea. Aug. 3, 14, 18, 1995
	Shane Spencer, AL:NY Sept. 18, 24, 27, 1998
	Manny Machado, AL:Balt. Aug. 7, 14, 18, 2017
	Eric Davis, NL:Cin. May 1, 3, 30, 1987
	Mike Piazza, NL:LA Apr. 9, 10, 24, 1998
	Devon White, NL:Mil. May 10, 15, 20, 2001
	Carlos Beltran, NL:NY July 16, 18, 30, 2006

Most Grand Slam Home Runs, Game
2	Tony Lazzeri, AL:NY May 24, 1936 (2nd, 5th)
	Jim Tabor, AL:Bos. July 4(2g), 1939 (3rd, 6th)
	Rudy York, AL:Bos. July 27, 1946 (2nd, 5th)
	Jim Gentile, AL:Balt. May 9, 1961 (1st, 2nd)
	Jim Northrup, AL:Det. June 24, 1968 (5th, 6th)
	Frank Robinson, AL:Balt. June 26, 1970 (5th, 6th)
	Robin Ventura, AL:Chi. Sept. 4, 1995 (4th, 5th)
	Chris Hoiles, AL:Balt. Aug. 14, 1998 (3rd, 8th)
	Nomar Garciaparra, AL:Bos. May 10, 1999 (1st, 8th)
	Bill Mueller, AL:Bos. July 29, 2003 (7th, 8th)
	Tony Cloninger, NL:Atl. July 3, 1966 (1st, 4th)
	Fernando Tatis, NL:StL. Apr. 23, 1999 (3rd, both)
	Josh Willingham, NL:Wash. July 27, 2009 (5th, 6th)

Most Grand Slam Home Runs, First Major League Game
1	Bill Duggleby, NL:Phil. Apr. 21, 1898 (2nd; first ab)
	Bobby Bonds, NL:SF June 25, 1968 (6th)
	Jeremy Hermida, NL:Fla. Aug. 31, 2005 (7th; first ab; ph)
	Brandon Crawford, NL:SF May 27, 2011 (7th)
	Kevin Kouzmanoff, AL:Clev. Sept. 2, 2006 (1st; first ab)
	Daniel Nava, AL:Bos. June 12, 2010 (2nd; first ab)

Most Consecutive Games with a Grand Slam Home Run
2	Jimmy Bannon, NL:Bos. Aug. 6-7, 1894
	Jimmy Sheckard, NL:Brk. Sept. 23-24, 1901
	Phil Garner, NL:Pitt. Sept. 14-15, 1978
	Fred McGriff, NL:SD Aug. 13-14, 1991
	Eric Davis, NL:Cin. May 4-5, 1996
	Mike Piazza, NL:LA Apr. 9-10, 1998
	Sammy Sosa, NL:Chi. July 27-28, 1998
	Robin Ventura, NL:NY May 20(1g)-20(2g), 1999
	Carlos Beltran, NL:NY July 16-18, 2006
	Tyler Saladino, NL:Mil. July 21-22, 2019
	Babe Ruth, AL:NY Sept. 27-29, 1927
	Babe Ruth, AL:NY Aug. 6-7, 1929
	Bill Dickey, AL:NY Aug. 3-4, 1937
	Jimmie Foxx, AL:Bos. May 20-21, 1940
	Jim Busby, AL:Clev. July 5-6, 1956
	Brooks Robinson, AL:Balt. May 6-9, 1962
	Willie Aikens, AL:Cal. June 13(2g)-14, 1979
	Greg Luzinski, AL:Chi. June 8-9, 1984
	Rob Deer, AL:Mil. Aug. 19-20, 1987
	Mike Blowers, AL:Sea. May 16-17, 1993
	Dan Gladden, AL:Det. Aug. 10-11, 1993
	Ken Griffey, Jr., AL:Sea. Apr. 29-30, 1999
	Albert Belle, AL:Balt. June 14-15, 2000
	David Eckstein, AL:Ana. Apr. 27-28, 2002
	Jorge Posada, AL:NY June 12-13, 2010

RUNS BATTED IN (Since 1920 - Prior seasons not compiled on official scores)

Most Seasons Leading Major Leagues
4	Babe Ruth, AL:NY 1920-21, 23, 26
	Lou Gehrig, AL:NY 1927-28, 31, 34
	Hank Aaron, NL:Mil./Atl. 1957, 60, 63, 66

Most Seasons, Consecutive, Leading Major Leagues
3	Cecil Fielder, AL:Det. 1990-92

Most Seasons Leading League
5	Lou Gehrig, AL:NY 1927-28, 30-31, 34
4	Rogers Hornsby, NL:StL. 1920-22, 25
	Hank Aaron, NL:Mil./Atl. 1957, 60, 63, 66
	Mike Schmidt, NL:Phil. 1980-81, 84, 86

Most Seasons, Consecutive, Leading League
3	Rogers Hornsby, NL:StL. 1920-22
	Joe Medwick, NL:StL. 1936-38
	George Foster, NL:Cin. 1976-78
	Cecil Fielder, AL:Det. 1990-92

Most Runs Batted In, Lifetime
2297	Hank Aaron, NL:Mil./Atl. 1954-74; AL:Mil. 75-76

Most Runs Batted In, League
2202	Hank Aaron, NL:Mil./Atl. 1954-74
2086	Alex Rodriguez, AL:Sea. 1994-2000; Tex. 01-03; NY 04-13, 15-16

Most Runs Batted In, Season
191	Hack Wilson, NL:Chi. 1930
184	Lou Gehrig, AL:NY 1931

Most Seasons, 150 or more Runs Batted In
7	Lou Gehrig, AL:NY 1927, 30-32, 34, 36-37
2	Rogers Hornsby, NL:StL. 1922; Chi. 1929
	Hack Wilson, NL:Chi. 1929-30
	Sammy Sosa, NL:Chi. 1998, 2001

Most Seasons, Consecutive, 150 or more Runs Batted In
3	Babe Ruth, AL:NY 1929-31
	Lou Gehrig, AL:NY 1930-32
2	Hack Wilson, NL:Chi. 1929-30

Most Seasons, 100 or more Runs Batted In
14	Alex Rodriguez, AL:Sea. 1996, 98-2000; Tex. 01-03; NY 04-10
	Albert Pujols, NL:StL. 2001-10; AL:LA 12, 14, 16-17
12	Barry Bonds, NL:Pitt. 1990-92; SF 93, 95-98, 2000-02, 04

Most Seasons, Consecutive, 100 or more Runs Batted In
13	Lou Gehrig, AL:NY 1926-38
	Jimmie Foxx, AL:Phil. 1929-35; Bos. 36-41
	Alex Rodriguez, AL:Sea. 1998-2000; Tex. 01-03; NY 04-10
10	Albert Pujols, NL:StL. 2001-10

Most Runs Batted In, Game
12	Jim Bottomley, NL:StL. Sept. 16, 1924
	Mark Whiten, NL:StL. Sept. 7(2g), 1993
11	Tony Lazzeri, AL:NY May 24, 1936

Most Runs Batted In, Game, All of Team's Runs
8	George Kelly, NL:NY June 14, 1924
	Bob Johnson, AL:Phil. June 12, 1938
	Extra-Inning Game:
9	Mike Greenwell, AL:Bos. Sept. 2, 1996 (10 inn)

Most Runs Batted In, Two Consecutive Games
15	Tony Lazzeri, AL:NY May 23-24, 1936
14	Sammy Sosa, NL:Chi. Aug. 10-11, 2002

Most Runs Batted In, Doubleheader
13	Nate Colbert, NL:SD Aug. 1, 1972
	Mark Whiten, NL:StL. Sept. 7, 1993
11	Earl Averill, AL:Clev. Sept. 17, 1930
	Jim Tabor, AL:Bos. July 4, 1939
	Boog Powell, AL:Balt. July 6, 1966 (20 inn)

Most Games, Consecutive, Runs Batted In
17	Ray Grimes, NL:Chi. June 27-July 23, 1922
14	Tris Speaker, AL:Phil. May 16-30(1g), 1928

Most Runs Batted In, Inning
8	Fernando Tatis, NL:StL. Apr. 23, 1999 (3rd)
7	Alex Rodriguez, AL:NY Oct. 4, 2009 (6th)

SACRIFICE HITS

Most Season Leading Major Leagues
4	Phil Rizzuto, AL:NY 1949-52

Most Seasons, Consecutive, Leading Major Leagues
4	Phil Rizzuto, AL:NY 1949-52

Most Seasons Leading League
6	Mule Haas, AL:Phil. 1930-32; Chi. 33-34, 36
4	Otto Knabe, NL:Phil. 1907-08, 10, 13

Most Seasons, Consecutive, Leading League
5	Mule Haas, AL:Phil. 1930-32; Chi. 33-34
2	By many in NL; last:
	Jack Wilson, NL:Pitt. 2001-02

Most Sacrifice Hits, Lifetime
515	Eddie Collins, AL:Phil. 1906-14, 27-30; Chi. 15-26
393	Jake Daubert, NL:Brk. 1910-18; Cin. 19-24

Most Sacrifice Hits, Season (including Sacrifice Flies)
67	Ray Chapman, AL:Clev. 1917
46	Jimmy Sheckard, NL:Chi. 1909

Most Sacrifice Hits, Season (not including Sacrifice Flies)
46	Bill Bradley, AL:Clev. 1907
43	Kid Gleason, NL:Phil. 1905

Most Sacrifice Hits, Game
4	Cy Seymour, NL:Cin. July 25, 1902
	Jake Daubert, NL:Brk. Aug. 15(2g), 1914
	Kris Benson, NL:Pitt. Apr. 18, 2004
	Cory Sullivan, NL:Col. June 14, 2006
	Red Killefer, AL:Wash. Aug. 27(1g), 1910
	Ray Chapman, AL:Clev. Aug. 31, 1919
	Felix Fermin, AL:Clev. Aug. 22, 1989 (10 inn)

Most Sacrifice Hits, Inning
2	Al Benton, AL:Det. Aug. 6, 1941 (3rd)

SACRIFICE FLIES (Since 1954)

Most Seasons Leading Major Leagues
3	Ron Santo, NL:Chi. 1963, 67, 69

Most Seasons, Consecutive, Leading Major Leagues
2	Carlos Lee, NL:Mil.-AL:Tex. 2006; NL:Hou. 2007
	Bengie Molina, NL:SF 2008-09

Most Seasons Leading League
4	Brooks Robinson, AL:Balt. 1962, 64, 67-68
3	Ron Santo, NL:Chi. 1963, 67, 69
	Johnny Bench, NL:Cin. 1970, 72-73
	Dante Bichette, NL:Col. 1996, 98-99

Most Seasons, Consecutive Leading League
2	Gil Hodges, NL:Brk. 1954-55
	Johnny Bench, NL:Cin. 1972-73
	Mike Schmidt, NL:Phil. 1979-80
	Dante Bichette, NL:Col. 1998-99
	Aramis Ramirez, NL:Pitt.-Chi. 2002-03
	Bengie Molina, NL:SF 2008-09
	Adrian Gonzalez, NL:LA 2013-14
	Jackie Jensen, AL:Bos. 1954-55
	Minnie Minoso, AL:Chi. 1960-61
	Dave Johnson, AL:Balt. 1966-67
	Brooks Robinson, AL:Balt. 1967-68
	Orlando Cabrera, AL:LA 2006-07

Most Sacrifice Flies, Lifetime
128	Eddie Murray, AL:Balt. 1977-88, 96; Clev. 94-96; Ana. 97; NL:LA 89-91, 97; NY 92-93

Most Sacrifice Flies, League
127	Cal Ripken, AL:Balt. 1981-2001
113	Hank Aaron, NL:Mil./Atl. 1954-74

Most Sacrifice Flies, Season
19	Gil Hodges, NL:Brk. 1954
17	Roy White, AL:NY 1971
	Bobby Bonilla, AL:Balt. 1996

Most Sacrifice Flies, Game
3	Ernie Banks, NL:Chi. June 2, 1961
	Vince Coleman, NL:StL. May 1, 1986
	Candy Maldonado, NL:SF Aug. 29, 1987
	Bob Meusel, AL:NY Sept. 15, 1926
	Russ Nixon, AL:Bos. Aug. 31(2g), 1965
	Don Mattingly, AL:NY May 3, 1986
	George Bell, AL:Tor. Aug. 14, 1990
	Chad Kreuter, AL:Det. July 30, 1994
	Juan Gonzalez, AL:Tex. July 3, 1999
	Edgar Martinez, AL:Sea. Aug. 3, 2002
	Jose Lopez, AL:Sea. Apr. 15, 2008

Most Sacrifice Flies, Inning
1	By many

WALKS (Since 1910 in NL; Since 1913 in AL)

Most Seasons Leading Major Leagues
11	Babe Ruth, AL:NY 1920-21, 23-24, 26-28, 30-33

Most Seasons, Consecutive, Leading Major Leagues
4	Babe Ruth, AL:NY 1930-33
	Barry Bonds, NL:SF 2001-04

Most Seasons Leading League
12	Barry Bonds, NL:Pitt. 1992; SF 94-97, 2000-04, 06-07
11	Babe Ruth, AL:NY 1920-21, 23-24, 26-28, 30-33

Most Seasons, Consecutive, Leading League
5	Mel Ott, NL:NY 1929-1933
	Barry Bonds, NL:SF 2000-04
4	Babe Ruth, AL:NY 1930-33
	Ted Williams, AL:Bos. 1946-49

Most Walks, Lifetime
2558	Barry Bonds, NL:Pitt. 1986-92; SF 93-2007
2043	Babe Ruth, AL:Bos. 1914-19; NY 20-34

Most Walks, Season
232	Barry Bonds, NL:SF 2004
170	Babe Ruth, AL:NY 1923

Most Seasons, 100 or more Walks
14	Barry Bonds, NL:Pitt. 1991-92; SF 93, 95-98, 2000-04, 06-07
13	Babe Ruth, AL:Bos. 1919; NY 20-21, 23-24, 26-28, 30-34

Most Seasons, Consecutive, 100 or more Walks
8	Max Bishop, AL:Phil. 1926-33
	Frank Thomas, AL:Chi. 1991-98
	Bobby Abreu, NL:Phil. 1999-2005; NL:Phil.-AL:NY 2006
7	Mel Ott, NL:NY 1936-42
	Jeff Bagwell, NL:Hou. 1996-2002
	Bobby Abreu, NL:Phil. 1998-2005

Most Walks, Game
6	Walter Wilmot, NL:Chi. Aug. 22, 1891 (cons)
	Jeff Bagwell, NL:Hou. Aug. 20, 1999 (16 inn)
	Bryce Harper, NL:Wash. May 8, 2016 (13 inn)
	Jimmie Foxx, AL:Bos. June 16, 1938 (cons)
	Andre Thornton, AL:Clev. May 2, 1984 (16 inn)
	NL Since 1900 (nine-inning game):
5	By many in NL; last:
	Christian Yelich, NL:Mil. Sept. 26, 2018 (cons)

Most Games, 5 or more Walks, League
4	Mel Ott, NL:NY Oct. 5, 1929(2g); Sept. 1(1g), 1933; June 17, 1943; Apr. 30(1g), 1944
2	Max Bishop, AL:Phil. Apr. 29, 1929; May 21(1g), 1930
	Larry Doby, AL:Clev. Sept. 19, 1951; July 1, 1952 (19 inn)
	Albie Pearson, AL:LA July 25, 1961 (14 inn); Apr. 24, 1963 (15 inn)
	Rickey Henderson, AL:Oak. Apr. 8, 1982 (16 inn); Sea. July 30, 2000
	Mark Teixeira, AL:Tex. Sept. 23, 2004; NY Apr. 25, 2009
	Alex Gordon, AL:KC July 30, 2008 (10 inn); June 17, 2012 (15 inn)

Most Games, Consecutive, 1 or more Walks, Lifetime
22	Roy Cullenbine, AL:Det. July 2-22, 1947
20	Barry Bonds, NL:SF Sept. 9, 2002-Apr. 1, 2003

Most Games, Consecutive, 1 or more Walks, Season
22	Roy Cullenbine, AL:Det. July 2-22, 1947
18	Barry Bonds, NL:SF Sept. 9-28, 2002

Most Walks, Consecutive, Season

7	Billy Rogell, AL:Det. Aug. 17-19, 1938
	Jose Canseco, AL:Oak. Aug. 4-5, 1992
	Mel Ott, NL:NY June 16-18, 1943
	Eddie Stanky, NL:NY Aug. 29-30, 1950
	Barry Bonds, NL:SF Sept. 24-26, 2004

Most Walks, Inning

2	By many

INTENTIONAL WALKS (Since 1955)

Most Seasons Leading Major Leagues

10	Barry Bonds, NL:Pitt. 1992; SF 93, 96-98, 2002-04, 06-07

Most Seasons, Consecutive, Leading Major Leagues

4	Frank Robinson, NL:Cin. 1961-64

Most Seasons Leading League

12	Barry Bonds, NL:Pitt. 1992; SF 93-98, 2002-04, 06-07
6	Wade Boggs, AL:Bos. 1987-92

Most Seasons, Consecutive, Leading League

7	Barry Bonds, NL:Pitt. 1992; SF 93-98
6	Wade Boggs, AL:Bos. 1987-92

Most Intentional Walks, Lifetime

688	Barry Bonds, NL:Pitt. 1986-92; SF 93-2007
228	George Brett, AL:KC 1973-93

Most Intentional Walks, Season

120	Barry Bonds, NL:SF 2004
34	Ted Williams, AL:Bos. 1957

Most Seasons, 20 or more Intentional Walks

15	Barry Bonds, NL:Pitt. 1989, 91-92; SF 93, 95-98, 2000-04, 06-07
3	Frank Thomas, AL:Chi. 1993, 95-96
	Ken Griffey Jr., AL:Sea. 1991, 93, 97
	Vladimir Guerrero, AL:LA 2005-07
	David Ortiz, AL:Bos. 2006, 13-14

Most Seasons Consecutive, 20 or more Intentional Walks

6	Albert Pujols, NL:StL. 2005-10
3	Vladimir Guerrero, AL:LA 2005-07

Most Intentional Walks, Game

4	Barry Bonds, NL:SF May 1, 2004; Sept. 22, 2004
3	By many in AL
	Extra-Inning Game:
5	Andre Dawson, NL:Chi. May 22, 1990 (16 inn)
4	Roger Maris, AL:NY May 22, 1962 (12 inn)
	Manny Ramirez, AL:Bos. June 5, 2001 (18 inn)

Most Intentional Walks, Inning

1	By many

HIT BY PITCH

Most Seasons Leading Major Leagues

9	Minnie Minoso, AL:Clev.-Chi. 1951; Chi. 53-54, 56-57, 60-61; Clev. 58-59

Most Seasons, Consecutive, Leading Major Leagues

6	Minnie Minoso, AL:Chi. 1956-57, 60-61; Clev. 58-59
	Ron Hunt, NL:SF 1968-70; Mtl. 71-73

Most Seasons Leading League

10	Minnie Minoso, AL:Clev.-Chi. 1951; Chi. 52-54, 56-57, 60-61; Clev. 58-59
7	Ron Hunt, NL:SF 1968-70; Mtl. 71-73; Mtl.-StL. 74

Most Seasons, Consecutive, Leading League

7	Ron Hunt, NL:SF 1968-70; Mtl. 71-73; Mtl.-StL. 74
6	Minnie Minoso, AL:Chi. 1956-57, 60-61; Clev. 58-59

Most Hit By Pitch, Lifetime

287	Hughie Jennings, AA:Lou. 1891; NL:Lou. 92-93; Balt. 93-99; Brk. 99-1900, 03; Phil. 01-02; AL:Det. 1907, 09, 12, 18

Most Hit By Pitch, League

285	Craig Biggio, NL:Hou. 1988-2007
267	Don Baylor, AL:Balt. 1970-75; Oak. 76, 88; Cal. 77-82; NY 83-85; Bos. 86-87; Minn. 87

Most Hit By Pitch, Season
51	Hughie Jennings, NL:Balt. 1896

Since 1900:
50	Ron Hunt, NL:Mtl. 1971
35	Don Baylor, AL:Bos. 1986

Most Hit By Pitch, Game
3	By many; last:
	Derek Dietrich, NL:Cin. June 21, 2019
	Jurickson Profar, AL:Tex. June 23, 2018

Most Hit By Pitch, Doubleheader
4	Frank Chance, NL:Chi. May 30, 1904
3	By many in AL

Most Hit By Pitch, Inning
2	Willard Schmidt, NL:Cin. Apr. 26, 1959 (3rd)
	Frank Thomas, NL:NY Apr. 29(1g), 1962 (4th)
	Andres Galarraga, NL:Col. July 12, 1996 (7th)
	Jose Guillen, NL:SF Sept. 23, 2010 (2nd)
	David DeJesus, NL:Chi. June 18, 2012 (7th)
	Brady Anderson, AL:Balt. May 23, 1999 (1st)
	Mike Hessman, AL:Det. Sept. 8, 2008 (2nd)
	Brandon Moss, AL:Oak. Apr. 25, 2014 (9th)

Most Plate Appearances, Season, No Hit By Pitch
739	Sandy Alomar Sr. AL:Cal. 1971
728	Cesar Izturis, NL:LA 2004

STRIKEOUTS (Since 1910 in NL; Since 1913 in AL)

Most Seasons Leading Major Leagues
4	Babe Ruth, AL:Bos. 1918; NY 23-24, 27
	Rob Deer, AL:Mil. 1987-88; Det. 91; Det.-Bos. 93
	Adam Dunn, NL:Cin. 2004-06; AL:Chi. 2012

Most Seasons, Consecutive, Leading Major Leagues
3	Hack Wilson, NL:Chi. 1928-30
	Mike Schmidt, NL:Phil. 1974-76
	Adam Dunn, NL:Cin. 2004-06
	Mark Reynolds, NL:Ari. 2008-10

Most Seasons Leading League
6	Vince DiMaggio, NL:Bos. 1937-38; Pitt. 42-44; Phil. 45
5	Jimmie Foxx, AL:Phil. 1930, 33, 35; Bos. 36, 41
	Mickey Mantle, AL:NY 1952, 54, 58-60
	Reggie Jackson, AL:Oak. 1968-71, Cal. 82

Most Seasons, Consecutive, Leading League
4	Hack Wilson, NL:Chi. 1927-30
	Vince DiMaggio, NL:Pitt. 1942-44; Phil. 45
	Juan Samuel, NL:Phil. 1984-87
	Reggie Jackson, AL:Oak. 1968-71
	Mark Reynolds, NL:Ari. 2008-10; AL:Balt. 11

Most Strikeouts, Lifetime
2596	Reggie Jackson, AL:Oak. 1968-75, 87; Balt. 76; NY 77-81; Cal. 82-86
1936	Willie Stargell, NL:Pitt. 1962-82

Most Strikeouts, Season
223	Mark Reynolds, NL:Ari. 2009
222	Adam Dunn, AL:Chi. 2012

Most Seasons, 100 or more Strikeouts, Lifetime
18	Reggie Jackson, AL:Oak. 1968-75; Balt. 76; NY 77-80; Cal. 82-86
13	Willie Stargell, NL:Pitt. 1965-76, 79

Most Seasons, Consecutive, 100 or more Strikeouts, Lifetime
14	Bobby Abreu, NL:Phil. 1998-2005; NL:Phil.-AL:NY 06; AL:NY 07-08; LA 09-11
13	Reggie Jackson, AL:Oak. 1968-75; Balt. 76; NY 77-80
12	Willie Stargell, NL:Pitt. 1965-76

Most Strikeouts, Consecutive At-Bats, Season
18	Sandy Alcantara, NL:Mia. Aug. 22-Sept. 29, 2019
14	Dean Chance, AL:Minn. May 6-June 1, 1968
	Vida Blue, AL:Oak. Aug. 13-Sept. 22, 1972

Most Strikeouts, Consecutive Plate Appearances, Season

13	Dean Chance, AL:Minn. May 10-June 1, 1968
	Roy Halladay, NL:Phil. Apr. 3-Aug. 25, 2013
	Non-Pitcher:
10	Rick Ankiel, AL:Hou. Apr. 2-8, 2013
	Jarrod Saltalamacchia, AL:Tor. Apr. 13-22, 2017
9	Adolfo Phillips, NL:Chi. June 8-11, 1966
	Eric Davis, NL:Cin. Apr. 24-25, 1987
	Mark Reynolds, NL:Ari. Aug. 18-21, 2007
	Wil Myers, NL:SD June 30-July 5, 2017
	Dylan Cozens, NL:Phil. July 1-Sept. 12, 2018

Most Strikeouts, Game

5	By many; last:
	Matt Chapman, AL:Oak. Sept. 5, 2020 (cons)
	Javier Baez, NL:Chi. May 27, 2019 (cons)
	Extra-Inning Game:
6	Carl Weilman, AL:StL. July 25, 1913 (15 inn; cons)
	Rick Reichardt, AL:Cal. May 31, 1966 (17 inn)
	Billy Cowan, AL:Cal. July 9, 1971 (20 inn)
	Cecil Cooper, AL:Bos. June 14, 1974 (15 inn)
	Sam Horn, AL:Balt. July 17, 1991 (15 inn)
	Alex Gonzalez, AL:Tor. Sept. 9, 1998 (13 inn)
	Don Hoak, NL:Chi. May 2, 1956 (17 inn)
	Geoff Jenkins, NL:Mil. June 8, 2004 (17 inn)

Most Strikeouts, Inning

2	By many

Most Games, Consecutive, No Strikeouts (Minimum: 1 pa)

115	Joe Sewell, AL:Clev. May 19-Sept. 19, 1929
93	Stuffy McInnis, NL:Bos. May 22-Aug. 30, 1924

GROUNDED INTO DOUBLE PLAYS (Since 1933 in NL; Since 1940 in AL)

Most Seasons Leading Major Leagues

4	Jim Rice, AL:Bos. 1982-85

Most Seasons, Consecutive, Leading Major Leagues

4	Jim Rice, AL:Bos. 1982-85

Most Seasons Leading League

5	Miguel Tejada, AL:Balt. 2004-06; NL:Hou. 08-09
4	Ernie Lombardi, NL:Cin. 1933-34, 38; NY 44
	Jim Rice, AL:Bos. 1982-85

Most Seasons, Consecutive, Leading League

4	Jim Rice, AL:Bos. 1982-85
2	Ernie Lombardi, NL:Cin. 1933-34
	Frank McCormick, NL:Cin. 1940-41
	Joe Torre, NL:Mil. 1964-65
	Willie Montanez, NL:Phil.-SF 1975; SF-Atl. 76
	Ray Knight, NL:Cin. 1980-81
	Miguel Tejada, NL:Hou. 2008-09

Most Grounded into Double Plays, Lifetime

399	Albert Pujols, NL:StL. 2001-11; AL:LA 12-20
350	Cal Ripken, AL:Balt. 1981-2001
310	Hank Aaron, NL:Mil./Atl. 1954-74

Most Grounded Into Double Plays, Season

36	Jim Rice, AL Bos. 1984
32	Miguel Tejada, NL:Hou. 2008

Most Grounded Into Double Plays, Game

4	Joe Torre, NL:NY July 21, 1975 (cons)
3	By many in AL

Most Grounded Into Double Plays, 2 Consecutive Games

5	Zeke Bonura, NL:NY July 8-9, 1939
4	By many in AL

Most At-Bats, No Grounded Into Double Plays, Season

646	Augie Galan, NL:Chi. 1935
570	Dick McAuliffe, AL:Det. 1968

STOLEN BASES (Prior to 1898 stolen bases credited on fielder's choice)

Most Seasons Leading Major Leagues

6	Lou Brock, NL:StL. 1966, 68, 71-74
	Rickey Henderson, AL:Oak. 1980, 82-83, 98; NY 88; NY-Oak. 89

Most Seasons, Consecutive, Leading Major Leagues
5 George Case, AL:Wash. 1939-43

Most Seasons Leading League
12 Rickey Henderson, AL:Oak. 1980-84, 90-91, 98; NY 85-86, 88; NY-Oak. 89
10 Max Carey, NL:Pitt. 1913, 15-18, 20, 22-25

Most Seasons, Consecutive, Leading League
9 Luis Aparicio, AL:Chi. 1956-62; Balt. 63-64
6 Maury Wills, NL:LA 1960-65
Vince Coleman, NL:StL. 1985-90

Most Stolen Bases, Lifetime
1406 Rickey Henderson, AL:Oak. 1979-84, 89-95, 98; NY 85-89; Tor. 93; Ana. 97; Sea. 2000; Bos. 02; NL:SD 96-97, 2001; NY 99-2000; LA 03

Most Stolen Bases, League
1270 Rickey Henderson, AL:Oak. 1979-84, 89-95, 98; NY 85-89; Tor. 93; Ana. 97; Sea. 2000; Bos. 02
938 Lou Brock, NL:Chi. 1961-64; StL. 64-79

Most Stolen Bases, Season
156 Harry Stovey, AA:Phil. 1888
Since 1900:
130 Rickey Henderson, AL:Oak. 1982
118 Lou Brock, NL:StL. 1974

Most Seasons, 100 or more Stolen Bases
3 Rickey Henderson, AL:Oak. 1980, 82-83
Vince Coleman, NL:StL. 1985-87

Most Seasons, Consecutive, 100 or more Stolen Bases
3 Vince Coleman, NL:StL. 1985-87
2 Rickey Henderson, AL:Oak. 1982-83

Most Seasons, 50 or more Stolen Bases
13 Rickey Henderson, AL:Oak. 1980-84, 90-91, 98; NY 85-86, 88; NY-Oak. 89; Oak.-Tor. 93
12 Lou Brock, NL:StL. 1965-76

Most Seasons, Consecutive, 50 or more Stolen Bases
12 Lou Brock, NL:StL. 1965-76
7 Rickey Henderson, AL:Oak. 1980-84; NY 85-86

Most Stolen Bases, Consecutive, Lifetime
50 Vince Coleman, NL:StL. Sept. 18, 1988-July 26, 1989
45 Ichiro Suzuki, AL:Sea. Apr. 29, 2006-May 16, 2007

Most Stolen Bases, Consecutive, Season
44 Vince Coleman, NL:StL. Apr. 3-July 26, 1989
39 Ichiro Suzuki, AL:Sea. Apr. 29-Sept. 30, 2006

Most Stolen Bases, Game
7 George Gore, NL:Chi. June 25, 1881
Billy Hamilton, NL:Phil. Aug. 31(2g), 1894
Since 1900:
6 Eddie Collins, AL:Phil. Sept. 11, 22(1g), 1912
Carl Crawford, AL:TB May 3, 2009
Otis Nixon, NL:Atl. June 16, 1991
Eric Young, NL:Col. June 30, 1996

Most Stolen Bases, Inning
3 By many; last:
Jon Berti, NL:Mia. Aug. 25(2g), 2020 (6th)
Mallex Smith, AL:Sea. May 27, 2019 (8th)

Most Stolen Home, Lifetime
54 Ty Cobb, AL:Det. 1905-26; Phil. 27-28
33 Max Carey, NL:Pitt. 1910-26, Brk. 26-29

Most Stolen Home, Season
8 Ty Cobb, AL:Det. 1912
7 Pete Reiser, NL:Brk. 1946

Most Stolen Home, Game
2 Honus Wagner, NL:Pitt. June 20, 1901
Ed Konetchy, NL:StL. Sept. 30, 1907
Joe Tinker, NL:Chi. June 28, 1910
Larry Doyle, NL:NY Sept. 18, 1911
Sherry Magee, NL:Phil. July 20, 1912
Doc Gautreau, NL:Bos. Sept. 3(1g), 1927
Joe Jackson, AL:Clev. Aug. 11, 1912
Guy Zinn, AL:NY Aug. 15, 1912
Eddie Collins, AL:Phil. Sept. 6, 1913
Ty Cobb, AL:Det. June 18, 1915
Bill Barrett, AL:Chi. May 1, 1924
Vic Power, AL:Clev. Aug. 14, 1958 (10 inn)

Highest Percentage Successful, Lifetime (Minimum: 300 stolen bases)
.864   Carlos Beltran, AL:KC 1998-2004; NY 14-16; Tex. 16; NL:Hou. 04; NY 05-11; SF 11; StL. 12-13 (312-361)

Highest Percentage Successful, League (Minimum: 300 stolen bases)
.857   Tim Raines, NL:Mtl. 1979-90, 2001; Fla. 2002 (635-741)
.833   Willie Wilson, AL:KC 1976-90; Oak. 91-92 (660-792)

Highest Percentage Successful, Season (Minimum: 30 stolen bases)
.969   Brady Anderson, AL:Balt. 1994 (31-32; ML record)
        Carlos Beltran, AL:KC 2001 (31-32; ML record)
.971   Dave Roberts, NL:LA 2004 (33-34)
        (.927, NL:LA-AL:Bos. 2004; 38-41)

Most Stolen Bases, None Caught, Season
23   Chase Utley, NL:Phil. 2009

Most Stolen Bases, None Caught, Season, League
28   Carlos Beltran, NL:Hou. 2004 (3 cs with AL:KC)
22   Alcides Escobar, AL:KC 2013

CAUGHT STEALING (Since 1920 in AL; Since 1951 in NL)

Most Seasons Leading Major Leagues
6   Maury Wills, NL:LA 1961-63, 65-66; Mtl.-LA 69

Most Seasons, Consecutive, Leading Major Leagues
3   Maury Wills, NL:LA 1961-63

Most Seasons Leading League
7   Maury Wills, NL:LA 1961-63, 65-66; Pitt. 68; Mtl.-LA 69
        Lou Brock, NL:Chi.-StL. 1964; StL. 67, 71, 73-74, 76-77
        Juan Pierre, NL:Col. 2001; Fla. 03-05; Chi. 06; AL:Chi. 10-11
6   Minnie Minoso, AL:Chi. 1952-54, 57, 60; Clev. 58

Most Seasons, Consecutive, Leading League
4   Ben Chapman, AL:NY 1931-34
        Rickey Henderson, AL:Oak. 1980-83
        Juan Pierre, NL:Fla. 2003-05; NL:Chi. 06

Most Caught Stealing, Lifetime
335   Rickey Henderson, AL:Oak. 1979-84, 89-95, 98; NY 85-89; Tor. 93; Ana. 97; Sea. 2000;
                         Bos. 02; NL:SD 97, 2001; NY 99-2000; LA 03

Most Caught Stealing, League
306   Lou Brock, NL:Chi. 1961-64; StL. 64-79
293   Rickey Henderson, AL:Oak. 1979-84, 89-95, 98; NY 85-89; Tor. 93; Ana. 97;
                         Sea. 2000; Bos. 02

Most Caught Stealing, Season
42   Rickey Henderson, AL:Oak. 1982 (172 attempts)
33   Lou Brock, NL:StL. 1974 (151 attempts)
        Omar Moreno, NL:Pitt. 1980 (129 attempts)

Most Caught Stealing, Game
3   By many
        Extra-Inning Game:
4   Robby Thompson, NL:SF June 27, 1986 (12 inn)

Most Caught Stealing, Inning
2   Bob Allison, AL:Minn. Sept. 8, 1969 (2nd)
        Don Baylor, AL:Balt. June 15, 1974 (9th)
        Roberto Kelly, AL:NY Apr. 17, 1990 (2nd)
        Kevin Kiermaier, AL:TB Apr. 16, 2019 (7th)
        Jim Morrison, NL:Pitt. June 15, 1987 (8th)
        Paul Noce, NL:Chi. June 26, 1987 (3rd)
        Donell Nixon, NL:SF July 6, 1988 (6th)
        Tony Fernandez, NL:SD June 26, 1992 (5th)
        Eric Young, NL:Col. May 1, 1993 (8th)
        Phil Plantier, NL:SD Sept. 25, 1993 (5th)
        Derek Bell, NL:Hou. June 19, 1995 (4th)
        Larry Walker, NL:Col. Apr. 30, 1998 (8th)
        Brandon Phillips, NL:Cin. July 7, 2011 (2nd)

PINCH HITTING

Most Games, Season
109   Ichiro Suzuki, NL:Mia. 2017
81   Elmer Valo, AL:NY-Wash. 1960

Most At-Bats, Lifetime
804   Lenny Harris, NL:Cin. 1988-89, 94-98; LA 89-93; NY 98, 2000-01; Col. 99; Ari. 2000;
                   Mil. 02; Chi. 03; Fla. 03-05
423   Gates Brown, AL:Det. 1963-75

Most At-Bats, Season
100	Ichiro Suzuki, NL:Mia. 2017
72	Dave Philley, AL:Balt. 1961

Most Hits, Lifetime
212	Lenny Harris, NL:Cin. 1988-89, 94-98; LA 89-93; NY 98, 2000-01; Col. 99; Ari. 2000; Mil. 02; Chi. 03; Fla. 03-05
106	Gates Brown, AL:Det. 1963-75

Most Hits, Season
28	John Vander Wal, NL:Col. 1995
24	Dave Philley, AL:Balt. 1961

Most Hits, Consecutive At-Bats, Major Leagues
9	Dave Philley, NL:Phil. Sept. 9, 1958-Apr. 16, 1959

Most Hits, Consecutive At-Bats, Season
8	Dave Philley, NL:Phil. Sept. 9-28, 1958
	Rusty Staub, NL:NY June 11-26(1g), 1983
7	Bill Stein, AL:Tex. Apr. 14-May 25, 1981
	Randy Bush, AL:Minn. July 5-Aug. 19, 1991
	Ross Gload, AL:Chi. July 2-Sept. 3, 2006

Most Home Runs, Lifetime
23	Matt Stairs, AL:Oak. 1996-98, KC 2005-06, Det. 06; Tor. 07; NL:Mil. 02, Pitt. 03, Phil. 08-09, SD 10

Most Home Runs, League
18	Jerry Lynch, NL:Cin.1957-59, 61-63; Pitt. 63-66
16	Gates Brown, AL:Det. 1963-66, 68, 70-72, 74-75

Most Home Runs, Season
7	Dave Hansen, NL:LA 2000
	Craig Wilson, NL:Pitt. 2001
5	Joe Cronin, AL:Bos. 1943

Most Home Runs, Consecutive At-Bats, Season
3	Lee Lacy, NL:LA May 2, 6, 17, 1978
	Del Unser, NL:Phil. June 30, July 5, 10, 1979
	Matthew LeCroy, AL:Minn. May 19, June 1, 17, 2004

Most Grand Slam Home Runs, Lifetime
3	Ron Northey, NL:StL. Sept. 3, 1947; May 30, 1948; Chi. Sept. 18, 1950
	Willie McCovey, NL:SF June 12, 1960; Sept. 10, 1965; SD May 30, 1975
	Rich Reese, AL:Minn. Aug. 3, 1969; June 7, 1970; July 9, 1972
	Ben Broussard, AL:Clev. June 23, Aug. 12, 2004; Sea. Apr. 21, 2007

Most Grand Slam Home Runs, Season
2	Dave Johnson, NL:Phil. Apr. 30, June 3, 1978
	Mike Ivie, NL:SF May 28, June 30, 1978
	Brooks Conrad, NL:Atl. May 20, July 24, 2010
	Darryl Strawberry, AL:NY May 2, Aug. 4, 1998
	Ben Broussard, AL:Clev. June 23, Aug. 12, 2004

Most Walks, Season
21	Matt Joyce, NL:Pitt. 2016
18	Earl Torgeson, AL:Chi. 1960
	Elmer Valo, AL:Wash. 1960

Most Runs Batted In, Season
25	Joe Cronin, AL:Bos. 1943
	Jerry Lynch, NL:Cin. 1961
	Rusty Staub, NL:NY 1983

ROOKIE BATTING

(No official rookie rule prior to 1958. Qualifiers based on 130 or fewer previous at-bats. Records listed are for a single season.)

Highest Batting Average (Minimum: 350 at-bats)
.408	Joe Jackson, AL:Clev. 1911
.373	George Watkins, NL:StL. 1930

Highest Slugging Percentage (Minimum: 350 at-bats)
.651	Rudy York, AL:Det. 1937
.634	Ryan Braun, NL:Mil. 2007

Most Games
163	Hideki Matsui, AL:NY 2003
162	Dick Allen, NL:Phil. 1964
	Johnny Ray, NL:Pitt. 1982
	Jeff Conine, NL:Fla. 1993

Most At-Bats
701	Juan Samuel, NL:Phil. 1984
692	Ichiro Suzuki, AL:Sea. 2001

Most Runs
152	Mike Griffin, AA:Balt. 1887
135	Roy Thomas, NL:Phil. 1899
	Since 1900:
133	Lloyd Waner, NL:Pitt. 1927
132	Joe DiMaggio, AL:NY 1936

Most Hits
242	Ichiro Suzuki, AL:Sea. 2001
223	Lloyd Waner, NL:Pitt. 1927

Most Games, Consecutive, Hits
34	Benito Santiago, NL:SD Aug. 25-Oct. 2, 1987
30	Nomar Garciaparra, AL:Bos. July 26-Aug. 29, 1997

Most Extra-Base Hits
89	Hal Trosky, AL:Clev. 1934
88	Albert Pujols, NL:StL. 2001

Most Total Bases
374	Hal Trosky, AL:Clev. 1934
	Tony Oliva, AL:Minn. 1964
360	Albert Pujols, NL:StL. 2001

Most Singles
198	Lloyd Waner, NL:Pitt. 1927
192	Ichiro Suzuki, AL:Sea. 2001

Most Doubles
52	Johnny Frederick, NL:Brk. 1929
47	Fred Lynn, AL:Bos. 1975
	Miguel Andujar, AL:NY 2018

Most Triples
27	Jimmy Williams, NL:Pitt. 1899
	Since 1900:
25	Tommy Long, NL:StL. 1915
19	Joe Cassidy, AL:Wash. 1904
	Frank Baker, AL:Phil. 1909
	Joe Jackson, AL:Clev. 1911

Most Home Runs
53	Pete Alonso, NL:NY 2019
52	Aaron Judge, AL:NY 2017

Most Runs Batted In
145	Ted Williams, AL:Bos. 1939
130	Albert Pujols, NL:StL. 2001

Most Sacrifice Hits (Since 1931)
28	Joe Hoover, AL:Det. 1943
	Jackie Robinson, NL:Brk. 1947
	Ozzie Smith, NL:SD 1978

Most Sacrifice Flies (Since 1954)
13	Willie Montanez, NL:Phil. 1971
	Gary Gaetti, AL:Minn. 1982

Most Walks (Since 1910 in NL; Since 1913 in AL)
127	Aaron Judge, AL:NY 2017
100	Jim Gilliam, NL:Brk. 1953

Most Intentional Walks (Since 1955)
16	Alvin Davis, AL:Sea. 1984
14	Willie Montanez, NL:Phil. 1971

Most Hit By Pitch
29	Tommy Tucker, AA:Balt. 1887
	Since 1900:
25	Victor Robles, NL:Wash. 2019
21	David Eckstein, AL:Ana. 2001

Most Strikeouts (Since 1910 in NL; Since 1913 in AL)
208	Aaron Judge, AL:NY 2017
199	Kris Bryant, NL:Chi. 2015

Most Stolen Bases (Since 1898)
110	Vince Coleman, NL:StL. 1985
66	Kenny Lofton, AL:Clev. 1992

Most Caught Stealing (Since 1920 in AL; Since 1951 in NL)
25	Vince Coleman, NL:StL. 1985
21	Jerry Remy, AL:Cal. 1975
	Mike Edwards, AL:Oak. 1978

Most Grounded Into Double Plays
28	George Kell, AL:Phil. 1944
26	Sid Gordon, NL:NY 1943

INDIVIDUAL FIELDING

(Career percentage leaders based on 1000-game minimum; pitchers' minimum: 300 tc)

FIRST BASE

Most Seasons, League
22	Willie McCovey, NL:SF 1959-73, 77-80; SD 74-76
20	Joe Judge, AL:Wash. 1915-32; Bos. 33-34

PERCENTAGE

Most Seasons Leading League
7	Ed Konetchy, NL:StL. 1910-11, 13; Pitt. 14; Bos. 17-18; Brk. 19
	Charlie Grimm, NL:Pitt. 1920, 23-24; Chi. 28, 30-31, 33
	Don Mattingly, AL:NY 1984-87, 92-94

Most Seasons, Consecutive, Leading League
5	Ted Kluszewski, NL:Cin. 1951-55
4	Don Mattingly, AL:NY 1984-87

Highest Percentage, Lifetime
.997	Travis Lee, NL:Ari. 1998-2000; Phil. 00-02; AL:TB 03, 05-06; NY 04

Highest Percentage, League
.997	Mark Teixeira, AL:Tex. 2003-07; LA 08; NY 09-16
.996	Paul Goldschmidt, NL:Ari. 2011-18; StL. 19-20

Highest Percentage, Season (Most Chances)
1.000	Steve Garvey, NL:SD 1984 (1319 tc)
	Kevin Youkilis, AL:Bos. 2007 (1080 tc)

Lowest Percentage, Season, Since 1900
.970	John Doyle, NL:NY 1900
.972	Pat Newnam, AL:StL. 1910

GAMES

Most Seasons Leading League
9	Steve Garvey, NL:LA 1975-81; SD 84-85
7	Lou Gehrig, AL:NY 1926-28, 32, 36-38

Most Games, Lifetime
2413	Eddie Murray, AL:Balt. 1977-88, 96; Clev. 94-96; NL:LA 1989-91; NY 92-93

Most Games, League
2247	Jake Beckley, NL:Pitt. 1888-89, 91-96; NY 96-97; Cin. 1897-1903; StL. 04-07
2227	Mickey Vernon, AL:Wash. 1939-43, 46-48, 50-55; Clev. 49-50, 58; Bos. 56-57

Most Games, Consecutive
885	Lou Gehrig, AL:NY June 2, 1925-Sept. 27, 1930
652	Frank McCormick, NL:Cin. Apr. 19, 1938-May 24, 1942

Most Games, Season
162	Norm Siebern, AL:KC 1962
	Bill Buckner, AL:Bos. 1985
	Carlos Delgado, AL:Tor. 2000
	Matt Olson, AL:Oak. 2018
	Bill White, NL:StL. 1963
	Ernie Banks, NL:Chi. 1965
	Steve Garvey, NL:LA 1976, 79-80; SD 85
	Pete Rose, NL:Phil. 1980, 82
	Jeff Bagwell, NL:Hou. 1996
	Eric Karros, NL:LA 1997
	Derrek Lee, NL:Fla. 2002
	Richie Sexson, NL:Mil. 2003
	Prince Fielder, NL:Mil. 2009
	Freddie Freeman, NL:Atl. 2014
	Joey Votto, NL:Cin. 2017

CHANCES ACCEPTED

Most Seasons Leading League
6	Bill Terry, NL:NY 1927-30, 32, 34
4	Wally Pipp, AL:NY 1915, 19-20, 22
	Carlos Delgado, AL:Tor. 2000-03

Most Chances Accepted, Lifetime
25,000   Jake Beckley, NL:Pitt. 1888-89, 91-96; NY 96-97; Cin. 1897-1903; StL. 04-07; PL:Pitt. 1890

Most Chances Accepted, League
23,687   Jake Beckley, NL:Pitt. 1888-89, 91-96; NY 96-97; Cin. 1897-1903; StL. 04-07
21,198   Mickey Vernon, AL:Wash. 1939-43, 46-48, 50-55; Clev. 49-50, 58; Bos. 56-57

Most Chances Accepted, Season
1986   Jiggs Donahue, AL:Chi. 1907
1862   George Kelly, NL:NY 1920

Most Chances Accepted, Game
22   By many; last:
      Alvin Davis, AL:Sea. May 28, 1988
      Ernie Banks, NL:Chi. May 9, 1963
      Extra-Inning Game:
43   Walter Holke, NL:Bos. May 1, 1920 (26 inn)
34   Rudy York, AL:Det. July 21, 1945 (24 inn)
      Mike Epstein, AL:Wash. June 12, 1967 (22 inn)
      Rod Carew, AL:Cal. Apr. 13, 1982 (20 inn)

Fewest Chances Accepted, Game (Complete Nine-Inning Game)
0   Guy Hecker, AA:Lou. Oct. 9, 1887
      Al McCauley, AA:Wash. Aug. 6, 1891
      Bud Clancy, AL:Chi. Apr. 27, 1930
      Norm Cash, AL:Det. June 27, 1963
      Gene Tenace, AL:Oak. Sept. 1, 1974
      Mark McGwire, AL:Oak. Sept. 12, 1995
      Scott Cooper, AL:KC May 31, 1997 (8 inn)
      Robb Quinlan, AL:Ana. Aug. 6, 2003 (8 inn)
      Chris Davis, AL:Tex. Aug. 9, 2008 (8 inn)
      Billy Butler, AL:KC June 3, 2010
      Edwin Encarnacion, AL:Tor. Aug. 25, 2012 (8 inn)
      Joe Mauer, AL:Minn. July 3, 2018 (8 inn)
      Ripper Collins, NL:Chi. June 29, 1937
      Fred McGriff, NL:Chi. Aug. 15, 2002
      Nomar Garciaparra, NL:LA May 11, 2007
      Jesus Aguilar, NL:Mil. Apr. 3, 2019

PUTOUTS

Most Seasons Leading League
6   Jake Beckley, NL:Pitt. 1892, 94-95; Cin. 1900, 02; StL. 04
      Frank McCormick, NL:Cin. 1939-42, 44-45
      Steve Garvey, NL:LA 1974-78; SD 85
5   Carlos Delgado, AL:Tor. 1999-2003

Most Putouts, Lifetime
23,696   Jake Beckley, NL:Pitt. 1888-89, 91-96; NY 96-97; Cin. 1897-1903; StL. 04-07; PL:Pitt. 1890

Most Putouts, League
22,438   Jake Beckley, NL:Pitt. 1888-89, 91-96; NY 96-97; Cin. 1897-1903; StL. 04-07
19,754   Mickey Vernon, AL:Wash. 1939-43, 46-48, 50-55; Clev. 49-50, 58; Bos. 56-57

Most Putouts, Season
1846   Jiggs Donahue, AL:Chi. 1907
1759   George Kelly, NL:NY 1920

Most Putouts, Game
22   Tom Jones, AL:StL. May 11, 1906
      Hal Chase, AL:NY Sept. 21(1g), 1906
      Don Mattingly, AL:NY July 20, 1987
      Alvin Davis, AL:Sea. May 28, 1988
      Ernie Banks, NL:Chi. May 9, 1963
      Extra-Inning Game:
42   Walter Holke, NL:Bos. May 1, 1920 (26 inn)
32   Mike Epstein, AL:Wash. June 12, 1967 (22 inn)
      Rod Carew, AL:Cal. Apr. 13, 1982 (20 inn)

Fewest Putouts, Game (Complete Nine-Inning Game)

0	Guy Hecker, AA:Lou. Oct. 9, 1887 (8 inn)
	Al McCauley, AA:Wash. Aug. 6, 1891
	Solly Hofman, NL:Chi. June 24, 1910 (8 inn)
	Ripper Collins, NL:StL. Aug. 21, 1935; Chi. June 29, 1937
	Dolph Camilli, NL:Phil. July 30, 1937
	Earl Torgeson, NL:Bos. May 30(1g), 1947
	Gary Thomasson, NL:SF July 31, 1977 (8 inn)
	Len Matuszek, NL:Phil. June 1, 1984
	Franklin Stubbs, NL:Hou. July 25, 1990
	Fred McGriff, NL:Chi. Aug. 15, 2002
	Nomar Garciaparra, NL:LA May 11, 2007
	Jesus Aguilar, NL:Mil. Apr. 3, 2019
	Bud Clancy, AL:Chi. Apr. 27, 1930
	Rudy York, AL:Det. June 18, 1943
	Norm Cash, AL:Det. June 27, 1963 (8 inn)
	Bill Skowron, AL:Chi. May 15, 1966 (8 inn)
	Gene Tenace, AL:Oak. Sept. 1, 1974
	Greg Brock, AL:Mil. June 28, 1987
	Mark McGwire, AL:Oak. Sept. 12, 1995
	Scott Cooper, AL:KC May 31, 1997 (8 inn)
	Rafael Palmeiro, AL:Balt. June 23, 1997
	John Olerud, AL:Sea. July 17, 2000 (8 inn)
	Robb Quinlan, AL:Ana. Aug. 6, 2003 (8 inn)
	Raul Ibanez, AL:Sea. Apr. 18, 2005 (8 inn)
	Justin Morneau, AL:Minn. Aug. 3, 2007
	Chris Davis, AL:Tex. Aug. 9, 2008 (8 inn)
	Billy Butler, AL:KC June 3, 2010
	Edwin Encarnacion, AL:Tor. Aug. 25, 2012 (8 inn)
	Joe Mauer, AL:Minn. July 3, 2018 (8 inn)

ASSISTS

Most Seasons Leading League

8	Fred Tenney, NL:Bos. 1899, 1901-07
6	George Sisler, AL:StL. 1919-20, 22, 24-25, 27
	Vic Power, AL:KC 1955, 57; Clev. 59-61; Minn. 62

Most Assists, Lifetime

1865	Eddie Murray, AL:Balt. 1977-88, 96; Clev. 94-96; NL:LA 89-91; NY 92-93

Most Assists, League

1726	Todd Helton, NL:Col. 1997-2013
1574	Rafael Palmeiro, AL:Tex. 1989-93, 99-2003; Balt. 94-98, 2004-05

Most Assists, Season

185	Albert Pujols, NL:StL. 2009
184	Bill Buckner, AL:Bos. 1985

Most Assists, Game

8	Bob Skinner, NL:Pitt. July 22, 1954 (14 inn)
	Bob Robertson, NL:Pitt. June 21, 1971
	Darrell Evans, NL:SF May 30, 1981 (14 inn)
7	George Stovall, AL:StL. Aug. 7, 1912
	Ferris Fain, AL:Phil. June 9, 1949 (12 inn)
	Don Mattingly, AL:NY May 11, 1984 (17 inn)

Fewest Assists, Game (Most Innings, Complete Game)

0	Todd Helton, NL:Col. Apr. 17, 2008 (22 inn)
	Bud Clancy, AL:Chi. May 24, 1929 (21 inn)

Most Assists, Inning

3	By many; last:
	Anthony Rizzo, NL:Chi. Aug. 31, 2019 (8th)
	Edwin Encarnacion, AL:Tor. May 2, 2015 (7th)

ERRORS

Most Seasons Leading League (Most Errors)

7	Dick Stuart, NL:Pitt. 1958-62; AL:Bos. 63-64
	Mo Vaughn, AL:Bos. 1992-94, 96-97; Ana. 2000; NL:NY 02
6	Mo Vaughn, AL:Bos. 1992-94, 96-97; Ana. 2000
5	Dick Stuart, NL:Pitt. 1958-62
	Willie McCovey, NL:SF 1967-68, 70-71, 77

Most Errors, League, Since 1900

285	Hal Chase, AL:NY 1905-13; Chi. 13-14
252	Fred Tenney, NL:Bos. 1900-07, 11; NY 08-09
	Fred Merkle, NL:NY 1907-16; Brk. 16-17; Cin. 17-20

Most Errors, Season

62	Joe Quinn, UA:StL. 1884	
58	Cap Anson, NL:Chi. 1884	
	Since 1900:	
43	Jack Doyle, NL:NY 1900	
41	Jerry Freeman, AL:Wash. 1908	

Fewest Errors, Season

	Minimum: 1500 total chances	
1	Stuffy McInnis, AL:Bos. 1921 (1652 tc)	
2	Todd Helton, NL:Col. 2007 (1545 tc)	
	Minimum: 150 games	
0	Steve Garvey, NL:SD 1984 (159 g)	
1	Stuffy McInnis, AL:Bos. 1921 (152 g)	

Most Errors, Game

5	John Carbine, NL:Lou. Apr. 29, 1876
	George Zettlein, NL:Phil. June 22, 1876
	Everett Mills, NL:Hart. Oct. 7, 1876
	Dude Esterbrook, NL:Buff. July 27, 1880
	Roger Connor, NL:Troy May 27, 1882
	Lew Brown, AA:Lou. Sept. 10, 1883
	Jack Gorman, UA:KC June 28, 1884
	Joe Quinn, UA:StL. July 4(1g), 1884
	Since 1900:
4	Jock Menefee, NL:Chi. Oct. 6, 1901
	Johnny Lush, NL:Phil. June 11 & Sept. 15(2g), 1904
	Fred Tenney, NL:Bos. July 12(1g), 1905
	Todd Zeile, NL:Phil. Aug. 7, 1996
	Buck Freeman, AL:Bos. Sept. 23(2g), 1901
	Hal Chase, AL:Chi. July 23, 1913
	George Sisler, AL:StL. Apr. 14, 1925
	Jimmy Wasdell, AL:Wash. May 3, 1939
	Glenn Davis, AL:Balt. Apr. 18, 1991

Most Errors, Inning

3	Dolph Camilli, NL:Phil. Aug. 2, 1935 (1st)
	Al Oliver, NL:Pitt. May 23, 1969 (4th)
	Jack Clark, NL:StL. May 25, 1987 (3rd)
	George Metkovich, AL:Bos. Apr. 17, 1945 (7th)
	Tom McCraw, AL:Chi. May 3, 1968 (3rd)
	Willie Upshaw, AL:Tor. July 1, 1986 (5th)
	Brandon Moss, AL:Oak. June 23, 2012 (6th)

Most Errorless Games, Consecutive, Lifetime

274	Casey Kotchman, AL:LA-Bos.-Sea.; NL:Atl. June 21, 2008-Aug. 20, 2010

Most Errorless Games, Consecutive, League

238	Kevin Youkilis, AL:Bos. July 5, 2006-June 6, 2008
193	Steve Garvey, NL:SD June 26, 1983-Apr. 14, 1985

Most Errorless Games, Consecutive, Season

159	Steve Garvey, NL:SD 1984 (entire season)
135	Kevin Youkilis, AL:Bos. 2007 (entire season)

Most Errorless Chances Accepted, Consecutive, Lifetime

2379	Casey Kotchman, AL:LA-Bos.-Sea.; NL:Atl. June 20, 2008-Aug. 21, 2010

Most Errorless Chances Accepted, Consecutive, League

2002	Kevin Youkilis, AL:Bos. July 4, 2006-June 6, 2008
1649	Steve Garvey, NL:SD June 26, 1983-Apr. 15, 1985

Most Errorless Chances Accepted, Consecutive, Season

1319	Steve Garvey, NL:SD 1984 (entire season)
1300	Stuffy McInnis, AL:Bos. May 31(1g)-Oct. 2, 1921

DOUBLE PLAYS

Most Seasons Leading League

6	Keith Hernandez, NL:StL. 1977, 79-81; NY 83-84
	Todd Helton, NL:Col. 1998-2000, 02-03, 06
4	Stuffy McInnis, AL:Phil. 1912, 14; Bos. 19-20
	Wally Pipp, AL:NY 1915-17, 20
	Vic Power, AL:KC 1955; Clev. 59-60; Minn. 62
	Cecil Cooper, AL:Mil. 1980-83
	Carlos Delgado, AL:Tor. 1999-2001, 03

Most Double Plays, Lifetime

2049	Mickey Vernon, AL:Wash. 1939-43, 46-48, 50-55; Clev. 49-50, 58; Bos. 56-57; NL:Mil. 1959

Most Double Plays, League

2046	Mickey Vernon, AL:Wash. 1939-43, 46-48, 50-55; Clev. 49-50, 58; Bos. 56-57
2028	Todd Helton, NL:Col. 1997-2013

Most Double Plays, Season

194	Ferris Fain, AL:Phil. 1949
182	Donn Clendenon, NL:Pitt. 1966

Most Double Plays, Unassisted, Season

9	Travis Lee, AL:TB 2005
8	Bill White, NL:StL. 1961

Most Double Plays, Game

7	Curt Blefary, NL:Hou. May 4, 1969
	Anthony Rizzo, NL:Chi. Aug. 17, 2018
6	Jimmie Foxx, AL:Phil. Aug. 24, 1935 (15 inn)
	Ferris Fain, AL:Phil. Sept. 1(2g), 1947
	George Vico, AL:Det. May 19, 1948
	Eddie Robinson, AL:Clev. Aug. 5, 1948
	Lee Thomas, AL:LA Aug. 23, 1963
	Bob Oliver, AL:KC May 14, 1971; NY Apr. 29, 1975
	John Mayberry, AL:KC May 16, 1972
	Rod Carew, AL:Minn. Aug. 29(1g), 1977 (10 inn)
	Dave Bergman, AL:Det. Apr. 13, 1984
	Kent Hrbek, AL:Minn. July 18, 1990
	Mark McGwire, AL:Oak. May 17, 1995
	Jason Giambi, AL:NY June 17(1g), 2003
	Lyle Overbay, AL:Tor. Aug. 12, 2006
	Ryan Garko, AL:Clev. Apr. 21, 2009
	Billy Butler, AL:KC Apr. 30, 2009
	Paul Konerko, AL:Chi. Aug. 7, 2009
	Mitch Moreland, AL:Tex. Apr. 15, 2011
	Adrian Gonzalez, AL:Bos. May 6, 2012 (17 inn)
	Yuli Gurriel, AL:Hou. Aug. 19, 2017

Most Double Plays, Unassisted, Game

2	By many; last:
	Prince Fielder, NL:Mil. June 24, 2008
	Adrian Gonzalez, AL:Bos. Sept. 3, 2011

TRIPLE PLAYS

Unassisted Triple Play

1	George Burns, AL:Bos. (Clev.) Sept. 14, 1923 (2nd)
	Johnny Neun, AL:Det. (Clev.) May 31, 1927 (9th)

SECOND BASE

Most Seasons, Lifetime

22	Joe Morgan, NL:Hou. 1963-71, 80; Cin. 72-79; SF 81-82; Phil. 83; AL:Oak. 1984

Most Seasons, League

22	Eddie Collins, AL:Phil. 1906, 08-14, 27-28; Chi. 15-26
21	Joe Morgan, NL:Hou. 1963-71, 80; Cin. 72-79; SF 81-82; Phil. 83

PERCENTAGE

Most Seasons Leading League

9	Eddie Collins, AL:Phil. 1909-10, 14; Chi. 15-16, 20-22, 24
6	Red Schoendienst, NL:StL. 1946, 49, 53, 55; StL.-NY 56; Mil. 58

Most Seasons, Consecutive, Leading League

3	Claude Ritchey, NL:Pitt. 1905-07
	Bret Boone, NL:Cin. 1995-97
	Nap Lajoie, AL:Clev. 1906-08
	Eddie Collins, AL:Phil. 1914; Chi. 15-16
	Eddie Collins, AL:Chi. 20-22
	Charlie Gehringer, AL:Det. 1935-37

Highest Percentage, Lifetime

.993	Placido Polanco, NL:StL. 1998-2002, Phil. 02-05, 10-11; AL:Det. 05-09

Highest Percentage, League

.991	Dustin Pedroia, AL:Bos. 2006-19
.989	Ryne Sandberg, NL:Phil. 1981; Chi. 82-94, 96-97

Highest Percentage, Season

1.000	Placido Polanco, AL:Det. 2007 (683 tc)
	David Eckstein, NL:SD 2010 (475 tc)

Lowest Percentage, Season, Since 1900

.914	Frank Truesdale, AL:StL. 1910
.927	John Farrell, NL:StL. 1903

GAMES

Most Seasons Leading League
8   Nellie Fox, AL:Chi. 1952-59
        Craig Biggio, NL:Hou. 1992-98, 2001

Most Games, Lifetime
2649   Eddie Collins, AL:Phil. 1906, 08-14, 27-28; Chi. 15-26
2426   Joe Morgan, NL:Hou. 1963-71, 80; Cin. 72-79; SF 81-82; Phil. 83

Most Games, Consecutive
798   Nellie Fox, AL:Chi. Aug. 7, 1955-Sept. 3, 1960
443   Dave Cash, NL:Pitt.-Phil. Sept. 20, 1973-Aug. 5, 1976

Most Games, Season
163   Bill Mazeroski, NL:Pitt. 1967
162   Jake Wood, AL:Det. 1961
        Bobby Grich, AL:Balt. 1973
        Jonathan Schoop, AL:Balt. 2016

CHANCES ACCEPTED

Most Seasons Leading League
9   Nellie Fox, AL:Chi. 1952-60
8   Bill Mazeroski, NL:Pitt. 1958, 60-64, 66-67

Most Chances Accepted, Lifetime
14,166   Eddie Collins, AL:Phil. 1906, 08-14, 27-28; Chi. 15-26
12,278   Joe Morgan, NL:Hou. 1963-71, 80; Cin. 72-79; SF 81-82; Phil. 83

Most Chances Accepted, Season
1037   Frankie Frisch, NL:StL. 1927
988   Nap Lajoie, AL:Clev. 1908

Most Chances Accepted, Game
18   Cupid Childs, AA:Syr. June 1, 1890
        Terry Harmon, NL:Phil. June 12, 1971
17   Jimmy Dykes, AL:Phil. Aug. 28, 1921
        Nellie Fox, AL:Chi. June 12, 1952
        Juan Uribe, AL:Chi. Apr. 6, 2008
        Gordon Beckham, AL:Chi. July 23, 2014
        Extra-Inning Game:
21   Eddie Moore, NL:Bos. May 17, 1927 (22 inn)
20   Willie Randolph, AL:NY Aug. 25, 1976 (19 inn)

Fewest Chances Accepted, Game (Most Innings, Complete Game)
0   Steve Yerkes, AL:Bos. June 11, 1913 (15 inn)
        Ken Boswell, NL:NY Aug. 7, 1972 (13 inn)

PUTOUTS

Most Seasons Leading League
10   Nellie Fox, AL:Chi. 1952-61
7   Fred Pfeffer, NL:Chi. 1884-89, 91
        Billy Herman, NL:Chi. 1933, 35-36, 38-40; Brk. 42

Most Putouts, Lifetime
6529   Eddie Collins, AL:Phil. 1906, 08-14, 27-28; Chi. 15-26
5540   Joe Morgan, NL:Hou. 1963-71, 80; Cin. 72-79; SF 81-82; Phil. 83

Most Putouts, Season
484   Bobby Grich, AL:Balt. 1974
466   Billy Herman, NL:Chi. 1933

Most Putouts, Game
12   Lou Bierbauer, AA:Phil. June 22, 1888
        Bobby Knoop, AL:Cal. Aug. 30, 1966
11   Sam Wise, NL:Wash. May 9, 1893
        Bid McPhee, NL:Cin. Apr. 21, 1894
        Nap Lajoie, NL:Phil. Apr. 25, 1899
        Billy Herman, NL:Chi. June 28(1g), 1933
        Gene Baker, NL:Chi. May 27, 1955
        Charlie Neal, NL:LA July 2, 1959
        Julian Javier, NL:StL. June 27, 1964
        Extra-Inning Game:
15   Jake Pitler, NL:Pitt. Aug. 22, 1917 (22 inn)
13   Roy Hughes, AL:Clev. May 10, 1936 (15 inn)

Fewest Putouts, Game (Most Innings, Complete Game)
0	Phil Garner, NL:Pitt. Aug. 10, 1977 (18 inn)
	Jason Kipnis, AL:Clev. Apr. 18, 2018 (16 inn)

ASSISTS

Most Seasons Leading League
9	Bill Mazeroski, NL:Pitt. 1958, 60-64, 66-68
7	Charlie Gehringer, AL:Det. 1927-28, 33-36, 38

Most Assists, Lifetime
7637	Eddie Collins, AL:Phil. 1906, 08-14, 27-28; Chi. 15-26
6738	Joe Morgan, NL:Hou. 1963-71, 80; Cin. 72-79; SF 81-82; Phil. 83

Most Assists, Season
641	Frankie Frisch, NL:StL. 1927
572	Oscar Melillo, AL:StL. 1930

Most Assists, Game
12	Monte Ward, NL:Brk. June 10(1g), 1892
	Frankie Frisch, NL:StL. Aug. 21, 1929
	Jim Gilliam, NL:Brk. July 21, 1956
	Jack Perconte, NL:LA Sept. 19, 1981
	Ryne Sandberg, NL:Chi. June 12, 1983
	Glenn Hubbard, NL:Atl. Apr. 14, 1985
	Juan Samuel, NL:Phil. Apr. 20, 1985
	DJ LeMahieu, NL:Col. Aug. 28, 2012
	Dick McAuliffe, AL:Det. May 3, 1970
	Don Money, AL:Mil. June 24, 1977
	Tony Phillips, AL:Oak. July 6, 1986
	Harold Reynolds, AL:Sea. Aug. 27, 1986
	Extra-Inning Game:
15	Lave Cross, NL:Phil. Aug. 5, 1897 (12 inn)
	Since 1900:
13	Lee Magee, NL:Brk. Apr. 30, 1919 (20 inn)
	Davey Lopes, NL:LA Apr. 12, 1980 (17 inn)
	Mark Loretta, NL:SD May 7, 2003 (10 inn)
	Chase Utley, NL:LA May 22, 2016 (17 inn)
	Bobby Avila, AL:Clev. July 1, 1952 (19 inn)
	Willie Randolph, AL:NY Aug. 25, 1976 (19 inn)

Fewest Assists, Game (Most Innings, Complete Game)
0	Gordon Slade, NL:Cin. July 1(1g), 1934 (18 inn)
	Delino DeShields, NL:LA Aug. 3, 1996 (18 inn)
	Jerry Browne, AL:Clev. Sept. 21, 1989 (17 inn)

Most Assists, Inning
4	Jason Kipnis, AL:Clev. June 22, 2014 (5th)
3	By many in NL

ERRORS

Most Seasons Leading League (Most Errors)
5	Fred Pfeffer, NL:Chi. 1884-88
	Rickie Weeks, NL:Mil. 2005-06, 08, 11-12
	Alfonso Soriano, AL:NY 2001-03, Tex. 04-05
	Ian Kinsler, AL:Tex. 2006-08, 12-13
	Rougned Odor, AL:Tex. 2015-17, 19-20

Most Errors, Lifetime
828	Fred Pfeffer, NL:Troy 1882; Chi. 83-89, 91, 96-97; Lou. 92-95; NY 96; PL:Chi. 1890

Most Errors, League
754	Fred Pfeffer, NL:Troy 1882; Chi. 83-89, 91, 96-97; Lou. 92-95; NY 96
	Since 1900:
443	Larry Doyle, NL:NY 1907-16, 18-20; Chi. 16-17
437	Eddie Collins, AL:Phil. 1906, 08-14, 27-28; Chi. 15-26

Most Errors, Season
92	Yank Robinson, AA:StL. 1886
88	Pop Smith, NL:Cin. 1880
	Bob Ferguson, NL:Phil. 1883
	Since 1900:
61	Kid Gleason, AL:Det. 1901
	Hobe Ferris, AL:Bos. 1901
55	George Grantham, NL:Chi. 1923

Fewest Errors, Season

Minimum: 800 tc

5	Jerry Adair, AL:Balt. 1964 (822 tc) 153 g
	Bobby Grich, AL:Balt. 1973 (945 tc) 162 g
	Mark Ellis AL:Oak. 2007 (806 tc) 150 g
	Ryne Sandberg NL:Chi. 1986 (806 tc) 153 g
	Jose Oquendo, NL:StL. 1989 (851 tc) 156 g

Minimum: 150 games

2	Placido Polanco, AL:Det. 2009 (151 g) 731 tc
	Darwin Barney, NL:Chi. 2012 (155 g) 731 tc

Most Errors, Game

9	Andy Leonard, NL:Bos. June 14, 1876

Since 1900:

5	Piano Legs Hickman, AL:Wash. Sept. 29, 1905
	Rollie Zeider, AL:Chi. June 15, 1910 (14 inn)
	Nap Lajoie, AL:Phil. Apr. 22, 1915
4	By many in NL; last:
	Casey Wise, NL:Chi. May 3, 1957

Fewest Errors, Game (Most Innings, Complete Game)

0	Felix Millan, NL:NY Sept. 11, 1974 (25 inn)
	Ted Sizemore, NL:StL. Sept. 11, 1974 (25 inn)
	Julio Cruz, AL:Chi. May 8, 1984 (25 inn)

Most Errors, Inning

3	Bid McPhee, NL:Cin. Sept. 23(1g), 1894 (6th)
	Claude Ritchey, NL:Pitt. Sept. 22, 1900 (6th)
	Bama Rowell, NL:Bos. Sept. 25, 1941 (3rd)
	Eddie Stanky, NL:Chi. June 20(1g), 1943 (8th)
	George Hausmann, NL:NY Aug. 13(2g), 1944 (4th)
	Kermit Wahl, NL:Cin. Sept. 18(1g), 1945 (11th)
	Davey Lopes, NL:LA June 2, 1973 (1st)
	Ted Sizemore, NL:StL. Apr. 17, 1975 (6th)
	Del Pratt, AL:StL. Sept. 1(2g), 1914 (4th)
	Bill Wambsganss, AL:Clev. May 15, 1923 (8th)
	Bobby Doerr, AL:Bos. May 11, 1949 (2nd)
	Tim Cullen, AL:Wash. Aug. 30, 1969 (8th)

Most Errorless Games, Consecutive, Lifetime

186	Placido Polanco, AL:Det. July 2, 2006-Apr. 5, 2008
141	Darwin Barney, NL:Chi. April 18-Sept. 27, 2012

Most Errorless Games. Consecutive, Season

141	Placido Polanco, AL:Det. 2007 (entire season)
	Darwin Barney, NL:Chi. April 18-Sept. 27, 2012

Most Errorless Chances Accepted, Consecutive, Lifetime

910	Placido Polanco, AL:Det. July 1, 2006-Apr. 5, 2008
679	Darwin Barney, NL:Chi. April 18-Sept. 28, 2012

Most Errorless Chances Accepted, Consecutive, Season

683	Placido Polanco, AL:Det. 2007 (entire season)
679	Darwin Barney, NL:Chi. April 18-Sept. 28, 2012

DOUBLE PLAYS

Most Seasons Leading League

8	Bill Mazeroski, NL:Pitt. 1960-67
5	Nap Lajoie, AL:Clev. 1903, 06-09
	Eddie Collins, AL:Phil. 1909-10, 12; Chi. 16, 19
	Bucky Harris, AL:Wash. 1921-25
	Bobby Doerr, AL:Bos. 1938, 40, 43, 46-47
	Nellie Fox, AL:Chi. 1954, 56-58, 60
	Harold Reynolds, AL:Sea. 1986-88, 91; Balt. 93

Most Double Plays, Lifetime

1707	Bill Mazeroski, NL:Pitt. 1956-72
1568	Nellie Fox, AL:Phil. 1947-49; Chi. 50-63

Most Double Plays, Season

161	Bill Mazeroski, NL:Pitt. 1966
150	Jerry Priddy, AL:Det. 1950

Most Double Plays, Game

6	Bobby Knoop, AL:Cal. May 1(1g), 1966
	Joe Gordon, AL:Clev. Aug. 31(1g), 1949 (14 inn)
	Alfonso Soriano, AL:NY June 17(1g), 2003
	Jayson Nix, AL:Chi. Aug. 7, 2009
	Felix Millan, NL:Atl. Aug. 5, 1971 (17 inn)
	Bill Doran, NL:Hou. May 8, 1988

Most Double Plays, Unassisted, Game

2	Davy Force, NL:Buff. Sept. 15, 1881
	Claude Ritchey, NL:Lou. July 9(1g), 1899
	Mike Edwards, AL:Oak. Aug. 10, 1978
	Luis Alicea, AL:Ana. Aug. 8, 1997

TRIPLE PLAYS

Unassisted Triple Play

1	Mickey Morandini, NL:Phil. (Pitt.) Sept. 20, 1992 (6th)
	Eric Bruntlett, NL:Phil. (NY) Aug. 23, 2009 (9th)
	Randy Velarde, AL:Oak. (NY) May 29, 2000 (6th)
	Asdrubal Cabrera, AL:Clev. (Tor.) May 12(2g), 2008 (5th)

THIRD BASE

Most Seasons, Lifetime

23	Brooks Robinson, AL:Balt. 1955-77

Most Seasons, League

23	Brooks Robinson, AL:Balt. 1955-77
18	Mike Schmidt, NL:Phil. 1972-89
	Lenny Harris, NL:Cin. 1988-89, 94-98; LA 89-93; NY 98, 2000-01; Col. 99; Ari. 2000; Mil. 02; Chi. 03; Fla. 03-05
	Aramis Ramirez, NL:Pitt. 1998-2003, 15; Chi. 03-11; Mil. 12-15

PERCENTAGE

Most Seasons Leading League

11	Brooks Robinson, AL:Balt. 1960-64, 66-69, 72, 75
6	Ken Reitz, NL:StL. 1973-74, 77-78, 80; Chi. 81

Most Seasons, Consecutive, Leading League

6	Willie Kamm, AL:Chi. 1924-29
4	Willie Jones, NL:Phil. 1953-56

Highest Percentage, Lifetime

.974	Mike Lowell, AL:NY 1998; Bos. 2006-10; NL:Fla. 1999-2005

Highest Percentage, League

.972	Nolan Arenado, NL:Col. 2013-20
.971	Brooks Robinson, AL:Balt. 1955-77

Highest Percentage, Season

.990	Kevin Kouzmanoff, NL:SD 2009

Highest Percentage, Season, League

.991	Steve Buechele, AL:Tex. 1991
.990	Kevin Kouzmanoff, NL:SD 2009 (ML record)

Lowest Percentage, Season, Since 1900

.836	Piano Legs Hickman, NL:NY 1900
.860	Hunter Hill, AL:Wash. 1904

GAMES

Most Seasons Leading League

8	Brooks Robinson, AL:Balt. 1960-64, 66, 68, 70
7	Ron Santo, NL:Chi. 1961, 63, 65-69

Most Games Lifetime

2870	Brooks Robinson, AL:Balt. 1955-77
2212	Mike Schmidt, NL:Phil. 1972-89

Most Games, Consecutive

576	Eddie Yost, AL:Wash. July 3, 1951-May 11, 1955
364	Ron Santo, NL:Chi. Apr. 19, 1964-May 31, 1966

Most Games, Season

164	Ron Santo, NL:Chi. 1965
163	Brooks Robinson, AL:Balt. 1961, 64

CHANCES ACCEPTED

Most Seasons Leading League

9	Ron Santo, NL:Chi. 1961-69
8	Frank Baker, AL:Phil. 1909-10, 12-14; NY 17-19
	Brooks Robinson, AL:Balt. 1960, 63-64, 66-69, 74

Most Chances Accepted, Lifetime
8908	Brooks Robinson, AL:Balt. 1955-77
6635	Mike Schmidt, NL:Phil. 1972-89

Most Chances Accepted, Season
603	Harlond Clift, AL:StL. 1937
601	Jimmy Collins, NL:Bos. 1899
	NL Since 1900:
583	Tommy Leach, NL:Pitt. 1904

Most Chances Accepted, Game
13	Willie Kuehne, NL:Pitt. May 24, 1889
	Jerry Denny, NL:NY May 29, 1890
	Bill Shindle, NL:Balt. Sept. 28, 1893
	Bill Joyce, NL:Wash. May 26, 1894
	Art Devlin, NL:NY May 23(1g), 1908
	Roy Hughes, NL:Chi. Aug. 29(2g), 1944
	Wid Conroy, AL:Wash. Sept. 25, 1911
	Extra-Inning Game:
16	Jerry Denny, NL:Prov. Aug. 17, 1882 (18 inn)
	Since 1900:
14	Jimmy Collins, AL:Bos. June 21, 1902 (15 inn)
	Ben Dyer, AL:Det. July 16, 1919 (14 inn)
	Frank Ellerbe, AL:StL. Aug. 9, 1921 (19 inn)
	Don Hoak, NL:Cin. May 4(2g), 1958 (14 inn)

Fewest Chances Accepted, Game (Most Innings, Complete Game)
0	Eduardo Escobar, NL:Ari. Sept. 24, 2019 (19 inn)
	Kyle Seager, AL:Sea. July 18, 2014 (16 inn)
	Eduardo Nunez, AL:Minn. Apr. 24, 2016 (16 inn)

PUTOUTS

Most Seasons Leading League
8	Eddie Yost, AL:Wash. 1948, 50-54, 56; Det. 59
7	Pie Traynor, NL:Pitt. 1923, 25-27, 31, 33-34
	Willie Jones, NL:Phil. 1949-50, 52-56
	Ron Santo, NL:Chi. 1962-67, 69
	Tim Wallach, NL:Mtl. 1982-85, 87-88; LA 94

Most Putouts, Lifetime
2702	Brooks Robinson, AL:Balt. 1955-77
2288	Pie Traynor, NL:Pitt. 1921-35, 37

Most Putouts, Season
252	Jimmy Collins, NL:Bos. 1900
243	Willie Kamm, AL:Chi. 1928

Most Putouts, Game
10	Willie Kuehne, NL:Pitt. May 24, 1889
	Since 1900:
9	Pat Dillard, NL:StL. June 18, 1900
	Randy Jackson, NL:Chi. June 4, 1955 (12 inn)
7	By many in AL

Fewest Putouts, Game (Most Innings, Complete Game)
0	Kevin Kouzmanoff, NL:SD Apr. 17, 2008 (22 inn)
	Vern Stephens, AL:Bos. July 13, 1951 (19 inn)
	Don Wert, AL:Det. Aug. 23(2g), 1968 (19 inn)
	Jim Gantner, AL:Mil. May 1, 1991 (19 inn)

ASSISTS

Most Seasons Leading League
8	Brooks Robinson, AL:Balt. 1960, 63-64, 66-69, 74
7	Ron Santo, NL:Chi. 1962-68
	Mike Schmidt, NL:Phil. 1974, 76-77, 80-83

Most Assists, Lifetime
6206	Brooks Robinson, AL:Balt. 1955-77
5045	Mike Schmidt, NL:Phil. 1972-89

Most Assists, Season
412	Graig Nettles, AL:Clev. 1971
404	Mike Schmidt, NL:Phil. 1974

Most Assists, Game

11	Deacon White, NL:Buff. May 16, 1884
	Jerry Denny, NL:NY May 29, 1890
	Damon Phillips, NL:Bos. Aug. 29, 1944
	Chris Sabo, NL:Cin. Apr. 7, 1988
	Kevin Young, NL:Pitt. June 25, 1995
	Carter Kieboom, NL:Wash. Aug. 14, 2020
	Frank Baker, AL:NY May 24, 1918 (19 inn)
	Ken McMullen, AL:Wash. Sept. 26(1g), 1966
	Mike Ferraro, AL:NY Sept. 14, 1968
	Doug DeCinces, AL:Cal. May 7, 1983 (12 inn)
	Extra-Inning Game:
12	Bobby Byrne, NL:Pitt. June 8(2g), 1910 (11 inn)

Fewest Assists, Game (Most Innings, Complete Game)

0	Sibby Sisti, NL:Bos. July 5, 1940 (20 inn)
	Toby Harrah, AL:Tex. Sept. 17, 1977 (17 inn)

Most Assists, Inning

3	By many

ERRORS

Most Seasons Leading League (Most)

5	Pie Traynor, NL:Pitt. 1926, 28, 31-33
	Jim Tabor, AL:Bos. 1939-43

Most Errors, Lifetime

359	Jimmy Austin, AL:NY 1909-10; StL. 11-22, 25-26, 29

Most Errors, League, Since 1900

359	Jimmy Austin, AL:NY 1909-10; StL. 11-22, 25-26, 29
324	Pie Traynor, NL:Pitt. 1921-35, 37

Most Errors, Season

91	Piano Legs Hickman, NL:NY 1900
64	Sammy Strang, AL:Chi. 1902

Fewest Errors, Season

	Minimum: 450 tc
5	Don Money, AL:Mil. 1974 (472 tc) 157 g
9	Ken Reitz, NL:StL. 1977 (450 tc) 157 g
	Robin Ventura, NL:NY 1999 (452 tc) 160 g
	Nolan Arenado, NL:Col. 2019 (457 tc) 154 g
	Minimum: 150 games
5	Don Money, AL:Mil. 1974 (157 g) 472 tc
6	Chris Johnson, NL:Atl. 2014 (150 g) 271 tc

Most Errors, Game

6	Jim Donnelly, UA:KC July 16, 1884
	Joe Moffett, AA:Tol. Aug. 2, 1884
	Joe Werrick, AA:Lou. July 28, 1888
	Billy Alvord, AA:Tol. May 22, 1890
	Joe Mulvey, NL:Phil. July 30, 1884
	Since 1900:
5	Dave Brain, NL:Bos. June 11, 1906
4	By many in AL; last:
	Marco Scutaro, AL:Oak. July 6, 2007

Fewest Errors, Game (Most Innings, Complete Game)

0	Tony Boeckel, NL:Bos. May 1, 1920 (26 inn)
	Jimmy Johnston, NL:Brk. May 1, 1920 (26 inn)
	Vance Law, AL:Chi. May 8, 1984 (25 inn)

Most Errors, Inning

4	Lew Whistler, NL:NY June 19, 1891 (4th)
	Bob Brenly, NL:SF Sept. 14, 1986 (4th)
	Jimmy Burke, AL:Mil. May 27, 1901 (4th)

Most Errorless Games, Consecutive, Lifetime

99	Jeff Cirillo, NL:Col.-AL:Sea. June 20, 2001-Apr. 19, 2002
	John Wehner, NL:Pitt.-Fla.-Pitt. Aug. 2, 1992-Sept. 29, 2000
	Jeff Cirillo, NL:Col.-SD-Mil. June 20, 2001-Apr. 15, 2005
	Gio Urshela, AL:NY July 5, 2019-Sept. 24, 2020

Most Errorless Games, Consecutive, Season

86	Don Money, AL:Mil. Apr. 5-July 16, 1974
85	Jeff Cirillo, NL:Col. June 20-Oct. 7, 2001

Most Errorless Chances Accepted, Consecutive, Lifetime

272	Vinny Castilla, NL:Col.-Wash. July 4, 2004-Apr. 22, 2005
261	Don Money, AL:Mil. Sept. 28(1g), 1973-July 16, 1974

Most Errorless Chances Accepted, Consecutive, Season
257   Don Money, AL:Mil. Apr. 5-July 16, 1974
230   Vinny Castilla, NL:Col. July 4 - Oct. 3, 2004

DOUBLE PLAYS

Most Seasons Leading League
6   Heinie Groh, NL:Cin. 1915-16, 18-20; NY 22
       Ron Santo, NL:Chi. 1961, 64, 66-68, 71
       Mike Schmidt, NL:Phil. 1978-80, 82-83, 87
5   Ken Keltner, AL:Clev. 1939, 41-42, 44, 47
       Frank Malzone, AL:Bos. 1957-61

Most Double Plays, Lifetime
619   Brooks Robinson, AL:Balt. 1955-77
449   Mike Schmidt, NL:Phil. 1972-89

Most Double Plays, Season
54   Graig Nettles, AL:Clev. 1971
45   Hank Thompson, NL:NY 1950
       Darrell Evans, NL:Atl. 1974
       Jeff Cirillo, NL:Mil. 1998

Most Double Plays, Game
4   Pie Traynor, NL:Pitt. July 9(1g), 1925
       Denny Walling, NL:Hou. May 8, 1988
       Edgardo Alfonzo, NL:NY May 14, 1997
       Shane Andrews, NL:Chi. Sept. 23, 2000
       Ryan Zimmerman, NL:Wash. Aug. 26, 2008
       Travis Shaw, NL:Mil. July 23, 2017
       Christian Villanueva, NL:SD July 3, 2018
       Alex Kampouris, AL:Wash. Aug. 18(1g), 1943 (14 inn)
       Andy Carey, AL:NY July 31(2g), 1955
       Brooks Robinson, AL:Balt. July 25, 1959 (17 inn)
       Felix Torres, AL:LA Aug. 23, 1963
       Ken McMullen, AL:Wash. Aug. 13, 1965
       Wade Boggs, AL:Bos. Aug. 9, 1985
       Jack Howell, AL:Cal. May 17, 1989
       Scott Brosius, AL:NY July 6, 2000
       Alex Rodriguez, AL:NY Apr. 2, 2008
       Michael Young, AL:Tex. Sept. 17, 2010
       Yangervis Solarte, AL:NY May 2, 2014 (14 inn)

Most Double Plays, Unassisted, Season
4   Joe Dugan, AL:NY 1924
3   Harry Wolverton, NL:Phil. 1902
       Heinie Groh, NL:Cin. 1915

Most Double Plays, Unassisted, Game
1   By many

SHORTSTOP

Most Seasons, Lifetime
24   Omar Vizquel, AL:Sea. 1989-93; Clev. 94-2004; Tex. 09; Chi. 10-11; Tor. 12; NL:SF 05-08

Most Seasons, League
20   Bill Dahlen, NL:Chi. 1891-98; Brk. 1899-1903, 11; NY 04-07; Bos. 08-09
       Luke Appling, AL:Chi. 1930-43, 45-50
       Alan Trammell, AL:Det. 1977-96
       Omar Vizquel, AL:Sea. 1989-93; Clev. 94-2004; Tex. 09; Chi. 10-11; Tor. 12
       Derek Jeter, AL:NY 1995-2014
       NL Since 1900:
19   Rabbit Maranville, NL:Bos. 1912-20, 29-31; Pitt. 21-23; Chi. 25; Brk. 26; StL. 27-28
       Chris Speier, NL:SF 1971-77, 87-89; Mtl. 77-84; StL. 84; Chi. 85-86
       Dave Concepcion, NL:Cin. 1970-88
       Ozzie Smith, NL:SD 1978-81, StL. 82-96
       Barry Larkin, NL:Cin. 1986-2004

PERCENTAGE

Most Seasons Leading League
8   Everett Scott, AL:Bos. 1916-21; NY 22-23
       Lou Boudreau, AL:Clev. 1940-44, 46-48
       Luis Aparicio, AL:Chi. 1959-62; Balt. 63-66
       Ozzie Smith, NL:SD 1981; StL. 82, 84-87, 91, 94

Most Seasons, Consecutive, Leading League
8	Everett Scott, AL:Bos. 1916-21; NY 22-23
	Luis Aparicio, AL:Chi. 1959-62; Balt. 63-66
5	Hughie Jennings, NL:Balt. 1894-98
	NL Since 1900:
4	Eddie Miller, NL:Bos. 1940-42; Cin. 43
	Ozzie Smith, NL:StL. 1984-87

Highest Percentage, Lifetime
.985	Omar Vizquel, AL:Sea. 1989-93; Clev. 94-2004; Tex. 09; Chi. 10-11; Tor. 12; NL:SF 05-08

Highest Percentage, League
.985	Troy Tulowitzki, NL:Col. 2006-15
.984	Omar Vizquel, AL:Sea. 1989-93; Clev. 94-2004; Tex. 09; Chi. 10-11; Tor. 12

Highest Percentage, Season
.998	Mike Bordick, AL:Balt. 2002
.994	Rey Ordonez, NL:NY 1999

Lowest Percentage, Season, Since 1900
.861	Bill Keister, AL:Balt. 1901
.891	Otto Kruger, NL:StL. 1902

GAMES

Most Seasons Leading League
12	Cal Ripken, AL:Balt. 1983-84, 87-96
6	Mickey Doolan, NL:Phil. 1906, 09-13
	Arky Vaughan, NL:Pitt. 1933-34, 36, 38-40
	Roy McMillan, NL:Cin. 1952-54, 56-57; Mil. 61

Most Games, Lifetime
2709	Omar Vizquel, AL:Sea. 1989-93; Clev. 94-2004; Tex. 09; Chi. 10-11; Tor. 12; NL:SF 05-08

Most Games, League
2674	Derek Jeter, AL:NY 1995-2014
2511	Ozzie Smith, NL:SD 1978-81; StL. 82-96

Most Games, Consecutive
2216	Cal Ripken, AL:Balt. July 1, 1982-July 14, 1996
584	Roy McMillan, NL:Cin. Sept. 16, 1951-Aug. 6, 1955

Most Games, Season
165	Maury Wills, NL:LA 1962
163	Tony Fernandez, AL:Tor. 1986

CHANCES ACCEPTED

Most Seasons Leading League
8	Ozzie Smith, NL:SD 1978, 80-81; StL. 83, 85, 87-89
7	Luis Aparicio, AL:Chi. 1956-61, 68

Most Chances Accepted, Lifetime
12,624	Ozzie Smith, NL:SD 1978-81; StL. 82-96
12,567	Luis Aparicio, AL:Chi. 1956-62, 68-70; Balt. 63-67; Bos. 71-73

Most Chances Accepted, Season
984	Dave Bancroft, NL:NY 1922
969	Donie Bush, AL:Det. 1914

Most Chances Accepted, Game
19	Danny Richardson, NL:Wash. June 20(1g), 1892
	Eddie Joost, NL:Cin. May 7, 1941
17	Bobby Wallace, AL:StL. June 10, 1902
	Extra-Inning Game:
21	Eddie Miller, NL:Bos. June 27, 1939 (23 inn)
20	Roy Smalley, AL:Minn. Aug. 25, 1976 (19 inn)

Fewest Chances Accepted, Game (Most Innings, Complete Game)
0	Trevor Story, NL:Col. Sept. 24, 2019 (16 inn)
	John Gochnaur, AL:Clev. July 14, 1903 (12 inn)
	Billy Rogell, AL:Det. June 16, 1937 (12 inn)
	Manuel Lee, AL:Tex. Apr. 29, 1994 (12 inn)
	Jorge Polanco, AL:Minn. Aug. 1, 2019 (12 inn)

PUTOUTS

Most Seasons Leading League
6 Rabbit Maranville, NL:Bos. 1914-17, 19; Pitt. 23
 Cal Ripken, AL:Balt. 1984-85, 88-89, 91-92

Most Putouts, Lifetime
5140 Rabbit Maranville, NL:Bos. 1912-20, 29-31; Pitt. 21-23; Chi. 25; Brk. 26; StL. 27-28
4547 Luis Aparicio, AL:Chi. 1956-62, 68-70; Balt. 63-67; Bos. 71-73

Most Putouts, Season
425 Hughie Jennings, NL:Balt. 1895
 Donie Bush, AL:Det. 1914
 NL Since 1900:
407 Rabbit Maranville, NL:Bos. 1914

Most Putouts, Game
11 Shorty Fuller, NL:NY Aug. 20, 1895
 Hod Ford, NL:Cin. Sept. 18, 1929
 John Cassidy, AL:Wash. Aug. 30(1g), 1904
 Extra-Inning Game:
15 Jake Pitler, NL:Pitt. Aug. 22, 1917 (22 inn)

Fewest Putouts, Game (Most Innings, Complete Game)
0 Jose Offerman, NL:LA July 7, 1993 (20 inn)
 Xander Bogaerts, AL:Bos. Aug. 9, 2014 (19 inn)
 Xander Bogaerts, AL:Bos. Sept. 5, 2017 (19 inn)

ASSISTS

Most Seasons Leading League
8 Ozzie Smith, NL:SD 1979-81; StL. 82, 85, 87-89
7 Luke Appling, AL:Chi. 1933, 35, 37, 39, 41, 43, 46
 Luis Aparicio, AL:Chi. 1956-61, 68
 Cal Ripken, AL:Balt. 1983-84, 86-87, 89, 91, 93

Most Assists, Lifetime
8375 Ozzie Smith, NL:SD 1978-81; StL. 82-96
8020 Luis Aparicio, AL:Chi. 1956-62, 68-70; Balt. 63-67; Bos. 71-73

Most Assists, Season
621 Ozzie Smith, NL:SD 1980
583 Cal Ripken, AL:Balt. 1984

Most Assists, Game
14 Herman Long, NL:Bos. May 6, 1892 (14 inn)
 Tommy Corcoran, NL:Cin. Aug. 7, 1903
 Bud Harrelson, NL:NY May 24, 1973 (19 inn)
13 Bobby Reeves, AL:Wash. Aug. 7, 1927
 Alex Gonzalez, AL:Tor. Apr. 26, 1996
 Extra-Inning Game:
15 Rick Burleson, AL:Cal. Apr. 13, 1982 (20 inn)

Fewest Assists, Game (Most Innings, Complete Game)
0 Jack Coffey, NL:Bos. July 26, 1909 (17 inn)
 Tony Batista, AL:Balt. Sept. 30, 2001 (15 inn)

Most Assists, Inning
4 Craig Grebeck, AL:Chi. May 2, 1995 (5th)
 Juan Uribe, NL:Col. May 21, 2002 (4th)

ERRORS

Most Seasons Leading League (Most)
6 Dick Groat, NL:Pitt. 1955-56, 59, 61-62; StL. 64
 Rafael Ramirez, NL:Atl. 1981-85; Hou. 89
5 Luke Appling, AL:Chi. 1933, 35, 37, 39, 46

Most Errors, League, Since 1900
694 Donie Bush, AL:Det. 1908-21; Wash. 21-23
675 Honus Wagner, NL:Pitt. 1901-17

Most Errors, Season
115 Bill Schindler, PL:Phil. 1890
106 Joe Sullivan, NL:Wash. 1893
 Since 1900:
95 John Gochnaur, AL:Clev. 1903
81 Rudy Hulswitt, NL:Phil. 1903

Fewest Errors, Season

Minimum: 700 tc

5	Omar Vizquel, AL:Clev. 1998 (720 tc) 151 g	
9	Larry Bowa, NL:Phil. 1972 (715 tc) 150 g	

Minimum: 150 games

3	Cal Ripken, AL:Balt. 1990 (161 g) 680 tc
	Omar Vizquel, AL:Clev. 2000 (156 g) 648 tc
4	Rey Ordonez, NL:NY 1999 (154 g) 640 tc
	Omar Vizquel, NL:SF 2006 (152 g) 599 tc

Most Errors, Game

7	Jimmy Hallinan, NL:NY July 29, 1876
	Germany Smith, AA:Brk. June 17, 1885

Since 1900:

5	Charlie Babb, NL:NY Aug. 24(1g), 1903
	Charlie Babb, NL:Brk. June 20, 1904
	Phil Lewis, NL:Brk. July 20, 1905
	Donie Bush, AL:Det. Aug. 25(1g), 1911

Extra-Inning Game:

6	Bill O'Neill, AL:Bos. May 21, 1904 (13 inn)

Fewest Errors, Game (Most Innings, Complete Game)

0	Rabbit Maranville, NL:Bos. May 1, 1920 (26 inn)
	Robin Yount, AL:Mil. May 8, 1984 (25 inn)

Most Errors, Inning

4	Shorty Fuller, NL:Wash. Aug. 17, 1888 (2nd)
	Len Merullo, NL:Chi. Sept. 13(2g), 1942 (2nd)
	Ray Chapman, AL:Clev. June 20, 1914 (5th)

Most Errorless Games, Consecutive, Lifetime

110	Mike Bordick, AL:Balt. Apr. 11-Sept. 29, 2002

Most Errorless Games, Consecutive, League

110	Mike Bordick, AL:Balt. Apr. 11-Sept. 29, 2002
	Omar Vizquel, AL:Clev.-Tex.-Chi.-Tor. July 26, 2004-Oct. 3, 2012
101	Rey Ordonez, NL:NY June 14, 1999-Mar. 29, 2000

Most Errorless Games, Consecutive, Season

110	Mike Bordick, AL:Balt. Apr. 11-Sept. 29, 2002
100	Rey Ordonez, NL:NY June 14-Oct. 4, 1999

Most Errorless Chances Accepted, Consecutive, Lifetime

544	Mike Bordick, AL:Balt.-Tor. Apr. 10, 2002-Apr. 2, 2003
419	Rey Ordonez, NL:NY June 13, 1999-Mar. 29, 2000

Most Errorless Chances Accepted, Consecutive, Season

543	Mike Bordick, AL:Balt.-Tor. Apr. 10-Sept. 29, 2002
412	Rey Ordonez, NL:NY June 13-Oct. 4, 1999

DOUBLE PLAYS

Most Seasons Leading League

8	Cal Ripken, AL:Balt. 1983-85, 89, 91-92, 94-95
5	Mickey Doolan, NL:Phil. 1907, 09-11, 13
	Dick Groat, NL:Pitt. 1958-59, 61-62; StL. 64
	Ozzie Smith, NL:SD 1980; StL. 84, 86-87, 91

Most Double Plays, Lifetime

1734	Omar Vizquel, AL:Sea. 1989-93; Clev. 94-2004; Tex. 09; Chi. 10-11; Tor. 12; NL:SF 05-08

Most Double Plays, League

1590	Ozzie Smith, NL:SD 1978-81; StL. 82-96
1566	Cal Ripken, AL:Balt. 1981-96

Most Double Plays, Season

147	Rick Burleson, AL:Bos. 1980
137	Bobby Wine, NL:Mtl. 1970

Most Double Plays, Game

6	Ozzie Smith, NL:SD Aug. 25, 1979 (19 inn)
	Rafael Ramirez, NL:Atl. June 27, 1982 (14 inn)
	Didi Gregorius, NL:Ari. Aug. 7, 2013
	Javier Baez, NL:Chi. May 11, 2019 (15 inn)
5	By many AL players; last:
	Adalberto Mondesi, AL:KC July 8, 2018

Extra-Inning Game:

6	Bert Campaneris, AL:Oak. Sept. 13(1g), 1970 (11 inn)

Most Double Plays, Unassisted, Game

2	Lee Tannehill, AL:Chi. Aug. 4(1g), 1911

TRIPLE PLAYS

Unassisted Triple Play
1	Neal Ball, AL:Clev. (Bos.) July 19(1g), 1909 (2nd)
	Ron Hansen, AL:Wash. (Clev.) July 30, 1968 (1st)
	John Valentin, AL:Bos. (Sea.) July 8, 1994 (6th)
	Ernie Padgett, NL:Bos. (Phil.) Oct. 6, 1923 (4th)
	Glenn Wright, NL:Pitt. (StL.) May 7, 1925 (9th)
	Jimmy Cooney, NL:Chi. (Pitt.) May 30, 1927 (4th)
	Rafael Furcal, NL:Atl. (StL.) Aug. 10, 2003 (5th)
	Troy Tulowitzki, NL:Col. (Atl.) Apr. 29, 2007 (7th)

OUTFIELD

Most Seasons, Lifetime
25	Rickey Henderson, AL:Oak. 1979-84, 89-95, 98; NY 85-89; Tor. 93; Ana. 97; Sea. 2000; Bos. 02; NL:SD 96-97, 2001; NY 99-2000; LA 03

Most Seasons, League
24	Ty Cobb, AL:Det. 1905-26; Phil. 27-28
22	Willie Mays, NL:NY/SF 1951-52, 54-72; NY 72-73
	Barry Bonds, NL:Pitt. 1986-92; SF 93-2007

PERCENTAGE

Most Seasons Leading League
5	Amos Strunk, AL:Phil. 1912, 14, 17; Bos. 18; Phil.-Chi. 20
4	Joe Hornung, NL:Bos. 1881-83, 87
	NL Since 1900:
3	Stan Musial, NL:StL. 1949, 54, 61
	Tony Gonzalez, NL:Phil. 1962, 64, 67

Most Seasons, Consecutive, Leading League
3	Joe Hornung, NL:Bos. 1881-83
	Gene Woodling, AL:NY 1951-53
	NL Since 1900:
2	By many

Highest Percentage, Lifetime
.996	Jon Jay, NL:StL. 2010-15; SD 16; Chi. 17; Ari. 18, 20; AL:KC 18; Chi. 19

Highest Percentage, League
.996	Shane Victorino, NL:SD 2003; Phil. 05-12; LA 12
.995	Jacoby Ellsbury, AL:Bos. 2007-13; NY 14-17

Highest Percentage, Season (Most Chances)
1.000	Mike Trout, AL:LA 2015 (435 tc)
	Curt Flood, NL:StL. 1966 (396 tc)

Lowest Percentage, Season
.843	John Manning, NL:Phil. 1884
	Since 1900:
.872	Bill O'Neill, AL:Wash. 1904
.900	Mike Donlin, NL:Cin. 1903

GAMES

Most Seasons Leading League
6	George Burns, NL:NY 1914, 16, 19-20; Cin. 22-23
	Billy Williams, NL:Chi. 1964-68, 70
	Dale Murphy, NL:Atl. 1982-85, 87-88
5	Rocky Colavito, AL:Clev. 1959, 65; Det. 61-63

Most Games, Lifetime
2935	Ty Cobb, AL:Det. 1905-26; Phil. 27-28
2874	Barry Bonds, NL:Pitt. 1986-92; SF 93-2007

Most Games, Consecutive
897	Billy Williams, NL:Chi.Sept. 22, 1963-June 13, 1969
511	Clyde Milan, AL:Wash. Aug. 12, 1910-Oct. 3, 1913

Most Games, Season
164	Billy Williams, NL:Chi. 1965
163	Leon Wagner, AL:Clev. 1964

CHANCES ACCEPTED

Most Seasons Leading League
9	Max Carey, NL:Pitt. 1912-13, 16-18, 21-24
	Richie Ashburn, NL:Phil. 1949-54, 56-58
8	Tris Speaker, AL:Bos. 1909-10, 12-15; Clev. 18-19

Most Chances Accepted, Lifetime
7288	Willie Mays, NL:NY/SF 1951-52, 54-72; NY 72-73
7244	Tris Speaker, AL:Bos. 1907-15; Clev. 16-26; Wash. 27; Phil. 28

Most Chances Accepted, Season
557	Taylor Douthit, NL:StL. 1928
524	Chet Lemon, AL:Chi. 1977

Most Chances Accepted, Game
13	Earl Clark, NL:Bos. May 10, 1929
	Rolando Roomes, NL:Cin. July 28, 1989 (17 inn)
12	By many in AL

Most Chances Accepted, Left Field, Game
11	Joseph Hornung, NL:Bos. Sept. 23, 1881
	Dick Harley, NL:StL. June 30, 1898
	Topsy Hartsel, NL:Chi. Sept. 10, 1901
	Phil Clark, NL:SD May 1, 1993
	Paul Lehner, AL:Phil. June 25(2g), 1950
	Willie Horton, AL:Det. July 18, 1969
	Extra-Inning Game:
12	Tom McBride, AL:Wash. July 2, 1948 (12 inn)
	Rickey Henderson, AL:NY Sept. 11, 1988 (18 inn)
	Darin Erstad, AL:Ana. July 24, 2000 (12 inn)

Most Chances Accepted, Center Field, Game
13	Earl Clark, NL:Bos. May 10, 1929
12	Happy Felsch, AL:Chi. June 23, 1919
	Johnny Mostil, AL:Chi. May 22, 1928
	Jacoby Ellsbury, AL:Bos. May 20, 2009
	AL Extra-Inning Game:
13	Oddibe McDowell, AL:Tex. July 20, 1985 (15 inn)

Most Chances Accepted, Right Field, Game
12	Tony Armas, AL:Oak. June 12, 1982
10	Greasy Neale, NL:Cin. July 13, 1920
	Casey Stengel, NL:Phil. July 30, 1920
	Bill Nicholson, NL:Chi. Sept. 17, 1945
	Bake McBride, NL:Phil. Sept. 8, 1978
	Raul Mondesi, NL:LA Sept. 25, 1995
	Jeromy Burnitz, NL:Mil. Sept. 17, 2001
	Jayson Werth, NL:Wash. May 3, 2012
	Extra-Inning Game:
13	Rolando Roomes, NL:Cin. July 28, 1989 (17 inn)

Fewest Chances Accepted, Left Field, Game (Most Innings, Complete Game)
0	Chuck Hinton AL:Wash. June 14(2g), 1963 (18 inn)
	Joe Delahanty, NL:StL. July 19, 1908 (16 inn)
	Gary Redus, NL:Cin. June 21, 1983 (16 inn)
	Vince Coleman, NL:StL. May 11, 1988 (16 inn)
	Justin Ruggiano, NL:LA Sept. 15, 2015 (16 inn)
	Matt Holliday, NL:StL. July 22, 2016 (16 inn)
	Joc Pederson, NL:LA July 24, 2018 (16 inn)

Fewest Chances Accepted, Center Field, Game (Most Innings, Complete Game)
0	Bill Bruton, AL:Det. June 24, 1962 (22 inn)
	Ernie Orsatti, NL:StL. July 2(1g), 1933 (18 inn)

Fewest Chances Accepted, Right Field, Game (Most Innings, Complete Game)
0	Cap Peterson, AL:Wash. June 12, 1967 (22 inn)
	Lance Richbourg, NL:Bos. May 14, 1927 (18 inn)
	Art Shamsky, NL:Cin. July 19, 1966 (18 inn)

Most Chances Accepted, Inning
3	By many

PUTOUTS

Most Seasons Leading League
9	Max Carey, NL:Pitt. 1912-13, 16-18, 21-24
	Richie Ashburn, NL:Phil. 1949-54, 56-58
7	Tris Speaker, AL:Bos. 1909-10, 13-15; Clev. 18-19

Most Putouts, Lifetime
7093	Willie Mays, NL:NY/SF 1951-52, 54-72; NY 72-73
6792	Tris Speaker, AL:Bos. 1907-15; Clev. 16-26; Wash. 27; Phil. 28

Most Putouts, Season
547	Taylor Douthit, NL:StL. 1928
512	Chet Lemon, AL:Chi. 1977

Most Putouts, Game
12	Earl Clark, NL:Bos. May 10, 1929
	Lyman Bostock, AL:Minn. May 25(2g), 1977
	Jacoby Ellsbury, AL:Bos. May 20, 2009
	Extra-Inning Game:
13	Rolando Roomes, NL:Cin. July 28, 1989 (17 inn)

Most Putouts, Left Field, Game
11	Dick Harley, NL:StL. June 30, 1898
	Topsy Hartsel, NL:Chi. Sept. 10, 1901
	Paul Lehner, AL:Phil. June 25(2g), 1950
	Willie Horton, AL:Det. July 18, 1969
	Extra-Inning Game:
12	Tom McBride, AL:Wash. July 2, 1948 (12 inn)
	Rickey Henderson, AL:NY Sept. 11, 1988 (18 inn)
	Darin Erstad, AL:Ana. July 24, 2000 (12 inn)

Most Putouts, Center Field, Game
12	Earl Clark, NL:Bos. May 10, 1929
	Carden Gillenwater, NL:Bos. Sept. 11, 1946 (17 inn)
	Lloyd Merriman, NL:Cin. Sept. 7, 1951 (18 inn)
	Garry Maddox, NL:Phil. June 10, 1984 (12 inn)
	Lyman Bostock, AL:Minn. May 25(2g), 1977
	Harry Bay, AL:Clev. July 19, 1904 (12 inn)
	Ruppert Jones, AL:Sea. May 16, 1978 (16 inn)
	Rick Manning, AL:Mil. July 11, 1983 (12 inn)
	Gary Pettis, AL:Cal. June 4, 1985 (15 inn)
	Oddibe McDowell, AL:Tex. July 20, 1985 (15 inn)
	Jacoby Ellsbury, AL:Bos. May 20, 2009

Most Putouts, Right Field, Game
11	Tony Armas, AL:Oak. June 12, 1982
10	Bill Nicholson, NL:Chi. Sept. 17, 1945
	Raul Mondesi, NL:LA Sept. 25, 1995
	Jayson Werth, NL:Wash. May 3, 2012
	Extra-Inning Game:
13	Rolando Roomes, NL:Cin. July 28, 1989 (17 inn)

Most Putouts, Consecutive, Game
7	Ben Chapman, AL:Bos. June 25, 1937 (rf)
	Brady Clark, NL:Mil. Apr. 24, 2005 (cf)

ASSISTS

Most Seasons Leading League
7	Carl Yastrzemski, AL:Bos. 1962-64, 66, 69, 71, 77
5	Roberto Clemente, NL:Pitt. 1958, 60-61, 66-67

Most Assists, Lifetime
448	Tris Speaker, AL:Bos. 1907-15; Clev. 16-26; Wash. 27; Phil. 28
356	Jimmy Ryan, NL:Chi. 1885-89, 1891-1900
	NL Since 1900:
339	Max Carey, NL:Pitt. 1910-26; Brk. 26-29

Most Assists, Season, Since 1900
44	Chuck Klein, NL:Phil. 1930
35	Tris Speaker, AL:Bos. 1909
	Tris Speaker, AL:Bos. 1912

Most Assists, Game
4	Bill Crowley, NL:Buff. May 24, 1880
	Bill Crowley, NL:Buff. Aug. 27, 1880
	Fred Clarke, NL:Pitt. Aug. 23, 1910
	Ducky Holmes, AL:Chi. Aug. 21, 1903
	Lee Magee, AL:NY June 28, 1916
	Happy Felsch, AL:Chi. Aug. 14, 1919
	Bob Meusel, AL:NY Sept. 5(2g), 1921
	Sam Langford, AL:Clev. May 1, 1928
	Extra-Inning Game:
5	Dusty Miller, NL:Cin. May 30(2g), 1895 (11 inn)

Most Assists, Inning
2   By many

ERRORS

Most Seasons Leading League (Most)
7	Lou Brock, NL:Chi.-StL. 1964; StL. 65-68, 72-73
	Vladimir Guerrero, NL:Mtl. 1997-2002; AL:LA 06
5	Burt Shotton, AL:StL. 1912, 14-16; Wash. 18
	Reggie Jackson, AL:Oak. 1968, 70, 72, 75; Balt. 76

Most Errors, Lifetime, Since 1900
271	Ty Cobb, AL:Det. 1905-26; Phil. 27-28
235	Max Carey, NL:Pitt. 1910-26; Brk. 26-29

Most Errors, Season
52	Ed Beecher, PL:Buff. 1890
47	George Van Haltren, NL:Balt.-Pitt. 1892
	Since 1900:
36	Cy Seymour, NL:Cin. 1903
31	Roy Johnson, AL:Det. 1929

Fewest Errors, Season
	Most total chances
0	Mike Trout, AL:LA 2015 (435 tc)
	Curt Flood, NL:StL. 1966 (396 tc)
	Most games
0	Rocky Colavito, AL:Clev. 1965 (162 g)
	Juan Pierre, NL:Chi. 2006 (162 g)

Most Errors, Game
5	Jack Manning, NL:Bos. May 1, 1876
	Pop Snyder, NL:Lou. July 29, 1876
	Jim O'Rourke, NL:Bos. June 21, 1877
	Charlie Bennett, NL:Mil. June 15, 1878
	Mike Dorgan, NL:NY May 24, 1884
	Mike Tiernan, NL:NY May 16, 1887
	Marty Sullivan, NL:Chi. May 18, 1887
	Jim Clinton, AA:Balt. May 3, 1884
	Fred Tenney, UA:Wash. May 29, 1884
	Since 1900:
4	Kip Selbach, AL:Balt. Aug. 19, 1902
	Fred Nicholson, NL:Bos. June 16, 1922

Fewest Errors, Game (Most Innings, Complete Game)
0	Walt Cruise, NL:Bos. May 1, 1920 (26 inn)
	Les Mann, NL:Bos. May 1, 1920 (26 inn)
	Ray Powell, NL:Bos. May 1, 1920 (26 inn)
	Bernie Nies, NL:Brk. May 1, 1920 (26 inn)
	Zack Wheat, NL:Brk. May 1, 1920 (26 inn)
	Harold Baines, AL:Chi. May 8, 1984 (25 inn)
	Rudy Law, AL:Chi. May 8, 1984 (25 inn)

Most Errors, Inning
3	Jim Donahue, AA:KC July 4(2g), 1889 (1st)
	George Gore, NL:Chi. Aug. 8, 1883 (1st)
	Larry Herndon, NL:SF Sept. 6, 1980 (4th)
	Kip Selbach, AL:Wash. June 23, 1904 (8th)
	Harry Bay, AL:Clev. June 29(2g), 1905 (9th)
	Harry Heilmann, AL:Det. May 22, 1914 (1st)
	Herschel Bennett, AL:StL. Apr. 24, 1925 (8th)
	Scott Lusader, AL:Det. Sept. 9, 1989 (1st)
	Ryan Doumit, AL:Minn. Sept. 12, 2012 (8th)

Most Errorless Games, Consecutive, Lifetime
398	Nick Markakis AL:Balt.-NL:Atl. Aug. 11, 2012-June 24, 2015

Most Errorless Games, Consecutive, League
369	Darren Lewis, NL:SF July 13, 1991-June 29, 1994
336	Rich Amaral, AL:Sea.-Balt. Apr. 30, 1995-June 14, 2000

Most Errorless Games, Consecutive, Season
162	Rocky Colavito, AL:Clev. 1965 (entire season)
	Juan Pierre, NL:Chi. 2006 (entire season)

Most Errorless Chances Accepted, Consecutive, Lifetime
938	Darren Lewis, AL:Oak. Aug. 21-Oct. 3, 1990; NL:SF July 13, 1991-June 29, 1994

Most Errorless Chances Accepted, Consecutive, League
905	Darren Lewis, NL:SF July 13, 1991-June 29, 1994
846	Franklin Gutierrez, AL:Sea. Aug. 21, 2009-Sept. 11, 2012

Most Errorless Chances Accepted, Consecutive, Season
458   Darin Erstad, AL:Ana. Mar. 31-Sept. 22, 2002
396   Curt Flood, NL:StL. 1966 (entire season)

DOUBLE PLAYS

Most Seasons Leading League
6   Tris Speaker, AL:Bos. 1909, 12, 14-15; Clev. 16, 25
5   Max Carey, NL:Pitt. 1912, 15-16, 18, 21

Most Double Plays, Lifetime
138   Tris Speaker, AL:Bos. 1907-15; Clev. 16-26; Wash. 27; Phil. 28
87   Max Carey, NL:Pitt. 1910-26; Brk. 26-29

Most Double Plays, Season
15   Happy Felsch, AL:Chi. 1919
14   Jimmy Sheckard, NL:Balt. 1899
                NL since 1900:
12   Cy Seymour, NL:Cin. 1905
                Ginger Beaumont, NL:Bos. 1907
                Jimmy Sheckard, NL:Chi. 1911
                Mel Ott, NL:NY 1929

Most Double Plays, Game
3   Candy Nelson, AA:NY June 9, 1887
                Jack McCarthy, NL:Chi. Apr. 26, 1905
                Ira Flagstead, AL:Bos. Apr. 19(2g), 1926

Most Double Plays, Unassisted, Lifetime
6   Tris Speaker, AL:Bos. 1909, 10, 14; Clev. 18

Most Double Plays, Unassisted, League
6   Tris Speaker, AL:Bos. 1909, 10, 14 (2); Clev. 18 (2)
2   By many in NL

Most Double Plays, Unassisted, Season
2   Socks Seybold, AL:Phil. Aug. 15; Sept. 10(1g), 1907
                Tris Speaker, AL:Bos. Apr. 21; Aug. 8, 1914
                Tris Speaker, AL:Clev. Apr. 18, 29, 1918
                Jose Cardenal, AL:Clev. June 8; July 16, 1968
                Adam Comorosky, NL:Pitt. May 31; June 13, 1931

Most Double Plays, Unassisted, Game
1   By many; last:
                Jake Marisnick, AL:Hou. May 7, 2015
                Jose Guillen, NL:Wash. May 8, 2005

CATCHER

Most Seasons, Lifetime
25   Deacon McGuire, AA:Tol. 1884; Clev. 88; Roch. 90; Wash. 91
                NL:Det. 1885, 88; Phil. 86-88; Wash. 92-99; Brk. 1899-1901
                AL:Det. 1902-03, 12; NY 04-06; Bos. 07; Clev. 10

Most Seasons, League
24   Carlton Fisk, AL:Bos. 1969, 71-80; Chi. 81-93
21   Bob O'Farrell, NL:Chi. 1915-25, 34; StL. 25-28, 33, 35; NY 28-32; Cin. 34

PERCENTAGE

Most Seasons Leading League
6   Gabby Hartnett, NL:Chi. 1928, 30, 34-37
                Jim Sundberg, AL:Tex. 1976-79; Mil. 84; KC 86

Most Seasons, Consecutive, Leading League
4   Gabby Hartnett, NL:Chi. 1934-37
                Jim Sundberg, AL:Tex. 1976-79

Highest Percentage, Lifetime
.995   A.J. Pierzynski, AL:Minn. 1998-2003; Chi. 05-12; Tex. 13; Bos. 14; NL: SF 04; StL. 14; Atl. 15-16

Highest Percentage, League
.995   Yadier Molina, NL:StL. 2004-20
.995   A.J. Pierzynski, AL:Minn. 1998-2003; Chi. 05-12; Tex. 13; Bos. 14

Highest Percentage, Season (Most Chances)
1.000   Charles Johnson, NL:Fla. 1997 (973 tc)
               James McCann, AL:Det. 2015 (777 tc)

GAMES

Most Seasons Leading League
8	Jason Kendall, NL:Pitt. 1997-98, 2000, 02-04; Mil. 08; AL:Oak. 05
	Yogi Berra, AL:NY 1950-57
7	Jason Kendall, NL:Pitt. 1997-98, 2000, 02-04; Mil. 08
	Yadier Molina, NL:StL. 2009, 11, 13, 15-17, 20

Most Games, Lifetime
2427	Ivan Rodriguez, AL:Tex. 1991-2002, 09; Det. 04-08; NY 08; NL:Fla. 2003; Hou. 09; Wash. 10-11

Most Games, League
2226	Carlton Fisk, AL:Bos. 1969, 71-80; Chi. 81-93
2056	Gary Carter, NL:Mtl. 1974-84, 92; NY 85-89; SF 90; LA 1991

Most Games, Consecutive
312	Frankie Hayes, AL:StL.-Phil.-Clev. Oct. 2, 1943-May 5, 1946
217	Ray Mueller, NL:Cin. July 31, 1943-Oct. 1, 1944

Most Seasons, 100 or more Games
17	Ivan Rodriguez, AL:Tex. 1992-93, 95-2002; Det. 04-07; Det.-NY 08; NL:Fla. 03; Wash. 10; NL:Hou.-AL:Tex. 09
15	Yadier Molina, NL:StL. 2005-19
14	Ivan Rodriguez, AL:Tex. 1992-93, 95-2002; Det. 04-07; Det.-NY 08

Most Seasons, Consecutive, 100 or more Games
15	Yadier Molina, NL:StL. 2005-19
13	Bill Dickey, AL:NY 1929-41

Most Games, Season
160	Randy Hundley, NL:Chi. 1968
155	Frankie Hayes, AL:Phil. 1944
	Jim Sundberg, AL:Tex. 1975

Most Games, Consecutive, Season
155	Ray Mueller, NL:Cin. 1944
	Frankie Hayes, AL:Phil. 1944

CHANCES ACCEPTED

Most Seasons Leading League
8	Ray Schalk, AL:Chi. 1913-17, 19-20, 22
	Yogi Berra, AL:NY 1950-52, 54-57, 59
	Gary Carter, NL:Mtl. 1977-82; NY 85, 88

Most Chances Accepted, Lifetime
16,091	Ivan Rodriguez, AL:Tex. 1991-2002, 09; Det. 04-08; NY 08; NL:Fla. 2003; Hou. 09; Wash. 10-11

Most Chances Accepted, League
14,729	Yadier Molina, NL:StL. 2004-20
13,443	Ivan Rodriguez, AL:Tex. 1991-2002, 09; Det. 04-08; NY 08

Most Chances Accepted, Season
1214	Johnny Edwards, NL:Hou. 1969
1134	Roberto Perez, AL:Clev. 2019

Most Chances Accepted, Game
23	George Bignal, UA:Mil. Oct. 3, 1884
22	Sandy Nava, NL:Prov. June 7, 1884
	Since 1900:
21	Miguel Montero, NL:Chi. June 5, 2016
	Yan Gomes, AL:Clev. Aug. 17(1g), 2017
	Welington Castillo, AL:Chi. Apr. 28, 2019
	Extra-Inning Game:
27	Jose Molina, AL:Ana. June 8, 2004 (17 inn)
	Erik Kratz, NL:SF Apr. 12, 2019 (18 inn)

Most Chances Accepted, Inning
5	Joe Garagiola, NL:StL. June 17, 1949 (8th)
4	By many in AL

PUTOUTS

Most Seasons Leading League
9	Ray Schalk, AL:Chi. 1913-20, 22
8	Gary Carter, NL:Mtl. 1977-82, NY 85, 88

Most Putouts, Lifetime
14,864	Ivan Rodriguez, AL:Tex. 1991-2002, 09; Det. 04-08; NY 08; NL:Fla. 2003; Hou. 09; Wash. 10-11

Most Putouts, League
13,741	Yadier Molina, NL:StL. 2004-20
12,377	Ivan Rodriguez, AL:Tex. 1991-2002, 09; Det. 04-08; NY 08

Most Putouts, Season

1169	Yasmani Grandal, NL:Mil. 2019
1082	Roberto Perez, AL:Clev. 2019

Most Putouts, Game

20	Jerry Grote, NL:NY Apr. 22, 1970
	Sandy Martinez, NL:Chi. May 6, 1998
	Wilson Ramos, NL:Wash. May 11, 2016
	Rich Gedman, AL:Bos. Apr. 29, 1986
	Dan Wilson, AL:Sea. Aug. 8, 1997
	Welington Castillo, AL:Chi. Apr. 28, 2019
	Extra-Inning Game:
26	Jose Molina, AL:Ana. June 8, 2004 (17 inn)
	Yasmani Grandal, NL:LA June 2, 2017 (12 inn)

Fewest Putouts, Game (Most Innings, Complete Game)

0	Wally Schang, AL:Bos. Sept. 13, 1920 (14 inn)
	Gene Desautels, AL:Clev. Aug. 11(1g), 1942 (14 inn)
	Jimmie Wilson, NL:Phil. Aug. 31(1g), 1927 (13 inn)
	Hal Finney, NL:Pitt. Sept. 22, 1931 (13 inn)

ASSISTS

Most Seasons Leading League

6	Bob Boone, NL:Phil. 1973; AL:Cal. 82-84, 86, 88
	Gabby Hartnett, NL:Chi. 1925, 27-28, 30, 34-35
	Del Crandall, NL:Mil. 1953-54, 57-60
	Jim Sundberg, AL:Tex. 1975-78, 80-81

Most Assists, Lifetime

1835	Deacon McGuire, AA:Tol. 1884; Clev. 88; Roch. 90; Wash. 91
	NL:Det. 85, 88; Phil. 86-88; Wash. 92-99; Brk. 1899-1901
	AL:Det. 02-03, 12; NY 04-06; Bos. 07; Clev. 08, 10

Most Assists, League

1807	Ray Schalk, AL:Chi. 1912-28
1593	Red Dooin, NL:Phil. 1902-14; Cin. 15; NY 15-16

Most Assists, Season

214	Pat Moran, NL:Bos. 1903
212	Oscar Stanage, AL:Det. 1911

Most Assists, Game

9	Mike Hines, NL:Bos. May 1, 1883
	Since 1900:
8	Wally Schang, AL:Bos. May 12, 1920
7	Ed McFarland, NL:Phil. May 7, 1901
	Fred Jacklitsch, NL:Brk. Apr. 21, 1903
	Bill Bergen, NL:Brk. Aug. 23(2g), 1909
	Jimmy Archer, NL:Pitt. May 24, 1918
	Bert Adams, NL:Phil. Aug. 21, 1919
	Benito Santiago, NL:SD May 15, 1989 (11 inn)

Fewest Assists, Game (Most Innings, Complete Game)

0	Bob Swift, AL:Det. July 21, 1945 (24 inn)
	Yorvit Torrealba, NL:Col. Apr. 17, 2008 (22 inn)

Most Assists, Inning

3	By many; last:
	Michael Perez, AL:TB Aug. 28, 2020 (1st)
	Will Smith, NL:LA Aug. 15, 2019 (5th)

ERRORS

Most Seasons Leading League (Most)

7	Ivey Wingo, NL:StL. 1912-13; Cin. 16-18, 20-21
6	Birdie Tebbetts, AL:Det. 1939-40, 42; Det.-Bos. 47; Bos. 48-49

Most Errors, Lifetime, Since 1900

234	Ivey Wingo, NL:StL. 1911-14; Cin. 15-26, 29

Most Errors, League, Since 1900

234	Ivey Wingo, NL:StL. 1911-14; Cin. 15-26, 29
223	Wally Schang, AL:Phil. 1913-17, 30; Bos. 18-20; NY 21-25; StL. 26-29; Det. 31

Most Errors, Season

94	Nat Hicks, NL:NY 1876
	Since 1900:
41	Oscar Stanage, AL:Det. 1911
40	Red Dooin, NL:Phil. 1909

Most Total Chances, No Errors, Season
973	Charles Johnson, NL:Fla. 1997 (123 g)
777	James McCann, AL:Det. 2015 (112 g)

Fewest Errors, Season (Minimum: 150 games)
4	Randy Hundley, NL:Chi. 1967 (152 g; 928 tc)
	Jim Sundberg, AL:Tex. 1979 (150 g; 833 tc)

Most Errors, Game
7	Jack Rowe, NL:Buff. May 16, 1883
	Dickie Lowe, NL:Det. June 26, 1884
	Billy Taylor, AA:Balt. May 29(1g), 1886
	Since 1900:
4	Gabby Street, NL:Bos. June 7, 1905
	John Peters, AL:Clev. May 16, 1918
	Lena Styles, AL:Phil. July 29, 1921
	Bill Moore, AL:Bos. Sept. 26(2g), 1927

Fewest Errors, Game (Most Innings, Complete Game)
0	Mike Powers, AL:Phil. Sept. 1, 1906 (24 inn)
	Buddy Rosar, AL:Phil. July 21, 1945 (24 inn)
	Bob Swift, AL:Det. July 21, 1945 (24 inn)
	Jerry Grote, NL:NY Apr. 15, 1968 (24 inn)
	Hal King, NL:Hou. Apr. 15, 1968 (24 inn)

Most Errors, Inning
4	Doggie Miller, NL:StL. May 24, 1895 (2nd)
	Since 1900:
3	Jeff Sweeney, AL:NY July 10, 1912 (1st)
	John Peters, AL:Clev. May 16, 1918 (1st)
	Andy Seminick, NL:Cin. July 16, 1952 (1st)
	Jeff Reed, NL:Mtl. July 28, 1987 (7th)

Most Errorless Games, Consecutive, Lifetime
253	Mike Redmond, NL:Fla.-AL:Minn.-Clev. July 22, 2004-May 18, 2010

Most Errorless Games, Consecutive, League
252	Mike Matheny, NL:StL. Aug. 2, 2002-Aug. 1, 2004
232	Mike Redmond, AL:Minn.-Clev. Apr. 6, 2005-May 18, 2010

Most Errorless Games, Consecutive, Season
138	Mike Matheny, NL:StL. 2003 (entire season)
117	Buddy Rosar, AL:Phil. Apr. 16-Sept. 29(1g), 1946
	A.J. Pierzynski, AL:Chi. Apr. 19-Oct. 2, 2005

Most Errorless Chances Accepted, Consecutive, League
1733	Chris Snyder, NL:Ari. Aug. 20, 2007-June 6, 2010
1474	Mike Redmond, AL:Minn. Apr. 6, 2005-May 22, 2010

Most Errorless Chances Accepted, Consecutive, Season
973	Charles Johnson, NL:Fla. 1997 (entire season)
913	Roberto Perez, AL:Clev. May 6-Sept. 27, 2019

PASSED BALLS

Most Seasons Leading League (Most)
9	Ernie Lombardi, NL:Cin. 1932, 35-41; NY 45
5	Mickey Cochrane, AL:Phil. 1925-26, 29, 31-32
	Rick Ferrell, AL:StL. 1931; Wash. 39-40, 44-46

Most Passed Balls, Season
99	Pop Snyder, NL:Bos. 1881
	Mike Hines, NL:Bos. 1883
	Since 1900:
35	Geno Petralli, AL:Tex. 1987
29	Frank Bowerman, NL:NY 1900

Most Passed Balls. Game
12	Alex Gardner, AA:Wash. May 10, 1884
10	Pat Dealy, NL:Bos. May 3, 1886
	Since 1900:
6	Rube Vickers, NL:Cin. Oct. 4, 1902
	Jerry Goff, NL:Hou. May 12, 1996
	Geno Petralli, AL:Tex. Aug. 30, 1987

Fewest Passed Balls, Game (Most Innings, Complete Game)
0	Carlton Fisk, AL:Chi. May 8, 1984 (25 inn)
	Jerry Grote, NL:NY Apr. 15, 1968 (24 inn)
	Hal King, NL:Hou. Apr. 15, 1968 (24 inn)

Most Passed Balls, Inning
5	Dan Sullivan, AA:StL. Aug. 9, 1885 (3rd)
4	Ray Katt, NL:NY Sept. 10, 1954 (8th)
	Geno Petralli, AL:Tex. Aug. 22, 1987 (7th)
	Ryan Lavarnway, AL:Bos. Aug. 6, 2013 (1st)

DOUBLE PLAYS

Most Seasons Leading League
6	Gabby Hartnett, NL:Chi. 1925, 27, 30-31, 34-35
	Yogi Berra, AL:NY 1949-52, 54, 56
	Jason Kendall, NL:Pitt. 1997, 99; 2002; Mil. 08; AL:Oak. 2006, KC 10

Most Double Plays, League
220	Ray Schalk, AL:Chi. 1912-28
163	Gabby Hartnett, NL:Chi. 1922-40; NY 41

Most Double Plays, Season
29	Frankie Hayes, AL:Phil.-Clev. 1945
24	Tom Haller, NL:LA 1968

Most Double Plays, Game
4	Chris Hoiles, AL:Balt. Apr. 9, 1998
3	Jack O'Neill, NL:Chi. Apr. 26, 1905
	John Bliss, NL:StL. Sept. 10(2g), 1909
	Bob O'Farrell, NL:Chi. July 9(2g), 1919 (11 inn)
	Shanty Hogan, NL:NY Aug. 19, 1931
	Ebba St. Claire, NL:Bos. Aug. 9, 1951
	Ron Hodges, NL:NY Apr. 23, 1978 (12 inn)
	Eddie Taubensee, NL:Cin. Apr. 23, 1999
	Damian Miller, NL:Ari. May 25, 1999
	Brian Schneider, NL:Mtl. June 11, 2004
	Henry Blanco, NL:Chi. July 22, 2006
	J.T. Realmuto, NL:Mia. May 21, 2016

RUNNERS CAUGHT STEALING

Most Runners Caught Stealing, Game
8	Duke Farrell, NL:Wash. May 11, 1897
	Since 1900:
6	Bill Bergen, NL:Brk. Aug. 23(2g), 1909
	Wally Schang, AL:Phil. May 12, 1915

Most Runners Caught Stealing, Inning
3	Jocko Milligan, AA:Phil. July 26, 1887 (3rd)
	Les Nunamaker, AL:NY Aug. 3, 1914 (7th)
2	By many in NL

PITCHER

Most Seasons, Lifetime
27	Nolan Ryan, NL:NY 1966, 68-71; Hou. 80-88; AL:Cal. 1972-79; Tex. 89-93

Most Seasons, Consecutive, Lifetime
26	Nolan Ryan, NL:NY 1968-71; Hou. 80-88; AL:Cal. 1972-79; Tex. 89-93

Most Seasons, League
23	Early Wynn, AL:Wash. 1939, 41-44, 46-48; Clev. 49-57, 63; Chi. 58-62
	Greg Maddux, NL:Chi. 1986-92, 2004-06; Atl. 1993-2003; LA 06, 08; SD 07-08

Most Seasons, Consecutive, League
23	Greg Maddux, NL:Chi. 1986-92, 2004-06; Atl. 1993-2003; LA 06, 08; SD 07-08
22	Sam Jones, AL:Clev. 1914-15; Bos. 16-21; NY 22-26; StL. 27; Wash. 28-31; Chi. 32-35

PERCENTAGE

Most Seasons Leading League
4	Claude Passeau, NL:Phil.-Chi. 1939; Chi. 42-43, 45
	Larry Jackson, NL:StL. 1957; Chi. 64-65; Phil. 68
3	Walter Johnson, AL:Wash. 1913, 17, 22

Most Seasons, Consecutive, Leading League
2   By many

Highest Percentage, Lifetime (Minimum: 300 tc)
.990   Don Mossi, AL:Clev. 1954-58, Det. 59-63, Chi. 64, KC 65
.990   Woody Fryman, NL:Pitt. 1966-77; Phil. 68-72; Mtl. 75-76, 78-83; Cin. 77; Chi. 78

Highest Percentage, Season, Most total chances:
1.000   Frank Owen, AL:Chi. 1904 (151 tc)
          Randy Jones, NL:SD 1976 (112 tc)

GAMES

Most Seasons Leading Major Leagues
5   Firpo Marberry, AL:Wash. 1924-26, 28, 32

Most Seasons Leading League
6   Joe McGinnity, AL:Balt. 1901; NL:NY 1903-07
        Firpo Marberry, AL:Wash. 1924-26, 28-29, 32
5   Joe McGinnity, NL:NY 1903-07

Most Games, Lifetime
1252   Jesse Orosco, NL:NY 1979, 81-87; LA 88, 2001-02; StL. 2000; SD 03;
          AL:Clev. 89-91, Mil. 92-94, Balt. 95-99; NY 03; Minn. 03

Most Games, League
1119   John Franco, NL:Cin. 1984-89; NY 90-2001, 03-04; Hou. 05
1115   Mariano Rivera, AL:NY 1995-2013

Most Games, Consecutive, Since 1900
13   Mike Marshall, NL:LA June 18-July 3(1g), 1974
       Dale Mohorcic, AL:Tex. Aug. 6-20, 1986

Most Games, Season
106   Mike Marshall, NL:LA 1974
90   Mike Marshall, AL:Minn. 1979

CHANCES ACCEPTED

Most Seasons Leading League
15   Greg Maddux, NL:Chi. 1989-92; Atl. 93-96, 98-2001, 03; SD 07; SD-LA 08
8   Bob Lemon, AL:Clev. 1948-54, 56

Most Chances Accepted, Lifetime, Since 1900
1761   Christy Mathewson, NL:NY 1900-16; Cin. 16
1606   Walter Johnson, AL:Wash. 1907-27

Most Chances Accepted, Season
262   Ed Walsh, AL:Chi. 1907
216   John Clarkson, NL:Bos. 1889
        NL Since 1900:
168   Christy Mathewson, NL:NY 1908

Most Chances Accepted, Game
13   Nick Altrock, AL:Chi. Aug. 6, 1904
       Ed Walsh, AL:Chi. Apr. 19, 1907
12   Rip Sewell, NL:Pitt. June 6(2g), 1941
        Extra-Inning Game:
15   Ed Walsh, AL:Chi. July 16, 1907 (13 inn)
13   Leon Cadore, NL:Brk. May 1, 1920 (26 inn)

Fewest Chances Accepted, Game (Most Innings, Complete Game)
0   Milt Watson, NL:Phil. July 17, 1918 (20 inn)
      Red Ruffing, AL:NY July 23(1g), 1932 (15 inn)

Most Chances Accepted, Inning
4   Phil Regan, NL:Chi. June 6, 1969 (6th)
     Fernando Valenzuela, NL:LA Apr. 20, 1983 (3rd)
     Hideo Nomo, NL:LA Sept. 17, 1996 (6th)
3   By many in AL

PUTOUTS

Most Seasons Leading League
8   Greg Maddux, NL:Chi. 1989-92, 2004; Atl. 93, 96, 98
5   Bob Lemon, AL:Clev. 1948-49, 52-54

Most Putouts, Lifetime

546	Greg Maddux, NL:Chi. 1986-92, 2004-06; Atl. 1993-2003; LA 06, 08; SD 07-08
387	Jack Morris, AL:Det. 1977-90; Minn. 1991; Tor. 92-93; Clev. 94

Most Putouts, Season

52	Al Spalding, NL:Chi. 1876
	Since 1900:
49	Mike Boddicker, AL:Balt. 1984
41	Kevin Brown, NL:LA 1999

Most Putouts, Game

7	Greg Maddux, NL:Chi. Apr. 29, 1990
6	Bert Blyleven, AL:Clev. June 24, 1984
	Eric King, AL:Det. July 8, 1986
	Kirk Saarloos, AL:Oak. Apr. 22, 2005
	Extra-Inning Game:
7	Dick Fowler, AL:Phil. June 9, 1949 (12 inn)

Fewest Putouts, Game (Most Innings, Complete Game)

0	Babe Adams, NL:Pitt. July 17, 1914 (21 inn)
	Rube Marquard, NL:NY July 17, 1914 (21 inn)
	Saul Rogovin, AL:Chi. July 12, 1951 (17 inn)

Most Putouts, Inning

3	By many; last:
	Peter Fairbanks, AL:TB Aug. 22, 2020 (7th)
	Brandon Kintzler, NL:Chi. Aug. 31, 2019 (8th)

ASSISTS

Most Seasons Leading League

12	Greg Maddux, NL:Chi. 1990; Atl. 92-93, 95-96, 98, 2000-01, 03; Chi.-LA 06; SD 07; LA-SD 08
6	Bob Lemon, AL:Clev. 1948-49, 51-53, 56

Most Assists, League, Since 1900

1489	Christy Mathewson, NL:NY 1900-16; Cin. 16
1337	Walter Johnson, AL:Wash. 1907-27

Most Assists, Season

225	Ed Walsh, AL:Chi. 1907
168	John Clarkson, NL:Bos. 1889
	NL Since 1900:
141	Christy Mathewson, NL:NY 1908

Most Assists, Game

11	Al Orth, AL:NY Aug. 12, 1906
	Ed Walsh, AL:Chi. Apr. 19 & Aug. 12, 1907
	George McConnell, AL:NY Sept. 2(2g), 1912
	Mellie Wolfgang, AL:Chi. Aug. 29, 1914
	Rip Sewell, NL:Pitt. June 6(2g), 1941
	Extra-Inning Game:
12	Ed Walsh, AL:Chi. July 16, 1907 (13 inn)
	Nick Altrock, AL:Chi. June 7, 1908 (10 inn)
	Leon Cadore, NL:Brk. May 1, 1920 (26 inn)

Fewest Assists, Game (Most Innings, Complete Game)

0	Milt Watson, NL:Phil. July 17, 1918 (20 inn)
	Red Ruffing, AL:NY July 23(1g), 1932 (15 inn)

Most Assists, Inning

3	By many; last:
	Shawn Armstrong, AL:Sea. Aug. 28, 2018 (8th)
	Scott Alexander, NL:LA June 5, 2018 (6th)

ERRORS

Most Seasons Leading League (Most)

5	Hippo Vaughn, NL:Chi. 1914-15, 17, 19-20
	Warren Spahn, NL:Bos. 1949-50, 52; Mil. 54, 64
4	Allen Sothoron, AL:StL. 1917-20
	Dizzy Trout, AL:Det. 1943-45, 48
	Dean Chance, AL:LA 1963; Minn. 67-68; Det. 71
	Nolan Ryan, AL:Cal. 1975-78

Most Errors, Lifetime, Since 1900

90	Joe McGinnity, NL:Brk. 1900; NY 1902-08; AL:Balt. 1901-02
	Nolan Ryan, NL:NY 1966, 68-71; Hou. 80-88; AL:Cal. 1972-79; Tex. 89-93

Most Errors, League, Since 1900

79	Rube Waddell, AL:Phil. 1902-07; StL. 08-10
75	Joe McGinnity, NL:Brk. 1900; 1902-08

Most Errors, Season
28	Jim Whitney, NL:Bos. 1881
	Since 1900:
17	Doc Newton, NL:Cin.-Brk. 1901
15	Jack Chesbro, AL:NY 1904
	Rube Waddell, AL:Phil. 1905
	Ed Walsh, AL:Chi. 1912

Most Errors, Game
5	Ed Doheny, NL:NY Aug. 15, 1899
	Since 1900:
4	Doc Newton, NL:Cin. Sept. 13(1g), 1900
	Lave Winham, NL:Pitt. Sept. 21(1g), 1903
	Bill Cramer, NL:Cin. June 25(1g), 1912
	Bert Husting, AL:Phil. July 11, 1902
	Jack Warhop, AL:NY Oct. 1(1g), 1914
	Buster Ross, AL:Bos. May 17, 1925

Fewest Errors, Game (Most Innings, Complete Game)
0	Leon Cadore, NL:Brk. May 1, 1920 (26 inn)
	Joe Oeschger, NL:Bos. May 1, 1920 (26 inn)
	Jack Coombs, AL:Phil. Sept. 1, 1906 (24 inn)
	Joe Harris, AL:Bos. Sept. 1, 1906 (24 inn)

Most Errors, Inning
3	Cy Seymour, NL:NY May 21, 1898 (6th)
	Tommy John, AL:NY July 27, 1988 (4th)
	Mike Sirotka, AL:Chi. Apr. 9, 1999 (5th)

Most Errorless Games, Consecutive, Lifetime
667	Dan Plesac, NL:Chi.-Pitt.-Ari.-Phil.; AL:Tor. July 30, 1993-Sept. 28, 2003

Most Errorless Games, Consecutive, League
551	Mariano Rivera, AL:NY Aug. 4, 2004-Sept. 26, 2013
549	Heath Bell, NL:NY-SD-Mia.-Ari. Aug.24, 2004-July 21, 2013

Most Errorless Games, Consecutive, Season
94	Salomon Torres, NL:Pitt. 2006
88	Wilbur Wood, AL:Chi. 1968
	Sean Runyan, AL:Det. 1998

Most Errorless Chances Accepted, Consecutive, Lifetime
273	Claude Passeau, NL:Chi. Sept. 21, 1941-May 20, 1946
231	Rick Langford, AL:Oak. Apr. 13, 1977-Oct. 2, 1980

DOUBLE PLAYS

Most Seasons Leading League
6	Greg Maddux, NL:Chi. 1987, 90-91; Atl. 94, 96; Chi.-LA 2006
4	Willis Hudlin, AL:Clev. 1929-31, 34
	Kenny Rogers, AL:Tex. 2000, 02, 05; Det. 08

Most Double Plays, Lifetime
98	Greg Maddux, NL:Chi. 1986-92, 2004-06; Atl. 1993-2003; LA 06, 08; SD 07-08
78	Bob Lemon, AL:Clev. 1941-42, 46-58

Most Double Plays, Season
15	Bob Lemon, AL:Clev. 1953
12	Curt Davis, NL:Phil. 1934
	Randy Jones, NL:SD 1976

Most Double Plays, Game
4	Milt Gaston, AL:Chi. May 17, 1932
	Hal Newhouser, AL:Det. May 19, 1948
3	By many in NL; last:
	Lance Lynn, NL:StL. July 25, 2013

Most Double Plays, Unassisted, League
2	Tex Carleton, NL:Chi. 1935; Brk. 40
	Claude Passeau, NL:Phil. 1938; Chi. 45

Most Double Plays, Unassisted, Game
1	By many; Last:
	Joe Jimenez, AL:Det. Apr. 2, 2019 (8th)
	Luis Perdomo, NL:SD Aug. 28, 2016 (7th)

INDIVIDUAL PITCHING RECORDS

SERVICE

Most Seasons, Lifetime
27   Nolan Ryan, NL:NY 1966, 68-71; Hou. 80-88; AL:Cal. 72-79; Tex. 89-93

Most Seasons, Consecutive, Lifetime
26   Nolan Ryan, NL:NY 1968-71; Hou. 80-88; AL:Cal. 72-79; Tex. 89-93

Most Seasons, League
23   Early Wynn, AL:Wash. 1939, 41-44, 46-48; Clev. 49-57, 63; Chi. 58-62
              Greg Maddux, NL:Chi. 1986-92, 2004-06; Atl. 93-03; LA 06; SD 07; SD-LA 08

Most Seasons, Consecutive, League
23   Greg Maddux, NL:Chi. 1986-92, 2004-06; Atl. 93-03; LA 06; SD 07; SD-LA 08
22   Sam Jones, AL:Clev. 1914-15; Bos. 16-21; NY 22-26; StL. 27; Wash. 28-31; Chi. 32-35

Most Leagues, Lifetime
4   Jerry Bakely, AA:1883, 88, 91; UA:84; NL:89; PL:90
              Cannonball Crane, UA:1884; NL:86, 88-89, 91-93; PL:90; AA:91
              Gus Weyhing, AA:1887-89, 91; PL:1890; NL:1892-1901; AL:1901
              Frank Foreman, UA:1884; AA:85, 89, 91; NL:90-93, 95-96; AL:1901-02

Most Leagues, Season
3   By many

CLUBS

Most Seasons, One Club
21   Walter Johnson, AL:Wash. 1907-27
              Ted Lyons, AL:Chi. 1923-42, 46
              Phil Niekro, NL:Mil./Atl. 1964-83, 87

Most Seasons, Consecutive, One Club
21   Walter Johnson, AL:Wash. 1907-27
20   Warren Spahn, NL:Bos.-Mil. 1942-64 (1943-45 Military Service)
              Phil Niekro, NL:Mil./Atl. 1964-83

Most Clubs, Lifetime
14   Edwin Jackson, NL:LA 2003-05; Ari. 10; StL. 11; Wash. 12, 17; Chi. 13-15; Atl. 15; Mia. 16; SD 17
              AL:TB 06-08; Det. 09; Chi. 10-11; Balt. 17; Oak. 18; Tor. 19

Most Clubs, League
9   Julian Tavarez, NL:SF 1997-99; Col. 2000; Chi. 01; Fla. 02; Pitt. 03; StL. 04-05; Mil. 08; Atl. 08; Wash. 09
8   Bartolo Colon, AL:Clev. 1997-2002; Chi. 03, 09; Ana./LA 04-07; Bos. 08; NY 11; Oak. 12-13; Minn. 17; Tex. 18

Most Clubs, Major Leagues, Season
5   Oliver Drake, NL:Mil.; AL:Clev.-LA-Tor.-Minn. 2018

Most Clubs, League, Season
4   Ted Gray, AL:Chi.-Clev.-NY-Balt. 1955
              Oliver Drake, AL:Clev.-LA-Tor.-Minn. 2018
3   By many in NL

GAMES

Most Seasons Leading Major Leagues
5   Firpo Marberry, AL:Wash. 1924-26, 28, 32

Most Seasons, Consecutive, Leading Major Leagues
3   Bill Hutchinson, NL:Chi. 1890-92
              Ace Adams, NL:NY 1942-44
              Steve Kline, NL:Mtl. 1999-2000; StL. 01
              Pedro Feliciano, NL:NY 2008-10
              Firpo Marberry, AL:Wash. 1924-26

Most Seasons Leading League
6   Joe McGinnity, AL:Balt. 1901; NL:NY 1903-07
              Firpo Marberry, AL:Wash. 1924-26, 28-29, 32
5   Joe McGinnity, NL:NY 03-07

Most Seasons, Consecutive, Leading League
5   Joe McGinnity, NL:NY 1903-07
3   Ed Walsh, AL:Chi. 1910-12
              Firpo Marberry, AL:Wash. 1924-26
              Wilbur Wood, AL:Chi. 1968-70

Most Games, Lifetime
1252   Jesse Orosco, NL:NY 1979, 81-87; LA 88, 2001-02; StL. 2000; SD 03
                AL:Clev. 89-91; Mil. 92-94; Balt. 95-99; NY 03; Minn. 03

Most Games, League
1119   John Franco, NL:Cin. 1984-89; NY 90-2001, 03-04; Hou. 05
1115   Mariano Rivera, AL:NY 1995-2013

Most Games, Season
106   Mike Marshall, NL:LA 1974 (0 starts)
90   Mike Marshall, AL:Minn. 1979 (1 start)

Most Games, Consecutive
13   Mike Marshall, NL:LA June 18-July 3(1g), 1974
             Dale Mohorcic, AL:Tex. Aug. 6-20, 1986

GAMES STARTED

Most Seasons Leading Major Leagues
6   Robin Roberts, NL:Phil. 1950-55
          Tom Glavine, NL:Atl. 1993, 96, 99-2002

Most Seasons, Consecutive, Leading Major Leagues
6   Robin Roberts, NL:Phil. 1950-55

Most Seasons Leading League
7   Greg Maddux, NL:Chi. 1990-92, 2005; Atl. 93, 2000, 03
5   Bob Feller, AL:Clev. 1940-41, 46-48
          Early Wynn, AL:Wash. 1943; Clev. 51, 54, 57; Chi. 59
          Justin Verlander, AL:Det. 2009, 11, 13; Hou. 18-19

Most Seasons, Consecutive, Leading League
6   Robin Roberts, NL:Phil. 1950-55
4   Wilbur Wood, AL:Chi. 1972-75
          Dave Stewart, AL:Oak. 1988-91

Most Games Started, Lifetime
815   Cy Young, NL:Clev. 1890-98; StL. 1899-1900; Bos. 11; AL:Bos. 1901-08; Clev. 09-11

Most Games Started, League
740   Greg Maddux, NL:Chi. 1986-92, 2004-06; Atl. 1994-2003; LA 06, 08; SD 07-08
666   Walter Johnson, AL:Wash. 1907-27

Most Games Started, Consecutive, Lifetime
712   Greg Maddux, NL:Chi.-Atl.-LA-SD Sept. 15, 1987-Sept. 27, 2008
597   Roger Clemens, AL:Bos.-Tor.-NY July 26, 1984-June 21, 2007

Most Games Started, Season
75   Will White, NL:Cin. 1879
          Since 1900:
51   Jack Chesbro, AL:NY 1904
48   Joe McGinnity, NL:NY 1903
          No relief appearances:
49   Wilbur Wood, AL:Chi. 1972
44   Phil Niekro, NL:Atl. 1979

Most Games Started, Incomplete, Season
37   Steve Bedrosian, NL:Atl. 1985 (37 starts)
36   Stan Bahnsen, AL:Chi. 1972 (41 starts)

Most Games Started, No Complete Games, Season
37   Steve Bedrosian, NL:Atl. 1985
35   Wilson Alvarez, AL:Chi. 1996
          Sterling Hitchcock, AL:Sea. 1996
          Rick Helling, AL:Tex. 2000
          Rodrigo Lopez, AL:Balt. 2005
          Barry Zito, AL:Oak. 2005

Most Games Started, Opening Day, Lifetime
16   Tom Seaver, NL:NY 1968-77, 83; Cin. 78-79, 81; AL:Chi. 1985-86

Most Games Started, Opening Day, League
14   Walter Johnson, AL:Wash. 1910, 12-21, 23-24, 26
          Jack Morris, AL:Det. 1980-90; Minn. 91; Tor. 92-93
          Tom Seaver, NL:NY 1968-77, 83; Cin. 78-79, 81
          Steve Carlton, NL:Phil. 72-75; 77-86

Most Games Started, Consecutive, Opening Day, League
14   Jack Morris, AL:Det. 1980-90; Minn. 91; Tor. 92-93
12   Robin Roberts, NL:Phil. 1950-61
          Tom Seaver, NL:NY 1968-77; Cin. 78-79

COMPLETE GAMES

Most Seasons Leading Major Leagues
7   Warren Spahn, NL:Bos. 1951; Mil. 57-60, 62-63

Most Seasons, Consecutive, Leading Major Leagues
5   Robin Roberts, NL:Phil. 1952-56

Most Seasons Leading League
9   Warren Spahn, NL:Bos. 1949, 51; Mil. 57-63
6   Walter Johnson, AL:Wash. 1910-11, 13-16

Most Seasons, Consecutive, Leading League
7   Warren Spahn, NL:Mil. 1957-63
4   Walter Johnson, AL:Wash. 1913-16

Most Complete Games, Lifetime
751   Cy Young, NL:Clev. 1890-98; StL. 1899-1900; Bos. 11; AL:Bos. 1901-08; Clev. 09-11

Most Complete Games, League
552   Pud Galvin, NL:Buff. 1879-85; Pitt. 87-89, 91-92; StL. 92
       Since 1900:
531   Walter Johnson, AL:Wash. 1907-27
437   Grover Alexander, NL:Phil. 1911-17, 30; Chi. 18-26; StL. 26-29

Most Complete Games, Season
75   Will White, NL:Cin. 1879 (75 starts)
       Since 1900:
48   Jack Chesbro, AL:NY 1904 (51 starts)
45   Vic Willis, NL:Bos. 1902 (46 starts)

Most Complete Games, Consecutive, Lifetime
198   Jack Lynch, NL:Buff. 1881; AA:NY 83-87, 90

Most Complete Games, Consecutive, League
197   Jack Lynch, AA:NY 1883-87, 90
187   Jack Taylor, NL:Chi. 1901-03, 06; StL. 04-06
54   Cy Young, AL:Bos. 1903-04
        Earl Moore, AL:Clev. 1902-04

Most Complete Games, Consecutive, Season, Since 1900
43   Vic Willis, NL:Bos. 1902 (five relief appearances during streak)
38   George Mullin, AL:Det. 1904 (one relief appearance during streak)

SHUTOUTS

Most Seasons Leading Major Leagues
6   Cy Young, NL:Clev. 1892, 95-96; StL. 1900; AL:Bos. 03-04
       Since 1900:
4   Christy Mathewson, NL:NY 1902, 05, 07-08
        Grover Alexander, NL:Phil. 1911, 15-16; Chi. 19
        Walter Johnson, AL:Wash. 1913-14, 18, 24
        Roger Clemens, AL:Bos. 1987-88, 90, 92

Most Seasons, Consecutive, Leading Major Leagues
3   Tommy Bond, NL:Bos. 1877-79
        Amos Rusie, NL:NY 1893-95
       Since 1900:
2   Jack Chesbro, NL:Pitt. 1901-02
        Christy Mathewson, NL:NY 1907-08
        Grover Alexander, NL:Phil. 1915-16
        Whitlow Wyatt, NL:Brk. 1940-41
        Jim Bunning, NL:Phil. 1966-67
        Jason Schmidt, NL:SF 2003-04
        Brandon Webb, NL:Ari. 2006-07
        Clayton Kershaw, NL:LA 2015-16
        Cy Young, AL:Bos. 1903-04
        Walter Johnson, AL:Wash. 1913-14
        Allie Reynolds, AL:NY 1951-52
        Camilo Pascual, AL:Minn. 1961-62
        Tommy John, AL:Chi. 1966-67
        Roger Clemens, AL:Bos. 1987-88
        Corey Kluber, AL:Clev. 2017-18
        Roy Halladay, AL:Tor. 2009-NL:Phil. 10

Most Seasons Leading League
7   Grover Alexander, NL:Phil. 1911, 13, 15-17; Chi. 19
        Walter Johnson, AL:Wash. 1911, 13-15, 18-19, 24

Most Seasons, Consecutive, Leading League
3   Tommy Bond, NL:Bos. 1877-79
           Amos Rusie, NL:NY 1893-95
           Grover Alexander, NL:Phil. 1915-17
           Walter Johnson, AL:Wash. 1913-15
           Roger Clemens, AL:Bos. 1990-92
           Corey Kluber, AL:Clev. 2016-18
           Roy Halladay, AL:Tor. 2008-09-NL:Phil. 10

Most Shutouts, Lifetime
110   Walter Johnson, AL:Wash. 1907-27
90   Grover Alexander, NL:Phil. 1911-17, 30; Chi. 18-26; StL. 26-29

Most Shutouts, Season
16   George Bradley, NL:StL. 1876
           Grover Alexander, NL:Phil. 1916
13   Jack Coombs, AL:Phil. 1910

Most Seasons, 10 or more Shutouts
2   Ed Walsh, AL:Chi. 1906, 08
           Grover Alexander, NL:Phil. 1915-16

Most Shutouts, Consecutive, Season
6   Don Drysdale, NL:LA May 14-18-22-26-31, June 4, 1968
5   Doc White, AL:Chi. Sept. 12-16-19-25-30, 1904

Most Shutouts, Doubleheader
2   Ed Reulbach, NL:Chi. vs. Brk. Sept. 26, 1908 (5-0, 3-0)

Most Shutouts, One Month
6   Doc White, AL:Chi. Sept. 1904
           Ed Walsh, AL:Chi. Aug. 1906 & Sept. 1908
5   George Bradley, NL:StL. May 1876
           Tommy Bond, NL:Hart. June 1876
           Pud Galvin, NL:Buff. Aug. 1884
           Jack Chesbro, NL:Pitt. July 1902
           Don Drysdale, NL:LA May 1968
           Bob Gibson, NL:StL. June 1968
           Orel Hershiser, NL:LA Sept. 1988

Most Shutouts vs. One Club, League
23   Walter Johnson, AL:Wash. vs. Phil. 1907-27
20   Grover Alexander, NL:Phil.-Chi.-StL. vs. Cin. 1911-30

Most Shutouts vs. One Club, Season
5   Tony Mullane, AA:Cin. vs. NY 1887
           Lady Baldwin, NL:Det. vs. Phil. 1886
           Grover Alexander, NL:Phil. vs. Cin. 1916
           Larry Jaster, NL:StL. vs. LA 1966 (cons)
           Tom Hughes, AL:Wash. vs. Clev. 1905

Most Clubs Shutout, Season
9   Denny McLain, AL:Det. 1969
8   Bob Gibson, NL:StL. 1968

Most Shutouts, Opening Game, Season
7   Walter Johnson, AL:Wash. 1910, 14-15, 17, 19, 24, 26
3   Rip Sewell, NL:Pitt. 1943, 47, 49
           Chris Short, NL:Phil. 1965, 68, 70
           Rick Mahler, NL:Atl. 1982, 86-87

Most Innings, Shutout Game
18   Monte Ward, NL:Prov. Aug. 17, 1882
           Carl Hubbell, NL:NY July 2(1g), 1933
           Ed Summers, AL:Det. July 19, 1909 (tie)
           Walter Johnson, AL:Wash. May 15, 1918

Most Scoreless Innings, Consecutive, Game
21   Joe Oeschger, NL:Bos. May 1, 1920
20   Joe Harris, AL:Bos. Sept. 1, 1906

Most Hits Allowed, Shutout (no more than nine innings)
14   Larry Cheney, NL:Chi. Sept. 14, 1913
           Milt Gaston, AL:Wash. July 10(2g), 1928

Most Walks Allowed, Shutout

11	Lefty Gomez, AL:NY Aug. 1, 1941
9	Gene Packard, NL:Cin. Sept. 28, 1913
	Vinegar Bend Mizell, NL:StL. Sept. 1(1g), 1958
	A.J. Burnett, NL:Fla. May 12, 2001
	Extra-Inning Game:
10	Jim Maloney, NL:Cin. Aug. 19(1g), 1965 (10 inn)
	J.R. Richard, NL:Hou. July 6, 1976 (10 inn)

Most Scoreless Innings, Consecutive. Season

59.0	Orel Hershiser, NL:LA Aug. 30-Sept. 28, 1988
55.2	Walter Johnson, AL:Wash. Apr. 10-May 14, 1913

Most Shutouts Lost, Starting Pitcher, Lifetime

63	Walter Johnson, AL:Wash. 1907-27
	Nolan Ryan, NL:NY 1966, 68-71; Hou. 80-88;
	AL: Cal. 72-79; Tex. 89-93
53	Phil Niekro, NL:Mil./Atl. 1964-83, 87

Most Shutouts Lost, Starting Pitcher, Season

14	Jim Devlin, NL:Lou. 1876
	Since 1900:
11	Bugs Raymond, NL:StL. 1908
10	Walter Johnson, AL:Wash. 1909

Most Shutouts Lost, Starting Pitcher, vs. One Club, Season

5	Jim Devlin, NL:Lou. (Hart.) 1876
	Walter Johnson, AL:Wash. (Chi.) 1909
	NL Since 1900:
4	Irv Young, NL:Bos. (Pitt.) 1906
	Lefty Leifield, NL:Pitt. (Chi.) 1906, 10
	Tom Zachary, NL:Brk. (Pitt.) 1935
	Bob Veale, NL:Pitt. (SF) 1968

Most Shutouts Lost, Starting Pitcher, One Month

5	Cherokee Fisher, NL:Cin. May 1876
	Walter Johnson, AL:Wash. July 1909
	NL Since 1900:
4	Irv Young, NL:Bos. July 1907
	George McQuillan, NL:Phil. June 1908
	Pete Schneider, NL:Cin. Aug. 1915
	Jesse Petty, NL:Brk. Aug. 1927
	Freddie Fitzsimmons, NL:NY Sept. 1934
	Max Butcher, NL:Phil. Sept. 1938
	Jim McAndrew, NL:NY Aug. 1968
	Ken Reynolds, NL:Phil. July 1972
	Ryan Vogelsong, NL:SF July 2014

GAMES FINISHED

Most Seasons Leading Major Leagues

4	Firpo Marberry, AL:Wash. 1924-27
	Mike Marshall, NL:Mtl. 1972-73, LA 74; AL:Minn. 79
	Dan Quisenberry, AL:KC 1980, 82-83, 85

Most Seasons, Consecutive, Leading Major Leagues

4	Firpo Marberry, AL:Wash. 1924-27

Most Seasons Leading League

5	Mike Marshall, NL:Mtl. 1971-73; LA 74; AL:Minn. 79
	Firpo Marberry, AL:Wash. 1924-28
4	Ace Adams, NL:NY 1942-45
	Roy Face, NL:Pitt. 1958, 60-62
	Mike Marshall, NL:Mtl. 1971-73; LA 74
	Rod Beck, NL:SF 1993-94, 97; Chi. 98

Most Seasons, Consecutive, Leading League

5	Firpo Marberry, AL:Wash. 1924-28
4	Ace Adams, NL:NY 1942-45
	Mike Marshall, NL:Mtl. 1971-73; LA 74

Most Games Finished, League

952	Mariano Rivera, AL:NY 1995-2013
856	Trevor Hoffman, NL:Fla. 1993; SD 93-2008; Mil. 09-10

Most Games Finished, Season

84	Mike Marshall, AL:Minn. 1979
83	Mike Marshall, NL:LA 1974

SAVES (Since 1969)

Most Seasons Leading Major Leagues
3   Rollie Fingers, NL:SD 1977-78; AL:Mil. 81
      Bruce Sutter, NL:Chi. 1979; StL. 82, 84
      Mariano Rivera, AL:NY 1999, 2001, 04

Most Seasons, Consecutive, Leading Major Leagues
2   Rollie Fingers, NL:SD 1977-78
      Jim Johnson, AL:Balt. 2012-13

Most Seasons Leading League
5   Bruce Sutter, NL:Chi. 1979-80; StL. 81-82, 84
      Dan Quisenberry, AL:KC 1980, 82-85

Most Seasons, Consecutive, Leading League
4   Bruce Sutter, NL:Chi. 1979-80; StL. 81-82
      Craig Kimbrel, NL:Atl. 2011-14
      Dan Quisenberry, AL:KC 1982-85

Most Saves, Lifetime
652   Mariano Rivera, AL:NY 1995-2013
601   Trevor Hoffman, NL:Fla. 1993; SD 93-2008; Mil. 09-10

Most Saves, Season
62   Francisco Rodriguez, AL:LA 2008
55   John Smoltz, NL:Atl. 2002
      Eric Gagne, NL:LA 2003

Most Saves, Month
15   Lee Smith, NL:StL. June 1993
      Chad Cordero, NL:Wash. June 2005
      John Wetteland, AL:NY June 1996

Most Saves, Consecutive Appearances, Season
24   John Wetteland, AL:NY May 31-July 14, 1996
23   Todd Jones, NL:Fla. July 19-Sept. 13, 2005

NO-HIT GAMES (Minimum: 9 innings pitched; additional listings on pages 373-379)

Most Perfect Games, Lifetime
1   Lee Richmond, NL:Wor. June 12, 1880 (vs. Clev.)
      Monte Ward, NL:Prov. June 17, 1880 (vs. Buff.)
      Jim Bunning, NL:Phil. June 21, 1964 (vs. NY)
      Sandy Koufax, NL:LA Sept. 9, 1965 (vs. Chi.)
      Tom Browning, NL:Cin. Sept. 16, 1988 (vs. LA)
      Dennis Martinez, NL:Mtl. July 28, 1991 (vs. LA)
      Randy Johnson, NL:Ari. May 18, 2004 (vs. Atl.)
      Roy Halladay, NL:Phil. May 29, 2010 (vs. Fla.)
      Matt Cain, NL:SF June 13, 2012 (vs. Hou.)
      Cy Young, AL:Bos. May 5, 1904 (vs. Phil.)
      Addie Joss, AL:Clev. Oct. 2, 1908 (vs. Chi.)
      Charlie Robertson, AL:Chi. Apr. 30, 1922 (vs. Det.)
      Catfish Hunter, AL:Oak. May 8, 1968 (vs. Minn.)
      Len Barker, AL:Clev. May 15, 1981 (vs. Tor.)
      Mike Witt, AL:Cal. Sept. 30, 1984 (vs. Tex.)
      Kenny Rogers, AL:Tex. July 28, 1994 (vs. Cal.)
      David Wells, AL:NY May 17, 1998 (vs. Minn.)
      David Cone, AL:NY July 18, 1999 (vs. NL:Mtl.)
      Mark Buehrle, AL:Chi. July 23, 2009 (vs. TB)
      Dallas Braden, AL:Oak. May 9, 2010 (vs. TB)
      Philip Humber, AL:Chi. Apr. 21, 2012 (vs. Sea.)
      Felix Hernandez, AL:Sea. Aug. 15, 2012 (vs. TB)

Most No-Hit Games, Lifetime
7   Nolan Ryan, AL:Cal. 1973, 74, 75; Tex. 90, 91; NL:Hou. 1981

Most No-Hit Games, League
6   Nolan Ryan, AL:Cal. 1973, 74, 75; Tex. 90, 91
4   Sandy Koufax, NL:LA 1962, 63, 64, 65

Most No-Hit Games, Season
2   Johnny Vander Meer, NL:Cin. June 11 (Bos.); June 15 (Brk.), 1938
      Max Scherzer, NL:Wash. June 20 (Pitt.); Oct. 3(2g) (NY) 2015
      Allie Reynolds, AL:NY July 12 (Clev.); Sept. 28 (Bos.), 1951
      Virgil Trucks, AL:Det. May 15 (Wash.); Aug. 25 (NY), 1952
      Nolan Ryan, AL:Cal. May 15 (KC); July 15 (Det.), 1973

Most No-Hit Games, Consecutive
2   Johnny Vander Meer, NL:Cin. June 11 (Bos.)-June 15 (Brk.), 1938

Most Innings, No-Hit Game
10	Sam Kimber, AA:Brk. (Tol.) Oct. 4, 1884 (0-0)
	Hooks Wiltse, NL:NY (Phil.) July 4(1g), 1908 (1-0)
	Fred Toney, NL:Cin. (Chi.) May 2, 1917 (1-0)
	Jim Maloney, NL:Cin. (Chi.) Aug. 19(1g), 1965 (1-0)

ONE-HIT GAMES

Most One-Hit Games, Lifetime
12	Bob Feller, AL:Clev. 1936-41, 45-56
	Nolan Ryan, NL:NY 1966, 68-71; Hou. 80-88; AL:Cal. 1972-79; Tex. 89-93

Most One-Hit Games, League
12	Bob Feller, AL:Clev. 1936-41, 45-56
7	Hoss Radbourn, NL:Prov. 1881-85; Bos. 86-89; Cin. 91
	NL Since 1900:
6	Steve Carlton, NL:StL. 1965-71; Phil. 72-86; SF 86

Most One-Hit Games, Season
4	Hugh Daily, UA:Chi. 1884
	Grover Alexander, NL:Phil. 1915
3	Dave Stieb, AL:Tor. 1988

Most One-Hit Games, Consecutive, Season
2	Hugh Daily, UA:Chi. July 7-10, 1884
	Toad Ramsey, AA:Lou. July 29-31, 1886
	Charlie Buffinton, NL:Phil. Aug. 6-9, 1887
	Rube Marquard, NL:NY Aug. 28-Sept. 1, 1911
	Lon Warneke, NL:Chi. Apr. 17-22, 1934
	Mort Cooper, NL:StL. May 31-June 4, 1943
	R.A. Dickey, NL:NY June 13-18, 2012
	Whitey Ford, AL:NY Sept. 2-7, 1955
	Sam McDowell, AL:Clev. Apr. 25-May 1, 1966
	Dave Stieb, AL:Tor. Sept. 24-30, 1988

Most Innings, One-Hit Game
12.2	Harvey Haddix, NL:Pitt. (Mil.) May 26, 1959
10.0	Doc White, AL:Chi. (Clev.) Sept. 6, 1903
	Bobo Newsom, AL:StL. (Bos.) Sept. 18, 1934
	Bert Blyleven, AL:Tex. (Oak.) June 21, 1976

EARNED RUN AVERAGE (Since 1912 in NL; Since 1913 in AL - Prior seasons not compiled on official scores)

Most Seasons Leading Major Leagues
5	Pedro Martinez, NL:Mtl. 1997; AL:Bos. 1999-2000, 02-03

Most Seasons, Consecutive, Leading Major Leagues
4	Clayton Kershaw, NL:LA 2011-14
3	Lefty Grove, AL:Phil. 1929-31

Most Seasons Leading League
9	Lefty Grove, AL:Phil. 1926, 29-32; Bos. 35-36, 38-39
5	Grover Alexander, NL:Phil. 1915-17; Chi. 19-20
	Sandy Koufax, NL:LA 1962-66
	Clayton Kershaw, NL:LA 2011-14, 17

Most Seasons, Consecutive, Leading League
5	Sandy Koufax, NL:LA 1962-66
	Lefty Grove, AL:Phil. 1929-32

Lowest Earned Run Average, Lifetime (Minimum: 2000 innings)
2.21	Eddie Cicotte, AL:Chi. 1913-20 (excluding AL:Det.-Bos.-Chi. 1905-12)
2.34	Hippo Vaughn, NL:Chi. 1913-21

Lowest Earned Run Average, Season (Qualifiers)
1.00	Dutch Leonard, AL:Bos. 1914
1.12	Bob Gibson, NL:StL. 1968

WINNING PERCENTAGE

Most Seasons Leading Major Leagues
5	Lefty Grove, AL:Phil. 1929-31, 33; Bos. 38

Most Seasons, Consecutive, Leading Major Leagues
3	Lefty Grove, AL:Phil. 1929-31

Most Seasons Leading League
5	Lefty Grove, AL:Phil. 1929-31, 33; Bos. 38	
3	Sam Leever, NL:Pitt. 1901, 03, 05	
	Ed Reulbach, NL:Chi. 1906-08	

Most Seasons, Consecutive, Leading League
3	Ed Reulbach, NL:Chi. 1906-08
	Lefty Grove, AL:Phil. 1929-31

Highest Winning Percentage, Lifetime (Minimum: 200 wins)
.690	Whitey Ford, AL:NY 1950, 53-67 (236-106)
.665	Christy Mathewson, NL:NY 1900-16; Cin. 16 (373-188)

Lowest Winning Percentage, Lifetime (Minimum: 100 wins)
.380	Si Johnson, NL:Cin. 1928-36; StL. 36-38; Phil. 40-43, 46; Bos. 46-47 (101-165)
.406	Sid Hudson, AL:Wash. 1940-42, 46-52; Bos. 52-54 (104-152)

Highest Winning Percentage, Season (Minimum: 15 decisions)
.947	Roy Face, NL:Pitt. 1959 (18-1)
.938	Johnny Allen, AL:Clev. 1937 (15-1)

GAMES WON

Most Seasons Leading Major Leagues
4	Cy Young, NL:Clev. 1892, 95; AL:Bos. 1901-02
	Joe McGinnity, NL:Balt. 1899; Brk. 1900; NY 03, 06
	Grover Alexander, NL:Phil. 1911, 15-17
	Robin Roberts, NL:Phil. 1952-55
	Warren Spahn, NL:Mil. 1953, 57-58, 60
	Tom Glavine, NL:Atl. 1991, 93, 98, 2000
	Roger Clemens, AL:Bos. 1986-87; Tor. 97-98

Most Seasons, Consecutive, Leading Major Leagues
4	Robin Roberts, NL:Phil. 1952-55

Most Seasons Leading League
8	Warren Spahn, NL:Bos. 1949-50; Mil. 53, 57-61
6	Walter Johnson, AL:Wash. 1913-16, 18, 24
	Bob Feller, AL:Clev. 1939-41, 46-47, 51

Most Seasons, Consecutive, Leading League
5	Warren Spahn, NL:Mil. 1957-61
4	Walter Johnson, AL:Wash. 1913-16

Most Games Won, Lifetime
511	Cy Young, NL:Clev. 1890-98; StL. 1899-1900; Bos. 11; AL:Bos. 1901-08; Clev. 09-11

Most Games Won, League
417	Walter Johnson, AL:Wash. 1907-27
373	Christy Mathewson, NL:NY 1900-16; Cin. 16
	Grover Alexander, NL:Phil. 1911-17, 30; Chi. 18-26; StL. 26-29

Most Games Won, Season
60	Hoss Radbourn, NL:Prov. 1884
	Since 1900:
41	Jack Chesbro, AL:NY 1904
37	Christy Mathewson, NL:NY 1908

Most Games Won, No Losses, Season
12	Tom Zachary, AL:NY 1929
10	Howie Krist, NL:StL. 1941

Most Seasons, 30 or more Games Won, Lifetime
7	Kid Nichols, NL:Bos. 1891-94, 96-98

Most Seasons, 30 or more Games Won, League
7	Kid Nichols, NL:Bos. 1891-94, 96-98
	Since 1900:
4	Christy Mathewson, NL:NY 1903-05, 08
2	Cy Young, AL:Bos. 1901-02
	Walter Johnson, AL:Wash. 1912-13

Most Seasons, Consecutive, 30 or more Games Won
6	Tim Keefe, AA:NY 1883-84; NL:NY 85-88
5	Amos Rusie, NL:NY 1890-94
	Since 1900:
3	Christy Mathewson, NL:NY 1903-05
	Grover Alexander, NL:Phil. 1915-17
2	Cy Young, AL:Bos. 1901-02
	Walter Johnson, AL:Wash. 1912-13

Most Seasons, 20 or more Games Won, Lifetime
16   Cy Young, NL:Clev. 1891-98; StL. 1899-1900; AL:Bos. 1901-04, 07-08

Most Seasons, 20 or more Games Won, League
13   Christy Mathewson, NL:NY 1901, 03-14
         Warren Spahn, NL:Bos. 1947, 49-51; Mil. 53-54, 56-61, 63
12   Walter Johnson, AL:Wash. 1910-19, 24-25

Most Seasons, Consecutive, 20 or more Games Won, Lifetime
14   Cy Young, NL:Clev. 1891-98; StL. 1899-1900; AL:Bos. 01-04

Most Seasons, Consecutive, 20 or more Games Won, League
12   Christy Mathewson, NL:NY 1903-14
10   Walter Johnson, AL:Wash. 1910-19

Most Games Won, Consecutive, Lifetime
24   Carl Hubbell, NL:NY July 17, 1936-May 27, 1937
20   Roger Clemens, AL:Tor.-NY June 3, 1998-June 1, 1999
         Gerrit Cole, AL:Hou.-NY May 27, 2019-Aug. 14, 2020

Most Games Won, Consecutive, Season
19   Tim Keefe, NL:NY June 23-Aug. 10, 1888
         Rube Marquard, NL:NY Apr. 11-July 3(1g), 1912
16   Walter Johnson, AL:Wash. July 3(2g)-Aug. 23(1g), 1912
         Smoky Joe Wood, AL:Bos. July 8-Sept. 15(2g), 1912
         Lefty Grove, AL:Phil. June 8-Aug. 19, 1931
         Schoolboy Rowe, AL:Det. June 15-Aug. 25, 1934
         Roger Clemens, AL:NY May 26-Sept. 19, 2001
         Gerrit Cole, AL:Hou. May 27-Sept. 29, 2019

Most Games Won, Consecutive, Start of Season
19   Rube Marquard, NL:NY Apr. 11-July 3(1g), 1912
15   Johnny Allen, AL:Clev. Apr. 23-Sept. 30(1g), 1937
         Dave McNally, AL:Balt. Apr. 12-July 30, 1969

Most Games Won, Consecutive, End of Season
17   Pat Luby, NL:Chi. Aug. 6(2g)-Oct. 3, 1890
         Since 1900:
16   Carl Hubbell, NL:NY July 17-Sept. 23, 1936
         Gerrit Cole, AL:Hou. May 27-Sept. 29, 2019

Most Games Won, Consecutive, Start of Career
12   Hooks Wiltse, NL:NY May 29-Sept. 15, 1904
         Butch Metzger, NL:SF-SD Sept. 21, 1974-Aug. 8, 1976
11   Joe Boehling, AL:Wash. May 31-July 23, 1913
         Jesse Crain, AL:Minn. Sept. 1, 2004-July 1, 2005

Most Games Won, vs. One Club
70   Grover Alexander, NL:Phil.-Chi.-StL. (vs. Cin.) 1911-30
66   Walter Johnson, AL:Wash. (vs. Det.) 1907-27

Most Games Won, vs. One Club, Season
12   Hoss Radbourn, NL:Prov. (vs. Clev.) 1884
         Since 1900:
9   Ed Reulbach, NL:Chi. (vs. Brk.) 1908
         Frank Smith, AL:Chi. (vs. Wash.) 1904
         Ed Walsh, AL:Chi. (vs. NY & Bos.) 1908
         Walter Johnson, AL:Wash. (vs. Chi.) 1912

Most Games Won, Consecutive, vs. One Club
27   Hoss Radbourn NL:Prov. (vs. Det.) June 2, 1882-Sept. 18, 1884
         Since 1900:
24   Christy Mathewson, NL:NY (vs. StL.) June 16, 1904-Sept. 15, 1908
         Carl Mays, AL:Bos.-NY (vs. Phil.) Aug. 30, 1918-July 24, 1923

GAMES LOST

Most Seasons Leading Major Leagues
3   Pedro Ramos, AL:Wash. 1958-59; Minn. 61

Most Seasons, Consecutive, Leading Major Leagues
2   Jim Devlin, NL:Lou. 1876-77
         Red Ruffing, AL:Bos. 1928-29
         Pedro Ramos, AL:Wash. 1958-59
         Roger Craig, NL:NY 1962-63

Most Seasons Leading League
4   Bobo Newsom, AL:StL. 1934; StL.-Wash. 35; Det. 41; Phil. 45
         Pedro Ramos, AL:Wash. 1958-60; Minn. 61
         Phil Niekro, NL:Atl. 1977-80

Most Seasons, Consecutive, Leading League
4	Pedro Ramos, AL:Wash. 1958-60; Minn. 61
	Phil Niekro, NL:Atl. 1977-80

Most Games Lost, Lifetime
315	Cy Young, NL:Clev. 1890-98; StL. 1899-1900; Bos. 11; AL:Bos. 1901-08; Clev. 09-11

Most Games Lost, League
279	Walter Johnson, AL:Wash. 1907-27
261	Pud Galvin, NL:Buff. 1879-85; Pitt. 87-89, 91-92; StL. 92
	NL Since 1900:
251	Eppa Rixey, NL:Phil. 1912-17, 19-20, Cin. 21-33

Most Games Lost, Season
48	John Coleman, NL:Phil. 1883
	Since 1900:
29	Vic Willis, NL:Bos. 1905
26	Jack Townsend, AL:Wash. 1904
	Bob Groom, AL:Wash. 1909

Most Games Lost, No Wins, Season
13	Terry Felton, AL:Minn. 1982
12	Russ Miller, NL:Phil. 1928

Most Games Lost, Consecutive, Lifetime
27	Anthony Young, NL:NY May 6, 1992-July 24, 1993
19	Jack Nabors, AL:Phil. Apr. 28-Sept. 28, 1916

Most Games Lost, Consecutive, Season
19	Jack Nabors, AL:Phil. Apr. 28-Sept. 28, 1916
18	Cliff Curtis, NL:Bos. June 13(1g)-Sept. 20(1g), 1910
	Roger Craig, NL:NY May 4-Aug. 4, 1963

Most Games Lost, Consecutive, Start of Season
14	Joe Harris, AL:Bos. May 10-July 25, 1906
	Matt Keough, AL:Oak. Apr. 15-Aug. 8, 1979
13	Anthony Young, NL:NY Apr. 9-July 24, 1993

Most Games Lost, Consecutive, End of Season
19	Jack Nabors, AL:Phil. Apr. 28-Sept. 28, 1916
18	Cliff Curtis, NL:Bos. June 13(1g)-Sept. 20(1g), 1910

Most Games Lost, Consecutive, Start of Career
16	Terry Felton, AL:Minn. Apr. 18, 1980-Sept. 12, 1982
14	Paul Sewald, NL:NY June 2, 2017-Sept. 8, 2019

Most Games Lost, vs. One Club, Season
7	By many; last:
	Cal McLish, NL:Cin. (vs. Pitt.) 1960
	Camilo Pascual, AL:Wash. (vs. NY) 1956

Most Games Lost, Consecutive, vs. One Club
14	Dupee Shaw, NL:Prov.-Wash. (vs. Det.) Sept. 28, 1885-July 10, 1888
	Fred Beebe, NL:StL. (vs. NY) July 15, 1906-Sept. 22, 1909
	Eppa Rixey, NL:Phil.-Cin. (vs. Bos.) Oct. 3, 1916-May 21, 1921
	George Smith, NL:Phil. (vs. Brk.) Sept. 3, 1920-June 25, 1922
	Bob Rush, NL:Chi. (vs. Phil.) June 14, 1951-June 17, 1955
	Herm Wehmeier, NL:Cin.-Phil. (vs. StL.) July 3, 1949-May 9, 1956
	Joe Bush, AL:Phil. (vs. Bos.) June 2, 1914-July 5, 1917
	Slim Harriss, AL:Phil. (vs. NY) July 2, 1920-May 30, 1924
	Danny MacFayden, AL:Bos. (vs. Wash.) Aug. 7, 1929-June 2, 1932

INNINGS PITCHED

Most Seasons Leading Major Leagues
5	Robin Roberts, NL:Phil. 1951-55

Most Seasons, Consecutive, Leading Major Leagues
5	Robin Roberts, NL:Phil. 1951-55

Most Seasons Leading League
7	Grover Alexander, NL:Phil. 1911-12, 14-17; Chi. 20
5	Walter Johnson, AL:Wash. 1910, 13-16
	Bob Feller, AL:Clev. 1939-41, 46-47

Most Seasons, Consecutive, Leading League
5	Robin Roberts, NL:Phil. 1951-55
	Greg Maddux, NL:Chi. 1991-92; Atl. 93-95
4	Walter Johnson, AL:Wash. 1913-16

Most Innings, Lifetime
7356	Cy Young, NL:Clev. 1890-98; StL. 1899-1900; Bos. 11; AL:Bos. 1901-08; Clev. 09-11

Most Innings, League
5916	Walter Johnson, AL:Wash. 1907-27
5246	Warren Spahn, NL:Bos./Mil. 1942, 46-64; NY 65; SF 65

Most Innings, Season
680	Will White, NL:Cin. 1879
	Since 1900:
464	Ed Walsh, AL:Chi. 1908
434	Joe McGinnity, NL:NY 1903

Most Seasons, 300 or more Innings, Lifetime
16	Cy Young, NL:Clev. 1891-98; StL. 1899-1900; AL:Bos. 1901-05, 07

Most Seasons, Consecutive, 300 or more Innings, Lifetime
15	Cy Young, NL:Clev. 1891-98; StL. 1899-1900; AL:Bos. 1901-05

Most Seasons, 300 or more Innings, League
12	Kid Nichols, NL:Bos. 1890-99, 1901, 04
	Since 1900:
11	Christy Mathewson, NL:NY 1901, 03-05, 07-08, 10-14
9	Walter Johnson, AL:Wash. 1910-18

Most Seasons, Consecutive, 300 or more Innings, League
10	Kid Nichols, NL:Bos. 1890-99
	Cy Young, NL:Clev. 1891-98; StL. 1899-1900
	Since 1900:
9	Walter Johnson, AL:Wash. 1910-18
7	Grover Alexander, NL:Phil. 1911-17

Most Seasons, 200 or more Innings, Lifetime
20	Don Sutton, NL:LA 1966-80, Hou. 82; AL:Mil. 1982-84; Oak. 85; Cal. 85-86

Most Seasons, Consecutive, 200 or more Innings, Lifetime
19	Cy Young, NL:Clev. 1891-98; StL. 1899-1900; AL:Bos. 1901-08; Clev. 09

Most Seasons, 200 or more Innings, League
18	Walter Johnson, AL:Wash. 1908-19, 21-26
	Greg Maddux, NL:Chi. 1988-91, 2004-05; Atl. 1993-2001, 03; Chi.-LA 2006

Most Seasons, Consecutive, 200 or more Innings, League
17	Warren Spahn, NL:Bos. 1947-52; Mil. 53-63
13	Eddie Plank, AL:Phil. 1901-13
	Red Ruffing, AL:Bos. 1928-30; NY 30-40

Most Innings, Game
26	Leon Cadore, NL:Brk. May 1, 1920
	Joe Oeschger, NL:Bos. May 1, 1920
24	Jack Coombs, AL:Phil. Sept. 1, 1906
	Joe Harris, AL:Bos. Sept. 1, 1906

BATTERS FACED

Most Seasons Leading League
7	Steve Carlton, NL:Phil. 1972-74, 80-83
5	Walter Johnson, AL:Wash. 1910, 13-16

Most Seasons, Consecutive, Leading League
4	Walter Johnson, AL:Wash. 1913-16
	Bob Lemon, AL:Clev. 1950-53
	Grover Alexander, NL:Phil. 1914-17
	Robin Roberts, NL:Phil. 1952-55
	Steve Carlton, NL:Phil. 1980-83
	Greg Maddux, NL:Chi. 1991-92; Atl. 93-94

Most Batters Faced, Lifetime
30,418	Cy Young, NL:Clev. 1890-98; StL. 1899-1900; AL:Bos. 1901-08, 11; Clev. 09-11

Most Batters Faced, League
23,433	Walter Johnson, AL:Wash. 1907-27
21,555	Warren Spahn, NL:Bos./Mil. 1942, 46-64; NY 65; SF 65

Most Batters Faced, Season
1807	Joe McGinnity, NL:NY 1903
1745	Ed Walsh, AL:Chi. 1908

Most Batters Faced, Game

67	George Derby, NL:Buff. July 3, 1883
	Since 1900:
57	Roy Patterson, AL:Chi. May 5, 1901
53	Bill Phillips, NL:Cin. June 24(2g), 1901
	Extra-Inning Game:
96	Leon Cadore, NL:Brk. May 1, 1920 (26 inn)
86	Jack Coombs, AL:Phil. Sept. 1, 1906 (24 inn)
	Joe Harris, AL:Bos. Sept. 1, 1906 (24 inn)

Most Batters Faced, Inning

22	Tony Mullane, NL:Balt. June 18(1g), 1894 (1st)
	Since 1900:
16	Doc Adkins, AL:Bos. July 8, 1902 (6th)
	Lefty O'Doul, AL:Bos. July 7(1g), 1923 (6th)
	Howard Ehmke, AL:Bos. Sept. 28, 1923 (6th)
	Hal Kelleher, NL:Phil. May 5, 1938 (8th)

Most Batters Retired, Consecutive, Season

46	Yusmeiro Petit, NL:SF July 22-Aug. 28, 2014
45	Mark Buehrle, AL:Chi. July 18-28, 2009

Most Batters Retired, Consecutive, Extra-Inning Game:

36	Harvey Haddix, NL:Pitt. (vs. Mil.) May 26, 1959
28	Walter Johnson, AL:Wash. (vs. NY) May 11, 1919
	Waite Hoyt, AL:Bos. (vs. NY) Sept. 24(2g), 1919

RUNS (Since 1900)

Most Seasons Leading Major Leagues

3	Phil Niekro, NL:Atl. 1977-79

Most Seasons, Consecutive, Leading Major Leagues

3	Phil Niekro, NL:Atl. 1977-79

Most Seasons Leading League

3	Burleigh Grimes, NL:Brk. 1923-24; Pitt. 28
	Hugh Mulcahy, NL:Phil. 1938-40
	Robin Roberts, NL:Phil. 1955-57
	Phil Niekro, NL:Atl. 1977-79
	Rick Mahler, NL:Atl. 1986, 88; Cin. 89
	George Mullin, AL:Det. 1905-07
	Wilbur Wood, AL:Chi. 1972-73, 75

Most Seasons, Consecutive, Leading League

3	George Mullin, AL:Det. 1905-07
	Hugh Mulcahy, NL:Phil. 1938-40
	Robin Roberts, NL:Phil. 1955-57
	Phil Niekro, NL:Atl. 1977-79

Most Runs, Lifetime

2337	Phil Niekro, NL:Mil./Atl. 1964-83, 87; AL:NY 1984-85; Clev. 86-87; Tor. 87

Most Runs, League

2115	Red Ruffing, AL:Bos. 1924-30; NY 30-42, 45-46; Chi. 47
2037	Burleigh Grimes, NL:Pitt. 1916-17, 28-29, 34; Brk. 18-26; NY 27; Bos. 30; StL. 30-31, 34; Chi. 32-33

Most Runs, Season

544	John Coleman, NL:Phil. 1883
	Since 1900:
224	Bill Carrick, NL:NY 1900
219	Joe McGinnity, AL:Balt. 1901

Most Runs, Game

24	Al Travers, AL:Det. May 18, 1912
21	Doc Parker, NL:Cin. June 21, 1901

Most Runs, Inning

13	Lefty O'Doul, AL:Bos. July 7(1g), 1923 (6th)
12	Hal Kelleher, NL:Phil. May 5, 1938 (8th)

EARNED RUNS (Since 1912 in NL; Since 1913 in AL – Prior seasons not compiled on official scores)

Most Seasons Leading Major Leagues

3	Burleigh Grimes, NL:Brk. 1922, 24-25
	Wilbur Wood, AL:Chi. 1972-73, 75

Most Seasons, Consecutive, Leading Major Leagues
2   Elmer Myers, AL:Phil. 1916-17
         Bump Hadley, AL:Chi.-StL. 1932-33
         Wilbur Wood, AL:Chi. 1972-73
         Burleigh Grimes, NL:Brk. 1924-25
         Robin Roberts, NL:Phil. 1955-56
         Sammy Ellis, NL:Cin. 1965-66

Most Seasons Leading League
3   Bobo Newsom, AL:StL. 1938; Wash. 42; Phil. 45
         Alex Kellner, AL:Phil. 1950-52
         Wilbur Wood, AL:Chi. 1972-73, 75
         Burleigh Grimes, NL:Brk. 1922, 24-25
         Jimmy Ring, NL:Phil. 1921, 23, 28
         Murry Dickson, NL:StL. 1948; Pitt. 51-52
         Robin Roberts, NL:Phil. 1955-57
         Jack Fisher, NL:NY 1964-65, 67

Most Seasons, Consecutive, Leading League
3   Alex Kellner, AL:Phil. 1950-52
         Robin Roberts, NL:Phil. 1955-57

Most Earned Runs, Lifetime
2011   Phil Niekro, NL:Mil./Atl. 1964-83, 87; AL:NY 1984-85; Clev. 86-87; Tor. 87

Most Earned Runs, League
1833   Red Ruffing, AL:Bos. 1924-30; NY 30-42, 45-46; Chi. 47
1804   Warren Spahn, NL:Bos./Mil. 1942, 46-64; NY 65; SF 65

Most Earned Runs, Season
186   Bobo Newsom, AL:StL. 1938
155   Guy Bush, NL:Chi. 1930

HITS

Most Seasons Leading Major Leagues
5   Robin Roberts, NL:Phil. 1952-56

Most Seasons, Consecutive, Leading Major Leagues
5   Robin Roberts, NL:Phil. 1952-56

Most Seasons Leading League
5   Robin Roberts, NL:Phil. 1952-56
         Livan Hernandez, NL:Fla. 1998; SF 2000-01; Wash. 05; Ari. 07
4   Jim Kaat, AL:Minn. 1965-67; Chi. 75
         Mark Buehrle, AL:Chi. 2005-06, 08, 10

Most Seasons, Consecutive, Leading League
5   Robin Roberts, NL:Phil. 1952-56
3   Wes Ferrell, AL:Bos. 1935-36; Bos.-Wash. 37
         Jim Kaat, AL:Minn. 1965-67

Most Hits, Lifetime
7090   Cy Young, NL:Clev. 1890-98; StL. 1899-1900; AL:Bos. 1901-08, 11; Clev. 09-11

Most Hits, League
5490   Pud Galvin, NL:Buff. 1879-85; Pitt. 87-89, 91-92; StL. 92
       Since 1900:
4910   Walter Johnson, AL:Wash. 1907-27
4865   Grover Alexander, NL:Phil. 1911-17, 30; Chi. 18-26; StL. 26-29

Most Hits, Season
809   John Coleman, NL:Phil. 1883
       Since 1900:
415   Bill Carrick, NL:NY 1900
412   Joe McGinnity, AL:Balt. 1901

Most Hits, Game
36   Jack Wadsworth, NL:Lou. Aug. 17, 1894
       Since 1900:
26   Al Orth, NL:Phil. Apr. 19, 1900
         Doc Parker, NL:Cin. June 21, 1901
         Al Travers, AL:Det. May 18, 1912
         Hod Lisenbee, AL:Phil. Sept. 11, 1936
       Extra-Inning Game:
29   Ed Rommel, AL:Phil. July 10, 1932 (last 17 inn of 18 inn game)

Most Hits, Inning
13   Stump Weidman, NL:Det. Sept. 6, 1883 (7th)
       Since 1900:
12   Doc Adkins, AL:Bos. July 8, 1902 (6th)
11   Reggie Grabowski, NL:Phil. Aug. 4(2g), 1934 (9th)

Most Hits, Consecutive, Game
10	Bill Reidy, AL:Mil. June 2, 1901
	Manny Banuelos, AL:Chi. May 4, 2019
	Heinie Meine, NL:Pitt. June 23, 1930

Most Hits, Consecutive, Inning
10	Bill Reidy, AL:Mil. June 2, 1901 (9th)
	Manny Banuelos, AL:Chi. May 4, 2019 (3rd)
	Heinie Meine, NL:Pitt. June 23, 1930 (6th)

Fewest Hits, 2 Consecutive Complete Games
0	Johnny Vander Meer, NL:Cin. June 11-15, 1938
1	Howard Ehmke, AL:Bos. Sept. 7-11, 1923

Fewest Hits, 3 Consecutive Complete Games
3	Johnny Vander Meer, NL:Cin. June 5-15, 1938
5	By many

Most Hitless Innings, Consecutive, Season
24	Cy Young, AL:Bos. Apr. 25-May 11, 1904
21	Johnny Vander Meer, NL:Cin. June 11-19, 1938

Most Extra-Base Hits, Game
16	George Derby, NL:Buff. July 3, 1883
11	Earl Whitehill, AL:Wash. July 10, 1935

SINGLES

Most Singles, Game
28	Jack Wadsworth, NL:Lou. Aug. 17, 1894
23	Bock Baker, AL:Clev. Apr. 28, 1901

Most Singles, Inning
10	Reggie Grabowski, NL:Phil. Aug. 4(2g), 1934 (9th)
	Elden Auker, AL:Det. Sept. 29(2g), 1935 (2nd)

DOUBLES

Most Doubles, Game
14	George Derby, NL:Buff. July 3, 1883
10	Earl Whitehill, AL:Wash. July 10, 1935

Most Doubles, Inning
6	Lefty Grove, AL:Bos. June 9, 1934 (8th)
	Mike Mussina, AL:NY July 31, 2002 (2nd)
	Dustin Hermanson, NL:Mtl. July 22, 1999 (2nd)

TRIPLES

Most Triples, Game
7	Tom Parrott, NL:Cin. Aug. 1, 1894
	Tony Kaufmann, NL:Chi. Apr. 22, 1925
6	Al Travers, AL:Det. May 18, 1912

Most Triples, Inning
4	Firpo Marberry, AL:Det. May 6, 1934 (4th)
3	By many in NL

HOME RUNS

Most Home Runs, Lifetime
522	Jamie Moyer, NL:Chi. 1986-88; StL. 91; Phil. 2006-10; Col. 12;
	AL:Tex. 89-90; Balt. 93-95; Bos. 96; Sea. 96-06

Most Home Runs, League
434	Warren Spahn, NL:Bos./Mil. 1942, 46-64; NY 65; SF 65
422	Frank Tanana, AL:Cal. 1973-80; Bos. 81; Tex. 82-85; Det. 85-92; NY 93

Most Home Runs, Season
50	Bert Blyleven, AL:Minn. 1986
48	Jose Lima, NL:Hou. 2000

Fewest Home Runs, Season (Most Innings), Since 1900
0	Walter Johnson, AL:Wash. 1916 (371 inn)
	Vic Willis, NL:Pitt. 1906 (322 inn)

Most Home Runs vs. One Club, Season
15	Jim Perry, AL:Clev. (vs. NY) 1960
13	Lee Sweetland, NL:Phil. (vs. Brk.) 1930
	Preacher Roe, NL:Brk. (vs. Cin.) 1953
	Warren Hacker, NL:Chi. (vs. Brk.) 1956
	Warren Spahn, NL:Mil. (vs. Chi.) 1958
	Greg Maddux, NL:Chi. (vs. Cin.) 2004

Most Home Runs, Game
7	Charlie Sweeney, NL:StL. June 12, 1886
	Since 1900:
6	Larry Benton, NL:NY May 12, 1930
	Sloppy Thurston, NL:Brk. Aug. 13(1g), 1932
	Bill Kerksieck, NL:Phil. Aug. 13(1g), 1939
	Michael Blazek, NL:Mil. July 27, 2017
	Tommy Thomas, AL:StL. June 27, 1936
	George Caster, AL:Phil. Sept. 24(1g), 1940
	Tim Wakefield, AL:Bos. Aug. 8, 2004
	R.A. Dickey, AL:Tex. Apr. 6, 2006
	James Shields, AL:TB Aug. 7, 2010

Most Home Runs, Inning
5	Michael Blazek, NL:Mil. July 27, 2017 (3rd)
	Chase Anderson, AL:Tor. Sept. 17, 2020 (5th)

Most Home Runs, Consecutive, Inning
4	Paul Foytack, AL:LA (Clev.) July 31(2g), 1963 (6th)
	Chase Wright, AL:NY (Bos.) Apr. 22, 2007 (3rd)
	Dave Bush, NL:Mil. Aug. 11, 2010 (4th)
	Michael Blazek, NL:Mil. July 27, 2017 (3rd)
	Craig Stammen, NL:SD June 9, 2019 (8th)
	Roel Ramirez, NL:StL. Aug. 16, 2020 (5th)

GRAND SLAM HOME RUNS

Most Grand Slam Home Runs, Lifetime
11	Kenny Rogers, AL:Tex. 1990, 92-93, 2000-01; Minn. 03; Det. 07-08
	Ryan Dempster, NL:Fla. 2002; Cin. 02; Chi. 05, 08, 11; AL:Tex. 12; Bos. 13
9	Jerry Reuss, NL:StL. 1971; Hou. 72-73; Pitt. 74, 76; LA 79-80
	Ryan Dempster, NL:Fla. 2002; Cin. 02; Chi. 05, 08, 11

Most Grand Slam Home Runs, Season
4	Ray Narleski, AL:Det. 1959
	Mike Schooler, AL:Sea. 1992
	Brian Bannister, AL:KC 2008
	J.A. Happ, AL:Tor.-NY 2018
	Tug McGraw, NL:Phil. 1979
	Chan Ho Park, NL:LA 1999
	Matt Clement, NL:SD 2000

Most Grand Slam Home Runs, Game
2 Bill Phillips, NL:Pitt. (Chi.) Aug. 16, 1890 (Tommy Burns, Malachi Kittredge)
  Charlie Petty, NL:Wash. (Bos.) May 28, 1894 (Bobby Lowe, Henry Staley)
  Archie Stimmel, NL:Cin. (Brk.) Sept. 23, 1901 (Joe Kelley, Jimmy Sheckard)
  Jock Menefee, NL:Chi. (Bos.) Aug. 12(2g), 1903 (Joe Stanley, Pat Moran)
  Jack Scott, NL:Bos. (Phil.) Apr. 28, 1921 (Ralph Miller, Lee Meadows)
  June Greene, NL:Phil. (StL.) July 6(2g), 1929 (Jim Bottomley, Chick Hafey)
  Luke Hamlin, NL:Brk. (NY) July 4(2g), 1938 (Dick Bartell, Gus Mancuso)
  Chan Ho Park, NL:LA (StL.) Apr. 23, 1999 (Fernando Tatis 2)
  Brandon Backe, NL:Hou. (Ari.) Aug. 16, 2008 (Miguel Montero, Chris Young)
  Mike Fiers, NL:Mil. (Cin.) Apr. 21, 2015 (Jay Bruce, Todd Frazier)
  Dillon Peters, NL:Mia. Apr. 7, 2018 (Mikael Franco, Aaron Altherr)
  Tex Shirley, AL:StL. (Bos.) July 27, 1946 (Rudy York 2)
  Jack Morris, AL:Det. (Bos.) Aug. 7(1g), 1984 (Bill Buckner, Tony Armas)
  Eric Plunk, AL:Oak. (Cal.) July 31, 1986 (Brian Downing, Bob Boone)
  Daniel Schlereth, AL:Det. (NL:NY) June 28, 2011 (Jason Bay, Carlos Beltran)

Most Games, Consecutive, Grand Slam Home Runs, Season
2 By many; last:
  Williams Perez, NL:Atl. Sept. 6-11, 2016
  Yoshinori Tateyama, AL:Tex. Sept. 3-10, 2011

Most Grand Slam Home Runs, Inning
2 Bill Phillips, NL:Pitt. (Chi.) Aug. 16, 1890 (5th)
  Chan Ho Park, NL:LA (StL.) Apr. 23, 1999 (3rd)

Most Consecutive Innings Allowing a Grand Slam Home Run, Game
2 Jock Menefee, NL:Chi. (Bos.) Aug. 12, 1903 (3rd, 4th)
  Mike Fiers, NL:Mil. (Cin.) Apr. 21, 2015 (3rd, 4th)
  Jack Morris, AL:Det. (Bos.) Aug. 7, 1984 (1st, 2nd)
  Eric Plunk, AL:Oak. (Cal.) July 31, 1986 (3rd, 4th)
  Daniel Schlereth, AL:Det. (NL:NY) June 28, 2011 (4th, 5th)

WALKS (Since 1889)

Most Seasons Leading Major Leagues
7 Nolan Ryan, AL:Cal. 1972-74, 76-78; NL:Hou. 82

Most Seasons, Consecutive, Leading Major Leagues
5 Amos Rusie, NL:NY 1890-94
  Since 1900:
3 Togie Pittinger, NL:Bos. 1902-04
  Tommy Byrne, AL:NY 1949-50; NY-StL. 51
  Nolan Ryan, AL:Cal. 1972-74; 76-78
  Randy Johnson, AL:Sea. 1990-92

Most Seasons Leading League
8 Nolan Ryan, AL:Cal. 1972-74, 76-78; NL:Hou. 80, 82
6 Nolan Ryan, AL:Cal. 1972-74; 76-78
5 Amos Rusie, NL:NY 1890-94
  NL Since 1900:
4 Jimmy Ring, NL:Phil. 1922-25
  Kirby Higbe, NL:Chi.-Phil. 1939; Phil. 40; Brk. 41; Brk.-Pitt. 47
  Sam Jones, NL:Chi. 1955-56; StL. 58; SF 59
  Bob Veale, NL:Pitt. 1964-65, 67-68

Most Seasons, Consecutive, Leading League
5 Amos Rusie, NL:NY 1890-94
  Since 1900:
4 George Mullin, AL:Det. 1903-06
  Jimmy Ring, NL:Phil. 1922-25

Most Walks, Lifetime
2795 Nolan Ryan NL:NY 1966, 68-71; Hou. 80-88; AL:Cal. 1972-79; Tex. 89-93

Most Walks, League
1775 Early Wynn, AL:Wash. 1939, 41-44, 46-48; Clev. 49-57, 63; Chi. 58-62
1717 Steve Carlton, NL:StL. 1965-71; Phil. 72-86; SF 86

Most Walks, Season
289 Amos Rusie, NL:NY 1890
  Since 1900:
208 Bob Feller, AL:Clev. 1938
185 Sam Jones, NL:Chi. 1955

Most Intentional Walks, Season (Since 1955)
24	Gene Garber, AL:KC-NL:Phil. 1974
23	Mike Garman, NL:StL. 1975
	Dale Murray, NL:Cin.-NY 1978
	Kent Tekulve, NL:Pitt. 1982
19	John Hiller, AL:Det. 1974

Most Walks, Game
16	Bill George, NL:NY May 30(1g), 1887
	George Van Haltren, NL:Chi. June 27, 1887
	Henry Gruber, PL:Clev. Apr. 19, 1890
	Bruno Haas, AL:Phil. June 23, 1915
	Tommy Byrne, AL:StL. Aug. 22, 1951 (13 inn)
	NL Since 1900:
14	Henry Mathewson, NL:NY Oct. 5, 1906

Most Walks, Inning
8	Dolly Gray, AL:Wash. Aug. 28(1g), 1909 (2nd)
7	Tony Mullane, NL:Balt. June 18(1g), 1894 (1st)
	Bob Ewing, NL:Cin. Apr. 19, 1902 (4th)

Most Walks, Consecutive, Inning
7	Dolly Gray, AL:Wash. Aug. 28(1g), 1909 (2nd)
6	Brickyard Kennedy, NL:Brk. Aug. 31, 1900 (2nd)

Fewest Walks, Game (Most Innings)
0	Babe Adams, NL:Pitt. July 17, 1914 (21 inn)
	Cy Young, AL:Bos. July 4(2g), 1905 (20 inn)

Most Innings, Consecutive, No Walks
84.1	Bill Fischer, AL:KC Aug. 3-Sept. 30, 1962
72.1	Greg Maddux, NL:Atl. June 20-Aug. 12, 2001

Most Innings, Consecutive, No Walks, Start Of Season
52.0	Grover Alexander, NL:Chi. Apr. 18-May 17, 1923
43.2	Cy Young, AL:Bos. Apr. 14-May 9, 1904

HIT BATTERS

Most Seasons Leading Major Leagues
6	Howard Ehmke, AL:Det. 1920-22; Bos. 23, 25; Phil. 27

Most Seasons, Consecutive, Leading Major Leagues
5	Tommy Byrne, AL:NY 1948-50; NY-StL. 51; StL. 52

Most Seasons Leading League
6	Howard Ehmke, AL:Det. 1920-22; Bos. 23, 25; Phil. 27
5	Don Drysdale, NL:LA 1958-61, 65

Most Seasons, Consecutive, Leading League
5	Tommy Byrne, AL:NY 1948-50; NY-StL. 51; StL. 52
4	Don Drysdale, NL:LA 1958-61

Most Hit Batters, Lifetime
205	Walter Johnson, AL:Wash. 1907-27
154	Don Drysdale, NL:Brk./LA 1956-69

Most Hit Batters, Season
41	Joe McGinnity, NL:Brk. 1900
31	Chick Fraser, AL:Phil. 1901

Most Hit Batters, Game
6	Ed Knouff, AA:Balt. Apr. 25, 1887
	John Grimes, NL:StL. July 31(1g), 1897
	Since 1900:
5	Oscar Jones, NL:Brk. Apr. 20, 1903
4	By many in AL; last:
	Charlie Morton, AL:Hou. June 9, 2018

Most Hit Batters, Inning

3	Pat Luby, NL:Chi. Sept. 5, 1890 (6th)
	Pink Hawley, NL:StL. July 4(1g), 1894 (1st; cons)
	Pink Hawley, NL:Pitt. May 9, 1896 (7th)
	Walter Thornton, NL:Chi. May 18, 1898 (4th; cons)
	Deacon Phillippe, NL:Pitt. Sept. 25, 1905 (1st)
	Ray Boggs, NL:Bos. Sept. 17, 1928 (9th)
	Raul Sanchez, NL:Cin. May 15(1g), 1960 (8th)
	Dock Ellis, NL:Pitt. May 1, 1974 (1st; cons)
	Mark Gardner, NL:Mtl. Aug. 15, 1992 (1st)
	Tom Candiotti, NL:LA Sept. 13, 1997 (1st)
	C.J. Nitkowski, NL:Hou. Aug. 3, 1998 (8th; cons)
	Brian Lawrence, NL:SD Apr. 22, 2003 (4th)
	Kazuhisa Ishii, NL:LA July 23, 2003 (4th)
	Matt Clement, NL:Chi. May 28(1g), 2004 (5th)
	Jeff Weaver, NL:LA Aug. 21, 2004 (1st; cons)
	Joe Kennedy, NL:Ari. Aug. 14, 2007 (4th)
	Sergio Mitre, NL:Fla. Aug. 31, 2007 (2nd)
	Oliver Perez, NL:NY Sept. 28, 2007 (3rd)
	Drew Storen, NL:Cin. May 8, 2017 (7th)
	John Lackey, NL:Chi. July 25, 2017 (5th)
	Jose Urena, NL:Mia. Mar. 29, 2018 (1st)
	Pat Venditte, NL:SF May, 6, 2019 (6th)
	Pablo Lopez, NL:Mia. Sept. 16, 2019 (1st)
	Bert Gallia, AL:Wash. June 20(2g), 1913 (1st)
	Harry Harper, AL:NY Aug. 25, 1921 (8th)
	Tom Morgan, AL:NY June 30, 1954 (3rd)
	Wilbur Wood, AL:Chi. Sept. 10, 1977 (1st; cons)
	Bud Black, AL:Clev. July 8(2g), 1988 (4th)
	Bert Blyleven, AL:Minn. Sept. 28, 1988 (2nd)
	Steve Sparks, AL:Ana. May 22, 1999 (3rd; cons)
	Javier Vazquez, AL:NY Sept. 22, 2010 (7th; cons)
	Cesar Cabral, AL:NY Apr. 18, 2014 (8th)
	Mike Pelfrey, AL:Minn. May 3, 2015 (4th)
	Kirby Yates, AL:NY June 27, 2016 (9th)
	Raul Alcantara, AL:Oak. Sept. 5, 2016 (1st)
	David Price, AL:Bos. July 7, 2018 (5th)

Fewest Hit Batters, Season (Most Innings)

0	General Crowder, AL:Wash. 1932 (327 inn)
	Sandy Koufax, NL:LA 1966 (323 inn)

Fewest Hit Batters, Game (Most Innings)

0	Leon Cadore, NL:Brk. May 1, 1920 (26 inn)
	Joe Oeschger, NL:Bos. May 1, 1920 (26 inn)
	Ted Lyons, AL:Chi. May 24, 1929 (21 inn)

STRIKEOUTS

Most Seasons Leading Major Leagues

9	Randy Johnson, AL:Sea. 1993-95; AL:Sea.-NL:Hou. 98; NL:Ari. 1999-2002, 04

Most Seasons, Consecutive, Leading Major Leagues

5	Rube Waddell, AL:Phil. 1903-07
	Randy Johnson, AL:Sea.-NL:Hou. 1998; NL:Ari. 1999-2002

Most Seasons Leading League

12	Walter Johnson, AL:Wash. 1910, 12-19, 21, 23-24
7	Dazzy Vance, NL:Brk. 1922-28

Most Seasons, Consecutive, Leading League

8	Walter Johnson, AL:Wash. 1912-19
7	Dazzy Vance, NL:Brk. 1922-28

Most Strikeouts, Lifetime

5714	Nolan Ryan, NL:NY 1966, 68-71; Hou. 80-88; AL:Cal. 1972-79; Tex. 89-93

Most Strikeouts, League

4167	Roger Clemens, AL:Bos. 1984-96; Tor. 97-98; NY 99-2003, 07
4000	Steve Carlton, NL:StL. 1965-71; Phil. 72-86; SF 86

Most Strikeouts, Season

513	Matt Kilroy, AA:Balt. 1886
	Since 1900:
383	Nolan Ryan, AL:Cal. 1973
382	Sandy Koufax, NL:LA 1965

Most Seasons, 300 or more Strikeouts, Lifetime

6	Nolan Ryan, AL:Cal. 1972-74, 76-77; Tex. 89
	Randy Johnson, AL:Sea. 1993; AL:Sea.-NL:Hou. 1998; NL:Ari. 1999-2002
4	Randy Johnson, NL:Ari. 1999-2002

Most Seasons, Consecutive, 300 or more Strikeouts, Lifetime

5	Randy Johnson, AL:Sea.-NL:Hou. 1998; NL:Ari. 99-2002
4	Randy Johnson, NL:Ari. 1999-2002
3	Nolan Ryan, AL:Cal. 1972-74

Most Seasons, 200 or more Strikeouts, Lifetime

15	Nolan Ryan, AL:Cal. 1972-74, 76-79; Tex. 89-91; NL:Hou. 80, 82, 85, 87-88

Most Seasons, 200 or more Strikeouts, League

11	Roger Clemens, AL:Bos. 1986-92, 96; Tor. 97-98; NY 2001
10	Tom Seaver, NL:NY 1968-76, 78

Most Seasons, Consecutive, 200 or more Strikeouts, League

9	Tom Seaver, NL:NY 1968-76
7	Walter Johnson, AL:Wash. 1910-16
	Roger Clemens, AL:Bos. 1986-92
	Chris Sale, AL:Chi. 2013-16; Bos. 17-19

Most Strikeouts, Game

20	Roger Clemens, AL:Bos. Apr. 29, 1986
	Roger Clemens, AL:Bos. Sept. 18, 1996
	Kerry Wood, NL:Chi. May 6, 1998
	Randy Johnson, NL:Ari. May 8, 2001 (first 9 inn of 11-inn game)
	Max Scherzer, NL:Wash. May 11, 2016
	Extra-Inning Game:
21	Tom Cheney, AL:Wash. Sept. 12, 1962 (16 inn)

Most Strikeouts, Consecutive, Game

10	Tom Seaver, NL:NY Apr. 22, 1970
9	Doug Fister, AL:Det. Sept. 27, 2012
	Tyler Alexander, AL:Det. Aug. 2(1g), 2020

Most Strikeouts, Consecutive, Start of Game

9	Mickey Welch, NL:NY Aug. 28, 1884
	Since 1900:
8	Jim Deshaies, NL:Hou. Sept. 23, 1986
	Jacob deGrom, NL:NY Sept. 15, 2014
	German Marquez, NL:Col. Sept. 26, 2018
7	Joe Cowley, AL:Chi. May 28, 1986
	Carlos Rodon, AL:Chi. Sept. 30, 2016
	Blake Snell, AL:TB June 3, 2018

Most Games, 10 or more Strikeouts, Lifetime

215	Nolan Ryan, NL:NY 1966, 68-71; Hou. 80-88; AL:Cal. 72-79; Tex. 89-93

Most Games, 10 or more Strikeouts, League

148	Nolan Ryan, AL:Cal. 72-79; Tex. 89-93
114	Randy Johnson, NL:Mtl. 1988-89; Hou. 98; Ari. 1999-2004, 07-08

Most Games, 10 or more Strikeouts, Season

23	Nolan Ryan, AL:Cal. 1973
	Randy Johnson, NL:Ari. 1999-2001

Most Strikeouts, 2 Consecutive Games

34	Dupee Shaw, UA:Bos. July 19 (18)-21 (16), 1884
33	Kerry Wood, NL:Chi. May 6 (20)-11 (13), 1998
32	Luis Tiant, AL:Clev. June 29 (13)-July 3 (19), 1968
	Nolan Ryan, AL:Cal. Aug. 7 (13)-12 (19), 1974
	Randy Johnson, AL:Sea. Aug. 8 (19)-15 (13), 1997
	Pedro Martinez, AL:Bos. Sept. 4 (15)-10 (17), 1999
	Pedro Martinez, AL:Bos. May 6 (17)-12 (15), 2000

Most Strikeouts, 3 Consecutive Games

48	Dupee Shaw, UA:Bos. July 16 (14)-19 (18)-21 (16), 1884
47	Nolan Ryan, AL:Cal. Aug. 12 (19)-16 (9)-20 (19), 1974
43	Dwight Gooden, NL:NY Sept. 7 (11)-12 (16)-17 (16), 1984
	Randy Johnson, NL:Ari. June 25 (14)-30 (17)-July 5 (12), 1999
	Randy Johnson, NL:Ari. Apr. 28 (12)-May 3 (11)-8 (20), 2001
	Randy Johnson, NL:Ari. May 3 (11)-May 8 (20)-13 (12), 2001

Most Strikeouts, Inning

4   Bobby Mathews, AA:Phil. Sept. 30, 1885 (7th)
Cannonball Crane, NL:NY Oct. 4, 1888 (5th; cons)
Doc White, NL:Phil. July 21, 1902 (5th)
Hooks Wiltse, NL:NY May 15, 1906 (5th; cons)
Jim Davis, NL:Chi. May 27(1g), 1956 (6th; cons)
Joe Nuxhall, NL:Cin. Aug. 11(1g), 1959 (6th)
Pete Richert, NL:LA Apr. 12, 1962 (3rd; cons)
Don Drysdale, NL:LA Apr. 17, 1965 (2nd; cons)
Bob Gibson, NL:StL. June 7, 1966 (4th)
Bill Bonham, NL:Chi. July 31(1g), 1974 (2nd)
Phil Niekro, NL:Atl. July 29, 1977 (6th)
Mario Soto, NL:Cin. May 17, 1984 (3rd; cons)
Mike Scott, NL:Hou. Sept. 3, 1986 (5th)
Paul Assenmacher, NL:Atl. Aug. 22, 1989 (5th)
Tim Birtsas, NL:Cin. June 4, 1990 (7th)
Mark Wohlers, NL:Atl. June 17, 1995 (9th; cons)
Bruce Ruffin, NL:Col. July 25, 1996 (9th)
Derek Wallace, NL:NY Sept. 13, 1996 (9th)
Kirt Ojala, NL:Fla. Sept. 16, 1998 (4th; cons)
Archie Corbin, NL:Fla. Apr. 28, 1999 (7th)
Jerry Spradlin, NL:SF July 22, 1999 (7th)
Steve Kline, NL:Mtl. Aug. 17, 1999 (7th; cons)
Frankie Rodriguez, NL:Cin. July 22, 2001 (7th)
A.J. Burnett, NL:Fla. July 5, 2002 (1st)
Kerry Wood, NL:Chi. Sept. 2(1g), 2002 (4th; cons)
Darren Dreifort, NL:LA May 22, 2003 (2nd)
Octavio Dotel, NL:Hou. June 11, 2003 (8th; cons)
Brad Lidge, NL:Hou. June 13, 2004 (7th)
Mike Stanton, NL:NY Aug. 3, 2004 (8th)
Jon Rauch, NL:Wash. Apr. 26, 2006 (8th)
Brad Penny, NL:LA Sept. 23, 2006 (2nd)
Ryan Dempster, NL:Chi. Oct. 4, 2009 (5th)
Luke Gregerson, NL:SD Oct. 4, 2009 (7th)
Manny Parra, NL:Mil. June 6, 2010 (4th)
Yovani Gallardo, NL:Mil. Sept. 17, 2011 (5th; cons)
Bud Norris, NL:Hou. Apr. 24, 2012 (3rd)
Jason Berken, NL:Chi. Sept. 20, 2012 (2nd; cons)
Craig Kimbrel NL:Atl. Sept. 26, 2012 (9th; cons)
Tony Cingrani, NL:Cin. Apr. 28, 2013 (4th)
Zack Greinke, NL:LA July 25, 2014 (3rd; cons)
Justin Grimm, NL:Chi. Aug. 29, 2014 (9th)
Oliver Perez, NL:Ari. Sept. 20, 2014 (7th; cons)
Kenley Jansen, NL:LA May 15, 2015 (8th; cons)
Sergio Santos NL:LA May 16, 2015 (8th)
Will Smith, NL:Mil. Oct. 4, 2015 (9th; cons)
Julio Teheran, NL:Atl. May 24, 2016 (2nd)
Jake Thompson, NL:Phil. Aug. 12, 2016 (2nd)
Jon Gray, NL:Col. Sept. 17, 2016 (2nd; cons)
Zack Godley, NL:Ari. Aug. 13, 2017 (1st)
Miguel Diaz, NL:SD July 8, 2018 (11th)
German Marquez, NL:Col. Oct. 1, 2018 (4th)
Ed Siever, AL:Det. Apr. 20, 1907 (5th)
Walter Johnson, AL:Wash. Apr. 15, 1911 (5th)
Guy Morton, AL:Clev. June 11, 1916 (6th; cons)
Ryne Duren, AL:LA May 18, 1961 (7th)
Lee Stange, AL:Clev. Sept. 2, 1964 (7th)
Mike Cuellar, AL:Balt. May 29, 1970 (4th; cons)
Mike Paxton, AL:Clev. July 21, 1978 (5th; cons)
Bobby Witt, AL:Tex. Aug. 2, 1987 (2nd; cons)
Charlie Hough, AL:Tex. July 4, 1988 (1st)
Matt Young, AL:Sea. Sept. 9, 1990 (1st)
Paul Shuey, AL:Clev. May 14, 1994 (9th)
Kevin Appier, AL:KC Sept. 3, 1996 (4th)
Wilson Alvarez, AL:Chi. July 21, 1997 (7th; cons)
Blake Stein, AL:Oak. July 27, 1998 (4th)
Chuck Finley, AL:Ana. May 12, 1999 (3rd)
Tim Wakefield, AL:Bos. Aug. 10, 1999 (9th)
Chuck Finley, AL:Ana. Aug. 15, 1999 (1st; cons)
Chuck Finley, AL:Clev. Apr. 16, 2000 (3rd)
Erik Hiljus, AL:Oak. June 30, 2001 (7th)
Kazuhiro Sasaki, AL:Sea. Apr. 4, 2003 (9th; cons)
Scott Baker, AL:Minn. June 15, 2008 (3rd; cons)
Scot Shields, AL:LA June 21, 2008 (8th)
Felix Hernandez, AL:Sea. June 3, 2010 (8th; cons)
A.J. Burnett, AL:NY June 24, 2011 (6th; cons)
Justin Masterson, AL:Clev. Aug. 4, 2011 (2nd; cons)
Jeremy Hellickson, AL:TB Aug. 25, 2011 (3rd; cons)
Ryan Cook, AL:Oak. Apr. 27, 2012 (8th; cons)
Francisco Liriano, AL:Minn. June 5, 2012 (4th; cons)
Steve Delabar, AL:Tor. Aug. 13, 2012 (10th; cons)
Phil Hughes, AL:NY Sept. 20, 2012 (4th; cons)
Zack Greinke, AL:LA Sept. 25, 2012 (4th)
Alex Cobb, AL:TB May 10, 2013 (3rd; cons)
Tyler Duffey, AL:Minn. May 8, 2016 (7th)
Ken Giles, AL:Hou. Aug. 7, 2016 (9th)
James Paxton, AL:Sea. Sept. 6, 2016 (1st)
Nate Karns, AL:KC May 3, 2017 (6th)
Craig Kimbrel, AL:Bos. May 25, 2017 (9th; cons)
Mike Bolsinger, Tor. July 18, 2017 (13th; cons)
Zach Duke, AL:Minn. Mar. 29, 2018 (7th)
Ryan Dull, AL:Oak. Apr. 17, 2018 (8th)
Luke Bard, AL:LA Apr. 22, 2019 (14th)

SACRIFICE HITS

Most Seasons Leading League
3   Eppa Rixey, NL:Phil. 1920; Cin. 21, 28
      Tom Glavine, NL:Atl. 1990, 99; NY 2005
      Earl Whitehill, AL:Det. 1931; Wash. 34-35
      Early Wynn, AL:Clev. 1951-52; Chi. 58
      Fritz Peterson, AL:NY 1966, 68-69
      Mark Buehrle, AL:Chi. 2002, 09; Tor. 15

Most Sacrifices, Season
      Including sacrifice flies:
55   Stan Coveleski, AL:Clev. 1921
50   Eppa Rixey, NL:Phil. 1920
      Excluding sacrifice flies:
35   Ed Brandt, NL:Bos. 1933
28   Earl Whitehill, AL:Det. 1931

SACRIFICE FLIES (Since 1954)

Most Seasons Leading Major Leagues
3   Charlie Hough, AL:Tex. 1987; Chi. 91; NL:Fla. 94
      Jaime Navarro, AL:Mil. 1992-93; Chi. 97

Most Seasons, Consecutive, Leading Major Leagues
2   Jaime Navarro, AL:Mil. 1992-93
      Chad Billingsley NL:LA 2009-10

Most Seasons Leading League
4   Charlie Hough, AL:Tex. 1987, 90; Chi. 91; NL:Fla. 94
3   Rick Reuschel, NL:Chi. 1976, 80; SF 88
      Charlie Hough, AL:Tex. 1987, 90; Chi. 91
      Jaime Navarro, AL:Mil. 1992-93; Chi. 97

Most Seasons, Consecutive, Leading League
2   Ferguson Jenkins, NL:Chi. 1973-AL:Tex. 74
      Jack Morris, AL:Det. 1980-81
      Charlie Hough, AL:Tex. 1990-Chi. 91
      Jaime Navarro, AL:Mil. 1992-93
      Chad Billingsley NL:LA 2009-10
      Jerad Eickhoff, NL:Phil. 2016-17

Most Sacrifice Flies, Lifetime
146   Nolan Ryan, NL:NY 1966, 68-71; Hou. 80-88; AL:Cal. 72-79; Tex. 89-93

Most Sacrifice Flies, League
119   Greg Maddux, NL:Chi. 1986-92, 2004-06; Atl. 93-2003; LA 06, 08; SD 07-08
114   Jack Morris, AL:Det. 1977-90; Minn. 91; Tor. 92-93; Clev. 94

Most Sacrifice Flies, Season
17   Larry Gura, AL:KC 1983
      Jaime Navarro, AL:Mil. 1993
15   Randy Lerch, NL:Phil. 1979

WILD PITCHES

Most Seasons Leading Major Leagues
6   Larry Cheney, NL:Chi. 1912-14; Brk. 16-18

Most Seasons, Consecutive, Leading Major Leagues
3   Larry Cheney, NL:Chi. 1912-14; Brk. 16-18
      Jimmy Ring, NL:Phil. 1921-23

Most Seasons Leading League
6   Nolan Ryan, AL:Cal. 1972, 77-78; Tex. 89; NL:Hou. 81, 86
      Larry Cheney, NL:Chi. 1912-14; Brk. 16-18
      Jack Morris, AL:Det. 1983-85, 87; Minn. 91; Clev. 94

Most Seasons, Consecutive, Leading League
3   Larry Cheney, NL:Chi. 1912-14; Brk. 16-18
      Jimmy Ring, NL:Phil. 1921-23
      John Smoltz, NL:Atl. 1990-92
      Jack Morris, AL:Det. 1983-85

Most Wild Pitches, Lifetime
277   Nolan Ryan, NL:NY 1966, 68-71; Hou. 80-88; AL:Cal. 72-79; Tex. 89-93

Most Wild Pitches, League
206   Jack Morris, AL:Det. 1977-90; Minn. 91; Tor. 92-93; Clev. 94
202   Phil Niekro, NL:Mil./Atl. 1964-83, 87

Most Wild Pitches, Season
64	Bill Stemmeyer, NL:Bos. 1886
	Since 1900:
30	Red Ames, NL:NY 1905
26	Juan Guzman, AL:Tor. 1993

Most Wild Pitches, Game
10	Johnny Ryan, NL:Lou. July 22, 1876
	Since 1900:
6	J.R. Richard, NL:Hou. Apr. 10, 1979
	Phil Niekro, NL:Atl. Aug. 4(2g), 1979
	Bill Gullickson, NL:Mtl. Apr. 10, 1982
5	Charlie Wheatley, AL:Det. Sept. 27, 1912
	Jack Morris, AL:Det. Aug. 3, 1987 (10 inn)
	Freddy Garcia, AL:NY Apr. 10, 2012 (12 inn)

Most Wild Pitches, Inning
4	Walter Johnson, AL:Wash. Sept. 21, 1914 (4th)
	Kevin Gregg, AL:Ana. July 25, 2004 (8th)
	R.A. Dickey, AL:Sea. Aug. 17, 2008 (5th)
	Phil Niekro, NL:Atl. Aug. 4(2g), 1979 (5th)
	Ryan Madson, NL:Phil. July 25, 2006 (3rd)

Fewest Wild Pitches, Season (Most Innings)
0	Joe McGinnity, NL:NY 1906 (338 inn)
	General Crowder, AL:Wash. 1932 (327 inn)

Fewest Wild Pitches, Game (Most Innings)
0	Leon Cadore, NL:Brk. May 1, 1920 (26 inn)
	Jack Coombs, AL:Phil. Sept. 1, 1906 (24 inn)
	Joe Harris, AL:Bos. Sept. 1, 1906 (24 inn)

BALKS

Most Balks, Season
16	Dave Stewart, AL:Oak. 1988
11	Steve Carlton, NL:Phil. 1979

Most Balks, Game
5	Bob Shaw, NL:Mil. May 4, 1963
4	Vic Raschi, AL:NY May 3, 1950
	Bobby Witt, AL:Tex. Apr. 12, 1988
	Rick Honeycutt, AL:Oak. Apr. 13, 1988
	Gene Walter, AL:Sea. July 18, 1988
	John Dopson, AL:Bos. June 13, 1989

Most Balks, Inning
3	Charlie Sweeney, NL:StL. Apr. 30, 1885 (1st)
	Jim Owens, NL:Cin. Apr. 24, 1963 (2nd)
	Bob Shaw, NL:Mil. May 4, 1963 (3rd)
	Jim Gott, NL:Pitt. Aug. 6, 1988 (8th)
	Milt Shoffner, AL:Clev. May 12, 1930 (3rd)
	Don Heinkel, AL:Det. May 3, 1988 (6th)

RELIEF PITCHING

Highest Percentage, Games Won, Lifetime (Minimum: 50 wins)
.708	Hugh Casey, NL:Chi. 1935; Brk. 39-42, 46-48; Pitt. 49; AL:NY 49 (51-21)

Highest Percentage, Games Won, League (Minimum: 50 wins)
.704	Hugh Casey, NL:Chi. 1935; Brk. 39-42, 46-48; Pitt. 49 (50-21)
.680	Eddie Rommel, AL:Phil. 1920-32 (51-24)

Most Games, Lifetime
1248	Jesse Orosco, NL:NY 1979, 81-87; LA 88, 2001-02; StL. 2000; SD 03
	AL:Clev. 89-91; Mil. 92-94; Balt. 95-99; NY 03; Minn. 03

Most Games, League
1119	John Franco, NL:Cin. 1984-89; NY 90-2001, 03-04; Hou. 05
1105	Mariano Rivera, AL:NY 1995-2013

Most Games, Consecutive, Lifetime
1199	Jesse Orosco, NL:NY-LA-StL.-SD; AL:Clev.-Mil.-Balt.-NY-Minn. July 20, 1982-Sept. 27, 2003

Most Games, Consecutive, League
1119	John Franco, NL:Cin. 1984-89; NY 90-2001, 03-04; Hou. 05
1102	Mariano Rivera, AL:NY 1995-2013

Most Games, Season
106	Mike Marshall, NL:LA 1974
89	Mike Marshall, AL:Minn. 1979
	Mark Eichhorn, AL:Tor. 1987

Most Games Won, Lifetime
124	Hoyt Wilhelm, NL:NY 1952-56; StL. 57; Atl. 69-71; Chi. 70; LA 71-72
	AL:Clev. 57-58; Balt. 58-62; Chi. 63-68; Cal. 69

Most Games Won, League
96	Roy Face, NL:Pitt. 1953, 55-68; Mtl. 69
87	Sparky Lyle, AL:Bos. 1967-71; NY 72-78; Tex. 79-80; Chi. 82

Most Games Won, Consecutive
22	Roy Face, NL:Pitt. June 7, 1958-Aug. 30, 1959
19	Rube Waddell, AL:Phil.-StL. July 21, 1902-June 11, 1908

Most Games Won, Consecutive, Start of Career
12	Butch Metzger, NL:SF-SD Sept. 21, 1974-Aug. 8, 1976
	(ML record)
19	Rube Waddell, AL:Phil.-StL. July 21, 1902-June 11, 1908
	(0-3 in NL prior to AL career)

Most Games Won, Season
18	Roy Face, NL:Pitt. 1959 (1 lost)
17	John Hiller, AL:Det. 1974 (14 lost)
	Bill Campbell, AL:Minn. 1976 (5 lost)

Most Games Lost, Lifetime
108	Gene Garber, NL:Pitt. 1969-72; Phil. 74-78; Atl. 78-87; AL:KC 1973-74, 87-88

Most Games Lost, League
98	Gene Garber, NL:Pitt. 1969-72; Phil. 74-78; Atl. 78-87
67	Hoyt Wilhelm, AL:Clev. 1957-58; Balt. 58-62; Chi. 63-68; Cal. 69
	Sparky Lyle, AL:Bos. 1967-71; NY 72-78; Tex. 79-80; Chi. 82

Most Games Lost, Consecutive
14	Skip Lockwood, NL:NY June 16, 1978-May 16, 1979
	Paul Sewald, NL:NY June 2, 2017-Sept. 8, 2019
11	Tom Murphy, AL:Mil.-Bos. May 17, 1975-June 10, 1976
	Mike Henneman, AL:Det.-Tex. May 28, 1994-July 4, 1996
	Heathcliff Slocumb, AL:Bos.-Sea. May 3, 1997-Apr. 14, 1998
	Matt Thornton, AL:Chi.-Bos.-NY Aug. 4, 2012-July 10, 2014
	Mychal Givens, AL:Balt. May 22, 2018-June 16, 2019

Most Games Lost, Season
16	Gene Garber, NL:Atl. 1979 (6 won)
14	Darold Knowles, AL:Wash. 1970 (2 won)
	John Hiller, AL:Det. 1974 (17 won)
	Mike Marshall, AL:Minn. 1979 (10 won)

Most Innings, Lifetime
1872.0	Hoyt Wilhelm, NL:NY 1952-56; StL. 57; Atl. 69-71; Chi. 70; LA 71-72
	AL:Clev. 57-58; Balt. 58-62; Chi. 63-68; Cal. 69

Most Innings, League
1436.2	Kent Tekulve, NL:Pitt. 1974-85; Phil. 85-88; Cin. 89
1264.2	Sparky Lyle, AL:Bos. 1967-71; NY 72-78; Tex. 79-80; Chi. 82

Most Innings, Season
208.0	Mike Marshall, NL:LA 1974
168.1	Bob Stanley, AL:Bos. 1982

Most Innings, Game
18.1	Zip Zabel, NL:Chi. June 17, 1915
17.0	Eddie Rommel, AL:Phil. July 10, 1932

Most Strikeouts, Consecutive, Game
9	Tyler Alexander, AL:Det. Aug. 2(1g), 2020
7	Randy Johnson, NL:Ari. July 18, 2001
	Aaron Harang, NL:Cin. May 25, 2008

DOUBLEHEADERS (Complete Games)

Most Doubleheaders, Lifetime
5	Joe McGinnity, AL:Balt. 1901; NL:NY 1903

Most Doubleheaders, League

3	Joe McGinnity, NL:NY 1903
2	Joe McGinnity, AL:Balt. 1901
	Ed Walsh, AL:Chi. 1905, 08
	Mule Watson, AL:Phil. 1918

Most Doubleheaders, Season

3	Joe McGinnity, NL:NY 1903
2	Joe McGinnity, AL:Balt. 1901
	Mule Watson, AL:Phil. 1918

Most Doubleheaders Won, League

3	Joe McGinnity, NL:NY 1903
1	By many

Most Doubleheaders Won, Season

3	Joe McGinnity, NL:NY 1903
1	By many; last:
	Dutch Levsen, AL:Clev. 1926

Fewest Runs, Doubleheader (two complete games)

0	Ed Reulbach, NL:Chi. Sept. 26, 1908
1	Ed Walsh, AL:Chi. Sept. 29, 1908
	Carl Mays, AL:Bos. Aug. 30, 1918

Fewest Hits, Doubleheader (two complete games)

3	Tim Keefe, AA:NY July 4, 1883
6	Fred Toney, NL:Cin. July 1, 1917
	Hi Bell, NL:StL. July 19, 1924
7	Frank Owen, AL:Chi. July 1, 1905
	Ed Walsh, AL:Chi. Sept. 29, 1908

Fewest Walks, Doubleheader (two complete games)

0	Guy Hecker, AA:Lou. July 4, 1884
1	Ed Walsh, AL:Chi. Sept. 29, 1908
	Grover Alexander, NL:Phil. Sept. 23, 1916 & Sept. 3, 1917

PITCHING – ROOKIE SEASON

(No official rookie rule prior to 1958. Qualifiers based on less than 45 previous innings pitched.)

Most Games

88	Sean Runyan, AL:Det. 1998
86	Oscar Villarreal, NL:Ari. 2003

Most Complete Games

66	Jim Devlin, NL:Lou. 1876
	Matt Kilroy, NL:Balt. 1886
	Since 1900:
41	Irv Young, NL:Bos. 1905
35	Roscoe Miller, AL:Det. 1901

Most Shutouts

16	George Bradley, NL:StL. 1876
	Since 1900:
8	Russ Ford, AL:NY 1910
	Reb Russell, AL:Chi. 1913
	Fernando Valenzuela, NL:LA 1981

Most Shutouts, Consecutive, Start of Career

2	Al Spalding, NL:Chi. Apr. 25-27, 1876
	Jim Hughes, NL:Balt. Apr. 18-22, 1898
	Al Worthington, NL:NY July 6-11, 1953
	Karl Spooner, NL:Brk. Sept. 22-26, 1954
	Slow Joe Doyle, AL:NY Aug. 25-30, 1906
	Johnny Marcum, AL:Phil. Sept. 7-11, 1933
	Boo Ferriss, AL:Bos. Apr. 29-May 6, 1945
	Tom Phoebus, AL:Balt. Sept. 15-20, 1966

Most Games Won

47	Al Spalding, NL:Chi. 1876 (13 lost)
	Since 1900:
28	Grover Alexander, NL:Phil. 1911 (13 lost)
26	Russ Ford, AL:NY 1910 (6 lost)

Most Games Won, Consecutive

17	Pat Luby, NL:Chi. Aug. 6-Oct. 3, 1890
	Since 1900:
12	Hooks Wiltse, NL:NY May 29-Sept. 15, 1904
	Russ Ford, AL:NY Aug. 9-Oct. 6, 1910
	Atley Donald, AL:NY May 9-July 25, 1939
	Ivan Nova, AL:NY June 10-Sept. 20, 2011

Most Games Lost
48	John Coleman, NL:Phil. 1883 (12 won)
	Since 1900:
26	Bob Groom, AL:Wash. 1909 (7 won)
25	Harry McIntire, NL:Brk. 1905 (8 won)

Most Games Lost, Consecutive
16	Dory Dean, NL:Cin. July 11-Sept. 12, 1876
	Since 1900:
15	Bob Groom, AL:Wash. July 6-Sept. 25, 1909
14	Anthony Young, NL:NY May 6-Sept. 29, 1992

Most Saves, Season
46	Craig Kimbrel, NL:Atl. 2011
40	Neftali Feliz, AL:Tex. 2010

Most Innings
591	Lee Richmond, NL:Wor. 1880
	Since 1900:
377	Irv Young, NL:Bos. 1905
332	Roscoe Miller, AL:Det. 1901
	Scott Perry, AL:Phil. 1918

Fewest Hits, First Game (complete game of 9 or more innings)
0	Bumpus Jones, NL:Cin. Oct. 15, 1892
	Since 1900:
1	Addie Joss, AL:Clev. Apr. 26, 1902
	Mike Fornieles, AL:Wash. Sept. 2(2g), 1952
	Billy Rohr, AL:Bos. Apr. 14, 1967
	Juan Marichal, NL:SF July 19, 1960
	Jimmy Jones, NL:SD Sept. 21, 1986

Most Scoreless Innings, Consecutive, Start of ML Career
39	Brad Ziegler, AL:Oak. May 31-Aug. 14, 2008
25	George McQuillan, NL:Phil. May 8-Sept. 29, 1907

Most Sacrifice Flies (Since 1954)
17	Arnie Portocarrero, AL:Phil. 1954
12	George O'Donnell, NL:Pitt. 1954

Most Intentional Walks (Since 1955)
20	Ron Willis, NL:StL. 1967
16	Ken Sanders, AL:Bos.-KC 1966

Most Strikeouts
513	Matt Kilroy, AA:Balt. 1886
	Since 1900:
276	Dwight Gooden, NL:NY 1984
245	Herb Score, AL:Clev. 1955

Most Strikeouts, First Game
15	Karl Spooner, NL:Brk. Sept. 22, 1954
	J.R. Richard, NL:Hou. Sept. 5(2g), 1971
12	Elmer Myers, AL:Phil. Oct. 6(2g), 1915
	Steve Woodard, AL:Mil. July 28(1g), 1997

Most Strikeouts, Consecutive, First Game
7	Sammy Stewart, AL:Balt. Sept. 1, 1978 (2-4 inn)
	Stephen Strasburg, NL:Wash. June 8, 2010 (5-7 inn)

Most Wild Pitches, First Game
5	Jake Seymour, AA:Pitt. Sept. 23, 1882
	Mike Corcoran, NL:Chi. July 15, 1884
	George Winkelman, NL:Wash. Aug. 2, 1886
	Since 1900:
4	Steve Hargan, AL:Clev. Aug. 3, 1965
3	Nap Rucker, NL:Brk. Apr. 15, 1907
	Bill Hoffman, NL:Phil. Aug. 13, 1939
	Tim Wakefield, NL:Pitt. July 31, 1992
	Chris Mabeus, NL:Mil. May 29, 2006

CLUB BATTING – SEASON

	AL:1901-1960 NL:1900-1961 8 clubs 154 games		AL:1961-1968 NL:1962-1968 10 clubs 162 games		AL:1969- NL:1969- 12-16 clubs 162 games	
Highest Batting Average						
AL:	.316	Det. 1921	.267	NY 1962	.293	Clev. 1996
NL:	.319	NY 1930	.279	Pitt. 1966	.294	Col. 2000
Lowest Batting Average						
AL:	.211	Chi. 1910	.214	NY 1968	.229	Mil. 1971
NL:	.213	Brk. 1908	.219	NY 1963	.225	SD 1969
Highest Slugging Percentage						
AL:	.488	NY 1927	.442	NY 1961	.495	Hou. 2019
NL:	.481	Chi. 1930	.441	SF 1962	.483	Col. 2001
Lowest Slugging Percentage						
AL:	.260	Chi. 1910	.311	Chi. 1968	.318	Cal. 1976
NL:	.277	Brk. 1908	.301	Hou. 1963	.327	StL. 1986
Most At-Bats						
AL:	5646	Clev. 1936	5705	NY 1964	5781	Bos. 1997
NL:	5667	Phil. 1930	5767	Cin. 1968	5734	StL. 1979
Fewest At-Bats						
AL:	4822	Chi. 1913	5275	Balt. 1968	5185	Mil. 1971
NL:	4725	Phil. 1907	5303	Hou. 1964	5294	SD 2014
Most Runs						
AL:	1067	NY 1931	841	Det. 1961	1009	Clev. 1999
NL:	1004	StL. 1930	878	SF 1962	968	Col. 2000
Fewest Runs						
AL:	380	Wash. 1909	463	Chi. 1968	511	Cal. 1971
NL:	372	StL. 1908	464	Hou. 1963	468	SD 1969
Most Hits						
AL:	1725	Det. 1921	1509	NY 1962	1684	Bos. 1997
NL:	1783	Phil. 1930	1586	Pitt. 1966	1664	Col. 2000
Fewest Hits						
AL:	1061	Chi. 1910	1137	NY 1968	1188	Mil. 1971
NL:	1044	Brk. 1908	1168	NY 1963	1199	SD 2014
Most Total Bases						
AL:	2703	NY 1936	2455	NY 1961	2832	Bos. 2003
						Minn. 2019
NL:	2684	Chi. 1930	2483	Cin. 1965	2748	Col. 2001
Fewest Total Bases						
AL:	1310	Chi. 1910	1681	Chi. 1968	1694	Cal. 1969
NL:	1358	Brk. 1908	1618	Hou. 1963	1756	StL. 1986
Most Extra-Base Hits						
AL:	580	NY 1936	494	Minn. 1964	649	Bos. 2003
NL:	566	StL. 1930	512	Cin. 1965	601	LA 2019
Fewest Extra-Base Hits						
AL:	173	StL. 1909	273	Chi. 1968	268	Cal. 1969
NL:	182	Bos. 1909	271	Hou. 1963	282	Atl. 1976
Most Singles						
AL:	1299	Det. 1921	1075	Chi. 1961	1202	Tex. 1980
NL:	1298	Pitt. 1922	1239	Pitt. 1967	1168	StL. 1971
Fewest Singles						
AL:	837	Wash. 1959	811	Balt. 1968	761	Tor. 2019
NL:	846	Brk. 1908	865	NY 1965	794	LA 2017

	AL:1901-1960 NL:1900-1961 8 clubs 154 games		AL:1961-1968 NL:1962-1968 10 clubs 162 games		AL:1969- NL:1969- 12-16 clubs 162 games

Most Doubles

AL:	357	Clev. 1936	257	Clev. 1961 Bos. 1962 Minn. 1965	376	Tex. 2008
NL:	373	StL. 1930	281	Cin. 1968	342	StL. 2003

Fewest Doubles

AL:	115	Chi. 1910	154	NY 1968	151	Cal. 1969
NL:	110	Brk. 1908	156	NY 1963	170	Atl. 1976

Most Triples

AL:	113	Bos. 1903	59	KC 1965	79	KC 1979
NL:	129	Pitt. 1912	66	StL. 1963 Pitt. 1966	70	Pitt. 1970

Fewest Triples

AL:	19	Balt. 1958	17	NY 1967 Bos. 1968	5	Tor. 2017
NL:	19	Bos. 1942	23	NY 1967	9	StL. 2018

Most Home Runs

AL:	193	NY 1960	240	NY 1961	307	Minn. 2019
NL:	221	NY 1947 Cin. 1956	207	Atl. 1966	279	LA 2019

Fewest Home Runs

AL:	3	Chi. 1908	69	KC 1967	55	Cal. 1975
NL:	9	Pitt. 1917	62	Hou. 1963	49	Hou. 1979

Most Grand Slam Home Runs

AL:	10	Det. 1938	8	Minn. 1961 Bos. 1964	14	Oak. 2000 Clev. 2006
NL:	9	Chi. 1929	8	Mil. 1962	12	Atl. 1997 StL. 2000

Most Home Runs, Pinch-Hitters

AL:	7	NY 1953-54, 60 Clev. & Det. 1958	10	NY 1961	11	Balt. 1982
NL:	12	Cin. 1957	9	Cin. 1962 NY 1962, 66	17	StL. 2016

Most Grand Slam Home Runs, Pinch-Hitters

AL:	2	Phil. 1931; Det. 1952 NY 1953; Bos. 1960	2	Chi.& NY 1961	3	Balt. 1982
NL:	2	NY 1934; Phil. 1945	1	By many	3	By many

Most Runs Batted In (Since 1920)

AL:	995	NY 1936	791	NY 1962	960	Clev. 1999
NL:	942	StL. 1930	807	SF 1962	909	Col. 1996

Fewest Runs Batted In (Since 1920)

AL:	440	Phil. 1945	431	Chi. 1968	477	Cal. 1971
NL:	354	Phil. 1942	421	Hou. 1963	431	SD 1969

Most Sacrifice Hits

AL:	207	Chi. 1906	109	Chi. 1966	142	Minn. 1979
NL:	231	Chi. 1906	120	LA 1964	133	SD 1975

Fewest Sacrifice Hits

AL:	41	Bos. 1957	35	Bos. 1964	4	LA 2019
NL:	32	NY 1957	46	NY 1963	20	Mil. 2019

Most Sacrifice Flies (Since 1954)

AL:	59	Clev. 1954-55 Chi. 1960	59	Minn. 1965	77	Oak. 1984
NL:	66	StL. 1954	53	LA 1963	75	Col. 2000

	AL:1901-1960 NL:1900-1961 8 clubs 154 games		AL:1961-1968 NL:1962-1968 10 clubs 162 games		AL:1969- NL:1969- 12-16 clubs 162 games	
Fewest Sacrifice Flies (Since 1954)						
AL:	27	Balt. 1955	23	Cal. 1967	25	TB 2001
						Minn. 2011
NL:	26	StL. 1959	26	NY 1964	19	SD 1971
Most Walks						
AL:	835	Bos. 1949	681	LA 1961	775	Sea. 2000
NL:	732	Brk. 1947	615	NY 1962	729	SF 1970
Fewest Walks						
AL:	283	Wash. 1904	397	Chi. 1968	363	Det. 2002
NL:	282	StL. 1908	345	StL. 1966	375	Mia. 2015
Most Intentional Walks (Since 1955)						
AL:	66	NY 1957	79	Minn. 1965	78	Minn. 1969
NL:	91	Brk. 1956	101	Phil. 1967	153	SF 2004
Fewest Intentional Walks (Since 1955)						
AL:	20	Wash. 1959	10	KC 1961	7	Sea. 2019
NL:	21	LA 1958	29	NY 1962	15	StL. 2019
Most Hit By Pitch						
AL:	82	Wash. 1910	61	Det. 1968	103	Clev. 2008
NL:	92	NY 1903	53	Phil. 1962	100	Hou. 1997
Fewest Hit By Pitch						
AL:	5	Phil. 1937	15	Wash. 1962	11	Clev. 1976
NL:	9	Phil. 1939	17	Pitt. 1962	9	SD 1989
Most Strikeouts						
AL:	883	Wash. 1960	1125	Wash. 1965	1595	Det. 2019
NL:	1054	Phil. 1960	1203	NY 1968	1581	SD 2019
Fewest Strikeouts						
AL:	326	Phil. 1927	612	Chi. 1961	589	Tex. 1980
NL:	308	Cin. 1921	782	Atl. 1968	649	StL. 1975
Most Stolen Bases						
AL:	292	Wash. 1913	153	Chi. 1966	341	Oak. 1976
NL:	347	NY 1911	198	LA 1962	314	StL. 1985
Fewest Stolen Bases						
AL:	13	Wash. 1957	18	Bos. 1964	19	Balt. 2016
NL:	17	StL. 1949	22	SF 1967	23	Pitt. 1973
Most Caught Stealing						
AL:	118	Chi. 1923	82	Chi. 1967	123	Oak. 1976
NL:	149	Chi. 1924	77	LA 1965	120	Pitt. 1977
Fewest Caught Stealing						
AL:	11	KC 1960	11	Clev. 1961	12	Bos. 2005
NL:	8	Mil. 1958	27	Mil. 1962	10	LA 2019
				SF 1965		
Most Grounded into Double Plays						
AL:	170	Phil. 1950	157	Bos. 1965	174	Bos. 1990
NL:	166	StL. 1958	149	SF 1965	169	StL. 2011
Fewest Grounded into Double Plays						
AL:	93	StL. 1944	79	KC 1967	81	Det. 1985
		NY 1952				
NL:	75	StL. 1945	79	LA 1965	76	Hou. 1983
Most Left on Base						
AL:	1334	StL. 1941	1246	Chi. 1964	1312	Det. 1993
NL:	1287	Brk. 1947	1218	NY 1962	1328	Cin. 1976
Fewest Left on Base						
AL:	925	KC 1957	995	KC 1966	975	Cal. 1992
NL:	973	Chi. 1924	1019	SF 1966	965	SD 2016

BATTING AVERAGE

Most Seasons Leading League
26 **AL:**Bos. 1903, 38-39, 41-42, 44, 46, 49-50, 64, 67, 75, 79, 81, 84-85, 87-90, 97, 2003, 05, 16, 18, 20
25 **NL:**StL. 1915, 20-21, 34, 38-39, 42-44, 46, 49, 52, 54, 56-57, 63, 71, 75, 79-80, 85, 92, 2004, 08, 11

Most Seasons, Consecutive, Leading League
8 **NL:**Col. 1995-2002
5 **AL:**Phil. 1910-14

Most Players, .300 or Higher, Season
(Minimum: 300 at-bats)
8 **NL:**Phil. 1894
  Balt. 1894
  StL. 1930
7 **AL:**Phil. 1927

SLUGGING PERCENTAGE

Most Seasons Leading League
32 **AL:**NY 1920-21, 23-24, 26-28, 30-31, 36-39, 43-45,47-48,51,53-58,60-62,86,2007,09,12
23 **NL:**NY/SF 1889, 91, 1904-05, 08, 10-11, 19, 23-24, 27-28, 35, 45, 47-48, 52, 61-63, 89, 93, 2002

Most Seasons, Consecutive, Leading League
6 **AL:**NY 1953-58
5 **NL:**Col. 1995-99

PLATE APPEARANCES

Most Plate Appearances, Game
71 **NL:**Chi. (Lou.) June 29, 1897
   Since 1900:
66 **NL:**Phil. (Chi.) Aug. 25, 1922
65 **AL:**Mil. (Tor.) Aug. 28, 1992
   Tex. (Balt.) Aug. 22(1g), 2007
   Extra-Inning Game
104 **AL:**Chi. (Mil.) May 8, 1984 (25 inn)
103 **NL:**NY(StL.) Sept. 11, 1974 (25 inn)

Most Plate Appearances, Both Clubs, Game
125 **NL:**Phil. (66) Chi. (59) Aug. 25, 1922
113 **AL:**Clev. (59) StL. (54) April 14, 1925
   Extra-Inning Game:
202 **NL:**NY (103) StL. (99) Sept. 11, 1974 (25 inn)
198 **AL:**Chi. (104) Mil. (94) May 8, 1984 (25 inn)

Most Plate Appearances, Inning
23 **NL:**Chi. (Det.) Sept. 6, 1883 (7th)
   Since 1900:
23 **AL:**Bos. (Det.) June 18, 1953 (7th)
21 **NL:**Brk. (Cin.) May 21, 1952 (1st)

Most Batters, 3 Appearances, Inning
5 **NL:**Chi. (Det.) Sept. 6, 1883 (7th)
  AL: Bos. (Det.) June 18, 1953 (7th)
  NL Since 1900:
3 **NL:**Brk. (Cin.) May 21, 1952 (1st)

Most Batters on Base, Inning
20 **AL:**Bos. (Det.) June 18, 1953 (7th)
19 **NL:**Bos. (Balt.) June 18(1g), 1894 (1st)
   Brk. (Cin.) May 21, 1952 (1st)

Most Batters, Consecutive, On Base, Inning
19 **NL:**Brk. (Cin.) May 21, 1952 (1st)
13 **AL:**KC (Chi.) Apr. 21, 1956 (2nd)
   KC (Det.) Sept. 9(1g), 2004 (3rd)

Most Batters, On Base 3 Times, Inning
3 **NL:**Chi. (Det.) Sept. 6, 1883 (7th)
  Bos. (Balt.) June 18(1g), 1894 (1st)
  AL: Bos. (Det.) June 18, 1953 (7th)
  NL Since 1900:
1 **NL:**Brk. (Cin.) May 21, 1952 (1st)

AT-BATS

Most At-Bats, Game
66 **NL:**Chi. (Buff.) July 3, 1883
   Since 1900:
58 **NL:**NY (Phil.) Sept. 2, 1925
   NY (Phil.) July 11, 1931
57 **AL:**Mil. (Tor.) Aug. 28, 1992
   Tex. (Balt.) Aug. 22(1g), 2007
   Extra-Inning Game:
95 **AL:**Chi. (Mil.) May 8, 1984 (25 inn)
89 **NL:**NY (StL.) Sept. 11, 1974 (25 inn)

Most At-Bats, Both Clubs, Game
106 **NL:**Chi. (64) Lou (42) July 22, 1876
   Since 1900:
99 **NL:**NY (56) Cin. (43) June 9, 1901
   NY (58) Phil. (41) July 11, 1931
   Cin. (52) Phil. (47) Aug. 3, 1969
96 **AL:**Clev. (51) Phil. (45) Apr. 29, 1952
   Extra-Inning Game:
175 **NL:**NY (89) StL. (86) Sept. 11, 1974 (25 inn)
   AL: Chi. (95) Mil. (80) May 8, 1984 (25 inn)

Fewest At-Bats, Game
9 innings:
22 **NL:**StL. (Cin.) Sept. 10, 1914
23 **AL:**NY (Bos.) Apr. 27, 1911
   Det. (Phil.) Aug. 4, 1915
   Chi. (StL.) May 6, 1917
   Chi. (Wash.) June 15, 1918
   Clev. (Chi.) May 9, 1961
   Det. (Balt.) May 6, 1968
8 innings:
19 **AL:**Balt. (KC) Sept. 12, 1964
21 **NL:**Pitt. (StL.) Sept. 8, 1908
   Cin. (Brk.) June 3, 1913
   Phil. (Bos.) May 29, 1914
   Bos. (Pitt.) July 21(1g), 1927
   Atl. (Pitt.) Sept. 6, 1986

Fewest At-Bats, Both Clubs, Game
9 innings:
46 **AL:**Balt. (19) KC (27) Sept. 12, 1964
48 **NL:**Bos. (25) Phil. (23) Apr. 22, 1910
   Brk. (24) Cin. (24) July 22, 1911
   StL. (22) Cin. (26) June 14, 1914
   Cin. (26) Atl. (22) Apr. 11, 1980

RUNS

Most Seasons Leading League
32 **AL:**NY 1921, 26-28, 30-33, 36-39, 42-43, 45, 47, 53-54, 56-58, 60, 62, 85, 98, 2002, 06-07, 09-10, 19-20
22 **NL:**Chi. 1876, 78, 80-86, 88, 1906, 11, 13, 18, 29, 31, 35, 37, 67, 84, 89, 2008

Most Seasons, Consecutive, Leading League
7 **NL:**Chi. 1880-86
  Since 1900:
5 **NL:**Brk. 1949-53
4 **AL:**Det. 1907-10
  NY 1930-33, 36-39
  Bos. 1948-51

Most Games, Consecutive, Scoring Runs
308 **AL:**NY Aug. 3, 1931-Aug. 2, 1933
208 **NL:**Cin. Apr. 3, 2000-May 23, 2001

Most Runs, Game
36 **NL:**Chi. (Lou.) June 29, 1897
  Since 1900:
30 **AL:**Tex. (Balt.) Aug. 22(1g), 2007
29 **NL:**Atl. (Mia.) Sept. 9, 2020

Most Runs, Both Clubs, Game
49 **NL:**Chi. (26) Phil. (23) Aug. 25, 1922
36 **AL:**Bos. (22) Phil. (14) June 29, 1950
    Bos. (19) Tex. (17) Aug. 12, 2008

Most Runs, 2 Consecutive Games
53 **NL:**Chi. July 22-25, 1876
  Since 1900:
49 **AL:**Bos. June 7-8, 1950
45 **NL:**Pitt. June 20-22, 1925

Most Runs, 3 Consecutive Games
71 **NL:**Chi. July 20-25, 1876
56 **AL:**Bos. June 7-9, 1950
  NL Since 1900:
54 **NL:**Pitt. June 19-22, 1925

Most Runs, 4 Consecutive Games
88 **NL:**Chi. July 20-27, 1876
65 **AL:**Bos. June 5-8, 1950
  Since 1900:
59 **NL:**Chi. June 1-5, 1930

Most Runs, Inning
18 **NL:**Chi. (Det.) Sept. 6, 1883 (7th)
  Since 1900:
17 **AL:**Bos. (Det.) June 18, 1953 (7th)
15 **NL:**Brk. (Cin.) May 21, 1952 (1st)

Most Runs, Both Clubs, Inning
19 **AA:**Wash. (14) Balt. (5) June 17, 1891 (1st)
  AL: Clev. (13) Bos. (6) Apr. 10, 1977 (8th)
18 **NL:**Chi. (18) Det. (0) Sept. 6, 1883 (7th)
  NL Since 1900:
17 **NL:**Bos. (10) NY (7) June 20, 1912 (9th)

Most Runs, Extra Inning
12 **AL:**Tex. (Oak.) July 3, 1983 (15th)
10 **NL:**KC (Det.) July 21, 1886 (11th)
    Bos. (NY) June 17(1g), 1887 (10th)
    Cin. (Brk.) May 15, 1919 (13th)

Most Runs, Both Clubs, Extra Inning
12 **AL:**Minn. (11) Oak. (1) June 21, 1969 (10th)
    Tex. (12) Oak. (0) July 3, 1983 (15th)
11 **NL:**NY (8) Pitt. (3) June 15, 1929 (14th)
    NY (6) Brk. (5) Apr. 24, 1955 (10th)
    NY (6) Chi. (5) June 30, 1979 (11th)
    Pitt. (6) Chi. (5) Apr. 21, 1991 (11th)
    Ari. (6) LA (5) Sept. 27, 2011 (10th)

Most Runs, 1st Inning
16 **NL:**Bos. (Balt.) June 18(1g), 1894
  Since 1900:
15 **NL:**Brk. (Cin.) May 21, 1952
14 **AL:**Clev. (Phil.) June 18(2g), 1950
    Bos. (Fla.) June 27, 2003

Most Runs, 2nd Inning
14 **AL:**Clev. (NY) Apr. 18, 2009
13 **NL:**Chi. (Cin.) Aug. 7, 1877
    NY (Clev.) July 19(1g), 1890
    Atl. (Hou.) Sept. 20, 1972
    SD (Pitt.) May 31, 1994

Most Runs, 3rd Inning
14 **NL:**Clev. (Wash.) Aug. 7, 1889
  Since 1900:
13 **NL:**SF (StL.) May 7, 1966
12 **AL:**NY (Wash.) Sept. 11(1g), 1949

Most Runs, 4th Inning
15 **NL:**Hart. (NY) May 13, 1876
  Since 1900:
14 **NL:**Chi. (Phil.) Aug. 25, 1922
13 **AL:**Chi. (Wash.) Sept. 26(1g), 1943

Most Runs, 5th Inning
14 **AL:**NY (Wash.) July 6, 1920
13 **NL:**Chi. (Pitt.) Aug. 16, 1890
    Col. (SF) May 5, 2016

Most Runs, 6th Inning
14 **PL:**Phil. (Buff.) June 26, 1890
13 **AL:**Clev. (Bos.) July 7(1g), 1923
    Det. (NY) June 17, 1925
  NL: Mtl. (SF) May 7, 1997

Most Runs, 7th Inning
18 **NL:**Chi. (Det.) Sept. 6, 1883
  Since 1900:
17 **AL:**Bos. (Det.) June 18, 1953
13 **NL:**SF (SD) July 15, 1997

Most Runs, 8th Inning
16 **AL:**Tex. (Balt.) Apr. 19, 1996
13 **NL:**Brk. (Cin.) Aug. 8, 1954

Most Runs, 9th Inning
14 **NL:**Balt. (Bos.) Apr. 24, 1894
  Since 1900:
13 **AL:**Cal. (Tex.) Sept. 14, 1978
    Det. (Tex.) Aug. 8, 2001
12 **NL:**SF (Cin.) Aug. 23, 1961
    SD (Col.) Sept. 12, 2004

Most Runs, 10th Inning
11 **AL:**Minn. (Oak.) June 21, 1969
10 **NL:**Bos. (NY) June 17(1g), 1887
  NL Since 1900:
9 **NL:**Cin. (Phil.) Aug. 24(1g), 1947
    SD (Phil.) May 28, 1995

Most Runs, 11th Inning
10 **NL:**KC (Det.) July 21, 1886
  Since 1900:
9 **NL:**SD (Col.) June 28(2g), 1994
8 **AL:**Phil. (Det.) May 1, 1951
    Tex. (Sea.) Sept. 23, 1991
    Sea. (KC) Sept. 8, 2002
    Tex. (Sea.) Aug. 8, 2015

Most Runs, 12th Inning
11 **AL:**NY (Det.) July 26(1g), 1928
9 **NL:**Chi. (Pitt.) July 23, 1923

Most Runs, 13th Inning
10 **NL:**Cin. (Brk.) May 15, 1919
9 **AL:**Clev. (Det.) Aug. 5(1g), 1933
    LA (Balt.) Aug. 16, 2009

Most Runs, 14th Inning
8 **NL:**NY (Pitt.) June 15, 1929
7 **AL:**Clev. (StL.) June 3, 1935
    Det. (Mil.) May 27, 1991

Most Runs, 15th Inning
12 **AL:**Tex. (Oak.) July 3, 1983
7 **NL:**StL. (Bos.) Sept. 28, 1928

Most Runs, 16th Inning
8 **AL:**Chi. (Wash.) May 20, 1920
5 **NL:**Cin. (NY) Aug. 20, 1973
    Hou. (Cin.) Apr. 8, 1988

Most Runs, 17th Inning
7 **NL:**NY (Pitt.) July 16, 1920
6 **AL:**NY (Det.) July 20, 1941

Most Runs, 18th Inning
5 **NL:**Chi. (Bos.) May 14, 1927
    Ari. (Phil.) Aug. 24, 2013
4 **AL:**Minn. (Sea.) July 19, 1969

Most Runs, 19th Inning
5 **NL:**NY (Atl.) July 4, 1985
4 **AL:**Clev. (Det.) Apr. 27, 1984

Most Runs, 20th Inning
4 **NL:**Brk. (Bos.) July 5, 1940
3 **AL:**Bos. (Sea.) July 27, 1969
Wash. (Clev.) Sept. 14(2g), 1971

Most Runs, 21st Inning
4 **AL:**Chi. (Clev.) May 26, 1973
3 **NL:**SD (Mtl.) May 21, 1977

Most Runs, 22nd Inning
2 **AL:**NY (Det.) June 24, 1962
1 **NL:**Brk. (Pitt.) Aug. 22, 1917
Chi. (Bos.) May 17, 1927
Hou. (LA) June 3, 1989
LA (Mtl.) Aug. 23, 1989
Col. (SD) Apr. 17, 2008

Most Runs, 23rd Inning
2 **NL:**SF (NY) May 31(2g), 1964
0 **AL:**Bos. (Phil.) Sept. 1, 1906
Phil. (Bos.) Sept. 1, 1906
Det. (Phil.) July 21, 1945
Phil. (Det.) July 21, 1945
Chi. (Mil.) May 8, 1984
Mil. (Chi.) May 8, 1984

Most Runs, 24th Inning
3 **AL:**Phil. (Bos.) Sept. 1, 1906
1 **NL:**Hou. (NY) Apr. 15, 1968

Most Runs, 25th Inning
1 **NL:**StL. (NY) Sept. 11, 1974
AL: Chi. (Mil.) May 8, 1984

Most Runs, 26th Inning
0 **NL:**Bos. (Brk.) May 1, 1920
Brk. (Bos.) May 1, 1920
AL: No games

Most Runs, Both Clubs, 1st Inning
19 **AA:**Wash. (14) Balt. (5) June 17, 1891
16 **NL:**Bos. (16) Balt. (0) June 18(1g), 1894
AL: Oak. (13) Cal. (3) July 5, 1996
NL Since 1900:
15 **NL:**Brk. (15) Cin. (0) May 21, 1952

Most Runs, Both Clubs, 2nd Inning
16 **AL:**Chi. (8) NY (8), Aug. 2, 2007
14 **NL:**Buff. (8) Wor. (6) July 4(2g), 1882
Clev. (10) Bos. (4) May 20, 1891
Bos. (9) Pitt. (5) Aug. 19(1g), 1893
Balt. (10) Chi. (4) Sept. 4, 1893
NL Since 1900:
13 **NL:**Chi. (10) Phil. (3) Aug. 25, 1922
Brk. (11) NY (2) Apr. 29, 1930
Atl. (13) Hou. (0) Sept. 20, 1972
SD (13) Pitt. (0) May 31, 1994
Atl. (11) Mia. (2) Sept. 9, 2020

Most Runs, Both Clubs, 3rd Inning
15 **NL:**NY (13) Phil. (2) Sept. 8, 1883
Since 1900:
13 **AL:**Clev. (8) StL. (5) July 6, 1917
Phil. (7) Bos. (6) July 4(2g), 1939
Bos. (8) Det. (5) July 2, 1995
NL: Brk. (9) Cin. (4) Aug. 22, 1929
SF (13) StL. (0) May 7, 1966
StL. (7) Atl. (6) Aug. 21, 1973
Col. (10) Cin. (3) July 26, 2015
ML:AL Clev. (10) NL:Ari. (3) June 17, 2005

Most Runs, Both Clubs, 4th Inning
15 **NL:**Hart. (15) NY (0) May 13, 1876
Chi. (14) Phil. (1) Aug. 25, 1922
14 **AL:**Chi. (12) Phil. (2) June 10, 1952

Most Runs, Both Clubs, 5th Inning
18 **AL:**Tex. (10) Det. (8) May 8, 2004
17 **NL:**Col. (13) SF (4) May 5, 2016

Most Runs, Both Clubs, 6th Inning
15 **AL:**Phil. (10) NY (5) Sept. 5(1g), 1912
Det. (10) Minn. (5) June 13, 1967
NL:NY (10) Cin. (5) June 12, 1979

Most Runs, Both Clubs, 7th Inning
18 **NL:**Chi. (18) Det. (0) Sept. 6, 1883
Since 1900:
17 **AL:**Bos. (17) Det. (0) June 18, 1953
13 **NL:**Chi. (12) Cin. (1) May 28, 1925
StL. (7) NY (6) June 26, 1940
Phil. (10) Chi. (3) July 22(2g), 1945
SF (13) SD (0) July 15, 1997

Most Runs, Both Clubs, 8th Inning
19 **AL:**Clev. (13) Bos. (6) Apr. 10, 1977
14 **NL:**NY (11) Pitt. (3) May 25, 1954
Brk. (13) Cin. (1) Aug. 8, 1954
Atl. (9) SD (5) Apr. 27(1g), 1975
Col. (8) LA (6) June 29, 1996

Most Runs, Both Clubs, 9th Inning
17 **NL:**Bos. (10) NY (7) June 20, 1912
15 **AL:**Tor. (11) Sea. (4) July 20, 1984

Most Runs, Both Clubs, 10th Inning
12 **AL:**Minn. (11) Oak. (1) June 21, 1969
11 **NL:**NY (6) Brk. (5) Apr. 24, 1955
Ari. (6) LA (5) Sept. 27, 2011

Most Runs, Both Clubs, 11th Inning
11 **AL:**Sea. (6) Bos. (5) May 16, 1969
NL:NY (6) Chi. (5) June 30, 1979
Pitt. (6) Chi. (5) Apr. 21, 1991

Most Runs, Both Clubs, 12th Inning
15 **FL:**StL. (8) Brk. (7) June 16. 1914
11 **AL:**NY (8) Det. (3) May 14, 1923
NY (11) Det. (0) July 26(1g), 1928
9 **NL:**Chi. (9) Pitt. (0) July 23, 1923
NY (8) Brk. (1) May 30(2g), 1940
Hou. (8) Cin. (1) June 2, 1966
SD (5) Hou. (4) July 5, 1969

Most Runs, Both Clubs, 13th Inning
10 **NL:**Cin. (10) Brk. (0) May 15, 1919
9 **AL:**Clev. (9) Det. (0) Aug. 5(1g), 1933
LA (9) Balt. (0) Aug. 16, 2009

Most Runs, Both Clubs, 14th Inning
11 **NL:**NY (8) Pitt. (3) May 15, 1929
10 **AL:**Chi. (5) Sea. (5) June 5, 2013

Most Runs, Both Clubs, 15th Inning
12 **AL:**Tex. (12) Oak. (0) July 3, 1983
7 **NL:**StL. (7) Bos. (0) Sept. 28, 1928
SF (4) LA (3) May 2, 1995

Most Runs, Both Clubs, 16th Inning
8 **AL:**Chi. (8) Wash. (0) May 20, 1920
5 **NL:**NY (4) Lou. (1) July 10, 1876
Cin. (4) Brk. (1) July 29, 1914
Cin. (5) NY (0) Aug. 20, 1973
Hou. (5) Cin. (0) Apr. 8, 1988
Ari. (3) LA (2) Apr. 13, 1999

Most Runs, Both Clubs, 17th Inning
7 **NL:**NY (7) Pitt. (0) July 16, 1920
6 **AL:**NY (3) Bos. (3) Sept. 5(1g), 1927
NY (6) Det. (0) July 20, 1941

Most Runs, Both Clubs, 18th Inning
5 **NL:**Chi. (5) Bos. (0) May 14, 1927
  Ari. (5) Phil. (0) Aug. 24, 2013
  AL: Oak. (3) Minn. (2) Aug. 8, 2004

Most Runs, Both Clubs, 19th Inning
7 **NL:**NY (5) Atl. (2) July 4, 1985
5 **AL:**Chi. (3) Bos. (2) July 13, 1951

Most Runs, Both Clubs, 20th Inning
4 **AL:**Bos. (3) Sea. (1) July 27, 1969
  Wash. (3) Clev. (1) Sept. 14(2g), 1971
  NL: Brk. (4) Bos. (0) July 5, 1940

Most Runs, Both Clubs, 21st Inning
6 **AL:**Mil. (3) Chi. (3) May 8, 1984
3 **NL:**SD (3) Mtl. (0) May 21, 1977

Most Runs, 2 Consecutive Innings, Game
21 **NL:**Pitt. (Bos.) June 6, 1894 (3rd-4th)
  Since 1900:
19 **AL:**Bos. (Phil.) May 2, 1901 (2nd-3rd)
  Bos. (Det.) June 18, 1953 (6th-7th)
  Mil. (Cal.) July 8, 1990 (4th-5th)
18 **NL:**Mtl. (SF) May 7, 1997 (5th-6th)

Most Runs, None Out, Inning
13 **NL:**Chi. (Det.) Sept. 6, 1883 (7th)
  Since 1900:
12 **NL:**Brk. (Phil.) May 24, 1953 (8th)
  AL: Bos. (Clev.) May 7, 2009 (6th)

Most Runs, Two Out, Inning
13 **AL:**Clev. (Bos.) July 7, 1923 (6th)
  KC (Chi.) Apr. 21, 1956 (2nd)
12 **NL:**Brk. (Cin.) May 21, 1952 (1st)
  Brk. (Cin.) Aug. 8, 1954 (8th)
  Col. (Chi.) July 30, 2010 (8th)

Most Runs, 2 Out, None On Base, Inning
12 **NL:**Brk. (Cin.) Aug. 8, 1954 (8th)
10 **AL:**Chi. (Det.) Sept. 2, 1959 (5th)

Most Runs, None Out, 1st Inning
10 **AL:**Bos. (Fla.) June 27, 2003
9 **NL:**Phil. (NY) Aug. 13, 1948

Most Innings Scored, Consecutive, Season
17 **AL:**Bos. Sept. 15-17, 1903 (3 g)
14 **NL:**Pitt. July 31-Aug. 2, 1894 (3 g)
  NY July 18-20, 1949 (3 g)
  Col. May 4-7, 1999 (3 g)

Most Innings, Consecutive, No Runs Scored
48 **AL:**Phil. Sept. 22-26, 1906
  NL: Chi. June 15-21, 1968

Scoring Each Inning, Game
9 **AA:**Colu. (Pitt.) June 14, 1883
  KC (Brk.) May 20, 1889
  NL: Clev. (Bos.) Aug. 15, 1889
  Wash. (Bos.) June 22, 1894
  Clev. (Phil.) July 12, 1894
  Chi. (Lou.) June 29, 1897
  NY (Phil.) June 1, 1923
  StL. (Chi.) Sept. 13, 1964
  Col. (Chi.) May 5, 1999
  FL: Pitt. (Balt.) July 1(2g), 1915
  AL:none

Scoring Each Inning, Game
(Did not bat in 9th)
8 **NL:**By many
  AL: Bos. (Clev.) Sept. 16, 1903
  Clev. (Bos.) July 7, 1923
  NY (StL.) July 26, 1939
  Chi. (Bos.) May 11, 1949
  KC (Oak.) Sept. 14, 1998
  NY (Tor.) Apr. 29, 2006
  Det. (NL:Col.) Aug. 2, 2014
  Chi. (Clev.) Sept. 12, 2016

Most Innings Scored, Both Clubs, Game
15 **NL:**Phil. (8) Det. (7) July 1, 1887
  Wash. (9) Bos. (6) June 22, 1894
  AA:KC (9) Brk. (6) May 20, 1889
  PL:NY (8) Chi. (7) May 23, 1890
  Since 1900:
14 **NL:**NY (9) Phil. (5) June 1, 1923
  StL. (8) Phil. (6) July 5, 1923
  Pitt. (8) Chi. (6) July 6, 1975
  LA (8) Chi. (6) May 5, 1976
  Col. (8) LA (6) June 30, 1996
  Col. (8) SD (6) Sept. 24, 2001
  AL: Balt. (8) Phil. (6) May 7, 1901
  StL. (7) Det. (7) Apr. 23, 1927
  Det. (7) Det. (7) July 2, 1940
  Chi. (7) Det. (7) May 28, 1995
  Minn. (7) Chi. (7) July 6, 2007
  ML: Sea. (7) SF (7) June 12, 1999
  Extra-Inning Game:
15 **NL:**Pitt. (8) NY (7) June 15, 1929 (14 inn)
  Phil. (8) Pitt. (7) July 23, 1930 (13 inn)
  Chi. (8) Brk. (7) July 22, 1935 (11 inn)
  NY (8) Atl. (7) July 4, 1985 (19 inn)
  Hou. (8) Chi. (7) Sept. 28, 1995 (11 inn)
  AL: Phil. (8) Clev. (7) July 10, 1932 (18 inn)

Most Runs Overcome to Win Game
12 **AL:**Det. (Chi.) June 18, 1911
  Phil. (Clev.) June 15, 1925
  Clev. (Sea.) Aug. 5, 2001 (11 inn)
11 **NL:**StL. (NY) June 15(1g), 1952
  Phil. (Chi.) Apr. 17, 1976 (10 inn)
  Hou. (StL.) July 18, 1994

Most Runs, Opening Game, Season
23 **PL:**Buff. (Clev.) Apr. 19, 1890
21 **AL:**Clev. (StL.) Apr. 14, 1925
18 **NL:**NY (Brk.) Apr. 11, 1912 (6 inn)
  Extra-Inning Game:
19 **NL:**Phil. (Bos.) Apr. 19, 1900 (10 inn)

Most Runs, Both Clubs, Opening Game
36 **NL:**Phil. (19) Bos. (17) Apr. 19, 1900 (10 inn)
35 **AL:**Clev. (21) StL. (14) Apr. 14, 1925

Most Players, 100 or more Runs, Season
7 **NL:**Bos. 1894
  Since 1900:
6 **NL:**Brk. 1953
5 **AL:**By many

Most Players Scoring Runs, Game
15 **NL:**Atl. (Fla.) Oct. 3, 1999
14 **AL:**Chi. (KC) Apr. 22, 1959
  Oak. (Tex.) Sept. 30, 2000

Most Players, 2 or more Runs, Game
10 **NL:**Chi. (Lou.) June 29, 1897
  Since 1900:
9 **NL:**StL. (Chi.) Apr. 16, 1912
  Chi. (Phil.) Aug. 25, 1922
  Cin. (Phil.) Aug. 11, 1926
  StL. (Phil.) July 6(2g), 1929
  NY (Phil.) July 11(1g), 1931
  Chi. (Col.) Aug. 18, 1995
  Wash. (NY) July 31, 2018
  AL: Bos. (Phil.) May 2, 1901
  NY (Clev.) July 14, 1904
  Clev. (Bos.) July 7(1g), 1923
  NY (Chi.) July 26(2g), 1931
  NY (Phil.) May 24, 1936
  Bos. (Phil.) June 29, 1950
  Cal. (Tor.) Aug. 25, 1979
  Minn. (Det.) June 4, 1994
  Tex. (Balt.) Aug. 22(1g), 2007

Most Players, 3 or more Runs, Game
9 **NL:**Chi. (Buff.) July 3, 1883
  Since 1900:
7 **AL:**Bos. (StL.) June 8, 1950
  NL:NY (Phil.) Aug. 16 (1g), 2018

Most Players, 4 or more Runs, Game
6 **NL:**Chi. (Clev.) July 24, 1882
Chi. (Lou.) June 29, 1897
Since 1900:
4 **NL:**StL. (Brk.) July 27(2g), 1918
StL. (Phil.) July 6(2g), 1929
Atl. (Mia.) Sept. 9, 2020
AL: Bos. (StL.) June 8, 1950
Tex. (Balt.) Aug. 22(1g), 2007

Most Players, 5 or more Runs, Game
3 **NL:**Chi. (Clev.) July 24, 1882
Bos. (Phil.) June 20, 1883
Bos. (Pitt.) Aug. 27, 1887
NY (Brk.) Apr. 30(1g), 1944
Chi. (Bos.) July 3, 1945
Atl. (Mia.) Sept. 9, 2020
2 **AL:**Clev. (Balt.) Sept. 2, 1902
Chi. (KC) Apr. 23, 1955
Tex. (Balt.) Aug. 22, 2007

Most Players, 6 or more Runs, Game
2 **NL:**Bos. (Pitt.) Aug. 27, 1887
Since 1900:
1 **AL:**By many teams
NL: By many teams
see individual batting, page 12

Most Runs, Two Players, Game
12 **NL:**Bos. (Pitt.) Aug. 27, 1887
Since 1900:
11 **NL:**NY (Brk.) Apr. 30(1g), 1944
10 **AL:**Clev. (Balt.) Sept. 2, 1902
Chi. (KC) Apr. 23, 1955
KC (Det.) Sept. 9(1g), 2004
Tex. (Balt.) Aug. 22(1g), 2007

Most Players, 2 or more Runs, Inning
7 **NL:**Chi. (Det.) Sept. 6, 1883 (7th)
Since 1900:
6 **NL:**Brk. (Cin.) May 21, 1952 (1st)
Cin. (Hou.) Aug. 3, 1989 (1st)
5 **AL:**NY (Wash.) July 6, 1920 (5th)
NY (Bos.) June 21, 1945 (5th)
Bos. (Phil.) July 4, 1948 (7th)
Clev. (Phil.) June 18, 1950 (1st)
Bos. (Det.) June 18, 1953 (7th)
Mil. (Cal.) July 8, 1990 (5th)
Ana. (Chi.) May 12, 1997 (7th)
Bos. (Fla.) June 27, 2003 (1st)
Clev. (NY) Apr. 18, 2009 (2nd)

HITS

Most Seasons Leading League
29 **NL:**StL. 1901, 20-21, 26, 34, 38-40, 42-47,
49, 54, 56-57, 63-64, 75, 79-80, 83,
92, 2004, 08, 11-12
28 **AL:**Bos. 1903, 39-42, 45-46, 49-50, 54, 67,
70,75,81,84-85,87-90,97,2003,05,11,16,18-20

Most Seasons, Consecutive, Leading League
8 **NL:**Col. 1995-2002
4 **AL:**Bos. 1939-42, 1987-90

Most Players, 200 or more Hits, Season
4 **NL:**Phil. 1929
AL: Det. 1937

Most Hits, Game
36 **NL:**Phil. (Lou.) Aug. 17, 1894
Since 1900:
31 **NL:**NY (Cin.) June 9, 1901
AL: Mil. (Tor.) Aug. 28, 1992
Extra-Inning Game:
33 **AL:**Clev. (Phil.) July 10, 1932 (18 inn)

Most Hits, Consecutive, Game
12 **NL:**StL. (Bos.) Sept. 17, 1920
Brk. (Pitt.) June 23, 1930
AL: Bos. (NL:Mia.) Aug. 29, 2018

Most Hits, Both Clubs, Game
51 **NL:**Phil. (26) Chi. (25) Aug. 25, 1922
45 **AL:**Phil. (27) Bos. (18) July 8, 1902
Det. (27) NY (18) Sept. 29, 1928
Extra-Inning Game:
58 **AL:**Clev. (33) Phil. (25) July 10, 1932 (18 inn)
52 **NL:**NY (28) Pitt. (24) June 15, 1929 (14 inn)

Most Hits, 2 Consecutive Games
55 **NL:**Phil. Aug. 16-17, 1894
Since 1900:
51 **AL:**Bos. June 7-8, 1950
49 **NL:**Pitt. Aug. 7-8, 1922

Fewest Hits, Game, 10 or more innings:
0 **AA:**See No-Hit Games
NL: See No-Hit Games
1 **AL:**Clev. (Chi.) Sept. 6, 1903 (10 inn)
Bos. (StL.) Sept. 18, 1934 (10 inn)
LA (NY) May 22, 1962 (12 inn)
Oak. (Tex.) June 21, 1976 (10 inn)
LA (Minn.) May 28, 2011 (10 inn)
Chi. (NL:NY) May 7, 2013 (10 inn)
Bos. (TB) Apr. 19, 2016 (10 inn)
Sea. (Chi.) May 19, 2017 (10 inn)

Fewest Hits, Both Clubs, Game
1 **NL:**Chi. (0) LA (1) Sept. 9, 1965
2 **AL:**Clev. (1) Wash. (1), July 27, 1915
Clev. (1) StL. (1) Apr. 23, 1952
Chi. (1) Balt. (1) June 21, 1956
Balt. (1) KC (1) Sept. 12, 1964
Det. (0) Balt. (2) Apr. 30(1g), 1967

Fewest Hits, 2 Consecutive Games
1 **NL:**Bos. Sept. 5(2g)-7(1g), 1908
Hou. Sept. 14-15, 2008
2 **AL:**StL. Sept. 25-27, 1910
Chi. Aug. 10-11, 1917
Mil. June 18-19, 1974
Clev. Apr. 12(1g)-12(2g), 1992
Det. May 3-4, 1996
Clev. June 29-30, 2014

Fewest Hits, Doubleheader
2 **AL:**Clev. (Bos.) Apr. 12, 1992
3 **NL:**Brk. (StL.) Sept. 21, 1934
NY (Phil.) June 21, 1964

Most Hits, No Runs, Game
14 **NL:**NY (Chi.) Sept. 14, 1913
AL: Clev. (Wash.) July 10(2g), 1928
Extra-Inning Game:
15 **NL:**Bos. (Pitt.) July 10, 1901 (12 inn)
Bos. (Pitt.) Aug. 1, 1918 (21 inn)
AL: Bos. (Wash.) July 3, 1913 (15 inn)

Most Players, 1 or more Hits, Game
15 **NL:**Atl. (Fla.) Oct. 3, 1999
StL. (NY) Sept. 28(2g), 1979 (11 inn)
14 **AL:**Clev. (StL.) Aug. 12(2g), 1948
NY (KC) Aug. 27(2g), 1972 (16 inn)

Most Players, 1 or more Hits, Both Clubs, Game
24 **NL:**StL. (15) NY (9) Sept. 28(2g), 1979 (11 inn)
SF (13) LA (11) Sept. 19, 1998
23 **AL:**Minn. (12) Clev. (11) July 13, 1996
Extra-Inning Game:
24 **AL:**NY (14) KC (10) Aug. 27(2g), 1972 (16 inn)

Most Players, 2 or more Hits, Game
- 10 **AA:**Brk. (Phil.) June 25, 1885
- **NL:**Pitt. (Phil.) Aug. 7, 1922
- NY (Phil.) Sept. 2 (2g), 1925
- 9 **AL:**By many; last:
- Oak. (Hou.) Sept. 10, 2019

Most Players, 3 or more Hits, Game
- 8 **NL:**Chi. (Det.) Sept. 6, 1883
- **Since 1900:**
- 7 **NL:**Cin. (Pitt.) May 13, 1902
- Pitt. (Phil.) June 12, 1928
- Phil. (Pitt.) July 23(2g), 1930 (13 inn)
- NY (Atl.) July 4, 1985 (19 inn)
- Cin. (Hou.) Aug. 3, 1989
- Cin. (Col.) May 19, 1999
- **AL:**NY (Phil.) June 28(1g), 1939
- Chi. (KC) Apr. 23, 1955
- Oak. (Tex.) July 1, 1979 (15 inn)
- Tex. (Minn.) July 25, 2011

Most Players, 4 or more Hits, Game
- 7 **NL:**Chi. (Clev.) July 24, 1882
- **Since 1900:**
- 5 **NL:**SF (LA) May 13, 1958
- 4 **AL:**By many; last:
- Minn. (Sea.) June 13, 2017

Most Players, 5 or more Hits, Game
- 4 **NL:**Phil. (Lou.) Aug. 17, 1894
- **Since 1900:**
- 3 **NL:**NY (Cin.) June 9, 1901
- NY (Phil.) June 1, 1923
- **AL:**Det. (Wash.) July 30, 1917
- Clev. (Phil.) July 10, 1932 (18 inn)
- Wash. (Clev.) May 16, 1933 (12 inn)
- Chi. (Phil.) Sept. 11, 1936

Most Players, 6 or more Hits, Game
- 2 **AA:**Cin. (Pitt.) Sept. 12, 1883
- **NL:**Balt. (StL.) Sept. 3, 1897
- Pitt. (NY) July 7, 1922 (18 inn)
- **Since 1900:**
- 1 By many in AL

Most Hits, Inning
- 18 **NL:**Chi. (Det.) Sept. 6, 1883 (7th)
- **Since 1900:**
- 16 **NL:**Cin. (Hou.) Aug. 3, 1989 (1st)
- 14 **AL:**Bos. (Det.) June 18, 1953 (7th)

Most Hits, Consecutive, Inning
- 12 **AL:**Bos.(NL:Mia.)Aug.29,2018(7th;sh,ibb)
- 11 **NL:**Col. (Chi.) July 30, 2010 (8th)

Most Hits, Consecutive, No Outs, 1st Inning
- 8 **NL:**Chi. (Pitt.) Apr. 21, 1973
- Phil. (Chi.) Aug. 5, 1975
- Pitt. (Atl.) Aug. 26, 1975
- Chi. (Pitt.) Sept. 8, 2009
- **AL:**Oak. (Chi.) Sept. 27, 1981
- NY (Balt.) Sept. 25, 1990
- Minn. (NL:SF) June 21, 2011

Most Players, 2 or more Hits, Inning
- 7 **NL:**Cin. (Hou.) Aug. 3, 1989 (1st)
- 5 **AL:**Phil. (Bos.) July 8, 1902 (6th)
- NY (Phil.) Sept. 10, 1921 (9th)
- Bos. (NL:Mia.) Aug. 29, 2018 (7th)

EXTRA-BASE HITS

Most Seasons Leading League
- 34 **AL:**Bos. 1903, 12-14, 40-42, 44, 46, 49-50,54-57, 65, 67, 69-72, 75-79, 89, 2003-04, 11, 13, 16, 18, 20
- 21 **NL:**StL. 1920-23, 26-28, 30, 34, 36-40, 42-44, 46, 49, 52, 80
- Phil. 1892-93, 95-96, 98-99, 1907, 13-14, 16-17, 29, 32, 75, 77, 84-86, 93, 2007, 09

Most Seasons, Consecutive, Leading League
- 5 **NL:**Chi. 1882-86
- StL. 1936-40
- Col. 1995-99
- **AL:**NY 1958-62
- Bos. 1975-79

Most Extra-Base Hits, Game
- 17 **AL:**Bos. (StL.) June 8, 1950
- 16 **NL:**Chi. (Buff.) July 3, 1883
- **NL Since 1900:**
- 15 **NL:**Phil. (Chi.) June 23, 1986
- Cin. (Col.) May 19, 1999
- NY (Phil.) Aug. 24, 2015

Most Extra-Base Hits, Both Clubs, Game
- 24 **NL:**StL. (13) Chi. (11) July 12, 1931
- **AL:**Clev. (15) Minn. (9) July 13, 1996

Fewest Extra-Base Hits, Game (Most Innings)
- 0 **NL:**Brk. (Bos.) May 1, 1920 (26 inn)
- **AL:**Wash. (Oak.) June 4, 1971 (21 inn)

Fewest Extra-Base Hits, Both Clubs, Game (Most Innings)
- 0 **AL:**Chi. (NY) Aug. 21, 1933 (18 inn)
- **NL:**Bos. (Chi.) Sept. 21, 1901 (17 inn)

Most Extra-Base Hits, Inning
- 8 **NL:**Chi. (Det.) Sept. 6, 1883 (7th)
- Col. (Chi.) July 30, 2010 (8th)
- StL. (Chi.) July 21, 2012 (7th)
- StL. (Pitt.) July 24, 2019 (2nd)
- **AL:**Clev. (NY) Apr. 18, 2009 (2nd)

TOTAL BASES

Most Seasons, Leading League
- 31 **AL:**NY 1921, 23-24, 26-28, 30-31, 36-39, 43-45, 47, 51, 53-62, 93, 2007, 09, 12
- 21 **NL:**Chi. 1876, 78, 80-82, 84-85, 88, 90, 1906, 16, 30-31, 37, 58, 61, 83, 88-89, 2004, 08

Most Seasons, Consecutive, Leading League
- 10 **AL:**NY 1953-62
- 7 **NL:**Brk. 1949-55

Most Total Bases, Game
- 60 **AL:**Bos. (StL.) June 8, 1950
- 58 **NL:**Mtl. (Atl.) July 30, 1978

Most Total Bases, Both Clubs, Game
- 81 **NL:**Cin. (55) Col. (26) May 19, 1999
- 77 **AL:**NY (50) Phil. (27) June 3, 1932
- NY (47) TB (30) June 21, 2005
- **Extra-Inning Game:**
- 97 **NL:**Chi. (49) Phil. (48) May 17, 1979 (10 inn)
- 85 **AL:**Clev. (45) Phil. (40) July 10, 1932 (18 inn)

Fewest Total Bases, Both Clubs, Game
- 2 **NL:**Chi.(1) Pitt. (1) July 4(1g), 1906
- Chi. (0) Cin. (2) May 2, 1917 (10 inn)
- Chi. (0) LA (2) Sept. 9, 1965
- **AL:**Clev. (1) Wash. (1) July 27, 1915
- Det. (0) Balt. (2) Apr. 30(1g), 1967

Most Total Bases, 2 Consecutive Games
- 102 **AL:**Bos. June 7-8, 1950
- 89 **NL:**Pitt. June 20-22, 1925

Most Total Bases, Inning
29 **NL:**Chi. (Det.) Sept. 6, 1883 (7th)
   Since 1900:
27 **NL:**SF (Cin.) Aug. 23, 1961 (9th)
   AL:NY (TB) June 21, 2005 (8th)
   Clev. (NY) Apr. 18, 2009 (2nd)

SINGLES

Most Seasons Leading League
29 **NL:**StL. 1900-01, 20, 23, 39, 41-43, 45, 49, 54,56-57,61-64,71,75,77,79,85,87-89,92, 93, 2008, 11
26 **AL:**Wash./Minn. 1918, 24, 26, 29, 32-33, 35, 37-39, 41-42, 44-45, 69, 71, 73-77, 89, 92, 96, 2006, 08

Most Seasons, Consecutive, Leading League
5 **AL:**Minn. 1973-77
   NL: Col. 1998-2002

Most Singles, Game
28 **NL:**Phil. (Lou.) Aug. 17, 1894
   Bos. (Balt.) Apr. 20, 1896
   Since 1900:
26 **AL:**Mil. (Tor.) Aug. 28, 1992
23 **NL:**NY (Chi.) Sept. 21, 1931
   Hou. (Atl.) May 30, 1976
   Extra-Inning Game:
25 **NL:**Brk. (Pitt.) Aug. 22, 1917 (22 inn)

Most Singles, Both Clubs, Game
37 **NL:**Balt. (21) Wash. (16) Aug. 8, 1896
   Since 1900:
36 **NL:**NY (22) Cin. (14) June 9, 1901
   AL: Chi. (21) Bos. (15) Aug. 15, 1922
   Extra-Inning Game:
42 **AL:**Oak. (25) Tex. (17) July 1, 1979 (15 inn)
41 **NL:**Brk. (25) Pitt. (16) Aug. 22, 1917 (22 inn)

Most Singles, Inning
12 **NL:**Cin. (Hou.) Aug. 3, 1989 (1st)
11 **AL:**Bos. (Det.) June 18, 1953 (7th)

Most Singles, Consecutive, Inning
10 **NL:**StL. (Bos.) Sept. 17, 1920 (4th)
8 **AL:**Wash. (Clev.) May 7, 1951 (4th)
   Oak. (Chi.) Sept. 27, 1981 (1st)
   Balt. (Tex.) May 18, 1990 (1st)

DOUBLES

Most Seasons Leading League
49 **AL:**Bos. 1912, 14, 41-42, 44, 46, 48-50, 52, 54-59, 62-64, 67, 70-72, 74-75, 79, 83, 85-86, 88-89, 91, 93, 95, 97-98, 2002-05, 07, 10-13, 16, 18-20
29 **NL:**StL. 1920-24, 28-31, 33-34, 36-39, 42, 44, 46, 49, 52-54, 56, 63, 69, 79-80, 2003, 12

Most Seasons, Consecutive, Leading League
8 **AL:**Clev. 1916-23
5 **NL:**StL. 1920-24

Most Doubles, Game
14 **NL:**Chi. (Buff.) July 3, 1883
   Since 1900:
13 **NL:**StL. (Chi.) July 12, 1931
12 **AL:**Bos. (Det.) July 29, 1990
   Clev. (Minn.) July 13, 1996

Most Doubles, Both Clubs, Game
23 **NL:**StL. (13) Chi. (10) July 12(2g), 1931
19 **AL:**KC (11) NY (8) Aug. 11, 2003

Most Doubles, Inning
7 **NL:**Bos. (StL.) Aug. 25, 1936 (1st)
   StL. (Chi.) July 21, 2012 (7th)
6 **AL:**Wash. (Bos.) June 9, 1934 (8th)
   Tex. (NY) July 31, 2002 (2nd)
   Tor. (NY) Aug. 2, 2010 (5th)
   Hou. (Sea.) Sept. 8, 2019 (3rd)

Most Doubles, Consecutive, Inning
5 **AL:**Wash. (Bos.) June 9, 1934 (8th)
   NL: StL. (Chi.) July 21, 2012 (7th)

Most Players, 2 or more Doubles, Inning
3 **NL:**Bos. (StL.) Aug. 25, 1936 (1st)
2 **AL:**NY (Bos.) July 3, 1932 (6th)
   Tor. (Balt.) June 26, 1978 (2nd)

TRIPLES

Most Seasons Leading League
46 **NL:**Pitt. 1893, 97, 99-1900, 1902-04, 08-09, 11-12, 16, 21-25, 28-30, 32-37, 43-44, 50, 55-56, 58, 61-62, 64, 66-67, 69-72, 78, 89, 92, 97, 2004
27 **AL:**Wash./Minn. 1923-24, 26, 31-37, 39, 45-46, 48, 53-54, 56, 60, 68, 70, 81, 96, 2000, 03, 08, 10, 16

Most Seasons, Consecutive, Leading League
7 **AL:**Wash. 1931-37
6 **NL:**Pitt. 1932-37

Most Triples, Game
8 **NL:**Pitt. (StL.) May 30(2g), 1925
6 **AL:**Chi. (Mil.) Sept. 15 (2g), 1901
   Phil. (Det.) May 18, 1912
   Chi. (Wash.) May 20, 1920 (16 inn)
   Chi. (NY) Sept. 17, 1920
   Det. (NY) June 17, 1922

Most Triples, Both Clubs, Game
9 **NL:**Wash. (6) Lou. (3) Aug. 24, 1893
   Pitt. (7) Cin. (2) Aug. 1, 1894
   Pitt. (6) Chi. (3) July 4(2g), 1894
   Pitt. (8) StL. (1) May 30(2g), 1925
   AL: Wash. (5) StL. (4) Aug. 9, 1921 (19 inn)
   Det. (6) NY (3) June 17, 1922

Fewest Triples, Game (Most Innings)
0 **NL:**Brk. (Bos.) May 1, 1920 (26 inn)
   AL: Mil. (Chi.) May 8, 1984 (25 inn)
   Chi. (Mil.) May 8, 1984 (25 inn)

Fewest Triples, Both Clubs, Game (Most Innings)
0 **NL:**Brk. (NY) Sept. 11, 1974 (25 inn)
   AL: Mil. (Chi.) May 8, 1984 (25 inn)

Most Triples, Inning
5 **AL:**Chi. (Mil.) Sept. 15, 1901 (8th)
4 **NL:**Bos. (Troy) May 6, 1882 (8th)
   Balt. (StL.) July 27, 1892 (7th)
   StL. (Chi.) July 2, 1895 (1st)
   Chi. (StL.) Apr. 17, 1899 (4th)
   Brk. (Pitt.) Aug. 23, 1902 (3rd)
   Cin. (Bos.) July 22, 1926 (2nd)
   NY (Pitt.) July 17, 1936 (1st)

Most Triples, Consecutive, Inning
4 **AL:**Bos. (Det.) May 6, 1934 (4th)
3 **NL:**By many; last:
   Mtl. (SD) May 6, 1981 (9th)

HOME RUNS

Most Seasons Leading League
41 **AL:**NY 1915-17, 19-21, 23-31, 33, 36-47, 51,
55-56, 58, 60-61, 2004, 07, 09, 11-12, 17-18
29 **NL:**NY/SF 1904-05, 07, 09, 12, 17, 24-25,
27-28, 31, 33-35, 37-39, 42-43, 45-48,
54, 62-64, 72, 2001

Most Seasons, Consecutive, Leading League
12 **AL:**NY 1936-47
7 **NL:**Brk. 1949-55

Most Home Runs, Home, Season
153 **AL:**Tex. 2005
149 **NL:**Col. 1996

Most Home Runs, Road, Season
170 **AL:**Minn. 2019
138 **NL:**SF 2001

Most Home Runs vs. One Club, Season
61 **AL:**NY (Balt.) 2019
44 **NL:**Cin. (Brk.) 1956
LA (Col.) 2019

Most Home Runs, One Month
74 **AL:**NY Aug. 2019
57 **NL:**LA Aug. 2020

Most Home Runs, Game
10 **AL:**Tor. (Balt.) Sept. 14, 1987
9 **NL:**Cin. (Phil.) Sept. 4, 1999

Most Home Runs, Both Clubs, Game
13 **NL:**Ari. (8) Phil. (5) June 10, 2019
12 **AL:**Det. (7) Chi. (5) May 28, 1995
Det. (6) Chi. (6) July 2, 2002

Fewest Home Runs, Both Clubs, Game (Most Innings)
0 **NL:**Bos. (Brk.) May 1, 1920 (26 inn)
AL: Bos. (Phil.) Sept. 1, 1906 (24 inn)
Det. (Phil.) July 21, 1945 (24 inn)

Most Home Runs, Opening Game
8 **NL:**LA (Ari.) Mar. 28, 2019
6 **AL:**Chi. (KC) Mar. 29, 2018

Most Home Runs, Both Clubs, Opening Game
10 **NL:**LA (8) Ari. (2) Mar. 28, 2019
7 **AL:**NY (5) Phil. (2) Apr. 12, 1932
Bos. (5) Wash. (2) Apr. 12, 1965
Mil. (5) Bos. (2) Apr. 10, 1980
Mil. (4) Cal. (3) Apr. 2, 1996
Chi. (6) KC (1) Mar. 29, 2018

Most Home Runs, Only Runs, Game
6 **AL:**Oak. (Minn.) Aug. 3, 1991
Tor. (NL:Ari.) May 21, 2010
5 **NL:**NY (Chi.) June 16, 1930
StL. (Brk.) Sept. 1, 1953
Cin. (Mil.) Apr. 16, 1955
Chi. (Pitt.) Apr. 21, 1964
Pitt. (LA) May 7, 1973
Col. (SF) May 9, 1994
Atl. (Col.) Apr. 19(1g), 1998
Phil. (Wash.) Sept. 8, 2009
Hou. (Cin.) Sept. 16, 2009
Col. (Cin.) May 27, 2012
Col. (AL:LA) June 9, 2012
Pitt. (Chi.) Apr. 9, 2014
Col. (Mia.) June 20, 2016

Most Home Runs, Both Clubs, Only Runs, Game
8 **NL:**Col. (5) Mia. (3) June 20, 2016
5 **AL:**Minn. (3) Chi. (2) Aug. 9 (2g), 2013
Sea. (3) LA (2) May 4, 2015
LA (3) Tex. (2) Sept. 11, 2016

Most Games, Consecutive, 1 or more HRs, Season
31 **AL:**NY May 26-June 30, 2019 (57 hr)
25 **NL:**Atl. Apr. 18-May 13, 1998 (45 hr)
SD June 28-July 27, 2016 (42 hr)
StL. Aug. 9-Sept. 6, 2016 (52 hr)

Most Games, Consecutive, 1 or more HRs, Start of Season
20 **AL:**Sea. Mar. 20-Apr. 16, 2019 (42 hr)
13 **NL:**Chi. Apr. 13-May 2, 1954 (28 hr)

Most Home Runs, 2-Game Span, Season
14 **NL:**Cin. Sept. 4-5, 1999
13 **AL:**NY June 28 (dh), 1939
Ana. June 3-4, 2003
NY July 31-Aug. 1, 2007
Tor. Aug. 12-14, 2020
NY Sept. 15-16, 16-17, 2020

Most Home Runs, 3-Game Span, Season
19 **AL:**NY Sept. 15-17, 2020
16 **NL:**Wash. Aug. 17-19, 2019

Most Home Runs, 4-Game Span, Season
20 **AL:**NY Sept. 13-17, 15-18, 2020
18 **NL:**Hou. Aug. 13-16, 2000
LA Aug. 11-15, 13-16, 2019

Most Home Runs, 5-Game Span, Season
22 **NL:**LA Aug. 11-16, 2019
21 **AL:**Bos. June 14-19, 1977
NY May 19-23, 2018
NY Aug. 4-8, 5-9, 2019
NY Sept. 13-18, 15-19, 2020

Most Home Runs, 6-Game Span, Season
24 **AL:**Bos. June 17-22, 1977
NL:LA Aug. 11-17, 2019

Most Home Runs, 7-Game Span, Season
27 **AL:**Chi. Aug. 16-22, 2020
26 **NL:**LA Aug. 13-20, 2019

Most Home Runs, 8-Game Span, Season
30 **NL:**LA Aug. 11-20, 2019
29 **AL:**Bos. June 14-22, 1977
Chi. Aug. 15(2g)-22, 2020

Most Home Runs, 9-Game Span, Season
32 **NL:**LA Aug. 11-21, 2019
30 **AL:**Bos. June 14-23, 16-24, 1977
NY Aug. 5-12, 2019
Chi. Aug. 15(2g)-23, 2020

Most Home Runs, 10-Game Span, Season
33 **AL:**Bos. June 14-24, 1977
NL: Atl. July 9-24, 2006
LA Aug. 10-21. 2019

Most Home Runs, 15-Game Span, Season
41 **AL:**Minn. July 22-Aug. 6, 2019
NY Aug. 3-15, 4-17, 2019
Chi. Aug. 11-28, 2020
39 **NL:**Chi. June 21-July 9, 1884
Mil. June 8-24, 1961
Atl. July 2-21, 6-26, 7-27, 2006

Most Home Runs, 20-Game Span, Season
52 **AL:**NY Aug. 4-23, 2019
49 **NL:**Atl. July 1-26, 2-27, 2006
LA June 11-July 1, 2017

Most Home Runs, 25-Game Span, Season
65 **AL:**NY Aug. 4-28, 2019
61 **NL:**LA Aug. 10-Sept. 6, 2019

Most Games, Consecutive, 2 or more HRs
10 **AL:**Balt. July 17-27, 2019
9 **NL:**StL. Aug. 9-19, 2016

Most Home Runs, Inning
5 **NL:**NY (Cin.) June 6, 1939 (4th)
   Phil. (Cin.) June 2, 1949 (8th)
   SF (Cin.) Aug. 23, 1961 (9th)
   Mil. (Cin.) Apr. 22, 2006 (4th)
   Wash. (Mil.) July 27, 2017 (3rd)
   AL: Minn. (KC) June 9, 1966 (7th)
   NY (Tor.) Sept. 17, 2020 (4th)

Most Home Runs, Consecutive, Inning
4 **NL:**Mil. (Cin.) June 8, 1961 (7th)
   LA (SD) Sept. 18, 2006 (9th)
   Ari. (Mil.) Aug. 11, 2010 (4th)
   Wash. (Mil.) July 27, 2017 (3rd)
   Wash. (SD) June 9, 2019 (8th)
   AL: Clev. (LA) July 31(2g), 1963 (6th)
   Minn. (KC) May 2, 1964 (11th)
   Bos. (NY) Apr. 22, 2007 (3rd)
   Chi. (KC) Aug. 14, 2008 (6th)
   Chi. (NL:StL.) Aug. 16, 2020 (5th)

Most Home Runs, Both Clubs, Inning
5 **AL:**StL. (3) Phil. (2) June 8, 1928 (9th)
   Det. (4) NY (1) June 23, 1950 (4th)
   Minn. (5) KC (0) June 9, 1966 (7th)
   Balt. (4) Bos. (1) May 17, 1967 (7th)
   Minn. (4) Oak. (1) May 16, 1983 (9th)
   Clev. (3) Tex. (2) June 29, 1984 (5th)
   Balt. (3) Bos. (2) Sept. 10, 1985 (8th)
   Clev. (3) Mil. (2) Apr. 25, 1997 (4th)
   Det. (3) Balt. (2) Apr. 7, 2000 (5th)
   Sea. (3) KC (2) Aug. 27, 2004 (5th)
   Balt. (4) Hou. (1) Aug. 19, 2016 (1st)
   KC (3) Minn. (2) Aug. 8, 2020 (4th)
   NY (5) Tor. (0) Sept. 17, 2020 (4th)
   NL:NY (5) Cin. (0) June 6, 1939 (4th)
   Phil. (5) Cin. (0) June 2, 1949 (8th)
   NY (3) Bos. (2) July 6, 1951 (3rd)
   Cin. (3) Brk. (2) June 11, 1954 (7th)
   SF (5) Cin. (0) Aug. 23, 1961 (9th)
   Phil. (3) Chi. (2) Apr. 17, 1964 (5th)
   Chi. (3) Atl. (2) July 3, 1967 (1st)
   Pitt. (3) Atl. (2) Aug. 1, 1970 (7th)
   Cin. (3) Chi. (2) July 28, 1977 (1st)
   SF (3) Atl. (2) May 25, 1979 (4th)
   Cin. (4) Atl. (1) June 19, 1994 (1st)
   SF (3) Pitt. (2) July 27(2g), 1997 (9th)
   Col. (3) StL. (2) July 31, 1999 (3rd)
   Atl. (4) SF (1) May 20, 2001 (7th)
   Mil. (5) Cin. (0) Apr. 22, 2006 (4th)
   Wash. (3) NY (2) July 7, 2016 (4th)
   Wash. (5) Mil. (0) July 27, 2017 (3rd)
   Chi. (3) Col. (2) June 10, 2019 (3rd)
   ML:NL:Chi. (4) AL:Chi. (1) June 21, 2008 (4th)

Most Home Runs, None on Base, Game
7 **AL:**Bos. (Tor.) July 4, 1977
   Balt. (NL:Phil.) June 16, 2015
   Chi. (Tor.) June 25, 2016
6 **NL:**NY (Phil.) Aug. 13, 1939
   NY (Cin.) June 24, 1950
   Atl. (Chi.) Aug. 3, 1967
   Chi. (SD) Aug. 19, 1970
   Atl. (Cin.) May 31, 1996
   Pitt. (Cin.) Apr. 14, 2014
   StL. (AL:Sea.) June 26, 2016
   Phil. (Cin.) July 26, 2018
   Cin. (Chi.) Aug. 10, 2019
   Extra-Inning Game:
7 **NL:**Atl. (Chi.) May 28, 2006 (11 inn)
   LA (NY) June 24, 2018 (11 inn)

Most Home Runs, None on Base,
Both Clubs, Game
10 **AL:**Det. (5) Chi. (5) May 28, 1995
9 **NL:**Phil. (5) Ari. (4) June 10, 2019

Most Home Runs, None on Base, Inning
4 **NL:**NY (Phil.) Aug. 13, 1939 (4th)
   Atl. (SF) May 20, 2001 (7th)
   LA (SD) Sept. 18, 2006 (9th)
   Ari. (Mil.) Aug. 11, 2010 (4th)
   Wash. (SD) June 9, 2019 (8th)
   Atl. (Pitt.) June 11, 2019 (2nd)
   Wash. (Mil.) July 27, 2017 (3rd)
   Wash. (SD) June 9, 2019 (8th)
   Atl. (Pitt.) June 11, 2019 (2nd)
   AL: Clev. (LA) July 31, 1963 (6th)
   Minn. (KC) May 2, 1964 (11th)
   Minn. (KC) June 9, 1966 (7th)
   Bos. (NY) June 17, 1977 (1st)
   Bos. (Tor.) July 4, 1977 (8th)
   Bos. (Mil.) May 31, 1980 (4th)
   Minn. (NY) May 2, 1992 (5th)
   Balt. (Cal.) Sept. 5, 1995 (2nd)
   Sea. (Oak.) Sept. 21, 1996 (3rd)
   Bos. (NY) Apr. 22, 2007 (3rd)
   TB (NY) Sept. 21, 2016 (3rd)
   NY (Tor.) June 3, 2017 (8th)
   NY (Tor.) Sept. 17, 2020 (4th)

Most Home Runs, Two Out, Inning
5 **NL:**NY (Cin.) June 6, 1939 (4th)
4 **AL:**Bos. (Det.) July 18, 1998 (4th)
   Tex. (NL:Hou.) May 21, 2005 (2nd)
   Bos. (NY) Apr. 22, 2007 (3rd)
   Chi. (KC) Aug. 14, 2008 (6th)
   Chi. (KC) July 11, 2010 (3rd)
   Chi. (NL:StL.) Aug. 16, 2020 (5th)

Most Players, 50 or more Home Runs, Season
2 **AL:**NY 1961
1 **NL:**By many

Most Players, 40 or more Home Runs, Season
3 **NL:**Atl. 1973
   Col. 1996, 97
2 **AL:**NY 1927, 30-31, 61
   Det. 1961
   Bos. 1969, 2004-05
   Sea. 1996-99
   Tor. 1999-2000, 15
   Tex. 2001-02
   Chi. 2006
   LA 2015

Most Players, 30 or more Home Runs, Season
5 **AL:**Minn. 2019
4 **NL:**LA 1977, 97
   Col. 1995-97, 99
   Atl. 1998
   Chi. 2004
   Phil. 2009

Most Players, 20 or more Home Runs, Season
8 **AL:**Minn. 2019
7 **NL:**LA 2018

Most Players, Home Run, Game
8 **NL:**Cin. (Phil.) Sept. 4, 1999
7 **AL:**Balt. (Bos.) May 17, 1967
   Oak. (Cal.) June 27, 1996
   Det. (Tor.) June 20, 2000
   Tex. (NL:Hou.) May 21, 2005
   NY (Chi.) July 31, 2007
   Bos. (Det.) Sept. 4, 2013

Most Players, Home Runs, Both Clubs, Game
10 **NL:**NY (7) Phil. (3) Aug. 24, 2015
        Ari. (6) Phil. (4) June 10, 2019
9 **AL:**NY (5) Det. (4) June 23, 1950
        Minn. (5) Bos. (4) May 25, 1965
        Balt. (7) Bos. (2) May 17, 1967
        Cal. (5) Clev. (4) Aug. 30, 1970
        Bos. (5) Mil. (4) May 22(1g), 1977
        Cal. (5) Oak. (4) Apr. 23, 1985
        Balt. (5) Cal. (4) July 1, 1994
        Det. (5) Balt. (4) Apr. 7, 2000
        Det. (7) Tor. (2) June 20, 2000
        Det. (5) Chi. (4) July 2, 2002
        Bos. (6) TB (3) Sept. 15, 2008
        Balt. (5) Hou. (4) Aug. 19, 2016
        Det. (5) Chi. (4) Apr. 26, 2019
        Minn. (6) LA (3) May 23, 2019
        Tor. (5) Balt. (4) Sept. 23, 2019 (15 inn)
        NY (6) Tor. (3) Sept. 27, 2019

Most Players, 2 or more Home Runs, Game
3 **NL:**Pitt. (StL.) Aug. 16, 1947
        Chi. (StL.) Apr. 16, 1955 (14 inn)
        NY (Pitt.) July 8, 1956
        Cin. (Mil.) Aug. 18, 1956
        Phil. (NY) Sept. 8, 1998
        Col. (Mtl.) Aug. 14, 1999
        Hou. (Chi.) Sept. 9, 2000
        SF (Col.) July 2, 2002
        Phil. (Cin.) July 26, 2018
        Chi. (Cin.) Aug. 30, 2020
    AL: Bos. (StL.) June 8, 1950
        NY (Bos.) May 30, 1961
        Tor. (Balt.) Sept. 14, 1987
        Tor. (Cal.) July 14, 1990
        Det. (Chi.) May 28, 1995
        Sea. (Mil.) July 31, 1996
        Ana. (TB) Apr. 21, 2000
        Minn. (Mil.) July 12, 2001
        Bos. (NY) July 4, 2003
        Minn. (Balt.) Apr. 20, 2019

Most Players, 2 or more Home Runs, Both Clubs, Game
4 **NL:**Pitt. (3) StL. (1) Aug. 16, 1947
        Col. (3) Mtl. (1) Aug. 14, 1999
    AL: Det. (3) Chi. (1) May 28, 1995
        Minn. (3) Balt. (1) Apr. 20, 2019
        Hou. (2) Oak. (2) Aug. 15, 2019
        Hou. (2) Oak. (2) Sept. 10, 2019

Most Players, 2 or more Home Runs, Inning
2 **AL:**Sea. (Chi.) May 2, 2002
1 **NL:**By many

Most Players, 3 or more Home Runs, Game
2 **NL:**Mil. (Ari.) Sept. 25, 2001
1 **AL:**By many

GRAND SLAM HOME RUNS

Most Grand Slam HRs, Game
3 **AL:**NY (Oak.) Aug. 25, 2011
2 **NL:**By many NL teams; Last:
        Phil. (Mia.) Apr. 7, 2018

Most Grand Slam HRs, Both Clubs, Game
3 **AL:**Balt. (2) Tex. (1) Aug. 6, 1986
        NY (3) Oak. (0) Aug. 25, 2011
    NL: Chi. (2) Hou. (1) June 3, 1987
        Cin. (2) Mil. (1) Apr. 21, 2015

Most Grand Slam HRs, 2 Consecutive Games
3 **NL:**Brk. Sept. 23(2g)-24, 1901
        Pitt. June 20-22(2g), 1925
        LA May 20-21, 2000
        NY July 16-18, 2006
    AL: Mil. Apr. 10-12(2g), 1980
        Chi. May 18-19, 1996
        Sea. Aug. 7-8(1g), 2000
        NY Aug. 24-25, 25-26, 2011

Most Games, Consecutive, Grand Slam HR
4 **NL:**SD Aug. 17-20, 2020
3 **AL:**Mil. Apr. 7-9, 1978
        Det. Aug. 10-12, 1993
        Chi. June 23-25, 2006

Most Grand Slam HRs, Inning
2 **NL:**Chi. (Pitt.) Aug. 16, 1890 (5th)
        Hou. (NY) July 30, 1969 (9th)
        StL. (LA) Apr. 23, 1999 (3rd)
        NY (Chi.) July 16, 2006 (6th)
    AL: Minn. (Clev.) July 18, 1962 (1st)
        Mil. (Bos.) Apr. 12, 1980 (2nd)
        Balt. (Tex.) Aug. 6, 1986 (4th)
        Balt. (KC) Sept. 11, 2015 (8th)

Grand Slam HRs, Both Clubs, Inning
2 **NL:**Chi. (NY) May 18, 1950 (6th)
        Atl. (Cin.) Sept. 12(1g), 1974 (2nd)
        Chi. (Pitt.) Sept. 9, 1992 (6th)
        Atl. (LA) May 13, 2005 (8th)
        StL. (NY) Aug. 22, 2006 (5th)
        Mia. (NY) Sept. 23, 2019 (6th)
    AL: Bos. (Wash.) June 18, 1961 (9th)
        Clev. (Tex.) Apr. 14, 1980 (1st)
        Det. (Chi.) Sept. 14(2g), 2008 (8th)
    ML:AL:Ana. (NL:Ari.) June 9, 1998 (3rd)
    (also see previous record)

RUNS BATTED IN (Since 1920)

Most Runs Batted In, Game
30 **AL:**Tex. (Balt.) Aug. 22(1g), 2007
28 **NL:**Atl. (Mia.) Sept. 9, 2020

Most Runs Batted In, Both Clubs, Game
43 **NL:**Chi. (24) Phil. (19) Aug. 25, 1922
35 **AL:**Bos. (21) Phil. (14) June 29, 1950
        Bos. (18) Tex. (17) Aug. 12, 2008
    Extra-Inning Game:
45 **NL:**Phil. (23) Chi. (22) May 17, 1979 (10 inn)

Fewest RBIs, Both Clubs, Game (Most Innings)
0 **NL:**Cin. (Brk.) Sept. 11, 1946 (19 inn)
    AL: Balt. (Clev.) May 14(1g), 1961 (15 inn)

Most Runs Batted In, 2 Consecutive Games
49 **AL:**Bos. June 7-8, 1950
39 **NL:**Pitt. June 20-22, 1925

Most Runs Batted In, Inning
17 **AL:**Bos. (Det.) June 18, 1953 (7th)
15 **NL:**Brk. (Cin.) May 21, 1952 (1st)

Most Players, 100 or more RBIs, Season
5 **AL:**NY 1936
4 **NL:**Pitt. 1925, 30
        Chi. 1929
        Phil. 1929
        Col. 1996-97, 99
        Ari. 1999
        Atl. 2003

SACRIFICE HITS

Most Sacrifice Hits, Game
8 **AL:**Chi. (Det.) May 1, 1910 (15 inn)
        NY (Bos.) May 4, 1918
        Chi. (Bos.) July 11, 1927
        StL. (Clev.) July 23, 1928
7 **NL:**By many; last:
        Cin. (Brk.) July 10, 1928

Most Sacrifice Hits, Both Clubs, Game
11 **AL:**Bos. (8) Clev. (3) Sept. 22, 1921 (12 inn)
      Wash. (7) Bos. (4) Sept. 1, 1926
 9 **NL:**By many; last:
      SF (6) SD (3) May 23, 1970 (15 inn)

Most Sacrifice Hits, Inning
 3 **AL:**Clev. (StL.) July 10, 1949 (5th)
      Det. (Balt.) July 12, 1970 (2nd)
      Cal. (Det.) June 5, 1977 (8th)
      Oak. (KC) June 26(1g), 1977 (5th)
      Clev. (Chi.) June 8, 1980 (6th)
      Sea. (Cal.) Apr. 29, 1984 (6th)
      Minn. (Mil.) July 26, 1991 (8th)
      Tex. (Tor.) July 23, 2011 (9th)
    NL: Chi. (Mil.) Aug. 26, 1962 (6th)
      Phil. (LA) Sept. 23, 1967 (7th)
      LA (SF) May 23, 1972 (6th)
      Hou. (SD) Apr. 29, 1975 (7th)
      Hou. (Atl.) July 6, 1975 (9th)
      Pitt. (StL.) Sept. 20, 1988 (8th)
      Hou. (AL:Tex.) June 26, 2005 (7th)

SACRIFICE FLIES (Since 1954)

Most Seasons Leading League
12 **NL:**Pitt. 1962, 65, 70, 82, 87-92, 2008, 18
 8 **AL:**NY 1962, 74-75, 85, 95-97, 2018

Most Seasons, Consecutive, Leading League
 6 **NL:**Pitt. 1987-92
 3 **AL:**Balt. 1967-69
      Mil. 1990-92
      NY 1995-97

Most Sacrifice Flies, Game
 5 **AL:**Sea. (Oak.) Aug. 7, 1988
      Sea. (KC) Apr. 15, 2008
    NL: Col. (Pitt.) June 7, 2006

Most Sacrifice Flies, Both Clubs, Game
 6 **AL:**Sea. (5) KC (1) Apr. 15, 2008
 5 **NL:**By many; last:
      Mil. (3) SF (2) June 15, 2019

Most Sacrifice Flies, Inning
 3 **AL:**Chi. (Clev.) July 1(2g), 1962 (5th)
      NY (Det.) June 29, 2000 (4th)
      NY (Ana.) Aug. 19, 2000 (3rd)
    NL:NY (AL:NY) June 24, 2005 (2nd)

WALKS

Most Seasons Leading League
31 **AL:**NY 1903, 10, 13-14, 26-28, 30-34, 36-39,
      43, 45, 53, 94-95, 97-98, 2002-04, 09, 11,
      17-18, 20
22 **NL:**NY/SF 1889, 1904-08, 20-21, 23, 50-51,
      64, 68-71, 81-82, 96, 98, 2000, 04
      Brk./LA 1892, 1903, 33-34, 38-39, 41-43,
      45-47, 52-57, 59, 61, 2017-18

Most Seasons, Consecutive, Leading League
 7 **AL:**Clev. 1917-23
 6 **NL:**Brk. 1952-57

Most Walks, Game
19 **AA:**Lou. (Clev.) Sept. 21, 1887
18 **AL:**Det. (Phil.) May 9, 1916
      Clev. (Bos.) May 20, 1948
17 **NL:**Chi. (NY) May 30, 1887
      Brk. (Phil.) Aug. 27, 1903
      NY (Brk.) Apr. 30, 1944
    Extra-Inning Game:
19 **AL:**Wash. (Clev.) Sept. 14, 1971 (20 inn)
18 **NL:**Phil. (AL:Balt.) July 2, 2004 (16 inn)
      Ari. (Phil.) Aug. 24, 2013 (18 inn)

Most Walks, Both Clubs, Game
30 **AL:**Det. (18) Phil. (12) May 9, 1916
      Wash.(19)Clev.(11)Sept.14(2g),1971(20inn)
26 **NL:**Hou. (13) SF (13) May 4(2g), 1975
    Extra-Inning Game:
28 **NL:**Ari. (18) Phil. (10) Aug. 24, 2013 (18 inn)

Fewest Walks, Game (Most Innings)
 0 **NL:**LA (Mtl.) Aug. 23, 1989 (22 inn)
    AL: Phil. (Bos.) July 4, 1905 (20 inn)

Fewest Walks, Both Clubs, Game (Most Innings)
 0 **AL:**Wash. (Det.) July 22, 1904 (13 inn)
      Bos. (Phil.) Sept. 9, 1907 (13 inn)
    NL: Brk. (Pitt.) July 25, 1917 (13 inn)

Most Walks, Doubleheader
25 **NL:**NY (Brk.) Apr. 30, 1944
23 **AL:**Clev. (NY) Aug. 18, 1943
      Clev. (Phil.) June 18, 1950
      Wash. (Clev.) Sept. 14, 1971

Most Walks, Both Clubs, Doubleheader
42 **NL:**Hou. (21) SF (21) May 4, 1975
32 **AL:**Balt. (18) Chi. (14) May 28, 1954
      Det. (20) KC (12) Aug. 1, 1962
      Tex. (17) Chi. (15) May 24, 1995
    Extra Innings:
39 **AL:**Wash. (23) Clev. (16) Sept. 14, 1971(29inn)

Fewest Walks, Doubleheader (Most Innings)
 0 **NL:**StL. (NY) July 2, 1933 (27 inn)
    AL: Det. (Phil.) Aug. 28, 1908 (20 inn)

Fewest Walks, Both Clubs, Doubleheader
 1 **NL:**Brk. (0) Cin. (1) Aug. 6, 1905
      Brk. (0) NY (1) Aug. 31, 1918
      Brk. (0) Chi. (1) Aug. 14, 1919
      Pitt. (0) Cin. (1) Sept. 7, 1924
      StL. (0) Brk. (1) Sept. 22, 1929
      Phil (0) StL. (1) Sept. 15, 1940
 2 **AL:**By many; last:
      Wash. (1) KC (1) July 13, 1958

Most Walks, 2 Consecutive Games
29 **AL:**Det. May 9-10, 1916
      Bos. Sept. 16-17, 1920 (22 inn)
26 **NL:**Chi. May 5-6, 1938
    Extra Innings:
27 **NL:**NY June 28-29, 1962 (22 inn)

Most Walks, No Runs, Game
11 **AL:**StL. (NY) Aug. 1, 1941
      Wash. (Clev.) June 4, 1948 (15 inn)
      Clev. (Chi.) Sept. 13, 1967 (17 inn)
      Wash. (NY) May 21, 1970
10 **NL:**Chi. (Cin.) Aug. 19(1g), 1965 (10 inn)
      NY (Hou.) July 6, 1976 (10 inn)
      Mtl. (NY) Apr. 24, 1982
      SF (Ari.) May 29, 2001 (18 inn)
      Ari. (SD) Sept. 2, 2001 (13 inn)
      Pitt. (StL.) Sept. 28, 2015

Most Walks, Inning
11 **AL:**NY (Wash.) Sept. 11(1g), 1949 (3rd)
 9 **NL:**Cin. (Chi.) Apr. 24, 1957 (5th)

Most Walks, Consecutive, Inning
 7 **AL:**Chi. (Wash.) Aug. 28, 1909 (2nd)
    NL: Atl. (Pitt.) May 25, 1983 (3rd)

INTENTIONAL WALKS (Since 1955)

Most Seasons, Leading League
13 **AL:**Bos. 1958, 86, 89-90, 97, 2003, 06, 11, 13, 16-19
12 **NL:**SF 1964, 70-71, 86, 93, 97, 2001-04, 06-07

Most Seasons, Consecutive, Leading League
 4 **NL:**SF 2001-04
    AL: Bos. 2016-19

Most Intentional Walks, Game
6 **NL:**SF (StL.) July 19, 1975
5 **AL:**Minn. (KC) Sept. 14, 1965
    Cal. (NY) May 10, 1967
    Wash. (Clev.) Sept. 2, 1970
  Extra-Inning Game:
7 **NL:**NY (Chi.) May 2, 1956 (17 inn)
    Cin. (SF) Apr. 15, 1969 (12 inn)
    Hou. (Phil.) July 15, 1984 (16 inn)
    Chi. (Cin.) May 22, 1990 (16 inn)
  AL:NY (LA) May 22, 1962 (12 inn)

Most Intentional Walks, Both Clubs, Game
7 **NL:**NY (4) Pitt. (3) June 27, 1979
6 **AL:**Cal. (5) NY (1) May 10, 1967
  Extra-Inning Game:
11 **NL:**NY (7) Chi. (4) May 2, 1956 (17 inn)
9 **AL:**Bos. (6) NY (3) Aug. 29, 1967 (20 inn)

Most Intentional Walks, Inning
4 **AL:**Chi. (KC) Oct. 1, 1965 (8th)
3 **NL:**By many; last:
    SF (SD) Sept. 19, 2004 (8th)

HIT BY PITCH

Most Hit By Pitch, Game
6 **AA:**Brk. (Balt.) Apr. 25, 1887
  NL: Lou. (StL.) July 31(1g), 1897
  AL:NY (Wash.) June 20(2g), 1913
    Tex. (Hou.) June 9, 2018
  NL Since 1900:
5   Atl. (Cin.) July 2, 1969
    Hou. (LA) Apr. 19, 2000
    Atl. (AL:Tor.) May 15, 2017
    StL. (SD) Aug. 23, 2017
    Cin. (SF) May 6, 2019
    Chi. (Cin.) July 27, 2020

Most Hit By Pitch, Both Clubs, Game
9 **NL:**Det. (5) Ind. (4) Apr. 30, 1887
  Since 1900:
8 **NL:**Chi. (5) Cin. (3) July 27, 2020
7 **AL:**Det. (4) Wash. (3) Aug. 24(2g), 1914
    Minn. (4) KC (3) Apr. 13, 1971
    KC (5) Tex. (2) Sept. 3, 1989
    Oak. (5) Ana. (2) June 7, 2001
    Bos. (4) NY (3) July 5, 2008

Most Hit By Pitch, Inning
4 **NL:**Bos. (Pitt.) Aug. 19(1g), 1893 (2nd)
    Cin. (Pitt.) May 6, 2019 (6th)
3 **AL:**By many teams; Last:
    KC (Bos.) July 7, 2018 (5th)

STRIKEOUTS

Most Strikeouts, Game
20 **AL:**Sea. (Bos.) Apr. 29, 1986
    Det. (Bos.) Sept. 18, 1996
    Sea. (LA) Sept. 25, 2012
    Det. (NL:Wash.) May 11, 2016
    Tex. (Bos.) May 25, 2017
    Det. (Chi.) Apr. 28, 2019
  NL: Hou. (Chi.) May 6, 1998
  Extra-Inning Game:
26 **AL:**Cal. (Oak.) July 9, 1971 (20 inn)
  NL: Mil. (Ana.) June 8, 2004 (17 inn)
    Chi. (AL:NY) May 7, 2017 (18 inn)
    Mil. (LA) June 2, 2017 (12 inn)
    Atl. (NY) Aug. 23, 2019 (14 inn)

Most Strikeouts, Both Clubs, Game
35 **NL:**Wash. (18) NY (17) Oct. 3(2g), 2015
31 **AL:**Tex. (18) Sea. (13) July 13, 1997
  Extra-Inning Game:
48 **ML:**NL:Chi. (26) AL:NY (22) May 7, 2017 (18 inn)
  NL: StL. (25) Ari. (23) Sept. 24, 2019 (19 inn)
43 **AL:**Cal. (26) Oak. (17) July 9, 1971 (20 inn)

Most Strikeouts, 2 Consecutive Games
36 **AL:**Sea. Apr. 29-30, 1986
33 **NL:**Mil. Apr. 6-7, 2002
    Ari. June 5-6, 2016
  Extra Innings:
40 **NL:**Mil. June 2-3, 2017 (21 inn)
    Col. May 14-15, 2019 (21 inn)
38 **AL:**Minn. Apr. 23-24, 2016 (25 inn)

Most Strikeouts, Doubleheader
29 **AL:**Det. (Chi.) May 27, 2017
27 **NL:**NY (Ari.) Apr. 27, 2003
  Extra Innings:
31 **NL:**Pitt. (Phil.) Sept. 22, 1958 (23 inn)
    NY (Phil.) Oct. 2, 1965 (27 inn)
27 **AL:**Clev. (Bos.) Aug. 25, 1963 (24 inn)

Most Strikeouts, Both Clubs, Doubleheader
47 **AL:**Det. (29) Chi. (18) May 27, 2017
    Chi. (26) Balt. (21) May 1, 2019
45 **NL:**Col. (24) Fla. (21) Aug. 16, 2009
  Extra Innings:
51 **NL:**NY (30) Phil. (21) Sept. 26, 1975 (24 inn)
48 **AL:**KC (24) Det. (24) June 17, 1967 (28 inn)

Most Strikeouts, Start of Game
9 **NL:**Clev. (NY) Aug. 28, 1884
  Since 1900:
8 **NL:**LA (Hou.) Sept. 23, 1986
    Mia. (NY) Sept. 15, 2014
    Phil. (Col.) Sept. 26, 2018
7 **AL:**Tex. (Chi.) May 28, 1986
    Minn. (Chi.) Sept. 30, 2016
    Sea. (TB) June 3, 2018

Most Strikeouts, Consecutive, Game
11 **AL:**TB (Bos.) Sept. 25, 2016
10 **NL:**SD (NY) Apr. 22, 1970

Fewest Strikeouts, Game (Most Innings)
0 **NL:**NY (Cin.) June 26, 1893 (17 inn)
    Cin. (NY) Aug. 27, 1920 (17 inn)
  AL: Clev. (NY) June 7, 1936 (16 inn)
    Phil. (Chi.) Sept. 24, 1943 (16 inn)

Fewest Strikeouts, Both Clubs, Game (Most Innings)
0 **AL:**Chi. (StL.) July 7, 1931 (12 inn)
  NL: Bos. (Pitt.) May 7, 1926 (11 inn)
    Cin. (StL.) July 6, 1926 (11 inn)

Fewest Strikeouts, Doubleheader (Most Innings)
0 **NL:**Pitt. (Phil.) July 12, 1924 (21 inn)
  AL: Bos. (StL.) July 28, 1917 (20 inn)

Fewest Strikeouts, Both Clubs, Doubleheader
1 **AL:**Bos. (0) Clev. (1) Aug. 28, 1926
2 **NL:**NY (0) Brk. (2) Aug. 13, 1932
    StL. (0) Pitt. (2) Sept. 6, 1948

Most Strikeouts, Inning
4 **AA:**Pitt. (Phil.) Sept. 30, 1885 (7th)
  AL: By many teams; Last:
    TB (Tor.) Sept. 27, 2019 (8th)
  NL: By many teams; Last:
    LA (Col.) Oct. 1, 2018 (4th)

GROUNDED INTO DOUBLE PLAYS

Most Grounded Into Double Plays, Game
7　**NL:**SF (Hou.) May 4, 1969
6　**AL:**Wash. (Clev.) Aug. 5, 1948
　　Bos. (Cal.) May 1, 1966
　　Balt. (KC) May 6, 1972
　　Clev. (NY) Apr. 29, 1975
　　Tor. (Minn.) Aug. 29(1g), 1977 (10 inn)
　　Bos. (Det.) Apr. 13, 1984
　　Mil. (Chi.) May 8, 1984 (25 inn)
　　Bos. (Chi.) Apr. 27, 1989 (16 inn)
　　Bos. (Minn.) July 18, 1990
　　Det. (Tor.) Apr. 16, 1996
　　TB (NY) June 17(1g), 2003
　　KC (Clev.) Apr. 21, 2009
　　Tor. (KC) Apr. 30, 2009
　　Clev. (Chi.) Aug. 7, 2009
　　NY (Tex.) Apr. 15, 2011
　　Balt. (Bos.) May 6, 2012 (17 inn)
　　Hou. (Sea.) Aug. 21, 2018

Most Grounded Into Double Plays, Both Clubs, Game
9　**AL:**Bos. (6) Cal. (3) May 1, 1966
　　Bos. (6) Minn. (3) July 18, 1990
8　**NL:**Bos. (5) Chi. (3) Sept. 18, 1928
　　SF (5) StL. (3) June 10, 1962
　　Extra-Inning Game:
10　**NL:**NY (6) SF (4) Aug. 21, 2004 (12 inn)

STOLEN BASES

Most Seasons Leading League
29　**AL:**Chi. 1901-04, 17, 19, 23-24, 28-29, 39,
　　41-43, 46-47, 49, 51-61, 66
26　**NL:**Brk./LA 1890-92, 1900, 03, 38, 42,
　　46-53, 55, 58-65, 70, 2014

Most Seasons, Consecutive, Leading League
11　**AL:**Chi. 1951-61
8　**NL:**Brk. 1946-53
　　LA 1958-65

Most Stolen Bases, Game
19　**AA:**Phil. (Syr.) Apr. 22, 1890
17　**NL:**NY (Pitt.) May 23, 1890
　　Since 1900:
15　**AL:**NY (StL.) Sept. 28, 1911
11　**NL:**StL. (Pitt.) Aug. 13(2g), 1916 (5 inn)

Most Stolen Bases, Both Clubs, Game
21　**AA:**Phil. (19) Syr. (2) Apr. 22, 1890
20　**NL:**NY (17) Pitt. (3) May 23, 1890
　　Since 1900:
15　**AL:**StL. (8) Det. (7) Oct. 1, 1916
　　NY (15) StL. (0) Sept. 28, 1911
14　**NL:**NY (9) Bos. (5) June 20, 1912
　　StL. (11) Pitt. (3) Aug. 13(2g), 1916 (5 inn)

Most Triple Steals, Game
2　**AL:**Phil. (Clev.) July 25, 1930
1　**NL:**By many

Fewest Stolen Bases, Game (Most Innings)
0　**NL:**Bos. (Brk.) May 1, 1920 (26 inn)
　　AL: Det. (Phil.) July 21, 1945 (24 inn)
　　Phil. (Det.) July 21, 1945 (24 inn)

Fewest Stolen Bases, Both Clubs, Game (Most Innings)
0　**AL:**Det. (Phil.) July 21, 1945 (24 inn)
　　NL:NY (SF) May 31(2g), 1964 (23 inn)

Most Stolen Bases, Inning
8　**AL:**Wash. (Clev.) July 19, 1915 (1st)
　　NL: Phil. (NY) July 7(1g), 1919 (9th)

Most Stealing Home, Season
16　**NL:**Chi. 1911
15　**AL:**Chi. 1906

Most Stealing Home, Game
3　**AL:**Chi. (StL.) July 2, 1909
　　NL: Chi. (Bos.) Aug. 23, 1909
　　NY (Pitt.) Sept. 18, 1911

Most Stealing Home, Inning
2　By many; last:
　　AL: Oak. (KC) May 28, 1980 (1st)
　　NL: StL. (Brk.) Sept. 19, 1925 (7th)

CAUGHT STEALING (AL since 1920; NL since 1951)

Most Caught Stealing, Game
6　**AL:**Wash. (Phil.) May 29 (1g), 1920
　　Clev. (Wash.) July 10(2g), 1920
5　**NL:**Pitt. (Chi.) July 6, 1980 (20 inn)
　　StL. (Chi.) Oct. 5(1g), 1991

Most Caught Stealing, Inning
3　**NL:**LA (Atl.) Aug. 6, 1982 (5th)
2　**AL:**By many

LEFT ON BASE

Most Left on Base, Game
20　**AL:**NY (Bos.) Sept. 21, 1956
18　**NL:**By many; last:
　　Pitt. (LA) Aug. 13, 2016
　　Extra-Inning Game:
27　**NL:**Atl. (Phil.) May 4, 1973 (20 inn)
25　**AL:**Wash. (Clev.) Sept. 14(2g), 1971 (20 inn)
　　KC (Tex.) June 6, 1991 (18 inn)

Most Left on Base, Both Clubs, Game
30　**NL:**Brk. (16) Pitt. (14) June 30, 1893
　　NY (17) Phil. (13) July 18(1g), 1943
　　Mia. (17) Wash. (13) July 8, 2018
　　AL:NY (15) Chi. (15) Aug. 27(1g), 1935
　　LA (15) Wash. (15) July 21, 1961
　　Extra-Inning Game:
45　**NL:**NY (25) StL. (20) Sept. 11, 1974 (25 inn)
　　AL:KC (25) Tex. (20) June 6, 1991 (18 inn)

Most Left on Base, No Runs, Game
16　**NL:**StL. (Phil.) May 24, 1994
　　Pitt. (StL.) Sept. 28, 2015
　　AL: Sea. (Tor.) May 7, 1998
　　Extra-Inning Game:
19　**NL:**Bos. (Pitt.) Aug. 1, 1918 (21 inn)
　　Ari. (SD) Sept. 2, 2001 (13 inn)
18　**AL:**Bos. (StL.) July 14, 1916 (17 inn)

Fewest Left on Base, Both Clubs, Game
1　**NL:**LA (0) Chi. (1) Sept. 9, 1965
2　**AL:**By many; last:
　　Det. (0) Hou. (2) July 15, 2018

Fewest Left on Base, 2 Consecutive Games
1　**AL:**Clev. June 23-24, 1976
　　Det. May 3-4, 1996
　　TB May 12-13, 2006
　　NL: Pitt. Aug. 3-4, 1999
　　NY Aug. 1-2, 2014
　　SD Aug. 12-13, 2016 (20 inn)

Most Left on Base, Doubleheader
30　**AL:**Phil. (StL.) June 12, 1949
29　**NL:**StL. (Phil.) Sept. 15, 1928
　　Phil. (Mil.) May 15, 1955
　　Extra Innings:
34　**NL:**Pitt. (StL.) May 30, 1938 (26 inn)
　　AL: Clev. (NY) Aug. 18, 1943 (23 inn)

Most Left on Base, Both Clubs, Doubleheader
49 **NL:**Brk. (25) Pitt. (24) July 24, 1926
AL:NY (27) Chi. (22) Aug. 27, 1935
Extra Innings:
60 **AL:**KC (31) Det. (29) June 17, 1967 (28 inn)
59 **NL:**Pitt. (34) StL. (25) May 30, 1938 (26 inn)

Fewest Left on Base, Doubleheader
3 **NL:**By many; last:
Pitt. (NY) Sept. 19, 2004
AL: By many; last:
NY (Clev.) Aug. 1, 1965

Fewest Left on Base, Both Clubs, Doubleheader
9 **NL:**StL. (5) Bos. (4) July 19, 1924
11 **AL:**NY (8) Phil. (3) Aug. 10, 1942
Balt. (6) Bos. (5) Sept. 2, 1974

PINCH-HITTERS

Most Pinch-Hitters, Game
9 **NL:**LA (StL.) Sept. 22, 1959
Mtl. (Pitt.) Sept. 5(2g), 1975
LA (StL.) Sept. 1, 1982 (13 inn)
LA (NY) Sept. 8, 1985 (14 inn)
SF (LA) Sept. 28, 1986 (16 inn)
Atl. (Mtl.) Sept. 21, 1993
StL. (Cin.) Sept. 25, 1997 (14 inn)
Ari. (StL.) Sept. 24, 2019 (19 inn)
8 **AL:**Balt. (Chi.) May 28, 1954
Balt. (NY) Sept. 25, 1984
Minn. (Sea.) Sept. 13, 1996
Extra-Inning Game:
10 **AL:**Oak. (Chi.) Sept. 19, 1972 (15 inn)

Most Pinch-Hitters, Both Clubs, Game
13 **NL:**LA (7) SD (6) Sept. 25, 1986
Atl. (9) Mtl. (4) Sept. 21, 1993
10 **AL:**Balt. (6) NY (4) Apr. 26, 1959
Tex. (6) Oak. (4) Sept. 7, 1975
Sea. (7) Chi. (3) Sept. 18, 1980
Extra-Inning Game:
14 **NL:**NY (7) Chi. (7) May 2, 1956 (17 inn)
LA (9) StL. (5) Sept. 1, 1982 (13 inn)
LA (7) Atl. (7) Sept. 18, 1986 (12 inn)
SF (9) LA (5) Sept. 28, 1986 (16 inn)
Ari. (9) StL. (5) Sept. 24, 2019 (19 inn)
AL: Oak. (10) Chi. (4) Sept. 19, 1972 (15 inn)

Most Pinch-Hitters, Doubleheader
10 **AL:**NY (Bos.) Sept. 6, 1954
Balt. (Wash.) Apr. 19, 1959
NL: StL. (Chi.) May 11, 1958
StL. (Pitt.) July 13, 1958
Mtl. (StL.) Sept. 18, 1976
Extra-Innings:
15 **NL:**Mtl. (Pitt.) Sept. 5, 1975 (19 inn)
Chi. (Mtl.) Sept. 4, 1978 (19 inn)

Most Pinch-Hitters, Both Clubs, Doubleheader
16 **NL:**SD (9) SF (7) May 30, 1977
14 **AL:**NY (10) Bos. (4) Sept. 6, 1954
Chi. (8) Minn. (6) Sept. 21, 1983
Extra innings:
19 **NL:**Mtl. (15) Pitt. (4) Sept. 5, 1975 (19 inn)
17 **AL:**NY (9) Wash. (8) Aug. 14, 1960 (24 inn)

Most Pinch-Hitters, Inning
6 **NL:**SF (Pitt.) May 5, 1958 (9th)
Mtl. (Cin.) May 31, 1970 (9th)
SD (SF) Sept. 16, 1986 (9th)
Atl. (Mtl.) Sept. 21, 1993 (7th)
LA (Col.) Sept. 14, 2002 (6th)
StL. (Pitt.) Sept. 23, 2017 (6th)
AL:KC (Det.) Sept. 9, 1966 (9th)
Det. (NY) Sept. 5, 1971 (7th)
Sea. (NY) Sept. 4, 2007 (8th)
TB (Bos) Sept. 6, 2010 (7th)

Most Pinch-Hitters, Both Clubs, Inning
8 **AL:**Chi. (5) Balt. (3) May 18, 1957 (7th)
NL: Phil. (5) StL. (3) Apr. 30, 1961 (8th)
NY (5) SF (3) Sept. 16, 1966 (9th)

Most Pinch-Hits, Game
5 **NL:**Brk. (Phil.) Sept. 9, 1926
4 **AL:**Clev. (Chi.) Apr. 22, 1930
Phil. (Det.) Sept. 18, 1940
Det. (Chi.) Apr. 22, 1953
KC (Det.) Sept. 1, 1958
NY (Clev.) Aug. 26, 1960 (11 inn)
Clev. (Bos.) Sept. 21, 1967
Oak. (Det.) Aug. 30, 1970
Chi. (Oak.) Sept. 7, 1970
Tex. (KC) June 8, 1995 (10 inn)
Bos. (NY) Sept. 8, 1995
Oak. (Hou.) Apr. 24, 2015 (11 inn)

Most Pinch-Hits, Inning
4 **NL:**Chi. (Brk.) May 21(2g), 1927 (9th)
Phil. (Pitt.) Sept. 12, 1974 (8th)
AL: Phil. (Det.) Sept. 18, 1940 (9th)
Tex. (KC) June 8, 1995 (8th)
Bos. (NY) Sept. 8, 1995 (8th)

Most Pinch-Hit Home Runs, Game
3 **NL:**StL. (Atl.) Apr. 8, 2016
2 **AL:**Clev. (Phil.) May 26, 1937
NY (KC) July 23, 1955
Clev. (Minn.) Aug. 15, 1965, (11 inn)
Balt. (Bos.) Aug. 26, 1966 (12 inn)
Det. (Bos.) Aug. 11, 1968 (14 inn)
Sea. (NY) Aug. 2, 1969
Minn. (Det.) July 31, 1970
Minn. (Cal.) July 28(2g), 1974
Sea. (NY) Apr. 27, 1979
Chi. (Oak.) July 6(2g), 1980
Minn. (Oak.) May 16, 1983
Balt. (Tex.) May 5, 1984
Balt. (Clev.) Aug. 12, 1985
Tor. (Det.) June 14, 1986
Tex. (Bos.) Sept. 1, 1986
Cal. (Chi.) June 28, 1987
Bos. (Chi.) Sept. 19, 1997 (10 inn)
Bos. (Mil.) June 7, 2003
Tor. (Tex.) Sept. 11, 2004
Minn. (NL:Phil.) June 19, 2010 (11 inn)
Det. (Chi.) Sept. 14, 2011 (10 inn)
Det. (Chi.) July 24, 2016
Balt. (NL:Wash.) Aug. 8, 2020

Most Pinch-Hit Home Runs, Both Clubs, Game
3 **ML:**AL:Minn. (2) NL:Phil. (1) June 19, 2010 (11 inn)
NL: Phil. (2) StL. (1) June 2, 1928
StL. (2) Brk. (1) July 21, 1930
Col. (2) LA (1) May 6, 1995
SD (2) Col. (1) July 2, 1999
StL. (3) Atl. (0) Apr. 8, 2016
Phil. (2) Cin. (1) Sept. 4, 2019
2 **AL:**By many; last:
Det. (1) Chi. (1) Sept. 28 (2g), 2019

Most Pinch-Hit Home Runs, 2 Cons. Games
3 **NL:**Mtl. July 13-13, 1973
SF Sept. 27-28, 1987
Chi. Sept. 11-12, 1998
Ari. Apr. 14-15, 2009
StL. Apr. 6-8, 2016
StL. April 8-9, 2016
AL: By many

Most Pinch-Hit Home Runs, Inning
2 **NL:**NY (StL.) June 20, 1954 (6th)
    SF (Mil.) June 4, 1958 (10th)
    LA (Chi.) Aug. 8, 1963 (5th)
    LA (StL.) July 23, 1975 (9th)
    NY (SF) May 4, 1991 (9th)
    Cin. (Atl.) June 22, 1995 (8th)
    NY (StL.) May 11, 1997 (9th)
    Atl. (Mil.) May 25, 1999 (9th)
    SD (Col.) July 2, 1999 (9th)
    SF (Mtl.) Aug. 23, 2001 (9th)
    Fla. (AL:Balt.) June 22, 2006 (9th)
    LA (Col.) Aug. 9, 2018 (7th)
    SF (Col.) Sept. 3, 2018 (8th)
    SF (Phil.) July 30, 2019 (8th)
  AL:NY (KC) July 23, 1955 (9th)
    Balt. (Bos.) Aug. 26, 1966 (9th)
    Sea. (NY) Apr. 27, 1979 (8th)
    Minn. (Oak.) May 16, 1983 (9th)
    Balt. (Clev.) Aug. 12, 1985 (9th)
    Tex. (Bos.) Sept. 1, 1986 (9th)
    Bos. (Chi.) Sept. 19, 1997 (9th)
    Tor. (Tex.) Sept. 11, 2004 (8th)
    Det. (Chi.) Sept. 14, 2011 (9th)
    Det. (Chi.) July 24, 2016 (9th)
    Balt. (NL:Wash.) Aug. 8, 2020 (8th)

Most Grand Slam HRs, Game
1 By many

Most Grand Slam HRs, Both Clubs, Game
2 **NL:**Bos. (1) NY (1) May 26, 1929
1 **AL:**By many

Most Walks, Inning
3 **NL:**Pitt. (Phil.) June 3, 1911 (9th)
    Brk. (NY) Apr. 22, 1922 (7th)
    Bos. (Brk.) June 2, 1932 (9th)
    Chi. (Phil.) July 29, 1947 (7th)
    StL. (NY) May 6, 1994 (9th)
    NY (Col.) May 18, 1997 (8th)
    Phil. (Pitt.) July 18, 1997 (6th)
    Chi. (Mil.) Aug. 30, 2012 (6th)
    LA (Mia.) Apr. 27, 2016 (8th)
    Mil. (Pitt.) Sept. 20, 2017 (7th)
  AL: Balt. (Wash.) Apr. 22, 1955 (7th)
    Wash. (Bos.) May 14, 1961 (9th)
    Minn. (Wash.) July 1, 1967 (8th)
    Cal. (Oak.) Sept. 4, 1973 (9th)
    Sea. (Bos.) June 3, 1995 (9th)
    Tex. (NL:Ari.) July 15, 1999 (9th)
    TB (NL:Fla.) May 21, 2011 (8th)

Most Strikeouts, Game
5 **AL:**Det. (NY) Sept. 8, 1979
  NL: Chi. (Cin.) May 22, 1990 (16 inn)
    Cin. (SF) Sept. 20, 2000
    SF (Col.) Sept. 2, 2008 (12 inn)
    LA (AL:TB) Sept. 18, 2019 (11 inn)

Most Strikeouts, Both Clubs, Game
6 **NL:**Ari. (4) Chi. (2) July 23, 2008
    Cin. (4) StL. (2) July 5, 2011
5 **AL:**NY (4) Bos. (1) July 4, 1955
    Wash. (4) Clev. (1) May 1, 1957
    Det. (4) Clev. (1) Aug. 4, 1967
    Det. (5) NY (0) Sept. 8, 1979
  Extra-Inning Game:
7 **NL:**Chi. (5) Cin. (2) May 22, 1990 (16 inn)
    Ari. (4) StL. (3) Sept. 24, 2019 (19 inn)

Most Strikeouts, Inning
3 By many; last:
  NL: Cin. (Pitt.) Apr. 4, 2019 (9th)
  AL: Hou. (Tex.) Sept. 26, 2017 (7th)

PINCH-RUNNERS

Most Pinch-Runners, Game
5 **AL:**Bos. (Balt.) Oct. 3, 2004
4 **NL:**By many; last:
    Col. (Wash.) Sept. 30, 2018
  Extra-Inning Game:
5 **NL:**Chi. (Hou.) Sept. 2, 1986 (18 inn)

Most Pinch-Runners, Inning
4 **AL:**Chi. (Minn.) Sept. 16, 1967 (9th)
    Oak. (Chi.) Sept. 24, 1975 (8th)
    Tex. (Cal.) Sept. 10, 1987 (9th)
    Ana. (Tex.) Sept. 23, 2000 (7th)
    NY (TB) Sept. 13, 2005 (6th)
  NL:SD (Cin.) Aug. 10, 1978 (7th)
    Col. (Wash.) Sept. 30, 2018 (8th)

Most Runs, Inning
3 **AL:**Chi. (Minn.) Sept. 16, 1967 (9th)
    Chi. (Oak.) May 19, 1968 (5th)
    Oak. (Cal.) May 7, 1975 (7th)
    Minn. (Balt.) June 19, 1991 (9th)
    Tex. (Balt.) Apr. 19, 1996 (8th)
    NY (TB) Sept. 13, 2005 (6th)
    Tex. (LA) Oct. 2, 2005 (3rd)
    NY (TB) Oct. 4, 2009 (6th)
    Sea. (LA) Sept. 14, 2015 (7th)
    Clev. (KC) Sept. 28, 2018 (7th)
2 **NL:**By many; last:
    Pitt. (Cin.) Aug. 23, 2019 (9th)

CLUB FIELDING – SEASON

	AL:1901-1960 NL:1900-1961 8 clubs 154 games		AL:1961-1968 NL:1962-1968 10 clubs 162 games		AL:1969- NL:1969- 12-16 clubs 162 games
Highest Fielding Average					
AL:	.983	Clev. 1949	.985	Balt. 1964	.991	Balt. 2013
NL:	.983	Cin. 1958	.982	Phil. 1966	.989	Col. 2007
Lowest Fielding Average					
AL:	.928	Det. 1901	.969	LA 1961	.970	Oak. 1977
NL:	.936	Phil. 1904	.967	NY 1963	.969	Chi. 1974
Most Total Chances					
AL:	6895	Chi. 1907	6557	Chi. 1967	6653	Cal. 1983
NL:	6682	NY 1920	6601	Pitt. 1968	6661	Chi. 1977
Fewest Total Chances					
AL:	5596	Clev. 1945	5930	Det. 1962	5718	Clev. 2019
NL:	5655	Phil. 1955	5964	Cin. 1966	5765	Wash. 2018
Most Chances Accepted					
AL:	6655	Chi. 1907	6419	Chi. 1967	6499	Cal. 1983
NL:	6472	NY 1920	6462	Pitt. 1968	6508	Chi. 1977
Fewest Chances Accepted					
AL:	5470	Clev. 1945	5774	Det. 1962	5635	Clev. 2019
NL:	5545	Phil. 1955	5842	Cin. 1966	5682	SD 2019
Most Putouts					
AL:	4396	Clev. 1910	4520	NY 1964	4493	Minn. 1969
NL:	4359	Phil. 1913	4471	Cin. 1968	4485	Ari. 2013
Fewest Putouts					
AL:	3907	Clev. 1945	4245	KC 1961	4188	Det. 1975
NL:	3887	Phil. 1907	4280	Phil. 1962	4223	Atl. 1979
Most Assists					
AL:	2446	Chi. 1907	1975	NY 1968	2077	Cal. 1983
NL:	2293	StL. 1917	2068	Chi. 1964	2104	Chi. 1977
Fewest Assists					
AL:	1493	NY 1948	1443	Det. 1962	1309	TB 2014
NL:	1437	Phil. 1957	1534	Cin. 1966	1363	Wash. 2018
Most Errors					
AL:	425	Det. 1901	192	LA 1961	191	Tex. 1975 Oak. 1977
NL:	408	Brk. 1905	210	NY 1962-63	199	Chi. 1974
Fewest Errors					
AL:	103	Clev. 1949	95	Balt. 1964	54	Balt. 2013
NL:	100	Cin. 1958	113	Phil. 1966	64	Wash. 2018
Most Double Plays					
AL:	218	Phil. 1949	186	Cal. 1966	206	Bos. & Tor. 1980
NL:	198	LA 1958	216	Pitt. 1966	202	Col. 1997
Fewest Double Plays					
AL:	74	Bos. 1913	114	Det. 1962	95	NY 2018
NL:	94	Pitt. 1935	100	Hou. 1963	97	SD 2012
Most Triple Plays					
AL:	3	Det. 1911 Bos. 1924	2	Wash. 1968	3	Bos. 1979 Oak. 1979 Chi. 2016
NL:	2	By many	3	Phil. 1964 Chi. 1965	2	Hou. 1971, 78, 91 NY 1982 Mtl. 1993 Cin. 1995 Phil. 2007 Mil. 2016
Most Passed Balls					
AL:	49	Balt. 1959	45	Chi. 1965	73	Tex. 1987
NL:	42	Bos. 1905	42	Atl. 1967	38	Atl. 1976 Hou. 1984
Fewest Passed Balls					
AL:	0	NY 1931	5	Minn. 1966	2	Tex. 1999, 2001 Clev. 2019
NL:	2	Bos. 1943	4	Chi. 1967	2	NY 1980 SD 1992 Pitt. 2004

AVERAGE

Most Seasons Leading League
22 **NL:**Bos./Mil./Atl. 1878-79, 82, 84, 91, 97,
 99-1900, 02, 15-16, 24, 32-33, 54, 61-63,
 69, 98, 2005, 12
 AL: StL./Balt. 1902, 63-64, 66, 69, 74-78,
 80, 82, 84, 89, 91, 94-95, 98-99, 2007, 13, 15

Most Seasons, Consecutive, Leading League
6 **AL:**Bos. 1916-21
 NL: StL. 1984-89

CHANCES ACCEPTED

Most Chances Accepted, Game
55 **NL:**Pitt. (NY) June 7, 1911
54 **AL:**StL. (Phil.) Aug. 16, 1919
 Extra-Inning game:
119 **NL:**Bos. (Brk.) May 1, 1920 (26 inn)
110 **AL:**Det. (Phil.) July 21, 1945 (24 inn)

PUTOUTS

Most Players, 1 or more Putouts, 9-Inning Game
15 **AL:**Bos. (Balt.) Oct. 3, 2004
 TB (Bos.) Sept. 15, 2008
 LA (Sea.) Sept. 16, 2014
14 **NL:**By many; last:
 NY (Atl.) Sept. 29, 2002

Most Players, 1 or more Putouts, Both Clubs, 9-Inning Game
25 By many; last:
 AL:TB (15) Bos. (10) Sept. 15, 2008
 NL:SD (14) SF (11) Sept. 26, 1997

ASSISTS

Most Assists, Game
28 **NL:**Cin. (NY) Aug. 1, 1905
 Pitt. (NY) June 7, 1911
27 **AL:**StL. (Phil.) Aug. 16, 1919
 Extra-Inning game:
42 **AL:**Minn. (Clev.) Aug. 31, 1993 (22 inn)
41 **NL:**Bos. (Brk.) May 1, 1920 (26 inn)

Fewest Assists, Game (9+ fielding innings)
0 **AL:**Clev. (NY) July 4(1g), 1945
 NY (Clev.) Sept. 11, 1995
 LA (Bos.) Aug. 10, 2014
 NY (Bos.) Sept. 2, 2014
 NL:NY (Phil.) June 25, 1989
 Cin. (Col.) Aug. 20, 1997

Most Assists, Both Clubs, Game
44 **AL:**Clev. (22) StL. (22) May 27, 1909
43 **NL:**Brk. (24) NY (19) Apr. 21, 1903
 Extra inning game:
72 **NL:**Bos. (41) Brk. (31) May 1, 1920 (26 inn)
 AL: Det. (38) Phil. (34) July 21, 1945 (24 inn)

Fewest Assists, Both Clubs, Game (9+ innings)
4 **AL:**Hou. (3) Tex. (1) Apr. 1, 2018
 Minn. (3) Balt. (1) Apr. 27, 2019
6 **NL:**Chi. (5) Phil. (1) May 2, 1957
 Phil. (3) SF (3) May 13, 1959
 Atl. (3) Hou. (3) Sept. 19, 1989
 LA (3) SF (3) Sept. 27, 1989
 Atl. (3) Mtl. (3) May 28, 1990
 Mtl. (3) NY (3) Sept. 10, 1991
 Cin. (5) Chi. (1) Aug. 26, 1998
 Cin. (5) SF (1) Sept. 6, 2006
 Chi. (3) NY (3) Sept. 23, 2008
 SD (3) SF (3) July 10, 2009

Most Assists, Infield, 9-Inning Game
22 **AL:**Sea. (NY) May 28, 1988
 Clev. (Minn.) May 15, 2012
21 **NL:**NY (Pitt.) July 13, 1919
 Phil. (Bos.) May 30(2g), 1931
 Brk. (Pitt.) Aug. 18(2g), 1935
 StL. (NY) June 27, 1993
 Phil. (Mtl.) Apr. 17, 1996

Fewest Assists, Infield, Game (9+ innings in field)
0 By many; last:
 AL:NY (NL:Col.) July 19, 2019
 NL: Mil. (Wash.) May 8, 2019

Most Assists, Infield, Both Clubs, 9-Inning Game
38 **NL:**Brk. (20) Cin. (18) June 10, 1917
35 **AL:**Det. (19) Clev. (16) Apr. 18, 1924
 Chi. (18) Bos. (17) Sept. 17(2g), 1945
 Det. (18) TB (17) Aug. 1, 1998

Fewest Assists, Infield, Both Clubs, Game (9+ innings)
2 **AL:**Wash. (0) Phil. (2) May 5, 1910
 Tor. (1) NY (1) Sept. 23, 2007
 NL: Phil. (0) Chi. (2) May 2, 1957

Most Assists, Outfield, Game
5 **NL:**Pitt. (Phil.) Aug. 23, 1910
 AL:NY (Bos.) Sept. 5(2g), 1921
 Clev. (StL.) May 1, 1928

Most Assists, Inning
10 **AL:**Clev. (Phil.) Aug. 17, 1921 (1st)
 Bos. (NY) May 10, 1952 (5th)
8 **NL:**Bos. (Phil.) May 1, 1911 (4th)
 Cin. (StL.) June 3, 1992 (3rd)
 Phil. (AL:Chi.) Aug. 30, 2004 (5th)

Most Players, 1 or more Assists, 9-Inning Game
12 **NL:**Chi. (Pitt.) Sept. 28, 2003
11 **AL:**Wash. (Phil.) Oct. 3, 1920
 Bos. (Phil.) May 1, 1929
 Wash. (Balt.) Apr. 29(1g), 1956
 Chi. (KC) Sept. 22(2g), 1970
 Balt. (LA) June 29, 2007
 KC (Oak.) Apr. 19, 2015

ERRORS – MOST

Most Seasons Leading League
21 **AL:**Phil./KC/Oak. 1915-16, 19-21, 36-41,
 64, 77-79, 82, 84, 98, 2011, 15, 17
19 **NL:**Pitt. 1890, 1925, 40-41, 46, 52, 54-57,
 59, 64, 78, 89, 2010, 14-15, 19-20

Most Seasons, Consecutive, Leading League
7 **NL:**Phil. 1930-36
6 **AL:**Phil. 1936-41
 StL. 1948-53

Most Errors, Game
24 **NL:**Bos. (StL.) June 14, 1876
 Since 1900:
12 **AL:**Det. (Chi.) May 1, 1901
 Chi. (Det.) May 6, 1903
11 **NL:**StL. (Pitt.) Apr. 19, 1902
 Bos. (StL.) June 11, 1906
 StL. (Cin.) July 3(2g), 1909

Most Errors, Both Clubs, Game
40 **NL:**Chi. (24) StL. (16) June 14, 1876
 Since 1900:
18 **AL:**Chi. (12) Det. (6) May 6, 1903
15 **NL:**StL. (11) Pitt. (4) Apr. 19, 1902
 Bos. (10) Chi. (5) Oct. 3, 1904

Most Errors, Inning, Since 1900
7 **AL:**Clev. (Chi.) Sept. 20, 1905 (8th)
6 **NL:**Pitt. (NY) Aug. 20(1g), 1903 (1st)

ERRORS – FEWEST

Most Seasons Leading League
27 **NL:**Cin. 1896, 1919, 27, 30, 40-41, 43,
57-58, 60, 64-65, 71-73, 75-77, 80-81, 83, 90,
95, 97, 2010, 14, 20
22 **AL:**StL./Balt. 1938, 43, 60, 63-64, 66, 69,
75-78, 80, 82, 89, 91, 94-95, 98-99, 2007, 13,
15

Most Seasons, Consecutive, Leading League
6 **AL:**Phil. 1909-14
Bos. 1916-21
4 **NL:**Chi. 1905-08
StL. 1984-87

Most Errorless Games, Season
119 **AL:**Balt. 2013
113 **NL:**Hou. 2008

Most Errorless Games, Consecutive, Season
18 **AL:**NY May 14-June 1, 2009
Bos. Sept. 13-Oct. 1, 2016
17 **NL:**SF Aug. 15-Sept. 2, 2016

Fewest Errors, Game (Most Innings)
0 **AL:**Chi. (Wash.) June 12, 1967 (22 inn)
Wash. (Chi.) June 12, 1967 (22 inn)
NL: Phil. (Chi.) July 17, 1918 (21 inn)
Bos. (Pitt.) Aug. 1, 1918 (21 inn)
SF (Cin.) Sept. 1, 1967 (21 inn)
SD (Mtl.) May 21, 1977 (21 inn)

Fewest Errors, Both Clubs, Game (Most Innings)
0 **AL:**Chi. (Wash.) June 12, 1967 (22 inn)
NL: Mia. (NY) June 8, 2013 (20 inn)

DOUBLE PLAYS

Most Seasons Leading League
25 **NL:**Pitt. 1904, 06, 11, 25, 38, 49, 55, 59-
67, 70, 72, 94, 2002, 04, 07-09, 16
17 **AL:**Chi. 1902, 04-05, 19-21, 32, 36, 47, 60,
70, 74, 87-88, 2000, 14, 19

Most Seasons, Consecutive, Leading League
9 **NL:**Pitt. 1959-67
5 **AL:**NY 1954-58

Most Double Plays, Game
7 **AL:**NY (Phil.) Aug. 14, 1942
NL: Hou. (SF) May 4, 1969
Atl. (Cin.) June 27, 1982 (14 inn)
StL. (Pitt.) June 16, 1994 (10 inn)
Chi. (Pitt.) Aug. 17, 2018

Most Double Plays, Both Clubs, Game
10 **AL:**Minn. (6) Bos. (4) July 18, 1990
9 **NL:**Chi. (5) Cin. (4) July 3, 1929
LA (5) Pitt. (4) Apr. 15, 1961
Chi. (7) Pitt. (2) Aug. 17, 2018
Extra-Inning Game:
10 **NL:**Bos. (5) Cin. (5) June 7, 1925 (12 inn)
Cin. (6) NY (4) May 1, 1955 (16 inn)
SF (6) NY (4) Aug. 21, 2004 (12 inn)
Chi. (6) Mil. (4) May 11, 2019 (15 inn)

Most Double Plays, Unassisted, Game
2 By many

Most Double Plays, Unassisted, Both Clubs, Game
3 **AL:**NY (2) Clev. (1) June 22, 1996
2 **NL:**By many

Most Double Plays, Doubleheader
9 **AL:**Phil. (Clev.) Sept. 14, 1931
Bos. (StL.) June 25, 1950
NL: StL. (Cin.) June 11, 1944
Including Extra-Inning Game:
10 **AL:**Wash. (Chi.) Aug. 18, 1943 (23 inn)

Most Double Plays, Both Clubs, Doubleheader
13 **NL:**NY (7) Phil. (6) Sept. 28, 1939
Pitt. (8) StL. (5) Sept. 6, 1948
12 **AL:**Phil. (9) Clev. (3) Sept. 14, 1931
Bos. (7) Chi. (5) Sept. 15, 1947
NY (7) KC (5) July 31, 1955
Cal. (8) Bos. (4) May 1, 1966
Cal. (7) Balt. (5) May 19, 1988 (19 inn)

Most Games, Consecutive, Double Plays
25 **AL:**Bos. May 7-June 4, 1951 (39)
Clev. Aug. 21(2g)-Sept. 12, 1953 (38)
23 **NL:**Brk. Aug. 7-27, 1952 (36)

Most Double Plays, 2 Consecutive Games
10 **NL:**NY Aug. 12-13(1g), 1932
Cin. Apr. 30-May 1, 1955
AL: Wash. Aug. 18(1g)-18(2g), 1943
Det. May 18-19, 1948
Clev. May 3-5, 1970
KC May 5-6, 1972

Most Double Plays, 3 Consecutive Games
13 **AL:**Phil. Sept. 12(2g)-14(2g), 1931
Wash. Aug. 16-18(2g), 1943
Bos. June 25(1g)-27, 1950
NL:SF Apr. 24-26, 1987

Most Double Plays, 4 Consecutive Games
15 **AL:**Phil. Sept. 12(2g)-15, 1931
NL:SF Apr. 24-27, 1987

Most Double Plays, 5 Consecutive Games
16 **NL:**Cin. May 13-18, 1928
SF Apr. 22-27, 1987
AL: Phil. Sept. 12(2g)-16, 1931
NY Apr. 19-23, 1952
Oak. Aug. 10-14, 1972
Clev. Sept. 11-16, 2005
Minn. May 25-29, 2012

TRIPLE PLAYS

Most Seasons, Consecutive, Triple Plays
6 **NL:**NY 1894-99
Since 1900:
4 **NL:**Pitt. 1968-71
3 **AL:**By many; Last:
Minn. 1982-84

Most Triple Plays, Season
3 **AA:**Cin. 1882
Brk. 1886
Roch. 1890
NL:NY 1885
Phil. 1964
Chi. 1965
AL: Det. 1911
Bos. 1924
Bos. 1979
Oak. 1979
Chi. 2016

Most Triple Plays, Game
2 **AL:**Minn. (Bos.) July 17, 1990 (4th, 8th)
1 **NL:**By many

Most Triple Plays, Both Clubs, Game
2 **AL:**Minn. (2) Bos. (0) July 17, 1990

Most Games, Consecutive, Triple Plays
2 **AL:**Det. June 6-7, 1908
1 **NL:**By many

PASSED BALLS

Most Seasons Leading League (Most)
Since 1903:
24 **NL:**Bos./Mil./Atl. 1904-05, 07, 24, 26,
28-30, 42, 65-67, 69-72, 74-79, 2017, 19
Since 1912:
21 **AL:**Bos. 1917, 19, 24-25, 31, 50, 54, 94,
96-2000, 03-04, 06, 08, 11, 14, 16, 18

Most Seasons, Consecutive, Leading League (Most)
7 **AL:**Tex. 1984-90
6 **NL:**Atl. 1974-79

Most Seasons Leading League (Fewest)
Since 1912:
22 **AL:**StL./Balt. 1912, 20-21, 29-30, 35, 45,
56, 65, 72, 83, 85-86, 90-91, 93-94, 2000,
10-11,16-17
Since 1903:
19 **NL:**NY/SF 1914, 16-17, 24, 28, 30, 42,
47-48, 60-64, 99, 2005, 12, 16-17

Most Seasons, Consecutive, Leading League (Fewest)
5 **NL:**SF 1960-64
3 **AL:**Clev. 1939-41

Most Passed Balls, Game
12 **AA:**Wash. (NY) May 10, 1884
10 **NL:**Bos. (Wash.) May 3, 1886
Since 1900:
6 **NL:**Cin. (Pitt.) Oct. 4, 1902
Hou. (Mtl.) May 12, 1996
AL: Tex. (Det.) Aug. 30, 1987

Fewest Passed Balls, Game (Most Innings)
0 **NL:**Bos. (Brk.) May 1, 1920 (26 inn)
Brk. (Bos.) May 1, 1920 (26 inn)
AL: Chi. (Mil.) May 8, 1984 (25 inn)
Mil. (Chi.) May 8, 1984 (25 inn)

Most Passed Balls, Both Clubs, Game
14 **AA:**Wash. (12) NY (2) May 10, 1884
11 **NL:**Troy (7) Clev. (4) June 16, 1880
Since 1900:
6 **NL:**Cin. (6) Pitt. (0) Oct. 4, 1902
Hou. (6) Mtl. (0) May 12, 1996
AL: Tex. (6) Det. (0) Aug. 30, 1987

Fewest Passed Balls, Both Clubs, Game
(Most Innings)
0 **NL:**Bos.-Brk. May 1, 1920 (26 inn)
AL: Mil.-Chi. May 8, 1984 (25 inn)

CLUB PITCHING – SEASON

	AL:1901-1960 NL:1900-1961 8 clubs 154 games		AL:1961-1968 NL:1962-1968 10 clubs 162 games		AL:1969- NL:1969- 12-16 clubs 162 games

Lowest Earned Run Average (Since 1912 in NL, 1913 in AL)

AL:	2.16	Chi. 1917	2.45	Chi. 1967	2.83	Balt. 1969
NL:	2.12	Brk. 1916	2.49	StL. 1968	2.91	NY 1988

Highest Earned Run Average (Since 1912 in NL, 1913 in AL)

AL:	6.24	StL. 1936	4.79	KC 1962	6.38	Det. 1996
NL:	6.70	Phil. 1930	5.04	NY 1962	6.01	Col. 1999

Most No-Hit Games

AL:	2	Bos. 1904, 16 Clev. 1908; StL. 1917 NY 1951; Det. 1952	2	Bos. 1962	2	Cal. 1973 Sea. 2012 Hou. 2019
NL:	2	Cin. 1938; Brk. 1956 Mil. 1960	1	By many	2	Chi. 1972 LA 2014 Wash. 2015

Most No-Hit Games Against

AL:	2	Chi. 1917 Phil. 1923	2	Det. 1967	2	Det. 1973 Cal. 1977 TB 2010 Tor. 2019
NL:	2	Phil. 1960	2	Chi. 1965	2	Cin. 1971 Col. 1996 SD 2001 LA & NY 2015

Most Complete Games

AL:	148	Bos. 1904	62	Det. 1961	94	Oak. 1980
NL:	146	StL. 1904	77	SF 1968	75	Chi. 1971

Fewest Complete Games

AL:	26	KC 1957	18	KC 1964-65	0	By many
NL:	27	Chi. 1958	24	Cin. 1968	0	By many

Most Shutouts Participating

AL:	47	Chi. 1910	44	LA 1964	40	TB 2014
NL:	46	Brk. 1907; StL. 1908	47	NY 1968	42	NY 1969

Fewest Shutouts Participating

AL:	7	NY 1926, 30; Chi. 1930	12	Chi. 1961	4	Tex. 2001
NL:	6	Phil. 1930	10	NY 1962	5	Col. & SF 1999; Hou. 2000

Most Shutouts

AL:	32	Chi. 1906	28	Cal. 1964	23	Mil. 1971 Oak. 1972
NL:	32	Chi. 1907, 09	30	StL. 1968	28	NY 1969

Most Times Shut Out

AL:	30	Wash. 1909	23	Chi. 1968	27	Tex. 1972
NL:	33	StL. 1908	30	NY 1963	24	Atl. 1978

Fewest Shutouts

AL:	1	Chi. 1924 Wash. 1956	3	Chi. 1961	1	Sea. 1977; Balt. 1996, Oak. 1997; Ana. & KC 2001
NL:	1	Bos. 1928	4	Chi. & NY 1962 Mil. 1965	0	Col. 1993

Fewest Times Shut Out

AL:	0	NY 1932	3	Minn. 1965	1	Mil. 1979, 82; Tor. 1993 Clev. 1996 Tex. 2001
NL:	1	Brk. 1953	6	By many	0	Cin. 2000

Most 1-0 Games Won

AL:	11	Wash. 1914	10	LA 1964	8	Balt. 1974
NL:	10	Pitt. 1908	8	StL. 1968	9	NY 1969 Hou. 1976

Most 1-0 Games Lost

AL:	9	NY 1914	9	Chi. 1968	7	Tex. 1976
NL:	10	Pitt. 1914 Chi. 1916	10	Phil. 1967	7	NY 1973 LA 1976, 89 StL. 1991

	AL:1901-1960 NL:1900-1961 8 clubs 154 games		AL:1961-1968 NL:1962-1968 10 clubs 162 games		AL:1969- NL:1969- 12-16 clubs 162 games
Most 1-Hit Games					
AL:	3	By many	5	Balt. 1964	6	Clev. 2015
NL:	4	Chi. 1906, 09	3	LA, Mil.,Pitt. 1965	4	Phil. 1979
		Phil. 1907, 11, 15				Cin. 1999
Most 1-Hit Games Against					
AL:	5	StL. 1910	4	Wash. 1963, 65	4	Tex. 2009, 15
		Clev. 1915				
NL:	3	By many	4	NY 1965	4	Stl. 1991
Most Games Decided By One Run					
AL:	65	Phil. 1908; StL. 1916	74	Chi. 1968	70	KC 1993
NL:	69	Cin. 1946	68	LA 1968	75	Hou. 1971
Fewest Games Decided By One Run					
AL:	22	StL. 1936	39	Bos. 1962; Minn. 1963	30	Det. 1993
				Det. 1967		Sea. 1998
						Tor. 2006
NL:	28	Brk. 1949	40	Phil. 1962	28	Mtl. 2001
Most 1-Run Games Won					
AL:	38	Clev. 1917	38	Chi. 1967	40	Balt. 1970, 74
		NY 1943				
NL:	41	Cin. 1940	37	Phil. 1968	42	SF 1978
Fewest 1-Run Games Won					
AL:	10	StL. 1937	13	Minn. 1963	10	Sea. 1998
		Clev. 1948				
NL:	7	Bos. 1935	17	NY 1964	10	Cin. 2018
Most 1-Run Games Lost					
AL:	40	Phil. 1908	44	Chi. 1968	36	Clev. 2005
						Chi. & Hou. 2013
NL:	41	Cin. 1916, 46	39	NY 1962	43	Hou. 1971
Fewest 1-Run Games Lost					
AL:	11	Wash. 1925	17	KC 1961	9	Balt. 2012
		StL. 1936		NY 1963		
		Bos. 1950		Det. 1966		
NL:	12	Pitt. 1908; Brk. 1949	14	Phil. 1962	12	SF 2003
						Atl. 2018
Most Saves (Since 1969)					
AL:	-	-	-	-	68	Chi. 1990
NL:	-	-	-	-	62	StL. 2015
Fewest Saves (Since 1969)					
AL:	-	-	-	-	11	Tor. 1979
NL:	-	-	-	-	13	Chi. 1971
Most Innings					
AL:	1465	Clev. 1910	1507	NY 1964	1498	Minn. 1969
NL:	1455	Phil. 1913	1490	Cin. 1968	1495	Ari. 2013
Fewest Innings					
AL:	1302	Clev. 1945	1415	KC 1961; NY 1966	1396	Det. 1975
NL:	1299	Phil. 1907	1427	Phil. 1962	1408	Atl. 1979
				NY 1963, 66		
Most Batters Faced					
AL:	6382	StL. 1936	6428	KC 1964	6713	Det. 1996
NL:	6549	Phil. 1930	6380	LA 1962	6574	Col. 1999
Fewest Batters Faced					
AL:	5559	Clev. 1945	5864	Balt. 1968	5799	Balt. 1971
NL:	5684	Brk. 1956	5941	LA 1966	5877	NY 1988
Most At-Bats					
AL:	5653	StL. 1936	5666	Clev. 1964	5770	Oak. 1997
NL:	5763	Phil. 1930	5664	LA 1962	5741	Chi. 1974
Fewest At-Bats					
AL:	4933	Clev. 1945	5237	Balt. 1968	5268	Balt. & Mil. 1971
NL:	5062	Phil. 1947	5363	Phil. 1963	5297	StL. 1978

	AL:1901-1960 / NL:1900-1961 / 8 clubs 154 games		AL:1961-1968 / NL:1962-1968 / 10 clubs 162 games		AL:1969- / NL:1969- / 12-16 clubs 162 games	
Most Runs						
AL:	1064	StL. 1936	863	KC 1961	1103	Det. 1996
NL:	1199	Phil. 1930	948	NY 1962	1028	Col. 1999
Fewest Runs						
AL:	408	Phil. 1909	491	Chi. 1967	517	Balt. 1969
NL:	381	Chi. 1906	472	StL. 1968	525	StL. 2015
Most Earned Runs (Since 1912 in NL, 1913 in AL)						
AL:	935	StL. 1936	764	KC 1962	1015	Det. 1996
NL:	1024	Phil. 1930	801	NY 1962	955	Col. 1999
Fewest Earned Runs (Since 1912 in NL, 1913 in AL)						
AL:	342	Chi. 1917	406	Chi. 1967	463	Balt. 1969
NL:	332	Phil. 1915	409	StL. 1968	465	NY 1988
Most Hits						
AL:	1776	StL. 1936	1519	KC 1961	1734	Oak. 1997
NL:	1994	Phil. 1930	1577	NY 1962	1700	Col. 1999
Fewest Hits						
AL:	1069	Phil. 1909	1087	Clev. 1968	1164	Hou. 2018
NL:	1018	Chi. 1906	1223	LA 1965	1125	Chi. 2016
Most Home Runs						
AL:	187	KC 1956	220	KC 1964	305	Balt. 2019
NL:	185	StL. 1955	192	NY 1962	270	Col. 2019
Fewest Home Runs						
AL:	6	Bos. 1913	87	Chi. 1967	80	Balt. 1976 / Clev. 1976
NL:	5	Cin. 1909	65	LA 1968	68	SF 1976
Most Grand Slam Home Runs						
AL:	9	Chi. 1934 / StL. 1938, 50	8	Clev. 1963	14	Det. 1996
NL:	8	Phil. 1933 / Pitt. 1951 / Chi. 1961	6	Chi. 1962 / LA 1962 / Phil. 1962 / Mil. 1965	12	Mtl. 2000 / NY 2010
Most Sacrifice Hits						
AL:	147	KC 1954	106	Chi. 1961	92	KC 1970 / Oak. 1978 / Tor. 1980
NL:	133	Brk. 1946	99	Hou. 1964	112	SD 1975
Fewest Sacrifice Hits						
AL:	46	NY 1958	51	Balt. 1968	7	NY 2019
NL:	44	Mil. 1958	53	Phil. 1966	25	Col. & LA 2018
Most Sacrifice Flies (Since 1954)						
AL:	63	Balt. & KC 1955	64	KC 1961	80	Oak. 1997
NL:	79	Pitt. 1954	58	Hou. 1963	78	Col. 1993
Fewest Sacrifice Flies (Since 1954)						
AL:	27	KC 1958	17	Det. 1968	20	Clev. & Hou. 2017
NL:	24	Brk. 1955	17	SF 1963	19	LA 2003
Most Walks						
AL:	827	Phil. 1915	713	LA 1961	784	Det. 1996
NL:	701	StL. 1911	600	Chi. 1962	737	Col. 1999
Fewest Walks						
AL:	233	Bos. 1904	392	Minn. 1966	348	Minn. 2005
NL:	258	Cin. 1933	344	SF 1968	352	Wash. 2014
Most Intentional Walks (Since 1955)						
AL:	59	Clev. 1957	78	Oak. 1968	94	Sea. 1980
NL:	85	Chi. 1956	101	LA 1967	116	SD 1974
Fewest Intentional Walks (Since 1955)						
AL:	18	Det. 1959	21	Bos. & KC 1961	0	Hou. 2019
NL:	33	Brk. 1957	19	Hou. 1962	9	LA 1974
Most Hit Batters						
AL:	81	Phil. 1911	66	Chi. 1968	95	TB 2003
NL:	68	Brk. 1903	61	Phil. 1966	92	Wash. 2006

	AL:1901-1961 NL:1900-1961 8 clubs 154 games		AL:1962-1968 NL:1962-1968 10 clubs 162 games		AL:1969- NL:1969- 12-16 clubs 162 games

Fewest Hit Batters

AL:	5	StL. 1945	12	Chi. 1961	10	Balt. 1983
NL:	9	Chi. 1944	17	Chi. 1964	11	Pitt. 1984

Most Strikeouts

AL:	896	Det. 1946	1189	Clev. 1967	1687	Hou. 2018
NL:	1122	LA 1960	1123	Cin. 1964	1565	LA 2018

Fewest Strikeouts

AL:	310	Bos. 1925	666	Wash. 1961	575	Mil. 1980
NL:	310	Cin. 1933	717	NY 1964	652	SD 1976

Most Wild Pitches

AL:	67	Phil. 1936	73	Minn. 1964 Bos. 1968	98	Hou. 2016 LA 2019
NL:	70	LA 1958	83	Cin. 1965 Atl. 1966	96	Cin. 2000

Fewest Wild Pitches

AL:	10	StL. 1930 Clev. 1943	27	Clev. 1962 NY 1962, 68	15	Bos. 1977
NL:	9	Cin. 1944	30	StL. 1964, 68 Phil. 1968	22	NY 2002 Hou. 2008

Most Balks

AL:	14	NY 1950	12	Bos. 1965 Balt. 1968	76	Oak. 1988
NL:	14	Phil. 1950	20	NY 1963	41	Mtl. 1988

Most Pitchers, 20 or more Games Won

AL:	4	Chi. 1920	2	NY 1963	4	Balt. 1971
NL:	3	Pitt. 1902 Chi. 1903 NY 1904-05, 13, 20 Cin. 1923	2	Cin. 1962, 65 LA 1965 SF 1966	2	LA & Chi. 1969 StL. 1985 Atl. & SF 1993 Hou. 1999 Ari. 2001-02

Most Pitchers, 20 or more Games Lost

AL:	3	Wash. 1904 StL. 1905 Phil. 1916	1	Minn. 1961 KC 1963 NY 1966	2	Chi. 1973
NL:	4	Bos. 1905-06	2	NY 1962, 65	1	SD 1969, 72, 74 Phil. 1973 Chi. & Mtl. 1974 NY 1977 Atl. 1977, 79

EARNED-RUN AVERAGE

Seasons Leading League
Lowest:
32 **NL:**Brk./LA 1916, 20, 27-28, 30, 41, 55, 57, 60, 63-66, 72-75, 77-78, 82-83, 85, 89, 91, 96, 2003, 08-09, 17-20
26 **AL:**NY 1919-23, 27, 32, 34-39, 42-43, 47, 52-53, 55, 57-58, 60, 78, 81, 97-98
Highest:
33 **NL:**Phil. 1914, 18-34, 36-42, 45-46, 56, 61, 81, 88-89, 92
19 **AL:**Phil./KC/Oak. 1915-16, 19, 22, 33,40-41, 43, 50, 54-55, 59, 61-62, 64, 67, 84, 93, 97
StL/Balt. 1917, 27, 30, 35-39, 46-49, 51, 88, 91, 2009, 11, 18-19

Seasons, Consecutive, Leading League
Lowest:
6 **AL:**NY 1934-39
NL: Atl. 1997-2002
Highest:
17 **NL:**Phil. 1918-34
5 **AL:**StL. 1935-39

COMPLETE GAMES

Seasons Leading League
Most:
32 **NL:**Bos./Mil./Atl. 1877, 85, 90-91, 93, 1905-06, 13-14, 16-18, 37-38, 47-51, 55-61, 63, 91, 94-96, 98
19 **AL:**Clev. 1903, 05-06, 24-26, 33, 51-54, 56, 59, 94, 2006, 15, 17-19
Fewest:
23 **NL:**Cin. 1893, 95, 97, 1934, 36, 48, 54-55, 60, 66-68, 71-72, 75, 78, 87, 91, 97, 2001, 05, 08, 19
20 **AL:**Phil./KC/Oak. 1902, 13, 25, 38-39, 45-46, 50, 55-57, 64-66, 78, 85, 92, 97, 2009, 12

Seasons, Consecutive, Leading League
Most:
7 **NL:**Mil. 1955-61
LA 1984-90
4 **AL:**Clev. 1951-54
Fewest:
7 **NL:**StL. 1916-22
6 **AL:**NY 1903-08

Most Incomplete Games, Consecutive
674 **AL:**TB May 15, 2016-Sept. 27, 2020
480 **NL:**Mia. June 4, 2014-June 2, 2017

Most Incomplete Games, Consecutive, Season
163 **NL:**Col. 2018 (entire season)
LA 2018 (entire season)
Mil. 2018 (entire season)
162 **AL:**By many

SHUTOUTS

Seasons Leading League
Most:
28 **NL:**Brk./LA 1928, 30, 40, 47, 49, 56-57, 63-66, 70-72, 75, 80-82, 85, 88-89, 91, 2002-03, 13, 16-17, 19
23 **AL:**NY 1905, 20, 24, 27, 32, 34, 37-39, 42, 50-53, 58-60, 80-81, 93, 96, 98, 2005
Fewest:
22 **AL:**Mil./StL/Balt. 1901, 05, 10, 15, 27, 31, 35-40, 47, 49, 51-52, 90-91, 96, 2002-03, 09
NL: Phil. 1883-84, 1920-23, 30-31, 38-42, 45, 56, 60, 68, 74, 76, 84, 92, 2013

Seasons, Consecutive, Leading League
Most:
6 **NL:**Chi. 1905-10
5 **AL:**Det. 1943-47
Fewest:
6 **AL:**StL. 1935-40
5 **NL:**Phil. 1938-42

Won, Consecutive, Season
6 **NL:**Pitt. June 2-8, 1903
5 **AL:**Balt. Sept. 2-6, 1974
Balt. Sept. 26-Oct. 1, 1995

Lost, Consecutive, Season
4 **NL:**Bos. May 19-23, 1906
Cin. July 30-Aug. 3, 1908
Cin. July 31-Aug. 3, 1931
Hou. June 20-23, 1963
Hou. Sept. 9-11, 1966
Chi. June 16-20, 1968
Atl. May 8-12, 1985
Chi. Apr. 27-May 1, 1992
AL: Bos. Aug. 2-6, 1906
StL. Aug. 25-30, 1913
Wash. Sept. 19-22, 1958
Wash. Sept. 1-5, 1964
KC Aug. 25-28, 2017

Won, vs. Opponent, Season
10 **NL:**Pitt. (Bos.) 1906
8 **AL:**Chi. (Bos.) 1906
Clev. (Wash.) 1956
Oak. (Clev.) 1968

1-0 Games Won, Consecutive, Season
3 **AL:**Chi. Apr. 25-27, 1909
NL: StL. Aug. 31-Sept. 1(2g), 1917

1-0 Games Lost, Consecutive, Season
3 **NL:**Brk. Sept. 7(1g)-8, 1908
Pitt. Aug. 31-Sept. 1(2g), 1917
Phil. May 11-13, 1960
AL: StL. Apr. 25-27, 1909
Wash. May 7-10, 1909

Most Runs Scored, Shutout Game
28 **NL:**Prov. (Phil.) Aug. 21, 1883
Since 1900:
22 **NL:**Pitt. (Chi.) Sept. 16, 1975
AL: Clev. (NY) Aug. 31, 2004

Most Runs Scored, Doubleheader Shutouts
26 **AL:**Det. (StL.) Sept. 22, 1936 (12, 14)
19 **NL:**NY (Cin.) July 31, 1949 (10, 9)

Most Innings, Consecutive, No Runs Allowed
56 **NL:**Pitt. June 1-9, 1903
54 **AL:**Balt. Sept. 1-7, 1974

SAVES (Since 1969)

Seasons Leading League
Most:
12 **NL:**Cin. 1969-70, 72, 74-76, 90, 92, 96-97,
99, 2012
AL:NY 1978, 80, 85-87, 96, 99, 2001, 03-04,
09, 19
Fewest:
8 **AL:**KC 1970, 90, 97, 99-2001, 04-05
7 **NL:**Chi. 1971, 81, 96, 99, 2002, 06, 12
Phil. 1973, 89, 91, 97, 99, 2013, 15

Seasons, Consecutive, Leading League
Most:
3 **NL:**Cin. 1974-76
AL:NY 1985-87
Bos. 1998-2000
Balt. 2012-14
Fewest:
4 **AL:**Cal. 1972-75
3 **NL:**StL. 1978-80
Atl. 1987-89

INNINGS

Seasons Leading League
21 **NL:**Brk./LA 1892, 1910, 16, 19, 39-41, 46,
48-49,51-52,59,62,64,73,76,82,93,2009,20
18 **AL:**Clev. 1906, 08, 10-11, 35, 42, 44,47-48,
54, 63, 73, 84, 92, 95, 99, 2007, 20

Seasons, Consecutive, Leading League
4 **NL:**Chi. 1905-08
3 **AL:**Chi. 1939-41, 65-67

One Day
32 **NL:**SF (NY) May 31, 1964 (dh)
29 **AL:**Bos. (Phil.) July 4, 1905 (dh)
Bos. (NY) Aug. 29, 1967 (dh)
Wash. (Clev.) Sept. 14, 1971 (dh)

RUNS

Seasons Leading League
Most:
32 **NL:**Phil. 1883-84, 1904, 14, 19-33, 35-39,
41-42, 45-46, 56, 58, 89, 92
22 **AL:**Phil./KC/Oak. 1915-17, 19-22, 33,
40-41, 43, 54-55, 59, 61-62, 64, 67,
82, 84, 93, 97
Fewest:
28 **NL:**Bos./Mil./Atl. 1877-79, 89-91, 97-99,
1916, 37, 47-48, 53, 56, 58, 92-2002, 13
24 **AL:**NY 1919-20, 22-23, 27, 34-39, 41-43,
46-47, 52-53, 57, 76-78, 81, 98

Seasons, Consecutive, Leading League
Most:
15 **NL:**Phil. 1919-33
6 **AL:**StL. 1946-51
Fewest:
11 **NL:**Atl. 1992-2002
6 **AL:**NY 1934-39
Chi. 1962-67

EARNED RUNS (Since 1912 in NL, 1913 in AL)

Seasons Leading League
Most:
33 **NL:**Phil. 1914, 18-34, 36-39, 41-42, 45-46,
56, 61, 79, 81, 88-89, 92
23 **AL:**Balt. 1917, 25, 27, 30, 32-33,
35-40, 46-49, 51, 88, 91, 2009, 11, 18-19
Fewest:
32 **NL:**Brk./LA 1916, 20, 27-28, 30, 55, 57, 60,
63-66, 72-75, 77-78, 83, 85, 87, 89, 91,
96, 2003, 08-09, 12, 17-20
28 **AL:**NY 1919-23, 27, 32, 34-39, 41-43,
46-47, 52-53, 55, 57-58, 76, 78, 81,
97-98

Seasons, Consecutive, Leading League
Most:
17 **NL:**Phil. 1918-34
6 **AL:**StL. 1935-40
Fewest:
6 **AL:**NY 1934-39
Balt. 1968-73
NL: Atl. 1997-2002

HITS

Seasons Leading League
Most:
33 **NL:**Phil. 1883, 96, 1900, 04, 14, 19, 21-33,
35-38,41,45-46,56,58,60,68-69,89,2015
21 **AL:**StL./Balt. 1909, 13, 17, 31-33, 36-41,
46-51, 2009, 11, 18
Fewest:
29 **NL:**Brk./LA 1902, 16, 27-28, 30, 41, 46-49,
56-57, 60, 62, 64-66, 72-75, 80, 85,
2000, 03, 09, 12, 17, 19
28 **AL:**NY 1919-23, 27, 34-37, 39, 41-42,
46-47, 49, 52-53, 55, 57-58, 63, 76,
78, 81, 96, 98, 2017

Seasons, Consecutive, Leading League
Most:
13 **NL:**Phil. 1921-33
6 **AL:**StL. 1936-41, 46-51
Fewest:
6 **NL:**Chi. 1905-10
5 **AL:**NY 1919-23

HOME RUNS

Seasons Leading League
Most:
25 **AL:**StL./Balt. 1924-31, 33, 37, 43, 47-49,
51, 87, 2006, 08-11, 13, 17-19
22 **NL:**Bos./Mil./Atl. 1878, 93-94, 96, 98-1900,
02-03, 05-08, 10-11, 45, 64, 70-72, 77-78
Fewest:
28 **NL:**Pitt. 1888, 95-96, 98, 1902-05, 12-13,
15-18, 20-21, 35, 40, 46, 58, 60-61, 65, 69, 75,
2004, 13, 15
25 **AL:**Clev. 1903-04, 07, 11, 14, 18, 20-21, 23,
25, 27, 32-34, 36-37, 39-40, 45, 51, 53, 76,
78, 94, 2017

Seasons, Consecutive, Leading League
Most:
8 **AL:**StL. 1924-31
5 **NL:**Phil. 1927-31
NY 1940-44
Fewest:
6 **AL:**Balt. 1956-61
5 **NL:**Cin. 1921-25
Mil. 1953-57

WALKS

Seasons Leading League
Most:
24 **NL:**Chi. 1880, 88, 94, 1914, 25-27, 31,
54-58, 60, 62, 80, 87, 92, 2003, 06, 10-13
22 **AL:**Phil./KC/Oak. 1913, 15-19, 24, 33-36,
42, 55, 62, 64, 66, 79, 82-83, 93-94, 97
Fewest:
23 **AL:**Chi. 1906-09, 11, 15-19, 30, 39-41, 51,
55-57, 63-65, 82-83
20 **NL:**Pitt. 1887, 89, 1900-02, 06-07, 09-10,
19-20, 35-36, 42, 59-61, 80, 90-91

Seasons, Consecutive, Leading League
Most:
5 **AL:**Phil. 1915-19
NL: Chi. 1954-58
Fewest:
6 **NL:**Cin. 1922-27
5 **AL:**Chi. 1915-19

INTENTIONAL WALKS (Since 1955)

Seasons Leading League
Most:
16 **AL:**Det. 1956, 74, 85-86, 88-96, 98, 2008, 17
9 **NL:**Brk./LA 1960-61, 64, 67, 91-92, 2009-10,
12
Pitt. 1957-59, 62-63, 75, 97, 2002, 14
Fewest:
15 **AL:**Minn. 1965-66, 73-75, 92-94, 96,
2000-02, 04, 10, 20
12 **NL:**Brk./LA 1955-57, 69, 71, 73-78, 2000

Seasons, Consecutive, Leading League
Most:
9 **AL:**Det. 1988-96
4 **NL:**Mia. 2016-19
Fewest:
6 **NL:**LA 1973-78
3 **AL:**NY 1956-58
KC 1969-71, 2014-2016
Minn. 1973-75, 92-94, 2000-02

STRIKEOUTS

Seasons Leading League
Most:
36 **NL:**Brk./LA 1920, 22-28, 36, 40, 45-46,
48-63, 66, 74, 84, 97, 2014, 16-18
19 **AL:**NY 1923-24, 31-36, 47, 49-51, 57, 59,
81, 84, 2001, 09, 11
Fewest:
23 **NL:**Bos./Mil./Atl. 1907-11, 20, 23, 25, 28,
35-40, 42, 47, 56, 61, 68, 72, 87, 2005
16 **AL:**StL./Balt. 1907, 11, 14, 16-17, 26, 35-37,
40, 49-50, 88-89, 2008-09

Seasons, Consecutive, Leading League
Most:
16 **NL:**Brk./LA 1948-63
9 **AL:**Phil. 1902-10
Fewest:
6 **NL:**Bos. 1935-40
5 **AL:**Minn. 2011-15

WILD PITCHES

Most Wild Pitches, Game
10 **NL:**Lou. (Chi.) July 22, 1876
Since 1900:
6 **NL:**Cin. (SD) May 3, 1969
Hou. (LA) Apr. 10, 1979
Atl. (Hou.) Aug. 4(2g), 1979
Mtl. (Phil.) Apr. 10, 1982
Atl. (Ari.) July 24, 2017
AL: Cal. (Minn.) Apr. 13, 1991
Bos. (Minn.) May 27, 2009
LA (NL:Col.) June 22, 2009

Most Wild Pitches, Inning
5 **NL:**Chi. (SF) Apr. 14, 2013 (6th)
4 **AL:**Wash. (Chi.) Sept. 21, 1914 (4th)
Ana. (Sea.) July 25, 2004 (8th)
Sea. (Minn.) Aug. 17, 2008 (5th)

BALKS

Most Balks, Game
6 **NL:**Mil. (Chi.) May 4, 1963
5 **AL:**Mil. (NY) Apr. 10, 1988
Oak. (Sea.) Apr. 13, 1988

Most Balks, Both Clubs, Game
7 **NL:**Pitt. (4) Cin. (3) Apr. 13, 1963
Mil. (6) Chi. (1) May 4, 1963
6 **AL:**Mil. (5) NY (1) Apr. 10, 1988
Chi. (4) Cal. (2) Apr. 12, 1988

Fewest Balks, Both Clubs, Game (Most Innings)
0 **NL:**Bos. (Brk.) May 1, 1920 (26 inn)
AL: Chi. (Mil.) May 8, 1984 (25 inn)

Most Balks, Inning
3 **AL:**Clev. (Phil.) May 12, 1930 (3rd)
Det. (Oak.) May 3, 1988 (6th)
NL: Cin. (LA) Apr. 24, 1963 (2nd)
Mil. (Chi.) May 4, 1963 (3rd)
Pitt. (NY) Aug. 6, 1988 (8th)

CLUB GENERAL – SEASON

	AL:1901-1960 NL:1900-1961 8 clubs 154 games		AL:1961-1968 NL:1962-1968 10 clubs 162 games		AL:1969- NL:1969- 12-16 clubs 162 games

Most Games Played

AL:	162	Det. 1904	164	By many	163	By many
NL:	160	Cin. 1915	165	LA & SF 1962	164	Pitt. & StL. 1989

Fewest Games Played

AL:	147	Clev. 1945	159	Wash. 1966	158	Balt. 1971
NL:	149	Phil. 1907, 34	160	Cin. 1966	160	By many

Highest Percentage Games Won

AL:	.721	Clev. 1954 (111-43)	.673	NY 1961 (109-53)	.716	Sea. 2001 (116-46)
NL:	.763	Chi. 1906 (116-36)	.627	StL. 1967 (101-60)	.667	Cin. 1975 (108-54) NY 1986 (108-54)

Lowest Percentage Games Won

AL:	.235	Phil. 1916 (36-117)	.346	Wash. 1963 (56-106)	.265	Det. 2003 (43-119)
NL:	.248	Bos. 1935 (38-115)	.250	NY 1962 (40-120)	.315	Ari. 2004 (51-111)

Lowest Percentage Games Won, First Place

AL:	.575	Det. 1945 (88-65)	.568	Bos. 1967 (92-70)	.519	KC 1984 (84-78)
NL:	.564	LA 1959 (88-68)	.574	StL. 1964 (93-69)	.506	SD 2005 (82-80)

Highest Percentage Games Won, Last Place

AL:	.431	Chi. 1924 (66-87)	.440	NY 1966 (70-89)	.500	Cal. 1991 (81-81)
NL:	.454	NY 1915 (69-83)	.444	Hou. 1968 (72-90)	.500	Wash. 2005 (81-81)

Most Games Won

AL:	111	Clev. 1954	109	NY 1961	116	Sea. 2001
NL:	116	Chi. 1906	103	SF 1962	108	Cin. 1975; NY 1986

Fewest Games Won

AL:	36	Phil. 1916	56	Wash. 1963	43	Det. 2003
NL:	38	Bos. 1935	40	NY 1962	51	Ari. 2004

Most Games Won, Home

AL:	62	NY 1932	65	NY 1961	62	NY 1998
NL:	60	StL. 1942 Brk. 1953	61	SF 1962	64	Cin. 1975

Fewest Games Won, Home

AL:	18	StL. 1939	26	KC 1964	22	Det. 2019
NL:	20	Phil. 1923	22	NY 1962	24	Mtl. 1969

Most Games Won, Road

AL:	54	NY 1939	51	Det. 1961 Minn. 1965	59	Sea. 2001
NL:	60	Chi. 1906	52	StL. 1967	53	Cin. 1972, 76; NY 1986 Atl. 1993; SF 1993

Fewest Games Won, Road

AL:	13	Phil. 1916	24	Cal. 1961	19	Balt. 2018
NL:	13	Bos. 1935	17	NY 1963	17	Pitt. 2010

Most Games Lost

AL:	117	Phil. 1916	106	Wash. 1963	119	Det. 2003
NL:	115	Bos. 1935	120	NY 1962	111	Ari. 2004

Fewest Games Lost

AL:	43	Clev. 1954	53	NY 1961	46	Sea. 2001
NL:	36	Chi. 1906	60	StL. 1967	54	Cin. 1975; NY 1986

Most Games Lost, Home

AL:	59	StL. 1939	55	KC 1964	59	Det. 2019
NL:	55	Phil. 1923, 40, 45 Bos. 1923	58	NY 1962	57	Mtl. 1969

Fewest Games Lost, Home

AL:	15	NY 1932	16	NY 1961	19	NY 1998
NL:	17	StL. 1942 Brk. 1953	21	SF 1962	17	Cin. 1975

Most Games Lost, Road

AL:	64	Phil. 1916	57	Wash. 1963	62	Balt. 2018
NL:	65	Bos. 1935	64	NY 1963	64	Pitt. 2010

	AL:1901-1960 NL:1900-1961 8 clubs 154 games		AL:1961-1968 NL:1962-1968 10 clubs 162 games		AL:1969- NL:1969- 12-16 clubs 162 games	
Fewest Games Lost, Road						
AL:	20	NY 1939	30	Det. 1961 Minn. 1965	22	Sea. 2001
NL:	15	Chi. 1906	28	StL. 1967	28	Cin. 1976 NY 1986 Atl. & SF 1993
Most Games Tied						
AL:	10	Det. 1904	2	By many	3	Chi. 1974
NL:	9	StL. 1911	2	By many	3	Chi. 1981
Most Night Games						
AL:	87	Balt. 1960	107	Cal. 1964, 68	133	Tex. 1979, 89-90
NL:	105	LA 1961	118	Hou. 1964	134	Hou. 1984
Fewest Night Games (Since 1935)						
AL:	2	Det. 1939	66	Minn. 1961 Bos. & NY 1962	62	Clev. 1973
NL:	0	NY 1935-39	43	Chi. 1962-65	46	Chi. 1969
Most Night Games Won						
AL:	47	Balt. 1960	64	Det. 1968	80	Balt. 1980
NL:	61	LA 1961	70	StL. 1967	77	Atl. 1993
Fewest Night Games Won						
AL:	1	By many	25	Bos. 1966	24	Det. 2019
NL:	1	By many	11	Chi. 1962	17	Chi. 1980
Most Night Games Lost						
AL:	48	KC 1956	68	Wash. 1963	83	Sea. 1980
NL:	67	Phil. 1961	68	Hou. 1964	83	Atl. 1977
Fewest Night Games Lost						
AL:	1	By many	26	Det. & NY 1962	32	Oak. 1971 NY 2002
NL:	0	By many	26	Chi. 1963, 65	21	Chi. 1969
Most Extra-Inning Games						
AL:	31	Bos. 1943	26	NY 1964	26	Tex. 1976
NL:	27	Bos. 1943	27	LA 1967	27	Hou. 1990
Fewest Extra-Inning Games						
AL:	3	StL. 1936	9	KC 1961-62 Minn. & NY 1966 Det. 1967	4	LA 2016
NL:	5	Chi. & Cin. 1948	7	Mil. 1964	5	Col. 2017
Most Extra-Inning Games Won						
AL:	18	Clev. 1949	16	Clev. 1967	16	Balt. 1970, 2012
NL:	19	Pitt. 1959	15	StL. 1968	18	Mtl. 1988
Fewest Extra-Inning Games Won						
AL:	1	By many	3	KC 1962, 65	0	LA 2016
NL:	1	By many	2	Pitt. 1964 NY 1968	0	Mtl. 1969
Most Extra-Inning Games Lost						
AL:	18	StL. 1943	16	Bos. 1966	15	Clev. 1977, 89 Chi. 1988, 2013 Sea. 2013
NL:	17	Phil. 1924 Cin. 1942	17	LA 1967	17	NY 1978 Pitt. 1984
Fewest Extra-Inning Games Lost						
AL:	0	Phil. 1928	2	NY 1961	1	Oak. 1975 Tor. 2006 Sea. 2018
NL:	0	Cin. 1948	2	Cin.& Mil. 1964 Phil. 1968	1	Pitt. 1969 NY 1984 Mtl. 1987 SD 2001 SF 2002
Most Extra-Inning Games Tied						
AL:	6	Det. 1904 Bos. 1907	1	By many	1	By many
NL:	6	Phil. 1913	1	By many	2	Chi. 1981

	AL:1901-1960 NL:1900-1961 8 clubs 154 games		AL:1961-1968 NL:1962-1968 10 clubs 162 games		AL:1969- NL:1969- 12-16 clubs 162 games	
Most Doubleheaders						
AL:	44	Chi. 1943; Wash. 1945	34	Chi. 1961	22	NY 1972
NL:	46	Bos. 1945	30	NY 1962	22	NY 1969
Fewest Doubleheaders						
AL:	8	Det. 1910	14	Bos. & Minn. 1968	0	By many
NL:	6	LA 1961	8	LA 1966; StL. 1968	0	By many
Most Doubleheaders Won						
AL:	14	Clev. 1943; NY 43, 47 Wash. 1945 Bos. 1946	15	Chi. 1961	10	NY 1972
NL:	20	Chi. 1945	8	Cin.& Mil. 1964	11	NY 1969
Fewest Doubleheaders Won						
AL:	0	By many	1	Minn. 1964, 68 Cal. & Wash. 1968	0	By many
NL:	1	By many	0	SF 1963	0	By many
Most Doubleheaders Lost						
AL:	19	StL. 1937	12	Cal. 1961, 65	13	Chi. 1970
NL:	18	Chi. 1950 Bos. 1935	15	NY 1962	11	NY 1974
Fewest Doubleheaders Lost						
AL:	0	By many	1	By many	0	By many
NL:	0	By many	0	Cin. 1967	0	By many
Most Doubleheaders Split						
AL:	19	By many	17	KC 1965, 67 Bos. 1966	14	Oak. 1969
NL:	25	Phil. 1944	13	NY 1967	12	Chi. 1973
Most Players						
AL:	56	Phil. 1915	52	KC 1961	67	Sea. 2019
NL:	53	Brk. 1944	54	NY 1967	64	SF 2019
Fewest Players						
AL:	18	Bos. 1904	30	NY 1963 Bos. 1965	30	Balt. 1969
NL:	20	Chi. 1905	30	LA 1962	29	Cin. 1975-76
Most Pitchers						
AL:	27	Phil. 1915 KC 1955	24	KC 1965	42	Sea. 2019
NL:	24	Cin. 1912 Brk. 1944 Phil. 1946	27	NY 1967	37	SD 2002 Atl. 2015 Mia. 2020
Fewest Pitchers						
AL:	5	Bos. 1904	12	Bos.& Chi. 1965 Minn. 1967	11	Balt. 1972, 74 Oak. 1974 Bos. 1976
NL:	5	Bos. 1901	12	LA 1962, 65 SF 1962, 68 Cin. 1963	11	Phil. 1976 Atl. 1980
Most Starting Pitchers						
AL:	24	Phil. 1915	17	Wash. 1963 Cal. 1967	21	Tor. 2019
NL:	19	Brk. 1944 Phil. 1946	20	NY 1967	18	Pitt. 1996
Most Appearances by Relief Pitchers						
AL:	263	NY 1960	378	KC 1965	632	Bos. 2019
NL:	293	Chi. 1958	321	Cin. 1968	607	LA 2016
Fewest Appearances by Relief Pitchers						
AL:	9	Bos. 1904	168	Balt. 1961	139	Bos. 1974
NL:	8	StL. 1904	167	SF 1968	170	LA 1975
Most Pinch Hitters						
AL:	309	Wash. 1960	277	Wash. 1962	326	Mil. 1970
NL:	300	Cin. 1958	363	NY 1965	362	LA 2018 SF 2019
Most Managers						
AL:	4	Bos. 1907	3	Det. 1966 Chi. 1968	4	Tex. 1977
NL:	4	Chi. 1961	3	Chi. 1962	4	StL. 1980

GAMES

Same Clubs, Consecutive
12 **NL:**Bos. vs. Phil. Sept. 2-8, 1903
11 **AL:**Det. vs. StL. Sept. 8-14, 1904

One Day
3 **NL:**Brk. vs. Pitt. Sept. 1, 1890
Balt. vs. Lou. Sept. 7, 1896
Cin. vs. Pitt. Oct. 2, 1920
2 **AL:**By many

TIME

Shortest Game (9 innings)
0:51 **NL:**NY 6 Phil. 1 Sept. 28(1g), 1919
0:55 **AL:**StL. 6 NY 2 Sept. 26(2g), 1926

Shortest Doubleheader (18 innings)
2:07 **AL:**NY vs. StL. Sept. 26, 1926
2:20 **NL:**Chi. vs. Brk. Aug. 14, 1919

Longest Game
4:45 **AL:**NY 14 Bos. 11 Aug. 18(2g), 2006
4:30 **NL:**Ari. 10 Col 9 June 24, 2016
Phil. 17 Pitt. 5 July 6, 2018
Extra Innings:
8:06 **AL:**Chi. 7 Mil. 6 May 8, 1984 (25 inn)
7:23 **NL:**SF 8 NY 6 May 31(2g), 1964 (23 inn)

Longest Doubleheader
7:53 **AL:**Clev. vs. Chi. June 28, 2013
6:46 **NL:**Brk. vs. NY Aug. 7, 1952
Extra Innings:
9:52 **NL:**SF vs. NY May 31, 1964 (32 inn)
9:05 **AL:**KC vs. Det. June 17, 1967 (28 inn)

INNINGS

Most Innings, Game
26 **NL:**Brk. (1) Bos. (1) May 1, 1920
25 **AL:**Chi. (7) Mil. (6) May 8, 1984

Most Innings, 2 Consecutive Games
45 **NL:**Bos. May 1-3, 1920
37 **AL:**Mil. May 12-13, 1972
Minn. May 12-13, 1972

Most Innings, 3 Consecutive Games
58 **NL:**Brk. May 1-3, 1920
46 **AL:**Mil. May 10-13, 12-14, 1972
Minn. May 10-13, 12-14, 1972

Most Innings, 2 Consecutive Games, Same Clubs
40 **NL:**Bos. vs. Chi. May 14-17, 1927
37 **AL:**Mil. vs. Minn. May 12-13, 1972

Most Innings, Opening-Day Game
16 **AL:**Tor. (7) Clev. (4) Apr. 5, 2012
14 **NL:**Phil. (5) Brk. (5) Apr. 17, 1923
Pitt. (4) Mil. (3) Apr. 15, 1958
Pitt. (6) StL. (2) Apr. 8, 1969
Cin. (2) LA (1) Apr. 7, 1975
Col. (11) NY (9) Apr. 26, 1995
NY (1) Phil. (0) Mar. 31, 1998

Most Innings, Shutout
24 **NL:**Hou. (1) NY (0) Apr. 15, 1968
20 **AL:**Oak. (1) Cal. (0) July 9, 1971

Most Innings, 0-0 Game
19 **NL:**Brk. vs. Cin. Sept. 11, 1946
18 **AL:**Det. vs. Wash. July 16, 1909

Most Innings, 1-0 Game
24 **NL:**Hou. vs. NY Apr. 15, 1968
20 **AL:**Oak. vs. Cal. July 9, 1971

Most Innings, Tie Game
26 **NL:**Brk. vs. Bos. May 1, 1920 (1-1)
24 **AL:**Det. vs. Phil. July 21, 1945 (1-1)

FIRST PLACE

Most Seasons
49 **AL:**NY 1921-23, 26-28, 32, 36-39, 41-43,
47, 49-53, 55-58, 60-64, 76-78, 80-81,
94, 96, 98-2006, 09, 11-12, 19
36 **NL:**Brk./LA 1890, 99-1900, 16, 20, 41, 47, 49,
52-53, 55-56, 59, 63, 65-66, 74, 77-78, 81,
83, 85, 88, 94-95, 2004, 08-09, 13-20

Most Seasons, Consecutive
11 **NL:**Atl. 1995-2005
9 **AL:**NY 1998-2006

Fewest Decisions to Clinch
136 **AL:**NY 1941 (Sept. 4)
137 **NL:**NY 1904 (Sept. 22)

Earliest Date To Clinch
Sept. 4 **AL:**NY 1941 (136 dec)
Sept. 7 **NL:**Cin. 1975 (142 dec)

Days In First Place
Most:
182 **AL:**Sea. 2001 162g (entire season)
(not including Sept. 11-16, 2001)
Chi. 2005 162g (entire season)
NL:SF 2003 161g (entire season)
Fewest (by team finishing in 1st place):
3 **NL:**NY 1951 154g (before playoff)
4 **AL:**Minn. 2006 162g

Largest Gain, Standings, From Previous Season
9 **NL:**Brk. 1899 (10th to 1st)
Since 1900:
8 **AL:**Bos. 1967 (9th to 1st)
NL:NY 1969 (9th to 1st)

LAST PLACE

Most Seasons
35 **NL:**Phil. 1883, 1904, 19-21, 23, 26-28, 30,
36, 38-42, 44-45, 47, 58-61, 71-73, 88-89,
92, 96-97, 2000, 14-15, 17
33 **AL:**Phil./KC/Oak. 1915-21, 35-36, 38, 40-
43, 45-46, 50, 54, 56, 60-61, 64-65, 67,
77, 79, 93, 97-98, 2009, 15-17

Most Seasons, Consecutive
7 **AL:**Phil. 1915-21
6 **NL:**SD 1969-74

GAMES AHEAD

Most, End of Season (since 1900)
30.0 **AL:**Clev. 1995
27.5 **NL:**Pitt. 1902

GAMES BEHIND

Most, End Of Season
84.0 **NL:**Clev. 1899
Since 1900:
66.5 **NL:**Bos. 1906
64.5 **AL:**StL. 1939

Fewest, End Of Season, Last Place Club
10.0 **AL:**Cal. 1987
AL: Tex. 1987
9.0 **NL:**Wash. 2005

PERCENTAGE

One Month (Minimum: 15 decisions)
Highest:
.947 **UA:**StL. May 1884 (18-1)
.944 **NL:**Prov. Aug. 1884 (17-1)
Since 1900:
.900 **AL:**Det. Apr. 1984 (18-2)
.897 **NL:**Chi. Aug. 1906 (26-3)
Lowest:
.036 **NL:**Pitt. Aug. 1890 (1-27)
Clev. Sept. 1899 (1-27)
Since 1900:
.043 **AL:**Balt. Apr. 1988 (1-22)
.111 **NL:**Hou. July 2012 (3-24)

PLAYOFF WINNERS

One-Game Playoff:
AL: Clev. (Bos.) 1948
NY (Bos.) 1978
Sea. (Cal.) 1995
Chi. (Minn.) 2008
Minn. (Det.) 2009
TB (Tex.) 2013
NL: Hou. (LA) 1980
Chi. (SF) 1998
NY (Cin.) 1999
Col. (SD) 2007
Mil. (Chi.) 2018
LA (Col.) 2018

Best-Of-Three Series:
NL: StL. (Brk.) 1946 (2-0)
NY (Brk.) 1951 (2-1)
LA (Mil.) 1959 (2-0)
SF (LA) 1962 (2-1)
AL:none

GAMES WON

Opening Games Won, Consecutive Seasons
10 **NL:**Bos. 1887-96
Since 1900:
9 **AL:**StL. 1937-45
Sea. 2007-15
NL:NY 1975-83
Cin. 1983-91

Most Seasons, 100 or more Games Won
21 **AL:**NY 1927-28, 32, 36-37, 39, 41-42, 54, 61, 63, 77-78, 80, 98, 2002-04, 09, 18-19
9 **NL:**StL. 1931, 42-44, 67, 85, 2004-05, 15

Most Seasons, Consecutive, 100 or more Wins
3 **AL:**Phil. 1929-31
Balt. 1969-71
NY 2002-04
Hou. 2017-19
NL: StL. 1942-44
Atl. 1997-99

Most Wins, 2 Consecutive Seasons
223 **NL:**Chi. 1906-07
217 **AL:**Balt. 1969-70

Most Wins, 3 Consecutive Seasons
322 **NL:**Chi. 1906-08
318 **AL:**Balt. 1969-71

Most Wins, Consecutive, Season
26 **NL:**NY Sept. 7-30, 1916 (excludes tie)
22 **AL:**Clev. Aug. 24-Sept. 14, 2017

Most Wins, Consecutive, Season (no ties)
22 **AL:**Clev. Aug. 24-Sept. 14, 2017
21 **NL:**Chi. Sept. 4-27, 1935

Most Wins, Consecutive, Start of Season
20 **UA:**StL. Apr. 20-May 22, 1884
13 **NL:**Atl. Apr. 6-21, 1982
AL: Mil. Apr. 6-20, 1987

Most Wins, vs. One Opponent, Season
21 **NL:**Chi. (Bos.) 1909 (lost 1)
Pitt. (Cin.) 1937 (lost 1)
Chi. (Cin.) 1945 (lost 1)
AL:NY (StL.) 1927 (lost 1)

Most Wins, Consecutive, vs. One Opponent
27 **NL:**Pro. (Det.) June 14, 1883-Sept. 18, 1884
23 **AL:**Balt. (KC) May 10, 1969-Aug. 2, 1970
NL Since 1900:
20 **NL:**StL. (Phil.) July 15, 1927-July 20, 1928
Pitt. (Cin.) May 31, 1937-Apr. 24, 1938

Most Wins, Consecutive Seasons, vs. One Opponent
40 **NL:**Pitt. (StL.) 1907-08
37 **AL:**Phil. (StL.) 1910-11
Chi. (Phil.) 1915-16
NY (Phil.) 1919-20
NY (StL.) 1926-27

Most Wins, vs. Pennant Winner, Season
16 **NL:**StL. (Chi.) 1945 (lost 6)
14 **AL:**Phil. (Det.) 1909 (lost 8)
Minn. (Oak.) 1973 (lost 4)

Most Home Wins, vs. One Club, Season
16 **NL:**Brk. (Pitt.) 1890 (lost 2)
Phil. (Pitt.) 1890 (lost 1)
Since 1900:
13 **NL:**NY (Phil.) 1904 (lost 2)
12 **AL:**Chi. (StL.) 1915 (lost 0)

Most Home Wins, Consecutive, vs. One Club
32 **NL:**Balt. (Lou.) June 7, 1894-July 11, 1899
Since 1900:
27 **AL:**Clev. (StL./Balt.) Aug. 13, 1952-Aug. 15, 1954
25 **NL:**StL. (Cin.) Apr. 27, 1929-May 31, 1931

Most Road Wins, Consecutive, vs. One Club
19 **NL:**Brk. (Cin.) June 22, 1947-May 22, 1949
18 **AL:**Bos. (NY) Oct. 3, 1911-June 2, 1913
NY (Balt.) July 11, 2018-Sept. 4(1g), 2020

Most Road Wins, vs. One Club, Season, No Losses
11 **NL:**Pitt. (StL.) 1908
Chi. (Bos.) 1909
Brk. (Phil.) 1945
AL: Chi. (Phil.) 1915
NY (StL.) 1927, 39
Clev. (Bos.) 1954

Most Home Wins, Consecutive, Season
27 **AA:**StL. Apr. 26-July 16, 1885
26 **NL:**NY Sept. 7-30, 1916 (excludes tie)
24 **AL:**Bos. June 25-Aug. 13, 1988

Most Road Wins, Consecutive, Season
17 **NL:**NY May 9-29, 1916
AL: Det. Apr. 3-May 24, 1984

Most Wins, One Month
29 **NL:**NY Sept. 1916 (lost 5)
28 **AL:**NY Aug. 1938 (lost 4)

Most Wins, One Day
3 **NL:**Brk. (Pitt.) Sept. 1, 1890
Balt. (Lou.) Sept. 7, 1896
2 **AL:**By many

Most Wins, 2 Consecutive Days
5 **NL:**Balt. Sept. 7-8, 1896
4 **AL:**By many

Most Days, 2 Wins vs. One Club, Season
7 **AL:**Chi. (Phil.) 1943
NL: Chi. (Cin.) 1945

GAMES LOST

Opening Games Lost, Consecutive Seasons
- 10 **AL:**Oak. 2005-14
- 9 **NL:**NY 1893-1901
-     Atl. 1972-80

Most Seasons, 100 or more Games Lost
- 16 **AL:**Phil./KC/Oak. 1915-16, 19-21, 36, 40, 43, 46, 50, 54, 56, 61, 64-65, 79
- 14 **NL:**Phil. 1904, 21, 23, 27-28, 30, 36, 38-42, 45, 61

Most Seasons, Consecutive, 100 or more Games Lost
- 5 **NL:**Phil. 1938-42
- 4 **AL:**Wash. 1961-64

Most Losses, 2 Consecutive Seasons
- 231 **NL:**NY 1962-63 (162 g)
- 226 **AL:**Phil. 1915-16
- 220 **NL:**Phil. 1941-42(154 g)

Most Losses, 3 Consecutive Seasons
- 340 **NL:**NY 1962-64 (162 g)
- 324 **AL:**Phil. 1915-17
- 323 **NL:**Phil. 1940-42 (154 g)

Most Losses, Consecutive, Season
- 26 **AA:**Lou. May 22-June 22, 1889
- 24 **NL:**Clev. Aug. 26-Sept. 16, 1899
-     **Since 1900:**
- 23 **NL:**Phil. July 29-Aug. 20, 1961
- 21 **AL:**Balt. Apr. 4-28, 1988

Most Losses, Consecutive, Start of Season
- 21 **AL:**Balt. Apr. 4-28, 1988
- 14 **NL:**Chi. Apr. 1-20, 1997

Most Home Losses, Consecutive, Season
- 20 **AL:**StL. June 3-July 7, 1953
- 15 **NL:**NY Aug. 1-Sept. 3, 2002

Most Road Losses, Consecutive, Season
- 41 **NL:**Pitt. July 18-Sept. 12, 1890
- 22 **AL:**Phil. July 11(2g)-Aug. 24(1g), 1943
-     **NL Since 1900:**
- 22 **NL:**NY June 16-July 28, 1963

Most Losses, One Month
- 29 **AL:**Wash. July 1909 (won 5)
- 27 **NL:**Pitt. Aug. 1890 (won 1)
-     Clev. Sept. 1899 (won 1)
-     StL. Sept. 1908 (won 7)
-     Brk. Sept. 1908 (won 6)
-     Phil. Sept. 1939 (won 6)

Most Losses, One Day
- 3 **NL:**Pitt. (Brk.) Sept. 1, 1890
-     Lou. (Balt.) Sept. 7, 1896
- 2 **AL:**By many

Most Losses, 2 Consecutive Days
- 5 **NL:**Lou. Sept. 7-8, 1896
- 4 **AL:**By many

NO-HIT GAMES

Most No-Hit Games, vs. One Club, Season
- 2 **AL:**StL. (Chi.) 1917
-    **NL:**Mil. (Phil.) 1960

EXTRA-INNING GAMES

Most Consecutive Extra-Inning Games, Season
- 5 **AL:**Det. Sept. 9-13, 1908
- 4 **NL:**Pitt. Aug. 18-22, 1917
-     Brk. Sept. 20-23, 1924
-     Cin. Aug. 21-23, 1926
-     Pitt. May 8-15, 1938
-     Cin. Sept. 5-7, 1939
-     SF July 7-10, 1987
-     Mil. Sept. 15-19, 1999

Most Consecutive Games, Season, Extra-Innings, Same Clubs
- 4 **AL:**Chi. vs. Det. Sept. 9-12, 1908
-     Clev. vs. StL. May 1-5, 1910
-     Bos. vs. StL. May 31-June 2, 1943
-     Tex. vs. Sea. Sept. 16-19, 2002
- 3 **NL:**Brk. vs. Pitt. Aug. 20-22, 1917
-     Cin. vs. Bos. June 4-7, 1925
-     Bos. vs. Cin. Aug. 21-22, 1926
-     Bos. vs. Phil. July 2-3, 1928
-     NY vs. Chi. Sept. 13-15, 1932
-     Pitt. vs. Cin. Sept. 6-7, 1939
-     Chi. vs. Pitt. Aug. 18-20, 1961
-     Mtl. vs. NY June 17-19, 1975
-     Cin. vs. NY May 5-7, 1980
-     Atl. vs. LA Aug. 5-7, 1982
-     Mil. vs. Chi. Sept. 17-19, 1999
-     NY vs. Hou. July 31-Aug. 2, 2001
-     Cin. vs. Phil. July 8-10, 2010
-     Phil. vs. AL:Chi. July 13-14, 2013
-     NY vs. Phil. May 30-June 1, 2014
-     Pitt. vs. StL. May 1-3, 2015
-     Chi. vs. Mil. Sept. 21-23, 2017

DOUBLEHEADERS

Most Consecutive Doubleheaders, Season
- 9 **NL:**Bos. Sept. 4-15, 1928
- 8 **AL:**Wash. July 27-Aug. 5, 1909

Most Doubleheaders Won, Consecutive, Season
- 5 **AL:**NY Aug. 30-Sept. 4, 1906
- 4 **NL:**Brk. Sept. 1-4, 1924
-     NY Sept. 10-14, 1928

Most Doubleheaders Lost, Consecutive, Season
- 5 **NL:**Bos. Sept. 8-14, 1928
- 4 **AL:**Bos. June 29-July 5, 1921

Most Doubleheaders, Consecutive, Same Clubs, Season
- 5 **AL:**Phil. vs. Wash. Aug. 5-10, 1901
- 4 **NL:**NY vs. Bos. Sept. 10-14, 1928

PERSONNEL

Most Players, Game
27 **AL:**KC (Cal.) Sept. 10, 1969
26 **NL:**LA (Cin.) Oct. 6, 1985
Extra-Inning Game:
30 **AL:**Oak. (Chi.) Sept. 19, 1972 (15 inn)
NL: Col. (LA) Sept. 15, 2015 (16 inn)
Ari. (StL.) Sept. 24, 2019 (19 inn)
Doubleheader:
42 **AL:**Tex. (Balt.) Sept. 7, 1989
Minn. (Chi.) Oct. 3, 1991 (22 inn)
41 **NL:**Pitt. (Phil.) May 13, 1956
SD (SF) May 30, 1977
Doubleheader, Extra Innings:
47 **NL:**Phil. (Wash.) Sept. 11, 2018 (19 inn)

Most Players, Both Clubs, Game
46 **AL:**NY (24) Bos. (22) Oct. 2, 2005
LA (25) Sea. (21) Sept. 16, 2014
45 **NL:**Chi. (24) Mtl. (21) Sept. 5, 1978
Atl. (24) NY (21) Sept. 29, 2002
Wash. (24) Pitt. (21) Sept. 25, 2016
LA (23) Col. (22) Sept. 30, 2017
Pitt. (23) Wash. (22) Oct. 1, 2017
LA (23) SF (22) Sept. 29, 2019
Extra-Inning Game:
58 **NL:**Col. (30) LA (28) Sept. 15, 2015 (16 inn)
54 **AL:**Sea. (29) Tex. (25) Sept. 25, 1992 (16 inn)
Doubleheader:
74 **NL:**SD (41) SF (33) May 30, 1977
71 **AL:**Tex. (42) Balt. (29) Sept. 7, 1989
TB (36) Balt. (35) Sept. 3, 2019
Doubleheader, Extra Innings:
85 **NL:**Phil. (47) Wash. (38) Sept. 11, 2018 (19 inn)
83 **AL:**Minn. (42) Chi. (41) Oct. 3, 1991 (22 inn)

Most Pitchers, Game
11 **NL:**SF (Col.) Oct. 4, 2015
10 **AL:**Balt. (NY) Sept. 12, 2004
Minn. (Clev.) Sept. 26, 2017
Extra-Inning Game:
13 **NL:**Col. (LA) Sept. 15, 2015 (16 inn)
SF (AL:Bos.) Sept. 17, 2019 (15 inn)
Ari. (StL.) Sept. 24, 2019 (19 inn)
SF (Col.) Sept. 24, 2019 (16 inn)
12 **AL:**LA (Oak.) Sept. 4, 2017 (11 inn)
Bos. (Tor.) Sept. 5, 2017 (19 inn)
TB (Bos.) Sept. 15, 2017 (15 inn)
Doubleheader:
13 **NL:**Mil. (Phil.) May 12, 1963 (23 inn)
SD (SF) May 30, 1977
Col. (SD) June 28 1994 (20 inn)
Fla. (Ari.) May 20, 2009 (22 inn)
12 **AL:**Clev. (Det.) Sept. 7, 1959
Cal. (Balt.) June 6, 1967
Cal. (Det.) Sept. 30, 1967
Chi. (Oak.) Sept. 7, 1970
Det. (NL:Pitt.) Apr. 25, 2018
Chi. (Clev.) July 28, 2020
Doubleheader, Extra Innings:
14 **AL:**Tor. (NY) Sept. 12, 2015 (20 inn)
NL: Phil. (Wash.) Sept. 11, 2018 (19 inn)
Wash. (Phil.) Sept. 11, 2018 (19 inn)

Most Pitchers, Both Clubs, Game
18 **NL:**StL. (10) Pitt. (8) Sept. 30, 2007
AL:LA (9) Tex. (9) Oct. 3, 2015
Bos. (9) Tor. (9) Sept. 11, 2016
Extra-Inning Game:
25 **NL:**SF (13) Col. (12) Sept. 24, 2019 (16 inn)
21 **AL:**TB (11) Balt. (10) Sept. 20, 2013 (18 inn)
TB (12) Bos. (9) Sept. 15, 2017 (15 inn)
Doubleheader:
22 **NL:**Mil. (11) NY (11) July 26, 1964
StL. (11) Phil. (11) June 20, 1989
Chi. (12) Phil. (10) Sept. 19, 2003
21 **AL:**Det. (11) KC (10) July 23, 1961
Doubleheader, Extra Innings:
28 **NL:**Phil. (14) Wash. (14) Sept. 11, 2018 (19 inn)
26 **AL:**Tor. (14) NY (12) Sept. 12, 2015 (20 inn)

Most Pitchers, Shutout Win
8 **AL:**TB (KC) Oct. 2, 2010
LA (Oak.) Aug. 30, 2014
LA (Tex.) Sept. 11, 2018
NL: Atl. (Pitt.) Oct. 3, 2012
LA (Ari.) May 3, 2015 (13 inn)
LA (SF) Sept. 29, 2019
Extra-Inning Game:
9 **AL:**Clev. (Det.) Sept. 17, 2016 (10 inn)

Most Pitchers, Inning
6 **AL:**Oak. (Clev.) Sept. 3, 1983 (9th)
Sea. (NY) Sept. 5, 2007 (7th)
5 **NL:**By many; last:
Col. (SD) Sept. 14, 2019 (8th)

Most Pitchers, Both Clubs, Inning
8 **NL:**LA (5) NY (3) Aug. 26, 1987 (8th)
LA (4) StL. (4) May 14, 1995 (8th)
StL. (4) SD (4) Aug. 22, 2015 (7th)
LA (5) Ari. (3) July 29, 2016 (7th)
AL:NY (4) Mil. (4) May 25, 1992 (8th)
Minn. (4) NY (4) Aug. 8, 1993 (7th)
Clev. (5) Minn. (3) May 10, 2000 (7th)
Tex. (4) Oak. (4) July 26, 2002 (7th)
Bos. (4) Tex. (4) Aug. 10, 2005 (8th)
ML: Fla. (4) Tex. (4), July 3, 2011 (8th)

LEAGUE RECORDS – SEASON

BATTING

	AL:1901-1960 NL:1900-1961 8 clubs 154 games		AL:1961-1968 NL:1962-1968 10 clubs 162 games		AL:1969- NL:1969- 12-16 clubs 162 games	
Highest Batting Average						
AL	.292	1921	.256	1961	.277	1996
NL	.303	1930	.261	1962	.268	1999
Lowest Batting Average						
AL	.239	1908	.230	1968	.239	1972
NL	.239	1908	.243	1968	.246	1989
Highest Slugging Percentage						
AL	.421	1936	.395	1961	.445	1996
NL	.448	1930	.393	1962	.432	2000
Lowest Slugging Percentage						
AL	.304	1908	.339	1968	.343	1972
NL	.306	1908	.341	1968	.361	1976
Most Tie Games						
AL	19	1910	4	1961, 64	3	1974, 80
NL	16	1913	4	1965	4	1981
Fewest Tie Games						
AL	0	1930	0	1963, 65	0	Many seasons
NL	0	1925, 54, 58	1	1963, 66-67	0	Many seasons
Most Extra-Inning Games						
AL	91	1943	91	1965	128	2014
NL	82	1920, 57	93	1967	144	2011
Most At-Bats						
AL	43,747	1936	55,239	1962	83,557	2019
NL	43,891	1936	55,449	1962	89,489	2007
Fewest At-Bats						
AL	39,914	1913	53,709	1968	64,642	1971
NL	39,326	1907	54,803	1963	65,156	1978
Most Runs						
AL	7,009	1936	7,342	1961	12,208	1996
NL	7,025	1930	7,278	1962	12,976	2000
Fewest Runs						
AL	4,267	1909	5,532	1968	7,472	1971
NL	4,136	1908	5,577	1968	7,522	1988
Most Hits						
AL	12,657	1936	14,068	1962	21,922	1996
NL	13,260	1930	14,453	1962	23,880	1999
Fewest Hits						
AL	9,703	1908	12,359	1968	15,957	1971
NL	9,566	1907	13,351	1968	16,215	1989
Most Total Bases						
AL	18,427	1936	21,762	1962	36,676	2019
NL	19,572	1930	21,781	1962	38,305	2000
Fewest Total Bases						
AL	12,337	1908	18,221	1968	23,537	1971
NL	12,142	1907	18,737	1968	23,767	1976
Most Extra-Base Hits						
AL	3,706	1936	4,190	1962	8,181	2019
NL	3,903	1930	3,977	1962	8,235	2006
Fewest Extra-Base Hits						
AL	1,879	1909	3,316	1968	4,177	1976
NL	1,793	1907	3,245	1968	4,264	1976
Most Singles						
AL	9,214	1921	9,878	1962	15,072	1980
NL	9,476	1922	10,476	1962	15,856	1999
Fewest Singles						
AL	7,573	1959	9,043	1968	11,696	1971
NL	7,466	1956	9,796	1963	11,536	1989

	AL:1901-1960 NL:1900-1961 8 clubs 154 games		AL:1961-1968 NL:1962-1968 10 clubs 162 games		AL:1969- NL:1969- 12-16 clubs 162 games	
Most Doubles						
AL	2,400	1936	2,238	1962	4,318	2019
NL	2,386	1930	2,161	1964	4,898	2007
Fewest Doubles						
AL	1,271	1909	1,874	1968	2,385	1969
NL	1,148	1907	1,984	1963	2,455	1969
Most Triples						
AL	694	1921	408	1966	644	1977
NL	684	1911, 12	453	1962	561	2006, 09
Fewest Triples						
AL	267	1959	333	1964	334	2017
NL	323	1942	359	1968	386	1973
Most Home Runs						
AL	1,091	1959	1,552	1962	3,478	2019
NL	1,263	1955	1,449	1962	3,298	2019
ML	2,294	1956	3,001	1962	6,776	2019
Fewest Home Runs						
AL	104	1907	1,104	1968	1,122	1976
NL	126	1906	891	1968	1,113	1976
ML	242	1907	1,995	1968	2,235	1976
Most Clubs, 100 or more Home Runs						
AL	8	1958, 60	10	1964	15	2013, 15-19
NL	8	1956, 58-59, 61	10	1962	16	1998-2010, 12
ML	16	1958	19	1962	30	1998-2010, 12, 16-19
Fewest Clubs, 100 or more Home Runs						
AL	0	Many seasons; last: 1945	6	1968	5	1976
NL	0	Many seasons; last: 1943	4	1968	5	1976
ML	0	Many seasons; last: 1924	10	1968	10	1976
Most Grand Slam Home Runs						
AL	37	1938	48	1961	89	2000
NL	35	1950	37	1962	87	2000
ML	68	1950	77	1961	176	2000
Fewest Grand Slam Home Runs						
AL	1	1907, 09, 15	20	1967	23	1976
NL	1	1920	16	1968	21	1976, 82
ML	3	1907	38	1968	44	1976
Most Home Runs, Pinch-hitters						
AL	27	1953, 58	51	1961	53	1980
NL	42	1958, 59	45	1962	144	2019
ML	69	1958	84	1962	190	2019
Most Grand Slam Home Runs, Pinch-hitters						
AL	5	1953	7	1961	7	2004
NL	4	1959	3	1963, 67	9	1978, 95
ML	8	1953	7	1961	13	1978, 2004
Most Runs Batted In						
AL	6,520	1936	6,841	1961	11,583	1996
NL	6,582	1930	6,760	1962	12,321	1999
Most Sacrifice Hits						
AL	1,731	1917	779	1965	1,016	1978
NL	1,655	1908	794	1968	1,190	2004, 06
Fewest Sacrifice Hits						
AL	531	1958	673	1964	245	2019
NL	511	1957	655	1962	531	2019
Most Sacrifice Flies (Since 1954)						
AL	370	1954	448	1961	765	1979
NL	425	1954	410	1962	809	2000
Fewest Sacrifice Flies (Since 1954)						
AL	312	1959	348	1967	484	1969
NL	304	1959	363	1966	430	1969

	AL:1901-1960 NL:1900-1961 8 clubs 154 games		AL:1961-1968 NL:1962-1968 10 clubs 162 games		AL:1969- NL:1969- 12-16 clubs 162 games	
Most Walks						
AL	5,627	1949	5,902	1961	8,592	1996
NL	4,545	1950	5,264	1962	9,735	2000
Fewest Walks						
AL	2,611	1904	4,881	1968	6,127	1976
NL	2,906	1921	4,275	1968	5,793	1988
Most Intentional Walks (since 1955)						
AL	353	1957	534	1965	734	1993
NL	506	1956	804	1967	964	2002
Fewest Intentional Walks (since 1955)						
AL	257	1959	290	1961	275	2019
NL	389	1957	451	1962	478	2019
Most Hit By Pitch						
AL	464	1911	426	1968	1,003	2018
NL	513	1900	404	1965	1,048	2019
Fewest Hit By Pitch						
AL	132	1947	316	1965	372	1982
NL	156	1943	327	1964	249	1984
Most Strikeouts						
AL	6,082	1959	9,956	1964	21,415	2019
NL	6,825	1960	9,649	1965	21,408	2019
Fewest Strikeouts						
AL	3,245	1924	8,330	1961	9,143	1976
NL	3,359	1926	9,032	1962	9,602	1976
Most Stolen Bases						
AL	1,809	1912	811	1968	1,734	1987
NL	1,692	1911	788	1962	1,959	1999
Fewest Stolen Bases						
AL	278	1950	540	1964	863	1970
NL	337	1954	636	1964	817	1969
Most Grounded into Double Plays						
AL	1,181	1950	1,256	1961	1,969	1980
NL	1,105	1933	1,251	1962	2,085	2002
Fewest Grounded into Double Plays						
AL	890	1945	1,060	1967	1,442	1976
NL	820	1945	1,120	1963	1,198	1991
Most Left on Base						
AL	9,628	1936	11,683	1961	16,844	2013
NL	9,424	1945	11,414	1962	18,939	2000
Fewest Left on Base						
AL	8,618	1958	10,667	1966	13,507	1976
NL	8,254	1920	10,994	1966	13,295	1988

FIELDING

	AL:1901-1960 NL:1900-1961 8 clubs 154 games		AL:1961-1968 NL:1962-1968 10 clubs 162 games		AL:1969- NL:1969- 12-16 clubs 162 games	
Highest Fielding Average						
AL	.979	1958	.980	1964	.985	2013
NL	.977	1956	.978	1968	.985	2013
Lowest Fielding Average						
AL	.937	1901	.976	1961	.975	1975
NL	.949	1903	.975	1962	.976	1974
Most Total Chances						
AL	53,194	1910	62,296	1968	90,415	2015
NL	52,196	1917	63,636	1968	99,083	1998
Fewest Total Chances						
AL	47,293	1958	62,042	1966	74,387	1971
NL	47,539	1955	62,857	1962	74,562	1991
Most Chances Accepted						
AL	50,870	1910	60,997	1964	89,008	2015
NL	50,419	1920	62,247	1968	97,233	1998
Fewest Chances Accepted						
AL	46,086	1938	60,550	1961	72,875	1971
NL	46,404	1955	61,302	1962	72,495	1990
Most Putouts						
AL	33,830	1916	43,847	1964	65,418	2013
NL	33,724	1917	44,042	1968	69,742	2007
Fewest Putouts						
AL	32,235	1938	43,281	1961	51,821	1975
NL	32,296	1906	43,470	1962	52,000	1978
Most Assists						
AL	17,167	1910	17,269	1961	25,626	1980
NL	16,759	1920	18,205	1968	27,513	1998
Fewest Assists						
AL	13,219	1958	17,048	1963	21,001	1971
NL	13,345	1956	17,681	1963	20,351	1990
Most Errors						
AL	2,889	1901	1,506	1961	1,989	1977
NL	2,590	1904	1,586	1964	1,915	1999
Fewest Errors						
AL	1,002	1958	1,261	1964	1,323	2009
NL	1,082	1956	1,389	1968	1,387	2017
Most Passed Balls						
AL	178	1914	211	1965	267	1987
NL	202	1905	216	1962	217	1969
Fewest Passed Balls						
AL	53	1949	147	1963, 66	127	1976
NL	65	1936	148	1968	122	1980
Most Double Plays						
AL	1,487	1949	1,585	1961	2,368	1980
NL	1,337	1951	1,596	1962	2,484	2002
Fewest Double Plays						
AL	818	1912	1,388	1967-68	1,821	1976
NL	1,007	1920	1,431	1963	1,527	1991
Most Triple Plays						
AL	7	1922, 36	5	1968	10	1979
NL	7	1905, 10, 29	5	1964-65	5	1991
Fewest Triple Plays						
AL	0	1904, 33, 42, 56	0	1961-62	0	1974, 75, 87, 93, 98, 2003, 05
NL	0	1928, 38, 41, 43, 45-46, 59, 61	1	1963	0	1974, 84, 2001, 06, 13, 18-19

PITCHING

	AL:1901-1960 NL:1900-1961 8 clubs 154 games		AL:1961-1968 NL:1962-1968 10 clubs 162 games		AL:1969- NL:1969- 12-16 clubs 162 games	
Lowest Earned Run Average						
AL	2.73	1914	2.98	1968	3.06	1972
NL	2.62	1916	2.99	1968	3.45	1988
Highest Earned Run Average						
AL	5.04	1936	4.02	1961	4.99	1996
NL	4.97	1930	3.94	1962	4.63	2000
Most Complete Games						
AL	1,100	1904	426	1968	650	1974
NL	1,089	1904	471	1968	546	1971
Fewest Complete Games						
AL	312	1960	323	1965	25	2018
NL	328	1961	402	1966	17	2018
Most Saves (since 1969)						
AL	–	–	–	–	644	2016
NL	–	–	–	–	707	2011
Fewest Saves (since 1969)						
AL	–	–	–	–	260	1974
NL	–	–	–	–	257	1974
Most Shutouts						
AL	146	1909	154	1968	193	1972
NL	164	1908	185	1968	202	2010
Fewest Shutouts						
AL	41	1930	100	1961	79	1996
NL	49	1925	95	1962	93	1999
Most No-Hit Games (9 or more innings)						
AL	5	1917	4	1962	5	1990
NL	3	1960	3	1963-64, 68	5	1969, 2014-15
ML	6	1915, 17	5	1962, 68	7	1990-91 2012, 15
Fewest No-Hit Games (9 or more innings)						
AL	0	Many seasons; last: 1960	0	1961, 63-64	0	Many seasons; last: 2017
NL	0	Many seasons; last: 1959	0	1966	0	Many seasons; last: 2019
ML	0	Many seasons; last: 1959	1	1961, 66	0	1982, 85, 89, 2000, 05
Most One-Hit Games						
AL	12	1910, 15	11	1968	19	2015
NL	12	1906, 11	15	1965	13	2010
Fewest One-Hit Games						
AL	0	1922, 26-27, 30	2	1962	3	1998, 2003, 05
NL	0	1924, 29, 32, 52	3	1962	2	1976
Most 1-0 Games Won						
AL	41	1908	38	1968	42	1971
NL	43	1907	44	1968	44	2010
Fewest 1-0 Games Won						
AL	4	1930, 36	16	1961	6	1996
NL	5	1932, 56	13	1962	12	1999
Most Games Won By One Run						
AL	217	1943	281	1967-68	368	1978
NL	223	1946	294	1968	413	1998
Fewest Games Won By One Run						
AL	157	1938	242	1963	272	2003
NL	170	1949	245	1968	286	1990
Most Earned Runs						
AL	6,120	1936	6,451	1961	11,241	1996
NL	6,046	1930	6,345	1962	11,884	2000
Fewest Earned Runs						
AL	3,414	1914	4,817	1968	6,650	1971
NL	3,258	1916	4,870	1968	6,695	1988

	AL:1901-1960 **NL:1900-1961** **8 clubs 154 games**			**AL:1961-1968** **NL:1962-1968** **10 clubs 162 games**		**AL:1969-** **NL:1969-** **12-16 clubs 162 games**
Most Wild Pitches						
AL	325	1936	513	1966	1,014	2018
NL	356	1961	550	1965	919	2016
Fewest Wild Pitches						
AL	166	1931	404	1962	491	1976
NL	174	1943	478	1967	443	1980
Most Balks						
AL	46	1950	51	1966	558	1988
NL	76	1950	147	1963	366	1988
Fewest Balks						
AL	18	1933, 41	29	1964	43	1973
NL	13	1936, 46, 56	25	1965	52	1971, 73
Most Pitchers 40 or more Games Won						
AL	1	1904, 08	0	1961-68	0	1969 to date
NL	0	1900-61	0	1962-68	0	1969 to date
Most Pitchers 30 or more Games Won						
AL	2	1912	1	1968	0	1969 to date
NL	2	1903-04	0	1962-68	0	1969 to date
Most Pitchers 20 or more Games Won						
AL	10	1907, 20	5	1963	12	1973
NL	9	1901, 03-04	7	1965	9	1969
Fewest Pitchers 20 or more Games Won						
AL	0	1955, 60	2	1961, 64-66	0	1982, 95, 2006, 09, 14, 17
NL	0	1931	2	1967	0	1983, 87, 95, 2006-07, 09, 13, 17-19
Most Pitchers 20 or more Games Lost						
AL	7	1904	1	1961, 63, 66	2	1973-74
NL	8	1905	4	1962	3	1974
Fewest Pitchers 20 or more Games Lost						
AL	0	17 seasons; last: 1960	0	1962, 64-65, 67-68	0	Many seasons; last: 2019
NL	0	22 seasons; last: 1961	0	1967-68	0	Many seasons; last: 2019

GENERAL

	AL:1901-1960 NL:1900-1961 8 clubs 154 games		AL:1961-1968 NL:1962-1968 10 clubs 162 games		AL:1969- NL:1969- 12-16 clubs 162 games	
Most Players						
AL	323	1955	369	1962	762	2019
NL	333	1946	373	1967	730	2018
Fewest Players						
AL	166	1904	351	1968	416	1976
NL	188	1905	336	1968	420	1979
Most Pitchers						
AL	133	1946	170	1962	456	2019
NL	149	1946	167	1967	431	2018
Most Pinch-Hitters						
AL	1,950	1960	2,403	1967	2,993	1970
NL	1,911	1960	2,448	1965	4,396	2008
ML	3,861	1960	4,723	1967	5,804	1970
Most Batters, .300 Batting Average (Minimum: 300 at-bats)						
AL	34	1921, 24	11	1962	37	1996
NL	45	1930	17	1962	38	2000
Fewest Batters, .300 Batting Average (Minimum: 300 at-bats)						
AL	3	1905	1	1968	6	1971-72
NL	4	1907, 09	5	1968	9	1982, 2018
Most Players 150 or more Games						
AL	19	1904, 21, 36	30	1962	49	2016
NL	23	1953	34	1965	42	1998, 2002
Most Players 600 or more At-Bats						
AL	15	1936	17	1962	24	2005, 13
NL	13	1929	19	1962	19	2007
Most Players 100 or more Runs						
AL	24	1936	6	1961	29	1999
NL	19	1929	10	1962	31	1999
Most Players 200 or more Hits						
AL	9	1936-37	1	1962, 64	6	1986
NL	12	1929-30	5	1963-64	6	1970
Most Players 300 or more Total Bases						
AL	12	1930, 37	7	1961	22	2000
NL	14	1930	9	1963, 65	20	1999, 2001
Most Players 40 or more Doubles						
AL	12	1937	3	1962, 65	15	2000, 06
NL	13	1929	3	1968	19	2007
Most Players 20 or more Triples						
AL	4	1912	0	1961-68	1	1979, 85, 2000, 07
NL	3	1911-12	0	1962-68	1	1996, 2007
Most Players 50 or more Home Runs						
AL	2	1938	2	1961	2	1996, 2002
NL	2	1947	1	1965	3	1998, 2001
Most Players 40 or more Home Runs						
AL	3	1936	6	1961	8	1996, 98
NL	6	1954-55	2	1961-63, 66	9	2000
Most Players 30 or more Home Runs						
AL	6	1937-38, 40, 58-59	9	1964	31	2019
NL	9	1953, 56	10	1965	26	2019
Most Players 20 or more Home Runs						
AL	18	1959	25	1964	70	2019
NL	23	1956	25	1962	56	2019
Most Players 100 or more Runs Batted In						
AL	18	1936	8	1962	31	1999-2000
NL	17	1930	10	1962	27	1999
Most Players 100 or more Walks						
AL	8	1949	5	1961-62	10	2000
NL	4	1949, 51	1	1962-63	9	2004

	AL:1901-1960 NL:1900-1961 8 clubs 154 games		AL:1961-1968 NL:1962-1968 10 clubs 162 games		AL:1969- NL:1969- 12-16 clubs 162 games	
Most Players 100 or more Strikeouts						
AL	3	1958-60	15	1967	81	2019
NL	4	1960	17	1965	75	2019
Most Managers						
AL	12	1933, 46	15	1966	20	1986
NL	12	1902, 48	12	1965-68	20	2009, 11, 15
ML	21	1902, 33	27	1966	38	2002

MISCELLANEOUS SERVICE

Oldest Player
AL: Satchel Paige, KC Sept. 25, 1965 (59 years, 78 days)
NL: Jim O'Rourke, NY Sept. 22, 1904 (52 years, 29 days)

Youngest Player
AA: Fred Chapman, Phil. July 22, 1887 (14 years, 140 days)
NL: Joe Nuxhall, Cin. June 10, 1944 (15 years, 316 days)
AL: Carl Scheib, Phil. Sept. 6, 1943 (16 years, 248 days)

Oldest Manager
AL: Connie Mack, Phil. Oct. 1, 1950 (87 years, 282 days)
NL: Jack McKeon, Fla. Sept. 28, 2011 (80 years, 309 days)

Youngest Manager
AL: Roger Peckinpaugh, NY Sept. 16, 1914 (23 years, 223 days)
NL: George Davis, NY Apr. 18, 1895 (24 years, 238 days)

Oldest Batting Leader
NL: Barry Bonds, SF 2004 (40 years, 71 days)
AL: Ted Williams, Bos. 1958 (40 years, 28 days)

Youngest Batting Leader
AL: Al Kaline, Det. 1955 (20 years, 280 days)
NL: Juan Soto, Wash. 2020 (21 years, 338 days)

Oldest Home Run Leader
NL: Cy Williams, Phil. 1927 (39 years, 286 days)
AL: Darrell Evans, Det. 1985 (38 years, 133 days)

Youngest Home Run Leader
AL: Tony Conigliaro, Bos. 1965 (20 years, 270 days)
NL: Sam Crawford, Cin. 1901 (21 years, 171 days)

CLUB SEASON RECORDS PRIOR TO 1900

(The following exceed or equal Major League records listed in preceding sections)

BATTING

Highest Batting Average
.343   **NL:**Phil. 1894

Lowest Batting Average
.208   **NL:**Wash. 1888

Most Runs Scored
1,220   **NL:**Bos. 1894

Most Singles
1,338   **NL:**Phil. 1894

Most Triples
153   **NL:**Balt. 1894

Most Hit By Pitch
121   **NL:**Balt. 1896

Most Stolen Bases
638   **AA:**Phil. 1887
426   **NL:**NY 1893

FIELDING

Most Errors
867   **NL:**Wash. 1886

Most Passed Balls
167   **NL:**Bos. 1883

PITCHING

Fewest Shutouts Won
0   **NL:**Brk., StL., Wash. 1898
        Clev. 1899

Most No-Hit Games
2   **AA:**Lou. 1882
        Colu. 1884
        Phil. 1888

Most No-Hit Games Against
2   **AA:**Pitt. 1884
        NL: Prov. 1885
        Bos. 1898

GENERAL

Highest Pct. Games Won, First Place
.850   **UA:**StL. 1884 (91-16)
.798   **NL:**Chi. 1880 (67-17)

Lowest Pct. Games Won, Last Place
.130   **NL:**Clev. 1899 (20-134)

Fewest Games Won
20   **NL:**Clev. 1899

Fewest Games Won, Road
11   **NL:**Clev. 1899

Most Games Lost
134   **NL:**Clev. 1899

Most Games Lost, Road
101   **NL:**Clev. 1899

MANAGERS

Most, Season
7   **AA:**Lou. 1889
4   **NL:**Wash. 1892, 98
        StL. 1895, 96, 97

MANAGERS

Most Seasons, Lifetime
53 Connie Mack, NL:Pitt. (3) 1894-96; AL:Phil. (50) 1901-50

Most Seasons, League
50 Connie Mack, AL:Phil. 1901-50
32 John McGraw, NL:Balt. 1899; NY 1902-32

Most Seasons, One Club
50 Connie Mack, AL:Phil. 1901-50
31 John McGraw, NL:NY 1902-32

Most Clubs, Lifetime
7 Frank Bancroft, NL:Wor. 1880; Det. 81-82; Clev. 83; Prov. 84-85; Ind. 89; Cin. 1902; AA:Phil. 1887
   Jack Chapman, NL:Lou. 1876-77; Mil. 78; Wor. 82; Det. 83-84; Buff. 85; Lou. 92; AA:Lou. 89-91
   Since 1900:
6 Jimmy Dykes, AL:Chi. 1934-46; Phil. 51-53; Balt. 54; Det. 59-60; Clev. 60-61; NL:Cin. 1958
   Dick Williams, AL:Bos. 1967-69; Oak. 71-73; Cal. 74-76; Sea. 86-88; NL:Mtl. 1977-81; SD 82-85
   John McNamara, AL:Oak. 1969-70; Cal. 83-84; Bos. 85-88; Clev. 90-91; NL:SD 1974-77; Cin. 79-82

Most Clubs, League
6 Frank Bancroft, NL:Wor. 1880; Det. 81-82; Clev. 83; Prov. 84-85; Ind. 89; Cin. 1902
   Jack Chapman, NL:Lou. 1876-77; Mil. 78; Wor. 82; Det. 83-84; Buff. 85; Lou. 92
5 Jimmy Dykes, AL:Chi. 1934-46; Phil. 51-53; Balt. 54; Det. 59-60; Clev. 60-61
   Billy Martin, AL:Minn. 1969; Det. 71-73; Tex. 73-75; NY 75-78, 79, 83, 85, 88; Oak. 80-82
   NL since 1900:
4 Bill McKechnie, NL:Pitt. 1922-26; StL. 28-29; Bos. 30-37; Cin. 38-46
   Rogers Hornsby, NL:StL. 1925-26; Bos. 28; Chi. 30-32; Cin. 52-53
   Leo Durocher, NL:Brk. 1939-46, 48; Chi. 66-72; Hou. 72-73
   Joe Torre, NL:NY 1977-81; Atl. 82-84; StL. 90-95; LA 2008-10
   Davey Johnson, NL:NY 1984-90; Cin. 93-95; LA 99-2000; Wash. 11-13
   Dusty Baker, NL:SF 1993-2002; Chi. 03-06; Cin. 08-13; Wash. 16-17
   Jim Riggleman, NL:SD 1992-94; Chi. 95-99; Wash. 2009-11; Cin. 2018

Most Clubs, Season
2 Joe Battin, AA:Pitt.-UA:Pitt. 1884
   Bill Watkins, NL:Det.-AA:KC 1888
   Gus Schmelz, NL:Clev.-AA:Colu. 1890
   John McGraw, AL:Balt.-NL:NY 1902
   Rogers Hornsby, AL:StL.-NL:Cin. 1952
   Bill Virdon, AL:NY-NL:Hou. 1975
   Pat Corrales, NL:Phil.-AL:Clev. 1983
   Buck Rodgers, NL:Mtl.-AL:Cal. 1991
   Also see following item

Most Clubs, League, Season
2 Ted Sullivan UA:StL.-KC 1884
   Leo Durocher. NL:Brk.-NY 1948; Chi.-Hou. 1972
   Jimmy Dykes, AL:Det.-Clev. 1960
   Joe Gordon, AL:Clev.-Det. 1960
   Billy Martin, AL:Det.-Tex. 1973; Tex.-NY 1975
   Bob Lemon, AL:Chi.-NY 1978
   Tony LaRussa, AL:Chi.-Oak. 1986

Most Different Terms, Same Club
5 Billy Martin, AL:NY 1975-78; 1979; 1983; 1985; 1988
4 Danny Murtaugh, NL:Pitt. 1957-64; 1967; 1970-71; 1973-76

Most Seasons, Manager, League Champion
10 John McGraw, NL:NY 1904-05, 11-13, 17, 21-24
    Casey Stengel, AL:NY 1949-53, 55-58, 60

Most Seasons, Consecutive, Manager, League Champion
5 Casey Stengel, AL:NY 1949-53
4 John McGraw, NL:NY 1921-24

AMERICAN LEAGUE WORLD SERIES

TEAM	No.	Series W	L	All Games G	W	L	Home Games G	W	L	Road Games G	W	L
New York Yankees	40	27	13	225	134	90	109	67	41	116	67	49
Phil./Oak. Athletics	14	9	5	75	41	34	37	22	15	38	19	19
Boston Red Sox	13	9	4	79	49	29	40	26	13	39	23	16
Detroit Tigers	11	4	7	65	27	37	32	13	19	33	14	18
St. Louis/Baltimore	7	3	4	39	21	18	20	11	9	19	10	9
Washington/Minnesota	6	3	3	40	19	21	22	17	5	18	2	16
Cleveland Indians	6	2	4	37	17	20	19	10	9	18	7	11
Chicago White Sox	5	3	2	30	17	13	15	8	7	15	9	6
Kansas City Royals	4	2	2	25	13	12	13	8	5	12	5	7
Toronto Blue Jays	2	2	0	12	8	4	6	4	2	6	4	2
*Houston Astros	2	1	1	14	7	7	7	2	5	7	5	2
Texas Rangers	2	0	2	12	4	8	6	3	3	6	1	5
Tampa Bay Rays	2	0	2	11	3	8	5	2	3	6	1	5
Anaheim Angels	1	1	0	7	4	3	4	3	1	3	1	2
Milwaukee Brewers	1	0	1	7	3	4	3	2	1	4	1	3
TOTALS	116	66	50	678	367	308	338	198	138	340	169	170

* Also played in the World Series for the National League.

NATIONAL LEAGUE WORLD SERIES

TEAM	No.	Series W	L	All Games G	W	L	Home Games G	W	L	Road Games G	W	L
Brk./LA Dodgers	21	7	14	123	53	70	61	35	26	62	18	44
NY/SF Giants	20	8	12	116	57	57	57	31	26	59	26	31
St. Louis Cardinals	19	11	8	118	58	60	59	31	28	59	27	32
Chicago Cubs	11	3	8	60	23	36	30	8	21	30	15	15
Bos./Mil./Atl. Braves	9	3	6	53	24	29	26	14	12	27	10	17
Cincinnati Reds	9	5	4	51	26	25	26	12	14	25	14	11
Pittsburgh Pirates	7	5	2	47	23	24	23	12	11	24	11	13
Philadelphia Phillies	7	2	5	37	14	23	20	9	11	17	5	12
New York Mets	5	2	3	29	13	16	16	9	7	13	4	9
Florida Marlins	2	2	0	13	8	5	7	4	3	6	4	2
San Diego Padres	2	0	2	9	1	8	4	1	3	5	0	5
Arizona Diamondbacks	1	1	0	7	4	3	4	4	0	3	0	3
Washington Nationals	1	1	0	7	4	3	3	0	3	4	4	0
Colorado Rockies	1	0	1	4	0	4	2	0	2	2	0	2
*Houston Astros	1	0	1	4	0	4	2	0	2	2	0	2
TOTALS	116	50	66	678	308	367	340	170	169	338	138	198

* Also played in the World Series for the American League.

TIE GAMES

1907 Oct. 8	Detroit AL at Chicago NL	3-3	12 innings	
1912 Oct. 9	New York NL at Boston AL	6-6	11 innings	
1922 Oct. 5	New York NL at New York AL	3-3	10 innings	

WORLD SERIES RECORDS

NOTE: Individual and Club records are listed under appropriate headings according to the duration of each annual Series, immediately preceding records for lifetime, game and inning. Players' complete names are found in the annual rosters.
8-Game Series records that tied or exceeded those shown are included under 7-Game Series

BATTING – INDIVIDUAL

4 Games	*5 Games*	*6 Games*	*7 Games*
Highest Batting Average (Minimum: 3.1 PA per game)			
.750 Hatcher, NL:Cin. 1990	.529 Casey, AL:Det. 2006	.688 Ortiz, AL:Bos. 2013	.500 Martin, NL:StL. 1931
			Lindell, AL:NY 1947
			Garner, NL:Pitt. 1979
Highest Slugging Percentage (Minimum: 3.1 PA per game)			
1.727 Gehrig, AL:NY 1928	1.167 Pearce, AL:Bos. 2018	1.250 Jackson, AL:NY 1977	1.294 Bonds, NL:SF 2002
Most At-Bats			
21 Damon, AL:Bos. 2004	26 Escobar, AL:KC 2015	29 Duncan, NL:Phil. 1993	36 Collins, AL:Bos. 1903 (8g)
Podsednik, AL:Chi. 2005			33 Harris, AL:Wash. 1924
			Rice, AL:Wash. 1925
			Moreno, NL:Pitt. 1979
			White, NL:Fla. 1997
			Altuve, AL:Hou. 2019
Most Runs			
9 Ruth, AL:NY 1928	6 Baker, AL:Phil. 1910	10 Jackson, AL:NY 1977	9 Berkman, NL:StL. 2011
Gehrig, AL:NY 1932	Murphy, AL:Phil. 1910	Molitor, AL:Tor. 1993	
	Hooper, AL:Bos. 1916		
	Simmons, AL:Phil. 1929		
	May, NL:Cin. 1970		
	Powell, AL:Balt 1970		
	Whitaker, AL:Det. 1984		
	Jeter, AL:NY 2000		
	Renteria, NL:SF 2010		
	Granderson, NL:NY 2015		
	Benintendi, AL:Bos. 2018		
Most Hits			
10 Ruth, AL:NY 1928	9 Baker, AL:Phil. 1910, 13	12 Martin, AL:NY 1953	13 Richardson, AL:NY 1964
	Collins, AL:Phil. 1910	Alomar, AL:Tor. 1993	Brock, NL:StL. 1968
	Groh, NL:NY 1922	Molitor, AL:Tor. 1993	Barrett, AL:Bos. 1986
	Moore, NL:NY 1937	Grissom, NL:Atl. 1996	
	Richardson, AL:NY 1961		
	Blair, AL:Balt 1970		
	B. Robinson, AL:Balt. 1970		
	Trammell, AL:Det. 1984		
	Jeter, AL:NY 2000		
	O'Neill, AL:NY 2000		
Most Extra-Base Hits			
6 Ruth, AL:NY 1928	5 Dempsey, AL:Balt. 1983	6 Jackson, AL:NY 1977	8 Springer, AL:Hou. 2017
	Jeter, AL:NY 2000	Molitor & White, AL:Tor. 1993	
	Torres, NL:SF 2010	Utley, NL:Phil. 2009	
		Turner, NL:LA 2020	
Most Total Bases			
22 Ruth, AL:NY 1928	19 Jeter, AL:NY 2000	25 Jackson, AL:NY 1977	29 Springer, AL:Hou. 2017
Most Singles			
9 Munson, AL:NY 1976	8 Chance, NL:Chi. 1908	10 Rolfe, AL:NY 1936	12 Rice, AL:Wash. 1925
	Baker, AL:Phil. 1913	Irvin, NL:NY 1951	
	Groh, NL:NY 1922		
	Moore, NL:NY 1937		
	Richardson, AL:NY 1961		
	Blair, AL:Balt. 1970		
	Garvey, NL:LA 1974		
Most Doubles			
4 Hatcher, NL:Cin. 1990	4 Collins, AL:Phil. 1910	5 Hafey, NL:StL. 1930	6 Fox, AL:Det. 1934
Boone, NL:Atl. 1999	Dempsey, AL:Balt. 1983		
Ellsbury, AL:Bos. 2007	Torres, NL:SF 2010		
	Zobrist, AL:KC 2015		

4 Games	5 Games	6 Games	7 Games

Most Triples

4 Games	5 Games	6 Games	7 Games
2 Gehrig, AL:NY 1927	2 Collins, AL:Phil. 1913	2 Rohe, AL:Chi. 1906	4 Leach, NL:Pitt. 1903 (8g)
Davis, NL:LA 1963	Brown, AL:NY 1949	Meusel, AL:NY 1923	3 Johnson, AL:NY 1947
R. Henderson, AL:Oak. 1989	O'Neill, AL:NY 2000	Martin, AL:NY 1953	Lemke, NL:Atl. 1991
Podsednik, AL:Chi. 2005		Molitor, AL:Tor. 1993	
		White, AL:Tor. 1993	

Most Home Runs .

4 Games	5 Games	6 Games	7 Games
4 Gehrig, AL:NY 1928	3 Clendenon, NL:NY 1969	5 Jackson, AL:NY 1977	5 Springer, AL:Hou. 2017
	Howard, NL:Phil. 2008	Utley, NL:Phil. 2009	
	Granderson, NL:NY 2015		
	Pearce, AL:Bos. 2018		

Most Runs Batted In

4 Games	5 Games	6 Games	7 Games
9 Gehrig, AL:NY 1928	8 Murphy, AL:Phil. 1910	10 Kluszewski, AL:Chi. 1959	12 Richardson, AL:NY 1960
	May, NL:Cin. 1970		
	Pearce, AL:Bos. 2018		

Most Sacrifice Hits

4 Games	5 Games	6 Games	7 Games
3 By many	4 Lewis, AL:Bos. 1916	3 Sheckard, NL:Chi. 1906	5 Clarke, NL:Pitt. 1909
		Steinfeldt, NL:Chi. 1906	Daubert, NL:Cin. 1919 (8g)
		Tinker, NL:Chi. 1906	
		Barry, AL:Phil. 1911	
		Lee, NL:Chi. 1935	

Most Sacrifice Flies (Since 1954)

4 Games	5 Games	6 Games	7 Games
2 Westrum, NL:NY 1954	2 Nettles, NL:SD 1984	3 Carter, AL:Tor. 1993	2 Campanella, NL:Brk. 1956
Matheny, NL:StL. 2004	Brosius, AL:NY 2000		B. Robinson, AL:Balt. 1971
Varitek, AL:Bos. 2007	Hosmer, AL:KC 2015		Stargell, NL:Pitt. 1979
			Ramirez, AL:Clev. 1997
			Williams, NL:Ari. 2001
			Sanders, NL:SF 2002

Most Walks

4 Games	5 Games	6 Games	7 Games
7 Thompson, NL:NY 1954	7 Sheckard, NL:Chi. 1910	9 Randolph, AL:NY 1981	13 Bonds, NL:SF 2002
	Cochrane, AL:Phil. 1929		
	Gordon, AL:NY 1941		

Most Intentional Walks (Since 1955)

4 Games	5 Games	6 Games	7 Games
3 Williams, AL:NY 1999	3 Posada, AL:NY 2000	4 Ortiz, AL:Bos. 2013	7 Bonds, NL:SF 2002

Most Strikeouts

4 Games	5 Games	6 Games	7 Games
8 Hawpe, Col. 2007	11 Burrell, NL:SF 2010	13 Howard, NL:Phil. 2009	17 Bellinger, NL:LA 2017

Most Stolen Bases

4 Games	5 Games	6 Games	7 Games
3 R. Henderson, AL:Oak. 1989-90	6 Slagle, NL:Chi. 1907	6 Lofton, AL:Clev. 1995	7 Brock, NL:StL. 1967-68
Jeter, AL:NY 1999			

Most Caught Stealing

4 Games	5 Games	6 Games	7 Games
2 Aparicio, AL:Balt. 1966	5 Schulte, NL:Chi. 1910	3 Devore, NL:NY 1911	4 Neale, NL:Cin. 1919 (8g)
Foster, NL:Cin. 1976			3 Brock, NL:StL. 1968
			Kinsler, AL:Tex. 2011

SERVICE

Most Series, Lifetime
14 Yogi Berra, AL:NY 1947, 49-53, 55-58, 60-63

Most Series, Consecutive
5 By many. See rosters AL:NY 1949-53; 60-64

Most Series, One Club, Lifetime
14 Yogi Berra, AL:NY 1947, 49-53, 55-58, 60-63

Most Series, Winning Club
10 Yogi Berra, AL:NY 1947, 49-53, 56, 58, 61-62

Most Series, Losing Club
6 Pee Wee Reese, NL:Brk. 1941, 47, 49, 52-53, 56
   Elston Howard, AL:NY 1955, 57, 60, 63-64; Bos. 67

Most Positions Played, Lifetime
4 Fred Snodgrass, NL:NY 1911-13 (cf, lf, rf, 1b)
   Babe Ruth, AL:Bos. 1915-16, 18 (p, lf); NY 21-23, 26-28, 32 (lf, rf, 1b)
   Jackie Robinson, NL:Brk. 1947, 49, 52-53, 55-56 (1b, 2b, lf, 3b)
   Tony Kubek, AL:NY 1957-58, 60-63 (lf, cf, ss)
   Elston Howard, AL:NY 1955-58, 60-64 (lf, rf, 1b, c); Bos. 67 (c)
   Pete Rose, NL:Cin. 1970, 72, 75-76 (rf, lf, 3b); Phil. 80, 83 (1b)

BATTING AVERAGE

Highest Batting Average (Minimum: 75 at-bats)
.391 Lou Brock, NL:StL. 1964, 67-68

Most Series, .300 or Higher Batting Average (Minimum: 3.1 PA per game)
5 Babe Ruth, AL:NY 1923, 26-28, 32
   Yogi Berra, AL:NY 1953, 55-57, 60
   Derek Jeter, AL:NY 1998-2000, 03, 09

Most Series Leading Club (Playing all games)
3 Frank Baker, AL:Phil. 1911, 13-14
   Pee Wee Reese, NL:Brk. 1947, 49, 52
   Duke Snider, NL:Brk. 1952, 55-56
   Gil Hodges, NL:Brk. 1953, 56; LA 59
   Steve Garvey, NL:LA 1974, 77, 81

SLUGGING PERCENTAGE

Highest Slugging Percentage (Minimum: 75 at-bats)
.755 Reggie Jackson, AL:Oak. 1973-74; NY 77-78, 81

GAMES

Most Games, Lifetime
75 Yogi Berra, AL:NY 1947, 49-53, 55-58, 60-63

Most Games, One Club
75 Yogi Berra, AL:NY 1947, 49-53, 55-58, 60-63

Most Games, Consecutive
30 Bobby Richardson, AL:NY 1960-64

AT-BATS

Most At-Bats, Lifetime
259 Yogi Berra, AL:NY 1947, 49-53, 55-58, 60-63

Most At-Bats, Game
6 Pat Dougherty, AL:Bos. Oct. 7, 1903
    Jimmy Collins, AL:Bos. Oct. 7, 1903
    Jimmy Sheckard, NL:Chi. Oct. 10, 1908
    Heinie Groh, NL:Cin. Oct. 9, 1919
    George Burns, NL:NY Oct. 7, 1921
    Mark Koenig, AL:NY Oct. 6, 1926
    Frankie Crosetti, AL:NY Oct. 2, 1932
    Bill Dickey, AL:NY Oct. 2, 1932
    Joe Sewell, AL:NY Oct. 2, 1932
    Red Rolfe, AL:NY Oct. 6, 1936
    Joe DiMaggio, AL:NY Oct. 6, 1936
    Jimmy Brown, NL:StL. Oct. 4, 1942
    Red Schoendienst, NL:StL. Oct. 10, 1946
    Enos Slaughter, NL:StL. Oct. 10, 1946
    Pee Wee Reese, NL:Brk. Oct. 5, 1956
    Tony Kubek, AL:NY Oct. 6, 1960
    Bill Skowron, AL:NY Oct. 6, 1960
    Clete Boyer, AL:NY Oct. 12, 1960
    Bobby Richardson, AL:NY Oct. 9, 1961
    Tony Kubek, AL:NY Oct. 9, 1961
    Paul Molitor, AL:Mil. Oct. 12, 1982
    Robin Yount, AL:Mil. Oct. 12, 1982
    Jim Rice, AL:Bos. Oct. 19, 1986
    Rickey Henderson, AL:Oak. Oct. 28, 1989
    Roberto Alomar, AL:Tor. Oct. 20, 1993
    Joe Carter, AL:Tor. Oct. 20, 1993
    Tony Fernandez, AL:Tor. Oct. 20, 1993
    Mariano Duncan, NL:Phil. Oct. 20, 1993
    Tony Womack, NL:Ari. Nov. 3, 2001
    Darin Erstad, AL:Ana. Oct. 22, 2002
    Garret Anderson, AL:Ana. Oct. 22, 2002
    Kenny Lofton, NL:SF Oct. 24, 2002
    Rich Aurilia, NL:SF Oct. 24, 2002
    Johnny Damon, AL:Bos. Oct. 23, 2004
    Rafael Furcal, NL:StL. Oct. 22, 2011
    Albert Pujols, NL:StL. Oct. 22, 2011
Extra-Inning Game:
8 Scott Podsednik, AL:Chi. Oct. 25, 2005 (14 inn)
    Xander Bogaerts, AL:Bos. Oct. 26, 2018 (18 inn)
    Justin Turner, NL:LA Oct. 26, 2018 (18 inn)

Most Plate Appearances, No At-Bats, Game
5 Fred Clarke, NL:Pitt. Oct. 16, 1909

Most At-Bats, Inning
2 By many

RUNS

Most Runs, Lifetime
42 Mickey Mantle, AL:NY 1951-53, 55-58, 60-64

Most Runs, Game
4 Babe Ruth, AL:NY Oct. 6, 1926
    Earle Combs, AL:NY Oct. 2, 1932
    Frankie Crosetti, AL:NY Oct. 2, 1936
    Enos Slaughter, NL:StL. Oct. 10, 1946
    Reggie Jackson, AL:NY Oct. 18, 1977
    Kirby Puckett, AL:Minn. Oct. 24, 1987
    Carney Lansford, AL:Oak. Oct. 27, 1989
    Len Dykstra, NL:Phil. Oct. 20, 1993
    Jeff Kent, NL:SF Oct. 24, 2002
    Albert Pujols, NL:StL. Oct. 22, 2011
    Lance Berkman, NL:StL. Oct. 27, 2011 (11 inn)

Most Runs, Inning
2 Frankie Frisch, NL:NY Oct. 7, 1921 (7th)
    Al Simmons, AL:Phil. Oct. 12, 1929 (7th)
    Jimmie Foxx, AL:Phil. Oct. 12, 1929 (7th)
    Dick McAuliffe, AL:Det. Oct. 9, 1968 (3rd)
    Mickey Stanley, AL:Det. Oct. 9, 1968 (3rd)
    Al Kaline, AL:Det. Oct. 9, 1968 (3rd)
    Greg Colbrunn, NL:Ari. Nov. 3, 2001 (3rd)

Most Games, Consecutive, Runs
9 Babe Ruth, AL:NY 1927-28, 32
    Frank Baker, AL:Phil. 1910-11

HITS

Most Hits, Lifetime
71 Yogi Berra, AL:NY 1947, 49-53, 55-58, 60-63

Most Hits, Game
5 Paul Molitor, AL:Mil. Oct. 12, 1982
   Albert Pujols, NL:StL. Oct. 22, 2011

Most Games, 4 or more Hits
2 Robin Yount, AL:Mil. Oct. 12, 17, 1982

Most Hits, 2 Consecutive Games
7 Frank Isbell, AL:Chi. Oct. 13-14, 1906
   Freddie Lindstrom, NL:NY Oct. 7-8, 1924
   Monte Irvin, NL:NY Oct. 4-5, 1951
   Thurman Munson, AL:NY Oct. 19-21, 1976
   Paul Molitor, AL:Mil. Oct. 12-13, 1982
   Billy Hatcher, NL:Cin. Oct. 16-17, 1990

Most Hits, Inning
2 Ross Youngs, NL:NY Oct. 7, 1921 (7th)
   Al Simmons, AL:Phil. Oct. 12, 1929 (7th)
   Jimmie Foxx, AL:Phil. Oct. 12, 1929 (7th)
   Jimmy Dykes, AL:Phil. Oct. 12, 1929 (7th)
   Joe Moore, NL:NY Oct. 4, 1933 (6th)
   Dizzy Dean, NL:StL. Oct. 9, 1934 (3rd)
   Joe DiMaggio, AL:NY Oct. 6, 1936 (9th)
   Hank Leiber, NL:NY Oct. 9, 1937 (2nd)
   Stan Musial, NL:StL. Oct. 4, 1942 (4th)
   Elston Howard, AL:NY Oct. 6, 1960 (6th)
   Bobby Richardson, AL:NY Oct. 6, 1960 (6th)
   Bob Cerv, AL:NY Oct. 8, 1960 (1st)
   Frank Quilici, AL:Minn. Oct. 6, 1965 (3rd)
   Al Kaline, AL:Det. Oct. 9, 1968 (3rd)
   Norm Cash, AL:Det. Oct. 9, 1968 (3rd)
   Merv Rettenmund, AL:Balt. Oct. 11, 1971 (5th)
   Gary Gaetti, AL:Minn. Oct. 17, 1987 (4th)
   Matt Williams, NL:Ari. Nov. 3, 2001 (3rd)
   Jacoby Ellsbury, AL:Bos. Oct. 27, 2007 (3rd)

Most Hits, Consecutive At-Bats
7 Thurman Munson, AL:NY 1976-77
   Billy Hatcher, NL:Cin. 1990

Most Hits, Consecutive At-Bats, One Series
7 Billy Hatcher, NL:Cin. 1990

Most Games, Consecutive, Hits
17 Hank Bauer, AL:NY 1956-58

Hitless At-Bats
Most At-Bats, No Hits, Lifetime
22 George Earnshaw, AL:Phil. 1929-31
Consecutive At-Bats, No Hits
31 Marv Owen, AL:Det. 1934-35
One Series, Most At-Bats, No Hits:
22 Dal Maxvill, NL:StL. 1968
Game, Most At-Bats, No Hits:
5 By many
   Extra-Inning game:
8 Xander Bogaerts, AL:Bos. Oct. 26, 2018 (18 inn)

EXTRA-BASE HITS

Most Extra-Base Hits, Lifetime
26 Mickey Mantle, AL:NY 1951-53, 55-58, 60-64

Most Extra-Base Hits, Game
4 Frank Isbell, AL:Chi. Oct. 13, 1906 (4-2b)

Most Extra-Base Hits, Inning
2   Ross Youngs, NL:NY Oct. 7, 1921 (7th; 2b, 3b)
    Matt Williams, NL:Ari. Nov. 3, 2001 (3rd; 2-2b)
    Jacoby Ellsbury, AL:Bos. Oct. 27, 2007 (3rd; 2-2b)

TOTAL BASES

Most Total Bases, Lifetime
123   Mickey Mantle, AL:NY 1951-53, 55-58, 60-64

Most Total Bases, Game
14   Albert Pujols, NL:StL. Oct. 22, 2011

Most Total Bases, Inning
5   Ross Youngs, NL:NY Oct. 7, 1921 (7th)
    Al Simmons, AL:Phil. Oct. 12, 1929 (7th)

SINGLES

Most Singles, Lifetime
49   Yogi Berra, AL:NY 1947, 49-53, 55-58, 60-63

Most Singles, Game
5   Paul Molitor, AL:Mil. Oct. 12, 1982

Most Singles, Inning
2   Jimmie Foxx, AL:Phil. Oct. 12, 1929 (7th)
    Joe Moore, NL:NY Oct. 4, 1933 (6th)
    Joe DiMaggio, AL:NY Oct. 6, 1936 (9th)
    Hank Leiber, NL:NY Oct. 9, 1937 (2nd)
    Bob Cerv, AL:NY Oct. 8, 1960 (1st)
    Al Kaline, AL:Det. Oct. 9, 1968 (3rd)
    Norm Cash, AL:Det. Oct. 9, 1968 (3rd)
    Merv Rettenmund, AL:Balt. Oct. 11, 1971 (5th)

DOUBLES

Most Doubles, Lifetime
10   Frankie Frisch, NL:NY 1921-24; StL. 28, 30-31, 34
     Yogi Berra, AL:NY 1947, 49-53, 55-58, 60-63

Most Doubles, Game
4   Frank Isbell, AL:Chi. Oct. 13, 1906

Most Doubles, Inning
2   Matt Williams, NL:Ari. Nov. 3, 2001 (3rd)
    Jacoby Ellsbury, AL:Bos. Oct. 27, 2007 (3rd)

TRIPLES

Most Triples, Lifetime
4   Tommy Leach, NL:Pitt. 1903, 09
    Tris Speaker, AL:Bos. 1912, 15; Clev. 20
    Billy Johnson, AL:NY 1943, 47, 49-50

Most Triples, Game
2   Tommy Leach, NL:Pitt. Oct. 1, 1903
    Patsy Dougherty, AL:Bos. Oct. 7, 1903
    Dutch Ruether, NL:Cin. Oct. 1, 1919
    Bobby Richardson, AL:NY Oct. 12, 1960
    Tommy Davis, NL:LA Oct. 3, 1963
    Mark Lemke, NL:Atl. Oct. 24, 1991

Most Triples, Inning
1   By many

HOME RUNS

Most Home Runs, Lifetime
18 Mickey Mantle, AL:NY 1951-53, 55-58, 60-64

Most Home Runs, Game
3 Babe Ruth, AL:NY Oct. 6, 1926
   Babe Ruth, AL:NY Oct. 9, 1928
   Reggie Jackson, AL:NY Oct. 18, 1977
   Albert Pujols, NL:StL. Oct. 22, 2011
   Pablo Sandoval, NL:SF Oct. 24, 2012

Most Home Runs, Game, Rookie
2 Charlie Keller, AL:NY Oct. 7, 1939
   Tony Kubek, AL:NY Oct. 5, 1957
   Willie McGee, NL:StL. Oct. 15, 1982
   Andruw Jones, NL:Atl. Oct. 20, 1996
   Michael Conforto, NL:NY Oct. 31, 2015

Most Games, Consecutive, Home Runs
5 George Springer, AL:Hou. Oct. 28, 29, 31; Nov. 1, 2017; Oct. 22, 2019

Most Home Runs, First Game
2 Ted Kluszewski, AL:Chi. Oct. 1, 1959
   Gene Tenace, AL:Oak. Oct. 14, 1972
   Willie Aikens, AL:KC Oct. 14, 1980
   Andruw Jones, NL:Atl. Oct. 20, 1996
   Greg Vaughn, NL:SD Oct. 17, 1998
   Troy Glaus, AL:Ana. Oct. 19, 2002
   Roberto Perez, AL:Clev. Oct 25, 2016

Most Games, 2 or more Home Runs
4 Babe Ruth, AL:NY Oct. 11, 1923; Oct. 6, 1926; Oct. 9, 1928; Oct. 1, 1932

Most Games, One Series, 2 or more Home Runs
2 Willie Aikens, AL:KC Oct. 14, 18, 1980
   Chase Utley, NL:Phil. Oct. 28, Nov. 2, 2009

Most Home Runs, Consecutive At-Bats
4 Reggie Jackson, AL:NY Oct. 16-18, 1977

Most Home Runs, Inning
1 By many

Most Consecutive Innings, Home Run, Game
2 Babe Ruth, AL:NY Oct. 11, 1923 (4th-5th)
   Babe Ruth, AL:NY Oct. 9, 1928 (7th-8th)
   Ted Kluszewski, AL:Chi. Oct. 1, 1959 (3rd-4th)
   Reggie Jackson, AL:NY Oct. 18, 1977 (4th-5th)
   Willie Aikens, AL:KC Oct. 18, 1980 (1st-2nd)
   Dave Henderson, AL:Oak. Oct. 27, 1989 (4th-5th)
   Chris Sabo, NL:Cin. Oct. 19, 1990 (2nd-3rd)
   Andruw Jones, NL:Atl. Oct. 20, 1996 (2nd-3rd)
   Scott Brosius, AL:NY Oct. 20, 1998 (7th-8th)
   Jeff Kent, NL:SF Oct. 24, 2002 (6th-7th)
   Albert Pujols, NL:StL. Oct. 22, 2011 (6th-7th)

Home Run, First Career At-Bat *(* = NOT first plate appearance)*

Chick Fewster, AL:NY Oct. 11, 1921*
Joe Harris, AL:Wash. Oct. 7, 1925
George Watkins, NL:StL. Oct. 2, 1930
Mel Ott, NL:NY Oct. 3, 1933
George Selkirk, AL:NY Sept. 30, 1936
Dusty Rhodes, NL:NY Sept. 29, 1954
Elston Howard, AL:NY Sept. 28, 1955
Roger Maris, AL:NY Oct. 5, 1960
Don Mincher, AL:Minn. Oct. 6, 1965
Brooks Robinson, AL:Balt. Oct. 5, 1966
Jose Santiago, AL:Bos. Oct. 4, 1967
Mickey Lolich, AL:Det. Oct. 3, 1968
Don Buford, AL:Balt. Oct. 11, 1969
Gene Tenace, AL:Oak. Oct. 14, 1972
Jim Mason, AL:NY Oct. 19, 1976
Doug DeCinces, AL:Balt. Oct. 10, 1979
Amos Otis, AL:KC Oct. 14, 1980
Bob Watson, AL:NY Oct. 20, 1981
Jim Dwyer, AL:Balt. Oct. 11, 1983
Jose Canseco, AL:Oak. Oct. 15, 1988*

Mickey Hatcher, NL:LA Oct. 15, 1988
Bill Bathe, NL:SF Oct. 27, 1989
Eric Davis, NL:Cin. Oct. 16, 1990
Ed Sprague, AL:Tor. Oct. 18, 1992
Fred McGriff, NL:Atl. Oct. 21, 1995
Andruw Jones, NL:Atl. Oct. 20, 1996
Barry Bonds, NL:SF Oct. 19, 2002
Troy Glaus, AL:Ana. Oct. 19, 2002
David Ortiz, AL:Bos. Oct. 23, 2004
Mike Lamb, NL:Hou. Oct. 22, 2005
Geoff Blum, AL:Chi. Oct. 25, 2005
Dustin Pedroia, AL:Bos. Oct. 24, 2007
Bobby Kielty, AL:Bos. Oct. 28, 2007
Chase Utley, NL:Phil. Oct. 22, 2008
Chris Taylor, NL:LA Oct. 24, 2017
Matt Kemp, NL:LA Oct. 23, 2018
Eduardo Nunez, AL:Bos. Oct. 23, 2018
Ryan Zimmerman, NL:Wash. Oct. 22, 2019
Michael Taylor, NL:Wash. Oct. 23, 2019

Home Run, Each of First Two Career At-Bats
2 Gene Tenace, AL:Oak. Oct. 14, 1972
   Andruw Jones, NL:Atl. Oct. 20, 1996

Home Run, Leading Off First Inning

Patsy Dougherty, AL:Bos. Oct. 2, 1903	Davey Lopes, NL:LA Oct. 17, 1978
Davy Jones, AL:Det. Oct. 13, 1909	Len Dykstra, NL:NY Oct. 21, 1986
Phil Rizzuto, AL:NY Oct. 5, 1942	Rickey Henderson, AL:Oak. Oct. 28, 1989
Dale Mitchell, AL:Clev. Oct. 10, 1948	Derek Jeter, AL:NY Oct. 25, 2000
Gene Woodling, AL:NY Oct. 4, 1953	Johnny Damon, AL:Bos. Oct. 27, 2004
Al Smith, AL:Clev. Sept. 30, 1954	Dustin Pedroia, AL:Bos. Oct. 24, 2007
Bill Bruton, NL:Mil. Oct. 2, 1958	Gregor Blanco, NL:SF Oct. 22, 2014
Lou Brock, NL:StL. Oct. 6, 1968	Alcides Escobar, AL:KC Oct. 27, 2015
Don Buford, AL:Balt. Oct. 11, 1969	Curtis Granderson, NL:NY Nov. 1, 2015
Tommie Agee, NL:NY Oct. 14, 1969	Dexter Fowler, NL:Chi. Nov. 2, 2016
Pete Rose, NL:Cin. Oct. 20, 1972	Chris Taylor, NL:LA Oct. 24, 2017
Wayne Garrett, NL:NY Oct. 16, 1973	David Freese, NL:LA Oct. 28, 2018

Grand Slam Home Runs
Elmer Smith (rf) AL:Clev. (Brk.) Oct. 10, 1920 (1st: Burleigh Grimes)
Tony Lazzeri (2b) AL:NY (NY) Oct. 2, 1936 (3rd: Dick Coffman)
Gil McDougald (2b) AL:NY (NY) Oct. 9, 1951 (3rd: Larry Jansen)
Mickey Mantle (cf) AL:NY (Brk.) Oct. 4, 1953 (3rd: Russ Meyer)
Yogi Berra (c) AL:NY (Brk.) Oct. 5, 1956 (2nd: Don Newcombe)
Bill Skowron (1b) AL:NY (Brk.) Oct. 10, 1956 (7th: Roger Craig)
Bobby Richardson (2b) AL:NY (Pitt.) Oct. 8, 1960 (1st: Clem Labine)
Chuck Hiller (2b) NL:SF (NY) Oct. 8, 1962 (7th: Marshall Bridges)
Ken Boyer (3b) NL:StL. (NY) Oct. 11, 1964 (6th: Al Downing)
Joe Pepitone (1b) AL:NY (StL.) Oct. 14, 1964 (8th: Gordie Richardson)
Jim Northrup (cf) AL:Det. (StL.) Oct. 9, 1968 (3rd: Larry Jaster)
Dave McNally (p) AL:Balt. (Cin.) Oct. 13, 1970 (6th: Wayne Granger)
Dan Gladden (lf) AL:Minn. (StL.) Oct. 17, 1987 (4th: Bob Forsch)
Kent Hrbek (1b) AL:Minn. (StL.) Oct. 24, 1987 (6th: Ken Dayley)
Jose Canseco (rf) AL:Oak. (LA) Oct. 15, 1988 (2nd: Tim Belcher)
Lonnie Smith (dh) NL:Atl. (Tor.) Oct. 22, 1992 (5th: Jack Morris)
Tino Martinez (1b) AL:NY (SD) Oct. 17, 1998 (7th: Mark Langston)
Paul Konerko (1b) AL:Chi. (Hou.) Oct. 23, 2005 (7th: Chad Qualls)
Addison Russell (ss) NL:Chi. (Clev.) Nov. 1, 2016 (3rd: Dan Otero)
Alex Bregman (3b) AL:Hou. (Wash.) Oct. 26, 2019 (7th: Fernando Rodney)

RUNS BATTED IN

Most Runs Batted In, Lifetime
40 Mickey Mantle, AL:NY 1951-53, 55-58, 60-64

Most Runs Batted In, Game
6 Bobby Richardson, AL:NY Oct. 8, 1960
   Hideki Matsui, AL:NY Nov. 4, 2009
   Albert Pujols, NL:StL. Oct. 22, 2011
   Addison Russell, NL:Chi. Nov. 1, 2016

Most Runs Batted In, Inning
4 By many

SACRIFICE HITS

Most Sacrifice Hits, Lifetime
8 Eddie Collins, AL:Phil. 1910-11, 13-14; Chi. 17, 19

Most Sacrifice Hits, Game
3 Joe Tinker, NL:Chi. Oct. 12, 1906
   Craig Counsell, NL:Ari. Oct. 31, 2001 (10 inn)

Most Sacrifice Hits, Inning
1 By many

SACRIFICE FLIES (Since 1954)

Most Sacrifice Flies, Lifetime
4 Joe Carter, AL:Tor. 1992-93

Most Sacrifice Flies, Game
2 Wes Westrum, NL:NY Oct. 2, 1954
   Manny Ramirez, AL:Clev. Oct. 25, 1997
   Mike Matheny, NL:StL. Oct. 23, 2004
   Mike Napoli, AL:Tex. Oct. 22, 2011
   Eric Hosmer, AL:KC Oct. 27, 2015 (14 inn)

Most Sacrifice Flies, Inning
  1 By many

Most Runs Batted In, Sacrifice Fly
  2 Tommy Herr, NL:StL. Oct. 16, 1982 (2nd)

WALKS

Most Walks, Lifetime
  43 Mickey Mantle, AL:NY 1951-53, 55-58, 60-64

Most Walks, Consecutive
  5 Lou Gehrig, AL:NY Oct. 7-9, 1928

Most Walks, Game
  4 Fred Clarke, NL:Pitt. Oct. 16, 1909
     Dick Hoblitzell, AL:Bos. Oct. 9, 1916 (14 inn)
     Ross Youngs, NL:NY Oct. 10, 1924 (12 inn)
     Babe Ruth, AL:NY Oct. 10, 1926
     Jackie Robinson, NL:Brk. Oct. 5, 1952 (11 inn)
     Doug DeCinces, AL:Balt. Oct. 13, 1979
     David Ortiz, AL:Bos. Oct. 30, 2013

Most Walks, Inning
  2 Lefty Gomez, AL:NY Oct. 6, 1937 (6th)
     Dick McAuliffe, AL:Det. Oct. 9, 1968 (3rd)

Most Intentional Walks. Lifetime
  7 Bernie Williams, AL:NY 1996, 98-2000
     Barry Bonds, NL:SF 2002
     Albert Pujols, NL:StL. 2004, 06, 11

HIT BY PITCH

Most Hit By Pitch, Lifetime
  4 Albert Pujols, NL:StL. 2004, 06, 11

Most Hit By Pitch, Game
  2 Max Carey, NL:Pitt. Oct. 7, 1925
     Yogi Berra, AL:NY Oct. 2, 1953
     Frank Robinson, NL:Cin. Oct. 8, 1961
     Todd Pratt, NL:NY Oct. 21, 2000 (12 inn)
     Jeff Bagwell, NL:Hou. Oct. 22, 2005
     Alex Rodriguez, AL:NY Oct. 31, 2009
     Justin Turner, NL:LA Nov. 1, 2017

Most Hit By Pitch, Inning
  1 By many

STRIKEOUTS

Most Strikeouts, Lifetime
  54 Mickey Mantle, AL:NY 1951-53, 55-58, 60-64

Most Strikeouts, Consecutive Plate Appearances
  8 Vida Blue, AL:Oak. Oct. 14, 1973-Oct. 17, 1974
     David Justice, AL:NY Oct. 27-31, 2001

Most Strikeouts, Game
  5 George Pipgras, AL:NY Oct. 1, 1932

Most Strikeouts, Inning
  2 Edgar Renteria, NL:Fla. Oct. 23, 1997 (6th)
     Freddy Sanchez, NL:SF Oct. 28, 2010 (8th)

GROUNDED INTO DOUBLE PLAYS

Most Grounded Into Double Plays, Lifetime
  8 George Kelly, NL:NY 1921-24

Most Grounded Into Double Plays, Game
  3 Willie Mays, NL:NY Oct. 8, 1951

STOLEN BASES

Most Stolen Bases, Lifetime
14 Eddie Collins, AL:Phil. 1910-11, 13-14; Chi. 17, 19
Lou Brock, NL:StL. 1964, 67-68

Most Stolen Bases, Game
3 Honus Wagner, NL:Pitt. Oct. 11, 1909
Willie Davis, NL:LA Oct. 11, 1965
Lou Brock, NL:StL. Oct. 12, 1967
Lou Brock, NL:StL. Oct. 5, 1968
B.J. Upton, AL:TB Oct. 25, 2008
Rajai Davis, AL:Clev. Oct. 30, 2016

Most Stolen Bases, Inning
2 George Browne, NL:NY Oct. 12, 1905 (9th)
Jimmy Slagle, NL:Chi. Oct. 8, 1907 (10th)
Ty Cobb, AL:Det. Oct. 12, 1908 (9th)
Honus Wagner, NL:Pitt. Oct. 13, 1909 (7th)
Eddie Collins, AL:Chi. Oct. 7, 1917 (6th)
Babe Ruth, AL:NY Oct. 6, 1921 (5th)
Lou Brock, NL:StL. Oct. 12, 1967 (5th)
Davey Lopes, NL:LA Oct. 15, 1974 (1st)
Roberto Alomar, AL:Tor. Oct. 19, 1993 (6th)
Kenny Lofton, AL:Clev. Oct. 21, 1995 (1st)
Omar Vizquel, AL:Clev. Oct. 26, 1997 (5th)
B.J. Upton, AL:TB Oct. 25, 2008 (8th)
Johnny Damon, AL:NY Nov. 1, 2009 (9th)
Rajai Davis, AL:Clev. Oct. 30, 2016 (8th)
Jason Heyward, NL:Chi. Oct 30, 2016 (8th)
Mookie Betts, NL:LA Oct. 20, 2020 (5th)

Most Steals of Home, Lifetime
2 Bob Meusel, AL:NY 1921, 28

Most Steals of Home, Game
1 Bill Dahlen, NL:NY Oct. 12, 1905 (5th)
George Davis, AL:Chi. Oct. 13, 1906 (3rd)
Jimmy Slagle, NL:Chi. Oct. 11, 1907 (7th)
Ty Cobb, AL:Det. Oct. 9, 1909 (3rd)
Buck Herzog, NL:NY Oct. 14, 1912 (1st)
Butch Schmidt, NL:Bos. Oct. 9, 1914 (8th)
Mike McNally, AL:NY Oct. 5, 1921 (5th)
Bob Meusel, AL:NY Oct. 6, 1921 (8th)
Bob Meusel, AL:NY Oct. 7, 1928 (6th)
Hank Greenberg, AL:Det. Oct. 6, 1934 (8th)
Monte Irvin, NL:NY Oct. 4, 1951 (1st)
Jackie Robinson, NL:Brk. Sept. 28, 1955 (8th)
Tim McCarver, NL:StL. Oct. 15, 1964 (4th)
Brad Fullmer, AL:Ana. Oct. 20, 2002 (1st)

CAUGHT STEALING

Most Caught Stealing, Lifetime
8 Frank Schulte, NL:Chi. 1906, 08, 10

Most Caught Stealing, Game
2 Frank Schulte, NL:Chi. Oct. 17, 23, 1910
Fred Luderus, NL:Phil. Oct. 8, 1915
Jimmy Johnston, NL:Brk. Oct. 9, 1916
Mickey Livingston, NL:Chi. Oct. 3, 1945
Billy Martin, AL:NY Sept. 28, 1955
Allen Craig, NL:StL. Oct. 24, 2011

Most Caught Stealing, Inning
1 By many

PINCH-HITTING

Most Games, Lifetime
12 Luis Polonia, AL:Oak. 1988, NY 2000; NL:Atl. 1995-96

Most Games, One Series
6 Luis Polonia, NL:Atl. 1996

Most At-Bats, Lifetime
11 Luis Polonia, AL:Oak. 1988, NY 2000; NL:Atl. 1995-96

Most Hits, Lifetime
4 Allen Craig, NL:StL. 2011, 13

Most Hits, One Series
3   Bobby Brown, AL:NY 1947
    Dusty Rhodes, NL:NY 1954
    Carl Warwick, NL:StL. 1964
    Gonzalo Marquez, AL:Oak. 1972
    Ken Boswell, NL:NY 1973

Most Total Bases, One Series
8   Chuck Essegian, NL:LA 1959
    Bernie Carbo, AL:Bos. 1975

Most Home Runs, Lifetime
2   Chuck Essegian, NL:LA 1959
    Bernie Carbo, AL:Bos. 1975

Most Runs Batted In, One Series
6   Dusty Rhodes, NL:NY 1954

Most Runs Batted In, Game
3   Dusty Rhodes, NL:NY Sept. 29, 1954
    Hank Majeski, AL:Clev. Oct. 2, 1954
    Bernie Carbo, AL:Bos. Oct. 21, 1975
    Bill Bathe, NL:SF Oct. 27, 1989
    Eduardo Nunez, AL:Bos. Oct. 23, 2018
    Mitch Moreland, AL:Bos. Oct. 27, 2018

Most Walks, One Series
3   Bennie Tate, AL:Wash. 1924

Most Strikeouts, One Series
3   Gabby Hartnett, NL:Chi. 1929
    Rollie Hemsley, NL:Chi. 1932
    Otto Velez, AL:NY 1976
    Luis Polonia, NL:Atl. 1996
    Ruben Sierra, AL:NY 2003
    Austin Meadows, AL:TB 2020

PINCH-RUNNING

Most Games, Lifetime
9   Allan Lewis, AL:Oak. 1972-73

Most Games, One Series
6   Allan Lewis, AL:Oak. 1972

MISCELLANY

Awarded First Base on Interference
1   Roger Peckinpaugh, AL:Wash. Oct. 15, 1925 (1st)
    Bud Metheny, AL:NY Oct. 6, 1943 (6th)
    Ken Boyer, NL:StL. Oct. 12, 1964 (1st)
    Pete Rose, NL:Cin. Oct. 10, 1970 (5th)
    George Hendrick, NL:StL. Oct. 15, 1982 (9th)

FIELDING — FIRST BASEMEN

4 Games	5 Games	6 Games	7 Games
Highest Average 1.000 (Most Chances)			
55 Schmidt, NL:Bos. 1914	73 Hoblitzell, AL:Bos. 1916	72 McInnis, AL:Bos. 1918	93 Pipp, AL:NY 1921 (8g)
			Kelly, NL:NY 1921 (8g)
			80 Bottomley, NL:StL. 1926
Chances Accepted			
55 Schmidt, NL:Bos. 1914	73 Hoblitzell, AL:Bos. 1916	87 Donahue, AL:Chi. 1906	93 Pipp, AL:NY 1921 (8g)
			Kelly, NL:NY 1921 (8g)
			81 Cooper, AL:Mil. 1982
Putouts			
52 Schmidt, NL:Bos. 1914	69 Hoblitzell, AL:Bos. 1916	79 Donahue, AL:Chi. 1906	92 Pipp, AL:NY 1921 (8g)
			79 Bottomley, NL:StL. 1926
Assists			
6 Wertz, AL:Clev. 1954	5 Rossman, AL:Det. 1908	9 Merkle, NL:Chi. 1918	10 Cooper, AL:Mil. 1982
Pepitone, AL:NY 1963	Camilli, NL:Brk. 1941		
	Sanders, NL:StL. 1943		
	Skowron, AL:NY 1961		
Errors			
2 McGwire, AL:Oak. 1990	3 Chance, NL:Chi. 1908	3 Greenberg, AL:Det. 1935	5 Abstein, NL:Pitt. 1909
Hunter, NL:Atl. 1999	Davis, AL:Phil. 1910		
Double Plays			
7 Pepitone, AL:NY 1963	7 Pipp, AL:NY 1922	8 Robinson, AL:Clev. 1948	11 Hodges, NL:Brk. 1955
		Rose, NL:Phil. 1980	
Double Plays Started			
2 Hunter, NL:Atl. 1999	2 May, NL:Cin. 1970	2 Garvey, NL:LA 1977	3 Hodges, NL:Brk. 1955
	Garvey, NL:SD 1984	McGriff, NL:Atl. 1996	

FIELDING – FIRST BASEMEN

Most Series
8 Bill Skowron, AL:NY 1955-58, 60-62; NL:LA 63

Games
38 Gil Hodges, NL:Brk. 1949, 52-53, 55-56; LA 59

Chances Accepted
Lifetime:
351 Gil Hodges, NL:Brk. 1949, 52-53, 55-56; LA 59
Game:
20 Fred McGriff, NL:Atl. Oct. 21, 1995
Extra-Inning Game:
23 Dick Hoblitzell, AL:Bos. Oct. 16, 1916 (14 inn)
Inning:
4 Bill Abstein, NL:Pitt. Oct. 12, 1909 (7th)
Wally Pipp, AL:NY Oct. 7, 1922 (5th)
George Kelly, NL:NY Oct. 11, 1923 (7th)
Steve Garvey, NL:LA Oct. 12, 1977 (4th)

Putouts
Lifetime:
326 Gil Hodges, NL:Brk. 1949, 52-53, 55-56; LA 59
Game:
19 George Kelly, NL:NY Oct. 15, 1923
Fred McGriff, NL:Atl. Oct. 21, 1995
Extra-Inning Game:
22 Dick Hoblitzell, AL:Bos. Oct. 16, 1916 (14 inn)
Inning:
3 By many

Assists
Lifetime:
29 Bill Skowron, AL:NY 1955-58, 60-62; NL:LA 63
Game:
4 Marv Owen, AL:Det. Oct. 6, 1935
Don Mincher, AL:Minn. Oct. 7, 1965
Inning:
2 By many

Errors
Lifetime:
8 Fred Merkle, NL:NY 1911-13; Brk. 16; Chi. 18
Game:
2 By many
Inning:
2 Claude Rossman, AL:Det. Oct. 12, 1908 (4th)
Hank Greenberg, AL:Det. Oct. 3, 1935 (5th)
Johnny McCarthy, NL:NY Oct. 8, 1937 (5th)
Frank Torre, NL:Mil. Oct. 9, 1958 (2nd)
Brian Hunter, NL:Atl. Oct. 23, 1999 (8th)

Double Plays
Lifetime:
31 Gil Hodges, NL:Brk. 1949, 52-53, 55-56; LA 59
Game:
4 Stuffy McInnis, AL:Phil. Oct. 9, 1914
Joe Collins, AL:NY Oct. 8, 1951
Gene Tenace, AL:Oak. Oct. 17, 1973
Pete Rose, NL:Phil. Oct. 15, 1980
Game, started:
2 Eddie Murray, AL:Balt. Oct. 11, 1979
Brian Hunter, NL:Atl. Oct. 26, 1999 (10 inn)
Game, unassisted:
1 George Grantham, NL:Pitt. Oct. 7, 1925
Joe Judge, AL:Wash. Oct. 13, 1925
Jimmie Foxx, AL:Phil. Oct. 8, 1930
Jim Bottomley, NL:StL. Oct. 1, 1931
Lou Gehrig, AL:NY Oct. 10, 1937
Ripper Collins, NL:Chi. Oct. 5, 1938
Joe Collins, AL:NY Oct. 7, 1956
Gordy Coleman, NL:Cin. Oct. 8, 1961
Tony Perez, NL:Cin. Oct. 11, 1975
Steve Garvey, NL:SD Oct. 9, 1984
Fred McGriff, NL:Atl. Oct. 24, 1996
Jim Thome, AL:Clev. Oct. 22, 1997
Tino Martinez, AL:NY Oct. 17, 1998
Brian Hunter, NL:Atl. Oct. 26, 1999
Todd Helton, NL:Col. Oct. 28, 2007

Triple Plays
None

FIELDING – SECOND BASEMEN

4 Games	5 Games	6 Games	7 Games
Highest Average 1.000 (Most Chances)			
26 Randolph, AL:Oak. 1990	43 Gordon, AL:NY 1943	39 Gehringer, AL:Det. 1935	49 Doerr, AL:Bos. 1946
Chances Accepted			
28 Lazzeri, AL:NY 1927	43 Gordon, AL:NY 1943	40 Lopes, NL:LA 1981	54 Harris, AL:Wash. 1924
Putouts			
14 Randolph, AL:Oak. 1990	20 Gordon, AL:NY 1943	26 Lopes, NL:LA 1981	26 Harris, AL:Wash. 1924
Assists			
18 Lazzeri, AL:NY 1927	23 Gordon, AL:NY 1943	27 Ward, AL:NY 1923	33 Ward, AL:NY 1921 (8g)
			Gantner, AL:Mil. 1982
Errors			
2 Lazzeri, AL:NY 1928	4 Murphy, AL:Phil. 1905	6 Lopes, NL:LA 1981	5 Gantner, AL:Mil. 1982
Gordon, AL:NY 1938			
Herman, NL:Chi. 1938			
Morgan, NL:Cin. 1976			
Double Plays			
6 Herman, NL:Chi. 1932	6 Green, AL:Oak. 1974	7 Frisch, NL:NY 1923	9 Garner, NL:Pitt. 1979
	Utley, NL:Phil. 2008	Gordon, AL:Clev. 1948	
		Neal, NL:LA 1959	
		Baerga, AL:Clev. 1995	
		Castillo, NL:Fla. 2003	
Double Plays Started			
5 Herman, NL:Chi. 1932	4 Gordon, AL:NY 1941	4 Castillo, NL:Fla. 2003	5 Herr, NL:StL. 1985
	Green, AL:Oak. 1974		Panik, NL:SF 2014

FIELDING – SECOND BASEMEN

Most Series
7   Frankie Frisch, NL:NY 1922-24; StL. 28, 30-31, 34

Games
42   Frankie Frisch, NL:NY 1922-24; StL. 28, 30-31, 34

Chances Accepted
Lifetime:
241   Frankie Frisch, NL:NY 1922-24; StL. 28, 30-31, 34
Game:
13   Claude Ritchey, NL:Pitt. Oct. 10, 1903
Bucky Harris, AL:Wash. Oct. 11, 1925
Davey Lopes, NL:LA Oct. 16, 1974
Extra-inning game:
14   Hughie Critz, NL:NY Oct. 6, 1933 (11 inn)
Inning:
4   Phil Garner, NL:Pitt. Oct. 11, 1979 (8th)

Putouts
Lifetime:
105   Frankie Frisch, NL:NY 1922-24; StL. 28, 30-31, 34
Game:
8   Bucky Harris, AL:Wash. Oct. 8, 1924
Davey Lopes, NL:LA Oct. 16, 1974
Extra-Inning Game:
9   Hughie Critz, NL:NY Oct. 6, 1933 (11 inn)
Inning:
3   Larry Doyle, NL:NY Oct. 9, 1913 (7th)
Bill Wambsganss, AL:Clev. Oct. 10, 1920 (5th)
Johnny Rawlings, NL:NY Oct. 11, 1921 (9th)
Frankie Frisch, NL:StL. Oct. 7, 1931 (7th)
Davey Lopes, NL:LA Oct. 16, 1974 (6th)
Davey Lopes, NL:LA Oct. 21, 1981 (4th)
Lou Whitaker, AL:Det. Oct. 14, 1984 (8th)

Assists
Lifetime:
136   Frankie Frisch, NL:NY 1922-24; StL. 28, 30-31, 34
Game:
8   Claude Ritchey, NL:Pitt. Oct. 10, 1903
Hal Janvrin, AL:Bos. Oct. 7, 1916
Eddie Collins, AL:Chi. Oct. 15, 1917
Bucky Harris, AL:Wash. Oct. 7, 1924
Joe Gordon, AL:NY Oct. 5, 1943
Bobby Doerr, AL:Bos. Oct. 9, 1946
Mark Lemke, NL:Atl. Oct. 21, 1995
Inning:
3   Eddie Collins, AL:Phil. Oct. 12, 1914 (4th)
Pete Kilduff, NL:Brk. Oct. 10, 1920 (3rd)
Aaron Ward, AL:NY Oct. 12, 1921 (6th)
Joe Gordon, AL:NY Oct. 11, 1943 (8th)
Jackie Robinson, NL:Brk. Oct. 8, 1949 (7th)
Gil McDougald, AL:NY Oct. 2, 1958 (2nd)
Phil Garner, NL:Pitt. Oct. 13, 1979 (9th)
Frank White, AL:KC Oct. 19, 1980 (8th)
Marty Barrett, AL:Bos. Oct. 23, 1986 (1st)
Akinori Iwamura, AL:TB Oct. 27, 2008 (7th)

Errors
Lifetime:
8   Larry Doyle, NL:NY 1911-13
Eddie Collins, AL:Phil. 1910-11, 13-14; Chi. 17, 19
Game:
3   Danny Murphy, AL:Phil. Oct. 12, 1905
Buddy Myer, AL:Wash. Oct. 3, 1933
Davey Lopes, NL:LA Oct. 25, 1981
Inning:
2   Danny Murphy, AL:Phil. Oct. 12, 1905 (5th)
Mike Andrews, AL:Oak. Oct. 14, 1973 (12th)
Davey Lopes, NL:LA Oct. 25, 1981 (4th)

Double Plays
Lifetime:
24   Frankie Frisch, NL:NY 1922-24; StL. 28, 30-31, 34
Game:
3   By many
Game, started:
3   Dick Green, AL:Oak. Oct. 15, 1974
Game, unassisted:
1   Hobe Ferris, AL:Bos. Oct. 2, 1903
Larry Doyle, NL:NY Oct. 9, 1913
Buck Herzog, NL:NY Oct. 7, 1917
Frank White, AL:KC Oct. 17, 1980
Mark Lemke, NL:Atl. Oct. 27, 1991

Triple Plays
1   Bill Wambsganss, AL:Clev. Oct. 10, 1920
(Unassisted, 5th)

FIELDING – THIRD BASEMEN

4 Games	5 Games	6 Games	7 Games
Highest Average 1.000 (Most Chances)			
25 Baker, AL:Phil. 1914	23 Moustakas, AL:KC 2015	26 Nettles, AL:NY 1978	29 Menke, NL:Cin. 1972
Chances Accepted			
25 Baker, AL:Phil. 1914	25 Gardner, AL:Bos. 1916	27 Thomson, NL:NY 1951	37 Frisch, NL:NY 1921 (8g)
			34 Higgins, AL:Det. 1940
Putouts			
10 Baker, AL:Phil. 1914	10 Steinfeldt, NL:Chi. 1907	14 Rolfe, AL:NY 1936	13 Kurowski, NL:StL. 1946
Assists			
15 Baker, AL:Phil. 1914	18 Gardner, AL:Bos. 1916	20 Nettles, AL:NY 1977	30 Higgins, AL:Det. 1940
Errors			
3 Mueller, AL:Bos. 2004	4 Steinfeldt, NL:Chi. 1910	3 Rohe, AL:Chi. 1906	4 Leach, NL:Pitt. 1903 (8g)
		Herzog, NL:NY 1911	Gardner, AL:Bos. 1912 (8g)
		Jackson, NL:NY 1936	Martin, NL:StL. 1934
		Elliott, NL:Bos. 1948	McDougald, AL:NY 1952
		Boone, AL:NY 2003	
Double Plays			
3 Nettles, AL:NY 1976	3 Uribe, NL:SF 2010	4 Nettles, AL:NY 1978	4 Davenport, NL:SF 1962
Mueller, AL:Bos. 2004	Moustakas, AL:KC 2015		Madlock, NL:Pitt. 1979
Double Plays Started			
2 Rolfe, AL:NY 1939	3 Uribe, NL:SF 2010	3 Nettles, AL:NY 1978	4 Davenport, NL:SF 1962
Nettles, AL:NY 1976	Moustakas, AL:KC 2015	Madlock, NL:Pitt. 1979	
Brosius, AL:NY 1999			
Mueller, AL:Bos. 2004			

FIELDING – THIRD BASEMEN

Most Series
6 Red Rolfe, AL:NY 1936-39, 41-42

Games
31 Gil McDougald, AL:NY 1951-53, 55, 60

Chances Accepted
Lifetime:
96 Graig Nettles, AL:NY 1976-78, 81; NL:SD 84
Game:
10 Larry Gardner, AL:Bos. Oct. 9, 1916 (14 inn)
     Pinky Higgins, AL:Det. Oct. 5, 1940
     Chris Sabo, NL:Cin. Oct. 19, 1990
Inning:
4 Eddie Mathews, NL:Mil. Oct. 5, 1957 (3rd)

Putouts
Lifetime:
37 Frank Baker, AL:Phil. 1910-11, 13-14; NY 21
Game:
4 Art Devlin, NL:NY Oct. 13, 1905
   Bill Coughlin, AL:Det. Oct. 10, 1907
   Bobby Byrne, NL:Pitt. Oct. 9, 1909
   Tommy Leach, NL:Pitt. Oct. 16, 1909
   Buck Herzog, NL:NY Oct. 17, 1911
   Frank Baker, AL:Phil. Oct. 24, 1911
   Frank Baker, AL:Phil. Oct. 12, 1914
   Heinie Zimmerman, NL:NY Oct. 7, 1917
   Jimmy Dykes, AL:Phil. Oct. 2, 1930
   Bob Elliott, NL:Bos. Oct. 11, 1948
   Willie Jones, NL:Phil. Oct. 4, 1950
   Bill Mueller, AL:Bos. Oct. 24, 2004
Inning:
3 Freddie Lindstrom, NL:NY Oct. 6, 1924 (9th)

Assists
Lifetime:
68 Graig Nettles, AL:NY 1976-78, 81; NL:SD 84
Game:
9 Pinky Higgins, AL:Det. Oct. 5, 1940
Inning:
3 Ossie Bluege, AL:Wash. Oct. 13, 1925 (3rd)
   Jose Pagan, NL:Pitt. Oct. 14, 1971 (9th)
   Sal Bando, AL:Oak. Oct. 16, 1974 (6th)
   Wade Boggs, AL:Bos. Oct. 19, 1986 (3rd)
   Terry Pendleton, NL:Atl. Oct. 27, 1991 (7th)

Errors
Lifetime:
8 Larry Gardner, AL:Bos. 1912, 15-16; Clev. 20
Game:
3 Pepper Martin, NL:StL. Oct. 6, 1934
   Buck Herzog, NL:NY Oct. 17, 1911 (11 inn)
   Bill Mueller, AL:Bos. Oct. 24, 2004
Inning:
2 Harry Steinfeldt, NL:Chi. Oct. 18, 1910 (3rd)
   Larry Gardner, AL:Bos. Oct. 16, 1912 (2nd)
   Doug DeCinces, AL:Balt. Oct. 10, 1979 (6th)
   Brandon Inge, AL:Det. Oct. 21, 2006 (6th)
   Kris Bryant, NL:Chi. Oct. 29, 2016 (2nd)

Double Plays
Lifetime:
8 Graig Nettles, AL:NY 1976-78, 81; NL:SD 84
Game:
2 By many
Game, started:
2 By many
Game, unassisted:
1 Bill Mueller, AL:Bos. Oct. 24, 2004

Triple Plays
None

FIELDING – SHORTSTOPS

4 Games	5 Games	6 Games	7 Games
Highest Average 1.000 (Most Chances)			
27 Wills, NL:LA 1966	29 Dahlen, NL:NY 1905 Scott, AL:NY 1922 Marion, NL:StL. 1942 Harrelson, NL:NY 1969	36 Scott, AL:Bos. 1918	42 Gelbert, NL:StL. 1931
Chances Accepted			
27 Wills, NL:LA 1966	38 Tinker, NL:Chi. 1907	37 Rizzuto, AL:NY 1951	51 Risberg, AL:Chi. 1919 (8g) 42 Gelbert, NL:StL. 1931
Putouts			
16 Crosetti, AL:NY 1938	15 Tinker, NL:Chi. 1907 Rizzuto, AL:NY 1942	16 Jurges, NL:Chi. 1935	24 Wagner, AL:Bos. 1912 (8g) 22 O. Smith, NL:StL. 1982
Assists			
21 Barry, AL:Phil. 1914	25 Scott, AL:Bos. 1916	26 Russell, NL:LA 1981	32 Foli, NL:Pitt. 1979
Errors			
4 Crosetti, AL:NY 1932	4 Olson, NL:Brk. 1916 English, NL:Chi. 1929	4 Fletcher, NL:NY 1911 Weaver, AL:Chi. 1917	8 Peckinpaugh, AL:Wash. 1925
Double Plays			
5 Jurges, NL:Chi. 1932 Kubek, AL:NY 1963 Everett, NL:Hou. 2005	6 Scott, AL:NY 1922 Rizzuto, AL:NY 1941	8 Rizzuto, AL:NY 1951	7 Reese, NL:Brk. 1955-56 Foli, NL:Pitt. 1979 Renteria, NL:Fla. 1997 Crawford, NL:SF 2014
Double Plays Started			
3 Koenig, AL:NY 1928 Uribe, AL:Chi. 2005	4 Tinker, NL:Chi. 1907	7 Bowa, NL:Phil. 1980	4 Reese, NL:Brk. 1947 McDougald, AL:NY 1957 Linz, AL:NY 1964 Wills, NL:LA 1965 Foli, NL:Pitt. 1979 Eckstein, AL:Ana. 2002

FIELDING – SHORTSTOPS

Most Series
9 Phil Rizzuto, AL:NY 1941-42, 47, 49-53, 55

Games
52 Phil Rizzuto, AL:NY 1941-42, 47, 49-53, 55

Chances Accepted
Lifetime:
250 Phil Rizzuto, AL:NY 1941-42, 47, 49-53, 55
Game:
13 Buck Weaver, AL:Chi. Oct. 7, 1917
Inning:
4 Charley Gelbert, NL:StL. Oct. 6, 1931 (3rd)
Alvin Dark, NL:NY Oct. 6, 1951 (3rd)

Putouts
Lifetime:
107 Phil Rizzuto, AL:NY 1941-42, 47, 49-53, 55
Game:
7 Buck Weaver, AL:Chi. Oct. 7, 1917
Phil Rizzuto, AL:NY Oct. 5, 1942
Inning:
3 Freddy Parent, AL:Bos. Oct. 1, 1903 (4th)
Art Fletcher, NL:NY Oct. 25, 1911 (9th)
Phil Rizzuto, AL:NY Oct. 5, 1947 (4th)
Mickey Stanley, AL:Det. Oct. 10, 1968 (6th)

Assists
Lifetime:
143 Phil Rizzuto, AL:NY 1941-42, 47, 49-53, 55
Game:
9 Roger Peckinpaugh, AL:NY Oct. 5, 1921
Extra-Inning Game:
10 Johnny Logan, NL:Mil. Oct. 6, 1957 (10 inn)
Inning:
3 Everett Scott, AL:Bos. Sept. 6, 1918 (6th)
Everett Scott, AL:Bos. Sept. 10, 1918 (3rd)
Joe Sewell, AL:Clev. Oct. 9, 1920 (6th)
Dave Bancroft, NL:NY Oct. 8, 1922 (3rd)
Ossie Bluege, AL:Wash. Oct. 7, 1924 (6th)
Glenn Wright, NL:Pitt. Oct. 8, 1927 (2nd)
Blondy Ryan, NL:NY Oct. 7, 1933 (3rd)
Phil Rizzuto, AL:NY Oct. 3, 1942 (2nd)
Ernie Bowman, NL:SF Oct. 8, 1962 (9th)
Bud Harrelson, NL:NY Oct. 14, 1969 (5th)
Mark Belanger, AL:Balt. Oct. 16, 1971 (7th)
Bud Harrelson, NL:NY Oct. 13, 1973 (7th)
Tim Foli, NL:Pitt. Oct. 12, 1979 (2nd)
Omar Vizquel, AL:Clev. Oct. 18, 1997 (5th)
Edgar Renteria, NL:SF Oct. 27, 2010 (4th)

Errors
Lifetime:
12 Art Fletcher, NL:NY 1911-13, 17
Game:
3 Jack Barry, AL:Phil. Oct. 26, 1911
Art Fletcher, NL:NY Oct. 9, 1912 (11 inn)
Buck Weaver, AL:Chi. Oct. 13, 1917
Inning:
2 Honus Wagner, NL:Pitt. Oct. 7, 1903 (6th)
Ivy Olson, NL:Brk. Oct. 12, 1916 (3rd)
Roger Peckinpaugh, AL:Wash. Oct. 8, 1925 (8th)
Woody English, NL:Chi. Oct. 8, 1929 (9th)
Dick Bartell, NL:NY Oct. 9, 1937 (3rd)
Pee Wee Reese, NL:Brk. Oct. 2, 1941 (8th)

Double Plays
Lifetime:
32 Phil Rizzuto, AL:NY 1941-42, 47, 49-53, 55
Game:
4 Phil Rizzuto, AL:NY, Oct. 8, 1951
Game, started:
3 Phil Rizzuto, AL:NY Oct. 10, 1951
Maury Wills, NL:LA Oct. 11, 1965
Larry Bowa, NL:Phil. Oct. 15, 1980
Game, unassisted:
1 Joe Tinker, NL:Chi. Oct. 10, 1907
Joe Tinker, NL:Chi. Oct. 11, 1907
Charlie Gelbert, NL:StL. Oct. 2, 1930
Eddie Kasko, NL:Cin. Oct. 7, 1961
Greg Gagne, AL:Minn. Oct. 26, 1991

Triple Plays
None

FIELDING – OUTFIELDERS

4 Games	5 Games	6 Games	7 Games
Highest Average 1.000 (Most Chances)			
16 Combs, AL:NY 1927	20 DiMaggio, AL:NY 1942	25 Rivers, AL:NY 1977	24 Murray, NL:NY 1912 (8g)
			Evans, AL:Bos. 1975
			Geronimo, NL:Cin. 1975
			Lynn, AL:Bos. 1975
			McGee, NL:StL. 1982
Chances Accepted			
16 Combs, AL:NY 1927	20 DiMaggio, AL:NY 1942	25 Rivers, AL:NY 1977	33 Roush, NL:Cin. 1919 (8g)
			26 Pafko, NL:Chi. 1945
			Gladden, AL:Minn. 1991
Putouts			
16 Combs, AL:NY 1927	20 DiMaggio, AL:NY 1942	24 Rivers, AL:NY 1977	30 Roush, NL:Cin. 1919 (8g)
			25 Gladden, AL:Minn. 1991
Assists			
2 By many	2 By many	2 By many	4 Rice, AL:Wash. 1924
Errors			
3 Davis, NL:LA 1966	2 By many	3 Murray, NL:NY 1911	4 Speaker, AL:Bos. 1912 (8g)
		J. Collins, AL:Chi. 1917	Devore, NL:NY 1912 (8g)
			Felsch, AL:Chi. 1919 (8g)
			Roush, NL:Cin. 1919 (8g)
			2 Crawford, AL:Det. 1909
			Wheat, NL:Brk. 1920
			Orsatti, NL:StL. 1934
			Goslin, AL:Det. 1934
			Mantle, AL:NY 1964
			Northrup, AL:Det. 1968
Double Plays			
1 Ramirez, AL:Bos. 2004	2 Murphy, AL:Phil. 1910	1 By many	2 Speaker, AL:Bos. 1912 (8g)
			Roush, NL:Cin. 1919 (8g)
			Howard, AL:NY 1958
Double Plays Started			
1 Ramirez, AL:Bos. 2004	2 Murphy, AL:Phil. 1910	1 By many	2 See preceding record

FIELDING – OUTFIELDERS

Most Series
12 Mickey Mantle, AL:NY 1951-53, 55-58, 60-64

Games
63 Mickey Mantle, AL:NY 1951-53, 55-58, 60-64

Chances Accepted
Lifetime:
150 Joe DiMaggio, AL:NY 1936-39, 41-42, 47, 49-51
Game, Left-fielder:
8 George Foster, NL:Cin. Oct. 21, 1976
Game, Center-fielder:
8 Edd Roush, NL:Cin. Oct. 1, 1919
Hank Leiber, NL:NY Oct. 2, 1936
Extra-Inning Game:
9 Edd Roush, NL:Cin. Oct. 7, 1919 (10 inn)
Mickey Rivers, AL:NY Oct. 11, 1977 (12 inn)
Amos Otis, AL:KC Oct. 17, 1980 (10 inn)
Game, Right-fielder:
7 Red Murray, NL:NY Oct. 14, 1912
Bing Miller, AL:Phil. Oct. 5, 1930
Ray Blades, NL:StL. Oct. 5, 1930
Tony Oliva, AL:Minn. Oct. 6, 1965
Al Kaline, AL:Det. Oct. 9, 1968
Frank Robinson, AL:Balt. Oct. 14, 1969
Mookie Betts, AL:Bos. Oct. 26, 2018 (18 inn)
Inning:
3 By many

Putouts
Lifetime:
150 Joe DiMaggio, AL:NY 1936-39, 41-42, 47, 49-51
Game, Left-fielder:
8 George Foster, NL:Cin. Oct. 21, 1976
Game, Center-fielder:
8 Edd Roush, NL:Cin. Oct. 1, 1919
Extra-Inning Game:
9 Amos Otis, AL:KC Oct. 17, 1980 (10 inn)
Game, Right-fielder:
7 Red Murray, NL:NY Oct. 14, 1912
Bing Miller, AL:Phil. Oct. 5, 1930
Ray Blades, NL:StL. Oct. 5, 1930
Tony Oliva, AL:Minn. Oct. 6, 1965
Al Kaline, AL:Det. Oct. 9, 1968
Frank Robinson, AL:Balt. Oct. 14, 1969
Mookie Betts, AL:Bos. Oct. 26, 2018 (18 inn)
Inning, Left-fielder:
3 By many; last:
Deion Sanders, NL:Atl. Oct. 22, 1992 (5th)
Inning, Center-fielder:
3 By many; last:
Curtis Granderson, AL:Det. Oct. 24, 2006 (3rd)
Inning, Right-fielder:
3 By many; last:
Curtis Granderson, NL:NY Oct. 28, 2015 (1st)

Assists
Lifetime:
5 Harry Hooper, AL:Bos. 1912, 15-16, 18
Ross Youngs, NL:NY 1921-24
Game:
2 By many
Inning:
1 By many

Errors
Lifetime:
4 Ross Youngs, NL:NY 1921-24
Game:
3 Willie Davis, NL:LA Oct. 6, 1966
Inning:
3 Willie Davis, NL:LA Oct. 6, 1966 (5th)

Double Plays
Lifetime:
2 By many
Game:
2 Edd Roush, NL:Cin. Oct. 7, 1919 (10 inn)
Game, started:
2 Edd Roush, NL:Cin. Oct. 7, 1919 (10 inn)
Game, unassisted:
1 Tris Speaker, AL:Bos. Oct. 15, 1912

Triple Plays
None

FIELDING – CATCHERS

4 Games	5 Games	6 Games	7 Games
Highest Average 1.000 (Most Chances)			
43 Roseboro, NL:LA 1963	61 Cochrane, AL:Phil. 1929	62 Molina, NL:StL. 2013	72 Grote, NL:NY 1973
Chances Accepted			
43 Roseboro, NL:LA 1963	61 Cochrane, AL:Phil. 1929	62 Molina, NL:StL. 2013	73 Posada, AL:NY 2001
Putouts			
43 Roseboro, NL:LA 1963	59 Cochrane, AL:Phil. 1929	59 Molina, NL:StL. 2013	69 Posada, AL:NY 2001
Assists			
7 Munson, AL:NY 1976	9 Kling, NL:Chi. 1907	12 Meyers, NL:NY 1911	15 Schalk, AL:Chi. 1919 (8g)
	Schmidt, AL:Det. 1907		11 Schmidt, AL:Det. 1909
	Burns, NL:Phil. 1915		
Errors			
3 Oliver, NL:Cin. 1990	2 Schmidt, AL:Det. 1907	2 Schalk, AL:Chi. 1917	5 Schmidt, AL:Det. 1909
	W. Cooper, NL:StL. 1943		
	Ferguson, NL:LA 1974		
	Ruiz, NL:Phil. 2008		
Double Plays			
2 Hartnett, NL:Chi. 1932	2 Burns, NL:Phil. 1915	3 Kling, NL:Chi. 1906	3 Schmidt, AL:Det. 1909
	Mancuso, NL:NY 1933		Schang, AL:NY 1921 (8g)
			Bench, NL:Cin. 1975
Double Plays Started			
1 By many	1 By many	2 Posada, AL:NY 2003	3 Schang, AL:NY 1921 (8g)
			2 Schmidt, AL:Det. 1909
			Crandall, NL:Mil. 1957-58
			Battey, AL:Minn. 1965
Passed Balls			
2 Schang, AL:Phil. 1914	2 Meyers, NL:Brk. 1916	2 Kling, NL:Chi. 1906	3 Burgess, NL:Pitt. 1960
		Killefer, AL:Chi. 1918	Howard, AL:NY 1964

FIELDING – CATCHERS

Most Series
12 Yogi Berra, AL:NY 1947, 49-53, 55-58, 60, 62

Games
63 Yogi Berra, AL:NY 1947, 49-53, 55-58, 60, 62

Chances Accepted
Lifetime:
457 Yogi Berra, AL:NY 1947, 49-53, 55-58, 60, 62
Game:
18 Johnny Roseboro, NL:LA Oct. 2, 1963
Tim McCarver, NL:StL. Oct. 2, 1968
Roberto Perez, AL:Clev. Oct. 25, 2016
Inning:
4 Boss Schmidt, AL:Det. Oct. 14, 1908 (8th)
Ira Thomas, AL:Phil. Oct. 14, 1911 (6th)
Steve O'Neill, AL:Clev. Oct. 6, 1920 (3rd)
Jimmie Wilson, NL:StL. Oct. 1, 1931 (3rd)
Roy Campanella, NL:Brk. Sept. 29, 1955 (2nd)
Tim McCarver, NL:StL. Oct. 9, 1967 (9th)
A.J. Pierzynski, AL:Chi. Oct. 25, 2005 (3rd)

Putouts
Lifetime:
421 Yogi Berra, AL:NY 1947, 49-53, 55-58, 60, 62
Game:
18 Johnny Roseboro, NL:LA Oct. 2, 1963
Roberto Perez, AL:Clev. Oct. 25, 2016
Inning:
3 By many

Assists
Lifetime:
36 Yogi Berra, AL:NY 1947, 49-53, 55-58, 60, 62
Game:
4 Roger Bresnahan, NL:NY Oct. 12, 1905
Johnny Kling, NL:Chi. Oct. 9, 1907
Boss Schmidt, AL:Det. Oct. 11, 1907
Boss Schmidt, AL:Det. Oct. 14, 1908
Bill Rariden, NL:NY Oct. 10, 1917
Sam Agnew, AL:Bos. Sept. 6, 1918
Bill DeLancey, NL:StL. Oct. 8, 1934
Extra-Inning Game:
6 Jack Lapp, AL:Phil. Oct. 17, 1911 (11 inn)
Inning:
2 By many

Errors
Lifetime:
7 Boss Schmidt, AL:Det. 1907-09
Game:
2 Lou Criger, AL:Bos. Oct. 1, 1903
Billy Sullivan Sr. AL:Chi. Oct. 10, 1906
Boss Schmidt, AL:Det. Oct. 8, 1907 (12 inn)
Jimmie Wilson, NL:StL. Oct. 7, 1928
Joe Ferguson, NL:LA Oct. 15, 1974
Carlton Fisk, AL:Bos. Oct. 14, 1975 (10 inn)
Inning:
2 Lou Criger, AL:Bos. Oct. 1, 1903 (1st)
Jimmie Wilson, NL:StL. Oct. 7, 1928 (6th)

Passed Balls
Lifetime:
4 Wally Schang, AL:Phil.1913-14; Bos.18; NY 21-23
Elston Howard, AL:NY 1955-58, 60-64; Bos. 67
Game:
2 Johnny Kling, NL:Chi. Oct. 9, 1906
Bill Killefer, NL:Chi. Sept. 9, 1918
Paul Richards, AL:Det. Oct. 3, 1945
Bruce Edwards, NL:Brk. Oct. 4, 1947
Smoky Burgess, NL:Pitt. Oct. 6, 1960
Elston Howard, AL:NY Oct. 7, 1964
Inning:
1 By many

Double Plays
Lifetime:
6 Yogi Berra, AL:NY 1947, 49-53, 55-58, 60, 62
Johnny Bench, NL:Cin. 1970, 72, 75
Game:
2 Boss Schmidt, AL:Det. Oct. 14, 1909
Wally Schang, AL:NY Oct. 11, 1921
Gabby Hartnett, NL:Chi. Sept. 29, 1932
Gus Mancuso, NL:NY Oct. 5, 1936 (10 inn)
Del Rice, NL:Mil. Oct. 9, 1957
Rich Gedman, AL:Bos. Oct. 22, 1986
Game, started:
2 Boss Schmidt, AL:Det. Oct. 14, 1909
Wally Schang, AL:NY Oct. 11, 1921
Game, unassisted:
1 Travis d'Arnaud, NL:NY Oct. 31, 2015

Triple Plays
None

FIELDING – PITCHERS

4 Games	5 Games	6 Games	7 Games
Highest Average 1.000 (Most Chances)			
6 Tyler, NL:Bos. 1914	8 Marquard, NL:NY 1913	17 Altrock, AL:Chi. 1906	13 Mathewson, NL:NY 1912 (8g)
Ruffing, AL:NY 1938	Shore, AL:Bos. 1916	Vaughn, NL:Chi. 1918	12 Mullin, AL:Det. 1909
	Smith, NL:Brk. 1916		
Chances Accepted			
6 Tyler, NL:Bos. 1914	10 Mathewson, NL:NY 1905	17 Altrock, AL:Chi. 1906	13 Mathewson, NL:NY 1912 (8g)
Ruffing, AL:NY 1938	Brown, NL:Chi. 1910	Vaughn, NL:Chi. 1918	12 Mullin, AL:Det. 1909
Putouts			
3 Ford, AL:NY 1963	5 Morris, AL:Det. 1984	6 Altrock, AL:Chi. 1906	5 Kaat, AL:Minn. 1965
Stewart, AL:Oak. 1989		Vaughn, NL:Chi. 1918	
Assists			
5 Bush, AL:Phil. 1914	10 Brown, NL:Chi. 1910	12 Brown, NL:Chi. 1906	12 Mullin, AL:Det. 1909
Tyler, NL:Bos. 1914			Mathewson, NL:NY 1912 (8g)
James, NL:Bos. 1914			
Moore, AL:NY 1927			
Pearson, AL:NY 1939			
Errors			
1 By many	2 Coombs, AL:Phil. 1910	2 Potter, AL:StL. 1944	2 Phillippe, NL:Pitt. 1909
	Lanier, NL:StL. 1942		Cicotte, AL:Chi. 1919 (8g)
	Verlander, AL:Det. 2006		Reynolds, AL:NY 1952
Double Plays			
2 Bender, AL:Phil. 1914	2 Bush, AL:NY 1922	2 Faber, AL:Chi. 1917	2 Johnson, AL:Wash. 1924
		Reynolds, AL:NY 1951	Stafford, AL:NY 1960
		Gura, AL:KC 1980	
Double Plays Started			
2 Bender, AL:Phil. 1914	2 Bush, AL:NY 1922	2 Faber, AL:Chi. 1917	2 Stafford, AL:NY 1960
		Reynolds, AL:NY 1951	

FIELDING – PITCHERS

Most Series
11 Whitey Ford, AL:NY 1950, 53, 55-58, 60-64

Games:
24 Mariano Rivera, AL:NY 1996, 98-2001, 03, 09

Chances Accepted
Lifetime:
40 Christy Mathewson, NL:NY 1905, 11-13
Game:
11 Nick Altrock, AL:Chi. Oct. 12, 1906
Inning:
3 By many

Putouts
Lifetime:
11 Whitey Ford, AL:NY 1950, 53, 55-58, 60-64
Game:
5 Jim Kaat, AL:Minn. Oct. 7, 1965
Inning:
2 Johnny Beazley, NL:StL. Oct. 5, 1942 (8th)
Bob Turley, AL:NY Oct. 9, 1957 (7th)
Whitey Ford, AL:NY Oct. 8, 1960 (9th)
Bob Purkey, NL:Cin. Oct. 7, 1961 (9th)
John Denny, NL:Phil. Oct. 15, 1983 (5th)
Dave Stewart, AL:Oak. Oct. 16, 1990 (3rd)
Jeff Nelson, AL:NY Oct. 23, 1996 (7th)
Joe Blanton, NL:Phil. Nov. 1, 2009 (6th)

Assists
Lifetime:
35 Christy Mathewson, NL:NY 1905, 11-13
Game:
8 Nick Altrock, AL:Chi. Oct. 12, 1906
Lon Warneke, NL:Chi. Oct. 2, 1935
Inning:
3 Eddie Plank, AL:Phil. Oct. 13, 1905 (8th)
Ed Reulbach, NL:Chi. Oct. 10, 1908 (6th)
Rube Marquard, NL:NY Oct. 7, 1913 (4th)
Lon Warneke, NL:Chi. Oct. 2, 1935 (3rd)
Johnny Murphy, AL:NY Oct. 8, 1939 (8th)
Bob Rush, NL:Mil. Oct. 4, 1958 (3rd)
Ray Washburn, NL:Cin. Oct. 15, 1970 (7th)

Errors
Lifetime:
3 Deacon Phillippe, NL:Pitt. 1903, 09
Eddie Cicotte, AL:Chi. 1917, 19
Max Lanier, NL:StL. 1942-44
Dave Stewart, NL:LA 1981; AL:Oak. 1989-90
Game:
2 Deacon Phillippe, NL:Pitt. Oct. 12, 1909
Jack Coombs, AL:Phil. Oct. 18, 1910
Eddie Cicotte, AL:Chi. Oct. 4, 1919
Max Lanier, NL:StL. Sept. 30, 1942
Nels Potter, AL:StL. Oct. 5, 1944 (11 inn)
Inning:
2 Jack Coombs, AL:Phil. Oct. 18, 1910 (5th)
Eddie Cicotte, AL:Chi. Oct. 4, 1919 (5th)
Max Lanier, NL:StL. Sept. 30, 1942 (9th)
Nels Potter, AL:StL. Oct. 5, 1944 (3rd)

Double Plays
Lifetime:
3 Chief Bender, AL:Phil. 1905, 10-11, 13-14
Joe Bush, AL:Phil.1913-14; Bos.18; NY 22-23
Allie Reynolds, AL:NY 1947, 49-53
Game:
2 Chief Bender, AL:Phil. Oct. 9, 1914
Joe Bush, AL:NY Oct. 8, 1922
Allie Reynolds, AL:NY Oct. 8, 1951
Larry Gura, AL:KC Oct. 19, 1980
Game, started:
2 Chief Bender, AL:Phil. Oct. 9, 1914
Joe Bush, AL:NY Oct. 8, 1922
Allie Reynolds, AL:NY Oct. 8, 1951
Game, unassisted:
None

Triple Plays
None

INDIVIDUAL PITCHING

	4 Games	5 Games	6 Games	7 Games

Earned Run Average 0.00 (Most Innings)

4 Games	5 Games	6 Games	7 Games
11.0 James, NL:Bos. 1914	27.0 Mathewson, NL:NY 1905	14.0 Benton, NL:NY 1917	27.0 Hoyt, AL:NY 1921 (8g)
			18.0 Ford, AL:NY 1960

Games

4 Games	5 Games	6 Games	7 Games
4 Nelson, AL:NY 1999	5 Marshall, NL:LA 1974	6 Quisenberry, AL:KC 1980	7 Knowles, AL:Oak. 1973
Foulke, AL:Bos. 2004	Reed, NL:NY 2015		Morrow, NL:LA 2017
Cotts, AL:Chi. 2005	Kelly, AL:Bos. 2018		
Jenks, AL:Chi. 2005			
Affeldt, NL:Col. 2007			

Games Started

4 Games	5 Games	6 Games	7 Games
2 By many; last:	3 Mathewson, NL:NY 1905	3 By many; last:	5 Phillippe, NL:Pitt. 1903 (8g)
Brown, NL:SD 1998	Coombs, AL:Phil. 1910	Wynn, AL:Chi. 1959	3 By many; last:
			Kluber, AL:Clev. 2016

Complete Games

4 Games	5 Games	6 Games	7 Games
2 Rudolph, NL:Bos. 1914	3 Mathewson, NL:NY 1905	3 Bender, AL:Phil. 1911	5 Phillippe, NL:Pitt. 1903 (8g)
Hoyt, AL:NY 1928	Coombs, AL:Phil. 1910	Vaughn, NL:Chi. 1918	3 Adams, NL:Pitt. 1909
Ruffing, AL:NY 1938			Mullin, AL:Det. 1909
Koufax, NL:LA 1963			Coveleski, AL:Clev. 1920
			Johnson, AL:Wash. 1925
			Newsom, AL:Det. 1940
			Burdette, NL:Mil. 1957
			Gibson, NL:StL. 1967-68
			Lolich, AL:Det. 1968

Shutouts

4 Games	5 Games	6 Games	7 Games
1 By many	3 Mathewson, NL:NY 1905	1 By many	2 Dineen, AL:Bos. 1903 (8g)
			Burdette, NL:Mil. 1957
			Ford, AL:NY 1960
			Koufax, NL:LA 1965

Games Finished

4 Games	5 Games	6 Games	7 Games
4 Foulke, AL:Bos. 2004	5 Marshall, NL:LA 1974	6 Quisenberry, AL:KC 1980	6 Casey, NL:Brk. 1947

Saves (Since 1969)

4 Games	5 Games	6 Games	7 Games
3 Rivera, AL:NY 1998	2 Fingers, AL:Oak. 1974	4 Wetteland, AL:NY 1996	3 Tekulve, NL:Pitt. 1979
Papelbon, AL:Bos. 2007	T. Martinez, AL:Balt. 1983		Percival, AL:Ana. 2002
Romo, NL:SF 2012	Hernandez, AL:Det. 1984		
	Rivera, AL:NY 2000		
	Lidge, NL:Phil. 2008		

Won

4 Games	5 Games	6 Games	7 Games
2 Rudolph, NL:Bos. 1914	3 Mathewson, NL:NY 1905	3 Faber, AL:Chi. 1917	3 Phillippe, NL:Pitt. 1903 (8g)
James, NL:Bos. 1914	Coombs, AL:Phil. 1910		Dinneen, AL:Bos. 1903 (8g)
Hoyt, AL:NY 1928			Adams, NL:Pitt. 1909
Ruffing, AL:NY 1938			Wood, AL:Bos. 1912 (8g)
Koufax, NL:LA 1963			Coveleski, AL:Clev. 1920
Stewart, AL:Oak. 1989			Brecheen, NL:StL. 1946
Moore, AL:Oak. 1989			Burdette, NL:Mil. 1957
Rijo, NL:Cin. 1990			Gibson, NL:StL. 1967
			Lolich, AL:Det. 1968
			Johnson, NL:Ari. 2001

Lost

4 Games	5 Games	6 Games	7 Games
2 Sherdel, NL:StL. 1928	2 By many; last:	3 Frazier, AL:NY 1981	3 Williams, AL:Chi. 1919 (8g)
Lee, NL:Chi. 1938	Kershaw, NL:LA 2018		2 By many; last:
Walters, NL:Cin. 1939			Verlander, AL:Hou. 2019
Lemon, AL:Clev. 1954			
Ford, AL:NY 1963			
Drysdale, NL:LA 1966			
Garrelts, NL:SF 1989			
Stewart, AL:Oak. 1990			
Lidge, NL:Hou. 2005			

4 Games	5 Games	6 Games	7 Games

Innings

18.0 Rudolph, NL:Bos. 1914	27.0 Mathewson, NL:NY 1905	27.0 Mathewson, NL:NY 1911	44.0 Phillippe, NL:Pitt. 1903 (8g)
Hoyt, AL:NY 1928	Coombs, AL:Phil. 1910	Faber, AL:Chi. 1917	32.0 Mullin, AL:Det. 1909
Ruffing, AL:NY 1938		Vaughn, NL:Chi. 1918	
Koufax, NL:LA 1963			

Runs

11 Alexander, NL:StL. 1928	16 Brown, NL:Chi. 1910	10 Sallee, NL:NY 1917	19 Phillippe, NL:Pitt. 1903 (8g)
Lemon, AL:Clev. 1954		Ruffing, AL:NY 1936	17 Burdette, NL:Mil. 1958
		Gullett, AL:NY 1977	
		Sutton, NL:LA 1978	
		Morris, AL:Tor. 1992	
		Glasnow, AL:TB 2020	

Hits

17 Ruffing, AL:NY 1938	23 Coombs, AL:Phil. 1910	25 Mathewson, NL:NY 1911	38 Phillippe, NL:Pitt. 1903 (8g)
	Brown, NL:Chi. 1910		30 Johnson, AL:Wash. 1924

Home Runs

4 Sherdel, NL:StL. 1928	4 Nolan, NL:Cin. 1970	4 Reynolds, AL:NY 1953	5 Burdette, NL:Mil. 1958
Root, NL:Chi. 1932	Hudson, NL:Phil. 1983		Hughes, NL:StL. 1967
Thompson, NL:Cin. 1939			
Garrelts, NL:SF 1989			

Walks

8 Lemon, AL:Clev. 1954	14 Coombs, AL:Phil. 1910	11 Tyler, NL:Chi. 1918	13 Nehf, NL:NY 1921 (8g)
		Gomez, AL:NY 1936	11 Johnson, AL:Wash. 1924
		Reynolds, AL:NY 1951	Bevens, AL:NY 1947
			Wilson, AL:Tex. 2011

Most Intentional Walks (since 1955)

2 Brown, NL:SD 1998	3 Brosnan, NL:Cin. 1961	2 By many	4 Lackey, AL:Ana. 2002
Francis, NL:Col. 2007	Colon, NL:NY 2015		Wilson, AL:Tex. 2011

Strikeouts

23 Koufax, NL:LA 1963	18 Mathewson, NL:NY 1905	20 Bender, AL:Phil. 1911	35 Gibson, NL:StL. 1968

SERVICE

Most Series, Lifetime
11 Whitey Ford, AL:NY 1950, 53, 55-58, 60-64

Most Series, Relief Pitcher, Lifetime
7 Mariano Rivera, AL:NY 1996, 98-2001, 03, 09

GAMES

Most Games, Lifetime
24 Mariano Rivera, AL:NY 1996, 98-2001, 03, 09

Most Games, Relief Pitcher, Lifetime
24 Mariano Rivera, AL:NY 1996, 98-2001, 03, 09

Most Games, Consecutive
7 Darold Knowles, AL:Oak. 1973
Jeff Nelson, AL:NY 1998-2000
Brandon Morrow, NL:LA 2017

GAMES STARTED

Most Games Started, Lifetime
22 Whitey Ford, AL:NY 1950, 53, 55-58, 60-64

Most Games Started, Consecutive
22 Whitey Ford, AL:NY 1950, 53, 55-58, 60-64

Most Opening Games Started, Lifetime
8 Whitey Ford, AL:NY 1955-58, 61-64

COMPLETE GAMES

Most Complete Games, Lifetime
10 Christy Mathewson, NL:NY 1905, 11-13

Most Complete Games, Consecutive
9 Chief Bender, AL:Phil. 1905, 10-11, 13

GAMES FINISHED

Most Games Finished, Lifetime
19 Mariano Rivera, AL:NY 1996, 98-2001, 03, 09

SAVES (since 1969)

Most Saves, Lifetime
11 Mariano Rivera, AL:NY 1996, 98-2001, 03, 09

SHUTOUTS

Most Shutouts
4 Christy Mathewson, NL:NY 1905, 13

Most Shutouts, Consecutive
3 Christy Mathewson, NL:NY 1905
Whitey Ford, AL:NY 1960-61

Most Consecutive Scoreless Innings
Complete game:
10 Christy Mathewson, NL:NY Oct. 8, 1913
Clem Labine, NL:Brk. Oct. 9, 1956
Jack Morris, AL:Minn. Oct. 27, 1991
Game, consecutive:
13 Babe Ruth, AL:Bos. Oct. 9, 1916 (14 inn)
Consecutive:
33 Whitey Ford, AL:NY 1960-62

GAMES WON

Most Won, Lifetime
10 Whitey Ford, AL:NY 1950, 53, 55-58, 60-64

Most Won, Consecutive
7 Bob Gibson, NL:StL. 1964, 67-68

GAMES LOST

Most Lost, Lifetime
8 Whitey Ford, AL:NY 1950, 53, 55-58, 60-64

Most Lost, Consecutive
6 Justin Verlander, AL:Det. 2006, 12; Hou. 17, 19

INNINGS PITCHED

Most Innings, Lifetime
146 Whitey Ford, AL:NY 1950, 53, 55-58, 60-64

Most Innings, Game
14 Babe Ruth, AL:Bos. Oct. 9, 1916

RUNS

Most Runs, Lifetime
51 Whitey Ford, AL:NY 1950, 53, 55-58, 60-64

Most Runs, Game
10 Brickyard Kennedy, NL:Pitt. Oct. 7, 1903

Most Runs, Inning
7 Hooks Wiltse, NL:NY Oct. 26, 1911 (7th)
Carl Hubbell, NL:NY Oct. 6, 1937 (6th)
Franklin Morales, NL:Col. Oct. 24, 2007 (5th)

EARNED RUNS

Most Earned Runs, Lifetime
44 Whitey Ford, AL:NY 1950, 53, 59-58, 60-64

Earned Runs, Game
8 Grover Alexander, NL:StL. Oct. 5, 1928
Guy Bush, NL:Chi. Sept. 28, 1932
Jay Witasick, AL:NY Nov. 3, 2001

Earned Runs, Inning
7 Franklin Morales, NL:Col. Oct. 24, 2007 (5th)

HITS

Most Hits, Lifetime
132 Whitey Ford, AL:NY 1950, 53, 55-58, 60-64

Most Hits, Game
15 Walter Johnson, AL:Wash. Oct. 15, 1925

Most Hits, Inning
8 Jay Witasick, AL:NY Nov. 3, 2001 (3rd)

Most Hits, Consecutive, Inning
6 Ed Summers, AL:Det. Oct. 10, 1908 (9th)

Most Hitless Innings, Consecutive
11.1 Don Larsen, AL:NY 1956-57

HOME RUNS

Most Home Runs, Lifetime
9 Catfish Hunter, AL:Oak. 1972-74; NY 76-78
Justin Verlander, AL:Det. 2006, 12; Hou: 17, 19

Most Home Runs, Game
4   Charlie Root, NL:Chi. Oct. 1, 1932
    Junior Thompson, NL:Cin. Oct. 7, 1939
    Dick Hughes, NL:StL. Oct. 11, 1967

Most Home Runs, Inning
3   Dick Hughes, NL:StL. Oct. 11, 1967 (4th)

Most Home Runs, Consecutive, Inning
2   By many; last:
    Josh Fields, NL:LA Oct. 25, 2017 (10th)

Most Grand Slam Home Runs, Lifetime
1   By many. See Batter's record.

WALKS

Most Walks, Lifetime
34   Whitey Ford, AL:NY 1950, 53, 55-58, 60-64

Most Walks, Game
10   Bill Bevens, AL:NY Oct. 3, 1947

Most Walks, Inning
4   Wild Bill Donovan, AL:Det. Oct. 16, 1909 (2nd)
    Art Reinhart, NL:StL. Oct. 6, 1926 (5th)
    Paul Derringer, NL:StL. Oct. 9, 1931 (5th)
    Guy Bush, NL:Chi. Sept. 28, 1932 (6th)
    Don Gullett, NL:Cin. Oct. 22, 1975 (3rd)
    Bobby Castillo, NL:LA Oct. 20, 1981 (4th)
    Tom Glavine, NL:Atl. Oct. 24, 1991 (6th)
    Todd Stottlemyre, AL:Tor. Oct. 20, 1993 (1st)
    Al Leiter, NL:Fla. Oct. 21, 1997 (4th)
    Jarrod Washburn, AL:Ana. Oct. 24, 2002 (1st)
    Tim Wakefield, AL:Bos. Oct. 23, 2004 (4th)
    Consecutive:
3   By many; last:
    Lance McCullers Jr., AL:Hou. Oct. 27, 2017 (3rd)

Most Intentional Walks, Lifetime (since 1955)
5   John Lackey, AL:Ana. 2002; NL:Chi. 2016

HIT BATTERS

Most Hit Batters, Lifetime
4   Wild Bill Donovan, AL:Det. 1907, 09
    Eddie Plank, AL:Phil. 1905, 11, 13-14
    Lance McCullers Jr., AL:Hou. 2017

Most Hit Batters, Game
4   Lance McCullers Jr., AL:Hou. Nov. 1, 2017
Most Hit Batters, Inning
2   Ed Willett, AL:Det. Oct. 11, 1909 (2nd)
    Wayne Granger, NL:StL. Oct. 9, 1968 (8th)
    Jose Contreras, AL:Chi. Oct. 22, 2005 (7th)
    Lance McCullers Jr., AL:Hou. Nov. 1, 2017 (1st)

STRIKEOUTS

Most Strikeouts, Lifetime
94   Whitey Ford, AL:NY 1950, 53, 55-58, 60-64

Most Strikeouts, Game
17   Bob Gibson, NL:StL. Oct. 2, 1968
    Relief pitcher:
11   Moe Drabowsky, AL:Balt. Oct. 5, 1966

Most Strikeouts, Inning
4   Orval Overall, NL:Chi. Oct. 14, 1908 (1st)

Most Strikeouts, Consecutive Batters Faced
7   Phil Coke, AL:Det. Oct. 25-28, 2012

Most Strikeouts, Consecutive Batters Faced, Game
6   Hod Eller, NL:Cin. Oct. 6, 1919
    Moe Drabowsky, AL:Balt. Oct. 5, 1966
    Todd Worrell, NL:StL. Oct. 24, 1985

Most Strikeouts, Consecutive, Start of Game:
5   Mort Cooper, NL:StL. Oct. 11, 1943
    Sandy Koufax, NL:LA, Oct. 2, 1963

WILD PITCHES

Most Wild Pitches, Lifetime
5   Hal Schumacher, NL:NY 1933, 36-37
    Jack Morris, AL:Det. 1984; Minn. 91; Tor. 92

Most Wild Pitches, Game
3   Tyler Glasnow, AL:TB Oct. 25, 2020

Most Wild Pitches, Inning
2   Bob Shawkey, AL:NY Oct. 5, 1922 (5th)
    Vic Aldridge, NL:Pitt. Oct. 15, 1925 (1st)
    Johnny Miljus, NL:Pitt. Oct. 8, 1927 (9th)
    Tex Carleton, NL:Chi. Oct. 9, 1938 (8th)
    Doc Medich, AL:Mil. Oct. 19, 1982 (6th)
    Justin Verlander, AL:Det. Oct. 27, 2006 (1st)
    Tyler Glasnow, AL:TB Oct. 25, 2020 (1st)

BALKS

1912	Oct.	14	AL:Bos	O'Brien, Buck
1919	Oct.	2	NL:Cin.	Sallee, Slim
1925	Oct.	8	NL:Pitt.	Aldridge, Vic
1926	Oct.	6	NL:StL.	Bell, Hi
1935	Oct.	5	NL:Chi.	Carleton, Tex
1947	Sept.	30	AL:NY	Shea, Spec
1948	Oct.	10	AL:Clev.	Paige, Satchel
1948	Oct.	11	AL:Clev.	Lemon, Bob
1952	Oct.	6	NL:Brk.	Loes, Billy
1953	Oct.	2	AL:NY	Raschi, Vic
1965	Oct.	7	NL:LA	Perranoski, Ron
1967	Oct.	4	AL:Bos.	Wyatt, John
1975	Oct.	11	AL:Bos.	Tiant, Luis
1979	Oct.	12	AL:Balt.	McGregor, Scott
1982	Oct.	19	AL:Mil.	Sutton, Don
1983	Oct.	15	AL:Balt.	Stewart, Sammy
1984	Oct.	10	AL:Det.	Petry, Dan
1985	Oct.	22	NL:StL.	Horton, Ricky
1987	Oct.	20	AL:Minn.	Straker, Les
1987	Oct.	22	AL:Minn.	Atherton, Keith
1988	Oct.	15	AL:Oak.	Stewart, Dave
1988	Oct.	18	NL:LA	Leary, Tim
1989	Oct.	27	NL:SF	Brantley, Jeff
1991	Oct.	20	NL:Atl.	Glavine, Tom
1993	Oct.	17	AL:Tor.	Stewart, Dave
1995	Oct.	25	NL:Atl.	Avery, Steve
1996	Oct.	23	AL:NY	Weathers, David
2007	Oct.	24	NL:Col.	Morales, Franklin
2013	Oct.	30	NL:StL.	Rosenthal, Trevor

CLUB BATTING – SERIES

BATTING AVERAGE

	4 Games	5 Games	6 Games	7 Games
Highest Batting Average, Winning Club				
	.333 AL:Bos. (Col.) 2007	.316 AL:Phil. (Chi.) 1910	.311 AL:Tor. (Phil.) 1993	.323 NL:Pitt. (Balt.) 1979
Highest Batting Average, Losing Club				
	.253 NL:Chi. (NY) 1932	.265 NL:SD (Det.) 1984	.300 NL:Brk. (NY) 1953	.338 AL:NY (Pitt.) 1960
Highest Batting Average, Both Clubs				
	.283 AL:NY (Chi.) 1932	.272 AL:Phil. (Chi.) 1910	.292 AL:Tor. (Phil.) 1993	.300 AL:NY (Pitt.) 1960
Lowest Batting Average, Winning Club				
	.200 AL:Balt. (LA) 1966	.209 NL:NY (Phil.) 1905	.186 AL:Bos. (Chi.) 1918	.199 AL:NY (SF) 1962
Lowest Batting Average, Losing Club				
	.142 NL:LA (Balt.) 1966	.146 AL:Balt. (NY) 1969	.175 NL:NY (Phil.) 1911	.183 AL:NY (Ari.) 2001
Lowest Batting Average, Both Clubs				
	.171 NL:LA (Balt.) 1966	.184 AL:Balt. (NY) 1969	.197 AL:Chi. (Chi.) 1906	.209 AL:Oak. (Cin.) 1972

SLUGGING PERCENTAGE

	4 Games	5 Games	6 Games	7 Games
Highest Slugging Percentage, Winning Club				
	.582 AL:Oak. (SF) 1989	.509 AL:Balt. (Cin.) 1970	.510 AL:Tor. (Phil.) 1993	.467 AL:Hou. (LA) 2017
Highest Slugging Percentage, Losing Club				
	.397 NL:Chi. (NY) 1932	.361 NL:SD (Det.) 1984	.484 NL:Brk. (NY) 1953	.528 AL:NY (Pitt.) 1960
Highest Slugging Percentage, Both Clubs				
	.468 AL:Oak. (SF) 1989	.433 AL:Balt. (Cin.) 1970	.483 NL:Brk. (NY) 1953	.481 AL:Ana. (SF) 2002
Lowest Slugging Percentage, Winning Club				
	.304 AL:NY (Phil.) 1950	.255 NL:NY (Phil.) 1905	.233 AL:Bos. (Chi.) 1918	.276 AL:NY (SF) 1962
Lowest Slugging Percentage, Losing Club				
	.192 NL:LA (Balt.) 1966	.194 AL:Phil. (NY) 1905	.243 NL:NY (Phil.) 1911	.237 NL:Brk. (Clev.) 1920
Lowest Slugging Percentage, Both Clubs				
	.267 AL:Balt. (LA) 1966	.224 NL:NY (Phil.) 1905	.241 NL:Chi. (Bos.) 1918	.285 AL:Clev. (Brk.) 1920

AT-BATS

	4 Games	5 Games	6 Games	7 Games
Most At-Bats				
	154 AL:Chi. (Hou.) 2005	197 AL:KC (NY) 2015	222 AL:NY (LA) 1978	282 AL:Bos. (Pitt.) 1903 (8g)
				269 AL:NY (Pitt.) 1960
Most At-Bats, Both Clubs				
	297 AL:Chi. (Hou.) 2005	378 AL:KC (NY) 2015	421 AL:NY (LA) 1978	552 AL:Bos. (Pitt.) 1903 (8g)
		AL:Bos. (LA) 2018		512 NL:StL. (Det.) 1934
Fewest At-Bats				
	117 NL:LA (NY) 1963	142 AL:Oak. (LA) 1974	172 AL:Bos. (Chi.) 1918	215 NL:Brk. (Clev.) 1920
				NL:Brk. (NY) 1956
				AL:Minn. (LA) 1965
Fewest At-Bats, Both Clubs				
	240 AL:Balt. (LA) 1966	300 AL:Oak. (LA) 1974	348 NL:Chi. (Bos.) 1918	432 AL:Clev. (Brk.) 1920

RUNS

	4 Games	5 Games	6 Games	7 Games
Most Runs				
	37 AL:NY (Chi.) 1932	35 AL:Phil. (Chi.) 1910	45 AL:Tor. (Phil.) 1993	55 AL:NY (Pitt.) 1960
Most Runs, Losing Club				
	19 NL:Chi. (NY) 1932	20 NL:Cin. (Balt.) 1970	36 NL:Phil. (Tor.) 1993	55 AL:NY (Pitt.) 1960
Most Runs, Both Clubs				
	56 AL:NY (Chi.) 1932	53 AL:Balt. (Cin.) 1970	81 AL:Tor. (Phil.) 1993	85 AL:Ana. (SF) 2002
Fewest Runs				
	2 NL:LA (Balt.) 1966	3 AL:Phil. (NY) 1905	9 AL:Bos. (Chi.) 1918	8 NL:Brk. (Clev.) 1920
Fewest Runs, Both Clubs				
	15 AL:Balt. (LA) 1966	18 NL:NY (Phil.) 1905	19 NL:Chi. (Bos.) 1918	29 AL:Clev. (Brk.) 1920

HITS

4 Games	5 Games	6 Games	7 Games
Most Hits			
47 AL:Bos. (Col.) 2007	56 AL:Phil. (Chi.) 1910	68 AL:NY (LA) 1978	91 AL:NY (Pitt.) 1960
Most Hits, Both Clubs			
82 AL:NY (Chi.) 1932	91 AL:Phil. (Chi.) 1910	122 AL:Tor. (Phil.) 1993	151 AL:NY (Pitt.) 1960
	AL:Phil. (Chi.) 1929		
Fewest Hits			
17 NL:LA (Balt.) 1966	23 AL:Balt. (NY) 1969	32 AL:Bos. (Chi.) 1918	40 NL:StL. (KC) 1985
Fewest Hits, Both Clubs			
41 AL:Balt. (LA) 1966	57 NL:NY (Phil.) 1905	69 NL:Chi. (Bos.) 1918	92 AL:Oak. (Cin.) 1972

EXTRA-BASE HITS

4 Games	5 Games	6 Games	7 Games
Most Extra-Base Hits			
21 AL:Bos. (Col.) 2007	21 AL:Phil. (Chi.) 1910	24 AL:Tor. (Phil.) 1993	28 AL:Hou. (LA) 2017
Most Extra-Base Hits, Both Clubs			
31 AL:Bos. (Col.) 2007	33 AL:Phil. (Chi.) 1910	41 NL:Brk. (NY) 1953	50 AL:Hou. (LA) 2017
		AL:NY (Phil.) 2009	
Fewest Extra-Base Hits			
4 NL:Cin. (NY) 1939	3 AL:Det. (Chi.) 1907	5 AL:Bos. (Chi.) 1918	6 NL:Brk. (Clev.) 1920
NL:LA (Balt.) 1966			
Fewest Extra-Base Hits, Both Clubs			
12 AL:Balt. (LA) 1966	10 NL:Chi. (Det.) 1907	11 NL:Chi. (Bos.) 1918	19 AL:Clev. (Brk.) 1920

TOTAL BASES

4 Games	5 Games	6 Games	7 Games
Most Total Bases			
85 AL:Oak. (SF) 1989	87 AL:Balt. (Cin.) 1970	105 AL:Tor. (Phil.) 1993	142 AL:NY (Pitt.) 1960
Most Total Bases, Both Clubs			
133 AL:NY (Chi.) 1932	145 AL:Balt. (Cin.) 1970	200 NL:Brk. (NY) 1953	231 AL:Ana. (SF) 2002
Fewest Total Bases			
23 NL:LA (Balt.) 1966	30 AL:Phil. (NY) 1905	40 AL:Bos. (Chi.) 1918	51 NL:Brk. (Clev.) 1920
Fewest Total Bases, Both Clubs			
64 AL:Balt. (LA) 1966	69 NL:NY (Phil.) 1905	84 NL:Chi. (Bos.) 1918	123 AL:Clev. (Brk.) 1920

SINGLES

4 Games	5 Games	6 Games	7 Games
Most Singles			
32 AL:NY (SD) 1998	46 NL:NY (NY) 1922	57 AL:NY (LA) 1978	64 AL:NY (Pitt.) 1960
Most Singles, Both Clubs			
55 AL:NY (Chi.) 1932	71 NL:Chi. (Phil.) 1929	95 AL:NY (LA) 1978	109 AL:NY (Pitt.) 1960
Fewest Singles			
13 AL:Phil. (Bos.) 1914	19 NL:Brk. (NY) 1941	17 AL:Phil. (StL) 1930	25 NL:LA (Hou.) 2017
NL:LA (Balt.) 1966	AL:Balt. (NY) 1969		
	AL:Det. (StL) 2006		
Fewest Singles, Both Clubs			
29 AL:Balt. (LA) 1966	40 NL:NY (Balt.) 1969	42 NL:StL. (Phil.) 1930	53 NL:LA (Hou.) 2017

DOUBLES

4 Games	5 Games	6 Games	7 Games
Most Doubles			
18 AL:Bos. (Col.) 2007	19 AL:Phil. (Chi.) 1910	15 AL:Phil. (NY) 1911	19 NL:StL. (Bos.) 1946
Most Doubles, Both Clubs			
24 AL:Bos. (Col.) 2007	30 AL:Phil. (Chi.) 1910	26 AL:Phil. (NY) 1911	29 AL:Det. (Pitt.) 1909
Fewest Doubles			
2 AL:Det. (SF) 2012	1 AL:Det. (Chi.) 1907	2 AL:Bos. (Chi.) 1918	3 AL:Balt. (Pitt.) 1971
	AL:Balt. (NY) 1969	NL:NY (NY) 1923	
	NL:NY (KC) 2015		
Fewest Doubles, Both Clubs			
6 NL:LA (NY) 1963	6 NL:Phil. (Bos.) 1915	7 NL:Chi. (Bos.) 1918	11 AL:Bos. (Pitt.) 1903 (8g)
AL:Balt. (LA) 1966			NL:StL. (Det.) 1968
AL:Det. (SF) 2012			

TRIPLES

4 Games	5 Games	6 Games	7 Games
Most Triples			
3 NL:Cin. (NY) 1976	6 AL:Bos. (Brk.) 1916	5 AL:Tor. (Phil.) 1993	16 AL:Bos. (Pitt.) 1903 (8g)
AL:Oak. (SF) 1989			5 NL:StL. (Det.) 1934
			AL:NY (Brk.) 1947
Most Triples, Both Clubs			
4 NL:Cin. (NY) 1976	11 AL:Bos. (Brk.) 1916	7 AL:NY (NY) 1923	25 AL:Bos. (Pitt.) 1903 (8g)
AL:Oak. (SF) 1989		AL:Tor. (Phil.) 1993	8 AL:Minn. (Atl.) 1991
Fewest Triples			
0 By many	0 By many	0 By many	0 By many
Fewest Triples, Both Clubs			
1 NL:StL. (NY) 1928	0 NL:NY (Phil.) 1905	0 AL:Clev. (Bos.) 1948	0 NL:StL. (Phil.) 1931
AL:Clev. (NY) 1954	NL:NY (Wash.) 1933	AL:NY (LA) 1978	AL:NY (Ari.) 2001
AL:Balt. (LA) 1966	NL:NY (Balt.) 1969	AL:Tor. (Atl.) 1992	
AL:NY (SD) 1998	NL:SD (Det.) 1984		
AL:NY (Atl.) 1999	NL:Phil. (TB) 2008		
AL:Bos. (Col.) 2007			

HOME RUNS

4 Games	5 Games	6 Games	7 Games
Most Home Runs			
9 AL:NY (StL.) 1928	10 AL:Balt. (Cin.) 1970	12 NL:LA (TB) 2020	15 AL:Hou. (LA) 2017
AL:Oak. (SF) 1989			
Most Home Runs, Both Clubs			
13 AL:Oak. (SF) 1989	15 AL:Balt. (Cin.) 1970	21 NL:LA (TB) 2020	25 AL:Hou. (LA) 2017
Fewest Home Runs			
0 By many	0 By many	0 By many	0 NL:Cin. (Chi.) 1919 (8g)
			NL:Brk. (Clev.) 1920
Fewest Home Runs, Both Clubs			
1 NL:Bos. (Phil.) 1914	0 NL:NY (Phil.) 1905	0 AL:Chi. (Chi.) 1906	1 AL:Chi. (Cin.) 1919 (8g)
	NL:Chi. (Det.) 1907	AL:Bos. (Chi.) 1918	

RUNS BATTED IN

4 Games	5 Games	6 Games	7 Games
Most Runs Batted In			
36 AL:NY (Chi.) 1932	32 AL:Balt. (Cin.) 1970	45 AL:Tor. (Phil.) 1993	54 AL:NY (Pitt.) 1960
Most Runs Batted In, Both Clubs			
52 AL:NY (Chi.) 1932	52 AL:Balt. (Cin.) 1970	80 AL:Tor. (Phil.) 1993	80 AL:NY (Pitt.) 1960
			AL:Ana. (SF) 2002
Fewest Runs Batted In			
2 NL:LA (Balt.) 1966	2 AL:Phil. (NY) 1905	6 AL:Bos. (Chi.) 1918	8 NL:Brk. (Clev.) 1920
Fewest Runs Batted In, Both Clubs			
12 NL:LA (Balt.) 1966	15 AL:Phil. (NY) 1905	16 AL:Bos. (Chi.) 1918	25 NL:Brk. (Clev.) 1920

SACRIFICE HITS

4 Games	5 Games	6 Games	7 Games
Most Sacrifice Hits			
6 By many	12 AL:Bos. (Brk.) 1916	13 NL:Chi. (Chi.) 1906	13 NL:Cin. (Chi.) 1919 (8g)
			12 NL:Pitt. (Det.) 1909
			NL:StL. (NY) 1926
Most Sacrifice Hits, Both Clubs			
12 AL:NY (Pitt.) 1927	18 AL:Bos. (Brk.) 1916	19 NL:Chi. (Chi.) 1906	22 NL:StL. (NY) 1926
Fewest Sacrifice Hits			
0 By many	0 By many	0 NL:NY (NY) 1923	0 NL:StL. (Bos.) 1967
		AL:NY (NY) 1951	NL:Chi. (Clev.) 2016
		NL:LA (NY) 1977	
		AL:Tor. (Phil.) 1993	
		AL:Clev. (Atl.) 1995	
		AL:Bos. (StL.) 2013	
		AL:TB (LA) 2020	
Fewest Sacrifice Hits, Both Clubs			
0 NL:Cin. (NY) 1976	0 AL:NY (Brk.) 1941	1 AL:Tor. (Phil.) 1993	2 NL:StL. (Mil.) 1982
AL:Oak. (SF) 1989	AL:Balt. (Phil.) 1983	AL:TB (LA) 2020	AL:Hou. (LA) 2017

SACRIFICE FLIES (Since 1954)

4 Games	5 Games	6 Games	7 Games
Most Sacrifice Flies			
3 NL:StL. (Bos.) 2004	4 NL:NY (KC) 2015	7 AL:Tor. (Phil.) 1993	5 NL:Pitt. (Balt.) 1979
Most Sacrifice Flies, Both Clubs			
3 NL:Cin. (NY) 1976	7 NL:NY (KC) 2015	8 AL:Tor. (Phil.) 1993	7 AL:Ana. (SF) 2002
AL:NY (SD) 1998			
NL:StL. (Bos.) 2004			
Fewest Sacrifice Flies			
0 By many	0 By many	0 By many	0 By many
Fewest Sacrifice Flies, Both Clubs			
0 AL:Balt. (LA) 1966	0 NL:StL. (Det.) 2006	0 AL:NY (LA) 1978	0 AL:Minn. (LA) 1965
AL:NY (Atl.) 1999			AL:KC (StL.) 1985

WALKS

4 Games	5 Games	6 Games	7 Games
Most Walks			
24 AL:Bos. (StL.) 2004	27 NL:Phil. (TB) 2008	34 NL:Phil. (Tor.) 1993	41 NL:StL. (Tex.) 2011
Most Walks, Both Clubs			
36 AL:Bos. (StL.) 2004	38 AL:Bos. (LA) 2018	59 NL:Phil. (Tor.) 1993	76 AL:Clev. (Fla.) 1997
Fewest Walks			
4 NL:Pitt. (NY) 1927	5 AL:Phil. (NY) 1905	4 AL:Phil. (NY) 1911	9 NL:StL. (Phil.) 1931
Fewest Walks, Both Clubs			
15 AL:NY (Cin.) 1939	15 NL:NY (Phil.) 1913	17 AL:Chi. (NY) 1917	27 AL:Bos. (Pitt.) 1903 (8g)
Most Intentional Walks			
4 NL:NY (Clev.) 1954	7 AL:NY (NY) 2000	7 AL:NY (LA) 1981	9 NL:SF (Ana.) 2002
			NL:StL. (Tex.) 2011

HIT BY PITCH

4 Games	5 Games	6 Games	7 Games
Most Hit By Pitch			
5 NL:Hou. (Chi.) 2005	4 NL:Chi. (Det.) 1907	6 AL:NY (Phil.) 2009	7 NL:LA (Hou.) 2017
Most Hit By Pitch, Both Clubs			
8 NL:Hou. (Chi.) 2005	6 AL:NY (NY) 2000	7 AL:NY (Phil.) 2009	10 NL:Pitt. (Det.) 1909
Fewest Hit By Pitch			
0 By many	0 By many	0 By many	0 By many
Fewest Hit By Pitch, Both Clubs			
0 NL:LA (Balt.) 1966	0 AL:Wash. (NY) 1933	0 AL:StL. (StL.) 1944	0 AL:Clev. (Brk.) 1920
AL:NY (Atl.) 1999	AL:NY (StL.) 1942-43		AL:Det. (Cin.) 1940
	AL:Balt. (Cin.) 1970		AL:NY (Brk.) 1956
			AL:NY (Mil.) 1958

STRIKEOUTS

4 Games	5 Games	6 Games	7 Games
Most Strikeouts			
41 NL:SF (Det.) 2012	56 NL:LA (Bos.) 2018	70 AL:TB (LA) 2020	70 NL:Ari. (NY) 2001
Most Strikeouts, Both Clubs			
77 NL:SF (Det.) 2012	109 NL:LA (Bos.) 2018	131 AL:TB (LA) 2020	133 AL:NY (Ari.) 2001
			AL:Clev. (Chi.) 2016
Fewest Strikeouts			
7 NL:Pitt. (NY) 1927	15 NL:NY (NY) 1922	14 NL:Chi. (Bos.) 1918	20 NL:Brk. (Clev.) 1920
Fewest Strikeouts, Both Clubs			
32 AL:NY (Pitt.) 1927	35 NL:NY(Phil.) 1913	35 AL:Bos. (Chi.) 1918	41 AL:Clev. (Brk.) 1920
NL:Cin. (NY) 1976	AL:NY (NY) 1922		

STOLEN BASES

4 Games	5 Games	6 Games	7 Games
Most Stolen Bases			
9 NL:Bos. (Phil.) 1914	18 NL:Chi. (Det.) 1907	15 NL:Atl. (Tor.) 1992	18 NL:Pitt. (Det.) 1909
Most Stolen Bases, Both Clubs			
11 NL:Bos. (Phil.) 1914	26 NL:Chi. (Det.) 1907	20 NL:Atl. (Tor.) 1992	24 NL:Pitt. (Det.) 1909
Fewest Stolen Bases			
0 By many	0 By many	0 By many	0 By many
Fewest Stolen Bases, Both Clubs			
1 NL:Cin. (NY) 1939	1 NL:Chi. (Phil.) 1929	0 NL:StL. (StL.) 1944	1 NL:Cin. (Det.) 1940
NL:NY (Clev.) 1954	AL:Wash. (NY) 1933		NL:StL. (Tex.) 2011
NL:LA (Balt.) 1966	NL:NY (NY) 1937		
NL:StL. (Bos.) 2004	AL:NY (Cin.) 1961		
	NL:Cin. (Balt.) 1970		
	AL:NY (NY) 2000		

CAUGHT STEALING

4 Games	5 Games	6 Games	7 Games
Most Caught Stealing			
5 NL:Cin. (NY) 1976	8 NL:Chi. (Phil.) 1910	10 NL:NY (Phil.) 1911	10 NL:Cin. (Chi.) 1919 (8g)
			8 NL:StL. (Det.) 1968
Most Caught Stealing, Both Clubs			
7 NL:Cin. (NY) 1976	15 NL:Chi. (Phil.) 1910	16 NL:NY (Phil.) 1911	15 AL:Chi. (Cin.) 1919 (8g)
			AL:NY (NY) 1921 (8g)
			10 NL:Pitt. (Det.) 1909
			AL:Det. (StL.) 1968
Fewest Caught Stealing (Most Attempts)			
0 AL:Oak. (Cin.) 1990 (7)	0 AL:KC (NY) 2015 (7)	0 AL:Tor. (Atl.) 1992 (5)	0 AL:Minn. (StL.) 1987 (6)
		NL:Phil. (NY) 2009 (5)	AL:Ana. (SF) 2002 (6)
Fewest Caught Stealing, Both Clubs (Most Attempts)			
0 AL:Bos. (Col.) 2007 (3)	0 AL:NY (Brk.) 1949 (3)	0 AL:NY (Phil.) 2009 (9)	0 AL:NY (StL.) 1964 (5)

LEFT ON BASE

4 Games	5 Games	6 Games	7 Games
Most Left on Base			
41 AL:Bos. (StL) 2004	52 AL:NY (NY) 2000	55 AL:NY (LA) 1981	72 NL:NY (Oak.) 1973
Most Left on Base, Both Clubs			
65 AL:Clev. (NY) 1954	88 AL:NY (NY) 2000	101 AL:NY (LA) 1981	130 NL:NY (Oak.) 1973
AL:Bos. (StL.) 2004			
Fewest Left on Base			
16 NY (Cin.) 1939	23 NL:Phil. (Bos.) 1915	28 AL:TB (LA) 2020	34 NL:LA (Hou.) 2017
	NL:Phil. (Balt.) 1983		
	AL:TB (Phil.) 2008		
Fewest Left on Base, Both Clubs			
39 NL:Cin. (NY) 1939	51 NL:Phil. (Balt.) 1983	61 NL:NY (Phil.) 1911	76 NL:LA (Hou.) 2017

PINCH-HITTING

4 Games	5 Games	6 Games	7 Games
Most Pinch-Hitters			
16 AL:Clev. (NY) 1954	16 NL:LA (Bos.) 2018	16 AL:TB (LA) 2020	23 AL:Balt. (Pitt.) 1979
Most Pinch-Hitters, Both Clubs			
19 AL:Clev. (NY) 1954	27 NL:LA (Bos.) 2018	24 NL:LA (NY) 1981	37 AL:Minn. (Atl.) 1991
Fewest Pinch-Hitters			
0 AL:NY (Cin.) 1939	0 AL:Phil. (Chi.) 1910	0 AL:Phil. (NY) 1911	1 NL:Pitt. (Bos.) 1903 (8g)
AL:Balt. (LA) 1966	AL:Phil. (NY) 1913		
NL:Cin. (NY) 1976			
Fewest Pinch-Hitters, Both Clubs			
3 NL:Cin. (NY) 1939	2 NL:NY (Phil.) 1905	6 NL:NY (Phil.) 1911	5 AL:Bos. (Pitt.) 1903 (8g)
		AL:Chi. (Chi.) 1906	AL:NY (NY) 1921 (8g)

PINCH-RUNNING

4 Games	5 Games	6 Games	7 Games
Most Pinch-Runners			
4 NL:Phil. (NY) 1950	5 NL:NY (Phil.) 1913	5 AL:NY (LA) 1981	8 AL:Oak. (Cin.) 1972
		AL:TB (LA) 2020	
Most Pinch-Runners, Both Clubs			
6 NL:Phil. (NY) 1950	6 AL:Oak. (LA) 1974	7 AL:NY (LA) 1981	10 AL:Oak. (Cin.) 1972
	AL:Balt. (Phil.) 1983		
Fewest Pinch-Runners			
0 By many	0 By many	0 By many	0 By many
Fewest Pinch-Runners, Both Clubs			
0 AL:NY (Chi.) 1938	0 NL:NY (Phil.) 1905	0 AL:Chi. (NY) 1917	0 AL:Bos. (Pitt.) 1903 (8g)
NL:LA (NY) 1963	AL:Phil. (Chi.) 1929	AL:Phil. (StL.) 1930	AL:NY (Brk.) 1956
NL:Cin. (NY) 1976	AL:NY (NY) 1937	AL:Det. (Chi.) 1935	NL:Cin. (Bos.) 1975
AL:Oak. (SF) 1989	AL:Balt. (Cin.) 1970	AL:NY (Brk.) 1953	
	NL:SF (Tex.) 2010		

PLATE APPEARANCES

Most Plate Appearances, Game
53 AL:NY (Chi.) Oct. 2, 1932
Extra-Inning Game:
66 NL:LA (Bos.) Oct. 26, 2018 (18 inn)
Fewest, 9-Inning Game:
26 NL:LA (NY) Oct. 6, 1963
AL:Balt. (LA) Oct. 8, 1966

Most Plate Appearances, Both Clubs, Game
101 AL:Tor. (Phil.) Oct. 20, 1993
Extra-Inning Game:
131 NL:LA (Bos.) Oct. 26, 2018 (18 inn)
Fewest, 9-Inning Game:
56 NL:Brk. (NY) Oct. 8, 1956

Most Plate Appearances, Inning
15 AL:Phil. (Chi.) Oct. 12, 1929 (7th)
AL:Det. (StL.) Oct. 9, 1968 (3rd)

Most Plate Appearances, Both Clubs, Inning
20 AL:Phil. (Chi.) Oct. 12, 1929 (7th)

AT-BATS

Most At-Bats, Game
46 NL:Ari. (NY) Nov. 3, 2001
Extra-Inning Game:
61 NL:LA (Bos.) Oct. 26, 2018 (18 inn)
Fewest, 9-Inning Game:
23 NL:Cin. (Chi.) Oct. 2, 1919

Most At-Bats, Both Clubs, Game
85 AL:Tor. (Phil.) Oct. 20, 1993
Extra-Inning Game:
118 NL:LA (Bos.) Oct. 26, 2018 (18 inn)
Fewest, 9-Inning Game:
53 NL:Brk. (Clev.) Oct. 7, 1920
AL:NY (NY) Oct. 6, 1921
AL:NY (Brk.) Oct. 8, 1956
NL:LA (NY) Oct. 5, 1963
AL:Det. (SF) Oct. 25, 2012

Most At-Bats, Inning
13 AL:Phil. (Chi.) Oct. 12, 1929 (7th)

Most At-Bats, Both Clubs, Inning
17 AL:Phil. (Chi.) Oct. 12, 1929 (7th)

RUNS

Most Runs, Game
18 AL:NY (NY) Oct. 2, 1936

Most Earned Runs, Game
17 AL:NY (NY) Oct. 2, 1936

Most Runs, Both Clubs, Game
29 AL:Tor. (Phil.) Oct. 20, 1993

Most Earned Runs, Both Clubs, Game
29 AL:Tor. (Phil.) Oct. 20, 1993

Most Runs, Inning
10 AL:Phil. (Chi.) Oct. 12, 1929 (7th)
AL:Det. (StL.) Oct. 9, 1968 (3rd)

Most Runs, Both Clubs, Inning
11 AL:Phil. (Chi.) Oct. 12, 1929 (7th)
NL:Brk. (NY) Oct. 5, 1956 (2nd)
NL:Fla. (Clev.) Oct. 21, 1997 (9th)

Most Innings Scoring Runs, Game
7 NL:StL. (Tex.) Oct. 22, 2011
NL:StL. (Tex.) Oct. 27, 2011 (11 inn)

Most Innings Scoring Runs, Both Clubs, Game
11 NL:LA (TB) Oct. 24, 2020
Extra-Inning Game:
13 NL:StL. (Tex.) Oct. 27, 2011 (11 inn)

Most Runs, Each Inning, Club

7	1st:	NL:Mil. (NY) Oct. 2, 1958
7	2nd:	AL:KC (SF) Oct. 28, 2014
10	3rd:	AL:Det. (StL.) Oct. 9, 1968
7	4th:	AL:Minn. (StL.) Oct. 17, 1987
7	5th:	AL:Bos. (Col.) Oct. 24, 2007
7	6th:	AL:NY (NY) Oct. 6, 1937
		AL:NY (Pitt.) Oct. 6, 1960
10	7th:	AL:Phil. (Chi.) Oct. 12, 1929
7	8th:	NL:SF (Tex.) Oct. 28, 2010
7	9th:	AL:NY (NY) Oct. 6, 1936
		NL:Fla. (Clev.) Oct. 21, 1997
3	10th:	NL:NY (Phil.) Oct. 8, 1913
		AL:NY (Cin.) Oct. 8, 1939
		NL:NY (Clev.) Sept. 29, 1954
		NL:Mil. (NY) Oct. 6, 1957
		NL:StL. (NY) Oct. 12, 1964
		NL:NY (Bos.) Oct. 25, 1986
2	11th:	AL:Phil. (NY) Oct. 17, 1911
		AL:Tor. (Atl.) Oct. 24, 1992
		AL:Hou. (LA) Oct. 25, 2017
5	12th:	AL:KC (NY) Nov. 1, 2015
1	13th:	AL:Bos. (LA) Oct. 26, 2018
		NL:LA (Bos.) Oct. 26, 2018
2	14th:	AL:Chi. (Hou.) Oct. 25, 2005
1	18th:ˋ	NL:LA (Bos.) Oct. 26, 2018

HITS

Most Hits, Game
22 NL:Ari. (NY) Nov. 3, 2001

Most Hits, Both Clubs, Game
32 AL:NY (Pitt.) Oct. 6, 1960
AL:Tor. (Phil.) Oct. 20, 1993

Most Hits, Inning
10 AL:Phil. (Chi.) Oct. 12, 1929 (7th)

Most Hits, Both Clubs, Inning
12 AL:Phil. (Chi.) Oct. 12, 1929 (7th)

Most Hits, Consecutive, Inning
8 NL:NY (NY) Oct. 7, 1921 (7th; 2 bb, sh)

Most Hitless Innings, Consecutive
11 NL:Cin. (NY) Oct. 4-5, 1939
Complete game:
9 NL:Brk. (NY) Oct. 8, 1956

EXTRA-BASE HITS

Most Extra-Base Hits, Game
9 NL:Pitt. (Wash.) Oct. 15, 1925
AL:Bos. (Col.) Oct. 24, 2007

Most Extra-Base Hits, Both Clubs, Game
13 NL:Phil. (Tor.) Oct. 20, 1993
AL:Bos. (Col.) Oct. 24, 2007
Extra-Inning Game:
16 AL:Hou. (LA) Oct. 29, 2017 (10 inn)

Most Extra-Base Hits, Inning
4 AL:Chi. (LA) Oct. 1, 1959 (3rd)
AL:NY (Cin.) Oct. 9, 1961 (1st)
AL:KC (Phil.) Oct. 18, 1980 (1st)

TOTAL BASES

Most Total Bases, Game
34 NL:Atl. (Minn.) Oct. 24, 1991

Most Total Bases, Both Clubs, Game
53 NL:Phil. (Tor.) Oct. 20, 1993
Extra-Inning Game:
59 AL:Hou. (LA) Oct. 29, 2017 (10 inn)

Most Total Bases, Inning
17 AL:Phil. (Chi.) Oct. 12, 1929 (7th)

Most Total Bases, Both Clubs, Inning
21 AL:Phil. (Chi.) Oct. 12, 1929 (7th)

SINGLES

Most Singles, Game
16 AL:NY (LA) Oct. 15, 1978
NL:Ari. (NY) Nov. 3, 2001

Most Singles, Both Clubs, Game
24 AL:NY (LA) Oct. 15, 1978

Most Singles, Inning
7 AL:Phil. (Chi.) Oct. 12, 1929 (7th)
NL:NY (Wash.) Oct. 4, 1933 (6th)
NL:NY (NY) Oct. 9, 1937 (2nd)
NL:Brk. (NY) Oct. 8, 1949 (6th)

Most Singles, Both Clubs, Inning
8 AL:Phil. (Chi.) Oct. 12, 1929 (7th)
NL:NY (Wash.) Oct. 4, 1933 (6th)
NL:NY (NY) Oct. 9, 1937 (2nd)
NL:Brk. (NY) Oct. 8, 1949 (6th)
AL:KC (SF) Oct. 25, 2014 (3rd)

DOUBLES

Most Doubles, Game
8 AL:Chi. (Chi.) Oct. 13, 1906
NL:Pitt. (Wash.) Oct. 15, 1925
AL:Bos. (Col.) Oct. 24, 2007

Most Doubles, Both Clubs, Game
12 AL:Bos. (Col.) Oct. 24, 2007

Most Doubles, Inning
3 AL:Chi. (Chi.) Oct. 13, 1906 (4th)
AL:Phil. (Chi.) Oct. 18, 1910 (7th)
AL:Phil. (NY) Oct. 24, 1911 (4th)
NL:Pitt. (Wash.) Oct. 15, 1925 (8th)
NL:StL. (Det.) Oct. 9, 1934 (3rd)
NL:Brk. (NY) Oct. 2, 1947 (2nd)
NL:Brk. (NY) Oct. 5, 1947 (3rd)
AL:NY (Brk.) Oct. 8, 1949 (4th)
AL:Chi. (LA) Oct. 1, 1959 (3rd)
NL:Cin. (Balt.) Oct. 15, 1970 (1st)
NL:StL. (KC) Oct. 20, 1985 (9th)
NL:Ari. (NY) Nov. 3, 2001 (3rd)
AL:Bos. (Col.) Oct. 24, 2007 (5th)
AL:Bos. (Col.) Oct. 27, 2007 (3rd)
AL:KC (SF) Oct. 28, 2014 (2nd)

TRIPLES

Most Triples, Game
5 AL:Bos. (Pitt.) Oct. 7, 1903
AL:Bos. (Pitt.) Oct. 10, 1903

Most Triples, Both Clubs, Game
7 AL:Bos. (Pitt.) Oct. 10, 1903

Most Triples, Inning
2 AL:Bos. (Pitt.) Oct. 1, 1903 (7th)
AL:Bos. (Pitt.) Oct. 7, 1903 (6th)
AL:Bos. (Pitt.) Oct. 10, 1903 (1st)
AL:Bos. (Pitt.) Oct. 10, 1903 (4th)
AL:Bos. (NY) Oct. 12, 1912 (3rd)
AL:Phil. (NY) Oct. 7, 1913 (4th)
AL:Bos. (Chi.) Sept. 6, 1918 (9th)
AL:NY (Brk.) Oct. 1, 1947 (3rd)
AL:NY (Brk.) Sept. 30, 1953 (1st)
AL:Det. (StL.) Oct. 7, 1968 (4th)

HOME RUNS

Most Home Runs, Game
5 AL:NY (StL.) Oct. 9, 1928
AL:Oak. (SF) Oct. 27, 1989
AL:Hou. (LA) Oct. 29, 2017 (10 inn)

Most Home Runs, Both Clubs, Game
7 AL:Oak. (SF) Oct. 27, 1989
Extra-Inning Game:
8 AL:Hou. (LA) Oct. 25, 2017 (11 inn)

Most Home Runs, Inning
3 AL:Bos. (StL.) Oct. 11, 1967 (4th)

Most Home Runs, Both Clubs, Inning
3 NL:NY (NY) Oct. 11, 1921 (2nd)
AL:Bos. (StL.) Oct. 11, 1967 (4th)
AL:Ana. (SF) Oct. 19, 2002 (2nd)
AL:Ana. (SF) Oct. 20, 2002 (2nd)
AL:Hou. (LA) Oct. 25, 2017 (10th)

Most Home Runs, Consecutive, Inning
2 AL:Wash. (Pitt.) Oct. 11, 1925 (3rd)
AL:NY (StL.) Oct. 9, 1928 (7th)
AL:NY (Chi.) Oct. 1, 1932 (5th)
AL:NY (StL.) Oct. 14, 1964 (6th)
AL:Balt. (LA) Oct. 5, 1966 (1st)
AL:Bos. (StL.) Oct. 11, 1967 (4th)
NL:Cin. (Bos.) Oct. 14, 1975 (5th)
AL:NY (LA) Oct. 16, 1977 (8th)
NL:LA (NY) Oct. 25, 1981 (7th)
AL:Bos. (NY) Oct. 27, 1986 (2nd)
NL:Fla. (Clev.) Oct. 18, 1997 (4th)
NL:SD (NY) Oct. 17, 1998 (5th)
NL:SF (Ana.) Oct. 20, 2002 (2nd)
NL:Phil. (TB) Oct. 25, 2008 (6th)
AL:Tex. (StL.) Oct. 27, 2011 (7th)
AL:Hou. (LA) Oct. 25, 2017 (10th)

Most Consecutive Games with a Home Run
14 AL:Hou. 2017-19

Games, One Series
7 AL:Wash. (Pitt.) 1925
AL:NY (Brk.) 1952
AL:Hou. (LA) 2017
AL:Hou. (Wash.) 2019

RUNS BATTED IN

Most Runs Batted In, Game
18 AL:NY (NY) Oct. 2, 1936

Most Runs Batted In, Both Clubs, Game
29 AL:Tor. (Phil.) Oct. 20, 1993

Most Runs Batted In, Inning
10 AL:Phil. (Chi.) Oct. 12, 1929 (7th)
AL:Det. (StL.) Oct. 9, 1968 (3rd)

Most Runs Batted In, Both Clubs, Inning
11 AL:Phil. (Chi.) Oct. 12, 1929 (7th)
NL:Brk. (NY) Oct. 5, 1956 (2nd)

SACRIFICE HITS

Most Sacrifice Hits, Game
5   NL:Chi. (Chi.) Oct. 12, 1906
    NL:Chi. (Det.) Oct. 10, 1908
    NL:Pitt. (Det.) Oct. 16, 1909

Most Sacrifice Hits, Both Clubs, Game
7   NL:Chi. (Det.) Oct. 10, 1908

Most Sacrifice Hits, Inning
2   By many

Most Sacrifice Hits, Consecutive, Inning
2   By many

SACRIFICE FLIES (Since 1954)

Most Sacrifice Flies, Game
3   AL:Tor. (Phil.) Oct. 19, 1993

Most Sacrifice Flies, Both Clubs, Game
3   AL:Tor. (Phil.) Oct. 19, 1993
    AL:Tor. (Phil.) Oct. 23, 1993
    AL:Clev. (Fla.) Oct. 25, 1997
    NL:SF (Ana.) Oct. 24, 2002
    AL:Tex. (StL.) Oct. 22, 2011
    NL:SF (KC) Oct. 29, 2014
    AL:KC (NY) Oct. 27, 2015 (14 inn)

Most Sacrifice Flies, Inning
2   AL:Balt. (Pitt.) Oct. 13, 1971 (1st)
    AL:Tex. (StL.) Oct. 20, 2011 (9th)
    NL:SF (KC) Oct. 29, 2014 (2nd)

Most Sacrifice Flies, Consecutive, Inning
2   AL:Balt. (Pitt.) Oct. 13, 1971 (1st)
    AL:Tex. (StL.) Oct. 20, 2011 (9th)
    NL:SF (KC) Oct. 29, 2014 (2nd)

Most Sacrifice Flies, Both Clubs, Inning
3   NL:SF (KC) Oct. 29, 2014 (2nd)

WALKS

Most Walks, Game
11   NL:Brk. (NY) Oct. 5, 1956
     AL:NY (Mil.) Oct. 5, 1957
     AL:Det. (SD) Oct. 12, 1984
     Extra-Inning Game:
12   NL:Hou. (Chi.) Oct. 25, 2005 (14 inn)

Most Walks, Both Clubs, Game
19   AL:NY (Mil.) Oct. 5, 1957
     Extra-Inning Game:
21   NL:Hou. (Chi.) Oct. 25, 2005 (14 inn)

Most Walks, Inning
5   AL:NY (StL.) Oct. 6, 1926 (5th)
    AL:Hou. (Wash.) Oct. 26, 2019 (7th)

Most Walks, Both Clubs, Inning
6   AL:NY (NY) Oct. 7, 1921 (3rd)
    AL:NY (StL.) Oct. 6, 1926 (5th)
    NL:LA (NY) Oct. 28, 1981 (6th)
    NL:Phil. (Tor.) Oct. 20, 1993 (1st)
    NL:StL. (Bos.) Oct. 23, 2004 (4th)
    AL: Hou. (Wash.) Oct. 26, 2019 (7th)

Fewest Walks, Both Clubs, Game
0   AL:Phil. (NY) Oct. 16, 1911
    NL:NY (Chi.) Oct. 10, 1917
    NL:NY (NY) Oct. 9, 1921
    AL:Bos. (StL.) Oct. 7, 1967
    NL:Phil. (Balt.) Oct. 11, 1983

HIT BY PITCH

Most Hit By Pitch, Game
4   NL:LA (Hou.) Nov. 1, 2017

Most Hit By Pitch, Both Clubs, Game
4   NL:LA (Hou.) Nov. 1, 2017

Most Hit By Pitch, Inning
2   NL:Pitt. (Det.) Oct. 11, 1909 (2nd)
    AL:Det. (StL.) Oct. 9, 1968 (8th)
    NL:Pitt. (Balt.) Oct. 17, 1979 (9th)
    NL:Hou. (Chi.) Oct. 22, 2005 (7th)
    NL:StL. (Tex.) Oct. 28, 2011 (5th)
    NL:LA (Hou.) Nov. 1, 2017 (1st)

STRIKEOUTS

Most Strikeouts, Game
17   AL:Det. (StL.) Oct. 2, 1968
     Extra-Inning Game:
19   AL:Bos. (LA) Oct. 26, 2018 (18 inn)

Most Strikeouts, Both Clubs, Game
27   AL:TB (LA) Oct. 27, 2020
     Extra-Inning Game:
34   AL:Bos. (LA) Oct. 26, 2018 (18 inn)

Most Strikeouts, Inning
4   AL:Det. (Chi.) Oct. 14, 1908 (1st)

Most Strikeouts, Both Clubs, Inning
6   NL:Cin. (Oak.) Oct. 18, 1972 (5th)
    AL:KC (StL.) Oct. 24, 1985 (7th)
    AL:NY (NY) Oct. 24, 2000 (2nd)

Most Strikeouts, Consecutive, Game
6   AL:Chi. (Cin.) Oct. 6, 1919
    NL:LA (Balt.) Oct. 5, 1966
    AL:KC (StL.) Oct. 24, 1985
    NL:LA (Bos.) Oct. 28, 2018

Fewest Strikeouts, Both Clubs, Game
0   NL:Pitt. (NY) Oct. 13, 1960

STOLEN BASES

Most Stolen Bases, Game
6   NL:Chi. (Chi.) Oct. 10, 1906
    Extra-Inning Game:
7   NL:Chi. (Det.) Oct. 8, 1907 (12 inn)

Most Stolen Bases, Both Clubs, Game
7   NL:Chi. (Det.) Oct. 12, 1907
    NL:Chi. (Clev.) Oct. 30, 2016
    Extra-Inning Game:
11   NL:Chi. (Det.) Oct. 8, 1907 (12 inn)

Most Stolen Bases, Inning
3   NL:Pitt. (Bos.) Oct. 1, 1903 (1st)
    NL:NY (Phil.) Oct. 12, 1905 (9th)
    NL:Chi. (Det.) Oct. 8, 1907 (10th)
    NL:Chi. (Det.) Oct. 11, 1908 (8th)
    AL:Det. (Chi.) Oct. 12, 1908 (9th)
    NL:NY (Bos.) Oct. 14, 1912 (1st)
    NL:LA (TB) Oct. 20, 2020 (5th)

CAUGHT STEALING

Most Caught Stealing, Game
3 By many; last:
NL:LA (Oak.) Oct. 19, 1988
Extra-Inning Game
5 NL:NY (Phil.) Oct. 17, 1911 (11 inn)

Most Caught Stealing, Both Clubs, Game
5 AL:Phil. (Chi.) Oct. 17, 1910
Extra-Inning Game:
6 NL:NY (Phil.) Oct. 17, 1911 (11 inn)

Most Caught Stealing Inning
2 NL:NY (Phil.) Oct. 12, 1905 (7th)
NL:NY (Phil.) Oct. 17, 1911 (10th)
NL:NY (Bos.) Oct. 9, 1912 (11th)
AL:Bos. (Phil.) Oct. 9, 1915 (1st)
AL:Bos. (Brk.) Oct. 12, 1916 (3rd)
AL:Chi. (Cin.) Oct. 3, 1919 (6th)
NL:Brk. (NY) Oct. 6, 1947 (1st)
AL:NY (Brk.) Oct. 2, 1952 (1st)
NL:StL. (Det.) Oct. 10, 1968 (6th)

LEFT ON BASE

Most Left on Base, Game
15 NL:NY (Oak.) Oct. 14, 1973 (12 inn)
NL:Phil. (KC) Oct. 17, 1980 (10 inn)
AL:NY (NY) Oct. 21, 2000 (12 inn)
AL:Ana. (SF) Oct. 22, 2002
AL:Chi. (Hou.) Oct. 25, 2005 (14 inn)
NL:Hou. (Chi.) Oct. 25, 2005 (14 inn)

Most Left on Base, Both Clubs, Game
24 AL:Det. (SD) Oct. 12, 1984
Extra-Inning Game:
30 AL:Chi. (Hou.) Oct. 25, 2005 (14 inn)

Fewest Left on Base, Game
0 NL:Brk. (NY) Oct. 8, 1956
NL:LA (NY) Oct. 6, 1963

Fewest Left on Base, Both Clubs, Game
3 NL:Brk. (NY) Oct. 8, 1956

PINCH-HITTING

Most Pinch-Hitters, Game
6 NL:LA (Chi.) Oct. 6, 1959
Extra-Inning Game:
8 AL:Minn. (Atl.) Oct. 22, 1991 (12 inn)

Most Pinch-Hitters, Both Clubs, Game
8 AL:Balt. (Phil.) Oct. 15, 1983
Extra-Inning Game:
12 AL:Minn. (Atl.) Oct. 22, 1991 (12 inn)

Most Pinch-Hitters, Inning
4 NL:NY (Oak.) Oct. 13, 1973 (9th)
AL:Balt. (Phil.) Oct. 15, 1983 (6th)
AL:KC (StL.) Oct. 26, 1985 (9th)
AL:Minn. (StL.) Oct. 22, 1987 (9th)
NL:SD (NY) Oct. 18, 1998 (8th)
NL:Atl. (NY) Oct. 23, 1999 (8th)
NL:NY (NY) Oct. 25, 2000 (7th)

Most Pinch-Hits, Series
6 AL:NY (Brk.) 1947 (7g)
AL:NY (Pitt.) 1960 (7g)
AL:Oak. (Cin.) 1972 (7g)
AL:Balt. (Pitt.) 1979 (7g)

Most Pinch-Hits, Both Clubs, Series
11 AL:NY (Brk.) 1947 (7g)

Most Pinch-Hits, Game
3 AL:Oak. (Cin.) Oct. 19, 1972
AL:Balt. (Pitt.) Oct. 13, 1979
NL:SD (NY) Oct. 18, 1998

Most Pinch-Hits, Both Clubs, Game
3 By many

Most Pinch-Hits, Inning
3 AL:Oak. (Cin.) Oct. 19, 1972 (9th)
NL:SD (NY) Oct. 18, 1998 (8th)

Most Pinch-Hit Home Runs, All-time
8 AL:NY 1947, 52, 55, 60-61, 99, 2003, 09

Most Pinch-Hit Home Runs, One Series
2 NL:LA (Chi.) 1959
AL:Bos. (Cin.) 1975
AL:Bos. (LA) 2018

Most Pinch-Hit HRs, Both Clubs, One Series
2 AL:Clev. (NY) 1954
NL:LA (Chi.) 1959
AL:Bos. (Cin.) 1975
AL:TB (Phil.) 2008
AL:Bos. (LA) 2018

Most Pinch-Hit Walks, Inning
2 AL:NY (NY) Oct. 15, 1923 (8th)
AL:Balt. (Pitt.) Oct. 11, 1979 (7th)
AL:Balt. (Phil.) Oct. 15, 1983 (6th)
AL:NY (Atl.) Oct. 23, 1999 (8th)

Most Pinch-Hit Strikeouts, Game
4 AL:StL. (StL.) Oct. 8, 1944
AL:StL. (StL.) Oct. 9, 1944

Most Pinch-Hit Strikeouts, Inning
3 AL:StL. (StL.) Oct. 8, 1944 (9th)
NL:LA (Bos.) Oct. 28. 2018 (8th)

PINCH-RUNNERS

Most Pinch-Runners, Game
2 By many

Most Pinch-Runners, Both Clubs, Game
4 NL:StL. (KC) Oct. 26, 1985

Most Pinch-Runners, Inning
2 NL:NY (NY) Oct. 10, 1923 (3rd)
AL:NY (NY) Oct. 15, 1923 (8th)
NL:Brk. (NY) Oct. 3, 1947 (9th)
NL:Bos. (Clev.) Oct. 6, 1948 (8th)
NL:Phil. (NY) Oct. 7, 1950 (9th)
NL:LA (Chi.) Oct. 6, 1959 (7th)
AL:Oak. (Cin.) Oct. 19, 1972 (9th)
NL:StL. (KC) Oct. 26, 1985 (8th)
AL:KC (StL.) Oct. 26, 1985 (9th)
NL:Ari. (NY) Nov. 4, 2001 (9th)
AL:Bos. (StL.) Oct. 27, 2004 (8th)
AL:TB (LA) Oct. 21, 2020 (9th)

CLUB FIELDING

AVERAGE

4 Games	5 Games	6 Games	7 Games
Highest Average (Most Chances)			
1.000 NL:Col. (Bos.) 2007	1.000 AL:NY (NY) 1937	1.000 AL:TB (LA) 2020	.993 NL:Cin. (Bos.) 1975
(149 tc)	(179 tc)	(198 tc)	
Highest Average, Both Clubs			
.993 NL:Col. (Bos.) 2007	.993 NL:LA (Bos.) 2018	.992 NL:LA (NY) 1977	.992 NL:SF (KC) 2014
Lowest Average			
.946 AL:Bos. (StL) 2004	.942 NL:Brk. (Bos.) 1916	.938 NL:NY (Phil.) 1911	.934 AL:Det. (Pitt.) 1909
Lowest Average, Both Clubs			
.954 AL:NY (Chi.) 1932	.946 NL:Chi. (Phil.) 1910	.947 NL:NY (Phil.) 1911	.941 AL:Det. (Pitt.) 1909

CHANCES ACCEPTED

4 Games	5 Games	6 Games	7 Games
Most Chances Accepted			
179 NL:Bos. (Phil.) 1914	237 AL:Bos. (Brk.) 1916	271 AL:Chi. (Chi.) 1906	329 NL:NY (Bos.) 1912 (8g)
			AL:Chi. (Cin.) 1919 (8g)
			300 AL:Wash. (NY) 1924
Most Chances Accepted, Both Clubs			
356 NL:Bos. (Phil.) 1914	449 AL:Bos. (Brk.) 1916	514 AL:Chi. (Chi.) 1906	649 NL:NY (Bos.) 1912 (8g)
			594 AL:Wash. (NY) 1924
Fewest Chances Accepted			
135 Det. (SF) 2012	165 AL:TB (Phil.) 2008	197 AL:Phil. (StL) 1930	232 AL:Hou. (Wash.) 2019
Fewest Chances Accepted, Both Clubs			
274 AL:NY (StL) 1928	348 NL:LA (Oak.) 1988	403 AL:NY (Phil.) 2009	487 AL:Hou. (Wash.) 2019
	AL:TB (Phil.) 2008		

PUTOUTS

4 Games	5 Games	6 Games	7 Games
Most Putouts			
123 AL:Chi. (Hou.) 2005	159 AL:Bos. (LA) 2018	168 AL:NY (LA) 1977	222 AL:Bos. (NY) 1912 (8g)
		AL:NY (Fla.) 2003	202 AL:Minn. (Atl.) 1991
Most Putouts, Both Clubs			
241 AL:Chi. (Hou.) 2005	315 AL:Bos. (LA) 2018	333 AL:NY (LA) 1977	443 AL:Bos. (NY) 1912 (8g)
			401 NL:NY (Wash.) 1924
Fewest Putouts			
102 NL:StL. (NY) 1928	126 NL:LA (Oak.) 1974	153 NL:NY (Chi.) 1917	177 NL:Brk. (Clev.) 1920
NL:Chi. (NY) 1932	NL:SD (Det.) 1984	AL:StL. (Phil.) 1930	NL:StL. (Minn.) 1987
NL:Chi. (NY) 1938	Al:Det. (StL.) 2006	AL:NY (LA) 1981	
AL:NY (LA) 1963	AL:TB (Phil.) 2008		
AL:LA (Balt.) 1966			
NL:SF (Oak.) 1989			
NL:SD (NY) 1998			
NL:StL. (Bos.) 2004			
NL:Col. (Bos.) 2007			
Fewest Putouts, Both Clubs			
210 NL:StL. (NY) 1928	258 NL:LA (Oak.) 1974	309 NL:NY (Chi.) 1917	357 NL:StL. (Minn.) 1987
NL:Chi. (NY) 1932, 38	NL:SD (Det.) 1984	NL:StL. (Phil.) 1930	
AL:NY (LA) 1963	NL:StL. (Det.) 2006	AL:NY (LA) 1981	
NL:LA (Balt.) 1966	AL:TB (Phil.) 2008		
NL:SF (Oak.) 1989			
AL:NY (SD) 1998			
NL:StL. (Bos.) 2004			
NL:Col. (Bos.) 2007			

ASSISTS

4 Games	5 Games	6 Games	7 Games
Most Assists			
67 NL:Phil. (Bos.) 1914	90 NL:Bos. (Brk.) 1916	99 AL:Chi. (Chi.) 1906	115 AL:Chi. (Cin.) 1919 (8g)
			99 AL:Wash. (NY) 1924
Most Assists, Both Clubs			
129 AL:Phil. (Bos.) 1914	160 AL:Bos. (Brk.) 1916	183 AL:Chi. (Chi.) 1906	211 AL:Chi. (Cin.) 1919 (8g)
			193 AL:Wash. (NY) 1924
Fewest Assists			
28 AL:NY (StL.) 1928	36 NL:LA (Oak.) 1988	35 NL:Phil. (NY) 2009	43 AL:Hou. (Wash.) 2019
Fewest Assists, Both Clubs			
64 AL:NY (StL.) 1928	76 NL:StL. (Det.) 2006	86 AL:NY (Phil.) 2009	109 AL:Hou. (Wash.) 2019

ERRORS

4 Games	5 Games	6 Games	7 Games
Most Errors			
8 AL:NY (Chi.) 1932	13 NL:Brk. (Bos.) 1916	16 NL:NY (Phil.) 1911	19 AL:Det. (Pitt.) 1909
AL:Bos. (StL.) 2004			
Most Errors, Both Clubs			
14 AL:NY (Chi.) 1932	23 NL:Chi. (Phil.) 1910	27 NL:NY (Phil.) 1911	34 AL:Det. (Pitt.) 1909
Fewest Errors			
0 AL:Balt. (LA) 1966	0 AL:NY (NY) 1937	0 AL:TB (LA) 2020	2 By many
NL:Col. (Bos.) 2007			
Fewest Errors, Both Clubs			
2 NL:Col. (Bos.) 2007	3 NL:LA (Bos.) 2018	4 NL:LA (NY) 1977	4 NL:SF (KC) 2014
AL:Det. (SF) 2012		AL:NY (Phil.) 2009	
		AL:TB (LA) 2020	
Most Errorless Games			
4 AL:Balt. (LA) 1966	5 AL:NY (NY) 1937	6 AL:TB (LA) 2020	5 NL:NY (NY) 1921 (8g)
NL:Col. (Bos.) 2007			AL:Phil. (StL.) 1931
			AL:NY (Brk.) 1955
			NL:Brk. (NY) 1956
			NL:StL. (Det.) 1968
			NL:Cin. (Bos.) 1975
			AL:KC (StL.) 1985
			NL:StL. (KC) 1985
			AL:Bos. (NY) 1986
			AL:Clev. (Fla.) 1997
			AL:KC (SF) 2014
			NL:SF (KC) 2014
			NL:Chi. (Clev.) 2016
			AL:Hou. (LA) 2017
			NL:Wash. (Hou.) 2019
Most Errorless Games, Both Clubs			
3 AL:Balt. (LA) 1966	3 AL:Bos. (LA) 2018	3 AL:NY (LA) 1977	4 AL:KC (StL.) 1985
NL:Cin. (NY) 1976		AL:Tor. (Atl.) 1992	
AL:Det. (SF) 2012		AL:NY (Phil.) 2009	
		AL:TB (LA) 2020	

DOUBLE PLAYS

4 Games	5 Games	6 Games	7 Games
Most Double Plays			
7 NL:Chi. (NY) 1932	7 AL:NY (NY) 1922	10 AL:NY (NY) 1951	12 NL:Brk. (NY) 1955
AL:NY (LA) 1963	AL:NY (Brk.) 1941		
	NL:Cin. (NY) 1961		
Most Double Plays, Both Clubs			
10 NL:Cin. (NY) 1976	12 AL:NY (Brk.) 1941	16 NL:Phil. (KC) 1980	19 NL:Brk. (NY) 1955
AL:Chi. (Hou.) 2005			
Fewest Double Plays			
1 AL:NY (Chi.) 1932	0 NL:NY (Balt.) 1969	2 AL:Chi. (Chi.) 1906	2 NL:StL. (Det.) 1934
NL:Cin. (NY) 1939		NL:NY (Phil.) 1911	AL:Balt. (Pitt.) 1971
NL:Phil. (NY) 1950		AL:Phil. (NY) 1911	NL:StL. (Minn.) 1987
NL:LA (NY) 1963		AL:Phil. (StL.) 1930	
AL:Oak. (SF) 1989		AL:NY (NY) 1936	
		AL:Chi. (LA) 1959	
		AL:NY (LA) 1977	
		AL:NY (LA) 1981	
		NL:Atl. (Clev.) 1995	
		AL:TB (LA) 2020	
Fewest Double Plays, Both Clubs			
4 NL:NY (Clev.) 1954	4 NL:NY (Balt.) 1969	4 AL:Phil. (NY) 1911	6 NL:StL. (Minn.) 1987
AL:Oak. (SF) 1989	AL:NY (NY) 2000		

TRIPLE PLAYS

Most Triple Plays			
none	none	none	1 AL:Clev. (Brk.) 1920

PASSED BALLS

Most Passed Balls			
2 AL:Phil. (Bos.) 1914	2 NL:Brk. (Bos.) 1916	2 NL:Chi. (Chi.) 1906	3 NL:Pitt. (NY) 1960
		NL:Chi. (Bos.) 1918	AL:NY (StL.) 1964
		NL:LA (NY) 1978	
Most Passed Balls, Both Clubs			
2 AL:Phil. (Bos.) 1914	3 NL:Brk. (Bos.) 1916	3 NL:Chi. (Chi.) 1906	4 NL:Brk. (NY) 1947
		NL:Chi. (Bos.) 1918	

CHANCES ACCEPTED

Chances Accepted, Game
48 AL:Chi. (Chi.) Oct. 12, 1906
AL:Chi. (NY) Oct. 7, 1917
AL:Bos. (Chi.) Sept. 9, 1918
Extra-Inning Game:
74 AL:Bos. (Brk.) Oct. 9, 1916 (14 inn)

Chances Accepted, Both Clubs, Game
91 AL:Chi. (Chi.) Oct. 12, 1906
Extra-Inning Game:
137 AL:Bos. (Brk.) Oct. 9, 1916 (14 inn)

PUTOUTS

Putouts, Game
54 NL:LA (Bos.) Oct. 26, 2018 (18 inn)

Putouts, Both Clubs, Game
105 NL:LA (Bos.) Oct. 26, 2018 (18 inn)

ASSISTS

Assists, Game
21 AL:Chi. (Chi.) Oct. 12, 1906
AL:Chi. (NY) Oct. 7, 1917
AL:Bos. (Chi.) Sept. 9, 1918
Extra-Inning Game:
32 AL:Bos. (Brk.) Oct. 9, 1916 (14 inn)

Assists, Both Clubs, Game
37 AL:Chi. (Chi.) Oct. 12, 1906
Extra-Inning Game:
55 NL:Brk. (Bos.) Oct. 9, 1916 (14 inn)

ERRORS

Errors, Game
6 AL:Chi. (Chi.) Oct. 13, 1906
NL:Pitt. (Det.) Oct. 12, 1909
AL:Chi. (NY) Oct. 13, 1917
NL:LA (Balt.) Oct. 6, 1966

Errors, Both Clubs, Game
9 AL:Chi. (NY) Oct. 13, 1917

Errors, Inning
3 By many; last:
AL:Det. (StL.) Oct. 21, 2006 (6th)

DOUBLE PLAYS

Double Plays, Game
5 AL:Phil. (Bos.) Oct. 9, 1914

Double Plays, Both Clubs, Game
6 AL:Phil. (Bos.) Oct. 9, 1914
AL:NY (Brk.) Sept. 29, 1955
NL:Phil. (KC) Oct. 15, 1980
AL:Ana. (SF) Oct. 23, 2002
NL:Hou. (Chi.) Oct. 25, 2005 (14 inn)

TRIPLE PLAYS

Triple Plays
1 AL:Clev. (Brk.) Oct. 10, 1920 (5th)

PASSED BALLS

Passed Balls, Game
2 NL:Chi. (Chi.) Oct. 9, 1906
NL:Chi. (Bos.) Sept. 9, 1918
AL:Det. (Chi.) Oct. 3, 1945
NL:Brk. (NY) Oct. 4, 1947
NL:Pitt. (NY) Oct. 6, 1960
AL:NY (StL.) Oct. 7, 1964
NL:LA (NY) Oct. 5, 1978

Passed Balls, Inning
1 By many

CLUB PITCHING

	4 Games	5 Games	6 Games	7 Games
Most Complete Games				
	4 AL:NY (StL.) 1928	5 AL:Phil. (NY) 1905, 13	5 AL:Phil. (NY) 1911	7 AL:Bos. (Pitt.) 1903 (8g)
		AL:Phil. (Chi.) 1910	AL:Bos. (Chi.) 1918	5 AL:Clev. (Brk.) 1920
		AL:Bos. (Phil.) 1915	AL:Det. (Chi.) 1935	AL:NY (Brk.) 1956
Most Complete Games, Both Clubs				
	5 AL:Bos. (Phil.) 1914	9 AL:Phil. (NY) 1905	9 AL:Bos. (Chi.) 1918	13 AL:Bos. (Pitt.) 1903 (8g)
		AL:Bos. (Phil.) 1915		8 1909, 20, 25, 34, 40, 56
Fewest Complete Games				
	0 By many	0 By many	0 By many	0 By many
Fewest Complete Games, Both Clubs				
	0 AL:NY (SD) 1998	0 AL:Oak. (LA) 1974	0 AL:Chi. (LA) 1959	0 AL:Oak. (Cin.) 1972
	AL:NY (Atl.) 1999	AL:NY (NY) 2000	AL:KC (Phil.) 1980	AL:Oak. (NY) 1973
	AL:Bos. (StL.) 2004	NL:StL. (Det.) 2006	AL:NY (Atl.) 1996	AL:Minn. (StL.) 1987
	AL:Chi. (Hou.) 2005	NL:Phil. (TB) 2008	AL:Bos. (StL.) 2013	AL:Clev. (Fla.) 1997
	AL:Bos. (Col.) 2007	NL:SF (Tex.) 2010	NL:LA (TB) 2020	AL:Ana. (SF) 2002
	AL:Det. (SF) 2012	AL:Bos. (LA) 2018		NL:StL. (Tex.) 2011
				NL:Chi. (Clev.) 2016
				AL:Hou. (LA) 2017
				NL:Wash. (Hou.) 2019
Most Saves (since 1969)				
	3 AL:NY (SD) 1998	3 AL:Oak. (LA) 1974	4 AL:NY (Atl.) 1996	4 AL:Oak. (NY) 1973
	AL:Chi. (Hou.) 2005			
	AL:Bos. (Col.) 2007			
	NL:SF (Det.) 2012			
Most Saves, Both Clubs (since 1969)				
	3 AL:NY (SD) 1998	4 AL:Oak. (LA) 1974	4 NL:Phil. (KC) 1980	7 AL:Oak. (NY) 1973
	AL:Chi. (Hou.) 2005		AL:Tor. (Atl.) 1992	
	AL:Bos. (Col.) 2007		NL:Atl. (Clev.) 1995	
	NL:SF (Det.) 2012		AL:NY (Atl.) 1996	
Fewest Saves (since 1969)				
	0 AL:NY (Cin.) 1976	0 AL:Balt. (NY) 1969	0 NL:LA(NY) 1977	0 AL:Bos. (Cin.) 1975
	NL:SF (Oak.) 1989	NL:Cin. (Balt.) 1970	AL:NY (LA) 1977-78	AL:Balt. (Pitt.) 1979
	AL:Oak. (Cin.) 1990	AL:Oak. (LA) 1988	NL:Atl. (NY) 1996	AL:KC (StL.) 1985
	NL:SD (NY) 1998	AL:TB (Phil.) 2008		NL:Atl. (Minn.) 1991
	NL:Atl. (NY) 1999	NL:NY (KC) 2015		NL:Ari. (NY) 2001
	NL:StL. (Bos.) 2004	NL:LA (Bos.) 2018		
	NL:Col. (Bos.) 2007			
	AL:Det. (SF) 2012			
Fewest Saves, Both Clubs (since 1969)				
	1 NL:SF (Oak.) 1989	1 AL:Oak. (LA) 1988	0 AL:NY (LA) 1977	1 NL:Ari. (NY) 2001
	AL:Oak. (Cin.) 1990	NL:NY (KC) 2015		
	AL:Bos. (StL.) 2004	NL:LA (Bos.) 2018		
Most Shutouts				
	3 AL:Balt. (LA) 1966	4 NL:NY (Phil.) 1905	2 NL:NY (Chi.) 1917	3 NL:LA (Minn.) 1965
			AL:Chi. (LA) 1959	
Most Shutouts, Both Clubs				
	3 AL:Balt. (LA) 1966	5 NL:NY (Phil.) 1905	2 By many	3 AL:Clev. (Brk.) 1920
				AL:NY (Brk.) 1956
				AL:NY (Mil.) 1958
				AL:Minn. (LA) 1965
Most Shutouts, Consecutive				
	3 AL:Balt. (LA) 1966	3 NL:NY (Phil.) 1905	2 NL:NY (Chi.) 1917	2 NL:Cin. (Chi.) 1919 (8g)
				AL:Clev. (Brk.) 1920
				NL:NY (NY) 1921 (8g)
Most Shutouts, Consecutive, Both Clubs				
	3 AL:Balt. (LA) 1966	5 NL:NY (Phil.) 1905	2 NL:Chi. (Chi.) 1906	3 NL:Cin. (Chi.) 1919 (8g)
			NL:NY (Chi.) 1917	AL:NY (Brk.) 1956
				AL:NY (Mil.) 1958

4 Games	5 Games	6 Games	7 Games

Fewest Shutouts

0 By many	0 By many	0 By many	0 By many

Fewest Shutouts, Both Clubs

0 1927, 28, 32, 38, 54, 76, 99, 2007	0 1910, 15, 16, 29, 37, 41, 70, 74, 84, 2000, 08, 15, 18	0 By many	0 1912, 24, 47, 64, 87, 97, 2002, 17, 19

Most Shutout Innings, Consecutive

33 AL:Balt. (LA) 1966	28 NL:NY (Phil.) 1905	24 NL:NY (Chi.) 1917	26 NL:Cin. (Chi.) 1919 (8g)
			22 NL:Pitt. (Balt.) 1971

Most Wild Pitches

3 NL:Pitt. (NY) 1927 AL:Clev. (NY) 1954	5 AL:Det. (StL.) 2006	6 AL:TB (LA) 2020	6 NL::Chi. (Clev.) 2016

Most Wild Pitches, Both Clubs

4 AL:Clev. (NY) 1954	7 NL:StL. (Det.) 2006	8 AL:TB (LA) 2020	8 AL:NY (Brk.) 1947 NL:Chi. (Clev.) 2016

CLUB GENERAL

4 Games	5 Games	6 Games	7 Games
Most Players, Club			
25 AL:Oak. (Cin.) 1990	25 NL:Brk. (NY) 1949	28 AL:TB (LA) 2020	26 AL:Det. (Chi.) 1945
NL:Atl. (NY) 1999	NL:NY (NY) 2000		AL:Bos. (StL.) 1946
NL:StL. (Bos.) 2004	AL:TB (Phil.) 2008		
AL:Det. (SF) 2012	AL:KC (NY) 2015		
	NL:LA (Bos.) 2018		
Most Players, Both Clubs			
48 AL:NY (Atl.) 1999	49 AL:KC (NY) 2015	55 AL:TB (LA) 2020	51 AL:Det. (Chi.) 1945
AL:Chi. (Hou.) 2005	NL:LA (Bos.) 2018		
Fewest Players			
13 NL:LA (NY) 1963	12 NL:NY (Phil.) 1905	14 NL:Chi. (Chi.) 1906	13 AL:Bos. (Pitt.) 1903 (8g)
AL:Balt. (LA) 1966	AL:Phil. (Chi.) 1910	AL:Phil. (NY) 1911	NL:NY (NY) 1921 (8g)
	AL:Phil. (NY) 1913		
Fewest Players, Both Clubs			
31 AL:Phil. (Bos.) 1914	25 AL:Phil. (NY) 1905	29 NL:NY (Phil.) 1911	27 AL:Bos. (Pitt.) 1903 (8g)
Most Pitchers			
11 NL:StL. (Bos.) 2004	12 NL:LA (Bos.) 2018	15 NL:LA (TB) 2020	12 NL:StL. (Tex.) 2011
AL:Chi. (Hou.) 2005			NL:SF (KC) 2014
NL:Hou. (Chi.) 2005			AL:Hou. (LA) 2017
NL:Col. (Bos.) 2007			NL:LA (Hou.) 2017
AL:Det. (SF) 2012			AL:Hou. (Wash.) 2019
Most Pitchers, Both Clubs			
22 AL:Chi. (Hou.) 2005	22 NL:SF (Tex.) 2010	28 NL:LA (TB) 2020	24 AL:Hou. (LA) 2017
	AL:KC (NY) 2015		
	NL:LA (Bos.) 2018		
Fewest Pitchers			
3 NL:Bos. (Phil.) 1914	2 AL:Phil. (Chi.) 1910	3 AL:Phil. (NY) 1911	3 AL:Bos. (Pitt.) 1903 (8g)
AL:NY (StL.) 1928			
Fewest Pitchers, Both Clubs			
9 NL:Bos. (Phil.) 1914	6 AL:Phil. (NY) 1905	8 AL:Chi. (Chi.) 1906	8 AL:Bos. (Pitt.) 1903 (8g)
AL:NY (StL.) 1928		AL:Phil. (NY) 1911	
		AL:Bos. (Chi.) 1918	
Most Extra-Inning Games			
1 NL:Bos. (Phil.) 1914	2 NL:NY (Wash.) 1933	2 AL:Phil. (NY) 1911	3 AL:Minn. (Atl.) 1991
AL:NY (Cin.) 1939	AL:KC (NY) 2015		
AL:NY (Phil.) 1950			
NL:NY (Clev.) 1954			
AL:Oak. (Cin.) 1990			
AL:NY (Atl.) 1999			
AL:Chi. (Hou.) 2005			
AL:Det. (SF) 2012			
Most 1-Run Decisions			
3 AL:NY (Phil.) 1950	4 AL:Bos. (Phil.) 1915	5 NL:Atl. (Clev.) 1995	6 AL:Oak. (Cin.) 1972
	AL:Oak. (LA) 1974		
Most 1-Run Decisions, Consecutive			
3 AL:NY (Phil.) 1950	4 AL:Bos. (Phil.) 1915	3 NL:LA (NY) 1981	5 AL:Oak. (Cin.) 1972
		AL:Tor. (Atl.) 1992	
		AL:Clev. (Atl.) 1995	
Most 1-Run Decisions Won			
3 AL:NY (Phil.) 1950	4 AL:Bos. (Phil.) 1915	4 AL:Bos. (Chi.) 1918	4 AL:Oak. (Cin.) 1972
		AL:Tor. (Atl.) 1992	
Most 1-Run Decisions Won, Consecutive			
3 AL:NY (Phil.) 1950	4 AL:Bos. (Phil.) 1915	3 NL:LA (NY) 1981	3 AL:NY (Ari.) 2001
		AL:Tor. (Atl.) 1992	
Most 1-0 Games Won (See Table)			
2 AL:Balt. (LA) 1966	1 By many	1 By many	1 By many

PERSONNEL

Most Players, Game
21 AL:NY (Brk.) Oct. 5, 1947
NL:Cin. (NY) Oct. 9, 1961
AL:TB (LA) Oct. 24, 2020
Extra-Inning Game:
23 AL:Minn. (Atl.) Oct. 22, 1991 (12 inn)
AL:Bos. (LA) Oct. 26, 2018 (18 inn)
NL:LA (Bos.) Oct. 26, 2018 (18 inn)

Most Players, Both Clubs, Game
38 AL:NY (Brk.) Oct. 5, 1947
NL:LA (TB) Oct. 27, 2020
Extra-Inning Game:
46 AL:Bos. (LA) Oct. 26, 2018 (18 inn)

Most Pitchers, Game
8 NL:Cin. (NY) Oct. 9, 1961
NL:StL. (Bos.) Oct. 11, 1967
Extra-Inning Game:
9 AL:Chi. (Hou.) Oct. 25, 2005 (14 inn)
NL:LA (Hou.) Oct. 25, 2017 (11 inn)
AL:Bos. (LA) Oct. 26, 2018 (18 inn)
NL:LA (Bos.) Oct. 26, 2018 (18 inn)

Most Pitchers, Both Clubs, Game
13 AL:TB (LA) Oct. 24, 2020
Extra-Inning Game:
18 AL:Bos. (LA) Oct. 26, 2018 (18 inn)

Most Pitchers, Inning
5 AL:Balt. (Pitt.) Oct. 17, 1979 (9th)
NL:StL. (KC) Oct. 27, 1985 (5th)
NL:SF (KC) Oct. 22, 2014 (6th)

DATES

Earliest Date, First Game
Sept. 5, 1918 AL:Bos. at Chi.

Earliest Date, Last Game
Sept. 11, 1918 NL:Chi. at Bos.

Latest Date, First Game
Oct. 28, 2009 NL:Phil. at NY

Latest Date, Final Game
Nov. 4, 2001 AL:NY at Ari.
Nov. 4, 2009 NL:Phil. at NY

ATTENDANCE

Game, Largest
92,706 AL:Chi. at LA Oct. 6, 1959

Game, Smallest
6,210 NL:Chi. at Det. Oct. 14, 1908

TIME

Longest Game
4:19 AL:Bos. at NL:Col. Oct. 27, 2007
Extra-Inning Game:
7:20 AL:Bos. at NL:LA Oct. 26, 2018 (18 inn)

Shortest Game
1:25 NL:Chi. at AL:Det. Oct. 14, 1908

SCORELESS INNINGS

Most, Consecutive, By Pitchers, Spanning Series:
39 AL:Balt. (LA) 1966 (33); (NY) 1969 (6)

LOW-HIT GAMES (Pitching)

No Hits

1956	Oct. 8	AL:NY Don Larsen

1 Hit

1906	Oct. 10	NL:Chi. Ed Reulbach
1945	Oct. 5	NL:Chi. Claude Passeau
1947	Oct. 3	AL:NY Bill Bevens (Lost)
1967	Oct. 5	AL:Bos. Jim Lonborg
1995	Oct. 28	NL:Atl. Tom Glavine & Mark Wohlers

2 Hits

1906	Oct. 11	AL:Chi. Ed Walsh
1906	Oct. 12	NL:Chi. Three Finger Brown
1913	Oct. 11	AL:Phil. Eddie Plank
1914	Oct. 10	NL:Bos. Bill James
1921	Oct. 6	AL:NY Waite Hoyt
1931	Oct. 5	NL:StL. Burleigh Grimes
1931	Oct. 6	AL:Phil. George Earnshaw
1939	Oct. 5	AL:NY Monte Pearson
1944	Oct. 4	NL:StL. Mort Cooper & Blix Donnelly (Lost)
1948	Oct. 6	AL:Clev. Bob Feller (Lost)
1949	Oct. 5	AL:NY Allie Reynolds
1950	Oct. 4	AL:NY Vic Raschi
1958	Oct. 5	NL:Mil. Warren Spahn
1961	Oct. 4	AL:NY Whitey Ford
1963	Oct. 6	AL:NY Whitey Ford & Hal Reniff (Lost)
1969	Oct. 12	NL:NY Jerry Koosman & Ron Taylor
1971	Oct. 14	NL:Pitt. Nelson Briles
1990	Oct. 20	NL:Cin. Jose Rijo & Randy Myers
1995	Oct. 21	NL:Atl. Greg Maddux
1999	Oct. 23	AL:NY Orlando Hernandez, Jeff Nelson, Mike Stanton & Mariano Rivera
2006	Oct. 21	NL:StL. Anthony Reyes & Braden Looper
2011	Oct. 23	AL:Tex. Derek Holland & Neftali Feliz
2012	Oct. 25	NL:SF Madison Bumgarner, Santiago Casilla & Sergio Romo
2015	Oct. 28	AL:KC Johnny Cueto
2017	Oct. 28	NL:LA Alex Wood, Brandon Morrow, Tony Watson & Kenley Jansen

HIGH-HIT GAMES (Batting)

22 Hits

2001	Nov. 3	NL:Ari. vs. NY

20 Hits

1921	Oct. 7	NL:NY vs. NY
1946	Oct. 10	NL:StL. vs. Bos.

19 Hits

1932	Oct. 2	AL:NY vs. Chi.
1960	Oct. 6	AL:NY vs. Pitt.

18 Hits

1978	Oct. 15	AL:NY vs. LA
1986	Oct. 19	AL:Bos. vs. NY
1993	Oct. 20	AL:Tor. vs. Phil.

17 Hits

1934	Oct. 9	NL:StL. vs. Det.
1936	Oct. 2	AL:NY vs. NY
1936	Oct. 6	AL:NY vs. NY
1960	Oct. 12	AL:NY vs. Pitt.
1979	Oct. 13	NL:Pitt. vs. Balt.
1982	Oct. 12	AL:Mil. vs. StL.
1991	Oct. 24	NL:Atl. vs. Minn.
2007	Oct. 24	AL:Bos. vs. Col.

16 Hits

1912	Oct. 15	NL:NY vs. Bos.
1919	Oct. 9	NL:Cin. vs. Chi.
1960	Oct. 8	AL:NY vs. Pitt.
1997	Oct. 21	NL:Fla. vs. Clev.
1998	Oct. 18	AL:NY vs. SD
2002	Oct. 20	AL:Ana. vs. SF
2002	Oct. 22	AL:Ana. vs. SF
2002	Oct. 24	NL:SF vs. Ana.
2014	Oct. 25	NL:SF vs. KC

EXTRA-INNING GAMES

18	NL:LA 3 Bos. 2 Oct. 26, 2018
14	AL:Bos. 2 Brk. 1 Oct. 9, 1916
	AL:Chi. 7 Hou. 5 Oct. 25, 2005
	AL:KC 5 NY 4 Oct. 27, 2015
12	NL:Chi. 3 Det. 3 Oct. 8, 1907
	NL:Bos. 5 Phil. 4 Oct. 12, 1914
	NL:NY 4 Wash. 3 Oct. 4, 1924
	AL:Wash. 4 NY 3 Oct. 10, 1924
	AL:Det. 3 StL. 2 Oct. 4 1934
	NL:Chi. 8 Det. 7 Oct. 8, 1945
	NL:NY 10 Oak. 7 Oct. 14, 1973
	AL:Bos. 7 Cin. 6 Oct. 21, 1975
	AL:NY 4 LA 3 Oct. 11, 1977
	NL:Atl. 5 Minn. 4 Oct. 22, 1991
	AL:NY 4 NY 3 Oct. 21, 2000
	AL:NY 3 Ari. 2 Nov. 1, 2001
	NL:Fla. 4 NY 3 Oct. 22, 2003
	AL:KC 7 NY 2 Nov. 1, 2015
11	AL:Phil. 3 NY 2 Oct. 17, 1911
	NL:NY 6 Bos. 6 Oct. 9, 1912
	NL:NY 2 Wash. 1 Oct. 6, 1933
	AL:Det. 6 Chi. 5 Oct. 4, 1935
	NL:StL. 3 StL. 2 Oct. 5, 1944
	NL:Brk. 6 NY 5 Oct. 5, 1952
	AL:Oak. 3 NY 2 Oct. 16, 1973
	AL:Minn. 4 Atl. 3 Oct. 26, 1991
	AL:Tor. 4 Atl. 3 Oct. 24, 1992
	AL:Clev. 7 Atl. 6 Oct. 24, 1995
	NL:Fla. 3 Clev. 2 Oct. 26, 1997
	NL:StL. 10 Tex. 9 Oct. 27, 2011
	AL:Hou. 7 LA 6 Oct. 25, 2017
10	NL:Chi. 4 Phil. 3 Oct. 22, 1910
	NL:NY 4 Phil. 3 Oct. 25, 1911
	AL:Bos. 3 NY 2 Oct. 16, 1912
	NL:NY 3 Phil. 0 Oct. 8, 1913
	AL:Chi. 5 Cin. 4 Oct. 7, 1919
	NL:NY 3 NY 3 Oct. 5, 1922
	AL:NY 3 StL. 2 Oct. 7, 1926
	NL:NY 4 Wash. 3 Oct. 7, 1933
	NL:NY 5 NY 4 Oct. 5, 1936
	AL:NY 7 Cin. 4 Oct. 8, 1939
	AL:Bos. 3 StL. 2 Oct. 6, 1946
	AL:NY 2 Phil. 1 Oct. 5, 1950
	NL:NY 5 Clev. 2 Sept. 29, 1954
	NL:Brk. 1 NY 0 Oct. 9, 1956
	NL:Mil. 7 NY 5 Oct. 6, 1957
	NL:Mil. 4 NY 3 Oct. 1, 1958
	AL:NY 4 Mil. 3 Oct. 8, 1958
	NL:StL. 5 NY 2 Oct. 12, 1964
	NL:NY 2 Balt. 1 Oct. 15, 1969
	AL:Balt. 3 Pitt. 2 Oct. 16, 1971
	NL:Cin. 6 Bos. 5 Oct. 14, 1975
	AL:NY 4 LA 3 Oct. 14, 1978
	AL:KC 4 Phil. 3 Oct. 17, 1980
	NL:NY 6 Bos. 5 Oct. 25, 1986
	NL:Cin. 5 Oak. 4 Oct. 17, 1990
	AL:Minn. 1 Atl. 0 Oct. 27, 1991
	AL:NY 8 Atl. 6 Oct. 23, 1996
	AL:NY 6 Atl. 5 Oct. 26, 1999
	AL:NY 4 Ari. 3 Oct. 31, 2001
	NL:SF 4 Det. 3 Oct. 28, 2012
	NL:Chi. 8 Clev. 7 Nov. 2, 2016
	AL:Hou. 13 LA 12, Oct. 29, 2017

WORLD SERIES – CLUB BATTING

AMERICAN LEAGUE	BA	SLG	G	AB	R	ER	H	TB	1B	2B	3B	HR	RBI	SH	SF	BB	HB	SO	SB	LOB
New York Yankees	.250	.386	225	7543	989	886	1883	2911	1339	276	52	216	935	109	22	787	54	1297	78	1556
Boston Red Sox	.243	.371	79	2654	312	263	646	985	449	105	42	50	290	60	12	259	21	458	24	565
Philadelphia/Oakland	.228	.338	75	2457	267	211	559	830	393	107	13	46	244	65	4	223	13	461	41	490
Detroit Tigers	.225	.319	65	2165	227	197	488	691	362	82	11	33	212	34	3	225	22	351	36	467
Washington/Minnesota	.238	.366	40	1340	145	128	319	491	228	46	9	36	140	24	2	128	6	229	23	279
St. Louis/Baltimore	.212	.329	39	1261	135	127	267	415	189	41	4	33	122	8	1	125	6	240	5	238
Cleveland Indians	.229	.347	37	1219	137	118	279	423	196	50	5	28	124	17	4	138	7	227	21	261
Chicago White Sox	.246	.343	30	1000	106	88	246	343	181	45	8	12	93	21	1	79	11	156	24	201
Kansas City Royals	.267	.386	25	869	105	100	232	335	164	48	5	15	100	8	7	82	4	185	21	183
*Houston Astros	.251	.460	14	494	64	62	124	227	73	25	0	26	62	2	2	49	2	105	9	102
Toronto Blue Jays	.271	.438	12	402	62	60	109	176	71	21	5	12	62	2	8	43	4	63	12	77
Texas Rangers	.229	.368	12	389	42	39	89	143	113	18	0	12	42	4	6	41	1	82	3	78
Tampa Bay Rays	.214	.360	11	350	37	35	75	126	51	10	1	13	35	2	2	26	1	106	3	51
Anaheim Angels	.310	.465	7	245	41	37	76	114	53	15	1	7	38	2	3	23	2	38	6	54
Milwaukee Brewers	.269	.399	7	238	33	26	64	95	45	12	2	5	29	1	1	19	1	28	1	44

* Also played in the World Series for the National League.

NATIONAL LEAGUE	BA	SLG	G	AB	R	ER	H	TB	1B	2B	3B	HR	RBI	SH	SF	BB	HB	SO	SB	LOB
Brooklyn/Los Angeles	.229	.357	123	4041	429	390	926	1442	649	145	25	107	403	56	15	384	26	766	63	799
St. Louis Cardinals	.240	.345	118	3931	430	353	943	1356	673	185	27	58	396	78	11	315	15	659	67	796
New York/San Francisco	.248	.350	116	3865	426	360	958	1351	722	143	29	64	395	74	11	314	24	638	65	760
Chicago Cubs	.243	.334	60	1998	205	160	486	668	363	85	17	21	181	63	12	161	12	365	61	401
Boston/Milwaukee/Atlanta	.235	.353	53	1760	188	174	414	622	296	68	10	40	182	35	12	189	9	316	41	367
Cincinnati Reds	.243	.358	51	1690	192	166	411	605	289	77	18	27	187	29	9	148	13	225	40	332
Pittsburgh Pirates	.254	.359	47	1576	175	135	400	565	289	76	16	19	162	39	5	109	19	226	42	337
Philadelphia Phillies	.239	.381	37	1210	138	126	289	461	193	55	6	35	132	16	8	126	9	233	26	253
New York Mets	.237	.350	29	1016	106	91	241	356	182	30	2	38	91	17	8	87	10	208	9	220
Florida Marlins	.254	.369	13	453	54	46	115	167	84	20	1	10	51	6	4	50	2	96	6	105
San Diego Padres	.253	.367	9	300	28	26	76	110	55	14	1	6	25	1	5	23	0	55	3	61
Arizona Diamondbacks	.264	.394	7	246	37	30	65	97	45	14	0	6	36	5	2	17	6	70	2	49
Washington Nationals	.241	.419	4	241	33	30	58	101	38	8	1	11	32	3	0	27	1	61	4	46
Colorado Rockies	.218	.346	4	133	10	10	29	46	36	6	1	3	10	3	1	10	2	36	1	28
*Houston Astros	.203	.336	4	143	14	12	29	48	36	8	1	3	14	5	1	17	5	36	5	34

* Also played in the World Series for the American League.

WORLD SERIES – CLUB FIELDING

AMERICAN LEAGUE	PCT	G	TC	CA	PO	A	E	DP	TP	PB
New York Yankees	.981	225	8554	8389	6022	2367	165	198	0	16
Boston Red Sox	.974	79	3134	3051	2159	892	83	54	0	6
Philadelphia/Oakland	.972	75	2870	2791	2016	775	79	56	0	5
Detroit Tigers	.964	65	2559	2467	1738	729	92	45	0	5
Washington/Minnesota	.976	40	1563	1526	1081	445	37	35	0	2
St. Louis/Baltimore	.972	39	1472	1431	1039	392	41	27	0	0
Cleveland Indians	.975	37	1407	1372	986	386	35	40	1	1
Chicago White Sox	.964	30	1263	1217	810	407	46	24	0	4
Kansas City Royals	.986	25	966	952	681	271	14	19	0	1
*Houston Astros	.990	14	491	486	381	105	5	11	0	1
Toronto Blue Jays	.974	12	427	416	324	92	11	10	0	0
Texas Rangers	.971	12	451	438	315	123	13	11	0	0
Tampa Bay Rays	.986	11	368	363	282	81	5	6	0	0
Anaheim Angels	.980	7	244	239	183	56	5	6	0	1
Milwaukee Brewers	.960	7	272	261	180	81	11	3	0	0

* Also played in the World Series for the National League.

NATIONAL LEAGUE	PCT	G	TC	CA	PO	A	E	DP	TP	PB
Brooklyn/Los Angeles	.977	123	4646	4537	3270	1267	109	104	0	10
St. Louis Cardinals	.977	118	4361	4261	3122	1139	100	93	0	5
New York/San Francisco	.969	116	4599	4458	3102	1356	141	95	0	8
Chicago Cubs	.970	60	2394	2322	1609	713	72	53	0	8
Boston/Milwaukee/Atlanta	.980	53	2092	2050	1436	614	42	50	0	1
Cincinnati Reds	.976	51	1946	1899	1367	532	47	47	0	2
Pittsburgh Pirates	.966	47	1834	1772	1235	537	62	39	0	5
Philadelphia Phillies	.984	37	1337	1315	976	339	22	29	0	2
New York Mets	.975	29	1109	1081	813	268	28	13	0	2
Florida Marlins	.980	13	509	499	360	139	10	17	0	0
San Diego Padres	.978	9	316	309	228	81	7	10	0	1
Arizona Diamondbacks	.988	7	259	256	195	61	3	6	0	0
Washington Nationals	.985	7	259	255	189	66	4	5	0	0
Colorado Rockies	1.000	4	149	149	102	47	0	3	0	0
*Houston Astros	.988	4	173	171	118	53	2	6	0	0

* Also played in the World Series for the American League.

WORLD SERIES – CLUB PITCHING

AMERICAN LEAGUE	ERA	BA	G	CG	SV	SHO	AB	IP	H	TB	2B	3B	HR	RBI	R	ER	BB	HP	SO	WP	BK
New York Yankees	3.09	.240	225	79	17	16	7469	2007.1	1790	2628	302	46	148	755	796	690	646	40	1295	27	3
Boston Red Sox	2.65	.229	79	30	9	7	2632	719.2	603	875	101	30	37	231	254	212	212	20	442	14	3
Philadelphia/Oakland	2.56	.228	75	34	11	3	2473	672.1	563	790	105	16	30	210	235	191	208	16	448	17	1
Detroit Tigers	3.21	.254	65	34	3	2	2192	579.2	557	785	103	19	29	231	260	207	165	15	364	15	1
Washington/Minnesota	3.07	.263	40	12	3	3	1374	360.1	361	511	54	9	26	138	147	123	105	11	207	10	2
St. Louis/Baltimore	2.52	.235	39	15	5	4	1295	346.1	304	454	57	6	27	112	117	97	111	5	240	8	2
Cleveland Indians	3.28	.243	37	10	4	5	1220	329.0	296	440	46	4	30	128	133	120	126	6	209	9	2
Chicago White Sox	2.83	.238	30	13	3	3	980	270.0	233	330	35	13	12	94	105	85	78	14	140	6	0
Kansas City Royals	3.29	.239	25	4	3	2	836	227.0	200	278	35	2	13	86	89	83	70	5	156	7	0
*Houston Astros	4.46	.223	14	0	2	0	470	127.0	105	191	19	2	21	63	67	63	48	8	126	5	1
Toronto Blue Jays	4.25	.248	12	0	5	0	412	108.0	102	149	13	2	10	54	56	51	54	2	98	5	0
Texas Rangers	5.14	.246	12	0	3	1	399	105.0	98	167	20	2	15	65	67	60	52	7	90	3	0
Tampa Bay Rays	5.07	.256	11	0	1	0	371	94.0	95	179	21	0	21	54	56	53	52	3	99	10	0
Anaheim Angels	5.75	.281	7	0	3	0	235	61.0	66	117	7	1	14	42	44	39	30	1	50	1	0
Milwaukee Brewers	4.80	.273	7	1	2	1	245	60.0	67	101	16	3	4	34	39	32	20	0	26	3	1

* Also played in the World Series for the National League.

NATIONAL LEAGUE	ERA	BA	G	CG	SV	SHO	AB	IP	H	TB	2B	3B	HR	RBI	R	ER	BB	HP	SO	WP	BK
Brooklyn/Los Angeles	3.64	.237	123	32	8	9	4043	1090.0	958	1527	145	29	122	459	491	441	424	24	787	28	3
St. Louis Cardinals	3.43	.239	118	36	10	11	3912	1040.2	935	1432	166	23	95	431	460	397	410	28	742	24	3
New York/San Francisco	3.29	.240	116	41	7	16	3869	1034.1	927	1353	158	29	70	407	446	378	332	20	592	28	1
Chicago Cubs	3.57	.242	60	23	4	8	1996	536.1	483	680	85	11	30	230	252	213	201	24	315	18	1
Boston/Milwaukee/Atlanta	2.90	.218	53	16	4	7	1750	478.2	382	601	62	8	47	169	176	154	171	4	322	10	2
Cincinnati Reds	3.34	.236	51	13	4	3	1687	455.2	398	608	56	11	44	179	190	169	173	6	259	8	1
Pittsburgh Pirates	4.08	.259	47	17	8	2	1597	412.1	413	620	60	24	33	202	221	187	127	17	224	14	1
Philadelphia Phillies	4.09	.256	37	7	8	1	1225	325.1	313	489	51	10	35	149	156	148	113	13	245	6	0
New York Mets	2.99	.232	29	2	8	0	1022	271.0	237	345	42	2	16	98	103	90	113	8	220	7	0
Florida Marlins	4.43	.278	13	1	4	1	454	120.0	126	191	22	0	13	63	65	59	62	3	100	2	0
San Diego Padres	5.21	.279	9	0	1	0	297	76.0	83	131	9	0	13	48	49	44	44	3	56	3	0
Arizona Diamondbacks	1.94	.183	7	1	0	1	229	65.0	42	66	6	0	6	14	14	14	16	0	63	4	0
Washington Nationals	4.29	.272	7	0	0	0	250	63.0	68	113	12	0	11	30	30	30	27	1	51	3	1
Colorado Rockies	7.68	.333	4	0	0	0	141	34.0	47	74	18	0	3	29	29	29	19	1	20	0	0
*Houston Astros	4.58	.286	4	0	0	0	154	39.1	44	75	9	2	6	20	20	20	15	3	30	0	0

* Also played in the World Series for the American League.

	AB	R	H	TB	1B	2B	3B	HR	RBI	SH	SF	BB	HP	SO	SB	LOB	BA	SLG
1903 (8)																		
AL:Bos.	282	39	71	113	49	4	16	2	35	6	-	13	2	27	5	55	.252	.401
NL:Pitt.	270	24	64	92	47	7	9	1	23	3	-	14	1	45	7	51	.237	.341
1905 (5)																		
NL:NY	153	15	32	39	25	7	0	0	13	5	-	15	2	26	11	31	.209	.255
AL:Phil.	155	3	25	30	20	5	0	0	2	3	-	5	1	25	2	26	.161	.194
1906 (6)																		
AL:Chi.	187	22	37	53	24	10	3	0	19	6	-	18	3	35	6	33	.198	.283
NL:Chi.	184	18	36	45	27	9	0	0	11	13	-	18	2	27	8	37	.196	.245
1907 (5)																		
NL:Chi.	167	19	43	51	36	6	1	0	16	9	-	12	4	25	18	35	.257	.305
AL:Det.	172	6	36	41	33	1	2	0	6	3	-	9	1	21	7	35	.209	.238
1908 (5)																		
NL:Chi.	164	24	48	59	41	4	2	1	21	9	-	13	0	26	13	30	.293	.360
AL:Det.	158	15	32	37	27	5	0	0	14	5	-	12	2	26	5	27	.203	.234
1909 (7)																		
NL:Pitt.	223	34	49	70	34	12	1	2	26	12	-	20	6	34	18	44	.220	.320
AL:Det.	233	28	55	77	37	16	0	2	25	4	-	20	4	22	6	50	.236	.330
1910 (5)																		
AL:Phil.	177	35	56	80	35	19	1	1	29	7	-	17	2	24	7	36	.316	.452
NL:Chi.	158	15	35	48	23	11	1	0	13	7	-	18	0	31	3	31	.222	.304
1911 (6)																		
AL:Phil.	205	27	50	74	32	15	0	3	21	9	-	4	0	31	4	29	.244	.361
NL:NY	189	13	33	46	21	11	1	0	10	6	-	14	3	44	4	32	.175	.243
1912 (8)																		
AL:Bos.	273	25	60	89	39	14	6	1	21	8	-	19	1	36	6	55	.220	.326
NL:NY	274	31	74	99	55	14	4	1	25	7	-	22	3	39	12	53	.270	.361
1913 (5)																		
AL:Phil.	174	23	46	64	36	4	4	2	21	7	-	7	0	16	5	30	.264	.368
NL:NY	164	15	33	41	28	3	1	1	15	2	-	8	3	19	5	24	.201	.250
1914 (4)																		
NL:Bos.	135	16	33	46	24	6	2	1	14	3	-	15	1	18	9	27	.244	.341
AL:Phil.	128	6	22	31	13	9	0	0	5	3	-	13	0	28	2	21	.172	.242
1915 (5)																		
AL:Bos.	159	12	42	57	35	2	2	3	11	7	-	11	1	25	1	35	.264	.358
NL:Phil.	148	10	27	36	21	4	1	1	9	5	-	10	2	25	2	23	.182	.243
1916 (5)																		
AL:Bos.	164	21	39	64	24	7	6	2	18	12	-	18	0	25	1	31	.238	.390
NL:Brk.	170	13	34	49	26	2	5	1	11	6	-	14	2	19	1	32	.200	.288
1917 (6)																		
AL:Chi.	197	21	54	63	47	6	0	1	18	3	-	11	0	28	6	37	.274	.320
NL:NY	199	17	51	70	40	5	4	2	16	3	-	6	2	27	4	37	.256	.352
1918 (6)																		
AL:Bos.	172	9	32	40	27	2	3	0	6	8	-	16	1	21	3	32	.186	.233
NL:Chi.	176	10	37	44	31	5	1	0	10	4	-	18	2	14	3	31	.210	.250
1919 (8)																		
NL:Cin.	251	35	64	88	47	10	7	0	34	13	-	25	5	22	7	46	.255	.351
AL:Chi.	263	20	59	78	45	10	3	1	17	7	-	15	3	30	5	52	.224	.297
1920 (7)																		
AL:Clev.	217	21	53	72	40	9	2	2	18	3	-	21	0	21	2	43	.244	.332
NL:Brk.	215	8	44	51	38	5	1	0	8	5	-	10	0	20	1	39	.205	.237
1921 (8)																		
NL:NY	264	29	71	98	52	13	4	2	28	6	-	22	1	38	7	54	.269	.371
AL:NY	241	22	50	65	40	7	1	2	20	9	-	27	1	44	6	43	.207	.270
1922 (5)																		
NL:NY	162	18	50	57	46	2	1	1	18	5	-	12	0	15	1	32	.309	.352
AL:NY	158	11	32	46	23	6	1	2	11	6	-	8	2	20	2	25	.203	.291
1923 (6)																		
AL:NY	205	30	60	91	43	8	4	5	29	6	-	20	1	22	1	43	.293	.444
NL:NY	201	17	47	70	37	2	3	5	17	0	-	12	1	18	1	35	.234	.348
1924 (7)																		
AL:Wash.	248	26	61	85	47	9	0	5	23	6	-	29	0	34	5	57	.246	.343
NL:NY	253	27	66	91	51	9	2	4	22	7	-	25	2	40	3	59	.261	.360
1925 (7)																		
NL:Pitt.	230	25	61	89	43	12	2	4	25	8	-	17	4	32	7	54	.265	.387
AL:Wash.	225	26	59	91	43	8	0	8	25	10	-	17	2	31	2	46	.262	.404
1926 (7)																		
NL:StL.	239	31	65	91	48	12	1	4	30	12	-	11	1	30	2	43	.272	.381
AL:NY	223	21	54	78	39	10	1	4	19	10	-	31	1	31	1	55	.242	.350
1927 (4)																		
AL:NY	136	23	38	54	28	6	2	2	20	6	-	13	1	25	2	29	.279	.397
NL:Pitt.	130	10	29	37	22	6	1	0	10	6	-	4	1	7	0	23	.223	.285

	AB	R	H	TB	1B	2B	3B	HR	RBI	SH	SF	BB	HP	SO	SB	LOB	BA	SLG
1928 (4)																		
AL:NY	134	27	37	71	21	7	0	9	25	5	-	13	1	12	4	24	.276	.530
NL:StL.	131	10	27	37	20	5	1	1	9	2	-	11	1	29	3	27	.206	.282
1929 (5)																		
AL:Phil.	171	26	48	71	37	5	0	6	26	7	-	13	1	27	0	35	.281	.415
NL:Chi.	173	17	43	56	34	6	2	1	15	2	-	13	0	50	1	36	.249	.324
1930 (6)																		
AL:Phil.	178	21	35	67	17	10	2	6	21	7	-	24	1	32	0	36	.197	.376
NL:StL.	190	12	38	56	25	10	1	2	11	4	-	11	0	33	1	37	.200	.295
1931 (7)																		
NL:StL.	229	19	54	71	41	11	0	2	17	4	-	9	0	41	8	40	.236	.310
AL:Phil.	227	22	50	64	42	5	0	3	20	4	-	28	1	46	0	52	.220	.282
1932 (4)																		
AL:NY	144	37	45	75	31	6	0	8	36	1	-	23	4	26	0	33	.313	.521
NL:Chi.	146	19	37	58	24	8	2	3	16	1	-	11	0	24	2	31	.253	.397
1933 (5)																		
NL:NY	176	16	47	61	39	5	0	3	16	6	-	11	0	21	0	39	.267	.347
AL:Wash.	173	11	37	47	31	4	0	2	11	3	-	13	0	24	1	37	.214	.272
1934 (7)																		
NL:StL.	262	34	73	103	52	14	5	2	32	4	-	11	1	31	2	49	.279	.393
AL:Det.	250	23	56	76	41	12	1	2	20	6	-	25	2	43	4	64	.224	.304
1935 (6)																		
AL:Det.	206	21	51	67	38	11	1	1	18	3	-	25	2	27	1	51	.248	.325
NL:Chi.	202	18	48	73	35	6	2	5	17	7	-	11	1	29	1	38	.238	.361
1936 (6)																		
AL:NY	215	43	65	96	49	8	1	7	41	3	-	26	1	35	1	43	.302	.447
NL:NY	203	23	50	71	37	9	0	4	20	7	-	21	0	33	0	46	.246	.350
1937 (5)																		
AL:NY	169	28	42	68	28	6	4	4	25	2	-	21	1	21	0	36	.249	.402
NL:NY	169	12	40	49	33	6	0	1	12	0	-	11	0	21	1	36	.237	.290
1938 (4)																		
AL:NY	135	22	37	60	25	6	1	5	21	1	-	11	1	16	3	24	.274	.444
NL:Chi.	136	9	33	45	26	4	1	2	8	1	-	6	0	26	0	26	.243	.331
1939 (4)																		
AL:NY	131	20	27	54	15	4	1	7	18	2	-	9	0	20	0	16	.206	.412
NL:Cin.	133	8	27	32	23	3	1	0	8	2	-	6	1	22	1	23	.203	.316
1940 (7)																		
NL:Cin.	232	22	58	78	42	14	0	2	21	4	-	15	0	30	1	49	.250	.336
AL:Det.	228	28	56	83	40	9	3	4	24	3	-	30	0	30	0	50	.246	.364
1941 (5)																		
AL:NY	166	17	41	54	33	5	1	2	16	0	-	23	2	18	2	42	.247	.325
NL:Brk.	159	11	29	43	19	7	2	1	11	0	-	14	0	21	0	27	.182	.270
1942 (5)																		
NL:StL.	163	23	39	53	31	4	2	2	23	7	-	17	0	19	0	32	.239	.325
AL:NY	178	18	44	59	35	6	0	3	14	1	-	8	0	22	3	34	.247	.331
1943 (5)																		
AL:NY	159	17	35	50	26	5	2	2	14	4	-	12	0	30	2	30	.220	.314
NL:StL.	165	9	37	48	30	5	0	2	8	5	-	11	0	26	1	37	.224	.291
1944 (6)																		
NL:StL.	204	16	49	69	36	9	1	3	15	7	-	19	0	43	0	51	.240	.338
AL:StL.	197	12	36	50	25	9	1	1	9	1	-	23	0	49	0	44	.183	.254
1945 (7)																		
AL:Det.	242	32	54	70	42	10	0	2	32	3	-	33	2	22	3	53	.223	.289
NL:Chi.	247	29	65	90	45	16	3	1	27	10	-	19	0	48	2	50	.263	.364
1946 (7)																		
NL:StL.	232	28	60	86	38	19	2	1	27	8	-	19	2	30	3	50	.259	.371
AL:Bos.	233	20	56	77	44	7	1	4	18	3	-	22	1	28	2	53	.240	.330
1947 (7)																		
AL:NY	238	38	67	100	47	11	5	4	36	3	-	38	2	37	2	63	.282	.420
NL:Brk.	226	29	52	70	37	13	1	1	26	3	-	30	1	32	7	46	.230	.310
1948 (6)																		
AL:Clev.	191	17	38	57	27	7	0	4	16	3	-	12	1	26	2	34	.199	.298
NL:Bos.	187	17	43	61	33	6	0	4	16	7	-	16	0	19	1	34	.230	.326
1949 (5)																		
AL:NY	164	21	37	57	23	10	2	2	20	3	-	18	0	27	2	32	.226	.348
NL:Brk.	162	14	34	55	22	7	1	4	14	2	-	15	1	38	1	31	.210	.340
1950 (4)																		
AL:NY	135	11	30	41	24	3	1	2	10	2	-	13	1	12	1	33	.222	.304
NL:Phil.	128	5	26	34	19	6	1	0	3	6	-	7	1	24	1	26	.203	.266
1951 (6)																		
AL:NY	199	29	49	75	35	7	2	5	25	0	-	26	1	23	0	41	.246	.377
NL:NY	194	18	46	61	36	7	1	2	15	2	-	25	1	22	2	45	.237	.314

	AB	R	H	TB	1B	2B	3B	HR	RBI	SH	SF	BB	HP	SO	SB	LOB	BA	SLG
1952 (7)																		
AL:NY	232	26	50	89	33	5	2	10	24	2	-	31	1	32	1	48	.216	.384
NL:Brk.	233	20	50	75	37	7	0	6	18	6	-	24	1	49	5	52	.215	.322
1953 (6)																		
AL:NY	201	33	56	97	37	6	4	9	32	4	-	25	4	43	2	47	.279	.483
NL:Brk.	213	27	64	103	42	13	1	8	26	2	-	15	2	30	2	49	.300	.484
1954 (4)																		
NL:NY	130	21	33	42	28	3	0	2	20	6	2	17	0	24	1	28	.254	.323
AL:Clev.	137	9	26	42	17	5	1	3	9	3	0	16	1	23	0	37	.190	.307
1955 (7)																		
NL:Brk.	223	31	58	95	40	8	1	9	30	6	2	33	2	38	2	55	.260	.426
AL:NY	222	26	55	87	41	4	2	8	25	1	0	22	2	39	3	41	.248	.392
1956 (7)																		
AL:NY	229	33	58	100	40	6	0	12	33	4	2	21	0	43	2	40	.253	.437
NL:Brk.	215	25	42	61	30	8	1	3	24	2	3	32	0	47	1	42	.199	.284
1957 (7)																		
NL:Mil.	225	23	47	79	32	6	1	8	22	6	0	22	3	40	1	46	.209	.351
AL:NY	230	25	57	87	42	7	1	7	25	3	1	22	0	34	1	45	.248	.378
1958 (7)																		
AL:NY	233	29	49	86	33	5	1	10	29	2	2	21	0	42	1	40	.210	.369
NL:Mil.	240	25	60	81	46	10	1	3	24	4	3	27	0	56	1	58	.250	.338
1959 (6)																		
NL:LA	203	21	53	79	42	3	1	7	19	4	0	12	0	27	5	42	.261	.389
AL:Chi.	199	23	52	74	38	10	0	4	19	3	1	20	2	33	2	43	.261	.372
1960 (7)																		
NL:Pitt.	234	27	60	83	45	11	0	4	26	3	0	12	3	26	2	42	.256	.355
AL:NY	269	55	91	142	64	13	4	10	54	2	1	18	2	40	0	51	.338	.528
1961 (5)																		
AL:NY	165	27	42	73	26	8	1	7	26	3	1	24	0	25	1	34	.255	.442
NL:Cin.	170	13	35	52	24	8	0	3	11	0	0	8	3	27	0	33	.206	.306
1962 (7)																		
AL:NY	221	20	44	61	34	6	1	3	17	1	1	21	2	39	4	43	.199	.276
NL:SF	226	21	51	80	34	10	2	5	19	4	0	12	1	39	1	39	.226	.354
1963 (4)																		
NL:LA	117	12	25	41	17	3	2	3	12	2	1	11	0	25	2	17	.214	.373
AL:NY	129	4	22	31	17	3	0	2	4	1	0	5	1	37	0	24	.171	.240
1964 (7)																		
NL:StL.	240	32	61	90	45	8	3	5	29	4	2	18	0	30	3	47	.254	.375
AL:NY	239	33	60	101	39	21	0	10	33	1	2	25	2	54	2	47	.251	.423
1965 (7)																		
NL:LA	234	24	64	91	48	10	1	5	21	6	0	13	3	31	9	52	.274	.389
AL:Minn.	215	20	42	71	27	7	2	6	19	2	0	19	0	54	2	36	.195	.330
1966 (4)																		
AL:Balt.	120	13	24	41	16	3	1	4	10	2	0	11	0	17	0	18	.200	.342
NL:LA	120	2	17	23	13	3	0	1	2	1	0	13	0	28	1	24	.142	.192
1967 (7)																		
NL:StL.	229	25	51	81	33	11	2	5	24	0	2	17	0	30	7	40	.223	.354
AL:Bos.	222	21	48	80	33	6	1	8	19	4	2	17	2	49	1	43	.216	.360
1968 (7)																		
AL:Det.	231	34	56	90	41	4	3	8	33	2	1	27	3	59	0	44	.242	.390
NL:StL.	239	27	61	95	44	7	3	7	27	1	0	21	1	40	11	49	.255	.397
1969 (5)																		
NL:NY	159	15	35	61	21	8	0	6	13	2	1	15	1	35	1	34	.220	.384
AL:Balt.	157	9	23	33	19	1	0	3	9	0	1	15	0	28	1	29	.146	.210
1970 (5)																		
AL:Balt.	171	33	50	87	33	7	0	10	32	2	0	20	0	33	0	31	.292	.509
NL:Cin.	164	20	35	58	23	6	1	5	20	2	1	15	0	23	1	28	.213	.354
1971 (7)																		
NL:Pitt.	238	23	56	84	40	9	2	5	21	4	0	26	1	47	5	63	.235	.353
AL:Balt.	219	24	45	65	36	3	1	5	22	2	3	20	4	35	1	39	.205	.297
1972 (7)																		
AL:Oak.	220	16	46	65	37	4	0	5	16	6	0	21	1	37	1	45	.209	.295
NL:Cin.	220	21	46	65	34	8	1	3	21	5	3	27	1	46	12	49	.209	.295
1973 (7)																		
AL:Oak.	241	21	51	75	34	12	3	2	20	2	1	28	2	62	3	58	.212	.311
NL:NY	261	24	66	89	53	7	2	4	16	4	0	26	3	36	0	72	.253	.341
1974 (5)																		
AL:Oak.	142	16	30	46	22	4	0	4	14	7	1	16	2	42	3	26	.211	.324
NL:LA	158	11	36	54	27	4	1	4	10	3	1	16	1	32	3	36	.228	.342
1975 (7)																		
NL:Cin.	244	29	59	95	40	9	3	7	29	2	2	25	2	30	9	50	.242	.389
AL:Bos.	239	30	60	89	45	7	2	6	30	4	3	30	1	40	0	52	.251	.372

	AB	R	H	TB	1B	2B	3B	HR	RBI	SH	SF	BB	HP	SO	SB	LOB	BA	SLG
1976 (4)																		
NL:Cin.	134	22	42	70	25	10	3	4	21	0	2	12	0	16	7	22	.313	.522
AL:NY	135	8	30	38	25	3	1	1	8	0	1	12	1	16	1	33	.222	.281
1977 (6)																		
AL:NY	205	26	50	84	32	10	0	8	25	4	1	11	2	37	1	32	.244	.410
NL:LA	208	28	48	86	31	5	3	9	28	0	2	16	1	36	2	31	.231	.413
1978 (6)																		
AL:NY	222	36	68	85	57	8	0	3	34	1	0	16	2	40	5	47	.306	.383
NL:LA	199	23	52	78	38	8	0	6	22	1	0	20	0	31	5	38	.261	.392
1979 (7)																		
NL:Pitt.	251	32	81	110	59	18	1	3	32	3	5	16	3	35	0	60	.323	.438
AL:Balt.	233	26	54	78	39	10	1	4	23	1	0	26	1	41	2	49	.232	.335
1980 (6)																		
NL:Phil.	201	27	59	81	43	13	0	3	26	2	4	15	2	17	3	41	.294	.403
AL:KC	207	23	60	97	41	9	2	8	22	2	3	26	0	49	6	54	.290	.469
1981 (6)																		
NL:LA	198	27	51	77	38	6	1	6	26	4	2	20	2	44	6	46	.258	.389
AL:NY	193	22	46	74	31	8	1	6	22	5	2	33	0	24	4	55	.238	.383
1982 (7)																		
NL:StL	245	39	67	101	44	16	3	4	34	1	1	20	0	26	7	49	.273	.412
AL:Mil.	238	33	64	95	45	12	2	5	29	1	1	19	1	28	1	44	.269	.399
1983 (5)																		
AL:Balt.	164	18	35	61	21	8	0	6	17	0	3	10	1	37	1	28	.213	.372
NL:Phil.	159	9	31	49	22	4	1	4	9	0	1	7	0	29	1	23	.195	.308
1984 (5)																		
AL:Det.	158	23	40	65	29	4	0	7	22	2	2	24	2	27	7	39	.253	.411
NL:SD	166	15	44	60	34	7	0	3	14	1	3	11	0	26	2	34	.265	.361
1985 (7)																		
AL:KC	236	28	68	90	52	12	2	2	26	3	0	28	1	56	7	56	.288	.381
NL:StL	216	13	40	58	27	10	1	2	13	3	0	18	0	42	2	38	.185	.269
1986 (7)																		
NL:NY	240	32	65	92	52	6	0	7	29	6	2	21	1	43	7	50	.271	.383
AL:Bos.	248	27	69	99	51	11	2	5	26	4	2	28	3	53	0	69	.278	.398
1987 (7)																		
AL:Minn.	238	38	64	101	44	10	3	7	38	1	0	29	3	36	6	56	.269	.424
NL:StL	232	26	60	74	50	8	0	2	25	2	1	13	1	44	12	43	.259	.319
1988 (5)																		
NL:LA	167	21	41	66	27	8	1	5	19	1	0	13	1	36	4	30	.246	.395
AL:Oak.	158	11	28	37	23	3	0	2	11	1	1	17	1	41	3	34	.177	.234
1989 (4)																		
AL:Oak.	146	32	44	85	24	8	3	9	30	0	0	18	1	22	4	31	.301	.582
NL:SF	134	14	28	46	19	4	1	4	14	0	1	8	0	27	2	21	.209	.343
1990 (4)																		
NL:Cin.	142	22	45	67	31	9	2	3	22	1	1	15	1	9	2	32	.317	.472
AL:Oak.	135	8	28	41	21	4	0	3	8	2	1	12	0	28	7	31	.207	.304
1991 (7)																		
AL:Minn.	241	24	56	96	36	8	4	8	24	2	2	21	1	48	7	47	.232	.398
NL:Atl.	249	29	63	105	41	10	4	8	29	4	3	26	1	39	5	52	.253	.422
1992 (6)																		
AL:Tor.	196	17	45	71	31	8	0	6	17	2	1	18	1	33	5	38	.230	.362
NL:Atl.	200	20	44	59	35	6	0	3	19	2	2	20	1	48	15	40	.220	.295
1993 (6)																		
AL:Tor.	206	45	64	105	40	13	5	6	45	0	7	25	3	30	7	39	.311	.510
NL:Phil.	212	36	58	90	42	7	2	7	35	1	1	34	1	50	7	54	.274	.425
1995 (6)																		
NL:Atl.	193	23	47	81	29	10	0	8	23	5	1	25	2	34	5	44	.244	.420
AL:Clev.	195	19	35	59	22	7	1	5	17	0	0	25	0	37	8	39	.179	303
1996 (6)																		
AL:NY	199	18	43	57	48	6	1	2	16	2	0	26	1	43	4	48	.216	.286
NL:Atl.	201	26	51	74	37	9	1	4	26	4	3	23	1	36	3	41	.254	.368
1997 (7)																		
NL:Fla.	250	37	68	106	47	12	1	8	34	1	2	36	1	48	4	62	.272	.424
AL:Clev.	247	44	72	107	52	12	1	7	42	5	3	40	0	51	5	59	.291	.433
1998 (4)																		
AL:NY	139	26	43	66	32	5	0	6	25	1	1	20	1	29	1	34	.309	.475
NL:SD	134	13	32	50	21	7	1	3	11	0	2	12	0	29	1	27	.239	.373
1999 (4)																		
AL:NY	137	21	37	57	27	5	0	5	20	3	0	13	0	31	5	27	.270	.416
NL:Atl.	130	9	26	36	19	5	1	1	9	0	0	15	0	26	1	25	.200	.277
2000 (5)																		
AL:NY	179	19	47	73	32	8	3	4	18	1	3	25	3	40	1	52	.263	.408
NL:NY	175	16	40	60	28	8	0	4	15	3	1	11	3	48	0	36	.229	.343

	AB	R	H	TB	1B	2B	3B	HR	RBI	SH	SF	BB	HP	SO	SB	LOB	BA	SLG
2001 (7)																		
NL:Ari.	246	37	65	97	45	14	0	6	36	5	2	17	6	70	2	49	.264	.394
AL:NY	229	14	42	66	30	6	0	6	14	1	0	16	1	63	1	38	.183	.288
2002 (7)																		
AL:Ana.	245	41	76	114	53	15	1	7	38	2	3	23	2	38	6	54	.310	.465
NL:SF	235	44	66	117	44	7	1	14	42	4	4	30	1	50	5	47	.281	.498
2003 (6)																		
NL:Fla.	203	17	47	61	37	8	0	2	17	5	2	14	1	48	2	43	.232	.300
AL:NY	207	21	54	84	37	10	1	6	21	2	2	22	3	49	2	47	.261	.406
2004 (4)																		
AL:Bos.	138	24	39	66	22	11	2	4	24	1	0	24	4	20	0	41	.283	.478
NL:StL.	126	12	24	38	14	8	0	2	8	2	3	12	1	32	1	24	.190	.302
2005 (4)																		
AL:Chi.	154	20	44	75	27	9	2	6	20	2	0	15	3	30	5	36	.286	.487
NL:Hou.	143	14	29	48	17	8	1	3	14	5	1	17	5	36	5	34	.203	.336
2006 (5)																		
NL:StL.	158	22	36	54	22	12	0	2	16	4	0	23	2	34	1	39	.228	.342
AL:Det.	161	11	32	54	19	8	1	4	11	3	0	8	2	37	1	31	.199	.335
2007 (4)																		
AL:Bos.	141	29	47	74	26	18	0	3	29	2	2	19	1	20	2	34	.333	.525
NL:Col.	133	10	29	46	19	6	1	3	10	1	0	10	2	36	1	28	.218	.346
2008 (5)																		
NL:Phil.	168	24	44	81	25	10	0	9	23	1	0	27	2	38	7	48	.262	.482
AL:TB	156	15	33	49	25	4	0	4	14	2	1	10	1	36	7	23	.212	.314
2009 (6)																		
AL:NY	198	32	49	79	31	12	0	6	30	1	2	18	6	56	4	37	.247	.399
NL:Phil.	194	27	44	90	21	11	1	11	27	1	2	26	1	50	5	38	.227	464
2010 (5)																		
NL:SF	169	29	42	76	57	11	1	7	29	1	0	11	3	43	1	26	.249	.450
AL:Tex.	153	12	29	44	35	6	0	3	12	1	2	15	0	31	2	27	.190	.288
2011 (7)																		
NL:StL.	230	38	56	91	38	9	1	8	36	6	1	41	4	47	0	58	.243	.396
AL:Tex.	236	30	60	99	39	12	0	9	30	3	4	26	1	51	1	51	.254	.419
2012 (4)																		
NL:SF	132	16	32	52	22	4	2	4	15	1	1	9	0	41	3	22	.242	.394
AL:Det.	126	6	20	31	15	2	0	3	6	0	0	12	2	36	0	23	.159	.246
2013 (6)																		
AL:Bos.	194	27	41	64	27	9	1	4	27	0	3	21	2	59	1	37	.211	.330
NL:StL.	201	14	45	60	35	7	1	2	12	2	1	13	1	43	3	43	.224	.299
2014 (7)																		
NL:SF	238	30	66	85	52	11	1	2	29	2	3	23	1	51	1	54	.277	.357
AL:KC	229	27	57	83	37	17	0	3	27	1	1	11	3	43	1	35	.249	.362
2015 (5)																		
AL:KC	197	27	47	65	34	10	1	2	25	2	3	17	0	37	7	38	.239	.330
NL:NY	181	19	35	54	28	1	0	6	18	2	4	14	2	46	1	28	.193	.298
2016 (7)																		
NL:Chi.	245	27	61	99	41	10	2	8	27	0	2	22	3	64	8	56	.249	.404
AL:Clev.	232	27	55	86	38	10	0	7	23	3	1	24	5	69	4	49	.237	.371
2017 (7)																		
AL:Hou.	244	34	56	114	28	13	0	15	32	1	1	22	2	54	3	42	.230	.467
NL:LA	229	34	47	90	25	11	1	10	31	1	2	21	7	65	1	34	.205	.393
2018 (5)																		
AL:Bos.	189	28	42	73	27	7	0	8	27	1	0	21	1	53	2	28	.222	.386
NL:LA	189	16	34	57	24	3	1	6	14	0	2	17	1	56	0	34	.180	.302
2019 (7)																		
NL:Wash.	241	33	58	101	38	8	1	11	32	3	0	27	1	61	4	46	.241	.419
AL:Hou	250	30	68	113	45	12	0	11	30	1	1	27	0	51	6	60	.272	.452
2020 (6)																		
NL:LA	203	32	51	98	28	11	0	12	31	1	0	25	1	61	5	42	.251	.483
AL:TB	194	22	42	77	26	6	1	9	21	0	1	16	0	70	2	28	.216	.397

WORLD SERIES CLUB FIELDING & PITCHING

[PL=Players Used   PI=Pitchers Used]

	Fielding:										Pitching:					
	PL	TC	CA	PO	A	E	DP	TP	PB	AVG	PI	IP	ER	ERA	CG	SHO
1903 (8)																
AL:Bos.	13	329	315	213	102	14	6	0	2	.957	3	71.0	16	2.03	7	2
NL:Pitt.	14	324	306	210	96	18	5	0	0	.944	5	70.0	29	3.73	6	0
1905 (5)																
NL:NY	12	219	213	135	78	6	3	0	0	.973	3	45.0	0	0.00	4	3
AL:Phil.	13	194	185	129	56	9	3	0	0	.954	3	43.0	4	0.83	5	1
1906 (6)																
AL:Chi.	16	275	261	162	99	14	2	0	1	.949	4	54.0	10	1.67	4	1
NL:Chi.	14	250	243	159	84	7	4	0	3	.972	4	53.0	19	3.22	4	1
1907 (5)																
NL:Chi.	15	219	209	144	65	10	6	0	1	.954	4	48.0	4	0.75	4	1
AL:Det.	14	217	208	138	70	9	2	0	0	.959	4	46.0	11	2.15	4	0
1908 (5)																
NL:Chi.	13	214	209	135	74	5	4	0	1	.977	4	45.0	13	2.60	3	2
AL:Det.	16	204	194	131	63	10	5	0	1	.951	5	44.0	18	3.68	3	0
1909 (7)																
NL:Pitt.	17	285	270	182	88	15	3	0	0	.947	6	61.0	18	2.65	4	1
AL:Det.	16	289	270	183	87	19	4	0	1	.934	5	61.0	20	2.95	4	1
1910 (5)																
AL:Phil.	12	206	195	136	59	11	6	0	0	.947	2	45.2	14	2.75	5	0
NL:Chi.	18	221	209	132	77	12	3	0	0	.946	7	44.0	23	4.70	1	0
1911 (6)																
AL:Phil.	14	250	239	167	72	11	2	0	0	.956	3	55.2	8	1.29	5	0
NL:NY	15	257	241	162	79	16	2	0	1	.938	5	54.0	17	2.83	2	0
1912 (8)																
AL:Bos.	17	337	323	222	101	14	5	0	0	.958	5	74.0	22	2.67	3	0
NL:NY	17	346	329	221	108	17	4	0	0	.951	5	73.2	15	1.83	6	0
1913 (5)																
AL:Phil.	12	197	192	138	54	5	6	0	0	.975	3	46.0	11	2.15	5	0
NL:NY	20	209	202	135	67	7	1	0	1	.967	5	45.0	19	3.80	3	1
1914 (4)																
NL:Bos.	15	183	179	117	62	4	4	0	0	.978	3	39.0	5	1.15	3	1
AL:Phil.	16	180	177	111	66	3	4	0	1	.983	6	37.0	15	3.55	2	0
1915 (5)																
AL:Bos.	17	194	190	132	58	4	2	0	0	.979	3	44.0	9	1.84	5	0
NL:Phil.	16	188	185	131	54	3	3	0	0	.984	4	43.2	10	2.06	4	0
1916 (5)																
AL:Bos.	20	243	237	147	90	6	5	0	1	.975	5	49.0	8	1.46	3	0
NL:Brk.	20	225	212	142	70	13	2	0	2	.942	7	47.1	16	3.04	1	0
1917 (6)																
AL:Chi.	16	250	238	156	82	12	7	0	1	.952	5	52.0	16	2.38	4	0
NL:NY	17	236	225	153	72	11	3	0	1	.953	6	51.0	17	3.00	3	2
1918 (6)																
AL:Bos.	15	247	246	159	88	1	4	0	1	.996	4	53.0	10	1.70	5	1
NL:Chi.	17	237	232	156	76	5	7	0	2	.979	4	52.0	6	1.04	4	1
1919 (8)																
NL:Cin.	17	324	312	216	96	12	7	0	0	.963	6	72.0	13	1.62	5	2
AL:Chi.	19	341	329	213	116	12	9	0	1	.965	7	71.0	28	3.54	5	1
1920 (7)																
AL:Clev.	20	283	271	182	89	12	8	1	0	.958	5	61.0	6	0.88	5	2
NL:Brk.	21	274	268	177	91	6	5	0	2	.978	7	59.0	16	2.44	3	1
1921 (8)																
NL:NY	13	319	314	212	102	5	5	0	2	.984	4	71.0	20	2.53	5	1
AL:NY	19	322	316	210	106	6	8	0	0	.981	8	70.0	24	3.08	6	2
1922 (5)																
NL:NY	16	214	208	138	70	6	4	0	0	.972	5	46.0	8	1.56	4	1
AL:NY	17	193	192	129	62	1	7	0	1	.995	5	43.0	16	3.35	2	0
1923 (6)																
AL:NY	17	242	239	162	77	3	6	0	0	.988	5	54.0	17	2.83	2	0
NL:NY	22	245	239	159	80	6	8	0	0	.976	8	53.0	25	4.24	1	1
1924 (7)																
AL:Wash.	21	312	300	201	99	12	10	0	1	.962	8	67.0	16	2.16	3	0
NL:NY	21	300	294	200	94	6	4	0	0	.980	9	66.2	23	3.07	2	0
1925 (7)																
NL:Pitt.	18	278	271	182	89	7	4	0	0	.975	7	61.0	25	3.69	4	0
AL:Wash.	21	264	255	180	75	9	8	0	1	.966	6	60.0	19	2.85	4	1
1926 (7)																
NL:StL.	19	292	287	189	98	5	6	0	0	.983	8	63.0	19	2.71	4	1
AL:NY	19	278	271	189	82	7	3	0	1	.975	7	63.0	22	3.14	3	0

	Fielding:										**Pitching:**					
	PL	**TC**	**CA**	**PO**	**A**	**E**	**DP**	**TP**	**PB**	**AVG**	**PI**	**IP**	**ER**	**ERA**	**CG**	**SHO**
1927 (4)																
AL:NY	15	155	152	108	44	3	4	0	0	.981	4	36.0	8	2.00	3	0
NL:Pitt.	21	156	150	104	46	6	2	0	0	.962	7	34.2	20	5.19	0	0
1928 (4)																
AL:NY	16	142	136	108	28	6	3	0	0	.958	3	36.0	9	2.25	4	0
NL:StL.	20	143	138	102	36	5	3	0	0	.965	6	34.0	23	6.08	0	0
1929 (5)																
AL:Phil.	17	179	175	135	40	4	2	0	0	.978	6	45.0	13	2.60	2	0
NL:Chi.	19	182	175	131	44	7	4	0	0	.962	6	43.2	21	4.33	2	0
1930 (6)																
AL:Phil.	15	200	197	156	41	3	2	0	0	.985	5	52.0	10	1.73	4	1
NL:StL.	21	212	207	153	54	5	4	0	1	.976	7	51.0	21	5.40	4	1
1931 (7)																
NL:StL.	21	263	259	186	73	4	7	0	0	.985	6	62.0	16	2.32	3	1
AL:Phil.	20	254	252	183	69	2	4	0	0	.992	6	61.0	18	2.66	4	1
1932 (4)																
AL:NY	16	157	149	108	41	8	1	0	0	.949	6	36.0	13	3.25	2	0
NL:Chi.	22	148	142	102	40	6	7	0	0	.959	8	34.0	35	9.26	1	0
1933 (5)																
NL:NY	15	212	208	141	67	4	5	0	0	.981	5	47.0	8	1.53	3	0
AL:Wash.	19	202	201	138	65	4	4	0	0	.981	7	46.0	14	2.73	1	1
1934 (7)																
NL:StL.	20	284	269	196	73	15	2	0	0	.947	8	65.1	17	2.34	4	1
AL:Det.	17	277	265	195	70	12	6	0	0	.957	6	65.0	27	3.74	4	0
1935 (6)																
AL:Det.	15	146	137	165	72	9	7	0	1	.963	5	55.0	14	2.29	5	0
NL:Chi.	18	244	238	164	74	6	5	0	0	.975	7	54.2	18	2.96	2	1
1936 (6)																
AL:NY	16	225	219	162	57	6	2	0	0	.973	6	54.0	20	3.33	3	0
NL:NY	22	228	221	159	62	7	7	0	0	.969	8	53.0	40	6.79	3	0
1937 (5)																
AL:NY	17	179	179	132	47	0	2	0	0	1.000	7	44.0	12	2.45	3	0
NL:NY	20	184	175	129	46	9	5	0	0	.951	7	43.0	23	4.81	1	0
1938 (4)																
AL:NY	14	153	147	108	39	6	4	0	0	.961	4	36.0	7	1.75	3	0
NL:Chi.	20	140	137	102	35	3	3	0	0	.979	8	34.0	19	5.03	0	0
1939 (4)																
AL:NY	15	163	161	111	50	2	5	0	0	.988	7	37.0	5	1.21	2	1
NL:Cin.	18	144	140	106	34	4	1	0	0	.972	5	35.1	17	4.34	2	0
1940 (7)																
NL:Cin.	23	257	249	183	66	8	9	0	1	.969	9	61.0	25	3.68	4	1
AL:Det.	20	264	260	180	80	4	4	0	0	.985	8	60.0	20	3.00	4	1
1941 (5)																
AL:NY	18	192	190	135	55	2	7	0	0	.990	7	45.0	9	1.80	3	0
NL:Brk.	20	196	192	132	60	4	5	0	0	.980	7	44.0	13	2.65	2	0
1942 (5)																
NL:StL.	18	190	180	135	45	10	3	0	0	.947	6	45.0	13	2.60	3	1
AL:NY	20	182	177	132	45	5	2	0	0	.973	7	44.0	22	4.50	2	0
1943 (5)																
AL:NY	16	203	198	135	63	5	3	0	0	.975	5	45.0	7	1.40	3	1
NL:StL.	20	192	182	129	53	10	4	0	0	.948	6	43.0	12	2.51	2	0
1944 (6)																
NL:StL.	20	225	224	165	59	1	3	0	1	.996	8	55.0	12	1.96	2	1
AL:StL.	22	233	223	163	60	10	4	0	0	.957	7	54.1	9	1.49	3	0
1945 (7)																
AL:Det.	26	287	282	197	85	5	4	0	2	.983	9	65.2	28	3.83	4	0
NL:Chi.	25	279	273	195	78	6	5	0	1	.978	8	65.0	30	4.15	2	2
1946 (7)																
NL:StL.	19	258	254	186	68	4	7	0	1	.984	7	62.0	16	2.32	4	1
AL:Bos.	26	269	259	183	76	10	5	0	0	.963	11	61.0	20	2.95	2	1
1947 (7)																
AL:NY	24	259	255	185	70	4	4	0	2	.985	9	61.2	28	4.09	3	0
NL:Brk.	24	259	251	180	71	8	8	0	2	.969	8	60.0	37	5.55	0	0
1948 (6)																
AL:Clev.	23	234	231	159	72	3	9	0	0	.987	8	53.0	16	2.72	4	1
NL:Bos.	20	216	210	156	54	6	3	0	0	.972	6	52.0	15	2.60	2	1
1949 (5)																
AL:NY	20	182	179	135	44	3	5	0	0	.984	5	45.0	14	2.80	2	1
NL:Brk.	25	177	172	132	40	5	1	0	0	.972	9	44.0	21	4.29	2	1
1950 (4)																
AL:NY	18	154	152	111	41	2	4	0	0	.987	5	37.0	3	0.73	2	1
NL:Phil.	20	146	142	107	35	4	1	0	0	.973	5	35.2	9	2.27	1	0

	Fielding:										Pitching:					
	PL	TC	CA	PO	A	E	DP	TP	PB	AVG	PI	IP	ER	ERA	CG	SHO
1951 (6)																
AL:NY	21	230	226	159	67	4	10	0	1	.982	8	53.0	11	1.87	3	0
NL:NY	24	231	221	156	65	10	4	0	0	.957	9	52.0	27	4.67	1	0
1952 (7)																
AL:NY	19	268	258	192	66	10	7	0	1	.963	8	64.0	20	2.81	2	1
NL:Brk.	19	267	263	192	71	4	4	0	0	.985	6	64.0	25	3.52	3	0
1953 (6)																
AL:NY	20	217	216	156	60	1	5	0	0	.995	9	52.0	26	4.50	2	0
NL:Brk.	23	223	216	154	62	7	3	0	0	.969	10	51.1	28	4.94	2	0
1954 (4)																
NL:NY	15	157	150	111	39	7	2	0	0	.955	6	37.0	6	1.46	1	0
AL:Clev.	24	150	146	106	40	4	2	0	0	.973	7	35.1	19	4.84	1	0
1955 (7)																
NL:Brk.	22	270	264	180	84	6	12	0	0	.978	10	60.0	25	3.75	2	1
AL:NY	24	254	252	180	72	2	7	0	0	.992	9	60.0	28	4.20	2	0
1956 (7)																
AL:NY	22	257	251	185	66	6	7	0	0	.977	8	61.2	17	2.48	5	2
NL:Brk.	21	254	252	183	69	2	8	0	0	.992	8	61.0	32	4.72	3	1
1957 (7)																
NL:Mil.	23	282	279	186	93	3	10	0	1	.989	8	62.0	24	3.48	4	2
AL:NY	23	265	259	187	72	6	5	0	0	.977	9	62.1	20	2.89	2	0
1958 (7)																
AL:NY	22	259	256	191	65	3	5	0	1	.988	9	63.2	24	3.39	1	2
NL:Mil.	19	274	267	189	78	7	5	0	0	.974	6	63.0	26	3.71	3	1
1959 (6)																
NL:LA	24	232	228	159	69	4	7	0	0	.983	9	53.0	19	3.23	0	0
AL:Chi.	21	222	218	156	62	4	2	0	1	.982	7	52.0	20	3.46	0	2
1960 (7)																
NL:Pitt.	25	257	253	186	67	4	7	0	3	.984	10	62.0	49	7.11	0	0
AL:NY	25	284	276	183	93	8	9	0	0	.972	10	61.0	24	3.54	2	2
1961 (5)																
AL:NY	18	190	185	135	50	5	1	0	1	.974	6	45.0	8	1.60	1	2
NL:Cin.	24	178	174	132	42	4	7	0	1	.978	9	44.0	24	4.91	2	0
1962 (7)																
AL:NY	18	255	250	183	67	5	5	0	0	.980	6	61.0	20	2.95	4	1
NL:SF	21	258	250	183	67	8	9	0	1	.969	7	61.0	18	2.66	2	1
1963 (4)																
NL:LA	13	142	139	108	31	3	1	0	0	.979	4	36.0	4	1.00	3	1
AL:NY	20	153	152	102	50	1	7	0	0	.993	7	34.0	11	2.91	0	0
1964 (7)																
NL:StL	21	257	253	189	64	4	6	0	0	.984	8	63.0	30	4.29	2	0
AL:NY	21	277	268	186	82	9	6	0	3	.986	9	62.0	26	3.77	2	0
1965 (7)																
NL:LA	20	258	252	180	72	6	7	0	0	.977	7	60.0	14	2.10	4	3
AL:Minn.	21	243	238	180	58	5	3	0	0	.979	9	60.0	21	3.15	3	0
1966 (4)																
AL:Balt.	13	141	141	108	33	0	4	0	0	1.000	4	36.0	2	0.50	3	3
NL:LA	23	152	146	102	44	6	4	0	0	.961	8	34.0	10	2.65	1	0
1967 (7)																
NL:StL	23	253	249	183	66	4	3	0	0	.984	10	61.0	18	2.66	4	1
AL:Bos.	25	253	249	183	66	4	4	0	1	.984	10	61.0	23	3.39	2	1
1968 (7)																
AL:Det.	24	269	258	186	72	11	4	0	0	.959	9	62.0	24	3.48	4	0
NL:StL.	25	236	234	186	48	2	7	0	0	.992	10	62.0	32	4.65	3	1
1969 (5)																
NL:NY	21	179	177	135	42	2	0	0	0	.989	6	45.0	9	1.80	2	1
AL:Balt.	21	184	180	129	51	4	4	0	0	.978	7	43.0	13	2.72	2	0
1970 (5)																
AL:Balt.	21	183	178	135	43	5	3	0	0	.973	9	45.0	17	3.40	2	0
NL:Cin.	24	182	179	129	50	3	4	0	0	.984	9	43.0	32	6.70	0	0
1971 (7)																
NL:Pitt.	25	258	255	185	70	3	7	0	1	.988	10	61.2	24	3.50	3	1
AL:Balt.	21	261	252	183	69	9	2	0	0	.966	10	61.0	18	2.66	1	0
1972 (7)																
AL:Oak.	23	260	251	186	65	9	4	0	0	.965	8	62.	21	3.05	0	0
NL:Cin.	22	280	275	187	88	5	4	0	0	.982	8	62.1	15	2.17	0	1
1973 (7)																
AL:Oak.	24	286	277	198	79	9	8	0	1	.969	8	66.0	17	2.32	0	1
NL:NY	22	275	265	195	70	10	3	0	1	.964	7	65.0	16	2.22	0	1
1974 (5)																
AL:Oak.	20	188	183	132	51	5	6	0	0	.973	5	44.0	10	2.05	0	0
NL:LA	19	182	176	126	50	6	5	0	0	.967	6	42.0	13	2.79	0	0

			Fielding:								Pitching:					
	PL	TC	CA	PO	A	E	DP	TP	PB	AVG	PI	IP	ER	ERA	CG	SHO
1975 (7)																
NL:Cin.	22	273	271	195	76	2	8	0	0	.993	9	65.0	28	3.88	0	0
AL:Bos.	23	274	268	196	72	6	6	0	0	.978	10	65.1	28	3.86	2	1
1976 (4)																
NL:Cin.	16	147	142	108	34	5	4	0	0	.966	7	36.0	8	2.00	0	0
AL:NY	21	146	144	104	40	2	6	0	0	.986	7	34.2	21	5.45	1	0
1977 (6)																
AL:NY	20	239	236	168	68	3	2	0	1	.987	7	56.0	25	4.02	3	0
NL:LA	25	235	234	165	69	1	4	0	0	.996	9	55.0	25	4.09	2	0
1978 (6)																
AL:NY	24	214	212	159	54	2	9	0	0	.991	8	53.0	22	3.74	2	0
NL:LA	23	229	222	158	64	7	2	0	2	.969	8	52.2	32	5.47	0	0
1979 (7)																
NL:Pitt.	24	274	265	186	79	9	11	0	0	.967	9	62.0	22	3.19	0	1
AL:Balt.	25	280	271	186	85	9	5	0	0	.968	8	62.0	30	4.35	2	0
1980 (6)																
NL:Phil.	22	231	229	161	68	2	8	0	0	.991	10	53.2	22	3.69	0	0
AL:KC	21	235	228	156	72	7	8	0	0	.970	7	52.0	24	4.15	0	0
1981 (6)																
NL:LA	24	230	221	156	65	9	6	0	0	.961	10	52.0	19	3.29	2	0
AL:NY	24	212	208	153	55	4	2	0	1	.981	9	51.0	24	4.24	0	1
1982 (7)																
NL:StL	22	264	257	183	74	7	9	0	0	.973	8	61.0	23	3.39	1	0
AL:Mi.l	21	272	261	180	81	11	3	0	0	.960	9	60.0	32	4.80	1	1
1983 (5)																
AL:Balt.	23	189	185	135	50	4	5	0	0	.979	7	45.0	8	1.60	2	1
NL:Phil.	23	177	174	132	42	3	3	0	0	.983	8	44.0	17	3.48	0	0
1984 (5)																
AL:Det.	22	188	184	132	52	4	2	0	0	.979	7	44.0	15	3.07	2	0
NL:SD	24	170	166	126	40	4	5	0	0	.976	10	42.0	22	4.71	0	0
1985 (7)																
AL:KC	22	269	266	186	80	3	3	0	1	.989	6	62.0	13	1.89	3	1
NL:StL	24	246	244	184	60	2	9	0	1	.992	9	61.1	27	3.96	1	1
1986 (7)																
NL:NY	22	257	252	189	63	5	4	0	1	.980	8	63.0	23	3.29	0	0
AL:Bos.	21	271	267	188	79	4	7	0	1	.985	8	62.2	30	4.31	1	1
1987 (7)																
AL:Minn.	24	256	253	180	73	3	4	0	0	.998	9	60.0	25	3.75	0	0
NL:StL	24	252	246	177	69	6	2	0	1	.976	9	59.0	37	5.64	0	0
1988 (5)																
NL:LA	22	172	169	133	36	3	3	0	1	.983	7	44.1	10	2.03	2	1
AL:Oak.	24	176	174	131	43	2	2	0	1	.989	10	43.2	19	3.92	0	0
1989 (4)																
AL:Oak.	19	144	143	108	35	1	1	0	1	.993	6	36.0	14	3.50	1	1
NL:SF	24	146	142	102	40	4	3	0	0	.973	9	34.0	31	8.21	0	0
1990 (4)																
NL:Cin.	21	157	153	111	42	4	2	0	0	.975	8	37.0	7	1.70	0	1
AL:Oak.	25	157	152	106	46	5	5	0	0	.968	10	35.1	15	3.82	1	0
1991 (7)																
AL:Minn.	25	280	276	202	74	4	6	0	1	.986	9	67.1	28	3.74	1	1
NL:Atl.	25	288	282	196	86	6	9	0	0	.979	10	65.1	21	2.89	1	0
1992 (6)																
AL:Tor.	23	216	212	165	47	4	5	0	0	.981	10	55.0	17	2.78	0	0
NL:Atl.	22	233	231	163	68	2	7	0	0	.991	8	54.1	16	2.65	2	0
1993 (6)																
AL:Tor.	23	211	204	159	45	7	5	0	0	.967	10	53.0	34	5.77	0	0
NL:Phil.	23	213	211	157	54	2	5	0	1	.991	10	52.1	44	7.57	1	1
1995 (6)																
NL:Atl.	23	238	232	162	73	6	2	0	0	.975	10	54.0	16	2.67	1	1
AL:Clev.	23	237	231	159	69	6	8	0	1	.975	9	53.0	21	3.57	0	0
1996 (6)																
AL:NY	25	233	228	165	63	5	7	0	0	.979	10	55.0	24	3.93	0	1
NL:Atl.	24	239	235	162	73	4	6	0	0	.983	10	54.0	14	2.33	0	1
1997 (7)																
NL:Fla.	25	282	274	192	82	8	9	0	0	.972	10	64.0	39	5.48	0	0
AL:Clev.	23	260	255	191	64	5	8	0	0	.981	11	63.2	32	4.52	0	0
1998 (4)																
AL:NY	19	146	144	108	36	2	4	0	0	.986	9	36.0	11	2.75	0	1
NL:SD	23	146	143	102	41	3	5	0	1	.979	10	34.0	22	5.82	0	0
1999 (4)																
AL:NY	20	160	159	111	48	1	5	0	0	.994	9	37.0	9	2.19	0	0
NL:Atl.	23	140	136	105	31	4	4	0	0	.971	9	35.0	17	4.37	0	0

	Fielding:									Pitching:					
	PL	TC	CA	PO	A	E	DP	TP	PB	AVG	PI	IP	ER	ERA	CG	SHO
2000 (5)																
AL:NY	22	189	187	141	46	2	1	0	1	.989	8	47.0	14	2.68	0	0
NL:NY	25	192	187	140	47	5	3	0	0	.974	10	46.2	18	3.47	0	0
2001 (7)																
NL:Ari.	25	259	256	195	61	3	6	0	0	.988	10	65.0	14	1.94	1	0
AL:NY	25	273	265	190	75	8	7	0	0	.971	10	63.1	30	4.26	0	0
2002 (7)																
AL:Ana.	22	244	239	183	56	5	6	0	1	.980	10	61.0	39	5.75	0	0
NL:SF	21	255	250	180	70	5	7	0	1	.980	11	60.0	37	5.55	0	0
2003 (6)																
NL:Fla.	20	227	225	168	57	2	8	0	0	.991	9	56.0	20	3.21	1	1
AL:NY	23	236	231	165	66	5	6	0	1	.979	9	55.0	13	2.13	0	0
2004 (4)																
AL:Bos.	21	148	140	108	32	8	5	0	1	.946	8	36.0	10	2.50	0	1
NL:StL.	25	140	139	102	37	1	3	0	0	.993	11	34.0	23	6.09	0	0
2005 (4)																
AL:Chi.	24	175	172	123	49	3	4	0	0	.983	11	41.0	12	2.63	0	1
NL:Hou.	24	173	171	118	53	2	6	0	0	.988	10	39.1	20	4.58	0	0
2006 (5)																
NL:StL.	23	179	175	132	43	4	3	0	0	.978	10	44.0	10	2.05	0	1
AL:Det.	24	185	177	126	51	8	4	0	0	.957	11	42.0	14	3.00	0	0
2007 (4)																
AL:Bos.	23	142	140	108	32	2	2	0	0	.986	10	36.0	10	2.50	0	0
NL:Col.	24	149	149	102	47	0	3	0	0	1.000	11	34.0	29	7.68	0	0
2008 (5)																
NL:Phil.	22	189	183	132	51	6	6	0	1	.968	9	44.0	14	2.86	0	0
AL:TB	25	170	165	126	39	5	4	0	0	.971	11	42.0	21	4.50	0	0
2009 (6)																
AL:NY	24	214	212	159	53	2	5	0	1	.991	11	53.0	27	4.58	0	0
NL:Phil.	22	193	191	156	35	2	3	0	0	.990	11	52.0	31	5.37	1	0
2010 (5)																
NL:SF	24	185	181	132	49	4	6	0	0	.978	11	44.0	12	2.45	0	2
AL:Tex.	24	175	170	129	41	5	3	0	0	.971	11	43.0	28	5.86	0	0
2011 (7)																
NL:StL.	25	267	261	189	72	6	7	0	0	.978	12	63.0	27	3.86	0	0
AL:Tex.	24	276	268	186	82	8	8	0	0	.971	11	62.0	32	4.65	0	1
2012 (4)																
NL:SF	22	152	151	111	40	1	4	0	0	.993	10	37.0	6	1.46	0	2
AL:Det.	25	136	135	105	30	1	3	0	0	.993	11	35.0	16	4.11	0	0
2013 (6)																
AL:Bos.	24	224	216	161	55	8	3	0	0	.964	10	53.2	11	1.84	0	0
NL:StL.	22	206	201	156	45	5	4	0	0	.976	10	52.0	23	3.98	0	0
2014 (7)																
NL:SF	25	295	253	183	70	2	9	0	0	.992	12	61.0	27	3.98	1	1
AL:KC	24	253	251	183	68	2	3	0	0	.992	11	61.0	29	4.28	0	1
2015 (5)																
AL:KC	25	209	207	156	51	2	5	0	0	.990	11	52.0	17	2.94	1	0
NL:NY	24	204	198	154	44	6	3	0	1	.971	11	51.1	24	4.21	0	0
2016 (7)																
NL:Chi.	25	261	256	189	67	5	5	0	2	.981	11	63.0	24	3.43	0	0
AL:Clev.	24	243	237	189	48	6	5	0	0	.975	11	63.0	26	3.71	0	2
2017 (7)																
AL:Hou.	24	256	254	192	62	2	6	0	0	.992	12	64.0	33	4.64	0	0
NL:LA	25	260	256	194	62	4	6	0	1	.985	12	64.2	32	4.45	0	0
2018 (5)																
AL:Bos.	24	207	205	159	46	2	1	0	0	.990	10	53.0	15	2.55	0	0
NL:LA	25	200	199	156	43	1	5	0	0	.995	12	52.0	28	4.85	0	0
2019 (7)																
NL:Wash.	25	259	255	189	66	4	5	0	0	.985	11	63.0	30	4.29	0	0
AL:Hou.	25	235	232	189	43	3	5	0	1	.987	12	63.0	30	4.29	0	0
2020 (6)																
NL:LA	27	211	207	161	46	4	4	0	0	.981	15	53.2	21	3.52	0	0
AL:TB	28	198	198	156	42	0	2	0	0	1.000	13	52.0	32	5.54	0	0

BATTING AVERAGE LEADERS

(Playing all games)

Year	Player	AB	H	AVG
1903				
AL	Chick Stahl, Bos.	33	10	.303
NL	Jimmy Sebring, Pitt.	30	11	.367
1905				
AL	Topsy Hartsel, Phil.	17	5	.294
NL	Mike Donlin, NY	19	6	.316
1906				
AL	George Rohe, Chi.	21	7	.333
AL	Jiggs Donahue, Chi.	18	6	.333
NL	Solly Hofman, Chi.	23	7	.304
1907				
AL	Claude Rossman, Det.	20	8	.400
NL	Harry Steinfeldt, Chi.	17	8	.471
1908				
AL	Ty Cobb, Det.	19	7	.368
NL	Frank Chance, Chi.	19	8	.421
1909				
AL	Jim Delahanty, Det.	26	9	.346
NL	Honus Wagner, Pitt.	24	8	.333
1910				
AL	Eddie Collins, Phil.	21	9	.429
NL	Frank Chance, Chi.	17	6	.353
NL	Frank Schulte, Chi.	17	6	.353
1911				
AL	Frank Baker, Phil.	24	9	.375
NL	Larry Doyle, NY	23	7	.304
1912				
AL	Tris Speaker, Bos.	30	9	.300
NL	Buck Herzog, NY	30	12	.400
1913				
AL	Frank Baker, Phil.	20	9	.450
NL	Larry McLean, NY	12	6	.500
1914				
AL	Frank Baker, Phil.	16	4	.250
NL	Hank Gowdy, Bos.	11	6	.545
1915				
AL	Duffy Lewis, Bos.	18	8	.444
NL	Fred Luderus, Phil.	16	7	.438
1916				
AL	Duffy Lewis, Bos.	17	6	.353
NL	Ivy Olson, Brk.	16	4	.250
1917				
AL	Eddie Collins, Chi.	22	9	.409
NL	Dave Robertson, NY	22	11	.500
1918				
AL	Stuffy McInnis, Bos.	20	5	.250
AL	George Whiteman, Bos.	20	5	.250
NL	Charlie Pick, Chi.	18	7	.389
1919				
AL	Joe Jackson, Chi.	32	12	.375
NL	Greasy Neale, Cin.	28	10	.357
1920				
AL	Steve O'Neill, Clev.	21	7	.333
NL	Zack Wheat, Brk.	27	9	.333
1921				
AL	Wally Schang, NY	21	6	.286
NL	Irish Meusel, NY	29	10	.345
1922				
AL	Bob Meusel, NY	20	6	.300
NL	Heinie Groh, NY	19	9	.474

YEAR	PLAYER	AB	H	AVG
1923				
AL	Aaron Ward, NY	24	10	.417
NL	Casey Stengel, NY	12	5	.417
1924				
AL	Joe Judge, Wash.	26	10	.385
NL	Frankie Frisch, NY	30	10	.333
NL	Freddie Lindstrom, NY	30	10	.333
1925				
AL	Bucky Harris, Wash.	25	11	.440
NL	Max Carey, Pitt.	24	11	.458
1926				
AL	Earle Combs, NY	28	10	.357
NL	Tommy Thevenow, StL.	24	10	.417
1927				
AL	Mark Koenig, NY	18	9	.500
NL	Lloyd Waner, Pitt.	15	6	.400
1928				
AL	Babe Ruth, NY	16	10	.625
NL	Rabbit Maranville, StL.	13	4	.308
1929				
AL	Jimmy Dykes, Phil.	19	8	.421
NL	Hack Wilson, Chi.	17	8	.471
1930				
AL	Al Simmons, Phil.	22	8	.364
NL	Charlie Gelbert, StL.	17	6	.353
1931				
AL	Jimmie Foxx, Phil.	23	8	.348
NL	Pepper Martin, StL.	24	12	.500
1932				
AL	Lou Gehrig, NY	17	9	.529
NL	Riggs Stephenson, Chi.	18	8	.444
1933				
AL	Fred Schulte, Wash.	21	7	.333
NL	Mel Ott, NY	18	7	.389
1934				
AL	Charlie Gehringer, Det.	29	11	.379
NL	Joe Medwick, StL.	29	11	.379
1935				
AL	Pete Fox, Det.	26	10	.385
NL	Billy Herman, Chi.	24	8	.333
1936				
AL	Jake Powell, NY	22	10	.455
NL	Dick Bartell, NY	21	8	.381
1937				
AL	Tony Lazzeri, NY	15	6	.400
NL	Joe Moore, NY	23	9	.391
1938				
AL	Bill Dickey, NY	15	6	.400
AL	Joe Gordon, NY	15	6	.400
NL	Stan Hack, Chi.	17	8	.471
1939				
AL	Charlie Keller, NY	16	7	.438
NL	Frank McCormick, Cin.	15	6	.400
1940				
AL	Bruce Campbell, Det.	25	9	.360
NL	Bill Werber, Cin.	27	10	.370
1941				
AL	Joe Gordon, NY	14	7	.500
NL	Joe Medwick, Brk.	17	4	.235
1942				
AL	Phil Rizzuto, NY	21	8	.381
NL	Jimmy Brown, StL.	20	6	.300
1943				
AL	Billy Johnson, NY	20	6	.300
NL	Marty Marion, StL.	14	5	.357

YEAR	PLAYER	AB	H	AVG		YEAR	PLAYER	AB	H	AVG
1944						**1965**				
AL	George McQuinn, StL.	16	7	.438		AL	Zoilo Versalles, Minn.	28	8	.286
NL	Emil Verban, StL.	17	7	.412		AL	Harmon Killebrew, Minn.	21	6	.286
1945						NL	Ron Fairly, LA	29	11	.379
AL	Doc Cramer, Det.	29	11	.379		**1966**				
NL	Phil Cavarretta, Chi.	26	11	.423		AL	Boog Powell, Balt.	14	5	.357
1946						NL	Lou Johnson, LA	15	4	.267
AL	Rudy York, Bos.	23	6	.261		**1967**				
NL	Harry Walker, StL.	17	7	.412		AL	Carl Yastrzemski, Bos.	25	10	.400
1947						NL	Lou Brock, StL.	29	12	.414
AL	Tommy Henrich, NY	31	10	.323		**1968**				
NL	Pee Wee Reese, Brk.	23	7	.304		AL	Norm Cash, Det.	26	10	.385
1948						NL	Lou Brock, StL.	28	13	.464
AL	Larry Doby, Clev.	22	7	.318		**1969**				
NL	Bob Elliott, Bos.	21	7	.333		AL	Boog Powell, Balt.	19	5	.263
1949						NL	Al Weis, NY	11	5	.455
AL	Tommy Henrich, NY	19	5	.263		**1970**				
NL	Pee Wee Reese, Brk.	19	6	.316		AL	Paul Blair, Balt.	19	9	.474
1950						NL	Lee May, Cin.	18	7	.389
AL	Gene Woodling, NY	14	6	.429		**1971**				
NL	Granny Hamner, Phil.	14	6	.429		AL	Brooks Robinson, Balt.	22	7	.318
1951						NL	Roberto Clement9e, Pitt.	29	12	.414
AL	Phil Rizzuto, NY	25	8	.320		**1972**				
NL	Monte Irvin, NY	24	11	.458		AL	Gene Tenace, Oak	23	8	.348
1952						NL	Tony Perez, Cin.	23	10	.435
AL	Gene Woodling, NY	23	8	.348		**1973**				
NL	Pee Wee Reese, Brk.	29	10	.345		AL	Joe Rudi, Oak.	27	9	.333
NL	Duke Snider, Brk.	29	10	.345		NL	Rusty Staub, NY	26	11	.423
1953						**1974**				
AL	Billy Martin, NY	24	12	.500		AL	Bert Campaneris, Oak.	17	6	.353
NL	Gil Hodges, Brk.	22	8	.364		NL	Steve Garvey, LA	21	8	.381
1954						**1975**				
AL	Vic Wertz, Clev.	16	8	.500		AL	Carl Yastrzemski, Bos.	29	9	.310
NL	Alvin Dark, NY	17	7	.412		NL	Pete Rose, Cin.	27	10	.370
1955						**1976**				
AL	Yogi Berra, NY	24	10	.417		AL	Thurman Munson, NY	17	9	.529
NL	Duke Snider, Brk.	25	8	.320		NL	Johnny Bench, Cin.	15	8	.533
1956						**1977**				
AL	Yogi Berra, NY	25	9	.360		AL	Reggie Jackson, NY	20	9	.450
NL	Gil Hodges, Brk.	23	7	.304		NL	Steve Garvey, LA	24	9	.375
NL	Duke Snider, Brk.	23	7	.304		**1978**				
1957						AL	Brian Doyle, NY	16	7	.438
AL	Jerry Coleman, NY	22	8	.364		NL	Bill Russell, LA	26	11	.423
NL	Hank Aaron, Mil.	28	11	.393		**1979**				
1958						AL	Kiko Garcia, Balt.	20	8	.400
AL	Hank Bauer, NY	31	10	.323		NL	Phil Garner, Pitt.	24	12	.500
NL	Bill Bruton, Mil.	17	7	.412		**1980**				
1959						AL	Amos Otis, KC	23	11	.478
AL	Ted Kluszewski, Chi.	23	9	.391		NL	Bob Boone, Phil.	17	7	.412
NL	Gil Hodges, LA	23	9	.391		**1981**				
1960						AL	Lou Piniella, NY	16	7	.438
AL	Mickey Mantle, NY	25	10	.400		NL	Steve Garvey, LA	24	10	.417
NL	Bill Mazeroski, Pitt.	25	8	.320		**1982**				
1961						AL	Robin Yount, Mil.	29	12	.414
AL	Bobby Richardson, NY	23	9	.319		NL	George Hendrick, StL.	28	9	.321
NL	Wally Post, Cin.	18	6	.333		NL	Lonnie Smith, StL.	28	9	.321
1962						**1983**				
AL	Tom Tresh, NY	28	9	.321		AL	John Shelby, Balt	9	4	.444
NL	Jose Pagan, SF	19	7	.368		NL	Bo Diaz, Phil.	15	5	.333
1963						**1984**				
AL	Elston Howard, NY	15	5	.333		AL	Alan Trammell, Det.	20	9	.450
NL	Tommy Davis, LA	15	6	.400		NL	Kurt Bevacqua, SD	17	7	.412
1964						**1985**				
AL	Bobby Richardson, NY	32	13	.406		AL	George Brett, KC	27	10	.370
NL	Tim McCarver, StL.	23	11	.478		NL	Tito Landrum, StL.	25	9	.360

YEAR	PLAYER	AB	H	AVG
1986				
AL	Marty Barrett, Bos.	30	13	.433
NL	Ray Knight, NY	23	9	.391
1987				
AL	Kirby Puckett, Minn.	28	10	.357
NL	Tony Pena, StL.	22	9	.409
1988				
AL	Dave Henderson, Oak.	20	6	.300
NL	Mickey Hatcher, LA	19	7	.368
1989				
AL	Rickey Henderson, Oak.	19	9	.474
NL	Kevin Mitchell, SF	17	5	.294
1990				
AL	Rickey Henderson, Oak.	15	5	.333
NL	Billy Hatcher, Cin.	12	9	.750
1991				
AL	Brian Harper, Minn.	21	8	.381
NL	Rafael Belliard, Atl.	16	6	.375
1992				
AL	Pat Borders, Tor.	20	9	.450
NL	Otis Nixon, Atl.	27	8	.296
1993				
AL	Paul Molitor, Tor.	24	12	.500
NL	Len Dykstra, Phil.	23	8	.348
NL	John Kruk, Phil.	23	8	.348
1995				
AL	Albert Belle, Clev.	17	4	.235
NL	Marquis Grissom, Atl.	25	9	.360
1996				
NL	Marquis Grissom, Atl.	27	12	.444
AL	Cecil Fielder, NY	23	9	.391
1997				
AL	Matt Williams, Clev.	26	10	.385
NL	Darren Daulton, Fla.	18	7	.389
1998				
AL	Ricky Ledee, NY	10	6	.600
NL	Tony Gwynn, SD	16	8	.500
1999				
AL	Scott Brosius, NY	16	6	.375
NL	Bret Boone, Atl.	13	7	.538
2000				
AL	Paul O'Neill, NY	19	9	.474
NL	Todd Zeile, NY	20	8	.400
2001				
AL	Alfonso Soriano, NY	25	6	.240
NL	Steve Finley, Ari.	19	7	.368
2002				
AL	Troy Glaus, Ana.	26	10	.385
NL	Barry Bonds, SF	17	8	.471
2003				
AL	Bernie Williams, NY	25	10	.400
NL	Jeff Conine, Fla.	21	7	.333
NL	Juan Pierre, Fla.	21	7	.333
2004				
AL	Bill Mueller, Bos.	14	6	.429
NL	Larry Walker, StL.	14	5	.357
2005				
AL	Carl Everett, Chi.	9	4	.444
NL	Lance Berkman, Hou.	13	5	.385
2006				
AL	Sean Casey, Det.	17	9	.529
NL	Scott Rolen, StL.	19	8	.421
2007				
AL	Jacoby Ellsbury, Bos.	16	7	.438
NL	Todd Helton, Col.	15	5	.333

YEAR	PLAYER	AB	H	AVG
2008				
AL	Dioner Navarro, TB	17	6	.353
NL	Jayson Werth, Phil.	18	8	.444
2009				
AL	Hideki Matsui, NY	13	8	.615
NL	Carlos Ruiz, Phil.	18	6	.333
2010				
AL	Mitch Moreland, Tex.	13	6	.462
NL	Edgar Renteria, SF	17	7	.412
2011				
AL	Ian Kinsler, Tex.	25	9	.360
NL	Lance Berkman, StL.	26	11	.423
2012				
AL	Delmon Young, Det.	14	5	.357
NL	Pablo Sandoval, SF	16	8	.500
2013				
AL	David Ortiz, Bos.	16	11	.688
NL	Allen Craig, StL.	16	6	.375
2014				
AL	Salvador Perez, KC	24	8	.333
NL	Hunter Pence, SF	27	12	.444
2015				
AL	Salvador Perez, KC	22	8	.364
NL	Michael Conforto, NY	15	5	.333
2016				
AL	Jose Ramirez, Clev.	29	9	.310
NL	Anthony Rizzo, Chi.	25	9	.360
2017				
AL	George Springer, Hou.	29	11	.379
NL	Logan Forsythe, LA	18	5	.278
2018				
AL	Andrew Benintendi, Bos.	18	6	.333
AL	Steve Pearce, Bos.	12	4	.333
NL	David Freese, LA	12	5	.417
2019				
AL	Yordan Alvarez, Hou.	17	7	.412
NL	Juan Soto, Wash.	27	9	.333
2020				
AL	Kevin Kiermaier, TB	19	7	.368
NL	Corey Seager, LA	20	8	.400
NL	Joc Pederson, LA	10	4	.400

HITTING SAFELY, EACH GAME

YEAR	PLAYER	AB	H	AVG
1907 - (5 games)				
NL	Frank Schulte, Chi.	20	5	.250
1908 - (5 games)				
NL	Frank Schulte, Chi.	18	7	.389
1910 - (5 games)				
AL	Eddie Collins, Phil.	21	9	.429
AL	Danny Murphy, Phil.	20	7	.350
1914 - (4 games)				
NL	Johnny Evers, Bos.	16	7	.438
NL	Butch Schmidt, Bos.	17	5	.294
1915 - (5 games)				
AL	Duffy Lewis, Bos	18	8	.444
AL	Harry Hooper, Bos.	20	7	.350
1916 - (5 games)				
AL	Harry Hooper, Bos.	21	7	.333
1917 - (6 games)				
NL	Dave Robertson, NY	22	11	.500
1922 - (5 games)				
AL	Bob Meusel, N. Y.	20	6	.300
AL	Wally Pipp, NY	21	6	.286
NL	Heinie Groh, NY	19	9	.474
NL	Irish Meusel, NY	20	5	.250
1923 - (6 games)				
AL	Aaron Ward, NY	24	10	.417
AL	Babe Ruth, NY	19	7	.368
AL	Wally Schang, NY	22	7	.318
1924 - (7 games)				
AL	Bucky Harris, Wash.	33	11	.333
NL	George Kelly, NY	31	9	.290
1925 - (7 games)				
AL	Joe Harris, Wash.	25	11	.440
1926 - (7 games)				
AL	Earle Combs, NY	28	10	.357
NL	Jim Bottomley, StL.	29	10	.345
1927 - (4 games)				
AL	Mark Koenig, NY	18	9	.500
NL	Lloyd Waner, Pitt.	15	6	.400
NL	Clyde Barnhart, Pitt.	16	5	.313
1928 - (4 games)				
AL	Babe Ruth, NY	16	10	.625
AL	Lou Gehrig, NY	11	6	.545
1929 - (5 games)				
AL	Bing Miller, Phil.	19	7	.368
NL	Riggs Stephenson, Chi.	19	6	.316
1930 - (6 games)				
AL	Jimmie Foxx, Phil.	21	7	.333
1932 - (4 games)				
AL	Lou Gehrig, NY	17	9	.529
AL	Bill Dickey, NY	16	7	.438
AL	Babe Ruth, NY	15	5	.333
NL	Riggs Stephenson, Chi.	18	8	.444
NL	Gabby Hartnett, Chi.	16	5	.313
1933 - (5 games)				
NL	Kiddo Davis, NY	19	7	.368
1934 - (7 games)				
AL	Charlie Gehringer, Det.	29	11	.379
NL	Pepper Martin, StL.	31	11	.355
1935 - (6 games)				
AL	Pete Fox, Det.	26	10	.385
1936 - (5 games)				
AL	George Selkirk, NY	24	8	.333
NL	Dick Bartell, NY	21	8	.381

YEAR	PLAYER	AB	H	AVG
1937 - (5 games)				
AL	Tony Lazzeri, NY	15	6	.400
NL	Joe Moore, NY	23	9	.391
1938 - (4 games)				
AL	Joe Gordon, NY	15	6	.400
AL	Lou Gehrig, NY	14	4	.286
NL	Stan Hack, Chi.	17	8	.471
NL	Phil Cavarretta, Chi.	13	6	.462
1939 - (4 games)				
AL	Charlie Keller, NY	16	7	.438
AL	Joe DiMaggio, NY	16	5	.313
AL	Bill Dickey, NY	15	4	.267
1941 - (5 games)				
AL	Joe Gordon, NY	14	7	.500
AL	Johnny Sturm, NY	21	6	.286
1943 - (5 games)				
NL	Walker Cooper, StL.	17	5	.294
1944 - (6 games)				
NL	Ray Sanders, StL.	21	6	.286
1947 - (7 games)				
AL	Tommy Henrich, NY	31	10	.323
1950 - (4 games)				
AL	Gene Woodling, NY	14	6	.429
1951 - (6 games)				
AL	Phil Rizzuto, NY	25	8	.320
NL	Alvin Dark, NY	24	10	.417
1953 - (6 games)				
AL	Billy Martin, NY	24	12	.500
1954 - (4 games)				
AL	Vic Wertz, Clev.	16	8	.500
NL	Alvin Dark, NY	17	7	.412
NL	Hank Thompson, NY	11	4	.364
1955 - (7 games)				
AL	Yogi Berra, NY	24	10	.417
1956 - (7 games)				
AL	Billy Martin, NY	27	8	.296
AL	Hank Bauer, NY	32	9	.281
1957 - (7 games)				
AL	Hank Bauer, NY	31	8	.258
NL	Hank Aaron, Mil.	28	11	.393
1960 - (7 games)				
NL	Roberto Clemente, Pitt.	29	9	.310
1961 - (5 games)				
AL	Bobby Richardson, NY	23	9	.391
1964 - (7 games)				
AL	Bobby Richardson, NY	32	13	.406
NL	Tim McCarver, StL.	23	11	.478
1965 - (7 games)				
NL	Ron Fairly, LA	29	11	.379
1966 - (4 games)				
AL	Boog Powell, Balt.	14	5	.357
1968 - (7 games)				
NL	Lou Brock, StL.	28	13	.464
1970 - (5 games)				
AL	Brooks Robinson, Balt.	21	9	.429
NL	Lee May, Cin.	18	7	.389
1971 - (7 games)				
NL	Roberto Clemente, Pitt.	29	12	.414
1972 - (7 games)				
NL	Tony Perez, Cin.	23	10	.435
1974 - (5 games)				
NL	Steve Garvey, LA	21	8	.381
1975 - (7 games)				
AL	Denny Doyle, Bos.	30	8	.267

YEAR	PLAYER	AB	H	AVG
1976 - (4 games)				
AL	Thurman Munson, NY	17	9	.529
AL	Chris Chambliss, NY	16	5	.313
NL	Johnny Bench, Cin.	15	8	.533
NL	George Foster, Cin.	14	6	.429
NL	Dave Concepcion, Cin.	14	5	.357
NL	Joe Morgan, Cin.	15	5	.333
1977 - (6 games)				
AL	Thurman Munson, NY	25	8	.320
1978 - (6 games)				
AL	Bucky Dent, NY	24	10	.417
AL	Reggie Jackson, NY	23	9	.391
AL	Roy White, NY	24	8	.333
AL	Lou Piniella, NY	25	7	.350
NL	Bill Russell, LA	26	11	.423
1979 - (7 games)				
NL	Phil Garner, Pitt.	24	12	.500
1980 - (6 games)				
AL	George Brett, KC	24	9	.375
NL	Mike Schmidt, Phil.	21	8	.381
NL	Larry Bowa, Phil.	24	9	.375
1981 - (6 games)				
NL	Steve Garvey, LA	24	10	.417
1984 - (5 games)				
NL	Kurt Bevacqua, SD	17	7	.412
1985 - (7 games)				
AL	Willie Wilson, KC	30	11	.367
NL	Tito Landrum, StL.	25	9	.360
1986 - (7 games)				
AL	Marty Barrett, Bos.	30	13	.433
1987 - (7 games)				
AL	Dan Gladden, Minn.	31	9	.290
1988 - (5 games)				
NL	Mickey Hatcher, LA	19	6	.368
NL	Steve Sax, LA	20	6	.300
1989 - (4 games)				
AL	Rickey Henderson, Oak.	19	9	.474
AL	Carney Lansford, Oak.	16	7	.438
AL	Terry Steinbach, Oak.	16	4	.250
NL	Kevin Mitchell, SF	17	5	.294
1990 - (4 games)				
NL	Chris Sabo, Cin.	16	9	.563
NL	Joe Oliver, Cin.	18	6	.333
1992 - (6 games)				
AL	Pat Borders, Tor.	20	9	.450
1993 - (6 games)				
AL	Paul Molitor, Tor.	24	12	.500
AL	Roberto Alomar, Tor.	25	12	.480
1995 - (6 games)				
NL	Marquis Grissom, Atl.	25	9	.350
1996 - (6 games)				
NL	Marquis Grissom, Atl.	27	12	.444
1998 - (4 games)				
AL	Scott Brosius, NY	17	8	.471
AL	Chuck Knoblauch, NY	16	6	.375
AL	Derek Jeter, NY	17	6	.353
NL	Tony Gwynn, SD	16	8	.500
1999 - (4 games)				
AL	Derek Jeter, NY	17	6	.353
NL	Bret Boone, Atl.	13	7	.538
2000 - (5 games)				
AL	Derek Jeter, NY	22	9	.409
NL	Jay Payton, NY	21	7	.333
NL	Mike Piazza, NY	22	6	.273

YEAR	PLAYER	AB	H	AVG
2002 - (7 games)				
AL	Garret Anderson, Ana.	32	9	.281
NL	J.T. Snow, SF	27	11	.407
2003 - (6 games)				
AL	Bernie Williams, NY	25	10	.400
2004 - (4 games)				
AL	Bill Mueller, Bos.	14	6	.429
AL	Manny Ramirez, Bos.	17	7	.412
AL	Johnny Damon, Bos.	21	6	.286
2005 - (4 games)				
AL	Jermaine Dye, Chi.	16	7	.438
AL	Joe Crede, Chi.	17	5	.294
AL	Aaron Rowand, Chi.	17	5	.294
AL	Scott Podsednik, Chi.	21	6	.286
AL	A.J. Pierzynski, Chi.	15	4	.267
2006 - (5 games)				
NL	Scott Rolen, StL.	19	8	.421
NL	Yadier Molina, StL.	17	7	.412
2007 - (4 games)				
AL	Mike Lowell, Bos.	15	6	.400
2008 - (5 games)				
NL	Jayson Werth, Phil.	18	8	.444
2009 - (6 games)				
AL	Derek Jeter, NY	27	11	.407
2010 - (5 games)				
AL	Mitch Moreland, Tex.	13	6	.462
NL	Andres Torres, SF	22	7	.318
NL	Buster Posey, SF	20	6	.300
2012 - (4 games)				
AL	Omar Infante, Det.	15	5	.333
NL	Pablo Sandoval, SF	16	8	.500
2014 - (7 games)				
NL	Hunter Pence, SF	27	12	.444
NL	Brandon Belt, SF	26	8	.308
2015 - (5 games)				
AL	Salvador Perez, KC	22	8	.364
AL	Mike Moustakas, KC	23	7	.304
AL	Alcides Escobar, KC	26	6	.231

1903 [3]
AL: BOSTON - 2
    Patsy Dougherty - lf (2)
NL: PITTSBURGH - 1
    Jimmy Sebring - rf

1904 No Series

1905 [0]
AL: PHILADELPHIA - 0
NL: NEW YORK - 0

1906 [0]
AL: CHICAGO - 0
NL: CHICAGO - 0

1907 [0]
AL: DETROIT - 0
NL: CHICAGO - 0

1908 [1]
AL: DETROIT - 0
NL: CHICAGO - 1
    Joe Tinker - ss

1909 [4]
AL: DETROIT - 2
    Sam Crawford - cf
    Davy Jones - lf
NL: PITTSBURGH - 2
    Fred Clarke - lf (2)

1910 [1]
AL: PHILADELPHIA - 1
    Danny Murphy - rf
NL: CHICAGO - 0

1911 [3]
AL: PHILADELPHIA - 3
    Frank Baker - 3b (2)
    Rube Oldring - cf
NL: NEW YORK - 0

1912 [2]
AL: BOSTON - 1
    Larry Gardner - 3b
NL: NEW YORK - 1
    Larry Doyle - 2b

1913 [3]
AL: PHILADELPHIA - 2
    Frank Baker - 3b
    Wally Schang - c
NL: NEW YORK - 1
    Fred Merkle - 1b

1914 [1]
AL: PHILADELPHIA - 0
NL: BOSTON - 1
    Hank Gowdy - c

1915 [4]
AL: BOSTON - 3
    Harry Hooper - rf (2)
    Duffy Lewis - lf
NL: PHILADELPHIA - 1
    Fred Luderus - 1b

1916 [3]
AL: BOSTON - 2
    Larry Gardner - 3b (2)
NL: BROOKLYN - 1
    Hy Myers - cf

1917 [3]
AL: CHICAGO - 1
    Happy Felsch - cf
NL: NEW YORK - 2
    Benny Kauff - cf (2)

1918 [0]
AL: BOSTON - 0
NL: CHICAGO - 0

1919 [1]
AL: CHICAGO - 1
    Joe Jackson - lf
NL: CINCINNATI - 0

1920 [2]
AL: CLEVELAND - 2
    Jim Bagby - p
    Elmer Smith - rf
NL: BROOKLYN - 0

1921 [4]
AL: NEW YORK - 2
    Chick Fewster - lf
    Babe Ruth - lf
NL: NEW YORK - 2
    Irish Meusel - lf
    Frank Snyder - c

1922 [3]
AL: NEW YORK - 2
    Aaron Ward - 2b (2)
NL: NEW YORK - 1
    Irish Meusel - lf

1923 [10]
AL: NEW YORK - 5
    Babe Ruth - rf (3)
    Joe Dugan - 3b
    Aaron Ward - 2b
NL: NEW YORK - 5
    Casey Stengel - cf (2)
    Irish Meusel - lf
    Frank Snyder - c
    Ross Youngs - rf

1924 [9]
AL: WASHINGTON - 5
    Goose Goslin - lf (3)
    Bucky Harris - 2b (2)
NL: NEW YORK - 4
    Jack Bentley - p
    George Kelly - cf
    Rosy Ryan - p
    Bill Terry - 1b

1925 [12]
AL: WASHINGTON - 8
    Goose Goslin - lf (3)
    Joe Harris - rf (3)
    Joe Judge - 1b
    Roger Peckinpaugh - ss
NL: PITTSBURGH - 4
    Kiki Cuyler - rf
    Eddie Moore - 2b
    Pie Traynor - 3b
    Glenn Wright - ss

1926 [8]
AL: NEW YORK - 4
    Babe Ruth - lf (3), rf
NL: ST. LOUIS - 4
    Les Bell - 3b
    Jesse Haines - p
    Billy Southworth - rf
    Tommy Thevenow - ss

1927 [2]
AL: NEW YORK - 2
    Babe Ruth - rf (2)
NL: PITTSBURGH - 0

1928 [10]
AL: NEW YORK - 9
    Lou Gehrig - 1b (4)
    Babe Ruth - lf (3)
    Cedric Durst - cf
    Bob Meusel - lf
NL: ST. LOUIS - 1
    Jim Bottomley - 1b

1929 [7]
AL: PHILADELPHIA - 6
    Jimmie Foxx - 1b (2)
    Mule Haas - cf (2)
    AL Simmons - lf (2)
NL: CHICAGO - 1
    Charlie Grimm - 1b

1930 [8]
AL: PHILADELPHIA - 6
    Mickey Cochrane - c (2)
    AL Simmons - lf, cf
    Jimmy Dykes - 3b
    Jimmie Foxx - 1b
NL: ST. LOUIS - 2
    Taylor Douthit - cf
    George Watkins - rf

1931 [5]
AL: PHILADELPHIA - 3
    AL Simmons - lf (2)
    Jimmie Foxx - 1b
NL: ST. LOUIS - 2
    Pepper Martin - cf
    George Watkins - rf

1932 [11]
AL: NEW YORK - 8
    Lou Gehrig - 1b (3)
    Tony Lazzeri - 2b (2)
    Babe Ruth - lf (2)
    Earle Combs - cf
NL: CHICAGO - 3
    Kiki Cuyler - rf
    Frank Demaree - cf
    Gabby Hartnett - c

1933 [5]
AL: WASHINGTON - 2
    Goose Goslin - rf
    Fred Schulte - cf
NL: NEW YORK - 3
    Mel Ott - rf (2)
    Bill Terry - 1b

1934 [4]
AL: DETROIT - 2
    Charlie Gehringer - 2b
    Hank Greenberg - 1b
NL: ST. LOUIS - 2
    Bill DeLancey - c
    Joe Medwick - lf

1935 [6]
AL: DETROIT - 1
    Hank Greenberg - 1b
NL: CHICAGO - 5
    Frank Demaree - rf (2)
    Gabby Hartnett - c
    Billy Herman - 2b
    Chuck Klein - cf

1936 [11]
AL: NEW YORK - 7
    Lou Gehrig - 1b (2)
    George Selkirk - rf (2)
    Bill Dickey - c
    Tony Lazzeri - 2b
    Jake Powell - lf
NL: NEW YORK - 4
    Dick Bartell - ss
    Joe Moore - lf
    Mel Ott - rf
    Jimmy Ripple - cf

1937 [5]
AL: NEW YORK - 4
    Joe DiMaggio - cf
    Lou Gehrig - 1b
    Myril Hoag - lf
    Tony Lazzeri - 2b
NL: NEW YORK - 1
    Mel Ott - 3b

1938 [7]
AL: NEW YORK - 5
  Frankie Crosetti - ss
  Bill Dickey - c
  Joe DiMaggio - cf
  Joe Gordon - 2b
  Tommy Henrich - rf
NL: CHICAGO - 2
  Joe Marty - cf
  Ken O'Dea - c

1939 [7]
AL: NEW YORK - 7
  Charlie Keller - rf (3)
  Bill Dickey - c (2)
  Babe Dahlgren - 1b
  Joe DiMaggio - cf
NL: CINCINNATI - 0

1940 [6]
AL: DETROIT - 4
  Bruce Campbell - rf
  Hank Greenberg - lf
  Pinky Higgins - 3b
  Rudy York - 1b
NL: CINCINNATI - 2
  Jimmy Ripple - lf
  Bucky Walters - p

1941 [3]
AL: NEW YORK - 2
  Joe Gordon - 2b
  Tommy Henrich - rf
NL: BROOKLYN - 1
  Pete Reiser - cf

1942 [5]
AL: NEW YORK - 3
  Charlie Keller - lf (2)
  Phil Rizzuto - ss
NL: ST. LOUIS - 2
  Whitey Kurowski - 3b
  Enos Slaughter - rf

1943 [4]
AL: NEW YORK - 2
  Bill Dickey - c
  Joe Gordon - 2b
NL: ST. LOUIS - 2
  Marty Marion - ss
  Ray Sanders - 1b

1944 [4]
AL: ST. LOUIS - 1
  George McQuinn - 1b
NL: ST. LOUIS - 3
  Danny Litwhiler - lf
  Stan Musial - rf
  Ray Sanders - 1b

1945 [3]
AL: DETROIT - 2
  Hank Greenberg - lf (2)
NL: CHICAGO - 1
  Phil Cavarretta - 1b

1946 [5]
AL: BOSTON - 4
  Rudy York - 1b (2)
  Leon Culberson - rf
  Bobby Doerr - 2b
NL: ST. LOUIS - 1
  Enos Slaughter - rf

1947 [5]
AL: NEW YORK - 4
  Joe DiMaggio - cf (2)
  Yogi Berra - ph
  Tommy Henrich - rf
NL: BROOKLYN - 1
  Dixie Walker - rf

1948 [8]
AL: CLEVELAND - 4
  Larry Doby - cf
  Joe Gordon - 2b
  Jim Hegan - c
  Dale Mitchell - lf
NL: BOSTON - 4
  Bob Elliott - 3b (2)
  Marv Rickert - lf
  Bill Salkeld - c

1949 [6]
AL: NEW YORK - 2
  Joe DiMaggio - cf
  Tommy Henrich - 1b
NL: BROOKLYN - 4
  Roy Campanella - c
  Gil Hodges - 1b
  Luis Olmo - lf
  Pee Wee Reese - ss

1950 [2]
AL: NEW YORK - 2
  Yogi Berra - c
  Joe DiMaggio - cf
NL: PHILADELPHIA - 0

1951 [7]
AL: NEW YORK - 5
  Joe Collins - 1b
  Joe DiMaggio - cf
  Gil McDougald - 2b
  Phil Rizzuto - ss
  Gene Woodling - lf
NL: NEW YORK - 2
  Alvin Dark - ss
  Whitey Lockman - 1b

1952 [16]
AL: NEW YORK - 10
  Johnny Mize - 1b (2), ph
  Yogi Berra - c (2)
  Mickey Mantle - cf (2)
  Billy Martin - 2b
  Gil McDougald - 3b
  Gene Woodling - lf
NL: BROOKLYN - 6
  Duke Snider - cf (4)
  Pee Wee Reese - ss
  Jackie Robinson - 2b

1953 [17]
AL: NEW YORK - 9
  Mickey Mantle - cf (2)
  Billy Martin - 2b (2)
  Gil McDougald - 3b (2)
  Yogi Berra - c
  Joe Collins - 1b
  Gene Woodling - lf
NL: BROOKLYN - 8
  Jim Gilliam - 2b (2)
  Roy Campanella - c
  Billy Cox - 3b
  Carl Furillo - rf
  Gil Hodges - 1b
  George Shuba - ph
  Duke Snider - cf

1954 [5]
AL: CLEVELAND - 3
  Hank Majeski - ph
  Al Smith - lf
  Vic Wertz - 1b
NL: NEW YORK - 2
  Dusty Rhodes - ph, lf

1955 [17]
AL: NEW YORK - 8
  Joe Collins - 1b (2)
  Yogi Berra - c
  Bob Cerv - ph
  Elston Howard - lf
  Mickey Mantle - cf
  Gil McDougald - 3b
  Bill Skowron - 1b
NL: BROOKLYN - 9
  Duke Snider - cf (4)
  Roy Campanella - c (2)
  Sandy Amoros - lf
  Carl Furillo - rf
  Gil Hodges - 1b

1956 [15]
AL: NEW YORK - 12
  Yogi Berra - c (3)
  Mickey Mantle - cf (3)
  Billy Martin - 2b (2)
  Hank Bauer - rf
  Elston Howard - lf
  Bill Skowron - 1b
  Enos Slaughter - lf
NL: BROOKLYN - 3
  Gil Hodges - 1b
  Jackie Robinson - 3b
  Duke Snider - cf

1957 [15]
AL: NEW YORK - 7
  Hank Bauer - rf (2)
  Tony Kubek - lf (2)
  Yogi Berra - c
  Elston Howard - 1b
  Mickey Mantle - cf
NL: MILWAUKEE - 8
  Hank Aaron - cf (3)
  Frank Torre - 1b (2)
  Del Crandall - c
  Johnny Logan - ss
  Eddie Mathews - 3b

1958 [13]
AL: NEW YORK - 10
  Hank Bauer - rf (4)
  Mickey Mantle - cf (2)
  Gil McDougald - 2b (2)
  Bill Skowron - 1b (2)
NL: MILWAUKEE - 3
  Bill Bruton - cf
  Lew Burdette - p
  Del Crandall - c

1959 [11]
AL: CHICAGO - 4
  Ted Kluszewski - 1b (3)
  Sherm Lollar - c
NL: LOS ANGELES - 7
  Chuck Essegian - ph (2)
  Charlie Neal - 2b (2)
  Gil Hodges - 1b
  Wally Moon - lf
  Duke Snider - cf

1960 [14]
AL: NEW YORK - 10
- Mickey Mantle - cf (3)
- Roger Maris - rf (2)
- Bill Skowron - 1b (2)
- Yogi Berra - lf
- Elston Howard - ph
- Bobby Richardson - 2b

NL: PITTSBURGH - 4
- Bill Mazeroski - 2b (2)
- Rocky Nelson - 1b
- Hal W. Smith - c

1961 [10]
AL: NEW YORK - 7
- Johnny Blanchard -ph, rf
- Yogi Berra - lf
- Elston Howard - c
- Hector Lopez - lf
- Roger Maris - rf
- Bill Skowron - 1b

NL: CINCINNATI - 3
- Gordy Coleman - 1b
- Wally Post - lf
- Frank Robinson - rf

1962 [8]
AL: NEW YORK - 3
- Clete Boyer - 3b
- Roger Maris - rf
- Tom Tresh - lf

NL: SAN FRANCISCO - 5
- Ed Bailey - c
- Tom Haller - c
- Chuck Hiller - 2b
- Willie McCovey - 1b
- Jose Pagan - ss

1963 [5]
AL: NEW YORK - 2
- Mickey Mantle - cf
- Tom Tresh - lf

NL: LOS ANGELES - 3
- Frank Howard - rf
- Johnny Roseboro - c
- Bill Skowron - 1b

1964 [15]
AL: NEW YORK - 10
- Mickey Mantle - rf (3)
- Phil Linz - ss (2)
- Tom Tresh - lf (2)
- Clete Boyer - 3b
- Roger Maris - cf
- Joe Pepitone - 1b

NL: ST. LOUIS - 5
- Ken Boyer - 3b (2)
- Lou Brock - lf
- Tim McCarver - c
- Mike Shannon - rf

1965 [11]
AL: MINNESOTA - 6
- Bob Allison - lf
- Mudcat Grant - p
- Harmon Killebrew - 3b
- Don Mincher - 1b
- Tony Oliva - rf
- Zoilo Versalles - ss

NL: LOS ANGELES - 5
- Ron Fairly - rf (2)
- Lou Johnson - lf (2)
- Wes Parker - 1b

1966 [5]
AL: BALTIMORE - 4
- Frank Robinson - rf (2)
- Paul Blair - cf
- Brooks Robinson - 3b

NL: LOS ANGELES - 1
- Jim Lefebvre - 2b

1967 [13]
AL: BOSTON - 8
- Carl Yastrzemski - lf (3)
- Rico Petrocelli - ss (2)
- Reggie Smith - cf (2)
- Jose Santiago - p

NL: ST. LOUIS - 5
- Lou Brock - lf
- Bob Gibson - p
- Julian Javier - 2b
- Roger Maris - rf
- Mike Shannon - 3b

1968 [15]
AL: DETROIT - 8
- AL Kaline - rf (2)
- Jim Northrup - cf (2)
- Norm Cash - 1b
- Willie Horton - lf
- Mickey Lolich - p
- Dick McAuliffe - 2b

NL: ST. LOUIS - 7
- Lou Brock - lf (2)
- Orlando Cepeda - 1b (2)
- Bob Gibson - p
- Tim McCarver - c
- Mike Shannon - 3b

1969 [9]
AL: BALTIMORE - 3
- Don Buford - lf
- Dave McNally - p
- Frank Robinson - rf

NL: NEW YORK - 6
- Donn Clendenon - 1b (3)
- Tommie Agee - cf
- Ed Kranepool - 1b
- AL Weis - 2b

1970 [15]
AL: BALTIMORE - 10
- Boog Powell - 1b (2)
- Brooks Robinson - 3b (2)
- Frank Robinson - rf (2)
- Don Buford - lf
- Ellie Hendricks - c
- Dave McNally - p
- Merv Rettenmund - lf

NL: CINCINNATI - 5
- Lee May - 1b (2)
- Johnny Bench - c
- Pete Rose - rf
- Bobby Tolan - cf

1971 [10]
AL: BALTIMORE - 5
- Don Buford - lf (2)
- Frank Robinson - rf (2)
- Merv Rettenmund - cf

NL: PITTSBURGH - 5
- Roberto Clemente - rf (2)
- Bob Robertson - 1b (2)
- Richie Hebner - 3b

1972 [8]
AL: OAKLAND - 5
- Gene Tenace - c (4)
- Joe Rudi - lf

NL: CINCINNATI - 3
- Johnny Bench - c
- Denis Menke - 3b
- Pete Rose - lf

1973 [6]
AL: OAKLAND - 2
- Bert Campaneris - ss
- Reggie Jackson - cf

NL: NEW YORK - 4
- Wayne Garrett - 3b (2)
- Cleon Jones - lf
- Rusty Staub - rf

1974 [8]
AL: OAKLAND - 4
- Ray Fosse - c
- Ken Holtzman - p
- Reggie Jackson - rf
- Joe Rudi - 1b

NL: LOS ANGELES - 4
- Bill Buckner - lf
- Willie Crawford - rf
- Joe Ferguson - rf
- Jimmy Wynn - cf

1975 [13]
AL: BOSTON - 6
- Bernie Carbo - ph (2)
- Carlton Fisk - c (2)
- Dwight Evans - rf
- Fred Lynn - cf

NL: CINCINNATI - 7
- Tony Perez - 1b (3)
- Cesar Geronimo - cf (2)
- Johnny Bench - c
- Dave Concepcion - ss

1976 [5]
AL: NEW YORK - 1
- Jim Mason - ss

NL: CINCINNATI - 4
- Johnny Bench - c (2)
- Dan Driessen - dh
- Joe Morgan - 2b

1977 [17]
AL: NEW YORK - 8
- Reggie Jackson - rf (5)
- Chris Chambliss - 1b
- Thurman Munson - c
- Willie Randolph - 2b

NL: LOS ANGELES - 9
- Reggie Smith - rf (3)
- Steve Yeager - c (2)
- Dusty Baker - lf
- Ron Cey - 3b
- Steve Garvey - 1b
- Davey Lopes - 2b

1978 [9]
AL: NEW YORK - 3
- Reggie Jackson - dh (2)
- Roy White - lf

NL: LOS ANGELES - 6
- Davey Lopes - 2b (3)
- Dusty Baker - lf
- Ron Cey - 3b
- Reggie Smith - rf

1979 [7]
AL: BALTIMORE - 4
- Benny Ayala - lf
- Rich Dauer - 2b
- Doug DeCinces - 3b
- Eddie Murray - 1b

NL: PITTSBURGH - 3
- Willie Stargell - 1b (3)

1980 [11]
AL: KANSAS CITY - 8
    Willie Aikens - 1b (4)
    Amos Otis - cf (3)
    George Brett - 3b
NL: PHILADELPHIA - 3
    Mike Schmidt - 3b (2)
    Bake McBride - rf

1981 [12]
AL: NEW YORK - 6
    Willie Randolph - 2b (2)
    Bob Watson - 1b (2)
    Rick Cerone - c
    Reggie Jackson - rf
NL: LOS ANGELES - 6
    Pedro Guerrero - rf (2)
    Steve Yeager - c (2)
    Ron Cey - 3b
    Jay Johnstone - ph

1982 [9]
AL: MILWAUKEE - 5
    Ted Simmons - c (2)
    Cecil Cooper - 1b
    Ben Oglivie - lf
    Robin Yount - ss
NL: ST. LOUIS - 4
    Willie McGee - cf (2)
    Keith Hernandez - 1b
    Darrell Porter - c

1983 [10]
AL: BALTIMORE - 6
    Eddie Murray - 1b (2)
    Rick Dempsey - c
    Jim Dwyer - rf
    Dan Ford - rf
    John Lowenstein - lf
NL: PHILADELPHIA - 4
    Joe Morgan - 2b (2)
    Garry Maddox - cf
    Gary Matthews Sr. - lf

1984 [10]
AL: DETROIT - 7
    Kirk Gibson - rf (2)
    Alan Trammell - ss (2)
    Marty Castillo - 3b
    Larry Herndon - lf
    Lance Parrish - c
NL: SAN DIEGO - 3
    Kurt Bevacqua - dh (2)
    Terry Kennedy - c

1985 [4]
AL: KANSAS CITY - 2
    Darryl Motley - rf
    Frank White - 2b
NL: ST. LOUIS - 2
    Tito Landrum - lf
    Willie McGee - cf

1986 [12]
AL: BOSTON - 5
    Dwight Evans - rf (2)
    Dave Henderson - cf (2)
    Rich Gedman - c
NL: NEW YORK - 7
    Gary Carter - c (2)
    Len Dykstra - cf (2)
    Ray Knight - 3b
    Darryl Strawberry - rf
    Tim Teufel - 2b

1987 [9]
AL: MINNESOTA - 7
    Don Baylor - dh
    Gary Gaetti - 3b
    Greg Gagne - ss
    Dan Gladden - lf
    Kent Hrbek - 1b
    Tim Laudner - c
    Steve Lombardozzi - 2b
NL: ST. LOUIS - 2
    Tommy Herr - 2b
    Tom Lawless - 3b

1988 [7]
AL: OAKLAND - 2
    Jose Canseco - rf
    Mark McGwire - 1b
NL: LOS ANGELES - 5
    Mickey Hatcher - lf (2)
    Mike Davis - dh
    Kirk Gibson - ph
    Mike Marshall - rf

1989 [13]
AL: OAKLAND - 9
    Dave Henderson - cf (2)
    Jose Canseco - rf
    Rickey Henderson - lf
    Carney Lansford - 3b
    Dave Parker - dh
    Tony Phillips - 2b
    Terry Steinbach - c
    Walt Weiss - ss
NL: SAN FRANCISCO - 4
    Bill Bathe - ph
    Greg Litton - 2b
    Kevin Mitchell - lf
    Matt Williams - ss

1990 [6]
AL: OAKLAND - 3
    Harold Baines - dh
    Jose Canseco - rf
    Rickey Henderson - lf
NL: CINCINNATI - 3
    Chris Sabo - 3b (2)
    Eric Davis - lf

1991 [16]
AL: MINNESOTA - 8
    Chili Davis - dh, ph
    Kirby Puckett - cf (2)
    Greg Gagne - ss
    Kent Hrbek - 1b
    Scott Leius - 3b
    Mike Pagliarulo - 3b
NL: ATLANTA - 8
    Lonnie Smith - lf (3)
    David Justice - rf (2)
    Terry Pendleton - 3b (2)
    Brian Hunter - 1b

1992 [9]
AL: TORONTO - 6
    Joe Carter - 1b, rf
    Pat Borders - c
    Kelly Gruber - 3b
    Candy Maldonado - lf
    Ed Sprague - ph
NL: ATLANTA - 3
    Damon Berryhill - c
    David Justice - rf
    Lonnie Smith - dh

1993 [13]
AL: TORONTO - 6
    Joe Carter - rf (2)
    Paul Molitor - 1b, dh
    John Olerud - 1b
    Devon White - cf
NL: PHILADELPHIA - 7
    Len Dykstra - cf (4)
    Darren Daulton - c
    Jim Eisenreich - rf
    Milt Thompson - lf

1994 No Series

1995 [13]
AL: CLEVELAND - 5
    Albert Belle - lf (2)
    Eddie Murray - 1b
    Manny Ramirez - rf
    Jim Thome - 3b
NL: ATLANTA - 8
    Ryan Klesko - dh (3)
    Fred McGriff - 1b (2)
    David Justice - rf
    Javier Lopez - c
    Luis Polonia - lf

1996 [6]
AL: NEW YORK - 2
    Jim Leyritz - c
    Bernie Williams - cf
NL: ATLANTA - 4
    Andruw Jones - lf (2)
    Fred McGriff - 1b (2)

1997 [15]
AL: CLEVELAND - 7
    Sandy Alomar Jr. - c (2)
    Manny Ramirez - rf (2)
    Jim Thome - 1b (2)
    Matt Williams - 3b
NL: FLORIDA - 8
    Moises Alou - lf (3)
    Bobby Bonilla - 3b
    Darren Daulton - 1b
    Jim Eisenreich - dh
    Charles Johnson - c
    Gary Sheffield - rf

1998 [9]
AL: NEW YORK - 6
    Scott Brosius - 3b (2)
    Chuck Knoblauch - 2b
    Tino Martinez - 1b
    Jorge Posada - c
    Bernie Williams - cf
NL: SAN DIEGO - 3
    Greg Vaughn - lf (2)
    Tony Gwynn - rf

1999 [6]
AL: NEW YORK - 5
    Chad Curtis - lf (2)
    Chuck Knoblauch - 2b
    Jim Leyritz - ph/dh
    Tino Martinez - 1b
NL: ATLANTA - 1
    Chipper Jones - 3b

2000 [8]
AL: NEW YORK - 4
    Derek Jeter - ss (2)
    Scott Brosius - 3b
    Bernie Williams - cf
NL: NEW YORK - 4
    Mike Piazza - c (2)
    Jay Payton - cf
    Robin Ventura - 3b

2001 [12]
AL: NEW YORK - 6
  Scott Brosius - 3b
  Derek Jeter - ss
  Tino Martinez - 1b
  Jorge Posada - c
  Alfonso Soriano - 2b
  Shane Spencer - lf
NL: ARIZONA - 6
  Rod Barajas - c
  Craig Counsell - 2b
  Steve Finley - cf
  Luis Gonzalez - lf
  Mark Grace - 1b
  Matt Williams - 3b

2002 [21]
AL: ANAHEIM - 7
  Troy Glaus - 3b (3)
  Tim Salmon - rf (2)
  Darin Erstad - cf
  Scott Spiezio - 1b
NL: SAN FRANCISCO - 14
  Barry Bonds - lf (4)
  Jeff Kent - 2b (3)
  Rich Aurilia - ss (2)
  Reggie Sanders - rf (2)
  David Bell - 3b
  Shawon Dunston - dh
  J.T. Snow - 1b

2003 [8]
AL: NEW YORK - 6
  Bernie Williams - cf (2)
  Aaron Boone - 3b
  Jason Giambi - ph
  Hideki Matsui - lf
  Alfonso Soriano - 2b
NL: FLORIDA - 2
  Miguel Cabrera - rf
  Alex Gonzalez - ss

2004 [6]
AL: BOSTON - 4
  Mark Bellhorn - 2b
  Johnny Damon - cf
  David Ortiz - dh
  Manny Ramirez - lf
NL: ST. LOUIS - 2
  Larry Walker - rf (2)

2005 [9]
AL: CHICAGO - 6
  Joe Crede - 3b (2)
  Geoff Blum - 2b
  Jermaine Dye - rf
  Paul Konerko - 1b
  Scott Podsednik - lf
NL: HOUSTON - 3
  Morgan Ensberg - 3b
  Mike Lamb - 1b
  Jason Lane - rf

2006 [6]
AL: DETROIT - 4
  Sean Casey - 1b (2)
  Craig Monroe - lf (2)
NL: ST. LOUIS - 2
  Albert Pujols - 1b
  Scott Rolen - 3b

2007 [6]
AL: BOSTON - 3
  Bobby Kielty - ph
  Mike Lowell - 3b
  Dustin Pedroia - 2b
NL: COLORADO - 3
  Garrett Atkins - 3b
  Brad Hawpe - rf
  Matt Holliday - lf

2008 [13]
AL: TAMPA BAY - 4
  Carl Crawford - lf (2)
  Rocco Baldelli - rf
  Eric Hinske - ph
NL: PHILADELPHIA - 9
  Ryan Howard -1b (3)
  Chase Utley - 2b (2)
  Joe Blanton - p
  Eric Bruntlett - ph
  Carlos Ruiz -c
  Jayson Werth - rf

2009 [17]
AL: NEW YORK - 6
  Hideki Matsui - dh (2), ph
  Alex Rodriguez - 3b
  Nick Swisher - rf
  Mark Teixeira - 1b
NL: PHILADELPHIA - 11
  Chase Utley - 2b (5)
  Jayson Werth - rf (2)
  Pedro Feliz - 3b
  Ryan Howard - 1b
  Raul Ibanez - lf
  Carlos Ruiz - c

2010 [10]
AL: TEXAS - 3
  Nelson Cruz - rf
  Josh Hamilton -cf
  Mitch Moreland - 1b
NL: SAN FRANCISCO -7
  Edgar Renteria - ss (2)
  Aubrey Huff - dh
  Buster Posey - c
  Cody Ross - rf
  Andres Torres - cf
  Juan Uribe - 3b

2011 [17]
AL: TEXAS - 9
  Adrian Beltre - 3b (2)
  Nelson Cruz - lf (2)
  Mike Napoli - c (2)
  Josh Hamilton - cf
  Mitch Moreland - 1b
  Michael Young - dh
NL: ST. LOUIS - 8
  Allen Craig - lf (2), rf
  Albert Pujols - 1b (3)
  Lance Berkman - rf
  David Freese - 3b

2012 [7]
AL: DETROIT - 3
  Miguel Cabrera - 3b
  Jhonny Peralta - ss
  Delmon Young - dh
NL: SAN FRANCISCO - 4
  Pablo Sandoval 3b (3)
  Buster Posey c

2013 [6]
AL: BOSTON - 4
  David Ortiz - dh (2)
  Stephen Drew - ss
  Jonny Gomes - lf
NL: ST. LOUIS - 2
  Matt Holliday - lf (2)

2014 [5]
AL: KANSAS CITY - 3
  Omar Infante - 2b
  Mike Moustakas - 3b
  Salvador Perez - c
NL: SAN FRANCISCO - 2
  Gregor Blanco - cf
  Hunter Pence - rf

2015 [8]
AL: KANSAS CITY - 2
  Alcides Escobar - ss
  Alex Gordon - lf
NL: NEW YORK - 6
  Curtis Granderson - rf (3)
  Michael Conforto - lf (2)
  David Wright - 3b

2016 [15]
AL: CLEVELAND - 7
  Jason Kipnis - 2b (2)
  Roberto Perez - c (2)
  Rajai Davis - cf
  Jose Ramirez - 3b
  Carlos Santana - 1b
NL: CHICAGO - 8
  Kris Bryant - 3b (2)
  Dexter Fowler - cf (2)
  Javier Baez - 2b
  Anthony Rizzo - 1b
  David Ross - c
  Addison Russell - ss

2017 [25]
AL: HOUSTON - 15
  George Springer - cf (4), rf
  Jose Altuve - 2b (2)
  Alex Bregman - 3b (2)
  Carlos Correa - ss (2)
  Yuli Gurriel - 1b (2)
  Marwin Gonzalez - lf
  Brian McCann - c
NL: LOS ANGELES - 10
  Joc Pederson - lf (2), dh
  Yasiel Puig - rf (2)
  Cody Bellinger - 1b
  Charlie Culberson - lf
  Corey Seager - ss
  Chris Taylor - cf
  Justin Turner - 3b

2018 [14]
AL: BOSTON - 8
  Steve Pearce - 1b (3)
  Mookie Betts - cf
  Jackie Bradley - cf
  J.D. Martinez - rf
  Mitch Moreland - ph
  Eduardo Nunez - ph
NL: LOS ANGELES - 6
  David Freese - 1b
  Kike Hernandez - lf
  Matt Kemp - dh
  Max Muncy - 2b
  Joc Pederson - lf
  Yasiel Puig - rf

2019 [22]
AL: HOUSTON - 11
  Alex Bregman -3b (3)
  Robinson Chirinos - c (2)
  George Springer - cf, rf
  Yordan Alvarez - dh
  Carlos Correa - ss
  Yuli Gurriel - 1b
  Martin Maldonado - c
NL: WASHINGTON - 11
  Juan Soto - lf (3)
  Adam Eaton - rf (2)
  Anthony Rendon - 3b (2)
  Howie Kendrick - dh
  Kurt Suzuki - c
  Michael Taylor - cf
  Ryan Zimmerman - 1b

2020 [21]
- AL: TAMPA BAY - 9
  - Randy Arozarena - lf (2), dh
  - Brandon Lowe - 2b (3)
  - Kevin Kiermaier - cf (2)
  - Hunter Renfroe - rf
- NL: LOS ANGELES - 12
  - Mookie Betts - rf (2)
  - Corey Seager - ss (2)
  - Justin Turner - 3b (2)
  - Austin Barnes - c
  - Cody Bellinger - cf
  - Max Muncy - 1b
  - Joc Pederson - lf
  - Will Smith - c
  - Chris Taylor - lf

1-0

1905	Oct. 13	NL:	NY vs. Phil.
			(Joe McGinnity)
1906	Oct. 12	NL:	Chi. vs. Chi.
			(Three Finger Brown)
1914	Oct. 10	NL:	Bos. vs. Phil.
			(Bill James)
1918	Sept. 5	AL:	Bos. vs. Chi.
			(Babe Ruth)
1920	Oct. 11	AL:	Clev. vs. Brk.
			(Duster Mails)
1921	Oct. 13	NL:	NY vs. NY
			(Art Nehf)
1923	Oct. 12	NL:	NY vs. NY
			(Art Nehf)
1948	Oct. 6	NL:	Bos. vs. Clev.
			(Johnny Sain)
1949	Oct. 5	AL:	NY vs. Brk.
			(Allie Reynolds)
1949	Oct. 6	NL:	Brk. vs. NY
			(Preacher Roe)
1950	Oct. 4	AL:	NY vs. Phil.
			(Vic Raschi)
1956	Oct. 9	NL:	Brk. vs. NY
			(Clem Labine, 10 inn)
1957	Oct. 7	NL:	Mil. vs. NY
			(Lew Burdette)
1959	Oct. 6	AL:	Chi. vs. LA
			(Bob Shaw, Billy Pierce & Dick Donovan)
1962	Oct. 16	AL:	NY vs. SF
			(Ralph Terry)
1963	Oct. 5	NL:	LA vs. NY
			(Don Drysdale)
1966	Oct. 8	AL:	Balt. vs. LA
			(Wally Bunker)
1966	Oct. 9	AL:	Balt. vs. LA
			(Dave McNally)
1972	Oct. 18	NL:	Cin. vs. Oak.
			(Jack Billingham & Clay Carroll)
1986	Oct. 18	AL:	Bos. vs. NY
			(Bruce Hurst & Calvin Schiraldi)
1991	Oct. 27	AL:	Minn. vs. Atl.
			(Jack Morris, 10 inn)
1995	Oct. 28	NL:	Atl. vs. Clev.
			(Tom Glavine & Mark Wohlers)
1996	Oct. 24	AL:	NY vs. Atl.
			(Andy Pettitte & John Wetteland)
2005	Oct. 26	AL:	Chi. vs. Hou.
			(Freddy Garcia, Cliff Politte, Neal Cotts & Bobby Jenks)
2016	Oct. 28	AL:	Clev. vs. Chi.
			(Josh Tomlin, Andrew Miller, Bryan Shaw & Cody Allen)

2-0

1905	Oct. 14	NL:	NY vs. Phil.
			(Christy Mathewson)
1907	Oct. 12	NL:	Chi. vs. Det.
			(Three Finger Brown)
1908	Oct. 14	NL:	Chi. vs. Det.
			(Orval Overall)
1917	Oct. 10	NL:	NY vs. Chi.
			(Rube Benton)
1919	Oct. 4	NL:	Cin. vs. Chi.
			(Jimmy Ring)
1930	Oct. 6	AL:	Phil. vs. StL.
			(George Earnshaw & Lefty Grove)
1931	Oct. 2	NL:	StL. vs. Phil.
			(Bill Hallahan)
1942	Oct. 3	NL:	StL. vs. NY
			(Ernie White)

1943	Oct. 11	AL:	NY vs. StL.
			(Spud Chandler)
1944	Oct. 8	NL:	StL. vs. StL.
			(Mort Cooper)
1948	Oct. 8	AL:	Clev. vs. Bos.
			(Gene Bearden)
1952	Oct. 4	AL:	NY vs. Brk.
			(Allie Reynolds)
1955	Oct. 4	NL:	Brk. vs. NY
			(Johnny Podres)
1956	Oct. 8	AL:	NY vs. Brk.
			(Don Larsen)
1961	Oct. 4	AL:	NY vs. Cin.
			(Whitey Ford)
1962	Oct. 5	NL:	SF vs. NY
			(Jack Sanford)
1965	Oct. 14	NL:	LA vs. Minn.
			(Sandy Koufax)
1973	Oct. 18	NL:	NY vs. Oak.
			(Jerry Koosman & Tug McGraw)
1993	Oct. 21	NL:	Phil. vs. Tor.
			(Curt Schilling)
2003	Oct. 25	NL:	Fla. vs. NY
			(Josh Beckett)
2012	Oct. 25	NL:	SF vs. Det.
			(Madison Bumgarner, Santiago Casilla & Sergio Romo)
2012	Oct. 27	NL:	SF vs. Det.
			(Ryan Vogelsong, Tim Lincecum & Sergio Romo)

3-0

1903	Oct. 2	AL:	Bos. vs. Pitt. (Bill Dinneen)
1903	Oct. 13	AL:	Bos. vs. Pitt. (Bill Dinneen)
1905	Oct. 9	NL:	NY vs. Phil. (Christy Mathewson)
1905	Oct. 10	AL:	Phil. vs. NY (Chief Bender)
1906	Oct. 11	AL:	Chi. vs. Chi. (Ed Walsh)
1908	Oct. 13	NL:	Chi. vs. Det. (Three Finger Brown)
1913	Oct. 8	NL:	NY vs. Phil. (Christy Mathewson, 10 inn)
1918	Sept. 10	NL:	Chi. vs. Bos. (Hippo Vaughn)
1919	Oct. 3	AL:	Chi. vs. Cin. (Dickie Kerr)
1920	Oct. 6	NL:	Brk. vs. Clev. (Burleigh Grimes)
1920	Oct. 12	AL:	Clev. vs. Brk. (Stan Coveleski)
1921	Oct. 5	AL:	NY vs. NY (Carl Mays)
1921	Oct. 6	AL:	NY vs. NY (Waite Hoyt)
1922	Oct. 6	NL:	NY vs. NY (Jack Scott)
1931	Oct. 6	AL:	Phil. vs. StL. (George Earnshaw)
1935	Oct. 2	NL:	Chi. vs. Det. (Lon Warneke)
1945	Oct. 5	NL:	Chi. vs. Det. (Claude Passeau)
1946	Oct. 7	NL:	StL. vs. Bos. (Harry Brecheen)
1958	Oct. 5	NL:	Mil. vs. NY (Warren Spahn)
1981	Oct. 21	AL:	NY vs. LA (Tommy John & Rich Gossage)
1985	Oct. 23	NL:	StL. vs. KC (John Tudor)
1998	Oct. 21	AL:	NY vs. SD (Andy Pettitte, Jeff Nelson & Mariano Rivera)
2004	Oct. 27	AL:	Bos. vs. StL. (Derek Lowe, Bronson Arroyo, Alan Embree & Keith Foulke)

4-0

1925	Oct. 11	AL:	Wash. vs. Pitt. (Walter Johnson)
1926	Oct. 5	NL:	StL. vs. NY (Jesse Haines)
1933	Oct. 5	AL:	Wash. vs. NY (Earl Whitehill)
1939	Oct. 5	AL:	NY vs. Cin. (Monte Pearson)
1940	Oct. 7	NL:	Cin. vs. Det. (Bucky Walters)
1946	Oct. 9	AL:	Bos. vs. StL. (Boo Ferriss)
1958	Oct. 4	AL:	NY vs. Mil. (Don Larsen & Ryne Duren)
1965	Oct. 9	NL:	LA vs. Minn. (Claude Osteen)
1968	Oct. 2	NL:	StL. vs. Det. (Bob Gibson)
1971	Oct. 14	NL:	Pitt. vs. Balt. (Nelson Briles)
1979	Oct. 16	NL:	Pitt. vs. Balt.

(John Candelaria & Kent Tekulve)

1996	Oct. 21	NL:	Atl. vs. NY (Greg Maddux)
2001	Oct. 28	NL:	Ari. vs. NY (Randy Johnson)
2010	Oct. 31	NL:	SF vs. Tex. (Madison Bumgarner & Brian Wilson)
2011	Oct. 23	AL:	Tex. vs. StL. (Derek Holland & Neftali Feliz)

5-0

1909	Oct. 12	AL:	Det. vs. Pitt. (George Mullin)
1917	Oct. 11	NL:	NY vs. Chi. (Ferdie Schupp)
1919	Oct. 6	NL:	Cin. vs. Chi. (Hod Eller)
1930	Oct. 4	NL:	StL. vs. Phil. (Bill Hallahan)
1957	Oct. 10	NL:	Mil. vs. NY (Lew Burdette)
1967	Oct. 5	AL:	Bos. vs. StL. (Jim Lonborg)
1969	Oct. 14	NL:	NY vs. Balt. (Gary Gentry & Nolan Ryan)
1983	Oct. 16	AL:	Balt. vs. Phil. (Scott McGregor)
1989	Oct. 14	AL:	Oak. vs. SF (Dave Stewart)
2006	Oct. 24	NL:	StL. vs. Det. (Chris Carpenter & Braden Looper)
2014	Oct. 26	NL:	SF vs. KC (Madison Bumgarner)

6-0

1966	Oct. 6	AL:	Balt. vs. LA (Jim Palmer)
1967	Oct. 8	NL:	StL. vs. Bos. (Bob Gibson)
1975	Oct. 11	AL:	Bos. vs. Cin. (Luis Tiant)
1988	Oct. 16	NL:	LA vs. Oak. (Orel Hershiser)
2016	Oct. 25	AL:	Clev. vs. Chi. (Corey Kluber, Andrew Miller & Cody Allen)

7-0

1958	Oct. 6	AL:	NY vs. Mil. (Bob Turley)
1961	Oct. 8	AL:	NY vs. Cin. (Whitey Ford & Jim Coates)
1965	Oct. 11	NL:	LA vs. Minn. (Sandy Koufax)
1990	Oct. 16	NL:	Cin. vs. Oak. (Jose Rijo, Rob Dibble & Randy Myers)

8-0

1909	Oct. 16	NL:	Pitt. vs. Det. (Babe Adams)
1940	Oct. 6	AL:	Det. vs. Cin. (Bobo Newsom)

9-0

1905	Oct. 12	NL:	NY vs. Phil.
			(Christy Mathewson)
1945	Oct. 3	NL:	Chi. vs. Det.
			(Hank Borowy)
1956	Oct. 10	AL:	NY vs. Brk.
			(Johnny Kucks)
2010	Oct. 28	NL:	SF vs. Tex.
			(Matt Cain, Javier Lopez &
			Guillermo Mota)

10-0

1960	Oct. 8	AL:	NY vs. Pitt.
			(Whitey Ford)
1982	Oct. 12	AL:	Mil. vs. StL.
			(Mike Caldwell)
2014	Oct. 28	AL:	KC vs. SF
			(Yordano Ventura, Jason Frasor &
			Tim Collins)

11-0

1934	Oct. 9	NL:	StL. vs. Det.
			(Dizzy Dean)
1959	Oct. 1	AL:	Chi. vs. LA
			(Early Wynn & Gerry Staley)
1985	Oct. 27	AL:	KC vs. StL.
			(Bret Saberhagen)

12-0

| 1960 | Oct. 12 | AL: | NY vs. Pitt. |
| | | | (Whitey Ford) |

PITCHER, CLUB, YEAR	W	L
Adams, Babe NL:Pitt. 1909	3	0
Adams, Mike AL:Tex. 2011	1	0
Affeldt, Jeremy NL:SF 2014	1	0
Aguilera, Rick NL:NY 1986 (1-0) AL:Minn. 1991 (1-1)	2	1
Aldridge, Vic NL:Pitt. 1925, 27	2	1
Alexander, Doyle AL:NY 1976	0	1
Alexander, Grover NL:Phil. 1915 (1-1) NL:StL. 1926, 28 (2-1)	3	2
Altrock, Nick AL:Chi. 1906	1	1
Ames, Red NL:NY 1911	0	1
Anderson, Brian NL:Ari. 2001	0	1
Anderson, Fred NL:NY 1917	0	1
Anderson, Nick AL:TB 2020	1	1
Andujar, Joaquin NL:StL. 1982, 85	2	1
Antonelli, Johnny NL:NY 1954	1	0
Arrieta, Jake NL:Chi. 2016	2	0
Arroyo, Luis AL:NY 1961	1	0
Ashby, Andy NL:SD 1998	0	1
Astacio, Ezequiel NL:Hou. 2005	0	1
Auker, Elden AL:Det. 1934	1	1
Avery, Steve NL:Atl. 1992, 95-96	1	2
Bagby, Jim AL:Clev. 1920	1	1
Bair, Doug NL:StL. 1982	0	1
Barnes, Jesse NL:NY 1921	2	0
Barnes, Matt AL:Bos. 2018	1	0
Barnes, Virgil NL:NY 1924	0	1
Barney, Rex NL:Brk. 1947, 49	0	2
Bauer, Trevor AL:Clev. 2016	0	2
Bearden, Gene AL:Clev. 1948	1	0
Beattie, Jim AL:NY 1978	1	0
Beazley, Johnny NL:StL. 1942	2	0
Beckett, Josh NL:Fla. 2003 (1-1) AL:Bos. 2007 (1-0)	2	1
Bedient, Hugh AL:Bos. 1912	1	0
Belcher, Tim NL:LA 1988	1	0
Bell, Gary AL:Bos. 1967	0	1
Bender, Chief AL:Phil. 1905, 10-11, 13-14	6	4
Bentley, Jack NL:NY 1923-24	1	3
Benton, Rube NL:NY 1917	1	1
Berenguer, Juan AL:Minn. 1987	0	1
Bessent, Don NL:Brk. 1956	1	0
Bevens, Bill AL:NY 1947	0	1
Bickford, Vern NL:Bos. 1948	0	1
Billingham, Jack NL:Cin. 1972, 76	2	0
Black, Bud AL:KC 1985	0	1
Black, Joe NL:Brk. 1952	1	2
Blake, Sheriff NL:Chi. 1929	0	1
Blanton, Joe NL:Phil. 2008	1	0
Blass, Steve NL:Pitt. 1971	2	0
Blue, Vida AL:Oak. 1972-74	0	3
Blyleven, Bert NL:Pitt. 1979 (1-0) AL:Minn. 1987 (1-1)	2	1
Boddicker, Mike AL:Balt. 1983	1	0
Bonham, Ernie AL:NY 1941-43	1	2
Borbon, Pedro Sr. NL:Cin. 1972	0	1
Borowy, Hank AL:NY 1943 (1-0) NL:Chi. 1945 (2-2)	3	2
Bouton, Jim AL:NY 1963-64	2	1
Boyd, Oil Can AL:Bos. 1986	0	1
Branca, Ralph NL:Brk. 1947, 49	1	2
Brazle, Al NL:StL. 1943, 46	0	2
Brecheen, Harry NL:StL. 1943-44, 46	4	1
Bridges, Tommy AL:Det. 1934-35, 40	4	1
Briles, Nelson NL:StL. 1967-68 (1-1) NL:Pitt. 1971 (1-0)	2	1
Brown, Kevin NL:Fla. 1997 (0-2) NL:SD 1998 (0-1)	0	3
Brown, Three Finger NL:Chi. 1906-08, 10	5	4
Browning, Tom NL:Cin. 1990	1	0
Bryant, Clay NL:Chi. 1935	0	1
Buehler, Walker NL:LA 2020	1	0
Buhl, Bob NL:Mil. 1957	0	1
Bumgarner, Madison NL:SF 2010, 12, 14	4	0
Bunker, Wally AL:Balt. 1966	1	0
Burdette, Lew NL:Mil. 1957-58	4	2
Burnett, A.J. AL:NY 2009	1	1
Burton, Jim AL:Bos. 1975	0	1
Bush, Guy NL:Chi. 1929, 32	1	1
Bush, Joe AL:Phil. 1913-14 (0-2) AL:Bos. 1918 (0-1) AL:NY 1922-23 (2-2)	2	5
Byrne, Tommy AL:NY 1955	1	1
Cadore, Leon NL:Brk. 1920	0	1
Cain, Matt NL:SF 2010	1	0

PITCHER, CLUB, YEAR	W	L
Caldwell, Mike AL:Mil. 1982	2	0
Caldwell, Ray AL:Clev. 1920	0	1
Camnitz, Howie NL:Pitt. 1909	0	1
Candelaria, John NL:Pitt. 1979	1	1
Carlton, Tex AL:Chi. 1935	0	1
Carlton, Steve NL:StL. 1967 (0-1) NL:Phil. 1980, 83 (2-1)	2	2
Carpenter, Chris NL:StL. 2006, 11	3	0
Carroll, Clay NL:Cin. 1970, 72, 75	2	1
Casey, Hugh NL:Brk. 1941, 47	2	2
Casilla, Santiago NL:SF 2012	1	0
Castillo, Tony AL:Tor. 1993	1	0
Chalmers, George NL:Phil. 1915	0	1
Chamberlain, Joba AL:NY 2009	1	0
Chandler, Spud AL:NY 1941-43	2	2
Chapman, Aroldis NL:Chi. 2016	1	0
Christenson, Larry NL:Phil. 1980	0	1
Cicotte, Eddie AL:Chi. 1917, 19	2	3
Clancy, Jim NL:Atl. 1991	1	0
Clemens, Roger AL:NY 1999-2001	3	0
Cleveland, Reggie AL:Bos. 1975	0	1
Clippard, Tyler NL:NY 2015	0	1
Cloninger, Tony NL:Cin. 1970	0	1
Coakley, Andy AL:Phil. 1905	0	1
Coates, Jim AL:NY 1962	0	1
Coke, Phil AL:Det. 2012	0	1
Cole, Gerrit AL:Hou. 2019	1	1
Colon, Bartolo NL:NY 2015	0	1
Cone, David AL:NY 1996, 99	2	0
Contreras, Jose AL:NY 2003 (0-1) AL:Chi. 2005 (1-0)	1	1
Cook, Aaron NL:Col. 2007	0	1
Cook, Dennis NL:Fla. 1997	1	0
Coombs, Jack AL:Phil. 1910-11 (4-0) NL:Brk. 1916 (1-0)	5	0
Cooper, Mort NL:StL. 1942-44	2	3
Corbin, Patrick NL:Wash. 2019	1	1
Cotts, Neal AL:Chi. 2005	1	0
Coveleski, Stan AL:Clev. 1920 (3-0) AL:Wash. 1925 (0-2)	3	2
Cox, Danny NL:StL. 1987	1	2
Craig, Roger NL:Brk./LA 1955-56, 59 (1-2) NL:StL. 1964 (1-0)	2	2
Crandall, Doc NL:NY 1911	1	0
Crawford, Steve AL:Bos. 1986	1	0
Crowder, General AL:Wash. 1933 (0-1) AL:Det. 1934-35 (1-1)	1	2
Cuellar, Mike AL:Balt. 1969-71	2	2
Cueto, Johnny AL:KC 2015	1	0
Curtiss, John AL:TB 2020	1	0
Daley, Bud AL:NY 1961	1	0
Darcy, Pat NL:Cin. 1975	0	1
Darling, Ron NL:NY 1986	1	1
Darvish, Yu NL:LA 2017	0	2
Davis, Curt NL:Brk. 1941	0	1
Davis, Storm AL:Balt. 1983 (1-0) AL:Oak. 1988 (0-2)	1	2
Dayley, Ken NL:StL. 1985	1	0
Dean, Dizzy NL:StL. 1934 (2-1) NL:Chi. 1938 (0-1)	2	2
Dean, Paul NL:StL. 1934	2	0
deGrom, Jacob NL:NY 2015	0	1
Demaree, Al NL:NY 1913	0	1
Denny, John NL:Phil. 1983	1	1
Derringer, Paul NL:StL. 1931 (0-2) NL:Cin. 1939-40 (2-2)	2	4
Devenski, Chris AL:Hou. 2017	1	0
Dibble, Rob NL:Cin. 1990	1	0
Dickson, Murry NL:StL. 1946	0	1
Dinneen, Bill AL:Bos. 1903	3	1
Ditmar, Art AL:NY 1960	0	2
Dobson, Joe AL:Bos. 1946	1	0
Donald, Atley AL:NY 1942	1	0
Donnelly, Blix NL:StL. 1944	1	0
Donnelly, Brendan AL:Ana. 2002	1	0
Donovan, Dick AL:Chi. 1959	0	1
Donovan, Wild Bill AL:Det. 1907-09	1	4
Dotel, Octavio NL:StL. 2011	0	1
Doubront, Felix AL:Bos. 2013	1	0
Douglas, Phil NL:Chi. 1918 (0-1) NL:NY 1921 (2-1)	2	2
Downing, Al AL:NY 1963-64 (0-2) NL:LA 1974 (0-1)	0	3
Drabowsky, Moe AL:Balt. 1966	1	0
Drago, Dick AL:Bos. 1975	0	1

PITCHER, CLUB, YEAR		W	L
Drysdale, Don NL:LA 1959, 63, 65-66		3	3
Duren, Ryne AL:NY 1958		1	1
Earnshaw, George AL:Phil. 1929-31		4	3
Eastwick, Rawly NL:Cin. 1975		2	0
Eckersley, Dennis AL:Oak. 1988, 90		0	2
Edwards, Carl Jr. NL:Chi. 2016		0	1
Ehmke, Howard AL:Phil. 1929		1	0
Eller, Hod NL:Cin. 1919		2	0
Ellis, Dock	NL:Pitt. 1971 (0-1)		
	AL:NY 1976 (0-1)	0	2
Eovaldi, Nathan AL:Bos. 2018		0	1
Erskine, Carl NL:Brk. 1952-53, 56		2	2
Faber, Red AL:Chi. 1917		3	1
Feller, Bob AL:Clev. 1948		0	2
Ferguson, Alex AL:Wash. 1925		1	1
Ferrick, Tom AL:NY 1950		1	0
Ferriss, Boo AL:Bos. 1946		1	0
Figueroa, Ed AL:NY 1976, 78		0	2
Fingers, Rollie AL:Oak. 1972-74		2	2
Finnegan, Brandon AL:KC 2014		0	1
Fisher, Ray NL:Cin. 1919		0	1
Fister, Doug AL:Det. 2012		0	1
Fitzsimmons, Freddie NL:NY 1933, 36		0	3
Flanagan, Mike AL:Balt. 1979		1	1
Floro, Dylan NL:LA 2018		0	1
Fogg, Josh NL:Col. 2007		0	1
Ford, Whitey AL:NY 1950, 53, 55-58, 60-64		10	8
Forsch, Bob NL:StL. 1982, 85, 87		1	3
Foster, Rube AL:Bos. 1915		2	0
Foulke, Keith AL:Bos. 2004		1	0
Francis, Jeff NL:Col. 2007		0	1
Franco, John NL:NY 2000		1	0
Frazier, George AL:NY 1981		0	3
French, Larry NL:Chi. 1935		0	2
Friend, Bob NL:Pitt. 1960		0	2
Gale, Rich AL:KC 1980		0	1
Galehouse, Denny AL:StL. 1944		1	1
Garcia, Freddy AL:Chi. 2005		1	0
Garcia, Mike AL:Clev. 1954		0	1
Garrelts, Scott NL:SF 1989		0	2
Gentry, Gary NL:NY 1969		1	0
Gibson, Bob NL:StL. 1964, 67-68		7	2
Giles, Ken AL:Hou. 2017		0	1
Glasnow, Tyler AL:TB 2020		0	2
Glavine, Tom NL:Atl. 1991-92, 95-96		4	3
Gomez, Lefty AL:NY 1932, 36-38		6	0
Gomez, Ruben NL:NY 1954		1	0
Gonsolin, Tony NL:LA 2020		0	1
Gonzalez, Victor NL:LA 2020		1	0
Gooden, Dwight NL:NY 1986		0	2
Gossage, Goose AL:NY 1978		1	0
Grant, Mudcat AL:Minn. 1965		2	1
Gregg, Hal NL:Brk. 1947		0	1
Grim, Bob AL:NY 1955, 57		0	2
Grimes, Burleigh	NL:Brk. 1920 (1-2)		
	NL:StL. 1930-31 (2-2)	3	4
Grimsley, Ross NL:Cin. 1972		2	1
Grissom, Marv NL:NY 1954		1	0
Gromek, Steve AL:Clev. 1948		1	0
Grove, Lefty AL:Phil. 1930-31		4	2
Guidry, Ron AL:NY 1977-78, 81		3	1
Gullett, Don	NL:Cin. 1975-76 (2-1)		
	AL:NY 1977 (0-1)	2	2
Guthrie, Jeremy AL:KC 2014		1	1
Guthrie, Mark AL:Minn. 1991		0	1
Guzman, Juan AL:Tor. 1993		0	1
Haddix, Harvey NL:Pitt. 1960		2	0
Hadley, Bump AL:NY 1936-37, 39		2	1
Haines, Jesse NL:StL. 1926, 28, 30		3	1
Hall, Dick AL:Balt. 1969		0	1
Hallahan, Bill NL:StL. 1930-31		3	1
Hamels, Cole NL:Phil. 2008-09		1	1
Hampton, Mike NL:NY 2000		0	1
Harris, Mickey AL:Bos. 1946		0	2
Harris, Will AL:Hou. 2019		0	1
Harrison, Matt AL:Tex. 2011		0	2
Hawkins, Andy NL:SD 1984		1	1
Hearn, Jim NL:NY 1951		1	0
Hentgen, Pat AL:Tor. 1993		1	0
Hernandez, Livan	NL:Fla. 1997 (2-0)		
	NL:SF 2002 (0-2)	2	2
Hernandez, Orlando AL:NY 1998-2000		2	1
Herrera, Kelvin AL:KC 2014		1	0
Hershiser, Orel	NL:LA 1988 (2-0)		
	AL:Clev. 1995, 97 (1-3)	3	3

PITCHER, CLUB, YEAR		W	L
Hill, Ken AL:Clev. 1995		0	1
Hitchcock, Sterling AL:NY 2001		1	0
Hochevar, Luke AL:KC 2015		1	0
Hoerner, Joe NL:StL. 1968		0	1
Hoffman, Trevor NL:SD 1998		0	1
Holland, Derek AL:Tex. 2011		1	0
Holtzman, Ken AL:Oak. 1972-74		4	1
Honeycutt, Rick AL:Oak. 1988		1	0
Hooton, Burt NL:LA 1977-78		3	3
Howe, Steve NL:LA 1981		1	0
Howell, Jay NL:LA 1988		0	1
Howell, J.P. AL:TB 2008		0	2
Hoyt, Waite	AL:NY 1921-22, 26-28 (6-3)		
	AL:Phil. 1931 (0-1)	6	4
Hubbell, Carl NL:NY 1933, 36-37		4	2
Hudson, Charles NL:Phil. 1983		0	2
Hudson, Tim NL:SF 2014		0	1
Hughes, Dick NL:StL. 1967		0	1
Hughes, Long Tom AL:Bos. 1903		0	1
Hughson, Tex AL:Bos. 1946		0	1
Hunter, Catfish	AL:Oak. 1972-74 (4-0)		
	AL:NY 1976-78 (1-3)	5	3
Hunter, Tommy AL:Tex. 2010		0	1
Hurst, Bruce AL:Bos. 1986		2	0
Jackson, Danny	AL:KC 1985 (1-1)		
	NL:Phil. 1993 (0-1)	1	2
Jackson, Edwin NL:StL. 2011		0	1
Jackson, Grant NL:Pitt. 1979		1	0
Jakucki, Sig AL:StL. 1944		0	1
James, Bill NL:Bos. 1914		2	0
James, Josh AL:Hou. 2019		0	1
Jansen, Kenley NL:LA 2017, 20		0	2
Jansen, Larry NL:NY 1951		0	2
Jay, Joey NL:Cin. 1961		1	1
Jimenez, Ubaldo NL:Col. 2007		0	1
John, Tommy	NL:LA 1977-78 (1-1)		
	AL:NY 1981 (1-0)	2	1
Johnson, Bob NL:Pitt. 1971		0	1
Johnson, Earl AL:Bos. 1946		1	0
Johnson, Ernie NL:Mil. 1957		0	0
Johnson, Randy NL:Ari. 2001		3	0
Johnson, Syl NL:StL. 1931		0	1
Johnson, Walter AL:Wash. 1924-25		3	3
Jones, Bobby J. NL:NY 2000		0	1
Jones, Sam	AL:Bos. 1918 (0-1)		
	AL:NY 1923 (0-1)	0	2
Kaat, Jim AL:Minn. 1965		1	2
Kazmir, Scott AL:TB 2008		0	1
Kelly, Joe AL:Bos. 2018		1	0
Kennedy, Brickyard NL:Pitt. 1903		0	1
Kerr, Dickie AL:Chi. 1919		2	0
Kershaw, Clayton NL:LA 2017-18, 20		3	2
Keuchel, Dallas AL:Hou. 2017		0	1
Key, Jimmy	AL:Tor. 1992 (2-0)		
	AL:NY 1996 (1-1)	3	1
Kim, Byung-Hyun NL:Ari. 2001		0	1
Kison, Bruce NL:Pitt. 1971, 79		1	1
Klinger, Bob AL:Bos. 1946		0	1
Kluber, Corey AL:Clev. 2016		2	0
Konstanty, Jim NL:Phil. 1950		0	1
Koosman, Jerry NL:NY 1969, 73		3	0
Koslo, Dave NL:NY 1951		1	1
Koufax, Sandy NL:LA 1959, 63, 65-66		4	3
Kramer, Jack AL:StL. 1944		1	0
Kremer, Ray NL:Pitt. 1925, 27		2	2
Kucks, Johnny AL:NY 1956		1	0
Labine, Clem NL:Brk. 1953, 55-56		2	2
Lackey, John	AL:Ana. 2002 (1-0)		
	AL:Bos. 2013 (1-1)		
	NL:Chi. 2016 (0-1)	2	2
Lamabe, Jack NL:StL. 1967		0	1
Lanier, Max NL:StL. 1942-44		2	1
Larsen, Don	AL:NY 1955-58 (3-2)		
	NL:SF 1962 (1-0)	4	2
Law, Vern NL:Pitt. 1960		2	0
Lee, Bill NL:Chi. 1938		0	2
Lee, Cliff	NL:Phil.2009 (2-0)		
	AL:Tex. 2010 (0-2)	2	2
Leever, Sam NL:Pitt. 1903		0	2
Leibrandt, Charlie	AL:KC 1985 (0-1)		
	NL:Atl. 1991-92 (0-3)	0	4
Leifield, Lefty NL:Pitt. 1909		0	1
Leiter, Al	AL:Tor. 1993 (1-0)		
	NL:NY 2000 (0-1)	1	1
Lemon, Bob AL:Clev. 1948, 54		2	2

PITCHER, CLUB, YEAR		W	L
Leonard, Dennis AL:KC 1980		1	1
Leonard, Dutch AL:Bos. 1915-16		2	0
Lester, Jon	AL:Bos. 2007, 13 (3-0)		
	NL:Chi. 2016 (1-1)	4	1
Lewis, Colby AL:Tex. 2010		1	0
Liddle, Don NL:NY 1954		1	0
Lidge, Brad	NL:Hou. 2005 (0-2)		
	NL:Phil. 2009 (0-1)	0	3
Lincecum, Tim NL:SF 2010		2	0
Lindblad, Paul AL:Oak. 1973		1	0
Lloyd, Graeme AL:NY 1996		1	0
Loes, Billy NL:Brk. 1952-53, 55		1	2
Lolich, Mickey AL:Det. 1968		3	0
Lollar, Tim NL:SD 1984		0	1
Lombardi, Vic NL:Brk. 1947		0	1
Lonborg, Jim AL:Bos. 1967		2	1
Looper, Braden NL:Fla. 2003		1	0
Lopat, Ed AL:NY 1949, 51-53		4	1
Lopez, Albie NL:Ari. 2001		0	1
Lopez, Aurelio AL:Det. 1984		1	0
Lowe, Derek AL:Bos. 2004		1	0
Lowe, Mark AL:Tex. 2011		0	1
Luque, Dolf NL:NY 1933		1	0
Lyle, Sparky AL:NY 1977		1	0
Lynn, Lance NL:StL. 2011, 13		1	1
Maddox, Nick NL:Pitt. 1909		1	0
Maddux, Greg NL:Atl. 1995-96, 99		2	3
Madson, Ryan AL:KC 2015		1	0
Maglie, Sal	NL:NY 1951 (0-1)		
	NL:Brk. 1956 (1-1)	1	2
Magrane, Joe NL:StL. 1987		0	1
Mails, Duster AL:Clev. 1920		1	0
Malone, Pat	NL:Chi. 1929 (0-2)		
	AL:NY 1936 (0-1)	0	3
Marberry, Firpo AL:Wash. 1924		0	1
Marquard, Rube	NL:NY 1911-13 (2-2)		
	NL:Brk. 1916, 20 (0-3)	2	5
Marquis, Jason NL:StL. 2004		0	1
Marshall, Mike NL:LA 1974		0	1
Marte, Damaso AL:Chi. 2005		1	0
Martinez, Dennis AL:Clev. 1995		0	1
Martinez, Pedro	AL:Bos. 2004 (1-0)		
	NL:Phil. 2009 (0-2)	1	2
Mathewson, Christy NL:NY 1905, 11-13		5	5
Matlack, Jon NL:NY 1973		1	2
Matsuzaka, Daisuke AL:Bos. 2007		1	0
May, Jakie NL:Chi. 1932		0	1
Mayer, Erskine NL:Phil. 1915		0	1
Mays, Carl	AL:Bos. 1916, 18 (2-1)		
	AL:NY 1921-22 (1-3)	3	4
McCarthy, Brandon NL:LA 2017		0	1
McClure, Bob AL:Mil. 1982		0	2
McCullers, Lance Jr. AL:Hou. 2017		1	0
McDonald, Jim AL:NY 1953		1	0
McDowell, Roger NL:NY 1986		1	0
McGinnity, Joe NL:NY 1905		1	1
McGraw, Tug	NL:NY 1973 (1-0)		
	NL:Phil. 1980 (1-1)	2	1
McGregor, Scott AL:Balt. 1979, 83		2	2
McIntire, Harry NL:Chi. 1910		0	1
McLain, Denny AL, Det. 1968		1	2
McNally, Dave AL:Balt. 1966, 69-71		4	2
McQuillan, Hugh NL:NY 1922-24		2	1
Meadow, Lee NL:Pitt. 1925, 27		0	2
Melton, Cliff NL:NY 1937		0	2
Mendoza, Ramiro AL:NY 1998		1	0
Merritt, Jim NL:Cin. 1970		0	1
Mesa, Jose AL:Clev. 1995		1	0
Messersmith, Andy NL:LA 1974		0	2
Meyer, Russ NL:Phil. 1950		0	1
Mikkelsen, Pete AL:NY 1964		0	1
Miljus, Johnny NL:Pitt. 1927		0	1
Miller, Andrew AL:Clev. 2016		1	0
Miller, Bob J. NL:Phil. 1950		0	1
Miller, Bob L. NL:Pitt. 1971		0	1
Millwood, Kevin NL:Atl. 1999		0	1
Mizell, Vinegar Bend NL:Pitt. 1960		0	1
Mogridge, George AL:Wash. 1924		1	0
Moore, Mike AL:Oak. 1989-90		2	1
Moore, Wilcy AL:NY 1927, 32		2	0
Morgan, Tom AL:NY 1956		0	1
Morris, Jack	AL:Det. 1984 (2-0)		
	AL:Minn. 1991 (2-0)		
	AL:Tor. 1992 (0-2)	4	2
Morris, Matt NL:StL. 2004		0	1

PITCHER, CLUB, YEAR		W	L
Morton, Charlie	AL:Hou. 2017 (1-0)		
	AL:TB 2020 (0-1)	1	1
Morton, Charlie AL:Hou. 2017			
Motte, Jason NL:StL. 2011		0	1
Mulholland, Terry NL:Phil. 1993		1	0
Mullin, George AL:Det. 1907-09		3	3
Muncrief, Bob AL:StL. 1944		0	1
Munger, George NL:StL. 1946		1	0
Murphy, Johnny AL:NY 1939, 41		2	0
Musgrove, Joe AL:Hou. 2017		1	0
Mussina, Mike AL:NY 2001, 03		1	1
Myers, Brett NL:Phil. 2008		0	1
Nagy, Charles AL:Clev. 1997		0	1
Nehf, Art NL:NY 1921-24		4	4
Nelson, Jeff AL:NY 2000		1	0
Newcombe, Don NL:Brk. 1949, 55-56		0	4
Newhouser, Hal AL:Det. 1945		2	1
Newsom, Bobo	AL:Det. 1940 (2-1)		
	AL:NY 1947 (0-1)	2	2
Nipper, Al AL:Bos. 1986		0	1
Nolan, Gary NL:Cin. 1970, 72, 76		1	2
Norman, Fred NL:Cin. 1975		0	1
O'Brien, Buck AL:Bos. 1912		0	2
O'Dell, Billy NL:SF 1962		0	1
Odom, Blue Moon AL:Oak. 1972, 74		1	1
Ogea, Chad AL:Clev. 1997		2	0
Ojeda, Bob NL:NY 1986		1	0
Oliver, Darren AL:Tex. 2011		1	0
Ortiz, Ramon AL:Ana. 2002		1	0
Osteen, Claude NL:LA 1965-66		1	2
O'Toole, Jim NL:Cin. 1961		0	2
Overall, Orval NL:Chi. 1907-08, 10		3	1
Overmire, Stubby AL:Det. 1945		0	1
Page, Joe AL:NY 1947, 49		2	1
Palmer, Jim AL:Balt. 1969-71, 79, 83		4	2
Parker, Harry NL:NY 1973		0	1
Pascual, Camilo AL:Minn. 1965		0	1
Passeau, Claude NL:Chi. 1945		1	0
Pearson, Monte AL:NY 1936-39		4	0
Peavy, Jake NL:SF 2014		0	2
Pena, Alejandro	NL:LA 1988 (1-0)		
	NL:Atl. 1991, 95 (0-2)	1	2
Pennock, Herb AL:NY 1923, 26-27		5	0
Penny, Brad NL:Fla. 2003		2	0
Petit, Yusmeiro NL:SF 2014		1	0
Petry, Dan AL:Det. 1984		0	1
Pettitte, Andy AL:NY 1996, 98, 2001, 03, 09		5	4
Pfeffer, Jeff NL:Brk. 1916		0	1
Pfiester, Jack NL:Chi. 1906-08		1	3
Phillippe, Deacon NL:Pitt. 1903		3	2
Phoebus, Tom AL:Balt. 1970		1	0
Pierce, Billy NL:SF 1962		1	1
Pipgras, George AL:NY 1927-28, 32		3	0
Plank, Eddie AL:Phil. 1905, 11, 13-14		2	5
Plunk, Eric AL:Clev. 1997		0	1
Podres, Johnny NL:Brk./LA 1953, 55, 59, 63		4	1
Pollet, Howie NL:StL. 1946		0	1
Poole, Jim AL:Clev. 1995		0	1
Potter, Nels AL:StL. 1944		0	1
Powell, Jay NL:Fla. 1997		1	0
Price, David AL:Bos. 2018		2	0
Prim, Ray NL:Chi. 1945		0	1
Purkey, Bob NL:Cin. 1961		0	1
Quinn, Jack AL:NY 1921		0	1
Quisenberry, Dan AL:KC 1980, 85		2	2
Raschi, Vic AL:NY 1949-53		5	3
Rau, Doug NL:LA 1977		0	1
Reardon, Jeff NL:Atl. 1992		0	1
Redman, Mark NL:Fla. 2003		0	1
Reed, Addison NL:NY 2015		0	1
Reinhart, Art NL:StL. 1926		0	1
Remlinger, Mike NL:Atl. 1999		0	1
Reulbach, Ed NL:Chi. 1906-07		2	0
Reuschel, Rick NL:SF 1989		0	1
Reuss, Jerry NL:LA 1981		1	1
Reyes, Anthony NL:StL. 2006		1	0
Reynolds, Allie AL:NY 1947, 49-53		7	2
Rhem, Flint NL:StL. 1930		0	1
Rhoden, Rick NL:LA 1977		0	1
Rijo, Jose NL:Cin. 1990		2	0
Ring, Jimmy NL:Cin. 1919		1	1
Rivera, Mariano AL:NY 1999, 2001		2	1
Rixey, Eppa NL:Phil. 1915		0	1
Roberts, Robin, NL:Phil. 1950		0	1
Robertson, Nate AL:Det. 2006		0	1

PITCHER, CLUB, YEAR	W	L
Robinson, Don NL:Pitt. 1979 (1-0)		
NL:SF 1989 (0-1)	1	1
Rodriguez, Felix NL:SF 2002	0	1
Rodriguez, Francisco AL:Ana. 2002	1	1
Rodriguez, Wandy NL:Hou. 2005	0	1
Roe, Preacher NL:Brk. 1949, 52-53	2	1
Rogers, Kenny AL:Det. 2006	1	0
Romero, J.C. NL:Phil. 2008	2	0
Rommel, Eddie AL:Phil. 1929	1	0
Root, Charlie NL:Chi. 1929, 32, 35	0	3
Rosenthal, Trevor NL:StL. 2013	1	0
Ross, Joe NL:Wash. 2019	0	1
Rowe, Schoolboy AL:Det. 1934-35, 40	2	5
Rudolph, Dick NL:Bos. 1914	2	0
Ruether, Dutch NL:Cin. 1919 (1-0)		
AL:NY 1926 (0-1)	1	1
Ruffing, Red AL:NY 1932, 36-39, 41-42	7	2
Rush, Bob NL:Mil. 1958	0	1
Russell, Jack AL:Wash. 1933	0	1
Russo, Marius AL:NY 1941, 43	2	0
Ruth, Babe AL:Bos. 1916, 18	3	0
Ryan, Rosy NL:NY 1922-23	2	0
Ryu, Hyun-Jin NL:LA 2018	0	1
Sabathia, CC AL:NY 2009	0	1
Saberhagen, Bret AL:KC 1985	2	0
Sadecki, Ray NL:StL. 1964	1	0
Sain, Johnny NL:Bos. 1948 (1-1)		
AL:NY 1952-53 (1-1)	2	2
Sallee, Slim NL:NY 1917 (0-2)		
NL:Cin. 1919 (1-1)	1	3
Sanchez, Anibal AL:Det. 2012 (0-1)		
NL:Wash. 2019 (0-1)	0	2
Sanchez, Jonathan NL:SF 2010	0	1
Sanford, Jack NL:SF 1962	1	2
Santiago, Jose AL:Bos. 1967	0	2
Saunders, Tony NL:Fla. 1997	0	1
Schatzeder, Dan AL:Minn. 1987	1	0
Scherzer, Max NL:Wash. 2019	1	0
Schilling, Curt NL:Phil. 1993 (1-1)		
NL:Ari. 2001 (1-0)		
AL:Bos. 2004, 07 (2-0)	4	1
Schiraldi, Calvin AL:Bos. 1986	0	2
Schmidt, Jason NL:SF 2002	1	0
Schultz, Barney NL:StL. 1964	0	1
Schumacher, Hal NL:NY 1933, 36-37	2	2
Schupp, Ferdie NL:NY 1917	1	0
Scott, Jack NL:NY 1922-23	1	1
Seaver, Tom NL:NY 1969, 73	1	2
Shantz, Bobby AL:NY 1957	0	1
Shaw, Bob AL:Chi. 1959	1	1
Shaw, Bryan AL:Clev. 2016	0	1
Shawkey, Bob AL:Phil. 1914 (0-1)		
AL:NY 1921, 23, 26 (1-2)	1	3
Shea, Spec AL:NY 1947	2	0
Sherdel, Bill NL:StL. 1926, 28	0	4
Sherry, Larry NL:LA 1959	2	0
Shields, James AL:TB 2008 (1-0)		
AL:KC 2014 (0-2)	1	2
Shocker, Urban AL:NY 1926	0	1
Shore, Ernie AL:Bos. 1915-16	3	1
Show, Eric NL:SD 1984	0	1
Siever, Ed AL:Det. 1907	0	1
Simmons, Curt NL:StL. 1964	0	1
Slaton, Jim AL:Mil. 1982	1	0
Smith, Sherry NL:Brk. 1916, 20	1	2
Smoltz, John NL:Atl. 1992, 96, 99	2	2
Sonnanstine, Andy AL:TB 2008	0	1
Spahn, Warren NL:Bos/Mil. 1948, 57-58	4	3
Spooner, Karl NL:Brk. 1955	0	1
Stafford, Bill AL:NY 1962	1	0
Staley, Gerry AL:Chi. 1959	0	1
Stanhouse, Don AL:Balt. 1979	0	1
Stanton, Mike NL Atl. 1991 (1-0)		
AL:NY 2000 (2-0)	3	0
Stewart, Dave AL:Oak. 1988-90 (2-3)		
AL:Tor. 1993 (0-1)	2	4
Stewart, Lefty AL:Wash. 1933	0	1
Stoddard, Tim AL:Balt. 1979	1	0
Stottlemyre, Mel AL:NY 1964	1	1
Strasburg, Stephen NL:Wash. 2019	2	0
Stuper, John NL:StL. 1982	1	0
Sturdivant, Tom AL:NY 1956	1	0
Summers, Ed AL:Det. 1908-09	0	4
Suppan, Jeff NL:StL. 2004	0	1
Sutter, Bruce NL:StL. 1982	1	0

PITCHER, CLUB, YEAR	W	L
Sutton, Don NL:LA 1974, 77-78 (2-2)		
AL:Mil. 1982 (0-1)	2	3
Syndergaard, Noah NL:NY 2015	1	0
Tapani, Kevin AL:Minn. 1991	1	1
Tavarez, Julian NL:StL. 2004	0	1
Tekulve, Kent NL:Pitt. 1979	0	1
Terry, Ralph AL:NY 1960-62	2	4
Tesreau, Jeff NL:NY 1912-13	1	3
Thompson, Junior NL:Cin. 1939-40	0	2
Thurmond, Mark NL:SD 1984	0	1
Tiant, Luis AL:Bos. 1975	2	0
Tomlin, Josh AL:Clev. 2016	0	1
Torrez, Mike AL:NY 1977	2	0
Trout, Dizzy AL:Det. 1940, 45	1	2
Trucks, Virgil AL:Det. 1945	1	0
Tudor, John NL:StL. 1985, 87	3	2
Turley, Bob AL:NY 1955, 58, 60	4	3
Turner, Jim NL:Cin. 1940	0	1
Tyler, Lefty NL:Chi. 1918	1	1
Urquidy, Jose AL:Hou. 2019	1	0
Valenzuela, Fernando NL:LA 1981	1	0
Vaughn, Hippo NL:Chi. 1918	1	2
Ventura, Yordano AL:KC 2014-15	1	1
Verlander, Justin AL:Det. 2006, 12 (0-3)		
AL:Hou. 2017, 19 (0-3)	0	6
Viola, Frank AL:Minn. 1987	2	1
Vogelsong, Ryan NL:SF 2012	1	0
Voiselle, Bill NL:Bos. 1948	0	1
Vuckovich, Pete AL:Mil. 1982	0	1
Wacha, Michael NL:StL. 2013	1	1
Wainwright, Adam NL:StL. 2006, 13	1	2
Walberg, Rube AL:Phil. 1929-30	1	1
Walk, Bob NL:Phil. 1980	1	0
Walker, Bill NL:StL. 1934	0	2
Wall, Donne NL:SD 1998	0	1
Walsh, Ed AL:Chi. 1906	2	0
Walters, Bucky NL:Cin. 1939-40	2	2
Ward, Duane AL:Tor. 1992-93	3	0
Warneke, Lon NL:Chi. 1932, 35	2	1
Washburn, Jarrod AL:Ana. 2002	0	2
Washburn, Ray NL:StL. 1968	1	1
Watson, Tony NL:LA 2017	2	0
Watt, Eddie AL:Balt. 1969-71	0	3
Weaver, Jeff AL:NY. 2003 (0-1)		
NL:StL. 2006 (1-1)	1	2
Weaver, Monte AL:Wash. 1933	0	1
Welch, Bob NL:LA 1978	0	1
Wells, David AL:NY 1998, 2003	1	1
Wendell, Turk NL:NY 2000	0	1
Westbrook, Jake NL:StL. 2011	1	0
White, Doc AL:Chi. 1906	1	1
White, Ernie NL:StL. 1942	1	0
Whitehill, Earl AL:Wash. 1933	1	0
Wilcox, Milt NL:Cin. 1970 (0-1)		
AL:Det. 1984 (1-0)	1	1
Wilks, Ted NL:StL. 1944	0	1
Williams, Lefty AL:Chi. 1919	0	3
Williams, Mitch NL:Phil. 1993	0	2
Willis, Vic NL:Pitt. 1909	0	1
Willoughby, Jim AL:Bos. 1975	0	1
Wilson, C.J. AL:Tex. 2010-11	0	2
Wilson, Earl AL:Det. 1968	1	1
Wise, Rick AL:Bos. 1975	1	0
Wood, Alex NL:LA 2018	1	0
Wood, Smoky Joe AL:Bos. 1912	3	1
Workman, Brandon AL:Bos. 2013	1	0
Worrell, Tim NL:SF 2002	1	1
Worrell, Todd NL:StL. 1985	0	1
Wright, Jaret NL:Clev. 1997	1	0
Wyatt, John AL:Bos. 1967	1	0
Wyatt, Whitlow NL:Brk. 1941	1	1
Wynn, Early AL:Clev. 1954 (0-1)		
AL:Chi. 1959 (1-1)	1	2
Wyse, Hank NL:Chi. 1945	0	1
Yde, Emil NL:Pitt. 1925	0	1
Young, Chris AL:KC 2015	1	0
Young, Cy AL:Bos. 1903	2	1
Zachary, Tom AL:Wash. 1924 (2-0)		
AL:NY 1928 (1-0)	3	0
Zachry, Pat NL:Cin. 1976	1	0
Zerbe, Chad NL:SF 2002	1	0
Zito, Barry NL:SF 2012	1	0
Zumaya, Joel AL:Det. 2006	0	1

AMERICAN LEAGUE WORLD SERIES MANAGERS

	SERIES			GAMES		YEARS	
	No.	**Won**	**Lost**	**Won**	**Lost**	**Won**	**Lost**
Altobelli, Joe Balt.	1	1	0	4	1	1983	
*Anderson, Sparky Det.	1	1	0	4	1	1984	
Baker, Del Det.	1	0	1	3	4		1940
Barrow, Ed Bos.	1	1	0	4	2	1918	
Bauer, Hank Balt.	1	1	0	4	0	1966	
*Berra, Yogi NY	1	0	1	3	4		1964
Boudreau, Lou Clev.	1	1	0	4	2	1948	
Carrigan, Bill Bos.	2	2	0	8	2	1915-16	
Cash, Kevin TB	1	0	1	2	4		2020
Cochrane, Mickey Det.	2	1	1	7	6	1935	1934
Collins, Jimmy Bos.	1	1	0	5	3	1903	
Cora, Alex, Bos.	1	1	0	4	1	2018	
Cronin, Joe Wash.	1	0	1	1	4		1933
Bos.	1	0	1	3	4		1946
Totals	(2)	(0)	(2)	(4)	(8)		
*Dark, Alvin Oak.	1	1	0	4	1	1974	
Farrell, John Bos.	1	1	0	4	2	2013	
Francona, Terry Bos.	2	2	0	8	0	2004, 07	
Clev.	1	0	1	3	4		2016
Totals	(3)	(2)	(1)	(11)	(4)		
Frey, Jim KC	1	0	1	2	4		1980
Gaston, Cito Tor.	2	2	0	8	4	1992-93	
Girardi, Joe NY	1	1	0	4	2	2009	
Gleason, Kid Chi.	1	0	1	3	5		1919
Guillen, Ozzie Chi.	1	1	0	4	0	2005	
Hargrove, Mike Clev.	2	0	2	5	8		1995, 97
Harris, Bucky Wash.	2	1	1	7	7	1924	1925
NY	1	1	0	4	3	1947	
Totals	(3)	(2)	(1)	(11)	(10)		
Hinch, A.J. Hou.	2	1	1	7	7	2017	2019
Houk, Ralph NY	3	2	1	8	8	1961-62	1963
Howser, Dick KC	1	1	0	4	3	1985	
Huggins, Miller NY	6	3	3	18	15	1923, 27-28	1921-22, 26
Jennings, Hughie Det.	3	0	3	4	12		1907-09
Johnson, Darrell Bos.	1	0	1	3	4		1975
Jones, Fielder Chi.	1	1	0	4	2	1906	
Kelly, Tom Minn.	2	2	0	8	6	1987, 91	
Kuenn, Harvey Mil.	1	0	1	3	4		1982
*LaRussa, Tony Oak.	3	1	2	5	8	1989	1988, 90
Lemon, Bob NY	2	1	1	6	6	1978	1981
*Leyland, Jim Det.	2	0	2	1	8		2006, 12
Lopez, Al Clev.	1	0	1	0	4		1954
Chi.	1	0	1	2	4		1959
Totals	(2)	(0)	(2)	(2)	(8)		
Mack, Connie Phil.	8	5	3	24	19	1910-11, 13, 29-30	1905, 14, 31
*Maddon, Joe TB	1	0	1	1	4		2008
Martin, Billy NY	2	1	1	4	6	1977	1976
*McCarthy, Joe NY	8	7	1	29	9	1932, 36-39, 41, 43	1942
McNamara, John Bos.	1	0	1	3	4		1986
Mele, Sam Minn.	1	0	1	3	4		1965
O'Neill, Steve Det.	1	1	0	4	3	1945	
Rowland, Pants Chi.	1	1	0	4	3	1917	
Scioscia, Mike Ana.	1	1	0	4	3	2002	
Sewell, Luke StL.	1	0	1	2	4		1944
Smith, Mayo Det.	1	1	0	4	3	1968	
Speaker, Tris Clev.	1	1	0	5	2	1920	
Stahl, Jake Bos.	1	1	0	4	3	1912	
Stengel, Casey NY	10	7	3	37	26	1949-53, 56, 58	1955, 57, 60
Torre, Joe NY	6	4	2	21	11	1996, 98-2000	2001, 03
Washington, Ron Tex.	2	0	2	4	8		2010-11
Weaver, Earl Balt.	4	1	3	11	13	1970	1969, 71, 79
*Williams, Dick Bos.	1	0	1	3	4		1967
Oak.	2	2	0	8	6	1972-73	
A.L. Totals	(3)	(2)	(1)	(11)	(10)		
Yost, Ned KC	2	1	1	7	5	2015	2014

* Also managed in the World Series for the National League (see next page)

NATIONAL LEAGUE WORLD SERIES MANAGERS

	SERIES			GAMES		YEARS	
	No.	Won	Lost	Won	Lost	Won	Lost
Alston, Walter Brk./LA	7	4	3	20	20	1955, 59, 63, 65	1956, 66, 74
*Anderson, Sparky Cin.	4	2	2	12	11	1975-76	1970, 72
Baker, Dusty SF	1	0	1	3	4		2002
*Berra, Yogi NY	1	0	1	3	4		1973
Bochy, Bruce SD	1	0	1	0	4		1998
SF	3	3	0	12	4	2010, 12, 14	
Totals	4	3	1	12	8		
Brenly, Bob Ari.	1	1	0	4	3	2001	
Bush, Donie Pitt.	1	0	1	0	4		1927
Chance, Frank Chi.	4	2	2	11	9	1907-08	1906, 10
Clarke, Fred Pitt.	2	1	1	7	8	1909	1903
Collins, Terry NY	1	0	1	1	4		2015
Cox, Bobby Atl.	5	1	4	11	18	1995	1991-92, 96, 99
Craig, Roger SF	1	0	1	0	4		1989
*Dark, Alvin SF	1	0	1	3	4		1962
Dressen, Chuck Brk.	2	0	2	5	8		1952-53
Durocher, Leo Brk.	1	0	1	1	4		1941
NY	2	1	1	6	4	1954	1951
Totals	(3)	(1)	(2)	(7)	(8)		
Dyer, Eddie StL.	1	1	0	4	3	1946	
Fregosi, Jim Phil.	1	0	1	2	4		1993
Frisch, Frankie StL.	1	1	0	4	3	1934	
Garner, Phil Hou.	1	0	1	0	4		2005
Green, Dallas Phil.	1	1	0	4	2	1980	
Grimm, Charlie Chi.	3	0	3	5	12		1932, 35, 45
Haney, Fred Mil.	2	1	1	7	7	1957	1958
Hartnett, Gabby Chi.	1	0	1	0	4		1938
Herzog, Whitey StL.	3	1	2	10	11	1982	1985, 87
Hodges, Gil NY	1	1	0	4	1	1969	
Hornsby, Rogers StL.	1	1	0	4	3	1926	
Hurdle, Clint Col.	1	0	1	0	4		2007
Hutchinson, Fred Cin.	1	0	1	1	4		1961
Johnson, Davey NY	1	1	0	4	3	1986	
Keane, Johnny StL.	1	1	0	4	3	1964	
*LaRussa, Tony, StL.	3	2	1	8	8	2006, 11	2004
Lasorda, Tommy LA	4	2	2	12	11	1981, 88	1977-78
*Leyland, Jim Fla.	1	1	0	4	3	1997	
*Maddon, Joe Chi.	1	1	0	4	3	2016	
Martinez, Dave Wash.	1	1	0	4	3	2019	
Matheny, Mike StL.	1	0	1	2	4		2013
Manuel, Charlie Phil.	2	1	1	6	5	2008	2009
*McCarthy, Joe Chi.	1	0	1	1	4		1929
McGraw, John NY	9	3	6	26	28	1905, 21-22	1911-13, 17, 23-24
McKeon, Jack Fla.	1	1	0	4	2	2003	
McKechnie, Bill Pitt.	1	1	0	4	3	1925	
Cin.	2	1	1	4	7	1940	1939
StL.	1	0	1	0	4		1928
Totals	(4)	(2)	(2)	(8)	(14)		
Mitchell, Fred Chi.	1	0	1	2	4		1918
Moran, Pat Phil.	1	0	1	1	4		1915
Cin.	1	1	0	5	3	1919	
Totals	(2)	(1)	(1)	(6)	(7)		
Murtaugh, Danny Pitt.	2	2	0	8	6	1960, 71	
Owens, Paul Phil.	1	0	1	1	4		1983
Piniella, Lou Cin.	1	1	0	4	0	1990	
Roberts, Dave LA	3	1	2	8	10	2020	2017-18
Robinson, Wilbert Brk.	2	0	2	3	9		1916, 20
Sawyer, Eddie Phil.	1	0	1	0	4		1950
Schoendienst, Red StL.	2	1	1	7	7	1967	1968
Shotton, Burt Brk.	2	0	2	4	8		1947, 49
Southworth, Billy StL.	3	2	1	9	7	1942, 44	1943
Bos.	1	0	1	2	4		1948
Totals	(4)	(2)	(2)	(11)	(11)		
Stallings, George Bos.	1	1	0	4	0	1914	
Street, Gabby StL.	2	1	1	6	7	1931	1930
Tanner, Chuck Pitt.	1	1	0	4	3	1979	
Terry, Bill NY	3	1	2	7	9	1933	1936-37
Valentine, Bobby NY	1	0	1	1	4		2000
*Williams, Dick SD	1	0	1	1	4		1984

* Also managed in the World Series for the American League (see previous page)

World Series Umpires

Ashford, Emmett 1970
Ballanfant, Lee 1940, 46, 51, 55
Barksdale, Lance 2019
Barlick, Al 1946, 50, 51, 54, 58, 62, 67
Barnett, Larry 1975, 81, 84, 90
Barr, George 1937, 42, 48-49
Barrett, Ted 2007, 11, 14, 18
Basil, Steve. 1937, 40
Bell, Wally 2006
Berry, Charlie 1946, 50, 54, 58, 62
Boggess, Dusty 1940, 52, 56, 60
Boyer, Jim 1947
Brémigan, Nick 1980
Brennan, Bill 1911
Brinkman, Joe 1978, 86, 95
Burkhart, Ken 1962, 64, 70
Byron, Bill 1914
Carlson, Mark 2015, 20
Cederstrom, Gary 2005, 11, 15, 19
Chill, Ollie 1921
Chylak, Nestor 1957, 60, 66, 71, 77
Clark, Al 1983, 89
Coble, Drew 1991
Colosi, Nick 1975, 81
Conlan, Jocko 1945, 50, 54, 57, 61
Connolly, Tom 1903, 08, 10-11, 13, 16, 20, 24
Cooney, Terry 1981
Cooper, Eric 2014
Cousins, Derryl 1988, 99, 2005
Crawford, Jerry 1988, 92, 98, 2000, 02
Crawford, Shag 1961, 63, 69
Culbreth, Fieldin 2008, 12, 18
Cuzzi, Phil 2017
Dale, Jerry 1977
Danley, Kerwin 2008, 18
Darling, Gary 2003, 10
Dascoli, Frank 1953, 55, 59
Davidson, Satch 1975, 82
Davidson, Bob 1992
Davis, Gerry 1996, 99, 2004, 09, 12, 17
Deegan, Bill 1976
DeMuth, Dana 1993, 98, 2001, 09, 13
Denkinger, Don 1974, 80, 85, 91
Diaz, Laz 2007, 17, 20
DiMuro, Lou 1969, 76
Dinneen, Bill 1911, 14, 16, 20, 26, 29, 32
Dixon, Hal 1959
Donatelli, Augie 1955, 57, 61, 67, 73
Drummond, Cal 1966
Dunn, Tom 1944
Eddings, Doug 2019
Egan, Rip 1913
Emmel, Paul 2013
Engel, Bob 1972, 79, 85
Evans, Jim 1977, 82, 86, 96
Evans, Billy 1909, 12, 15, 17, 19, 23
Everitt, Mike 2007, 09, 15
Fairchild, Chad 2018
Flaherty, Red 1955, 58, 65, 70
Ford, Dale 1986, 97
Frantz, Art 1975
Froemming, Bruce 1976, 84, 88, 95
Garcia, Rich 1981, 84, 89, 98
Geisel, Harry 1930, 34, 36
Gibson, Greg 2011
Goetz, Larry 1941, 47, 52
Goetz, Russ 1973, 79
Gore, Artie 1951, 53
Gorman, Brian 2004, 09, 12
Gorman, Tom 1956, 58, 63, 68, 74, 12
Gregg, Eric 1989
Grieve, Bill 1941, 48, 53
Guccione, Chris 2016, 20
Haller, Bill 1968, 72, 78, 82
Hallion, Tim 2008
Hart, Bob 1923
Harvey, Doug 1968, 74, 81, 84, 88
Hendry, Ted 1965
Hernandez, Angel 2002, 05
Hildebrand, George 1914, 18, 22, 26
Hirschbeck, John 1995, 2006, 10, 13, 16
Hirschbeck, Mark 1998, 2001
Holbrook, Sam 2010, 16, 19
Honochick, Jim 1952, 55, 60, 62, 68, 72
Hoye, James 2019
Hubbard, Cal 1938, 42, 46, 49
Hudson, Marvin 2016, 20
Hurley, Ed 1949, 53, 59, 65
Iassogna, Dan 2012, 17
Jackowski, Bill 1958, 60, 66
Johnson, Mark 1993
Johnstone, Jim 1906, 09
Jorda, Lou 1945, 49
Joyce, Jim 1999, 2001, 13
Kaiser, Ken 1987, 97
Kellogg, Jeff 2000, 03, 08, 10, 14
Kibler, John 1971, 78, 82, 86
Kinnamon, Bill 1968
Klem, Bill 1908-09, 11-15, 17-18, 20, 22, 24, 26, 29, 31-32, 34, 40
Kolls, Lou 1938
Kosc, Greg 1987, 97
Kulpa, Ron 2011

Kunkel, Bill 1974, 80
Landes, Stan 1960, 62, 68
Layne, Jerry 2005, 11
Luciano, Ron 1974
Magerkurth, George 1932, 36, 42, 47
Maloney, George 1975
Marsh, Randy 1990, 97, 99, 2003, 06
Marquez, Alfonso 2006, 11, 15
McClelland, Tim 1993, 2000, 02, 06
McCormick, Barry 1922, 25
McCoy, Larry 1977, 88
McGowan, Bill 1928, 31, 35, 39, 41, 44, 47, 50
McKean, Jim 1979, 85, 95
McKinley, Bill 1950, 52, 57, 64
McSherry, John 1977, 87
Meals, Jerry 2014, 20
Meriwether, Chuck 2004, 07
Merrill, Durwood 1988
Miller, Bill 2010, 13, 17, 20
Montague, Ed 1986, 91, 97, 2000, 04, 07
Moran, Charlie 1927, 29, 33, 38
Moriarty, George 1921, 25, 30, 33, 35
Morrison, Dan 1992
Nallin, Dick 1919, 23, 27, 31
Napp, Larry 1954, 56, 63, 69
Nauert, Paul 2017
Nelson, Jeff 2005, 09, 14, 18
Neudecker, Jerry 1973, 79
O'Day, Hank 1903, 05, 07-08, 10, 16, 18, 20, 23, 26
Odom, Jim 1971
O'Loughlin, Silk 1906, 09, 12, 15, 17
Olsen, Andy 1974
O'Nora, Brian 2012
Ormsby, Red 1927, 33, 37, 40
Owens, Brick 1918, 22, 25, 28, 34
Palermo, Steve 1983
Paparella, Joe 1948, 51, 57, 63
Passarella, Art 1945, 49, 52
Pelekoudas, Chris 1966, 72
Pfirman, Cy 1928, 33, 36
Phillips, Dave 1976, 82, 87, 93
Pinelli, Babe 1939, 41, 47-48, 52, 56
Pipgras, George 1944
Porter, Alan 2019
Pryor, Paul 1967, 73, 80
Pulli, Frank 1978, 83, 90, 95
Quick, Jim 1985, 90
Quigley, Ernie 1916, 19, 21, 24, 27, 35
Randazzo, Tony 2016
Rapuano, Ed 2001, 03
Reardon, Beans 1930, 34, 39, 43, 49
Reed, Rick 1991
Reilly, Mike 1984, 92, 2002, 07
Reliford, Charlie 2000, 04
Rennert, Dutch 1980, 83, 89
Reynolds, Jim 2014, 18
Rice, John 1959, 63, 66, 71
Rigler, Cy 1910, 12-13, 15, 17, 19, 21, 25, 28, 30
Rippley, Steve 1996, 99, 2001
Roe, Rocky 1990, 99
Rommel, Ed 1943, 47
Rue, Joe 1943
Runge, Ed 1956, 61, 67
Runge, Paul 1979, 84, 89, 93
Scott, Dale 1998, 2001, 04
Sears, Ziggy 1938, 44
Secory, Frank 1957, 59, 64, 69
Sheridan, Jack 1905, 07-08, 10
Shulock, John 1985, 92
Smith, Vinnie 1964
Smith, Al 1964
Soar, Hank 1953, 56, 62, 64, 69
Springstead, Marty 1973, 78, 83
Stark, Dolly 1931, 35
Steiner, Mel 1966, 72
Stello, Dick 1975, 81
Stevens, Johnny 1951, 54, 60, 67
Stewart, Bob 1961, 65, 70
Stewart, Bill 1937, 43, 48, 53
Sudol, Ed 1965, 71, 77
Summers, Bill 1936, 39, 42, 45, 48, 51, 55, 59
Tata, Terry 1979, 87, 91, 96
Tichenor, Todd 2020
Timmons, Tim 2018
Tschida, Tim 1998, 2002, 08
Umont, Frank 1958, 61, 67, 72
Van Graflan, Roy 1929, 32
Vanover, Larry 2016
Vargo, Ed 1965, 71, 78, 83
Venzon, Tony 1963, 65, 70
Voltaggio, Vic 1989
Warneke, Lon 1954
Wegner, Mark 2013, 17
Welke, Bill 2015
Welke, Tim 1996, 2000, 03, 08
Wendelstedt, Harry 1973, 80, 86, 91, 95
Wendelstedt, Hunter 2014
West, Joe 1992, 97, 2005, 09, 12, 16
Weyer, Lee 1969, 76, 82, 87
Williams, Charlie 1993
Williams, Billy 1970, 76, 85
Winters, Mike 2002, 06, 10, 15
Wolf, Jim 2015, 19
Young, Larry 1996, 2003

1903 – BOSTON RED SOX A.L. (5) vs. PITTSBURGH PIRATES N.L. (3)
(Huntington Grounds / Exposition Park)

Oct. 1	at Bos.	Pittsburgh (Phillippe)	7	Boston (Young)	3
Oct. 2	at Bos.	Boston (Dinneen)	3	Pittsburgh (Leever)	0
Oct. 3	at Bos.	Pittsburgh (Phillippe)	4	Boston (Hughes)	2
Oct. 6	at Pitt.	Pittsburgh (Phillippe)	5	Boston (Dinneen)	4
Oct. 7	at Pitt.	Boston (Young)	11	Pittsburgh (Kennedy)	2
Oct. 8	at Pitt.	Boston (Dinneen)	6	Pittsburgh (Leever)	3
Oct. 10	at Pitt.	Boston (Young)	7	Pittsburgh (Phillippe)	3
Oct. 13	at Bos.	Boston (Dinneen)	3	Pittsburgh (Phillippe)	0

POSTPONED: (Rain) Oct. 5, 12 (Cold) Oct. 9

MANAGERS: Jimmy Collins, Red Sox; Fred Clarke, Pirates

Red Sox – Lou Criger, Duke Farrell, catchers; Bill Dinneen, Long Tom Hughes, Cy Young, pitchers; Jimmy Collins, Hobe Ferris, Candy LaChance, Freddy Parent, infielders; Patsy Dougherty, Buck Freeman, Jack O'Brien, Chick Stahl, outfielders.

Pirates – Ed Phelps, Harry Smith, catchers; Brickyard Kennedy, Sam Leever, Deacon Phillippe, Gus Thompson, Bucky Veil, pitchers; Kitty Bransfield, Tommy Leach, Claude Ritchey, Honus Wagner, infielders; Ginger Beaumont, Fred Clarke, Jimmy Sebring, outfielders.

1904 – NO WORLD SERIES PLAYED

1905 – NEW YORK GIANTS N.L. (4) vs. PHILADELPHIA ATHLETICS A.L. (1)
(Polo Grounds / Columbia Park)

Oct. 9	at Phil.	New York (Mathewson)	3	Philadelphia (Plank)	0
Oct. 10	at NY	Philadelphia (Bender)	3	New York (McGinnity)	0
Oct. 12	at Phil.	New York (Mathewson)	9	Philadelphia (Coakley)	0
Oct. 13	at NY	New York (McGinnity)	1	Philadelphia (Plank)	0
Oct. 14	at NY	New York (Mathewson)	2	Philadelphia (Bender)	0

POSTPONED: (Rain) Oct. 11

MANAGERS: John McGraw, Giants; Connie Mack, Athletics

Giants – Frank Bowerman, Roger Bresnahan, Boileryard Clarke, catchers; Red Ames, Claude Elliott, Christy Mathewson, Joe McGinnity, Dummy Taylor, Hooks Wiltse, pitchers; Bill Dahlen, Art Devlin, Billy Gilbert, Dan McGann, Sammy Strang, infielders; George Browne, Mike Donlin, Sam Mertes, outfielders.

Athletics – Mike Powers, Ossee Schreckengost, catchers; Chief Bender, Andy Coakley, Jimmy Dygert, Weldon Henley, Eddie Plank, Rube Waddell, pitchers; Lave Cross, Monte Cross, Harry Davis, John Knight, Danny Murphy, infielders; Harry Barton, Topsy Hartsel, Danny Hoffman, Bris Lord, Socks Seybold, outfielders.

1906 – CHICAGO WHITE SOX A.L. (4) vs. CHICAGO CUBS N.L. (2)
(South Side Park / West Side Park)

Oct. 9	at Cubs	White Sox (Altrock)	2	Cubs (Brown)	1
Oct. 10	at White Sox	Cubs (Reulbach)	7	White Sox (White)	1
Oct. 11	at Cubs	White Sox (Walsh)	3	Cubs (Pfiester)	0
Oct. 12	at White Sox	Cubs (Brown)	1	White Sox (Altrock)	0
Oct. 13	at Cubs	White Sox (Walsh)	8	Cubs (Pfiester)	6
Oct. 14	at White Sox	White Sox (White)	8	Cubs (Brown)	3

MANAGERS: Fielder Jones, White Sox; Frank Chance, Cubs

White Sox – Hub Hart, Ed McFarland, Billy Sullivan Sr., Babe Towne, catchers; Nick Altrock, Lou Fiene, Frank Owen, Roy Patterson, Frank Smith, Ed Walsh, Doc White, pitchers; George Davis, Jiggs Donahue, Gus Dundon, Frank Isbell, Bill O'Neill, George Rohe, Lee Tannehill, infielders; Patsy Dougherty, Ed Hahn, Fielder Jones, outfielders.

Cubs – Johnny Kling, Pat Moran, Tom Walsh, catchers; Three Finger Brown, Jack Harper, Carl Lundgren, Orval Overall, Jack Pfiester, Ed Reulbach, Jack Taylor, pitchers; Frank Chance, Johnny Evers, Barry McCormick, Harry Steinfeldt, Joe Tinker, infielders; Doc Gessler, Solly Hofman, Frank Schulte, Jimmy Sheckard, Jimmy Slagle, outfielders.

1907 - CHICAGO CUBS N.L. (4) vs. DETROIT TIGERS A.L. (0) 1 tie

(West Side Park / Bennett Park)

Oct. 8	at Chi.	Chicago (tie)	3	Detroit (tie)	3	(12 Innings, tie)
Oct. 9	at Chi.	Chicago (Pfiester)	3	Detroit (Mullin)	1	
Oct. 10	at Chi.	Chicago (Reulbach)	5	Detroit (Siever)	1	
Oct. 11	at Det.	Chicago (Overall)	6	Detroit (Donovan)	1	
Oct. 12	at Det.	Chicago (Brown)	2	Detroit (Mullin)	0	

MANAGERS: Frank Chance, Cubs; Hughie Jennings, Tigers

Cubs — Johnny Kling, Pat Moran, Tom Walsh, catchers; Three Finger Brown, Chick Fraser, Carl Lundgren, Orval Overall, Jack Pfiester, Ed Reulbach, pitchers; Frank Chance, Johnny Evers, Del Howard, Harry Steinfeldt, Joe Tinker, Heinie Zimmerman, infielders; Kid Durbin, Solly Hofman, Frank Schulte, Jimmy Sheckard, Jimmy Slagle, outfielders.

Tigers — Jimmy Archer, Fred Payne, Boss Schmidt, catchers; Wild Bill Donovan, Ed Killian, George Mullin, Ed Siever, Ed Willett, pitchers; Bill Coughlin, Red Downs, Bobby Lowe, Charley O'Leary, Claude Rossman, Germany Schaefer, infielders; Ty Cobb, Sam Crawford, Davy Jones, Matty McIntyre, outfielders.

1908 - CHICAGO CUBS N.L. (4) vs. DETROIT TIGERS A.L. (1)

(West Side Park / Bennett Park)

Oct. 10	at Det.	Chicago (Brown)	10	Detroit (Summers)	6
Oct. 11	at Chi.	Chicago (Overall)	6	Detroit (Donovan)	1
Oct. 12	at Chi.	Detroit (Mullin)	8	Chicago (Pfiester)	3
Oct. 13	at Det.	Chicago (Brown)	3	Detroit (Summers)	0
Oct. 14	at Det.	Chicago (Overall)	2	Detroit (Donovan)	0

MANAGERS: Frank Chance, Cubs; Hughie Jennings, Tigers

Cubs — Johnny Kling, Doc Marshall, Pat Moran, catchers; Three Finger Brown, Chick Fraser, Rube Kroh, Carl Lundgren, Orval Overall, Jack Pfiester, Ed Reulbach, pitchers; Frank Chance, Johnny Evers, Del Howard, Harry Steinfeldt, Joe Tinker, Heinie Zimmerman, infielders; Kid Durbin, Solly Hofman, Frank Schulte, Jimmy Sheckard, Jimmy Slagle, outfielders.

Tigers — Boss Schmidt, Ira Thomas, catchers; Wild Bill Donovan, Ed Killian, George Mullin, George Suggs, Ed Summers, Ed Willett, George Winter, pitchers; Bill Coughlin, Red Downs, Red Killefer, Charley O'Leary, Claude Rossman, Germany Schaefer, infielders; Ty Cobb, Sam Crawford, Davy Jones, Matty McIntyre, outfielders.

1909 - PITTSBURGH PIRATES N.L. (4) vs. DETROIT TIGERS A.L. (3)

(Forbes Field / Bennett Park)

Oct. 8	at Pitt.	Pittsburgh (Adams)	4	Detroit (Mullin)	1
Oct. 9	at Pitt.	Detroit (Donovan)	7	Pittsburgh (Camnitz)	2
Oct. 11	at Det.	Pittsburgh (Maddox)	8	Detroit (Summers)	6
Oct. 12	at Det.	Detroit (Mullin)	5	Pittsburgh (Leifield)	0
Oct. 13	at Pitt.	Pittsburgh (Adams)	8	Detroit (Summers)	4
Oct. 14	at Det.	Detroit (Mullin)	5	Pittsburgh (Willis)	4
Oct. 16	at Det.	Pittsburgh (Adams)	8	Detroit (Donovan)	0

MANAGERS: Fred Clarke, Pirates; Hughie Jennings, Tigers

Pirates — George Gibson, Paddy O'Connor, Mike Simon, catchers; Babe Adams, Chick Brandom, Howie Camnitz, Sam Frock, Sam Leever, Lefty Leifield, Nick Maddox, Gene Moore, Deacon Phillippe, Bill Powell, Vic Willis, pitchers; Ed Abbaticchio, Bill Abstein, Bobby Byrne, Dots Miller, Honus Wagner, infielders; Fred Clarke, Ham Hyatt, Tommy Leach, Owen Wilson, outfielders.

Tigers — Heinie Beckendorf, Boss Schmidt, Oscar Stanage, catchers; Wild Bill Donovan, Ed Killian, George Mullin, George Speer, Ed Summers, Ed Willett, Ralph Works, pitchers; Donie Bush, Jim Delahanty, Tom Jones, George Moriarty, Charley O'Leary, infielders; Ty Cobb, Sam Crawford, Davy Jones, Matty McIntyre, outfielders.

1910 – PHILADELPHIA ATHLETICS A.L. (4) vs. CHICAGO CUBS N.L. (1)
(Shibe Park / West Side Park)

Oct. 17	at Phil.	Philadelphia (Bender)	4	Chicago (Overall)	1	
Oct. 18	at Phil.	Philadelphia (Coombs)	9	Chicago (Brown)	3	
Oct. 20	at Chi.	Philadelphia (Coombs)	12	Chicago (McIntire)	5	
Oct. 22	at Chi.	Chicago (Brown)	4	Philadelphia (Bender)	3	(10 innings)
Oct. 23	at Chi.	Philadelphia (Coombs)	7	Chicago (Brown)	2	

POSTPONED: (Rain) Oct. 21

MANAGERS: Connie Mack, Athletics; Frank Chance, Cubs

Athletics – Pat Donahue, Jack Lapp, Paddy Livingston, Ira Thomas, catchers; Tommy Atkins, Chief Bender, Jack Coombs, Jimmy Dygert, Harry Krause, Cy Morgan, Eddie Plank, pitchers; Frank Baker, Jack Barry, Eddie Collins, Harry Davis, Claud Derrick, Ben Houser, Stuffy McInnis, infielders; Topsy Hartsel, Bristol Lord, Danny Murphy, Rube Oldring, Amos Strunk, outfielders.

Cubs – Jimmy Archer, Johnny Kling, Tom Needham, catchers; Three Finger Brown, King Cole, Bill Foxen, Harry McIntire, Orval Overall, Big Jeff Pfeffer, Jack Pfiester, Ed Reulbach, Lew Richie, Orlie Weaver, pitchers; Frank Chance, Johnny Evers, Harry Steinfeldt, Joe Tinker, Heinie Zimmerman, infielders; Ginger Beaumont, Solly Hofman, John Kane, Frank Schulte, Jimmy Sheckard, outfielders.

1911 – PHILADELPHIA ATHLETICS A.L. (4) vs. NEW YORK GIANTS N.L. (2)
(Shibe Park / Polo Grounds)

Oct. 14	at NY	New York (Mathewson)	2	Philadelphia (Bender)	1	
Oct. 16	at Phil.	Philadelphia (Plank)	3	New York (Marquard)	1	
Oct. 17	at NY	Philadelphia (Coombs)	3	New York (Mathewson)	2	(11 innings)
Oct. 24	at Phil.	Philadelphia (Bender)	4	New York (Mathewson)	2	
Oct. 25	at NY	New York (Crandall)	4	Philadelphia (Plank)	3	(10 innings)
Oct. 26	at Phil.	Philadelphia (Bender)	13	New York (Ames)	2	

POSTPONED: (Rain) Oct. 18, 19, 20, 21, 23

MANAGERS: Connie Mack, Athletics; John McGraw, Giants

Athletics – Jack Lapp, Paddy Livingston, Ira Thomas, catchers; Chief Bender, Jack Coombs, Dave Danforth, Harry Krause, Doc Martin, Cy Morgan, Eddie Plank, pitchers; Frank Baker, Jack Barry, Eddie Collins, Harry Davis, Claud Derrick, Stuffy McInnis, infielders; Topsy Hartsel, Bristol Lord, Danny Murphy, Rube Oldring, Amos Strunk, outfielders.

Giants – Grover Hartley, Chief Meyers, Art Wilson, catchers; Red Ames, Doc Crandall, Louis Drucke, Rube Marquard, Christy Mathewson, Hooks Wiltse, pitchers; Art Devlin, Larry Doyle, Art Fletcher, Buck Herzog, Fred Merkle, Gene Paulette, infielders; Beals Becker, Josh DeVore, Red Murray, Fred Snodgrass, outfielders.

1912 – BOSTON RED SOX A.L. (4) vs. NEW YORK GIANTS N.L. (3) 1 tie
(Fenway Park / Polo Grounds)

Oct. 8	at NY	Boston (Wood)	4	New York (Tesreau)	3	
Oct. 9	at Bos.	Boston (tie)	6	New York (tie)	6	(11 innings, tie)
Oct. 10	at Bos.	New York (Marquard)	2	Boston (O'Brien)	1	
Oct. 11	at NY	Boston (Wood)	3	New York (Tesreau)	1	
Oct. 12	at Bos.	Boston (Bedient)	2	New York (Mathewson)	1	
Oct. 14	at NY	New York (Marquard)	5	Boston (O'Brien)	2	
Oct. 15	at Bos.	New York (Tesreau)	11	Boston (Wood)	4	
Oct. 16	at Bos.	Boston (Wood)	3	New York (Mathewson)	2	(10 innings)

MANAGERS: Jake Stahl, Red Sox; John McGraw, Giants

Red Sox – Hick Cady, Bill Carrigan, Les Nunamaker, Pinch Thomas, catchers; Hugh Bedient, Ray Collins, Charley Hall, Buck O'Brien, Larry Pape, Smoky Joe Wood, pitchers; Neal Ball, Hugh Bradley, Clyde Engle, Larry Gardner, Marty Krug, Jake Stahl, Heinie Wagner, Steve Yerkes, infielders; Olaf Henriksen, Harry Hooper, Duffy Lewis, Tris Speaker, outfielders.

Giants – Grover Hartley, Chief Meyers, Art Wilson, catchers; Red Ames, Doc Crandall, Rube Marquard, Christy Mathewson, Jeff Tesreau, Hooks Wiltse, pitchers; Larry Doyle, Art Fletcher, Heinie Groh, Buck Herzog, Fred Merkle, Tillie Shafer, infielders; Beals Becker, George Burns, Josh DeVore, Red Murray, Moose McCormick, Fred Snodgrass, outfielders.

1913 – PHILADELPHIA ATHLETICS A.L. (4) vs. NEW YORK GIANTS N.L. (1)
(Shibe Park / Polo Grounds)

Oct. 7	at NY	Philadelphia (Bender)	6	New York (Marquard)	4	
Oct. 8	at Phil.	New York (Mathewson)	3	Philadelphia (Plank)	0	(10 innings)
Oct. 9	at NY	Philadelphia (Bush)	8	New York (Tesreau)	2	
Oct. 10	at Phil.	Philadelphia (Bender)	6	New York (Demaree)	5	
Oct. 11	at NY	Philadelphia (Plank)	3	New York (Mathewson)	1	

MANAGERS: Connie Mack, Athletics; John McGraw, Giants

Athletics – Jack Lapp, Wally Schang, Ira Thomas, catchers; Chief Bender, Boardwalk Brown, Joe Bush, Jack Coombs, Byron Houck, Herb Pennock, Eddie Plank, Bob Shawkey, John Wyckoff, pitchers; Frank Baker, Jack Barry, Eddie Collins, Harry Davis, Doc Lavan, Stuffy McInnis, Bill Orr, infielders; Tom Daley, Danny Murphy, Eddie Murphy, Rube Oldring, Amos Strunk, James Walsh, outfielders.

Giants – Grover Hartley, Chief Meyers, Larry McLean, Art Wilson, catchers; Doc Crandall, Al Demaree, Art Fromme, Rube Marquard, Christy Mathewson, Jeff Tesreau, Hooks Wiltse, pitchers; Larry Doyle, Art Fletcher, Eddie Grant, Buck Herzog, Fred Merkle, Tillie Shafer, infielders; George Burns, Claude Cooper, Moose McCormick, Red Murray, Fred Snodgrass, Jim Thorpe, outfielders.

1914 – BOSTON BRAVES N.L. (4) vs. PHILADELPHIA ATHLETICS A.L. (0)
(Fenway Park / Shibe Park)

Oct. 9	at Phil.	Boston (Rudolph)	7	Philadelphia (Bender)	1	
Oct. 10	at Phil.	Boston (James)	1	Philadelphia (Plank)	0	
Oct. 12	at Bos.	Boston (James)	5	Philadelphia (Bush)	4	(12 innings)
Oct. 13	at Bos.	Boston (Rudolph)	3	Philadelphia (Shawkey)	1	

MANAGERS: George Stallings, Braves; Connie Mack, Athletics

Braves – Hank Gowdy, Bert Whaling, catchers; Gene Cocreham, Ensign Cottrell, Dick Crutcher, George Davis, Otto Hess, Bill L. James, Dick Rudolph, Paul Strand, Lefty Tyler, pitchers; Charlie Deal, Oscar Dugey, Johnny Evers, Rabbit Maranville, Bill Martin, Butch Schmidt, Red Smith, infielders; Ted Cather, Joe Connolly, Josh DeVore, Larry Gilbert, Les Mann, Herbie Moran, Possum Whitted, outfielders.

Athletics – Jack Lapp, Wickey McAvoy, Wally Schang, Ira Thomas, catchers; Chief Bender, Rube Bressler, Joe Bush, Jack Coombs, Chick Davies, Herb Pennock, Eddie Plank, Bob Shawkey, John Wyckoff, pitchers; Frank Baker, Jack Barry, Eddie Collins, Harry Davis, Larry Kopf, Stuffy McInnis, infielders; Eddie Murphy, Rube Oldring, Amos Strunk, Shag Thompson, Jimmy Walsh, outfielders.

1915 – BOSTON RED SOX A.L. (4) vs. PHILADELPHIA PHILLIES N.L. (1)
(Braves Field / Baker Bowl)

Oct. 8	at Phil.	Philadelphia (Alexander)	3	Boston (Shore)	1
Oct. 9	at Phil.	Boston (Foster)	2	Philadelphia (Mayer)	1
Oct. 11	at Bos.	Boston (Leonard)	2	Philadelphia (Alexander)	1
Oct. 12	at Bos.	Boston (Shore)	2	Philadelphia (Chalmers)	1
Oct. 13	at Phil.	Boston (Foster)	5	Philadelphia (Rixey)	4

MANAGERS: Bill Carrigan, Red Sox; Pat Moran, Phillies

Red Sox – Hick Cady, Bill Carrigan, Pinch Thomas, catchers; Ray Collins, Rube Foster, Vean Gregg, Dutch Leonard, Carl Mays, Babe Ruth, Ernie Shore, Smoky Joe Wood, pitchers; Jack Barry, Del Gainer, Larry Gardner, Dick Hoblitzell, Hal Janvrin, Mike McNally, Everett Scott, Heinie Wagner, infielders; Olaf Henriksen, Harry Hooper, Duffy Lewis, Tris Speaker, outfielders.

Phillies – Bert Adams, Ed Burns, Bill Killefer, catchers; Grover Alexander, Stan Baumgartner, George Chalmers, Al Demaree, Erskine Mayer, George McQuillan, Eppa Rixey, Ben Tincup, pitchers; Dave Bancroft, Bobby Byrne, Oscar Dugey, Fred Luderus, Bert Niehoff, Milt Stock, infielders; Beals Becker, Gavvy Cravath, Dode Paskert, Bud Weiser, Possum Whitted, outfielders.

1916 – BOSTON RED SOX A.L. (4) vs. BROOKLYN DODGERS N.L. (1)
(Braves Field / Ebbets Field)

Oct. 7	at Bos.	Boston (Shore)	6	Brooklyn (Marquard)	5	
Oct. 9	at Bos.	Boston (Ruth)	2	Brooklyn (Smith)	1	(14 innings)
Oct. 10	at Brk.	Brooklyn (Coombs)	4	Boston (Mays)	3	
Oct. 11	at Brk.	Boston (Leonard)	6	Brooklyn (Marquard)	2	
Oct. 12	at Bos.	Boston (Shore)	4	Brooklyn (Pfeffer)	1	

MANAGERS: Bill Carrigan, Red Sox; Wilbert Robinson, Dodgers

Red Sox – Sam Agnew, Hick Cady, Bill Carrigan, Pinch Thomas, catchers; Rube Foster, Vean Gregg, Sam Jones, Dutch Leonard, Carl Mays, Babe Ruth, Ernie Shore, John Wyckoff, pitchers; Jack Barry, Del Gainer, Larry Gardner, Dick Hoblitzell, Hal Janvrin, Mike McNally, Everett Scott, Heinie Wagner, infielders; Olaf Henriksen, Harry Hooper, Duffy Lewis, Chick Shorten, Tilly Walker, Jimmy Walsh, outfielders.

Dodgers – Chief Meyers, Otto Miller, catchers; Ed Appleton, Larry Cheney, Jack Coombs, Wheezer Dell, Duster Mails, Rube Marquard, Jeff Pfeffer, Nap Rucker, Sherry Smith, pitchers; George Cutshaw, Jake Daubert, Gus Getz, Fred Merkle, Mike Mowrey, Ivy Olson, Ollie O'Mara, infielders; Jimmy Johnston, Hy Myers, Casey Stengel, Zack Wheat, outfielder,

1917 – CHICAGO WHITE SOX A.L. (4) vs. NEW YORK GIANTS N.L. (2)
(Comiskey Park / Polo Grounds)

Oct. 6	at Chi.	Chicago (Cicotte)	2	New York (Sallee)	1
Oct. 7	at Chi.	Chicago (Faber)	7	New York (Anderson)	2
Oct. 10	at NY	New York (Benton)	2	Chicago (Cicotte)	0
Oct. 11	at NY	New York (Schupp)	5	Chicago (Faber)	0
Oct. 13	at Chi.	Chicago (Faber)	8	New York (Sallee)	5
Oct. 15	at NY	Chicago (Faber)	4	New York (Benton)	2

MANAGERS: Pants Rowland, White Sox; John McGraw, Giants

White Sox – Joe Jenkins, Byrd Lynn, Ray Schalk, catchers; Joe Benz, Eddie Cicotte, Dave Danforth, Red Faber, Reb Russell, Jim Scott, Lefty Williams, Red Wolfgang, pitchers; Bobby Byrne, Eddie Collins, Chick Gandil, Ziggy Hasbrook, Ted Jourdan, Fred McMullin, Swede Risberg, Buck Weaver, infielders; Shano Collins, Happy Felsch, Joe Jackson, Nemo Leibold, Eddie Murphy, outfielders.

Giants – George Gibson, Lew McCarty, Jack Onslow, Bill Rariden, catchers; Fred Anderson, Rube Benton, Al Demaree, Pol Perritt, Slim Sallee, Ferdie Schupp, Jeff Tesreau, pitchers; Al Baird, Art Fletcher, Buck Herzog, Walter Holke, Hans Lobert, Jimmy Smith, Heinie Zimmerman, infielders; George Burns, Benny Kauff, Red Murray, Dave Robertson, Jim Thorpe, Joe Wilhoit, outfielders.

1918 – BOSTON RED SOX A.L. (4) vs. CHICAGO CUBS N.L. (2)
(Fenway Park / Comiskey Park)

Sept. 5	at Chi.	Boston (Ruth)	1	Chicago (Vaughn)	0
Sept. 6	at Chi.	Chicago (Tyler)	3	Boston (Bush)	1
Sept. 7	at Chi.	Boston (Mays)	2	Chicago (Vaughn)	1
Sept. 9	at Bos.	Boston (Ruth)	3	Chicago (Douglas)	2
Sept. 10	at Bos.	Chicago (Vaughn)	3	Boston (Jones)	0
Sept. 11	at Bos.	Boston (Mays)	2	Chicago (Tyler)	1

POSTPONED: (Rain) Sept. 4

MANAGERS: Ed Barrow, Red Sox; Fred Mitchell, Cubs

Red Sox – Sam Agnew, Wally Mayer, Wally Schang, catchers; Joe Bush, Jean Dubuc, Sam Jones, Walt Kinney, Carl Mays, Bill Pertica, Babe Ruth, pitchers; George Cochran, Jack Coffey, Stuffy McInnis, Everett Scott, Dave Shean, Fred Thomas, Heinie Wagner, infielders; Harry Hooper, Hack Miller, Amos Strunk, George Whiteman, outfielders.

Cubs – Tommy Clarke, Bill Killefer, Bob O'Farrell, catchers; Paul Carter, Phil Douglas, Claude Hendrix, Speed Martin, Lefty Tyler, Hippo Vaughn, Roy Walker, pitchers; Charlie Deal, Charlie Hollocher, Otto Knabe, Bill McCabe, Fred Merkle, Charlie Pick, Chuck Wortman, Rollie Zeider, infielders; Turner Barber, Max Flack, Les Mann, Dode Paskert, outfielders.

1919 – CINCINNATI REDS N.L. (5) vs. CHICAGO WHITE SOX A.L. (3)
(Redland Field / Comiskey Park)

Oct. 1	at Cin.	Cincinnati (Ruether)	9	Chicago (Cicotte)	1	
Oct. 2	at Cin.	Cincinnati (Sallee)	4	Chicago (Williams)	2	
Oct. 3	at Chi.	Chicago (Kerr)	3	Cincinnati (Fisher)	0	
Oct. 4	at Chi.	Cincinnati (Ring)	2	Chicago (Cicotte)	0	
Oct. 6	at Chi.	Cincinnati (Eller)	5	Chicago (Williams)	0	
Oct. 7	at Cin.	Chicago (Kerr)	5	Cincinnati (Ring)	4	(10 Innings)
Oct. 8	at Cin.	Chicago (Cicotte)	4	Cincinnati (Sallee)	1	
Oct. 9	at Chi.	Cincinnati (Eller)	10	Chicago (Williams)	5	

MANAGERS: Pat Moran, Reds; Kid Gleason, White Sox

Reds – Nick Allen, Bill Rariden, Ivy Wingo, catchers; Hod Eller, Ray Fisher, Ed Gerner, Dolf Luque, Roy Mitchell, Jimmy Ring, Dutch Ruether, Slim Sallee, pitchers; Jake Daubert, Heinie Groh, Larry Kopf, Morrie Rath, Hank Schreiber, Jimmy Smith, infielders; Rube Bressler, Pat Duncan, Sherry Magee, Greasy Neale, Edd Roush, Charlie See, outfielders.

White Sox – Joe Jenkins, Byrd Lynn, Ray Schalk, catchers; Eddie Cicotte, Red Faber, Bill James, Dickie Kerr, Grover Lowdermilk, Erskine Mayer, John Sullivan, Roy Wilkinson, Lefty Williams, pitchers; Eddie Collins, Chick Gandil, Hervey McClellan, Fred McMullin, Swede Risberg, Buck Weaver, infielders; Shano Collins, Happy Felsch, Joe Jackson, Nemo Leibold, Eddie Murphy, outfielders.

1920 – CLEVELAND INDIANS A.L. (5) vs. BROOKLYN DODGERS N.L. (2)
(League Park / Ebbets Field)

Oct. 5	at Brk.	Cleveland (Coveleski)	3	Brooklyn (Marquard)	1
Oct. 6	at Brk.	Brooklyn (Grimes)	3	Cleveland (Bagby)	0
Oct. 7	at Brk.	Brooklyn (Smith)	2	Cleveland (Caldwell)	1
Oct. 9	at Clev.	Cleveland (Coveleski)	5	Brooklyn (Cadore)	1
Oct. 10	at Clev.	Cleveland (Bagby)	8	Brooklyn (Grimes)	1
Oct. 11	at Clev.	Cleveland (Mails)	1	Brooklyn (Smith)	0
Oct. 12	at Clev.	Cleveland (Coveleski)	3	Brooklyn (Grimes)	0

MANAGERS: Tris Speaker, Indians; Wilbert Robinson, Dodgers

Indians – Les Nunamaker, Steve O'Neill, Pinch Thomas, catchers; Jim Bagby, Ray Caldwell, Bob Clark, Stan Coveleski, George Ellison, Duster Mails, Guy Morton, George Uhle, pitchers; George Burns, Larry Gardner, Doc Johnston, Harry Lunte, Joe Sewell, Bill Wambsganss, infielders; Joe Evans, Jack Graney, Charlie Jamieson, Elmer Smith, Tris Speaker, Smoky Joe Wood, outfielders.

Dodgers – Rowdy Elliott, Ernie Krueger, Otto Miller, Zack Taylor, catchers; Leon Cadore, Burleigh Grimes, Al Mamaux, Rube Marquard, Johnny Miljus, Clarence Mitchell, George Mohart, Jeff Pfeffer, Sherry Smith, pitchers; Jimmy Johnston, Pete Kilduff, Ed Konetchy, Bill McCabe, Ivy Olson, Ray Schmandt, Jack Sheehan, Chuck Ward, infielders; Tommy Griffith, Bill Lamar, Hy Myers, Bernie Neis, Zack Wheat, outfielders.

1921 – NEW YORK GIANTS N.L. (5) vs. NEW YORK YANKEES A.L. (3)
(Polo Grounds / Polo Grounds)

Oct. 5	at Giants	Yankees (Mays)	3	Giants (Douglas)	0
Oct. 6	at Yankees	Yankees (Hoyt)	3	Giants (Nehf)	0
Oct. 7	at Giants	Giants (Barnes)	13	Yankees (Quinn)	5
Oct. 9	at Yankees	Giants (Douglas)	4	Yankees (Mays)	2
Oct. 10	at Giants	Yankees (Hoyt)	3	Giants (Nehf)	1
Oct. 11	at Yankees	Giants (Barnes)	8	Yankees (Shawkey)	5
Oct. 12	at Giants	Giants (Douglas)	2	Yankees (Mays)	1
Oct. 13	at Yankees	Giants (Nehf)	1	Yankees (Hoyt)	0

MANAGERS: John McGraw, Giants; Miller Huggins, Yankees

Giants – Alex Gaston, Earl Smith, Frank Snyder, catchers; Jesse Barnes, Red Causey, Phil Douglas, Art Nehf, Rosy Ryan, Slim Sallee, Red Shea, Fred Toney, pitchers; Dave Bancroft, Frankie Frisch, Mike Gonzalez, George Kelly, Wally Kopf, Johnny Rawlings, infielders; Eddie Brown, George Burns, Bill Cunningham, Irish Meusel, Casey Stengel, Ross Youngs, outfielders.

Yankees – Al DeVormer, Wally Schang, catchers; Rip Collins, Alex Ferguson, Harry Harper, Waite Hoyt, Carl Mays, Bill Piercy, Jack Quinn, Tom Rogers, Bob Shawkey, pitchers; Frank Baker, Mike McNally, Johnny Mitchell, Roger Peckinpaugh, Wally Pipp, Aaron Ward, infielders; Chick Fewster, Chicken Hawks, Bob Meusel, Elmer Miller, Braggo Roth, Babe Ruth, outfielders.

1922 – NEW YORK GIANTS N.L. (4) vs. NEW YORK YANKEES A.L. (0) 1 tie
(Polo Grounds / Polo Grounds)

Oct. 4	at Giants	Giants (Ryan)	3	Yankees (Bush)	2	
Oct. 5	at Yankees	Giants (tie)	3	Yankees (tie)	3	(10 Innings, tie)
Oct. 6	at Giants	Giants (Scott)	3	Yankees (Hoyt)	0	
Oct. 7	at Yankees	Giants (McQuillan)	4	Yankees (Mays)	3	
Oct. 8	at Giants	Giants (Nehf)	5	Yankees (Bush)	3	

MANAGERS: John McGraw, Giants; Miller Huggins, Yankees

Giants – Alex Gaston, Earl Smith, Frank Snyder, catchers; Jesse Barnes, Virgil Barnes, Clint Blume, Carmen Hill, Claude Jonnard, Hugh McQuillan, Art Nehf, Rosy Ryan, Jack Scott, pitchers; Dave Bancroft, Frankie Frisch, Heinie Groh, George Kelly, Johnny Rawlings, infielders; Bill Cunningham, Lee King, Irish Meusel, Dave Robertson, Casey Stengel, Ross Youngs, outfielders.

Yankees – Al DeVormer, Fred Hofmann, Wally Schang, catchers; Joe Bush, Waite Hoyt, Sam Jones, Carl Mays, George Murray, Lefty O'Doul, Bob Shawkey, pitchers; Frank Baker, Joe Dugan, Mike McNally, Wally Pipp, Everett Scott, Aaron Ward, infielders; Norm McMillan, Bob Meusel, Babe Ruth, Camp Skinner, Elmer Smith, Whitey Witt, outfielders.

1923 – NEW YORK YANKEES A.L. (4) vs. NEW YORK GIANTS N.L. (2)
(Yankee Stadium / Polo Grounds)

Oct. 10	at Yankees	Giants (Ryan)	5	Yankees (Bush)	4
Oct. 11	at Giants	Yankees (Pennock)	4	Giants (McQuillan)	2
Oct. 12	at Yankees	Giants (Nehf)	1	Yankees (Jones)	0
Oct. 13	at Giants	Yankees (Shawkey)	8	Giants (Scott)	4
Oct. 14	at Yankees	Yankees (Bush)	8	Giants (Bentley)	1
Oct. 15	at Giants	Yankees (Pennock)	6	Giants (Nehf)	4

MANAGERS: Miller Huggins, Yankees; John McGraw, Giants

Yankees – Benny Bengough, Fred Hofmann, Wally Schang, catchers; Joe Bush, Waite Hoyt, Sam Jones, Carl Mays, Herb Pennock, George Pipgras, Oscar Roettger, Bob Shawkey, pitchers; Joe Dugan, Mike Gazella, Ernie Johnson, Mike McNally, Wally Pipp, Everett Scott, Aaron Ward, infielders; Hinkey Haines, Harvey Hendrick, Bob Meusel, Babe Ruth, Elmer Smith, Whitey Witt, outfielders.

Giants – Alex Gaston, Hank Gowdy, Frank Snyder, catchers; Virgil Barnes, Jack Bentley, Dinty Gearin, Claude Jonnard, Hugh McQuillan, Art Nehf, Rosy Ryan, Jack Scott, Mule Watson, pitchers; Dave Bancroft, Frankie Frisch, Heinie Groh, Travis Jackson, George Kelly, Freddie Maguire, infielders; Bill Cunningham, Irish Meusel, Jimmy O'Connell, Ralph Shinners, Casey Stengel, Ross Youngs, outfielders.

1924 – WASHINGTON SENATORS A.L. (4) vs. NEW YORK GIANTS N.L. (3)
(Griffith Stadium / Polo Grounds)

Oct. 4	at Wash.	New York (Nehf)	4	Washington (Johnson)	3	(12 innings)
Oct. 5	at Wash.	Washington (Zachary)	4	New York (Bentley)	3	
Oct. 6	at NY	New York (McQuillan)	6	Washington (Marberry)	4	
Oct. 7	at NY	Washington (Mogridge)	7	New York (Barnes)	4	
Oct. 8	at NY	New York (Bentley)	6	Washington (Johnson)	2	
Oct. 9	at Wash.	Washington (Zachary)	2	New York (Nehf)	1	
Oct. 10	at Wash.	Washington (Johnson)	4	New York (Bentley)	3	(12 innings)

MANAGERS: Bucky Harris, Senators; John McGraw, Giants

Senators – Pinky Hargrave, Muddy Ruel, Bennie Tate, catchers; Walter Johnson, Firpo Marberry, Joe Martina, George Mogridge, Curly Ogden, Allan Russell, Byron Speece, Tom Zachary, Paul Zahniser, pitchers; Ossie Bluege, Bucky Harris, Joe Judge, Ralph Miller, Roger Peckinpaugh, Mule Shirley, Tommy Taylor, infielders; Showboat Fisher, Goose Goslin, Nemo Leibold, Earl McNeely, Sam Rice, outfielders.

Giants – Hank Gowdy, Frank Snyder, catchers; Harry Baldwin, Virgil Barnes, Jack Bentley, Wayland Dean, Walter Huntzinger, Claude Jonnard, Ernie Maun, Hugh McQuillan, Art Nehf, Rosy Ryan, Mule Watson, pitchers; Frankie Frisch, Heinie Groh, Travis Jackson, George Kelly, Fred Lindstrom, Bill Terry, infielders; Irish Meusel, Jimmy O'Connell, Billy Southworth, Hack Wilson, Ross Youngs, outfielders.

1925 – PITTSBURGH PIRATES N.L. (4) vs. WASHINGTON SENATORS A.L. (3)

(Forbes Field / Griffith Stadium)

Oct. 7	at Pitt.	Washington (Johnson)	4	Pittsburgh (Meadows)	1
Oct. 8	at Pitt.	Pittsburgh (Aldridge)	3	Washington (Coveleski)	2
Oct. 10	at Wash.	Washington (Ferguson)	4	Pittsburgh (Kremer)	3
Oct. 11	at Wash.	Washington (Johnson)	4	Pittsburgh (Yde)	0
Oct. 12	at Wash.	Pittsburgh (Aldridge)	6	Washington (Coveleski)	3
Oct. 13	at Pitt.	Pittsburgh (Kremer)	3	Washington (Ferguson)	2
Oct. 15	at Pitt.	Pittsburgh (Kremer)	9	Washington (Johnson)	7

POSTPONED: (Rain) Oct. 14

MANAGERS: Bill McKechnie, Pirates; Bucky Harris, Senators

Pirates – Johnny Gooch, Earl Smith, Roy Spencer, catchers; Babe Adams, Vic Aldridge, Bud Culloton, Remy Kremer, Lee Meadows, Johnny Morrison, Red Oldham, Tom Sheehan, Emil Yde, pitchers; Jewel Ens, George Grantham, Stuffy McInnis, Eddie Moore, Johnny Rawlings, Fresco Thompson, Pie Traynor, Glenn Wright, infielders; Clyde Barnhart, Carson Bigbee, Max Carey, Kiki Cuyler, Mule Haas, outfielders.

Senators – Muddy Ruel, Hank Severeid, Bennie Tate, catchers; Win Ballou, Stan Coveleski, Alex Ferguson, Walter Johnson, Firpo Marberry, Dutch Ruether, Allan Russell, Tom Zachary, pitchers; Spencer Adams, Ossie Bluege, Bucky Harris, Joe Judge, Buddy Myer, Roger Peckinpaugh, Everett Scott, infielders; Goose Goslin, Joe Harris, Tex Jeanes, Nemo Leibold, Earl McNeely, Sam Rice, Bobby Veach, outfielders.

1926 – ST. LOUIS CARDINALS N.L. (4) vs. NEW YORK YANKEES A.L. (3)

(Sportsman's Park / Yankee Stadium)

Oct. 2	at NY	New York (Pennock)	2	St. Louis (Sherdel)	1	
Oct. 3	at NY	St. Louis (Alexander)	6	New York (Shocker)	2	
Oct. 5	at StL.	St. Louis (Haines)	4	New York (Ruether)	0	
Oct. 6	at StL.	New York (Hoyt)	10	St. Louis (Reinhart	5	
Oct. 7	at StL.	New York (Pennock)	3	St. Louis (Sherdel)	2	(10 innings)
Oct. 9	at NY	St. Louis (Alexander)	10	New York (Shawkey)	2	
Oct. 10	at NY	St. Louis (Haines)	3	New York (Hoyt)	2	

MANAGERS: Rogers Hornsby, Cardinals; Miller Huggins, Yankees

Cardinals – Bob O'Farrell, Ernie Vick, catchers; Grover Alexander, Hi Bell, Ed Clough, Jesse Haines, Bill Hallahan, Syl Johnson, Vic Keen, Art Reinhart, Flint Rhem, Bill Sherdel, Allen Sothoron, pitchers; Les Bell, Jim Bottomley, Jake Flowers, Rogers Hornsby, Tommy Thevenow, Specs Toporcer, infielders; Ray Blades, Taylor Douthit, Chick Hafey, Roscoe Holm, Billy Southworth, outfielders.

Yankees – Benny Bengough, Pat Collins, Hank Severeid, catchers; Walter Beall, Garland Braxton, Waite Hoyt, Sam Jones, Herb McQuaid, Herb Pennock, Dutch Ruether, Bob Shawkey, Urban Shocker, Myles Thomas, pitchers; Spencer Adams, Joe Dugan, Michael Gazella, Lou Gehrig, Mark Koenig, Tony Lazzeri, Aaron Ward, infielders; Roy Carlyle, Earle Combs, Bob Meusel, Ben Paschal, Babe Ruth, outfielders.

1927 – NEW YORK YANKEES A.L. (4) vs. PITTSBURGH PIRATES N.L. (0)

(Yankee Stadium / Forbes Field)

Oct. 5	at Pitt.	New York (Hoyt)	5	Pittsburgh (Kremer)	4
Oct. 6	at Pitt.	New York (Pipgras)	6	Pittsburgh (Aldridge)	2
Oct. 7	at NY	New York (Pennock)	8	Pittsburgh (Meadows)	1
Oct. 8	at NY	New York (Moore)	4	Pittsburgh (Miljus)	3

MANAGERS: Miller Huggins, Yankees; Donie Bush, Pirates

Yankees – Benny Bengough, Pat Collins, Johnny Grabowski, catchers; Joe Giard, Waite Hoyt, Wilcy Moore, Herb Pennock, George Pipgras, Dutch Ruether, Bob Shawkey, Urban Shocker, Myles Thomas, pitchers; Joe Dugan, Mike Gazella, Lou Gehrig, Mark Koenig, Tony Lazzeri, Ray Morehart, Julie Wera, infielders; Earle Combs, Cedric Durst, Bob Meusel, Ben Paschal, Babe Ruth, outfielders.

Pirates – Johnny Gooch, Earl Smith, Roy Spencer, catchers; Vic Aldridge, Mike Cvengros, Joe Dawson, Carmen Hill, Remy Kremer, Lee Meadows, Johnny Miljus, Emil Yde, pitchers; Joe Cronin, George Grantham, Heinie Groh, Joe Harris, Hal Rhyne, Pie Traynor, Glenn Wright, infielders; Clyde Barnhart, Fred Brickell, Kiki Cuyler, Lloyd Waner, Paul Waner, outfielders.

1928 – NEW YORK YANKEES A.L. (4) vs. ST. LOUIS CARDINALS N.L. (0)

(Yankee Stadium / Sportsman's Park)

Oct. 4	at NY	New York (Hoyt)	4	St. Louis (Sherdel)	1
Oct. 5	at NY	New York (Pipgras)	9	St. Louis (Alexander)	3
Oct. 7	at StL.	New York (Zachary)	7	St. Louis (Haines)	3
Oct. 9	at StL.	New York (Hoyt)	7	St. Louis (Sherdel)	3

MANAGERS: Miller Huggins, Yankees; Bill McKechnie, Cardinals

Yankees – Benny Bengough, Pat Collins, Bill Dickey, Johnny Grabowski, catchers; Fred Heimach, Waite Hoyt, Herb Pennock, George Pipgras, Rosy Ryan, Myles Thomas, Tom Zachary, pitchers; Joe Dugan, Leo Durocher, Mike Gazella, Lou Gehrig, Mark Koenig, Tony Lazzeri, Gene Robertson, infielders; Earle Combs, Cedric Durst, Bob Meusel, Ben Paschal, Babe Ruth, outfielders.

Cardinals – Earl Smith, Jimmie Wilson, catchers; Grover Alexander, Fred Frankhouse, Hal Haid, Jesse Haines, Syl Johnson, Clarence Mitchell, Art Reinhart, Flint Rhem, Bill Sherdel, pitchers; Jim Bottomley, Frankie Frisch, Andy High, Wattie Holm, Rabbit Maranville, Tommy Thevenow, infielders; Ray Blades, Taylor Douthit, Chick Hafey, George Harper, Pepper Martin, Ernie Orsatti, Wally Roettger, Howie Williamson, outfielders.

1929 – PHILADELPHIA ATHLETICS A.L. (4) vs. CHICAGO CUBS N.L. (1)

(Shibe Park / Wrigley Field)

Oct. 8	at Chi.	Philadelphia (Ehmke)	3	Chicago (Root)	1
Oct. 9	at Chi.	Philadelphia (Earnshaw)	9	Chicago (Malone)	3
Oct. 11	at Phil.	Chicago (Bush)	3	Philadelphia (Earnshaw)	1
Oct. 12	at Phil.	Philadelphia (Rommel)	10	Chicago (Blake)	8
Oct. 14	at Phil.	Philadelphia (Walberg)	3	Chicago (Malone)	2

MANAGERS: Connie Mack, Athletics; Joe McCarthy, Cubs

Athletics – Mickey Cochrane, Cy Perkins, catchers; Bill Breckinridge, George Earnshaw, Howard Ehmke, Lefty Grove, Jack Quinn, Ed Rommel, Bill Shores, Rube Walberg, Carroll Yerkes, pitchers; Max Bishop, Joe Boley, George Burns, Eddie Collins, Jim Cronin, Jimmie Dykes, Jimmie Foxx, Sammy Hale, infielders; Walter French, Mule Haas, Bevo LeBourveau, Bing Miller, Al Simmons, Homer Summa, outfielders.

Cubs – Mike Gonzalez, Gabby Hartnett, Johnny Schulte, Zack Taylor, catchers; Sheriff Blake, Guy Bush, Hal Carlson, Mike Cvengros, Henry Grampp, Pat Malone, Art Nehf, Ken Penner, Charlie Root, pitchers; Clyde Beck, Footsie Blair, Woody English, Charlie Grimm, Rogers Hornsby, Norm McMillan, Chick Tolson, infielders; Kiki Cuyler, Cliff Heathcote, Johnny Moore, Riggs Stephenson, Hack Wilson, outfielders.

1930 – PHILADELPHIA ATHLETICS A.L. (4) vs. ST. LOUIS CARDINALS N.L. (2)

(Shibe Park / Sportsman's Park)

Oct. 1	at Phil.	Philadelphia (Grove)	5	St. Louis (Grimes)	2
Oct. 2	at Phil.	Philadelphia (Earnshaw)	6	St. Louis (Rhem)	1
Oct. 4	at StL.	St. Louis (Hallahan)	5	Philadelphia (Walberg)	0
Oct. 5	at StL.	St. Louis (Haines)	3	Philadelphia (Grove)	1
Oct. 6	at StL.	Philadelphia (Grove)	2	St. Louis (Grimes)	0
Oct. 8	at Phil.	Philadelphia (Earnshaw)	7	St. Louis (Hallahan)	1

MANAGERS: Connie Mack, Athletics; Gabby Street, Cardinals

Athletics – Mickey Cochrane, Cy Perkins, Wally Schang, catchers; George Earnshaw, Lefty Grove, Lee Roy Mahaffey, Jack Quinn, Ed Rommel, Bill Shores, Rube Walberg, pitchers; Max Bishop, Joe Boley, Eddie Collins, Jimmy Dykes, Jimmie Foxx, Pinky Higgins, Eric McNair, Dib Williams, infielders; Mule Haas, Bing Miller, Jimmy Moore, Al Simmons, Homer Summa, outfielders.

Cardinals – Gus Mancuso, Jimmie Wilson, catchers; Hi Bell, Al Grabowski, Burleigh Grimes, Jesse Haines, Bill Hallahan, Syl Johnson, Jim Lindsey, Flint Rhem, pitchers; Sparky Adams, Jim Bottomley, Frankie Frisch, Charley Gelbert, Andy High, infielders; Ray Blades, Taylor Douthit, Showboat Fisher, Chick Hafey, Ernie Orsatti, George Puccinelli, George Watkins, outfielders

1931- ST. LOUIS CARDINALS N.L. (4) vs. PHILADELPHIA ATHLETICS A.L. (3)

(Sportsman's Park / Shibe Park)

Oct. 1	at StL.	Philadelphia (Grove)	6	St. Louis (Derringer)	2
Oct. 2	at StL.	St. Louis (Hallahan)	2	Philadelphia (Earnshaw)	0
Oct. 5	at Phil.	St. Louis (Grimes)	5	Philadelphia (Grove)	2
Oct. 6	at Phil.	Philadelphia (Earnshaw)	3	St. Louis (Johnson)	0
Oct. 7	at Phil.	St. Louis (Hallahan)	5	Philadelphia (Hoyt)	1
Oct. 9	at StL.	Philadelphia (Grove)	8	St. Louis (Derringer)	1
Oct. 10	at StL.	St. Louis (Grimes)	4	Philadelphia (Earnshaw)	2

POSTPONED: (Rain) Oct. 4

MANAGERS: Gabby Street, Cardinals; Connie Mack, Athletics

Cardinals — Mike Gonzalez, Gus Mancuso, Jimmie Wilson, catchers; Paul Derringer, Burleigh Grimes, Jesse Haines, Bill Hallahan, Syl Johnson, Tony Kaufman, Jim Lindsey, Flint Rhem, Allyn Stout, pitchers; Sparky Adams, Jim Bottomley, Ripper Collins, Jake Flowers, Frankie Frisch, Charley Gelbert, Andy High, infielders; Ray Blades, Chick Hafey, Pepper Martin, Ernie Orsatti, Wally Roettger, George Watkins, outfielders.

Athletics — Mickey Cochrane, Johnnie Heving, Joe Palmisano, catchers; George Earnshaw, Lefty Grove, Waite Hoyt, Lew Krausse, Lee Roy Mahaffey, Hank McDonald, Jim Peterson, Ed Rommel, Rube Walberg, pitchers; Max Bishop, Joe Boley, Jimmy Dykes, Jimmie Foxx, Eric McNair, Philip Todt, Dib Williams, infielders; Doc Cramer, Mule Haas, Bing Miller, Jimmy Moore, Al Simmons, outfielders.

1932 – NEW YORK YANKEES A.L. (4) vs. CHICAGO CUBS N.L. (0)

(Yankee Stadium / Wrigley Field)

Sept. 28	at NY	New York (Ruffing)	12	Chicago (Bush)	6
Sept. 29	at NY	New York (Gomez)	5	Chicago (Warneke)	2
Oct. 1	at Chi.	New York (Pipgras)	7	Chicago (Root)	5
Oct. 2	at Chi.	New York (Moore)	13	Chicago (May)	6

MANAGERS: Joe McCarthy, Yankees; Charlie Grimm, Cubs

Yankees — Bill Dickey, Arndt Jorgens, catchers; Johnny Allen, Jumbo Brown, Charlie Devens, Lefty Gomez, Danny MacFayden, Wilcy Moore, Herb Pennock, George Pipgras, Red Ruffing, Ed Wells, pitchers; Frankie Crosetti, Doc Farrell, Lou Gehrig, Lyn Lary, Tony Lazzeri, Joe Sewell, infielders; Sammy Byrd, Ben Chapman, Earle Combs, Myril Hoag, Babe Ruth, outfielders.

Cubs — Gabby Hartnett, Rollie Hemsley, Zack Taylor, catchers; Guy Bush, Burleigh Grimes, LeRoy Herrmann, Pat Malone, Frank May, Charlie Root, Bob Smith, Bud Tinning, Lon Warneke, pitchers; Woody English, Charlie Grimm, Stan Hack, Billy Herman, Billy Jurges, Mark Koenig, infielders; Kiki Cuyler, Frank Demaree, Marv Gudat, Johnny Moore, Riggs Stephenson, outfielders.

1933 – NEW YORK GIANTS N.L. (4) vs. WASHINGTON SENATORS A.L. (1)

(Polo Grounds / Griffith Stadium)

Oct. 3	at NY	New York (Hubbell)	4	Washington (Stewart)	2	
Oct. 4	at NY	New York (Schumacher)	6	Washington (Crowder)	1	
Oct. 5	at Wash.	Washington (Whitehill)	4	New York (Fitzsimmons)	0	
Oct. 6	at Wash.	New York (Hubbell)	2	Washington (Weaver)	1	(11 innings)
Oct. 7	at Wash.	New York (Luque)	4	Washington (Russell)	3	(10 innings)

MANAGERS: Bill Terry, Giants; Joe Cronin, Senators

Giants — Harry Danning, Gus Mancuso, Paul Richards, catchers; Hi Bell, Watty Clark, Freddie Fitzsimmons, Carl Hubbell, Dolf Luque, Roy Parmelee, Jack Salveson, Hal Schumacher, Glenn Spencer, pitchers; Hughie Critz, Chuck Dressen, Travis Jackson, Bernie James, Blondy Ryan, Bill Terry, Johnny Vergez, infielders; Kiddo Davis, Joe Moore, Lefty O'Doul, Mel Ott, Homer Peel, outfielders.

Senators — Moe Berg, Cliff Bolton, Luke Sewell, catchers; Bobby Burke, Ed Chapman, General Crowder, Alex McColl, Jack Russell, Lefty Stewart, Tommy Thomas, Monte Weaver, Earl Whitehill, pitchers; Ossie Bluege, Bob Boken, Joe Cronin, John Kerr, Joe Kuhel, Buddy Myer, infielders. Goose Goslin, Dave Harris, Heinie Manush, Sam Rice, Fred Schulte, outfielders.

1934 – ST. LOUIS CARDINALS N.L. (4) vs. DETROIT TIGERS A.L. (3)
(Sportsman's Park / Navin Field)

Oct. 3	at Det.	St. Louis (Dizzy Dean)	8	Detroit (Crowder)	3	
Oct. 4	at Det.	Detroit (Rowe)	3	St. Louis (Walker)	2	(12 innings)
Oct. 5	at StL.	St. Louis (Daffy Dean)	4	Detroit (Bridges)	1	
Oct. 6	at StL.	Detroit (Auker)	10	St. Louis (Walker)	4	
Oct. 7	at StL.	Detroit (Bridges)	3	St. Louis (Dizzy Dean)	1	
Oct. 8	at Det.	St. Louis (Daffy Dean)	4	Detroit (Rowe)	3	
Oct. 9	at Det.	St. Louis (Dizzy Dean)	11	Detroit (Auker)	0	

MANAGERS: Frankie Frisch, Cardinals; Mickey Cochrane, Tigers

Cardinals – Spud Davis, Bill DeLancey, Francis Healy, catchers; Tex Carleton, Dizzy Dean, Daffy Dean, Jesse Haines, Bill Hallahan, Jim Mooney, Dazzy Vance, Bill Walker, pitchers; Ripper Collins, Pat Crawford, Leo Durocher, Frankie Frisch, Pepper Martin, Burgess Whitehead, infielders; Chick Fullis, Joe Medwick, Ernie Orsatti, Jack Rothrock, outfielders.

Tigers – Mickey Cochrane, Ray Hayworth, catchers; Elden Auker, Tommy Bridges, General Crowder, Carl Fischer, Luke Hamlin, Chief Hogsett, Firpo Marberry, Schoolboy Rowe, Vic Sorrell, pitchers; Flea Clifton, Charlie Gehringer, Hank Greenberg, Marv Owen, Billy Rogell, Heinie Schuble, infielders; Frank Doljack, Pete Fox, Goose Goslin, Gee Walker, Jo-Jo White, outfielders

1935 – DETROIT TIGERS A.L. (4) vs. CHICAGO CUBS N.L. (2)
(Navin Field / Wrigley Field)

Oct. 2	at Det.	Chicago (Warneke)	3	Detroit (Rowe)	0	
Oct. 3	at Det.	Detroit (Bridges)	8	Chicago (Root)	3	
Oct. 4	at Chi.	Detroit (Rowe)	6	Chicago (French)	5	(11 innings)
Oct. 5	at Chi.	Detroit (Crowder)	2	Chicago (Carleton)	1	
Oct. 6	at Chi.	Chicago (Warneke)	3	Detroit (Rowe)	1	
Oct. 7	at Det.	Detroit (Bridges)	4	Chicago (French)	3	

MANAGERS: Mickey Cochrane, Tigers; Charlie Grimm, Cubs

Tigers – Mickey Cochrane, Ray Hayworth, Frank Reiber, catchers; Elden Auker, Tommy Bridges, General Crowder, Chief Hogsett, Roxie Lawson, Schoolboy Rowe, Vic Sorrell, Joe Sullivan, pitchers; Flea Clifton, Charlie Gehringer, Hank Greenberg, Marv Owen, Billy Rogell, Heinie Schuble, infielders; Pete Fox, Goose Goslin, Hugh Shelley, Gee Walker, Jo-Jo White, outfielders.

Cubs – Gabby Hartnett, Ken O'Dea, Walter Stephenson, catchers; Tex Carleton, Hugh Casey, Larry French, Roy Henshaw, Fabian Kowalik, Bill Lee, Charlie Root, Clyde Shoun, Lon Warneke, pitchers; Phil Cavarretta, Woody English, Charlie Grimm, Stan Hack, Billy Herman, Bill Jurges, infielders; Frank Demaree, Augie Galan, Chuck Klein, Freddie Lindstrom, Tuck Stainback, outfielders.

1936 – NEW YORK YANKEES A.L. (4) vs. NEW YORK GIANTS N.L. (2)
(Yankee Stadium / Polo Grounds)

Sept. 30	at Giants	Giants (Hubbell)	6	Yankees (Ruffing)	1	
Oct. 2	at Giants	Yankees (Gomez)	18	Giants (Schumacher)	4	
Oct. 3	at Yankees	Yankees (Hadley)	2	Giants (Fitzsimmons)	1	
Oct. 4	at Yankees	Yankees (Pearson)	5	Giants (Hubbell)	2	
Oct. 5	at Yankees	Giants (Schumacher)	5	Yankees (Malone)	4	(10 innings)
Oct. 6	at Giants	Yankees (Gomez)	13	Giants (Fitzsimmons)	5	

POSTPONED: (Rain) Oct. 1

MANAGERS: Joe McCarthy, Yankees; Bill Terry, Giants

Yankees – Bill Dickey, Joe Glenn, Arndt Jorgens, catchers; Johnny Broaca, Jumbo Brown, Lefty Gomez, Bump Hadley, Pat Malone, Johnny Murphy, Monte Pearson, Red Ruffing, Kemp Wicker, pitchers; Frankie Crosetti, Lou Gehrig, Don Heffner, Tony Lazzeri, Red Rolfe, Jack Saltzgaver, infielders; Joe DiMaggio, Roy Johnson, Jake Powell, Bob Seeds, George Selkirk, outfielders.

Giants – Harry Danning, Gus Mancuso, Roy Spencer, catchers; Slick Castleman, Dick Coffman, Freddie Fitzsimmons, Frank Gabler, Harry Gumbert, Carl Hubbell, Hal Schumacher, Al Smith, pitchers; Dick Bartell, Travis Jackson, Mark Koenig, Sam Leslie, Eddie Mayo, Bill Terry, Burgess Whitehead, infielders; Kiddo Davis, Hank Leiber, Joe Moore, Mel Ott, Jimmy Ripple, outfielders.

1937 - NEW YORK YANKEES A.L. (4) vs. NEW YORK GIANTS N.L. (1)
(Yankee Stadium / Polo Grounds)

Oct. 6	at Yankees	Yankees (Gomez)	8	Giants (Hubbell)	1
Oct. 7	at Yankees	Yankees (Ruffing)	8	Giants (Melton)	1
Oct. 8	at Giants	Yankees (Pearson)	5	Giants (Schumacher)	1
Oct. 9	at Giants	Giants (Hubbell)	7	Yankees (Hadley)	3
Oct. 10	at Giants	Yankees (Gomez)	4	Giants (Melton)	2

MANAGERS: Joe McCarthy, Yankees; Bill Terry, Giants

Yankees — Bill Dickey, Joe Glenn, Arndt Jorgens, catchers; Ivy Andrews, Spud Chandler, Lefty Gomez, Bump Hadley, Frank Makosky, Pat Malone, Johnny Murphy, Monte Pearson, Red Ruffing, Kemp Wicker, pitchers; Frankie Crosetti, Lou Gehrig, Don Heffner, Tony Lazzeri, Red Rolfe, Jack Saltzgaver, infielders; Joe DiMaggio, Tommy Henrich, Myril Hoag, Jake Powell, George Selkirk, outfielders.

Giants — Harry Danning, Ed Madjeski, Gus Mancuso, catchers; Tom Baker, Don Brennan, Slick Castleman, Dick Coffman, Harry Gumbert, Carl Hubbell, Cliff Melton, Hal Schumacher, Al Smith, pitchers; Dick Bartell, Lou Chiozza, Mickey Haslin, Sam Leslie, Johnny McCarthy, Mel Ott, Blondy Ryan, Burgess Whitehead, infielders; Wally Berger, Hank Leiber, Joe Moore, Jimmy Ripple, outfielders.

1938 - NEW YORK YANKEES A.L. (4) vs. CHICAGO CUBS N.L. (0)
(Yankee Stadium / Wrigley Field)

Oct. 5	at Chi.	New York (Ruffing)	3	Chicago (Lee)	1
Oct. 6	at Chi.	New York (Gomez)	6	Chicago (Dean)	3
Oct. 8	at NY	New York (Pearson)	5	Chicago (Bryant)	2
Oct. 9	at NY	New York (Ruffing)	8	Chicago (Lee)	3

MANAGERS: Joe McCarthy, Yankees; Gabby Hartnett, Cubs

Yankees — Bill Dickey, Joe Glenn, Arndt Jorgens, catchers; Ivy Andrews, Spud Chandler, Wes Ferrell, Lefty Gomez, Bump Hadley, Johnny Murphy, Monte Pearson, Red Ruffing, Steve Sundra, pitchers; Frankie Crosetti, Babe Dahlgren, Lou Gehrig, Joe Gordon, Billy Knickerbocker, Red Rolfe, infielders; Joe DiMaggio, Tommy Henrich, Myril Hoag, Jake Powell, George Selkirk, outfielders.

Cubs — Bob Garbark, Gabby Hartnett, Ken O'Dea, catchers; Clay Bryant, Tex Carleton, Dizzy Dean, Larry French, Bill Lee, Vance Page, Charlie Root, Jack Russell, pitchers; Phil Cavarretta, Ripper Collins, Stan Hack, Billy Herman, Billy Jurges, Tony Lazzeri, infielders; Jim Asbell, Frank Demaree, Augie Galan, Joe Marty, Carl Reynolds, outfielders.

1939 - NEW YORK YANKEES A.L. (4) vs. CINCINNATI REDS N.L. (0)
(Yankee Stadium / Crosley Field)

Oct. 4	at NY	New York (Ruffing)	2	Cincinnati (Derringer)	1	
Oct. 5	at NY	New York (Pearson)	4	Cincinnati (Walters)	0	
Oct. 7	at Cin.	New York (Hadley)	7	Cincinnati (Thompson)	3	
Oct. 8	at Cin.	New York (Murphy)	7	Cincinnati (Walters)	4	(10 innings)

MANAGERS: Joe McCarthy, Yankees; Bill McKechnie, Reds

Yankees — Bill Dickey, Arndt Jorgens, Buddy Rosar, catchers; Spud Chandler, Atley Donald, Lefty Gomez, Bump Hadley, Oral Hildebrand, Johnny Murphy, Monte Pearson, Red Ruffing, Marius Russo, Steve Sundra, pitchers; Frankie Crosetti, Babe Dahlgren, Lou Gehrig, Joe Gordon, Billy Knickerbocker, Red Rolfe, infielders; Joe DiMaggio, Tommy Henrich, Charlie Keller, Jake Powell, George Selkirk, outfielders.

Reds — Willard Hershberger, Ernie Lombardi, catchers; Paul Derringer, Lee Grissom, Hank Johnson, Whitey Moore, Johnny Niggeling, Milt Shoffner, Junior Thompson, Johnny Vander Meer, Bucky Walters, pitchers; Lonny Frey, Eddie Joost, Frank McCormick, Billy Myers, Lew Riggs, Les Scarsella, Bill Werber, infielders; Wally Berger, Tony Bongiovanni, Frenchy Bordagaray, Harry Craft, Lee Gamble, Ival Goodman, Al Simmons, outfielders.

1940 – CINCINNATI REDS N.L. (4) vs. DETROIT TIGERS A.L. (3)
(Crosley Field / Briggs Stadium)

Oct. 2	at Cin.	Detroit (Newsom)	7	Cincinnati (Derringer)	2
Oct. 3	at Cin.	Cincinnati (Walters)	5	Detroit (Rowe)	3
Oct. 4	at Det.	Detroit (Bridges)	7	Cincinnati (Turner)	4
Oct. 5	at Det.	Cincinnati (Derringer)	5	Detroit (Trout)	2
Oct. 6	at Det.	Detroit (Newsom)	8	Cincinnati (Thompson)	0
Oct. 7	at Cin.	Cincinnati (Walters)	4	Detroit (Rowe)	0
Oct. 8	at Cin.	Cincinnati (Derringer)	2	Detroit (Newsom)	1

MANAGERS: Bill McKechnie, Reds; Del Baker, Tigers

Reds – Bill Baker, Ernie Lombardi, Jimmie Wilson, catchers; Joe Beggs, Paul Derringer, Witt Guise, Johnny Hutchings, Whitey Moore, Elmer Riddle, Milt Shoffner, Junior Thompson, Jim Turner, Johnny Vander Meer, Bucky Walters, pitchers; Lonny Frey, Eddie Joost, Frank McCormick, Billy Myers, Lew Riggs, Bill Werber, infielders; Morris Arnovich, Harry Craft, Ival Goodman, Myron McCormick, Jimmy Ripple, outfielders.

Tigers – Billy Sullivan Jr., Birdie Tebbetts, catchers; Al Benton, Tommy Bridges, Johnny Gorsica, Fred Hutchinson, Archie McKain, Hal Newhouser, Bobo Newsom, Schoolboy Rowe, Tom Seats, Clay Smith, Dizzy Trout, pitchers; Dick Bartell, Frank Croucher, Charlie Gehringer, Pinky Higgins, Dutch Meyer, Rudy York, infielders; Earl Averill, Bruce Campbell, Pete Fox, Hank Greenberg, Barney McCosky, Tuck Stainback, outfielders

1941 – NEW YORK YANKEES A.L. (4) vs. BROOKLYN DODGERS N.L. (1)
(Yankee Stadium / Ebbets Field)

Oct. 1	at NY	New York (Ruffing)	3	Brooklyn (Davis)	2
Oct. 2	at NY	Brooklyn (Wyatt)	3	New York (Chandler)	2
Oct. 4	at Brk.	New York (Russo)	2	Brooklyn (Casey)	1
Oct. 5	at Brk.	New York (Murphy)	7	Brooklyn (Casey)	4
Oct. 6	at Brk.	New York (Bonham)	3	Brooklyn (Wyatt)	1

POSTPONED: (Rain) Oct. 3

MANAGERS: Joe McCarthy, Yankees; Leo Durocher, Dodgers

Yankees – Bill Dickey, Buddy Rosar, Ken Silvestri, catchers; Ernie Bonham, Norm Branch, Marv Breuer, Spud Chandler, Atley Donald, Lefty Gomez, Johnny Murphy, Steve Peek, Red Ruffing, Marius Russo, Charley Stanceu, pitchers; Frankie Crosetti, Joe Gordon, Gerry Priddy, Phil Rizzuto, Red Rolfe, Johnny Sturm, infielders; Frenchy Bordagaray, Joe DiMaggio, Tommy Henrich, Charlie Keller, George Selkirk, outfielders.

Dodgers – Herman Franks, Mickey Owen, catchers; Ed Albosta, Johnny Allen, Hugh Casey, Curt Davis, Tom Drake, Freddie Fitzsimmons, Larry French, Luke Hamlin, Kirby Higbe, Newt Kimball, Whit Wyatt, pitchers; Dolph Camilli, Pete Coscarart, Leo Durocher, Billy Herman, Cookie Lavagetto, Pee Wee Reese, Lew Riggs, infielders; Augie Galan, Joe Medwick, Pete Reiser, Dixie Walker, Jimmy Wasdell, outfielders.

1942 – ST. LOUIS CARDINALS N.L. (4) vs. NEW YORK YANKEES A.L. (1)
(Sportsman's Park / Yankee Stadium)

Sept. 30	at StL.	New York (Ruffing)	7	St. Louis (M. Cooper)	4
Oct. 1	at StL.	St. Louis (Beazley)	4	New York (Bonham)	3
Oct. 3	at NY	St. Louis (White)	2	New York (Chandler)	0
Oct. 4	at NY	St. Louis (Lanier)	9	New York (Donald)	6
Oct. 5	at NY	St. Louis (Beazley)	4	New York (Ruffing)	2

MANAGERS: Billy Southworth, Cardinals; Joe McCarthy, Yankees

Cardinals – Walker Cooper, Sam Narron, Ken O'Dea, catchers; Johnny Beazley, Mort Cooper, Murry Dickson, Harry Gumbert, Howie Krist, Max Lanier, Whitey Moore, Howie Pollet, Ernie White, pitchers; Jimmy Brown, Creepy Crespi, Johnny Hopp, Whitey Kurowski, Marty Marion, Ray Sanders, infielders; Terry Moore, Stan Musial, Enos Slaughter, Coaker Triplett, Harry Walker, outfielders.

Yankees – Bill Dickey, Rollie Hemsley, Buddy Rosar, catchers; Ernie Bonham, Hank Borowy, Marv Breuer, Spud Chandler, Atley Donald, Lefty Gomez, Johnny Lindell, Johnny Murphy, Red Ruffing, Marius Russo, Jim Turner, pitchers; Frankie Crosetti, Joe Gordon, Buddy Hassett, Gerry Priddy, Phil Rizzuto, Red Rolfe, infielders; Roy Cullenbine, Joe DiMaggio, Charlie Keller, George Selkirk, Tuck Stainback, outfielders.

1943 – NEW YORK YANKEES A.L. (4) vs. ST. LOUIS CARDINALS N.L. (1)

(Yankee Stadium / Sportsman's Park)

Oct. 5	at NY	New York (Chandler)	4	St. Louis (Lanier)	2
Oct. 6	at NY	St. Louis (M. Cooper)	4	New York (Bonham)	3
Oct. 7	at NY	New York (Borowy)	6	St. Louis (Brazle)	2
Oct. 10	at StL.	New York (Russo)	2	St. Louis (Brecheen)	1
Oct. 11	at StL.	New York (Chandler)	2	St. Louis (M. Cooper)	0

MANAGERS: Joe McCarthy, Yankees; Billy Southworth, Cardinals

Yankees – Bill Dickey, Rollie Hemsley, Ken Sears, catchers; Ernie Bonham, Hank Borowy, Marv Breuer, Tommy Byrne, Spud Chandler, Atley Donald, Johnny Murphy, Marius Russo, Jim Turner, Butch Wensloff, Bill Zuber, pitchers; Frankie Crosetti, Nick Etten, Joe Gordon, Oscar Grimes, Billy Johnson, Snuffy Stirnweiss, infielders; Charlie Keller, Johnny Lindell, Bud Metheny, Tuck Stainback, Roy Weatherly, outfielders.

Cardinals – Walker Cooper, Sam Narron, Ken O'Dea, catchers; Al Brazle, Harry Brecheen, Mort Cooper, Murry Dickson, Harry Gumbert, Howie Krist, Max Lanier, George Munger, Ernie White, pitchers; George Fallon, Debs Garms, Lou Klein, Whitey Kurowski, Marty Marion, Ray Sanders, infielders; Frank Demaree, Johnny Hopp, Danny Litwhiler, Stan Musial, Harry Walker, outfielders.

1944 – ST. LOUIS CARDINALS N.L. (4) vs. ST. LOUIS BROWNS A.L. (2)

(Sportsman's Park / Sportsman's Park)

Oct. 4	at Cardinals	Browns (Galehouse)	2	Cardinals (M. Cooper)	1	
Oct. 5	at Cardinals	Cardinals (Donnelly)	3	Browns (Muncrief)	2	(11 innings)
Oct. 6	at Browns	Browns (Kramer)	6	Cardinals (Wilks)	2	
Oct. 7	at Browns	Cardinals (Brecheen)	5	Browns (Jakucki)	1	
Oct. 8	at Browns	Cardinals (M. Cooper)	2	Browns (Galehouse)	0	
Oct. 9	at Cardinals	Cardinals (Lanier)	3	Browns (Potter)	1	

MANAGERS: Billy Southworth, Cardinals; Luke Sewell, Browns

Cardinals – Walker Cooper, Bob Keely, Ken O'Dea, catchers; Harry Brecheen, Bud Byerly, Mort Cooper, Blix Donnelly, Al Jurisich, Max Lanier, Freddy Schmidt, Ted Wilks, pitchers; George Fallon, Whitey Kurowski, Marty Marion, Ray Sanders, Emil Verban, infielders; Augie Bergamo, Debs Garms, Johnny Hopp, Danny Litwhiler, Pepper Martin, Stan Musial, outfielders.

Browns – Red Hayworth, Frank Mancuso, Tom Turner, catchers; George Caster, Denny Galehouse, Al Hollingsworth, Willis Hudlin, Sig Jakucki, Jack Kramer, Bob Muncrief, Nels Potter, Tex Shirley, Sam Zoldak, pitchers; Floyd Baker, Mark Christman, Ellis Clary, Don Gutteridge, George McQuinn, Vern Stephens, infielders; Milt Byrnes, Mike Chartak, Mike Kreevich, Chet Laabs, Gene Moore, Al Zarilla, outfielders.

1945 – DETROIT TIGERS A.L. (4) vs. CHICAGO CUBS N.L. (3)

(Briggs Stadium / Wrigley Field)

Oct. 3	at Det.	Chicago (Borowy)	9	Detroit (Newhouser)	0	
Oct. 4	at Det.	Detroit (Trucks)	4	Chicago (Wyse)	1	
Oct. 5	at Det.	Chicago (Passeau)	3	Detroit (Overmire)	0	
Oct. 6	at Chi.	Detroit (Trout)	4	Chicago (Prim)	1	
Oct. 7	at Chi.	Detroit (Newhouser)	8	Chicago (Borowy)	4	
Oct. 8	at Chi.	Chicago (Borowy)	8	Detroit (Trout)	7	(12 innings)
Oct. 10	at Chi.	Detroit (Newhouser)	9	Chicago (Borowy)	3	

MANAGERS: Steve O'Neill, Tigers; Charlie Grimm, Cubs

Tigers – Hack Miller, Paul Richards, Bob Swift, catchers; Al Benton, Tommy Bridges, George Caster, Zeb Eaton, Art Houtteman, Les Mueller, Hal Newhouser, Stubby Overmire, Billy Pierce, Jim Tobin, Dizzy Trout, Virgil Trucks, Walter Wilson, pitchers; Red Borom, Joe Hoover, Bob Maier, Eddie Mayo, John McHale, Jimmy Outlaw, Skeeter Webb, Rudy York, infielders; Doc Cramer, Roy Cullenbine, Hank Greenberg, Chuck Hostetler, Ed Mierkowicz, Hub Walker, outfielders.

Cubs – Paul Gillespie, Mickey Livingston, Clyde McCullough, Len Rice, Dewey Williams, catchers; Hi Bithorn, Hank Borowy, Bob Chipman, Paul Derringer, Paul Erickson, Ed Hanyzewski, Claude Passeau, Ray Prim, Walter Signer, Ray Starr, Hy Vandenburg, Lon Warneke, Hank Wyse, pitchers; Heinz Becker, Cy Block, Phil Cavarretta, Stan Hack, Roy Hughes, Don Johnson, Lennie Merullo, Bill Schuster, infielders; Peanuts Lowrey, Bill Nicholson, Andy Pafko, Ed Sauer, Frank Secory, outfielders.

1946 – ST. LOUIS CARDINALS N.L. (4) vs. BOSTON RED SOX A.L. (3)
(Sportsman's Park / Fenway Park)

Oct. 6	at StL.	Boston (Johnson)	3	St. Louis (Pollet)	2	(10 innings)
Oct. 7	at StL.	St. Louis (Brecheen)	3	Boston (Harris)	0	
Oct. 9	at Bos.	Boston (Ferriss)	4	St. Louis (Dickson)	0	
Oct. 10	at Bos.	St. Louis (Munger)	12	Boston (Hughson)	3	
Oct. 11	at Bos.	Boston (Dobson)	6	St. Louis (Brazle)	3	
Oct. 13	at StL.	St. Louis (Brecheen)	4	Boston (Harris)	1	
Oct. 15	at StL.	St. Louis (Brecheen)	4	Boston (Klinger)	3	

MANAGERS: Eddie Dyer, Cardinals; Joe Cronin, Red Sox

Cardinals – Joe Garagiola, Clyde Kluttz, Del Rice, catchers; Red Barrett, Johnny Beazley, Al Brazle, Harry Brecheen, Ken Burkhart, Murry Dickson, Johnny Grodzicki, Howie Krist, George Munger, Howie Pollet, Freddy Schmidt, Ted Wilks, pitchers; Jeff Cross, Nippy Jones, Whitey Kurowski, Marty Marion, Stan Musial, Red Schoendienst, infielders; Buster Adams, Erv Dusak, Bill Endicott, Terry Moore, Walter Sessi, Dick Sisler, Enos Slaughter, Harry Walker, outfielders.

Red Sox – Ed McGah, Roy Partee, Hal Wagner, catchers; Jim Bagby, Mace Brown, Joe Dobson, Clem Dreisewerd, Boo Ferriss, Mickey Harris, Tex Hughson, Earl Johnson, Bob Klinger, Mike Ryba, Charlie Wagner, Bill Zuber, pitchers; Paul Campbell, Bobby Doerr, Don Gutteridge, Pinky Higgins, Eddie Pellagrini, Johnny Pesky, Rip Russell, Rudy York, infielders; Leon Culberson, Dom DiMaggio, Johnny Lazor, Tom McBride, George Metkovich, Wally Moses, Ted Williams, outfielders.

1947 – NEW YORK YANKEES A.L. (4) vs. BROOKLYN DODGERS N.L. (3)
(Yankee Stadium / Ebbets Field)

Sept. 30	at NY	New York (Shea)	5	Brooklyn (Branca)	3
Oct. 1	at NY	New York (Reynolds)	10	Brooklyn (Lombardi)	3
Oct. 2	at Brk.	Brooklyn (Casey)	9	New York (Newsom)	8
Oct. 3	at Brk.	Brooklyn (Casey)	3	New York (Bevens)	2
Oct. 4	at Brk	New York (Shea)	2	Brooklyn (Barney)	1
Oct. 5	at NY	Brooklyn (Branca)	8	New York (Page)	6
Oct. 6	at NY	New York (Page)	5	Brooklyn (Gregg)	2

MANAGERS: Bucky Harris, Yankees; Burt Shotton, Dodgers

Yankees – Yogi Berra, Ralph Houk, Sherm Lollar, Aaron Robinson, catchers; Bill Bevens, Spud Chandler, Karl Drews, Randy Gumpert, Don Johnson, Bobo Newsom, Joe Page, Vic Raschi, Allie Reynolds, Spec Shea, Butch Wensloff, pitchers; Bobby Brown, Lonny Frey, Billy Johnson, George McQuinn, Jack Phillips, Phil Rizzuto, Snuffy Stirnweiss, infielders; Allie Clark, Joe DiMaggio, Tommy Henrich, Charlie Keller, Johnny Lindell, outfielders.

Dodgers – Bobby Bragan, Bruce Edwards, Gil Hodges, catchers; Dan Bankhead, Rex Barney, Hank Behrman, Ralph Branca, Hugh Casey, Hal Gregg, Joe Hatten, Clyde King, Vic Lombardi, Harry Taylor, pitchers; Tommy Brown, Spider Jorgensen, Cookie Lavagetto, Eddie Miksis, Pee Wee Reese, Jackie Robinson, Stan Rojek, Eddie Stanky, Arky Vaughan, infielders; Carl Furillo, Al Gionfriddo, Gene Hermanski, Pete Reiser, Dixie Walker, outfielders.

1948 – CLEVELAND INDIANS A.L. (4) vs. BOSTON BRAVES N.L. (2)
(Cleveland Stadium / Braves Field)

Oct. 6	at Bos.	Boston (Sain)	1	Cleveland (Feller)	0
Oct. 7	at Bos.	Cleveland (Lemon)	4	Boston (Spahn)	1
Oct. 8	at Clev.	Cleveland (Bearden)	2	Boston (Bickford)	0
Oct. 9	at Clev.	Cleveland (Gromek)	2	Boston (Sain)	1
Oct. 10	at Clev.	Boston (Spahn)	11	Cleveland (Feller)	5
Oct. 11	at Bos.	Cleveland (Lemon)	4	Boston (Voiselle)	3

MANAGERS: Lou Boudreau, Indians; Billy Southworth, Braves

Indians – Jim Hegan, Joe Tipton, catchers; Gene Bearden, Russ Christopher, Bob Feller, Steve Gromek, Eddie Klieman, Bob Lemon, Bob Muncrief, Satchel Paige, Sam Zoldak, pitchers; Johnny Berardino, Ray Boone, Lou Boudreau, Joe Gordon, Ken Keltner, Eddie Robinson, Al Rosen, infielders; Allie Clark, Larry Doby, Walt Judnich, Bob Kennedy, Dale Mitchell, Hal Peck, Thurman Tucker, outfielders.

Braves – Phil Masi, Bill Salkeld, catchers; Red Barrett, Vern Bickford, Bobby Hogue, Al Lyons, Nels Potter, Johnny Sain, Clyde Shoun, Warren Spahn, Bill Voiselle, Ernie White, pitchers; Alvin Dark, Bob Elliott, Frank McCormick, Connie Ryan, Ray Sanders, Sibby Sisti, Eddie Stanky, Bobby Sturgeon, Earl Torgeson, infielders; Clint Conatser, Tommy Holmes, Mike McCormick, Marv Rickert, outfielders.

1949 – NEW YORK YANKEES A.L. (4) vs. BROOKLYN DODGERS N.L. (1)

(Yankee Stadium / Ebbets Field)

Oct. 5	at NY	New York (Reynolds)	1	Brooklyn (Newcombe)	0
Oct. 6	at NY	Brooklyn (Roe)	1	New York (Raschi)	0
Oct. 7	at Brk.	New York (Page)	4	Brooklyn (Branca)	3
Oct. 8	at Brk.	New York (Lopat)	6	Brooklyn (Newcombe)	4
Oct. 9	at Brk.	New York (Raschi)	10	Brooklyn (Barney)	6

MANAGERS: Casey Stengel, Yankees; Burt Shotton, Dodgers

Yankees – Yogi Berra, Gus Niarhos, Charlie Silvera, catchers; Ralph Buxton, Tommy Byrne, Ed Lopat, Cuddles Marshall, Joe Page, Duane Pillette, Vic Raschi, Allie Reynolds, Fred Sanford, pitchers; Bobby Brown, Jerry Coleman, Tommy Henrich, Billy Johnson, Johnny Mize, Phil Rizzuto, Snuffy Stirnweiss, infielders; Hank Bauer, Joe DiMaggio, Charlie Keller, Johnny Lindell, Cliff Mapes, Gene Woodling, outfielders.

Dodgers – Roy Campanella, Bruce Edwards, catchers; Jack Banta, Rex Barney, Ralph Branca, Carl Erskine, Joe Hatten, Paul Minner, Don Newcombe, Erv Palica, Preacher Roe, pitchers; Billy Cox, Gil Hodges, Spider Jorgensen, Eddie Miksis, Pee Wee Reese, Jackie Robinson, infielders; Tommy Brown, Carl Furillo, Gene Hermanski, Mike McCormick, Luis Olmo, Marv Rackley, Duke Snider, Dick Whitman, outfielders.

1950 – NEW YORK YANKEES A.L. (4) vs. PHILADELPHIA PHILLIES N.L. (0)

(Yankee Stadium / Shibe Park)

Oct. 4	at Phil.	New York (Raschi)	1	Philadelphia (Konstanty)	0	
Oct. 5	at Phil.	New York (Reynolds)	2	Philadelphia (Roberts)	1	(10 innings)
Oct. 6	at NY	New York (Ferrick)	3	Philadelphia (Meyer)	2	
Oct. 7	at NY	New York (Ford)	5	Philadelphia (Miller)	2	

MANAGERS: Casey Stengel, Yankees; Eddie Sawyer, Phillies

Yankees – Yogi Berra, Ralph Houk, Charlie Silvera, catchers; Tommy Byrne, Tom Ferrick, Whitey Ford, Ed Lopat, Joe Ostrowski, Joe Page, Vic Raschi, Allie Reynolds, Fred Sanford, pitchers; Bobby Brown, Jerry Coleman, Joe Collins, Johnny Hopp, Billy Johnson, Billy Martin, Johnny Mize, Phil Rizzuto, infielders; Hank Bauer, Joe DiMaggio, Jackie Jensen, Cliff Mapes, Gene Woodling, outfielders.

Phillies – Stan Lopata, Andy Seminick, Ken Silvestri, catchers; Milo Candini, Bubba Church, Blix Donnelly, Ken Heintzelman, Ken Johnson, Jim Konstanty, Russ Meyer, Bob Miller, Robin Roberts, Jocko Thompson, pitchers; Jimmy Bloodworth, Ralph Caballero, Mike Goliat, Granny Hamner, Willie Jones, Eddie Waitkus, infielders; Richie Ashburn, Del Ennis, Stan Hollmig, Jackie Mayo, Dick Sisler, Dick Whitman, outfielders.

1951 – NEW YORK YANKEES A.L. (4) vs. NEW YORK GIANTS N.L. (2)

(Yankee Stadium / Polo Grounds)

Oct. 4	at Yankees	Giants (Koslo)	5	Yankees (Reynolds)	1
Oct. 5	at Yankees	Yankees (Lopat)	3	Giants (Jansen)	1
Oct. 6	at Giants	Giants (Hearn)	6	Yankees (Raschi)	2
Oct. 8	at Giants	Yankees (Reynolds)	6	Giants (Maglie)	2
Oct. 9	at Giants	Yankees (Lopat)	13	Giants (Jansen)	1
Oct. 10	at Yankees	Yankees (Raschi)	4	Giants (Koslo)	3

POSTPONED: (Rain) Oct. 7

MANAGERS: Casey Stengel, Yankees; Leo Durocher, Giants

Yankees – Yogi Berra, Ralph Houk, Charlie Silvera, catchers; Bobby Hogue, Bob Kuzava, Ed Lopat, Tom Morgan, Joe Ostrowski, Stubby Overmire, Vic Raschi, Allie Reynolds, Johnny Sain, Art Schallock, Spec Shea, pitchers; Bobby Brown, Jerry Coleman, Joe Collins, Johnny Hopp, Billy Martin, Gil McDougald, Johnny Mize, Phil Rizzuto, infielders; Hank Bauer, Joe DiMaggio, Mickey Mantle, Gene Woodling, outfielders.

Giants – Ray Noble, Wes Westrum, Sal Yvars, catchers; Al Corwin, Jim Hearn, Larry Jansen, Sheldon Jones, Monte Kennedy, Alex Konikowski, Dave Koslo, Sal Maglie, George Spencer, pitchers; Alvin Dark, Whitey Lockman, Jack Lohrke, Bill Rigney, Hank Schenz, Eddie Stanky, Hank Thompson, Bobby Thomson, Davey Williams, infielders; Clint Hartung, Monte Irvin, Willie Mays, Don Mueller, outfielders.

1952 - NEW YORK YANKEES A.L. (4) vs. BROOKLYN DODGERS N.L. (3)
(Yankee Stadium / Ebbets Field)

Oct. 1	at Brk.	Brooklyn (Black)	4	New York (Reynolds)	2	
Oct. 2	at Brk.	New York (Raschi)	7	Brooklyn (Erskine)	1	
Oct. 3	at NY	Brooklyn (Roe)	5	New York (Lopat)	3	
Oct. 4	at NY	New York (Reynolds)	2	Brooklyn (Black)	0	
Oct. 5	at NY	Brooklyn (Erskine)	6	New York (Sain)	5	(11 innings)
Oct. 6	at Brk.	New York (Raschi)	3	Brooklyn (Loes)	2	
Oct. 7	at Brk.	New York (Reynolds)	4	Brooklyn (Black)	2	

MANAGERS: Casey Stengel, Yankees; Chuck Dressen, Dodgers

Yankees — Yogi Berra, Ralph Houk, Charlie Silvera, catchers; Ewell Blackwell, Tom Gorman, Bob Kuzava, Ed Lopat, Jim McDonald, Bill Miller, Joe Ostrowski, Vic Raschi, Allie Reynolds, Johnny Sain, Ray Scarborough, pitchers; Loren Babe, Jim Brideweser, Joe Collins, Billy Martin, Gil McDougald, Johnny Mize, Phil Rizzuto, infielders; Hank Bauer, Mickey Mantle, Irv Noren, Gene Woodling, outfielders.

Dodgers — Roy Campanella, Rube Walker, catchers; Joe Black, Ralph Branca, Carl Erskine, Clyde King, Clem Labine, Joe Landrum, Ken Lehman, Billy Loes, Ray Moore, Preacher Roe, Johnny Rutherford, Ben Wade, pitchers; Rocky Bridges, Billy Cox, Gil Hodges, Bobby Morgan, Rocky Nelson, Pee Wee Reese, Jackie Robinson, infielders; Sandy Amoros, Carl Furillo, Tommy Holmes, Andy Pafko, George Shuba, Duke Snider, outfielders.

1953 - NEW YORK YANKEES A.L. (4) vs. BROOKLYN DODGERS N.L. (2)
(Yankee Stadium / Ebbets Field)

Sept. 30	at NY	New York (Sain)	9	Brooklyn (Labine)	5
Oct. 1	at NY	New York (Lopat)	4	Brooklyn (Roe)	2
Oct. 2	at Brk.	Brooklyn (Erskine)	3	New York (Raschi)	2
Oct. 3	at Brk.	Brooklyn (Loes)	7	New York (Ford)	3
Oct. 4	at Brk.	New York (McDonald)	11	Brooklyn (Podres)	7
Oct. 5	at NY	New York (Reynolds)	4	Brooklyn (Labine)	3

MANAGERS: Casey Stengel, Yankees; Chuck Dressen, Dodgers

Yankees — Yogi Berra, Charlie Silvera, Gus Triandos, catchers; Whitey Ford, Tom Gorman, Steve Kraly, Bob Kuzava, Ed Lopat, Jim McDonald, Bill Miller, Vic Raschi, Allie Reynolds, Johnny Sain, Art Schallock, pitchers; Don Bollweg, Andy Carey, Jerry Coleman, Joe Collins, Billy Martin, Gil McDougald, Willie Miranda, Johnny Mize, Phil Rizzuto, infielders; Hank Bauer, Mickey Mantle, Irv Noren, Bill Renna, Gene Woodling, outfielders.

Dodgers — Roy Campanella, Rube Walker, catchers; Joe Black, Carl Erskine, Jim Hughes, Clem Labine, Billy Loes, Russ Meyer, Bob Milliken, Erv Palica, Johnny Podres, Preacher Roe, Ben Wade, pitchers; Wayne Belardi, Billy Cox, Jim Gilliam, Gil Hodges, Bobby Morgan, Pee Wee Reese, infielders; Bill Antonello, Carl Furillo, Jackie Robinson, George Shuba, Duke Snider, Don Thompson, Dick Williams, outfielders.

1954 - NEW YORK GIANTS N.L. (4) vs. CLEVELAND INDIANS A.L. (0)
(Polo Grounds / Cleveland Stadium)

Sept. 29	at NY	New York (Grissom)	5	Cleveland (Lemon)	2	(10 innings)
Sept. 30	at NY	New York (Antonelli)	3	Cleveland (Wynn)	1	
Oct. 1	at Clev.	New York (Gomez)	6	Cleveland (Garcia)	2	
Oct. 2	at Clev.	New York (Liddle)	7	Cleveland (Lemon)	4	

MANAGERS: Leo Durocher, Giants; Al Lopez, Indians

Giants — Ray Katt, Wes Westrum, catchers; Johnny Antonelli, Al Corwin, Paul Giel, Ruben Gomez, Marv Grissom, Jim Hearn, Alex Konikowski, Don Liddle, Sal Maglie, Windy McCall, Hoyt Wilhelm, Al Worthington, pitchers; Joey Amalfitano, Foster Castleman, Alvin Dark, Billy Gardner, Bobby Hofman, Whitey Lockman, Hank Thompson, Davey Williams, infielders; Monte Irvin, Willie Mays, Don Mueller, Dusty Rhodes, Bill Taylor, outfielders.

Indians — Mickey Grasso, Jim Hegan, Hal Naragon, catchers; Bob Feller, Mike Garcia, Bob Hooper, Art Houtteman, Bob Lemon, Don Mossi, Ray Narleski, Hal Newhouser, Early Wynn, pitchers; Bobby Avila, Sam Dente, Bill Glynn, Hank Majeski,, Rudy Regalado, Al Rosen, George Strickland, Vic Wertz, infielders; Larry Doby, Dale Mitchell, Dave Philley, David Pope, Al Smith, Wally Westlake, outfielders.

1955 – BROOKLYN DODGERS N.L. (4) vs. NEW YORK YANKEES A.L. (3)

(Ebbets Field / Yankee Stadium)

Sept. 28	at NY	New York (Ford)	6	Brooklyn (Newcombe)	5	
Sept. 29	at NY	New York (Byrne)	4	Brooklyn (Loes)	2	
Sept. 30	at Brk.	Brooklyn (Podres)	8	New York (Turley)	3	
Oct. 1	at Brk.	Brooklyn (Labine)	8	New York (Larsen)	5	
Oct. 2	at Brk.	Brooklyn (Craig)	5	New York (Grim)	3	
Oct. 3	at NY	New York (Ford)	5	Brooklyn (Spooner)	1	
Oct. 4	at NY	Brooklyn (Podres)	2	New York (Byrne)	0	

MANAGERS: Walter Alston, Dodgers; Casey Stengel, Yankees

Dodgers – Roy Campanella, Dixie Howell, Rube Walker, catchers; Don Bessent, Roger Craig, Carl Erskine, Sandy Koufax, Clem Labine, Billy Loes, Russ Meyer, Don Newcombe, Johnny Podres, Ed Roebuck, Karl Spooner, pitchers; Jim Gilliam, Don Hoak, Gil Hodges, Frank Kellert, Jackie Robinson, Pee Wee Reese, Don Zimmer, infielders; Sandy Amoros, Carl Furillo, George Shuba, Duke Snider, outfielders.

Yankees – Yogi Berra, Charlie Silvera, catchers; Tommy Byrne, Rip Coleman, Whitey Ford, Bob Grim, Johnny Kucks, Don Larsen, Tom Morgan, Tom Sturdivant, Bob Turley, Bob Wiesler, pitchers; Andy Carey, Tommy Carroll, Jerry Coleman, Joe Collins, Frank Leja, Gil McDougald, Billy Martin, Phil Rizzuto, Eddie Robinson, Bill Skowron, infielders; Hank Bauer, Bob Cerv, Elston Howard, Mickey Mantle, Irv Noren, outfielders.

1956 – NEW YORK YANKEES A.L. (4) vs. BROOKLYN DODGERS N.L. (3)

(Yankee Stadium / Ebbets Field)

Oct. 3	at Brk.	Brooklyn (Maglie)	6	New York (Ford)	3	
Oct. 5	at Brk.	Brooklyn (Bessent)	13	New York (Morgan)	8	
Oct. 6	at NY	New York (Ford)	5	Brooklyn (Craig)	3	
Oct. 7	at NY	New York (Sturdivant)	6	Brooklyn (Erskine)	2	
Oct. 8	at NY	New York (Larsen)	2	Brooklyn (Maglie)	0	
Oct. 9	at Brk.	Brooklyn (Labine)	1	New York (Turley)	0	(10 innings)
Oct. 10	at Brk.	New York (Kucks)	9	Brooklyn (Newcombe)	0	
POSTPONED: (Rain) Oct. 4						

MANAGERS: Casey Stengel, Yankees; Walter Alston, Dodgers

Yankees – Yogi Berra, Charlie Silvera, catchers; Tommy Byrne, Rip Coleman, Whitey Ford, Bob Grim, Johnny Kucks, Don Larsen, Mickey McDermott, Tom Morgan, Tom Sturdivant, Bob Turley, pitchers; Andy Carey, Tommy Carroll, Jerry Coleman, Joe Collins, Billy Hunter, Billy Martin, Gil McDougald, Bill Skowron, infielders; Hank Bauer, Bob Cerv, Elston Howard, Mickey Mantle, Norm Siebern, Enos Slaughter, Ted Wilson, outfielders.

Dodgers – Roy Campanella, Dixie Howell, Rube Walker, catchers; Don Bessent, Roger Craig, Don Drysdale, Carl Erskine, Sandy Koufax, Clem Labine, Ken Lehman, Sal Maglie, Don Newcombe, Ed Roebuck, pitchers; Chico Fernandez, Jim Gilliam, Gil Hodges, Randy Jackson, Charlie Neal, Pee Wee Reese, Jackie Robinson, infielders; Sandy Amoros, Gino Cimoli, Carl Furillo, Dale Mitchell, Duke Snider, outfielders.

1957 – MILWAUKEE BRAVES N.L. (4) vs. NEW YORK YANKEES A.L. (3)

(County Stadium / Yankee Stadium)

Oct. 2	at NY	New York (Ford)	3	Milwaukee (Spahn)	1	
Oct. 3	at NY	Milwaukee (Burdette)	4	New York (Shantz)	2	
Oct. 5	at Mil.	New York (Larsen)	12	Milwaukee (Buhl)	3	
Oct. 6	at Mil.	Milwaukee (Spahn)	7	New York (Grim)	5	(10 innings)
Oct. 7	at Mil.	Milwaukee (Burdette)	1	New York (Ford)	0	
Oct. 9	at NY	New York (Turley)	3	Milwaukee (Johnson)	2	
Oct. 10	at NY	Milwaukee (Burdette)	5	New York (Larsen)	0	

MANAGERS: Fred Haney, Braves; Casey Stengel, Yankees

Braves – Del Crandall, Del Rice, Carl Sawatski, catchers; Bob Buhl, Lew Burdette, Gene Conley, Ernie Johnson, Dave Jolly, Don McMahon, Taylor Phillips, Juan Pizarro, Warren Spahn, Bob Trowbridge, pitchers; Joe Adcock, Nippy Jones, Johnny Logan, Felix Mantilla, Eddie Mathews, Mel Roach, Red Schoendienst, Frank Torre, infielders; Hank Aaron, Wes Covington, John DeMerit, Bob Hazle, Andy Pafko, outfielders.

Yankees – Yogi Berra, Darrell Johnson, catchers; Tommy Byrne, Al Cicotte, Art Ditmar, Whitey Ford, Bob Grim, Johnny Kucks, Don Larsen, Bobby Shantz, Tom Sturdivant, Bob Turley, pitchers; Andy Carey, Jerry Coleman, Joe Collins, Tony Kubek, Jerry Lumpe, Gil McDougald, Bobby Richardson, Bill Skowron, infielders; Hank Bauer, Elston Howard, Mickey Mantle, Harry Simpson, Enos Slaughter, outfielders.

1958 – NEW YORK YANKEES A.L. (4) vs. MILWAUKEE BRAVES N.L. (3)
(Yankee Stadium / County Stadium)

Oct. 1	at Mil.	Milwaukee (Spahn)	4	New York (Duren)	3	(10 innings)
Oct. 2	at Mil.	Milwaukee (Burdette)	13	New York (Turley)	5	
Oct. 4	at NY	New York (Larsen)	4	Milwaukee (Rush)	0	
Oct. 5	at NY	Milwaukee (Spahn)	3	New York (Ford)	0	
Oct. 6	at NY	New York (Turley)	7	Milwaukee (Burdette)	0	
Oct. 8	at Mil.	New York (Duren)	4	Milwaukee (Spahn)	3	(10 innings)
Oct. 9	at Mil.	New York (Turley)	6	Milwaukee (Burdette)	2	

MANAGERS: Casey Stengel, Yankees; Fred Haney, Braves

Yankees – Yogi Berra, Elston Howard, Darrell Johnson, catchers; Murry Dickson, Art Ditmar, Ryne Duren, Whitey Ford, Johnny Kucks, Don Larsen, Duke Maas, Zack Monroe, Bobby Shantz, Tom Sturdivant, Bob Turley, pitchers; Andy Carey, Tony Kubek, Jerry Lumpe, Gil McDougald, Bobby Richardson, Bill Skowron, Marv Throneberry, infielders; Hank Bauer, Mickey Mantle, Norm Siebern, Enos Slaughter, outfielders.

Braves – Del Crandall, Del Rice, catchers; Bob Buhl, Lew Burdette, Gene Conley, Ernie Johnson, Don McMahon, Juan Pizarro, Humberto Robinson, Bob Rush, Warren Spahn, Bob Trowbridge, Carl Willey, pitchers; Joe Adcock, Harry Hanebrink, Johnny Logan, Felix Mantilla, Eddie Mathews, Red Schoendienst, Frank Torre, Casey Wise, infielders; Hank Aaron, Bill Bruton, Wes Covington, Andy Pafko, outfielders.

1959 – LOS ANGELES DODGERS N.L. (4) vs. CHICAGO WHITE SOX A.L. (2)
(Memorial Coliseum / Comiskey Park)

Oct. 1	at Chi.	Chicago (Wynn)	11	Los Angeles (Craig)	0
Oct. 2	at Chi.	Los Angeles (Podres)	4	Chicago (Shaw)	3
Oct. 4	at LA	Los Angeles (Drysdale)	3	Chicago (Donovan)	1
Oct. 5	at LA	Los Angeles (Sherry)	5	Chicago (Staley)	4
Oct. 6	at LA	Chicago (Shaw)	1	Los Angeles (Koufax)	0
Oct. 8	at Chi.	Los Angeles (Sherry)	9	Chicago (Wynn)	3

MANAGERS: Walter Alston, Dodgers; Al Lopez, White Sox

Dodgers – Joe Pignatano, Johnny Roseboro, catchers; Chuck Churn, Roger Craig, Don Drysdale, Johnny Klippstein, Sandy Koufax, Clem Labine, Danny McDevitt, Johnny Podres, Larry Sherry, Stan Williams, pitchers; Jim Gilliam, Gil Hodges, Charlie Neal, Maury Wills, Don Zimmer, infielders; Don Demeter, Chuck Essegian, Ron Fairly, Carl Furillo, Norm Larker, Wally Moon, Rip Repulski, Duke Snider, outfielders.

White Sox – Earl Battey, Sherm Lollar, Johnny Romano, catchers; Rudy Arias, Dick Donovan, Barry Latman, Turk Lown, Ken McBride, Ray Moore, Billy Pierce, Bob Shaw, Gerry Staley, Early Wynn, pitchers; Luis Aparicio, Norm Cash, Sammy Esposito, Nellie Fox, Billy Goodman, Ted Kluszewski, Bubba Phillips, Earl Torgeson, infielders; Jim Landis, Jim McAnany, Jim Rivera, Al Smith, outfielders.

1960 – PITTSBURGH PIRATES N.L. (4) vs. NEW YORK YANKEES A.L. (3)
(Forbes Field / Yankee Stadium)

Oct. 5	at Pitt.	Pittsburgh (Law)	6	New York (Ditmar)	4
Oct. 6	at Pitt.	New York (Turley)	16	Pittsburgh (Friend)	3
Oct. 8	at NY	New York (Ford)	10	Pittsburgh (Mizell)	0
Oct. 9	at NY	Pittsburgh (Law)	3	New York (Terry)	2
Oct. 10	at NY	Pittsburgh (Haddix)	5	New York (Ditmar)	2
Oct. 12	at Pitt.	New York (Ford)	12	Pittsburgh (Friend)	0
Oct. 13	at Pitt.	Pittsburgh (Haddix)	10	New York (Terry)	9

MANAGERS: Danny Murtaugh, Pirates; Casey Stengel, Yankees

Pirates – Smoky Burgess, Bob Oldis, Hal W. Smith, catchers; Tom Cheney, Roy Face, Bob Friend, Joe Gibbon, Fred Green, Harvey Haddix, Clem Labine, Vern Law, Vinegar Bend Mizell, George Witt, pitchers; Gene Baker, Dick Groat, Don Hoak, Bill Mazeroski, Rocky Nelson, Dick Schofield, Dick Stuart, infielders; Joe Christopher, Gino Cimoli, Roberto Clemente, Bob Skinner, Bill Virdon, outfielders.

Yankees – Yogi Berra, Johnny Blanchard, Elston Howard, catchers; Luis Arroyo, Jim Coates, Art Ditmar, Ryne Duren, Whitey Ford, Eli Grba, Duke Maas, Bobby Shantz, Bill Stafford, Ralph Terry, Bob Turley, pitchers; Clete Boyer, Joe DeMaestri, Tony Kubek, Dale Long, Gil McDougald, Bobby Richardson, Bill Skowron, infielders; Bob Cerv, Hector Lopez, Mickey Mantle, Roger Maris, outfielders.

1961 – NEW YORK YANKEES A.L. (4) vs. CINCINNATI REDS N.L. (1)
(Yankee Stadium / Crosley Field)

Oct. 4	at NY	New York (Ford)	2	Cincinnati (O'Toole)	0
Oct. 5	at NY	Cincinnati (Jay)	6	New York (Terry)	2
Oct. 7	at Cin.	New York (Arroyo)	3	Cincinnati (Purkey)	2
Oct. 8	at Cin.	New York (Ford)	7	Cincinnati (O'Toole)	0
Oct. 9	at Cin.	New York (Daley)	13	Cincinnati (Jay)	5

MANAGERS: Ralph Houk, Yankees; Fred Hutchinson, Reds

Yankees – Johnny Blanchard, Elston Howard, catchers; Luis Arroyo, Tex Clevenger, Jim Coates, Bud Daley, Al Downing, Whitey Ford, Hal Reniff, Rollie Sheldon, Bill Stafford, Ralph Terry, Bob Turley, pitchers; Clete Boyer, Joe DeMaestri, Billy Gardner, Bob Hale, Tony Kubek, Bobby Richardson, Bill Skowron, infielders; Yogi Berra, Hector Lopez, Mickey Mantle, Roger Maris, Jack Reed, outfielders.

Reds – Johnny Edwards, Darrell Johnson, Jerry Zimmerman, catchers; Jim Brosnan, Bill Henry, Jay Hook, Ken Hunt, Joey Jay, Ken Johnson, Sherman Jones, Jim Maloney, Jim O'Toole, Bob Purkey, pitchers; Don Blasingame, Leo Cardenas, Elio Chacon, Gordy Coleman, Gene Freese, Dick Gernert, Eddie Kasko, infielders; Gus Bell, Jerry Lynch, Vada Pinson, Wally Post, Frank Robinson, outfielders.

1962 – NEW YORK YANKEES A.L. (4) vs. SAN FRANCISCO GIANTS N.L. (3)
(Yankee Stadium / Candlestick Park)

Oct. 4	at SF	New York (Ford)	6	San Francisco (O'Dell)	2
Oct. 5	at SF	San Francisco (Sanford)	2	New York (Terry)	0
Oct. 7	at NY	New York (Stafford)	3	San Francisco (Pierce)	2
Oct. 8	at NY	San Francisco (Larsen)	7	New York (Coates)	3
Oct. 10	at NY	New York (Terry)	5	San Francisco (Sanford)	3
Oct. 15	at SF	San Francisco (Pierce)	5	New York (Ford)	2
Oct. 16	at SF	New York (Terry)	1	San Francisco (Sanford)	0

POSTPONED: (Rain) Oct. 9, 12, 13, 14

MANAGERS: Ralph Houk, Yankees; Alvin Dark, Giants

Yankees – Johnny Blanchard, Elston Howard, catchers; Luis Arroyo, Jim Bouton, Marshall Bridges, Tex Clevenger, Jim Coates, Bud Daley, Whitey Ford, Rollie Sheldon, Bill Stafford, Ralph Terry, Bob Turley, pitchers; Clete Boyer, Tony Kubek, Phil Linz, Dale Long, Bobby Richardson, Bill Skowron, infielders; Yogi Berra, Hector Lopez, Mickey Mantle, Roger Maris, Jack Reed, Tom Tresh, outfielders.

Giants – Ed Bailey, Tom Haller, John Orsino, catchers; Bobby Bolin, Jim Duffalo, Bob Garibaldi, Don Larsen, Juan Marichal, Mike McCormick, Stu Miller, Billy O'Dell, Billy Pierce, Jack Sanford, pitchers; Ernie Bowman, Orlando Cepeda, Jim Davenport, Chuck Hiller, Willie McCovey, Jose Pagan, infielders; Felipe Alou, Matty Alou, Carl Boles, Harvey Kuenn, Willie Mays, Bob Nieman, outfielders.

1963 – LOS ANGELES DODGERS N.L. (4) vs. NEW YORK YANKEES A.L. (0)
(Dodger Stadium / Yankee Stadium)

Oct. 2	at NY	Los Angeles (Koufax)	5	New York (Ford)	2
Oct. 3	at NY	Los Angeles (Podres)	4	New York (Downing)	1
Oct. 5	at LA	Los Angeles (Drysdale)	1	New York (Bouton)	0
Oct. 6	at LA	Los Angeles (Koufax)	2	New York (Ford)	1

MANAGERS: Walter Alston, Dodgers; Ralph Houk, Yankees

Dodgers – Doug Camilli, Johnny Roseboro, catchers; Dick Calmus, Don Drysdale, Sandy Koufax, Bob Miller, Ron Perranoski, Johnny Podres, Pete Richert, Ken Rowe, Larry Sherry, pitchers; Marv Breeding, Ron Fairly, Jim Gilliam, Ken McMullen, Bill Skowron, Dick Tracewski, Maury Wills, infielders; Tommy Davis, Willie Davis, Al Ferrara, Frank Howard, Wally Moon, Lee Walls, outfielders.

Yankees – Yogi Berra, Elston Howard, catchers; Jim Bouton, Marshall Bridges, Al Downing, Whitey Ford, Steve Hamilton, Bill Kunkel, Tom Metcalf, Hal Reniff, Bill Stafford, Ralph Terry, Stan Williams, pitchers; Clete Boyer, Harry Bright, Tony Kubek, Phil Linz, Joe Pepitone, Bobby Richardson, infielders; Johnny Blanchard, Hector Lopez, Mickey Mantle, Roger Maris, Jack Reed, Tom Tresh, outfielders.

1964 – ST. LOUIS CARDINALS N.L. (4) vs. NEW YORK YANKEES A.L. (3)

(Busch Stadium / Yankee Stadium)

Oct. 7	at StL.	St. Louis (Sadecki)	9	New York (Ford)	5
Oct. 8	at StL.	New York (Stottlemyre)	8	St. Louis (Gibson)	3
Oct. 10	at NY	New York (Bouton)	2	St. Louis (Schultz)	1
Oct. 11	at NY	St. Louis (Craig)	4	New York (Downing)	3
Oct. 12	at NY	St. Louis (Gibson)	5	New York (Mikkelsen)	2 (10 innings)
Oct. 14	at StL.	New York (Bouton)	8	St. Louis (Simmons)	3
Oct. 15	at StL.	St. Louis (Gibson)	7	New York (Stottlemyre)	5

MANAGERS: Johnny Keane, Cardinals; Yogi Berra, Yankees

Cardinals – Tim McCarver, Bob Uecker, catchers; Roger Craig, Mike Cuellar, Bob Gibson, Bob Humphreys, Gordie Richardson, Ray Sadecki, Barney Schultz, Curt Simmons, Ron Taylor, Ray Washburn, pitchers; Ken Boyer, Jerry Buchek, Dick Groat, Julian Javier, Dal Maxvill, Ed Spiezio, Bill White, infielders; Lou Brock, Curt Flood, Charlie James, Mike Shannon, Bob Skinner, Carl Warwick, outfielders.

Yankees – Johnny Blanchard, Elston Howard, catchers; Jim Bouton, Al Downing, Whitey Ford, Steve Hamilton, Pete Mikkelsen, Hal Reniff, Rollie Sheldon, Bill Stafford, Mel Stottlemyre, Ralph Terry, Stan Williams, pitchers. Clete Boyer, Pedro Gonzalez, Mike Hegan, Phil Linz, Joe Pepitone, Bobby Richardson, Chet Trail, infielders; Hector Lopez, Mickey Mantle, Roger Maris, Archie Moore, Tom Tresh, outfielders.

1965 – LOS ANGELES DODGERS N.L. (4) vs. MINNESOTA TWINS A.L. (3)

(Dodger Stadium / Metropolitan Stadium)

Oct. 6	at Minn.	Minnesota (Grant)	8	Los Angeles (Drysdale)	2
Oct. 7	at Minn.	Minnesota (Kaat)	5	Los Angeles (Koufax)	1
Oct. 9	at LA	Los Angeles (Osteen)	4	Minnesota (Pascual)	0
Oct. 10	at LA	Los Angeles (Drysdale)	7	Minnesota (Grant)	2
Oct. 11	at LA	Los Angeles (Koufax)	7	Minnesota (Kaat)	0
Oct. 13	at Minn.	Minnesota (Grant)	5	Los Angeles (Osteen)	1
Oct. 14	at Minn.	Los Angeles (Koufax)	2	Minnesota (Kaat)	0

MANAGERS: Walter Alston, Dodgers; Sam Mele, Twins

Dodgers – Johnny Roseboro, Jeff Torborg, catchers; Jim Brewer, Don Drysdale, Mike Kekich, Sandy Koufax, Bob Miller, Claude Osteen, Ron Perranoski, Johnny Podres, John Purdin, Howie Reed, Nick Willhite, pitchers; Ron Fairly, Jim Gilliam, John Kennedy, Jim Lefebvre, Don LeJohn, Wes Parker, Dick Tracewski, Maury Wills, infielders; Willie Crawford, Willie Davis, Lou Johnson, Wally Moon, outfielders.

Twins – Earl Battey, John Sevcik, Jerry Zimmerman, catchers; Dave Boswell, Mudcat Grant, Jim Kaat, Johnny Klippstein, Jim Merritt, Mel Nelson, Camilo Pascual, Jim Perry, Bill Pleis, Dick Stigman, Al Worthington, pitchers; Harmon Killebrew, Jerry Kindall, Don Mincher, Frank Quilici, Rich Rollins, Zoilo Versalles, infielders; Bob Allison, Jimmie Hall, Joe Nossek, Tony Oliva, Sandy Valdespino, outfielders.

1966 – BALTIMORE ORIOLES A.L. (4) vs. LOS ANGELES DODGERS N.L. (0)

(Memorial Stadium / Dodger Stadium)

Oct. 5	at LA	Baltimore (Drabowsky)	5	Los Angeles (Drysdale)	2
Oct. 6	at LA	Baltimore (Palmer)	6	Los Angeles (Koufax)	0
Oct. 8	at Balt.	Baltimore (Bunker)	1	Los Angeles (Osteen)	0
Oct. 9	at Balt.	Baltimore (McNally)	1	Los Angeles (Drysdale)	0

MANAGERS: Hank Bauer, Orioles; Walter Alston, Dodgers

Orioles – Andy Etchebarren, Larry Haney, Vic Roznovsky, catchers; Frank Bertaina, Gene Brabender, Wally Bunker, Moe Drabowsky, Eddie Fisher, Dick Hall, Dave McNally, John Miller, Stu Miller, Jim Palmer, Eddie Watt, pitchers; Luis Aparicio, Woody Held, Dave Johnson, Bob Johnson, Boog Powell, Brooks Robinson, Infielders; Paul Blair, Curt Blefary, Sam Bowens, Frank Robinson, Russ Snyder, outfielders.

Dodgers – Johnny Roseboro, Jeff Torborg, catchers; Jim Brewer, Don Drysdale, Sandy Koufax, Bob Miller, Joe Moeller, Claude Osteen, Ron Perranoski, Phil Regan, Don Sutton, pitchers; Jim Gilliam, John Kennedy, Jim Lefebvre, Nate Oliver, Wes Parker, Dick Stuart, Maury Wills, infielders; Jim Barbieri, Wes Covington, Tommy Davis, Willie Davis, Ron Fairly, Al Ferrara, Lou Johnson, outfielders.

1967 - ST. LOUIS CARDINALS N.L. (4) vs. BOSTON RED SOX A.L. (3)
(Busch Memorial Stadium / Fenway Park)

Oct. 4	at Bos.	St. Louis (Gibson)	2	Boston (Santiago)	1
Oct. 5	at Bos.	Boston (Lonborg)	5	St. Louis (Hughes)	0
Oct. 7	at StL.	St. Louis (Briles)	5	Boston (Bell)	2
Oct. 8	at StL.	St. Louis (Gibson)	6	Boston (Santiago)	0
Oct. 9	at StL.	Boston (Lonborg)	3	St. Louis (Carlton)	1
Oct. 11	at Bos.	Boston (Wyatt)	8	St. Louis (Lamabe)	4
Oct. 12	at Bos.	St. Louis (Gibson)	7	Boston (Lonborg)	2

MANAGERS: Red Schoendienst, Cardinals; Dick Williams, Red Sox

Cardinals — Tim McCarver, Dave Ricketts, catchers; Nelson Briles, Steve Carlton, Bob Gibson, Joe Hoerner, Dick Hughes, Al Jackson, Larry Jaster, Jack Lamabe, Ray Washburn, Ron Willis, Hal Woodeshick, pitchers; Eddie Bressoud, Orlando Cepeda, Phil Gagliano, Julian Javier, Dal Maxvill, Mike Shannon, Ed Spiezio, infielders; Lou Brock, Curt Flood, Alex Johnson, Roger Maris, Bobby Tolan, outfielders.

Red Sox — Russ Gibson, Elston Howard, Mike Ryan, catchers; Gary Bell, Ken Brett, Jim Lonborg, Dave Morehead, Dan Osinski, Jose Santiago, Lee Stange, Jerry Stephenson, Gary Waslewski, John Wyatt, pitchers; Jerry Adair, Mike Andrews, Joe Foy, Dalton Jones, Rico Petrocelli, George Scott, infielders; Ken Harrelson, Norm Siebern, Reggie Smith, Jose Tartabull, George Thomas, Carl Yastrzemski, outfielders.

1968 - DETROIT TIGERS A.L. (4) vs. ST. LOUIS CARDINALS N.L. (3)
(Tiger Stadium / Busch Memorial Stadium)

Oct. 2	at StL.	St. Louis (Gibson)	4	Detroit (McLain)	0
Oct. 3	at StL.	Detroit (Lolich)	8	St. Louis (Briles)	1
Oct. 5	at Det.	St. Louis (Washburn)	7	Detroit (Wilson)	3
Oct. 6	at Det.	St. Louis (Gibson)	10	Detroit (McLain)	1
Oct. 7	at Det.	Detroit (Lolich)	5	St. Louis (Hoerner)	3
Oct. 9	at StL.	Detroit (McLain)	13	St. Louis (Washburn)	1
Oct. 10	at StL.	Detroit (Lolich)	4	St. Louis (Gibson)	1

MANAGERS: Mayo Smith, Tigers; Red Schoendienst, Cardinals

Tigers — Bill Freehan, Jim Price, catchers; Pat Dobson, John Hiller, Fred Lasher, Mickey Lolich, Dennis McLain, Don McMahon, Daryl Patterson, Joe Sparma, Jon Warden, Earl Wilson, pitchers; Norm Cash, Tommy Matchick, Eddie Mathews, Dick McAuliffe, Ray Oyler, Mickey Stanley, Dick Tracewski, Don Wert, infielders; Gates Brown, Wayne Comer, Willie Horton, Al Kaline, Jim Northrup, outfielders.

Cardinals — Johnny Edwards, Tim McCarver, Dave Ricketts, catchers; Nelson Briles, Steve Carlton, Bob Gibson, Wayne Granger, Joe Hoerner, Dick Hughes, Larry Jaster, Mel Nelson, Ray Washburn, Ron Willis, pitchers; Orlando Cepeda, Phil Gagliano, Julian Javier, Dal Maxvill, Dick Schofield, Mike Shannon, Ed Spiezio, infielders; Lou Brock, Ron Davis, Curt Flood, Roger Maris, Bobby Tolan, outfielders.

1969 - NEW YORK METS N.L. (4) vs. BALTIMORE ORIOLES A.L. (1)
(Shea Stadium / Memorial Stadium)

Oct. 11	at Balt.	Baltimore (Cuellar)	4	New York (Seaver)	1	
Oct. 12	at Balt.	New York (Koosman)	2	Baltimore (McNally)	1	
Oct. 14	at NY	New York (Gentry)	5	Baltimore (Palmer)	0	
Oct. 15	at NY	New York (Seaver)	2	Baltimore (Hall)	1	(10 innings)
Oct. 16	at NY	New York (Koosman)	5	Baltimore (Watt)	3	

MANAGERS: Gil Hodges, Mets; Earl Weaver, Orioles

Mets — Duffy Dyer, Jerry Grote, J.C. Martin, catchers; Don Cardwell, Jack DiLauro, Gary Gentry, Cal Koonce, Jerry Koosman, Jim McAndrew, Tug McGraw, Nolan Ryan, Tom Seaver, Ron Taylor, pitchers; Ken Boswell, Ed Charles, Donn Clendenon, Wayne Garrett, Bud Harrelson, Ed Kranepool, Al Weis, infielders; Tommie Agee, Rod Gaspar, Cleon Jones, Art Shamsky, Ron Swoboda, outfielders.

Orioles — Clay Dalrymple, Andy Etchebarren, Elrod Hendricks, catchers; Mike Cuellar, Dick Hall, Jim Hardin, Dave Leonhard, Marcelino Lopez, Dave McNally, Jim Palmer, Tom Phoebus, Pete Richert, Eddie Watt, pitchers; Mark Belanger, Bobby Floyd, Dave Johnson, Boog Powell, Brooks Robinson, Chico Salmon, infielders; Paul Blair, Don Buford, Dave May, Curt Motton, Merv Rettenmund, Frank Robinson, outfielders.

1970 – BALTIMORE ORIOLES A.L. (4) vs. CINCINNATI REDS N.L. (1)
(Memorial Stadium / Riverfront Stadium)

Oct. 10	at Cin.	Baltimore (Palmer)	4	Cincinnati (Nolan)	3	
Oct. 11	at Cin.	Baltimore (Phoebus)	6	Cincinnati (Wilcox)	5	
Oct. 13	at Balt.	Baltimore (McNally)	9	Cincinnati (Cloninger)	3	
Oct. 14	at Balt.	Cincinnati (Carroll)	6	Baltimore (Watt)	5	
Oct. 15	at Balt.	Baltimore (Cuellar)	9	Cincinnati (Merritt)	3	

MANAGERS: Earl Weaver, Orioles; Sparky Anderson, Reds

Orioles – Andy Etchebarren, Elrod Hendricks, catchers; Mike Cuellar, Moe Drabowsky, Dick Hall, Jim Hardin, Dave Leonhard, Marcelino Lopez, Dave McNally, Jim Palmer, Tom Phoebus, Pete Richert, Eddie Watt, pitchers; Mark Belanger, Bobby Grich, Dave Johnson, Boog Powell, Brooks Robinson, Chico Salmon, infielders; Paul Blair, Don Buford, Terry Crowley, Curt Motton, Merv Rettenmund, Frank Robinson, outfielders.

Reds – Johnny Bench, Pat Corrales, catchers; Mel Behney, Clay Carroll, Tony Cloninger, Wayne Granger, Don Gullett, Jim McGlothlin, Jim Merritt, Gary Nolan, Ray Washburn, Milt Wilcox, pitchers; Darrel Chaney, Dave Concepcion, Tommy Helms, Lee May, Tony Perez, Jim Stewart, Woody Woodward, infielders; Angel Bravo, Bernie Carbo, Ty Cline, Hal McRae, Pete Rose, Bobby Tolan, outfielders.

1971 – PITTSBURGH PIRATES N.L. (4) vs. BALTIMORE ORIOLES A.L. (3)
(Three Rivers Stadium / Memorial Stadium)

Oct. 9	at Balt.	Baltimore (McNally)	5	Pittsburgh (Ellis)	3	
Oct. 11	at Balt.	Baltimore (Palmer)	11	Pittsburgh (Johnson)	3	
Oct. 12	at Pitt.	Pittsburgh (Blass)	5	Baltimore (Cuellar)	1	
Oct. 13n	at Pitt.	Pittsburgh (Kison)	4	Baltimore (Watt)	3	
Oct. 14	at Pitt.	Pittsburgh (Briles)	4	Baltimore (McNally)	0	
Oct. 16	at Balt.	Baltimore (McNally)	3	Pittsburgh (Miller)	2	(10 innings)
Oct. 17	at Balt.	Pittsburgh (Blass)	2	Baltimore (Cuellar)	1	

POSTPONED: (Rain) Oct. 10

MANAGERS: Danny Murtaugh, Pirates; Earl Weaver, Orioles

Pirates – Milt May, Charlie Sands, Manny Sanguillen, catchers; Steve Blass, Nelson Briles, Dock Ellis, Dave Giusti, Bob Johnson, Bruce Kison, Bob Miller, Bob Moose, Bob Veale, Luke Walker, pitchers; Gene Alley, Dave Cash, Richie Hebner, Jackie Hernandez, Bill Mazeroski, Jose Pagan, Bob Robertson, infielders; Roberto Clemente, Gene Clines, Vic Davalillo, Al Oliver, Willie Stargell, outfielders.

Orioles – Clay Dalrymple, Andy Etchebarren, Elrod Hendricks, catchers; Mike Cuellar, Pat Dobson, Tom Dukes, Dick Hall, Grant Jackson, Dave Leonhard, Dave McNally, Jim Palmer, Pete Richert, Eddie Watt, pitchers; Mark Belanger, Jerry DaVanon, Dave Johnson, Boog Powell, Brooks Robinson, Chico Salmon, infielders; Paul Blair, Don Buford, Curt Motton, Merv Rettenmund, Frank Robinson, Tom Shopay, outfielders.

1972 – OAKLAND ATHLETICS A.L. (4) vs. CINCINNATI REDS N.L. (3)
(Oakland Coliseum / Riverfront Stadium)

Oct. 14	at Cin.	Oakland (Holtzman)	3	Cincinnati (Nolan)	2
Oct. 15	at Cin.	Oakland (Hunter)	2	Cincinnati (Grimsley)	1
Oct. 18n	at Oak.	Cincinnati (Billingham)	1	Oakland (Odom)	0
Oct. 19n	at Oak.	Oakland (Fingers)	3	Cincinnati (Carroll)	2
Oct. 20	at Oak.	Cincinnati (Grimsley)	5	Oakland (Fingers)	4
Oct. 21	at Cin.	Cincinnati (Grimsley)	8	Oakland (Blue)	1
Oct. 22	at Cin.	Oakland (Hunter)	3	Cincinnati (Borbon Sr.)	2

POSTPONED: (Rain) Oct. 17

MANAGERS: Dick Williams, Athletics; Sparky Anderson, Reds

Athletics – Dave Duncan, Gene Tenace, catchers; Vida Blue, Rollie Fingers, Dave Hamilton, Ken Holtzman, Joel Horlen, Catfish Hunter, Bob Locker, Blue Moon Odom, pitchers; Sal Bando, Bert Campaneris, Tim Cullen, Mike Epstein, Dick Green, Mike Hegan, Ted Kubiak, Gonzalo Marquez, Dal Maxvill, Don Mincher, infielders; Matty Alou, George Hendrick, Allan Lewis, Angel Mangual, Joe Rudi, outfielders.

Reds – Johnny Bench, Bill Plummer, catchers; Jack Billingham, Pedro Borbon Sr., Clay Carroll, Ross Grimsley, Don Gullett, Tom Hall, Jim McGlothlin, Gary Nolan, Wayne Simpson, Ed Sprague, pitchers; Darrell Chaney, Dave Concepcion, Julian Javier, Denis Menke, Joe Morgan, Tony Perez, infielders; George Foster, Cesar Geronimo, Joe Hague, Hal McRae, Pete Rose, Bobby Tolan, Ted Uhlaender, outfielders.

1973 – OAKLAND ATHLETICS A.L. (4) vs. NEW YORK METS N.L. (3)

(Oakland Coliseum / Shea Stadium)

Oct. 13	at Oak.	Oakland (Holtzman)	2	New York (Matlack)	1	
Oct. 14	at Oak.	New York (McGraw)	10	Oakland (Fingers)	7	(12 innings)
Oct. 16n	at NY	Oakland (Lindblad)	3	New York (Parker)	2	(11 innings)
Oct. 17n	at NY	New York (Matlack)	6	Oakland (Holtzman)	1	
Oct. 18n	at NY	New York (Koosman)	2	Oakland (Blue)	0	
Oct. 20	at Oak.	Oakland (Hunter)	3	New York (Seaver)	1	
Oct. 21	at Oak.	Oakland (Holtzman)	5	New York (Matlack)	2	

MANAGERS: Dick Williams, Athletics; Yogi Berra, Mets

Athletics – Ray Fosse, catcher; Vida Blue, Rollie Fingers, Ken Holtzman, Catfish Hunter, Darold Knowles, Paul Lindblad, Blue Moon Odom, Horacio Pina, pitchers; Mike Andrews, Sal Bando, Pat Bourque, Bert Campaneris, Vic Davalillo, Dick Green, Deron Johnson, Ted Kubiak, Gene Tenace infielders; Jesus Alou, Billy Conigliaro, Reggie Jackson, Allan Lewis, Angel Mangual, Joe Rudi, outfielders.

Mets – Duffy Dyer, Jerry Grote, Ron Hodges, catchers; Buzz Capra, Jerry Koosman, Jon Matlack, Jim McAndrew, Tug McGraw, Harry Parker, Ray Sadecki, Tom Seaver, George Stone, pitchers; Jim Beauchamp, Ken Boswell, Wayne Garrett, Bud Harrelson, Ed Kranepool, Teddy Martinez, Felix Millan, infielders; Don Hahn, Cleon Jones, Willie Mays, John Milner, Rusty Staub, George Theodore, outfielders.

1974 – OAKLAND ATHLETICS A.L. (4) vs. LOS ANGELES DODGERS N.L. (1)

(Oakland Coliseum / Dodger Stadium)

Oct. 12	at LA	Oakland (Fingers)	3	Los Angeles (Messersmith)	2
Oct. 13	at LA	Los Angeles (Sutton)	3	Oakland (Blue)	2
Oct. 15n	at Oak.	Oakland (Hunter)	3	Los Angeles (Downing)	2
Oct. 16n	at Oak.	Oakland (Holtzman)	5	Los Angeles (Messersmith)	2
Oct. 17n	at Oak.	Oakland (Odom)	3	Los Angeles (Marshall)	2

MANAGERS: Alvin Dark, Athletics; Walter Alston, Dodgers

Athletics – Ray Fosse, Larry Haney, catchers; Glenn Abbott, Vida Blue, Rollie Fingers, Dave Hamilton, Ken Holtzman, Catfish Hunter, Darold Knowles, Paul Lindblad, Blue Moon Odom, pitchers; Sal Bando, Bert Campaneris, Dick Green, Jim Holt, Ted Kubiak, Dal Maxvill, Gene Tenace, infielders; Jesus Alou, Reggie Jackson, Angel Mangual, Billy North, Joe Rudi, Claudell Washington, Herb Washington, outfielders.

Dodgers – Joe Ferguson, Steve Yeager, catchers; Jim Brewer, Al Downing, Charlie Hough, Mike Marshall, Andy Messersmith, Doug Rau, Eddie Solomon, Don Sutton, Geoff Zahn, pitchers; Rick Auerbach, Ron Cey, Steve Garvey, Gail Hopkins, Lee Lacy, Davey Lopes, Ken McMullen, Bill Russell, infielders; Bill Buckner, Willie Crawford, Von Joshua, Manny Mota, Tom Paciorek, Jimmy Wynn, outfielders.

1975 – CINCINNATI REDS N.L. (4) vs. BOSTON RED SOX A.L. (3)

(Riverfront Stadium / Fenway Park)

Oct. 11	at Bos.	Boston (Tiant)	6	Cincinnati (Gullett)	0	
Oct. 12	at Bos.	Cincinnati (Eastwick)	3	Boston (Drago)	2	
Oct. 14n	at Cin.	Cincinnati (Eastwick)	6	Boston (Willoughby)	5	(10 innings)
Oct. 15n	at Cin.	Boston (Tiant)	5	Cincinnati (Norman)	4	
Oct. 16n	at Cin.	Cincinnati (Gullett)	6	Boston (Cleveland)	2	
Oct. 21n	at Bos.	Boston (Wise)	7	Cincinnati (Darcy)	6	(12 innings)
Oct. 22n	at Bos.	Cincinnati (Carroll)	4	Boston (Burton)	3	

POSTPONED: (Rain) Oct. 18, 19, 20

MANAGERS: Sparky Anderson, Reds; Darrell Johnson, Red Sox

Reds – Johnny Bench, Bill Plummer, catchers; Jack Billingham, Pedro Borbon Sr., Clay Carroll, Pat Darcy, Rawly Eastwick, Don Gullett, Clay Kirby, Will McEnaney, Gary Nolan, Fred Norman, pitchers; Darrel Chaney, Dave Concepcion, Dan Driessen, Doug Flynn, Joe Morgan, Tony Perez, Pete Rose, infielders; Ed Armbrister, Terry Crowley, George Foster, Cesar Geronimo, Ken Griffey Sr., Merv Rettenmund, outfielders.

Red Sox – Tim Blackwell, Carlton Fisk, Bob Montgomery, catchers; Jim Burton, Reggie Cleveland, Dick Drago, Bill Lee, Roger Moret, Dick Pole, Diego Segui, Luis Tiant, Jim Willoughby, Rick Wise, pitchers; Rick Burleson, Cecil Cooper, Denny Doyle, Doug Griffin, Bob Heise, Rico Petrocelli, Carl Yastrzemski, infielders; Juan Beniquez, Bernie Carbo, Dwight Evans, Fred Lynn, Rick Miller, outfielders.

1976 – CINCINNATI REDS N.L. (4) vs. NEW YORK YANKEES A.L. (0)
(Riverfront Stadium / Yankee Stadium)

Oct. 16	at Cin.	Cincinnati (Gullett)	5	New York (Alexander)	1	
Oct. 17n	at Cin.	Cincinnati (Billingham)	4	New York (Hunter)	3	
Oct. 19n	at NY	Cincinnati (Zachry)	6	New York (Ellis)	2	
Oct. 21n	at NY	Cincinnati (Nolan)	7	New York (Figueroa)	2	

POSTPONED: (Rain) Oct. 20

MANAGERS: Sparky Anderson, Reds; Billy Martin, Yankees

Reds – Johnny Bench, Bill Plummer, catchers; Santo Alcala, Jack Billingham, Pedro Borbon Sr., Rawly Eastwick, Don Gullett, Will McEnaney, Gary Nolan, Fred Norman, Manny Sarmiento, Pat Zachry, pitchers; Bob Bailey, Dave Concepcion, Dan Driessen, Doug Flynn, Joe Morgan, Tony Perez, Pete Rose, infielders; Ed Armbrister, George Foster, Cesar Geronimo, Ken Griffey Sr., Mike Lum, Joel Youngblood, outfielders.

Yankees – Fran Healy, Elrod Hendricks, Thurman Munson, catchers; Doyle Alexander, Dock Ellis, Ed Figueroa, Ron Guidry, Ken Holtzman, Catfish Hunter, Grant Jackson, Sparky Lyle, Dick Tidrow, pitchers; Sandy Alomar Sr. Chris Chambliss, Jim Mason, Graig Nettles, Willie Randolph, Fred Stanley, infielders; Oscar Gamble, Elliott Maddox, Carlos May, Lou Piniella, Mickey Rivers, Otto Velez, Roy White, outfielders.

1977 – NEW YORK YANKEES A.L. (4) vs. LOS ANGELES DODGERS N.L. (2)
(Yankee Stadium / Dodger Stadium)

Oct. 11n	at NY	New York (Lyle)	4	Los Angeles (Rhoden)	3	(12 innings)
Oct. 12n	at NY	Los Angeles (Hooton)	6	New York (Hunter)	1	
Oct. 14n	at LA	New York (Torrez)	5	Los Angeles (John)	3	
Oct. 15	at LA	New York (Guidry)	4	Los Angeles (Rau)	2	
Oct. 16	at LA	Los Angeles (Sutton)	10	New York (Gullett)	4	
Oct. 18n	at NY	New York (Torrez)	8	Los Angeles (Hooton)	4	

MANAGERS: Billy Martin, Yankees; Tommy Lasorda, Dodgers

Yankees – Fran Healy, Cliff Johnson, Thurman Munson, catchers; Ken Clay, Ed Figueroa, Ron Guidry, Don Gullett, Ken Holtzman, Catfish Hunter, Sparky Lyle, Dick Tidrow, Mike Torrez, pitchers; Chris Chambliss, Bucky Dent, Mickey Klutts, Graig Nettles, Willie Randolph, Fred Stanley, George Zeber, infielders; Paul Blair, Reggie Jackson, Lou Piniella, Mickey Rivers, Roy White, outfielders.

Dodgers – Jerry Grote, Johnny Oates, Steve Yeager, catchers; Mike Garman, Burt Hooton, Charlie Hough, Tommy John, Doug Rau, Lance Rautzhan, Rick Rhoden, Elias Sosa, Don Sutton, pitchers; Ron Cey, Steve Garvey, Ed Goodson, Rafael Landestoy, Davey Lopes, Bill Russell, infielders; Dusty Baker, Glenn Burke, Vic Davalillo, Lee Lacy, Rick Monday, Manny Mota, Reggie Smith, outfielders.

1978 – NEW YORK YANKEES A.L. (4) vs. LOS ANGELES DODGERS N.L. (2)
(Yankee Stadium / Dodger Stadium)

Oct. 10n	at LA	Los Angeles (John)	11	New York (Figueroa)	5	
Oct. 11n	at LA	Los Angeles (Hooton)	4	New York (Hunter)	3	
Oct. 13n	at NY	New York (Guidry)	5	Los Angeles (Sutton)	1	
Oct. 14	at NY	New York (Gossage)	4	Los Angeles (Welch)	3	(10 innings)
Oct. 15	at NY	New York (Beattie)	12	Los Angeles (Hooton)	2	
Oct. 17n	at LA	New York (Hunter)	7	Los Angeles (Sutton)	2	

MANAGERS: Bob Lemon, Yankees; Tommy Lasorda, Dodgers

Yankees – Mike Heath, Cliff Johnson, Thurman Munson, catchers; Jim Beattie, Ken Clay, Ed Figueroa, Rich Gossage, Ron Guidry, Catfish Hunter, Paul Lindblad, Sparky Lyle, Dick Tidrow pitchers; Chris Chambliss, Bucky Dent, Brian Doyle, Graig Nettles, Jim Spencer, Fred Stanley, infielders; Paul Blair, Reggie Jackson, Jay Johnstone, Lou Piniella, Mickey Rivers, Gary Thomasson, Roy White, outfielders.

Dodgers – Joe Ferguson, Jerry Grote, Johnny Oates, Steve Yeager, catchers; Terry Forster, Burt Hooton, Charlie Hough, Tommy John, Doug Rau, Lance Rautzhan, Rick Rhoden, Don Sutton, Bob Welch, pitchers; Ron Cey, Steve Garvey, Davey Lopes, Teddy Martinez, Bill Russell, infielders; Dusty Baker, Vic Davalillo, Lee Lacy, Rick Monday, Manny Mota, Billy North, Reggie Smith, outfielders.

1979 – PITTSBURGH PIRATES N.L. (4) vs. BALTIMORE ORIOLES A.L. (3)

(Three Rivers Stadium / Memorial Stadium)

Oct. 10n	at Balt.	Baltimore (Flanagan)	5	Pittsburgh (Kison)	4
Oct. 11n	at Balt.	Pittsburgh (D. Robinson)	3	Baltimore (Stanhouse)	2
Oct. 12n	at Pitt.	Baltimore (McGregor)	8	Pittsburgh (Candelaria)	4
Oct. 13	at Pitt.	Baltimore (Stoddard)	9	Pittsburgh (Tekulve)	6
Oct. 14	at Pitt.	Pittsburgh (Blyleven)	7	Baltimore (Flanagan)	1
Oct. 16n	at Balt.	Pittsburgh (Candelaria)	4	Baltimore (Palmer)	0
Oct. 17n	at Balt.	Pittsburgh (Jackson)	4	Baltimore (McGregor)	1

POSTPONED: (Rain) Oct. 9

MANAGERS: Chuck Tanner, Pirates; Earl Weaver, Orioles

Pirates – Steve Nicosia, Ed Ott, Manny Sanguillen, catchers; Jim Bibby, Bert Blyleven, John Candelaria, Grant Jackson, Bruce Kison, Dave Roberts, Don Robinson, Enrique Romo, Jim Rooker, Kent Tekulve, pitchers; Tim Foli, Phil Garner, Bill Madlock, Willie Stargell, Rennie Stennett, infielders; Matt Alexander, Mike Easler, Lee Lacy, John Milner, Omar Moreno, Dave Parker, Bill Robinson, outfielders.

Orioles – Rick Dempsey, Dave Skaggs, catchers; Mike Flanagan, Dennis Martinez, Tippy Martinez, Scott McGregor, Jim Palmer, Don Stanhouse, Sammy Stewart, Tim Stoddard, Steve Stone, pitchers; Mark Belanger, Terry Crowley, Rich Dauer, Doug DeCinces, Kiko Garcia, Lee May, Eddie Murray, Billy Smith, infielders; Benny Ayala, Al Bumbry, Pat Kelly, John Lowenstein, Gary Roenicke, Ken Singleton, outfielders.

1980 – PHILADELPHIA PHILLIES N.L. (4) vs. KANSAS CITY ROYALS A.L. (2)

(Veterans Stadium / Royals Stadium)

Oct. 14n	at Phil.	Philadelphia (Walk)	7	Kansas City (Leonard)	6
Oct. 15n	at Phil.	Philadelphia (Carlton)	6	Kansas City (Quisenberry)	4
Oct. 17n	at KC	Kansas City (Quisenberry)	4	Philadelphia (McGraw)	3 (10 innings)
Oct. 18	at KC	Kansas City (Leonard)	5	Philadelphia (Christenson)	3
Oct. 19	at KC	Philadelphia (McGraw)	4	Kansas City (Quisenberry)	3
Oct. 21n	at Phil.	Philadelphia (Carlton)	4	Kansas City (Gale)	1

MANAGERS: Dallas Green, Phillies; Jim Frey, Royals

Phillies – Bob Boone, Keith Moreland, catchers; Warren Brusstar, Marty Bystrom, Steve Carlton, Larry Christenson, Tug McGraw, Dickie Noles, Ron Reed, Dick Ruthven, Kevin Saucier, Bob Walk, pitchers; Ramon Aviles, Larry Bowa, Pete Rose, Mike Schmidt, Manny Trillo, John Vukovich, infielders; Greg Gross, Greg Luzinski, Garry Maddox, Bake McBride, Lonnie Smith, Del Unser, George Vukovich, outfielders.

Royals – Darrell Porter, Jamie Quirk, John Wathan, catchers; Ken Brett, Rich Gale, Larry Gura, Dennis Leonard, Renie Martin, Marty Pattin, Dan Quisenberry, Paul Splittorff, Jeff Twitty, pitchers; Willie Aikens, George Brett, Dave Chalk, Onix Concepcion, Pete LaCock, Rance Mulliniks, U.L. Washington, Frank White, infielders; Jose Cardenal, Clint Hurdle, Hal McRae, Amos Otis, Willie Wilson, outfielders.

1981 – LOS ANGELES DODGERS N.L. (4) vs. NEW YORK YANKEES A.L. (2)

(Dodger Stadium / Yankee Stadium)

Oct. 20n	at NY	New York (Guidry)	5	Los Angeles (Reuss)	3
Oct. 21n	at NY	New York (John)	3	Los Angeles (Hooton)	0
Oct. 23n	at LA	Los Angeles (Valenzuela)	5	New York (Frazier)	4
Oct. 24	at LA	Los Angeles (Howe)	8	New York (Frazier)	7
Oct. 25	at LA	Los Angeles (Reuss)	2	New York (Guidry)	1
Oct. 28n	at NY	Los Angeles (Hooton)	9	New York (Frazier)	2

POSTPONED: (Rain) Oct. 27

MANAGERS: Tommy Lasorda, Dodgers; Bob Lemon, Yankees

Dodgers – Mike Scioscia, Steve Yeager, catchers; Bobby Castillo, Terry Forster, Dave Goltz, Burt Hooton, Steve Howe, Tom Niedenfuer, Alejandro Pena, Jerry Reuss, Dave Stewart, Fernando Valenzuela, Bob Welch, pitchers; Ron Cey, Steve Garvey, Davey Lopes, Bill Russell, Steve Sax, Derrel Thomas, infielders; Dusty Baker, Pedro Guerrero, Jay Johnstone, Ken Landreaux, Rick Monday, Reggie Smith, outfielders.

Yankees – Rick Cerone, Barry Foote, catchers; Ron Davis, George Frazier, Rich Gossage, Ron Guidry, Tommy John, Dave LaRoche, Rudy May, Rick Reuschel, Dave Righetti, pitchers; Larry Milbourne, Graig Nettles, Willie Randolph, Dave Revering, Andre Robertson, Aurelio Rodriguez, Bob Watson, infielders; Bobby Brown, Oscar Gamble, Reggie Jackson, Jerry Mumphrey, Bobby Murcer, Lou Piniella, Dave Winfield, outfielders.

1982 – ST. LOUIS CARDINALS N.L. (4) vs. MILWAUKEE BREWERS A.L. (3)
(Busch Stadium / County Stadium)

Oct. 12n	at StL.	Milwaukee (Caldwell)	10	St. Louis (Forsch)	0
Oct. 13n	at StL.	St. Louis (Sutter)	5	Milwaukee (McClure)	4
Oct. 15n	at Mil.	St. Louis (Andujar)	6	Milwaukee (Vuckovich)	2
Oct. 16	at Mil.	Milwaukee (Slaton)	7	St. Louis (Bair)	5
Oct. 17	at Mil.	Milwaukee (Caldwell)	6	St. Louis (Forsch)	4
Oct. 19n	at StL.	St. Louis (Stuper)	13	Milwaukee (Sutton)	1
Oct. 20n	at StL.	St. Louis (Andujar)	6	Milwaukee (McClure)	3

MANAGERS: Whitey Herzog, Cardinals; Harvey Kuenn, Brewers

Cardinals – Glenn Brummer, Darrell Porter, Gene Tenace, catchers; Joaquin Andujar, Doug Bair, Bob Forsch, Jim Kaat, Jeff Lahti, Dave LaPoint, John Martin, Steve Mura, John Stuper, Bruce Sutter, pitchers; Julio Gonzalez, Keith Hernandez, Tommy Herr, Ken Oberkfell, Mike Ramsey, Ozzie Smith, infielders; Steve Braun, David Green, George Hendrick, Dane Iorg, Willie McGee, Lonnie Smith, outfielders.

Brewers – Ted Simmons, Ned Yost, catchers; Dwight Bernard, Pete Ladd, Bob McClure, Doc Medich, Mike Caldwell, Rollie Fingers, Moose Haas, Jim Slaton, Don Sutton, Pete Vuckovich, pitchers; Roy Howell, Paul Molitor, Cecil Cooper, Jim Gantner, Don Money, Rob Picciolo, Ed Romero, Robin Yount, infielders; Mark Brouhard, Marshall Edwards, Charlie Moore, Ben Oglivie, Gorman Thomas, outfielders.

1983 – BALTIMORE ORIOLES A.L. (4) vs. PHILADELPHIA PHILLIES N.L. (1)
(Memorial Stadium / Veterans Stadium)

Oct. 11n	at Balt.	Philadelphia (Denny)	2	Baltimore (McGregor)	1
Oct. 12n	at Balt.	Baltimore (Boddicker)	4	Philadelphia (Hudson)	1
Oct. 14n	at Phil.	Baltimore (Palmer)	3	Philadelphia (Carlton)	2
Oct. 15	at Phil.	Baltimore (Davis)	5	Philadelphia (Denny)	4
Oct. 16	at Phil.	Baltimore (McGregor)	5	Philadelphia (Hudson)	0

MANAGERS: Joe Altobelli, Orioles; Paul Owens, Phillies

Orioles – Rick Dempsey, Joe Nolan, catchers; Mike Boddicker, Storm Davis, Mike Flanagan, Dennis Martinez, Tippy Martinez, Scott McGregor, Jim Palmer, Sammy Stewart, Tim Stoddard, pitchers; Todd Cruz, Rich Dauer, Eddie Murray, Cal Ripken, Lenn Sakata, infielders; Benny Ayala, Al Bumbry, Jim Dwyer, Dan Ford, Tito Landrum, John Lowenstein, Gary Roenicke, John Shelby, Ken Singleton, outfielders.

Phillies – Bo Diaz, Ozzie Virgil, catchers; Larry Andersen, Marty Bystrom, Steve Carlton, John Denny, Kevin Gross, Willie Hernandez, Al Holland, Charles Hudson, Tug McGraw, Ron Reed, pitchers; Ivan DeJesus, Kiko Garcia, Joe Morgan, Tony Perez, Pete Rose, Juan Samuel, Mike Schmidt, infielders; Bob Dernier, Greg Gross, Von Hayes, Joe Lefebvre, Sixto Lezcano, Garry Maddox, Gary Matthews Sr., outfielders.

1984 – DETROIT TIGERS A.L. (4) vs. SAN DIEGO PADRES N.L. (1)
(Tiger Stadium / Jack Murphy Stadium)

Oct. 9n	at SD	Detroit (Morris)	3	San Diego (Thurmond)	2
Oct. 10n	at SD	San Diego (Hawkins)	5	Detroit (Petry)	3
Oct. 12n	at Det.	Detroit (Wilcox)	5	San Diego (Lollar)	2
Oct. 13	at Det.	Detroit (Morris)	4	San Diego (Show)	2
Oct. 14	at Det.	Detroit (Lopez)	8	San Diego (Hawkins)	4

MANAGERS: Sparky Anderson, Tigers; Dick Williams, Padres

Tigers – Marty Castillo, Lance Parrish, catcher; Doug Bair, Juan Berenguer, Willie Hernandez, Aurelio Lopez, Jack Morris, Dan Petry, Dave Rozema, Bill Scherrer, Milt Wilcox, pitchers; Doug Baker, Dave Bergman, Tom Brookens, Darrell Evans, Howard Johnson, Alan Trammell, Lou Whitaker, infielders; Barbaro Garbey, Kirk Gibson, Johnny Grubb, Larry Herndon, Ruppert Jones, Rusty Kuntz, Chet Lemon, outfielders.

Padres – Bruce Bochy, Terry Kennedy, catchers; Greg Booker, Dave Dravecky, Rich Gossage, Greg Harris, Andy Hawkins, Craig Lefferts, Tim Lollar, Eric Show, Mark Thurmond, Ed Whitson, pitchers; Kurt Bevacqua, Tim Flannery, Steve Garvey, Graig Nettles, Mario Ramirez, Luis Salazar, Garry Templeton, Alan Wiggins, infielders; Bobby Brown, Tony Gwynn, Carmelo Martinez, Ron Roenicke, Champ Summers, outfielders.

1985 – KANSAS CITY ROYALS A.L. (4) vs. ST. LOUIS CARDINALS N.L. (3)

(Royals Stadium / Busch Stadium)

Oct. 19n	at KC	St. Louis (Tudor)	3	Kansas City (Jackson)	1
Oct. 20n	at KC	St. Louis (Daley)	4	Kansas City (Leibrandt)	2
Oct. 22n	at StL.	Kansas City (Saberhagen)	6	St. Louis (Andujar)	1
Oct. 23n	at StL.	St. Louis (Tudor)	3	Kansas City (Black)	0
Oct. 24n	at StL.	Kansas City (Jackson)	6	St. Louis (Forsch)	1
Oct. 26n	at KC	Kansas City (Quisenberry)	2	St. Louis (Worrell)	1
Oct. 27n	at KC	Kansas City (Saberhagen)	11	St. Louis (Tudor)	0

MANAGERS: Dick Howser, Royals; Whitey Herzog, Cardinals

Royals – Jamie Quirk, Jim Sundberg, John Wathan, catchers; Joe Beckwith, Bud Black, Steve Farr, Mark Gubicza, Danny Jackson, Charlie Leibrandt, Dan Quisenberry, Bret Saberhagen, pitchers; Steve Balboni, Buddy Biancalana, George Brett, Onix Concepcion, Greg Pryor, Frank White, infielders; Dane Iorg, Lynn Jones, Hal McRae, Darryl Motley, Jorge Orta, Pat Sheridan, Lonnie Smith, Willie Wilson, outfielders.

Cardinals – Tom Nieto, Darrell Porter, catchers; Joaquin Andujar, Bill Campbell, Danny Cox, Ken Dayley, Bob Forsch, Rick Horton, Jeff Lahti, John Tudor, Todd Worrell, pitchers; Jack Clark, Ivan DeJesus, Tommy Herr, Mike Jorgensen, Tom Lawless, Terry Pendleton, Ozzie Smith, infielders; Steve Braun, Cesar Cedeno, Vince Coleman, Brian Harper, Terry Landrum, Willie McGee, Andy Van Slyke, outfielders.

1986 – NEW YORK METS N.L. (4) vs. BOSTON RED SOX A.L. (3)

(Shea Stadium / Fenway Park)

Oct. 18n	at NY	Boston (Hurst)	1	New York (Darling)	0	
Oct. 19n	at NY	Boston (Crawford)	9	New York (Gooden)	3	
Oct. 21n	at Bos.	New York (Ojeda)	7	Boston (Boyd)	1	
Oct. 22n	at Bos.	New York (Darling)	6	Boston (Nipper)	2	
Oct. 23n	at Bos.	Boston (Hurst)	4	New York (Gooden)	2	
Oct. 25n	at NY	New York (Aguilera)	6	Boston (Schiraldi)	5	(10 innings)
Oct. 27n	at NY	New York (McDowell)	8	Boston (Schiraldi)	5	

POSTPONED: (Rain) Oct. 26

MANAGERS: Davey Johnson, Mets; John McNamara, Red Sox

Mets – Gary Carter, Ed Hearn, catchers; Rick Aguilera, Ron Darling, Sid Fernandez, Dwight Gooden, Roger McDowell, Randy Niemann, Bob Ojeda, Jesse Orosco, Doug Sisk, pitchers; Wally Backman, Kevin Elster, Keith Hernandez, Howard Johnson, Ray Knight, Lee Mazzilli, Kevin Mitchell, Rafael Santana, Tim Teufel, infielders; Len Dykstra, Danny Heep, Darryl Strawberry, Mookie Wilson, outfielders.

Red Sox – Rich Gedman, Marc Sullivan, catchers; Oil Can Boyd, Roger Clemens, Steve Crawford, Bruce Hurst, Tim Lollar, Al Nipper, Joe Sambito, Calvin Schiraldi, Bob Stanley, Sammy Stewart, pitchers; Marty Barrett, Wade Boggs, Bill Buckner, Spike Owen, Ed Romero, Dave Stapleton, infielders; Tony Armas, Don Baylor, Dwight Evans, Mike Greenwell, Dave Henderson, Jim Rice, outfielders.

1987 – MINNESOTA TWINS A.L. (4) vs. ST. LOUIS CARDINALS N.L. (3)

(Metrodome / Busch Stadium)

Oct. 17n	at Minn.	Minnesota (Viola)	10	St. Louis (Magrane)	1
Oct. 18n	at Minn.	Minnesota (Blyleven)	8	St. Louis (Cox)	4
Oct. 20n	at StL.	St. Louis (Tudor)	3	Minnesota (Berenguer)	1
Oct. 21n	at StL.	St. Louis (Forsch)	7	Minnesota (Viola)	2
Oct. 22n	at StL.	St. Louis (Cox)	4	Minnesota (Blyleven)	2
Oct. 24	at Minn.	Minnesota (Schatzeder)	11	St. Louis (Tudor)	5
Oct. 25n	at Minn.	Minnesota (Viola)	4	St. Louis (Cox)	2

MANAGERS: Tom Kelly, Twins; Whitey Herzog, Cardinals

Twins – Sal Butera, Tim Laudner, catchers; Keith Atherton, Juan Berenguer, Bert Blyleven, George Frazier, Joe Niekro, Jeff Reardon, Dan Schatzeder, Les Straker, Frank Viola, pitchers; Don Baylor, Gary Gaetti, Greg Gagne, Kent Hrbek, Gene Larkin, Steve Lombardozzi, Al Newman, Roy Smalley, infielders; Tom Brunansky, Randy Bush, Mark Davidson, Dan Gladden, Kirby Puckett, outfielders.

Cardinals – Steve Lake, Tom Pagnozzi, Tony Pena, catchers; Danny Cox, Bill Dawley, Ken Dayley, Bob Forsch, Ricky Horton, Joe Magrane, Greg Mathews, John Tudor, Lee Tunnell, Todd Worrell, pitchers; Dan Driessen, Tommy Herr, Tom Lawless, Jim Lindeman, Jose Oquendo, Terry Pendleton, Ozzie Smith, infielders; Vince Coleman, Curt Ford, Lance Johnson, Willie McGee, John Morris, outfielders.

1988 – LOS ANGELES DODGERS N.L. (4) vs. OAKLAND ATHLETICS A.L. (1)
(Dodger Stadium / Oakland Coliseum)

Oct. 15n	at LA	Los Angeles (Pena)	5	Oakland (Eckersley)	4	
Oct. 16n	at LA	Los Angeles (Hershiser)	6	Oakland (Davis)	0	
Oct. 18n	at Oak.	Oakland (Honeycutt)	2	Los Angeles (J. Howell)	1	
Oct. 19n	at Oak.	Los Angeles (Belcher)	4	Oakland (Stewart)	3	
Oct. 20n	at Oak.	Los Angeles (Hershiser)	5	Oakland (Davis)	2	

MANAGERS: Tommy Lasorda, Dodgers; Tony LaRussa, Athletics

Dodgers – Rick Dempsey, Mike Scioscia, catchers; Tim Belcher, Orel Hershiser, Brian Holton, Ricky Horton, Jay Howell, Tim Leary, Jesse Orosco, Alejandro Pena, John Tudor, pitchers; Dave Anderson, Alfredo Griffin, Jeff Hamilton, Danny Heep, Steve Sax, Mike Sharperson, Franklin Stubbs, Tracy Woodson, infielders; Mike Davis, Kirk Gibson, Jose Gonzalez, Mickey Hatcher, Mike Marshall, John Shelby, outfielders.

Athletics – Ron Hassey, Terry Steinbach, catchers; Todd Burns, Greg Cadaret, Storm Davis, Dennis Eckersley, Rick Honeycutt, Gene Nelson, Eric Plunk, Dave Stewart, Bob Welch, Curt Young, pitchers; Mike Gallego, Glenn Hubbard, Carney Lansford, Mark McGwire, Tony Phillips, Walt Weiss, infielders; Don Baylor, Jose Canseco, Dave Henderson, Stan Javier, Doug Jennings, Dave Parker, Luis Polonia, outfielders.

1989 – OAKLAND ATHLETICS A.L. (4) vs. SAN FRANCISCO GIANTS N.L. (0)
(Oakland Coliseum / Candlestick Park)

Oct. 14n	at Oak.	Oakland (Stewart)	5	San Francisco (Garrelts)	0
Oct. 15n	at Oak.	Oakland (Moore)	5	San Francisco (Reuschel)	1
Oct. 27n	at SF	Oakland (Stewart)	13	San Francisco (Garrelts)	7
Oct. 28n	at SF	Oakland (Moore)	9	San Francisco (Robinson)	6

POSTPONED: (Earthquake) Oct. 17 through Oct. 26

MANAGERS: Tony LaRussa, Athletics; Roger Craig, Giants

Athletics – Ron Hassey, Terry Steinbach, catchers; Todd Burns, Storm Davis, Dennis Eckersley, Rick Honeycutt, Mike Moore, Gene Nelson, Dave Stewart, Bob Welch, Curt Young, Matt Young, pitchers; Lance Blankenship, Mike Gallego, Carney Lansford, Mark McGwire, Ken Phelps, Tony Phillips, Walt Weiss, infielders; Jose Canseco, Dave Henderson, Rickey Henderson, Stan Javier, Dave Parker, outfielders.

Giants – Bill Bathe, Terry Kennedy, Kirt Manwaring, catchers; Steve Bedrosian, Jeff Brantley, Kelly Downs, Scott Garrelts, Atlee Hammaker, Mike LaCoss, Craig Lefferts, Rick Reuschel, Don Robinson, pitchers; Will Clark, Greg Litton, Ken Oberkfell, Ernest Riles, Rob Thompson, Jose Uribe, Matt Williams, infielders; Brett Butler, Candy Maldonado, Kevin Mitchell, Donell Nixon, Pat Sheridan, outfielders.

1990 – CINCINNATI REDS N.L. (4) vs. OAKLAND ATHLETICS A.L. (0)
(Riverfront Stadium / Oakland Coliseum)

Oct. 16n	at Cin.	Cincinnati (Rijo)	7	Oakland (Stewart)	0	
Oct. 17n	at Cin.	Cincinnati (Dibble)	5	Oakland (Eckersley)	4	(10 innings)
Oct. 19n	at Oak.	Cincinnati (Browning)	8	Oakland (Moore)	3	
Oct. 20n	at Oak.	Cincinnati (Rijo)	2	Oakland (Stewart)	1	

MANAGERS: Lou Piniella, Reds; Tony LaRussa, Athletics

Reds – Joe Oliver, Jeff Reed, catchers; Jack Armstrong, Tom Browning, Norm Charlton, Rob Dibble, Danny Jackson, Rick Mahler, Randy Myers, Jose Rijo, Scott Scudder, pitchers; Billy Bates, Todd Benzinger, Mariano Duncan, Barry Larkin, Terry Lee, Hal Morris, Ron Oester, Luis Quinones, Chris Sabo, infielders; Glenn Braggs, Eric Davis, Billy Hatcher, Paul O'Neill, Herm Winningham, outfielders.

Athletics – Ron Hassey, Jamie Quirk, Terry Steinbach, catchers; Todd Burns, Dennis Eckersley, Rick Honeycutt, Joe Klink, Mike Moore, Gene Nelson, Scott Sanderson, Dave Stewart, Bob Welch, Curt Young, pitchers; Lance Blankenship, Mike Bordick, Mike Gallego, Carney Lansford, Mark McGwire, Willie Randolph, infielders; Harold Baines, Jose Canseco, Dave Henderson, Rickey Henderson, Doug Jennings, Willie McGee, outfielders.

1991 – MINNESOTA TWINS A.L. (4) vs. ATLANTA BRAVES N.L. (3)

(Metrodome / Atlanta-Fulton County Stadium)

Oct. 19n	at Minn.	Minnesota (Morris)	5	Atlanta (Leibrandt)	2	
Oct. 20n	at Minn.	Minnesota (Tapani)	3	Atlanta (Glavine)	2	
Oct. 22n	at Atl.	Atlanta (Clancy)	5	Minnesota (Aguilera)	4	(12 innings)
Oct. 23n	at Atl.	Atlanta (Stanton)	3	Minnesota (Guthrie)	2	
Oct. 24n	at Atl.	Atlanta (Glavine)	14	Minnesota (Tapani)	5	
Oct. 26n	at Minn.	Minnesota (Aguilera)	4	Atlanta (Leibrandt)	3	(11 innings)
Oct. 27n	at Minn.	Minnesota (Morris)	1	Atlanta (Pena)	0	(10 innings)

MANAGERS: Tom Kelly, Twins; Bobby Cox, Braves

Twins – Brian Harper, Junior Ortiz, catchers; Rick Aguilera, Steve Bedrosian, Scott Erickson, Mark Guthrie, Terry Leach, Jack Morris, Kevin Tapani, David West, Carl Willis, pitchers; Greg Gagne, Kent Hrbek, Chuck Knoblauch, Scott Leius, Al Newman, Mike Pagliarulo, Paul Sorrento, infielders; Jarvis Brown, Randy Bush, Chili Davis, Dan Gladden, Gene Larkin, Shane Mack, Kirby Puckett, outfielders.

Braves – Francisco Cabrera, Greg Olson, Jerry Willard, catchers; Steve Avery, Jim Clancy, Tom Glavine, Charlie Leibrandt, Kent Mercker, Alejandro Pena, John Smoltz, Mike Stanton, Randy St. Claire, Mark Wohlers, pitchers; Rafael Belliard, Jeff Blauser, Sid Bream, Brian Hunter, Mark Lemke, Terry Pendleton, Jeff Treadway, infielders; Ron Gant, Tommy Gregg, David Justice, Keith Mitchell, Lonnie Smith, outfielders.

1992 – TORONTO BLUE JAYS A.L. (4) vs. ATLANTA BRAVES N.L. (2)

(SkyDome / Atlanta-Fulton County Stadium)

Oct. 17n	at Atl.	Atlanta (Glavine)	3	Toronto (Morris)	1	
Oct. 18n	at Atl.	Toronto (D. Ward)	5	Atlanta (Reardon)	4	
Oct. 20n	at Tor.	Toronto (D. Ward)	3	Atlanta (Avery)	2	
Oct. 21n	at Tor.	Toronto (Key)	2	Atlanta (Glavine)	1	
Oct. 22n	at Tor.	Atlanta (Smoltz)	7	Toronto (Morris)	2	
Oct. 24n	at Atl.	Toronto (Key)	4	Atlanta (Leibrandt)	3	(11 innings)

MANAGERS: Cito Gaston, Blue Jays; Bobby Cox, Braves

Blue Jays – Pat Borders, Randy Knorr, Ed Sprague, catchers; David Cone, Mark Eichhorn, Juan Guzman, Tom Henke, Jimmy Key, Jack Morris, Todd Stottlemyre, Mike Timlin, Duane Ward, David Wells, pitchers; Roberto Alomar, Alfredo Griffin, Kelly Gruber, Manuel Lee, Rance Mulliniks, John Olerud, Pat Tabler, infielders; Derek Bell, Joe Carter, Candy Maldonado, Devon White, Dave Winfield, outfielders.

Braves – Damon Berryhill, Francisco Cabrera, Javier Lopez, catchers; Steve Avery, Tom Glavine, Charlie Leibrandt, Kent Mercker, David Nied, Jeff Reardon, Pete Smith, John Smoltz, Mike Stanton, Mark Wohlers, pitchers; Rafael Belliard, Jeff Blauser, Sid Bream, Brian Hunter, Mark Lemke, Terry Pendleton, Jeff Treadway, infielders; Ron Gant, David Justice, Otis Nixon, Deion Sanders, Lonnie Smith, outfielders.

1993 – TORONTO BLUE JAYS A.L. (4) vs. PHILADELPHIA PHILLIES N.L. (2)

(SkyDome / Veterans Stadium)

Oct. 16n	at Tor.	Toronto (Leiter)	8	Philadelphia (Schilling)	5
Oct. 17n	at Tor.	Philadelphia (Mulholland)	6	Toronto (Stewart)	4
Oct. 19n	at Phil.	Toronto (Hentgen)	10	Philadelphia (Jackson)	3
Oct. 20n	at Phil.	Toronto (Castillo)	15	Philadelphia (Williams)	14
Oct. 21n	at Phil.	Philadelphia (Schilling)	2	Toronto (Guzman)	0
Oct. 23n	at Tor.	Toronto (D. Ward)	8	Philadelphia (Williams)	6

MANAGERS: Cito Gaston, Blue Jays; Jim Fregosi, Phillies

Blue Jays – Pat Borders, Randy Knorr, catchers; Tony Castillo, Danny Cox, Mark Eichhorn, Juan Guzman, Pat Hentgen, Al Leiter, Dave Stewart, Todd Stottlemyre, Mike Timlin, Duane Ward, pitchers; Roberto Alomar, Tony Fernandez, Alfredo Griffin, Paul Molitor, John Olerud, Dick Schofield, Ed Sprague, infielders; Rob Butler, William Canate, Joe Carter, Darnell Coles, Rickey Henderson, Devon White, outfielders.

Phillies – Darren Daulton, Todd Pratt, catchers; Larry Andersen, Tommy Greene, Danny Jackson, Roger Mason, Terry Mulholland, Ben Rivera, Curt Schilling, Bobby Thigpen, David West, Mitch Williams, pitchers; Kim Batiste, Mariano Duncan, Dave Hollins, Ricky Jordan, John Kruk, Mickey Morandini, Kevin Stocker, infielders; Wes Chamberlain, Len Dykstra, Jim Eisenreich, Pete Incaviglia, Tony Longmire, Milt Thompson, outfielders.

1994 - No World Series Played

1995 - ATLANTA BRAVES N.L. (4) vs. CLEVELAND INDIANS A.L. (2)
(Atlanta-Fulton County Stadium / Jacobs Field)

Oct. 21n	at Atl.	Atlanta (Maddux)	3	Cleveland (Hershiser)	2	
Oct. 22n	at Atl.	Atlanta (Glavine)	4	Cleveland (Martinez)	3	
Oct. 24n	at Clev.	Cleveland (Mesa)	7	Atlanta (Pena)	6	(11 innings)
Oct. 25n	at Clev.	Atlanta (Avery)	5	Cleveland (Hill)	2	
Oct. 26n	at Clev.	Cleveland (Hershiser)	5	Atlanta (Maddux)	4	
Oct. 28n	at Atl.	Atlanta (Glavine)	1	Cleveland (Poole)	0	

MANAGERS: Bobby Cox, Braves; Mike Hargrove, Indians

Braves – Javier Lopez, Charlie O'Brien, Eduardo Perez, catchers; Steve Avery, Pedro Borbon Jr., Brad Clontz, Tom Glavine, Greg Maddux, Greg McMichael, Kent Mercker, Alejandro Pena, John Smoltz, Mark Wohlers, pitchers; Rafael Belliard, Jeff Blauser, Chipper Jones, Mark Lemke, Fred McGriff, Mike Mordecai, infielders; Mike Devereaux, Marquis Grissom, David Justice, Ryan Klesko, Luis Polonia, Dwight Smith, outfielders.

Indians – Sandy Alomar Jr., Tony Pena, catchers; Paul Assenmacher, Alan Embree, Orel Hershiser, Ken Hill, Dennis Martinez, Jose Mesa, Charles Nagy, Chad Ogea, Eric Plunk, Jim Poole, Julian Tavarez, pitchers; Carlos Baerga, Alvaro Espinoza, Eddie Murray, Herbert Perry, Paul Sorrento, Jim Thome, Omar Vizquel, infielders; Ruben Amaro Jr., Albert Belle, Wayne Kirby, Kenny Lofton, Manny Ramirez, outfielders.

1996 - NEW YORK YANKEES A.L. (4) vs. ATLANTA BRAVES N.L. (2)
(Yankee Stadium / Atlanta-Fulton County Stadium)

Oct. 20n	at NY	Atlanta (Smoltz)	12	New York (Pettite)	1	
Oct. 21n	at NY	Atlanta (Maddux)	4	New York (Key)	0	
Oct. 22n	at Atl.	New York (Cone)	5	Atlanta (Glavine)	2	
Oct. 23n	at Atl.	New York (Lloyd)	8	Atlanta (Avery)	6	(10 innings)
Oct. 24n	at Atl.	New York (Pettitte)	1	Atlanta (Smoltz)	0	
Oct. 26n	at NY	New York (Key)	3	Atlanta (Maddux)	2	

POSTPONED: (Rain) Oct. 19

MANAGERS: Joe Torre, Yankees; Bobby Cox, Braves

Yankees – Joe Girardi, Jim Leyritz, catchers; Brian Boehringer, David Cone, Jimmy Key, Graeme Lloyd, Jeff Nelson, Andy Pettitte, Mariano Rivera, Kenny Rogers, David Weathers, John Wetteland, pitchers; Wade Boggs, Mariano Duncan, Cecil Fielder, Andy Fox, Charlie Hayes, Derek Jeter, Tino Martinez, Luis Sojo, infielders; Mike Aldrete, Paul O'Neill, Tim Raines, Darryl Strawberry, Bernie Williams, outfielders.

Braves – Joe Ayrault, Javier Lopez, Eduardo Perez, catchers; Steve Avery, Mike Bielecki, Brad Clontz, Tom Glavine, Greg Maddux, Greg McMichael, Denny Neagle, John Smoltz, Terrell Wade, Mark Wohlers, pitchers; Rafael Belliard, Jeff Blauser, Chipper Jones, Mark Lemke, Fred McGriff, Mike Mordecai, Terry Pendleton, infielders; Jermaine Dye, Marquis Grissom, Andruw Jones, Ryan Klesko, Luis Polonia, outfielders.

1997 - FLORIDA MARLINS N.L. (4) vs. CLEVELAND INDIANS A.L. (3)
(Pro Player Stadium / Jacobs Field)

Oct. 18n	at Fla.	Florida (Hernandez)	7	Cleveland (Hershiser)	4	
Oct. 19n	at Fla.	Cleveland (Ogea)	6	Florida (Brown)	1	
Oct. 21n	at Clev.	Florida (Cook)	14	Cleveland (Plunk)	11	
Oct. 22n	at Clev.	Cleveland (Wright)	10	Florida (Saunders)	3	
Oct. 23n	at Clev.	Florida (Hernandez)	8	Cleveland (Hershiser)	7	
Oct. 25n	at Fla.	Cleveland (Ogea)	4	Florida (Brown)	1	
Oct. 26n	at Fla.	Florida (Powell)	3	Cleveland (Nagy)	2	(11 innings)

MANAGERS: Jim Leyland, Marlins; Mike Hargrove, Indians

Marlins – Charles Johnson, Gregg Zaun, catchers; Antonio Alfonseca, Kevin Brown, Dennis Cook, Felix Heredia, Livan Hernandez, Al Leiter, Robb Nen, Jay Powell, Tony Saunders, Ed Vosberg, pitchers; Kurt Abbott, Alex Arias, Bobby Bonilla, Jeff Conine, Darren Daulton, Cliff Floyd, Edgar Renteria, infielders; Moises Alou, John Cangelosi, Craig Counsell, Jim Eisenreich, Gary Sheffield, Devon White, outfielders.

Indians – Sandy Alomar Jr., Pat Borders, catchers; Brian Anderson, Paul Assenmacher, Orel Hershiser, Mike Jackson, Jeff Juden, Jose Mesa, Alvin Morman, Charles Nagy, Chad Ogea, Eric Plunk, Jaret Wright, pitchers; Jeff Branson, Tony Fernandez, Jeff Manto, Bip Roberts, Kevin Seitzer, Jim Thome, Omar Vizquel, Matt Williams, infielders; Brian Giles, Marquis Grissom, David Justice, Manny Ramirez, outfielders.

1998 – NEW YORK YANKEES A.L. (4) vs. SAN DIEGO PADRES N.L. (0)

(Yankee Stadium / Qualcomm Stadium)

Oct. 17n	at NY	New York (Wells)	9	San Diego (Wall)	6	
Oct. 18n	at NY	New York (Hernandez)	9	San Diego (Ashby)	3	
Oct. 20n	at SD	New York (Mendoza)	5	San Diego (Hoffman)	4	
Oct. 21n	at SD	New York (Pettitte)	3	San Diego (Brown)	0	

MANAGERS: Joe Torre, Yankees; Bruce Bochy, Padres

Yankees – Joe Girardi, Jorge Posada, catchers; David Cone, Orlando Hernandez, Hideki Irabu, Graeme Lloyd, Ramiro Mendoza, Jeff Nelson, Andy Pettitte, Mariano Rivera, Mike Stanton, David Wells, pitchers; Scott Brosius, Homer Bush, Derek Jeter, Chuck Knoblauch, Tino Martinez, Luis Sojo, infielders; Chad Curtis, Chili Davis, Ricky Ledee, Paul O'Neill, Tim Raines, Shane Spencer, Bernie Williams, outfielders.

Padres – Carlos Hernandez, Jim Leyritz, Greg Myers, catchers; Andy Ashby, Brian Boehringer, Kevin Brown, Joey Hamilton, Sterling Hitchcock, Trevor Hoffman, Mark Langston, Dan Miceli, Randy Myers, Donne Wall, pitchers; George Arias, Ken Caminiti, Chris Gomez, Wally Joyner, Andy Sheets, Quilvio Veras, infielders; Steve Finley, Tony Gwynn, Ruben Rivera, Mark Sweeney, John Vander Wal, Greg Vaughn, outfielders.

1999 – NEW YORK YANKEES A.L. (4) vs. ATLANTA BRAVES N.L. (0)

(Yankee Stadium / Turner Field)

Oct. 23n	at Atl.	New York (Hernandez)	4	Atlanta (Maddux)	1	
Oct. 24n	at Atl.	New York (Cone)	7	Atlanta (Millwood)	2	
Oct. 26n	at NY	New York (Rivera)	6	Atlanta (Remlinger)	5	(10 innings)
Oct. 27n	at NY	New York (Clemens)	4	Atlanta (Smoltz)	1	

MANAGERS: Joe Torre, Yankees; Bobby Cox, Braves

Yankees – Joe Girardi, Jorge Posada, catchers; Roger Clemens, David Cone, Jason Grimsley, Orlando Hernandez, Ramiro Mendoza, Jeff Nelson, Andy Pettitte, Mariano Rivera, Mike Stanton, Allen Watson, pitchers; Clay Bellinger, Scott Brosius, Derek Jeter, Chuck Knoblauch, Jim Leyritz, Tino Martinez, Luis Sojo, infielders; Chad Curtis, Chili Davis, Ricky Ledee, Paul O'Neill, Darryl Strawberry, Bernie Williams, outfielders.

Braves – Jorge Fabregas, Greg Myers, Eddie Perez, catchers; Tom Glavine, Greg Maddux, Kevin McGlinchy, Kevin Millwood, Terry Mulholland, Mike Remlinger, John Rocker, John Smoltz, Russ Springer, pitchers; Howard Battle, Bret Boone, Ozzie Guillen, Jose Hernandez, Brian Hunter, Chipper Jones, Ryan Klesko, Keith Lockhart, Walt Weiss, infielders; Andruw Jones, Brian Jordan, Otis Nixon, Gerald Williams, outfielders.

2000 – NEW YORK YANKEES A.L. (4) vs. NEW YORK METS N.L. (1)

(Yankee Stadium / Shea Stadium)

Oct. 21n	at Yankees	Yankees (Stanton)	4	Mets (Wendell)	3	(12 innings)
Oct. 22n	at Yankees	Yankees (Clemens)	6	Mets (Hampton)	5	
Oct. 24n	at Mets	Mets (J. Franco)	4	Yankees (Hernandez)	2	
Oct. 25n	at Mets	Yankees (Nelson)	3	Mets (Jones)	2	
Oct. 26n	at Mets	Yankees (Stanton)	4	Mets (Leiter)	2	

MANAGERS: Joe Torre, Yankees; Bobby Valentine, Mets

Yankees – Jorge Posada, Chris Turner, catchers; Roger Clemens, David Cone, Dwight Gooden, Jason Grimsley, Orlando Hernandez, Denny Neagle, Jeff Nelson, Andy Pettitte, Mariano Rivera, Mike Stanton, pitchers; Clay Bellinger, Scott Brosius, Derek Jeter, Chuck Knoblauch, Tino Martinez, Luis Sojo, Jose Vizcaino, infielders; Jose Canseco, Glenallen Hill, David Justice, Paul O'Neill, Luis Polonia, Bernie Williams, outfielders.

Mets – Mike Piazza, Todd Pratt, catchers; Armando Benitez, Dennis Cook, John Franco, Mike Hampton, Bobby J. Jones, Al Leiter, Rick Reed, Glendon Rusch, Turk Wendell, Rick White, pitchers; Kurt Abbott, Edgardo Alfonzo, Mike Bordick, Matt Franco, Lenny Harris, Robin Ventura, Todd Zeile, infielders; Benny Agbayani, Darryl Hamilton, Joe McEwing, Jay Payton, Timo Perez, Bubba Trammell, outfielders.

2001 - ARIZONA DIAMONDBACKS N.L. (4) vs. NEW YORK YANKEES A.L. (3)

(Bank One Ballpark / Yankee Stadium)

Oct. 27n	at Ari.	Arizona (Schilling)	9	New York (Mussina)	1	
Oct. 28n	at Ari.	Arizona (Johnson)	4	New York (Pettitte)	0	
Oct. 30n	at NY	New York (Clemens)	2	Arizona (Anderson)	1	
Oct. 31n	at NY	New York (Rivera)	4	Arizona (Kim)	3	(10 innings)
Nov. 1n	at NY	New York (Hitchcock)	3	Arizona (Lopez)	2	(12 innings)
Nov. 3n	at Ari.	Arizona (Johnson)	15	New York (Pettitte)	2	
Nov. 4n	at Ari.	Arizona (Johnson)	3	New York (Rivera)	2	

MANAGERS: Bob Brenly, Diamondbacks; Joe Torre, Yankees

Diamondbacks – Rod Barajas, Damian Miller, catchers; Brian Anderson, Miguel Batista, Troy Brohawn, Randy Johnson, Byung-Hyun Kim, Albie Lopez, Mike Morgan, Curt Schilling, Greg Swindell, Bobby Witt, pitchers; Jay Bell, Greg Colbrunn, Craig Counsell, Erubiel Durazo, Mark Grace, Matt Williams, Tony Womack, infielders; Danny Bautista, Midre Cummings, David Dellucci, Steve Finley, Luis Gonzalez, Reggie Sanders, outfielders.

Yankees – Todd Greene, Jorge Posada, catchers; Randy Choate, Roger Clemens, Orlando Hernandez, Sterling Hitchcock, Ramiro Mendoza, Mike Mussina, Andy Pettitte, Mariano Rivera, Mike Stanton, Jay Witasick, pitchers; Scott Brosius, Derek Jeter, Tino Martinez, Luis Sojo, Alfonso Soriano, Randy Velarde, Enrique Wilson, infielders; Clay Bellinger, David Justice, Chuck Knoblauch, Paul O'Neill, Shane Spencer, Bernie Williams, outfielders.

2002 - ANAHEIM ANGELS A.L. (4) vs. SAN FRANCISCO GIANTS N.L. (3)

(Edison International Field of Anaheim / Pacific Bell Park)

Oct. 19n	at Ana.	San Francisco (Schmidt)	4	Anaheim (Washburn)	3
Oct. 20n	at Ana.	Anaheim (Rodriguez)	11	San Francisco (Rodriguez)	10
Oct. 22n	at SF	Anaheim (Ortiz)	10	San Francisco (Hernandez)	4
Oct. 23n	at SF	San Francisco (Worrell)	4	Anaheim (Rodriguez)	3
Oct. 24n	at SF	San Francisco (Zerbe)	16	Anaheim (Washburn)	4
Oct. 26n	at Ana.	Anaheim (Donnelly)	6	San Francisco (Worrell)	5
Oct. 27n	at Ana.	Anaheim (Lackey)	4	San Francisco (Hernandez)	1

MANAGERS: Mike Scioscia, Angels; Dusty Baker, Giants

Angels – Bengie Molina, Jose Molina, catchers; Kevin Appier, Brendan Donnelly, John Lackey, Ramon Ortiz, Troy Percival, Francisco Rodriguez, Scott Schoeneweis, Scot Shields, Jarrod Washburn, Ben Weber, pitchers; David Eckstein, Chone Figgins, Brad Fullmer, Benji Gil, Troy Glaus, Adam Kennedy, Scott Spiezio, Shawn Wooten, infielders; Garret Anderson, Darin Erstad, Alex Ochoa, Orlando Palmeiro, Tim Salmon, outfielders.

Giants – Benito Santiago, Yorvit Torrealba, catchers; Scott Eyre, Aaron Fultz, Livan Hernandez, Robb Nen, Russ Ortiz, Felix Rodriguez, Kirk Rueter, Jason Schmidt, Jay Witasick, Tim Worrell, Chad Zerbe, pitchers; Rich Aurilia, David Bell, Pedro Feliz, Jeff Kent, Ramon Martinez, J.T. Snow, infielders; Barry Bonds, Shawon Dunston, Tom Goodwin, Kenny Lofton, Reggie Sanders, Tsuyoshi Shinjo, outfielders.

2003 - FLORIDA MARLINS N.L. (4) vs. NEW YORK YANKEES A.L. (2)

(Pro Player Stadium / Yankee Stadium)

Oct. 18n	at NY	Florida (Penny)	3	New York (Wells)	2	
Oct. 19n	at NY	New York (Pettitte)	6	Florida (Redman)	1	
Oct. 21n	at Fla.	New York (Mussina)	6	Florida (Beckett)	1	
Oct. 22n	at Fla.	Florida (Looper)	4	New York (Weaver)	3	(12 innings)
Oct. 23n	at Fla.	Florida (Penny)	6	New York (Contreras)	4	
Oct. 25n	at NY	Florida (Beckett)	2	New York (Pettitte)	0	

MANAGERS: Jack McKeon, Marlins; Joe Torre, Yankees

Marlins – Mike Redmond, Ivan Rodriguez, catchers; Josh Beckett, Nate Bump, Chad Fox, Rick Helling, Braden Looper, Carl Pavano, Brad Penny, Mark Redman, Michael Tejera, Ugueth Urbina, Dontrelle Willis, pitchers; Luis Castillo, Alex Gonzalez, Lenny Harris, Derrek Lee, Mike Lowell, Mike Mordecai, infielders; Brian Banks, Miguel Cabrera, Jeff Conine, Juan Encarnacion, Todd Hollandsworth, Juan Pierre, outfielders.

Yankees – John Flaherty, Jorge Posada, catchers; Roger Clemens, Jose Contreras, Chris Hammond, Felix Heredia, Mike Mussina, Jeff Nelson, Andy Pettitte, Mariano Rivera, Jeff Weaver, David Wells, Gabe White, pitchers; Aaron Boone, Jason Giambi, Derek Jeter, Nick Johnson, Alfonso Soriano, Enrique Wilson, infielders; David Dellucci, Karim Garcia, Hideki Matsui, Juan Rivera, Ruben Sierra, Bernie Williams, outfielders.

2004 – BOSTON RED SOX A.L. (4) vs. ST. LOUIS CARDINALS N.L. (0)

(Fenway Park / Busch Stadium)

Oct. 23n	at Bos.	Boston (Foulke)	11	St. Louis (Tavarez)	9	
Oct. 24n	at Bos.	Boston (Schilling)	6	St. Louis (Morris)	2	
Oct. 26n	at StL.	Boston (Martinez)	4	St. Louis (Suppan)	1	
Oct. 27n	at StL.	Boston (Lowe)	3	St. Louis (Marquis)	0	

MANAGERS: Terry Francona, Red Sox; Tony LaRussa, Cardinals

Red Sox – Doug Mirabelli, Jason Varitek, catchers; Bronson Arroyo, Alan Embree, Keith Foulke, Curtis Leskanic, Derek Lowe, Pedro Martinez, Mike Myers, Curt Schilling, Mike Timlin, Tim Wakefield, pitchers; Mark Bellhorn, Orlando Cabrera, Doug Mientkiewicz, Kevin Millar, Bill Mueller, David Ortiz, Pokey Reese, Kevin Youkilis, infielders; Johnny Damon, Gabe Kapler, Trot Nixon, Manny Ramirez, Dave Roberts, outfielders.

Cardinals – Mike Matheny, Yadier Molina, catchers; Kiko Calero, Cal Eldred, Dan Haren, Jason Isringhausen, Ray King, Jason Marquis, Matt Morris, Al Reyes, Jeff Suppan, Julian Tavarez, Woody Williams, pitchers; Marlon Anderson, Hector Luna, Albert Pujols, Edgar Renteria, Scott Rolen, Tony Womack, infielders; Roger Cedeno, Jim Edmonds, John Mabry, Reggie Sanders, So Taguchi, Larry Walker, outfielders.

2005 – CHICAGO WHITE SOX A.L. (4) vs. HOUSTON ASTROS N.L. (0)

(U.S. Cellular Field / Minute Maid Park)

Oct. 22n	at Chi.	Chicago (Contreras)	5	Houston (Rodriguez)	3	
Oct. 23n	at Chi.	Chicago (Cotts)	7	Houston (Lidge)	6	
Oct. 25n	at Hou.	Chicago (Marte)	7	Houston (Astacio)	5	(14 innings)
Oct. 26n	at Hou.	Chicago (Garcia)	1	Houston (Lidge)	0	

MANAGERS: Ozzie Guillen, White Sox; Phil Garner, Astros

White Sox – A.J. Pierzynski, Chris Widger, catchers; Mark Buehrle, Jose Contreras, Neal Cotts, Freddy Garcia, Jon Garland, Dustin Hermanson, Orlando Hernandez, Bobby Jenks, Damaso Marte, Cliff Politte, Luis Vizcaino, pitchers; Geoff Blum, Joe Crede, Willie Harris, Tadahito Iguchi, Paul Konerko, Juan Uribe, Pablo Ozuna, infielders; Jermaine Dye, Carl Everett, Timo Perez, Scott Podsednik, Aaron Rowand, outfielders.

Astros – Brad Ausmus, Raul Chavez, catchers; Ezequiel Astacio, Brandon Backe, Roger Clemens, Mike Gallo, Brad Lidge, Roy Oswalt, Andy Pettitte, Chad Qualls, Wandy Rodriguez, Russ Springer, Dan Wheeler, pitchers; Jeff Bagwell, Lance Berkman, Craig Biggio, Eric Bruntlett, Morgan Ensberg, Adam Everett, Mike Lamb, Jose Vizcaino, infielders; Chris Burke, Jason Lane, Orlando Palmeiro, Willy Taveras, outfielders.

2006 – ST. LOUIS CARDINALS N.L. (4) vs. DETROIT TIGERS A.L. (1)

(Busch Stadium / Comerica Park)

Oct. 21n	at Det.	St. Louis (Reyes)	7	Detroit (Verlander)	2
Oct. 22n	at Det.	Detroit (Rogers)	3	St. Louis (Weaver)	1
Oct. 24n	at StL.	St. Louis (Carpenter)	5	Detroit (Robertson)	0
Oct. 26n	at StL.	St. Louis (Wainright)	5	Detroit (Zumaya)	4
Oct. 27n	at StL.	St. Louis (Weaver)	4	Detroit (Verlander)	2
POSTPONED: (Rain) Oct. 25					

MANAGERS: Tony LaRussa, Cardinals; Jim Leyland, Tigers

Cardinals – Gary Bennett, Yadier Molina, catchers; Chris Carpenter, Randy Flores, Josh Hancock, Tyler Johnson, Josh Kinney, Braden Looper, Anthony Reyes, Jeff Suppan, Brad Thompson, Adam Wainwright, Jeff Weaver, pitchers; Ronnie Belliard, David Eckstein, Aaron Miles, Albert Pujols, Scott Rolen, Scott Spiezio, infielders; Chris Duncan, Jim Edmonds, Juan Encarnacion, John Rodriguez, So Taguchi, Preston Wilson, outfielders.

Tigers – Ivan Rodriguez, Vance Wilson, catchers; Jeremy Bonderman, Jason Grilli, Todd Jones, Wil Ledezma, Zach Miner, Nate Robertson, Fernando Rodney, Kenny Rogers, Justin Verlander, Jamie Walker, Joel Zumaya, pitchers; Sean Casey, Carlos Guillen, Omar Infante, Brandon Inge, Neifi Perez, Placido Polanco, Ramon Santiago, infielders; Alexis Gomez, Curtis Granderson, Craig Monroe, Magglio Ordonez, Marcus Thames, outfielders.

2007 – BOSTON RED SOX A.L. (4) vs. COLORADO ROCKIES N.L. (0)
(Fenway Park / Coors Field)

Oct. 24n	at Bos.	Boston (Beckett)	13	Colorado (Francis)	1
Oct. 25n	at Bos.	Boston (Schilling)	2	Colorado (Jimenez)	1
Oct. 27n	at Col.	Boston (Matsuzaka)	10	Colorado (Fogg)	5
Oct. 28n	at Col.	Boston (Lester)	4	Colorado (Cook)	3

MANAGERS: Terry Francona, Red Sox; Clint Hurdle, Rockies

Red Sox – Doug Mirabelli, Jason Varitek, catchers; Josh Beckett, Manny Delcarmen, Eric Gagne, Jon Lester, Javier Lopez, Daisuke Matsuzaka, Hideki Okajima, Jonathan Papelbon, Curt Schilling, Kyle Snyder, Mike Timlin, pitchers; Alex Cora, Eric Hinske, Mike Lowell, Julio Lugo, David Ortiz, Dustin Pedroia, Kevin Youkilis, infielders; Coco Crisp, J.D. Drew, Jacoby Ellsbury, Bobby Kielty, Manny Ramirez, outfielders.

Rockies – Chris Iannetta, Yorvit Torrealba, catchers; Jeremy Affeldt, Aaron Cook, Manny Corpas, Josh Fogg, Jeff Francis, Brian Fuentes, LaTroy Hawkins, Matt Herges, Ubaldo Jimenez, Franklin Morales, Ryan Speier, pitchers; Garrett Atkins, Jamey Carroll, Todd Helton, Kazuo Matsui, Troy Tulowitzki, infielders; Jeff Baker, Brad Hawpe, Matt Holliday, Seth Smith, Ryan Spilborghs, Cory Sullivan, Willy Taveras, outfielders.

2008 – PHILADELPHIA PHILLIES N.L. (4) vs. TAMPA BAY RAYS A.L. (1)
(Citizens Bank Park / Tropicana Field)

Oct. 22n	at TB	Philadelphia (Hamels)	3	Tampa Bay (Kazmir)	2
Oct. 23n	at TB	Tampa Bay (Shields)	4	Philadelphia (Myers)	2
Oct. 25n	at Phil.	Philadelphia (Romero)	5	Tampa Bay (Howell)	4
Oct. 26n	at Phil.	Philadelphia (Blanton)	10	Tampa Bay (Sonnanstine)	2
Oct. 27n	at Phil.	Philadelphia (Romero)	4	Tampa Bay (Howell)	3

Game Five suspended in the sixth inning (rain); resumed and completed on Oct. 29

MANAGERS: Charlie Manuel, Phillies; Joe Maddon, Rays

Phillies – Chris Coste, Carlos Ruiz, catchers; Joe Blanton, Clay Condrey, Chad Durbin, Scott Eyre, Cole Hamels, J.A. Happ, Brad Lidge, Ryan Madson, Jamie Moyer, Brett Myers, J.C. Romero, pitchers; Eric Bruntlett, Greg Dobbs, Pedro Feliz, Ryan Howard, Jimmy Rollins, Chase Utley, infielders; Pat Burrell, Geoff Jenkins, Matt Stairs, So Taguchi, Shane Victorino, Jayson Werth, outfielders.

Rays – Michel Hernandez, Dioner Navarro, catchers; Grant Balfour, Chad Bradford, Matt Garza, J.P. Howell, Edwin Jackson, Scott Kazmir, Trever Miller, David Price, James Shields, Andy Sonnanstine, Dan Wheeler, pitchers; Willy Aybar, Jason Bartlett, Akinori Iwamura, Evan Longoria, Carlos Pena, infielders; Rocco Baldelli, Carl Crawford, Cliff Floyd, Gabe Gross, Eric Hinske, Fernando Perez, B.J. Upton, Ben Zobrist, outfielders. *Hinske replaced Floyd (injured).*

2009 - NEW YORK YANKEES A.L. (4) vs. PHILADELPHIA PHILLIES N.L. (2)
(Yankee Stadium / Citizens Bank Park)

Oct. 28n	at NY	Philadelphia (Lee)	6	New York (Sabathia)	1
Oct. 29n	at NY	New York (Burnett)	3	Philadelphia (Martinez)	1
Oct. 31n	at Phil.	New York (Pettitte)	8	Philadelphia (Hamels)	5
Nov. 1n	at Phil.	New York (Chamberlain)	7	Philadelphia (Lidge)	4
Nov. 2n	at Phil.	Philadelphia (Lee)	8	New York (Burnett)	6
Nov. 4n	at NY	New York (Pettitte)	7	Philadelphia (Martinez)	3

MANAGERS: Joe Girardi, Yankees; Charlie Manuel, Phillies

Yankees – Jose Molina, Jorge Posada, catchers; Alfredo Aceves, Brian Bruney, A.J. Burnett, Joba Chamberlain, Phil Coke, Chad Gaudin, Phil Hughes, Damaso Marte, Andy Pettitte, Mariano Rivera, David Robertson, CC Sabathia, pitchers; Robinson Cano, Derek Jeter, Ramiro Pena, Alex Rodriguez, Mark Teixeira, infielders; Melky Cabrera, Johnny Damon, Brett Gardner, Jerry Hairston Jr., Eric Hinske, Hideki Matsui, Nick Swisher, outfielders. *Pena replaced Cabrera (injured).*

Phillies – Paul Bako, Carlos Ruiz, catchers; Antonio Bastardo, Joe Blanton, Chad Durbin, Scott Eyre, Cole Hamels, J.A. Happ, Cliff Lee, Brad Lidge, Ryan Madson, Pedro Martinez, Brett Myers, Chan Ho Park, pitchers; Eric Bruntlett, Greg Dobbs, Pedro Feliz, Ryan Howard, Jimmy Rollins, Chase Utley, infielders; Ben Francisco, Raul Ibanez, Matt Stairs, Shane Victorino, Jayson Werth, outfielders.

2010 – SAN FRANCISCO GIANTS N.L. (4) vs. TEXAS RANGERS A.L. (1)

(AT&T Park / Rangers Ballpark in Arlington)

Oct. 27	at SF	San Francisco (Lincecum)	11	Texas (Lee)	7
Oct. 28	at SF	San Francisco (Cain)	9	Texas (Wilson)	0
Oct. 30n	at Tex.	Texas (Lewis)	4	San Francisco (J. Sanchez)	2
Oct. 31n	at Tex.	San Francisco (Bumgarner)	4	Texas (Hunter)	0
Nov. 1n	at Tex.	San Francisco (Lincecum)	3	Texas (Lee)	1

MANAGERS: Bruce Bochy, Giants; Ron Washington, Rangers

Giants – Buster Posey, Eli Whiteside, catchers; Jeremy Affeldt, Madison Bumgarner, Matt Cain, Santiago Casilla, Tim Lincecum, Javier Lopez, Guillermo Mota, Ramon Ramirez, Sergio Romo, Jonathan Sanchez, Brian Wilson, pitchers; Mike Fontenot, Aubrey Huff, Travis Ishikawa, Edgar Renteria, Freddy Sanchez, Pablo Sandoval, Juan Uribe, infielders; Pat Burrell, Cody Ross, Aaron Rowand, Nate Schierholtz, Andres Torres, outfielders.

Rangers – Bengie Molina, Matt Treanor, catchers; Neftali Feliz, Derek Holland, Tommy Hunter, Michael Kirkman, Cliff Lee, Colby Lewis, Mark Lowe, Dustin Nippert, Darren O'Day, Darren Oliver, C.J. Wilson, pitchers; Elvis Andrus, Andres Blanco, Jorge Cantu, Ian Kinsler, Mitch Moreland, Michael Young, infielders; Julio Borbon, Nelson Cruz, Jeff Francoeur, Vladimir Guerrero, Josh Hamilton, David Murphy, outfielders. *Nippert replaced Ogando (injured).*

2011– ST. LOUIS CARDINALS N.L. (4) vs. TEXAS RANGERS A.L. (3)

(Busch Stadium / Rangers Ballpark in Arlington)

Oct. 19n	at StL.	St. Louis (Carpenter)	3	Texas (Wilson)	2	
Oct. 20n	at StL.	Texas (Adams)	2	St. Louis (Motte)	1	
Oct. 22n	at Tex.	St. Louis (Lynn)	16	Texas (Harrison)	7	
Oct. 23n	at Tex.	Texas (Holland)	4	St. Louis (Jackson)	0	
Oct. 24n	at Tex.	Texas (Oliver)	4	St. Louis (Dotel)	2	
Oct. 27n	at StL.	St. Louis (Westbrook)	10	Texas (Lowe)	9	(11 innings)
Oct. 28n	at StL.	St. Louis (Carpenter)	6	Texas (Harrison)	2	

POSTPONED: (Rain) Oct. 26

MANAGERS: Tony LaRussa, Cardinals; Ron Washington, Rangers

Cardinals – Yadier Molina, Gerald Laird, catchers; Mitchell Boggs, Chris Carpenter, Octavio Dotel, Jaime Garcia, Edwin Jackson, Kyle Lohse, Lance Lynn, Jason Motte, Arthur Rhodes, Marc Rzepczynski, Fernando Salas, Jake Westbrook, pitchers; Daniel Descalso, David Freese, Rafael Furcal, Albert Pujols, Nick Punto, Ryan Theriot, infielders; Lance Berkman, Adron Chambers, Allen Craig, Matt Holliday, Jon Jay, Skip Schumaker, outfielders. *Chambers replaced Holliday (injured).*

Rangers – Mike Napoli, Yorvit Torrealba, Matt Treanor, catchers; Mike Adams, Scott Feldman, Neftali Feliz, Mike Gonzalez, Matt Harrison, Derek Holland, Colby Lewis, Mark Lowe, Alexi Ogando, Darren Oliver, C.J. Wilson, pitchers; Elvis Andrus, Adrian Beltre, Ian Kinsler, Mitch Moreland, Michael Young, infielders; Endy Chavez, Nelson Cruz, Craig Gentry, Esteban German, Josh Hamilton, David Murphy, outfielders.

2012– SAN FRANCISCO GIANTS N.L. (4) vs. DETROIT TIGERS A.L. (0)

(AT&T Park / Comerica Park)

Oct. 24n	at SF	San Francisco (Zito)	8	Detroit (Verlander)	3	
Oct. 25n	at SF	San Francisco (Bumgarner)	2	Detroit (Fister)	0	
Oct. 27n	at Det.	San Francisco (Vogelsong)	2	Detroit (Sanchez)	0	
Oct. 28n	at Det.	San Francisco (Casilla)	4	Detroit (Coke)	3	(10 innings)

MANAGERS: Bruce Bochy, Giants; Jim Leyland, Tigers

Giants – Buster Posey, Hector Sanchez, catchers; Jeremy Affeldt, Madison Bumgarner, Matt Cain, Santiago Casilla, George Kontos, Tim Lincecum, Javier Lopez, Jose Mijares, Guillermo Mota, Sergio Romo, Ryan Vogelsong, Barry Zito, pitchers; Joaquin Arias, Brandon Belt, Brandon Crawford, Aubrey Huff, Pablo Sandoval, Marco Scutaro, Ryan Theriot, infielders; Gregor Blanco, Xavier Nady, Angel Pagan, Hunter Pence, outfielders.

Tigers – Alex Avila, Gerald Laird, catchers; Al Alburquerque, Joaquin Benoit, Phil Coke, Octavio Dotel, Doug Fister, Rick Porcello, Anibal Sanchez, Max Scherzer, Drew Smyly, Jose Valverde, Justin Verlander, pitchers; Miguel Cabrera, Prince Fielder, Omar Infante, Jhonny Peralta, Ramon Santiago, Danny Worth, infielders; Quintin Berry, Andy Dirks, Avisail Garcia, Austin Jackson, Don Kelly, Delmon Young, outfielders.

2013 - BOSTON RED SOX A.L. (4) vs. ST. LOUIS CARDINALS N.L. (2)
(Fenway Park / Busch Stadium)

Oct. 23n	at Bos.	Boston (Lester)	8	St. Louis (Wainwright)	1
Oct. 24n	at Bos.	St. Louis (Wacha)	4	Boston (Lackey)	2
Oct. 26n	at StL.	St. Louis (Rosenthal)	5	Boston (Workman)	4
Oct. 27n	at StL.	Boston (Doubront)	4	St. Louis (Lynn)	2
Oct. 28n	at StL.	Boston (Lester)	3	St. Louis (Wainwright)	1
Oct. 30n	at Bos.	Boston (Lackey)	6	St. Louis (Wacha)	1

MANAGERS: John Farrell, Red Sox; Mike Matheny, Cardinals

Red Sox — David Ross, Jarrod Saltalamacchia, catchers; Craig Breslow, Clay Buchholz, Ryan Dempster, Felix Doubront, John Lackey, Jon Lester, Franklin Morales, Jake Peavy, Junichi Tazawa, Koji Uehara, Brandon Workman, pitchers; Xander Bogaerts, Stephen Drew, Will Middlebrooks, Mike Napoli, David Ortiz, Dustin Pedroia, infielders; Quintin Berry, Mike Carp, Jacoby Ellsbury, Jonny Gomes, Daniel Nava, Shane Victorino, outfielders.

Cardinals — Tony Cruz, Yadier Molina, catchers; John Axford, Randy Choate, Joe Kelly, Lance Lynn, Seth Maness, Carlos Martinez, Shelby Miller, Edward Mujica, Trevor Rosenthal, Kevin Siegrist, Michael Wacha, Adam Wainwright, pitchers; Matt Adams, Matt Carpenter, Allen Craig, Daniel Descalso, David Freese, Pete Kozma, Kolten Wong, infielders; Carlos Beltran, Matt Holliday, Jon Jay, Shane Robinson, outfielders.

2014 - SAN FRANCISCO GIANTS N.L. (4) vs. KANSAS CITY ROYALS A.L. (3)
(AT&T Park / Kauffman Stadium)

Oct. 21n	at KC	San Francisco (Bumgarner)	7	Kansas City (Shields)	1
Oct. 22n	at KC	Kansas City (Herrera)	7	San Francisco (Peavy)	2
Oct. 24n	at SF	Kansas City (Guthrie)	3	San Francisco (Hudson)	2
Oct. 25n	at SF	San Francisco (Petit)	11	Kansas City (Finnegan)	4
Oct. 26n	at SF	San Francisco (Bumgarner)	5	Kansas City (Shields)	0
Oct. 28n	at KC	Kansas City (Ventura)	10	San Francisco (Peavy)	0
Oct. 29n	at KC	San Francisco (Affeldt)	3	Kansas City (Guthrie)	2

MANAGERS: Bruce Bochy, Giants; Ned Yost, Royals

Giants — Buster Posey, Andrew Susac, catchers; Jeremy Affeldt, Madison Bumgarner, Santiago Casilla, Tim Hudson, Tim Lincecum, Javier Lopez, Jean Machi, Jake Peavy, Yusmeiro Petit, Sergio Romo, Hunter Strickland, Ryan Vogelsong, pitchers; Joaquin Arias, Brandon Belt, Brandon Crawford, Matt Duffy, Joe Panik, Pablo Sandoval, infielders; Gregor Blanco, Travis Ishikawa, Michael Morse, Hunter Pence, Juan Perez, outfielders.

Royals — Erik Kratz, Salvador Perez, catchers; Tim Collins, Wade Davis, Danny Duffy, Brandon Finnegan, Jason Frasor, Jeremy Guthrie, Kelvin Herrera, Greg Holland, James Shields, Jason Vargas, Yordano Ventura, pitchers; Billy Butler, Alcides Escobar, Eric Hosmer, Omar Infante, Mike Moustakas, Jayson Nix, infielders; Nori Aoki, Lorenzo Cain, Jarrod Dyson, Alex Gordon, Terrance Gore, Josh Willingham, outfielders.

2015 - KANSAS CITY ROYALS A.L. (4) vs. NEW YORK METS N.L. (1)
(Kauffman Stadium / Citi Field)

Oct. 27n	at KC	Kansas City (Young)	5	New York (Colon)	4	(14 innings)
Oct. 28n	at KC	Kansas City (Cueto)	7	New York (deGrom)	1	
Oct. 30n	at NY	New York (Syndergaard)	9	Kansas City (Ventura)	3	
Oct. 31n	at NY	Kansas City (Madson)	5	New York (Clippard)	3	
Nov. 1n	at NY	Kansas City (Hochevar)	7	New York (Reed)	2	(12 innings)

MANAGERS: Ned Yost, Royals; Terry Collins, Mets

Royals — Drew Butera, Salvador Perez, catchers; Johnny Cueto, Wade Davis, Danny Duffy, Kelvin Herrera, Luke Hochevar, Ryan Madson, Kris Medlen, Franklin Morales, Yordano Ventura, Edinson Volquez, Chris Young, pitchers; Christian Colon, Alcides Escobar, Eric Hosmer, Raul Mondesi, Kendrys Morales, Mike Moustakas, Ben Zobrist, infielders; Lorenzo Cain, Jarrod Dyson, Alex Gordon, Paulo Orlando, Alex Rios, outfielders.

Mets — Travis d'Arnaud , Kevin Plawecki, catchers; Tyler Clippard, Bartolo Colon, Jacob deGrom, Jeurys Familia, Sean Gilmartin, Matt Harvey, Steven Matz, Jonathon Niese, Addison Reed, Hansel Robles, Noah Syndergaard, pitchers; Lucas Duda, Wilmer Flores, Kelly Johnson, Daniel Murphy, Juan Uribe, David Wright, infielders; Yoenis Cespedes, Michael Conforto, Michael Cuddyer, Curtis Granderson, Juan Lagares, Kirk Nieuwenhuis, outfielders.

2016 – CHICAGO CUBS N.L. (4) vs. CLEVELAND INDIANS A.L. (3)
(Wrigley Field / Progressive Field)

Oct. 25n	at Clev.	Cleveland (Kluber)	6	Chicago (Lester)	0	
Oct. 26n	at Clev.	Chicago (Arrieta)	5	Cleveland (Bauer)	1	
Oct. 28n	at Chi.	Cleveland (Miller)	1	Chicago (Edwards)	0	
Oct. 29n	at Chi.	Cleveland (Kluber)	7	Chicago (Lackey)	2	
Oct. 30n	at Chi.	Chicago (Lester)	3	Cleveland (Bauer)	2	
Nov. 1n	at Clev.	Chicago (Arrieta)	9	Cleveland (Tomlin)	3	
Nov. 2n	at Clev.	Chicago (Chapman)	8	Cleveland (Shaw)	7	(10 innings)

MANAGERS: Joe Maddon, Cubs; Terry Francona, Indians

Cubs – Willson Contreras, Miguel Montero, David Ross, catchers; Jake Arrieta, Aroldis Chapman, Carl Edwards Jr., Justin Grimm, Kyle Hendricks, John Lackey, Jon Lester, Mike Montgomery, Hector Rondon, Pedro Strop, Travis Wood, pitchers; Javier Baez, Kris Bryant, Anthony Rizzo, Addison Russell, infielders; Albert Almora, Chris Coghlan, Dexter Fowler, Jason Heyward, Kyle Schwarber, Jorge Soler, Ben Zobrist, outfielders.

Indians – Yan Gomes, Roberto Perez, catchers; Cody Allen, Trevor Bauer, Mike Clevinger, Corey Kluber, Jeff Manship, Zach McAllister, Ryan Merritt, Andrew Miller, Dan Otero, Danny Salazar, Bryan Shaw, Josh Tomlin, pitchers; Jason Kipnis, Francisco Lindor, Michael Martinez, Mike Napoli, Jose Ramirez, Carlos Santana, infielders; Lonnie Chisenhall, Coco Crisp, Rajai Davis, Brandon Guyer, Tyler Naquin, outfielders.

2017 – HOUSTON ASTROS A.L. (4) vs. LOS ANGELES DODGERS N.L. (3)
(Minute Maid Park / Dodger Stadium)

Oct. 24n	at LA	Los Angeles (Kershaw)	3	Houston (Keuchel)	1	
Oct. 25n	at LA	Houston (Devenski)	7	Los Angeles (McCarthy)	6	(11 innings)
Oct. 27n	at Hou.	Houston (McCullers Jr.)	5	Los Angeles (Darvish)	3	
Oct. 28n	at Hou.	Los Angeles (Watson)	6	Houston (Giles)	2	
Oct. 29n	at Hou.	Houston (Musgrove)	13	Los Angeles (Jansen)	12	(10 innings)
Oct. 31n	at LA	Los Angeles (Watson)	3	Houston (Verlander)	1	
Nov. 1n	at LA	Houston (Morton)	5	Los Angeles (Darvish)	1	

MANAGERS: A.J. Hinch, Astros; Dave Roberts, Dodgers

Astros – Juan Centeno, Evan Gattis, Brian McCann, catchers; Chris Devenski, Ken Giles, Luke Gregerson, Will Harris, Dallas Keuchel, Francisco Liriano, Lance McCullers Jr., Collin McHugh, Charlie Morton, Joe Musgrove, Brad Peacock, Justin Verlander, pitchers; Jose Altuve, Alex Bregman, Carlos Correa, Marwin Gonzalez, Yuli Gurriel, infielders; Carlos Beltran, Derek Fisher, Cameron Maybin, Josh Reddick, George Springer, outfielders.

Dodgers – Austin Barnes, Yasmani Grandal, catchers; Tony Cingrani, Yu Darvish, Josh Fields, Rich Hill, Kenley Jansen, Clayton Kershaw, Kenta Maeda, Brandon McCarthy, Brandon Morrow, Ross Stripling, Tony Watson, Alex Wood, pitchers; Cody Bellinger, Charlie Culberson, Logan Forsythe, Corey Seager, Justin Turner, Chase Utley, infielders; Andre Ethier, Kike Hernandez, Joc Pederson, Yasiel Puig, Chris Taylor, outfielders.

2018 – BOSTON RED SOX A.L. (4) vs. LOS ANGELES DODGERS N.L. (1)
(Fenway Park / Dodger Stadium)

Oct. 23n	at Bos.	Boston (Barnes)	8	Los Angeles (Kershaw)	4	
Oct. 24n	at Bos.	Boston (Price)	4	Los Angeles (Ryu)	2	
Oct. 26n	at LA	Los Angeles (Wood)	3	Boston (Eovaldi)	2	(18 innings)
Oct. 27n	at LA	Boston (Kelly)	9	Los Angeles (Floro)	6	
Oct. 28n	at LA	Boston (Price)	5	Los Angeles (Kershaw)	1	

MANAGERS: Alex Cora, Red Sox; Dave Roberts, Dodgers

Red Sox – Sandy Leon, Blake Swihart, Christian Vazquez, catchers; Matt Barnes, Ryan Brasier, Nathan Eovaldi, Heath Hembree, Joe Kelly, Craig Kimbrel, Drew Pomeranz, Rick Porcello, David Price, Eduardo Rodriguez, Chris Sale, pitchers; Xander Bogaerts, Rafael Devers, Brock Holt, Ian Kinsler, Mitch Moreland, Eduardo Nunez, infielders; Andrew Benintendi, Mookie Betts, Jackie Bradley, J.D. Martinez, Steve Pearce, outfielders.

Dodgers – Austin Barnes, Yasmani Grandal, catchers; Scott Alexander, Pedro Baez, Walker Buehler, Dylan Floro, Rich Hill, Kenley Jansen, Clayton Kershaw, Ryan Madson, Kenta Maeda, Hyun-Jin Ryu, Julio Urias, Alex Wood, pitchers; Brian Dozier, David Freese, Manny Machado, Max Muncy, Justin Turner, infielders; Cody Bellinger, Kike Hernandez, Matt Kemp, Joc Pederson, Yasiel Puig, Chris Taylor, outfielders.

2019 – WASHINGTON NATIONALS N.L. (4) vs. HOUSTON ASTROS A.L. (3)

(Nationals Park / Minute Maid Park)

Oct. 22n	at Hou.	Washington (Scherzer)	5	Houston (Cole)	4
Oct. 23n	at Hou.	Washington (Strasburg)	12	Houston (Verlander)	3
Oct. 25n	at Wash.	Houston (James)	4	Washington (Sanchez)	1
Oct. 26n	at Wash.	Houston (Urquidy)	8	Washington (Corbin)	1
Oct. 27n	at Wash.	Houston (Cole)	7	Washington (Ross)	1
Oct. 29n	at Hou.	Washington (Strasburg)	7	Houston (Verlander)	2
Oct. 30n	at Hou.	Washington (Corbin)	6	Houston (Harris)	2

MANAGERS: Dave Martinez, Nationals; A.J. Hinch, Astros

Nationals – Yan Gomes, Kurt Suzuki, catchers; Patrick Corbin, Sean Doolittle, Javy Guerra, Daniel Hudson, Tanner Rainey, Fernando Rodney, Joe Ross, Anibal Sanchez, Max Scherzer, Stephen Strasburg, Wander Suero, pitchers; Matt Adams, Asdrubal Cabrera, Brian Dozier, Howie Kendrick, Anthony Rendon, Trea Turner, Ryan Zimmerman, infielders; Adam Eaton, Gerardo Parra, Victor Robles, Juan Soto, Michael Taylor, outfielders.

Astros – Robinson Chirinos, Martin Maldonado, catchers; Gerrit Cole, Chris Devenski, Zack Greinke, Will Harris, Josh James, Roberto Osuna, Brad Peacock, Ryan Pressly, Hector Rondon, Joe Smith, Jose Urquidy, Justin Verlander, pitchers; Jose Altuve, Alex Bregman, Carlos Correa, Aledmys Diaz, Yuli Gurriel, infielders; Yordan Alvarez, Michael Brantley, Jake Marisnick, Josh Reddick, George Springer, Kyle Tucker, outfielders.

2020 – LOS ANGELES DODGERS N.L. (4) vs. TAMPA BAY RAYS A.L. (2)

(All games at Globe Life Field – Arlington, TX)

Oct. 20n	at LA	Los Angeles (Kershaw)	8	Tampa Bay (Glasnow)	3
Oct. 21n	at LA	Tampa Bay (Anderson)	6	Los Angeles (Gonsolin)	4
Oct. 23n	at TB	Los Angeles (Buehler)	6	Tampa Bay (Morton)	2
Oct. 24n	at TB	Tampa Bay (Curtiss)	8	Los Angeles (Jansen)	7
Oct. 25n	at TB	Los Angeles (Kershaw)	4	Tampa Bay (Glasnow)	2
Oct. 27n	at LA	Los Angeles (Gonzalez)	3	Tampa Bay (Anderson)	1

MANAGERS: Dave Roberts, Dodgers; Kevin Cash, Rays

Dodgers – Austin Barnes, Will Smith, catchers; Pedro Baez, Walker Buehler, Dylan Floro, Tony Gonsolin, Victor Gonzalez, Brusdar Graterol, Kenley Jansen, Joe Kelly, Clayton Kershaw, Adam Kolarek, Dustin May, Jake McGee, Blake Treinen, Julio Urias, Alex Wood, pitchers; Matt Beaty, Kike Hernandez, Max Muncy, Edwin Rios, Corey Seager, Chris Taylor, Justin Turner, infielders; Cody Bellinger, Mookie Betts, Joc Pederson, A.J. Pollock, outfielders.

Rays – Michael Perez, Mike Zunino, catchers; Nick Anderson, Diego Castillo, John Curtiss, Peter Fairbanks, Josh Fleming, Tyler Glasnow, Aaron Loup, Shane McClanahan, Charlie Morton, Ryan Sherriff, Blake Snell, Ryan Thompson, Ryan Yarbrough, pitchers; Willy Adames, Mike Brosseau, Ji-Man Choi, Yandy Diaz, Brandon Lowe, Joey Wendle, infielders; Randy Arozarena, Kevin Kiermaier, Manuel Margot, Austin Meadows, Brett Phillips, Hunter Renfroe, Yoshitomo Tsutsugo, outfielders.

AMERICAN LEAGUE CHAMPIONSHIP SERIES

	SERIES			GAMES			WON	LOST
	No.	W	L	No.	W	L		
New York	17	11	6	90	50	40	1976-78, 81, 96, 98-2001, 03, 09	1980, 2004, 10, 12, 17, 19
Boston	11	6	5	62	30	32	1975, 86, 2004, 07, 13, 18	1988, 90, 99, 2003, 08
Oakland	11	6	5	46	23	23	1972-74, 88-90	1971, 75, 81, 92, 2006
Baltimore	10	5	5	41	21	20	1969-71, 79, 83	1973-74, 96, 97, 2014
Kansas City	8	4	4	37	20	17	1980, 85, 2014-15	1976-78, 84
Detroit	7	3	4	33	18	15	1984, 2006, 12	1972, 87, 2011, 13
Toronto	7	2	5	40	16	24	1992-93	1985, 89, 91, 2015-16
Cal./Ana./LA	6	1	5	32	13	19	2002	1979, 82, 86, 2005, 09
Cleveland	5	3	2	30	17	13	1995, 97, 2016	1998, 2007
Minnesota	5	2	3	21	9	12	1987, 91	1969-70, 2002
*Houston	4	2	2	25	12	13	2017, 19	2018, 20
Seattle	3	0	3	17	5	12		1995, 2000-01
Chicago	3	1	2	15	7	8	2005	1983, 93
Tampa Bay	2	2	0	14	8	6	2008, 20	
Texas	2	2	0	12	8	4	2010-11	
*Milwaukee	1	1	0	5	3	2	1982	

* Also played in the National League Championship Series.

Note: 1994 Championship Series not played;

NATIONAL LEAGUE CHAMPIONSHIP SERIES

	SERIES			GAMES				
	No.	W	L	No.	W	L	WON	LOST
Los Angeles	14	8	6	75	37	38	1974, 77-78, 81, 88, 2017-18, 20	1983, 85, 2008-09, 13, 16
St. Louis	14	7	7	81	38	43	1982, 85, 87, 2004, 06, 11, 13	1996, 2000, 02, 05, 12, 14, 19
Atlanta	12	5	7	67	30	37	1991-92, 95-96, 99	1969, 82, 93, 97-98, 2001, 20
Philadelphia	9	5	4	42	22	20	1980, 83, 93, 2008-09	1976-78, 2010
Pittsburgh	9	2	7	42	17	25	1971, 79	1970, 72, 74-75, 90-92
New York	8	5	3	43	26	17	1969, 73, 86, 2000, 15	1988, 99, 2006
Cincinnati	8	5	3	32	18	14	1970, 72, 75-76, 90	1973, 79, 95
San Francisco	7	5	2	39	24	15	1989, 2002, 10, 12, 14	1971, 87
Chicago	6	1	5	32	11	21	2016	1984, 89, 2003, 15, 17
*Houston	4	1	3	24	11	13	2005	1980, 86, 2004
Florida	2	2	0	13	8	5	1997, 2003	
San Diego	2	2	0	11	7	4	1984, 98	
Mtl./Wash.	2	1	1	9	6	3	2019	1981
Arizona	2	1	1	9	4	5	2001	2007
*Milwaukee	2	0	2	13	5	8		2011, 18
Colorado	1	1	0	4	4	0	2007	

* Also played in the American League Championship Series.

Note: 1994 Championship Series not played;

LEAGUE CHAMPIONSHIP SERIES - YEARLY RESULTS

(=Wild Card, since 1995)*

American League   National League

1969

Baltimore 3, Minnesota 0

10/4	at Balt.	Balt.	4	Minn.	3	(12 inn)
10/5	at Balt.	Balt.	1	Minn.	0	(11 inn)
10/6	at Minn.	Balt.	11	Minn.	2	

New York 3, Atlanta 0

10/4	at Atl.	NY	9	Atl.	5
10/5	at Atl.	NY	11	Atl.	6
10/6	at NY	NY	7	Atl.	4

1970

Baltimore 3, Minnesota 0

10/3	at Minn.	Balt.	10	Minn.	6	
10/4	at Minn.	Balt.	11	Minn.	3	
10/5	at Balt.	Balt.	6	Minn.	1	

Cincinnati 3, Pittsburgh 0

10/3	at Pitt.	Cin.	3	Pitt.	0	(10 inn)
10/4	at Pitt.	Cin.	3	Pitt.	1	
10/5	at Cin.	Cin.	3	Pitt.	2	

1971

Baltimore 3, Oakland 0

10/3	at Balt.	Balt.	5	Oak.	3
10/4	at Balt.	Balt.	5	Oak.	1
10/5	at Oak.	Balt.	5	Oak.	3

Pittsburgh 3, San Francisco 1

10/2	at SF	SF	5	Pitt.	4
10/3	at SF	Pitt.	9	SF	4
10/5	at Pitt.	Pitt.	2	SF	1
10/6	at Pitt.	Pitt.	9	SF	5

1972

Oakland 3, Detroit 2

10/7	at Oak.	Oak.	3	Det.	2	(11 inn)
10/8	at Oak.	Oak.	5	Det.	0	
10/10	at Det.	Det.	3	Oak.	0	
10/11	at Det.	Det.	4	Oak.	3	(10 inn)
10/12	at Det.	Oak.	2	Det.	1	

Cincinnati 3, Pittsburgh 2

10/7	at Pitt.	Pitt.	5	Cin.	1
10/8	at Pitt.	Cin.	5	Pitt.	3
10/9	at Cin.	Pitt.	3	Cin.	2
10/10	at Cin.	Cin.	7	Pitt.	1
10/11	at Cin.	Cin.	4	Pitt.	3

1973

Oakland 3, Baltimore 2

10/6	at Balt.	Balt.	6	Oak.	0	
10/7	at Balt.	Oak.	6	Balt.	3	
10/9	at Oak.	Oak.	2	Balt.	1	(11 inn)
10/10	at Oak.	Balt.	5	Oak.	4	
10/11	at Oak.	Oak.	3	Balt.	0	

New York 3, Cincinnati 2

10/6	at Cin.	Cin.	2	NY	1	
10/7	at Cin.	NY	5	Cin.	0	
10/8	at NY	NY	9	Cin.	2	
10/9	at NY	Cin.	2	NY	1	(12 inn)
10/10	at NY	NY	7	Cin.	2	

1974

Oakland 3, Baltimore 1

10/5	at Oak.	Balt.	6	Oak.	3
10/6	at Oak.	Oak.	5	Balt.	0
10/8	at Balt.	Oak.	1	Balt.	0
10/9	at Balt.	Oak.	2	Balt.	1

Los Angeles 3, Pittsburgh 1

10/5	at Pitt.	LA	3	Pitt.	0
10/6	at Pitt.	LA	5	Pitt.	2
10/8	at LA	Pitt.	7	LA	0
10/9	at LA	LA	12	Pitt.	1

1975

Boston 3, Oakland 0

10/4	at Bos.	Bos.	7	Oak.	1
10/5	at Bos.	Bos.	6	Oak.	3
10/7	at Oak.	Bos.	5	Oak.	3

Cincinnati 3, Pittsburgh 0

10/4	at Cin.	Cin.	8	Pitt.	3	
10/5	at Cin.	Cin.	6	Pitt.	1	
10/7	at Pitt.	Cin.	5	Pitt.	3	(10 inn)

1976

New York 3, Kansas City 2

10/9	at KC	NY	4	KC	1
10/10	at KC	KC	7	NY	3
10/12	at NY	NY	5	KC	3
10/13	at NY	KC	7	NY	4
10/14	at NY	NY	7	KC	6

Cincinnati 3, Philadelphia 0

10/9	at Phil.	Cin.	6	Phil.	3
10/10	at Phil.	Cin.	6	Phil.	2
10/12	at Cin.	Cin.	7	Phil.	6

1977

New York 3, Kansas City 2

10/5	at NY	KC	7	NY	2
10/6	at NY	NY	6	KC	2
10/7	at KC	KC	6	NY	2
10/8	at KC	NY	6	KC	4
10/9	at KC	NY	5	KC	3

Los Angeles 3, Philadelphia 1

10/4	at LA	Phil.	7	LA	5
10/5	at LA	LA	7	Phil.	1
10/7	at Phil.	LA	6	Phil.	5
10/8	at Phil.	LA	4	Phil.	1

American League

(*=Wild Card, since 1995)

National League

1978

New York 3, Kansas City 1

10/3	at KC	NY	7	KC	1
10/4	at KC	KC	10	NY	4
10/6	at NY	NY	6	KC	5
10/7	at NY	NY	2	KC	1

Los Angeles 3, Philadelphia 1

10/4	at Phil.	LA	9	Phil.	5	
10/5	at Phil.	LA	4	Phil.	0	
10/6	at LA	Phil.	9	LA	4	
10/7	at LA	LA	4	Phil.	3	(10 inn)

1979

Baltimore 3, California 1

10/3	at Balt.	Balt.	6	Cal.	3	(10 inn)
10/4	at Balt.	Balt.	9	Cal.	8	
10/5	at Cal.	Cal.	4	Balt.	3	
10/6	at Cal.	Balt.	8	Cal.	0	

Pittsburgh 3, Cincinnati 0

10/2	at Cin.	Pitt.	5	Cin.	2	(11 inn)
10/3	at Cin.	Pitt.	3	Cin.	2	(10 inn)
10/5	at Pitt.	Pitt.	7	Cin.	1	

1980

Kansas City 3, New York 0

10/8	at KC	KC	7	NY	2
10/9	at KC	KC	3	NY	2
10/10	at NY	KC	4	NY	2

Philadelphia 3, Houston 2

10/7	at Phil.	Phil.	3	Hou.	1	
10/8	at Phil.	Hou.	7	Phil.	4	(10 inn)
10/10	at Hou.	Hou.	1	Phil.	0	(11 inn)
10/11	at Hou.	Phil.	5	Hou.	3	(10 inn)
10/12	at Hou.	Phil.	8	Hou.	7	(10 inn)

1981

New York 3, Oakland 0

10/13	at NY	NY	3	Oak.	1
10/14	at NY	NY	13	Oak.	3
10/15	at Oak.	NY	4	Oak.	0

Los Angeles 3, Montreal 2

10/13	at LA	LA	5	Mtl.	1
10/14	at LA	Mtl.	3	LA	0
10/16	at Mtl.	Mtl.	4	LA	1
10/17	at Mtl.	LA	7	Mtl.	1
10/19	at Mtl.	LA	2	Mtl.	1

1982

Milwaukee 3, California 2

10/5	at Cal.	Cal.	8	Mil.	3
10/6	at Cal.	Cal.	4	Mil.	2
10/8	at Mil.	Mil.	5	Cal.	3
10/9	at Mil.	Mil.	9	Cal.	5
10/10	at Mil.	Mil.	4	Cal.	3

St. Louis 3, Atlanta 0

10/7	at StL.	StL.	7	Atl.	0
10/9	at StL.	StL.	4	Atl.	3
10/10	at Atl.	StL.	6	Atl.	2

1983

Baltimore 3, Chicago 1

10/5	at Balt.	Chi.	2	Balt.	1	
10/6	at Balt.	Balt.	4	Chi.	0	
10/7	at Chi.	Balt.	11	Chi.	1	
10/8	at Chi.	Balt.	3	Chi.	0	(10 inn)

Philadelphia 3, Los Angeles 1

10/4	at LA	Phil.	1	LA	0
10/5	at LA	LA	4	Phil.	1
10/7	at Phil.	Phil.	7	LA	2
10/8	at Phil.	Phil.	7	LA	2

1984

Detroit 3, Kansas City 0

10/2	at KC	Det.	8	KC	1	
10/3	at KC	Det.	5	KC	3	(11 inn)
10/5	at Det.	Det.	1	KC	0	

San Diego 3, Chicago 2

10/2	at Chi.	Chi.	13	SD	0
10/3	at Chi.	Chi.	4	SD	2
10/4	at SD	SD	7	Chi.	1
10/6	at SD	SD	7	Chi.	5
10/7	at SD	SD	6	Chi.	3

1985

Kansas City 4, Toronto 3

10/8	at Tor.	Tor.	6	KC	1	
10/9	at Tor.	Tor.	6	KC	5	(10 inn)
10/11	at KC	KC	6	Tor.	5	
10/12	at KC	Tor.	3	KC	1	
10/13	at KC	KC	2	Tor.	0	
10/15	at Tor.	KC	5	Tor.	3	
10/16	at Tor.	KC	6	Tor.	2	

St. Louis 4, Los Angeles 2

10/9	at LA	LA	4	StL.	1
10/10	at LA	LA	8	StL.	2
10/12	at StL.	StL.	4	LA	2
10/13	at StL.	StL.	12	LA	2
10/14	at StL.	StL.	3	LA	2
10/16	at LA	StL.	7	LA	5

American League
(=Wild Card, since 1995)*

National League

1986
Boston 4, California 3

10/7	at Bos.	Cal.	8	Bos.	1		
10/8	at Bos.	Bos.	9	Cal.	2		
10/10	at Cal.	Cal.	5	Bos.	3		
10/11	at Cal.	Cal.	4	Bos.	3	(11 inn)	
10/12	at Cal.	Bos.	7	Cal.	6	(11 inn)	
10/14	at Bos.	Bos.	10	Cal.	4		
10/15	at Bos.	Bos.	8	Cal.	1		

New York 4, Houston 2

10/8	at Hou.	Hou.	1	NY	0		
10/9	at Hou.	NY	5	Hou.	1		
10/11	at NY	NY	6	Hou.	5		
10/12	at NY	Hou.	3	NY	1		
10/14	at NY	NY	2	Hou.	1	(12 inn)	
10/15	at Hou.	NY	7	Hou.	6	(16 inn)	

1987
Minnesota 4, Detroit 1

10/7	at Minn.	Minn.	8	Det.	5
10/8	at Minn.	Minn.	6	Det.	3
10/10	at Det.	Det.	7	Minn.	6
10/11	at Det.	Minn.	5	Det.	3
10/12	at Det.	Minn.	9	Det.	5

St. Louis 4, San Francisco 3

10/6	at StL.	StL.	5	SF	3
10/7	at StL.	SF	5	StL.	0
10/9	at SF	StL.	6	SF	5
10/10	at SF	SF	4	StL.	2
10/11	at SF	SF	6	StL.	3
10/13	at StL.	StL.	1	SF	0
10/14	at StL.	StL.	6	SF	0

1988
Oakland 4, Boston 0

10/5	at Bos.	Oak.	2	Bos.	1
10/6	at Bos.	Oak.	4	Bos.	3
10/8	at Oak.	Oak.	10	Bos.	6
10/9	at Oak.	Oak.	4	Bos.	1

Los Angeles 4, New York 3

10/4	at LA	NY	3	LA	2	
10/5	at LA	LA	6	NY	3	
10/8	at NY	NY	8	LA	4	
10/9	at NY	LA	5	NY	4	(12 inn)
10/10	at NY	LA	7	NY	4	
10/11	at LA	NY	5	LA	1	
10/12	at LA	LA	6	NY	0	

1989
Oakland 4, Toronto 1

10/3	at Oak.	Oak.	7	Tor.	3
10/4	at Oak.	Oak.	6	Tor.	3
10/6	at Tor.	Tor.	7	Oak.	3
10/7	at Tor.	Oak.	6	Tor.	5
10/8	at Tor.	Oak.	4	Tor.	3

San Francisco 4, Chicago 1

10/4	at Chi.	SF	11	Chi.	3
10/5	at Chi.	Chi.	9	SF	5
10/7	at SF	SF	5	Chi.	4
10/8	at SF	SF	6	Chi.	4
10/9	at SF	SF	3	Chi.	2

1990
Oakland 4, Boston 0

10/6	at Bos.	Oak.	9	Bos.	1
10/7	at Bos.	Oak.	4	Bos.	1
10/9	at Oak.	Oak.	4	Bos.	1
10/10	at Oak.	Oak.	3	Bos.	1

Cincinnati 4, Pittsburgh 2

10/4	at Cin.	Pitt.	4	Cin.	3
10/5	at Cin.	Cin.	2	Pitt.	1
10/8	at Pitt.	Cin.	6	Pitt.	3
10/9	at Pitt.	Cin.	5	Pitt.	3
10/10	at Pitt.	Pitt.	3	Cin.	2
10/12	at Cin.	Cin.	2	Pitt.	1

1991
Minnesota 4, Toronto 1

10/8	at Minn.	Minn.	5	Tor.	4	
10/9	at Minn.	Tor.	5	Minn.	2	
10/11	at Tor.	Minn.	3	Tor.	2	(10 inn)
10/12	at Tor.	Minn.	9	Tor.	3	
10/13	at Tor.	Minn.	8	Tor.	5	

Atlanta 4, Pittsburgh 3

10/9	at Pitt.	Pitt.	5	Atl.	1	
10/10	at Pitt.	Atl.	1	Pitt.	0	
10/12	at Atl.	Atl.	10	Pitt.	3	
10/13	at Atl.	Pitt.	3	Atl.	2	(10 inn)
10/14	at Atl.	Pitt.	1	Atl.	0	
10/16	at Pitt.	Atl.	1	Pitt.	0	
10/17	at Pitt.	Atl.	4	Pitt.	0	

1992
Toronto 4, Oakland 2

10/7	at Tor.	Oak.	4	Tor.	3	
10/8	at Tor.	Tor.	3	Oak.	1	
10/10	at Oak.	Tor.	7	Oak.	5	
10/11	at Oak.	Tor.	7	Oak.	6	(11 inn)
10/12	at Oak.	Oak.	6	Tor.	2	
10/14	at Tor.	Tor.	9	Oak.	2	

Atlanta 4, Pittsburgh 3

10/6	at Atl.	Atl.	5	Pitt.	1
10/7	at Atl.	Atl.	13	Pitt.	5
10/9	at Pitt.	Pitt.	3	Atl.	2
10/10	at Pitt.	Atl.	6	Pitt.	4
10/11	at Pitt.	Pitt.	7	Atl.	1
10/13	at Atl.	Pitt.	13	Atl.	4
10/14	at Atl.	Atl.	3	Pitt.	2

American League

(=Wild Card, since 1995)*

National League

1993

Toronto 4, Chicago 2

10/5	at Chi.	Tor.	7	Chi.	3	
10/6	at Chi.	Tor.	3	Chi.	1	
10/8	at Tor.	Chi.	6	Tor.	1	
10/9	at Tor.	Chi.	7	Tor.	4	
10/10	at Tor.	Tor.	5	Chi.	3	
10/12	at Chi.	Tor.	6	Chi.	3	

Philadelphia 4, Atlanta 2

10/6	at Phil.	Phil.	4	Atl.	3	(10 inn)
10/7	at Phil.	Atl.	14	Phil.	3	
10/9	at Atl.	Atl.	9	Phil.	4	
10/10	at Atl.	Phil.	2	Atl.	1	
10/11	at Atl.	Phil.	4	Atl.	3	(10 inn)
10/13	at Phil.	Phil.	6	Atl.	3	

1995

Cleveland 4, Seattle 2

10/10	at Sea.	Sea.	3	Clev.	2	
10/11	at Sea.	Clev.	5	Sea.	2	
10/13	at Clev.	Clev.	2	Sea.	2	(11 inn)
10/14	at Clev.	Clev.	7	Sea.	0	
10/15	at Clev.	Clev.	3	Sea.	2	
10/17	at Sea.	Clev.	4	Sea.	0	

Atlanta 4, Cincinnati 0

10/10	at Cin.	Atl.	2	Cin.	1	(11 inn)
10/11	at Cin.	Atl.	6	Cin.	2	(10 inn)
10/13	at Atl.	Atl.	5	Cin.	2	
10/14	at Atl.	Atl.	6	Cin.	0	

1996

New York 4, Baltimore* 1

10/9	at NY	NY	5	Balt.	4	(11 inn)
10/10	at NY	Balt.	5	NY	3	
10/11	at Balt.	NY	5	Balt.	2	
10/12	at Balt.	NY	8	Balt.	4	
10/13	at Balt.	NY	6	Balt.	4	

Atlanta 4, St. Louis 3

10/9	at Atl.	Atl.	4	StL.	2	
10/10	at Atl.	StL.	8	Atl.	3	
10/12	at StL.	StL.	3	Atl.	2	
10/13	at StL.	StL.	4	Atl.	3	
10/14	at StL.	Atl.	14	StL.	0	
10/16	at Atl.	Atl.	3	StL.	1	
10/17	at Atl.	Atl.	15	StL.	0	

1997

Cleveland 4, Baltimore 2

10/8	at Balt.	Balt.	3	Clev.	0	
10/9	at Balt.	Clev.	5	Balt.	4	
10/11	at Clev.	Clev.	2	Balt.	1	(12 inn)
10/12	at Clev.	Clev.	8	Balt.	7	
10/13	at Clev.	Balt.	4	Clev.	2	
10/15	at Balt.	Clev.	1	Balt.	0	(11 inn)

Florida* 4, Atlanta 2

10/7	at Atl.	Fla.	5	Atl.	3	
10/8	at Atl.	Atl.	7	Fla.	1	
10/10	at Fla.	Fla.	5	Atl.	2	
10/11	at Fla.	Atl.	4	Fla.	0	
10/12	at Fla.	Fla.	2	Atl.	1	
10/14	at Atl.	Fla.	7	Atl.	4	

1998

New York 4, Cleveland 2

10/6	at NY	NY	7	Clev.	2	
10/7	at NY	Clev.	4	NY	1	(12 inn)
10/9	at Clev.	Clev.	6	NY	1	
10/10	at Clev.	NY	4	Clev.	0	
10/11	at Clev.	NY	5	Clev.	3	
10/13	at NY	NY	9	Clev.	5	

San Diego 4, Atlanta 2

10/7	at Atl.	SD	3	Atl.	2	(10 inn)
10/8	at Atl.	SD	3	Atl.	0	
10/10	at SD	SD	4	Atl.	1	
10/11	at SD	Atl.	8	SD	3	
10/12	at SD	Atl.	7	SD	6	
10/14	at Atl.	SD	5	Atl.	0	

1999

New York 4, Boston* 1

10/13	at NY	NY	4	Bos.	3	(10 inn)
10/14	at NY	NY	3	Bos.	2	
10/16	at Bos.	Bos.	13	NY	1	
10/17	at Bos.	NY	9	Bos.	2	
10/18	at Bos.	NY	6	Bos.	1	

Atlanta 4, New York* 2

10/12	at Atl.	Atl.	4	NY	2	
10/13	at Atl.	Atl.	4	NY	3	
10/15	at NY	Atl.	1	NY	0	
10/16	at NY	NY	3	Atl.	2	
10/17	at NY	NY	4	Atl.	3	(15 inn)
10/19	at Atl.	Atl.	10	NY	9	(11 inn)

2000

New York 4, Seattle* 2

10/10	at NY	Sea.	2	NY	0	
10/11	at NY	NY	7	Sea.	1	
10/13	at Sea.	NY	8	Sea.	2	
10/14	at Sea.	NY	5	Sea.	0	
10/15	at Sea.	Sea.	6	NY	2	
10/17	at NY	NY	9	Sea.	7	

New York* 4, St. Louis 1

10/11	at StL.	NY	6	StL.	2	
10/12	at StL.	NY	6	StL.	5	
10/14	at NY	StL.	8	NY	2	
10/15	at NY	NY	10	StL.	6	
10/16	at NY	NY	7	StL.	0	

American League

(*=Wild Card, since 1995)

National League

2001

New York 4, Seattle 1

10/17	at Sea.	NY	4	Sea.	2
10/18	at Sea.	NY	3	Sea.	2
10/20	at NY	Sea.	14	NY	3
10/21	at NY	NY	3	Sea.	1
10/22	at NY	NY	12	Sea.	3

Arizona 4, Atlanta 1

10/16	at Ari.	Ari.	2	Atl.	0
10/17	at Ari.	Atl.	8	Ari.	1
10/19	at Atl.	Ari.	5	Atl.	1
10/20	at Atl.	Ari.	11	Atl.	4
10/21	at Atl.	Ari.	3	Atl.	2

2002

Anaheim* 4, Minnesota 1

10/8	at Minn.	Minn.	2	Ana.	1
10/9	at Minn.	Ana.	6	Minn.	3
10/11	at Ana.	Ana.	2	Minn.	1
10/12	at Ana.	Ana.	7	Minn.	1
10/13	at Ana.	Ana.	13	Minn.	5

San Francisco* 4, St. Louis 1

10/9	at StL.	SF	9	StL.	6
10/10	at StL.	SF	4	StL.	1
10/12	at SF	StL.	5	SF	4
10/13	at SF	SF	4	StL.	3
10/14	at SF	SF	2	StL.	1

2003

New York 4, Boston* 3

10/8	at NY	Bos.	5	NY	2	
10/9	at NY	NY	6	Bos.	2	
10/11	at Bos.	NY	4	Bos.	3	
10/13	at Bos.	Bos.	3	NY	2	
10/14	at Bos.	NY	4	Bos.	2	
10/15	at NY	Bos.	9	NY	6	
10/16	at NY	NY	6	Bos.	5	(11 inn)

Florida* 4, Chicago 3

10/7	at Chi.	Fla.	9	Chi.	8	(11 inn)
10/8	at Chi.	Chi.	12	Fla.	3	
10/10	at Fla.	Chi.	5	Fla.	4	(11 inn)
10/11	at Fla.	Chi.	8	Fla.	3	
10/12	at Fla.	Fla.	4	Chi.	0	
10/14	at Chi.	Fla.	8	Chi.	3	
10/15	at Chi.	Fla.	9	Chi.	6	

2004

Boston* 4, New York 3

10/12	at NY	NY	10	Bos.	7	
10/13	at NY	NY	3	Bos.	1	
10/16	at Bos.	NY	19	Bos.	8	
10/17	at Bos.	Bos.	6	NY	4	(12 inn)
10/18	at Bos.	Bos.	5	NY	4	(14 inn)
10/19	at NY	Bos.	4	NY	2	
10/20	at NY	Bos.	10	NY	3	

St. Louis 4, Houston* 3

10/13	at StL.	StL.	10	Hou.	7	
10/14	at StL.	StL.	6	Hou.	4	
10/16	at Hou.	Hou.	5	StL.	2	
10/17	at Hou.	Hou.	6	StL.	5	
10/18	at Hou.	Hou.	3	StL.	0	
10/20	at StL.	StL.	6	Hou.	4	(12 inn)
10/21	at StL.	StL.	5	Hou.	2	

2005

Chicago 4, Los Angeles 1

10/11	at Chi.	LA	3	Chi.	2
10/12	at Chi.	Chi.	2	LA	1
10/14	at LA	Chi.	5	LA	2
10/15	at LA	Chi.	8	LA	2
10/16	at LA	Chi.	6	LA	3

Houston* 4, St. Louis 2

10/12	at StL.	StL.	5	Hou.	3
10/13	at StL.	Hou.	4	StL.	1
10/15	at Hou.	Hou.	4	StL.	3
10/16	at Hou.	Hou.	2	StL.	1
10/17	at Hou.	StL.	5	Hou.	4
10/19	at StL.	Hou.	5	StL.	1

2006

Detroit* 4, Oakland 0

10/10	at Oak.	Det.	5	Oak.	1
10/11	at Oak.	Det.	8	Oak.	5
10/13	at Det.	Det.	3	Oak.	0
10/14	at Det.	Det.	6	Oak.	3

St. Louis 4, New York 3

10/12	at NY	NY	2	StL.	0
10/13	at NY	StL.	9	NY	6
10/14	at StL.	StL.	5	NY	0
10/15	at StL.	NY	12	StL.	5
10/17	at StL.	StL.	4	NY	2
10/18	at NY	NY	4	StL.	2
10/19	at NY	StL.	3	NY	1

2007

Boston 4, Cleveland 3

10/12	at Bos.	Bos.	10	Clev.	3	
10/13	at Bos.	Clev.	13	Bos.	6	(11 inn)
10/15	at Clev.	Clev.	4	Bos.	2	
10/16	at Clev.	Clev.	7	Bos.	3	
10/18	at Clev.	Bos.	7	Clev.	1	
10/20	at Bos.	Bos.	12	Clev.	2	
10/21	at Bos.	Bos.	11	Clev.	2	

Colorado* 4, Arizona 0

10/11	at Ari.	Col.	5	Ari.	1	
10/12	at Ari.	Col.	3	Ari.	2	(11 inn)
10/14	at Col.	Col.	4	Ari.	1	
10/15	at Col.	Col.	6	Ari.	4	

American League

(=Wild Card, since 1995)*

National League

2008

Tampa Bay 4, Boston* 3

10/10	at TB	Bos.	2	TB	0
10/11	at TB	TB	9	Bos.	8 (11 inn)
10/13	at Bos.	TB	9	Bos.	1
10/14	at Bos.	TB	13	Bos.	4
10/16	at Bos.	Bos.	8	TB	7
10/18	at TB	Bos.	4	TB	2
10/19	at TB	TB	3	Bos.	1

Philadelphia 4, Los Angeles 1

10/9	at Phil.	Phil.	3	LA	2
10/10	at Phil.	Phil.	8	LA	5
10/12	at LA	LA	7	Phil.	2
10/13	at LA	Phil.	7	LA	5
10/15	at LA	Phil.	5	LA	1

2009

New York 4, Los Angeles 2

10/16	at NY	NY	4	LA	1
10/17	at NY	NY	4	LA	3 (13 inn)
10/19	at LA	LA	5	NY	4 (11 inn)
10/20	at LA	NY	10	LA	1
10/22	at LA	LA	7	NY	6
10/25	at NY	NY	5	LA	2

Philadelphia 4, Los Angeles 1

10/15	at LA	Phil.	8	LA	6
10/16	at LA	LA	2	Phil.	1
10/18	at Phil.	Phil.	11	LA	0
10/19	at Phil.	Phil.	5	LA	4
10/21	at Phil.	Phil.	10	LA	4

2010

Texas 4, New York* 2

10/15	at Tex.	NY	6	Tex.	5
10/16	at Tex.	Tex.	7	NY	2
10/18	at NY	Tex.	8	NY	0
10/19	at NY	Tex.	10	NY	3
10/20	at NY	NY	7	Tex.	2
10/22	at Tex.	Tex.	6	NY	1

San Francisco 4, Philadelphia 2

10/16	at Phil.	SF	4	Phil.	3
10/17	at Phil.	Phil.	6	SF	1
10/19	at SF	SF	3	Phil.	0
10/20	at SF	SF	6	Phil.	5
10/21	at SF	Phil.	4	SF	2
10/23	at Phil.	SF	3	Phil.	2

2011

Texas 4, Detroit 2

10/8	at Tex.	Tex.	3	Det.	2
10/10	at Tex.	Tex.	7	Det.	3 (11 inn)
10/11	at Det.	Det.	5	Tex.	2
10/12	at Det.	Tex.	7	Det.	3 (11 inn)
10/13	at Det.	Det.	7	Tex.	5
10/15	at Tex.	Tex.	15	Det.	5

St. Louis* 4, Milwaukee 2

10/9	at Mil.	Mil.	9	StL.	6
10/10	at Mil.	StL.	12	Mil.	3
10/12	at StL.	StL.	4	Mil.	3
10/13	at StL.	Mil.	4	StL.	2
10/14	at StL.	StL.	7	Mil.	1
10/16	at Mil.	StL.	12	Mil.	6

2012

Detroit 4, New York 0

10/13	at NY	Det.	6	NY	4 (12 inn)
10/14	at NY	Det.	3	NY	0
10/16	at Det.	Det.	2	NY	1
10/18	at Det.	Det.	8	NY	1

San Francisco 4, St. Louis* 3

10/14	at SF	StL.	6	SF	4
10/15	at SF	SF	7	StL.	1
10/17	at StL.	StL.	3	SF	1
10/18	at StL.	StL.	8	SF	3
10/19	at StL.	SF	5	StL.	0
10/21	at SF	SF	6	StL.	1
10/22	at SF	SF	9	StL.	0

2013

Boston 4, Detroit 2

10/12	at Bos.	Det.	1	Bos.	0
10/13	at Bos.	Bos.	6	Det.	5
10/15	at Det.	Bos.	1	Det.	0
10/16	at Det.	Det.	7	Bos.	3
10/17	at Det.	Bos.	4	Det.	3
10/19	at Bos.	Bos.	5	Det.	2

St. Louis 4, Los Angeles 2

10/11	at StL.	StL.	3	LA	2 (13 inn)
10/12	at StL.	StL.	1	LA	0
10/14	at LA	LA	3	StL.	0
10/15	at LA	StL.	4	LA	2
10/16	at LA	LA	6	StL.	4
10/18	at StL.	StL.	9	LA	0

2014

Kansas City* 4, Baltimore 0

10/10	at Balt.	KC	8	Balt.	6 (10 inn)
10/11	at Balt.	KC	6	Balt.	4
10/14	at KC	KC	2	Balt.	1
10/15	at KC	KC	2	Balt.	1

San Francisco 4*, St. Louis 1

10/11	at StL.	SF	3	StL.	0
10/12	at StL.	StL.	5	SF	4
10/14	at SF	SF	5	StL.	4 (10 inn)
10/15	at SF	SF	6	StL.	4
10/16	at SF	SF	6	StL.	3

American League
(*=Wild Card, since 1995)

National League

2015

Kansas City 4, Toronto 2

10/16	at KC	KC	5	Tor.	0
10/17	at KC	KC	6	Tor.	3
10/19	at Tor.	Tor.	11	KC	8
10/20	at Tor.	KC	14	Tor.	2
10/21	at Tor.	Tor.	7	KC	1
10/23	at KC	KC	4	Tor.	3

New York 4, Chicago* 0

10/17	at NY	NY	4	Chi.	2
10/18	at NY	NY	4	Chi.	1
10/20	at Chi.	NY	5	Chi.	2
10/21	at Chi.	NY	8	Chi.	3

2016

Cleveland 4, Toronto* 1

10/14	at Clev.	Clev.	2	Tor.	0
10/15	at Clev.	Clev.	2	Tor.	1
10/17	at Tor.	Clev.	4	Tor.	2
10/18	at Tor.	Tor.	5	Clev.	1
10/19	at Tor.	Clev.	3	Tor.	0

Chicago 4, Los Angeles 2

10/15	at Chi	Chi.	8	LA	4
10/16	at Chi.	LA	1	Chi.	0
10/18	at LA	LA	6	Chi.	0
10/19	at LA	Chi.	10	LA	2
10/20	at LA	Chi.	8	LA	4
10/22	at Chi.	Chi.	5	LA	0

2017

Houston 4, New York* 3

10/13	at Hou.	Hou.	2	NY	1
10/14	at Hou.	Hou.	2	NY	1
10/16	at NY	NY	8	Hou.	1
10/17	at NY	NY	6	Hou.	4
10/18	at NY	NY	5	Hou.	0
10/20	at Hou.	Hou.	7	NY	1
10/21	at Hou.	Hou.	4	NY	0

Los Angeles 4, Chicago 1

10/14	at LA	LA	5	Chi.	2
10/15	at LA	LA	4	Chi.	1
10/17	at Chi.	LA	6	Chi.	1
10/18	at Chi.	Chi.	3	LA	2
10/19	at Chi.	LA	11	Chi.	1

2018

Boston 4, Houston 1

10/13	at Bos.	Hou.	7	Bos.	2
10/14	at Bos.	Bos.	7	Hou.	5
10/16	at Hou.	Bos.	8	Hou.	2
10/17	at Hou.	Bos.	8	Hou.	6
10/18	at Hou.	Bos.	4	Hou.	1

Los Angeles 4, Milwaukee 3

10/12	at Mil.	Mil.	6	LA	5	
10/13	at Mil.	LA	4	Mil.	3	
10/15	at LA	Mil.	4	LA	0	
10/16	at LA	LA	2	Mil.	1	(13 inn)
10/17	at LA	LA	5	Mil.	2	
10/19	at Mil.	Mil.	7	LA	2	
10/20	at Mil.	LA	5	Mil.	1	

2019

Houston 4, New York 2

10/12	at Hou.	NY	7	Hou.	0	
10/13	at Hou.	Hou.	3	NY	2	(11 inn)
10/15	at NY	Hou.	4	NY	1	
10/17	at NY	Hou.	8	NY	3	
10/18	at NY	NY	4	Hou.	1	
10/19	at Hou.	Hou.	6	NY	4	

Washington* 4, St. Louis 0

10/11	at StL.	Wash. 2	StL.	0
10/12	at StL.	Wash. 3	StL.	1
10/14	at Wash.	Wash. 8	StL.	1
10/15	at Wash.	Wash. 7	StL.	4

2020

Tampa Bay 4, Houston 3

10/11	at TB	TB	2	Hou.	1
10/12	at TB	TB	4	Hou.	2
10/13	at Hou.	TB	5	Hou.	2
10/14	at Hou.	Hou.	4	TB	3
10/15	at Hou.	Hou.	4	TB	3
10/16	at TB	Hou.	7	TB	4
10/17	at TB	TB	4	Hou.	2

All games at PETCO Park – San Diego, CA

Los Angeles 4, Atlanta 3

10/12	at LA	Atl.	5	LA	1
10/13	at LA	Atl.	8	LA	7
10/14	at Atl.	LA	15	Atl.	3
10/15	at Atl.	Atl.	10	LA	2
10/16	at Atl.	LA	7	Atl.	3
10/17	at LA	LA	3	Atl.	1
10/18	at LA	LA	4	Atl.	3

All games at Globe Life Field – Arlington, TX

AMERICAN LEAGUE CLUB CHAMPIONSHIP SERIES RECORDS

(Winning club first. IB = innings batted)

YEAR	G	IB	AB	R	ER	H	TB	1B	2B	3B	HR	RBI	SH	SF	BB	HP	SO	SB	CS	GDP	BA	SLG	LOB	PO	A	E	DP	ERA	CG	SHO
1969	3																													
Balt.		31.1	123	16	14	36	58	23	8	1	4	15	2	0	13	0	14	0	4	3	.293	.472	28	96	31	1	2	1.13	2	1
Minn.		32	110	5	4	17	25	12	3	1	1	5	0	1	12	0	27	2	0	2	.155	.227	22	94	34	5	3	4.02	0	0
1970	3																													
Balt.		26	109	27	22	36	61	23	7	0	6	24	1	2	12	1	19	1	0	4	.330	.560	20	81	29	0	3	3.33	2	0
Minn.		27	101	10	10	24	39	16	4	1	3	10	1	0	9	0	22	0	0	3	.238	.386	20	78	28	6	5	7.62	0	0
1971	3																													
Balt.		25	95	15	15	26	47	14	7	1	4	14	0	1	13	0	22	0	0	3	.274	.495	19	81	30	1	3	2.33	2	0
Oak.		27	96	7	7	22	41	10	8	0	3	7	2	0	5	0	16	0	1	3	.229	.427	15	75	15	0	4	5.40	1	0
1972	5																													
Oak.		46.1	170	13	11	38	49	29	8	0	1	10	4	1	12	3	35	7	2	2	.224	.288	38	138	60	3	5	1.76	1	1
Det.		46	162	10	9	32	52	21	6	1	4	10	3	0	13	0	25	0	2	5	.198	.321	30	139	48	7	4	2.14	1	1
1973	5																													
Oak.		45	160	15	14	32	54	21	5	1	5	15	4	1	17	2	39	3	1	2	.200	.338	34	138	47	4	4	2.74	2	1
Balt.		46	171	15	14	36	52	26	7	0	3	15	0	0	16	2	25	1	4	2	.211	.304	36	135	52	2	2	2.80	2	1
1974	4																													
Oak.		35	120	11	7	22	37	14	4	1	3	11	2	1	22	1	16	3	3	3	.183	.308	30	108	43	2	4	1.75	2	2
Balt.		36	124	7	7	22	32	18	1	0	3	7	2	0	5	0	20	0	3	3	.177	.258	16	105	50	4	4	1.80	1	0
1975	3																													
Bos.		25	98	18	12	31	45	21	8	0	2	14	5	1	3	0	12	3	0	3	.316	.459	14	81	33	4	3	1.67	1	0
Oak.		27	98	7	5	19	28	12	6	0	1	7	0	0	9	1	14	0	3	2	.194	.286	19	75	40	6	4	4.32	0	0
1976	5																													
NY		43	174	23	21	55	84	36	13	2	4	21	2	1	16	0	15	4	3	4	.316	.483	41	132	60	6	3	4.70	1	0
KC		44	162	24	23	40	60	28	6	4	2	24	0	4	11	1	18	5	5	2	.247	.370	22	129	51	4	5	4.40	0	0
1977	5																													
NY		44	175	21	16	46	64	32	12	0	2	17	1	2	9	0	16	2	0	1	.263	.366	34	132	51	2	2	4.50	1	0
KC		44	163	22	22	42	66	27	9	3	3	21	2	2	15	0	22	5	4	2	.258	.405	28	132	54	5	2	3.27	1	0
1978	4																													
NY		34	140	19	18	42	62	33	3	1	5	18	0	1	7	0	18	0	1	3	.300	.443	27	105	35	1	2	3.86	0	0
KC		35	133	17	15	35	59	22	6	3	4	16	1	2	14	0	21	6	3	0	.263	.444	28	102	36	4	4	4.76	1	0
1979	4																													
Balt.		35.2	133	26	23	37	53	28	5	1	3	25	1	3	18	1	24	5	1	4	.278	.398	23	109	52	5	5	2.97	1	1
Cal.		36.1	137	15	12	32	48	22	7	0	3	14	0	2	7	0	13	2	1	4	.234	.350	22	107	37	2	7	5.80	0	0
1980	3																													
KC		25	97	14	12	28	45	18	6	3	3	14	0	0	9	1	15	3	5	2	.289	.464	18	81	29	1	3	1.67	1	0
NY		27	102	6	5	26	44	15	7	1	3	5	1	0	6	0	16	0	0	2	.255	.431	22	75	42	1	2	4.32	1	0

AMERICAN LEAGUE CLUB CHAMPIONSHIP SERIES RECORDS

(Winning club first. IB = innings batted)

YEAR	Team	G	IB	AB	R	ER	H	TB	1B	2B	3B	HR	RBI	SH	SF	BB	HP	SO	SB	CS	GDP	BA	SLG	LOB	PO	A	E	DP	ERA	CG	SHO
1981	NY	3	25	107	20	19	36	49	29	4	0	3	20	2	1	13	2	10	2	1		.336	.458	30	81	30	1	6	1.33	0	1
	Oak.		27	99	4	4	22	28	17	4	1	0	4	0	0	6	0	23	2	0	6	.222	.283	20	75	33	4	1	6.84	0	0
1982	Mil.	5	42	151	23	20	33	52	24	4	0	5	20	2	3	15	2	28	2	2	2	.219	.344	24	129	45	8	6	4.19	1	0
	Cal.		43	157	23	20	40	62	27	8	1	4	23	5	2	16	1	34	1	2	4	.255	.395	29	126	47	4	3	4.29	2	0
1983	Balt.	4	36	129	19	16	28	46	16	9	0	3	17	1	3	16	2	24	2	0	5	.217	.357	24	111	49	2	4	0.49	1	2
	Chi.		37	133	3	2	28	32	24	4	0	0	2	0	0	12	3	26	4	1	2	.211	.241	35	108	51	3	5	4.00	1	0
1984	Det.	3	28	107	14	11	25	43	16	4	1	4	14	2	1	8	0	17	4	0	2	.234	.402	20	87	27	1	0	1.24	0	1
	KC		29	106	4	4	18	21	16	1	1	0	4	0	0	6	0	21	0	1	0	.170	.198	21	84	26	7	2	3.54	1	0
1985	KC	7	62	227	26	26	51	83	34	9	1	7	26	4	2	22	1	51	2	4	2	.225	.366	44	188	87	6	7	3.16	1	1
	Tor.		62.2	242	25	22	65	90	44	19	0	2	23	0	2	16	3	37	2	2	4	.269	.372	50	186	61	4	4	3.77	0	0
1986	Bos.	7	64	254	41	28	69	102	50	11	2	6	35	3	2	19	3	31	1	0	7	.272	.402	48	196	73	7	5	3.58	1	0
	Cal.		65.1	256	30	26	71	103	53	11	0	7	29	4	2	20	4	44	1	4	5	.277	.402	60	192	78	8	7	3.94	1	0
1987	Minn.	5	43	171	34	32	46	85	24	13	1	8	33	0	1	20	5	25	4	1	1	.269	.497	37	132	41	3	3	4.50	0	0
	Det.		44	167	23	22	40	65	29	4	0	7	21	2	2	18	3	35	5	0	3	.240	.389	37	129	56	5	1	6.70	1	0
1988	Oak.	4	34	137	20	20	41	70	26	8	0	7	20	0	1	10	0	35	1	3	1	.299	.511	26	108	30	3	5	2.00	0	0
	Bos.		36	126	11	8	26	36	20	4	0	2	10	2	2	18	1	23	0	0	3	.206	.286	30	102	34	1	2	5.29	1	0
1989	Oak.	5	43	158	26	24	43	75	26	9	1	7	23	3	2	20	1	32	9	2	2	.272	.475	29	132	45	3	4	3.89	0	0
	Tor.		44	165	21	19	40	54	32	5	0	3	19	0	3	15	0	24	1	0	3	.242	.327	30	129	40	2	5	5.02	0	0
1990	Oak.	4	34	127	20	17	38	42	34	4	0	0	18	1	3	19	4	21	8	3	4	.299	.331	35	108	43	1	3	1.00	0	0
	Bos.		36	126	4	4	23	31	17	5	0	1	4	3	2	6	0	16	7	0	3	.183	.246	23	102	47	5	6	4.50	1	0
1991	Minn.	5	45	181	27	23	50	70	37	9	1	3	25	1	2	15	1	37	7	4	4	.276	.387	38	138	51	4	3	3.33	0	0
	Tor.		46	173	19	17	43	52	36	6	0	1	18	3	1	15	0	30	16	1	3	.249	.301	35	135	49	7	5	4.60	1	0
1992	Tor.	6	54	210	31	27	59	99	40	8	3	10	30	1	4	23	0	29	7	2	4	.281	.471	45	165	60	8	7	3.44	1	0
	Oak.		55	207	24	21	52	71	42	5	1	4	23	3	2	24	1	33	3	2	3	.251	.343	48	162	55	7	5	4.50	1	0
1993	Tor.	6	53	216	26	21	65	85	52	8	1	2	24	1	1	21	2	36	7	2	5	.301	.394	56	162	57	2	7	3.67	0	0
	Chi.		54	194	23	22	46	68	35	5	1	5	22	5	1	32	3	43	3	2	4	.237	.351	50	159	56	7	5	3.57	1	0

AMERICAN LEAGUE CLUB CHAMPIONSHIP SERIES RECORDS

(Winning club first. IB = innings batted)

YEAR G	IB	AB	R	ER	H	TB	1B	2B	3B	HR	RBI	SH	SF	BB	HP	SO	SB	CS	GDP	BA	SLG	LOB	PO	A	E	DP	ERA	CG	SHO
1995 6																													
Clev.	54	206	23	20	53	86	37	6	3	7	21	1	2	25	1	37	9	1	6	.257	.417	50	165	66	7	4	1.64	0	2
Sea.	55	201	12	10	37	60	24	8	0	5	10	1	0	15	3	46	9	2	2	.184	.299	43	162	59	6	7	3.33	0	0
1996 5																													
NY	46	183	27	21	50	91	30	9	1	10	24	0	0	20	2	37	3	0	6	.273	.497	40	141	44	1	2	3.64	0	0
Balt.	47	176	19	19	39	70	26	4	0	9	19	3	3	15	0	33	0	0	1	.222	.398	34	138	58	4	7	4.11	0	0
1997 6																													
Clev.	58	207	18	17	40	63	27	8	0	5	15	2	0	23	4	62	5	0	3	.193	.304	44	174	61	5	11	2.95	0	1
Balt.	58	218	19	19	54	86	36	11	0	7	19	2	0	23	1	47	3	1	10	.248	.394	50	174	60	5	4	2.64	0	1
1998 6																													
NY	55	197	27	22	43	65	30	8	1	4	25	3	3	35	2	42	9	2	7	.218	.330	48	168	54	2	5	3.21	0	1
Clev.	56	205	20	20	45	77	32	3	1	9	19	0	1	16	5	51	6	1	5	.220	.376	39	165	77	7	7	3.60	1	0
1999 5																													
NY	45	176	23	18	42	72	29	4	1	8	21	2	0	18	1	44	3	1	0	.239	.409	42	135	38	5	7	3.80	0	0
Bos.	45	184	21	19	54	86	34	13	2	5	19	2	0	15	1	38	4	1	6	.293	.467	45	132	40	10	0	3.68	0	0
2000 6																													
NY	52	204	31	31	57	85	41	10	0	6	31	1	3	25	3	41	4	2	4	.279	.417	49	159	54	1	5	3.06	1	1
Sea.	53	191	18	18	41	68	24	12	0	5	18	2	1	21	0	48	3	2	2	.215	.356	38	156	58	3	4	5.37	0	1
2001 5																													
NY	43.1	159	25	21	42	70	28	7	0	7	24	4	1	23	2	31	3	3	4	.264	.440	34	135	47	4	4	3.80	0	0
Sea.	45	171	22	19	36	59	25	4	2	5	20	1	0	18	1	35	3	0	2	.211	.345	34	130	45	1	5	4.36	0	0
2002 5																													
Ana.	42	171	29	28	49	82	34	5	2	8	26	2	2	9	2	26	3	1	2	.287	.480	29	132	38	2	4	2.45	0	0
Minn.	44	160	12	12	37	46	28	9	0	0	11	2	2	7	1	38	1	1	4	.231	.287	28	126	43	4	4	6.00	0	0
2003 7																													
NY	63	238	30	28	54	90	34	12	0	8	29	0	1	21	4	49	5	1	4	.227	.378	45	192	73	5	12	3.94	0	0
Bos.	64	250	29	28	68	117	45	9	2	12	26	0	0	17	3	60	5	5	9	.272	.468	49	189	67	3	5	4.00	0	0
2004 7																													
Bos.	69.2	271	41	40	75	119	52	12	1	10	40	1	2	28	1	53	4	2	8	.277	.439	53	207	66	1	4	5.87	0	0
NY	69	277	45	45	78	130	46	21	2	9	44	3	1	33	7	51	3	0	3	.282	.469	69	209	74	4	9	5.17	0	0
2005 5																													
Chi.	44.2	165	23	17	41	68	25	10	1	5	23	2	2	16	4	36	5	4	2	.248	.412	33	135	66	3	4	2.20	4	0
LA	45	154	11	11	27	41	19	5	0	3	11	3	1	4	1	22	2	0	4	.175	.266	17	134	47	7	5	3.43	0	0
2006 4																													
Det.	34.2	137	22	22	39	67	25	7	0	7	22	1	0	19	0	25	2	0	3	.285	.489	33	108	37	1	7	2.25	1	0
Oak.	36	131	9	9	29	48	18	7	0	4	9	0	0	14	1	28	0	0	7	.221	.366	29	104	44	3	4	5.71	0	0
2007 7																													
Bos.	62	242	51	47	77	126	49	17	1	10	48	2	5	31	3	43	2	0	14	.318	.521	46	189	57	3	5	4.57	0	0
Clev.	63	244	32	32	62	100	41	12	1	8	30	0	3	16	2	63	3	0	5	.254	.410	44	186	69	4	14	6.82	0	0

AMERICAN LEAGUE CLUB CHAMPIONSHIP SERIES RECORDS

(Winning club first. IB = innings batted)

YEAR	G	IB	AB	R	ER	H	TB	1B	2B	3B	HR	RBI	SH	SF	BB	HP	SO	SB	CS	GDP	BA	SLG	LOB	PO	A	E	DP	ERA	CG	SHO
2008	7																													
TB		63.2	242	43	42	61	123	33	10	2	16	43	0	1	25	2	57	10	1	5	.252	.508	36	194	56	6	6	3.62	0	0
Bos.		64.2	244	28	27	57	102	33	13	1	10	27	0	2	35	4	56	2	1	5	.234	.418	63	191	69	0	5	5.94	0	1
2009	6																													
NY		57.1	222	33	28	62	99	43	9	2	8	30	4	2	38	3	47	2	3	6	.279	.446	64	176	78	3	8	2.91	0	0
LA		58.2	216	19	19	51	76	33	14	1	3	18	4	1	18	2	38	4	1	7	.236	.352	46	172	71	8	7	4.40	0	0
2010	6																													
Tex.		52	207	38	38	63	106	39	14	1	9	36	3	1	24	1	43	9	1	5	.304	.512	42	159	56	2	4	3.06	0	1
NY		53	189	18	18	38	70	20	10	2	6	17	1	1	25	2	52	2	1	4	.201	.370	40	156	56	1	6	6.58	0	0
2011	6																													
Tex.		55	220	39	37	63	103	38	17	1	7	39	1	2	20	2	42	3	3	5	.286	.468	41	168	60	2	8	4.02	0	0
Det.		56	209	25	25	51	101	28	9	1	13	24	2	0	22	2	50	2	1	7	.244	.483	42	165	63	5	6	6.05	0	0
2012	4																													
Det.		37	158	19	17	46	73	32	7	1	6	19	1	2	12	0	30	3	0	2	.291	.462	40	117	35	3	1	1.38	0	1
NY		39	140	6	6	22	37	14	4	1	3	6	2	0	12	0	36	4	1	1	.157	.264	29	111	40	3	2	4.14	0	0
2013	6																													
Bos.		52	193	19	16	39	64	23	11	1	4	18	0	0	18	2	73	5	1	3	.202	.332	39	159	65	3	10	3.06	0	1
Det.		53	197	18	18	50	65	39	9	0	2	17	1	0	18	4	42	2	0	9	.254	.330	44	156	42	4	3	2.77	0	1
2014	4																													
KC		35	132	18	17	37	55	27	6	0	4	17	2	2	15	3	28	1	2	3	.280	.417	31	111	34	2	3	2.92	0	0
Balt.		37	138	12	12	30	41	23	5	0	2	12	1	1	13	0	29	2	0	3	.217	.297	29	105	39	1	4	4.37	0	0
2015	6																													
KC		51	201	38	37	59	91	42	9	1	7	35	0	6	12	3	35	3	2	3	.294	.453	31	156	50	1	4	4.50	0	1
Tor.		52	197	26	26	46	76	28	12	0	6	26	1	0	24	2	56	5	0	3	.234	.386	42	153	61	1	3	6.53	0	0
2016	5																													
Clev.		43	149	12	11	25	49	13	6	0	6	11	3	0	9	0	39	1	1	1	.168	.329	20	132	52	1	4	1.43	0	2
Tor.		44	159	8	7	32	45	25	3	2	2	8	0	1	11	0	50	0	0	4	.201	.283	31	129	41	2	1	2.30	1	0
2017	7																													
Hou.		59.1	214	20	18	40	63	25	11	1	4	19	0	1	24	1	45	1	0	6	.187	.294	43	180	59	2	2	3.30	0	1
NY		60	219	22	22	45	76	27	11	1	6	21	1	1	19	2	70	0	1	2	.205	.347	39	178	71	6	6	2.73	0	1
2018	5																													
Bos.		44	172	29	27	40	66	24	11	0	5	27	0	0	20	4	38	0	1	2	.233	.384	35	135	43	2	1	4.00	0	0
Hou.		45	169	21	20	37	65	21	10	0	6	21	0	0	25	5	43	2	2	1	.219	.385	43	132	54	3	2	5.52	0	0
2019	6																													
Hou.		54.2	201	22	19	36	64	24	4	0	8	19	0	1	27	2	54	2	0	4	.179	.318	45	165	35	2	3	344	0	0
NY		55	206	21	21	44	79	29	5	0	10	21	0	0	22	0	64	3	0	1	.214	.383	42	164	50	5	5	3.13	0	1
2020	7																													
TB		60	219	25	21	44	83	27	6	0	11	25	1	1	24	6	81	0	1	6	.201	.379	46	184	70	1	12	3.08	0	0
Hou.		61.1	227	22	21	59	91	45	5	0	9	21	1	1	29	3	54	1	2	10	.260	.401	55	180	57	4	6	3.15	0	0

NATIONAL LEAGUE CLUB CHAMPIONSHIP SERIES RECORDS

(Winning club first. IB = innings batted)

YEAR	G	IB	AB	R	ER	H	TB	1B	2B	3B	HR	RBI	SH	SF	BB	HP	SO	SB	CS	GDP	BA	SLG	LOB	PO	A	E	DP	ERA	CG	SHO
1969																														
NY	3	26	113	27	20	37	65	22	8	1	6	24	1	0	10	0	25	5	1	2	.327	.575	19	81	23	2	2	5.00	0	0
Atl		27	106	15	15	27	51	13	9	0	5	15	1	1	11	1	20	1	0	2	.255	.481	23	78	37	6	4	6.92	0	0
1970																														
Cin	3	27	100	9	8	22	36	15	3	1	3	8	2	0	8	0	12	1	1	2	.220	.360	18	84	39	1	1	0.96	0	1
Pitt		28	102	3	3	23	29	17	6	0	0	3	2	0	12	0	19	0	2	1	.225	.284	29	81	37	2	3	2.67	0	0
1971																														
Pitt	4	34	144	24	23	39	67	27	4	0	8	23	3	0	5	2	33	2	1	0	.271	.465	26	105	32	3	3	3.34	1	0
SF		35	132	15	13	30	51	21	5	0	5	14	4	0	16	1	28	2	0	3	.235	.386	33	102	37	4	1	6.09	2	0
1972																														
Cin	5	43.2	166	19	16	42	67	27	9	2	4	16	3	1	10	0	28	4	1	0	.253	.404	30	132	53	4	3	3.07	1	0
Pitt		44	158	15	15	30	47	20	6	1	3	14	2	0	9	2	27	0	0	2	.190	.297	24	131	38	4	3	3.30	0	0
1973																														
NY	5	46	168	23	23	37	51	29	5	0	3	22	3	1	19	0	28	0	1	3	.220	.304	30	142	44	4	3	1.33	3	1
Cin		47.1	167	8	7	31	52	20	6	0	5	8	1	0	13	1	42	0	0	3	.186	.311	35	138	59	2	3	4.50	0	0
1974																														
LA	4	35	138	20	19	37	56	25	8	1	4	19	0	0	30	0	16	11	0	2	.268	.406	44	108	46	7	8	2.00	1	1
Pitt		36	129	10	8	25	35	21	1	0	3	10	2	0	8	2	17	1	0	5	.194	.271	24	105	38	4	2	4.89	0	0
1975																														
Cin	3	26	102	19	19	29	45	21	4	0	4	18	0	0	9	0	28	11	0	2	.284	.441	17	84	31	1	2	2.25	1	0
Pitt		28	101	7	7	20	26	16	3	0	1	7	0	0	9	1	18	0	0	2	.198	.257	21	78	20	2	3	6.58	0	0
1976																														
Cin	3	26.1	99	19	15	25	45	14	5	3	3	17	3	3	15	0	16	5	1	1	.253	.455	20	81	32	2	3	3.33	0	0
Phil		27	100	11	10	27	40	17	8	1	1	11	3	2	12	0	9	0	1	2	.270	.400	25	79	34	2	3	5.13	0	0
1977																														
LA	4	35	133	22	21	35	52	25	6	0	6	20	2	0	14	1	22	3	1	2	.263	.391	22	108	44	5	3	2.25	2	0
Phil		36	138	14	9	31	40	26	3	0	2	12	2	1	11	3	21	1	0	3	.225	.290	32	105	49	3	3	5.40	0	0
1978																														
LA	4	36.2	147	21	19	42	80	23	8	3	8	21	2	0	9	1	22	2	2	4	.286	.544	28	111	50	3	4	3.41	1	1
Phil		37	140	17	14	35	57	25	3	2	5	16	2	1	9	0	21	0	1	4	.250	.407	24	110	46	4	4	4.66	0	0
1979																														
Pitt	3	29	105	15	14	28	47	19	3	2	4	14	3	1	13	0	13	4	0	2	.267	.448	24	90	34	0	2	1.50	1	0
Cin		30	107	5	5	23	35	16	4	1	2	5	1	1	11	0	26	4	2	2	.215	.327	25	87	39	1	2	4.34	0	0
1980																														
Phil	5	49	190	20	19	55	68	45	8	1	1	19	5	2	13	1	37	7	3	2	.289	.358	43	148	71	6	7	3.28	0	0
Hou		49.1	172	19	18	40	57	28	7	5	0	18	7	2	31	0	19	4	1	4	.233	.331	45	147	52	3	4	3.49	1	0
1981																														
LA	5	44	163	15	14	38	55	30	3	1	4	15	4	0	12	1	23	5	0	7	.233	.337	33	132	53	2	5	1.84	0	0
Mtl		44	158	10	9	34	44	26	7	0	1	8	3	0	12	2	25	2	1	4	.215	.278	31	132	52	4	8	2.86	2	1
1982																														
StL	3	25.1	103	17	17	34	45	27	4	2	1	16	5	3	12	1	16	1	0	0	.330	.437	31	81	35	2	3	1.33	1	1
Atl		27	89	5	4	15	16	14	1	0	0	3	2	0	6	0	15	1	2	3	.169	.180	12	76	39	1	0	6.04	0	1

NATIONAL LEAGUE CLUB CHAMPIONSHIP SERIES RECORDS

(Winning club first. IB = innings batted)

YEAR	G	IB	AB	R	ER	H	TB	1B	2B	3B	HR	RBI	SH	SF	BB	HP	SO	SB	CS	GDP	BA	SLG	LOB	PO	A	E	DP	ERA	CG	SHO
1983	4																													
Phil.		34	130	16	15	34	53	25	4	0	5	15	3	1	15	0	22	2	1	3	.262	.408	31	105	36	5	0	1.03	1	1
LA		35	129	8	4	27	40	19	5	1	2	7	2	0	11	2	31	3	3	0	.209	.310	31	102	38	1	3	3.97	0	0
1984	5																													
SD		42.1	155	22	20	41	54	33	5	1	2	20	2	4	14	1	22	2	2	6	.265	.348	27	129	43	1	4	5.23	0	0
Chi.		43	162	26	25	42	80	22	11	0	9	25	1	2	20	2	28	6	3	3	.259	.494	32	127	48	3	6	4.25	0	1
1985	6																													
StL		51.1	201	29	22	56	77	42	10	1	3	26	2	1	30	0	34	6	6	3	.279	.383	51	156	54	4	4	3.46	0	0
LA		52	197	23	20	46	75	28	12	1	5	23	1	1	19	0	31	4	1	3	.234	.381	40	154	71	6	3	3.51	1	0
1986	6																													
NY		62.2	227	21	20	43	60	34	4	2	3	19	1	3	14	0	57	4	0	3	.189	.264	36	189	94	1	6	2.29	1	0
Hou.		63	225	17	16	49	70	38	6	0	5	17	2	0	17	1	40	8	4	4	.218	.311	39	188	66	7	3	2.87	2	1
1987	7																													
StL		60	215	23	22	56	74	46	4	4	2	22	5	4	16	0	42	4	4	7	.260	.344	37	183	67	3	5	2.95	2	2
SF		61	226	23	20	54	90	37	7	1	9	20	3	1	17	2	51	5	4	5	.239	.398	43	180	77	6	10	3.30	2	1
1988	7																													
LA		64	243	31	28	52	70	41	7	1	3	30	1	2	25	2	54	9	1	2	.214	.288	50	195	61	4	9	3.32	1	1
NY		65	240	27	24	58	87	40	12	1	5	27	3	1	28	4	42	6	2	8	.242	.363	54	192	62	8	2	3.94	1	0
1989	5																													
SF		42	165	30	26	44	78	28	6	2	8	29	2	1	17	1	29	2	1	1	.267	.473	30	132	49	5	7	4.09	0	0
Chi.		44	175	22	20	53	77	38	9	3	3	21	1	1	16	1	27	3	0	4	.303	.440	43	126	40	3	1	5.57	0	0
1990	6																													
Cin.		52	192	20	19	49	70	36	9	0	4	20	3	3	10	1	37	6	3	4	.255	.365	33	159	45	2	3	2.38	0	0
Pitt.		53	186	15	14	36	58	22	9	2	3	14	0	1	27	1	49	6	2	2	.194	.312	41	156	71	5	4	3.29	1	0
1991	7																													
Atl.		63	229	19	18	53	80	37	10	1	5	19	5	1	22	2	42	10	4	2	.231	.349	51	189	62	4	6	1.57	1	1
Pitt.		63	228	12	11	51	70	38	10	0	3	11	4	1	22	0	57	6	2	4	.224	.307	54	189	75	6	3	2.57	1	1
1992	7																													
Atl.		60.2	234	34	30	57	90	38	11	2	6	32	2	2	29	0	28	5	0	3	.244	.385	51	183	73	2	3	4.72	0	0
Pitt.		61	231	35	32	59	100	31	20	3	5	32	3	3	29	2	42	1	2	3	.255	.433	50	182	63	5	6	4.45	3	0
1993	6																													
Phil.		54.1	207	23	19	47	87	25	11	4	7	22	3	2	26	0	51	2	0	1	.227	.420	52	165	47	7	2	4.75	0	0
Atl.		55	215	33	29	59	88	40	14	0	5	32	5	2	22	2	54	0	3	2	.274	.409	47	163	55	5	1	3.15	0	0
1995	4																													
Atl.		37	149	19	19	42	62	31	6	1	4	17	1	0	16	0	22	2	0	3	.282	.416	36	117	54	3	8	1.15	0	1
Cin.		39	134	5	5	28	35	22	5	1	0	4	1	1	12	2	31	4	3	8	.209	.261	28	111	43	2	4	4.62	0	0
1996	7																													
Atl.		60	249	44	44	77	118	55	11	3	8	43	2	3	25	3	51	4	1	3	.309	.474	58	183	55	4	6	1.92	0	2
StL		61	221	18	13	45	65	35	4	2	4	15	3	1	11	1	53	1	1	5	.204	.294	34	180	62	6	5	6.60	0	0

NATIONAL LEAGUE CLUB CHAMPIONSHIP SERIES RECORDS

(Winning club first. IB = innings batted)

YEAR	G	IB	AB	R	ER	H	TB	1B	2B	3B	HR	RBI	SH	SF	BB	HP	SO	SB	CS	GDP	BA	SLG	LOB	PO	A	E	DP	ERA	CG	SHO
1997	6																													
Fla.		52	181	20	15	36	47	27	8	0	1	20	5	0	23	3	52	2	1	4	.199	.260	36	159	57	3	4	3.57	2	0
Atl.		53	194	21	21	49	76	36	5	2	6	21	5	3	16	2	49	1	1	3	.253	.392	40	156	57	4	7	2.60	1	1
1998	6																													
SD		54	208	24	21	53	75	41	7	0	5	20	2	0	27	1	48	2	1	6	.255	.361	52	165	60	1	6	2.78	1	2
Atl.		55	200	18	17	47	65	38	4	1	4	17	2	1	26	0	54	3	1	4	.235	.325	46	162	74	8	6	3.50	0	0
1999	6																													
Atl.		60	206	24	23	46	72	31	9	1	5	22	7	1	31	4	47	14	3	5	.223	.350	47	181	55	7	4	2.69	0	1
NY		61	225	21	18	49	70	36	9	0	4	21	3	2	14	0	49	7	3	3	.218	.311	42	178	82	8	9	3.49	0	0
2000	5																													
NY		43	164	31	28	43	69	26	12	1	4	27	3	3	27	3	24	2	1	3	.262	.421	40	135	39	4	1	3.60	1	1
StL.		45	177	21	18	47	64	34	11	0	2	18	4	1	11	1	39	3	0	0	.266	.362	39	129	49	7	3	5.86	0	0
2001	5																													
Ari.		44	172	22	13	40	52	32	6	0	2	19	2	0	18	1	32	3	1	5	.233	.302	39	135	43	3	3	3.00	2	1
Atl.		45	169	15	15	35	56	24	6	0	5	14	0	0	11	0	39	0	1	3	.207	.331	30	132	53	7	5	2.66	0	0
2002	5																													
SF		43.2	158	23	23	39	67	27	3	2	7	23	8	2	21	3	36	1	0	3	.247	.424	38	135	49	1	4	3.20	1	1
StL.		45	171	16	16	44	73	29	8	0	7	16	5	2	10	2	23	1	1	3	.257	.427	39	131	40	1	4	4.74	0	0
2003	7																													
Fla.		66	256	40	32	68	116	43	12	3	10	39	3	2	28	2	45	4	0	4	.266	.453	53	198	70	3	4	5.59	1	1
Chi.		66	252	42	41	65	122	38	10	4	13	41	7	1	23	2	57	1	1	4	.258	.484	45	198	82	4	6	4.36	0	0
2004	7																													
StL.		62.1	235	34	34	60	107	36	12	1	11	33	6	1	17	2	56	2	0	2	.255	.455	40	190	66	1	5	4.26	0	0
Hou.		63.1	233	31	30	53	105	29	10	0	14	30	1	1	25	5	42	6	4	3	.227	.451	44	187	71	2	2	4.91	0	1
2005	6																													
Hou.		52	198	22	17	55	81	41	7	2	5	19	8	2	15	1	33	1	1	2	.278	.409	46	159	77	3	4	2.72	0	0
StL.		53	187	16	16	39	54	30	6	0	3	16	3	4	16	3	42	3	1	4	.209	.289	38	156	73	5	3	2.94	0	0
2006	7																													
StL.		61	226	28	27	56	98	36	7	4	9	27	4	0	29	3	33	4	1	6	.248	.434	51	183	73	4	4	3.84	0	1
NY		61	234	27	26	54	92	33	12	1	8	27	2	0	24	3	36	5	0	3	.231	.393	53	183	77	4	10	3.98	0	1
2007	4																													
Col.		36	135	18	12	30	42	24	3	0	3	16	2	1	18	1	39	2	0	1	.222	.311	31	114	41	2	6	1.89	0	0
Ari.		38	142	8	8	36	51	26	7	1	2	8	0	0	8	4	28	0	2	4	.254	.359	32	108	29	3	2	3.00	0	0
2008	5																													
Phil.		43	169	25	21	45	68	33	6	1	5	22	1	0	19	0	37	2	2	5	.266	.402	35	132	48	2	8	3.89	0	0
LA		44	165	20	19	43	64	31	7	1	4	19	2	1	25	2	42	1	2	7	.261	.388	43	129	49	5	5	4.40	0	0

NATIONAL LEAGUE CLUB CHAMPIONSHIP SERIES RECORDS

(Winning club first. IB = innings batted)

YEAR	G	IB	AB	R	ER	H	TB	1B	2B	3B	HR	RBI	SH	SF	BB	HP	SO	SB	CS	GDP	BA	SLG	LOB	PO	A	E	DP	ERA	CG	SHO
2009 Phil.	5	42.2	156	35	35	36	78	17	6	3	10	34	3	0	23	5	33	2	1	3	.231	.500	24	132	45	3	2	3.07	0	1
LA		44	164	16	15	38	59	29	3	0	6	15	2	1	12	1	33	3	2	2	.232	.360	32	128	41	0	4	7.38	0	0
2010 SF	6	52.2	201	19	17	48	70	34	10	0	4	17	2	1	14	3	56	1	1	3	.239	.348	44	159	52	3	5	3.06	0	1
Phil.		53	190	20	18	41	61	27	11	0	3	18	4	2	21	7	56	7	1	3	.216	.321	45	158	43	4	4	2.91	0	0
2011 StL	6	52	216	43	38	67	107	43	16	0	8	37	4	2	19	2	43	2	1	5	.310	.495	44	159	64	2	6	4.25	0	0
Mil.		53	201	26	25	51	93	27	15	0	9	26	3	1	14	4	40	0	1	5	.254	.463	38	156	62	9	7	6.58	0	0
2012 SF	7	60	241	35	25	63	94	45	10	3	5	31	3	0	23	0	51	1	0	3	.261	.390	52	183	60	4	3	2.80	0	2
StL		61	230	19	19	50	71	35	12	0	3	19	1	1	15	3	49	5	1	3	.217	.309	48	180	63	6	3	3.75	0	0
2013 StL	6	55.1	199	21	20	42	60	30	8	2	2	20	1	2	18	1	50	1	0	5	.211	.302	35	168	68	1	9	2.09	0	1
LA		56	199	13	13	42	67	28	7	3	4	13	1	0	11	1	50	1	0	8	.211	.337	31	166	63	3	7	3.25	0	0
2014 SF	5	43.1	166	24	22	42	59	31	8	0	3	21	3	2	19	1	27	1	0	3	.253	.355	37	135	49	0	6	3.20	0	1
StL		45	163	16	16	38	69	24	5	1	8	15	3	0	13	2	32	1	1	5	.233	.423	30	130	46	2	4	4.57	0	0
2015 NY	4	34	130	21	21	35	65	20	7	0	7	20	3	1	11	2	37	7	1	0	.269	.500	24	108	32	1	0	2.00	0	0
Chi.		36	128	8	8	21	38	12	5	1	4	8	0	0	9	1	37	1	0	0	.164	.297	22	102	33	1	3	5.56	0	0
2016 Chi.	6	52	202	31	25	48	86	25	15	1	7	29	1	2	16	2	50	3	0	1	.238	.426	36	159	62	3	7	2.89	0	1
LA		53	186	17	17	39	56	30	5	0	4	17	1	1	19	3	42	8	0	6	.210	.301	35	156	39	7	1	4.33	0	2
2017 LA	5	43.2	163	28	26	42	84	22	8	2	10	27	2	2	28	1	41	1	2	6	.258	.515	37	132	36	0	1	1.64	0	0
Chi.		44	154	8	8	24	46	16	1	0	7	8	1	0	5	2	53	1	0	1	.156	.299	22	131	53	2	6	5.36	0	0
2018 LA	7	65.2	238	23	23	53	78	39	8	1	5	23	2	0	23	5	82	5	2	7	.223	.328	48	195	68	4	5	3.18	0	0
Mil.		65	246	24	23	57	94	33	17	1	6	22	2	1	22	1	79	3	2	4	.232	.382	52	197	65	2	8	3.15	0	1
2019 Wash.	4	34	135	20	17	37	56	23	11	1	2	20	3	1	11	0	44	0	0	1	.274	.415	28	108	21	2	1	1.25	0	1
StL		36	123	6	5	16	22	12	3	0	1	5	0	0	7	3	48	3	0	1	.130	.179	19	102	30	1	1	4.50	0	0
2020 LA	7	61	240	39	38	61	121	34	10	1	16	39	0	1	31	3	67	2	0	4	.254	.504	53	186	52	3	6	4.35	0	0
Atl.		62	237	33	30	58	100	35	13	1	9	33	0	2	27	2	64	4	0	4	.245	.422	49	183	51	1	4	5.61	0	0

CHAMPIONSHIP SERIES – INDIVIDUAL BATTING

		3 Games	4 Games	5 Games	6 Games	7 Games
Batting Average (Minimum: 3.1 PA per game)						
	AL:	.583 B. Robinson Balt. 1970	.533 Cain KC 2014	.611 Lynn Cal. 1982	.478 Escobar KC 2015	.500 Youkilis Bos. 2007
	NL:	.778 Johnstone Phil. 1976	.529 Murphy NY 2015	.650 Clark SF 1989	.545 Freese StL 2011	.542 Lopez Atl. 1996
Slugging Percentage (Minimum: 3.1 PA per game)						
	AL:	1.000 Buford Balt. 1970	1.056 Brett KC 1978	1.000 Brunansky Minn. 1987; Henderson Oak. 1989	1.273 Cruz Tex. 2011	.929 Youkilis Bos. 2007
	NL:	1.182 Stargell Pitt. 1979	1.294 Murphy NY 2015	1.200 Clark SF 1989	1.091 Freese StL 2011	1.000 Lopez Atl. 1996; Pujols StL 2004
Plate Appearances						
	AL:	17 Blair & Buford Balt. 1969	20 Bumbry Balt. 1979	25 Offerman Bos. 1999; Valentin Bos. 1999; Betts Bos. 2018	33 Jeter NY 2009	38 Jeter NY 2004
	NL:	16 Agee NY 1969	20 Lopes LA 1974; Taveras Col. 2007	25 Rose & Schmidt Phil. 1980; Cabell Hou. 1980; Sandberg Chi. 1989	31 Williams Atl. 1999	36 Pierre Fla. 2003
At-Bats						
	AL:	15 Belanger Balt. 1969; Blair Balt. 1969; Law Chi. 1983	18 By many	24 Puckett Minn. 1987; Jeter NY 1996; Offerman Bos. 1999; Benintendi Bos. 2018	30 Damon NY 2009	36 Williams NY 2004
	NL:	15 Oberkfell StL 1982	19 Cash Pitt. 1971; Maddox Phil. 1978; Grissom Atl. 1995	24 Schmidt Phil. 1980	28 Williams Atl. 1999	35 Grissom Atl. 1996
Runs						
	AL:	5 Belanger Balt. 1970	7 Brett KC 1978	8 R. Henderson Oak. 1989	8 Zobrist KC 2015	10 Youkilis Bos. 2007
	NL:	4 By many	6 Garvey LA 1978; Murphy NY 2015	8 Clark SF 1989; Perez NY 2000	7 Freese StL 2011; Jay StL 2011	12 Beltran Hou. 2004
Hits						
	AL:	7 B. Robinson Balt. 1969-70	9 Bradley Oak. 2006; Polanco Det. 2006	11 Chambliss NY 1976; Lynn Cal. 1982; Offerman Bos. 1999	12 Raines Chi. & White Tor. 1993	14 Matsui NY 2004; Youkilis Bos. 2007
	NL:	7 Shamsky NY 1969; Johnstone Phil. 1976	9 Murphy NY 2015	13 Clark SF 1989	12 Freese StL 2011	14 Pujols StL 2004; Scutaro SF 2012
Extra-Base Hits						
	AL:	4 Watson NY 1980	5 Brett KC 1978	6 Brunansky Minn. 1987	8 Cruz Tex. 2011	9 Matsui NY 2004
	NL:	5 Aaron Atl. 1969	6 Garvey LA 1978	6 Clark SF 1989	6 Ross SF 2010; Pujols StL 2011	7 Lopez Atl. 1996; Seager LA 2020
Total Bases						
	AL:	11 By many	19 Brett KC 1978	20 Chambliss NY 1976	28 Cruz Tex. 2011	28 Matsui NY 2004
	NL:	16 H. Aaron Atl. 1969	22 Garvey LA 1978; Murphy NY 2015	24 Clark SF 1989	24 Freese StL 2011	28 Pujols StL 2004

CHAMPIONSHIP SERIES – INDIVIDUAL BATTING

		3 Games	4 Games	5 Games	6 Games	7 Games
Singles						
AL:		6 B. Robinson Balt. 1969	8 Polanco Det. 2006	10 Offerman Bos. 1999	10 Raines Chi. 1993 Vizquel Clev. 1998	9 Barrett Bos. 1986 Boone Cal. 1986 Cabrera Bos. 2004 Youkilis Bos. 2007
NL:		7 Shamsky NY 1969	7 Russell LA 1974	8 Puhl Hou. 1980 Rose Phil. 1980 Walton Chi. 1989 Jay StL 2014	8 Biggio Hou. 2005	11 Scutaro SF 2012
Doubles						
AL:		3 Watson NY 1980	3 Carew Cal. 1979	4 Alou Oak. 1972 Brunansky Minn. 1987	5 Mathis LA 2009	6 Matsui NY 2004
NL:		3 Morgan Cin. 1975 Porter StL 1982	4 McGriff Atl. 1995 Kendrick Wash. 2019	4 Rose Cin. 1972	4 Herr StL. 1985 Alfonzo NY 1999 Howard Phil. 2010 Hairston Jr. Mil. 2011 Pujols StL 2011 Baez Chi. 2016	5 Lopez Atl. 1996
Triples						
AL:		1 By many	1 By many	2 Brett KC 1977 Carrera Tor. 2016	2 Lofton Clev. 1995 Cano NY 2009	1 By many
NL:		2 McGee StL. 1982	1 By many	1 By many	2 Duncan Phil. 1993	2 Pierre Fla. 2003 Spiezio StL. 2006
Home Runs						
AL:		2 By many	3 Brett KC 1978 Canseco Oak. 1988	3 Strawberry NY 1996 Zeile Balt. 1996 Williams NY 2001 Kennedy Ana. 2002	6 Cruz Tex. 2011	4 Longoria TB 2008 Upton TB 2008 Arozarena TB 2020
NL:		3 H. Aaron Atl. 1969	4 Robertson Pitt. 1971 Garvey LA 1978 Murphy NY 2015	3 Staub NY 1973 Werth Phil. 2009 Hernandez LA 2017	3 Madlock LA 1985 Ross SF 2010 Freese StL. 2011	5 Seager LA 2020
Runs Batted In						
AL:		9 Nettles NY 1981	6 Jackson NY 1978 Ordonez Det. 2006 Young Det. 2012	10 Baylor Cal. 1982	13 Cruz Tex. 2011	11 Ortiz Bos. 2004 Upton TB 2008
NL:		7 H. Aaron Atl. 1969	8 Baker LA 1977 Matthews Sr. Phil. 1983	9 Williams SF 1989	9 Freese StL. 2011 Pujols StL. 2011	11 Seager LA 2020
Walks						
AL:		6 Killebrew Minn. 1969	5 By many	7 Whitaker Det. 1987 R. Henderson Oak. 1989 Bregman Hou. 2018	10 Thomas Chi. 1993	9 Ramirez Bos. 2007 Adames TB 2020
NL:		6 Morgan Cin. 1976	9 Wynn LA 1974	10 Bonds SF 2002	9 C. Jones Atl. 1999	9 Muncy LA 2020

CHAMPIONSHIP SERIES – INDIVIDUAL BATTING

	3 Games	4 Games	5 Games	6 Games	7 Games
Intentional Walks					
AL:	1 By many	2 Rudi Oak. 1974 Murray Balt. 1979 Baines Oak.F 1990	2 By many	5 Hamilton Tex. 2010	3 Brett KC 1985
NL:	2 Morgan Cin. 1976 Hernandez StL. 1982	3 McCovey SF 1971 Cey LA 1974	4 Cruz Hou. 1980	5 Guerrero LA 1985	4 Pujols StL. 2006
Hit By Pitch					
AL:	1 By many	2 Gordon KC 2014	2 Gladden Minn. 1987 Sheridan Det. 1987 Bregman Hou. 2018	2 Cora Sea. 1995 Grich Cal. 1986 Cano NY 2009 Victorino Bos. 2013 Escobar KC 2015	4 Cairo NY 2004
NL:	1 By many	2 Upton Ari. 2007 Molina StL. 2019	2 Martin LA 2008 Rollins Phil. 2009 Victorino Phil. 2009	3 Ruiz Phil. 2010	2 Dykstra NY 1986 Blauser Atl. 1996 Ensberg Hou. 2004 Kent Hou. 2004 Eckstein StL. 2006 Beaty LA 2020
Strikeouts					
AL:	7 Cardenas Minn. 1969	7 D. Henderson Oak. 1988 Granderson NY 2012 Gordon KC 2014	9 Martin Tor. 2016	12 Alvarez Hou. 2019 Sanchez NY 2019	12 Hafner Clev. 2007
NL:	7 Geronimo Cin. 1975	10 R. Sanders Cin. 1995	9 Edmonds StL. 2000	12 Strawberry NY 1986 Howard Phil. 2010	13 Muncy LA 2018
Stolen Bases					
AL:	2 By many	4 Otis KC 1978	8 R. Henderson Oak. 1989	7 Wilson Oak. 1992	3 Crawford TB 2008
NL:	4 Morgan Cin. 1975	3 Lopes LA 1974 Granderson NY 2015	5 Lopes LA 1981	3 By many	7 Gant Atl. 1991
Caught Stealing					
AL:	3 McRae KC 1980	2 By many	3 Patek KC 1976	4 White Tor. 1992	2 Pettis Cal. 1986 Nixon Bos. 2003
NL:	1 By many	2 Marshall LA 1983 Young Ari. 2007	2 Rose Phil. 1980	3 McGee StL. 1985 Bass Hou. 1986	3 Pierre Fla. 2003
Grounded into Double Plays					
AL:	2 Thompson Minn. 1970	2 Anderson Cal. 1979 Singleton Balt. 1983 Benzinger Bos. 1988 Pena Bos. 1990 Guillen Det. 2006 Kotsay Oak. 2006 Young Balt. 2014	3 Taylor Det. 1972	3 Sorrento Clev. 1995 Raburn Det. 2011	4 Lugo Bos. 2007
NL:	2 Jones NY 1969 Royster Atl. 1982	2 Bowa Phil. 1977 Boone Cin. 1995 Devereaux Atl. 1995	4 Guerrero LA 1981	3 Gomez SD 1998 Uribe LA 2013	3 Herr StL. 1987 Machado LA 2018

Most Series (non-pitchers)
- 11 Reggie Jackson, AL:Oak. 1971-75, NY 77-78, 80-81, Cal. 82, 86
- 8 Richie Hebner, NL:Pitt. 1970-72,74-75; Phil. 77-78; Chi. 84
    Yadier Molina, NL:StL. 2004-06, 11-14, 19

Most Games
- 54 Derek Jeter, AL:NY
- 39 Yadier Molina, NL:StL.

Highest Batting Average (50 or more at-bats)
- .468 Will Clark, NL:SF-StL. (62ab-29h)
- .414 Kevin Youkilis, AL:Bos. (58ab-24h)

Highest Slugging Percentage (50 or more at-bats)
- .845 Nelson Cruz, AL:Tex.-Balt. (58ab-49tb)
- .806 Will Clark, NL:SF-StL. (62ab-50tb)

Most Plate Appearances
- 261 Derek Jeter, AL:NY
- 154 Chipper Jones, NL:Atl.

Most Plate Appearances, Game
- 6 By many
- **Extra-Inning Game:**
- 8 Mookie Wilson, NL:NY Oct. 15, 1986 (16 inn)
    Chipper Jones, NL:Atl. Oct. 17, 1999 (15 inn)
    Brian Jordan, NL:Atl. Oct. 17, 1999 (15 inn)
    Gerald Williams, NL:Atl. Oct. 17, 1999 (15inn)
    Derek Jeter, AL:NY Oct. 18, 2004 (14 inn)

Most Plate Appearances, Inning
- 2 By many

Most At-Bats
- 226 Derek Jeter, AL:NY
- 141 Yadier Molina, NL:StL.

Most At-Bats, Game
- 6 By many
- **Extra-Inning Game:**
- 7 Mookie Wilson, NL:NY Oct. 15, 1986 (16 inn)
    Keith Hernandez, NL:NY Oct. 15, 1986 (16 inn)
    Bill Doran, NL:Hou. Oct. 15, 1986 (16 inn)
    Billy Hatcher, NL:Hou. Oct. 15, 1986 (16 inn)
    Glenn Davis, NL:Hou. Oct. 15, 1986 (16 inn)
    Brian Jordan, NL:Atl. Oct. 17, 1999 (15 inn)
    Robin Ventura, NL:NY Oct. 17, 1999 (15 inn)
    Gerald Williams, NL:Atl. Oct. 17, 1999 (15 inn)
    Derek Jeter, AL:NY Oct. 18, 2004 (14 inn)
    Hideki Matsui, AL:NY Oct. 18, 2004 (14 inn)
    Bernie Williams, AL:NY Oct. 18, 2004 (14 inn)
    Tony Clark, AL:NY Oct. 18, 2004 (14 inn)
    Vladimir Guerrero, AL:LA Oct. 17, 2009 (13 inn)

Most At-Bats, Inning
- 2 By many

Most Runs
- 32 Derek Jeter, AL:NY
- 25 Albert Pujols, NL:StL.

Most Runs, Game
- 5 Alex Rodriguez, AL:NY Oct. 16, 2004
    Hideki Matsui, AL:NY Oct. 16, 2004
- 4 Bob Robertson, NL:Pitt. Oct. 3, 1971
    Steve Garvey, NL:LA Oct. 9, 1974
    Will Clark, NL:SF Oct. 4, 1989
    Javier Lopez, NL:Atl. Oct. 14, 1996
    Fred McGriff, NL:Atl. Oct. 17, 1996
    Carlos Beltran, NL:NY Oct. 15, 2006

Most Runs, Inning
- 2 Jack Clark, NL:StL. Oct. 13, 1985 (2nd)
    Cesar Cedeno, NL:StL. Oct. 13, 1985 (2nd)
    Mookie Betts, NL:LA Oct. 14, 2020 (1st)
    Corey Seager, NL:LA Oct. 14, 2020 (1st)
    Chone Figgins, AL:Ana. Oct. 13, 2002 (7th)
    Scott Spiezio, AL:Ana. Oct. 13, 2002 (7th)
    Elvis Andrus, AL:Tex. Oct. 15, 2011 (3rd)

Most Hits
- 59 Manny Ramirez, AL:Clev.-Bos.; NL:LA
- 58 Derek Jeter, AL:NY
- 45 Pete Rose, NL:Cin.-Phil.

Most Hits, Game
- 5 Paul Blair, AL:Balt. Oct. 6, 1969
    Hideki Matsui, AL:NY Oct. 16, 2004
    Carl Crawford, AL:TB Oct. 14, 2008
- 4 Bob Robertson, NL:Pitt. Oct. 3, 1971
    Ron Cey, NL:LA Oct. 6, 1974
    Steve Garvey, NL:LA Oct. 9, 1974
    Dusty Baker, NL:LA Oct. 7, 1978 (10 inn)
    Terry Puhl, NL:Hou. Oct. 12, 1980 (10 inn)
    Steve Garvey, NL:SD Oct. 6, 1984
    Tito Landrum, NL:StL. Oct. 13, 1985
    Kevin McReynolds, NL:NY Oct. 11, 1988
    Will Clark, NL:SF Oct. 4, 1989
    Otis Nixon, NL:Atl. Oct. 10, 1992
    Chipper Jones, NL:Atl. Oct. 9, 1996
    Mark Lemke, NL:Atl. Oct. 14, 1996
    Javier Lopez, NL:Atl. Oct. 14, 1996
    Keith Lockhart, NL:Atl. Oct. 14, 1997
    Kenny Lofton, NL:Chi. Oct. 8, 2003
    Buster Posey, NL:SF Oct. 20, 2010
    Albert Pujols, NL:StL. Oct. 10, 2011
    Yadier Molina, NL:StL. Oct. 22, 2012
    Daniel Murphy, NL:NY Oct. 21, 2015
    Joc Pederson, NL:LA Oct. 14, 2020
    Marcell Ozuna, NL:Atl. Oct. 15, 2020

Most Hits, Inning
- 2 Graig Nettles, AL:NY Oct. 14, 1981 (4th)
    Rickey Henderson, AL:Oak. Oct. 6, 1990 (9th)
    Adam Kennedy, AL:Ana. Oct. 13, 2002 (7th)
    Scott Spiezio, AL:Ana. Oct. 13, 2002 (7th)
    Casey Blake, AL:Clev. Oct. 16, 2007 (5th)
    Michael Young, AL:Tex. Oct. 15, 2011 (3rd)
    Jack Clark, NL:StL. Oct. 13, 1985 (2nd)
    Tito Landrum, NL:StL. Oct. 13, 1985 (2nd)
    Jerome Walton, NL:Chi. Oct. 5, 1989 (1st)
    Barry Bonds, NL:Pitt. Oct. 13, 1992 (2nd)
    Lloyd McClendon, NL:Pitt. Oct. 13, 1992 (2nd)
    Juan Pierre, NL:Fla. Oct. 14, 2003 (8th)
    Trea Turner, NL:Wash. Oct. 15, 2019 (1st)
    Corey Seager, NL:LA Oct. 14, 2020 (1st)

Most Extra-Base Hits
- 20 Manny Ramirez, AL:Clev.-Bos.; NL:LA
- 19 Bernie Williams, AL:NY
    Derek Jeter, AL:NY
- 18 Albert Pujols, NL:StL.

Most Extra-Base Hits, Game
- 4 Bob Robertson, NL:Pitt. Oct. 3, 1971
    Albert Pujols, NL:StL. Oct. 10, 2011
    Hideki Matsui, AL:NY Oct. 16, 2004

Most Extra-Base Hits, Inning
- 2 Michael Young, AL:Tex. Oct. 15, 2011 (3rd)
- 1 By many in NL

Most Total Bases
- 105 Manny Ramirez, AL:Clev.-Bos.; NL:LA
- 93 Derek Jeter, AL:NY
- 82 Albert Pujols, NL:StL.

Most Total Bases, Game
- 14 Bob Robertson, NL:Pitt. Oct. 3, 1971
- 13 Adam Kennedy, AL:Ana. Oct. 13, 2002
    Hideki Matsui, AL:NY Oct. 16, 2004

Most Total Bases, Inning
- 5 Barry Bonds, NL:Pitt. Oct. 13, 1992 (2nd)
    Adam Kennedy, AL:Ana. Oct. 13, 2002 (7th)
    Casey Blake, AL:Clev. Oct. 16, 2007 (5th)

Most Singles
- 39 Manny Ramirez, AL:Clev.-Bos.; NL:LA
    Derek Jeter, AL:NY
- 34 Pete Rose, NL:Cin.-Phil.

Most Singles, Game

4   Brooks Robinson, AL:Balt. Oct. 4, 1969 (12 inn)
    Chris Chambliss, AL:NY Oct. 4, 1978
    Kelly Gruber, AL:Tor. Oct. 7, 1989
    Jerry Browne, AL:Oak. Oct. 12, 1992
    Terry Puhl, NL:Hou. Oct. 12, 1980 (10 inn)
    Tito Landrum, NL:StL. Oct. 13, 1985
    Chipper Jones, NL:Atl. Oct. 9, 1996
    Keith Lockhart, NL:Atl. Oct. 14, 1997
    Kenny Lofton, NL:Chi. Oct. 8, 2003
    Yadier Molina, NL:StL. Oct. 22, 2012

Most Singles, Inning

2   Graig Nettles, AL:NY Oct. 14, 1981 (4th)
    Rickey Henderson, AL:Oak. Oct. 6, 1990 (9th)
    Scott Spiezio, AL:Ana. Oct. 13, 2002 (7th)
    Jack Clark, NL:StL. Oct. 13, 1985 (2nd)
    Tito Landrum, NL:StL. Oct. 13, 1985 (2nd)
    Jerome Walton, NL:Chi. Oct. 5, 1989 (1st)
    Lloyd McClendon, NL:Pitt. Oct. 13, 1992 (2nd)
    Trea Turner, NL:Wash. Oct. 15, 2019 (1st)

Most Doubles

10   Bernie WIlliams, AL:NY
    Hideki Matsui, AL:NY
    Derek Jeter, AL:NY
    Jorge Posada, AL:NY
8   Albert Pujols, NL:StL.
    Yadier Molina, NL:StL.

Most Doubles, Game

3   Fred McGriff, NL:Atl. Oct. 11, 1995 (10 inn)
    Albert Pujols, NL:StL. Oct. 10, 2011
    Howie Kendrick, NL:Wash. Oct. 14, 2019
    Ben Zobrist, AL:KC Oct. 19, 2015

Most Doubles, Inning

2   Michael Young, AL:Tex. Oct. 15, 2011 (3rd)
1   By many in NL

Most Triples

4   George Brett, AL:KC
3   Willie McGee, NL:StL.
    Mariano Duncan, NL:LA-Phil.
    Keith Lockhart, NL:Atl.

Most Triples, Game

2   Mariano Duncan, NL:Phil. Oct. 9, 1993
1   By many in AL

Most Triples, Inning

1   By many

Most Home Runs

13   Manny Ramirez, AL:Clev.-Bos.; NL:LA
10   Manny Ramirez, AL:Clev.-Bos.
    Albert Pujols, NL:StL.

Most Home Runs, Game

3   Bob Robertson, NL:Pitt. Oct. 3, 1971
    Kike Hernandez, NL:LA Oct. 19, 2017
    George Brett, AL:KC Oct. 6, 1978
    Adam Kennedy, AL:Ana. Oct. 13, 2002

Most Home Runs, Inning

1   By many

Most Games, Consecutive, Home Runs

4   Gary Matthews Sr., NL:Phil.-Chi. Oct. 5, 1983-Oct. 2, 1984
    Jeffrey Leonard, NL:SF Oct. 6-10, 1987
    Carlos Beltran, NL:Hou. Oct. 13-17, 2004
    Daniel Murphy, NL:NY Oct. 17-21, 2015
    Evan Longoria, AL:TB Oct. 11-16, 2008

Most Grand Slam Home Runs, Game

1   Mike Cuellar, AL:Balt. Oct. 3, 1970 (4th)
    Don Baylor, AL:Cal. Oct. 9, 1982 (8th)
    Jim Thome, AL:Clev. Oct. 13, 1998 (5th)
    Ricky Ledee, AL:NY Oct. 17, 1999 (9th)
    Johnny Damon, AL:Bos. Oct. 20, 2004 (2nd)
    J.D. Drew, AL:Bos. Oct. 20, 2007 (1st)
    Nelson Cruz, AL:Tex. Oct. 10, 2011 (11th)
    David Ortiz, AL:Bos. Oct. 13, 2013 (8th)
    Shane Victorino, AL:Bos. Oct. 19, 2013 (7th)
    Jackie Bradley, AL:Bos. Oct. 16, 2018 (8th)
    Ron Cey, NL:LA Oct. 4, 1977 (7th)
    Dusty Baker, NL:LA Oct. 5, 1977 (4th)
    Will Clark, NL:SF Oct. 4, 1989 (4th)
    Ron Gant, NL:Atl. Oct. 7, 1992 (5th)
    Gary Gaetti, NL:StL. Oct. 10, 1996 (7th)
    Andres Galarraga, NL:Atl. Oct. 11, 1998 (7th)
    Aramis Ramirez, NL:Chi. Oct. 11, 2003 (1st)
    Miguel Montero, NL:Chi. Oct. 15, 2016 (8th)
    Kike Hernandez, NL:LA Oct. 19, 2017 (3rd)
    Max Muncy, NL:LA Oct. 14, 2020 (1st)

Most Runs Batted In

33   Bernie Williams, AL:NY
27   Albert Pujols, NL:StL.

Most Runs Batted In, Game

7   Kike Hernandez, NL:LA Oct. 19, 2017
6   Johnny Damon, AL:Bos. Oct. 20, 2004

Most Runs Batted In, Inning

4   Mike Cuellar, AL:Balt. Oct. 3, 1970 (4th)
    Don Baylor, AL:Cal. Oct. 9, 1982 (8th)
    Jim Thome, AL:Clev. Oct. 13, 1998 (5th)
    Ricky Ledee, AL:NY Oct. 17, 1999 (9th)
    Johnny Damon, AL:Bos. Oct. 20, 2004 (2nd)
    J.D. Drew, AL:Bos. Oct. 20, 2007 (1st)
    Nelson Cruz, AL:Tex. Oct. 10, 2011 (11th)
    Michael Young, AL:Tex. Oct. 15, 2011 (3rd)
    David Ortiz, AL:Bos. Oct. 13, 2013 (8th)
    Shane Victorino, AL:Bos. Oct. 19, 2013 (7th)
    Jackie Bradley, AL:Bos. Oct. 16, 2018 (8th)
    Ron Cey, NL:LA Oct. 4, 1977 (7th)
    Dusty Baker, NL:LA Oct. 5, 1977 (4th)
    Will Clark, NL:SF Oct. 4, 1989 (4th)
    Ron Gant, NL:Atl. Oct. 7, 1992 (5th)
    Gary Gaetti, NL:StL. Oct. 10, 1996 (7th)
    Andres Galarraga, NL:Atl. Oct. 11, 1998 (7th)
    Aramis Ramirez, NL:Chi. Oct. 11, 2003 (1st)
    Miguel Montero, NL:Chi. Oct. 15, 2016 (8th)
    Kike Hernandez, NL:LA Oct. 19, 2017 (3rd)
    Max Muncy, NL:LA Oct. 14, 2020 (1st)

Most Sacrifice Hits

6   Greg Maddux, NL:Chi.-Atl.
5   Derek Jeter, AL:NY

Most Sacrifice Hits, Game

2   Dock Ellis, NL:Pitt. Oct. 3, 1970 (10 inn)
    Gaylord Perry, NL:SF Oct. 2, 1971
    Jim Bibby, NL:Pitt. Oct. 3, 1979 (10 inn)
    Manny Trillo, NL:Phil. Oct. 8, 1980 (10 inn)
    Joaquin Andujar, NL:StL. Oct. 10, 1982
    Greg Mathews, NL:StL. Oct. 6, 1987
    Tim Wakefield, NL:Pitt. Oct. 13, 1992
    Otis Nixon, NL:Atl. Oct. 10, 1993
    Greg Maddux, NL:Atl. Oct. 13, 1993
    Tommy Greene, NL:Phil. Oct. 13, 1993
    Mark Prior, NL:Chi. Oct. 8, 2003
    Edgar Renteria, NL:StL. Oct. 21, 2004
    Chris Carpenter, NL:StL. Oct. 12, 2005
    Jeff Suppan, NL:StL. Oct. 14, 2006
    Vicente Padilla, NL:LA Oct. 16, 2009
    Stephen Strasburg, NL:Wash. Oct. 14, 2019
    Freddie Patek, AL:KC Oct. 7, 1977
    Mike Gallego, AL:Oak. Oct. 8, 1989
    Joey Cora, AL:Chi. Oct. 8, 1993
    Melky Cabrera, AL:NY Oct. 25, 2009
    Coco Crisp, AL:Clev. Oct. 14, 2016

Most Sacrifice Flies

3   Robin Ventura, AL:Chi.; NL:NY
2   By many in AL & NL

Most Sacrifice Flies, Game
2 David Ortiz, AL:Bos. Oct. 18, 2007
   Alcides Escobar, AL:KC Oct. 20, 2015
1 By many in NL

Most Walks
34 Manny Ramirez, AL:Clev.-Bos.; NL:LA
32 Jorge Posada, AL:NY
24 Chipper Jones, NL:Atl.
    Barry Bonds, NL:Pitt.-SF

Most Walks, Game
4 Ruppert Jones, AL:Cal. Oct. 11, 1986 (11 inn)
   Frank Thomas, AL:Chi. Oct. 5, 1993
   Josh Hamilton, AL:Tex. Oct. 16, 2010
   Darren Daulton, NL:Phil. Oct. 10, 1993
   Ken Caminiti, NL:SD Oct. 8, 1998
   Chase Utley, NL:Phil. Oct. 10, 2008

Most Walks, Inning
2 Manny Ramirez, AL:Bos. Oct. 20, 2007 (3rd)
1 By many in NL

Most Intentional Walks
6 Keith Hernandez, NL:StL.-NY
   Albert Pujols, NL:StL.
   Josh Hamilton, AL:Tex.

Most Intentional Walks, Game
3 Josh Hamilton, AL:Tex. Oct. 22, 2010
2 By many NL players
   NL Extra-Inning Game:
3 Jose Cruz, NL:Hou. Oct. 10, 1980 (11 inn)

Most Intentional Walks, Inning
1 By many

Most Hit By Pitch
5 David Eckstein, AL:Ana.-NL:StL.
   Shane Victorino, NL:Phil.-AL:Bos.
4 Richie Hebner, NL:Pitt.-Phil.-Chi.
   David Eckstein, NL:StL.
   Carlos Ruiz, NL:Phil.
   Justin Turner, NL:LA
   Miguel Cairo, AL:NY
   Alex Bregman, AL:Hou.

Most Hit By Pitch, Game
2 Dan Gladden, AL:Minn. Oct. 11, 1987
   Pat Sheridan, AL:Det. Oct. 12, 1987
   Jason Bartlett, AL:TB Oct. 18, 2008
   Russell Martin, NL:LA Oct. 12, 2008
   Jimmy Rollins, NL:Phil. Oct. 21, 2009
   Matt Beaty, NL:LA Oct. 14, 2020

Most Strikeouts
42 Derek Jeter, AL:NY
32 Reggie Sanders, NL:Cin.-Ari.-SF-StL.

Most Strikeouts, Game
4 Dave Boswell, AL:Minn. Oct. 5, 1969 (11 inn)
   Bobby Bonilla, AL:Balt. Oct. 10, 1996
   Marquis Grissom, AL:Clev. Oct. 11, 1997 (12 inn)
   Rafael Palmeiro, AL:Balt. Oct. 11, 1997 (12 inn)
   Marquis Grissom, AL:Clev. Oct. 15, 1997 (11 inn)
   Corey Koskie, AL:Minn. Oct. 11, 2002
   Alfonso Soriano, AL:NY Oct. 16, 2003 (11 inn)
   Johnny Damon, AL:Bos. Oct. 12, 2004
   Mark Bellhorn, AL:Bos. Oct. 16, 2004
   Tony Clark, AL:NY Oct. 18, 2004 (14 inn)
   Casey Blake, AL:Clev. Oct. 13, 2007 (11 inn)
   Travis Hafner, AL:Clev. Oct. 16, 2007
   Austin Jackson, AL:Det. Oct. 13, 2011
   Alex Gordon, AL:KC Oct. 11, 2014
   Didi Gregorius, AL:NY Oct. 21, 2017
   Hunter Renfroe, AL:TB Oct. 11, 2020
   John Kruk, NL:Phil. Oct. 10, 1993
   Reggie Sanders, NL:Cin. Oct. 11, 1995 (10 inn)
   Gerald Williams, NL:Atl. Oct. 10, 1998
   Jimmy Rollins, NL:Phil. Oct. 10, 2008
   Andres Torres, NL:SF Oct. 17, 2010
   Nick Punto, NL:StL. Oct. 16, 2011
   Yasiel Puig, NL:LA Oct. 12, 2013
   Curtis Granderson, NL:LA Oct. 18, 2017
   Justin Turner, NL:LA Oct. 12, 2018
   Jesus Aguilar, NL:Mil. Oct. 20, 2018
   Paul Goldschmidt, NL:StL. Oct. 14, 2019

Most Strikeouts, Inning
2 Ron Karkovice, AL:Chi. Oct. 8, 1993 (3rd)
   Casey Blake, AL:Clev. Oct. 13, 2007 (11th)

Most Stolen Bases
17 Rickey Henderson, AL:Oak.-Tor.; NL:NY
16 Rickey Henderson, AL:Oak.-Tor.
9 Davey Lopes, NL:LA-Hou.

Most Stolen Bases, Game
4 Rickey Henderson, AL:Oak. Oct. 4, 1989
3 Joe Morgan, NL:Cin. Oct. 4, 1975
   Ken Griffey Sr. NL:Cin. Oct. 5, 1975
   Steve Sax, NL:LA Oct. 9, 1988 (12 inn)
   Ron Gant, NL:Atl. Oct. 10, 1991
   Edgar Renteria, NL:StL. Oct. 12, 2000

Most Stolen Bases, Inning
2 Bert Campaneris, AL:Oak. Oct. 8, 1972 (1st)
   Reggie Jackson, AL:Oak. Oct. 12, 1972 (2nd)
   Juan Beniquez, AL:Bos. Oct. 4, 1975 (7th)
   Randy Bush, AL:Minn. Oct. 8, 1987 (4th)
   Rickey Henderson, AL:Oak. Oct. 4, 1989 (4th)
   Rickey Henderson, AL:Oak. Oct. 4, 1989 (7th)
   Willie Wilson, AL:Oak. Oct. 8, 1992 (5th)
   Elvis Andrus, AL:Tex. Oct. 16, 2010 (1st)
   Brett Gardner, AL:NY Oct. 13, 2012 (10th)
   Dalton Pompey, AL:Tor. Oct. 23, 2015 (9th)
   Joe Morgan, NL:Cin. Oct. 4, 1975 (3rd)
   Ken Griffey Sr. NL:Cin. Oct. 5, 1975 (6th)
   Steve Sax, NL:LA Oct. 9, 1988 (3rd)
   Barry Bonds, NL:Pitt. Oct. 10, 1991 (2nd)
   Ron Gant, NL:Atl. Oct. 10, 1991 (3rd)
   Roger Cedeno, NL:NY Oct. 16, 1999 (8th)
   Jimmy Rollins, NL:Phil. Oct. 21, 2010 (7th)
   Curtis Granderson, NL:NY Oct. 18, 2015 (3rd)
   Josh Reddick, NL:LA Oct 18, 2016 (4th)

Most Times Stealing Home
1 Reggie Jackson, AL:Oak. Oct. 12, 1972
   Marquis Grissom, AL:Clev. Oct. 11, 1997
   Scott Spiezio, AL:Ana. Oct. 9, 2002
   Elvis Andrus, AL:Tex. Oct. 16, 2010
   Jeff Branson, NL:Cin. Oct. 11, 1995
   Javier Baez, NL:Chi. Oct. 15, 2016

Most Caught Stealing
6 Hal McRae, AL:KC
   Devon White, AL:Cal.-Tor.
4 Vince Coleman, NL:StL.
   Willie McGee, NL:StL.
   Juan Pierre, NL:Fla.-LA

Most Caught Stealing, Game
2 Brooks Robinson, AL:Balt. Oct. 4, 1969 (12 inn)
   Trot Nixon, AL:Bos. Oct. 13, 2003
1 By many in NL
   NL Extra-Inning Game:
2 Kevin Bass, NL:Hou. Oct. 15, 1986 (16 inn)

Most Caught Stealing, Inning
1 By many

Most Grounded into Double Plays
8 Manny Ramirez, AL:Clev.-Bos.
6 Yasiel Puig, NL:LA
   Yadier Molina, NL:StL.

Most Grounded into Double Plays, Game
3 Tony Taylor, AL:Det. Oct. 10, 1972
2 Cleon Jones, NL:NY Oct. 4, 1969
   Garry Maddox, NL:Phil. Oct. 12, 1980 (10 inn)
   Pedro Guerrero, NL:LA Oct. 16, 1981
   Jerry Royster, NL:Atl. Oct. 10, 1982
   Bret Boone, NL:Cin. Oct. 10, 1995 (11 inn)
   Chris Gomez, NL:SD Oct. 7, 1998 (10 inn)
   Gerald Williams, NL:Atl. Oct. 13, 1999
   Damian Miller, NL:Ari. Oct. 20, 2001
   Blake DeWitt, NL:LA Oct. 15, 2008
   Yadier Molina, NL:StL. Oct. 16, 2013
   Jhonny Peralta, NL:StL. Oct. 15, 2014
   Pablo Sandoval, NL:SF Oct. 15, 2014
   Manny Machado, NL:LA Oct. 17, 2018

Most Bases on Interference, Game
1 Richie Hebner, NL:Pitt. Oct. 8, 1974
   Mike Scioscia, NL:LA Oct. 14, 1985
   Jon Jay, NL:StL. Oct. 15, 2013
   Josh Reddick, NL:LA Oct 19, 2016
   Jesus Aguilar, NL:Mil. Oct. 12, 2018
   Josh Reddick, AL:Hou. Oct. 17, 2017

CHAMPIONSHIP SERIES FIELDING RECORDS
FIRST BASEMEN – FIELDING

	3 Games	4 Games	5 Games	6 Games	7 Games
Highest Percentage 1.000 (Most Chances)					
AL:	34 Powell Balt. 1969	40 McGwire Oak. 1990	58 Konerko Chi. 2005	73 Teixeira NY 2009	64 Johnson NY 2003
NL:	36 Hernandez StL. 1982	49 Garvey LA 1978	60 Rose Phil. 1980	79 Hernandez NY 1986	72 Lee Fla. 2003
Games					
AL:	3 By many	4 By many	5 By many	6 By many	7 By many
NL:	3 By many	4 By many	5 By many	6 By many	7 By many
Total Chances					
AL:	34 Powell Balt. 1969 / Watson NY 1980	49 Murray Balt. 1979	58 Konerko Chi. 2005	73 Teixeira NY 2009	81 Balboni KC 1985
NL:	36 Hernandez StL. 1982	49 Garvey LA 1978	60 Rose Phil. 1980	79 Hernandez NY 1986	72 Lee Fla. 2003
Chances Accepted					
AL:	34 Powell Balt. 1969	47 Murray Balt. 1979	58 Konerko Chi. 2005	73 Teixeira NY 2009	79 Balboni KC 1985
NL:	36 Hernandez StL. 1982	49 Garvey LA 1978	60 Rose Phil. 1980	79 Hernandez NY 1986	72 Lee Fla. 2003
Putouts					
AL:	34 Powell Balt. 1969	44 Murray Balt. 1979	57 Konerko Chi. 2005	71 Teixeira NY 2009	72 Balboni KC 1985
NL:	35 Hernandez StL. 1982	44 Garvey LA 1978	53 Rose Phil. 1980	67 Hernandez NY 1986	66 Lee Fla. 2003
Assists					
AL:	5 Reese Minn. 1969	3 Murray Balt. 1979, 83 / Paciorek Chi. 1983 / Fielder Det. 2012 / Teixeira NY 2012 / Pierce Balt. 2014	8 Hrbek Minn. 1991	11 Morales LA 2009	8 Millar Bos. 2003
NL:	5 Perez Cin. 19755 / Chambliss Atl. 1982	5 Garvey LA 1978	7 Rose Phil. 1980 / Franco Atl. 2001 / Belt SF 2014 / Rizzo Chi. 2017	12 Hernandez NY 1986	8 Pujols StL. 2004
Errors					
AL:	1 By many	2 Murray Balt. 1979	2 Mayberry KC 1977 / Cooper Mil. 1982	2 Sorrento Clev. 1995 / LeMahieu NY 2019	2 Balboni KC 1985
NL:	2 Cepeda Atl. 1969	2 Jackson Ari. 2007	2 Clark StL. 2000	4 Galarraga Atl. 1998	2 Hatcher LA 1988 / Redus Pitt. 1991
Double Plays					
AL:	5 Watson NY 1981	6 Carew Cal. 1979	6 Palmeiro Balt. 1996 / Martinez NY 1999	8 Thome Clev. 1997 / Teixeira NY 2009 / Napoli Bos. 2013	13 Garko Clev. 2007
NL:	3 Hernandez StL. 1982	8 McGriff Atl. 1995	7 Howard Phil. 2008	8 Adams StL. 2013	10 Clark SF 1987

FIRST BASEMEN

Most Series
7 Tino Martinez, AL:Sea. 1995; NY 96, 98-2001;
    NL:StL. 02
    John Olerud, AL:Tor. 1991-93; Sea. 2000-01;
    NY 04; NL:NY 99
6 Tino Martinez, AL:Sea. 1995; NY 96, 98-2001
    John Olerud, AL:Tor. 1991-93; NY 04
5 Bob Robertson, NL:Pitt. 1970-72, 74-75
    Tony Perez, NL:Cin. 1970,72-73, 75-76
    Steve Garvey, NL:LA 1974, 77-78, 81; SD 84
    Albert Pujols, NL:StL. 2002, 04-06, 11

Most Games
38 John Olerud, AL:Tor.-Sea.-NY; NL:NY
33 Tino Martinez, AL:Sea.-NY
27 Albert Pujols, NL:StL.

Highest Percentage (Most Chances)
1.000 Albert Pujols, NL:StL. (264 tc)
        Yuli Gurriel, AL:Hou. (184 tc)

Most Total Chances
346 John Olerud, AL:Tor.-Sea.-NY; NL:NY
285 Tino Martinez, AL:Sea.-NY
264 Albert Pujols, NL:StL.

Most Total Chances, Game
18 Steve Garvey, NL:LA Oct. 6, 1978
16 Steve Balboni, AL:KC Oct. 12, 1985
    Mark McGwire, AL:Oak. Oct. 4, 1989
    Kevin Millar, AL:Bos. Oct. 9, 2003
    Kevin Millar, AL:Bos. Oct. 14, 2003
    Extra-Inning Game:
27 Keith Hernandez, NL:NY Oct. 15, 1986 (16 inn)
17 Kendry Morales, AL:LA Oct. 17, 2009 (13 inn)

Most Total Chances, Inning
4 Dick Allen, NL:Phil. Oct. 10, 1976 (6th)
    Enos Cabell, NL:LA Oct. 9, 1985 (4th)
    Mark McGwire, AL:Oak. Oct. 4, 1989 (3rd)
    Will Clark, NL:StL. Oct. 12, 2000 (9th)
    Mike Lamb, NL:Hou. Oct. 17, 2005 (7th)

Most Chances Accepted
343 John Olerud, AL:Tor.-Sea.-NY; NL:NY
283 Tino Martinez, AL:Sea.-NY
264 Albert Pujols, NL:StL.

Most Chances Accepted, Game
18 Steve Garvey, NL:LA Oct. 6, 1978
16 Steve Balboni, AL:KC Oct. 12, 1985
    Kevin Millar, AL:Bos. Oct. 9, 2003
    Extra-Inning Game:
27 Keith Hernandez, NL:NY Oct. 15, 1986 (16 inn)
17 Kendry Morales, AL:LA Oct. 17, 2009 (13 inn)

Most Chances Accepted, Inning
4 Enos Cabell, NL:LA Oct. 9, 1985 (4th)

Most Putouts
313 John Olerud, AL:Tor.-Sea.-NY; NL:NY
256 Tino Martinez, AL:Sea.-NY
246 Albert Pujols, NL:StL.

Most Putouts, Game
17 Andres Galarraga, NL:Atl. Oct. 14, 1998
    Albert Pujols, NL:StL. Oct. 12, 2005
15 Chris Chambliss, AL:NY Oct. 14, 1976
    Mark McGwire, AL:Oak. Oct. 4, 1989
    Extra-Inning Game:
21 Glenn Davis, NL:Hou. Oct. 15, 1986 (16 inn)
16 John Olerud, AL:Tor. Oct. 11, 1991 (10 inn)
    Herbert Perry, AL:Clev. Oct. 13, 1995 (11 inn)

Most Assists
33 Tino Martinez, AL:Sea.-NY; NL:StL.
27 Tino Martinez, AL:Sea.-NY
18 Albert Pujols, NL:StL.

Most Assists, Game
5 Tino Martinez, NL:StL. Oct. 12, 2002
4 Steve Balboni, AL:KC Oct. 12, 1985
    Kevin Millar, AL:Bos. Oct. 9, 2003
    Extra-Inning Game:
7 Keith Hernandez, NL:NY Oct. 15, 1986 (16 inn)

Most Assists, Inning
2 By many

Most Errors
4 Andres Galarraga, NL:Atl.
3 Cecil Cooper, AL:Bos.-Mil.
    Eddie Murray, AL:Balt.
    Steve Balboni, AL:KC

Most Errors, Game
2 Paul Sorrento, AL:Clev. Oct. 15, 1995
    DJ LeMahieu, AL:NY Oct. 17, 2019
    Andres Galarraga, NL:Atl. Oct. 7, 1998 (10 inn)
    Ryan Klesko, NL:Atl. Oct. 17, 1999 (15 inn)

Most Errors, Inning
2 Paul Sorrento, AL:Clev. Oct. 15, 1995 (7th)
    Andres Galarraga, NL:Atl. Oct. 7, 1998 (8th)
    Ryan Klesko, NL:Atl. Oct. 17, 1999 (6th)

Most Double Plays
31 John Olerud, AL:Tor.-Sea.-NY; NL:NY
27 Tino Martinez, AL:Sea.-NY
21 Steve Garvey, NL:LA-SD

Most Double Plays, Game
4 Will Clark, NL:SF Oct. 10, 1987
    Ji-Man Choi, AL:TB Oct. 14, 2020
    Extra-Inning Game:
5 Fred McGriff, NL:Atl. Oct. 10, 1995 (11 inn)

Double Plays, Unassisted
1 Tino Martinez, AL:NY Oct. 11, 1996 (5th)
    Tino Martinez, AL:NY Oct. 22, 2001 (4th)
    Kevin Millar, AL:Bos. Oct. 13, 2003 (1st)
    John Olerud, AL:NY Oct. 16, 2004 (4th)
    Yuli Gurriel, AL:Hou. Oct. 12, 2019 (2nd)
    John Mabry, NL:StL. Oct. 14, 1996 (2nd)
    Will Clark, NL:StL. Oct. 14, 2000 (4th)
    Tony Clark, NL:Ari. Oct. 12, 2007 (1st)
    Aubrey Huff, NL:SF Oct. 21, 2010 (7th)

SECOND BASEMEN – FIELDING

	3 Games	4 Games	5 Games	6 Games	7 Games
Highest Percentage 1.000 (Most Chances)					
AL:	25 Randolph NY 1981	23 Cruz Chi. 1983	30 Iguchi Chi. 2005	39 Pedroia Bos. 2013	40 Barrett Bos. 1986
NL:	23 Helms Cin. 1970 Morgan Cin. 1979	29 Lemke Atl. 1995	40 Morgan Cin. 1973	38 Lind Pitt. 1990	46 Valentin NY 2006
Games					
AL:	3 By many	4 By many	5 By many	6 By many	7 By many
NL:	3 By many	4 By many	5 By many	6 By many	7 By many
Total Chances					
AL:	25 Randolph NY 1981	26 Grich Balt. 1974	42 Alomar Balt. 1996	41 Cora Chi. 1993	40 Barrett Bos. 1986
NL:	23 Helms Cin. 1970	29 Lemke Atl. 1995	44 Trillo Phil. 1980	38 Lind Pitt. 1990	46 Valentin NY 2006
Chances Accepted					
AL:	25 Randolph NY 1981	25 Grich Balt. 1974	40 Alomar Balt. 1996	38 Cora Chi. 1993	40 Barrett Bos. 1986
NL:	23 Helms Cin. 1970	29 Lemke Atl. 1995	43 Trillo Phil. 1980	38 Lind Pitt. 1990	46 Valentin NY 2006
Putouts					
AL:	12 Randolph NY 1981	13 Grich Balt. 1974 Jimenez Oak. 2006	16 Grich Balt. 1973 Alomar Balt. 1996 Offerman Bos. 1999	18 Cora Chi. 1993	19 Barrett Bos. 1986 Cabrera Clev. 2007
NL:	12 Morgan Cin. 1979	13 Lemke Atl. 1995	18 Trillo Phil. 1980	19 Lind Pitt. 1990	20 Grudzielanek Chi. 2003
Assists					
AL:	13 Randolph NY 1981	14 Cruz Chi. 1983	25 Alomar Balt. 1996	24 Pedroia Bos. 2013	28 White KC 1985
NL:	12 Helms Cin. 1970	18 Lopes LA 1974	28 Morgan Cin. 1973	21 Sax LA 1985	31 Valentin NY 2006
Errors					
AL:	1 By many	2 Green Oak. 1974 Jimenez Oak. 2006	2 Green Oak. 1973 Alomar Balt. 1996 Offerman Bos. 1999	3 Cora Chi. 1993	3 Altuve Hou. 2020
NL:	1 By many	2 Sizemore Phil. 1977 Lopes LA 1978	2 Giles Atl. 2001 Utley Phil. 2009	3 Weeks Mil. 2011	2 Backman NY 1988 Lind Pitt. 1992 Grudzielanek Chi. 2003 Belliard StL. 2006
Double Plays					
AL:	4 Randolph NY 1981	6 Polanco Det. 2006	7 Alomar Balt. 1996	9 Pedroia Bos. 2013	10 Cabrera Clev. 2007
NL:	3 Cash Pitt. 1970	6 Matsui Col. 2007	7 Scott Mtl. 1981 Utley Phil. 2008	6 Alfonzo NY 1999 Weeks Mil. 2011	9 Valentin NY 2006

SECOND BASEMEN

Most Series
7   Joe Morgan, NL:Cin. 1972-73, 75-76, 79; Hou. 80; Phil. 83
6   Frank White, AL:KC 1976-78, 80, 84-85

Most Games
31   Mark Lemke, NL:Atl.
28   Roberto Alomar, AL:Tor.-Balt.

Highest Percentage (Most Chances)
1.000   Joe Morgan, NL:Cin.-Hou.-Phil. (148 tc)
       Dustin Pedroia, AL:Bos. (105 tc)

Most Total Chances
158   Roberto Alomar, AL:Tor.-Balt.
148   Joe Morgan, NL:Cin.-Hou.-Phil.

Most Total Chances, Game
13   Bobby Grich, AL:Balt. Oct. 6, 1974
       Roberto Alomar, AL:Tor. Oct. 11, 1992 (11 inn)
       Asdrubal Cabrera, AL:Clev. Oct. 13, 2007 (11 inn)
       Manny Trillo, NL:Phil. Oct. 7, 1980

Most Total Chances, Inning
4   Dick Green, AL:Oak. Oct. 9, 1973 (7th)
      Rodney Scott, NL:Mtl. Oct. 16, 1981 (2nd)

Most Chances Accepted
154   Roberto Alomar, AL:Tor.-Balt.
148   Joe Morgan, NL:Cin.-Hou.-Phil.

Most Chances Accepted, Game
13   Manny Trillo, NL:Phil. Oct. 7, 1980
12   Bobby Grich, AL:Balt. Oct. 6, 1974
       Willie Randolph, AL:NY Oct. 13, 1981
Extra-Inning Game:
13   Roberto Alomar, AL:Tor. Oct. 11, 1992 (11 inn)
       Asdrubal Cabrera, AL:Clev. Oct. 13, 2007 (11 inn)

Most Chances Accepted, Inning
3   By many

Most Putouts
69   Roberto Alomar, AL:Tor.-Balt.
62   Joe Morgan, NL:Cin.-Hou.-Phil.

Most Putouts, Game
10   Brock Holt, AL:Bos. Oct. 13, 2018
6   Dave Cash, NL:Phil. Oct. 12, 1976
      Davey Lopes, NL:LA Oct. 13, 1981
      Jose Lind, NL:Pitt. Oct. 12, 1990
      Chase Utley, NL:Phil. Oct. 15, 2009
Extra-Inning Game:
7   Steve Sax, NL:LA Oct. 9, 1988 (12 inn)

Most Putouts, Inning
3   Dick Green, AL:Oak. Oct. 8, 1974 (7th)
      Joe Morgan, NL:Cin. Oct. 10, 1976 (8th)
      Ryne Sandberg, NL:Chi. Oct. 4, 1984 (5th)

Most Assists
86   Joe Morgan, NL:Cin.-Hou.-Phil.
85   Roberto Alomar, AL:Tor.-Balt.

Most Assists, Game
9   Joey Cora, AL:Chi. Oct. 6, 1993
      Wally Backman, NL:NY Oct. 14, 1986 (12 inn)
      Jose Valentin, NL:NY Oct. 13, 2006

Most Assists, Inning
3   Tony Phillips, AL:Oak. Oct. 4, 1989 (5th)
      Joey Cora, AL:Chi. Oct. 6, 1993 (6th)
      Jason Kipnis, AL:Clev. Oct 15, 2016 (1st)
      Mark Lemke, NL:Atl. Oct. 13, 1993 (1st)
      Edgardo Alfonzo, NL:NY Oct. 11, 2000 (1st)
      Jose Valentin, NL:NY Oct. 13, 2006 (9th)

Most Errors
4   Dick Green, AL:Oak.
      Bobby Grich, AL:Balt.-Cal.
      Joey Cora, AL:Chi.-Sea.
      Roberto Alomar, AL:Tor.-Balt.
      Jose Altuve, AL:Hou.
      Davey Lopes, NL:LA
      Chase Utley, NL: Phil.-LA

Most Errors, Game
2   Dick Green, AL:Oak. Oct. 9, 1973 (11 inn)
      Dick Green, AL:Oak. Oct. 8, 1974
      Lance Blankenship, AL:Oak. Oct. 10, 1992
      Robinson Cano, AL:NY Oct. 17, 2009 (13 inn)
      Starlin Castro, AL:NY Oct. 17, 2017
      Gleyber Torres, AL:NY Oct. 17, 2019
      Jose Altuve, AL:Hou. Oct. 12, 2020
1   By many in NL

Most Errors, Inning
1   By many

Most Double Plays
20   Roberto Alomar, AL:Tor.-Balt.
14   Joe Morgan, NL:Cin.-Hou.-Phil.
      Mark Lemke, NL:Atl.

Most Double Plays, Game
4   Davey Lopes, NL:LA Oct. 13, 1981
3   Rob Wilfong, AL:Cal. Oct. 14, 1986
      Bip Roberts, AL:Clev. Oct. 11, 1997 (12 inn)
      Alfonso Soriano, AL:NY Oct. 13, 2003
      Placido Polanco, AL:Det. Oct. 10, 2006
      Asdrubal Cabrera, AL:Clev. Oct. 13, 2007 (11 inn)
      Asdrubal Cabrera, AL:Clev. Oct. 21, 2007

Double Plays, Unassisted
1   Joe Morgan, NL:Cin. Oct. 10, 1976 (8th)
      Chase Utley, NL:Phil. Oct. 13, 2008 (6th)

THIRD BASEMEN — FIELDING

	3 Games	4 Games	5 Games	6 Games	7 Games
Highest Percentage 1.000 (Most Chances)					
AL:	16 B Robinson Balt. 1969	19 Cruz Balt. 1983	22 Bando Oak. 1972	22 Inge Det. 2011	26 Youkilis Bos. 2008
NL:	8 Madlock Pitt. 1979	19 Schmidt Phil. 1977	17 Williams SF 1989	21 Ventura NY 1999 / Turner LA 2016	23 Rolen StL 2004
Games					
AL:	3 By many	4 By many	5 By many	6 By many	7 By many
NL:	3 By many	4 By many	5 By many	6 By many	7 By many
Total Chances					
AL:	16 B. Robinson Balt. 1969	19 Cruz Balt. 1983	24 DeCinces Cal. 1982	26 Williams Clev. 1997	26 DeCinces Cal. 1986 / Youkilis Bos. 2008
NL:	14 Schmidt Phil. 1976	23 Schmidt Phil. 1978	22 Cey LA 1981	25 Pendleton StL 1985 / Knight NY 1986	31 King Pitt. 1992
Chances Accepted					
AL:	16 B. Robinson Balt. 1969	19 Cruz Balt. 1983	22 Bando Oak. 1972 / Bregman Hou. 2018	24 Williams Clev. 1997	24 DeCinces Cal. 1986
NL:	13 Schmidt Phil. 1976	21 Cey LA 1977 / Schmidt Phil. 1978	21 Cey LA 1981	24 Pendleton StL 1985 / Knight NY 1986	30 King Pitt. 1992
Putouts					
AL:	6 By many	7 Lansford Oak. 1988 / Cey LA 1977	9 Decinces Cal. 1982	7 Bregman Hou. 2019	12 Youkilis Bos. 2008
NL:	5 Perez Cin. 1970	7 Cey LA 1977	5 By many	7 Sabo Cin. 1990 / Pendleton Atl. 1993 / Polanco Phil. 2010 / Turner LA 2016	11 King Pitt. 1992
Assists					
AL:	10 B. Robinson Balt. 1969 / Bando Oak. 1975	13 Robinson Balt. 1974 / Cruz Balt. 1983	20 Bregman Hou. 2018	18 Williams Clev. 1997	18 DeCinces Cal. 1986 / Bregman Hou. 2017
NL:	9 Schmidt Phil. 1976	18 Schmidt Phil. 1978	17 Schmidt Phil. 1978	19 Knight NY 1986	19 King Pitt. 1992 / Turner LA 2018
Errors					
AL:	1 By many	1 By many	3 Brett KC 1976 / DeCinces Cal. 1982 / Gruber Tor. 1991	2 Williams Clev. 1997	3 Longoria TB 2008
NL:	1 By many	2 Cey LA 1974 / Schmidt Phil. 1978	3 Williams Ari. 2001	3 Hairston Jr. Mil. 2011	2 Hamilton LA 1988 / Rolen StL 2006 / Sandoval SF 2012
Double Plays					
AL:	2 Bando Oak. 1971 / Nettles NY 1981	3 Lansford Cal. 1979	3 DeCinces Cal. 1982	4 Beltre Tex. 2011	3 DeCinces Cal. 1986
NL:	2 Schmidt Phil. 1976	2 Jones Atl. 1995 / Atkins Col. 2007	3 Parrish Mtl. 1981 / Sandoval SF 2014	4 Ventura NY 1999	5 King Pitt. 1992

THIRD BASEMEN

Most Series
6 Graig Nettles, AL:NY 1976-78, 80-81; NL:SD 84
George Brett, AL:KC 1976-78, 80, 84-85
Terry Pendleton, NL:StL. 1985, 87; Atl. 91-93, 96
Chipper Jones, NL:Atl. 1995-99, 2001

Most Games
34 Terry Pendleton, NL:StL.-Atl.
Chipper Jones, NL:Atl.
27 George Brett, AL:KC

Highest Percentage (Minimum: 40 chances)
.989 Terry Pendleton, NL:StL.-Atl. (90 tc)
.986 Sal Bando, AL:Oak. (73 tc)

Most Total Chances
91 Mike Schmidt, NL:Phil.
79 George Brett, AL:KC
Alex Bregman, AL:Hou.

Most Total Chances, Game
10 Ron Cey, NL:LA Oct. 16, 1981
9 Todd Cruz, AL:Balt. Oct. 5, 1983
Wade Boggs, AL:Bos. Oct. 10, 1990

Most Total Chances, Inning
3 By many

Most Chances Accepted
89 Terry Pendleton, NL:StL.-Atl.
76 Alex Bregman, AL:Hou.

Most Chances Accepted, Game
10 Ron Cey, NL:LA Oct. 16, 1981
9 Todd Cruz, AL:Balt. Oct. 5, 1983
Wade Boggs, AL:Bos. Oct. 10, 1990

Most Chances Accepted, Inning
3 Denis Menke, NL:Cin. Oct. 11, 1972 (9th)
Ron Cey, NL:LA Oct. 4, 1977 (4th)
Ron Cey, NL:LA Oct. 16, 1981 (8th)
Jeff King, NL:Pitt. Oct. 6, 1992 (1st)
Gary Gaetti, NL:StL. Oct. 17, 1996 (1st)
Miguel Cairo, NL:StL. Oct. 14, 2002 (6th)
David Wright, NL:NY Oct. 12, 2006 (3rd)
Justin Turner, NL:LA Oct. 18, 2020 (4th)
Todd Cruz, AL:Balt. Oct. 5, 1983 (5th)
Mike Lowell, AL:Bos. Oct. 21, 2007 (2nd)
Alex Bregman, AL:Hou. Oct. 14, 2020 (3rd)

Most Putouts
25 Sal Bando, AL:Oak.
Terry Pendleton, NL:StL.-Atl.

Most Putouts, Game
4 Carney Lansford, AL:Cal. Oct. 6, 1979
Wade Boggs, AL:Bos. Oct. 10, 1990
Mike Lowell, AL:Bos. Oct. 13, 2007 (11 inn)
Kevin Youkilis, AL:Bos. Oct. 18, 2008
3 By many in NL

Most Putouts, Inning
2 By many

Most Assists
66 Mike Schmidt, NL:Phil.
59 Alex Bregman, AL:Hou.

Most Assists, Game
8 Ron Cey, NL:LA Oct. 16, 1981
7 Aurelio Rodriguez, AL:Det. Oct. 11, 1972 (11 inn)
Alex Bregman, AL:Hou. Oct. 13, 2018

Most Assists, Inning
3 Ron Cey, NL:LA Oct. 4, 1977 (4th)
Ron Cey, NL:LA Oct. 16, 1981 (8th)
Todd Cruz, AL:Balt. Oct. 5, 1983 (5th)

Most Errors
8 George Brett, AL:KC
5 Mike Schmidt, NL:Phil.

Most Errors, Game
2 Ron Cey, NL:LA Oct. 5, 1974
Fernando Tatis, NL:StL. Oct. 15, 2000
Jerry Hairston Jr., NL:Mil. Oct. 16, 2011
George Brett, AL:KC Oct. 9, 1976
Doug DeCinces, AL:Cal. Oct. 9, 1982
Darrell Evans, AL:Det. Oct. 11, 1987
Kelly Gruber, AL:Tor. Oct. 8, 1991
Evan Longoria, AL:TB Oct. 14, 2008

Most Errors, Inning
2 George Brett, AL:KC Oct. 9, 1976 (1st)
Evan Longoria, AL:TB Oct. 14, 2008 (2nd)
Fernando Tatis, NL:StL. Oct. 15, 2000 (6th)
Jerry Hairston Jr., NL:Mil. Oct. 16, 2011 (5th)

Most Double Plays
8 Terry Pendleton, NL:StL.-Atl.
7 Doug DeCinces, AL:Balt.-Cal.
Carney Lansford, AL:Cal.-Oak.

Most Double Plays, Game
2 Mike Schmidt, NL:Phil. Oct. 9, 1976
Mike Schmidt, NL:Phil. Oct. 11, 1980 (10 inn)
Larry Parrish, NL:Mtl. Oct. 16, 1981
Jeff King, NL:Pitt. Oct. 9, 1992
Jeff King, NL:Pitt. Oct. 10, 1992
Robin Ventura, NL:NY Oct. 17, 1999 (15 inn)
Garrett Atkins, NL:Col. Oct. 11, 2007
Pablo Sandoval, NL:SF Oct. 15, 2014
Kris Bryant, NL:Chi. Oct. 16, 2016
Mike Moustakas, NL:Mil. Oct. 13, 2018
Justin Turner, NL:LA Oct. 16, 2020
Doug DeCinces, AL:Cal. Oct. 14, 1986
Adrian Beltre, AL:Tex. Oct. 8, 2011

Double Plays, Unassisted
1 Mike Schmidt, NL:Phil. Oct. 9, 1976 (5th)
Jeff King, NL:Pitt. Oct. 14, 1992 (6th)

SHORTSTOP – FIELDING

	3 Games	4 Games	5 Games	6 Games	7 Games
Highest Percentage 1.000 (Most Chances)					
AL:	21 Dent NY 1980	20 Campaneris Oak. 1974	31 Patek KC 1976	36 Aybar LA 2009	44 Jeter NY 2003
NL:	17 Concepcion Cin. 1979	29 Russell LA 1974	26 Harrelson NY 1973 Peralta StL. 2014	31 Santana NY 1986 Ordonez NY 1999	40 Eckstein StL. 2006
Games					
AL:	3 By many	4 By many	5 By many	6 By many	7 By many
NL:	3 By many	4 By many	5 By many	6 By many	7 By many
Total Chances					
AL:	26 Cardenas Minn. 1969	24 Garcia Balt. 1979	34 Uribe Chi. 2005	38 Vizquel Clev. 1998	45 Jeter NY 2004
NL:	18 RamirezAtl. 1982	29 Russell LA 1974	33 Speier Mtl. 1981	37 Larkin Cin. 1990	40 Eckstein StL. 2006
Chances Accepted					
AL:	25 Cardenas Minn. 1969	22 Garcia Balt. 1979	33 Uribe Chi. 2005	37 Vizquel Clev. 1998	44 Jeter NY 2003
NL:	17 Concepcion Cin. 1979	29 Russell LA 1974	31 Speier Mtl. 1981	36 Larkin Cin. 1990	40 Eckstein StL. 2006
Putouts					
AL:	13 Cardenas Minn. 1969	9 Patek KC 1978	13 Patek KC 1976	19 Aybar LA 2009	23 Jeter NY 2004
NL:	16 By many	13 Russell LA 1974	19 Templeton SD 1984	21 Larkin Cin. 1990	19 Renteria StL. 2004 Eckstein StL. 2006
Assists					
AL:	14 Belanger Balt. 1970	17 Campaneris Oak. 1974	26 Uribe Chi. 2005	26 Vizquel Clev. 1998	25 Jeter NY 2003
NL:	14 Concepcion Cin. 1979	17 Bowa Phil. 1977	17 Rollins Phil. 2008	24 Ordonez NY 1999	26 Gonzalez Fla. 2003
Errors					
AL:	2 Cardenas Minn. 1970	2 Patek KC 1978 Garcia Balt. 1979	4 Garciaparra Bos. 1999	3 Lee Tor. 1992	5 Owen Bos. 1986
NL:	1 By many	2 Russell LA 1977 DeJesus Phil. 1983	4 Furcal LA 2008	2 Reynolds Hou. 1986	2 Elster NY 1988 Blauser Atl. 1992 Kozma StL. 2012
Double Plays					
AL:	3 By many	3 Ripken Balt. 1983 Weiss Oak. 1988 Rivera Bos. 1990 Santiago Det. 2006 Guillen Det. 2006 Escobar KC 2014 Hardy Balt. 2014	5 Ripken Balt. 1996 Jeter NY 1999	8 Vizquel Clev. 1997	11 Peralta Clev. 2007
NL:	3 Garrido Atl. 1969 Alley Pitt. 1970	6 Russell LA 1974	7 Rollins Phil. 2008	5 Betancourt Mil. 2011 Kozma StL. 2013 Russell Chi. 2016	7 Uribe SF 1987 Griffin LA 1988

SHORTSTOPS

Most Series
10 Derek Jeter, AL:NY 1996, 98-2001, 03-04, 09-10, 12
6 Jeff Blauser, NL:Atl. 1991-93, 95-97

Most Games
54 Derek Jeter, AL:NY
29 Jeff Blauser, NL:Atl.

Highest Percentage (Most Chances)
1.000 Jhonny Peralta, AL:Clev.-Det.; NL:StL. (106 tc)
Jhonny Peralta, AL:Clev.-Det. (80 tc)
Brandon Crawford, NL:SF (49 tc)
Addison Russell, NL:Chi. (49 tc)

Most Total Chances
252 Derek Jeter, AL:NY
109 Bill Russell, NL:LA

Most Total Chances, Game
13 Bill Russell, NL:LA Oct. 8, 1974
11 Kiko Garcia, AL:Balt. Oct. 4, 1979
Omar Vizquel, AL:Clev. Oct. 9, 1998
Extra-Inning Game:
12 Leo Cardenas, AL:Minn. Oct. 5, 1969 (11 inn)

Most Total Chances, Inning
4 Rafael Furcal, NL:LA Oct. 15, 2008 (5th)
Pete Kozma, NL:StL. Oct. 22, 2012 (7th)
Addison Russsell, NL:Chi. Oct 16, 2016 (6th)
3 By many in AL

Most Chances Accepted
239 Derek Jeter, AL:NY
106 Bill Russell, NL:LA

Most Chances Accepted, Game
13 Bill Russell, NL:LA Oct. 8, 1974
11 Leo Cardenas, AL:Minn. Oct. 5, 1969 (11 inn)
Kiko Garcia, AL:Balt. Oct. 4, 1979
Omar Vizquel, AL:Clev. Oct. 9, 1998
Erick Aybar, AL:LA Oct. 17, 2009 (13 inn)

Most Chances Accepted, Inning
4 Addison Russell, NL:Chi. Oct 16, 2016 (6th)
3 By many in AL

Most Putouts
105 Derek Jeter, AL:NY
48 Edgar Renteria, NL:Fla.-StL.-SF

Most Putouts, Game
7 Garry Templeton, NL:SD Oct. 4, 1984
6 By many in AL

Most Putouts, Inning
3 Mark Belanger, AL:Balt. Oct. 5, 1974 (3rd)
Freddie Patek, AL:KC Oct. 5, 1977 (2nd)
Omar Vizquel, AL:Clev. Oct. 15, 1995 (8th)
Derek Jeter, AL:NY Oct. 19, 2004 (9th)
Chris Speier, NL:Mtl. Oct. 14, 1981 (5th)

Most Assists
142 Derek Jeter, AL:NY
70 Larry Bowa, NL:Phil.-Chi.

Most Assists, Game
9 Bill Russell, NL:LA Oct. 5, 1978
Kiko Garcia, AL:Balt. Oct. 4, 1979

Most Assists, Inning
3 Mark Belanger, AL:Balt. Oct. 7, 1973 (7th)
Walt Weiss, AL:Oak. Oct. 8, 1989 (1st)
Manuel Lee, AL:Tor. Oct. 13, 1991 (5th)
Omar Vizquel, AL:Clev. Oct. 10, 1995 (2nd)
Dave Concepcion, NL:Cin. Oct. 3, 1979 (4th)
Barry Larkin, NL:Cin. Oct. 10, 1990 (6th)
Jeff Blauser, NL:Atl. Oct. 13, 1993 (7th)
Alex Gonzalez, NL:Chi. Oct. 12, 2003 (3rd)
Jimmy Rollins, NL:Phil. Oct. 20, 2010 (3rd)

Most Errors
5 Spike Owen, AL:Bos.
Nomar Garciaparra, AL:Bos.
Derek Jeter, AL:NY
Jeff Blauser, NL:Atl.

Most Errors, Game
3 Rafael Furcal, NL:LA Oct. 15, 2008
2 Leo Cardenas, AL:Minn. Oct. 4, 1970
Manuel Lee, AL:Tor. Oct. 11, 1992 (11 inn)
Nomar Garciaparra, AL:Bos. Oct. 13, 1999 (10 inn)

Most Errors, Inning
3 Rafael Furcal, NL:LA Oct. 15, 2008 (5th)
1 By many in AL

Most Double Plays
40 Derek Jeter, AL:NY
18 Bill Russell, NL:LA

Most Double Plays, Game
4 Willy Adames, AL:TB Oct. 14, 2020
3 Bill Russell, NL:LA Oct. 8, 1974
Bill Russell, NL:LA Oct. 5, 1983
Jose Uribe, NL:SF Oct. 10, 1987
Ozzie Smith, NL:StL. Oct. 14, 1987
Jeff Blauser, NL:Atl. Oct. 10, 1995 (11 inn)
Jose Reyes, NL:NY Oct. 15, 2006
Yuniesky Betancourt, NL:Mil. Oct. 12, 2011

Double Plays, Unassisted
1 Bill Russell, NL:LA Oct. 8, 1974 (6th)
Alfredo Griffin, NL:LA Oct. 5, 1988 (1st)
Walt Weiss, NL:Atl. Oct. 19, 1999 (6th)
Robin Yount, AL:Mil. Oct. 5, 1982 (4th)
Buddy Biancalana, AL:KC Oct. 12, 1985 (6th)
Tony Fernandez, AL:Tor. Oct. 4, 1989 (1st)
Omar Vizquel, AL:Clev. Oct. 15, 1995 (8th)
Willy Adames, AL:TB Oct. 11, 2020 (4th)

OUTFIELDERS – FIELDING

	3 Games	4 Games	5 Games	6 Games	7 Games
Highest Percentage 1.000 (Most Chances)					
AL:	12 Oliva Minn. 1970	16 Miller Cal. 1979	22 D. Henderson Oak. 1989	20 Swisher NY 2009 / Pillar Tor. 2015	26 Hicks NY 2017
NL:	14 Parker Pitt. 1975	13 Stargell Pitt. 1974	23 Maddox Phil. 1980	25 Jay StL 2011	27 Lofton Chi. 2003
Games					
AL:	3 By many	4 By many	5 By many	6 By many	7 By many
NL:	3 By many	4 By many	5 By many	6 By many	7 By many
Total Chances					
AL:	14 Lynn Bos. 1975	16 Miller Cal. 1979	22 D. Henderson Oak. 1989	23 Springer Hou. 2019	34 Upton TB 2008
NL:	14 Parker Pitt. 1975	17 Maddox Phil. 1978	23 Maddox Phil. 1980	25 Jay StL 2011	27 Lofton Chi. 2003
Chances Accepted					
AL:	13 Lynn Bos. 1975	16 Miller Cal. 1979	22 D. Henderson Oak. 1989	22 Springer Hou. 2019	33 Upton TB 2008
NL:	14 Parker Pitt. 1975	16 Maddox Phil. 1978	23 Maddox Phil. 1980	25 Jay StL 2011	27 Lofton Chi. 2003
Putouts					
AL:	12 Lynn Bos. 1975	15 Jackson Det. 2012 / Cain KC 2014	22 D. Henderson Oak. 1989	22 Springer Hou. 2019	33 Upton TB 2008
NL:	13 Parker Pitt. 1975 / Geronimo Cin. 1975	16 Maddox Phil. 1978	23 Maddox Phil. 1980	25 Jay StL 2011	26 Lofton Chi. 2003 / Pache Atl. 2020
Assists					
AL:	2 By many	2 Miller Cal. 1979	2 Betts Bos. 2018	2 Raines Chi. 1993	3 Smith KC 1985
NL:	2 Foster Cin. 1979	2 McBride Phil. 1977	3 McBride Phil. 1980	3 Mora NY 1999	3 Justice Atl. 1992
Errors					
AL:	2 Oliva Minn. 1969 / Washington Oak. 1975	2 D. Henderson Oak. 1988	2 Gamble NY 1976 / Oglivie Mil. 1982	3 R. Henderson Oak. 1992	2 Barfield Tor. 1985 / Smith KC 1985
NL:	1 By many	1 By many	1 By many	2 Lofton Atl. 1997 / Puig LA 2013 / Toles LA 2016	1 By many
Double Plays					
AL:	1 By many	2 Miller Cal. 1979	1 O'Neill NY 1996 / Guerrero LA 2005 / Anderson LA 2005	1 Carter & Maldonado Tor. 1992 / Swisher NY 2009 / Hunter LA 2009 / Francoeur & Hamilton Tex. 2010 / Cruz Tex. 2011 / Brantley Hou. 2019 / Judge NY 2019	0
NL:	1 Parker Pitt. 1975	1 McBride Phil. 1977	2 McBride Phil. 1980	1 By many	1 By many

OUTFIELDERS

Most Series
10 Reggie Jackson, AL:Oak. 1971-75;
NY 77-78, 80-81; Cal. 82
5 Cesar Geronimo, NL:Cin. 1972-73, 75-76, 79
Garry Maddox, NL:Phil. 1976-78, 80, 83
Ron Gant, NL:Atl. 1991-93; Cin. 95; StL. 96
Andruw Jones, NL:Atl. 1996-99, 2001
Reggie Sanders, NL:Cin. 1995; Ari. 2001;
SF 02; StL. 04-05
Jim Edmonds, NL:StL. 2000, 02, 04-06
Matt Holliday, NL:Col. 2007, StL. 11-14
Jon Jay, NL:StL. 2011-14; Chi. 17

Most Games
49 Manny Ramirez, AL:Clev.-Bos.; NL:LA
41 Bernie Williams, AL:NY
31 Ron Gant, NL:Atl.-Cin.-StL.

Highest Percentage (Most chances)
1.000 Paul O'Neill, NL:Cin; AL:NY (64 tc)
Andruw Jones, NL:Atl. (63 tc)
Paul O'Neill, AL:NY (53 tc)

Most Total Chances
106 Bernie Williams, AL:NY
83 Jim Edmonds, NL:StL.

Most Total Chances, Game
9 Jesse Barfield, AL:Tor. Oct. 11, 1985
Gary Pettis, AL:Cal. Oct. 10, 1986
Darin Erstad, AL:Ana. Oct. 13, 2002
B.J. Upton, AL:TB Oct. 11, 2008 (11 inn)
8 Al Oliver, NL:Pitt. Oct. 7, 1972
Don Hahn, NL:NY Oct. 8, 1973
Brian Jordan, NL:Atl. Oct. 21, 2001
Michael Taylor, NL:Wash. Oct. 11, 2019

Most Total Chances, Inning
3 By many

Most Chances Accepted
105 Bernie Williams, AL:NY
80 Jim Edmonds, NL:StL.

Most Chances Accepted, Game
9 Jesse Barfield, AL:Tor. Oct. 11, 1985
Gary Pettis, AL:Cal. Oct. 10, 1986
Darin Erstad, AL:Ana. Oct. 13, 2002
B.J. Upton, AL:TB Oct. 11, 2008 (11 inn)
8 Al Oliver, NL:Pitt. Oct. 7, 1972
Don Hahn, NL:NY Oct. 8, 1973
Brian Jordan, NL:Atl. Oct. 21, 2001
Michael Taylor, NL:Wash. Oct. 11, 2019

Most Chances Accepted, Inning
3 By many

Most Putouts
103 Bernie Williams, AL:NY
79 Jim Edmonds, NL:StL.

Most Putouts, Game
9 Jesse Barfield, AL:Tor. Oct. 11, 1985
Gary Pettis, AL:Cal. Oct. 10, 1986
Darin Erstad, AL:Ana. Oct. 13, 2002
B.J. Upton, AL:TB Oct. 11, 2008 (11 inn)
8 Al Oliver, NL:Pitt. Oct. 7, 1972
Don Hahn, NL:NY Oct. 8, 1973
Brian Jordan, NL:Atl. Oct. 21, 2001
Michael Taylor, NL:Wash. Oct. 11, 2019

Most Putouts, Inning
3 By many

Most Assists
6 Lonnie Smith, NL:Phil.-StL.-Atl.; AL:KC
5 Bake McBride, NL:Phil.
4 Reggie Jackson, AL:Oak.-NY-Cal.

Most Assists, Game
2 Tony Oliva, AL:Minn. Oct. 4, 1970
Rickey Henderson, NL:NY Oct. 15, 1999
George Foster, NL:Cin. Oct. 3, 1979 (10 inn)
Bake McBride, NL:Phil. Oct. 11, 1980 (10 inn)
Wes Chamberlain, NL:Phil. Oct. 11, 1993 (10 inn)

Most Assists, Inning
1 By many

Most Errors
7 Rickey Henderson, AL:Oak.-Tor.; NL:NY
6 Rickey Henderson, AL:Oak.-Tor.
3 Jim Edmonds, NL:StL.

Most Errors, Game
2 Tony Oliva, AL:Minn. Oct. 6, 1969
Ben Oglivie, AL:Mil. Oct. 10, 1982
Albert Belle, AL:Chi. Oct. 15, 1995
Yasiel Puig, NL:LA Oct. 18, 2013

Most Errors, Inning
2 Albert Belle, AL:Clev. Oct. 15, 1995 (5th)
1 By many in NL

Most Double Plays
3 Bake McBride, NL:Phil.
2 Rick Miller, AL:Cal.
Nick Swisher, AL:NY

Most Double Plays, Game
1 By many
Extra-Inning Game:
2 Bake McBride, NL:Phil. Oct. 11, 1980 (10 inn)

Double Plays, Unassisted
None

CATCHERS – FIELDING

	3 Games	4 Games	5 Games	6 Games	7 Games
Highest Percentage 1.000 (Most Chances)					
AL:	25 Cerone NY 1981	39 Gedman Bos. 1988	51 Perez Clev. 2016	70 Avila Det. 2013	79 Maldonado Hou. 2020
NL:	28 Ott Pitt. 1979	47 Molina StL 2019	45 Contreras Chi. 2017	61 Ruiz Phil. 2010	63 Olson Atl. 1991
Games					
AL:	3 By many	4 By many	5 By many	6 By many	7 By many
NL:	3 By many	4 By many	5 By many	6 By many	7 By many
Total Chances					
AL:	25 Cerone NY 1981	39 Gedman Bos. 1988	51 Perez Clev. 2016	70 Avila Det. 2013	79 Maldonado Hou. 2020
NL:	31 Sanguillen Pitt. 1975	47 Molina StL 2019	45 Contreras Chi. 2017	60 Ashby Hou. 1986	63 Olson Atl. 1991
Chances Accepted					
AL:	25 Cerone NY 1981	39 Gedman Bos. 1988	51 Perez Clev. 2016	70 Avila Det. 2013	79 Maldonado Hou. 2020
NL:	30 Sanguillen Pitt. 1975	47 Molina StL 2019	45 Contreras Chi. 2017	61 Ruiz Phil. 2010	63 Olson Atl. 1991
Putouts					
AL:	23 Cerone NY 1981	34 Gedman Bos. 1988	51 Perez Clev. 2016	68 Avila Det. 2013	77 Maldonado Hou. 2020
NL:	29 Sanguillen Pitt. 1975	45 Molina StL 2019	42 Grote NY 1973 Contreras Chi. 2017	59 Ashby Hou. 1986 Ruiz Phil. 2010	62 Olson Atl. 1991
Assists					
AL:	4 Mitterwald Minn. 1969 Cerone NY 1980	5 Gedman Bos. 1988 Dempsey Balt. 1983	7 B. Molina LA 2005	7 Steinbach Oak. 1992	6 Posada NY 2003
NL:	4 Bench Cin. 1975-76	3 Montero Chi. 2015	4 By many	7 Ausmus Hou. 2005	5 By many
Errors					
AL:	3 Slaught KC 1984	1 Dempsey Balt. 1983 Pena Bos. 1990 Joseph Balt. 2014	2 Munson NY 1976 Borders Tor. 1991 Pierzynski Minn. 2002	2 Webster Balt. 1997 Alomar Clev. 1998	1 Sundberg KC 1985 Romine NY 2017
NL:	1 Sanguillen Pitt. 1970, 75	2 Sanguillen Pitt. 1974	1 By many	3 Piazza NY 1999	2 Grandal LA 2018
Passed Balls					
AL:	1 Cerone NY 1981	1 By many	2 Borders Tor. 1991 Pierzynski Chi. 2005 Maldonado Hou. 2018	3 Borders Tor. 1992	5 Zunino TB 2020
NL:	2 Sanguillen Pitt. 1975	1 By many	1 By many	2 Ashby Hou. 1986 Daulton Phil. 1993	3 Grandal LA 2018
Double Plays					
AL:	2 Mitterwald Minn. 1970	1 By many	2 Fosse Oak. 1973	1 Borders Tor. 1992-93 Alomar Clev. 1997 Posada NY 2000 Avila Det. & Napoli Tex. 2011 Saltalamacchia Bos. 2013	3 Posada NY 2003
NL:	1 By many	1 By many	2 Kennedy SF 1989	2 Lopez Atl. 1997 Piazza NY 1999	2 Olson Atl. 1991 Smith LA 2020

CATCHERS

Most Series
8 Jorge Posada, AL:NY 1998-2001, 03-04, 09-10
   Yadier Molina, NL:StL. 2004-06, 11-14, 19

Most Games
45 Jorge Posada, AL:NY
39 Yadier Molina, NL:StL.

Highest Percentage (Most Chances)
1.000 Yadier Molina, NL:StL. (285 tc)
       Alex Avila, AL:Det. (140 tc)

Most Total Chances
347 Jorge Posada, AL:NY
285 Yadier Molina, NL:StL.

Most Total Chances, Game
17 Kurt Suzuki, NL:Wash. Oct. 14, 2019
16 Rick Dempsey, AL:Balt. Oct. 6, 1983
    Chris Hoiles, AL:Balt. Oct. 11, 1997 (12 inn)
    Jorge Posada, AL:NY Oct. 18, 2004 (14 inn)
    Alex Avila, AL:Det. Oct. 12, 2013
    Extra-Inning Game:
18 Mike Piazza, NL:NY Oct. 17, 1999 (15 inn)

Most Total Chances, Inning
4 Pat Borders, AL:Tor. Oct. 8, 1991 (3rd)
   Jorge Posada, AL:NY Oct. 16, 1999 (5th)
3 By many in NL

Most Chances Accepted
346 Jorge Posada, AL:NY
285 Yadier Molina, NL:StL.

Most Chances Accepted, Game
17 Kurt Suzuki, NL:Wash. Oct. 14, 2019
16 Rick Dempsey, AL:Balt. Oct. 6, 1983
    Chris Hoiles, AL:Balt. Oct. 11, 1997 (12 inn)
    Jorge Posada, AL:NY Oct. 18, 2004 (14 inn)
    Alex Avila, AL:Det. Oct. 12, 2013
    Extra-Inning Game:
18 Mike Piazza, NL:NY Oct. 17, 1999 (15 inn)

Most Chances Accepted, Inning
4 Pat Borders, AL:Tor. Oct. 8, 1991 (3rd)
3 By many in NL

Most Putouts
322 Jorge Posada, AL:NY
270 Yadier Molina, NL:StL.

Most Putouts, Game
17 Kurt Suzuki, NL:Wash. Oct. 14, 2019
16 Alex Avila, AL:Det. Oct. 12, 2013

Most Putouts, Inning
3 By many

Most Assists
24 Jorge Posada, AL:NY
18 Johnny Bench, NL:Cin.

Most Assists, Game
4 Bengie Molina, AL:LA Oct. 16, 2005
3 Johnny Bench, NL:Cin. Oct. 3, 1970 (10 inn)
   Johnny Bench, NL:Cin. Oct. 5, 1975
   Gary Carter, NL:NY Oct. 15, 1986 (16 inn)
   Mike Matheny, NL:StL. Oct. 12, 2002
   Brad Ausmus, NL:Hou. Oct. 17, 2005
   Hector Sanchez, NL:SF Oct. 18, 2012

Most Assists, Inning
3 Bengie Molina, AL:LA Oct. 16, 2005 (9th)
2 Johnny Bench, NL:Cin. Oct. 7, 1973 (8th)
   Mike Scioscia, NL:LA Oct. 10, 1985 (1st)
   Gary Carter, NL:NY Oct. 15, 1986 (12th)
   Raul Chavez, NL:Hou. Oct. 20, 2004 (10th)
   Yorvit Torrealba, NL:Col. Oct. 12, 2007 (3rd)

Most Errors
5 Manny Sanguillen, NL:Pitt.
3 Don Slaught, AL:KC
   Pat Borders, AL:Tor.
   Sandy Alomar Jr., AL:Clev.

Most Errors, Game
2 Manny Sanguillen, NL:Pitt. Oct. 6, 1974
   Mike Piazza, NL:NY Oct. 19, 1999 (11 inn)
   Yasmani Grandal, NL:LA Oct. 12, 2018
   Thurman Munson, AL:NY Oct. 10, 1976
   Don Slaught, AL:KC Oct. 5, 1984
   Sandy Alomar Jr., AL:Clev. Oct. 10, 1998

Most Errors, Inning
2 Yasmani Grandal, NL:LA Oct. 12, 2018 (3rd)
1 By many in AL

Most Passed Balls
6 Jason Varitek, AL:Bos.
4 Manny Sanguillen, NL:Pitt.
   Yasmani Grandal, NL:LA

Most Passed Balls, Game
2 Manny Sanguillen, NL:Pitt. Oct. 4, 1975
   Alan Ashby, NL:Hou. Oct. 11, 1986
   Don Slaught, NL:Pitt. Oct. 13, 1992
   Yasmani Grandal, NL:LA Oct. 12, 2018
   Pat Borders, AL:Tor. Oct. 13, 1991
   Pat Borders, AL:Tor. Oct. 14, 1992
   Martin Maldonado, AL:Hou. Oct. 14, 2018
   Mike Zunino, AL:TB Oct. 16, 2020
   Extra-Inning Game:
3 Jason Varitek, AL:Bos. Oct. 18, 2004 (14 inn)

Most Passed Balls, Inning
3 Jason Varitek, AL:Bos. Oct. 18, 2004 (13th)
1 By many in NL

Most Double Plays
5 Jorge Posada, AL:NY
3 Manny Sanguillen, NL:Pitt.
   Terry Kennedy, NL:SD-SF

Most Double Plays, Game
1 By many

Double Plays, Unassisted
None

PITCHERS – FIELDING

	3 Games	4 Games	5 Games	6 Games	7 Games
Highest Percentage 1.000 (Most Chances)					
AL:	5 By many	5 By many	5 John Cal. 1982 Flanagan Tor. 1989 Rivera NY 2001	5 Erickson Balt. 1997 Wood NY 2010	10 Leibrandt KC 1985
NL:	5 Gullett Cin. 1975	6 Marichal SF 1971 Carlton Phil. 1983	5 Blass Pitt. 1972 Ryan Hou. 1980 Kile StL 2000 Glavine Atl. 2001 Rueter SF 2002 Wainwright StL 2014	9 Oswalt Hou. 2005	9 Cox StL 1987
Games					
AL:	3 By many	4 Eckersley Oak. 1988 Kennedy Oak. 2006 Coke Det. 2012 Eppley & Rapada NY 2012 Davis, Herrera & Holland KC 2014	5 Acker Tor. 1989 Barnes Bos. 2018	6 Alburquerque Det. 2013	6 Embree Bos. 2004 Gordon NY 2004 Howell TB 2008
NL:	3 By many	4 Giusti Pitt. 1971 Wohlers Atl. 1995 Fuentes Col. 2007 Corpas Col. 2007 Familia NY 2015 Richard Chi. 2015	5 McGraw Phil. 1980	6 Rocker Atl. 1998-99	6 Petkovsek StL 1996 Isringhausen StL 2004 Knebel Mil. 2018
Total Chances					
AL:	5 By many	5 By many	6 Contreras Chi. 2005	5 Erickson Balt. 1997 Wood NY 2010 Workman Bos. 2013	10 Leibrandt KC 1985
NL:	5 Gullett Cin. 1975	6 Marichal SF 1971 Carlton Phil. 1983	6 Maddux Atl. 2001	10 Maddux Atl. 1993	9 Cox StL 1987

PITCHERS – FIELDING

	3 Games	4 Games	5 Games	6 Games	7 Games
Chances Accepted					
AL:	5 By many	5 By many	5 John Cal. 1982 Flanagan Tor. 1989 Morris Minn. 1991 Rivera NY 2001 Contreras Chi. 2005	5 Erickson Balt. 1997 Wood NY 2010	10 Leibrandt KC 1985
NL:	5 Gullett Cin. 1975	6 Marichal SF 1971 Carlton Phil. 1983	5 Blass Pitt. 1972 Ryan Hou. 1980 Kile StL 2000 Glavine Atl. 2001 Maddux Atl. 2001 Rueter SF 2002 Wainwright StL 2014	9 Maddux Atl. 1993 Oswalt Hou. 2005	9 Cox StL 1987
Putouts					
AL:	2 By many	3 Hunter Oak. 1974	4 Rivera NY 2001	4 Tomko Sea. 2000	4 Lowe Bos. 2004
NL:	4 Gullett Cin. 1975	2 By many	3 Wainwright StL 2014	4 Maddux Atl. 1993 Ashby SD 1998 Oswalt Hou. 2005	4 Cox StL 1987
Assists					
AL:	4 By many	5 Cuellar Balt. 1974	4 Contreras Chi. 2005	5 Erickson Balt. 1997	7 Leibrandt KC 1985
NL:	3 By many	5 Carlton Phil. 1983	4 Kile StL 2000	8 Carpenter StL 2005	5 Cox StL 1987
Errors					
AL:	1 Saberhagen KC 1984	1 Clemens Bos. 1988 Gray & Boddicker Bos. 1990 Sanchez Det. 2012 Herrera KC 2014	1 By many	1 By many	1 Beckett Bos. 2007 Perez Clev. 2007 Slegers TB 2020
NL:	1 Walker Pitt. 1970	1 By many	1 By many	2 Andujar StL 1985	1 Reuschel SF 1987 Munro Hou. 2004 Cain SF 2012 C. Carpenter & Lynn StL 2012
Double Plays					
AL:	1 By many	1 Loaiza Oak. 2006 Harden Oak. 2006 Rodney Det. 2006 Gonzalez Balt. 2014	2 Flanagan Tor. 1989	2 Nelson Sea. 1995 Saunders LA 2009	1 By many
NL:	1 Jarvis & Upshaw Atl. 1969	1 By many	2 Maddux Atl. 2001	2 Mahomes NY 1999	2 Cox StL 1987

PITCHERS

Most Series
10   Tom Glavine, NL:Atl. 1991-93, 95-99, 2001;
     NY 2006
     Andy Pettitte, AL:NY 1996, 98-2001, 03, 09-10, 12;
     NL:Hou. 2005
9   Mariano Rivera, AL:NY 1996, 98-2001, 03-04, 09-10
     Andy Pettitte, AL:NY 1996, 98-2001, 03, 09-10, 12

Most Games
33   Mariano Rivera, AL:NY
18   Mark Wohlers, NL:Atl.
     Brad Lidge, NL:Hou.-Phil.
     Ryan Madson, NL:Phil.-LA

Highest Percentage (Most Chances)
1.000   Tom Glavine, NL:Atl.-NY (29 tc)
      Mariano Rivera, AL:NY (23 tc)

Most Total Chances
39   Greg Maddux, NL:Chi.-Atl.
23   Mariano Rivera, AL:NY

Most Total Chances, Game
8   Charlie Leibrandt, AL:KC Oct. 12, 1985
6   Juan Marichal, NL:SF Oct. 5, 1971

Most Total Chances, Inning
3   Pat Zachry, NL:Cin. Oct. 10, 1976 (4th)
    John Smoltz, NL:Atl. Oct. 7, 1998 (1st)
    Bud Black, AL:KC Oct. 9, 1985 (7th)
    Mariano Rivera, AL:NY Oct. 17, 2001 (9th)

Most Chances Accepted
36   Greg Maddux, NL:Chi.-Atl.
23   Mariano Rivera, AL:NY

Most Chances Accepted, Game
8   Charlie Leibrandt, AL:KC Oct. 12, 1985
6   Juan Marichal, NL:SF Oct. 5, 1971

Most Chances Accepted, Inning
3   Pat Zachry, NL:Cin. Oct. 10, 1976 (4th)
    Bud Black, AL:KC Oct. 9, 1985 (7th)
    Mariano Rivera, AL:NY Oct. 17, 2001 (9th)

Most Putouts
13   Mariano Rivera, AL:NY
11   Greg Maddux, NL:Chi.-Atl.

Most Putouts, Game
4   Don Gullett, NL:Cin. Oct. 4, 1975
3   Tommy John, AL:Cal. Oct. 5, 1982
    Charlie Leibrandt, AL:KC Oct. 12, 1985
    Charles Nagy, AL:Clev. Oct. 7, 1998 (12 inn)
    Derek Lowe, AL:Bos. Oct. 20, 2004

Most Putouts, Inning
2   Don Gullett, NL:Cin. Oct. 4, 1975 (3rd)
    Dwight Gooden, NL:NY Oct. 8, 1986 (3rd)
    Roger McDowell, NL:NY Oct. 15, 1986 (10th)
    Brandon Webb, NL:Ari. Oct. 11, 2007 (5th)
    Mike Torrez, AL:NY Oct. 7, 1977 (2nd)
    Charlie Leibrandt, AL:KC Oct. 12, 1985 (5th)
    Bret Saberhagen, AL:KC Oct. 16, 1985 (3rd)
    Mike Witt, AL:Cal. Oct. 12, 1986 (1st)
    Andy Pettitte, AL:NY Oct. 13, 1996 (2nd)
    Mariano Rivera, AL:NY Oct. 17, 2001 (9th)
    Derek Lowe, AL:Bos. Oct. 20, 2004 (4th)
    Bud Norris, AL:Balt. Oct. 11, 2014 (1st)

Most Assists
25   Greg Maddux, NL:Chi.-Atl.
12   Mike Cuellar, AL:Balt.

Most Assists, Game
5   Charlie Leibrandt, AL:KC Oct. 12, 1985
4   Juan Marichal, NL:SF Oct. 5, 1971
    Greg Maddux, NL:Atl. Oct. 7, 1997
    Tom Glavine, NL:Atl. Oct. 14, 1997
    Andy Ashby, NL:SD Oct. 7, 1998 (10 inn)
    Greg Maddux, NL:Atl. Oct. 12, 1999
    Kenny Rogers, NL:NY Oct. 13, 1999
    Chris Carpenter, NL:StL. Oct. 12, 2005
    Chris Carpenter, NL:StL. Oct. 17, 2005

Most Assists, Inning
3   Pat Zachry, NL:Cin. Oct. 10, 1976 (4th)
2   By many in AL

Most Errors
3   Greg Maddux, NL:Chi.-Atl.
2   Bret Saberhagen, AL:KC-Bos.
    Rick Porcello, Det.-Bos.

Most Errors, Game
1   By many

Most Errors, Inning
1   By players

Most Double Plays
3   Greg Maddux, NL:Chi.-Atl.
2   Mike Flanagan, AL:Tor.
    Jeff Nelson, AL:Sea.
    Mariano Rivera, AL:NY
    Joe Saunders, AL:LA

Most Double Plays, Game
2   Danny Cox, NL:StL. Oct. 14, 1987
    Greg Maddux, NL:Atl. Oct. 16, 2001
    Mike Flanagan, AL:Tor. Oct. 7, 1989
    Jeff Nelson, AL:Sea. Oct. 14, 1995
    Joe Saunders, AL:LA Oct. 17, 2009 (13 inn)

Double Plays, Unassisted
None

CHAMPIONSHIP SERIES PITCHING RECORDS

	3 Games	4 Games	5 Games	6 Games	7 Games
Games					
AL:	3 Perranoski Minn. 1969 / Todd Oak. 1975 / Hernandez Det. 1984	5 Eckersley Oak. 1988 / Kennedy Oak. 2006 / Coke Det. 2012 / Eppley & Rapada NY 2012 / Davis, Herrera & Holland KC 2014	5 Acker Tor. 1989 / Barnes Bos. 2018	6 Alburquerque Det. 2013	6 Embree Bos. 2004 / Gordon NY 2004 / Howell TB 2008
NL:	3 By many	5 Giusti Pitt. 1971 / Wohlers Atl. 1995 / Corpas & Fuentes Col. 2007 / Familia NY 2015 / Richard Chi. 2015	5 McGraw Phil. 1980	6 Rocker Atl. 1998-99	6 Petkovsek StL. 1996 / Isringhausen StL. 2004 / Knebel Mil. 2018
Games Started					
AL:	2 Holtzman Oak. 1975	2 By many	2 By many	2 By many	3 Stieb Tor. 1985 / Clemens Bos. 1986
NL:	1 By many	2 By many	2 By many	2 By many	3 Hershiser LA 1988 / Drabek Pitt.; Smoltz Atl. 1992 / Miley Mil. 2018
Complete Games					
AL:	1 By many	1 By many	1 By many	1 By many	1 By many
NL:	1 By many	1 By many	1 By many	2 Scott Hou. 1986	2 Cox StL. 1987 / Wakefield Pitt. 1992
Games Finished					
AL:	3 Perranoski Minn. 1969	4 Eckersley Oak. 1988 / Holland KC 2014	4 Lyle NY 1977 / Reardon Minn. 1987 / Eckersley Oak. 1989 / Rivera NY 2001 / Osuna Tor. 2016	5 Uehara Bos. 2013	4 Quisenberry KC 1985 / Schiraldi Bos. 1986 / Rivera NY 2003 / Borowski Clev. 2007
NL:	2 By many	4 Giusti Pitt. 1971 / Familia NY 2015	4 Borbon Sr. Cin. 1973 / Bedrosian SF 1989 / Lidge Phil. 2008 / Jansen LA 2017	4 Orosco NY 1986 / Wohlers Atl. 1993 / Lidge Hou. 2005 / Wilson SF 2010 / Motte StL. 2011	5 Isringhausen StL. 2004
Saves					
AL:	2 Drago Bos. 1975	4 Eckersley Oak. 1988 / Holland KC 2014	3 Eckersley Oak. 1989 / Aguilera Minn. 1991 / Allen Clev. 2016 / Kimbrel Bos. 2018	3 Henke Tor. 1992 / Uehara Bos. 2013	3 Williamson Bos. 2003
NL:	2 Gullett Cin. 1970	3 Giusti Pitt. 1971 / Familia NY 2015	3 Bedrosian SF 1989 / Nen SF 2002 / Lidge Phil. 2008	3 Myers Cin. 1990 / Lidge Hou. 2005 / Wilson SF 2010	3 Pena Atl. 1991 / Isringhausen StL. 2004
Most Decisions					
AL:	2 Holtzman Oak. 1975	2 By many	2 By many	2 By many	3 Leibrandt KC 1985 / Wakefield Bos. 2003
NL:	1 By many	2 By many	2 By many	3 Orosco NY 1986	3 Drabek Pitt. 1992 / Tavarez StL. 2004

CHAMPIONSHIP SERIES PITCHING RECORDS

	3 Games	4 Games	5 Games	6 Games	7 Games
Most Won					
AL:	1 By many	2 Nelson Oak. 1988 / Stewart Oak. 1990 / Davis KC 2014	2 By many	2 By many	2 Henke Tor. 1985 / Wakefield Bos. 2003 / Beckett Bos. 2007 / Garza TB 2008 / Verlander Hou. 2017 / Morton TB 2020
NL:	1 By many	2 Sutton LA 1974 / Carlton Phil. 1983	2 Hooton LA 1981 / Lefferts SD 1984 / Hampton NY 2000 / Johnson Ari. 2001 / Worrell SF 2002 / Hamels Phil. 2008	3 Orosco NY 1986	2 Myers NY 1988 / Belcher LA 1988 / Avery Atl. 1991 / Smoltz Atl. 1991-92, 96 / Wakefield Pitt. 1992 / Tavarez StL. 2004 / Vogelsong SF 2012 / Urias LA 2020
Most Lost					
AL:	2 Holtzman Oak. 1975	2 Leonard KC 1978 / Hurst Bos. 1988 / O'Day Balt. 2014	2 Fryman Det. 1972 / Alexander Det. 1987 / Stieb Tor. 1989 / Sele Sea. 2001 / Escobar LA 2005 / Estrada Tor. 2016	2 Moore Oak. 1992 / Fernandez & McDowell Chi. 1993 / Benitez Balt. 1997 / Ogea Clev. 1997 / Neagle NY 2000 / Hughes NY 2010	2 Leibrandt KC 1985 / McCaskill Cal. 1986 / Mussina NY 2003 / Lowe Bos. 2003 / Sabathia Clev. 2007 / Lester Bos. 2008 / Shields TB 2008 / McCullers Hou. 2020
NL:	1 By many	2 Reuss Pitt. 1974; LA 83	2 Gullickson Mtl. 1981 / Kile StL. 2000 / Maddux Atl. 2001 / Morris StL. 2002 / Billingsley LA 2008	2 Niedenfuer LA 1985 / Smith Pitt. 1990 / Maddux Atl. 1997 / Glavine Atl. 1998 / Rogers NY 1999 / Mulder StL. 2005 / Marcum Mil. 2011 / Kershaw LA 2013 / Blanton LA 2016	3 Drabek Pitt. 1992
Innings					
AL:	11.0 McNally Balt. 1969 / Holtzman Oak. 1975	16.0 Stewart Oak. 1990	19.0 Lolich Det. 1972	16.2 Stewart Oak. 1992	22.2 Clemens Bos. 1986
NL:	9.2 Ellis Pitt. 1970	17.0 Sutton LA 1974	17.0 Burris Mtl. 1981	18.0 Scott Hou. 1986	24.2 Hershiser LA 1988
Runs					
AL:	9 Perry Minn. 1970	10 Frost Cal. 1979	10 Alexander Det. 1987	11 Hughes NY 2010	13 McCaskill Cal. 1986
NL:	9 Niekro Atl. 1969	11 Perry SF 1971	12 Maddux Chi. 1989	11 Greinke Mil. 2011	11 Drabek Pitt. 1992
Earned Runs					
AL:	8 Perry Minn. 1970	9 Frost Cal. 1979	10 Alexander Det. 1987	11 Hughes NY 2010	12 Sabathia Clev. 2007
NL:	6 Jarvis Atl. 1969 / Koosman NY 1969	10 Perry SF 1971	11 Maddux Chi. 1989	10 Greene Phil. 1993	11 Stottlemyre StL. 1996

CHAMPIONSHIP SERIES PITCHING RECORDS

	3 Games	4 Games	5 Games	6 Games	7 Games
Hits					
AL:	12 Holtzman Oak. 1975	13 Leonard KC 1978	18 Gura KC 1976	18 McDowell Chi. 1993	22 Clemens Bos. 1986
NL:	10 Jarvis Atl. 1969	19 Perry SF 1971 Perez Atl. 1982	16 Ryan Hou. 1980 Morris StL. 2002	17 Hershiser LA 1985	19 Andy Benes StL. 1996
Home Runs					
AL:	4 Hunter Oak. 1971	3 Hunter Oak. 1974 & NY 1978	4 McNally 1973	4 Pettitte NY 1998	5 Mussina NY 2003 Beckett Bos. 2008
NL:	3 Jarvis Atl. 1969	4 Boddicker Bos. 1988 Blass Pitt. 1971	5 Pettitte NY 1996 Show SD 1984 Hamels Phil. 2009	4 Holland Tex. 2011 Jackson StL. 2011	4 Wakefield Pitt. 1992 Zambrano Chi. 2003
Walks					
AL:	7 Boswell Minn. 1969	13 Cuellar Balt. 1974	8 Palmer Balt. 1973 Abbott Sea. 2001	9 Morris Tor. 1992	10 Stieb Tor. 1985
NL:	5 Norman Cin. 1974 Carlton Phil. 1978	8 Reuss Pitt. 1974 Carlton Phil. 1977	8 Carlton Phil. 1980 Sutcliffe Chi. 1984	11 Guzman Tor. 1993 Glavine Atl. 1997	10 Smoltz Atl. 1992
Intentional Walks					
AL:	2 Segui Oak. 1971	2 Gardner Bos. 1988	3 Henneman Det. 1987	3 Fernandez Chi. 1993 Hughes NY 2010	2 Stieb Tor. 1985 Schiraldi Bos. 1986
NL:	2 By many	4 Giusti Pitt. 1974	3 McGraw Phil. 1980 Christenson Phil. 1980	3 Welch LA 1985 Lopez Hou. 1986 Avery Atl. 1993 Glavine Atl. 1997	2 Tudor StL. 1987 Gooden NY 1988 Glavine Atl. 1991 Smoltz Atl. 1992 Farnsworth Chi. 2003 Isringhausen StL. 2004 Wood LA 2018
Hit Batters					
AL:	1 By many	2 Boddicker Balt. 1983 Boddicker Bos. 1990 Gonzalez Balt. 2014	3 Tanana Det. 1987	3 Key Balt. 1997	3 Martinez Bos. 2004 Sabathia Clev. 2007
NL:	1 By many	2 John LA 1977 Francis Col. 2007 Sanchez Wash. 2019	3 Morris StL. 2002	2 Leiter NY 1999 Oswalt Hou. 2005 Cain SF 2010 Strop Chi. 2016	2 Hershiser LA 1988 Glavine Atl. 1992 Cain SF 2012 Woodruff Mil. 2018
Strikeouts					
AL:	12 Palmer Balt. 1970	14 Boddicker Balt. 1983	15 Palmer Balt. 1973	25 Mussina Balt. 1997	21 Verlander Hou. 2017
NL:	14 Candelaria Pitt. 1975	13 Sutton LA 1974 Carlton Phil. 1983 Schourek Cin. 1995	19 Johnson Ari. 2001	19 Scott Hou. 1986	20 Gooden NY 1988
Wild Pitches					
AL:	1 By many	2 Haren Oak. 2006	3 John Cal. 1982	3 Guzman Tor. 1993 Sanchez Det. 2013	2 Black KC 1985 Contreras NY 2003 Matsuzaka Bos. 2007 Tanaka NY 2017 Pressly Hou. 2020
NL:	2 By many	2 By many	4 Ankiel StL. 2000	3 Gallardo Mil. 2011	2 By many

INDIVIDUAL PITCHING

Most Series
10 Tom Glavine, NL:Atl. 1991-93, 95-99, 2001;
      NY 2006
      Andy Pettitte, AL:NY 1996, 98-2001, 03, 09-10, 12;
      NL:Hou. 2005
9   Mariano Rivera, AL:NY 1996, 98-2001, 03-04, 09-10
      Andy Pettitte, AL:NY 1996, 98-2001, 03, 09-10, 12

Lowest Earned Run Average (Minimum: 30 IP)
0.92 Mariano Rivera, AL:NY (48.2 inn)
1.69 Jeff Suppan, NL:StL. (32 inn)

Most Games
33 Mariano Rivera, AL:NY
18 Mark Wohlers, NL:Atl.
      Brad Lidge, NL:Hou.-Phil.
      Ryan Madson, NL:Phil.-LA

Most Games Started
17 Tom Glavine, NL:Atl.-NY
13 Andy Pettitte, AL:NY

Most Complete Games
5   Jim Palmer, AL:Balt.
2   Kevin Brown, NL:Fla.-SD
      Danny Cox, NL:StL.
      Doug Drabek, NL:Pitt.
      Orel Hershiser, NL:LA
      Tommy John, NL:LA
      Mike Scott, NL:Hou.
      Don Sutton, NL:LA
      Tim Wakefield, NL:Pitt.

Most Games Finished
27 Mariano Rivera, AL:NY
17 Brad Lidge, NL:Hou.-Phil.

Most Shutouts
1   By many

Most Games Won
8   Dave Stewart, AL:Oak.-Tor.
6   John Smoltz, NL:Atl.
      Tom Glavine, NL:Atl.-NY

Most Games Lost
10 Tom Glavine, NL:Atl.-NY
4   Doyle Alexander, AL:Balt.-Tor.-Det.
      Phil Hughes, AL:NY
      CC Sabathia, AL:Clev.-NY
      Justin Verlander, AL:Det.-Hou.

Most Saves
13 Mariano Rivera, AL:NY
10 Brad Lidge, NL:Hou.-Phil.

Most Innings
103.1 Tom Glavine, NL:Atl.-NY
86.0   Andy Pettitte, AL:NY

Most Innings, Game
11.0 Dave McNally, AL:Balt. Oct. 5, 1969
        Ken Holtzman, AL:Oak. Oct. 9, 1973
10.0 Joe Niekro, NL:Hou. Oct. 10, 1980
        Dwight Gooden, NL:NY Oct. 14, 1986

Most Runs
52 Greg Maddux, NL:Chi.-Atl.-LA
34 Andy Pettitte, AL:NY

Most Runs, Game
9   Phil Niekro, NL:Atl. Oct. 4, 1969
8   Jim Perry, AL:Minn. Oct. 3, 1970
      Roger Clemens, AL:Bos. Oct. 7, 1986
      Hideki Irabu, AL:NY Oct. 16, 1999
      CC Sabathia, AL:Clev. Oct. 12, 2007
      Josh Beckett, AL:Bos. Oct. 11, 2008 (11 inn)
      Johnny Cueto, AL:KC Oct. 19, 2015

Most Runs, Inning
8   Tom Glavine, NL:Atl. Oct. 13, 1992 (2nd)
6   Jim Perry, AL:Minn. Oct. 3, 1970 (4th)
      Scott Erickson, AL:Balt. Oct. 13, 1996 (3rd)
      Max Scherzer, AL:Det. Oct. 15, 2011 (3rd)

Most Earned Runs
41 Andy Pettitte, AL:NY; NL:Hou.
37 Tom Glavine, NL:Atl.-NY
34 Andy Pettitte, AL:NY

Most Earned Runs, Game
8   Greg Maddux, NL:Chi. Oct. 4, 1989
      Grant Dayton, NL:Atl. Oct. 14, 2020
      CC Sabathia, AL:Clev. Oct. 12, 2007
      Josh Beckett, AL:Bos. Oct. 11, 2008 (11 inn)
      Johnny Cueto, AL:KC Oct. 19, 2015

Most Earned Runs, Inning
7   Tom Glavine, NL:Atl. Oct. 13, 1992 (2nd)
      Kyle Wright, NL:Atl. Oct. 14, 2020 (1st)
6   Jim Perry, AL:Minn. Oct. 3, 1970 (4th)
      Max Scherzer, AL:Det. Oct. 15, 2011 (3rd)

Most Hits
104 Andy Pettitte, AL:NY; NL:Hou.
102 Tom Glavine, NL:Atl.-NY
89   Andy Pettitte, AL:NY

Most Hits, Game
13 Jack McDowell, AL:Chi. Oct. 5, 1993
      Hideki Irabu, AL:NY Oct. 16, 1999
11 Kevin Brown, NL:Fla. Oct. 14, 1997

Fewest Hits, Complete Game
1   Roger Clemens, AL:NY Oct. 14, 2000
2   Ross Grimsley, NL:Cin. Oct. 10, 1972
      Jon Matlack, NL:NY Oct. 7, 1973
      Dave Dravecky, NL:SF Oct. 7, 1987
      Josh Beckett, NL:Fla. Oct. 12, 2003

Most Hits, Inning
6   Jim Perry, AL:Minn. Oct. 3, 1970 (4th)
      Kirk McCaskill, AL:Cal. Oct. 14, 1986 (3rd)
      Greg Harris, NL:SD Oct. 2, 1984 (5th)
      Tom Glavine, NL:Atl. Oct. 13, 1992 (2nd)
      Todd Stottlemyre, NL:StL. Oct. 14, 1996 (1st)
      Matt Morris, NL:StL. Oct. 9, 2002 (2nd)
      Kameron Loe, NL:Mil. Oct. 10, 2011 (7th)

Most Home Runs
14 Andy Pettitte, AL:NY; NL:Hou.
13 Andy Pettitte, AL:NY
9   Tom Glavine, NL:Atl.-NY

Most Home Runs, Game
4   Catfish Hunter, AL:Oak. Oct. 4, 1971
      Dave McNally, AL:Balt. Oct. 7, 1973
      Andy Pettitte, AL:NY Oct. 9, 1998
3   Pat Jarvis, NL:Atl. Oct. 6, 1969
      Eric Show, NL:SD Oct. 2, 1984
      Danny Cox, NL:StL. Oct. 10, 1987
      Carlos Zambrano, NL:Chi. Oct. 7, 2003 (11 inn)
      Oliver Perez, NL:NY Oct. 15, 2006
      Cole Hamels, NL:Phil. Oct. 21, 2009
      Edwin Jackson, NL:StL. Oct. 16, 2011
      Alex Wood, NL:LA Oct. 18, 2017
      Grant Dayton, NL:Atl. Oct. 14, 2020

Most Home Runs, Inning
3   Scott Erickson, AL:Balt. Oct. 13, 1996 (3rd)
      Jaret Wright, AL:Clev. Oct. 12, 1997 (3rd)
      Andy Pettitte, AL:NY Oct. 9, 1998 (5th)
      Carlos Zambrano, NL:Chi. Oct. 7, 2003 (3rd)

Most Grand Slam Home Runs
2 Greg Maddux, NL:Atl.
1 Jim Perry, AL:Minn.
  Moose Haas, AL:Mil.
  David Cone, AL:NY
  Rod Beck, AL:Bos.
  Javier Vazquez, AL:NY
  Fausto Carmona, AL:Clev.
  Ryan Perry, AL:Det.
  Joaquin Benoit, AL:Det.
  Jose Veras, AL:Det.
  Roberto Osuna, AL:Hou.

Most Walks
42 Tom Glavine, NL:Atl.-NY
26 Orlando Hernandez, AL:NY

Most Walks, Game
9 Mike Cuellar, AL:Balt. Oct. 9, 1974
8 Fernando Valenzuela, NL:LA Oct. 14, 1985

Most Walks, Inning
4 Mike Cuellar, AL:Balt. Oct. 9, 1974 (5th)
  Burt Hooton, NL:LA Oct. 7, 1977 (2nd)
  Bob Welch, NL:LA Oct. 12, 1985 (1st)

Most Walks, Consecutive
4 Mike Cuellar, AL:Balt. Oct. 9, 1974
  Manny Delcarmen, AL:Bos. Oct. 14-16, 2008
  Burt Hooton, NL:LA Oct. 7, 1977

Most Intentional Walks
8 Tom Glavine, NL:Atl.-NY
  Greg Maddux, NL:Chi.-Atl.-LA
3 Mike Henneman, AL:Det.
  Alex Fernandez, AL:Chi.
  Mike Timlin, AL:Tor.-Bos.
  Phil Hughes, AL:NY
  David Robertson, AL:NY

Most Intentional Walks, Game
3 Dave Giusti, NL:Pitt. Oct. 5, 1974
  Tug McGraw, NL:Phil. Oct. 10, 1980 (11 inn)
  Bob Welch, NL:LA Oct. 12, 1985
  Steve Avery, NL:Atl. Oct. 6, 1993 (10 inn)
  Tom Glavine, NL:Atl. Oct. 14, 1997
2 Diego Segui, AL:Oak. Oct. 5, 1971
  Mark Littell, AL:KC Oct. 5, 1977
  Dave Stieb, AL:Tor. Oct. 12, 1985
  Calvin Schiraldi, AL:Bos. Oct. 11, 1986 (11 inn)
  Mike Henneman, AL:Det. Oct. 10, 1987
  Wes Gardner, AL:Bos. Oct. 8, 1988
  Alex Fernandez, AL:Chi. Oct. 6, 1993
  Danny Cox, AL:Tor. Oct. 8, 1993
  David Robertson, AL:NY Oct. 17, 2009 (13 inn)
  Phil Hughes, AL:NY Oct. 22, 2010
  Kerry Wood, AL:NY Oct. 22, 2010

Most Intentional Walks, Inning
2 Tom Seaver, NL:NY Oct. 4, 1969 (3rd)
  Dave Giusti, NL:Pitt. Oct. 5, 1974 (9th)
  Lance Rautzhan, NL:LA Oct. 6, 1978 (7th)
  Tug McGraw, NL:Phil. Oct. 10, 1980 (11th)
  Joe Beckwith, NL:LA Oct. 8, 1983 (5th)
  Bob Welch, NL:LA Oct. 12, 1985 (1st)
  Dwight Gooden, NL:NY Oct. 12, 1988 (2nd)
  Rick Sutcliffe, NL:Chi. Oct. 7, 1989 (1st)
  Steve Avery, NL:Atl. Oct. 6, 1993 (6th)
  Mike Jackson, NL:Cin. Oct. 14, 1995 (7th)
  John Smoltz, NL:Atl. Oct. 10, 1997 (6th)
  Kenny Rogers, NL:NY Oct. 19, 1999 (11th)
  Jason Isringhausen, NL:StL. Oct. 10, 2002 (9th)
  Kyle Farnsworth, NL:Chi. Oct. 14, 2003 (8th)
  Joe Blanton, NL:LA Oct. 15, 2016 (8th)

Most Hit Batters
5 Pedro Martinez, AL:Bos.; NL:Phil.
  Tom Glavine, NL:Atl.
  Greg Maddux, NL:Chi.-Atl.
4 Frank Tanana, AL:Cal.-Det.
  Mike Boddicker, AL:Balt.-Bos.
  David Wells, AL:Balt.-NY
  Jeff Nelson, AL:NY
  Pedro Martinez, AL:Bos.
  CC Sabathia, AL:Clev.-NY

Most Hit Batters, Game
3 Frank Tanana, AL:Det. Oct. 11, 1987
  Jimmy Key, AL:Balt. Oct. 9, 1997
  Matt Morris, NL:StL. Oct. 14, 2002

Most Hit Batters, Inning
3 Jimmy Key, AL:Balt. Oct. 9, 1997 (1st)
2 Al Leiter, NL:NY Oct. 19, 1999 (1st)

Most Strikeouts
89 John Smoltz, NL:Atl.
79 Justin Verlander, AL:Det.-Hou.

Most Strikeouts, Game
15 Livan Hernandez, NL:Fla. Oct. 12, 1997
   Mike Mussina, AL:Balt. Oct. 11, 1997 (12 inn)
   Roger Clemens, AL:NY Oct. 14, 2000

Most Strikeouts, Inning
4 Anibal Sanchez, AL:Det. Oct. 12, 2013 (1st)
3 By many in NL

Most Strikeouts, Consecutive Batters Faced
7 Andrew Miller, AL:Clev. Oct. 14-15, 2016
6 Tony Pena, NL:Ari. Oct. 11-12. 2007
  Ryan Madson, NL:Phil. Oct. 20-23, 2010

Most Strikeouts, Consecutive Batters Faced, Game
6 Justin Verlander, AL:Det. Oct. 15, 2013
5 Curt Schilling, NL:Phil. Oct. 6, 1993
  A.J. Minter, NL:Atl. Oct. 16, 2020

Most Strikeouts, 2 Consecutive Innings, Game
6 Jim Palmer, AL:Balt. Oct. 6, 1973 (1st-2nd)
  Justin Verlander, AL:Det. Oct. 15, 2013 (2nd-3rd)
5 By many in NL

Most Wild Pitches
5 Clayton Kershaw, NL:LA
  Justin Verlander, AL:Det.-Hou.

Most Wild Pitches, Game
3 Tommy John, AL:Cal. Oct. 9, 1982
  Juan Guzman, AL:Tor. Oct. 5, 1993
  Clayton Kershaw, NL:LA Oct. 15, 2009
  Yovani Gallardo, NL:Mil. Oct. 12, 2011

Most Wild Pitches, Inning
3 Clayton Kershaw, NL:LA Oct. 15, 2009 (5th)
2 Chris Zachary, AL:Det. Oct. 8, 1972 (5th)
  Tommy John, AL:Cal. Oct. 9, 1982 (4th)
  David West, AL:Minn. Oct. 11, 1991 (5th)
  Juan Guzman, AL:Tor. Oct. 5, 1993 (1st)
  Mariano Rivera, AL:NY Oct. 17, 2001 (9th)
  Jonathan Loaisiga, AL:NY Oct. 17, 2019 (9th)

Most Balks
1 By many

Most Balks, Game
1 By many

SHUTOUTS

American League: *(* = Winning Pitcher)*

1-0	1969 Oct. 5	Dave McNally, Balt. (vs. Minn.)
5-0	1972 Oct. 8	Blue Moon Odom, Oak. (vs. Det.)
3-0	1972 Oct. 10	Joe Coleman, Det. (vs. Oak.)
6-0	1973 Oct. 6	Jim Palmer, Balt. (vs. Oak.)
3-0	1973 Oct. 11	Catfish Hunter, Oak. (vs. Balt.)
5-0	1974 Oct. 6	Ken Holtzman, Oak. (vs. Balt.)
1-0	1974 Oct. 8	Vida Blue, Oak. (at Balt.)
8-0	1979 Oct. 6	Scott McGregor, Balt. (at Cal.)
4-0	1981 Oct. 15	Dave Righetti*, Ron Davis, Rich Gossage, NY (at Oak.)
4-0	1983 Oct. 6	Mike Boddicker, Balt. (vs. Chi.)
3-0	1983 Oct. 8	Storm Davis, Tippy Martinez*, Balt. (at Chi.)
1-0	1984 Oct. 5	Milt Wilcox*, Willie Hernandez, Det. (vs. KC)
2-0	1985 Oct. 13	Danny Jackson, KC (vs. Tor.)
7-0	1995 Oct. 14	Ken Hill*, Jim Poole, Chad Ogea, Alan Embree, Clev. (vs. Sea.)
4-0	1995 Oct. 17	Dennis Martinez*, Julian Tavarez, Jose Mesa, Clev. (at Sea.)
3-0	1997 Oct. 8	Scott Erickson*, Randy Myers, Balt. (vs. Clev.)
1-0	1997 Oct. 15	Charles Nagy, Paul Assenmacher, Mike Jackson, Brian Anderson*, Jose Mesa, Clev. (at Balt.)
4-0	1998 Oct. 10	Orlando Hernandez*, Mike Stanton, Mariano Rivera, NY (at Clev.)
2-0	2000 Oct. 10	Freddy Garcia*, Jose Paniagua, Arthur Rhodes, Kazuhiro Sasaki, Sea. (at NY)
5-0	2000 Oct. 14	Roger Clemens, NY (at Sea.)
3-0	2006 Oct. 13	Kenny Rogers*, Fernando Rodney, Todd Jones, Det. (vs. Oak)
2-0	2008 Oct. 10	Daisuke Matzusaka*, Hideki Okajima, Justin Masterson, Jonathan Papelbon, Bos. (at TB)
8-0	2010 Oct. 18	Cliff Lee*, Neftali Feliz, Tex. (at NY)
3-0	2012 Oct. 14	Anibal Sanchez*, Phil Coke, Det. (at NY)
1-0	2103 Oct. 12	Anibal Sanchez*, Al Alburquerque, Jose Veras, Drew Smyly, Joaquin Benoit, Det. (at Bos.)
1-0	2013 Oct. 15	John Lackey*, Craig Breslow, Junichi Tazawa, Koji Uehara, Bos. (at Det.)
5-0	2015 Oct. 16	Edinson Volquez*, Kelvin Herrera, Ryan Madson, Luke Hochevar, KC (vs. Tor.)
2-0	2016 Oct. 14	Corey Kluber*, Andrew Miller, Cody Allen, Clev. (vs. Tor.)
3-0	2016 Oct .19	Ryan Merritt, Bryan Shaw*, Andrew Miller, Cody Allen, Clev. (at Tor.)
5-0	2017 Oct. 18	Masahiro Tanaka*, Tommy Kahnle, NY (vs. Hou.)
4-0	2017 Oct. 21	Charlie Morton*, Lance McCullers Jr. Hou. (vs. NY)
7-0	2019 Oct. 12	Masahiro Tanaka*, Adam Ottavino, Zack Britton, Jonathan Loaisiga, NY (at Hou.)

National League: *(* = Winning Pitcher)*

3-0	1970 Oct. 3	Gary Nolan*, Clay Carroll, Cin. (at Pitt.)
5-0	1973 Oct. 7	Jon Matlack, NY (at Cin.)
3-0	1974 Oct. 5	Don Sutton, LA (at Pitt.)
7-0	1974 Oct. 8	Bruce Kison*, Ramon Hernandez, Pitt. (at LA)
4-0	1978 Oct. 5	Tommy John, LA (at Phil.)
1-0	1980 Oct. 10	Joe Niekro, Dave Smith*, Hou. (vs. Phil.)
3-0	1981 Oct. 14	Ray Burris, Mtl. (at LA)
7-0	1982 Oct. 7	Bob Forsch, StL. (vs. Atl.)

1-0	1983 Oct. 4	Steve Carlton*, Al Holland, Phil. (at LA)
13-0	1984 Oct. 2	Rick Sutcliffe*, Warren Brusstar, Chi. (vs. SD)
1-0	1986 Oct. 8	Mike Scott, Hou. (vs. NY)
5-0	1987 Oct. 7	Dave Dravecky, SF (at StL.)
1-0	1987 Oct. 13	John Tudor*, Todd Worrell, Ken Dayley, StL. (vs. SF)
6-0	1987 Oct. 14	Danny Cox, StL. (vs. SF)
6-0	1988 Oct. 12	Orel Hershiser, LA (vs. NY)
1-0	1991 Oct. 10	Steve Avery*, Alejandro Pena, Atl. (at Pitt.)
1-0	1991 Oct. 14	Zane Smith*, Roger Mason, Pitt. (at Atl.)
1-0	1991 Oct. 16	Steve Avery*, Alejandro Pena, Atl. (at Pitt.)
4-0	1991 Oct. 17	John Smoltz, Atl. (at Pitt.)
6-0	1995 Oct. 14	Steve Avery*, Greg McMichael, Alejandro Pena, Mark Wohlers, Atl. (vs. Cin.)
14-0	1996 Oct. 14	John Smoltz*, Mike Bielecki, Terrell Wade, Brad Clontz, Atl. (at StL.)
15-0	1996 Oct. 17	Tom Glavine*, Mike Bielecki, Steve Avery, Atl. (vs. StL.)
4-0	1997 Oct. 11	Denny Neagle, Atl. (at Fla.)
3-0	1998 Oct. 8	Kevin Brown, SD (at Atl.)
5-0	1998 Oct. 14	Sterling Hitchcock*, Brian Boehringer, Mark Langston, Joey Hamilton, Trevor Hoffman, SD (at Atl.)
1-0	1999 Oct. 15	Tom Glavine*, Mike Remlinger, John Rocker, Atl. (at NY)
7-0	2000 Oct. 16	Mike Hampton, NY (vs. StL.)
2-0	2001 Oct. 16	Randy Johnson, Ari. (vs. Atl.)
4-0	2003 Oct. 12	Josh Beckett, Fla. (vs. Chi.)
3-0	2004 Oct. 18	Brandon Backe, Brad Lidge*, Hou. (vs. StL.)
2-0	2006 Oct. 14	Tom Glavine*, Guillermo Mota, Billy Wagner, NY (vs. StL.)
5-0	2006 Oct. 14	Jeff Suppan*, Josh Kinney, StL. (vs. NY)
11-0	2009 Oct. 18	Cliff Lee*, Chad Durbin, Phil. (vs. LA)
3-0	2010 Oct. 19	Matt Cain*, Javier Lopez, Brian Wilson, SF (vs. Phil.)
5-0	2012 Oct. 19	Barry Zito*, Santiago Casilla, Sergio Pena, SF (at StL.)
9-0	2012 Oct. 22	Matt Cain*, Jeremy Affeldt, Santiago Casilla, Javier Lopez, Sergio Romo, SF (vs. StL.)
1-0	2013 Oct. 12	Michael Wacha*, Kevin Siegrist, Randy Choate, Carlos Martinez, Trevor Rosenthal, StL. (vs. LA)
3-0	2013 Oct. 14	Hyun-Jin Ryu*, Brian Wilson, Kenley Jansen, LA (vs. StL.)
9-0	2013 Oct. 18	Michael Wacha*, Carlos Martinez, Trevor Rosenthal, StL. (vs. LA)
3-0	2014 Oct. 11	Madison Bumgarner*, Sergio Romo, Santiago Casilla, SF (at StL.)
1-0	2016 Oct. 16	Clayton Kershaw*, Kenley Jansen, LA (at Chi.)
6-0	2016 Oct. 18	Rich Hill*, Joe Blanton, Grant Dayton, Kenley Jansen, LA (vs. Chi.)
5-0	2016 Oct. 22	Kyle Hendricks*, Aroldis Chapman, Chi. (vs. LA)
4-0	2018 Oct. 15	Jhoulys Chacin*, Corey Knebel, Joakim Soria, Josh Hader, Jeremy Jeffress, Mil. (vs. LA)
2-0	2019 Oct. 11	Anibal Sanchez*, Sean Doolittle, Wash. (at StL.)

CHAMPIONSHIP SERIES – CLUB BATTING

	3 Games	4 Games	5 Games	6 Games	7 Games
Batting Average					
AL:	.336 New York 1981	.300 New York 1978	.316 New York 1976	.304 Texas 2010	.318 Boston 2007
NL:	.330 St. Louis 1982	.286 Los Angeles 1978	.303 Chicago 1989	.310 St. Louis 2011	.309 Atlanta 1996
Batting Average Both Clubs					
AL:	.286 Balt. .330 Minn. .238 1970	.282 NY .300 KC .263 1978	.283 NY .316 KC .247 1976	.271 Tor. .301 Chi. .237 1993	.286 Bos. .318 Clev. .254 2007
NL:	.292 NY .327 Atl. .255 1969	.268 LA .286 Phil. .250 1978	.285 Chi. .303 SF .267 1989	.283 StL .310 Mil. .254 2011	.262 Fla. .266 Chi. .258 2003
Slugging Percentage					
AL:	.560 Baltimore 1970	.511 Oakland 1988	.497 New York 1996	.512 Texas 2010	.521 Boston 2007
NL:	.575 New York 1969	.544 Los Angeles 1978	.515 Los Angeles 2017	.495 St. Louis 2011	.504 Los Angeles 2020
Slugging Percentage Both Clubs					
AL:	.476 Balt. .560 & Minn. .386 1970	.443 KC .444 NY .443 1978	.448 NY .497 Balt. .398 1996	.476 Det. .483 Tex. .468 2011	.465 Bos. .521 Clev. .410 2007
NL:	.530 NY .575 Atl. .481 1969	.477 LA .544 Phil. .407 1978	.456 SF .473 Chi. .440 1989	.480 StL .495 Mil. .463 2011	.469 Fla. .453 Chi. .484 2003
At-Bats					
AL:	123 Baltimore 1969	158 Detroit 2012	184 Boston 1999	222 New York 2009	277 New York 2004
NL:	113 New York 1969	149 Atlanta 1995	190 Philadelphia 1980	227 New York 1986	256 Florida 2003
At-Bats, Both Clubs					
AL:	233 Balt. 123 Minn. 110 1969	298 Det. 158 NY 140	360 NY 176 Bos. 184 1999	438 NY 222 LA 216 2009	548 Bos. 271 NY 277 2004
NL:	219 NY 113 Atl. 106 1969	287 LA 147 Phil. 140 1978	362 Phil. 190 Hou. 172 1980	452 NY 227 Hou. 225 1986	508 Fla. 256 Chi. 252 2003
Runs					
AL:	27 Baltimore 1970	26 Baltimore 1979	34 Minnesota 1987	39 Texas 2011	51 Boston 2007
NL:	27 New York 1969	24 Pittsburgh 1971	35 Philadelphia 2009	43 St. Louis 2011	44 Atlanta 1996
Runs, Both Clubs					
AL:	37 Balt. 27 Minn. 10 1970	41 Balt. 26 Cal. 15 1979	57 Minn. 34 Det. 23 1987	64 Tex. 39 Det. 25 2011 KC 38 Tor. 26 2015	86 Bos. 41 NY 45 2004
NL:	42 NY 27 Atl. 15 1969	39 Pitt. 24 SF 15 1971	52 SF 30 Chi. 22 1989 NY 31 StL 21 2000	69 StL 43 Mil. 26 2011	82 Fla. 40 Chi. 42 2003
Hits					
AL:	36 Balt. 1969-70; NY 1981	46 Detroit 2012	55 New York 1976	65 Toronto 1993	78 New York 2004
NL:	37 New York 1969	42 Los Angeles 1978 Atlanta 1995	55 Philadelphia 1980	67 St. Louis 2011	77 Atlanta 1996
Hits, Both Clubs					
AL:	60 Balt. 36 Minn. 24 1970	77 NY 42 KC 35 1978	96 NY 42 Bos. 54 1999	114 Tex. 63 Det. 51 2011	153 Bos. 75 NY 78 2004
NL:	64 NY 37 Atl. 27 1969	77 LA 42 Phil. 35 1978	97 Chi. 53 SF 44 1989	118 StL 67 Mil. 51 2011	133 Fla. 68 Chi. 65 2003
Extra-Base Hits					
AL:	13 Baltimore 1969-70	15 Oakland 1988	22 Minnesota 1987	25 Texas 2011	32 New York 2004
NL:	15 New York 1969	19 Los Angeles 1978	20 Chicago 1984 Los Angeles 2017	24 St. Louis 2011 Milwaukee 2011	28 Pittsburgh 1992

CHAMPIONSHIP SERIES – CLUB BATTING

	3 Games	4 Games	5 Games	6 Games	7 Games
Extra-Base Hits, Both Clubs					
AL:	24 Balt. 12 Oak. 12 1971	25 Det. 14 Oak. 11 2006	33 Minn. 22 Det. 11 1987 NY 20 Balt. 13 1996 Bos. 20 NY 13 1999	48 Tex. 25 Det. 23 2011	55 Bos. 23 NY 32 2004
NL:	29 NY 15 Atl. 14 1969	29 LA 19 Phil. 10 1978	31 SF 16 Chi. 15 1989	48 StL 24 Mil. 24 2011	52 Chi. 27 Fla. 25 2003
Total Bases					
AL:	61 Baltimore 1970	73 Detroit 2012	91 New York 1996	106 Texas 2010	130 New York 2004
NL:	65 New York 1969	80 Los Angeles 1978	84 Los Angeles 2017	107 St. Louis 2011	122 Chicago 2003
Total Bases, Both Clubs					
AL:	100 Balt. 61 Minn. 39 1970	121 NY 62 KC 59 1978	161 NY 91 Balt. 70 1996	204 Tex. 103 Det. 101 2011	249 Bos. 119 NY 130 2004
NL:	116 NY 65 Atl. 51 1969	137 LA 80 Phil. 57 1978	155 SF 78 Chi. 77 1989	200 StL 107 Mil. 93 2011	238 Fla. 116 Chi. 122 2003
Singles					
AL:	29 New York 1981	34 Oakland 1990	37 Minnesota 1991	52 Toronto 1993	53 California 1986
NL:	27 St. Louis 1982	31 Atlanta 1995	45 Philadelphia 1980	42 St. Louis 1985	55 Atlanta 1996
Singles, Both Clubs					
AL:	46 NY 29 Oak. 17 1981	55 NY 33 KC 22 1978	73 Minn. 37 Tor. 36 1991	87 Tor. 52 Chi. 35 1993	103 Cal. 53 Bos. 50 1986
NL:	41 StL 27 Atl. 14 1982	53 Atl. 31 Cin. 22 1995	73 Phil. 45 Hou. 28 1980	79 SD 41 Atl. 38 1998	90 Atl. 55 StL. 35 1996
Doubles					
AL:	8 By many	9 Baltimore 1983	13 NY 1976 Minn. 1987 Boston 1999	17 Texas 2011	21 New York 2004
NL:	9 Atlanta 1969	11 Washington 2019	12 New York 2000	16 St. Louis 2011	20 Pittsburgh 1992
Doubles, Both Clubs					
AL:	15 Oak. 8 Balt. 7 1971	14 Det. 7 Oak. 7 2006	21 NY 12 KC 9 1977 Bos. 11 Hou. 10 2018	26 Tex. 17 Det. 9 2011	33 Bos. 12 NY 21 2004
NL:	17 Atl. 9 NY 8 1969	14 Wash. 11 StL. 3 2019	23 NY 12 StL. 11 2000	31 StL. 16 Mil. 15 2011	31 Pitt. 20 Atl. 11 1992
Triples					
AL:	1 By many	3 Kansas City 1978	4 Kansas City 1976	3 Toronto 1993 Cleveland 1995	2 Boston 1986 & 2003 New York 2004 Tampa Bay 2008
NL:	3 Cincinnati 1976	3 Los Angeles 1978	5 Houston 1980	4 Philadelphia 1993	4 St. Louis 1987 Chicago 2003 St. Louis 2006
Triples, Both Clubs					
AL:	2 Balt. 1 Minn. 1 1969 Balt. 1 Oak. 1 1971 KC 1 NY 1 1980	4 KC 3 NY 1 1978	6 KC 4 NY 2 1976	4 Tor. 3 Chi. 1 1993	3 Bos. 1 NY 2 2004 TB 2 Bos. 1 2008
NL:	4 Cin. 3 Phil. 1 1976	5 LA 3 Phil. 2 1978	6 Hou. 5 Phil. 1 1980	5 LA 3 StL. 2 2013	7 Chi. 4 Fla. 3 2003

CHAMPIONSHIP SERIES – CLUB BATTING

	3 Games	4 Games	5 Games	6 Games	7 Games
Home Runs					
AL:	6 Baltimore 1970	7 Oakland 1988 Detroit 2006	10 New York 1996	13 Detroit 2011	16 Tampa Bay 2008
NL:	6 New York 1969	8 By many	10 Philadelphia 2009 Los Angeles 2017	9 Milwaukee 2011	16 Los Angeles 2020
Home Runs, Both Clubs					
AL:	9 Balt. 6 Minn. 3 1970	11 Det. 7 Oak. 4 2006	19 NY 10 Balt. 9 1996	20 Det. 13 Tex. 7 2011	26 TB 16 Bos. 10 2008
NL:	11 NY 6 Atl. 5 1969	13 Pitt. 8 SF 5 1971 LA 8 Phil. 5 1978	17 LA 10 Chi. 7 2017	17 Mil. 9 StL 8 2011	25 StL 11 Hou. 14 2004 LA 16 Atl. 9 2020
Runs Batted In					
AL:	24 Baltimore 1970	25 Baltimore 1979	33 Minnesota 1987	39 Texas 2011	48 Boston 2007
NL:	24 New York 1969	23 Pittsburgh 1971	34 Philadelphia 2009	37 St. Louis 2011	43 Atlanta 1996
Runs Batted In, Both Clubs					
AL:	34 Balt. 24 Minn. 10 1970	39 Balt. 25 Cal. 14 1979	54 Minn. 33 Det. 21 1987	63 Tex. 39 Det. 24 2011	84 Bos. 40 NY 44 2004
NL:	39 NY 24 Atl. 15 1969	37 Pitt. 23 SF 14 1971 LA 21 Phil. 16 1978	50 SF 29 Chi. 21 1989	63 StL. 37 Mil. 26 2011	80 Chi. 41 Fla. 39 2003
Sacrifice Hits					
AL:	5 Boston 1975	4 Oakland 1990	5 California 1982	5 Chicago 1993	4 KC 1985 Cal. 1986
NL:	5 Pitt. 1979; StL. 1982	4 San Francisco 1971	8 San Francisco 2002	8 Houston 2005	7 Chicago 2003
Sacrifice Hits, Both Clubs					
AL:	5 Bos. 5 Oak. 0 1975	5 Oak. 4 Bos. 1 1990	7 Oak. 4 Det. 3 1972 Cal. 5 Mil. 2 1982	8 NY 4 LA 4 2009	7 Cal. 4 Bos. 3 1986
NL:	7 StL 5 Atl. 2 1982	5 SF 4 Pitt. 1 1971 Phil. 3 LA 2 1983	13 SF 8 StL 5 2002	11 Hou. 8 StL. 3 2005	10 Fla. 3 Chi. 7 2003
Sacrifice Flies					
AL:	2 Baltimore 1970	3 Baltimore 1979 Oakland 1990	4 Kansas City 1976	6 Kansas City 2015	5 Boston 2007
NL:	3 By many	1 Philadelphia 1978, 83 Cincinnati 1995 Colorado 2007 New York 2015 Washington 2019	4 San Diego 1984	4 St. Louis 2005	4 St. Louis 1987
Sacrifice Flies, Both Clubs					
AL:	2 Balt. 2 Minn. 0 1970	5 Balt. 3 Cal. 2 1979 Oak. 3 Bos. 2 1990	5 KC 4 NY 1 1976 Mil. 3 Cal. 2 1982 Tor. 3 Oak. 2 1989	6 Tor. 4 Oak. 2 1992 KC 6 Tor. 0 2015	8 Bos. 5 Clev. 3 2007
NL:	5 Cin. 3 Phil. 2 1976	1 Phil. 1 LA 0 1978, 83 Cin. 1 Atl. 0 1995 Col. 1 Ari. 0 2007 NY 1 Chi. 0 2015 Wash. 1 StL. 0 2019	6 SD 4 Chi. 2 1984	6 StL. 4 Hou. 2 2005	5 StL. 4 SF 1 1987 Pitt. 3 Atl. 2 1992

CHAMPIONSHIP SERIES – CLUB BATTING

	3 Games	4 Games	5 Games	6 Games	7 Games
Walks					
AL:	13 Balt. 1969, 71; NY 81	22 Oakland 1974	25 Houston 2018	38 New York 2009	35 Boston 2008
NL:	15 Cincinnati 1976	30 Los Angeles 1974	31 Houston 1980	31 Atlanta 1999	31 Los Angeles 2020
Walks, Both Clubs					
AL:	25 Balt. 13 Minn. 12 1969	33 Det. 19 Oak. 14 2006	45 Hou. 25 Bos. 20 2018	56 NY 38 LA 18 2009	61 Bos. 28 NY 33 2004
NL:	27 Cin. 15 Phil. 12 1976	38 LA 30 Pitt. 8 1974	44 Hou. 31 Phil. 13 1980 / LA 25 Phil. 19 2008	53 SD 27 Atl. 26 1998	58 Atl. 29 Pitt. 29 1992 / LA 31 Atl. 27 2020
Intentional Walks					
AL:	2 By many	3 By many	3 Oak. 1973; Minn. 1987 / New York 1999	8 Texas 2010	4 KC 1985 Cal. 1986
NL:	4 By many	8 Los Angeles 1984	9 Houston 1980	10 Atlanta 1999	5 St. Louis 2006 / Milwaukee 2018
Hit By Pitch					
AL:	2 New York 1981	4 Oakland 1990	5 Minnesota 1987 / Houston 2018	5 Cleveland 1998	7 New York 2004
NL:	1 By many	4 Arizona 2007	5 Philadelphia 2009	7 Philadelphia 2010	5 Houston 2004 / Los Angeles 2018
Hit By Pitch, Both Clubs					
AL:	2 NY 2 Oak. 0 1981	5 Oak. 3 Balt. 2 1983	9 Hou. 5 Bos. 4 2018	7 NY 2 Clev. 5 1998	9 TB 6 Hou. 3 2020
NL:	1 Atl. 1 NY 0 1969 / Pitt. 1 Cin. 0 1975	5 Ari. 4 Col. 1 2007	6 Phil. 5 LA 1 2009	10 Phil. 7 SF 3 2010	7 StL 2 Hou. 5 2004
Strikeouts					
AL:	27 Minnesota 1969	36 New York 2012	50 Toronto 2016	73 Boston 2013	81 Tampa Bay 2020
NL:	28 Cincinnati 1975	48 St. Louis 2019	53 Chicago 2017	57 New York 1986	82 Los Angeles 2018
Strikeouts, Both Clubs					
AL:	41 Minn. 27 Balt. 14 1969 / Minn. 22 Balt. 19 1970	66 NY 36 Det. 30 2012	89 Tor. 50 Clev. 39 2016	118 NY 64 Hou. 54 2019	135 TB 81 Hou. 54 2020
NL:	46 Cin. 28 Pitt. 18 1975	92 StL. 48 Wash. 44 2019	94 Chi. 53 LA 41 2017	112 SF 56 Phil. 56 2010	161 LA 82 Mil. 79 2018
Stolen Bases					
AL:	4 Detroit 1984	9 Oakland 1990	13 Oakland 1989	16 Oakland 1992	10 Tampa Bay 2008
NL:	11 Cincinnati 1975	7 New York 2015	7 Philadelphia 1980	14 Atlanta 1999	10 Atlanta 1991

CHAMPIONSHIP SERIES – CLUB BATTING

	3 Games	4 Games	5 Games	6 Games	7 Games
Stolen Bases, Both Clubs					
AL:	4 NY 2 Oak. 2 1981 Det. 4 KC 0 1984	10 Oak. 9 Bos. 1 1990	24 Oak. 13 Tor. 11 1989	23 Oak. 16 Tor. 7 1992	12 TB 10 Bos. 2 2008
NL:	11 Cin. 11 Pitt. 0 1975	8 NY 7 Chi. 1 2015	11 Phil. 7 Hou. 4 1980	21 Atl. 14 NY 7 1999	16 Atl. 10 Pitt. 6 1991
Caught Stealing					
AL:	5 Kansas City 1980	3 By many	5 Kansas City 1976	5 Toronto 1992	5 Boston 2003
NL:	2 By many	3 Los Angeles 1983 Cincinnati 1995	3 Philadelphia 1980 Chicago 1984	6 St. Louis 1985	4 StL. & SF 1987 Atlanta 1991 Houston 2004
Caught Stealing, Both Clubs					
AL:	5 KC 5 NY 0 1980	6 Oak. 3 Balt. 3 1974	8 KC 5 NY 3 1976	7 Tor. 5 Oak. 2 1992	6 KC 4 Tor. 2 1985 NY 1 Bos. 5 2003
NL:	3 Pitt. 2 Cin. 1 1970	4 Cin. 3 Atl. 1 1995	5 Chi. 3 SD 2 1984	7 StL. 6 LA 1 1985	8 SF 4 StL. 4 1987
Grounded into Double Plays					
AL:	6 Oakland 1981	7 Oakland 2006	6 New York 1996 Boston 1999	10 Baltimore 1997	14 Boston 2007
NL:	3 Atlanta 1982	8 Cincinnati 1995	7 Los Angeles 1981 Los Angeles 2008	8 Los Angeles 2013	8 St. Louis 1987
Grounded into Double Plays, Both Clubs					
AL:	7 Balt. 4 Minn. 3 1970 Oak. 6 NY 1 1981	10 Oak. 7 Det. 3 2006	7 Det. 5 Oak. 2 1972 Minn. 4 Tor. 3 1991 NY 6 Balt. 1 1996 NY 4 Sea. 3 2001	13 Balt. 10 Clev. 3 1997 LA 7 NY 6 2009	19 Bos. 14 Clev. 5 2007
NL:	4 NY 2 Atl. 2 1969 Cin. 2 Pitt. 2 1975 Pitt. 2 Cin. 2 1979	11 Cin. 8 Atl. 3 1995	12 LA 7 Phil. 5 2008	13 LA 8 StL. 5 2013	13 StL. 8 SF 5 1987
Left on Base					
AL:	30 New York 1981	40 Detroit 2012	45 Boston 1999	64 New York 2009	69 New York 2004
NL:	31 St. Louis 1982	44 Los Angeles 1974	45 Houston 1980	52 Philadelphia 1993 San Diego 1998	58 Atlanta 1996
Left on Base, Both Clubs					
AL:	50 Balt. 28 Minn. 22 1969 NY 30 Oak. 20 1981	69 Det. 40 NY 29 2012	87 Bos. 45 NY 42 1999	110 NY 64 LA 46 2009	122 Bos. 53 NY 69 2004
NL:	49 Cin. 25 Pitt. 24 1979	68 LA 44 Pitt. 24 1974	88 Hou. 45 Phil. 43 1980	99 Phil. 52 Atl. 47 1993	105 Pitt. 54 Atl. 51 1991

BATTING

Highest Batting Average, Game
.468 Atlanta NL Oct. 14, 1996
.468 New York AL Oct. 16, 2004

Highest Slugging Percentage, Game
.936 New York AL Oct. 16, 2004
.895 Chicago NL Oct. 2, 1984

Most Plate Appearances, Game
54 Los Angeles NL Oct. 14, 2020
53 New York AL Oct. 16, 2004
Extra-Inning Game:
67 Atlanta NL Oct. 17, 1999 (15 inn)
64 New York AL Oct. 18, 2004 (14 inn)

Most Plate Appearances, Both Clubs, Game
97 NY (53) Bos. (44) AL Oct. 16, 2004
90 Ari. (50) Atl. (40) NL Oct. 20, 2001
    LA (54) Atl. (36) NL Oct. 14, 2020
Extra-Inning Game:
126 NY (59) Atl. (67) NL Oct. 17, 1999 (15 inn)
122 NY (64) Bos. (58) AL Oct. 18, 2004 (14 inn)

Most Plate Appearances, Inning
15 Anaheim AL Oct. 13, 2002 (7th)
14 St. Louis NL Oct. 13, 1985 (2nd)
    Los Angeles NL Oct. 14, 2020 (1st)

Most At-Bats, Game
47 Atlanta NL Oct. 14, 1996
    New York AL Oct. 16, 2004
Extra-Inning Game:
56 Houston NL Oct. 15, 1986 (16 inn)
53 New York AL Oct. 18, 2004 (14 inn)

Most At-Bats, Both Clubs, Game
87 NY (47) Bos. (40) AL Oct. 16, 2004
80 Atl. (47) StL. (33) NL Oct. 14, 1996
    Ari. (42) Atl. (38) NL Oct. 20, 2001
Extra-Inning Game:
110 Hou. (56) NY (54) NL Oct. 15, 1986 (16 inn)
103 NY (53) Bos. (50) AL Oct. 18, 2004 (14 inn)

Most At-Bats, Inning
13 Anaheim AL Oct. 13, 2002 (7th)
12 St. Louis NL Oct. 13, 1985 (2nd)

Most Runs, Game
19 New York AL Oct. 16, 2004
15 Atlanta NL Oct. 17, 1996
    Los Angeles NL Oct. 14, 2020

Most Runs, Both Clubs, Game
27 NY (19) Bos. (8) AL Oct. 16, 2004
18 Atl. (13) Pitt. (5) NL Oct. 7, 1992
    StL. (12) Mil. (6) NL Oct. 16, 2011
    LA (15) Atl. (3) NL Oct. 14, 2020
Extra-Inning Game:
19 Atl. (10) NY (9) NL Oct. 19, 1999 (11 inn)

Most Runs, Inning
11 Los Angeles NL Oct. 14, 2020 (1st)
10 Anaheim AL Oct. 13, 2002 (7th)

Most Earned Runs, Game
19 New York AL Oct. 16, 2004
15 Atlanta NL Oct. 17, 1996
    Los Angeles NL Oct. 14, 2020

Most Earned Runs, Both Clubs, Game
26 NY (19) Bos. (7) AL Oct. 16, 2004
18 Atl. (10) NY (8) NL Oct. 19, 1999 (11 inn)
    LA (15) Atl. (3) NL Oct. 14, 2020

Most Earned Runs, Inning
11 Los Angeles NL Oct. 14, 2020 (1st)
10 Anaheim AL Oct. 13, 2002 (7th)

Most Innings Scoring, Game
6 New York NL Oct. 5, 1969
   Los Angeles NL Oct. 9, 1974
   Atlanta NL Oct. 14, 1996
   Philadelphia NL Oct. 21, 2009
   St. Louis NL Oct. 10, 2011
   Detroit AL Oct. 2, 1984
   Toronto AL Oct. 10, 1992
   Boston AL Oct. 16, 1999
   New York AL Oct. 16, 2004
   Boston AL Oct. 17, 2018

Most Innings Scoring, Consecutive, Game
5 New York NL Oct. 5, 1969
   Seattle AL Oct. 20, 2001

Most Innings Scoreless, Consecutive, Series
30 Baltimore AL Oct. 5-9, 1974
26 Atlanta NL Oct. 13-16, 1991

Most Hits, Game
22 Atlanta NL Oct. 14, 1996
    New York AL Oct. 16, 2004

Most Hits, Both Clubs, Game
37 NY (22) Bos. (15) AL Oct. 16, 2004
29 Atl. (22) StL. (7) NL Oct. 14, 1996

Fewest Hits, Game
1 Oakland AL Oct. 9, 1974
   Seattle AL Oct. 14, 2000
   Boston AL Oct. 12, 2013
   Pittsburgh NL Oct. 12, 1990
   St. Louis NL Oct. 18, 2004
   St. Louis NL Oct. 11, 2019

Most Hits, Inning
10 Anaheim AL Oct. 13, 2002 (7th)
8   St. Louis NL Oct. 13, 1985 (2nd)
    Pittsburgh NL Oct. 13, 1992 (2nd)

Most Total Bases, Game
44 New York AL Oct. 16, 2004
34 Chicago NL Oct. 2, 1984
    Atlanta NL Oct. 14, 1996
    Los Angeles NL Oct. 14, 2020

Most Total Bases, Both Clubs, Game
70 NY (44) Bos. (26) AL Oct. 16, 2004
50 NY (28) StL. (22) NL Oct. 15, 2006
Extra-Inning Game:
60 Fla. (32) Chi. (28) NL Oct. 7, 2003 (11 inn)

Fewest Total Bases, Game
1 St. Louis NL Oct. 18, 2004
   St. Louis NL Oct. 11, 2019
   Boston AL Oct. 12, 2013

Most Total Bases, Inning
18 Los Angeles NL Oct. 14, 2020 (1st)
16 Baltimore AL Oct. 3, 1970 (4th)

Most Extra-Base Hits, Game
13 New York AL Oct. 16, 2004
8   Cincinnati NL Oct. 9, 1976
    Chicago NL Oct. 2, 1984
    Milwaukee NL Oct. 9, 2011
    Chicago NL Oct. 15, 2016
    Los Angeles NL Oct. 14, 2020
Extra-Inning Game:
9 Chicago NL Oct. 7, 2003 (11 inn)

Most Extra-Base Hits, Both Clubs, Game
20 NY (13) Bos. (7) AL Oct. 16, 2004
12 Phil. (7) Atl. (5) NL Oct. 9, 1993
NL Extra-Inning Game:
17 Chi. (9) Fla. (8) NL Oct. 7, 2003 (11 inn)

Most Extra-Base Hits, Inning
5 New York NL Oct. 15, 2000 (1st)
   Milwaukee NL Oct. 9, 2011(5th)
4 Baltimore AL Oct. 12, 1997 (3rd)
   Seattle AL Oct. 20, 2001 (6th)
   Boston AL Oct. 16, 2007 (8th)
   Detroit AL Oct. 13, 2013 (6th)

Most Singles, Game
15 New York AL Oct. 14, 1981
    Atlanta NL Oct. 14, 1996

Most Singles, Both Clubs, Game
25 KC (13) NY (12) AL Oct. 4, 1978
22 Atl. (15) StL. (7) NL Oct. 14, 1996

Most Singles, Inning
9 Anaheim AL Oct. 13, 2002 (7th)
8 St. Louis NL Oct. 13, 1985 (2nd)

Most Doubles, Game
8 New York AL Oct. 16, 2004
6 Philadelphia NL Oct. 12, 1976
   Atlanta NL Oct. 17, 1999 (15 inn)
   New York NL Oct. 15, 2000

Most Doubles, Both Clubs, Game
13 NY (8) Bos. (5) AL Oct. 16, 2004
 8 LA (5) StL. (3) NL Oct. 12, 1985
   Phil. (5) Atl. (3) NL Oct. 6, 1993 (10 inn)
   Atl. (5) Phil. (3) NL Oct. 9, 1993
   NY (6) StL. (2) NL Oct. 15, 2000
   Chi. (5) LA (3) NL Oct. 20, 2016

Most Doubles, Inning
5 New York NL Oct. 15, 2000 (1st)
3 Oakland AL Oct. 10, 1973 (2nd)
   Boston AL Oct. 4, 1975 (7th)
   Minnesota AL Oct. 8, 1987 (2nd)
   New York AL Oct. 16, 2003 (8th)
   Boston AL Oct. 21, 2007 (8th)
   Texas AL Oct. 16, 2010 (3rd)

Most Triples, Game
3 Philadelphia NL Oct. 9, 1993
2 Kansas City AL Oct. 13, 1976
   Kansas City AL Oct. 8, 1977
   Seattle AL Oct. 20, 2001
   Tampa Bay AL Oct. 14, 2008

Most Triples, Both Clubs, Game
3 LA (2) Phil. (1) NL Oct. 4, 1978
   Phil. (3) Atl. (0) NL Oct. 9, 1993
   TB (2) Bos. (1) AL Oct. 14, 2008
   Extra-Inning Game:
4 Fla. (2) Chi. (2) NL Oct. 7, 2003 (11 inn)

Most Triples, Inning
2 Kansas City AL Oct. 8, 1977 (3rd)
   Philadelphia NL Oct. 9, 1993 (4th)
   Chicago NL Oct. 7, 2003 (1st)

Most Home Runs, Game
5 Chicago NL Oct. 2, 1984
   Los Angeles NL Oct. 14, 2020
4 Baltimore AL Oct. 4, 1971
   Oakland AL Oct. 7, 1973
   Oakland AL Oct. 9, 1988
   New York AL Oct. 12, 1996
   Cleveland AL Oct. 9, 1998
   Anaheim AL Oct. 13, 2002
   New York AL Oct. 16, 2004
   Boston AL Oct. 20, 2004
   Boston AL Oct. 11, 2008 (11 inn)
   Tampa Bay AL Oct. 13, 2008
   New York AL Oct. 19, 2009 (11 inn)
   Texas AL Oct. 19, 2010
   Detroit AL Oct. 13, 2011
   Detroit AL Oct. 15, 2011
   Detroit AL Oct. 18, 2012

Most Home Runs, Both Clubs, Game
7 Fla. (4) Chi. (3) NL Oct. 7, 2003 (11 inn)
   NY (4) StL. (3) NL Oct. 15, 2006
   Phil. (4) LA (3) NL Oct. 21, 2009
6 Balt. (3) NY (3) AL Oct. 13, 1996
   NY (4) Bos. (2) AL Oct. 16, 2004
   Det. (4) Tex. (2) AL Oct. 15, 2011
   Extra-Inning Game:
7 Bos. (4) TB (3) AL Oct. 11, 2008 (11 inn)

Most Home Runs, Inning
3 Baltimore AL Oct. 3, 1970 (4th)
   New York AL Oct. 13, 1996 (3rd)
   Baltimore AL Oct. 12, 1997 (3rd)
   Cleveland AL Oct. 9, 1998 (5th)
   Boston AL Oct. 16, 2007 (6th)
   Tampa Bay AL Oct. 11, 2008 (5th)
   Florida NL Oct. 7, 2003 (3rd)
   Los Angeles NL Oct. 14, 2020 (1st)

Most Grand Slam Home Runs, Game
1 By many (see individual batting)

Most Runs Batted In, Game
18 New York AL Oct. 16, 2004
15 Los Angeles NL Oct. 14, 2020

Most Runs Batted In, Both Clubs, Game
25 NY (18) Bos. (7) AL Oct. 16, 2004
18 Atl. (9) NY (9) NL Oct. 19, 1999 (11 inn)
   LA (15) Atl. (3) NL Oct. 14, 2020

Most Runs Batted In, Inning
11 Los Angeles NL Oct. 14, 2020 (1st)
 9 Anaheim AL Oct. 13, 2002 (7th)
   Texas AL Oct. 15, 2011 (3rd)

Most Sacrifice Hits, Game
3 By many; last:
   New York AL Oct. 25, 2009
   Houston NL Oct. 19, 2005

Most Sacrifice Hits, Both Clubs, Game
4 LA (3) Mtl. (1) NL Oct. 17, 1981
   StL. (2) Atl. (2) NL Oct. 9, 1982
   Atl. (2) Phil. (2) NL Oct. 13, 1993
3 Cal. (3) Mil. (0) AL Oct. 10, 1982
   Bos. (2) Cal. (1) AL Oct. 11, 1986 (11 inn)
   Cal. (3) Bos. (0) AL Oct. 12, 1986 (11 inn)
   Oak. (2) Bos. (1) AL Oct. 6, 1990
   NY (2) Bos. (1) AL Oct. 17, 2004 (12 inn)
   LA (2) NY (1) AL Oct. 17, 2009 (13 inn)
   NY (3) LA (0) AL Oct. 25, 2009
   Extra-Inning Game:
5 Phil. (3) Hou. (2) NL Oct. 8, 1980 (10 inn)
   Chi. (2) Fla. (3) NL Oct. 10, 2003 (11 inn)

Most Sacrifice Hits, Inning
2 Philadelphia NL Oct. 10, 1976 (4th)
   New York AL Oct. 25, 2009 (8th)

Most Sacrifice Flies, Game
4 Kansas City AL Oct. 20, 2015
3 St. Louis NL Oct. 7, 1982

Most Sacrifice Flies, Both Clubs, Game
4 KC (4) Tor. (0) AL Oct. 20, 2015
3 StL. (3) Atl. (0) NL Oct. 7, 1982
   StL. (2) SF (1) NL Oct. 11, 1987
   NY (2) Atl. (1) NL Oct. 19, 1999 (11 inn)

Most Sacrifice Flies, Inning
2 Milwaukee AL Oct. 8, 1982 (4th)
   Baltimore AL Oct. 7, 1983 (9th)
   Detroit AL Oct. 7, 1987 (8th)
   Kansas City AL Oct. 20, 2015 (7th)
   San Diego NL Oct. 7, 1984 (6th)

Most Walks, Game
11 Oakland AL Oct. 9, 1974
   New York AL Oct. 11, 1998
   Los Angeles NL Oct. 9, 1974

Most Walks, Both Clubs, Game
15 NY (10) Sea. (5) AL Oct. 21, 2001
   Bos. (8) NY (7) AL Oct. 17, 2004 (12 inn)
   NY (8) Bos. (7) AL Oct. 18, 2004 (14 inn)
   Hou. (9) TB (6) AL Oct. 16, 2020
14 Phil. (7) LA (7) NL Oct. 10, 2008
   Extra-Inning Game:
15 Atl. (10) NY (5) NL Oct. 17, 1999 (15 inn)

Most Walks, Inning
4 Oakland AL Oct. 9, 1974 (5th)
   Boston AL Oct. 20, 2007 (3rd)
   Texas AL Oct. 15, 2011 (3rd)
   Philadelphia NL Oct. 7, 1977 (2nd)
   St. Louis NL Oct. 12, 1985 (1st)
   San Francisco NL Oct. 9, 1989 (8th)
   Atlanta NL Oct. 13, 2020 (5th)

Most Walks, Consecutive, Inning
4 Oakland AL Oct. 9, 1974 (5th)
   Philadelphia NL Oct. 7, 1977 (2nd)

Most Intentional Walks, Game
5 Houston NL Oct. 10, 1980 (11 inn)
   St. Louis NL Oct. 12, 1985
   Atlanta NL Oct. 17, 1999 (15 inn)
4 Texas AL Oct. 22, 2010

Most Intentional Walks, Both Clubs, Game
6 StL. (5) LA (1) NL Oct. 12, 1985
4 Tex. (4) NY (0) AL Oct. 22, 2010
   Extra-Inning Game:
7 Hou. (5) Phil. (2) NL Oct. 10, 1980 (11 inn)
5 LA (3) NY (2) AL Oct. 17, 2009 (13 inn)

Most Intentional Walks, Inning
2 By many

Most Hit By Pitch, Game
3 Minnesota AL Oct. 11, 1987
   Cleveland AL Oct. 9, 1997
   Houston AL Oct. 13, 2018
   Atlanta NL Oct. 19, 1999 (11 inn)
   San Francisco NL Oct. 14, 2002
   Philadelphia NL Oct. 21, 2009
   Los Angeles NL Oct. 14, 2020

Most Hit By Pitch, Both Clubs, Game
4 Det. (2) Minn. (2) AL Oct. 12, 1987
   NY (2) Clev. (2) AL Oct. 11, 1998
   Bos. (2) Hou. (2) AL Oct. 17, 2018
3 Atl. (2) Fla. (1) NL Oct. 7, 1997
   Atl. (3) NY (0) NL Oct. 19, 1999 (11 inn)
   SF (3) StL. (0) NL Oct. 14, 2002
   Phil. (3) LA (0) NL Oct. 21, 2009
   Phil. (2) SF (1) NL Oct. 20, 2010
   LA (3) Atl. (0) NL Oct. 14, 2020

Most Hit By Pitch, Inning
3 Cleveland AL Oct. 9, 1997 (1st)
2 Atlanta NL Oct. 19, 1999 (1st)
   Philadelphia NL Oct. 21, 2009 (4th)

Most Strikeouts, Game
17 Boston AL Oct. 12, 2013
16 St. Louis NL:Oct. 14, 2019
   Extra-Inning Game:
21 Cleveland AL Oct. 11, 1997 (12 inn)
19 Atlanta NL Oct. 17, 1999 (15 inn)

Most Strikeouts, Both Clubs, Game
27 StL. (16) Wash. (11) NL Oct. 14, 2019
24 TB (13) Hou. (11) AL Oct. 16, 2020
   Extra-Inning Game:
33 Clev. (21) Balt. (12) AL Oct. 11, 1997 (12 inn)
32 Atl. (19) NY (13) NL Oct. 17, 1999 (15 inn)
   LA (17) Mil. (15) NL Oct. 16, 2018 (13 inn)

Fewest Strikeouts, Game
0 Pittsburgh NL Oct. 6, 1974
1 Baltimore AL Oct. 11, 1973
   New York AL Oct. 13, 1976
   Kansas City AL Oct. 4, 1978
   Toronto AL Oct. 12, 1985
   Boston AL Oct. 10, 1990

Most Strikeouts, Consecutive, Game
6 Oakland AL Oct. 11, 2006
   Boston AL Oct. 15, 2013
   Colorado NL Oct. 15, 2007

Most Stolen Bases, Game
7 Cincinnati NL Oct. 5, 1975
6 Oakland AL Oct. 4, 1989
   Oakland AL Oct. 8, 1992

Most Stolen Bases, Both Clubs, Game
8 Oak. (6) Tor. (2) AL Oct. 4, 1989
   Oak. (6) Tor. (2) AL Oct. 8, 1992
7 Cin. (7) Pitt. (0) NL Oct. 5, 1975
   Extra-Inning Game:
8 Atl. (6) NY (2) NL Oct. 19, 1999 (11 inn)

Most Stolen Bases, Inning
3 Oakland AL Oct. 12, 1972 (2nd)
   Oakland AL Oct. 4, 1989 (7th)
   Oakland AL Oct. 8, 1992 (5th)
   Texas AL Oct. 16, 2010 (1st)
   Toronto AL Oct. 23, 2015 (9th)
   New York NL Oct. 16, 1999 (8th)

Most Caught Stealing, Game
2 By many

Most Caught Stealing, Both Clubs, Game
3 Balt. (2) Oak. (1) AL Oct. 10, 1973
   KC (2) NY (1) AL Oct. 12, 1976
   Mil. (2) Cal. (1) AL Oct. 9, 1982
   Chi. (2) SD (1) NL Oct. 7, 1984
   StL. (2) LA (1) NL Oct. 12, 1985
   SF (2) StL. (1) NL Oct. 7, 1987

Most Caught Stealing, Inning
2 St. Louis NL Oct. 10, 1985 (1st)
   St. Louis NL Oct. 12, 1985 (2nd)
1 By many in AL

Most Grounded into Double Plays, Game
4 Oakland AL Oct. 10, 2006
   Houston AL Oct. 14, 2020
3 By many in NL
   Extra Innings:
5 Cincinnati NL Oct. 10, 1995 (11 inn)

Most Grounded into Double Plays, Both Clubs, Game
5 Cin. (5) Atl. (0) NL Oct. 10, 1995 (11 inn)
   StL. (3) SF (2) NL Oct. 15, 2014
   Hou. (4) TB (1) AL Oct. 14, 2020

Most Left on Base, Game
15 Philadelphia NL Oct. 10, 1993
   New York AL Oct. 15, 2000
   Extra-Inning Game:
19 Atlanta NL Oct. 17, 1999 (15 inn)
18 New York AL Oct. 18, 2004 (14 inn)

Most Left on Base, Both Clubs, Game
26 Phil. (15) Atl. (11) NL Oct. 10, 1993
25 Chi. (13) Tor. (12) AL Oct. 5, 1993
   Extra-Inning Game:
31 Atl. (19) NY (12) NL Oct. 17, 1999 (15 inn)
30 NY (18) Bos. (12) AL Oct. 18, 2004 (14 inn)

Fewest Left on Base, Game
0 Atlanta NL Oct. 16, 1999
   Los Angeles NL Oct. 22, 2016
1 Baltimore AL Oct. 11, 1996
   Los Angeles AL Oct. 14, 2005
   New York AL Oct. 18, 2019

PITCHING

Most Wild Pitches, Game
3 California AL Oct. 9, 1982
   Oakland AL Oct. 10, 1992
   Toronto AL Oct. 5, 1993
   Anaheim AL Oct. 13, 2002
   Oakland AL Oct. 14, 2006
   Houston AL Oct. 17, 2018
   St. Louis NL Oct. 19, 2005
   Los Angeles NL Oct. 15, 2009
   Milwaukee NL Oct. 12, 2011
   Los Angeles NL Oct. 18, 2013

Most Wild Pitches, Both Clubs, Game
4 Ana. (3) Minn. (1) AL Oct. 13, 2002
   Oak. (3) Det. (1) AL Oct. 14, 2006
   Hou. (3) Bos. (1) AL Oct. 17, 2018
3 StL. (2) NY (1) NL Oct. 12, 2000
   StL. (3) Hou. (0) NL Oct. 19, 2005
   LA (3) Phil. (0) NL Oct. 15, 2009
   Phil. (2) SF (1) NL Oct. 20, 2010
   Mil. (3) StL. (0) NL Oct. 12, 2011
   LA (3) StL. (0) NL Oct. 18, 2013

Most Wild Pitches, Inning
3 Los Angeles NL Oct. 15, 2009 (5th)
2 Detroit AL Oct. 8, 1972 (5th)
   California AL Oct. 9, 1982 (4th)
   Minnesota AL Oct. 11, 1991 (5th)
   Toronto AL Oct. 5, 1993 (1st)
   New York AL Oct. 17, 2001 (9th)
   New York AL Oct. 15, 2003 (7th)
   New York AL Oct. 18, 2010 (9th)
   New York AL Oct. 17, 2019 (9th)

CLUB FIELDING

Highest Percentage (1.000 Most Chances)

	3 Games	4 Games	5 Games	6 Games	7 Games
AL:	1.000 Baltimore 1970 (110 tc)	.993 Oakland 1990	.995 New York 1996	.995 Toronto 2015	1.000 Boston 2008 (260 tc)
NL:	1.000 Pittsburgh 1979 (124 tc)	.993 Los Angeles 1983 / New York 2015	1.000 San Francisco 2014 (184 tc)	.996 New York 1986	.996 St. Louis 2004

Highest Percentage, Both Clubs

	3 Games	4 Games	5 Games	6 Games	7 Games
AL:	.995 Oak. 1.000 Balt. .991 1971	.987 Det. .993 Oak. .980 2006	.992 Clev. .995 Tor. .988 2016	.995 Tor. .995 KC .995 2015	.991 Bos. .997 NY .986 2004
NL:	.996 Pitt. 1.000 Cin. .992 1979	.993 NY .993 Chi. .993 2015	.994 SF 1.000 StL. .989 2014	.991 StL. .996 LA .987 2013	.994 StL. .996 Hou. .992 2004

Total Chances

	3 Games	4 Games	5 Games	6 Games	7 Games
AL:	133 Minnesota 1969	166 Baltimore 1979	204 Chicago 2005	257 New York 2009	287 New York 2004
NL:	127 Cincinnati 1979	174 Atlanta 1995	225 Philadelphia 1980	284 New York 1986	284 Chicago 2003

Total Chances, Both Clubs

	3 Games	4 Games	5 Games	6 Games	7 Games
AL:	261 Minn. 133 Balt. 128 1969	323 Balt. 162 Chi. 161 1983	395 Oak. 201 Det. 194 1972	508 NY 257 LA 251 2009	561 NY 287 Bos. 274 2004
NL:	244 Cin. 124 Pitt. 120 1970	330 Atl. 174 Cin. 156 1995	427 Phil. 225 Hou. 202 1980	545 NY 284 Hou. 261 1986	555 Fla. 271 Chi. 284 2003

Chances Accepted

	3 Games	4 Games	5 Games	6 Games	7 Games
AL:	128 Minnesota 1969	161 Baltimore 1979	201 Chicago 2005	254 New York 2009	283 New York 2004
NL:	126 Cincinnati 1979	171 Atlanta 1995	219 Philadelphia 1980	283 New York 1986	280 Chicago 2003

Chances Accepted, Both Clubs

	3 Games	4 Games	5 Games	6 Games	7 Games
AL:	255 Minn. 128 Balt. 127 1969	318 Balt. 160 Chi. 158 1983	385 Oak. 198 Det. 187 1972	497 NY 254 LA 243 2009	556 NY 283 Bos. 273 2004
NL:	241 Cin. 123 Pitt. 118 1970	325 Atl. 171 Cin. 154 1995	418 Phil. 219 Hou. 199 1980	537 NY 283 Hou. 254 1986	548 Fla. 268 Chi. 280 2003

Putouts

	3 Games	4 Games	5 Games	6 Games	7 Games
AL:	96 Baltimore 1969	117 Detroit 2012	141 New York 1996	176 New York 2009	209 New York 2004
NL:	90 Pittsburgh 1979 / 90 Atlanta 1982	117 Atlanta 1995	148 Philadelphia 1980	189 New York 1986	198 Chicago & Florida 2003

Putouts, Both Clubs

	3 Games	4 Games	5 Games	6 Games	7 Games
AL:	190 Balt. 96 Minn. 94 1969	228 Det. 117 NY 111 2012	279 NY 141 Balt. 138 1996	348 Balt. 174 Clev. 174 1997 / NY 176 LA 172 2009	416 NY 209 Bos. 207 2004
NL:	177 Pitt. 90 Cin. 87 1979	228 Atl. 117 Cin. 111 1995	295 Phil. 148 Hou. 147 1980	377 NY 189 Hou. 188 1986	396 Fla. 198 Chi. 198 2003

Assists

	3 Games	4 Games	5 Games	6 Games	7 Games
AL:	41 New York 1980	52 Baltimore 1979	66 Chicago 2005	78 New York 2009	87 Kansas City 1985
NL:	39 Cincinnati 1979 / Atlanta 1982	54 Atlanta 1995	71 Philadelphia 1980	94 New York 1986	82 Chicago 2003

Assists, Both Clubs

	3 Games	4 Games	5 Games	6 Games	7 Games
AL:	73 Oak. 40 Bos. 33 1975	100 Chi. 51 Balt. 49 1983	113 Chi. 66 LA 47 2005	149 NY 78 LA 71 2009	151 Cal. 78 Bos. 73 1986
NL:	76 Cin. 39 Pitt. 37 1970	97 Atl. 54 Cin. 43 1995	123 Phil. 71 Hou. 52 1980	160 NY 94 Hou. 66 1986	152 Fla. 70 Hou. 82 2003

CHAMPIONSHIP SERIES – CLUB FIELDING

	3 Games	4 Games	5 Games	6 Games	7 Games
Errors					
AL:	7 Kansas City 1984	5 Baltimore 1979 Boston 1990	10 Boston 1999	8 Toronto 1992 Los Angeles 2009	8 California 1986
NL:	6 Atlanta 1969	7 Los Angeles 1974	7 St. Louis 2000 Atlanta 2001	9 Milwaukee 2011	8 New York 1988
Errors, Both Clubs					
AL:	10 Oak. 6 Bos. 4 1975	7 Balt. 5 Cal. 2 1979	15 Bos. 10 NY 5 1999	15 Tor. 8 Oak. 7 1992	15 Cal. 8 Bos. 7 1986
NL:	8 Atl. 6 NY 2 1969	11 LA 7 Pitt. 4 1974	11 StL. 7 NY 4 2000	15 NY 8 Atl. 7 1999	13 NY 8 LA 5 1988
Passed Balls					
AL:	1 New York 1981	1 By many	2 Toronto 1991 Chicago 2005 Houston 2018	3 Toronto 1992	5 Tampa Bay 2020
NL:	2 Pittsburgh 1975	1 By many	2 Chicago 1989	2 Houston 1986 Philadelphia 1993	3 Los Angeles 2018
Passed Balls, Both Clubs					
AL:	1 By many	2 NY 1 KC 1 1978 Bos. 1 Oak. 1 1988	3 Hou. 2 Bos. 1 2018	3 Tor. 3 Oak. 0 1992	6 TB 5 Hou. 1 2020
NL:	2 NY 1 Atl. 1 1969 Pitt. 2 Cin. 0 1975 Pitt. 2 Atl. 1 1992	2 Pitt. 1 SF 1 1971	3 Chi. 2 SF 1 1989	2 Hou. 2 NY 0 1986 Phil. 2 Atl. 0 1993	4 LA 3 Mil. 1 2018
Double Plays					
AL:	6 New York 1981	7 California 1979 Detroit 2006	7 Baltimore 1996 New York 1999	11 Cleveland 1997	14 Cleveland 2007
NL:	4 Atlanta 1969	8 Los Angeles 1974 Atlanta 1995	8 Montreal 1981 Philadelphia 2008	9 New York 1999 St. Louis 2013	10 San Francisco 1987 New York 2006
Double Plays, Both Clubs					
AL:	8 Minn. 5 Balt. 3 1970	12 Cal. 7 Balt. 5 1979	9 Oak. 5 Det. 4 1972 Balt. 6 Cal. 3 1982 Tor. 5 Oak. 4 1989 Balt. 7 NY 2 1996 Sea. 5 NY 4 2001 LA 5 Chi. 4 2005	15 Clev. 11 Balt. 4 1997	19 Clev. 14 Bos. 5 2007
NL:	6 Atl. 4 NY 2 1969 Cin. 3 Phil. 3 1976	12 Atl. 8 Cin. 4 1995	13 Pitt. 8 LA 5 1981 Phil. 8 LA 5 2008	16 StL. 9 LA 7 2013	15 SF 10 StL. 5 1987

FIELDING

Most Total Chances, Game
48 Atlanta NL Oct. 4, 1969
    Los Angeles NL Oct. 5, 1978
46 Boston AL Oct. 7, 1975
Extra-Inning Game:
79 New York NL Oct. 15, 1986 (16 inn)
60 Los Angeles AL Oct. 17, 2009 (13 inn)

Most Total Chances, Inning
10 New York AL Oct. 10, 1976 (7th)
    Houston NL Oct. 17, 2005 (7th)

Most Chances Accepted, Game
48 Los Angeles NL Oct. 5, 1978
45 Boston AL Oct. 7, 1975
Extra-Inning Game:
79 New York NL Oct. 15, 1986 (16 inn)
58 Los Angeles AL Oct. 17, 2009 (13 inn)

Most Chances Accepted, Inning
8 New York AL Oct. 10, 1976 (7th)
  Los Angeles NL Oct. 7, 1978 (5th)
  Los Angeles NL Oct. 9, 1985 (4th)
  San Francisco NL Oct. 14, 1987 (1st)
  Atlanta NL Oct. 13, 1992 (2nd)
  New York NL Oct. 13, 1999 (2nd)
  Houston NL Oct. 17, 2005 (7th)
  New York NL Oct. 13, 2006 (9th)

Most Assists, Game
21 Los Angeles NL Oct. 5, 1978
19 Boston AL Oct. 9, 2003
Extra-Inning Game:
31 New York NL Oct. 15, 1986 (16 inn)
21 Los Angeles AL Oct. 17, 2009 (13 inn)

Most Assists, Both Clubs, Game
33 Bos. (18) Oak. (15) AL Oct. 7, 1975
30 LA (21) Phil. (9) NL Oct. 5, 1978
Extra-Inning Game:
56 NY (31) Hou. (25) NL Oct. 15, 1986 (16 inn)
38 LA (21) NY (17) AL Oct. 17, 2009 (13 inn)

Most Assists, Inning
5 New York AL Oct. 10, 1976 (7th)
  Los Angeles NL Oct. 7, 1978 (5th)
  Los Angeles NL Oct. 9, 1985 (4th)
  San Francisco NL Oct. 14, 1987 (1st)
  Atlanta NL Oct. 13, 1992 (2nd)
  New York NL Oct. 13, 1999 (2nd)
  Houston NL Oct. 17, 2005 (7th)
  New York NL Oct. 13, 2006 (9th)

Most Errors, Game
5 Los Angeles NL Oct. 8, 1974
  New York NL Oct. 10, 1976

Most Errors, Both Clubs, Game
7 Oak. (4) Bos. (3) AL Oct. 4, 1975
6 LA (4) Chi. (2) NL Oct. 19, 2016

Most Errors, Inning
3 Oakland AL Oct. 4, 1975 (1st)
  California AL Oct. 8, 1986 (7th)
  Atlanta NL Oct. 20, 2001 (3rd)
  Los Angeles NL Oct. 15, 2008 (5th)
  Milwaukee NL Oct. 16, 2011 (5th)

Most Double Plays, Game
4 Oakland AL Oct. 5, 1975
  Cleveland AL Oct. 11, 1997 (12 inn)
  Detroit AL Oct. 10, 2006
  Tampa Bay AL Oct. 14, 2020
  Los Angeles NL Oct. 13, 1981
  San Francisco NL Oct. 10, 1987
Extra Inning Game:
5 Atlanta NL Oct. 10, 1995 (11 inn)

Most Double Plays, Both Clubs, Game
6 Oak. (4) Bos. (2) AL Oct. 5, 1975
5 Pitt. (3) Cin. (2) NL Oct. 5, 1975
  Mil. (3) StL. (2) NL Oct. 12, 2011
  SF (3) StL. (2) NL Oct. 15, 2014
Extra-Inning Game:
6 Atl. (5) Cin. (1) NL Oct. 10, 1995 (11 inn)

Most Passed Balls, Game
3 Boston AL Oct. 18, 2004 (14 inn)
  Tampa Bay AL Oct. 16, 2020
2 Pittsburgh NL Oct. 4, 1975
  Houston NL Oct. 11, 1986
  Pittsburgh NL Oct. 13, 1992
  Los Angeles NL Oct. 12, 2018

Most Passed Balls, Both Clubs, Game
4 TB (3) Hou. (1) AL Oct. 16, 2020
3 LA (2) Mil. (1) NL Oct. 12, 2018

Most Passed Balls, Inning
3 Boston AL Oct. 18, 2004 (13th)
1 By many in NL

CLUB PITCHING

	3 Games	4 Games	5 Games	6 Games	7 Games
Earned Run Average, Lowest					
AL:	1.13 Baltimore 1969	0.49 Baltimore 1983	1.43 Cleveland 2016	1.64 Cleveland 1995	2.73 New York 2017
NL:	0.96 Cincinnati 1970	1.03 Philadelphia 1983	1.33 New York 1973	2.09 St. Louis 2013	1.57 Atlanta 1991
Earned Run Average, Lowest, Both Clubs					
AL:	2.37 Det. 1.24 KC 3.54 1984	1.77 Oak. 1.75 Balt. 1.80 1974	1.86 Clev. 1.43 Tor. 2.30 2016	2.47 Clev. 1.64 Sea. 3.33 1995	3.02 NY 2.73 Hou. 3.30 2017
NL:	1.80 Cin. 0.96 Pitt. 2.67 1970	2.43 Col. 1.89 Ari. 3.00 2007	2.35 LA 1.84 Mtl. 2.86 1981	2.58 NY 2.29 Hou. 2.87 1986	2.07 Atl. 1.57 Pitt. 2.57 1991
Earned Run Average, Highest					
AL:	7.62 Minnesota 1970	5.80 California 1979	6.70 Detroit 1987	6.58 New York 2010	6.82 Cleveland 2007
NL:	6.92 Atlanta 1969	6.09 San Francisco 1971	7.38 Los Angeles 2009	6.58 Milwaukee 2011	6.60 St. Louis 1996
Earned Run Average, Highest, Both Clubs					
AL:	5.43 Minn. 7.62 Balt. 3.33 1970	4.38 Cal. 5.80 Balt. 2.97 1979	5.59 Det. 6.70 Minn. 4.50 1987	5.50 Tor. 6.53 KC 4.50 2015	5.69 Clev. 6.82 Bos. 4.57 2007
NL:	5.94 Atl. 6.92 NY 5.00 1969	4.70 SF 6.09 Pitt. 3.34 1971	5.19 LA 7.38 Phil. 3.07 2009	5.40 Mil. 6.58 StL. 4.25 2011	4.98 Fla. 5.59 Chi. 4.36 2003
Complete Games					
AL:	2 Baltimore 1969-71	2 Oakland 1974	4 Chicago AL 2005	1 By many	1 Kansas City 1985 Bos. & Cal. 1986 Houston 2017
NL:	1 By many	2 San Francisco 1971 Los Angeles 1977	3 New York 1973	2 Houston 1986 Florida 1997	3 Pittsburgh 1992
Complete Games, Both Clubs					
AL:	3 Balt. 2 Oak. 1 1971	3 Oak. 2 Balt. 1 1974	4 Balt. 2 Oak. 2 1973 Chi. 4 LA 0 2005	2 Tor. 1 Oak. 1 1992	2 Cal. 1 Bos. 1 1986
NL:	1 Cin. 1 Pitt. 0 1975 Pitt. 1 Cin. 0 1979 StL. 1 Atl. 0 1982	2 SF 2 Pitt. 0 1971 LA 2 Phil. 0 1977 LA 1 Phil. 1 1978	3 NY 3 Cin. 0 1973 Fla. 2 Atl. 1 1997	3 Hou. 2 NY 1 1986 Fla. 2 Atl. 1 1997	4 SF 2 StL. 2 1987
Saves					
AL:	2 Boston 1975	4 Oakland 1988 Kansas City 2014	4 Cleveland 2016	3 Toronto 1992 Boston 2013	4 Tampa Bay 2020
NL:	3 Cincinnati 1970	3 Pittsburgh 1971 Colorado 2007 New York 2015 Washington 2019	3 San Francisco 1989, 2002 Philadelphia 2008	4 Cincinnati 1990	3 St. Louis 1987, 2004 Los Angeles 1988 Atlanta 1991
Saves, Both Clubs					
AL:	2 Bos. 2 Oak. 0 1975	4 Oak. 4 Bos. 0 1988 KC 4 Balt. 0 2014	4 Minn. 3 Tor. 1 1991	4 Tor. 3 Oak. 1 1992 Bos. 3 Det. 1 2013	6 TB 4 Hou. 2 2020
NL:	3 Cin. 3 Pitt. 0 1970	3 Pitt. 3 SF 0 1971 Col. 3 Ari. 0 2007 NY 3 Chi. 0 2015 Wash. 3 StL. 0 2019	4 SF 3 StL. 1 2002	6 Cin. 4 Pitt. 2 1990	5 Atl. 3 Pitt. 2 1991 StL. 3 Hou. 2 2004

CLUB PITCHING

	3 Games	4 Games	5 Games	6 Games	7 Games
Shutouts					
AL:	1 Balt. 1969; NY 1981; Det. 1984	2 Oak. 1974; Balt. 1983	2 Cleveland 2016	2 Cleveland 1995	1 Kansas City 1985 / Boston 2008 / Houston & New York 2017
NL:	1 Cin. 1970; StL. 1982	1 LA 1974, 78; Phil. 1983 / Washington 2019	1 By many	2 San Diego 1998 / St. Louis 2013 / Los Angeles 2016	3 Atlanta 1991, 1997
Shutouts, Both Clubs					
AL:	1 Balt. 1 Minn. 0 1969 / Oak. 0 1981 / Det. 1 KC 0 1984	2 Oak. 2 Balt. 0 1974 / Balt. 2 Chi. 0 1983	2 Oak. 1 Det. 1 1972 / Oak. 1 Balt. 1 1973 / Clev. 2 Tor. 0 2016	2 Clev. 2 Sea. 0 1995 / Balt. 1 Clev. 1 1997 / NY 1 Sea. 1 2000 / Bos. 1 Det. 1 2013	2 Hou. 1 NY 1 2017
NL:	1 Cin. 1 Pitt. 0 1970 / StL. 1 Atl. 0 1982	2 LA 1 Pitt. 1 1974 / Hou. 1 Phil. 0 1980	1 By many	3 StL. 2 LA 1 2013 / LA 2 Chi. 1 2016	4 Atl. 3 Pitt. 1 1991
Total Batters Faced					
AL:	138 Minnesota 1969	170 New York 2012	205 Baltimore 1996	269 Los Angeles 2009	321 Boston 2004
NL:	126 Cincinnati 1979	169 Pitt. 1974; Phil. 1993	212 Philadelphia 1980	249 New York 1999	291 Chicago 2003
Total Batters Faced, Both Clubs					
AL:	261 Minn. 138 Balt. 123 1969	322 NY 170 Det. 152	399 Balt. 205 NY 194 1996	510 LA 269 NY 241 2009	624 Bos. 321 NY 303 2004
NL:	246 Cin. 126 Pitt. 120 1979	316 Cin. 166 Atl. 150 1995	422 Phil. 212 Hou. 210 1980	493 NY 249 Atl. 244 1999	576 Fla. 285 Chi. 291 2003
Innings					
AL:	32.0 Baltimore 1969	39.0 Detroit 2012	47.0 New York 1996	58.2 New York 2009	69.2 New York 2004
NL:	30.0 Pittsburgh 1979	39.0 Atlanta 1995	49.1 Philadelphia 1980	63.0 New York 1986	66.0 Chicago & Florida 2003
Innings, Both Clubs					
AL:	63.1 Balt. 32.0 Minn. 31.1 1969	76.0 Det. 39.0 NY 37.0 2012	93.0 NY 47.0 Balt. 46.0 1996	116.0 Balt. 58 Clev. 58 1997 / NY 58.2 LA 57.1 2009	138.2 NY 69.2 Bos. 69.0 2004
NL:	59.0 Pitt. 30.0 Cin. 29.0 1979	76.0 Atl. 39.0 Cin. 37.0 1995	98.1 Phil. 49.1 Hou. 49.0 1980	125.2 NY 63.0 Hou. 62.2 1986	132.0 Chi. 66.0 Fla. 66.0 2003
Earned Runs, Most					
AL:	22 Minnesota 1970	23 California 1979	32 Detroit 1987	38 New York 2010	47 Cleveland 2007
NL:	20 Atlanta 1969	23 San Francisco 1971	35 Los Angeles 2009	38 Milwaukee 2011	44 St. Louis 1996
Earned Runs, Most, Both Clubs					
AL:	32 Minn. 22 Balt. 10 1970	35 Cal. 23 Balt. 12 1979	54 Det. 32 Minn. 22 1987	63 Tor. 37 KC 26 2015	85 Bos. 45 NY 40 2004
NL:	35 Atl. 20 NY 15 1969	36 SF 23 Pitt. 13 1971	50 LA 35 Phil. 15 2009	63 Mil. 38 StL. 25 2011	73 Fla. 41 Chi. 32 2003
Earned Runs, Fewest					
AL:	4 Balt. 1969; NY 1981; Det. 1984	2 Baltimore 1983	7 Cleveland 2016	10 Cleveland 1995	18 New York 2017
NL:	3 Cincinnati 1970	4 Philadelphia 1983	7 New York 1973	13 St. Louis 2013	11 Atlanta 1991
Earned Runs, Fewest, Both Clubs					
AL:	15 Det. 4 KC 11 1984	14 Oak. 7 Balt. 7 1974	18 Clev. 7 Tor. 11 2016	30 Clev. 10 Sea. 20 1995	40 NY 18 Hou. 22 2017
NL:	11 Cin. 3 Pitt. 8 1970	19 Phil. 4 LA 15 1983	23 LA 9 Mtl. 14 1981	33 Cin. 14 Pitt. 19 1990 / Hou. 16 StL. 17 2005 / StL. 13 LA 20 2013	29 Atl. 11 Pitt. 18 1991

CLUB PITCHING

	3 Games	4 Games	5 Games	6 Games	7 Games
Wild Pitches					
AL:	2 By many	3 California 1979 Oakland 2006	7 Houston 2018	7 New York 2010	4 Boston 2007 Houston 2017
NL:	2 By many	4 Los Angeles 1983	6 Los Angeles 2009	4 San Diego 1998 St. Louis 2005 Milwaukee 2011 Los Angeles 2013	4 Atlanta 1996 Florida 2003 New York 2006
Wild Pitches, Both Clubs					
AL:	3 Balt. 2 Minn. 1 1969	5 Oak. 3 Det. 2 2006	10 Hou. 7 Bos. 3 2018	9 NY 7 Tex. 2 2010	7 Hou. 4 NY 3 2017
NL:	4 Cin. 2 Phil. 2 1976 Atl. 2 StL. 2 1982	6 LA 4 Phil. 2 1983	7 StL. 5 NY 2 2000 LA 6 Phil. 1 2009	7 LA 4 StL. 3 2013	7 Fla. 4 Chi. 3 2003
Balks					
AL:	1 Kansas City 1980	2 Baltimore 1983	1 Detroit 1972 Kansas City 1977 Minnesota 1987 New York 1996	1 Toronto 1993 New York 2010 Texas 2010	1 California 1986 Boston 2004
NL:	2 Pittsburgh 1975	1 Los Angeles 1977 Philadelphia 1977 Cincinnati 1995	1 Chicago 1989	1 Atlanta 1998 Los Angeles 2013	2 New York 1988
Balks, Both Clubs					
AL:	1 KC 1 NY 0 1980	2 Balt. 2 Chi. 0 1983 Bos. 1 Oak. 1 1988	1 Det. 1 Oak. 0 1972 KC 1 NY 0 1977 Minn. 1 Det. 0 1987 NY 1 Balt. 0 1996	2 NY 1 Tex. 1 2010	1 Cal. 1 Bos. 0 1986 Bos. 1 NY 0 2004
NL:	2 Pitt. 2 Cin. 0 1975	2 LA 1 Phil. 1 1977	1 Chi. 1 SF 0 1989	1 Atl. 1 SD 0 1998 1 LA 1 StL. 0 2013	2 NY 2 LA 0 1988

CLUB MISCELLANEOUS

	3 Games	4 Games	5 Games	6 Games	7 Games
Players					
AL:	24 Minnesota 1970 Oakland 1981	26 New York 2012	25 Oakland 1972 Seattle 2001 Los Angeles 2005 Houston 2018	25 Oakland 1992 Cleveland 1995, 98 Seattle 1995, 2000 New York 2009 Detroit 2011 Boston 2013 Toronto 2015 Houston 2019	28 Tampa Bay 2020
NL:	24 Pittsburgh 1975	25 St. Louis 2019	25 St. Louis 2000 Philadelphia 2008 Chicago 2013 Los Angeles 2017	25 Los Angeles 1985, 2016 Atlanta 1993 New York & Atlanta 1999 Milwaukee 2011	29 Atlanta 2020

CLUB MISCELLANEOUS

	3 Games	4 Games	5 Games	6 Games	7 Games
Players, Both Clubs					
AL:	46 Oak. 24 NY 22 1981	47 NY 26 Det. 21 2012	49 Oak. 25 Det. 24 1972 / Hou. 25 Bos. 24 2018	50 Clev. 25 Sea. 25 1995	54 TB 28 Hou. 26 2020
NL:	42 Pitt. 24 Cin. 18 1975	46 Cin. 24 Atl. 22 1995 / Ari. 23 Col. 23 2007 / StL. 25 Wash. 21 2019	50 LA 25 Chi. 25 2017	50 Atl. 25 NY 25 1999	57 Atl. 29 LA 28 2020
Pitchers					
AL:	9 Minnesota 1969-70	12 New York 2012	12 Houston 2018	13 New York 2019	14 Tampa Bay 2020
NL:	10 Pittsburgh 1975	12 St. Louis 2019	11 Atlanta 2001 / Philadelphia 2008-09 / Los Angeles 2008-09 / St. Louis & San Francisco 2014 / Los Angeles & Chicago 2017	12 Los Angeles 2016	15 Atlanta 2020 / Los Angeles 2020
Pitchers, Both Clubs					
AL:	16 Minn. 9 Balt. 7 1969	21 NY 12 Det. 9 2012	23 Hou. 12 Bos. 11 2018	25 NY 13 Hou. 12 2019	26 TB 14 Hou. 12 2020
NL:	17 Pitt. 10 Cin. 7 1975 / Cin. 9 Pitt. 8 1979	20 Col. 10 Ari. 10 2007 / Chi. 11 NY 9 2015 / StL. 12 Wash. 8 2019	22 Phil. 11 LA 11 2008-09 / StL. 11 SF 11 2014 / LA 11 Chi. 11 2017	23 LA 12 Chi. 11 2016	30 Atl. 15 LA 15 2020
Pinch-Hitters					
AL:	10 Minnesota 1970	8 Baltimore 1983	14 Oakland 1972	10 Seattle 1995	13 Toronto 1985
NL:	9 Pittsburgh 1975	13 Cincinnati 1995	18 St. Louis 2000	20 New York 1999 / Los Angeles 2016	23 Los Angeles 2018
Pinch-Hitters, Both Clubs					
AL:	13 Oak. 8 NY 5 1981	13 Balt. 8 Chi. 5 1983	22 Oak. 14 Det. 8 1972	14 Balt. 8 Clev. 6 1997	21 Tor. 13 KC 8 1985
NL:	12 Pitt. 9 Cin. 3 1975	21 Cin. 13 Atl. 8 1995	28 StL. 18 NY 10 2000	33 LA 20 Chi. 13 2016	40 LA 23 Mil. 17 2018
Pinch-Runners					
AL:	4 Kansas City 1984	5 Oakland 1974, 1990	5 Anaheim 2002	7 New York 2009	4 Boston 2003-04
NL:	3 New York 1969	1 By many	4 Houston 1980 / New York 2000	5 Atlanta 1998	2 SF 1987; NY 1988 / LA 1988; Atl. 1996
Pinch-Runners, Both Clubs					
AL:	5 KC 4 Det. 1 1984	8 Oak. 5 Balt. 3 1974	6 NY 3 Bos. 3 1999	10 NY 7 LA 3 2009	7 Bos. 4 NY 3 2003
NL:	3 NY 3 Atl. 0 1969 / Pitt. 2 Cin. 1 1970	2 LA 1 Pitt. 1 1974 / Atl. 1 Cin. 1 1995	7 Hou. 4 Phil. 3 1980 / NY 4 StL. 3 2000	5 Atl. 5 SD 0 1998	4 LA 2 NY 2 1988
Extra-Inning Games					
AL:	2 Balt. & Minn. 1969	1 Balt. & Chi. 1983 / Det. & NY 2012 / Balt. & KC 2014	2 Det. & Oak. 1972	2 Balt. & Clev. 1997 / NY & LA 2009 / Tex. & Det. 2011	2 Bos. & Cal. 1986 / Bos. & NY 2004
NL:	2 Cin. & Pitt. 1979	2 Atl. & Cin. 1995	4 Hou. & Phil. 1980	2 NY & Hou. 1986 / Atl. & Phil. 1993 / Atl. & NY 1999	2 Fla. & Chi. 2003

PERSONNEL

Most Players, Game
- 21 St. Louis NL Oct. 16, 2000
  - St. Louis NL Oct. 10, 2011
  - Los Angeles NL Oct. 13, 2018
- 20 Oakland AL Oct. 10, 1972
  - **Extra-Inning Game:**
- 23 New York NL Oct. 17, 1999 (15 inn)
- 21 New York AL Oct. 17, 2009 (13 inn)

Most Players, Both Clubs, Game
- 39 SD (20) Atl. (19) NL Oct. 12, 1998
  - LA (21) Mil. (18) NL Oct. 13, 2018
- 37 Minn. (19) Ana. (18) AL Oct. 13, 2002
  - **Extra-Inning Game:**
- 45 NY (23) Atl. (22) NL Oct. 17, 1999 (15 inn)
- 38 NY (21) LA (17) AL Oct. 17, 2009 (13 inn)
  - NY (20) Det. (18) AL Oct. 13, 2012 (12 inn)

Most Pitchers, Game
- 8 Los Angeles NL Oct. 13, 2018
- 7 Minnesota AL Oct. 6, 1969
  - Boston AL Oct. 12, 2004
  - Cleveland AL Oct. 17, 2016
  - Houston AL Oct. 16, 2018
  - New York AL Oct. 17, 2019
  - New York AL Oct. 19, 2019
  - Houston AL Oct. 19, 2019
  - Houston AL Oct. 15, 2020
  - **Extra-Inning Game:**
- 9 New York NL Oct. 17, 1999 (15 inn)
  - Los Angeles NL Oct. 16, 2018 (13 inn)
  - New York AL Oct. 13, 2019 (11 inn)

Most Pitchers, Both Clubs, Game
- 14 LA (8) Mil. (6) NL Oct. 13, 2018
  - Atl. (7) LA (7) NL Oct. 13, 2020
  - Hou. (7) NY (7) AL Oct. 19, 2019
  - **Extra-Inning Game:**
- 16 LA (9) Mil. (7) NL Oct. 16, 2018 (13 inn)
- 15 NY (9) Hou. (6) AL Oct. 13, 2019 (11 inn)

Most Pitchers, Inning
- 5 Kansas City AL Oct. 12, 1976 (6th)
  - New York AL Oct. 18, 1999 (8th)
  - Minnesota AL Oct. 12, 2002 (8th)
  - Tampa Bay AL Oct. 19, 2008 (8th)
  - Texas AL Oct. 15, 2010 (8th)
  - New York AL Oct. 14, 2012 (8th)
  - Philadelphia NL Oct. 16, 2009 (8th)

Most Pinch-Hitters, Game
6   Oakland AL Oct. 10, 1972
     Los Angeles NL Oct. 9, 1988 (12 inn)
     Atlanta NL Oct. 19, 1999 (11 inn)
     St. Louis NL Oct. 15, 2006

Most Pinch-Hitters, Both Clubs, Game
9   Mil. (5) StL. (4) NL Oct. 16, 2011
7   Oak. (6) Det. (1) AL Oct. 10, 1972
     Extra-Inning Game:
11 Atl. (6) NY (5) NL Oct. 19, 1999 (11 inn)

Most Pinch-Hitters, Inning
4   Philadelphia NL Oct. 5, 1983 (9th)
     Atlanta NL Oct. 7, 1998 (8th)
     Baltimore AL Oct. 7, 1983 (9th)

Most Pinch-Runners, Game
2   By many
     Extra-Inning Game:
3   Kansas City AL Oct. 3, 1984 (11 inn)

Most Pinch-Runners, Both Clubs, Game
3   Oak. (2) Balt. (1) AL Oct. 6, 1974
     Balt. (2) Oak. (1) AL Oct. 9, 1974
     Bos. (2) Oak. (1) AL Oct. 5, 1988
     Oak. (2) Bos. (1) AL Oct. 6, 1990
     NY (2) Bos. (1) AL Oct. 18, 1999
     NY (2) LA (1) AL Oct. 22, 2009
     KC (2) Tor. (1) AL Oct. 23, 2015
     Phil. (2) Hou. (1) NL Oct. 12, 1980 (10 inn)
     Atl. (2) NY (1) NL Oct. 17, 1999 (15 inn)
     NY (2) StL. (1) NL Oct. 11, 2000
     Extra-Inning Game:
4   Bos. (2) Cal. (2) AL Oct. 12, 1986 (11 inn)

Most Pinch-Runners, Inning
2   Oakland AL Oct. 7, 1972 (11th)
     Baltimore AL Oct. 9, 1974 (9th)
     Boston AL Oct. 14, 1999 (8th)
     New York AL Oct. 13, 2000 (9th)
     Anaheim AL Oct. 13, 2002 (7th)
     Boston AL Oct. 18, 2004 (8th)
     New York AL Oct. 22, 2009 (9th)
     New York NL Oct. 11, 2000 (9th)
     Los Angeles NL Oct. 16, 2009 (8th)

INNINGS – TIME

Most Innings, Game
NL: 16 NY 7 at Hou. 6 Oct. 15, 1986
AL: 14 NY 4 at Bos. 5 Oct. 18, 2004

Longest Game, Time
AL: 4:33 Bos. at Hou. Oct. 17, 2018
NL: 4:16 Chi. at LA Oct. 20, 2016
     Extra-Inning Game:
AL: 5:49 NY at Bos. Oct. 18, 2004 (14 inn)
NL: 5:46 Atl. at NY Oct. 17, 1999 (15 inn)

Shortest Game, Time
AL: 1:57 Oak. at Balt. Oct. 8, 1974
NL: 1:57 Cin. at Pitt. Oct. 7, 1972

AMERICAN LEAGUE DIVISION SERIES

(*=Wild Card, since 1995)

	SERIES			GAMES			WON	LOST
	No.	W	L	No.	W	L		
New York	22	13	9	93	53	40	1981, 96, 98-2001, 03-04, 09-10, 12, 17, 19 1995, 97, 2002, 05-07, 11, 18, 20
Boston	13	7	6	48	23	25	1999, 2003-04, 07-08, 13, 18	1995, 98, 2005, 09, 16-17
Cleveland	10	5	5	41	22	19	1995, 97-98, 2007, 16	1996, 99, 2001, 17-18
Oakland	9	2	7	40	19	21	1981, 2006	2000-03, 12-13, 20
Texas	7	2	5	27	9	18	2010-11	1996, 98-99, 2015-16
Ana./LA	7	3	4	25	10	15	2002, 05, 09	2004, 07-08, 14
Minnesota	7	1	6	25	5	20	2002	2003-04, 06, 09-10, 19
Tampa Bay	6	2	4	27	12	15	2008, 20	2010-11, 13, 19
Detroit	5	4	1	22	12	10	2006, 11-13	2014
Houston	5	4	1	21	14	7	2017-20	2015
Seattle	4	3	1	17	10	7	1995, 2000-01	1997
Baltimore	4	3	1	16	11	5	1996-97, 2014	2012
Kansas City	3	2	1	11	6	5	2014-15	1981
Chicago	3	1	2	10	4	6	2005	2000, 08
Toronto	2	2	0	8	6	2	2015-16	
Milwaukee	1	0	1	5	2	3		1981

1981

New York 3, Milwaukee 2

10/7	at Mil.	NY	5	Mil.	3
10/8	at Mil.	NY	3	Mil.	0
10/9	at NY	Mil.	5	NY	3
10/10	at NY	Mil.	2	NY	1
10/11	at NY	NY	7	Mil.	3

Oakland 3, Kansas City 0

10/6	at KC	Oak.	4	KC	0
10/7	at KC	Oak.	2	KC	1
10/9	at Oak.	Oak.	4	KC	1

1995

Cleveland 3, Boston 0

10/3	at Clev.	Clev.	5	Bos.	4	(13 inn)
10/4	at Clev.	Clev.	4	Bos.	0	
10/6	at Bos.	Clev.	8	Bos.	2	

Seattle 3, New York* 2

10/3	at NY	NY	9	Sea.	6	
10/4	at NY	NY	7	Sea.	5	(15 inn)
10/6	at Sea.	Sea.	7	NY	4	
10/7	at Sea.	Sea.	11	NY	8	
10/8	at Sea.	Sea.	6	NY	5	(11 inn)

1996

New York 3, Texas 1

10/1	at NY	Tex.	6	NY	2	
10/2	at NY	NY	5	Tex.	4	(12 inn)
10/4	at Tex.	NY	3	Tex.	2	
10/5	at Tex.	NY	6	Tex.	4	

Baltimore* 3, Cleveland 1

10/1	at Balt.	Balt.	10	Clev.	4	
10/2	at Balt.	Balt.	7	Clev.	4	
10/4	at Clev.	Clev.	9	Balt.	4	
10/5	at Clev.	Balt.	4	Clev.	3	(12 inn)

1997

Cleveland 3, New York* 2

9/30	at NY	NY	8	Clev.	6
10/2	at NY	Clev.	7	NY	5
10/4	at Clev.	NY	6	Clev.	1
10/5	at Clev.	Clev.	3	NY	2
10/6	at Clev.	Clev.	4	NY	3

Baltimore 3, Seattle 1

10/1	at Sea.	Balt.	9	Sea.	3
10/2	at Sea.	Balt.	9	Sea.	3
10/4	at Balt.	Sea.	4	Balt.	2
10/5	at Balt.	Balt.	3	Sea.	1

1998

New York 3, Texas 0

9/29	at NY	NY	2	Tex.	0
9/30	at NY	NY	3	Tex.	1
10/2	at Tex.	NY	4	Tex.	0

Cleveland 3, Boston* 1

9/29	at Clev.	Bos.	11	Clev.	3
9/30	at Clev.	Clev.	9	Bos.	5
10/2	at Bos.	Clev.	4	Bos.	3
10/3	at Bos.	Clev.	2	Bos.	1

1999

New York 3, Texas 0

10/5	at NY	NY	8	Tex.	0
10/7	at NY	NY	3	Tex.	1
10/9	at Tex.	NY	3	Tex.	0

Boston* 3, Cleveland 2

10/6	at Clev.	Clev.	3	Bos.	2
10/7	at Clev.	Clev.	11	Bos.	1
10/9	at Bos.	Bos.	9	Clev.	3
10/10	at Bos.	Bos.	23	Clev.	7
10/11	at Clev.	Bos.	12	Clev.	8

2000

New York 3, Oakland 2

10/3	at Oak.	Oak.	5	NY	3
10/4	at Oak.	NY	4	Oak.	0
10/6	at NY	NY	4	Oak.	2
10/7	at NY	Oak.	11	NY	1
10/8	at Oak.	NY	7	Oak.	5

Seattle* 3, Chicago 0

10/3	at Chi.	Sea.	7	Chi.	4	(10 inn)
10/4	at Chi.	Sea.	5	Chi.	2	
10/6	at Sea.	Sea.	2	Chi.	1	

(=Wild Card, since 1995)*

2001

New York 3, Oakland* 2

10/10	at NY	Oak.	5	NY	3
10/11	at NY	Oak.	2	NY	0
10/13	at Oak.	NY	1	Oak.	0
10/14	at Oak.	NY	9	Oak.	2
10/15	at NY	NY	5	Oak.	3

Seattle 3, Cleveland 2

10/9	at Sea.	Clev.	5	Sea.	0
10/11	at Sea.	Sea.	5	Clev.	1
10/13	at Clev.	Clev.	17	Sea.	2
10/14	at Clev.	Sea.	6	Clev.	2
10/15	at Sea.	Sea.	3	Clev.	1

2002

Anaheim* 3, New York 1

10/1	at NY	NY	8	Ana.	5
10/2	at NY	Ana.	8	NY	6
10/4	at Ana.	Ana.	9	NY	6
10/5	at Ana.	Ana.	9	NY	5

Minnesota 3, Oakland 2

10/1	at Oak.	Minn.	7	Oak.	5
10/2	at Oak.	Oak.	9	Minn.	1
10/4	at Minn.	Oak.	6	Minn.	3
10/5	at Minn.	Minn.	11	Oak.	2
10/6	at Oak.	Minn.	5	Oak.	4

2003

New York 3, Minnesota 1

9/30	at NY	Minn.	3	NY	1
10/2	at NY	NY	4	Minn.	1
10/4	at Minn.	NY	3	Minn.	1
10/5	at Minn.	NY	8	Minn.	1

Boston* 3, Oakland 2

10/1	at Oak.	Oak.	5	Bos.	4 (12 inn)
10/2	at Oak.	Oak.	5	Bos.	1
10/4	at Bos.	Bos.	3	Oak.	1 (11 inn)
10/5	at Bos.	Bos.	5	Oak.	4
10/6	at Oak.	Bos.	4	Oak.	3

2004

Boston* 3, Anaheim 0

10/5	at Ana.	Bos.	9	Ana.	3
10/6	at Ana.	Bos.	8	Ana.	3
10/8	at Bos.	Bos.	8	Ana.	6 (10 inn)

New York 3, Minnesota 1

10/5	at NY	Minn.	2	NY	0
10/6	at NY	NY	7	Minn.	6 (12 inn)
10/8	at Minn.	NY	8	Minn.	4
10/9	at Minn.	NY	6	Minn.	5 (11 inn)

2005

Chicago 3, Boston* 0

10/4	at Chi.	Chi.	14	Bos.	2
10/5	at Chi.	Chi.	5	Bos.	4
10/7	at Bos.	Chi.	5	Bos.	3

Los Angeles 3, New York 2

10/4	at LA	NY	4	LA	2
10/5	at LA	LA	5	NY	3
10/7	at NY	LA	11	NY	7
10/9	at NY	NY	3	LA	2
10/10	at LA	LA	5	NY	3

2006

Detroit* 3, New York 1

10/3	at NY	NY	8	Det.	4
10/5	at NY	Det.	4	NY	3
10/6	at Det.	Det.	6	NY	0
10/7	at Det.	Det.	8	NY	3

Oakland 3, Minnesota 0

10/3	at Minn.	Oak.	3	Minn.	2
10/4	at Minn.	Oak.	5	Minn.	2
10/6	at Oak.	Oak.	8	Minn.	3

2007

Boston 3, Los Angeles 0

10/3	at Bos.	Bos.	4	LA	0
10/5	at Bos.	Bos.	6	LA	3
10/7	at LA	Bos.	9	LA	1

Cleveland 3, New York* 1

10/4	at Clev.	Clev.	12	NY	3
10/5	at Clev.	Clev.	2	NY	1 (11 inn)
10/7	at NY	NY	8	Clev.	4
10/8	at NY	Clev.	6	NY	4

2008

Tampa Bay 3, Chicago 1

10/2	at TB	TB	6	Chi.	4
10/3	at TB	TB	6	Chi.	2
10/5	at Chi.	Chi.	5	TB	3
10/6	at Chi.	TB	6	Chi.	2

Boston* 3, Los Angeles 1

10/1	at LA	Bos.	4	LA	1
10/3	at LA	Bos.	7	LA	5
10/5	at Bos.	LA	5	Bos.	4 (12 inn)
10/6	at Bos.	Bos.	3	LA	2

2009

New York 3, Minnesota 0

10/7	at NY	NY	7	Minn.	2
10/9	at NY	NY	4	Minn.	3 (11 inn)
10/11	at Minn.	NY	4	Minn.	1

Los Angeles 3, Boston* 0

10/8	at LA	LA	5	Bos.	0
10/9	at LA	LA	4	Bos.	1
10/11	at Bos.	LA	7	Bos.	6

2010

Texas 3, Tampa Bay 2

10/6	at T.B.	Tex.	5	T.B.	1
10/7	at T.B.	Tex.	6	T.B.	0
10/9	at Tex.	T.B.	6	Tex.	3
10/10	at Tex.	T.B.	5	Tex.	2
10/12	at T.B.	Tex.	5	T.B.	1

New York* 3, Minnesota 0

10/6	at Minn.	NY	6	Minn.	4
10/7	at Minn.	NY	5	Minn.	2
10/9	at NY	NY	6	Minn.	1

(*=Wild Card, since 1995)

2011

Texas 3, Tampa Bay* 1

9/30	at Tex.	T.B.	9	Tex.	0
10/1	at Tex.	Tex.	8	T.B.	6
10/3	at T.B.	Tex.	4	T.B.	3
10/4	at T.B.	Tex.	4	T.B.	3

Detroit 3, New York 2

9/30	at NY	NY	9	Det.	3
10/2	at NY	Det.	5	NY	3
10/3	at Det.	Det.	5	NY	4
10/4	at Det.	NY	10	Det.	1
10/6	at NY	Det.	3	NY	2

Game 1 suspended; resumed and completed on Oct. 1

2012

Detroit 3, Oakland 2

10/6	at Det.	Det.	3	Oak.	1
10/7	at Det.	Det.	5	Oak.	4
10/9	at Oak.	Oak.	2	Det.	0
10/10	at Oak.	Oak.	4	Det.	3
10/11	at Oak.	Det.	6	Oak.	0

New York 3, Baltimore* 2

10/7	at Balt.	NY	7	Balt.	2
10/8	at Balt.	Balt.	3	NY	2
10/10	at NY	NY	3	Balt.	2 (12 inn)
10/11	at NY	Balt.	2	NY	1 (13 inn)
10/12	at NY	NY	3	Balt.	1

2013

Boston 3, Tampa Bay*1

10/4	at Bos.	Bos.	12	T.B.	2
10/5	at Bos.	Bos.	7	T.B.	4
10/7	at T.B.	T.B.	5	Bos.	4
10/8	at T.B.	Bos.	3	T.B.	1

Detroit 3, Oakland 2

10/4	at Oak.	Det.	3	Oak.	2
10/5	at Oak.	Oak.	1	Det.	0
10/7	at Det.	Oak.	6	Det.	3
10/8	at Det.	Det.	8	Oak.	6
10/10	at Oak.	Det.	3	Oak.	0

2014

Kansas City* 3, Los Angeles 0

10/2	at LA	KC	3	LA	2 (11 inn)
10/3	at LA	KC	4	LA	1 (11 inn)
10/5	at KC	KC	8	LA	3

Baltimore 3, Detroit 0

10/2	at Balt.	Balt.	12	Det.	3
10/3	at Balt.	Balt.	7	Det.	6
10/5	at Det.	Balt.	2	Det.	1

2015

Kansas City 3, Houston* 2

10/8	at KC	Hou.	5	KC	2
10/9	at KC	KC	5	Hou.	4
10/11	at Hou.	Hou.	4	KC	2
10/12	at Hou.	KC	9	Hou.	6
10/14	at KC	KC	7	Hou.	2

Toronto 3, Texas 2

10/8	at Tor.	Tex.	5	Tor.	3
10/9	at Tor.	Tex.	6	Tor.	4 (14 inn)
10/11	at Tex.	Tor.	5	Tex.	1
10/12	at Tex.	Tor.	8	Tex.	4
10/14	at Tex.	Tor.	6	Tex.	3

2016

Cleveland 3, Boston 0

10/6	at Clev.	Clev.	5	Bos.	4
10/7	at Clev.	Clev.	6	Bos.	0
10/10	at Bos.	Clev.	4	Bos.	3

Toronto* 3, Texas 0

10/6	at Tex.	Tor.	10	Tex.	1
10/7	at Tex.	Tor.	5	Tex.	3
10/9	at Tor.	Tor.	7	Tex.	6 (10 inn)

2017

Houston 3, Boston 1

10/5	at Hou.	Hou.	8	Bos.	2
10/6	at Hou.	Hou.	8	Bos.	2
10/8	at Bos.	Bos.	10	Hou.	3
10/9	at Bos.	Hou.	5	Bos.	4

New York* 3, Cleveland 2

10/5	at Clev.	Clev.	4	NY	0
10/6	at Clev.	Clev.	9	NY	8 (13 inn)
10/8	at NY	NY	1	Clev.	0
10/9	at NY	NY	7	Clev.	3
10/11	at Clev.	NY.	5	Clev.	2

2018

Boston 3, New York* 1

10/5	at Bos.	Bos.	5	NY	4
10/6	at Bos.	NY	6	Bos.	2
10/8	at NY	Bos.	16	NY	1
10/9	at NY	Bos.	4	NY	3

Houston 3, Cleveland 0

10/5	at Hou.	Hou.	7	Clev.	2
10/6	at Hou.	Hou.	3	Clev.	1
10/8	at Clev.	Hou.	11	Clev.	3

2019

Houston 3, Tampa Bay* 2

10/4	at Hou.	Hou.	6	TB	2
10/5	at Hou.	Hou.	3	TB	1
10/7	at TB	TB	10	Hou.	3
10/8	at TB	TB	4	Hou.	1
10/10	at Hou.	Hou.	6	TB	1

New York 3, Minnesota 0

10/4	at NY	NY	10	Minn.	4
10/5	at NY	NY	8	Minn.	2
10/7	at Minn.	NY	5	Minn.	1

2020

Tampa Bay 3, New York 2

10/5	at TB	NY	9	TB	3
10/6	at TB	TB	7	NY	5
10/7	at NY	TB	8	NY	4
10/8	at NY	NY	5	TB	1
10/9	at TB	TB	2	NY	1

Houston 3, Oakland 1

10/5	at Oak.	Hou.	10	Oak.	5
10/6	at Oak.	Hou.	5	Oak.	2
10/7	at Hou.	Oak.	9	Hou.	7
10/8	at Hou.	Hou.	11	Oak.	6

All games at PETCO Park – San Diego, CA

All games at Dodger Stadium – Los Angeles, CA

NATIONAL LEAGUE DIVISION SERIES

(=Wild Card, since 1995)*

	SERIES No.	W	L	GAMES No.	W	L	WON	LOST
Atlanta	16	7	9	62	33	29	1995-99, 2001, 20	2000, 02-05, 10, 13, 18-19
Los Angeles	15	8	7	57	30	27	1981, 2008-09, 13, 16-18, 20	1995-96, 2004, 06, 14-15, 19
St. Louis	14	11	3	56	36	20	1996, 2000, 02, 04-06, 11-14, 19	2001, 09, 15
San Francisco	8	4	4	33	15	18	2002, 10, 12, 14	1997, 2000, 03, 16
Houston	7	2	5	28	10	18	2004-05	1981, 97-99, 2001
Chicago	7	4	3	27	12	15	2003, 15-17	1998, 2007-08
Mtl./Wash.	6	2	4	29	13	16	1981, 2019	2012, 14, 16-17
Philadelphia	6	3	3	24	13	11	2008-10	1981, 2007, 11
Arizona	6	2	4	23	9	14	2001, 07	1999, 2002, 11, 17
San Diego	5	1	4	17	4	13	1998	1996., 2005-06, 20
New York	4	4	0	16	12	4	1999-2000, 06, 15	
Colorado	4	1	3	14	5	9	2007	1995, 2009, 18
Milwaukee	3	2	1	12	7	5	2011, 18	2008
Florida/Miami	3	2	1	10	6	4	1997, 2003	2020
Cincinnati	3	1	2	11	5	6	1995	2010, 12
Pittsburgh	1	0	1	5	2	3		2013

1981

Los Angeles 3, Houston 2

10/6	at Hou.	Hou.	3	LA	1
10/7	at Hou.	Hou.	1	LA	0 (11 inn)
10/9	at LA	LA	6	Hou.	1
10/10	at LA	LA	2	Hou.	1
10/11	at LA	LA	4	Hou.	0

Montreal 3, Philadelphia 2

10/7	at Mtl.	Mtl.	3	Phil.	1
10/8	at Mtl.	Mtl.	3	Phil.	1
10/9	at Phil.	Phil.	6	Mtl.	2
10/10	at Phil.	Phil.	6	Mtl.	5 (10 inn)
10/11	at Phil.	Mtl.	3	Phil.	0

1995

Atlanta 3, Colorado* 1

10/3	at Col.	Atl.	5	Col.	4
10/4	at Col.	Atl.	7	Col.	4
10/6	at Atl.	Col.	7	Atl.	5 (10 inn)
10/7	at Atl.	Atl.	10	Col.	4

Cincinnati 3, Los Angeles 0

10/3	at LA	Cin.	7	LA	2
10/4	at LA	Cin.	5	LA	4
10/6	at Cin.	Cin.	10	LA	1

1996

Atlanta 3, Los Angeles* 0

10/2	at LA	Atl.	2	LA	1 (10 inn)
10/3	at LA	Atl.	3	LA	2
10/5	at Atl.	Atl.	5	LA	2

St. Louis 3, San Diego 0

10/1	at StL.	StL.	3	SD	1
10/3	at StL.	StL.	5	SD	4
10/5	at SD	StL.	7	SD	5

1997

Florida* 3, San Francisco 0

9/30	at Fla.	Fla.	2	SF	1
10/1	at Fla.	Fla.	7	SF	6
10/3	at SF	Fla.	6	SF	2

Atlanta 3, Houston 0

9/30	at Atl.	Atl.	2	Hou.	1
10/1	at Atl.	Atl.	13	Hou.	3
10/3	at Hou.	Atl.	4	Hou.	1

1998

San Diego 3, Houston 1

9/29	at Hou.	SD	2	Hou.	1
10/1	at Hou.	Hou.	5	SD	4
10/3	at SD	SD	2	Hou.	1
10/4	at SD	SD	6	Hou.	1

Atlanta 3, Chicago* 0

9/30	at Atl.	Atl.	7	Chi.	1
10/1	at Atl.	Atl.	2	Chi.	1 (10 inn)
10/3	at Chi.	Atl.	6	Chi.	2

1999

Atlanta 3, Houston 1

10/5	at Atl.	Hou.	6	Atl.	1
10/6	at Atl.	Atl.	5	Hou.	1
10/8	at Hou.	Atl.	5	Hou.	3 (12 inn)
10/9	at Hou.	Atl.	7	Hou.	5

New York* 3, Arizona 1

10/5	at Ari.	NY	8	Ari.	4
10/6	at Ari.	Ari.	7	NY	1
10/8	at NY	NY	9	Ari.	2
10/9	at NY	NY	4	Ari.	3 (10 inn)

2000

New York* 3, San Francisco 1

10/4	at SF	SF	5	NY	1
10/5	at SF	NY	5	SF	4 (10 inn)
10/7	at NY	NY	3	SF	2 (13 inn)
10/8	at NY	NY	4	SF	0

St. Louis 3, Atlanta 0

10/3	at StL.	StL.	7	Atl.	5
10/5	at StL.	StL.	10	Atl.	4
10/7	at Atl.	StL.	7	Atl.	1

(*=Wild Card, since 1995)

2001

Arizona 3, St. Louis* 2

10/9	at Ari.	Ari. 1	StL.	0
10/10	at Ari.	StL. 4	Ari.	1
10/12	at StL.	Ari. 5	StL.	3
10/13	at StL.	StL. 4	Ari.	1
10/14	at Ari.	Ari. 2	StL.	1

Atlanta 3, Houston 0

10/9	at Hou.	Atl. 7	Hou.	4
10/10	at Hou.	Atl. 1	Hou.	0
10/12	at Atl.	Atl. 6	Hou.	2

2002

San Francisco* 3, Atlanta 2

10/2	at Atl.	SF 8	Atl.	5
10/3	at Atl.	Atl. 7	SF	3
10/5	at SF	Atl. 10	SF	2
10/6	at SF	SF 8	Atl.	3
10/7	at Atl.	SF 3	Atl.	1

St. Louis 3, Arizona 0

10/1	at Ari.	StL. 12	Ari.	2
10/3	at Ari.	StL. 2	Ari.	1
10/5	at StL.	StL. 6	Ari.	3

2003

Florida* 3, San Francisco 1

9/30	at SF	SF 2	Fla.	0
10/1	at SF	Fla. 9	SF	5
10/3	at Fla.	Fla. 4	SF	3 (11 inn)
10/4	at Fla.	Fla. 7	SF	6

Chicago 3, Atlanta 2

9/30	at Atl.	Chi. 4	Atl.	2
10/1	at Atl.	Atl. 5	Chi.	3
10/3	at Chi.	Chi. 3	Atl.	1
10/4	at Chi.	Atl. 6	Chi.	4
10/5	at Atl.	Chi. 5	Atl.	1

2004

St. Louis 3, Los Angeles 1

10/5	at StL.	StL. 8	LA	3
10/7	at StL.	StL. 8	LA	3
10/9	at LA	LA 4	StL.	0
10/10	at LA	StL. 6	LA	2

Houston* 3, Atlanta 2

10/6	at Atl.	Hou. 9	Atl.	3
10/7	at Atl.	Atl. 4	Hou.	2 (11 inn)
10/9	at Hou.	Hou. 8	Atl.	5
10/10	at Hou.	Atl. 6	Hou.	5
10/11	at Atl.	Hou. 12	Atl.	3

2005

Houston* 3, Atlanta 1

10/5	at Atl.	Hou. 10	Atl.	5
10/6	at Atl.	Atl. 7	Hou.	1
10/8	at Hou.	Hou. 7	Atl.	3
10/9	at Hou.	Hou. 7	Atl.	6 (18 inn)

St. Louis 3, San Diego 0

10/4	at StL.	StL. 8	SD	5
10/6	at StL.	StL. 6	SD	2
10/8	at SD	StL. 7	SD	4

2006

St. Louis 3, San Diego 1

10/3	at SD	StL. 5	SD	1
10/5	at SD	StL. 2	SD	0
10/7	at StL.	SD 3	StL.	1
10/8	at StL.	StL. 6	SD	2

New York 3, Los Angeles* 0

10/4	at NY	NY 6	LA	5
10/5	at NY	NY 4	LA	1
10/7	at LA	NY 9	LA	5

2007

Colorado* 3, Philadelphia 0

10/3	at Phil.	Col. 4	Phil.	2
10/4	at Phil.	Col. 10	Phil.	5
10/6	at Col.	Col. 2	Phil.	1

Arizona 3, Chicago 0

10/3	at Ari.	Ari. 3	Chi.	1
10/4	at Ari.	Ari. 8	Chi.	4
10/6	at Chi.	Ari. 5	Chi.	1

2008

Philadelphia 3, Milwaukee* 1

10/1	at Phil.	Phil. 3	Mil.	1
10/2	at Phil.	Phil. 5	Mil.	2
10/4	at Mil.	Mil. 4	Phil.	1
10/5	at Mil.	Phil. 6	Mil.	2

Los Angeles 3, Chicago 0

10/1	at Chi.	LA 7	Chi.	2
10/2	at Chi.	LA 10	Chi.	3
10/4	at LA	LA 3	Chi.	1

2009

Philadelphia 3, Colorado* 1

10/7	at Phil.	Phil. 5	Col.	1
10/8	at Phil.	Col. 5	Phil.	4
10/11	at Col.	Phil. 6	Col.	5
10/12	at Col.	Phil. 5	Col.	4

Los Angeles 3, St. Louis 0

10/7	at LA	LA 5	StL.	3
10/8	at LA	LA 3	StL.	2
10/10	at StL.	LA 5	StL.	1

2010

San Francisco 3, Atlanta* 1

10/7	at SF	SF 1	Atl.	0
10/8	at SF	Atl. 5	SF	4 (11 inn)
10/10	at Atl.	SF 3	Atl.	2
10/11	at Atl.	SF 3	Atl.	2

Philadelphia 3, Cincinnati 0

10/6	at Phil.	Phil. 4	Cin.	0
10/8	at Phil.	Phil. 7	Cin.	4
10/10	at Cin.	Phil. 2	Cin.	0

(=Wild Card, since 1995)*

2011

St. Louis* 3, Philadelphia 2

10/1	at Phil.	Phil. 11	StL.	6
10/2	at Phil.	StL. 5	Phil.	4
10/4	at StL.	Phil. 3	StL.	2
10/5	at StL.	StL. 5	Phil.	3
10/7	at Phil.	StL. 1	Phil.	0

Milwaukee 3, Arizona 2

10/1	at Mil.	Mil. 4	Ari.	1	
10/2	at Mil.	Mil. 9	Ari.	4	
10/4	at Ari.	Ari. 8	Mil.	1	
10/5	at Ari.	Ari. 10	Mil.	6	
10/7	at Mil.	Mil. 3	Ari.	2	(10 inn)

2012

San Francisco 3, Cincinnati 2

10/6	at SF	Cin. 5	SF	2	
10/7	at SF	Cin. 9	SF	0	
10/9	at Cin.	SF 2	Cin.	1	(10 inn)
10/10	at Cin.	SF 8	Cin.	3	
10/11	at Cin.	SF 6	Cin.	4	

St. Louis* 3, Washington 2

10/7	at StL.	Wash. 3	StL.	2
10/8	at StL.	StL. 12	Wash.	4
10/10	at Wash.	StL. 8	Wash.	0
10/11	at Wash.	Wash. 2	StL.	1
10/12	at Wash.	StL. 9	Wash.	7

2013

St. Louis 3, Pittsburgh* 2

10/3	at StL.	StL. 9	Pitt.	1
10/4	at StL.	Pitt. 7	StL.	1
10/6	at Pitt.	Pitt. 5	StL.	3
10/7	at Pitt.	StL. 2	Pitt.	1
10/9	at StL.	StL. 6	Pitt.	1

Los Angeles 3, Atlanta 1

10/3	at Atl.	LA 6	Atl.	1
10/4	at Atl.	Atl. 4	LA	3
10/6	at LA	LA 13	Atl.	6
10/7	at LA	LA 4	Atl.	3

2014

San Francisco* 3, Washington 1

10/3	at Wash.	SF 3	Wash.	2	
10/4	at Wash.	SF 2	Wash.	1	(18 inn)
10/6	at SF	Wash. 4	SF	1	
10/7	at SF	SF 3	Wash.	2	

St. Louis 3, Los Angeles 1

10/3	at LA	StL. 10	LA	9
10/4	at LA	LA 3	StL.	2
10/6	at StL.	StL. 3	LA	1
10/7	at StL.	StL. 3	LA	2

2015

New York 3, Los Angeles 2

10/9	at LA	NY 3	LA	1
10/10	at LA	LA 5	NY	2
10/12	at NY	NY 13	LA	7
10/13	at NY	LA 3	NY	1
10/15	at LA	NY 3	LA	2

Chicago* 3, St. Louis 1

10/9	at StL.	StL. 4	Chi.	0
10/10	at StL.	Chi. 6	StL.	3
10/12	at Chi.	Chi. 8	StL.	6
10/13	at Chi.	Chi. 6	StL.	4

2016

Chicago 3, San Francisco* 1

10/7	at Chi.	Chi. 1	SF	0	
10/8	at Chi.	Chi. 5	SF	2	
10/10	at SF	SF 6	Chi.	5	(13 inn)
10/11	at SF	Chi. 6	SF	5	

Los Angeles 3, Washington 2

10/7	at Wash.	LA 4	Wash.	3
10/9	at Wash.	Wash. 5	LA	2
10/10	at LA	Wash. 8	LA	3
10/11	at LA	LA 6	Wash.	5
10/13	at Wash.	LA 4	Wash.	3

2017

Los Angeles 3, Arizona* 0

10/6	at LA	LA 9	Ari.	5
10/7	at LA	LA 8	Ari.	5
10/9	at Ari.	LA 3	Ari.	1

Chicago 3, Washington 2

10/6	at Wash.	Chi. 3	Wash.	0
10/7	at Wash.	Wash. 6	Chi.	3
10/9	at Chi.	Chi. 2	Wash.	1
10/11	at Chi.	Wash. 5	Chi.	0
10/12	at Wash.	Chi. 9	Wash.	8

2018

Los Angeles 3, Atlanta 1

10/4	at LA	LA 6	Atl.	0
10/5	at LA	LA 3	Atl.	0
10/7	at Atl.	Atl. 6	LA	5
10/8	at Atl.	LA 6	Atl.	2

Milwaukee 3, Colorado* 0

10/4	at Mil.	Mil. 3	Col.	2	(10 inn)
10/5	at Mil.	Mil. 4	Col.	0	
10/7	at Col.	Mil. 6	Col.	0	

2019

Washington* 3, Los Angeles 2

10/3	at LA	LA 6	Wash.	0	
10/4	at LA	Wash. 4	LA	2	
10/6	at Wash.	LA 10	Wash.	4	
10/7	at Wash.	Wash. 6	LA	1	
10/9	at LA	Wash. 7	LA	3	(10 inn)

St. Louis 3, Atlanta 2

10/3	at Atl.	StL. 7	Atl.	6	
10/4	at Atl.	Atl. 3	StL.	0	
10/6	at StL.	Atl. 3	StL.	1	
10/7	at StL.	StL. 5	Atl.	4	(10 inn)
10/9	at Atl.	StL. 13	Atl.	1	

2020

Los Angeles 3, San Diego 0

10/6	at LA	LA 5	SD	1
10/7	at LA	LA 6	SD	5
10/8	at SD	LA 12	SD	3

All games at Globe Life Field – Arlington, TX

Atlanta 3, Miami 0

10/6	at Atl.	Atl. 9	Mia.	5
10/7	at Atl.	Atl. 2	Mia.	0
10/8	at Mia.	Atl. 7	Mia.	0

All games at Minute Maid Park – Houston, TX

INDIVIDUAL BATTING

Most Series, Lifetime (non-pitchers)
16 Derek Jeter, AL:NY 1996-2007, 09-12
11 Chipper Jones, NL:Atl. 1995-2005

Most Games, Lifetime
66 Derek Jeter, AL:NY
42 Chipper Jones, NL:Atl.

Highest Batting Average, Lifetime (min: 50 AB)
.446 Hanley Ramirez, NL:LA; AL:Bos. (56ab-25h)
.400 Mike Stanley, AL:NY-Bos. (55ab-22h)
.372 Justin Turner, NL:LA (94ab-35h)

Highest Batting Average, Series (min: 3.1 PA/G)
.714 David Ortiz, AL:Bos. 2007 (7ab-5h)
.615 Jeff Kent, NL:LA 2006 (13ab-8h)

Highest Slugging Percentage, Lifetime (min: 50 AB)
.806 Carlos Beltran, NL:Hou.-NY-StL. (67ab-54tb)
.781 Edgar Martinez, AL:Sea. (64ab-50tb)
       (ML record)

Highest Slugging Percentage, Series (min: 3.1 PA/G)
1.571 David Ortiz, AL:Bos. 2007 (7ab-11tb)
       Jorge Soler, NL:Chi. 2015 (7ab-11tb)

Most Plate Appearances, Lifetime
300 Derek Jeter, AL:NY
189 Chipper Jones, NL:Atl.

Most Plate Appearances, Series
28 Bernie Williams, AL:NY 1995
26 Rafael Furcal, NL:Atl. 2004

Most Plate Appearances, Game
7 Jose Offerman, AL:Bos. Oct. 10, 1999
6 By many in NL
   Extra-Inning Game:
9 By many in NL
7 By many in AL

Most Plate Appearances, Inning
2 By many

Most At-Bats, Lifetime
268 Derek Jeter, AL:NY
152 Rafael Furcal, NL:Atl.-LA-StL.

Most At-Bats, Series
24 Jay Buhner, AL:Sea. 1995
    Don Mattingly, AL:NY 1995
    Elvis Andrus, AL:Tex. 2010
    Derek Jeter, AL:NY 2011
    Delino DeShields, AL:Tex. 2015
    Rafael Furcal, NL:Atl. 2002
    Marcus Giles, NL:Atl. 2004
    Brandon Phillips, NL:Cin. 2012

Most At-Bats, Game
6 By many
   Extra-Inning Game:
8 Brian McCann, NL:Atl. Oct. 9, 2005 (18 inn)
   Jayson Werth, NL:Wash. Oct. 4, 2014 (18 inn)
7 By many in AL

Most At-Bats, Inning
2 By many

Most Runs, Lifetime
47 Derek Jeter, AL:NY
30 Chipper Jones, NL:Atl.

Most Runs, Series
9 Ken Griffey Jr., AL:Sea. 1995
   Carlos Beltran, NL:Hou. 2004

Most Runs, Game
5 Jason Varitek, AL:Bos. Oct. 10, 1999
3 By many in NL

Most Runs, Inning
2 Shawn Wooten, AL:Ana. Oct. 5, 2002 (5th)
   Matt Holliday, NL:StL. Oct. 3, 2014 (7th)
   Dexter Fowler, NL:StL. Oct. 9, 2019 (1st)

Most Hits, Lifetime
92 Derek Jeter, AL:NY
41 Chipper Jones, NL:Atl.

Most Hits, Series
12 Edgar Martinez, AL:Sea. 1995
    Ichiro Suzuki, AL:Sea. 2001
11 Marquis Grissom, NL:Atl. 1995

Most Hits, Game
5 Marquis Grissom, NL:Atl. Oct. 7, 1995
   Will Smith, NL:LA Oct. 8, 2020
   Mike Stanley, AL:Bos. Oct. 10, 1999
   Derek Jeter, AL:NY Oct. 3, 2006

Most Hits, Inning
2 Chuck Knoblauch, AL:NY Oct. 8, 2000 (1st)
   Doug Mientkiewicz, AL:Minn. Oct. 5, 2002 (4th)
   Shawn Wooten, AL:Ana. Oct. 5, 2002 (5th)
   Benji Gil, AL:Ana. Oct. 5, 2002 (5th)
   Alex Rodriguez, AL:NY Oct. 4, 2011 (8th)
   Alejandro De Aza, AL:Balt. Oct. 2, 2014 (8th)
   Brock Holt, AL:Bos. Oct. 8, 2018 (4th)
   Aaron Judge, AL:NY Oct. 5, 2019 (3rd)
   Matt Holliday, NL:StL. Oct. 3, 2014 (7th)
   Cody Bellinger, NL:LA Oct. 6, 2019 (6th)

Most Extra-Base Hits, Lifetime
25 Derek Jeter, AL:NY
17 Jayson Werth, NL:LA-Phil.-Wash.

Most Extra-Base Hits, Series
6 Jim Edmonds, NL:StL. 2000
   Carlos Beltran, NL:Hou. 2004
   Hanley Ramirez, NL:LA 2013
   Matt Carpenter, NL:StL. 2014
   Justin Turner, NL:LA 2015
   Paul Goldschmidt, NL:StL. 2019
5 By many in AL

Most Extra-Base Hits, Game
3 By many; last:
   Anthony Rendon, NL:Wash. Oct. 9, 2019 (10 inn)
   Gleyber Torres, AL:NY Oct. 7, 2019

Most Extra-Base Hits, Inning
2 Alejandro De Aza, AL:Balt. Oct. 2, 2014 (8th)
1 By many in NL

Most Total Bases, Lifetime
139 Derek Jeter, AL:NY
73 Chipper Jones, NL:Atl.

Most Total Bases, Series
24 Ken Griffey Jr., AL:Sea. 1995
    Carlos Beltran, NL:Hou. 2004

Most Total Bases, Game
12 Adrian Beltre, AL:Tex. Oct. 4, 2011
    Jose Altuve, AL:Hou. Oct. 5, 2017
10 Eric Karros, NL:LA Oct. 4, 1995
    Carlos Beltran, NL:Hou. Oct. 11, 2004

Most Total Bases, Inning
5 Shawn Wooten, AL:Ana. Oct. 5, 2002 (5th)
   Matt Holliday, NL:StL. Oct. 3, 2014 (7th)

Most Singles, Lifetime
67 Derek Jeter, AL:NY
31 Rafael Furcal, NL:Atl.-LA-StL.

Most Singles, Series
11 Ichiro Suzuki, AL:Sea. 2001
9 Fernando Vina, NL:StL. 2002
   Moises Alou, NL:Chi. 2003

Most Singles, Game
4 Chad Fonville, NL:LA Oct. 4, 1995
   Marquis Grissom, NL:Atl. Oct. 7, 1995
   Fernando Vina, NL:StL. Oct. 3, 2002
   Ryan Theriot, NL:StL. Oct. 4, 2011
   Anthony Rendon, NL:Wash. Oct. 4, 2014 (18 inn)
   Conor Gillaspie, NL:SF Oct. 11, 2016
   Johnny Damon, AL:Oak. Oct. 10, 2001
   Jason Giambi, AL:Oak. Oct. 15, 2001
   Jermaine Dye, AL:Chi. Oct. 3, 2008
   Yuli Gurriel, AL:Hou. Oct. 8, 2017
   Avisail Garcia, AL:TB Oct. 8, 2019

Most Singles, Inning
2 Chuck Knoblauch, AL:NY Oct. 8, 2000 (1st)
   Doug Mientkiewicz, AL:Minn. Oct. 5, 2002 (4th)
   Benji Gil, AL:Ana. Oct. 5, 2002 (5th)
   Alex Rodriguez, AL:NY Oct. 4, 2011 (8th)
   Aaron Judge, AL:NY Oct. 5, 2019 (3rd)
1 By many in NL

Most Doubles, Lifetime
16 Bernie Williams, AL:NY
9 Justin Turner, NL:LA

Most Doubles, Series
6 Justin Turner, NL:LA 2015
4 Don Mattingly, AL:NY 1995
David Justice, AL:Clev. 1998
Roberto Alomar, AL:Clev. 1999
Torii Hunter, AL:Minn. 2002
Derek Jeter, AL:NY 2006
Marco Scutaro, AL:Oak. 2006
Josh Donaldson, AL:Tor. 2016
Luis Arraez, AL:Minn. 2019

Most Doubles, Game
3 Jim Edmonds, NL:StL. Oct. 5, 2000
Craig Biggio, NL:Hou. Oct. 8, 2005
Albert Pujols, NL:StL. Oct. 4, 2011
2 By many in AL

Most Doubles, Inning
2 Alejandro De Aza, AL:Balt. Oct. 2, 2014 (8th)
1 By many in NL

Most Triples, Lifetime
5 Rafael Furcal, NL:Atl.-LA-StL.
3 Curtis Granderson, AL:Det.-NY

Most Triples, Series
2 Kazuo Matsui, NL:Col. 2007
Rafael Furcal, NL:StL. 2011
1 By many in AL

Most Triples, Game
1 By many

Most Home Runs, Lifetime
12 Manny Ramirez, AL:Clev.-Bos.; NL:LA
10 Manny Ramirez, AL:Clev.-Bos.
Derek Jeter, AL:NY
9 Chipper Jones, NL:Atl.

Most Home Runs, Series
5 Ken Griffey Jr., AL:Sea. 1995
Juan Gonzalez, AL:Tex. 1996
4 Carlos Beltran, NL:Hou. 2004

Most Home Runs, Game
3 Adrian Beltre, AL:Tex. Oct. 4, 2011
Jose Altuve, AL:Hou. Oct. 5, 2017
2 By many in NL; last:
Marcell Ozuna, NL:StL. Oct. 7, 2019 (10 inn)

Most Consecutive Games, Home Run
4 Juan Gonzalez, AL:Tex. Oct. 1-5, 1996
Manny Ramirez, AL:Bos-NL:LA Oct. 5, 2007-Oct. 2, 2008
3 Jim Leyritz, NL:SD Oct. 1-4, 1998
Vinny Castilla, NL:Col.-Hou. Oct. 6, 1995-Oct. 9, 2001
Matt Carpenter, NL:StL. Oct. 3-6, 2014

Most Home Runs, Inning
1 By many

Most Grand Slam Home Runs, Lifetime
1 Mark Lewis, NL:Cin. Oct. 6, 1995 (6th)
Devon White, NL:Fla. Oct. 3, 1997 (6th)
Ryan Klesko, NL:Atl. Sept. 30, 1998 (7th)
Eddie Perez, NL:Atl. Oct. 3, 1998 (8th)
Edgardo Alfonzo, NL:NY Oct. 5, 1999 (9th)
Reggie Sanders, NL:StL. Oct. 4, 2005 (5th)
Adam LaRoche, NL:Atl. Oct. 9, 2005 (3rd)
Lance Berkman, NL:Hou. Oct. 9, 2005 (8th)
Kazuo Matsui, NL:Col. Oct. 4, 2007 (4th)
James Loney, NL:LA Oct. 1, 2008 (5th)
Shane Victorino, NL:Phil. Oct. 2, 2008 (2nd)
Paul Goldschmidt, NL:Ari. Oct. 4, 2011 (5th)
Ryan Roberts, NL:Ari. Oct. 5, 2011 (1st)
Buster Posey, NL:SF Oct. 11, 2012 (5th)
Michael Taylor, NL:Wash. Oct. 11, 2017 (8th)
Ronald Acuna, NL:Atl. Oct. 7, 2018 (2nd)
Howie Kendrick, NL:Wash. Oct. 9, 2019 (10th)
Edgar Martinez, AL:Sea. Oct. 7, 1995 (8th)
Bobby Bonilla, AL:Balt. Oct. 1, 1996 (6th)
Albert Belle, AL:Clev. Oct. 4, 1996 (7th)
Paul O'Neill, AL:NY Oct. 4, 1997 (4th)
Jim Thome, AL:Clev. Oct. 7, 1999 (4th)
Troy O'Leary, AL:Bos. Oct. 11, 1999 (3rd)
Vladimir Guerrero, AL:Ana. Oct. 8, 2004 (7th)
Robinson Cano, AL:NY Sept. 30, 2011 (6th)
Francisco Lindor, AL:Clev. Oct. 6, 2017 (6th)
Didi Gregorius, AL:NY Oct. 5, 2019 (3rd)
Giancarlo Stanton, AL:NY Oct. 5, 2020 (9th)

Most Runs Batted In, Lifetime
33 Bernie Williams, AL:NY
26 Chipper Jones, NL:Atl.

Most Runs Batted In, Series
12 John Valentin, AL:Bos. 1999
10 Reggie Sanders, NL:StL. 2005

Most Runs Batted In, Game
7 Edgar Martinez, AL:Sea. Oct. 7, 1995
Mo Vaughn, AL:Bos. Sept. 29, 1998
John Valentin, AL:Bos. Oct. 10, 1999
Troy O'Leary, AL:Bos. Oct. 11, 1999
6 Reggie Sanders, NL:StL. Oct. 4, 2005

Most Runs Batted In, Inning
4 Mark Lewis, NL:Cin. Oct. 6, 1995 (6th)
Devon White, NL:Fla. Oct. 3, 1997 (6th)
Ryan Klesko, NL:Atl. Sept. 30, 1998 (7th)
Eddie Perez, NL:Atl. Oct. 3, 1998 (8th)
Edgardo Alfonzo, NL:NY Oct. 5, 1999 (9th)
Reggie Sanders, NL:StL. Oct. 4, 2005 (5th)
Adam LaRoche, NL:Atl. Oct. 9, 2005 (3rd)
Lance Berkman, NL:Hou. Oct. 9, 2005 (8th)
Kazuo Matsui, NL:Col. Oct. 4, 2007 (4th)
James Loney, NL:LA Oct. 1, 2008 (5th)
Shane Victorino, NL:Phil. Oct. 2, 2008 (2nd)
Paul Goldschmidt, NL:Ari. Oct. 4, 2011 (5th)
Ryan Roberts, NL:Ari. Oct. 5, 2011 (1st)
Buster Posey, NL:SF Oct. 11, 2012 (5th)
Michael Taylor, NL:Wash. Oct. 11, 2017 (8th)
Ronald Acuna, NL:Atl. Oct. 7, 2018 (2nd)
Howie Kendrick, NL:Wash. Oct. 9, 2019 (10th)
Edgar Martinez, AL:Sea. Oct. 7, 1995 (8th)
Bobby Bonilla, AL:Balt. Oct. 1, 1996 (6th)
Albert Belle, AL:Clev. Oct. 4, 1996 (7th)
Paul O'Neill, AL:NY Oct. 4, 1997 (4th)
Jim Thome, AL:Clev. Oct. 7, 1999 (4th)
Troy O'Leary, AL:Bos. Oct. 11, 1999 (3rd)
Vladimir Guerrero, AL:Ana. Oct. 8, 2004 (7th)
Robinson Cano, AL:NY Sept. 30, 2011 (6th)
Francisco Lindor, AL:Clev. Oct. 6, 2017 (6th)
Didi Gregorius, AL:NY Oct. 5, 2019 (3rd)
Giancarlo Stanton, AL:NY Oct. 5, 2020 (9th)

Most Sacrifice Hits, Lifetime
5 Clayton Kershaw, NL:LA
4 Omar Vizquel, AL:Clev.
Steve Finley, AL:LA

Most Sacrifice Hits, Series
4 Steve Finley, AL:LA 2005
3 Placido Polanco, NL:StL. 2001
Clayton Kershaw, NL:LA 2014

Most Sacrifice Hits, Game
3 Placido Polanco, NL:StL. Oct. 13, 2001
2 Stan Javier, AL:Sea. Oct. 15, 2001
Asdrubal Cabrera, AL:Clev. Oct. 5, 2007 (11 inn)
Ramon Santiago, AL:Det. Oct. 2, 2011
Erick Aybar, AL:LA Oct. 2, 2014 (11 inn)

Most Sacrifice Hits, Inning
1 By many

Most Sacrifice Flies, Lifetime
4 Bernie Williams, AL:NY
3 Barry Bonds, NL:SF

Most Sacrifice Flies, Series
2 By many

Most Sacrifice Flies, Game
2 Dexter Fowler, NL:Col. Oct. 8, 2009
Anthony Rendon, NL:Wash. Oct. 7, 2019
1 By many in AL

Most Walks, Lifetime
36 Chipper Jones, NL:Atl.
26 Bernie Williams, AL:NY

Most Walks, Series
8 Barry Bonds, NL:SF 2003
7 Bernie Williams, AL:NY 1995
Jose Offerman, AL:Bos. 1999
Jason Giambi, AL:Oak. 2000
Ji-Man Choi, AL:TB 2019

Most Walks, Game
4 Bernie Williams, AL:NY Oct. 8, 1995 (11 inn)
   David Ortiz, AL:Bos. Oct. 5, 2007
   Bobby Abreu, AL:LA Oct. 8, 2009
3 Chris Speier, NL:Mtl. Oct. 7, 1981
   Bill Russell, NL:LA Oct. 7, 1981 (11 inn)
   Chipper Jones, NL:Atl. Oct. 1, 1997
   Andruw Jones, NL:Atl. Oct. 3, 1998
   Jeff Bagwell, NL:Hou. Oct. 8, 1999 (12 inn)
   Andruw Jones, NL:Atl. Oct. 2, 2000
   Richard Hidalgo, NL:Atl. Oct. 9, 2001
   Gary Sheffield, NL:Atl. Oct. 5, 2002
   Gary Sheffield, NL:Atl. Oct. 7, 2002
   Barry Bonds, NL:SF Sept. 30, 2003
   Scott Rolen, NL:StL. Oct. 10, 2004
   Lance Berkman, NL:Hou. Oct. 5, 2005
   Chipper Jones, NL:Atl. Oct. 9, 2005 (18 inn)
   Carlos Beltran, NL:NY Oct. 4, 2006
   Ryan Howard, NL:Phil. Oct. 1, 2008
   Raul Ibanez, NL:Phil. Oct. 11, 2009
   Chase Utley, NL:Phil. Oct. 12, 2009
   Pete Kozma, NL:StL. Oct. 11, 2012
   Max Muncy, NL:LA Oct. 4, 2018
   Yasmani Grandal, NL:LA Oct. 7, 2018
   Will Smith, NL:LA Oct. 6, 2020
   Max Muncy, NL:LA Oct. 8, 2020

Most Walks, Inning
1 By many

Most Intentional Walks, Lifetime
10 Barry Bonds, NL:SF
6 David Ortiz, AL:Bos.

Most Intentional Walks, Series
6 Barry Bonds, NL:SF 2003
3 David Ortiz, AL:Bos. 2004
   Miguel Cabrera, AL:Det. 2011
   Edwin Encarnacion, AL:Tor. 2015

Most Intentional Walks, Game
2 Edgar Martinez, AL:Sea. Oct. 6, 1995
   Nomar Garciaparra, AL:Bos. Oct. 11, 1999
   David Ortiz, AL:Bos. Oct. 6, 2004
   David Ortiz, AL:Bos. Oct. 5, 2007
   Jose Altuve, AL:Hou. Oct. 6, 2017
   Tyler White, AL:Hou. Oct. 6, 2018
   Barry Bonds, NL:SF Sept. 30, 2003
   Barry Bonds, NL:SF Oct. 3, 2003 (11 inn)
   Mike Lamb, NL:Hou. Oct. 8, 2005
   Albert Pujols, NL:StL. Oct. 8, 2005
   Manny Ramirez, NL:LA, Oct. 4, 2008
   Albert Pujols, NL:StL. Oct. 7, 2009
   Yasiel Puig, NL:LA Oct. 7, 2016
   Daniel Murphy, NL:Wash. Oct. 13, 2016

Most Intentional Walks, Inning
1 By many

Most Hit By Pitch, Lifetime
5 Russell Martin, NL:LA; AL:NY-Tor.
   Jon Jay, NL:StL.-Chi.
   Justin Turner, NL:LA
4 Manny Ramirez, AL:Clev.
   Shane Victorino, AL:Bos.
   Russell Martin, AL:NY-Tor.

Most Hit By Pitch, Series
4 Shane Victorino, AL:Bos. 2013
3 Danny Espinosa, NL:Wash. 2016
   Jon Jay, NL:Chi. 2017

Most Hit By Pitch, Game
2 Manny Ramirez, AL:Clev. Sept. 30, 1998
   Jason Giambi, AL:NY Oct. 3, 2006
   Matt Treanor, AL:Tex. Oct. 7, 2010
   Shane Victorino, AL:Bos. Oct. 8, 2013
   Rougned Odor, AL:Tex. Oct. 8, 2015
   Marwin Gonzalez, AL:Hou. Oct. 9, 2017
   Derrek Lee, NL:Fla. Oct. 4, 2003
   Xavier Nady, NL:SD Oct. 6, 2005
   Danny Espinosa, NL:Wash. Oct. 9, 2016

Most Strikeouts, Lifetime
54 Derek Jeter, AL:NY
44 Jayson Werth, NL:LA-Phil.-Wash.

Most Strikeouts, Series
16 Aaron Judge, AL:NY 2017
11 Lucas Duda, NL:NY 2015
   Trea Turner, NL:Wash. 2016
   A.J. Pollock, NL:LA 2019

Most Strikeouts, Game
5 Reggie Sanders, NL:Cin. Oct. 6, 1995
4 Rafael Palmeiro, AL:Balt. Oct. 5, 1996 (12 inn)
   Bobby Bonilla, AL:Balt. Oct. 5, 1996 (12 inn)
   Pete Incaviglia, AL:Balt. Oct. 5, 1996 (12 inn)
   Dan Wilson, AL:Sea. Oct. 2, 1997
   Brady Anderson, AL:Balt. Oct. 5, 1997
   Ben Grieve, AL:Oak. Oct. 8, 2000
   Bret Boone, AL:Sea. Oct. 13, 2001
   Derek Jeter, AL:NY Oct. 9, 2004 (11 inn)
   Howie Kendrick, AL:LA Oct. 3, 2008
   Jason Kubel, AL:Minn. Oct. 9, 2009 (11 inn)
   Johnny Damon, AL:NY Oct. 11, 2009
   Stephen Drew, AL:Oak. Oct. 11, 2012
   Austin Jackson, AL:Det. Oct. 5, 2013
   George Springer, AL:Hou. Oct. 12, 2015
   Aaron Judge, AL:NY Oct. 5, 2017
   Jay Bruce, AL:Clev. Oct. 8, 2017
   Aaron Judge, AL:NY Oct. 9, 2017
   Lonnie Chisenhall, AL:Clev. Oct. 9, 2017
   Aaron Judge, AL:NY Oct. 11, 2017
   Giancarlo Stanton, AL:NY Oct. 5, 2018
   Miguel Sano, AL:Minn. Oct. 5, 2019
   Austin Meadows, AL:TB Oct. 8, 2019
   Khris Davis, AL:Oak. Oct. 8, 2020

Most Strikeouts, Inning
1 By many

Most Stolen Bases, Lifetime
14 Kenny Lofton, AL:Clev.; NL:Atl.-SF-Chi.
12 Rafael Furcal, NL:Atl.-LA-StL.
10 Omar Vizquel, AL:Clev.
   Kenny Lofton, AL:Clev.

Most Stolen Bases, Series
6 Rickey Henderson, NL:NY 1999
5 Kenny Lofton, AL:Clev. 1996

Most Stolen Bases, Game
3 Kenny Lofton, AL:Clev. Oct. 4, 1996
   Rickey Henderson, NL:NY Oct. 6, 1999

Most Stolen Bases, Inning
2 Barry Larkin, NL:Cin. Oct. 3, 1995 (9th)
   Reggie Sanders, NL:Cin. Oct. 4, 1995 (9th)
   Barry Larkin, NL:Cin. Oct. 6, 1995 (1st)
   Rafael Furcal, NL:Atl. Oct. 9, 2005 (11th)
   Kenny Lofton, AL:Clev. Oct. 2, 1996 (6th)
   Howie Kendrick, AL:LA Oct. 5, 2007 (8th)
   Carl Crawford, AL:TB Oct. 6, 2008 (6th)
   Craig Gentry, AL:Tex. Oct. 3, 2011 (7th)
   Yoenis Cespedes, AL:Oak. Oct. 7, 2012 (8th)
   Dalton Pompey, AL:Tor. Oct. 9, 2015 (12th)
   Cameron Maybin, AL:NY Oct. 4, 2019 (7th)

Most Caught Stealing, Lifetime
4 Elvis Andrus, AL:Tex.
3 Yasiel Puig, NL:LA

Most Caught Stealing, Series
2 Cesar Cedeno, NL:Hou. 1981
   Jerry White, NL:Mtl. 1981
   Luis Alicea, NL:StL. 1996
   Sammy Sosa, NL:Chi. 1998
   Andres Torres, NL:SF 2010
   Omar Vizquel, AL:Clev. 1996
   Ichiro Suzuki, AL:Sea. 2001
   Michael Cuddyer, AL:Minn. 2004
   Adam Kennedy, AL:LA 2005
   Scott Podsednik, AL:Chi. 2005
   B.J. Upton, AL:TB 2011

Most Caught Stealing, Game
1 By many

Most Grounded Into Double Plays, Lifetime
11 Bernie Williams, AL:NY
7 Chipper Jones, NL:Atl.

Most Grounded Into Double Plays, Series
4 Bernie Williams, AL:NY 2004
3 Kurt Suzuki, NL:Wash. 2019

Most Grounded Into Double Plays, Game
2 Chipper Jones, NL:Atl. Oct. 3, 1995
   Lance Berkman, NL:Hou. Oct. 10, 2001
   Jeff Kent, NL:Hou. Oct. 10, 2004
   Kolten Wong, NL:StL. Oct. 6, 2014
   David Wright, NL:NY Oct. 10, 2015
   Brandon Drury, NL:Ari. Oct. 6, 2017
   Ben Zobrist, NL:Chi. Oct. 7, 2017
   Kurt Suzuki, NL:Wash. Oct. 7, 2019
   Paul O'Neill, AL:NY Oct. 4, 1996
   Sandy Alomar Jr., AL:Clev. Sept. 30, 1998
   Roberto Alomar, AL:Clev. Oct. 15, 2001
   Darin Erstad, AL:Ana. Oct. 5, 2002
   Bernie Williams, AL:NY Oct. 8, 2004
   Placido Polanco, AL:Det. Oct. 3, 2006
   Derek Jeter, AL:NY Oct. 7, 2007
   Tommy Pham, AL:TB Oct. 4, 2019

INDIVIDUAL FIELDING

GAMES

Most Games, First Base, Lifetime
37 Tino Martinez, AL:Sea.-NY; NL:StL.
34 Tino Martinez, AL:Sea.-NY
24 Albert Pujols, NL:StL.

Most Games, Second Base, Lifetime
29 Robinson Cano, AL:NY
25 Chase Utley, NL:Phil.-LA

Most Games, Third Base, Lifetime
32 Chipper Jones, NL:Atl.
31 Alex Rodriguez, AL:NY

Most Games, Shortstop, Lifetime
65 Derek Jeter, AL:NY
36 Rafael Furcal, NL:Atl.-LA-StL.

Most Games, Outfield, Lifetime
45 Bernie Williams, AL:NY
38 Andruw Jones, NL:Atl.

Most Games, Catcher, Lifetime
45 Jorge Posada, AL:NY
37 Yadier Molina, NL:StL.

Most Games, Pitcher, Lifetime
39 Mariano Rivera, AL:NY
20 Kenley Jansen, NL:LA

ERRORS

Most Errors, First Base, Lifetime
3 Paul Sorrento, AL:Clev.-Sea.
   Jeff Bagwell, NL:Hou.

Most Errors, Second Base, Lifetime
4 Brooks Conrad, NL:Atl.
   Chase Utley, NL:Phil.-LA
3 Robinson Cano, AL:NY

Most Errors, Third Base, Lifetime
4 Ken Caminiti, NL:SD-Hou.-Atl.
   Chipper Jones, NL:Atl.
   Scott Rolen, NL:Cin.
   Kris Bryant, NL:Chi.
   Todd Zeile, AL:Balt.-Tex.

Most Errors, Shortstop, Lifetime
9 Derek Jeter, AL:NY
5 Edgar Renteria, NL:Fla.-StL.

Most Errors, Outfield, Lifetime
3 Kenny Lofton, AL:Clev.
2 Ryan Klesko, NL:Atl.
   Tony Womack, NL:Ari.
   Marquis Grissom, NL:Atl.-SF
   Kyle Schwarber, NL:Chi.

Most Errors, Catcher, Lifetime
4 Sandy Alomar Jr., AL:Clev.
3 Willson Contreras, NL:Chi.

Most Errors, Pitcher, Lifetime
2 LaTroy Hawkins, AL:Minn.
   Trevor Bauer, AL:Clev.
1 By many in NL

Most Errors, Series
4 Brooks Conrad, NL:Atl. 2010
3 Charlie Hayes, AL:NY 1997
   Scott Brosius, AL:NY 2001

Most Errors, Game
3 Brooks Conrad, NL:Atl. Oct. 10, 2010 (2b)
2 Eric Chavez, AL:Oak. Oct. 4, 2003 (3b; 11 inn)
   Elvis Andrus, AL:Tex. Oct. 14, 2015 (ss)
   Todd Frazier, AL:NY Oct. 6, 2017 (3b; 13 inn)
   Giovanny Urshela, AL:Clev. Oct. 9, 2017 (3b)
   Trevor Bauer, AL:Clev. Oct. 8, 2018 (p)
   Willy Adames, AL:TB Oct. 7, 2020 (ss)

Most Errors, Inning
2 Eric Chavez, AL:Oak. Oct. 4, 2003 (3b; 2nd)
   Elvis Andrus, AL:Tex. Oct. 14, 2015 (ss; 7th)
   Trevor Bauer, AL:Clev. Oct. 8, 2018 (p; 7th)
   Chase Utley, NL:Phil. Oct. 8, 2010 (2b; 2nd)
   Kris Bryant, NL:Chi. Oct. 8, 2016 (3b; 5th)
   Willson Contreras, NL:Chi. Oct. 10, 2016 (c; 8th)
   Kyle Schwarber, NL:Chi. Oct. 9, 2017 (lf; 6th)
   Matt Wieters, NL:Wash. Oct. 12, 2017 (c; 5th)

INDIVIDUAL PITCHING

Most Series
16 Mariano Rivera, AL:NY 1995-2007, 09-11
11 Greg Maddux, NL:Atl. 1995-2003; LA 06, 08
   John Smoltz, NL:Atl. 1995-99, 2001-05; StL. 09

Lowest ERA, Lifetime (Minimum: 20 innings)
0.32 Mariano Rivera, AL:NY (56 inn)
0.72 Curt Schilling, NL:Ari. (25 inn)

Most Games, Lifetime
39 Mariano Rivera, AL:NY
20 Kenley Jansen, NL:LA

Most Games, Series
5 Kevin Gryboski, NL:Atl. 2003
   Kevin Gryboski, NL:Atl. 2004
   Santiago Casilla, NL:SF 2012
   Sammy Solis, NL:Wash. 2016
   Carl Edwards Jr. NL:Chi. 2017
   Scott Williamson, AL:Bos. 2003
   Brian Matusz, AL:Balt. 2012
   Aaron Sanchez, AL:Tor. 2015
   Tony Sipp, AL:Hou. 2015
   Colin Poche, AL:TB 2019

Most Games Started, Lifetime
16 Andy Pettitte, AL:NY-NL:Hou.
15 Andy Pettitte, AL:NY
13 Clayton Kershaw, NL:LA

Most Games Started, Series
2 By many

Most Complete Games, Lifetime
2 Cliff Lee, NL:Phil-AL:Tex.
   Curt Schilling, NL:Ari.
1 By many in AL

Most Complete Games, Series
2 Curt Schilling, NL:Ari. 2001
1 By many in AL

Most Games Finished, Lifetime
32 Mariano Rivera, AL:NY
17 Kenley Jansen, NL:LA

Most Games Finished, Series
4 Trevor Hoffman, NL:SD 1998
   Steve Kline, NL:StL. 2001
   Ryan Madson, NL:Phil. 2011
   Drew Storen, NL:Wash. 2012
   Jeurys Familia, NL:NY 2015
   Mark Melancon, NL:Wash. 2016
3 By many in AL

Most Saves, Lifetime
18 Mariano Rivera, AL:NY
9 Kenley Jansen, NL:LA

Most Saves, Series
3 Rich Gossage, AL:NY 1981
Mike Jackson, AL:Clev. 1998
Mariano Rivera, AL:NY 2000
Neftali Feliz, AL:Tex. 2011
Dennis Eckersley, NL:StL. 1996
Mark Wohlers, NL:Atl. 1996
Manny Corpas, NL:Col. 2007
Trevor Rosenthal, NL:StL. 2014
Aroldis Chapman, NL:Chi. 2016
Wade Davis, NL:Chi. 2017

Most Shutouts, Lifetime
1 Mike Norris, AL:Oak. Oct. 6, 1981
Josh Beckett, AL:Bos. Oct. 3, 2007
Justin Verlander, AL:Det. Oct. 11, 2012
Jerry Reuss, NL:LA Oct. 11, 1981
Steve Rogers, NL:Mtl. Oct. 11, 1981
Bobby J. Jones, NL:NY Oct. 8, 2000
Curt Schilling, NL:Ari. Oct. 9, 2001
Jason Schmidt, NL:SF Sept. 30, 2003
Jose Lima, NL:LA Oct. 9, 2004
Roy Halladay, NL:Phil. Oct. 6, 2010
Tim Lincecum, NL:SF Oct. 7, 2010
Cole Hamels, NL:Phil. Oct. 10, 2010
Chris Carpenter, NL:StL. Oct. 7, 2011

Most Games Won, Lifetime
8 Justin Verlander, AL:Det.-Hou.
7 John Smoltz, NL:Atl.

Most Games Won, Series
2 By many

Most Games Lost, Lifetime
8 Randy Johnson, AL:Sea.-NY; NL:Hou.-Ari.
David Price, AL:TB-Det.-Tor.-Bos.
5 Randy Johnson, NL:Hou.-Ari.

Most Games Lost, Series
2 By many

Most Innings Pitched, Lifetime
100.2 Andy Pettitte, AL:NY-NL:Hou.
93.2 Andy Pettitte, AL:NY
85.0 Clayton Kershaw, NL:LA

Most Innings Pitched, Series
18.0 Jerry Reuss, NL:LA 1981
Curt Schilling, NL:Ari. 2001
17.2 CC Sabathia, AL:NY 2012

Most Innings Pitched, Game
9.0 By many

Most Runs, Lifetime
41 Randy Johnson, AL:Sea.-NY; NL:Hou.-Ari.
Andy Pettitte, AL:NY; NL:Hou.
40 Clayton Kershaw, NL:LA
38 Andy Pettitte, AL:NY

Most Runs, Series
13 Tom Glavine, NL:Atl. 2002
12 Chien-Ming Wang, AL:NY 2007

Most Runs, Game
8 Steve Reed, AL:Clev. Oct. 10, 1999
Charles Nagy, AL:Clev. Oct. 11, 1999
Paul Abbott, AL:Sea. Oct. 13, 2001
David Wells, AL:NY Oct. 5, 2002
Matt Clement, AL:Bos. Oct. 4, 2005
Chien-Ming Wang, AL:NY Oct. 4, 2007
C.J. Wilson, AL:Tex. Sept. 30, 2011
Matt Moore, AL:TB Oct. 4, 2013
Jake Peavy, NL:SD Oct. 4, 2005
Clayton Kershaw, NL:LA Oct. 3, 2014

Most Runs, Inning
7 David Wells, AL:NY Oct. 5, 2002 (5th)
A.J. Burnett, NL:Pitt. Oct. 3, 2013 (3rd)
Mike Foltynewicz, NL:Atl. Oct. 9, 2019 (1st)

Most Earned Runs, Lifetime
41 Andy Pettitte, AL:NY; NL:Hou.
38 Andy Pettitte, AL:NY
Clayton Kershaw, NL:LA

Most Earned Runs, Series
13 Tom Glavine, NL:Atl. 2002
12 Chien-Ming Wang, AL:NY 2007

Most Earned Runs, Game
8 Steve Reed, AL:Clev. Oct. 10, 1999
Paul Abbott, AL:Sea. Oct. 13, 2001
David Wells, AL:NY Oct. 5, 2002
Matt Clement, AL:Bos. Oct. 4, 2005
Chien-Ming Wang, AL:NY Oct. 4, 2007
Jake Peavy, NL:SD Oct. 4, 2005
Clayton Kershaw, NL:LA Oct. 3, 2014

Most Earned Runs, Inning
7 David Wells, AL:NY Oct. 5, 2002 (5th)
A.J. Burnett, NL:Pitt. Oct. 3, 2013 (3rd)

Most Hits, Lifetime
98 Andy Pettitte, AL:NY-NL:Hou.
94 Andy Pettitte, AL:NY
78 Greg Maddux, NL:Atl.-LA

Most Hits, Series
19 Greg Maddux, NL:Atl. 1995
17 David Price, AL:TB 2010

Most Hits, Game
12 Nate Roberston, AL:Det. Oct. 3, 2006
Cliff Lee, NL:Phil. Oct. 2, 2011

Fewest Hits, Complete Game
0 Roy Halladay, NL:Phil. Oct. 6, 2010
4 Mike Norris, AL:Oak. Oct. 6, 1981
Erik Hanson, AL:Bos. Oct. 4, 1995 (8 inn)
Josh Beckett, AL:Bos. Oct. 3, 2007
Justin Verlander, AL:Det. Oct. 11, 2012
CC Sabathia, AL:NY Oct. 12, 2012

Most Hits, Inning
7 David Wells, AL:NY Oct. 5, 2002 (5th)
6 Clayton Kershaw, NL:LA Oct. 3, 2014 (7th)

Most Home Runs, Lifetime
14 Clayton Kershaw, NL:LA
11 David Price, AL:TB-Det.-Tor.-Bos.

Most Home Runs, Series
5 Jaret Wright, NL:Atl. 2004
4 David Cone, AL:NY 1995
Charles Nagy, AL:Clev. 1996
Rick Reed, AL:Minn. 2002
Yu Darvish, AL:Tex. 2016
Corey Kluber, AL:Clev. 2017
Chris Sale, AL:Bos. 2017
Jose Urquidy, AL:Hou. 2020

Most Home Runs, Game
4 Rick Reed, AL:Minn. Oct. 4, 2002
Yu Darvish, AL:Tex. Oct. 7, 2016
Jose Urquidy, AL:Hou. Oct. 7, 2020
Clayton Kershaw, NL:LA Oct. 6, 2017

Most Home Runs, Inning
3 Rick Porcello, AL:Bos. Oct. 6, 2016 (3rd)
Yu Darvish, AL:Tex. Oct. 7, 2016 (5th)
2 By many in NL

Most Grand Slam Home Runs, Lifetime
1 Mark Guthrie, NL:LA Oct. 6, 1995 (6th)
Wilson Alvarez, NL:SF Oct. 3, 1997 (6th)
Matt Karchner, NL:Chi. Sept. 30, 1998 (7th)
Rod Beck, NL:Chi. Oct. 3, 1998 (8th)
Bobby Chouinard, NL:Ari. Oct. 5, 1999 (9th)
Jake Peavy, NL:SD Oct. 4, 2005 (5th)
Brandon Backe, NL:Hou. Oct. 9, 2005 (3rd)
Kyle Farnsworth, NL:Atl. Oct. 9, 2005 (8th)
Kyle Lohse, NL:Phil. Oct. 4, 2007 (4th)
Ryan Dempster, NL:Chi. Oct. 1, 2008 (5th)
CC Sabathia, NL:Mil. Oct. 2, 2008 (2nd)
Shaun Marcum, NL:Mil. Oct. 4, 2011 (5th)
Randy Wolf, NL:Mil. Oct. 5, 2011 (1st)
Mat Latos, NL:Cin. Oct. 11, 2012 (5th)
Wade Davis, NL:Chi. Oct. 11, 2017 (8th)
Walker Buehler, NL:LA Oct. 7, 2018 (2nd)
Joe Kelly, NL:LA Oct. 9, 2019 (10th)
John Wetteland, AL:NY Oct. 7, 1995 (8th)
Paul Shuey, AL:Clev. Oct. 1, 1996 (6th)
Armando Benitez, AL:Balt. Oct. 4, 1996 (7th)
Chad Ogea, AL:Clev. Oct. 4, 1997 (4th)
John Wasdin, AL:Bos. Oct. 7, 1999 (4th)
Charles Nagy, AL:Clev. Oct. 11, 1999 (3rd)
Mike Timlin, AL:Bos. Oct. 8, 2004 (7th)
Al Alburquerque, AL:Det. Sept. 30, 2011 (6th)
Chad Green, AL:NY Oct. 6, 2017 (6th)
Tyler Duffey, AL:Minn. Oct. 5, 2019 (3rd)
John Curtiss, AL:TB Oct. 5, 2020 (9th)

Most Walks, Lifetime
- 34 CC Sabathia, AL:Clev.-NY; NL:Mil.
- 30 CC Sabathia, AL:Clev.-NY
- 25 Tom Glavine, NL:Atl.-NY

Most Walks, Series
- 11 Gio Gonzalez, NL:Wash. 2012
- 9 David Cone, AL:NY 1995
  - Andy Benes, AL:Sea. 1995
  - John Lackey, AL:LA 2005

Most Walks, Game
- 8 Mike Hampton, NL:Hou. Oct. 1, 1997
- 6 David Cone, AL:NY Oct. 3, 1995
  - Andy Benes, AL:Sea. Oct. 8, 1995 (11 inn)
  - Andy Pettitte, AL:NY Oct. 2, 1996 (12 inn)
  - Charles Nagy, AL:Clev. Oct. 4, 1997
  - Orlando Hernandez, AL:NY Oct. 5, 1999
  - CC Sabathia, AL:Clev. Oct. 4, 2007
  - CC Sabathia, AL:NY Oct. 3, 2011

Most Walks, Inning
- 4 Andy Benes, AL:Sea. Oct. 8, 1995 (6th)
  - Mike Hampton, NL:Hou. Oct. 1, 1997 (5th)
  - Rick Ankiel, NL:StL. Oct. 3, 2000 (3rd)
  - Gio Gonzalez, NL:Wash. Oct. 7, 2012 (2nd)
  - Patrick Corbin, NL:Wash. Oct. 3, 2019 (1st)

Most Intentional Walks, Lifetime
- 7 Greg Maddux, NL:Atl.-LA
- 5 CC Sabathia, AL:Clev.-NY

Most Intentional Walks, Series
- 3 Tom Glavine, NL:Atl. 2002
- 2 Aaron Sele, AL:Tex. 1999
  - Chad Bradford, AL:Oak. 2003
  - Derek Lowe, AL:Bos. 2003
  - Brendan Donnelly, AL:Ana. 2004
  - Joe Nathan, AL:Minn. 2004
  - CC Sabathia, AL:NY 2011
  - Jason Hammel, AL:Balt. 2012
  - Dallas Keuchel, AL:Hou. 2015
  - Cody Allen, AL:Clev. 2018

Most Intentional Walks, Game
- 2 Steve Carlton, NL:Phil. Oct. 7, 1981
  - Greg Maddux, NL:Atl. Oct. 5, 1999
  - Jose Lima, NL:Hou. Oct. 6, 1999
  - Greg Maddux, NL:Atl. Oct. 3, 2000
  - Andy Ashby, NL:Atl. Oct. 5, 2000
  - Tom Glavine, NL:Atl. Oct. 6, 2002
  - Jake Peavy, NL:SD Oct. 4, 2005
  - Jorge Sosa, NL:Atl. Oct. 8, 2005
  - Rich Harden, NL:Chi. Oct. 4, 2008
  - Randy Wolf, NL:LA Oct. 7, 2009
  - Nick Masset, NL:Cin. Oct. 8, 2010
  - Jaime Garcia, NL:StL. Oct. 4, 2011
  - Aaron Sele, AL:Tex. Oct. 5, 1999
  - Brendan Donnelly, AL:Ana. Oct. 6, 2004
  - Cody Allen, AL:Clev. Oct. 8, 2018

Most Intentional Walks, Inning
- 2 Aaron Sele, AL:Tex. Oct. 5, 1999 (5th)
  - Brendan Donnelly, AL:Ana. Oct. 6, 2004 (9th)
  - Cody Allen, AL:Clev. Oct. 8, 2018 (8th)
  - Jake Peavy, NL:SD Oct. 4, 2005 (3rd)
  - Nick Masset, NL:Cin. Oct. 8, 2010 (8th)

Most Hit Batters, Lifetime
- 6 Tim Wakefield, AL:Bos.
  - James Shields, AL:TB-KC
- 3 Kevin Brown, NL:SD
  - Greg Maddux, NL:Atl.-LA
  - Ian Kennedy, NL:Ari.
  - Craig Stammen, NL:Wash.
  - Rich Hill, NL:Chi.-LA
  - Max Scherzer, NL:Wash.
  - Clayton Kershaw, NL:LA

Most Hit Batters, Series
- 3 Kevin Brown, NL:SD 1998
  - Ian Kennedy, NL:Ari. 2011
  - Craig Stammen NL:Wash. 2012
- 2 By many in AL

Most Hit Batters, Game
- 2 Kevin Brown, NL:SD Oct. 3, 1998
  - Jeff Weaver, NL:LA Oct. 7, 2004
  - Mark Mulder, NL:StL. Oct. 6, 2005
  - Ian Kennedy, NL:Ari. Oct. 1, 2011
  - Craig Stammen NL:Wash. Oct. 7, 2012
  - Rich Hill NL:LA Oct. 9, 2016
  - Joe Ross NL:Wash. Oct. 11, 2016
  - Clayton Kershaw, NL:LA Oct. 4, 2019
  - Steve Reed, AL:Clev. Oct. 10, 1999
  - Dwight Gooden, AL:NY Oct. 7, 2000
  - Barry Zito, AL:Oak. Oct. 13, 2001
  - Mark Mulder, AL:Oak. Oct. 15, 2001
  - Tim Wakefield, AL:Bos. Oct. 2, 2003
  - Felix Heredia, AL:NY Oct. 8, 2004
  - Javier Vazquez, AL:NY Oct. 9, 2004 (11 inn)
  - Matt Clement, AL:Bos. Oct. 4, 2005
  - Tim Wakefield, AL:Bos. Oct. 7, 2005
  - Nate Robertson, AL:Det. Oct. 3, 2006
  - A.J. Burnett, AL:NY Oct. 9, 2009 (11 inn)
  - James Shields, AL:TB Oct. 7, 2010
  - James Shields, AL:TB Oct. 1, 2011
  - Rick Porcello, AL:Det. Oct. 4, 2011
  - Doug Fister, AL:Det. Oct. 7, 2012
  - Hiroki Kuroda, AL:NY Oct. 10, 2012 (12 inn)
  - David Price, AL:Tor. Oct. 8, 2015
  - Lance McCullers, AL:Hou. Oct. 12, 2015
  - Corey Kluber, AL:Clev. Oct. 5, 2018

Most Hit Batters, Inning
- 2 Jeff Weaver, NL:LA Oct. 7, 2004 (5th)
  - Felix Heredia, AL:NY Oct. 8, 2004 (9th)
  - Tim Wakefield, AL:Bos. Oct. 7, 2005 (1st)
  - A.J. Burnett, AL:NY Oct. 9, 2009 (4th)
  - James Shields, AL:TB Oct. 1, 2011 (4th)
  - Corey Kluber, AL:Clev. Oct. 5, 2018 (2nd)

Most Strikeouts, Lifetime
- 100 Clayton Kershaw, NL:LA
- 87 Justin Verlander, AL:Det.-Hou.

Most Strikeouts, Series
- 25 Gerrit Cole, AL:Hou. 2019
- 22 Stephen Strasburg, NL:Wash. 2017

Most Strikeouts, Game
- 16 Kevin Brown, NL:SD Sept. 29, 1998
- 15 Gerrit Cole, AL:Hou. Oct. 5, 2019

Most Strikeouts, Inning
- 3 By many

Most Wild Pitches, Lifetime
- 5 Roger Clemens, AL:Bos.-NY; NL:Hou.
  - Rick Ankiel, NL:StL.
- 4 John Lackey, AL:LA

Most Wild Pitches, Series
- 5 Rick Ankiel, NL:StL. 2000
- 2 David Cone, AL:NY 1995
  - Steve Karsay, AL:Clev. 1999
  - Francisco Rodriguez, AL:Ana. 2004
  - Kelvim Escobar, AL:LA 2005
  - John Lackey, AL:LA 2005
  - Joba Chamberlain, AL:NY 2007
  - James Shields, AL:TB 2011
  - Jarrod Parker, AL:Oak. 2012
  - Jaime Garcia, AL:NY 2017

Most Wild Pitches, Game
- 5 Rick Ankiel, NL:StL. Oct. 3, 2000
- 2 David Cone, AL:NY Oct. 8, 1995 (11 inn)
  - Steve Karsay, AL:Clev. Oct. 10, 1999
  - Francisco Rodriguez, AL:Ana. Oct. 6, 2004
  - Kelvim Escobar, AL:LA Oct. 9, 2005
  - Joba Chamberlain, AL:NY Oct. 5, 2007 (11 inn)
  - James Shields, AL:TB Oct. 1, 2011
  - Jarrod Parker, AL:Oak. Oct. 11, 2012
  - Jaime Garcia, AL:NY Oct. 5, 2017

Most Wild Pitches, Inning
- 5 Rick Ankiel, NL:StL. Oct. 3, 2000 (3rd)
- 2 Kelvim Escobar, AL:LA Oct. 9, 2005 (8th)
  - Joba Chamberlain, AL:NY Oct. 5, 2007 (8th)
  - James Shields, AL:TB Oct. 1, 2011 (4th)
  - Jarrod Parker, AL:Oak. Oct. 11, 2012 (3rd)

Most Balks, Lifetime
1 Kevin Tapani, NL:Chi. Oct. 1, 1998 (5th)
  Kevin Millwood, NL:Atl. Oct. 7, 2000 (5th)
  Andy Benes, NL:StL. Oct. 5, 2002 (1st)
  Brett Tomko, NL:LA Oct. 7, 2006 (8th)
  Brad Ziegler, NL:Ari. Oct. 2, 2011 (6th)
  Fernando Salas, NL:StL. Oct. 5, 2011 (5th)
  Scott Oberg, NL:Col. Oct. 7, 2018 (6th)
  Brusdar Graterol. NL:LA Oct. 7, 2020 (7th)
  Yimi Garcia, NL:Mia. Oct. 8, 2020 (6th)
  Brad Boxberger, NL:Mia. Oct. 8, 2020 (8th)
  Julio Urias, NL:LA Oct. 8, 2020 (6th)
  Clay Buchholz, AL:Bos. Oct. 11, 2009 (6th)
  Doug Fister, AL:Det. Sept. 30, 2011 (2nd)
  Boone Logan, AL:NY Oct. 2, 2011 (6th)
  Al Alburquerque, AL:Det. Oct. 4, 2011 (8th)
  Adam Cimber, AL:Clev. Oct. 8, 2018 (9th)

CLUB BATTING

Most At-Bats, Series
200 Seattle, AL 1995
180 Atlanta, NL 2004
    Houston, NL 2004
    Cincinnati NL 2012

Most At-Bats, Game
48 Boston, AL Oct. 10, 1999
42 Florida, NL Oct. 1, 2003
   Los Angeles, NL Oct. 7, 2006
   Extra-Inning Game:
62 Atlanta, NL Oct. 9, 2005 (18 inn)
   Washington, NL Oct. 4, 2014 (18 inn)
56 Seattle, AL Oct. 4, 1995 (15 inn)

Most At-Bats, Inning
13 Anaheim, AL Oct. 5, 2002 (5th)
10 St. Louis, NL Oct. 3, 2014 (7th)

Most Runs, Series
47 Boston, AL 1999
36 Houston, NL 2004

Most Runs, Game
23 Boston, AL Oct. 10, 1999
13 Atlanta, NL Oct. 1, 1997
   Los Angeles, NL Oct. 6, 2013
   New York, NL Oct. 12, 2015
   St. Louis, NL Oct. 9, 2019

Most Runs, Both Clubs, Game
30 Bos. (23) Clev. (7) AL Oct. 10, 1999
20 NY (13) LA (7) NL Oct. 12, 2015

Most Runs, Inning
10 St. Louis, NL Oct. 9, 2019 (1st)
8 Anaheim, AL Oct. 5, 2002 (5th)
  Baltimore, AL Oct. 2, 2014 (8th)

Most Hits, Series
63 Seattle, AL 1995
58 Houston, NL 2004

Most Hits, Game
24 Boston, AL Oct. 10, 1999
17 Houston, NL Oct. 11, 2004

Most Hits, Both Clubs, Game
32 Bos. (24) Clev. (8) AL Oct. 10, 1999
30 LA (16) NY (14) NL Oct. 7, 2006

Most Hits, Inning
10 Anaheim, AL Oct. 5, 2002 (5th)
7 Atlanta, NL Oct. 9, 1999 (6th)
  St. Louis, NL Oct. 3, 2014 (7th)

Most Total Bases, Series
105 Boston, AL 1999
103 Houston, NL 2004

Most Total Bases, Game
45 Boston, AL Oct. 10, 1999
33 Chicago, NL Oct. 12, 2015

Most Total Bases, Both Clubs, Game
57 Bos. (45) Clev. (12) AL Oct. 10, 1999
49 Chi. (33) StL. (16) NL Oct. 12, 2015

Most Total Bases, Inning
14 New York, AL Sept. 30, 1997 (6th)
   Anaheim, AL Oct. 5, 2002 (5th)
12 Washington, NL Oct. 12, 2017 (2nd)
   Los Angeles, NL Oct. 6, 2019 (6th)
   Atlanta, NL Oct. 6, 2020 (7th)

Most Extra-Base Hits, Series
28 Boston, AL 1999
23 Houston, NL 2004

Most Extra-Base Hits, Game
12 Boston, AL Oct. 10, 1999
8 Houston, NL Oct. 8, 2005
  Atlanta, NL Oct. 9, 2005 (18 inn)
  Colorado, NL Oct. 4, 2007
  St. Louis, NL Oct. 8, 2012
  San Francisco, NL Oct. 10, 2012
  Los Angeles, NL Oct. 6, 2019

Most Extra-Base Hits, Both Clubs, Game
14 Bos. (12) Clev. (2) AL Oct. 10, 1999
12 Atl. (8) Hou. (4) NL Oct. 9, 2005 (18 inn)
   Col. (8) Phil. (4) NL Oct. 4, 2007
   StL. (7) Atl. (5) NL Oct. 3, 2019

Most Extra-Base Hits, Inning
4 New York, AL Oct. 5, 2003 (4th)
  St. Louis, NL Oct. 8, 2012 (8th)
  Los Angeles, NL Oct. 6, 2019 (6th)

Most Singles, Series
45 Seattle, AL 1995
39 Atlanta, NL 1999

Most Singles, Game
14 Los Angeles, NL Oct. 7, 2006
13 Boston, AL Oct. 8, 2018

Most Singles, Both Clubs, Game
25 LA (14) NY (11) NL Oct. 7, 2006
23 Hou. (12) Bos. (11) AL Oct. 8, 2017

Most Singles, Inning
8 Anaheim, AL Oct. 5, 2002 (5th)
7 Atlanta, NL Oct. 9, 1999 (6th)

Most Doubles, Series
17 Boston, AL 1999
16 St. Louis, NL 2019

Most Doubles, Game
7 Boston, AL Oct. 10, 1999
  Houston, NL Oct. 8, 2005

Most Doubles, Both Clubs, Game
9 Clev. (5) Sea. (4) AL Oct. 13, 2001
  Hou. (7) Atl. (2) NL Oct. 8, 2005
  StL. (6) Atl. (3) NL Oct. 3, 2019

Most Doubles, Inning
4 New York, AL Oct. 5, 2003 (4th)
3 Cincinnati, NL Oct. 3, 1995 (5th)
  Los Angeles, NL Oct. 6, 2019 (6th)
  St. Louis, NL Oct. 9, 2019 (1st)

Most Triples, Series
3 Los Angeles, AL 2005
  Oakland, AL 2013
  Colorado, NL 2007
  St. Louis, NL 2011

Most Triples, Game
2 Chicago, AL Oct. 3, 2000 (10 inn)
  Los Angeles, AL Oct. 7, 2005
  San Diego, NL Oct. 3, 2006
  Arizona, NL Oct. 4, 2007
  St. Louis, NL Oct. 2, 2011
  San Francisco, NL Oct. 10, 2016 (13 inn)
  Los Angeles, NL Oct. 6, 2017

Most Triples, Both Clubs, Game
2 Mtl. (1) Phil. (1) NL Oct. 7, 1981
  SD (2) StL. (0) NL Oct. 3, 2006
  Col. (1) Phil. (1) NL Oct. 4, 2007
  Ari. (2) Chi. (0) NL Oct. 4, 2007
  StL. (2) Phil. (0) NL Oct. 2, 2011
  SF (2) Chi. (0) NL Oct 10, 2016 (13 inn)
  LA (2) Ari. (0) NL Oct. 6, 2017
  Chi. (2) Sea. (0) AL Oct. 3, 2000 (10 inn)
  LA (2) NY (0) AL Oct. 7, 2005
  Bos. (1) LA (1) AL Oct. 9, 2009
  Tex. (1) Tor. (1) AL Oct. 6, 2016

Most Triples, Inning
1 By many

Most Home Runs, Series
12 Houston, AL 2020
   Cleveland, AL 2020
11 Houston, NL 2004

Most Home Runs, Game
6 Chicago, NL Oct. 12, 2015
5 Chicago, AL Oct. 4, 2005
  Oakland, AL Oct. 7, 2020

Most Home Runs, Both Clubs, Game
8 Chi. (6) StL. (2) NL Oct. 12, 2015
7 Oak. (5) Hou. (2) AL Oct. 7, 2020

Most Home Runs, Inning
3 New York, AL Sept. 30, 1997 (6th)
  Cleveland, AL Oct. 6, 2016 (3rd)
  Toronto, AL Oct. 7, 2016 (5th)
2 By many in NL

Most Grand Slam Home Runs, Series
2 Atlanta, NL 1998
  Arizona, NL 2011
1 By many in AL

Most Grand Slam Home Runs, Game
1 By many (see individual batting)

Most Runs Batted In, Series
47 Boston, AL 1999
36 Houston, NL 2004

Most Runs Batted In, Game
23 Boston, AL Oct. 10, 1999
13 Los Angeles, NL Oct. 6, 2013
   New York, NL Oct. 12, 2015

Most Runs Batted In, Both Clubs, Game
30 Bos. (23) Clev. (7) AL Oct. 10, 1999
19 LA (13) Atl. (6) NL Oct. 6, 2013
   StL. (10) LA (9) NL Oct. 3, 2014
   NY (13) LA (6) NL Oct. 12, 2015

Most Runs Batted In, Inning
9 St. Louis, NL Oct. 9, 2019 (1st)
8 Anaheim, AL Oct. 5, 2002 (5th)

Most Sacrifice Hits, Series
8 St. Louis, NL 2001
5 Los Angeles, AL 2005
  Cleveland, AL 2007

Most Sacrifice Hits, Game
4 Houston, NL Oct. 5, 2005
3 Oakland, AL Oct. 7, 1981
  Seattle, AL Oct. 6, 2000
  Extra-Inning AL Game:
4 Cleveland, AL Oct. 5, 2007 (11 inn)

Most Sacrifice Hits, Both Clubs, Game
4 Oak. (3) KC (1) AL Oct. 7, 1981
  NY (2) Tex. (2) AL Oct. 2, 1996 (12 inn)
  Sea. (3) Chi. (1) AL Oct. 6, 2000
  Clev. (4) NY (0) AL Oct. 5, 2007 (11 inn)
  Hou. (4) Atl. (0) NL Oct. 5, 2005
  Extra-Inning NL Game:
5 Chi. (3) Atl. (2) NL Oct. 1, 1998 (10 inn)

Most Sacrifice Hits, Inning
2 Los Angeles, AL Oct. 5, 2005 (7th)
  Chicago, AL Oct. 7, 2005 (9th)
  Chicago, NL Oct. 10, 2015 (2nd)

Most Sacrifice Flies, Series
4 Cleveland, AL 1999
  Minnesota, AL 2004
  Houston, NL 2005
  San Francisco, NL 2016

Most Sacrifice Flies, Game
2 Atlanta, NL Oct. 6, 1999
  San Francisco, NL Oct. 4, 2003
  Houston, NL Oct. 8, 2005
  Milwaukee, NL Oct. 4, 2008
  Colorado, NL Oct. 8, 2009
  San Francisco, NL Oct. 11, 2016
  Washington, NL Oct. 7, 2019
  Cleveland, AL Oct. 10, 1999
  New York, AL Oct. 8, 2000
  Oakland, AL Oct. 8, 2000
  Oakland, AL Oct. 10, 2001
  New York, AL Oct. 4, 2002
  Minnesota, AL Oct. 9, 2004 (11 inn)
  New York, AL Oct. 9, 2018
  Oakland, AL Oct. 7, 2020

Most Sacrifice Flies, Both Clubs, Game
4 NY (2) Oak. (2) AL Oct. 8, 2000
3 SF (2) Chi. (1) NL Oct. 11, 2016

Most Sacrifice Flies, Inning
2 New York, AL Oct. 8, 2000 (1st)
  Oakland, AL Oct. 8, 2000 (4th)
1 By many in NL

Most Walks, Series
32 New York, AL 1995
29 St. Louis, NL 2012

Most Walks, Game
10 Atlanta, NL Oct. 1, 1997
   Los Angeles, NL Oct. 6, 2020
9 Cleveland, AL Oct. 7, 1999
  Cleveland, AL Oct. 9, 1999
  Boston, AL Oct. 5, 2007
  Extra-Inning Game:
11 Atlanta, NL Oct. 9, 2005 (18 inn)
10 New York, AL Oct. 8, 1995 (11 inn)
   Oakland, AL Oct. 1, 2003 (12 inn)

Most Walks, Both Clubs, Game
16 Atl. (10) Hou. (6) NL Oct. 1, 1997
14 Tex. (7) NY (7) AL Oct. 5, 1999
   Clev. (9) Bos. (5) AL Oct. 10, 1999
   Bos. (9) LA (5) AL Oct. 5, 2007
   NY (8) Minn. (6) AL Oct. 4, 2019
   Extra-Inning Game:
17 Bos. (7) Oak. (10) AL Oct. 1, 2003 (12 inn)
   Atl. (11) Hou. (6) NL Oct. 9, 2005 (18 inn)

Most Walks, Inning
5 Florida, NL Oct. 1, 1997 (4th)
  Cleveland, AL Oct. 10, 1999 (5th)

Most Intentional Walks, Series
8 San Francisco, NL 2003
  Houston, NL 2005
6 Boston, AL 2004

Most Intentional Walks, Game
3 Montreal, NL Oct. 7, 1981
  Houston, NL Oct. 5, 1999
  St. Louis, NL Oct. 3, 2000
  San Francisco, NL Oct. 6, 2002
  Houston, NL Oct. 5, 2005
  Houston, NL Oct. 8, 2005
  St. Louis, NL Oct. 3, 2019
  Boston, AL Oct. 11, 1999
  Boston, AL Oct. 1, 2003 (12 inn)
  Boston, AL Oct. 6, 2004
  Extra-Inning NL Game:
4 San Francisco, NL Oct. 3, 2003 (11 inn)

Most Intentional Walks, Both Clubs, Game
4 Mtl. (3) Phil. (1) NL Oct. 7, 1981
  StL. (3) Atl. (1) NL Oct. 3, 2019
3 Bos. (3) Clev. (0) AL Oct. 11, 1999
  Bos. (3) Ana. (0) AL Oct. 6, 2004
  Extra-Inning Game:
5 SF (4) Fla. (1) NL Oct. 3, 2003 (11 inn)
4 Bos. (3) Oak. (1) AL Oct. 1, 2003 (11 inn)

Most Intentional Walks, Inning
2 Baltimore, AL Oct. 2, 1996 (8th)
   New York, AL Oct. 5, 1999 (5th)
   New York, AL Oct. 4, 2003 (7th)
   Boston, AL Oct. 6, 2004 (9th)
   Boston, AL Oct. 4, 2013 (5th)
   Houston, AL Oct. 8, 2018 (8th)
   St. Louis, NL Oct. 4, 2005 (3rd)
   Houston, NL Oct. 5, 2005 (8th)
   Philadelphia NL Oct. 8, 2010 (8th)

Most Hit By Pitch, Series
6 Los Angeles, NL 2016
5 Chicago, AL 2005
   Cleveland, AL 2007
   Houston AL 2020

Most Hit By Pitch, Game
4 Los Angeles, NL Oct. 11, 2016
3 Cleveland, AL Sept. 30, 1998
   Chicago, AL Oct. 4, 2005
   Texas, AL Oct. 1, 2011

Most Hit By Pitch, Both Clubs, Game
5 LA (4) Wash. (1) NL Oct. 11, 2016
3 Balt. (2) Clev. (1) AL Oct. 1, 1996
   Clev. (3) Bos. (0) AL Sept. 30, 1998
   NY (2) Oak. (1) AL Oct. 15, 2001
   Ana. (2) NY (1) AL Oct. 4, 2002
   Chi. (3) Bos. (0) AL Oct. 4, 2005
   Tex. (2) TB (1) AL Oct. 7, 2010
   Tex. (3) TB (0) AL Oct. 1, 2011
   Oak. (2) Det. (1) AL Oct. 7, 2012
   KC (2) Hou. (1) AL Oct. 12, 2015

Most Hit By Pitch, Inning
2 St. Louis NL Oct. 7, 2004 (5th)
   Philadelphia NL Oct. 8, 2010 (6th)
   Minnesota, AL Oct. 4, 2004 (9th)
   Chicago, AL Oct. 4, 2005 (1st)
   Minnesota, AL Oct. 9, 2009 (4th)
   Texas, AL Oct. 1, 2011 (4th)
   Houston, AL Oct. 5, 2018 (2nd)

Most Strikeouts, Series
64 New York, AL 2017
    Los Angeles, NL 2019

Most Strikeouts, Game
18 New York, AL Oct. 6, 2020
17 Houston, NL Sept. 29, 1998
    Los Angeles, NL Oct. 4, 2019
    Extra-Inning Game:
23 Baltimore, AL Oct. 5, 1996 (12 inn)
20 Washington, NL Oct. 4, 2014 (18 inn)

Most Strikeouts, Both Clubs, Game
31 NY (16) Clev. (15) AL Oct. 11, 2017
28 Hou. (17) SD (11) NL Sept. 29, 1998
    Extra-Inning Game:
34 Wash. (20) SF (14) NL Oct. 4, 2014 (18 inn)
33 Balt. (23) Clev. (10) AL Oct. 5, 1996 (12 inn)

Most Strikeouts, Inning
3 By many

Most Stolen Bases, Series
11 Cleveland, AL 1996
9 Cincinnati, NL 1995

Most Stolen Bases, Game
5 Cleveland, AL Oct. 4, 1996
   Los Angeles, AL Oct. 5, 2007
4 Montreal, NL Oct. 7, 1981
   Cincinnati, NL Oct. 4, 1995
   New York, NL Oct. 6, 1999
   Atlanta, NL Oct. 10, 2004
   Philadelphia, NL Oct. 2, 2008
   Washington, NL Oct. 13, 2016
   Los Angeles, NL:Oct. 7, 2017

Most Stolen Bases, Both Clubs, Game
6 Clev. (5) Balt. (1) AL Oct. 4, 1996
   LA (5) Bos. (1) AL Oct. 5, 2007
4 Mtl. (4) Phil. (0) NL Oct. 7, 1981
   Cin. (4) LA (0) NL Oct. 4, 1995
   StL. (2) SD (2) NL Oct. 1, 1996
   NY (4) Ari. (0) NL Oct. 6, 1999
   StL. (3) Atl. (1) NL Oct. 7, 2000
   Atl. (4) Hou. (0) NL Oct. 10, 2004
   Ari. (3) Chi. (1) NL Oct. 6, 2007
   Phil. (4) Mil. (0) NL Oct. 2, 2008
   StL. (3) Phil. (1) NL Oct. 4, 2011
   Wash. (4) LA (0) NL Oct. 13, 2016
   LA (4) Ari. (0) NL Oct. 7, 2017
   Extra-Inning Game:
5 Atl. (3) Hou. (2) NL Oct. 9, 2005 (18 inn)

Most Stolen Bases, Inning
3 Cincinnati, NL Oct. 4, 1995 (9th)
   Los Angeles, AL Oct. 5, 2007 (8th)
   Texas, AL Oct. 3, 2011 (7th)
   New York, AL Oct. 4, 2019 (7th)

Most Caught Stealing, Series
5 Montreal, NL 1981
4 New York, AL 2001
   Minnesota, AL 2004
   Los Angeles, AL 2005
   NL since 1995:
3 By many

Most Caught Stealing, Game
2 By many
   Extra-Inning Game:
3 Atlanta, NL Oct. 2, 1996 (10 inn)
   Minnesota, AL Oct. 9, 2004 (11 inn)

Most Caught Stealing, Both Clubs, Game
3 Clev. (2) Balt. (1) AL Oct. 5, 1996 (12 inn)
   Minn. (3) NY (0) AL Oct. 9, 2004 (11 inn)
   Tex. (2) TB (1) AL Oct. 3, 2011
2 By many in NL
   Extra-Inning Game:
4 Atl. (3) LA (1) NL Oct. 2, 1996 (10 inn)

Most Caught Stealing, Inning
2 Oakland, AL Oct. 9, 1981 (3rd)
   New York, AL Oct. 15, 2001 (4th)
1 By many in NL

Most Grounded Into Double Plays, Series
7 Chicago, NL 2003
   Houston, NL 2005
   San Diego, NL 2005
   St. Louis, NL 2006
   New York, AL 2004

Most Grounded Into Double Plays, Game
4 Colorado, NL Oct. 3, 1995
   San Diego, NL Oct. 6, 2005
   Chicago, NL Oct. 6, 2007
   New York, AL Oct. 1, 2002

Most Grounded Into Double Plays, Both Clubs, Game
6 Col. (4) Atl. (2) NL Oct. 3, 1995
   NY (4) Ana. (2) AL Oct. 1, 2002

CLUB FIELDING

Most Errors, Series
9 Cleveland, AL 2017
7 Colorado, NL 1995
   San Francisco, NL 2003
   Atlanta, NL 2010
   Cincinnati, NL 2010
   Chicago, NL 2017

Most Errors, Game
4 Montreal, NL Oct. 9, 1981
   Colorado, NL Oct. 3, 1995
   Atlanta, NL Oct. 3, 2003
   Chicago, NL Oct. 2, 2008
   Cincinnati, NL Oct. 8, 2010
   Chicago, NL Oct. 9, 2017
   Oakland, AL Oct. 4, 2003 (11 inn)
   Cleveland, AL Oct. 9, 2017

Most Errors, Both Clubs, Game
6 Cin. (4) Phil. (2) NL Oct. 8, 2010
4 Mil. (3) NY (1) AL Oct. 7, 1981
    Oak. (3) NY (1) AL Oct. 15, 2001
    Minn. (3) Oak. (1) AL Oct. 6, 2006
    Bos. (3) LA (1) AL Oct. 8, 2009
    Balt. (2) NY (2) AL Oct. 8, 2012
    Tex. (3) Tor. (1) AL Oct. 14, 2015
    Clev. (4) NY (0) AL Oct. 9, 2017
    Extra-Inning Game:
6 Oak. (4) Bos. (2) AL Oct. 4, 2003 (11 inn)

Most Errors, Inning
3 Kansas City, AL Oct. 9, 1981 (3rd)
    Oakland, AL Oct. 4, 2003 (2nd)
    Toronto, AL Oct. 14, 2015 (7th)
    NL Since 1995:
2 By many

Most Double Plays, Series
9 Minnesota, AL 2004
8 Atlanta, NL 2003
    San Diego, NL 2006

Most Double Plays, Game
5 Minnesota, AL Oct. 5, 2004
4 Atlanta, NL Oct. 3, 1995
    Houston, NL Oct. 10, 2001
    St. Louis, NL Oct. 6, 2005
    Arizona, NL Oct. 6, 2007

Most Double Plays, Both Clubs, Game
7 Hou. (4) Atl. (3) NL Oct. 10, 2001
6 Ana. (4) NY (2) AL Oct. 1, 2002
    Minn. (5) NY (1) AL Oct. 5, 2004

CLUB PITCHING

Most Earned Runs, Series
46 Cleveland, AL 1999
36 Atlanta, NL 2004

Most Earned Runs, Game
23 Cleveland, AL Oct. 10, 1999
13 Los Angeles, NL Oct. 12, 2015

Most Earned Runs, Both Clubs, Game
30 Clev. (23) Bos. (7) AL Oct. 10, 1999
19 LA (10) StL. (9) NL Oct. 3, 2014
    LA (13) NY (6) NL Oct. 12, 2015

Most Consecutive Scoreless Innings, Series
21 San Francisco, NL 2014
20 Detroit, AL 2006
    Oakland, AL 2013

Most Wild Pitches, Series
5 St. Louis, NL 2000
4 Oakland, AL 2002
    Anaheim, AL 2004
    Los Angeles, AL 2005
    Tampa Bay, AL 2011
    Texas, AL 2011
    Oakland, AL 2012
    Tampa Bay, AL 2013
    Boston, AL 2017
    New York, AL 2017

Most Wild Pitches, Game
5 St. Louis, NL Oct. 3, 2000
4 New York, AL Oct. 5, 2017

Most Wild Pitches, Both Clubs, Game
5 StL. (5) Atl. (0) NL Oct. 3, 2000
    NY (4) Clev. (1) AL Oct. 5, 2017

Most Wild Pitches, Inning
5 St. Louis, NL Oct. 3, 2000 (3rd)
2 Oakland, AL Oct. 5, 2002 (4th)
    Los Angeles, AL Oct. 9, 2005 (8th)
    New York, AL Oct. 5, 2007 (8th)
    Texas, AL Oct. 1, 2011 (4th)
    Oakland, AL Oct. 11, 2012 (3rd)
    New York, AL Oct. 5, 2017 (5th)
    Cleveland, AL Oct. 8, 2018 (8th)

Most Balks, Game
2 Miami, NL Oct. 8, 2020
1 By many AL teams

CLUB MISCELLANEOUS

Most Players, Game
24 San Diego, NL Oct. 8, 2020
22 Tampa Bay, AL Oct. 8, 2013

Most Players, Both Clubs, Game
41 Wash. (22) LA (19) NL Oct. 13, 2016
    SD (24) LA (17) NL Oct. 8, 2020
39 Tex. (20) NY (19) AL Oct. 5, 1996
    Extra-Inning Game:
42 Hou. (23) Atl. (19) NL Oct. 9, 2005 (18 inn)
40 Balt. (20) NY (20) AL Oct. 11, 2012 (13 inn)

Most Pitchers, Game
11 San Diego, NL Oct. 8, 2020
9 Tampa Bay, AL Oct. 8, 2013
    Tampa Bay, AL Oct. 10, 2019)

Most Pitchers, Both Clubs, Game
17 Wash. (9) SF (8) NL Oct. 4, 2014 (18 inn)
    SD (11) LA (6) NL Oct. 8, 2020
13 Tex. (8) NY (5) AL Oct. 5, 1996
    TB (9) Bos. (4) AL Oct. 8, 2013
    NY (7) Minn. (6) AL Oct. 4, 2019
    Oak. (8) Hou. (5) AL Oct. 5, 2020
    Extra-Inning Game:
16 Balt. (8) NY (8) AL Oct. 11, 2012 (13 inn)

Most Pitchers, Inning
6 Washington, NL Oct. 13, 2016 (7th)
4 By many AL teams

Most Left On Base, Series
49 Seattle, AL 1995
43 Atlanta, NL 2004

Most Left On Base, Game
16 Los Angeles, NL Oct. 7, 2009
13 Texas, AL Oct. 7, 2016
    Houston, AL Oct. 9, 2017
    Tampa Bay, AL Oct. 8, 2019
    Extra-Inning Game:
18 San Francisco, NL Oct. 3, 2003 (11 inn)
    Atlanta, NL Oct. 9, 2005 (18 inn)
17 Minnesota, AL Oct. 9, 2009 (11 inn)

Most Left On Base, Both Clubs, Game
30 Fla. (12) SF (18) NL Oct. 3, 2003 (11 inn)
    LA (16) StL. (14) NL Oct. 7, 2009
22 Bos. (12) Clev. (10) AL Oct. 6, 1995
    NY (12) Sea. (10) AL Oct. 7, 1995
    Extra-Inning Game:
27 LA (16) Bos. (11) AL Oct. 5, 2008 (12 inn)

Longest Game, Innings
18 Atlanta at Houston, NL Oct. 9, 2005
    San Francisco at Washington, NL Oct. 4, 2014
15 Seattle at New York, AL Oct. 4, 1995

Longest Game, Time
4:37 Chicago at Washington, NL Oct. 12, 2017
4:19 Boston at Tampa Bay, AL Oct. 7, 2013
    Extra-Inning Game:
6:23 San Francisco at Washington, NL Oct. 4, 2014 (18 inn)
5:19 Los Angeles at Boston, AL Oct. 5, 2008 (12 inn)

Shortest Game, Time
2:00 Houston at Los Angeles, NL Oct. 10, 1981
2:19 Oakland at Minnesota, AL Oct. 3, 2006
    NL since 1995:
2:08 Atlanta at Los Angeles, NL Oct. 3, 1996

AMERICAN LEAGUE WILD CARD GAMES / SERIES

	No.	W	L	WON	LOST
New York	4	3	1	2017-18, 20	2015
Oakland	4	1	3	2020	2014, 18-19
Tampa Bay	3	3	0	2013, 19-20	
Houston	2	2	0	2015, 20	
Baltimore	2	1	1	2012	2016
Toronto	2	1	1	2016	2020
Cleveland	2	0	2		2013, 20
Minnesota	2	0	2		2017, 20
Kansas City	1	1	0	2014	
Chicago	1	0	1		2020
Texas	1	0	1		2012

2012
10/5   at Tex.   Balt.   5   Tex.   1

2013
10/2   at Clev.   TB   4   Clev.   0

2014
9/30   at KC   KC   9   Oak.   8   (12 inn)

2015
10/6   at NY   Hou.   3   NY   0

2016
10/4   at Tor.   Tor.   5   Balt.   2   (11 inn)

2017
10/3   at NY   NY   8   Minn.   4

2018
10/3   at NY   NY   7   Oak.   2

2019
10/2   at Oak.   TB   5   Oak.   1

2020

Tampa Bay 2, Toronto 0
9/29   at TB   TB   3   Tor.   1
9/30   at TB   TB   8   Tor.   2

Oakland 2, Chicago 1
9/29   at Oak.   Chi.   4   Oak.   1
9/30   at Oak.   Oak.   5   Chi.   3
10/1   at Oak.   Oak.   6   Chi.   4

Houston 2, Minnesota 0
9/29   at Minn.   Hou.   4   Minn.   1
9/30   at Minn.   Hou.   3   Minn.   1

New York 2, Cleveland 0
9/29   at Clev.   NY   12   Clev.   3
9/30   at Clev.   NY   10   Clev.   9

NATIONAL LEAGUE WILD CARD GAMES / SERIES

	No.	W	L	WON	LOST
Chicago	3	1	2	2015	2018, 20
Pittsburgh	3	1	2	2013	2014-15
San Francisco	2	2	0	2014, 16	
Atlanta	2	1	1	2020	2012
Colorado	2	1	1	2018	2017
St. Louis	2	1	1	2012	2020
Cincinnati	2	0	2		2013, 20
Milwaukee	2	0	2		2019-20
Arizona	1	1	0	2017	
Los Angeles	1	1	0	2020	
Miami	1	1	0	2020	
San Diego	1	1	0	2020	
Washington	1	1	0	2019	
New York	1	0	1		2016

2012
10/5 at Atl.. StL. 6 Atl. 3

2013
10/1 at Pitt. Pitt. 6 Cin. 2

2014
10/1 at Pitt. SF 8 Pitt. 0

2015
10/7 at Pitt. Chi. 4 Pitt. 0

2016
10/5 at NY SF 3 NY 0

2017
10/4 at Ari. Ari. 11 Col. 8

2018
10/2 at Chi. Col. 2 Chi. 1 (13 inn)

2019
10/1 at Wash. Wash. 4 Mil. 3

2020

Los Angeles 2, Milwaukee 0
9/30 at LA LA 4 Mil. 2
10/1 at LA LA 3 Mil. 0

Miami 2, Chicago 0
9/30 at Chi. Mia. 5 Chi. 1
10/2 at Chi. Mia. 2 Chi. 0

Atlanta 2, Cincinnati 0
9/30 at Atl. Atl. 1 Cin. 0 (13 inn)
10/1 at Atl. Atl. 5 Cin. 0

San Diego 2, St. Louis 1
9/30 at SD StL. 7 SD 4
10/1 at SD SD 11 StL. 9
10/2 ar SD SD 4 StL. 0

ALL-STAR GAME

No. 1 AL: Chicago July 6, 1933

NL	000	002	000	2	8	0
AL	012	001	00x	4	9	1

HALLAHAN, Warneke (3), Hubbell (7)
GOMEZ, Crowder (4), Grove (7)
A-47,595   T-2:05

No. 2 NL: New York July 10, 1934

AL	000	261	000	9	14	1
NL	103	030	000	7	8	1

Gomez, Ruffing (4), HARDER (5)
Hubbell, Warneke (4), MUNGO (5), Dean (6),
    Frankhouse (9)
A-48,363   T-2:44

No. 3 AL: Cleveland July 8, 1935

NL	000	100	000	1	4	1
AL	210	010	00x	4	8	0

WALKER, Schumacher (3), Derringer (7), Dean (8)
GOMEZ, Harder (7)
A-69,831   T-2:06

No. 4 NL: Boston July 7, 1936

AL	000	000	300	3	7	1
NL	020	020	00x	4	9	0

GROVE, Rowe (4), Harder (7)
DEAN, Hubbell (4), Davis (7), Warneke (7)
A-25,556   T-2:00

No. 5 AL: Washington July 7, 1937

NL	000	111	000	3	13	0
AL	002	312	00x	8	13	2

DEAN, Hubbell (4), Blanton (4), Grissom (5), Mungo
    (6), Walters (8)
GOMEZ, Bridges (4), Harder (7)
A-31,391   T-2:30

No. 6 NL: Cincinnati July 6, 1938

AL	000	000	001	1	7	4
NL	100	100	20x	4	8	0

GOMEZ, Allen (4), Grove (7)
VANDER MEER, Lee (4), Brown (7)
A-27,067   T-1:58

No. 7 AL: New York July 11, 1939

NL	001	000	000	1	7	1
AL	000	210	00x	3	6	1

Derringer, LEE (4), Fette (7)
Ruffing, BRIDGES (4), Feller (6)
A-62,892   T-1:55

No. 8 NL: St. Louis July 9, 1940

AL	000	000	000	0	3	1
NL	300	000	01x	4	7	0

RUFFING, Newsom (4), Feller (7)
DERRINGER, Walters (3), Wyatt (5), French (7), Hubbell (9)
A-32,373   T-1:53

No. 9 AL: Detroit July 8, 1941

NL	000	001	220	5	10	2
AL	000	101	014	7	11	3

Wyatt, Derringer (3), Walters (5), PASSEAU (7)
Feller, Lee (4), Hudson (7), SMITH (8)
A-54,674   T-2:23

No. 10 NL: New York July 6n, 1942

AL	300	000	000	3	7	0
NL	000	000	010	1	6	1

CHANDLER, Benton (5)
COOPER, Vander Meer (4), Passeau (7), Walters (9)
A-33,694   T-2:07

No. 11 AL: Philadelphia July 13n, 1943

NL	100	000	101	3	10	3
AL	031	010	00x	5	8	1

COOPER, Vander Meer (3), Sewell (6), Javery (7)
LEONARD, Newhouser (4), Hughson (7)
A-31,938   T-2:07

No. 12 NL: Pittsburgh July 11n, 1944

AL	010	000	000	1	6	3
NL	000	040	21x	7	12	1

Borowy, HUGHSON (4), Muncrief (5), Newhouser (7),
    Newsom (8)
Walters, RAFFENSBERGER (4), Sewell (6), Tobin (9)
A-29,589   T-2:11

1945 No Game (World War II)

No. 13 AL: Boston July 9, 1946

NL	000	000	000	0	3	0
AL	200	130	24x	12	14	1

PASSEAU, Higbe (4), Blackwell (5), Sewell (8)
FELLER, Newhouser (4), Kramer(7)
A-34,906   T-2:19

No. 14 NL: Chicago July 8, 1947

AL	000	001	100	2	8	0
NL	000	100	000	1	5	1

Newhouser, SHEA (4), Masterson (7), Page (8)
Blackwell, Brecheen (4), SAIN (7), Spahn (8)
A-41,123   T-2:19

No. 15 AL: St. Louis July 13, 1948

NL	200	000	000	2	8	0
AL	011	300	00x	5	6	0

Branca, SCHMITZ (4), Sain (4), Blackwell (6)
Masterson, RASCHI (4), Coleman (7)
A-34,009   T-2:27

No. 16 NL: Brooklyn July 12, 1949

AL	400	202	300	11	13	1
NL	212	002	000	7	12	5

Parnell, TRUCKS (2), Brissie (4), Raschi (7)
Spahn, NEWCOMBE (2), Munger (5), Bickford (6), Pollet
    (7), Blackwell (8), Roe (9)
A-32,577   T-3:04

No. 17 AL: Chicago July 11, 1950

NL	020	000	001	000	01	4	10	0
AL	001	020	000	000	00	3	8	1

Roberts, Newcombe (4), Konstanty (6), Jansen (7),
    BLACKWELL (12)
Raschi, Lemon (4), Houtteman (7), Reynolds (10), GRAY
    (13), Feller (14)
A-46,127   T-3:19

No. 18 AL: Detroit July 10, 1951

NL	100	302	110	8	12	1
AL	010	110	000	3	10	2

Roberts, MAGLIE (3), Newcombe (6), Blackwell (9)
Garver, LOPAT (4), Hutchinson (5), Parnell (8), Lemon (9)
A-52,075   T-2:41

No. 19 NL: Philadelphia July 8, 1952 (rain)

AL	000	20	2	5	0
NL	100	20	3	3	0

Raschi, LEMON (3), Shantz (5)
Simmons, RUSH (4)
A-32,785   T-1:29

No. 20 NL: Cincinnati July 14, 1953

AL	000	000	001	1	5	0
NL	000	020	12x	5	10	0

Pierce, REYNOLDS (4), Garcia (6), Paige (8)
Roberts, SPAHN (4), Simmons (6), Dickson (8)
A-30,846   T-2:19

No. 21 AL: Cleveland July 13, 1954

NL	000	520	020	9	14	0
AL	004	121	03x	11	17	1

Roberts, Antonelli (4), Spahn (6), Grissom (6), CONLEY (8), Erskine (8)
Ford, Consuegra (4), Lemon (4), Porterfield (5), Keegan (8), STONE (8), Trucks (9)
A-68,751   T-3:10

No. 22 NL: Milwaukee July 12, 1955

AL	400	001	000	000	5	10	2
NL	000	000	230	001	6	13	1

Pierce, Wynn (4), Ford (7), SULLIVAN (8)
Roberts, Haddix (4), Newcombe (7), Jones (8), Nuxhall (8), CONLEY (12)
A-45,314   T-3:17

No. 23 AL: Washington July 10, 1956

NL	001	211	200	7	11	0
AL	000	003	000	3	11	0

FRIEND, Spahn (4), Antonelli (6)
PIERCE, Ford (4), Wilson (5), Brewer (6), Score (8), Wynn (9)
A-28,843   T-2:45

No. 24 NL: St. Louis July 9, 1957

AL	020	001	003	6	10	0
NL	000	000	203	5	9	1

BUNNING, Loes (4), Wynn (7), Pierce (7), Mossi (9), Grim (9)
SIMMONS, Burdette (2), Sanford (6), Jackson (7), Labine (9)
A-30,693   T-2:43

No. 25 AL: Baltimore July 8, 1958

NL	210	000	000	3	4	2
AL	110	011	00x	4	9	2

Spahn, FRIEND (4), Jackson (6), Farrell (7)
Turley, Narleski (2), WYNN (6), O'Dell (7)
A-48,829   T-2:13

No. 26 NL: Pittsburgh July 7, 1959

AL	000	100	030	4	8	0
NL	100	000	22x	5	9	1

Wynn, Duren (4), Bunning (7), FORD (8), Daley (8)
Drysdale, Burdette (4), Face (7), ANTONELLI (8), Elston (9)
A-35,277   T-2:33

No. 27 NL: Los Angeles August 3, 1959

AL	012	000	110	5	6	0
NL	100	100	100	3	6	3

WALKER, Wynn (4), Wilhelm (6), O'Dell (7), McLish (8)
DRYSDALE, Conley (4), Jones (6), Face (9)
A-55,105   T-2:42

No. 28 AL: Kansas City July 11, 1960

NL	311	000	000	5	12	4
AL	000	001	020	3	6	1

FRIEND, McCormick (4), Face (6), Buhl (8), Law (9)
MONBOUQUETTE, Estrada (3), Coates (4), Bell (6), Lary (8), Daley (9)
A-30,619   T-2:39

No. 29 AL: New York July 13, 1960

NL	021	000	102	6	10	0
AL	000	000	000	0	8	0

LAW, Podres (3), Williams (5), Jackson (7), Henry (8), McDaniel (9)
FORD, Wynn (4), Staley (6), Lary (8), Bell (9)
A-38,362   T-2:42

No. 30 NL: San Francisco July 11, 1961

AL	000	001	002	1	4	4	2
NL	010	100	010	2	5	11	5

Ford, Lary (4), Donovan (4), Bunning (6), Fornieles (8), WILHELM (8)
Spahn, Purkey (4), McCormick (6), Face (9), Koufax (9), MILLER (9)
A-44,115   T-2:53

No. 31 AL: Boston July 31, 1961 (rain)

NL	000	001	000	1	5	1
AL	100	000	000	1	4	0

Purkey, Mahaffey (3), Koufax (5), Miller (7)
Bunning, Schwall (4), Pascual (7)
A-31,851   T-2:27

No. 32 AL: Washington July 10, 1962

NL	000	002	010	3	8	0
AL	000	001	000	1	4	0

Drysdale, MARICHAL (4), Purkey (6), Shaw (8)
Bunning, PASCUAL (4), Donovan (7), Pappas (9)
A-45,480   T-2:33

No. 33 NL: Chicago July 30, 1962

AL	001	201	302	9	10	0
NL	010	000	111	4	10	4

Stenhouse, HERBERT (3), Aguirre (6), Pappas (9)
Podres, MAHAFFEY (3), Gibson (5), Farrell (7), Marichal (8)
A-38,359   T-2:28

No. 34 AL: Cleveland July 9, 1963

NL	012	010	010	5	6	0
AL	012	000	000	3	11	1

O'Toole, JACKSON (3), Culp (5), Woodeshick (6), Drysdale (8)
McBride, BUNNING (4), Bouton (6), Pizarro (7), Radatz (8)
A-44,160   T-2:20

No. 35 NL: New York July 7, 1964

AL	100	002	100	4	9	1
NL	000	210	004	7	8	0

Chance, Wyatt (4), Pascual (5), RADATZ (7)
Drysdale, Bunning (4), Short (6), Farrell (7), MARICHAL(9)
A-50,844   T-2:27

No. 36 AL: Minnesota July 13, 1965

NL	320	000	100	6	11	0
AL	000	140	000	5	8	0

Marichal, Maloney (4), Drysdale (5), KOUFAX (6), Farrell (7), Gibson (8)
Pappas, Grant (2), Richert (4), McDOWELL (6), Fisher (8)
A-46,706   T-2:45

No. 37 NL: St. Louis July 12, 1966

AL	010	000	000	0	1	6	0
NL	100	100	000	1	2	6	0

McLain, Kaat (4), Stottlemyre (6), Siebert (8), RICHERT (10)
Koufax, Bunning (4), Marichal (6), PERRY (9)
A-49,936   T-2:19

No. 38 AL: California July 11, 1967

NL	010	000	000	000	001	2	9	0
AL	000	001	000	000	000	1	8	0

Marichal, Jenkins (4), Gibson (7), Short (9), Cuellar (11), DRYSDALE (13), Seaver (15)
Chance, McGlothlin (4), Peters (6), Downing (9), HUNTER (11)
A-46,309   T-3:41

No. 39 NL: Houston July 9n, 1968

AL	000	000	000	0	3	1
NL	100	000	00x	1	5	0

TIANT, Odom (3), McLain (5), McDowell (7),
Stottlemyre (8), John (8)
DRYSDALE, Marichal (4), Carlton (6), Seaver (7), Reed
(9), Koosman (9)
A-48,321   T-2:10

No. 40 AL: Washington July 23, 1969

NL	125	100	000	9	11	0
AL	011	100	000	3	6	2

CARLTON, Gibson (4), Singer (5), Koosman (7), Dierker
(8), Niekro (9)
STOTTLEMYRE, Odom (3), Knowles (3), McLain (4),
McNally (5), McDowell (7), Culp (9)
A-45,259   T-2:38

No. 41 NL: Cincinnati July 14n, 1970

AL	000	001	120 000	4	12	0
NL	000	000	103 001	5	10	0

Palmer, McDowell (4), J. Perry (7), Hunter (9), Peterson
(9), Stottlemyre (9), WRIGHT (11)
Seaver, Merritt (4), G. Perry (6), Gibson (8), OSTEEN (10)
A-51,838   T-3:19

No. 42 AL: Detroit July 13n, 1971

NL	021	000	010	4	5	0
AL	004	002	00x	6	7	0

ELLIS, Marichal (4), Jenkins (6), Wilson (7)
BLUE, Palmer (4), Cuellar (6), Lolich (8)
A-53,559   T-2:05

No. 43 NL: Atlanta July 25n, 1972

AL	001	000	020	0	3	6	0
NL	000	000	001	1	4	8	0

Palmer, Lolich (4), G. Perry (6), Wood (8), McNALLY (10)
Gibson, Blass (3), Sutton (4), Carlton (6), Stoneman
(7), McGRAW (9)
A-53,107   T-2:26

No. 44 NL: Kansas City July 24n, 1973

NL	002	122	000	7	10	0
AL	010	000	000	1	5	0

WISE, Osteen (3), Sutton (5), Twitchell (6), Giusti (7),
Seaver (8), Brewer (9)
Hunter, Holtzman (2), BLYLEVEN (3), Singer (4), Ryan
(6), Lyle (8), Fingers (9)
A-40,849   T-2:45

No. 45 NL: Pittsburgh July 23n, 1974

AL	002	000	000	2	4	1
NL	010	210	12x	7	10	1

G. Perry, TIANT (4), Hunter (6), Fingers (8)
Messersmith, BRETT (4), Matlack (6), McGlothen (7),
Marshall (8)
A-50,706   T-2:37

No. 46 AL: Milwaukee July 15n, 1975

NL	021	000	003	6	13	1
AL	000	003	000	3	10	1

Reuss, Sutton (4), Seaver (6), MATLACK (7), R. Jones (9)
Blue, Busby (3), Kaat (5), HUNTER (7), Gossage (9)
A-51,480   T-2:35

No. 47 NL: Philadelphia July 13n, 1976

AL	000	100	000	1	5	0
NL	202	000	03x	7	10	0

FIDRYCH, Hunter (3), Tiant (5), Tanana (7)
R. JONES, Seaver (4), Montefusco (6), Rhoden (8),
Forsch (9)
A-63,974   T-2:12

No. 48 AL: New York July 19n, 1977

NL	401	000	020	7	9	1
AL	000	002	102	5	8	0

SUTTON, Lavelle (4), Seaver (6), Reuschel (8), Gossage (9)
PALMER, Kern (3), Eckersley (4), LaRoche (6), Campbell
(7), Lyle (8)
A-56,683   T-2:34

No. 49 NL: San Diego July 11n, 1978

AL	201	000	000	3	8	1
NL	003	000	04x	7	10	0

Palmer, Keough (3), Sorensen (4), Kern (7), Guidry (7),
GOSSAGE (8)
Blue, Rogers (4), Fingers (6), SUTTER (8), P. Niekro (9)
A-51,549   T-2:37

No.50 AL: Seattle July 17n, 1979

NL	211	001	011	7	10	1
AL	302	001	000	6	10	0

Carlton, Andujar (2), Rogers (4), Perry (6), Sambito (6),
LaCoss (6), SUTTER (7)
Ryan, Stanley (3), Clear (5), KERN (7), Guidry (9)
A-58,905   T-3:11

No. 51 NL: Los Angeles July 8n, 1980

AL	000	020	000	2	7	2
NL	000	012	10x	4	7	0

Stone, JOHN (4), Farmer (6), Stieb (7), Gossage (8)
Richard, Welch (3), REUSS (6), Bibby (7), Sutter (8)
A-58,088   T-2:33

No.52 AL: Cleveland August 9n, 1981

NL	000	011	120	5	9	1
AL	010	003	000	4	11	1

Valenzuela, Seaver (2), Knepper (3), Hooton (5),
Ruthven (6), BLUE (7), Ryan (8), Sutter (9)
Morris, Barker (3), K. Forsch (5), Norris (6), Davis (7),
FINGERS (8), Stieb (8)
A-72,086   T-2:59

No. 53 NL: Montreal July 13n, 1982

AL	100	000	000	1	8	2
NL	021	001	00x	4	8	1

ECKERSLEY, Clancy (4), Bannister (5), Quisenberry (6),
Fingers (8)
ROGERS, Carlton (4), Soto (6), Valenzuela (8), Minton
(8), Howe (9), Hume (9)
A-59,057   T-2:53

No. 54 AL: Chicago July 6n, 1983

NL	100	110	000	3	8	3
AL	117	000	22x	13	15	2

SOTO, Hammaker (3), Dawley (3), Dravecky (5), Perez
(7), Orosco (7), L. Smith (8)
STIEB, Honeycutt (4), Stanley (6), Young (8),
Quisenberry (9)
A-43,801   T-3:05

No. 55 NL: San Francisco July 10n, 1984

AL	010	000	000	1	7	2
NL	110	000	01x	3	8	0

STIEB, Morris (3), Dotson (5), Caudill (7), Hernandez (8)
LEA, Valenzuela (3), Gooden (5), Soto (7), Gossage (9)
A-57,756   T-2:29

No. 56 AL: Minnesota July 16n, 1985

NL	011	020	002	6	9	1
AL	100	000	000	1	5	0

HOYT, Ryan (4), Valenzuela (7), Reardon (8), Gossage (9)
MORRIS, Key (3), Blyleven (4), Stieb (6), Moore (7),
Petry (9), Hernandez (9)
A-54,960   T-2:54

No. 57 NL: Houston July 15n, 1986

AL	020	000	100	3	5	0
NL	000	000	020	2	5	1

CLEMENS, Higuera (4), Hough (7), Righetti (8), Aase (9)
GOODEN, Valenzuela (4), Scott (7), Fernandez (8), Krukow (9)
A-45,774   T-2:28

No. 58 AL: Oakland July 14n, 1987

NL	000	000	000	000	2	2	8	2
AL	000	000	000	000	0	0	6	1

Scott, Sutcliffe (3), Hershiser (5), Reuschel (7), Franco (8), Bedrosian (9), L. SMITH (10), Fernandez (13)
Saberhagen, Morris (4), Langston (6), Plesac (8), Righetti (9), Henke (9), HOWELL (12)
A-44,671   T-3:39

No. 59 NL: Cincinnati July 12n, 1988

AL	001	100	000	2	6	2
NL	000	100	000	1	5	0

VIOLA, Clemens (3), Gubicza (4), Stieb (6), Russell (7), D. Jones (8), Plesac (8), Eckersley (9)
GOODEN, Knepper (4), Cone (5), Gross (6), Davis (7), Walk (7), Hershiser (8), Worrell (9)
A-55,837   T-2:26

No. 60 AL: California July 11n, 1989

NL	200	000	010	3	9	1
AL	212	000	00x	5	12	0

Reuschel, SMOLTZ (2), Sutcliffe (3),Burke (4), M. Davis (6), Howell (7), M. Williams (8)
Stewart, RYAN (2), Gubicza (4), Moore (5), Swindell (6), Russell (7), Plesac (8), D. Jones (8)
A-64,036   T-2:48

No. 61 NL: Chicago July 10n, 1990

AL	000	000	200	2	7	0
NL	000	000	000	0	2	1

Welch, Stieb (3), SABERHAGEN (5), Thigpen (7), Finley (8), Eckersley (9)
Armstrong, R. Martinez (3), D. Martinez (4), Viola (5), D. Smith (6), BRANTLEY (6), Dibble (7), Myers (8), Franco (9)
A-39,071   T-2:53

No. 62 AL: Toronto July 9n, 1991

NL	100	100	000	2	10	1
AL	003	000	10x	4	8	0

Glavine, D. MARTINEZ (3), Viola (5), Harnisch (6), Smiley (7), Dibble (7), Morgan (8)
Morris, KEY (3), Clemens (4), McDowell (5), Reardon (7), Aguilera (7), Eckersley (9)
A-52,313   T-3:04

No. 63 NL: San Diego July 14n, 1992

AL	411	004	030	13	19	1
NL	000	001	032	6	12	1

BROWN, McDowell (2), Guzman (3), Clemens (3), Mussina (5), Langston (6), Nagy (7), Montgomery (8), Aguilera (8), Eckersley (9)
GLAVINE, Maddux (2), Cone (4), Tewksbury (5), Smoltz (6), D. Martinez (7), Jones (8), Charlton (9)
A-59,372   T-2:55

No. 64 AL: Baltimore July 13n, 1993

NL	200	001	000	3	7	2
AL	011	033	10x	9	11	0

Mulholland, Benes (3), BURKETT (5), Avery (6), Smoltz (6), Beck (7), Harvey (8)
Langston, R. Johnson (3), McDOWELL (5), Key (6), Montgomery (7), Aguilera (8), Ward (9)
A-48,147   T-2:49

No. 65 NL: Pittsburgh July 12n, 1994

AL	100	003	300	0	7	15	0
NL	103	001	002	1	8	12	1

Key, Cone (3), Mussina (5), Johnson (6), Hentgen (7), Alvarez (8), L. Smith (9), BERE (10)
Maddux, Hill (4), Drabek (6), Hudek (6), Jackson (7), Beck (7), Myers (9), JONES (10)
A-59, 568   T-3:14

No. 66 AL: Texas July 11n, 1995

NL	000	001	110	3	3	0
AL	000	200	000	2	8	0

Nomo, Smiley (3), Green (5), Neagle (6), Perez (7), SLOCUMB (7), Henke (8), Myers (9)
Johnson, Appier (3), D. Martinez (5), Rogers (7), ONTIVEROS (8), Wells (8), Mesa (9)
A-50,920   T-2:40

No. 67 NL: Philadelphia July 9n, 1996

AL	000	000	000	0	7	0
NL	121	002	00x	6	12	1

NAGY, Finley (3), Pavlik (5), Percival (7), R. Hernandez (8)
SMOLTZ, Brown (3), Glavine (4), Bottalico (5), P. Martinez (6), Trachsel (7), Worrell (8), Wohlers (9), Leiter (9)
A-62,670   T-2:35

No. 68 AL: Cleveland July 8n, 1997

NL	000	000	100	1	3	0
AL	010	000	20x	3	7	0

Maddux, Schilling (3), Brown (5), P. Martinez (6), ESTES (7), B. Jones (8)
Johnson, Clemens (3), Cone (4), Thompson (5), Hentgen (6), ROSADO (7), Myers (8), Rivera (9)
A-44,916   T-2:36

No. 69 NL: Colorado July 7n, 1998

AL	000	413	113	13	19	2
NL	002	130	020	8	12	1

Wells, Clemens (3), Radke (4), COLON (5), Arrojo (6), Wetteland (7), Gordon (8), Percival (9)
Maddux, Glavine (3), Brown (4), Ashby (5), URBINA (6), Hoffman (7), Shaw (8), Nen (9)
A-51,267   T-3:38

No. 70 AL: Boston July 13n, 1999

NL	001	000	000	1	7	1
AL	200	200	00x	4	6	2

SCHILLING, Johnson (3), Bottenfield (4), Lima (5), Millwood (6), Ashby (7), Hampton (7), Hoffman (8), Wagner (8)
MARTINEZ, Cone (3), Mussina (5), Rosado (6), Zimmerman (7), Hernandez (8), Wetteland (9)
A-34,187   T-2:53

No. 71 NL: Atlanta July 11n, 2000

AL	001	200	003	6	10	2
NL	001	010	001	3	9	2

Wells, BALDWIN (3), Sele (4), Isringhausen (5), Lowe (6), Jones (7), Hudson (8), Rivera (9)
Johnson, Graves (3), Brown (3), LEITER (4), Glavine (5), Kile (6), Wickman (8), Hoffman (9)
A-51,323   T-2:56

No. 72 AL: Seattle July 10n, 2001

NL	000	001	000	1	3	1
AL	001	012	00x	4	8	0

Johnson, PARK (3), Burkett (4), Hampton (5), Lieber (6), Morris (7), Shaw (8), Wagner (8), Sheets (9)
Clemens, GARCIA (3), Pettitte (4), Mays (5), Quantrill (6), Stanton (6), Nelson (7), Percival (8), Sasaki (9)
A-47,364   T-2:48

No. 73 NL: Milwaukee July 9n, 2002 (called)
```
AL    000   110   410   00    7   12   0
NL    013   010   200   00    7   13   0
```
Lowe, Halladay (3), Buehrle (4), Zito (6), Guardado (6), Sasaki (7), Urbina (8), Rivera (9), Garcia (10)
Schilling, Williams (3), Perez (4), Gagne (5), Hoffman (6), Remlinger (7), Kim (7), Nen (8), Smoltz (9), Padilla (10)
A-41,871   T-3:29

No. 74 AL: Chicago July 15n, 2003
```
NL    000   050   100    6   11   1
AL    001   002   13x    7    9   0
```
Schmidt, Wolf (3), Wood (4), Ortiz (5), Williams (6), Wagner (7), GAGNE (8)
Loaiza, Clemens (4), Moyer (4), Hasegawa (5), Guardado (5), Mulder (6), DONNELLY (8), Foulke (9)
A-47,609   T-2:38

No. 75 NL: Houston July 13n, 2004
```
AL    600   102   000    9   14   0
NL    100   300   000    4    9   1
```
MULDER, Loaiza (3), Sabathia (4), Vazquez (5), Lilly (6), Nathan (7), Gordon (8), F. Rodriguez (8), Rivera (9)
CLEMENS, Kolb (2), Johnson (3), Zambrano (4), Pavano (5), Glavine (7), Sheets (9), Gagne (9)
A-41,886   T-2:59

No. 76 AL: Detroit July 12n, 2005
```
NL    000   000   212    5   11   0
AL    012   202   00x    7   11   1
```
Carpenter, SMOLTZ (3), Oswalt (3), Hernandez (4), Clemens (5), Willis (6), Lidge (7), Peavy (8), Cordero (8)
BUEHRLE, Colon (3), Santana (4), Clement (5), Garland (6), Rogers (7), Nathan (8), Wickman (9), Ryan (9), Rivera (9)
A-41,617   T-2:41

No. 77 NL: Pittsburgh July 11n, 2006
```
AL    010   000   002    3    7   1
NL    011   000   000    2    6   0
```
Rogers, Halladay (3), Zito (5), Kazmir (6), Santana (7), RYAN (8), Rivera (9)
Penny, Oswalt (3), Webb (4), Arroyo (5), Fuentes (6), Turnbow (7), Gordon (8), HOFFMAN (9)
A-38,904   T-2:33

No. 78 NL: San Francisco July 10n, 2007
```
AL    000   021   020    5   10   0
NL    100   001   002    4    9   1
```
Haren, BECKETT (3), Sabathia (5), Verlander (6), Santana (7), Papelbon (8), Putz (9), F. Rodriguez (9)
Peavy, Penny (2), Sheets (3), Hamels (4), C. YOUNG (5), Cordero (6), Saito (7), Wagner (8), Hoffman (9)
A-43,965   T-3:06

No. 79 AL: New York July 15n, 2008
```
NL    000   011   010   000   000    3   13   4
AL    000   000   210   000   001    4   14   1
```
Sheets, Zambrano (3), Haren (5), Volquez (7), Wilson (8), Wagner (8), Dempster (9), Cook (10), Marmol (13), Webb (14), LIDGE (15)
Lee, Saunders (3), Halladay (4), Santana (5), Duchscherer (6), Nathan (7), Papelbon (8), F. Rodriguez (9), Rivera (9), Soria (11), Sherrill (12), KAZMIR (15)
A-55,632   T-4:50

No. 80 NL: St. Louis July 14n, 2009
```
AL    200   010   010    4    8   1
NL    030   000   000    3    5   1
```
Halladay, Buehrle (3), Greinke (4), Jackson (5), Hernandez (6), PAPELBON (7), Nathan (8), Rivera (9)
Lincecum, Franklin (3), Haren (5), Billingsley (5), Hoffman (6), Cordero (7), BELL (8), Rodriguez (9)
A-46,760   T-2:31

No. 81 AL: Los Angeles July 13n, 2010
```
NL    000   000   300    3    7   1
AL    000   000   010    1    6   0
```
Jimenez, Johnson (3), Kuo (5), Bell (5), Halladay (6), CAPPS (6), Wainwright (7), Wilson (8), Broxton (9)
Price, Pettitte (3), Lee (4), Verlander (5), Lester (6), HUGHES (7), Thornton (7), Bailey (7), Soriano (8), Valverde (9)
A-45,408   T-2:59

No. 82 NL: Arizona July 12n, 2011
```
AL    000   100   000    1    6   0
NL    000   310   10x    5    9   2
```
Weaver, Robertson (2), Pineda (3), WILSON (4), Walden (5), Perez (6), League (7), Ogando (8), G. Gonzalez (8)
Halladay, Lee (3), CLIPPARD (4), Kershaw (5), Jurrjens (6), Kimbrel (7), Venters (8), Bell (8), Hanrahan (9), Wilson (9)
A-47,994   T-2:50

No. 83 AL: Kansas City July 10n, 2012
```
NL    500   300   000    8   10   0
AL    000   000   000    0    6   0
```
CAIN, G. Gonzalez (3), Strasburg (4), Kershaw (5), Dickey (6), Hamels (7), Kimbrel (8), Chapman (8), Miley (9), Hanrahan (9), Papelbon (9)
VERLANDER, Nathan (2), Price (3), Harrison (4), Weaver (5), Sale (6), Coke (7), Johnson (8), Rodney (9)
A-40,933   T-2:59

No. 84 NL: New York July 16n, 2013
```
AL    000   110   010    3    9   0
NL    000   000   000    0    3   0
```
Scherzer, SALE (2), Hernandez (4), Moore (5), Balfour (6), Holland (7), Cecil (7), Delabar (7), Rivera (8), Nathan (9)
Harvey, Kershaw (3), CORBIN (4), Lee (5), Fernandez (6), Chapman (7), Kimbrel (8), Grilli (9)
A-45,186   T-3:06

No. 85 AL: Minnesota July 15n, 2014
```
NL    020   100   000    3    8   1
AL    300   000   00x    5    7   0
```
Wainwright, Kershaw (2), Simon (3), Greinke (4), NESHEK (5), Clippard (5), Rodriguez (6), Kimbrel (7), Watson (8), Chapman (8)
Hernandez, Lester (2), Darvish (3), Sele (4), SCHERZER (5), Kazmir (6), Uehara (6), Holland (7), Doolittle (8), Rodney (8), Perkins (9)
A-41,048   T-3:13

No. 86 NL: Cincinnati July 14n, 2015
```
AL    100   020   210    6    7   2
NL    010   001   001    3    6   0
```
Keuchel, Hernandez (3), PRICE (4), Archer (5), Britton (6), Betances (7), Davis (8) Perkins (9)
Greinke, Cole (3), Bumgarner (4), KERSHAW (5), deGrom (6), Rodriguez (7), Melancon (8), Chapman (9)
A-43,656   T-3:02

No. 87 NL: San Diego July 12n, 2016
```
NL    100   100   000    2   10   1
AL    031   000   00x    4    8   1
```
CUETO, Fernandez (2), Pomeranz (4), Teheran (5), Scherzer (6), Lester (7), Melancon (7), Rodney (8), Jansen (8)
Sale, KLUBER (2), Hamels (3), Sanchez (4), Quintana (5), Herrera (6), Betances (7), Miller (8), Harris (8), Britton (9)
A-42,386   T-3:05

No. 88 NL: Miami July 11n, 2017
```
AL    000   010   000    1    2   10   0
NL    000   001   000    0    1    7   0
```
Sale, Betances (3), Vargas (4), Kintzler (5), Santana (6), Osuna (7), Devenski (8), KIMBREL (9), Miller (10)
Scherzer, Neshek (2), Martinez (3), Wood (5), Greinke (6), Hand (7), Holland (8), Jansen (9), DAVIS (10)
A-37,188   T-3:16

No. 89 NL: Washington July 17n, 2018
```
AL    011   000   030    3    8   13   0
NL    001   000   112    1    6    7   1
```
Sale, Severino (2), Snell (3), Jimenez (4), Berrios (5), Treinen (6), Morton (7), DIAZ (9), Happ (10)
Scherzer, deGrom (3), Foltynewicz (4), Nola (5), Jeffress (6), Vazquez (7), Hader (8), Hand (8), STRIPLING (9)
A-43,843   T-3:34

No. 90 AL: Cleveland July 9n, 2019
```
NL    000   001   020    3    5   0
AL    010   010   20x    4    8   0
```
Ryu, KERSHAW (2), deGrom (3), Castillo (4), Buehler (5), Soroka (6), Woodruff (7), Smith (7), Alcantara (8)
Verlander, TANAKA (3), Berrios (3), Giolito (4), Bieber (5), Hendriks (6), Greene (7), Hand (8), Chapman (9)
A-36,747   T-2:48

2020 No Game (COVID-19)

ALL-STAR GAME CLUB BATTING

YEAR	AB	R	ER	H	TB	1B	2B	3B	HR	RBI	SH	SF	BB	HP	SO	SB	CS	BAT	SLG
1933																			
NL	34	2	2	8	14	5	1	1	1	2	0	0	0	0	4	0	0	.235	.412
AL	31	4	4	9	12	8	0	0	1	4	1	0	6	0	4	1	0	.290	.387
1934																			
AL	39	9	9	14	23	7	5	2	0	9	0	0	9	0	12	2	0	.359	.590
NL	36	7	7	8	15	5	1	0	2	6	0	0	3	0	5	2	0	.222	.417
1935																			
NL	31	1	1	4	6	2	2	0	0	1	0	0	2	0	5	1	0	.129	.194
AL	32	4	4	8	15	4	2	1	1	4	0	0	3	0	9	0	0	.250	.469
1936																			
AL	32	3	3	7	11	5	1	0	1	3	0	0	7	0	7	0	1	.219	.344
NL	31	4	3	9	14	7	0	1	1	4	0	0	3	0	6	0	0	.290	.452
1937																			
NL	41	3	3	13	16	10	3	0	0	3	0	0	0	0	0	0	0	.317	.390
AL	35	8	8	13	21	8	3	1	1	8	0	0	4	0	7	0	0	.371	.600
1938																			
AL	34	1	1	7	9	5	2	0	0	1	0	0	2	0	5	1	0	.206	.265
NL	33	4	1	8	10	7	0	1	0	2	0	0	0	1	7	1	0	.242	.303
1939																			
NL	34	1	1	7	8	6	1	0	0	1	0	0	3	0	9	0	0	.206	.235
AL	31	3	2	6	9	5	0	0	1	2	0	0	4	0	6	0	0	.194	.290
1940																			
AL	29	0	0	3	4	2	1	0	0	0	0	0	2	0	7	0	0	.103	.138
NL	29	4	4	7	10	6	0	0	1	4	2	0	3	1	6	0	0	.241	.345
1941																			
NL	35	5	5	10	19	5	3	0	2	5	2	0	1	0	7	0	1	.286	.543
AL	36	7	7	11	17	7	3	0	1	7	0	0	4	0	6	0	0	.306	.472
1942																			
AL	35	3	3	7	14	4	1	0	2	3	0	0	0	0	8	0	0	.200	.400
NL	31	1	1	6	9	5	0	0	1	1	0	0	2	1	3	0	0	.194	.290
1943																			
NL	37	3	3	10	16	7	1	1	1	3	0	0	1	0	3	0	0	.270	.432
AL	29	5	4	8	13	5	2	0	1	4	2	0	3	1	10	0	0	.276	.448
1944																			
AL	32	1	1	6	6	6	0	0	0	1	0	0	1	0	5	0	0	.188	.188
NL	33	7	5	12	16	9	2	1	0	7	3	0	4	0	4	1	0	.364	.485
1945																			
No Game (World War II)																			
1946																			
NL	31	0	0	3	3	3	0	0	0	0	0	0	1	0	10	0	0	.097	.097
AL	36	12	12	14	25	9	2	0	3	12	0	0	4	0	3	0	0	.389	.694
1947																			
AL	34	2	2	8	10	6	2	0	0	1	0	0	1	0	8	1	0	.235	.294
NL	32	1	1	5	8	4	0	0	1	1	0	0	4	0	6	0	0	.156	.250
1948																			
NL	35	2	2	8	11	7	0	0	1	2	0	0	4	0	7	1	0	.229	.314
AL	29	5	5	6	9	5	0	0	1	5	1	0	7	0	7	3	0	.207	.310
1949																			
AL	41	11	7	13	18	8	5	0	0	10	0	0	5	0	5	1	0	.317	.439
NL	37	7	7	12	20	8	2	0	2	6	0	0	8	1	3	0	0	.324	.541
1950 (14 innings)																			
NL	52	4	4	10	19	6	1	1	2	4	0	0	3	0	7	0	0	.192	.365
AL	49	3	3	8	12	5	2	1	0	3	0	0	2	0	12	0	0	.163	.245
1951																			
NL	39	8	7	12	25	7	1	0	4	7	0	0	4	0	3	0	1	.308	.641
AL	35	3	3	10	21	5	1	2	2	3	1	0	3	0	7	0	1	.286	.600
1952 (Five innings, rain)																			
AL	18	2	2	5	7	3	2	0	0	2	0	0	2	0	4	0	1	.278	.389
NL	18	3	3	3	10	0	1	0	2	3	0	0	2	1	6	0	0	.167	.556
1953																			
AL	31	1	1	5	5	5	0	0	0	1	0	0	3	0	5	0	1	.161	.161
NL	32	5	5	10	11	9	1	0	0	5	0	0	3	1	3	1	0	.313	.344
1954																			
NL	40	9	9	14	23	9	3	0	2	9	0	0	2	0	2	0	1	.350	.575
AL	39	11	11	17	29	13	0	0	4	11	0	1	4	0	10	0	0	.436	.744
1955 (12 innings)																			
AL	44	5	5	10	14	8	1	0	1	4	2	0	6	1	12	0	0	.227	.318
NL	45	6	4	13	17	11	1	0	1	4	0	0	2	0	8	0	0	.289	.378

ALL-STAR GAME CLUB BATTING

YEAR	AB	R	ER	H	TB	1B	2B	3B	HR	RBI	SH	SF	BB	HP	SO	SB	CS	BAT	SLG
1956																			
NL	36	7	7	11	19	7	2	0	2	6	1	0	4	0	12	1	1	.306	.528
AL	37	3	3	11	17	9	0	0	2	3	0	0	0	0	5	0	0	.297	.459
1957																			
AL	37	6	4	10	12	8	2	0	0	6	1	0	4	0	1	0	0	.270	.324
NL	34	5	5	9	13	6	2	1	0	4	0	0	2	0	6	0	0	.265	.382
1958																			
NL	30	3	3	4	4	4	0	0	0	2	0	1	3	1	2	1	0	.133	.133
AL	31	4	2	9	9	9	0	0	0	3	1	0	3	0	4	0	0	.290	.290
1959 #1																			
AL	36	4	4	8	12	6	1	0	1	4	0	0	3	0	9	0	0	.222	.333
NL	30	5	5	9	16	5	2	1	1	5	1	0	2	0	9	0	0	.300	.533
1959 #2																			
AL	33	5	4	6	15	3	0	0	3	5	0	0	6	0	12	1	1	.182	.455
NL	31	3	3	6	13	3	1	0	2	3	0	1	5	0	4	0	0	.194	.419
1960 #1																			
NL	38	5	5	12	23	6	3	1	2	5	0	0	1	1	6	1	0	.316	.605
AL	34	3	1	6	9	5	0	0	1	3	0	0	5	0	7	0	0	.176	.265
1960 #2																			
NL	34	6	6	10	22	6	0	0	4	6	1	0	3	0	3	1	1	.294	.647
AL	33	0	0	8	9	7	1	0	0	0	0	0	6	0	4	0	0	.242	.273
1961 #1 (10 innings)																			
AL	38	4	2	4	8	2	1	0	1	3	0	0	2	0	12	0	0	.105	.211
NL	37	5	4	11	18	7	2	1	1	5	0	2	1	1	6	1	0	.297	.486
1961 #2 (Nine innings, rain)																			
NL	32	1	1	5	6	4	1	0	0	1	0	0	2	1	7	0	0	.156	.188
AL	30	1	1	4	7	3	0	0	1	1	0	0	3	0	8	1	0	.133	.233
1962 #1																			
NL	33	3	3	8	9	7	1	0	0	3	0	1	1	0	3	2	1	.242	.273
AL	29	1	1	4	6	3	0	1	0	1	0	1	3	2	5	0	0	.138	.207
1962 #2																			
AL	37	9	8	10	21	5	2	0	3	9	0	1	4	0	8	0	0	.270	.568
NL	35	4	4	10	17	6	2	1	1	4	0	0	2	1	3	0	0	.286	.486
1963																			
NL	34	5	4	6	6	6	0	0	0	5	0	0	3	0	6	3	0	.176	.176
AL	34	3	3	11	12	10	1	0	0	3	1	0	1	1	9	0	0	.324	.353
1964																			
AL	35	4	3	9	12	7	1	1	0	4	0	1	1	1	10	0	0	.257	.343
NL	34	7	7	8	18	4	1	0	3	6	0	0	2	0	8	1	0	.235	.529
1965																			
NL	36	6	6	11	20	8	0	0	3	6	1	0	3	0	7	0	0	.306	.556
AL	34	5	5	8	15	5	1	0	2	5	0	0	6	0	5	0	0	.235	.441
1966 (10 innings)																			
AL	35	1	1	6	8	5	0	1	0	0	0	0	1	0	6	0	0	.171	.229
NL	33	2	2	6	7	5	1	0	0	2	1	0	1	0	5	0	0	.182	.212
1967 (15 innings)																			
NL	51	2	2	9	16	6	1	0	2	2	1	0	0	0	13	1	0	.176	.314
AL	49	1	1	8	12	6	1	0	1	1	2	0	2	0	17	0	2	.163	.245
1968																			
AL	30	0	0	3	6	0	3	0	0	0	0	0	0	0	11	0	0	.100	.200
NL	27	1	0	5	6	4	1	0	0	0	0	0	6	0	9	1	0	.185	.231
1969																			
NL	40	9	7	11	22	6	2	0	3	8	0	0	3	0	10	0	0	.275	.550
AL	33	3	3	6	13	3	1	0	2	3	0	0	2	0	7	0	0	.182	.394
1970 (12 innings)																			
AL	44	4	4	12	16	9	2	1	0	4	1	1	3	0	7	0	1	.273	.364
NL	43	5	5	10	13	9	0	0	1	4	0	1	5	1	11	0	0	.233	.302
1971																			
NL	31	4	4	5	14	2	0	0	3	4	0	0	1	1	8	0	0	.161	.452
AL	29	6	6	7	16	4	0	0	3	6	0	0	3	0	5	0	0	.241	.552
1972 (10 innings)																			
AL	33	3	3	6	11	3	2	0	1	3	1	0	2	0	8	0	0	.182	.333
NL	33	4	4	8	11	7	0	0	1	4	1	0	3	0	5	1	0	.242	.333
1973																			
NL	34	7	7	10	21	5	2	0	3	7	1	0	5	0	6	0	0	.294	.618
AL	32	1	1	5	9	2	2	1	0	1	0	0	3	0	5	1	0	.156	.281
1974																			
AL	30	2	2	4	5	3	1	0	0	1	1	0	6	0	7	1	0	.133	.167
NL	33	7	6	10	18	5	3	1	1	6	0	1	3	0	7	1	0	.303	.545
1975																			
NL	37	6	6	13	20	10	1	0	2	6	0	1	0	1	3	1	1	.351	.541
AL	36	3	3	10	13	9	0	0	1	3	0	0	1	1	10	3	1	.278	.361

ALL-STAR GAME CLUB BATTING

YEAR	AB	R	ER	H	TB	1B	2B	3B	HR	RBI	SH	SF	BB	HP	SO	SB	CS	BAT	SLG
1976																			
AL	29	1	1	5	8	4	0	0	1	1	0	0	3	0	5	1	0	.172	.276
NL	33	7	7	10	20	6	0	2	2	7	0	0	1	0	5	0	0	.303	.606
1977																			
NL	33	7	7	9	21	3	3	0	3	7	1	0	3	1	9	0	1	.273	.636
AL	35	5	4	8	12	6	1	0	1	5	0	0	3	1	10	0	0	.229	.343
1978																			
AL	31	3	3	8	13	5	1	2	0	3	0	2	1	0	7	1	2	.258	.419
NL	32	7	7	10	13	8	1	1	0	6	0	0	6	0	6	1	1	.313	.406
1979																			
NL	35	7	7	10	18	5	3	1	1	7	0	1	6	0	5	0	0	.286	.514
AL	35	6	5	10	16	6	3	0	1	5	1	0	5	1	5	0	0	.286	.457
1980																			
AL	32	2	2	7	11	5	1	0	1	2	0	0	4	0	11	1	0	.219	.344
NL	31	4	3	7	10	6	0	0	1	2	0	0	2	0	4	2	0	.226	.323
1981																			
NL	35	5	5	9	23	3	2	0	4	5	0	0	4	0	6	2	0	.257	.657
AL	37	4	4	11	15	9	1	0	1	4	0	1	2	0	8	0	1	.297	.405
1982																			
AL	33	1	1	8	9	7	1	0	0	1	0	1	5	0	10	1	0	.242	.273
NL	29	4	4	8	14	5	1	1	1	4	0	1	2	0	2	2	3	.276	.483
1983																			
NL	35	3	2	8	9	7	1	0	0	2	0	0	1	0	6	2	0	.229	.257
AL	38	13	10	15	28	8	3	2	2	13	1	3	4	0	8	0	0	.395	.737
1984																			
AL	32	1	1	7	13	3	3	0	1	1	0	0	0	0	11	0	0	.219	.406
NL	32	3	2	8	15	5	1	0	2	2	0	0	2	0	10	4	0	.250	.469
1985																			
NL	35	6	6	9	13	5	4	0	0	6	0	0	7	1	8	2	0	.257	.371
AL	30	1	0	5	5	5	0	0	0	1	0	1	4	0	6	3	0	.167	.167
1986																			
AL	33	3	3	5	12	2	1	0	2	3	0	0	2	0	12	2	0	.152	.364
NL	32	2	1	5	6	4	1	0	0	1	0	0	1	0	7	1	0	.156	.188
1987 (13 innings)																			
NL	46	2	2	8	11	6	1	1	0	2	0	0	1	0	10	1	1	.174	.239
AL	42	0	0	6	7	5	1	0	0	0	3	0	5	0	7	0	0	.143	.167
1988																			
AL	31	2	2	6	11	3	2	0	1	2	0	1	2	0	3	0	0	.194	.355
NL	33	1	1	5	5	5	0	0	0	0	0	0	1	0	7	2	0	.152	.152
1989																			
NL	33	3	3	9	9	9	0	0	0	3	0	0	3	0	8	3	1	.273	.273
AL	35	5	5	12	20	8	2	0	2	5	0	0	1	0	5	1	0	.343	.571
1990																			
AL	32	2	2	7	8	6	1	0	0	2	0	0	7	0	5	4	0	.219	.250
NL	29	0	0	2	2	2	0	0	0	0	0	0	2	0	6	1	0	.069	.069
1991																			
NL	35	2	2	10	14	8	1	0	1	2	0	0	2	0	6	1	0	.286	.400
AL	30	4	3	8	11	7	0	0	1	4	1	1	3	0	6	0	0	.267	.367
1992																			
AL	44	13	13	19	29	13	4	0	2	13	0	0	1	0	7	2	0	.432	.659
NL	39	6	4	12	17	9	2	0	1	6	0	0	2	0	7	0	0	.308	.436
1993																			
NL	33	3	3	7	13	3	3	0	1	3	0	1	1	0	9	0	0	.212	.394
AL	35	9	6	11	21	5	4	0	2	7	0	0	4	1	7	1	0	.314	.600
1994 (10 innings)																			
AL	44	7	5	15	18	12	3	0	0	6	0	0	2	0	8	3	0	.341	.409
NL	36	8	8	12	21	7	3	0	2	8	0	1	1	1	5	0	0	.333	.583
1995																			
NL	29	3	3	3	12	0	0	0	3	3	0	0	3	0	1	0	1	.103	.414
AL	34	2	2	8	12	6	1	0	1	2	0	0	2	0	2	1	1	.235	.353
1996																			
AL	34	0	0	7	8	6	1	0	0	0	0	0	0	0	8	2	0	.206	.235
NL	35	6	6	12	23	6	3	1	2	6	0	0	0	0	8	1	2	.343	.657
1997																			
NL	29	1	1	3	6	0	0	0	1	1	0	0	4	0	7	1	0	.103	.207
AL	30	3	3	7	14	0	1	0	2	3	0	0	1	0	8	0	1	.233	.467
1998																			
AL	43	13	11	19	26	16	1	0	2	11	0	2	6	0	5	5	0	.442	.605
NL	36	8	7	12	17	10	0	1	1	8	1	0	5	1	8	0	0	.333	.472
1999																			
NL	32	1	1	7	9	5	2	0	0	1	0	0	4	0	12	0	2	.219	.281
AL	31	4	4	6	6	6	0	0	0	4	0	0	2	1	10	1	0	.194	.194

ALL-STAR GAME CLUB BATTING

YEAR	AB	R	ER	H	TB	1B	2B	3B	HR	RBI	SH	SF	BB	HP	SO	SB	CS	BAT	SLG
2000																			
AL	38	6	5	10	13	7	3	0	0	6	0	1	4	0	7	1	0	.263	.342
NL	36	3	2	9	12	8	0	0	1	3	0	0	1	0	4	0	0	.250	.333
2001																			
NL	29	1	1	3	4	2	1	0	0	1	0	1	2	0	5	1	0	.103	.138
AL	33	4	3	8	19	3	2	0	3	4	0	0	0	0	7	1	0	.242	.576
2002 (11 innings, called)																			
AL	45	7	6	12	20	7	3	1	1	7	0	0	2	0	12	3	0	.267	.489
NL	45	7	7	13	18	10	2	0	1	7	0	0	1	0	11	2	0	.289	.422
2003																			
NL	36	6	6	11	19	7	2	0	2	6	0	0	1	0	7	0	0	.306	.528
AL	33	7	7	9	20	4	2	0	3	7	0	0	2	1	11	0	0	.273	.606
2004																			
AL	41	9	6	14	28	8	1	2	3	9	0	0	2	0	8	0	0	.341	.683
NL	36	4	4	9	12	6	3	0	0	4	0	0	1	1	6	0	0	.250	.333
2005																			
NL	35	5	5	11	17	7	3	0	1	5	0	0	5	0	6	0	0	.314	.486
AL	32	7	7	11	19	7	2	0	2	7	0	0	3	0	6	0	0	.344	.594
2006																			
AL	33	3	3	7	13	4	1	1	1	3	0	0	0	0	7	0	0	.212	.393
NL	30	2	2	6	10	4	1	0	1	1	0	0	1	0	4	2	0	.200	.333
2007																			
AL	36	5	5	10	20	6	1	0	3	5	0	0	1	0	1	1	0	.278	.556
NL	35	4	4	9	15	6	1	1	1	4	0	1	4	0	9	2	0	.257	.429
2008 (15 innings)																			
NL	52	3	2	13	16	12	0	0	1	3	1	2	4	0	17	1	1	.250	.308
AL	57	4	4	14	20	10	3	0	1	4	0	1	7	0	17	6	1	.246	.351
2009																			
AL	34	4	3	8	11	6	1	1	0	3	0	1	1	1	3	0	0	.235	.314
NL	32	3	2	5	6	4	1	0	0	2	0	0	1	0	5	1	0	.156	.188
2010																			
NL	33	3	3	7	8	6	1	0	0	3	0	0	2	0	10	1	0	.212	.242
AL	31	1	0	6	8	4	2	0	0	1	0	3	0	8	1	1	1	.194	.258
2011																			
AL	33	1	1	6	9	5	0	0	1	1	0	0	1	0	5	0	0	.182	.273
NL	31	5	5	9	14	6	2	0	1	5	0	0	1	0	9	3	1	.290	.452
2012																			
NL	37	8	8	10	20	5	1	3	1	8	0	0	3	0	6	0	0	.270	.541
AL	31	0	0	6	6	6	0	0	0	0	0	0	3	1	7	1	0	.194	.194
2013																			
AL	31	3	3	9	15	4	4	1	0	3	0	1	1	1	7	0	0	.290	.484
NL	30	0	0	3	4	2	1	0	0	0	0	0	1	0	8	1	0	.100	.133
2014																			
NL	35	3	3	8	13	3	5	0	0	3	0	0	1	1	13	1	0	.229	.371
AL	31	5	5	7	14	3	2	1	1	5	0	1	1	0	9	1	0	.226	.452
2015																			
AL	34	6	6	7	15	3	2	0	2	6	0	1	4	0	15	1	0	.206	.444
NL	33	3	2	6	11	4	0	1	1	3	0	1	2	0	9	1	0	.182	.333
2016																			
NL	37	2	2	10	15	7	2	0	1	2	0	0	2	0	9	0	0	.270	.405
AL	32	4	4	8	15	5	1	0	2	4	0	0	3	0	5	0	0	.250	.469
2017 (10 innings)																			
AL	39	2	2	10	14	8	1	0	1	2	0	0	1	0	14	2	0	.256	.359
NL	34	1	1	7	10	6	0	0	1	1	0	0	5	0	9	0	0	.206	.294
2018 (10 innings)																			
AL	42	8	6	13	28	8	0	0	5	8	0	1	4	0	13	0	0	.310	.667
NL	37	6	6	7	23	1	1	0	5	6	0	0	5	1	12	0	0	.189	.622
2019																			
NL	32	3	3	5	9	3	1	0	1	3	0	0	3	0	16	2	0	.156	.281
AL	30	4	4	8	13	5	2	0	1	3	0	0	1	0	7	0	0	.267	.433
2020																			
No Game (COVID-19)																			

ALL-STAR GAME – INDIVIDUAL RECORDS

BATTING – GAME

Most At-Bats
5 By many
   Extra-Inning Game:
7 Willie Jones, NL:Phil. 1950 (14 inn)

Most Runs
4 Ted Williams, AL:Bos. 1946
3 Frankie Frisch, NL:StL. 1934
   Jackie Robinson, NL:Brk. 1949

Most Hits
4 Joe Medwick, NL:StL. 1937
   Ted Williams, AL:Bos.1946
   Carl Yastrzemski, AL:Bos. 1970 (12 inn)

Most Total Bases
10 Ted Williams, AL:Bos. 1946
9 Arky Vaughan, NL:Pitt. 1941

Most Singles
3 By many; last:
   Derek Jeter, AL:NY 2004
   Ken Boyer, NL:StL. 1956

Most Doubles
2 Joe Medwick, NL:StL. 1937
   Ted Kluszewski, NL:Cin. 1956
   Ernie Banks, NL:Chi. 1959
   Barry Bonds, NL:SF 1993
   Damian Miller, NL:Ari. 2002
   Albert Pujols, NL:StL. 2004
   Jonathan Lucroy, NL:Mil. 2014
   Al Simmons, AL:Chi. 1934
   Paul Konerko, AL:Chi. 2002

Most Triples
2 Rod Carew, AL:Minn. 1978
1 By many in NL

Most Home Runs
2 Arky Vaughan, NL:Pitt. 1941 (cons)
   Willie McCovey, NL:SF 1969 (cons)
   Gary Carter, NL:Mtl. 1981 (cons)
   Ted Williams, AL:Bos. 1946
   Al Rosen, AL:Clev. 1954 (cons)

Most Runs Batted In
5 Ted Williams, AL:Bos. 1946
   Al Rosen, AL:Clev. 1954
4 Arky Vaughan, NL:Pitt. 1941

Most Walks
3 Charlie Gehringer, AL:Det. 1934
   Phil Cavarretta, NL:Chi. 1944

Most Strikeouts
3 Lou Gehrig, AL:NY 1934
   Bob Johnson, AL:Phil. 1935
   Joe Gordon, AL:NY 1942
   Ken Keltner, AL:Clev. 1943
   Jim Hegan, AL:Clev. 1950 (14 inn)
   Mickey Mantle, AL:NY 1956
   Tony Oliva, AL:Minn. 1967 (15 inn)
   Kirby Puckett, AL:Minn. 1987 (12 inn)
   Albert Belle, AL:Clev. 1996
   Stan Hack, NL:Chi. 1939
   John Roseboro, NL:LA 1961(2g)
   Willie McCovey, NL:SF 1968
   Craig Biggio, NL:Hou. 1998
   Yasiel Puig, NL:LA 2014
   Extra-Inning Game:
4 Roberto Clemente, NL:Pitt. 1967 (15 inn)

Most Stolen Bases
2 Willie Mays, NL:SF 1963
   Starlin Castro, NL:Chi. 2011
   Kelly Gruber, AL:Tor. 1990
   Roberto Alomar, AL:Tor. 1992
   Kenny Lofton, AL:Clev. 1996

Most Stolen Bases, Inning
2 Roberto Alomar, AL:Tor. 1992 (2nd)
   Starlin Castro, NL:Chi. 2011 (5th)

Most Caught Stealing
2 Stan Musial, NL:StL. 1951
   Tony Oliva, AL:Minn. 1967

Most Hit By Pitch
1 By many

Most Grounded Into Double Plays
2 Bobby Richardson, AL:NY 1963
1 By many in NL

PITCHING – GAME

Most Innings
6 Lefty Gomez, AL:NY 1935
5 Larry Jansen, NL:NY 1950

Most Runs
7 Atlee Hammaker, NL:SF 1983
5 Sandy Consuegra, AL:Chi. 1954
   Whitey Ford, AL:NY 1955 (12 inn)
   Blue Moon Odom, AL:Oak. 1969
   Jim Palmer, AL:Balt. 1977
   Justin Verlander, AL Det. 2012

Most Earned Runs
7 Atlee Hammaker, NL:SF 1983
5 Sandy Consuegra, AL:Chi. 1954
   Jim Palmer, AL:Balt. 1977
   Justin Verlander, AL Det. 2012

Most Hits
9 Tom Glavine, NL:Atl. 1992
7 Tommy Bridges, AL:Det. 1937

Most Hits, Inning
7 Tom Glavine, NL:Atl. 1992 (1st)
5 Tex Hughson, AL:Bos. 1944 (5th)
   Sandy Consuegra, AL:Chi. 1954 (4th)
   Blue Moon Odom, AL:Oak. 1969 (3rd)

Most Walks
5 Bill Hallahan, NL:StL. 1933
4 Jim Palmer, AL:Balt. 1978

Most Walks, Inning
3 Early Wynn, AL:Chi. 1959 (5th)
   Jim Palmer, AL:Balt. 1978 (3rd)
   Jim Kern, AL:Tex. 1979 (9th)
   Dan Petry, AL:Det. 1985 (9th)
   Kevin Brown, NL:LA 2000 (3rd)

Most Strikeouts
6 Carl Hubbell, NL:NY 1934
   Johnny Vander Meer, NL:Cin. 1943
   Larry Jansen, NL:NY 1950 (14 inn)
   Ferguson Jenkins, NL:Chi. 1967 (15 inn)
5 Billy Pierce, AL:Chi. 1956
   Dick Radatz, AL:Bos. 1963-64
   Pedro Martinez, AL:Bos. 1999

Most Strikeouts, Consecutive
5 Carl Hubbell, NL:NY 1934
   Fernando Valenzuela, NL:LA 1986
4 Pedro Martinez, AL:Bos. 1999

ALL-STAR GAME – INDIVIDUAL RECORDS

Most Strikeouts, Consecutive Innings
6   Carl Hubbell, NL:NY 1934
5   Dick Radatz, AL:Bos. 1963
    Pedro Martinez, AL:Bos. 1999

Most Strikeouts, Inning (only batters faced)
3   Johnny Sain, NL:Bos. 1948 (5th)
    Gene Conley, NL:Mil. 1955 (12th)
    Jerry Reuss, NL:LA 1980 (6th)
    Fernando Valenzuela, NL:LA 1984 (4th)
    Fernando Valenzuela, NL:LA 1986 (4th)
    Dwight Gooden, NL:NY 1984 (5th)
    Brad Lidge, NL:Hou. 2005 (7th)
    Brad Penny, NL:LA 2006 (1st)
    Ryan Dempster, AL:Chi. 2008 (9th)
    Jacob deGrom, NL:NY 2015 (6th)
    Aroldis Chapman, NL:Cin. 2015 (9th)
    Bobby Shantz, AL:Phil. 1952 (5th)
    Bill Caudill, AL:Oak. 1984 (7th)
    Pedro Martinez, AL:Bos. 1999 (1st)
    Jose Valverde, AL:Det. 2010 (9th)
    Shane Bieber, AL:Clev. 2019 (5th)
    Aroldis Chapman, AL:NY 2019 (9th)

Most Home Runs Allowed
3   Jim Palmer, AL:Balt. 1977
2   By many in NL; last:
    Ross Stripling, NL:LA 2018

Most Home Runs Allowed, Inning
2   By many; last:
    Ross Stripling, NL:LA 2018 (10th)
    Jim Palmer, AL:Balt. 1977 (1st)

Most Hit Batters
1   By many

Most Wild Pitches
2   Tom Brewer, AL:Bos. 1956
    Dave Stieb, AL:Tor. 1980
    Dellin Betances, AL:NY 2017
    Juan Marichal, NL:SF 1962
    John Smoltz, NL:Atl. 1993

Most Balks
1   Bob Friend, NL:Pitt. 1960
    Stu Miller, NL:SF 1961
    Dwight Gooden, NL:NY 1986, 88
    Kenley Jansen, NL:LA 2017
    Steve Busby, AL:KC 1975
    Jim Kern, AL:Tex. 1979
    Charlie Hough, AL:Tex. 1986
    Derek Lowe, AL:Bos. 2002

BATTING – LIFETIME

Most Games
24   Hank Aaron, NL:Mil./Atl; AL:Mil.
     Stan Musial, NL:StL.
     Willie Mays, NL:NY/SF-NY
18   Ted Williams, AL:Bos.
     Brooks Robinson, AL:Balt.
     Cal Ripken, AL:Balt.

Most Games, Consecutive
24   Stan Musial, NL:StL. 1943-63
     Willie Mays, NL:NY/SF 1954-71; NY 72-73
18   Brooks Robinson, AL:Balt. 1960(1g)-74

Most Winning Teams
17   Willie Mays, NL:NY/SF-NY
     Hank Aaron, NL:Mil./Atl.
12   Cal Ripken, AL:Balt.

Most Losing Teams
15   Brooks Robinson, AL:Balt.
10   Stan Musial, NL:StL.

Highest Batting Avg. (Minimum: 20 at-bats)
.500   Charlie Gehringer, AL:Det. (20-10)
.433   Billy Herman, NL:Chi.-Brk. (30-13)

Highest Slugging Pct. (Minimum: 20 at-bats)
.900   Fred Lynn, AL:Bos.-Cal. (20-18)
.821   Steve Garvey, NL:LA-SD (28-23)

Most At-Bats
75   Willie Mays, NL:NY/SF-NY
49   Cal Ripken, AL:Balt.

Most Runs
20   Willie Mays, NL:NY/SF
10   Ted Williams, AL:Bos.

Most Hits
23   Willie Mays, NL:NY/SF
14   Ted Williams, AL:Bos.
     Nellie Fox, AL:Chi.

Most Extra Base Hits
8   Stan Musial, NL:StL.
    Willie Mays, NL:NY/SF
7   Ted Williams, AL:Bos.

Most Total Bases
40   Stan Musial, NL:StL.
     Willie Mays, NL:NY/SF
30   Ted Williams, AL:Bos.

Most Singles
15   Willie Mays, NL:NY/SF
14   Nellie Fox, AL:Chi.

Most Doubles
7   Dave Winfield, NL-SD AL:NY
5   Dave Winfield, AL:NY
3   Ted Kluszewski, NL:Cin.
    Ernie Banks, NL:Chi.
    Al Oliver, NL:Pitt.-Mtl.
    Barry Bonds, NL:Pitt.-SF

Most Triples
3   Willie Mays, NL:NY/SF
    Brooks Robinson, AL:Balt.

Most Home Runs
6   Stan Musial, NL:StL.
4   Ted Williams, AL:Bos.
    Fred Lynn, AL:Bos.-Cal.

Most Runs Batted In
12   Ted Williams, AL:Bos.
10   Stan Musial, NL:StL.

Most Walks
11   Ted Williams, AL:Bos.
7   Stan Musial, NL:StL.
    Willie Mays, NL:NY/SF

Most Strikeouts
17   Mickey Mantle, AL:NY
14   Willie Mays, NL:NY/SF-NY

Most Stolen Bases
6   Willie Mays, NL:NY/SF
5   Roberto Alomar, AL:Tor.-Balt.
    Kenny Lofton, AL:Clev.

Most Hit By Pitch
1   By many

PITCHING – LIFETIME

Most Games
10   Roger Clemens, AL:Bos.-Tor.-NY; NL:Hou.
9   Mariano Rivera, AL:NY
8   Don Drysdale, NL:LA
    Juan Marichal, NL:SF
    Tom Seaver, NL:NY-Cin.

ALL-STAR GAME – INDIVIDUAL RECORDS

Most Games, Consecutive
6 Ewell Blackwell, NL:Cin. 1946-51
    Early Wynn, AL:Clev. 1955-57; Chi. 58-59(2g)

Most Games Started
5 Lefty Gomez, AL:NY
    Robin Roberts, NL:Phil.
    Don Drysdale, NL:LA

Most Games Finished
6 Rich Gossage, NL:Pitt.-SD; AL:Chi.-NY
    Mariano Rivera, AL:NY
3 Ewell Blackwell, NL:Cin.
    Bruce Sutter, NL:Chi.-StL.
    Rich Gossage, NL:Pitt.-SD
    Trevor Hoffman, NL:SD

Most Games Won
3 Lefty Gomez, AL:NY
2 Bob Friend, NL:Pitt.
    Juan Marichal, NL:SF
    Don Drysdale, NL:LA
    Bruce Sutter, NL:Chi.

Most Games Lost
2 Mort Cooper, NL:StL.
    Claude Passeau, NL:Chi.
    Dwight Gooden, NL:NY
    John Smoltz, NL:Atl.
    Whitey Ford, AL:NY
    Luis Tiant, AL:Clev.-Bos.
    Catfish Hunter, AL:Oak.-NY

Most Saves (Since 1969)
4 Mariano Rivera, AL:NY
2 Bruce Sutter, NL:Chi.-StL.

Lowest Earned Run Average (Minimum: 12 IP)
0.00 Mel Harder, AL:Clev. (13 inn)
0.50 Juan Marichal, NL:SF (18 inn)

Most Innings
19.1 Don Drysdale, NL:LA
18.0 Lefty Gomez, AL:NY

Most Runs
13 Whitey Ford, AL:NY
10 Robin Roberts, NL:Phil.
    Warren Spahn, NL:Bos./Mil.

Most Earned Runs
11 Whitey Ford, AL:NY
10 Robin Roberts, NL:Phil.

Most Hits
19 Whitey Ford, AL:NY
17 Robin Roberts, NL:Phil.
    Warren Spahn, NL:Bos.-Mil.

Most Home Runs
4 Vida Blue, AL:Oak.
    Catfish Hunter, AL:KC-Oak.-NY
3 Robin Roberts, NL:Phil.
    Mort Cooper, NL:StL.
    Tom Seaver, NL:NY-Cin.
    Steve Carlton, NL:StL.-Phil.

Most Walks
7 Jim Palmer, AL:Balt.
6 Lon Warneke, NL:Chi.
    Carl Hubbell, NL:NY
    Robin Roberts, NL:Phil.

Most Strikeouts
19 Don Drysdale, NL:LA
14 Jim Palmer, AL:Balt.

Most Hit Batters
1 By many

Most Wild Pitches
3 Dellin Betances, AL:NY
2 Ewell Blackwell, NL:Cin.
    Robin Roberts, NL:Phil.
    Juan Marichal, NL:SF
    Steve Rogers, NL:Mtl.
    John Smoltz, NL:Atl.

Most Balks
2 Dwight Gooden, NL:NY
1 Steve Busby, AL:KC
    Jim Kern, AL:Tex.
    Charlie Hough, AL:Tex.
    Derek Lowe, AL:Bos.

ALL-STAR GAME – MOST VALUABLE PLAYER

1962(1g)	Maury Wills, NL:LA
1962(2g)	Leon Wagner, AL:LA
1963	Willie Mays, NL:SF
1964	Johnny Callison, NL:Phil.
1965	Juan Marichal, NL:SF
1966	Brooks Robinson, AL:Balt.
1967	Tony Perez, NL:Cin.
1968	Willie Mays, NL:SF
1969	Willie McCovey, NL:SF
1970	Carl Yastrzemski, AL:Bos.
1971	Frank Robinson, AL:Balt.
1972	Joe Morgan, NL:Cin.
1973	Bobby Bonds, NL:SF
1974	Steve Garvey, NL:LA
1975	Bill Madlock, NL:Chi. & Jon Matlack, NL:NY
1976	George Foster, NL:Cin.
1977	Don Sutton, NL:LA
1978	Steve Garvey, NL:LA
1979	Dave Parker, NL:Pitt.
1980	Ken Griffey Sr., NL:Cin.
1981	Gary Carter, NL:Mtl.
1982	Dave Concepcion, NL:Cin.
1983	Fred Lynn, AL:Cal.
1984	Gary Carter, NL:Mtl.
1985	LaMarr Hoyt, NL:SD
1986	Roger Clemens, AL:Bos.
1987	Tim Raines, NL:Mtl.
1988	Terry Steinbach, AL:Oak.
1989	Bo Jackson, AL:KC
1990	Julio Franco, AL:Tex.
1991	Cal Ripken, AL:Balt.
1992	Ken Griffey Jr., AL:Sea.
1993	Kirby Puckett, AL:Minn.
1994	Fred McGriff, NL:Atl.
1995	Jeff Conine, NL:Fla.
1996	Mike Piazza, NL:LA
1997	Sandy Alomar Jr., AL:Clev.
1998	Roberto Alomar, AL:Balt.
1999	Pedro Martinez, AL:Bos.
2000	Derek Jeter, AL:NY
2001	Cal Ripken, AL:Balt.
2002	no selection
2003	Garrett Anderson, AL:Ana.
2004	Alfonso Soriano, AL:Tex.
2005	Miguel Tejada, AL:Balt.
2006	Michael Young, AL:Tex.
2007	Ichiro Suzuki, AL:Sea.
2008	J.D. Drew, AL:Bos.
2009	Carl Crawford, AL:TB
2010	Brian McCann, NL:Atl.
2011	Prince Fielder, NL:Mil.
2012	Melky Cabrera, NL:SF
2013	Mariano Rivera, AL:NY
2014	Mike Trout, AL:LA
2015	Mike Trout, AL:LA
2016	Eric Hosmer, AL:KC
2017	Robinson Cano, AL:Sea.
2018	Alex Bregman, AL:Hou.
2019	Shane Bieber, AL:Clev.
2020	No Game (COVID-19)

AMERICAN LEAGUE CLUB STANDINGS - 1901-1968

	BALT	BOS	CAL	CHI	CLEV	DET	KC	MIL	MINN	NY	OAK	PHIL	STL	WASH	WASH
1901	5	2	-	1	7	3	-	8	-	-	-	4	-	6	-
1902	8	3	-	4	5	7	-	-	-	-	-	1	2	6	-
1903	-	1	-	7	3	5	-	-	-	4	-	2	6	8	-
1904	-	1	-	3	4	7	-	-	-	2	-	5	6	8	-
1905	-	4	-	2	5	3	-	-	-	6	-	1	8	7	-
1906	-	8	-	1	3	6	-	-	-	2	-	4	5	7	-
1907	-	7	-	3	4	1	-	-	-	5	-	2	6	8	-
1908	-	5	-	3	2	1	-	-	-	8	-	6	4	7	-
1909	-	3	-	4	6	1	-	-	-	5	-	2	7	8	-
1910	-	4	-	6	5	3	-	-	-	2	-	1	8	7	-
1911	-	5	-	4	3	2	-	-	-	6	-	1	8	7	-
1912	-	1	-	4	5	6	-	-	-	8	-	3	7	2	-
1913	-	4	-	5	3	6	-	-	-	7	-	1	8	2	-
1914	-	2	-	6	8	4	-	-	-	6	-	1	5	3	-
1915	-	1	-	3	7	2	-	-	-	5	-	8	6	4	-
1916	-	1	-	2	6	3	-	-	-	4	-	8	5	7	-
1917	-	2	-	1	3	4	-	-	-	6	-	8	7	5	-
1918	-	1	-	6	2	7	-	-	-	4	-	8	5	3	-
1919	-	6	-	1	2	4	-	-	-	3	-	8	5	7	-
1920	-	5	-	2	1	7	-	-	-	3	-	8	4	6	-
1921	-	5	-	7	2	6	-	-	-	1	-	8	3	4	-
1922	-	8	-	5	4	3	-	-	-	1	-	7	2	6	-
1923	-	8	-	7	3	2	-	-	-	1	-	6	5	4	-
1924	-	7	-	8	6	3	-	-	-	2	-	5	4	1	-
1925	-	8	-	5	6	4	-	-	-	7	-	2	3	1	-
1926	-	8	-	5	2	6	-	-	-	1	-	3	7	4	-
1927	-	8	-	5	6	4	-	-	-	1	-	2	7	3	-
1928	-	8	-	5	7	6	-	-	-	1	-	2	3	4	-
1929	-	8	-	7	3	6	-	-	-	2	-	1	4	5	-
1930	-	8	-	7	4	5	-	-	-	3	-	1	6	2	-
1931	-	6	-	8	4	7	-	-	-	2	-	1	5	3	-
1932	-	8	-	7	4	5	-	-	-	1	-	2	6	3	-
1933	-	7	-	6	4	5	-	-	-	2	-	3	8	1	-
1934	-	4	-	8	3	1	-	-	-	2	-	5	6	7	-
1935	-	4	-	5	3	1	-	-	-	2	-	8	7	6	-
1936	-	6	-	3	5	2	-	-	-	1	-	8	7	4	-
1937	-	5	-	3	4	2	-	-	-	1	-	7	8	6	-
1938	-	2	-	6	3	4	-	-	-	1	-	8	7	5	-
1939	-	2	-	4	3	5	-	-	-	1	-	7	8	6	-
1940	-	4	-	4	2	1	-	-	-	3	-	8	6	7	-
1941	-	2	-	3	4	4	-	-	-	1	-	8	6	6	-
1942	-	2	-	6	4	5	-	-	-	1	-	8	3	7	-
1943	-	7	-	4	3	5	-	-	-	1	-	8	6	2	-
1944	-	4	-	7	5	2	-	-	-	3	-	5	1	8	-
1945	-	7	-	6	5	1	-	-	-	4	-	8	3	2	-
1946	-	1	-	5	6	2	-	-	-	3	-	8	7	4	-
1947	-	3	-	6	4	2	-	-	-	1	-	5	8	7	-
1948	-	2	-	8	1	5	-	-	-	3	-	4	6	7	-
1949	-	2	-	6	3	4	-	-	-	1	-	5	7	8	-
1950	-	3	-	6	4	2	-	-	-	1	-	8	7	5	-
1951	-	3	-	4	2	5	-	-	-	1	-	6	8	7	-
1952	-	6	-	3	2	8	-	-	-	1	-	4	7	5	-
1953	-	4	-	3	2	6	-	-	-	1	-	7	8	5	-
1954	7	4	-	3	1	5	-	-	-	2	-	8	-	6	-
1955	7	4	-	3	2	5	6	-	-	1	-	-	-	8	-
1956	6	4	-	3	2	5	8	-	-	1	-	-	-	7	-
1957	5	3	-	2	6	4	7	-	-	1	-	-	-	8	-
1958	6	3	-	2	4	5	7	-	-	1	-	-	-	8	-
1959	6	5	-	1	2	4	7	-	-	3	-	-	-	8	-
1960	2	7	-	3	4	6	8	-	-	1	-	-	-	5	-
1961	3	6	8	4	5	2	9	-	7	1	-	-	-	-	9
1962	7	8	3	5	6	4	9	-	2	1	-	-	-	-	10
1963	4	7	9	2	5	5	8	-	3	1	-	-	-	-	10
1964	3	8	5	2	6	4	10	-	6	1	-	-	-	-	9
1965	3	9	7	2	5	4	10	-	1	6	-	-	-	-	8
1966	1	9	6	4	5	3	7	-	2	10	-	-	-	-	8
1967	6	1	5	4	8	2	10	-	2	9	-	-	-	-	6
1968	2	4	8	8	3	1	-	-	7	5	6	-	-	-	10

AMERICAN LEAGUE CLUB STANDINGS (since 1969)

(1969 Seattle listed under MIL.)

| | EAST | | | | | | WEST | | | | | |
	BALT	BOS	CLEV	DET	NY	WASH	CAL	CHI	KC	MIL	MINN	OAK
1969	1	3	6	2	5	4	3	5	4	6	1	2
1970	1	3	5	4	2	6	3	6	4	4	1	2
1971	1	3	6	2	4	5	4	3	2	6	5	1

	BALT	BOS	CLEV	DET	MIL	NY	CAL	CHI	KC	MINN	OAK	TEX
1972	3	2	5	1	6	4	5	2	4	3	1	6
1973	1	2	6	3	5	4	4	5	2	3	1	6
1974	1	3	4	6	5	2	6	4	5	3	1	2
1975	2	1	4	6	5	3	6	5	2	4	1	3
1976	2	3	4	5	6	1	4	6	1	3	2	4

	BALT	BOS	CLEV	DET	MIL	NY	TOR	CAL	CHI	KC	MINN	OAK	TEX	SEA
1977	2	2	5	4	6	1	7	5	3	1	4	7	2	6
1978	4	2	6	5	3	1	7	2	5	1	4	6	2	7
1979	1	3	6	5	2	4	7	1	5	2	4	7	3	6
1980	2	4	6	5	3	1	7	6	5	1	3	2	4	7
1981 *Split Season*														
1st Half	2	5	6	4	3	1	7	4	3	5	7	1	2	6
2nd Half	4	2	5	2	1	6	7	7	6	1	4	2	3	5
1982	2	3	6	4	1	5	6	1	3	2	7	5	6	4
1983	1	6	7	2	5	3	4	5	1	2	5	4	3	7
1984	5	4	6	1	7	3	2	2	5	1	2	4	7	5
1985	4	5	7	3	6	2	1	2	3	1	4	4	7	6
1986	7	1	5	3	6	2	4	1	5	3	6	3	2	7
1987	6	5	7	1	3	4	2	6	5	2	1	3	6	4
1988	7	1	6	2	3	5	3	4	5	3	2	1	6	7
1989	2	3	6	7	4	5	1	3	7	2	5	1	4	6
1990	5	1	4	3	6	7	2	4	2	6	7	1	3	5
1991	6	2	7	2	4	5	1	7	2	6	1	4	3	5
1992	3	7	4	6	2	4	1	5	3	5	2	1	4	7
1993	3	5	6	3	7	2	1	5	1	3	5	7	2	4

| | EAST | | | | | CENTRAL | | | | | WEST | | | |
	BALT	BOS	DET	NY	TOR	CHI	CLEV	KC	MIL	MINN	ANA	OAK	SEA	TEX
1994	2	4	5	1	3	1	2	3	5	4	4	2	3	1
1995	3	1	4	2	5	3	1	2	4	5	2	4	1	3
1996	2	3	5	1	4	2	1	5	3	4	4	3	2	1
1997	1	4	3	2	5	2	1	5	3	4	2	4	1	3

| | EAST | | | | | CENTRAL | | | | | WEST | | | |
	BALT	BOS	NY	TB	TOR	CHI	CLEV	DET	KC	MINN	ANA	OAK	SEA	TEX
1998	4	2	1	5	3	2	1	5	3	4	2	4	3	1
1999	4	2	1	5	3	2	1	3	4	5	4	2	3	1
2000	4	2	1	5	3	1	2	3	4	5	3	1	2	4
2001	4	2	1	5	3	3	1	4	5	2	3	2	1	4
2002	4	2	1	5	3	2	3	5	4	1	2	1	3	4
2003	4	2	1	5	3	2	4	5	3	1	3	1	2	4
2004	3	2	1	4	5	2	3	4	5	1	1	2	4	3

| | EAST | | | | | CENTRAL | | | | | WEST | | | |
	BALT	BOS	NY	TB	TOR	CHI	CLEV	DET	KC	MINN	LA	OAK	SEA	TEX
2005	4	2	1	5	3	1	2	4	5	3	1	2	4	3
2006	4	3	1	5	2	3	4	2	5	1	2	1	4	3
2007	4	1	2	5	3	4	1	2	5	3	1	3	2	4
2008	5	2	3	1	4	1	3	5	4	2	1	3	4	2
2009	5	2	1	3	4	3	4	2	4	1	1	4	3	2
2010	5	3	2	1	4	2	4	3	5	1	3	2	4	1
2011	5	3	1	2	4	3	2	1	4	5	2	3	4	1
2012	2	5	1	3	4	2	4	1	3	5	3	1	4	2

| | EAST | | | | | CENTRAL | | | | | WEST | | | | |
	BALT	BOS	NY	TB	TOR	CHI	CLEV	DET	KC	MINN	HOU	LA	OAK	SEA	TEX
2013	3	1	3	2	5	5	2	1	3	4	5	3	1	4	2
2014	1	5	2	4	3	4	3	1	2	5	4	1	2	3	5
2015	3	5	2	4	1	4	3	5	1	2	2	3	5	4	1
2016	2	1	4	5	3	4	1	2	3	5	3	4	5	2	1
2017	5	1	2	3	4	4	1	5	3	2	1	2	5	3	3
2018	5	1	2	3	4	4	1	3	5	2	1	4	2	3	5
2019	5	3	1	2	4	3	2	5	4	1	1	4	2	5	3
2020	4	5	2	1	3	3	2	5	4	1	2	4	1	3	5

NATIONAL LEAGUE CLUB STANDINGS 1876-1899

	BALT	BOS	BRK	BUFF	CHI	CIN	CLEV	DET	HART	IND	KC	LOU	MIL	NY	PHIL	PITT	PROV	STL	SYR	TROY	WASH	WOR
1876		4			1	8			2			5		6	7			3				
1877		1			5	6			3			2						4				
1878		1			4	2				5			6				3					
1879		2		3	4	5	6										1		7	8		
1880		6		7	1	8	3										2			4		5
1881		6		3	1		7	4									2			5		8
1882		3		4	1		5	6									2			7		8
1883		1		5	2		4	7						6	8		3					
1884		2		3	4		7	8						5	6		1					
1885		5		7	1			6						2	3		4	8				
1886		5			1			2			7			3	4			6			8	
1887		5			3			1		8				4	2	6					7	
1888		4			2			5		7				1	3	6					8	
1889		2			3		6			7				1	4	5					8	
1890		5	1		2	4	7							6	3	8						
1891		1	6		2	7	5							3	4	8						
1892-1st	12	1	2		7	4	5					10		8	3	6		9			11	
1892-2nd	10	2	3		8	5	1					9		6	7	4		11			12	
1893	8	1	6		9	7	3					11		5	4	2		10			12	
1894	1	3	5		8	10	6					12		2	4	7		9			11	
1895	1	5	6		4	8	2					12		9	3	7		11			10	
1896	1	4	9		5	3	2					12		7	8	6		11			10	
1897	2	1	6		9	4	5					11		3	10	8		12			7	
1898	2	1	10		4	3	5					9		7	6	8		12			11	
1899	4	2	1		8	6	12					9		10	3	7		5			11	

NOTE: 1892 Split season. Boston defeated Cleveland, 5 games to 0 (1 tie) in best-of-nine playoff.

NATIONAL LEAGUE CHAMPIONS 1876-1899

	Club & Manager	W	L	PCT	GA
1876	Chicago (Al Spalding)	52	14	.788	6
1877	Boston (Harry Wright)	31	17	.646	7
1878	Boston (Harry Wright)	41	19	.683	4
1879	Providence (George Wright)	55	23	.705	5
1880	Chicago (Cap Anson)	67	17	.798	15
1881	Chicago (Cap Anson)	56	28	.667	9
1882	Chicago (Cap Anson)	55	29	.655	3
1883	Boston (John Morrill)	63	35	.643	4
1884	Providence (Frank Bancroft)	84	28	.750	10.5
1885	Chicago (Cap Anson)	87	25	.777	2
1886	Chicago (Cap Anson)	90	34	.726	21
1887	Detroit (Bill Watkins)	79	45	.637	31
1888	New York (Jim Mutrie)	84	47	.641	9
1889	New York (Jim Mutrie)	83	43	.659	1
1890	Brooklyn (Bill McGunnigle)	86	43	.667	6
1891	Boston (Frank Selee)	87	51	.630	3.5
1892	Boston (Frank Selee)	102	48	.680	8.5
1893	Boston (Frank Selee)	86	44	.662	5
1894	Baltimore (Ned Hanlon)	89	39	.695	3
1895	Baltimore (Ned Hanlon)	87	43	.669	3
1896	Baltimore (Ned Hanlon)	90	39	.698	9.5
1897	Boston (Frank Selee)	93	39	.705	2
1898	Boston (Frank Selee)	102	47	.685	6
1899	Brooklyn (Ned Hanlon)	89	41	.685	5

NATIONAL LEAGUE CLUB STANDINGS 1900-1968

	ATL	BOS	BRK	CHI	CIN	HOU	LA	MIL	NYG	NYM	PHIL	PITT	STL	SF
1900	-	4	1	5	7	-	-	-	8	-	3	2	5	-
1901	-	5	3	6	8	-	-	-	7	-	2	1	4	-
1902	-	3	2	5	4	-	-	-	8	-	7	1	6	-
1903	-	6	5	3	4	-	-	-	2	-	7	1	8	-
1904	-	7	6	2	3	-	-	-	1	-	8	4	5	-
1905	-	7	8	3	5	-	-	-	1	-	4	2	6	-
1906	-	8	5	1	6	-	-	-	2	-	4	3	7	-
1907	-	7	5	1	6	-	-	-	4	-	3	2	8	-
1908	-	6	7	1	5	-	-	-	2	-	4	2	8	-
1909	-	8	6	2	4	-	-	-	3	-	5	1	7	-
1910	-	8	6	1	5	-	-	-	2	-	4	3	7	-
1911	-	8	7	2	6	-	-	-	1	-	4	3	5	-
1912	-	8	7	3	4	-	-	-	1	-	5	2	6	-
1913	-	5	6	3	7	-	-	-	1	-	2	4	8	-
1914	-	1	5	4	8	-	-	-	2	-	6	7	3	-
1915	-	2	3	4	7	-	-	-	8	-	1	5	6	-
1916	-	3	1	5	7	-	-	-	4	-	2	6	7	-
1917	-	6	7	5	4	-	-	-	1	-	2	8	3	-
1918	-	7	5	1	3	-	-	-	2	-	6	4	8	-
1919	-	6	5	3	1	-	-	-	2	-	8	4	7	-
1920	-	7	1	5	3	-	-	-	2	-	8	4	5	-
1921	-	4	5	7	6	-	-	-	1	-	8	2	3	-
1922	-	8	6	5	2	-	-	-	1	-	7	3	3	-
1923	-	7	6	4	2	-	-	-	1	-	8	3	5	-
1924	-	8	2	5	4	-	-	-	1	-	7	3	6	-
1925	-	5	6	8	3	-	-	-	2	-	6	1	4	-
1926	-	7	6	4	2	-	-	-	5	-	8	3	1	-
1927	-	7	6	4	5	-	-	-	3	-	8	1	2	-
1928	-	7	6	3	5	-	-	-	2	-	8	4	1	-
1929	-	8	6	1	7	-	-	-	3	-	5	2	4	-
1930	-	6	4	2	7	-	-	-	3	-	8	5	1	-
1931	-	7	4	3	8	-	-	-	2	-	6	5	1	-
1932	-	5	3	1	8	-	-	-	6	-	4	2	6	-
1933	-	4	6	3	8	-	-	-	1	-	7	2	5	-
1934	-	4	6	3	8	-	-	-	2	-	7	5	1	-
1935	-	8	5	1	6	-	-	-	3	-	7	4	2	-
1936	-	6	7	2	5	-	-	-	1	-	8	4	2	-
1937	-	5	6	2	8	-	-	-	1	-	7	3	4	-
1938	-	5	7	1	4	-	-	-	3	-	8	2	6	-
1939	-	7	3	4	1	-	-	-	5	-	8	6	2	-
1940	-	7	2	5	1	-	-	-	6	-	8	4	3	-
1941	-	7	1	6	3	-	-	-	5	-	8	4	2	-
1942	-	7	2	6	4	-	-	-	3	-	8	5	1	-
1943	-	6	3	5	2	-	-	-	8	-	7	4	1	-
1944	-	6	7	4	3	-	-	-	5	-	8	2	1	-
1945	-	6	3	1	7	-	-	-	5	-	8	4	2	-
1946	-	4	2	3	6	-	-	-	8	-	5	7	1	-
1947	-	3	1	6	5	-	-	-	4	-	7	7	2	-
1948	-	1	3	8	7	-	-	-	5	-	6	4	2	-
1949	-	4	1	8	7	-	-	-	5	-	3	6	2	-
1950	-	4	2	7	6	-	-	-	3	-	1	8	5	-
1951	-	4	2	8	6	-	-	-	1	-	5	7	3	-
1952	-	7	1	5	6	-	-	-	2	-	4	8	3	-
1953	-	-	1	7	6	-	-	2	5	-	3	8	3	-
1954	-	-	2	7	5	-	-	3	1	-	4	8	6	-
1955	-	-	1	6	5	-	-	2	3	-	4	8	7	-
1956	-	-	1	8	3	-	-	2	6	-	5	7	4	-
1957	-	-	3	7	4	-	-	1	6	-	5	7	2	-
1958	-	-	-	5	4	-	7	1	-	-	8	2	5	3
1959	-	-	-	5	5	-	1	2	-	-	8	4	7	3
1960	-	-	-	7	6	-	4	2	-	-	8	1	3	5
1961	-	-	-	7	1	-	2	4	-	-	8	6	5	3
1962	-	-	-	9	3	8	2	5	-	10	7	4	6	1
1963	-	-	-	7	5	9	1	6	-	10	4	8	2	3
1964	-	-	-	8	2	9	6	5	-	10	2	6	1	4
1965	-	-	-	8	4	9	1	5	-	10	6	3	7	2
1966	5	-	-	10	7	8	1	-	-	9	4	3	6	2
1967	7	-	-	3	4	9	8	-	-	10	5	6	1	2
1968	5	-	-	3	4	10	7	-	-	9	7	6	1	2

NATIONAL LEAGUE CLUB STANDINGS (since 1969)

	EAST						WEST					
	CHI	MTL	NY	PHIL	PITT	STL	ATL	CIN	HOU	LA	SD	SF
1969	2	6	1	5	3	4	1	3	5	4	6	2
1970	2	6	3	5	1	4	5	1	4	2	6	3
1971	3	5	3	6	1	2	3	4	4	2	6	1
1972	2	5	3	6	1	4	4	1	2	3	6	5
1973	5	4	1	6	3	2	5	1	4	2	6	3
1974	6	4	5	3	1	2	3	2	4	1	6	5
1975	5	5	3	2	1	3	5	1	6	2	4	3
1976	4	6	3	1	2	5	6	1	3	2	5	4
1977	4	5	6	1	2	3	6	2	3	1	5	4
1978	3	4	6	1	2	5	6	2	5	1	4	3
1979	5	2	6	4	1	3	6	1	2	3	5	4
1980	6	2	5	1	3	4	4	3	1	2	6	5
1981 *Split Season*												
1st Half	6	3	5	1	4	2	4	2	3	1	6	5
2nd Half	5	1	4	3	6	2	5	2	1	4	6	3
1982	5	3	6	2	4	1	1	6	5	2	4	3
1983	5	3	6	1	2	4	2	6	3	1	4	5
1984	1	5	2	4	6	3	2	5	2	4	1	6
1985	4	3	2	5	6	1	5	2	3	1	3	6
1986	5	4	1	2	6	3	6	2	1	5	4	3
1987	6	3	2	4	4	1	5	2	3	4	6	1
1988	4	3	1	6	2	5	6	2	5	1	3	4
1989	1	4	2	6	5	3	6	5	3	4	2	1
1990	4	3	2	4	1	6	6	1	4	2	4	3
1991	4	6	5	3	1	2	1	5	6	2	3	4
1992	4	2	5	6	1	3	1	2	4	6	3	5

	CHI	FLA	MTL	NY	PHI	PITT	STL	ATL	CIN	COL	HOU	LA	SD	SF
1993	4	6	2	7	1	5	3	1	5	6	3	4	7	2

	EAST					CENTRAL					WEST			
	ATL	FLA	MTL	NY	PHI	CHI	CIN	HOU	PITT	STL	COL	LA	SD	SF
1994	2	5	1	3	4	5	1	2	3	3	3	1	4	2
1995	1	4	5	2	2	3	1	2	5	4	2	1	3	4
1996	1	3	2	4	5	4	3	2	5	1	3	2	1	4
1997	1	2	4	3	5	5	3	1	2	4	3	2	4	1

	ATL	FLA	MTL	NY	PHI	CHI	CIN	HOU	MIL	PITT	STL	ARI	COL	LA	SD	SF
1998	1	5	4	2	3	2	4	1	5	6	3	5	4	3	1	2
1999	1	5	4	2	3	6	2	1	5	3	4	1	5	3	4	2
2000	1	3	4	2	5	6	2	4	3	5	1	3	4	2	5	1
2001	1	4	5	3	2	3	5	1	4	6	2	1	5	3	4	2
2002	1	4	2	5	3	5	3	2	6	4	1	1	4	3	5	2
2003	1	2	4	5	3	1	5	2	6	4	3	3	4	2	5	1
2004	1	3	5	4	2	3	4	2	6	5	1	5	4	1	3	2

	ATL	FLA	WASH	NY	PHI	CHI	CIN	HOU	MIL	PITT	STL	ARI	COL	LA	SD	SF
2005	1	3	5	3	2	4	5	2	3	6	1	2	5	4	1	3
2006	3	4	5	1	2	6	3	2	4	5	1	4	4	2	1	3
2007	3	5	4	2	1	1	5	4	2	6	3	1	2	4	3	5
2008	4	3	5	2	1	1	5	3	2	6	4	2	3	1	5	4
2009	3	2	5	4	1	2	4	5	3	6	1	5	2	1	4	3
2010	2	3	5	4	1	5	1	4	3	6	2	5	3	4	2	1
2011	2	5	3	4	1	5	3	6	1	4	2	1	4	3	5	2

	ATL	MIA	WASH	NY	PHI	CHI	CIN	HOU	MIL	PITT	STL	ARI	COL	LA	SD	SF
2012	2	5	1	4	3	5	1	6	3	4	2	3	5	2	4	1

	ATL	MIA	WASH	NY	PHI	CHI	CIN	MIL	PITT	STL	ARI	COL	LA	SD	SF
2013	1	5	2	3	4	5	3	4	2	1	2	5	1	3	3
2014	2	4	1	2	5	5	4	3	2	1	5	4	1	3	2
2015	4	3	2	1	5	3	5	4	2	1	3	5	1	4	2
2016	5	3	1	2	4	1	5	4	3	2	4	3	1	5	2
2017	3	2	1	4	5	1	5	2	4	3	2	3	1	4	5
2018	1	5	2	4	3	2	5	1	4	3	3	2	1	5	4
2019	1	5	2	3	4	3	4	2	5	1	2	4	1	5	3
2020	1	2	4	4	3	1	3	4	5	2	5	4	1	2	3

AMERICAN LEAGUE CHAMPIONS (1901 to 1968)
(* = mid-season replacement)

YEAR	CLUB (MANAGER)	WON	LOST	PCT.	GA
1901	Chicago (Clark Griffith)	83	53	.610	4
1902	Philadelphia (Connie Mack)	83	53	.610	5
1903	Boston (Jimmy Collins)	91	47	.659	14.5
1904	Boston (Jimmy Collins)	95	59	.617	1.5
1905	Philadelphia (Connie Mack)	92	56	.622	2
1906	Chicago (Fielder Jones)	93	58	.616	3
1907	Detroit (Hughie Jennings)	92	58	.613	1.5
1908	Detroit (Hughie Jennings)	90	63	.588	0.5
1909	Detroit (Hughie Jennings)	98	54	.645	3.5
1910	Philadelphia (Connie Mack)	102	48	.680	14.5
1911	Philadelphia (Connie Mack)	101	50	.669	13.5
1912	Boston (Jake Stahl)	105	47	.691	14
1913	Philadelphia (Connie Mack)	96	57	.627	6.5
1914	Philadelphia (Connie Mack)	99	53	.651	8.5
1915	Boston (Bill Carrigan)	101	50	.669	2.5
1916	Boston (Bill Carrigan)	91	63	.591	2
1917	Chicago (Pants Rowland)	100	54	.649	9
1918	Boston (Ed Barrow)	75	51	.595	3.5
1919	Chicago (Kid Gleason)	88	52	.629	3.5
1920	Cleveland (Tris Speaker)	98	56	.636	2
1921	New York (Miller Huggins)	98	55	.641	4.5
1922	New York (Miller Huggins)	94	60	.610	1
1923	New York (Miller Huggins)	98	54	.645	16
1924	Washington (Bucky Harris)	92	62	.597	2
1925	Washington (Bucky Harris)	96	55	.636	8.5
1926	New York (Miller Huggins)	91	63	.591	3
1927	New York (Miller Huggins)	110	44	.714	19
1928	New York (Miller Huggins)	101	53	.656	2.5
1929	Philadelphia (Connie Mack)	104	46	.693	18
1930	Philadelphia (Connie Mack)	102	52	.662	8
1931	Philadelphia (Connie Mack)	107	45	.704	13.5
1932	New York (Joe McCarthy)	107	47	.695	13
1933	Washington (Joe Cronin)	99	53	.651	7
1934	Detroit (Mickey Cochrane)	101	53	.656	7
1935	Detroit (Mickey Cochrane)	93	58	.616	3
1936	New York (Joe McCarthy)	102	51	.667	19.5
1937	New York (Joe McCarthy)	102	52	.662	13
1938	New York (Joe McCarthy)	99	53	.651	9.5
1939	New York (Joe McCarthy)	106	45	.702	17
1940	Detroit (Del Baker)	90	64	.584	1
1941	New York (Joe McCarthy)	101	53	.656	17
1942	New York (Joe McCarthy)	103	51	.669	9
1943	New York (Joe McCarthy)	98	56	.636	13.5
1944	St. Louis (Luke Sewell)	89	65	.578	1
1945	Detroit (Steve O'Neill)	88	65	.575	1.5
1946	Boston (Joe Cronin)	104	50	.675	12
1947	New York (Bucky Harris)	97	57	.630	12
1948	Cleveland (Lou Boudreau)	97	58	.626	1
1949	New York (Casey Stengel)	97	57	.630	1
1950	New York (Casey Stengel)	98	56	.636	3
1951	New York (Casey Stengel)	98	56	.636	5
1952	New York (Casey Stengel)	95	59	.617	2
1953	New York (Casey Stengel)	99	52	.656	8.5
1954	Cleveland (Al Lopez)	111	43	.721	8
1955	New York (Casey Stengel)	96	58	.623	3
1956	New York (Casey Stengel)	97	57	.630	9
1957	New York (Casey Stengel)	98	56	.636	8
1958	New York (Casey Stengel)	92	62	.597	10
1959	Chicago (Al Lopez)	94	60	.610	5
1960	New York (Casey Stengel)	97	57	.630	8
1961	New York (Ralph Houk)	109	53	.673	8
1962	New York (Ralph Houk)	96	66	.593	5
1963	New York (Ralph Houk)	104	57	.646	10.5
1964	New York (Yogi Berra)	99	63	.611	1
1965	Minnesota (Sam Mele)	102	60	.630	7
1966	Baltimore (Hank Bauer)	97	63	.606	9
1967	Boston (Dick Williams)	92	70	.568	1
1968	Detroit (Mayo Smith)	103	59	.636	12

AMERICAN LEAGUE DIVISION CHAMPIONS (1969 to 1993)

(Championship Series Winner Capitalized)
(E = East; W = West)
(* = mid-season replacement)

YEAR	CLUB (MANAGER)	WON	LOST	PCT.	GA
1969	(E) BALTIMORE (Earl Weaver)	109	53	.673	19
	(W) Minnesota (Billy Martin)	97	65	.599	9
1970	(E) BALTIMORE (Earl Weaver)	108	54	.667	15
	(W) Minnesota (Bill Rigney)	98	64	.605	9
1971	(E) BALTIMORE (Earl Weaver)	101	57	.639	12
	(W) Oakland (Dick Williams)	101	60	.627	16
1972	(W) OAKLAND (Dick Williams)	93	62	.600	5.5
	(E) Detroit (Billy Martin)	86	70	.551	0.5
1973	(W) OAKLAND (Dick Williams)	94	68	.580	6
	(E) Baltimore (Earl Weaver)	97	65	.599	8
1974	(W) OAKLAND (Alvin Dark)	90	72	.556	5
	(E) Baltimore (Earl Weaver)	91	71	.562	2
1975	(E) BOSTON (Darrell Johnson)	95	65	.594	4.5
	(W) Oakland (Alvin Dark)	98	64	.605	7
1976	(E) NEW YORK (Billy Martin)	97	62	.610	10.5
	(W) Kansas City (Whitey Herzog)	90	72	.556	2.5
1977	(E) NEW YORK (Billy Martin)	100	62	.617	2.5
	(W) Kansas City (Whitey Herzog)	102	60	.630	8
1978	(E) NEW YORK (Bob Lemon*)	100	63	.613	1
	(W) Kansas City (Whitey Herzog)	92	70	.568	5
1979	(E) BALTIMORE (Earl Weaver)	102	57	.642	8
	(W) California (Jim Fregosi)	88	74	.543	3
1980	(W) KANSAS CITY (Jim Frey)	97	65	.599	14
	(E) New York (Dick Howser)	103	59	.636	3
1981	(E) NEW YORK (Bob Lemon*)	59	48	.551	--
	(W) Oakland (Billy Martin)	64	45	.587	--

Due to players' strike, 1981 season was divided into two halves. Leaders of each half met in a best-of-five series to determine the ALCS participants. East: New York 3, Milwaukee 2; West: Oakland 3, Kansas City 0.

YEAR	CLUB (MANAGER)	WON	LOST	PCT.	GA
1982	(E) MILWAUKEE (Harvey Kuenn*)	95	67	.586	1
	(W) California (Gene Mauch)	93	69	.574	3
1983	(E) BALTIMORE (Joe Altobelli)	98	64	.605	6
	(W) Chicago (Tony LaRussa)	99	63	.611	20
1984	(E) DETROIT (Sparky Anderson)	104	58	.642	15
	(W) Kansas City (Dick Howser)	84	78	.519	3
1985	(W) KANSAS CITY (Dick Howser)	91	71	.562	1
	(E) Toronto (Bobby Cox)	99	62	.615	2
1986	(E) BOSTON John (McNamara)	95	66	.590	5.5
	(W) California (Gene Mauch)	92	70	.568	5
1987	(W) MINNESOTA (Tom Kelly)	85	77	.525	2
	(E) Detroit (Sparky Anderson)	98	64	.605	2
1988	(W) OAKLAND (Tony LaRussa)	104	58	.642	13
	(E) Boston (Joe Morgan*)	89	73	.549	1
1989	(W) OAKLAND (Tony LaRussa)	99	63	.611	7
	(E) Toronto (Cito Gaston*)	89	73	.549	2
1990	(W) OAKLAND (Tony LaRussa)	103	59	.636	9
	(E) Boston (Joe Morgan)	88	74	.543	2
1991	(W) MINNESOTA (Tom Kelly)	95	67	.586	8
	(E) Toronto (Cito Gaston)	91	71	.562	7
1992	(E) TORONTO (Cito Gaston)	96	66	.593	4
	(W) Oakland (Tony LaRussa)	96	66	.593	6
1993	(E) TORONTO (Cito Gaston)	95	67	.586	7
	(W) Chicago (Gene Lamont)	94	68	.580	8

AMERICAN LEAGUE POSTSEASON PARTICIPANTS (since 1995)

*Championship Series Winner Capitalized; E = East; C = Central; W = West; WC = Wild Card; * = mid-season replacement*

YEAR	CLUB (MANAGER)	WON	LOST	PCT.	GA
1995	(C) CLEVELAND (Mike Hargrove)	100	44	.694	30
	(W) Seattle (Lou Piniella)	79	66	.545	1
	(E) Boston (Kevin Kennedy)	86	58	.597	7
	(WC) New York (Buck Showalter)	79	65	.549	--
1996	(E) NEW YORK (Joe Torre)	92	70	.568	4
	(WC) Baltimore (Davey Johnson)	88	74	.543	--
	(C) Cleveland (Mike Hargrove)	99	62	.615	14.5
	(W) Texas (Johnny Oates)	90	72	.556	4.5
1997	(C) CLEVELAND (Mike Hargrove)	86	75	.534	6
	(E) Baltimore (Davey Johnson)	98	64	.605	2
	(W) Seattle (Lou Piniella)	90	72	.556	6
	(WC) New York (Joe Torre)	96	66	.593	--
1998	(E) NEW YORK (Joe Torre)	114	48	.704	22
	(C) Cleveland (Mike Hargrove)	89	73	.549	9
	(W) Texas (Johnny Oates)	88	74	.543	3
	(WC) Boston (Jimy Williams)	92	70	.568	--
1999	(E) NEW YORK (Joe Torre)	98	64	.605	4
	(WC) Boston (Jimy Williams)	94	68	.580	--
	(C) Cleveland (Mike Hargrove)	97	65	.599	21.5
	(W) Texas (Johnny Oates)	95	67	.586	8
2000	(E) NEW YORK (Joe Torre)	87	74	.540	2.5
	(WC) Seattle (Lou Piniella)	91	71	.562	--
	(W) Oakland (Art Howe)	91	70	.565	0.5
	(C) Chicago (Jerry Manuel)	95	67	.586	5
2001	(E) NEW YORK (Joe Torre)	95	65	.594	13.5
	(W) Seattle (Lou Piniella)	116	46	.716	14
	(C) Cleveland (Charlie Manuel)	91	71	.562	6
	(WC) Oakland (Art Howe)	102	60	.630	--
2002	(WC) ANAHEIM (Mike Scioscia)	99	63	.611	--
	(W) Oakland (Art Howe)	103	59	.636	4
	(E) New York (Joe Torre)	103	58	.640	10.5
	(C) Minnesota (Ron Gardenhire)	94	67	.584	13.5
2003	(E) NEW YORK (Joe Torre)	101	61	.623	6
	(WC) Boston (Grady Little)	95	67	.586	--
	(W) Oakland (Ken Macha)	96	66	.593	3
	(C) Minnesota (Ron Gardenhire)	90	72	.556	4
2004	(WC) BOSTON (Terry Francona)	98	64	.605	--
	(E) New York (Joe Torre)	101	61	.623	3
	(C) Minnesota (Ron Gardenhire)	92	70	.568	9
	(W) Anaheim (Mike Scioscia)	92	70	.568	1
2005	(C) CHICAGO (Ozzie Guillen)	99	63	.611	6
	(W) Los Angeles (Mike Scioscia)	95	67	.586	7
	(E) New York (Joe Torre)	95	67	.586	--
	(WC) Boston (Terry Francona)	95	67	.586	--
2006	(WC) DETROIT (Jim Leyland)	95	67	.586	--
	(W) Oakland (Ken Macha)	93	69	.574	4
	(E) New York (Joe Torre)	97	65	.599	10
	(C) Minnesota (Ron Gardenhire)	96	66	.593	1
2007	(E) BOSTON (Terry Francona)	96	66	.593	2
	(C) Cleveland (Eric Wedge)	96	66	.593	8
	(W) Los Angeles (Mike Scioscia)	94	68	.580	6
	(WC) New York (Joe Torre)	94	68	.580	--
2008	(E) TAMPA BAY (Joe Maddon)	97	65	.599	2
	(WC) Boston (Terry Francona)	95	67	.586	--
	(C) Chicago (Ozzie Guillen)	89	74	.546	1
	(W) Los Angeles (Mike Scioscia)	100	62	.617	21
2009	(E) NEW YORK (Joe Girardi)	103	59	.636	8
	(W) Los Angeles (Mike Scioscia)	97	65	.599	10
	(C) Minnesota (Ron Gardenhire)	87	76	.534	1
	(WC) Boston (Terry Francona)	95	67	.586	--
2010	(W) TEXAS (Ron Washington)	90	72	.556	9
	(WC) New York (Joe Girardi)	95	67	.586	--
	(E) Tampa Bay (Joe Maddon)	96	66	.593	1
	(C) Minnesota (Ron Gardenhire)	94	68	.580	6

AMERICAN LEAGUE POSTSEASON PARTICIPANTS (continued)

*Championship Series Winner Capitalized; E = East; C = Central; W = West; WC = Wild Card; * = mid-season replacement*

YEAR	CLUB (MANAGER)	WON	LOST	PCT.	GA
2011	(W) TEXAS (Ron Washington)	96	66	.593	10
	(C) Detroit (Jim Leyland)	95	67	.586	15
	(E) New York (Joe Girardi)	97	65	.599	6
	(WC) Tampa Bay (Joe Maddon)	91	71	.562	--
2012	(C) DETROIT (Jim Leyland)	88	74	.543	3
	(E) New York (Joe Girardi)	95	67	.586	2
	(W) Oakland (Bob Melvin)	94	68	.580	1
	(WC) Baltimore (Buck Showalter)	93	69	.569	--
	(WC) Texas (Ron Washington)	93	69	.569	--
2013	(E) BOSTON (John Farrell)	97	65	.599	5.5
	(C) Detroit (Jim Leyland)	93	69	.574	1
	(W) Oakland (Bob Melvin)	96	66	.593	5.5
	(WC) Tampa Bay (Joe Maddon)	92	71	.564	--
	(WC) Cleveland (Terry Francona)	92	70	.568	--
2014	(WC) KANSAS CITY (Ned Yost)	89	73	.549	--
	(E) Baltimore (Buck Showalter)	96	66	.593	12
	(C) Detroit (Brad Ausmus)	90	72	.556	1
	(W) Los Angeles (Mike Scioscia)	98	64	.605	10
	(WC) Oakland (Bob Melvin)	88	74	.543	--
2015	(C) KANSAS CITY (Ned Yost)	95	67	.586	12
	(E) Toronto (John Gibbons)	93	69	.574	6
	(W) Texas (Jeff Banister)	88	74	.543	2
	(WC) Houston (A.J. Hinch)	86	76	.531	--
	(WC) New York (Joe Girardi)	87	75	.537	--
2016	(C) CLEVELAND (Terry Francona)	94	67	.584	8
	(WC) Toronto (John Gibbons)	89	73	.549	--
	(W) Texas (Jeff Banister)	95	67	.586	9
	(E) Boston (John Farrell)	93	69	.574	4
	(WC) Baltimore (Buck Showalter)	89	73	.549	--
2017	(W) HOUSTON (A.J. Hinch)	101	61	.623	21
	(WC) New York (Joe Girardi)	91	71	.562	--
	(C) Cleveland (Terry Francona)	102	60	.630	17
	(E) Boston (John Farrell)	93	69	.574	2
	(WC) Minnesota (Paul Molitor)	85	77	.525	--
2018	(E) BOSTON (Alex Cora)	108	54	.667	8
	(W) Houston (A.J. Hinch)	103	59	.636	6
	(C) Cleveland (Terry Francona)	91	71	.562	13
	(WC) New York (Aaron Boone)	100	62	.617	--
	(WC) Oakland (Bob Melvin)	97	65	.599	--
2019	(W) HOUSTON (A.J. Hinch)	107	55	.660	10
	(E) New York (Aaron Boone)	103	59	.636	7
	(C) Minnesota (Rocco Baldelli)	101	61	.623	8
	(WC) Tampa Bay (Kevin Cash)	96	66	.593	--
	(WC) Oakland (Bob Melvin)	97	65	.599	--
2020	(E) TAMPA BAY (Kevin Cash)	40	20	.667	7
	(W2) Houston (Dusty Baker)	29	31	.483	--
	(W) Oakland (Bob Melvin)	36	24	.600	7
	(E2) New York (Aaron Boone)	33	27	.550	--
	(C) Minnesota (Rocco Baldelli)	36	24	.600	1
	(C2) Cleveland (Terry Francona)	35	25	.583	--
	(WC) Chicago (Rick Renteria)	35	25	.583	--
	(WC) Toronto (Charlie Montoyo)	32	28	.533	--

NATIONAL LEAGUE CHAMPIONS (1900 to 1968)

(* = mid-season replacement)

YEAR	CLUB (MANAGER)	WON	LOST	PCT.	GA
1900	Brooklyn (Ned Hanlon)	82	54	.603	4.5
1901	Pittsburgh (Fred Clarke)	90	49	.647	7.5
1902	Pittsburgh (Fred Clarke)	103	36	.741	27.5
1903	Pittsburgh (Fred Clarke)	91	49	.650	6.5
1904	New York (John McGraw)	06	47	.693	13
1905	New York (John McGraw)	105	48	.686	9
1906	Chicago (Frank Chance)	116	36	.763	20
1907	Chicago (Frank Chance)	107	45	.704	17
1908	Chicago (Frank Chance)	99	55	.643	1
1909	Pittsburgh (Fred Clarke)	110	42	.724	6.5
1910	Chicago (Frank Chance)	104	50	.675	13
1911	New York (John McGraw)	99	54	.647	7.5
1912	New York (John McGraw)	103	48	.682	10
1913	New York (John McGraw)	101	51	.664	12.5
1914	Boston (George Stallings)	94	59	.614	10.5
1915	Philadelphia (Pat Moran)	90	62	.592	7
1916	Brooklyn (Wilbert Robinson)	94	60	.610	2.5
1917	New York (John McGraw)	98	56	.636	10
1918	Chicago (Fred Mitchell)	84	45	.651	10.5
1919	Cincinnati (Pat Moran)	96	44	.686	9
1920	Brooklyn (Wilbert Robinson)	93	61	.604	7
1921	New York (John McGraw)	94	59	.614	4
1922	New York (John McGraw)	93	61	.604	7
1923	New York (John McGraw)	95	58	.621	4.5
1924	New York (John McGraw)	93	60	.608	1.5
1925	Pittsburgh (Bill McKechnie)	95	58	.621	8.5
1926	St. Louis (Rogers Hornsby)	89	65	.578	2
1927	Pittsburgh (Donie Bush)	94	60	.610	1.5
1928	St. Louis (Bill McKechnie)	95	59	.617	2
1929	Chicago (Joe McCarthy)	98	54	.645	10.5
1930	St. Louis (Gabby Street)	92	62	.597	2
1931	St. Louis (Gabby Street)	101	53	.656	13
1932	Chicago (Charlie Grimm*)	90	64	.584	4
1933	New York (Bill Terry)	91	61	.599	5
1934	St. Louis (Frankie Frisch)	95	58	.621	2
1935	Chicago (Charlie Grimm)	100	54	.649	4
1936	New York (Bill Terry)	92	62	.597	5
1937	New York (Bill Terry)	95	57	.625	3
1938	Chicago (Gabby Hartnett*)	89	63	.586	2
1939	Cincinnati (Bill McKechnie)	97	57	.630	4.5
1940	Cincinnati (Bill McKechnie)	100	53	.654	12
1941	Brooklyn (Leo Durocher)	100	54	.649	2.5
1942	St. Louis (Billy Southworth)	106	48	.688	2
1943	St. Louis (Billy Southworth)	105	49	.682	18
1944	St. Louis (Billy Southworth)	105	49	.682	14.5
1945	Chicago (Charlie Grimm)	98	56	.636	3
1946	St. Louis (Eddie Dyer)	98	58	.628	2
1947	Brooklyn (Burt Shotton*)	94	60	.610	5
1948	Boston (Billy Southworth)	91	62	.595	6.5
1949	Brooklyn (Burt Shotton)	97	57	.630	1
1950	Philadelphia (Eddie Sawyer)	91	63	.591	2
1951	New York (Leo Durocher)	98	59	.624	1
1952	Brooklyn (Chuck Dressen)	96	57	.627	4.5
1953	Brooklyn (Chuck Dressen)	105	49	.682	13
1954	New York (Leo Durocher)	97	57	.630	5
1955	Brooklyn (Walter Alston)	98	55	.641	13.5
1956	Brooklyn (Walter Alston)	93	61	.604	1
1957	Milwaukee (Fred Haney)	95	59	.617	8
1958	Milwaukee (Fred Haney)	92	62	.597	8
1959	Los Angeles (Walter Alston)	88	68	.564	2
1960	Pittsburgh (Danny Murtaugh)	95	59	.617	7
1961	Cincinnati (Fred Hutchinson)	93	61	.604	4
1962	San Francisco (Alvin Dark)	103	62	.624	1
1963	Los Angeles (Walter Alston)	99	63	.611	6
1964	St. Louis (Johnny Keane)	93	69	.574	1
1965	Los Angeles (Walter Alston)	97	65	.599	2
1966	Los Angeles (Walter Alston)	95	67	.586	1.5
1967	St. Louis (Red Schoendienst)	101	60	.627	10.5
1968	St. Louis (Red Schoendienst)	97	65	.599	9

NATIONAL LEAGUE DIVISION CHAMPIONS (1969 to 1993)

(Championship Series Winner Capitalized)
(E = East; W = West)
(* = mid-season replacement)

YEAR	CLUB (MANAGER)	WON	LOST	PCT.	GA
1969	(E) NEW YORK (Gil Hodges)	100	62	.617	8
	(W) Atlanta (Lum Harris)	93	69	.574	3
1970	(W) CINCINNATI (Sparky Anderson)	102	60	.630	14.5
	(E) Pittsburgh (Danny Murtaugh)	89	73	.549	5
1971	(E) PITTSBURGH (Danny Murtaugh)	97	65	.599	7
	(W) San Francisco (Charlie Fox)	90	72	.556	1
1972	(W) CINCINNATI (Sparky Anderson)	95	59	.617	10.5
	(E) Pittsburgh (Bill Virdon)	96	59	.619	11
1973	(E) NEW YORK (Yogi Berra)	82	79	.509	1.5
	(W) Cincinnati (Sparky Anderson)	99	63	.611	3.5
1974	(W) LOS ANGELES (Walter Alston)	102	60	.630	4
	(E) Pittsburgh (Danny Murtaugh)	88	74	.543	1.5
1975	(W) CINCINNATI (Sparky Anderson)	108	54	.667	20
	(E) Pittsburgh (Danny Murtaugh)	92	69	.571	6.5
1976	(W) CINCINNATI (Sparky Anderson)	102	60	.630	10
	(E) Philadelphia (Danny Ozark)	101	61	.623	9
1977	(W) LOS ANGELES (Tommy Lasorda)	98	64	.605	10
	(E) Philadelphia (Danny Ozark)	101	61	.623	5
1978	(W) LOS ANGELES (Tommy Lasorda)	95	67	.586	2.5
	(E) Philadelphia (Danny Ozark)	90	72	.556	1.5
1979	(E) PITTSBURGH (Chuck Tanner)	98	64	.605	2
	(W) Cincinnati (John McNamara)	90	71	.559	1.5
1980	(E) PHILADELPHIA (Dallas Green)	91	71	.562	1
	(W) Houston (Bill Virdon)	93	70	.571	1
1981	(W) LOS ANGELES (Tommy Lasorda)	63	47	.573	--
	(E) Montreal (Jim Fanning*)	60	48	.556	--

Due to players' strike, 1981 season was divided into two halves. Leaders of each half met in a best-of-five
series to determine the NLCS participants. West: Los Angeles 3, Houston 2; East: Montreal 3, Philadelphia 2.

1982	(E) ST. LOUIS (Whitey Herzog)	92	70	.568	3
	(W) Atlanta (Joe Torre)	89	73	.549	1
1983	(E) PHILADELPHIA (Paul Owens*)	90	72	.556	6
	(W) Los Angeles (Tommy Lasorda)	91	71	.562	3
1984	(W) SAN DIEGO (Dick Williams)	92	70	.568	12
	(E) Chicago (Jimmy Frey)	96	65	.596	6.5
1985	(E) ST. LOUIS (Whitey Herzog)	101	61	.623	3
	(W) Los Angeles (Tommy Lasorda)	95	67	.586	5.5
1986	(E) NEW YORK (Davey Johnson)	108	54	.667	21.5
	(W) Houston (Hal Lanier)	96	66	.593	10
1987	(E) ST. LOUIS (Whitey Herzog)	95	67	.586	3
	(W) San Francisco (Roger Craig)	90	72	.556	6
1988	(W) LOS ANGELES (Tommy Lasorda)	94	67	.584	7
	(E) New York (Davey Johnson)	100	60	.625	15
1989	(W) SAN FRANCISCO (Roger Craig)	92	70	.568	3
	(E) Chicago (Don Zimmer)	93	69	.574	6
1990	(W) CINCINNATI (Lou Piniella)	91	71	.562	5
	(E) Pittsburgh (Jim Leyland)	95	67	.586	4
1991	(W) ATLANTA (Bobby Cox)	94	68	.580	1
	(E) Pittsburgh (Jim Leyland)	98	64	.605	14
1992	(W) ATLANTA (Bobby Cox)	98	64	.605	8
	(E) Pittsburgh (Jim Leyland)	96	66	.593	9
1993	(E) PHILADELPHIA (Jim Fregosi)	97	65	.599	3
	(W) Atlanta (Bobby Cox)	104	58	.642	1

NATIONAL LEAGUE POSTSEASON PARTICIPANTS (since 1995)

Championship Series Winner Capitalized; E = East; C = Central; W = West; WC = Wild Card; * = mid-season replacement

YEAR	CLUB (MANAGER)	WON	LOST	PCT.	GA
1995	(E) ATLANTA (Bobby Cox)	90	54	.625	21
	(C) Cincinnati (Davey Johnson)	85	59	.590	9
	(W) Los Angeles (Tommy Lasorda)	78	66	.542	1
	(WC) Colorado (Don Baylor)	77	67	.535	--
1996	(E) ATLANTA (Bobby Cox)	96	66	.593	8
	(C) St. Louis (Tony LaRussa)	88	74	.543	6
	(W) San Diego (Bruce Bochy)	91	71	.562	1
	(WC) Los Angeles (Bill Russell*)	90	72	.556	--
1997	(WC) FLORIDA (Jim Leyland)	92	70	.568	--
	(E) Atlanta (Bobby Cox)	101	61	.623	9
	(C) Houston (Larry Dierker)	84	78	.519	5
	(W) San Francisco (Dusty Baker)	90	72	.556	2
1998	(W) SAN DIEGO (Bruce Bochy)	98	64	.605	9.5
	(E) Atlanta (Bobby Cox)	106	56	.654	18
	(C) Houston (Larry Dierker)	102	60	.630	12.5
	(WC) Chicago (Jim Riggleman)	90	73	.552	--
1999	(E) ATLANTA (Bobby Cox)	103	59	.636	6.5
	(WC) New York (Bobby Valentine)	97	66	.595	--
	(C) Houston (Larry Dierker)	97	65	.599	1.5
	(W) Arizona (Buck Showalter)	100	62	.617	14
2000	(WC) NEW YORK (Bobby Valentine)	94	68	.580	--
	(C) St. Louis (Tony LaRussa)	95	67	.586	10
	(E) Atlanta (Bobby Cox)	95	67	.586	1
	(W) San Francisco (Dusty Baker)	97	65	.599	11
2001	(W) ARIZONA (Bob Brenly)	92	70	.568	2
	(E) Atlanta (Bobby Cox)	88	74	.543	2
	(C) Houston (Larry Dierker)	93	69	.574	--
	(WC) St. Louis (Tony LaRussa)	93	69	.574	--
2002	(WC) SAN FRANCISCO (Dusty Baker)	95	66	.590	--
	(C) St. Louis (Tony LaRussa)	97	65	.599	13
	(E) Atlanta (Bobby Cox)	101	59	.631	19
	(W) Arizona (Bob Brenly)	98	64	.605	2.5
2003	(WC) FLORIDA (Jack McKeon*)	91	71	.562	--
	(C) Chicago (Dusty Baker)	88	74	.543	1
	(E) Atlanta (Bobby Cox)	101	61	.623	10
	(W) San Francisco (Felipe Alou)	100	61	.621	15.5
2004	(C) ST. LOUIS (Tony LaRussa)	105	57	.648	13
	(WC) Houston (Phil Garner*)	92	70	.568	--
	(E) Atlanta (Bobby Cox)	96	66	.593	10
	(W) Los Angeles (Jim Tracy)	93	69	.574	2
2005	(WC) HOUSTON (Phil Garner)	89	73	.549	--
	(C) St. Louis (Tony LaRussa)	100	62	.617	11
	(E) Atlanta (Bobby Cox)	90	72	.556	2
	(W) San Diego (Bruce Bochy)	82	80	.506	5
2006	(C) ST. LOUIS (Tony LaRussa)	83	78	.516	1.5
	(E) New York (Willie Randolph)	97	65	.599	12
	(W) San Diego (Bruce Bochy)	88	74	.543	--
	(WC) Los Angeles (Grady Little)	88	74	.543	--
2007	(WC) COLORADO (Clint Hurdle)	90	73	.552	--
	(W) Arizona (Bob Melvin)	90	72	.556	0.5
	(E) Philadelphia (Charlie Manuel)	89	73	.549	1
	(C) Chicago (Lou Piniella)	85	77	.525	2
2008	(E) PHILADELPHIA (Charlie Manuel)	92	70	.568	3
	(W) Los Angeles (Joe Torre)	84	78	.519	2
	(C) Chicago (Lou Piniella)	97	64	.602	7.5
	(WC) Milwaukee (Dale Sveum*)	90	72	.556	--
2009	(E) PHILADELPHIA (Charlie Manuel)	93	69	.574	6
	(W) Los Angeles (Joe Torre)	95	67	.586	3
	(C) St. Louis (Tony LaRussa)	91	71	.562	7.5
	(WC) Colorado (Jim Tracy*)	92	70	.568	--
2010	(W) SAN FRANCISCO (Bruce Bochy)	92	70	.568	2
	(E) Philadelphia (Charlie Manuel)	97	65	.599	6
	(C) Cincinnati (Dusty Baker)	91	71	.562	5
	(WC) Atlanta (Bobby Cox)	91	71	.562	--

NATIONAL LEAGUE POSTSEASON PARTICIPANTS (continued)

Championship Series Winner Capitalized; E = East; C = Central; W = West; WC = Wild Card; * = mid-season replacement

YEAR	CLUB (MANAGER)	WON	LOST	PCT.	GA
2011	(WC) ST. LOUIS (Tony LaRussa)	90	72	.556	--
	(C) Milwaukee (Ron Roenicke)	96	66	.593	6
	(E) Philadelphia (Charlie Manuel)	102	60	.630	13
	(W) Arizona (Kirk Gibson)	94	68	.580	8
2012	(W) SAN FRANCISCO (Bruce Bochy)	94	68	.580	8
	(WC) St. Louis (Mike Matheny)	88	74	.543	--
	(E) Washington (Davey Johnson)	98	64	.605	4
	(C) Cincinnati (Dusty Baker)	97	65	.599	9
	(WC) Atlanta (Fredi Gonzalez)	94	68	.580	--
2013	(C) ST. LOUIS (Mike Matheny)	97	65	.599	3
	(W) Los Angeles (Don Mattingly)	92	70	.568	11
	(E) Atlanta (Fredi Gonzalez)	96	66	.593	10
	(WC) Pittsburgh (Clint Hurdle)	94	68	.580	--
	(WC) Cincinnati (Dusty Baker)	90	72	.556	--
2014	(WC) SAN FRANCISCO (Bruce Bochy)	88	74	.543	--
	(C) St. Louis (Mike Matheny)	90	72	.556	2
	(E) Washington (Matt Williams)	96	66	.593	17
	(W) Los Angeles (Don Mattingly)	94	68	.580	6
	(WC) Pittsburgh (Clint Hurdle)	88	74	.543	--
2015	(E) NEW YORK (Terry Collins)	90	72	.556	7
	(WC) Chicago (Joe Maddon)	97	65	.599	--
	(C) St. Louis (Mike Matheny)	100	62	.617	2
	(W) Los Angeles (Don Mattingly)	92	70	.568	8
	(WC) Pittsburgh (Clint Hurdle)	98	64	.605	--
2016	(C) CHICAGO (Joe Maddon)	103	58	.640	17.5
	(W) Los Angeles (Dave Roberts)	91	71	.562	4
	(E) Washington (Dusty Baker)	95	67	.586	8
	(WC) San Francisco (Bruce Bochy)	87	75	.537	--
	(WC) New York (Terry Collins)	87	75	.537	--
2017	(W) LOS ANGELES (Dave Roberts)	104	58	.642	11
	(C) Chicago (Joe Maddon)	92	70	.568	6
	(E) Washington (Dusty Baker)	97	65	.599	20
	(WC) Arizona (Torey Lovullo)	93	69	.574	--
	(WC) Colorado (Bud Black)	87	75	.537	--
2018	(W) LOS ANGELES (Dave Roberts)	92	71	.564	1
	(C) Milwaukee (Craig Counsell)	96	67	.589	1
	(E) Atlanta (Brian Snitker)	90	72	.556	8
	(WC) Colorado (Bud Black)	91	72	.558	--
	(WC) Chicago (Joe Maddon)	95	68	.583	--
2019	(WC) WASHINGTON (Dave Martinez)	93	69	.574	--
	(C) St. Louis (Mike Shildt)	91	71	.562	2
	(W) Los Angeles (Dave Roberts)	106	56	.654	21
	(E) Atlanta (Brian Snitker)	97	65	.599	4
	(WC) Milwaukee (Craig Counsell)	89	73	.549	--
2020	(W) LOS ANGELES (Dave Roberts)	43	17	.717	6
	(E) Atlanta (Brian Snitker)	35	25	.583	4
	(W2) San Diego (Jayce Tingler)	37	23	.617	--
	(E2) Miami (Don Mattingly)	31	29	.517	--
	(C) Chicago (David Ross)	34	26	.567	3
	(C2) St. Louis (Mike Shildt)	30	28	.517	--
	(WC) Cincinnati (David Bell)	31	29	.517	--
	(WC) Milwaukee (Craig Counsell)	29	31	.483	--

CONSECUTIVE VICTORIES

SINGLE SEASON

NATIONAL LEAGUE

No.	Club	H	A	Year
26	New York	26	0	1916
21	Chicago	11	10	1880
	Chicago	18	3	1935
20	Providence	16	4	1884
18	Chicago	14	4	1885
	Boston	16	2	1891
	Baltimore	13	5	1894
	New York	13	5	1904
17	Boston	16	1	1897
	New York	14	3	1907
	New York	0	17	1916
16	Philadelphia	5	11	1887
	Philadelphia	14	2	1890
	Philadelphia	11	5	1892
	Pittsburgh	12	4	1909
	New York	11	5	1912
	New York	13	3	1951
15	Detroit	12	3	1886
	Pittsburgh	11	4	1903
	Brooklyn	3	12	1924
	Chicago	11	4	1936
	New York	8	7	1936
	Atlanta	9	6	2000

AMERICAN LEAGUE

No.	Club	H	A	Year
22	Cleveland	11	11	2017
20	Oakland	10	10	2002
19	Chicago	11	8	1906
	New York	6	13	1947
18	New York	3	15	1953
17	Washington	1	16	1912
	Philadelphia	5	12	1931
16	New York	12	4	1926
	Kansas City	9	7	1977
15	New York	12	3	1906
	Philadelphia	13	2	1913
	Boston	11	4	1946
	New York	9	6	1960
	Minnesota	8	7	1991
	Seattle	5	10	2001

AMERICAN ASSOCIATION

No.	Club	H	A	Year
15	St. Louis	15	0	1887

UNION ASSOCIATION

No.	Club	H	A	Year
20	St. Louis	16	4	1884

CONSECUTIVE LOSSES

SINGLE SEASON

NATIONAL LEAGUE

No.	Club	H	A	Year
24	Cleveland	5	19	1899
23	Pittsburgh	1	22	1890
	Philadelphia	6	17	1961
20	Louisville	0	20	1894
	Montreal	12	8	1969
19	Boston	3	16	1906
	Cincinnati	6	13	1914
18	Cincinnati	9	9	1876
	Louisville	0	18	1894
	St. Louis	4	14	1897
17	Washington	7	10	1894
	New York	7	10	1962
	Atlanta	8	9	1977
16	Troy	5	11	1882
	Buffalo	12	4	1885
	Cleveland	0	16	1899
	Boston	5	11	1907
	Boston	8	8	1911
	Brooklyn	0	16	1944
15	Louisville	10	5	1895
	St. Louis	11	4	1909
	Boston	0	15	1909
	Boston	0	15	1927
	Boston	0	15	1935
	New York	8	7	1963
	New York	6	9	1982

AMERICAN LEAGUE

No.	Club	H	A	Year
21	Baltimore	8	13	1988
20	Boston	19	1	1906
	Philadelphia	1	19	1916
	Philadelphia	3	17	1943
19	Detroit	9	10	1975
	Kansas City	8	11	2005
18	Philadelphia	0	18	1920
	Washington	8	10	1948
	Washington	3	15	1959
17	Boston	14	3	1926
16	Boston	9	7	1907
15	Boston	10	5	1927
	Philadelphia	10	5	1937
	Texas	5	10	1972
	Tampa Bay	9	6	2002

AMERICAN ASSOCIATION

No.	Club	H	A	Year
26	Louisville	5	21	1889
22	Philadelphia	6	16	1890
15	Baltimore	0	15	1882
	Washington	0	15	1884
	Louisville	0	15	1891

UNION ASSOCIATION

No.	Club	H	A	Year
15	Kansas City	3	12	1884

LONGEST GAMES, 18 OR MORE INNINGS

AMERICAN LEAGUE

25 Chi. 7 Mil. 6, May 8, 1984
24 Phil. 4 Bos. 1, Sept. 1, 1906
    Det. 1 Phil. 1, July 21, 1945
22 NY 9 Det. 7, June 24, 1962
    Wash. 6 Chi. 5, June 12, 1967
    Mil. 4 Minn. 3, May 12, 1972
    Minn. 5 Clev. 4, Aug. 31, 1993
21 Det. 6 Chi. 5, May 24, 1929
    Oak. 5 Wash. 3, June 4, 1971
    Chi. 6 Clev. 3, May 26, 1973
20 Phil. 4 Bos. 2, July 4, 1905
    Wash. 9 Minn. 7, Aug. 9, 1967
    NY 4 Bos. 3, Aug. 29(2g), 1967
    Bos. 5 Sea. 3, July 27, 1969
    Oak. 1 Cal. 0, July 9, 1971
    Wash. 8 Clev. 6, Sept. 14(2g), 1971
    Sea. 8 Bos. 7, Sept. 3, 1981
    Cal. 4 Sea. 3, Apr. 13, 1982
19 Wash. 5 Phil. 4, Sept. 27, 1912
    Chi. 5 Clev. 4, June 24, 1915
    Clev. 3 NY 2, May 24, 1918
    StL. 8 Wash. 6, Aug. 9, 1920
    Chi. 5 Bos. 4, July 13, 1951
    Clev. 4 StL. 3, July 1, 1952
    Clev. 3 Wash. 2, June 14(2g), 1963
    Balt. 7 Wash. 5, June 4, 1967
    KC 6 Det. 5, June 17(2g), 1967
    NY 3 Det. 3, Aug. 23(2g), 1968
    Oak. 5 Chi. 3, Aug. 10, 1972
    NY 5 Minn. 4, Aug. 25, 1976
    Clev. 8 Det. 4, Apr. 27, 1984
    Mil. 10 Chi. 9, May 1, 1991
    Bos. 7 Clev. 5, Apr. 11, 1992
    Sea. 5 Bos. 4, Aug. 1, 2000
    Chi. 6 Bos. 5, July 9, 2006
    Oak. 10 LA 8, Apr. 29, 2013
    LA 5 Bos. 4, Aug. 9, 2014
    Tor. 6 Det. 5, Aug. 10, 2014
    Bos. 6 NY 5, Apr. 10, 2015
    Clev. 2 Tor. 1, July 1, 2016
    Bos. 3 Tor. 2 Sept. 5, 2017
18 Chi. 6 NY 4, June 25, 1903
    Det. 0 Wash. 0, July 16, 1909
    Wash. 1 Chi. 0, May 15, 1918
    Det. 7 Wash. 6, Aug. 4(2g), 1918
    Bos. 12 NY 11, Sept. 5(1g), 1927
    Phil. 18 Clev. 17, July 10, 1932
    NY 3 Chi. 3, Aug. 21, 1933
    Wash. 1 Chi. 0, June 8(1g), 1947
    Wash. 5 StL. 5, June 20, 1952
    Chi. 1 Balt. 1, Aug. 6, 1959
    NY 7 Bos. 6, Apr. 16, 1967
    Minn. 3 NY 2, July 26(2g), 1967
    Balt. 3 Bos. 2, Aug. 25, 1968
    Minn. 11 Sea. 7, July 19, 1969
    Oak. 9 Balt. 8, Aug. 9(1g), 1969
    Minn. 8 Oak. 6, Sept. 6, 1969
    Wash. 2 NY 1, Apr. 22, 1970
    Tex. 4 KC 3, May 17, 1972
    Det. 4 Clev. 3, June 9(2g), 1982
    NY 5 Det. 4, Sept. 11, 1988
    KC 4 Tex. 3, June 6, 1991
    Bos. 4 Det. 3, June 5, 2001
    Tex. 8 Bos. 7, Aug. 25, 2001
    Tex. 9 Sea. 7, June 24, 2004
    Oak. 6 Minn. 5, Aug. 8, 2004
    Tor. 2 LA 1, July 28, 2005
    Balt. 4 Sea. 2, Sept. 18, 2012
    Tor. 4 Tex. 3, June 8, 2013
    Oak. 3 NY 2, June 13, 2013
    TB 5 Balt. 4, Sept. 20, 2013
    TB 5 Minn. 2, June 27, 2019

NATIONAL LEAGUE

26 Brk. 1 Bos. 1, May 1, 1920
25 StL. 4 NY 3, Sept. 11 1974
24 Hou. 1 NY 0, Apr. 15, 1968
23 Brk. 2 Bos. 2, June 27, 1939
    SF 8 NY 6, May 31(2g), 1964
22 Brk. 6 Pitt. 5, Aug. 22, 1917
    Chi. 4 Bos. 3, May 17 1927
    Hou. 5 LA 4, June 3, 1989
    LA 1 Mtl. 0, Aug. 23, 1989
    Col. 2 SD 1, Apr. 17, 2008

21 NY 3 Pitt. 1, July 17, 1914
    Chi. 2 Phil. 1, July 17, 1918
    Pitt. 2 Bos. 0, Aug. 1, 1918
    SF 1 Cin. 0, Sept. 1, 1967
    Hou. 2 SD 1, Sept. 24(1g), 1971
    SD 11 Mtl. 8, Aug. 15, 1977
    LA 2 Chi. 1, Aug. 17, 1982
20 Chi. 7 Cin. 7, June 30, 1892
    Chi. 2 Phil. 1, Aug. 24, 1905
    Brk. 9 Phil. 9, Apr. 30, 1919
    StL. 8 Chi. 7, Aug. 28, 1930
    Brk. 6 Bos. 2, July 5, 1940
    Phil. 5 Atl. 4, May 4, 1973
    Pitt. 5 Chi. 4, July 6, 1980
    Hou. 3 SD 1, Aug. 15, 1980
    Phil. 7 LA 6, July 7, 1993
    StL. 7 Fla. 6, Apr. 27, 2003
    NY 2 StL. 1, Apr. 17, 2010
    Mia. 2 NY 1, June 8, 2013
19 Chi. 3 Pitt. 2, June 22, 1902
    Pitt. 7 Bos. 6, July 31, 1912
    Chi. 4 Brk. 3, June 17, 1915
    StL. 8 Phil. 8, June 13, 1918
    Bos. 2 Brk. 1, May 3, 1920
    Chi. 3 Bos. 2, Aug. 17, 1932
    Brk. 9 Chi. 9, May 17, 1939
    Cin. 0 Brk. 0, Sept. 11, 1946
    Phil. 8 Cin. 7, Sept. 15(2g), 1950
    Pitt. 4 Mil. 3, July 19, 1955
    Cin. 2 LA 1, Aug. 8, 1972
    NY 7 LA 3, May 24, 1973
    Pitt. 4 SD 3, Aug. 25, 1979
    NY 16 Atl. 13, July 4, 1985
    Mtl. 6 Hou. 3, July 7, 1985
    Atl. 7 StL. 5, May 14, 1988
    Phil. 5 Cin. 4, May 25, 2011
    Atl. 4 Pitt. 3, July 26, 2011
    Pitt. 6 StL. 3, Aug. 19, 2012
    Ari. 3 StL. 2, Sept. 24, 2019
18 Prov. 1 Det. 0, Aug. 17, 1882
    Brk. 7 StL.7, Aug. 17, 1902
    Chi. 2 StL. 1, June 24, 1905
    Pitt. 3 Chi. 2, June 28(2g), 1916
    Phil. 10 Brk. 9, June 1, 1919
    NY 9 Pitt. 8, July 7, 1922
    Chi. 7 Bos. 2, May 14, 1927
    NY 1 StL. 0, July 2(1g), 1933
    StL. 8 Cin. 6, July 1(1g), 1934
    Chi. 10 Cin. 8, Aug. 9(1g), 1942
    Phil. 4 Pitt. 3, June 9, 1949
    Cin. 7 Chi. 6, Sept. 7, 1951
    NY 0 Phil. 0, Oct. 2(2g), 1965
    Cin. 3 Chi. 2, July 19, 1966
    Phil. 2 Cin. 1, May 21, 1967
    Pitt. 1 SD 0, June 7(2g), 1972
    NY 3 Phil. 2, Aug. 1(1g), 1972
    Mtl. 5 Chi. 4, June 27(2g), 1973
    Chi. 8 Mtl. 7, June 28(1g), 1974
    NY 4 Mtl. 3, Sept. 16, 1975
    Pitt. 2 Chi. 1, Aug. 20, 1977
    Chi. 9 Cin. 8, May 10, 1979
    Hou. 3 NY 2, June 18, 1979
    SD 8 NY 6, Aug. 26, 1980
    StL. 3 Hou. 1, May 27, 1983
    Pitt. 4 SF 3, July 13(2g), 1984
    Atl. 3 LA 2, Sept. 6, 1984
    NY 5 Pitt. 4, Apr. 28, 1985
    SF 5 Atl. 4, June 11, 1985
    Hou. 8 Chi. 7, Sept. 2, 1986
    Pitt. 5 Chi. 4, Aug. 6, 1989
    Atl. 5 LA 3, Aug. 3, 1996
    Ari. 1 SF 0, May 29, 2001
    Pitt. 8 Hou. 7, May 27, 2006
    Chi. 8 Hou. 6, Aug. 15, 2006
    Ari. 2 Col. 1, Aug. 15, 2006
    SD 12 Cin. 9, May 25, 2008
    Ari. 9 SD 6, June 7, 2009
    Ari. 12 Phil. 7, Aug. 24, 2013
    NY 3 StL. 1, July 19, 2015
    Pitt. 2 Wash. 1, July 17, 2016
    SF 3 Col. 2, Apr. 12, 2019
    Mil. 4 NY 3, May 4, 2019

INTERLEAGUE

18 AL:NY 5 NL:Chi. 4 May 7, 2017

AMERICAN LEAGUE CLUB HOME RUNS

(* = Leader)

(1901 Milwaukee total under StL.)

	BALT	BOS	CHI	CLEV	DET	KC	NY	PHIL	STL	WASH	TOTAL
1901	24	*37	32	12	29	-	-	35	26	33	228
1902	33	42	14	33	22	-	-	38	29	*47	258
1903	-	*48	14	31	12	-	18	32	12	17	184
1904	-	26	14	27	11	-	27	*31	10	10	156
1905	-	*29	11	18	13	-	23	24	16	22	156
1906	-	13	7	12	10	-	17	*32	20	26	137
1907	-	18	5	11	11	-	15	*22	10	12	104
1908	-	14	3	18	19	-	13	*21	20	8	116
1909	-	20	4	10	19	-	16	*21	10	9	109
1910	-	*43	7	9	28	-	20	19	12	9	147
1911	-	*35	20	20	30	-	25	*35	17	16	198
1912	-	*29	17	11	19	-	18	22	19	20	155
1913	-	17	23	16	24	-	8	*33	18	19	158
1914	-	18	19	10	25	-	12	*29	17	18	148
1915	-	14	25	20	23	-	*31	16	19	12	160
1916	-	14	17	16	17	-	*35	19	14	12	144
1917	-	14	18	13	25	-	*27	17	15	4	133
1918	-	15	8	9	13	-	20	*22	5	4	96
1919	-	33	25	24	23	-	*45	35	31	24	240
1920	-	22	37	35	30	-	*115	44	50	36	369
1921	-	17	35	42	58	-	*134	82	67	42	477
1922	-	45	45	32	54	-	95	*111	98	45	525
1923	-	34	42	59	41	-	*105	53	82	26	442
1924	-	30	41	41	35	-	*98	63	67	22	397
1925	-	41	38	52	50	-	*110	76	*110	56	533
1926	-	32	32	27	36	-	*121	61	72	43	424
1927	-	28	36	26	51	-	*158	56	55	29	439
1928	-	38	24	34	62	-	*133	89	63	40	483
1929	-	28	37	62	110	-	*142	122	46	48	595
1930	-	47	63	72	82	-	*152	125	75	57	673
1931	-	37	27	71	43	-	*155	118	76	49	576
1932	-	53	36	78	80	-	160	*172	67	61	707
1933	-	50	43	50	57	-	*144	139	64	60	607
1934	-	51	71	100	74	-	135	*144	62	51	688
1935	-	69	74	93	106	-	104	*112	73	32	663
1936	-	86	60	123	94	-	*182	72	79	62	758
1937	-	100	67	103	150	-	*174	94	71	47	806
1938	-	98	67	113	137	-	*174	98	92	85	864
1939	-	124	64	85	124	-	*166	98	91	44	796
1940	-	145	73	101	134	-	*155	105	118	52	883
1941	-	124	47	103	81	-	*151	85	91	52	734
1942	-	103	25	50	76	-	*108	33	98	40	533
1943	-	57	33	55	77	-	*100	26	78	47	473
1944	-	69	23	70	60	-	*96	36	72	33	459
1945	-	50	22	65	77	-	*93	33	63	27	430
1946	-	109	37	79	108	-	*136	40	84	60	653
1947	-	103	53	112	103	-	*115	61	90	42	679
1948	-	121	55	*155	78	-	139	68	63	31	710
1949	-	*131	43	112	88	-	115	82	117	81	769
1950	-	161	93	*164	114	-	159	100	106	76	973
1951	-	127	86	*140	104	-	*140	102	86	54	839
1952	-	113	80	*148	103	-	129	89	82	50	794
1953	-	101	74	*160	108	-	139	116	112	69	879
1954	52	123	94	*156	90	-	133	94	-	81	823
1955	54	137	116	148	130	121	*175	-	-	80	961
1956	91	139	128	153	150	112	*190	-	-	112	1075
1957	87	153	106	140	116	*166	145	-	-	111	1024
1958	108	155	101	161	109	138	*164	-	-	121	1057
1959	109	125	97	*167	160	117	153	-	-	163	1091
1960	123	124	112	127	150	110	*193	-	-	147	1086

AMERICAN LEAGUE CLUB HOME RUNS

(* = Leader)

(1969 Seattle listed under MIL.)

	ANA	BALT	BOS	CHI	CLEV	DET	KC	MIL	MINN	NY	OAK	SEA	TEX	TOR	WASH	TOTAL
1961	189	149	112	138	150	130	90	-	167	*240	-	-	-	-	119	1534
1962	137	156	146	92	180	*209	116	-	185	199	-	-	-	-	132	1552
1963	95	146	171	114	169	148	95	-	*225	188	-	-	-	-	138	1489
1964	102	162	186	106	164	157	166	-	*221	162	-	-	-	-	125	1551
1965	92	125	*165	125	156	162	110	-	150	149	-	-	-	-	136	1370
1966	122	175	145	87	155	*179	110	-	144	162	-	-	-	-	126	1365
1967	114	138	*158	89	131	152	69	-	131	100	-	-	-	-	115	1197
1968	83	133	125	71	75	*185	-	-	105	109	94	-	-	-	124	1104
1969	88	175	*197	112	119	182	98	125	163	94	148	-	-	-	148	1649
1970	114	179	*203	123	183	148	97	126	153	111	171	-	-	-	138	1746
1971	96	158	161	138	109	*179	80	124	116	97	160	-	-	-	86	1484
1972	78	100	124	108	91	122	78	88	93	103	*134	-	56	-	-	1175
1973	93	119	147	111	*158	157	114	145	120	131	147	-	110	-	-	1552
1974	95	116	109	*135	131	131	89	120	111	101	132	-	99	-	-	1369
1975	55	124	134	94	*153	125	118	146	124	110	151	-	134	-	-	1465
1976	63	119	*134	73	85	101	65	88	81	120	113	-	80	-	-	1122
1977	131	148	*213	192	100	166	146	125	123	184	117	133	135	100	-	2013
1978	108	154	172	106	106	129	98	*173	82	125	100	97	132	98	-	1680
1979	164	181	*194	127	138	164	116	185	112	150	108	132	140	95	-	2006
1980	106	156	162	91	89	143	115	*203	99	189	137	104	124	126	-	1844
1981	97	88	90	76	39	65	61	96	47	100	*104	89	49	61	-	1062
1982	186	179	136	136	109	177	132	*216	148	161	149	130	115	106	-	2080
1983	154	*168	142	157	86	156	109	132	141	153	121	111	106	167	-	1903
1984	150	160	181	172	123	*187	117	96	114	130	158	129	120	143	-	1980
1985	153	*214	162	146	116	202	154	101	141	176	155	171	129	158	-	2178
1986	167	169	144	121	157	*198	137	127	196	188	163	158	184	181	-	2290
1987	172	211	174	173	187	*225	168	163	196	196	199	161	194	215	-	2634
1988	124	137	124	132	134	143	121	113	151	148	156	148	112	*158	-	1901
1989	*145	129	108	94	127	116	101	126	117	130	127	134	122	142	-	1718
1990	147	132	106	106	110	*172	100	128	100	147	164	107	110	167	-	1796
1991	115	170	126	139	79	*209	117	116	140	147	159	126	177	133	-	1953
1992	88	148	84	110	127	*182	75	82	104	163	142	149	159	163	-	1776
1993	114	157	114	162	141	178	125	125	121	178	158	161	*181	159	-	2074
1994	120	139	120	121	*167	161	100	99	103	139	113	153	124	115	-	1774
1995	186	173	175	146	*207	159	119	128	120	122	169	182	138	140	-	2164
1996	192	*257	209	195	218	204	123	178	118	162	243	245	221	177	-	2742
1997	161	196	185	158	220	176	158	135	132	161	197	*264	187	147	-	2477

	ANA	BALT	BOS	CHI	CLEV	DET	KC	MINN	NY	OAK	SEA	TEX	TOR	TB	TOTAL
1998	147	214	205	198	198	165	134	115	207	149	*234	201	221	111	2499
1999	158	203	176	162	209	212	151	105	193	235	*244	230	212	145	2635
2000	236	184	167	216	221	177	150	116	205	239	198	173	*244	162	2688
2001	158	136	198	214	212	139	152	164	203	199	169	*246	195	121	2506
2002	152	165	177	217	192	124	140	167	223	205	152	*230	187	133	2464
2003	150	152	238	220	158	153	162	155	230	176	139	*239	190	137	2499
2004	162	169	222	*242	184	201	150	191	*242	189	136	227	145	145	2605

	LA	BALT	BOS	CHI	CLEV	DET	KC	HOU	MINN	NY	OAK	SEA	TEX	TOR	TB	TOTAL
2005	147	189	199	200	207	168	126	-	134	229	155	130	*260	136	157	2437
2006	159	164	192	*236	196	203	124	-	143	210	175	172	183	199	190	2456
2007	123	142	166	190	178	177	102	-	118	*201	171	153	179	165	187	2252
2008	159	172	173	*235	171	200	120	-	111	180	125	124	194	126	180	2270
2009	173	160	212	184	161	183	144	-	172	*244	135	160	224	209	199	2560
2010	155	133	211	177	128	152	121	-	142	201	109	101	162	*257	160	2209
2011	155	191	203	154	154	169	129	-	103	*222	114	109	210	186	172	2271
2012	187	214	165	211	136	163	131	-	131	*245	195	149	200	198	175	2500
2013	164	*212	178	148	171	176	112	148	151	144	186	188	176	185	165	2504
2014	155	*211	123	155	142	155	95	163	128	147	146	136	111	177	117	2161
2015	176	217	161	136	141	151	139	230	156	212	146	198	172	*232	167	2634
2016	156	*253	208	168	185	211	147	198	200	183	169	223	215	221	216	2953
2017	186	232	168	186	212	187	193	238	206	*241	234	200	237	222	228	3170
2018	214	188	208	182	216	135	155	205	166	*267	227	176	194	217	150	2900
2019	220	213	245	182	223	149	162	288	*307	306	257	239	223	247	217	3478
2020	85	77	81	*96	59	62	68	69	91	94	71	60	62	88	80	1143

NATIONAL LEAGUE CLUB HOME RUNS

(* = Leader)

	BOS	BRK	CHI	CIN	LA	MIL	NY	PHIL	PITT	STL	SF	TOTAL
1900	*48	26	33	33	-	-	23	29	26	36	-	254
1901	28	32	18	38	-	-	19	24	28	*39	-	226
1902	14	*19	6	18	-	-	6	5	18	10	-	96
1903	25	15	9	28	-	-	20	12	*34	8	-	151
1904	24	15	22	21	-	-	*31	23	15	24	-	175
1905	17	29	12	27	-	-	*39	16	22	20	-	182
1906	16	*25	20	16	-	-	15	12	12	10	-	126
1907	22	18	13	15	-	-	*23	12	19	18	-	140
1908	17	*28	19	14	-	-	20	11	25	17	-	151
1909	14	16	20	22	-	-	*26	12	25	15	-	150
1910	31	25	*34	23	-	-	31	22	33	15	-	214
1911	37	28	54	21	-	-	41	*60	49	26	-	316
1912	35	32	42	21	-	-	*48	42	39	27	-	286
1913	32	39	59	27	-	-	31	*73	35	15	-	311
1914	35	31	42	16	-	-	30	*62	18	33	-	267
1915	17	14	53	15	-	-	24	*58	24	20	-	225
1916	22	28	*46	14	-	-	42	42	20	25	-	239
1917	22	25	17	26	-	-	*39	38	9	26	-	202
1918	13	10	21	15	-	-	13	25	15	*27	-	139
1919	24	25	21	20	-	-	40	*42	17	18	-	207
1920	23	28	34	18	-	-	46	*64	16	32	-	261
1921	61	59	37	20	-	-	75	*88	37	83	-	460
1922	32	56	42	45	-	-	80	*116	52	107	-	530
1923	32	62	90	45	-	-	85	*112	49	63	-	538
1924	25	72	66	36	-	-	*95	94	44	67	-	499
1925	41	64	86	44	-	-	*114	100	78	109	-	636
1926	16	40	66	35	-	-	73	75	44	*90	-	439
1927	37	39	74	29	-	-	*109	57	54	84	-	483
1928	52	66	92	32	-	-	*118	85	52	113	-	610
1929	33	99	139	34	-	-	136	*153	60	100	-	754
1930	66	122	*171	74	-	-	143	126	86	104	-	892
1931	34	71	84	21	-	-	*101	81	41	60	-	493
1932	63	110	69	47	-	-	116	*122	48	76	-	651
1933	54	62	72	34	-	-	*82	60	39	57	-	460
1934	83	79	101	55	-	-	*126	56	52	104	-	656
1935	75	59	88	73	-	-	*123	92	66	86	-	662
1936	67	33	76	82	-	-	97	*103	60	88	-	606
1937	63	37	96	73	-	-	*111	103	47	94	-	624
1938	54	61	65	110	-	-	*125	40	65	91	-	611
1939	56	78	91	98	-	-	*116	49	63	98	-	649
1940	59	93	86	89	-	-	91	75	76	*119	-	688
1941	48	*101	99	64	-	-	95	64	56	70	-	597
1942	68	62	75	66	-	-	*109	44	54	60	-	538
1943	39	39	52	43	-	-	*81	66	42	70	-	432
1944	79	56	71	51	-	-	93	55	70	*100	-	575
1945	101	57	57	56	-	-	*114	56	72	64	-	577
1946	44	55	56	65	-	-	*121	80	60	81	-	562
1947	85	83	71	95	-	-	*221	60	156	115	-	886
1948	95	91	87	104	-	-	*164	91	108	105	-	845
1949	103	*152	97	86	-	-	147	122	126	102	-	935
1950	148	*194	161	99	-	-	133	125	138	102	-	1100
1951	130	*184	103	88	-	-	179	108	137	95	-	1024
1952	110	*153	107	104	-	-	151	93	92	97	-	907
1953	-	*208	137	166	-	156	176	115	99	140	-	1197
1954	-	*186	159	147	-	139	*186	102	76	119	-	1114
1955	-	*201	164	181	-	182	169	132	91	143	-	1263
1956	-	179	142	*221	-	177	145	121	110	124	-	1219
1957	-	147	147	187	-	*199	157	117	92	132	-	1178
1958	-	-	*182	123	172	167	-	124	134	111	170	1183
1959	-	-	163	161	148	*177	-	113	112	118	167	1159
1960	-	-	119	140	126	*170	-	99	120	138	130	1042
1961	-	-	176	158	157	*188	-	103	128	103	183	1196

NATIONAL LEAGUE CLUB HOME RUNS

(* = Leader)

	ATL	CHI	CIN	HOU	LA	MIL	MTL	NY	PHIL	PITT	STL	SD	SF	TOTAL
1962	-	126	167	105	140	181	-	139	142	108	137	-	*204	1449
1963	-	127	122	62	110	139	-	96	126	108	128	-	*197	1215
1964	-	145	130	70	79	159	-	103	130	121	109	-	*165	1211
1965	-	134	183	97	78	*196	-	107	144	111	109	-	159	1318
1966	*207	140	149	112	108	-	-	98	117	158	108	-	181	1378
1967	*158	128	109	93	82	-	-	83	103	91	115	-	140	1102
1968	80	*130	106	66	67	-	-	81	100	80	73	-	108	891
1969	141	142	*171	104	97	-	125	109	137	119	90	99	136	1470
1970	160	179	*191	129	87	-	136	120	101	130	113	172	165	1683
1971	153	128	138	71	95	-	88	98	123	*154	95	96	104	1379
1972	144	133	124	134	98	-	91	105	98	110	70	102	*150	1359
1973	*206	117	137	134	110	-	125	85	134	154	75	112	161	1550
1974	120	110	135	110	*139	-	86	96	95	114	83	99	93	1280
1975	107	95	124	84	118	-	98	101	125	*138	81	78	84	1233
1976	82	105	*141	66	91	-	94	102	110	110	63	64	85	1113
1977	139	111	181	114	*191	-	138	88	186	133	96	120	134	1631
1978	123	72	136	70	*149	-	121	86	133	115	79	75	117	1276
1979	126	135	132	49	*183	-	143	74	119	148	100	93	125	1427
1980	144	107	113	75	*148	-	114	61	117	116	101	67	80	1243
1981	64	57	64	45	*82	-	81	57	69	55	50	32	63	719
1982	*146	102	82	74	138	-	133	97	112	134	67	81	133	1299
1983	130	140	107	97	*146	-	102	112	125	121	83	93	142	1398
1984	111	136	106	79	102	-	96	107	*147	98	75	109	112	1278
1985	126	*150	114	121	129	-	118	134	141	80	87	109	115	1424
1986	138	*155	144	125	130	-	110	148	154	111	58	136	114	1523
1987	152	*209	192	122	125	-	120	192	169	131	94	113	205	1824
1988	96	113	122	96	99	-	107	*152	106	110	71	94	113	1279
1989	128	124	128	97	89	-	100	*147	123	95	73	120	141	1365
1990	162	136	125	94	129	-	114	*172	103	138	73	123	152	1521
1991	141	159	*164	79	108	-	95	117	111	126	68	121	141	1430
1992	*138	104	99	96	72	-	102	93	118	106	94	135	105	1262

	ATL	CHI	CIN	COL	FLA	HOU	LA	MTL	NY	PHIL	PITT	STL	SD	SF	TOTAL
1993	*169	161	137	142	94	138	130	122	158	156	110	118	153	168	1956
1994	*137	109	124	125	94	120	115	108	117	80	80	108	92	123	1532
1995	168	158	161	*200	144	109	140	118	125	94	125	107	116	152	1917
1996	197	175	191	*221	150	129	150	148	147	132	138	142	147	153	2220
1997	174	127	142	*239	136	133	174	172	153	116	129	144	152	172	2163

	ARI	ATL	CHI	CIN	COL	FLA	HOU	LA	MIL	MTL	NY	PHIL	PITT	STL	SD	SF	TOTAL
1998	159	215	212	138	183	114	166	159	152	147	136	126	107	*223	167	161	2565
1999	216	197	189	209	*223	128	168	187	165	163	181	161	171	194	153	188	2893
2000	179	179	183	200	161	160	*249	211	177	178	198	144	168	235	157	226	3005
2001	208	174	194	176	213	166	208	206	209	131	147	164	161	199	161	*235	2952
2002	165	164	*200	169	152	146	167	155	139	162	160	165	142	175	136	198	2595
2003	152	*235	172	182	198	157	191	124	196	144	124	166	163	196	128	180	2708
2004	135	178	*235	194	202	148	187	203	135	151	185	215	142	214	139	183	2846

	ARI	ATL	CHI	CIN	COL	FLA	HOU	LA	MIL	WASH	NY	PHIL	PITT	STL	SD	SF	TOTAL
2005	191	184	194	*222	150	128	161	149	175	117	175	167	139	170	130	128	2580
2006	160	*222	166	217	157	182	174	153	180	164	200	216	141	184	161	163	2840
2007	171	176	151	204	171	201	167	129	*231	123	177	213	148	141	171	131	2705
2008	159	130	184	187	160	208	167	137	198	117	172	*214	153	174	154	94	2608
2009	173	149	161	158	190	159	142	145	182	156	95	*224	125	160	141	122	2482
2010	180	139	149	*188	173	152	108	120	182	149	128	166	126	150	132	162	2404
2011	172	173	148	183	163	149	95	117	*185	154	108	153	107	162	91	121	2281

	ARI	ATL	CHI	CIN	COL	MIA	HOU	LA	MIL	WASH	NY	PHIL	PITT	STL	SD	SF	TOTAL
2012	165	149	137	172	166	130	146	116	*202	194	139	158	170	159	121	103	2434
2013	130	*181	172	155	159	95	-	138	157	161	130	140	161	125	146	107	2157
2014	118	123	157	131	*186	122	-	134	150	152	125	125	156	105	109	132	2025
2015	154	100	171	167	186	120	-	*187	145	177	177	130	140	137	148	136	2275
2016	190	122	199	164	204	128	-	189	194	203	218	161	153	*225	177	130	2657
2017	220	165	223	219	192	194	-	221	*224	215	*224	174	151	196	189	128	2935
2018	176	175	167	172	210	128	-	*235	218	191	170	186	157	205	162	133	2685
2019	220	249	256	227	224	146	-	*279	250	231	242	215	163	210	219	167	3298
2020	58	103	74	90	63	60	-	*118	75	66	86	82	59	51	95	81	1161

MANAGERS – AMERICAN LEAGUE

*(*also listed in NL)*

*Acta, Manny Clev. 2010-12
Adcock, Joe Clev. 1967
Alomar, Sandy Jr. Clev. 2012
*Altobelli, Joe Balt. 1983-85
*Anderson, Sparky Det. 1979-95
Appling, Luke KC 1967
Armour, Bill Clev. 1902-04
    Det. 1905-06
Aspromonte, Ken Clev. 1972-74
Ausmus, Brad Det. 2014-17
    LA 2019
Austin, Jimmy StL. 1923
Baker, Del Det. 1933, 38-42
*Baker, Dusty Hou. 2020-
Baldelli, Rocco Minn. 2019-
*Bamberger, George Mil. 1978-80; 85-86
Banister, Jeff Tex. 2015-18
Barrow, Ed Det. 1903-04
    Bos. 1918-20
Barry, Jack Bos. 1917
Bauer, Hank KC 1961-62
    Balt. 1964-68
    Oak. 1969
*Bell, Buddy Det. 1996-98
    KC 2005-07
*Berra, Yogi NY 1964; 84-85
Bevington, Terry Chi. 1995-97
Birmingham, Joe Clev. 1912-15
Blackburne, Lena Chi. 1928-29
Bluege, Ossie Wash. 1943-47
Bogar, Tim Tex. 2014
Boone, Aaron NY 2018-
*Boone, Bob KC 1995-97
*Boros, Steve Oak. 1983-84
Bottomley, Jim StL. 1937
*Boudreau, Lou Clev. 1942-50
    Bos. 1952-54
    KC 1955-57
*Bragan, Bobby Clev. 1958
*Bristol, Dave Mil. 1970-72
Brown, Daren Sea. 2010
*Burke, Jimmy StL. 1918-20
*Bush, Donie Wash. 1923
    Chi. 1930-31
*Callahan, Nixey Chi. 1903-04; 12-14
Cantillon, Joe Wash. 1907-09
Carrigan, Bill Bos. 1913-16; 27-29
Cash, Kevin TB 2015-
*Chance, Frank NY 1913-14
    Bos. 1923
Chase, Hal NY 1910-11
Cobb, Ty Det. 1921-26
Cochrane, Mickey Det. 1934-38
Collins, Eddie Chi. 1925-26
Collins, Jimmy Bos. 1901-06
Collins, Shano Bos. 1931-32
*Collins, Terry Ana. 1997-99
Cooper, Don Chi. 2011
Cora, Alex Bos. 2018-19
*Corrales, Pat Tex. 1978-80
    Clev. 1983-87
Corriden, Red Chi. 1950
Cottier, Chuck Sea. 1984-86
*Cox, Bobby Tor. 1982-85
*Craft, Harry KC 1957-59
Crandall, Del Mil. 1972-75
    Sea. 1983-84
Cronin, Joe Wash. 1933-34
    Bos. 1935-47
*Dark, Alvin KC /Oak. 1966-67; 74-75
    Clev. 1968-71
Davis, Harry Clev. 1912
Dent, Bucky NY 1989-90
Dickey, Bill NY 1946
Doby, Larry Chi. 1978
*Donovan, Patsy Wash. 1904
    Bos. 1910-11
*Donovan, Wild Bill NY 1915-17
Dressen, Chuck Wash. 1955-57
    Det. 1963-66
*Duffy, Hugh Mil. 1901
    Chi. 1910-11
    Bos. 1921-22
Dwyer, Frank Det. 1902
*Dykes, Jimmy Chi. 1934-46
    Phil. 1951-53
    Balt. 1954
    Det. 1959-60
    Clev. 1960-61

Edwards, Doc Clev. 1987-89
Elberfeld, Kid NY 1908
Elliot, Bob KC 1960
Ermer, Cal Minn. 1967-68
*Evers, Johnny Chi. 1924
Farrell, John Tor. 2011-12
    Bos. 2013-17
Farrell, Kerby Clev. 1957
Ferraro, Mike Clev. 1983
    KC 1986
*Fletcher, Art NY 1929
Fohl, Lee Clev. 1915-19
    StL. 1921-23
    Bos. 1924-26
Fonseca, Lew Chi. 1932-34
*Francona, Terry Bos. 2004-11
    Clev. 2013-
*Fregosi, Jim Cal. 1978-81
    Chi. 1986-88
    Tor. 1999-2000
*Frey, Jim KC 1980-81
Garcia, Dave Cal. 1977-78
    Clev. 1979-82
Gardenhire, Ron Minn. 2002-14
    Det. 2018-20
Gardner, Billy Minn. 1981-85
    KC 1987
*Garner, Phil Mil. 1992-97
    Det. 2000-02
Gaston, Cito Tor. 1989-97, 2008-10
Geren, Bob Oak. 2007-11
Gibbons, John Tor. 2004-08; 13-18
*Girardi, Joe NY 2008-17
Gleason, Kid Chi. 1919-23
Gordon, Joe Clev. 1958-60
    Det. 1960
    KC 1961; 69
Goryl, John Minn. 1980-81
Grammas, Alex Mil. 1976-77
*Green, Dallas NY 1989
*Griffith, Clark Chi. 1901-02
    NY 1903-08
    Wash. 1912-20
*Guillen, Ozzie Chi. 2004-11
Gutteridge, Don Chi. 1969-70
*Haney, Fred StL. 1939-41
Hargrove, Mike Clev. 1991-99
    Balt. 2000-03
    Sea. 2005-07
Harrah, Toby Tex. 1992
*Harris, Lum Balt. 1961
*Harris, Bucky Det. 1929-33; 1955-56
    Bos. 1934
    NY 1947-48
Hart, John Clev. 1989
Hartsfield, Roy Tor. 1977-79
*Herman, Billy Bos. 1965-66
*Herzog, Whitey Tex. 1973
    Cal. 1974
    KC 1975-79
Higgins, Pinky Bos. 1955-62
Hillman, Trey KC 2008-10
*Hinch, A.J. Hou. 2015-19
*Hitchcock, Billy Balt. 1962-63
Hobson, Butch Bos. 1992-1994
*Hodges, Gil Wash. 1963-67
*Hornsby, Rogers StL. 1933-37; 52
Houk, Ralph NY 1961-63; 66-73
    Det. 1974-78
    Bos. 1981-84
*Howe, Art Oak. 1996-2002
*Howley, Dan StL. 1927-29
Howser, Dick NY 1980
    KC 1981-86
Huff, George Bos. 1907
*Huggins, Miller NY 1918-29
Hunter, Billy Tex. 1977-78
*Hutchinson, Fred Det. 1952-54
*Hyde, Brandon Balt. 2019-
Jennings, Hughie Det. 1907-20
Johnson, Darrell Bos. 1974-76
    Sea. 1977-80
    Tex. 1982
*Johnson, Davey Balt. 1996-97
Johnson, Tim Tor. 1998
Johnson, Walter Wash. 1929-32
    Clev. 1933-35
Jones, Fielder Chi. 1904-08
    StL. 1916-18
Joost, Eddie Phil. 1954
Jurges, Billy Bos. 1959-60

Kasko, Eddie Bos. 1970-73
*Keane, Johnny NY 1965-66
Kelly, Tom Minn. 1986-2001
*Kennedy, Bob Oak. 1968
Kennedy, Kevin Tex. 1993-1994
    Bos. 1995-96
Kerrigan, Joe Bos. 2001
Kessinger, Don Chi. 1979
*Killefer, Bill StL. 1930-33
*King, Clyde NY 1982
Kittredge, Malachi Wash. 1904
Kuenn, Harvey Mil. 1982-83
Kuhel, Joe Wash. 1948-49
Lachemann, Marcel Cal. 1994-96
*Lachemann, Rene Sea. 1981-83
    Mil. 1984
Lajoie, Nap Clev. 1905-09
*Lake, Fred Bos. 1908-09
*Lamont, Gene Chi. 1992-95
*LaRussa, Tony Chi. 1979-86
    Oak. 1986-95
Lavagetto, Cookie Wash./Minn.1957-61
Lawless, Tom Hou. 2014
*Lefebvre, Jim Sea. 1989-91
Lemon, Jim Wash. 1968
Lemon, Bob KC 1970-72
    Chi. 1977-78
    NY 1978-79; 81-82
*Leyland, Jim Det. 2006-13
Lipon, Johnny Clev. 1971
*Little, Grady Bos. 2002-03
*Loftus, Tom Wash. 1902-03
Lopat, Ed KC 1963-64
Lopez, Al Clev. 1951-56
    Chi. 1957-65; 68-69
Lowe, Bobby Det. 1904
*Lucchesi, Frank Tex. 1975-77
Lyons, Ted Chi. 1946-48
*Macha, Ken Oak. 2003-06
*Mack, Connie Phil. 1901-50
*Maddon, Joe Ana./LA 1999; 2020-
    TB 2006-14
Manning, Jimmy Wash. 1901
*Manuel, Charlie Clev. 2000-02
*Manuel, Jerry Chi. 1998-2003
*Marion, Marty StL. 1952-53
    Chi. 1954-56
*Marshall Jim Oak. 1979
Martin, Billy Minn. 1969
    Det. 1971-73
    Tex. 1973-75
    NY 1975-78; 79; 83; 85; 88
    Oak. 1980-82
Martinez, Buck Tor. 2001-02
*Matheny, Mike KC 2020-
Mattick, Bobby Tor. 1980-81
*Mauch, Gene Minn. 1976-80
    Cal. 1981-82; 85-87
Mazzilli, Lee Balt. 2004-05
McAleer, Jimmy Clev. 1901
    StL. 1902-09
    Wash. 1910-11
McBride, George Wash. 1921
McCallister, Jack Clev. 1927
*McCarthy, Joe NY 1931-46
    Bos. 1948-50
*McClendon, Lloyd Sea. 2014-15
    Det. 2020
McGaha, Mel Clev. 1962
    KC 1964-65
*McGraw, John Balt. 1901-02
McGuire, Deacon Bos. 1907-08
    Clev. 1909-11
*McKeon, Jack KC 1973-75
    Oak. 1977-78
*McLaren, John Sea. 2007-08
McManus, Marty Bos. 1932-33
*McNamara, John Oak. 1969-70
    Cal. 1983-84; 96
    Bos. 1985-88
    Clev. 1990-91
McRae, Hal KC 1991-1994
    TB 2001-02
Mele, Sam Minn. 1961-67
*Melvin, Bob Sea. 2003-04
    Oak. 2011-
Merrill, Stump NY 1990-91
*Metro, Charlie KC 1970
*Michael, Gene NY 1981; 82
Milan, Clyde Wash. 1922
Miller, Ray Minn. 1985-86
    Balt. 1998-99

Mizerock, John KC 2002
Molitor, Paul Minn. 2015-18
Montoyo, Charlie Tor. 2019-
Moore, Jackie, Oak. 1984-86
Morgan, Joe M. Bos. 1988-91
Moriarty, George Det. 1927-28
Moss, Les Det. 1979
Muser, Tony KC 1997-2002
*Narron, Jerry Tex. 2001-02
*Neun, Johnny NY 1946
Norman, Bill Det. 1958-59
Oates, Johnny Balt. 1991-1994
    Tex. 1995-2001
O'Connor, Jack StL. 1910
*O'Neill, Steve Clev. 1935-37
    Det. 1943-48
    Bos. 1950-51
Onslow, Jack Chi. 1949-50
Parrish, Larry Det. 1998-99
Peckinpaugh, Roger NY 1914
    Clev. 1928-33; 41
Pena, Tony KC 2002-05
Perlozzo, Sam Balt. 2005-07
Pesky, Johnny Bos. 1963-64
Phillips, Lefty Cal. 1969-71
*Piniella, Lou NY 1986-87; 88
    Sea. 1993-2002
    TB 2003-05
Plummer, Bill Sea. 1992
Porter, Bo Hou. 2013-14
Pujols, Luis Det. 2002
Queen, Mel Tor. 1997
Quilici, Frank Minn. 1972-75
Rader, Doug Tex. 1983-85
    Cal. 1989-91
Regan, Phil Balt. 1995
*Renteria, Rick Chi. 2017-20
Rice, Del Cal. 1972
Richards, Paul Chi. 1951-54; 76
    Balt. 1955-61
*Rickey, Branch StL. 1913-15
*Riggleman, Jim Sea. 2008
*Rigney, Bill Cal. 1961-69
    Minn. 1970-72
Ripken, Cal Sr. Balt. 1987-88
*Robinson, Frank Clev. 1975-77
    Balt. 1988-91
*Robinson, Wilbert Balt. 1902
*Rodgers, Buck Mil. 1980-82
    Cal. 1991-1994
*Roenicke, Ron Bos. 2020
*Rojas, Cookie Cal. 1988
Rolfe, Red Det. 1949-52
Rothschild, Larry TB 1998-2001
Rowland, Pants Chi. 1915-18
Ruel, Muddy StL. 1947
Ryan, Connie Tex. 1977
Samuel, Juan Balt. 2010
Schaeffer, Bob KC 1991; 2005
Schalk, Ray Chi. 1927-28
*Scheffing, Bob Det. 1961-63
Schultz, Joe Sea. 1969
Scioscia, Mike Ana./LA 2000-18
Servais, Scott Sea. 2016-
*Sewell, Luke StL. 1941-46
Shawkey, Bob NY 1930
Sherry, Norm Cal. 1976-77
*Showalter, Buck NY 1992-95
    Tex. 2003-06
    Balt. 2010-18
Sisler, George StL. 1924-26
Skaff, Frank Det. 1966
Skinner, Joel Clev. 2002
*Smith, Mayo Det. 1967-70
Snyder, Jimmy Sea. 1988
Speaker, Tris Clev. 1919-26
Stahl, Jake Wash. 1905-06
    Bos. 1912-13
Stahl, Chick Bos. 1906
*Stallings, George Det. 1901
    NY 1909-10
*Stanky, Eddie Chi. 1966-68
    Tex. 1977
*Stengel, Casey NY 1949-60
Stovall, George Clev. 1911
    StL. 1912-13
*Street, Gabby StL. 1938
Strickland, George Clev. 1966
Stubing, Moose Cal. 1988
Sullivan, Haywood, KC 1965
Sullivan, Billy Sr. Chi. 1909
Swift, Bob Det. 1965-66

*Tanner, Chuck Chi. 1970-75
    Oak. 1976
Taylor, Zack StL. 1948-51
*Tebbetts, Birdie Clev. 1963-66
Tighe, Jack Det. 1957-58
*Torborg, Jeff Clev. 1977-79
    Chi. 1989-1991
*Torre, Joe NY 1996-2007
Tosca, Carlos Tor. 2002-04
*Trammell, Alan Det. 2003-05
*Trebelhorn, Tom Mil. 1986-91
Trembley, Dave Balt. 2007-10
Unglaub, Bob Bos. 1907
*Valentine, Bobby Tex. 1985-92
    Bos. 2012
Ventura, Robin Chi. 2012-16
Vernon, Mickey Wash. 1961-63
*Virdon, Bill NY 1974-75
Vitt, Ossie Clev. 1938-40
Wagner, Heinie Bos. 1930
Wakamatsu, Don Sea. 2009-10
    Tex. 18
*Wallace, Bobby StL. 1911-12
Washington, Ron Tex. 2007-14
Wathan, John KC 1987-1991
Weaver, Earl Balt. 1968-82; 85-86
Wedge, Eric Clev. 2003-09
    Sea. 2011-13
*Williams, Dick Bos. 1967-69
    Oak. 1971-73
    Cal. 1974-76
    Sea. 1986-88
*Williams, Jimy Tor. 1986-89
    Bos. 1997-2001
Williams, Ted Wash./Tex. 1969-72
Wills, Maury Sea. 1980-81
Winkles, Bobby Cal. 1973-74
    Oak. 1977-78
Wolverton, Harry NY 1912
Woodward, Chris Tex. 2019-
*Yost, Ned KC 2010-19
*Zimmer, Don Bos. 1976-80
    Tex. 1981-82

MANAGERS – NATIONAL LEAGUE

Since 1901 (* also listed in AL)

*Acta, Manny Wash. 2007-09
Alou, Felipe Mtl. 1992-2001
    SF 2003-06
Alston, Walter Brk./LA 1954-76
*Altobelli, Joe SF 1977-79
Amalfitano, Joey Chi. 1980-81
*Anderson, Sparky Cin. 1970-78
*Baker, Dusty SF 1993-2002
    Chi. 2003-06
    Cin. 2008-13
    Wash. 2016-17
*Bamberger, George NY 1982-83
Bancroft, Dave Bos. 1924-27
Bancroft, Frank Cin. 1902
Barajas, Rod SD 2019
Baylor, Don Col. 1993-98
    Chi. 2000-02
*Bell, Buddy Col. 2000-02
Bell, David Cin. 2019-
*Berra, Yogi NY 1972-75
Bezdek, Hugo Pitt. 1917-19
Bissonette, Del Bos. 1945
Black, Bud SD 2007-15
    Col. 2017-
Blades, Ray StL. 1939-40
Bochy, Bruce SD 1995-06
    SF 2007-19
Boles, John Fla. 1996, 99-2001
*Boone, Bob Cin. 2001-03
*Boros, Steve SD 1986
*Boudreau, Lou Chi. 1960
Bowa, Larry SD, 1987-88
    Phil. 2001-04
Bowerman, Frank Bos. 1909
Boyer, Ken StL. 1978-80
*Bragan, Bobby Pitt. 1956-57
    Mil./Atl. 1963-66
Brenly, Bob Ari. 2001-04
Bresnahan, Roger StL. 1909-12
    Chi. 1915
*Bristol, Dave Cin. 1966-69
    Atl. 1976-77
    SF 1979-80

Buckenberger, Al Bos. 1902-04
*Burke, Jimmy StL. 1905
*Bush, Donie Pitt. 1927-29
    Cin. 1933
*Callahan, Nixey Pitt. 1916-17
Callaway, Mickey NY 2018-19
Carey, Max Brk. 1932-33
Cavarretta, Phil Chi. 1951-53
*Chance, Frank Chi. 1905-12
Chapman, Ben Phil. 1945-48
Clark, Dave Hou. 2009
Clarke, Fred Pitt. 1901-15
Coleman, Bob Bos. 1944-45
Coleman, Jerry SD 1980
*Collins, Terry Hou. 1994-96
    NY 2011-17
Coombs, Jack Phil. 1919
Cooper, Cecil, Hou. 2007-09
*Corrales, Pat Phil. 1982-83
Counsell, Craig Mil. 2015-
*Cox, Bobby Atl. 1978-81; 90-2010
*Craft, Harry Chi. 1961
    Hou. 1962-64
Craig, Roger SD 1978-79
    SF 1985-92
Cravath, Gavvy Phil. 1919-20
Dahlen, Bill Brk. 1910-13
*Dark, Alvin SF 1961-64
    SD 1977
Davenport, Jim SF 1985
Davis, George NY 1901
DeFrancesco, Tony Hou. 2012
Dierker, Larry Hou. 1997-2001
*Donovan, Patsy StL. 1901-03
    Brk. 1906-08
*Donovan, Wild Bill Phil. 1921
Dooin, Red Phil. 1910-14
*Dressen, Chuck Cin. 1934-37
    Brk. 1951-53
    Mil. 1960-61
*Duffy, Hugh Phil. 1904-06
Durocher, Leo Brk. 1939-46; 48
    NY 1948-55
    Chi. 1966-72
    Hou. 1972-73
Dyer, Eddie StL. 1946-50
*Dykes, Jimmy Cin. 1958
Elia, Lee Chi. 1982-83
    Phil. 1987-88
Ens, Jewel Pitt. 1929-31
Essian, Jim Chi. 1991
*Evers, Johnny Chi. 1913; 21
Fanning, Jim Mtl. 1981-82; 84
Felske, John Phil. 1985-87
Fitzsimmons, Freddie Phil. 1943-45
*Fletcher, Art Phil. 1923-26
Fogel, Horace NY 1902
Fox, Charlie SF 1970-74
    Mtl. 1976
    Chi. 1983
*Francona, Terry Phil. 1997-2000
Franks, Herman SF 1965-68
    Chi. 1977-79
Frazier, Joe NY 1976-77
*Fregosi, Jim Phil. 1991-96
*Frey, Jim Chi. 1984-86
Frisch, Frankie StL. 1933-38
    Pitt. 1940-46
    Chi. 1949-51
Fuchs, Judge Bos. 1929
Ganzel, John Cin. 1908
*Garner, Phil Mil. 1998-99
    Hou. 2004-07
Gibson, George Pitt. 1920-22; 32-34
    Chi. 1925
Gibson, Kirk Ari. 2010-14
*Girardi, Joe Fla. 2006
    Phil. 2020-
Gomez, Preston SD 1969-72
    Hou. 1974-75
    Chi. 1980
Gonzales, Mike StL. 1938; 40
Gonzalez, Fredi Fla. 2007-10
    Atl. 2011-16
Green, Andy SD 2016-19
*Green, Dallas Phil. 1979-81
    NY 1993-96
*Griffith, Clark Cin. 1909-11
Grimes, Burleigh Brk. 1937-38
Grimm, Charlie Chi. 1932-38; 44-49; 60
    Bos./Mil. 1952-56
*Guillen, Ozzie Mia. 2012

Haas, Eddie Atl. 1985
Hack, Stan Chi. 1954-56
   StL. 1958
Hale, Chip Ari. 2015-16
*Haney, Fred Pitt. 1953-55
   Mil. 1956-59
Hanlon, Ned Brk. 1901-05
   Cin. 1906-07
Harrelson, Bud NY 1990-91
*Harris, Lum Hou. 1964-65
   Atl. 1968-72
*Harris, Bucky Phil. 1943
Hartnett, Gabby Chi. 1938-40
Hatton, Grady Hou. 1966-68
Heffner, Don Cin. 1966
Helms, Tommy Cin. 1989
Hemus, Solly StL. 1959-61
Hendricks, Jack StL. 1918
   Cin. 1924-29
*Herman, Billy Pitt. 1947
Herzog, Buck Cin. 1914-16
*Herzog, Whitey StL. 1980-90
Himsl, Vedie Chi. 1961
*Hinch, A.J. Ari. 2009-10
*Hitchcock, Billy Atl. 1966-67
*Hodges, Gil NY 1968-71
Hoffman, Glenn LA 1998
Holmes, Tommy Bos. 1951-52
*Hornsby, Rogers StL. 1925-26
   Bos. 1928
   Chi. 1930-32
   Cin. 1952-53
Howard, Frank SD 1981
   NY 1983
*Howe, Art Hou. 1989-93
   NY 2003-04
*Howley, Dan Cin. 1930-32
*Huggins, Miller StL. 1913-17
Hurdle, Clint Col. 2002-09
   Pitt. 2011-19
*Hutchinson, Fred StL. 1956-58
   Cin. 1959-64
*Hyde, Brandon Fla. 2011
Jennings, Dan Mia. 2015
*Johnson, Davey NY 1984-90
   Cin. 1993-95
   LA 1999-2000
   Wash. 2011-13
Jorgensen, Mike StL. 1995
Kapler, Gabe Phil. 2018-19
   SF 2020-
*Keane, Johnny StL. 1961-64
Kelley, Joe Cin. 1902-05
   Bos. 1908
*Kennedy, Bob Chi. 1963-65
*Killefer, Bill Chi. 1921-25
Kimm, Bruce Chi. 2002
*King, Clyde SF 1969-70
   Atl. 1974-75
Klein, Lou Chi. 1961;62;65
Kling, Johnny Bos. 1912
Knight, Ray Cin. 1996-97
Krol, Jack StL. 1980
Kuehl, Karl Mtl. 1976
*Lachemann, Rene Fla. 1993-96
*Lake, Fred Bos. 1910
*Lamont, Gene Pitt. 1997-2000
Lanier, Hal Hou. 1986-88
*LaRussa, Tony StL. 1996-2011
Lasorda, Tommy LA 1977-96
*Lefebvre, Jim Chi. 1992-93
   Mil. 1999
*Leyland, Jim Pitt. 1986-96
   Fla. 1997-98
   Col. 1999
Leyva, Nick Phil. 1989-91
Lillis, Bob Hou. 1982-85
*Little, Grady LA 2006-07
Lobert, Hans Phil. 1938; 42
Lockman, Whitey Chi. 1972-74
*Loftus, Tom Chi. 1901
Lopes, Davey Mil. 2000-02
Lovullo, Torey Ari. 2017-
*Lucchesi, Frank Phil. 1970-72
   Chi. 1987
Lumley, Harry Brk. 1909
*Macha, Ken Mil. 2009-10
Mackanin, Pete Cin. 2005
   Cin. 2007
   Phil. 2015-17
*Maddon, Joe Chi. 2015-19
*Manuel, Charlie Phil. 2005-13

*Manuel, Jerry NY 2008-10
Maranville, Rabbit Chi. 1925
*Marion, Marty StL. 1951
*Marshall, Jim Chi. 1974-76
Martinez, Dave Wash. 2018-
*Matheny, Mike StL. 2012-18
Mathews, Eddie Atl. 1972-74
Mathewson, Christy Cin. 1916-18
Mattingly, Don LA 2011-15
   Mia. 2016-
*Mauch, Gene Phil. 1960-68
   Mtl. 1969-75
*McCarthy, Joe Chi. 1926-30
*McClendon, Lloyd Pitt. 2001-05
McCloskey, John StL. 1906-08
*McGraw, John NY 1902-32
McInnis, Stuffy Phil. 1927
McKechnie, Bill Pitt. 1922-26
   StL. 1928-29
   Bos. 1930-37
   Cin. 1938-46
*McKeon, Jack SD 1988-90
   Cin. 1997-2000
   Fla. 2003-05; 11
*McLaren, John Wash. 2011
McMillan, Roy NY 1975
*McNamara, John SD 1974-77
   Cin. 1979-82
McPhee, Bid Cin. 1901-02
*Melvin, Bob Ari. 2005-09
*Metro, Charlie Chi. 1962
Meyer, Billy Pitt. 1948-52
*Michael, Gene Chi. 1986-87
Miley, Dave Cin. 2003-05
Mills, Brad Hou. 2010-12
Mitchell, Fred Chi. 1917-20
   Bos. 1921-23
Moore, Terry Phil. 1954
Moran, Pat Phil. 1915-18
   Cin. 1919-23
Murphy, Pat SD 2015
Murray, Billy Phil. 1907-09
Murtaugh, Danny Pitt.1957-64; 67,
   70-71; 73-76
Myatt, George Phil. 1969
*Narron, Jerry Cin. 2005-07
*Neun, Johnny Cin. 1947-48
Nichols, Kid StL. 1904-05
Nixon, Russ Cin. 1982-83
   Atl. 1988-90
O'Day, Hank Cin. 1912
   Chi. 1914
O'Farrell, Bob StL. 1927
   Cin. 1934
*O'Neill, Steve Phil. 1952-54
Ott, Mel NY 1942-48
Owens, Paul Phil. 1972; 83-84
Ozark, Danny Phil. 1973-79
   SF 1984
Pedroque, Al Ari. 2004
Perez, Tony Cin. 1993
   Fla. 2001
*Piniella, Lou Cin. 1990-92
   Chi. 2007-10
Price, Bryan Cin. 2014-18
Prince, Tom Pitt. 2019
Prothro, Doc Phil. 1939-41
Quade, Mike Chi. 2010-11
Randolph, Willie NY 2005-08
Rapp, Vern StL. 1977-78
   Cin. 1984
Redmond, Mike Mia. 2013-15
*Renteria, Rick Chi. 2014
*Rickey, Branch StL. 1919-25
Riddoch, Greg SD 1990-92
*Riggleman, Jim SD 1992-1994
   Chi. 1995-99
   Wash. 2009-11
   Cin. 2018
*Rigney, Bill NY/SF 1956-60; 76
Roberts, Dave SD 2015
   LA 2016-
*Robinson, Frank SF 1981-84
   Mtl./Wash. 2002-06
*Robinson, Wilbert Brk. 1914-31
*Rodgers, Buck Mtl. 1985-91
Rodriguez, Edwin Fla. 2010-11
*Roenicke, Ron Mil. 2011-15
*Rojas, Cookie Fla. 1996
Rojas, Luis NY 2020-
Rose, Pete Cin. 1984-89
Ross, David Chi. 2020-

Royster, Jerry Mil. 2002
Runnells, Tom Mtl. 1991-92
Russell, Bill LA 1996-98
Russell, John Pitt. 2008-10
Ryan, Connie Atl. 1975
Sandberg, Ryne Phil. 2013-15
Sawyer, Eddie Phil. 1948-52; 58-60
*Scheffing, Bob Chi. 1957-59
Schoendienst, Red StL. 1965-76; 80; 90
Selee, Frank Bos. 1901
   Chi. 1902-05
*Sewell, Luke Cin. 1950-52
Sheehan, Tom SF 1960
Shelton, Derek Pitt. 2020-
Shepard, Larry Pitt. 1968-69
Shettsline, Bill Phil. 1901-02
Shildt, Mike StL. 2018-
Shotton, Burt Phil. 1928-33
   Brk. 1947-50
*Showalter, Buck Ari. 1998-2000
Sisler, Dick Cin. 1964-65
Skinner, Bob Phil. 1968-69
Slattery, Jack Bos. 1928
Smith, Heinie NY 1902
Smith, Harry Bos. 1909
*Smith, Mayo Phil. 1955-58
   Cin. 1959
Snitker, Brian Atl. 2016-
Southworth, Billy StL. 1929; 40-45
   Bos. 1946-51
*Stallings, George Bos. 1913-20
*Stanky, Eddie StL. 1952-55
*Stengel, Casey Brk. 1934-36
   Bos. 1938-43
   NY 1962-65
*Street, Gabby StL. 1930-33
Sveum, Dale Mil. 2008
   Chi. 2012-13
*Tanner, Chuck Pitt. 1977-85
   Atl. 1986-88
Tappe, El Chi. 1961; 62
*Tebbetts, Birdie Cin. 1954-58
   Mil. 1961-62
Tenney, Fred Bos. 1905-07; 11
Terry, Bill NY 1932-41
Tingler, Jayce SD 2020-
Tinker, Joe Cin. 1913
   Chi. 1916
*Torborg, Jeff NY 1992-93
   Mtl. 2001
   Fla. 2002-03
*Torre, Joe NY 1977-81
   Atl. 1982-84
   StL. 1990-95
   LA 2008-10
Tracy, Jim LA 2001-05
   Pitt. 2006-07
   Col. 2009-12
*Trammell, Alan Ari. 2014
Traynor, Pie Pitt. 1934-39
*Trebelhorn, Tom Chi. 1994
*Valentine, Bobby NY 1996-2002
*Virdon, Bill Pitt. 1972-73
   Hou. 1975-82
   Mtl. 1983-84
Wagner, Honus Pitt. 1917
Walker, Harry StL. 1955
   Pitt. 1965-67
   Hou. 1968-72
*Wallace, Bobby Cin. 1937
Walters, Bucky Cin. 1948-49
Weiss, Walt Col. 2013-16
Westrum, Wes NY 1965-67
   SF 1974-75
Wilhelm, Kaiser Phil. 1921-22
*Williams, Dick Mtl. 1977-81
   SD 1982-85
*Williams, Jimy Hou. 2002-04
Williams, Matt Wash. 2014-15
Wilson, Jimmie Phil.1934-38
   Chi. 1941-44
Wine, Bobby Atl. 1985
*Yost, Ned Mil. 2003-08
Zimmer, Chief Phil. 1903
*Zimmer, Don SD 1972-73
   Chi. 1988-91

HOME RUN
FIRST MAJOR LEAGUE AT-BAT

= Pinch-hitter
* = NOT first plate appearance

Joe Harrington, NL:Bos. Sept. 10, 1895
Bill Duggleby, NL:Phil. Apr. 21, 1898
Johnny Bates, NL:Bos. Apr. 12, 1906
Luke Stuart, AL:StL. Aug. 8, 1921
Walter Mueller, NL:Pitt. May 7, 1922
Earl Averill, AL:Clev. Apr. 16, 1929
Clise Dudley, NL:Brk. Apr. 27, 1929
Gordon Slade, NL:Brk. May 24, 1930
Eddie Morgan, NL:StL. Apr. 14, 1936#
Ace Parker, AL:Phil. Apr. 30, 1937#
Gene Hasson, AL:Phil. Sept. 9, 1937
Emmett Mueller, NL:Phil. Apr. 19, 1938
Ernie Koy, NL:Brk. Apr. 19, 1938
Bill LeFebvre, AL:Bos. June 10, 1938
Clyde Vollmer, NL:Cin. May 31, 1942
Paul Gillespie, NL:Chi. Sept. 11, 1942
Buddy Kerr, NL:NY Sept. 8, 1943
Hack Miller, AL:Det. Apr. 23, 1944
Whitey Lockman, NL:NY July 5, 1945
Eddie Pellagrini, AL:Bos. Apr. 22, 1946
Dan Bankhead, NL:Brk. Aug. 26, 1947
George Vico, AL:Det. Apr. 20, 1948
Les Layton, NL:NY May 21, 1948#
Ed Sanicki, NL:Phil. Sept. 14, 1949
Ted Tappe, NL:Cin. Sept. 14, 1950#
Bob Nieman, AL:StL. Sept. 14, 1951
Hoyt Wilhelm, NL:NY Apr. 23, 1952
Wally Moon, NL:StL. Apr. 13, 1954
Chuck Tanner, NL:Mil. Apr. 12, 1955#
Bill White, NL:NY May 7, 1956
Frank Ernaga, NL:Chi. May 24, 1957
Don Leppert, NL:Pitt. June 18, 1961
Cuno Barragan, NL:Chi. Sept. 1, 1961
Bob Tillman, AL:Bos. May 19, 1962*
John Kennedy, AL:Wash. Sept. 5, 1962#
Buster Narum, AL:Balt. May 3, 1963
Gates Brown, AL:Det. June 19, 1963#
Bert Campaneris, AL:KC July 23, 1964
Bill Roman, AL:Det. Sept. 30, 1964#
Brant Alyea, AL:Wash. Sept. 12, 1965#
John Miller, AL:NY Sept. 11, 1966
Rick Renick, AL:Minn. July 11, 1968
Joe Keough, AL:Oak. Aug. 7, 1968#
Gene Lamont, AL:Det. Sept. 2, 1970
Don Rose, AL:Cal. May 24, 1972
Benny Ayala, NL:NY Aug. 27, 1974
Reggie Sanders, AL:Det. Sept. 1, 1974
John Montefusco, NL:SF Sept. 3, 1974*
Jose Sosa, NL:Hou. July 30, 1975
Dave McKay, AL:Minn. Aug. 22, 1975
Johnnie LeMaster, NL:SF Sept. 2, 1975
Al Woods, AL:Tor. Apr. 7, 1977#
Dave Machemer, AL:Cal. June 21, 1978
Tim Wallach, NL:Mtl. Sept. 6, 1980*
Gary Gaetti, AL:Minn. Sept. 20, 1981
Carmelo Martinez, NL:Chi. Aug. 22, 1983*
Mike Fitzgerald, NL:NY Sept. 13, 1983
Andre David, AL:Minn. June 29, 1984
Will Clark, NL:SF Apr. 8, 1986
Terry Steinbach, AL:Oak. Sept. 12, 1986
Jay Bell, AL:Clev. Sept. 29, 1986
Ricky Jordan, NL:Phil. July 17, 1988*
Junior Felix, AL:Tor. May 4, 1989
Jose Offerman, NL:LA Aug. 19, 1990
Dave Eiland, NL:SD Apr. 10, 1992
Jim Bullinger, NL:Chi. June 8, 1992
Jay Gainer, NL:Col. May 14, 1993
Mitch Lyden, NL:Fla. June 16, 1993
Garey Ingram, NL:LA May 19, 1994#
Jon Nunnally, AL:KC Apr. 29, 1995

Jermaine Dye, NL:Atl. May 17, 1996
Dustin Hermanson, NL:Mtl. Apr. 16, 1997
Brad Fullmer, NL:Mtl. Sept. 2, 1997#
Marlon Anderson, NL:Phil. Sept. 8, 1998#
Carlos Lee, AL:Chi. May 7, 1999
Guillermo Mota, NL:Mtl. June 9, 1999
Esteban Yan, AL:TB June 4, 2000
Alex Cabrera, NL:Ari. June 26, 2000#
Keith McDonald, NL:StL. July 4, 2000#
Chris Richard, NL:StL. July 17, 2000
Gene Stechschulte, NL:StL. Apr. 17, 2001#
Marcus Thames, AL:NY June 10, 2002
Miguel Olivo, AL:Chi. Sept. 15, 2002
David Matranga, NL:Hou. June 27, 2003#
Kazuo Matsui, NL:NY Apr. 6, 2004
Hector Luna, NL:StL. Apr. 8, 2004
Greg Dobbs, AL:Sea. Sept. 8, 2004#
Andy Phillips, AL:NY Sept. 26, 2004#
Mike Jacobs, NL:NY Aug. 21, 2005#
Jeremy Hermida, NL:Fla. Aug. 31, 2005#
Mike Napoli, AL:LA May 4, 2006
Adam Wainwright, NL:StL. May 24, 2006
Kevin Kouzmanoff, AL:Clev. Sept. 2, 2006
Charlton Jimerson, NL:Hou. Sept. 4, 2006#
Josh Fields, AL:Chi. Sept. 18, 2006#
Elijah Dukes, AL:TB Apr. 2, 2007*
Mark Worrell, NL:StL. June 5, 2008
Lou Montanez, AL:Balt. Aug. 6, 2008
Mark Saccomanno, NL:Hou. Sept. 8, 2008#
Jordan Schafer, NL:Atl. Apr. 5, 2009
Gerardo Parra, NL:Ari. May 13, 2009
John Hester, NL:Ari. Aug. 28, 2009#
Jason Heyward, NL:Atl. Apr. 5, 2010
Luke Hughes, AL:Minn. Apr. 28, 2010
Starlin Castro, NL:Chi. May 7, 2010
Daniel Nava, AL:Bos. June 12, 2010
J.P. Arencibia, AL:Tor. Aug. 7, 2010
Brandon Guyer, AL:TB May 6, 2011
Tommy Milone, NL:Wash. Sept. 3, 2011
Brett Pill, NL:SF Sept. 6, 2011
Starling Marte, NL:Pitt. July 26, 2012
Eddy Rodriguez, NL:SD Aug. 2, 2012
Jurickson Profar, AL:Tex. Sept. 2, 2012
Jorge Soler, NL:Chi. Aug. 27, 2014
Eddie Rosario, AL:Minn. May 6, 2015
Daniel Norris, AL:Det. Aug. 19, 2015
Willson Contreras, NL:Chi. June 19, 2016#
Tyler Austin, AL:NY Aug. 13, 2016
Aaron Judge, AL:NY Aug. 13, 2016
Paul DeJong, NL:StL. May 28, 2017#
Lane Thomas, NL:StL. Apr. 19, 2019#
Zack Collins, AL:Chi. June 21, 2019*'
Tyler Stephenson, NL:Cin. July 27, 2020
Keibert Ruiz, NL:LA Aug. 16, 2020
Sergio Alcantara, AL:Det. Sept. 6, 2020

TRIPLE CROWN WINNERS
(Led league in Batting Average, Home Runs & Runs Batted In)

Rogers Hornsby, NL:StL. 1922
Rogers Hornsby, NL:StL. 1925
Jimmie Foxx, AL:Phil. 1933
Chuck Klein, NL:Phil. 1933
Lou Gehrig, AL:NY 1934
Joe Medwick, NL:StL. 1937
Ted Williams, AL:Bos. 1942
Ted Williams, AL:Bos. 1947
Mickey Mantle, AL:NY 1956
Frank Robinson, AL:Balt. 1966
Carl Yastrzemski, AL:Bos. 1967
Miguel Cabrera, AL:Det. 2012

50 OR MORE HOME RUNS, SEASON

73 Barry Bonds, NL:SF 2001
70 Mark McGwire, NL:StL. 1998
66 Sammy Sosa, NL:Chi. 1998
65 Mark McGwire, NL:StL. 1999
64 Sammy Sosa, NL:Chi. 2001
63 Sammy Sosa, NL:Chi. 1999
61 Roger Maris, AL:NY 1961
60 Babe Ruth, AL:NY 1927
59 Babe Ruth, AL:NY 1921
   Giancarlo Stanton, NL:Mia. 2017
58 Jimmie Foxx, AL:Phil. 1932
   Hank Greenberg, AL:Det. 1938
   Mark McGwire, AL:Oak.-NL:StL. 1997
   Ryan Howard, NL:Phil. 2006
57 Luis Gonzalez, NL:Ari. 2001
   Alex Rodriguez, AL:Tex. 2002
56 Hack Wilson, NL:Chi. 1930
   Ken Griffey Jr., AL:Sea. 1997
   Ken Griffey Jr., AL:Sea. 1998
54 Babe Ruth, AL:NY 1920
   Babe Ruth, AL:NY 1928
   Ralph Kiner, NL:Pitt. 1949
   Mickey Mantle, AL:NY 1961
   David Ortiz, AL:Bos. 2006
   Alex Rodriguez, AL:NY 2007
   Jose Bautista, AL:Tor. 2010
53 Chris Davis, AL:Balt. 2013
   Pete Alonso, NL:NY 2019
52 Mickey Mantle, AL:NY 1956
   Willie Mays, NL:SF 1965
   Mark McGwire, AL:Oak. 1996
   George Foster, NL:Cin. 1977
   Alex Rodriguez, AL:Tex. 2001
   Jim Thome, AL:Clev. 2002
   Aaron Judge, AL:NY 2017
51 Ralph Kiner, NL:Pitt. 1947
   Johnny Mize, NL:NY 1947
   Willie Mays, NL:NY 1955
   Cecil Fielder, AL:Det. 1990
   Andruw Jones, NL:Atl. 2005
50 Jimmie Foxx, AL:Bos. 1938
   Albert Belle, AL:Clev. 1995
   Brady Anderson, AL:Balt. 1996
   Greg Vaughn, NL:SD 1998
   Sammy Sosa, NL:Chi. 2000
   Prince Fielder, NL:Mil. 2007

MOST HRs, LIFETIME, BY POSITION

First Base
566 Mark McGwire, AL:Oak. (349); NL:StL. (217)
493 Lou Gehrig, AL:NY
446 Jeff Bagwell, NL:Hou.
Second Base
351 Jeff Kent, AL:Tor.-Clev. (2); NL:NY-SF-Hou.-LA (349)
349 Jeff Kent, NL:NY-SF-Hou.-LA
296 Robinson Cano, AL:NY-Sea.
Third Base
509 Mike Schmidt, NL:Phil.
317 Graig Nettles, AL:Clev.-NY
Shortstop
345 Cal Ripken, AL:Balt.
277 Ernie Banks, NL:Chi.
Outfield
748 Barry Bonds, NL:Pitt.-SF
686 Babe Ruth, AL:Bos.-NY
Catcher
396 Mike Piazza, NL:LA-NY-SD
351 Carlton Fisk, AL:Bos.-Chi.
Pitcher
37 Wes Ferrell, AL:Clev.-Bos.-Wash. (36); NL:Bos. (1)
36 Wes Ferrell, AL:Clev.-Bos.-Wash.
35 Warren Spahn, NL:Bos./Mil.
Designated Hitter
485 David Ortiz, AL:Minn.-Bos.
14 Marcell Ozuna, NL:Atl.

MOST HRs, SEASON, BY POSITION

National League
1B: 69 Mark McGwire, StL. 1998
2B: 42 Rogers Hornsby, StL. 1922
    Davey Johnson, Atl. 1973
3B: 49 Eugenio Suarez, Cin. 2019
SS: 47 Ernie Banks, Chi. 1958
OF: 71 Barry Bonds, SF 2001
C: 42 Javy Lopez, Atl. 2003
P: 7 Don Newcombe, Brk. 1955
       Don Drysdale, LA 1958
       Don Drysdale, LA 1965
       Mike Hampton, Col. 2001
DH: 14 Marcell Ozuna, NL:Atl. 2020

American League
1B: 58 Hank Greenberg, Det. 1938
2B: 40 Brian Dozier, Minn. 2016
3B: 52 Alex Rodriguez, NY 2007
SS: 57 Alex Rodriguez, Tex. 2002
OF: 61 Roger Maris, NY 1961
C: 35 Ivan Rodriguez, Tex. 1999
P: 9 Wes Ferrell, Clev. 1931
DH: 47 David Ortiz, Bos. 2006

CLUB HOME RUN LEADERS, SEASON

National League

Team	HR	Player
ARIZONA	57	Luis Gonzalez 2001
ATLANTA	51	Andruw Jones 2005
CHICAGO	66	Sammy Sosa 1998
CINCINNATI	52	George Foster 1977
COLORADO	49	Larry Walker 1997
		Todd Helton 2001
LOS ANGELES	49	Shawn Green 2001
MIAMI	59	Giancarlo Stanton 2017
MILWAUKEE	50	Prince Fielder 2007
NEW YORK	53	Pete Alonso 2019
PHILADELPHIA	58	Ryan Howard 2006
PITTSBURGH	54	Ralph Kiner 1949
ST. LOUIS	70	Mark McGwire 1998
SAN DIEGO	50	Greg Vaughn 1998
SAN FRANCISCO	73	Barry Bonds 2001
WASHINGTON	46	Alfonso Soriano 2006

American League

Team	HR	Player
BALTIMORE	53	Chris Davis 2013
BOSTON	54	David Ortiz 2006
CHICAGO	49	Albert Belle 1998
CLEVELAND	52	Jim Thome 2002
DETROIT	58	Hank Greenberg 1938
KANSAS CITY	48	Jorge Soler 2019
HOUSTON	47	Jeff Bagwell 2000 (NL)
LOS ANGELES	47	Troy Glaus 2000
MINNESOTA	49	Harmon Killebrew 1964
		Harmon Killebrew 1969
NEW YORK	61	Roger Maris 1961
OAKLAND	58	Jimmie Foxx (Phil.) 1932
SEATTLE	56	Ken Griffey Jr. 1997-98
TAMPA BAY	46	Carlos Pena 2007
TEXAS	57	Alex Rodriguez 2002
TORONTO	54	Jose Bautista 2010

250 OR MORE HOMERS

(At-Bats per Home Run in parentheses;
players active in 2020 in boldface)

762 Barry Bonds (12.92)
755 Hank Aaron (16.38)
714 Babe Ruth (11.76)
696 Alex Rodriguez (15.18)
662 Albert Pujols (16.37)
660 Willie Mays (16.49)
630 Ken Griffey Jr. (15.56)
612 Jim Thome (13.76)
609 Sammy Sosa (14.47)
586 Frank Robinson (17.08)
583 Mark McGwire (10.61)
573 Harmon Killebrew (14.22)
569 Rafael Palmeiro (18.40)
563 Reggie Jackson (17.52)
555 Manny Ramirez (14.85)
548 Mike Schmidt (15.24)
541 David Ortiz (15.97)
536 Mickey Mantle (15.11)
534 Jimmie Foxx (15.23)
521 Willie McCovey (15.73)
521 Frank Thomas (15.74)
521 Ted Williams (14.79)
512 Ernie Banks (18.40)
512 Eddie Mathews (16.67)
511 Mel Ott (18.50)
509 Gary Sheffield (18.11)
504 Eddie Murray (22.49)
493 Lou Gehrig (16.23)
493 Fred McGriff (17.76)
487 Miguel Cabrera (18.79)
477 Adrian Beltre (23.20)
475 Stan Musial (23.10)
475 Willie Stargell (16.69)
473 Carlos Delgado (15.40)
468 Chipper Jones (19.20)
465 Dave Winfield (23.66)
462 Jose Canseco (15.27)
462 Adam Dunn (14.90)
452 Carl Yastrzemski (26.52)
449 Jeff Bagwell (17.37)
449 Vladimir Guerrero (18.16)
442 Dave Kingman (15.11)
440 Jason Giambi (16.52)
439 Paul Konerko (19.12)
438 Andre Dawson (22.66)
435 Carlos Beltran (22.46)
434 Juan Gonzalez (15.11)
434 Andruw Jones (17.51)
431 Cal Ripken (26.80)
427 Mike Piazza (16.19)
426 Billy Williams (21.95)
424 Edwin Encarnacion (16.60)
417 Nelson Cruz (15.34)
414 Darrell Evans (21.67)
412 Alfonso Soriano (18.81)
409 Mark Teixeira (16.96)
407 Duke Snider (17.59)
399 Andres Galarraga (20.29)
399 Al Kaline (25.35)
398 Dale Murphy (20.00)
396 Joe Carter (21.27)
393 Jim Edmonds (17.45)
390 Graig Nettles (23.04)
389 Johnny Bench (19.69)
386 Aramis Ramirez (21.08)
385 Dwight Evans (23.37)
384 Harold Baines (25.80)
383 Larry Walker (18.03)
382 Frank Howard (16.98)
382 Ryan Howard (14.94)
382 Jim Rice (21.53)
381 Albert Belle (15.36)
379 Orlando Cepeda (20.92)
379 Tony Perez (25.80)
378 Matt Williams (18.52)
377 Norm Cash (17.79)
377 Jeff Kent (22.54)
376 Carlton Fisk (23.29)

374 Rocky Colavito (17.39)
370 Gil Hodges (19.00)
369 Todd Helton (21.58)
369 Ralph Kiner (14.11)
366 Lance Berkman (17.73)
361 Joe DiMaggio (18.89)
360 Gary Gaetti (24.86)
359 Johnny Mize (17.94)
358 Yogi Berra (21.10)
358 Carlos Lee (22.30)
355 Greg Vaughn (17.19)
354 Luis Gonzalez (25.87)
354 Lee May (21.49)
353 Torii Hunter (25.09)
352 Ryan Braun (18.81)
352 Ellis Burks (20.55)
351 Dick Allen (18.04)
350 Chili Davis (24.78)
348 George Foster (20.18)
344 Jose Bautista (17.59)
344 Curtis Granderson (21.03)
342 Ron Santo (23.81)
340 Jack Clark (20.14)
339 Tino Martinez (20.98)
339 Dave Parker (27.60)
339 Boog Powell (19.71)
338 Don Baylor (24.25)
336 Joe Adcock (19.66)
335 Darryl Strawberry (16.17)
334 Robinson Cano (25.97)
332 Moises Alou (21.20)
332 Bobby Bonds (21.21)
331 Hank Greenberg (15.69)
331 Derrek Lee (21.03)
328 Shawn Green (21.59)
328 Mo Vaughn (16.87)
325 Jermaine Dye (19.96)
325 Willie Horton (22.46)
324 Gary Carter (24.60)
324 Lance Parrish (21.81)
321 Ron Gant (20.09)
320 Vinny Castilla (21.32)
320 Troy Glaus (18.25)
319 Cecil Fielder (16.17)
319 Prince Fielder (18.25)
318 Jay Bruce (18.65)
318 Roy Sievers (20.08)
317 George Brett (32.65)
317 Adrian Gonzalez (22.52)
316 Ron Cey (22.66)
316 Matt Holliday (22.18)
316 Scott Rolen (23.41)
315 Jeromy Burnitz (18.13)
314 Reggie Smith (22.40)
312 Giancarlo Stanton (13.88)
311 Ivan Rodriguez (30.84)
310 Jay Buhner (16.17)
309 Edgar Martinez (23.34)
307 Greg Luzinski (21.59)
307 Al Simmons (28.53)
307 Miguel Tejada (27.47)
307 Justin Upton (20.70)
306 Fred Lynn (22.63)
306 Richie Sexson (16.10)
306 Ruben Sierra (26.29)
305 Raul Ibanez (24.50)
305 David Justice (18.44)
305 Reggie Sanders (20.46)
304 Steve Finley (30.91)
304 Evan Longoria (21.63)
302 Mike Trout (15.03)
301 Rogers Hornsby (27.15)
300 Chuck Klein (21.62)
299 Tim Salmon (19.85)
298 Mark Reynolds (18.23)
297 Rickey Henderson (36.91)
295 Chris Davis (16.87)
295 Joey Votto (21.27)
294 Magglio Ordonez (23.73)
294 Robin Ventura (24.03)
293 Kent Hrbek (21.13)
292 Pat Burrell (18.85)

292 Rusty Staub (33.29)
291 Craig Biggio (37.37)
291 Jimmy Wynn (22.86)
288 Bobby Abreu (29.44)
288 Del Ennis (25.19)
288 Bob Johnson (24.03)
288 Hank Sauer (16.65)
287 Garret Anderson (30.10)
287 Bobby Bonilla (25.13)
287 Brian Giles (22.74)
287 Matt Kemp (22.18)
287 Bernie Williams (27.42)
286 Carlos Pena (17.30)
286 Frank J. Thomas (21.98)
284 Will Clark (25.26)
284 Eric Karros (22.68)
282 Ken Boyer (26.44)
282 Eric Davis (18.87)
282 Adam Jones (24.85)
282 Brian McCann (21.51)
282 Ryne Sandberg (29.73)
281 Paul O'Neill (26.04)
279 Ted Kluszewski (21.25)
278 Mike Cameron (24.60)
278 Ryan Klesko (20.18)
277 Rudy York (21.27)
275 Brian Downing (28.56)
275 Roger Maris (18.55)
275 Dean Palmer (17.83)
275 Jorge Posada (22.15)
274 Dante Bichette (23.29)
272 Steve Garvey (32.48)
271 Tom Brunansky (23.21)
271 Raul Mondesi (21.45)
271 Hanley Ramirez (23.43)
271 George Scott (27.43)
270 Vernon Wells (24.60)
270 Ryan Zimmerman (23.70)
268 Joe Morgan (34.62)
268 Brooks Robinson (39.75)
268 Gorman Thomas (17.45)
267 George Hendrick (26.70)
267 Mike Napoli (17.12)
266 Vic Wertz (22.94)
265 George Bell (23.11)
265 Matt Stairs (19.64)
264 Bobby Thomson (23.88)
262 Danny Tartabull (19.13)
260 Eric Chavez (21.22)
260 Derek Jeter (43.06)
260 Javy Lopez (20.46)
260 Tim Wallach (31.15)
259 Chase Utley (26.47)
257 Ian Kinsler (28.88)
256 Bob Allison (19.66)
256 Larry Parrish (26.53)
256 Vada Pinson (37.67)
255 Kirk Gibson (22.74)
255 Adam LaRoche (21.93)
255 John Mayberry (21.36)
255 John Olerud (29.77)
253 Larry Doby (21.13)
253 Joe Gordon (22.55)
253 Andre Thornton (20.91)
253 Todd Zeile (29.93)
252 Bret Boone (26.52)
252 Bobby Murcer (26.71)
252 Joe Torre (31.25)
251 Tony Armas (20.57)
251 Tony Clark (18.06)
251 Cy Williams (27.01)
251 Robin Yount (43.86)

3 OR MORE HOME RUNS, GAME
(4-HR Games in Boldface)

AMERICAN ASSOCIATION
Guy Hecker, Lou., Aug. 15(2g), 1886

AMERICAN LEAGUE
Jose Abreu, Chi., Aug. 22, 2020
Bob Allison, Minn., May 17, 1963
Roberto Alomar, Balt., Apr. 26, 1997
Yordan Alvarez, Hou., Aug. 10, 2019
Garret Anderson, Ana., June 4, 2003
Earl Averill, Clev., Sept. 17(1g), 1930
Bobby Avila, Clev., June 20, 1951
Carlos Baerga, Clev., June 17, 1993
Harold Baines, Chi., July 7, 1982
Harold Baines, Chi., Sept. 17, 1984 #2
Harold Baines, Oak., May 7, 1991 #3
Jose Bautista, Tor., May 15, 2011
Don Baylor, Balt., July 2, 1975
George Bell, Tor., Apr. 4, 1988
Albert Belle, Clev., Sept. 6, 1992 (12 inn)
Albert Belle, Clev., Sept. 19, 1995 #2
Albert Belle, Balt., July 25, 1999 (11 inn) #3
Adrian Beltre, Tex., Aug. 22, 2012
Juan Beniquez, Balt., June 12, 1986
Geronimo Berroa, Oak., May 22, 1996
Geronimo Berroa, Oak., Aug. 12, 1996 #2
Mookie Betts, Bos., May 31, 2016
Mookie Betts, Bos., Aug. 14, 2016 #2
Mookie Betts, Bos., Apr. 17, 2018 #3
Mookie Betts, Bos., May 2, 2018 #4
Mookie Betts, Bos., July 26, 2019 #5 NL:1
Paul Blair, Balt., Apr. 29, 1970
Curt Blefary, Balt., June 6(1g), 1967
Steve Boros, Det., Aug. 6, 1962
Mickey Brantley, Sea., Sept. 14, 1987
George Brett, KC, July 22, 1979
George Brett, KC, Apr. 20, 1983 #2
Tom Brunansky, Bos., Sept. 29, 1990
John Buck, Tor., Apr. 29, 2010
Ellis Burks, Clev., June 19, 2001 (12 inn)
Jeff Burroughs, Sea., Aug. 14(2g), 1981
Byron Buxton, Minn., Aug. 27, 2017
Miguel Cabrera, Det., May 28, 2010
Miguel Cabrera, Det., May 19, 2013 #2
Lorenzo Cain, KC, May 10, 2016
Mike Cameron, Sea., May 2, 2002
Jose Canseco, Oak., July 3, 1988 (16 inn)
Jose Canseco, Tex., June 13, 1994 #2
Joe Carter, Clev., Aug. 29, 1986
Joe Carter, Clev., May 28, 1987 #2
Joe Carter, Clev., June 24, 1989 #3
Joe Carter, Clev., July 19, 1989 #4
Joe Carter, Tor., Aug. 23, 1993 #5
Bob Cerv, KC, Aug. 20, 1959
Sam Chapman, Phil., Aug. 15, 1946
Ben Chapman, NY, July 9(2g), 1932
Lonnie Chisenhall, Clev., June 9, 2014
Shin-Soo Choo, Clev., Sept. 17, 2010
Tony Clark, NY, Aug. 28, 2004
Jack Clark, Bos., July 31, 1991 (14 inn)
Ty Cobb, Det., May 5, 1925
Mickey Cochrane, Phil., May 21, 1925
Rocky Colavito, Clev., June 10, 1959
Rocky Colavito, Det., Aug. 27(2g), 1961 #2
Rocky Colavito, Det., July 5, 1962 #3
Ed Coleman, Phil., Aug. 17(1g), 1934 (10 inn)
Darnell Coles, Tor., July 5, 1994 NL:1
Merv Connors, Chi., Sept. 17(2g), 1938
Cecil Cooper, Mil., July 27, 1979
Nelson Cruz, Minn., July 25, 2019
Nelson Cruz, Minn., Aug. 3, 2019 #2
Travis d'Arnaud, TB, July 15, 2019
Matt Davidson, Chi., Mar. 29, 2018
Chris Davis, Balt., Aug. 24, 2012
Chris Davis, Balt., May 20, 2014 #2
Khris Davis, Oak., May 17, 2016
Doug DeCinces, Cal., Aug. 3, 1982
Doug DeCinces, Cal., Aug. 8, 1982 #2
Carlos Delgado, Tor., Aug. 4, 1998
Carlos Delgado, Tor., Aug. 6, 1999 #2

Carlos Delgado, Tor., Apr. 4, 2001 #3
Carlos Delgado, Tor., Apr. 20, 2001 #4
Carlos Delgado, Tor., Sept. 25, 2003 #5
Bill Dickey, NY, July 26, 1939
Joe DiMaggio, NY, June 13(2g), 1937 (11 inn)
Joe DiMaggio, NY, May 23(1g), 1948 #2
Joe DiMaggio, NY, Sept. 10, 1950 #3
Larry Doby, Clev., Aug. 2, 1950
Bobby Doerr, Bos., June 8, 1950
Josh Donaldson, Tor., Aug. 28, 2016
Brian Dozier, Minn., Sept. 5, 2016
Erubiel Durazo, Oak., Aug. 18, 2004 NL:1
Edwin Encarnacion, Tor., May 21, 2010
Edwin Encarnacion, Tor., Aug. 29, 2015 #2
Edwin Encarnacion, Clev., May 2, 2018 #3
Mike Epstein, Wash., May 16, 1969
Cecil Fielder, Det., May 6, 1990
Cecil Fielder, Det., June 6, 1990 #2
Cecil Fielder, Det., Apr. 16, 1996 #3
Darrin Fletcher, Tor., Aug. 27, 2000
Dan Ford, Balt., July 20, 1983
Jimmie Foxx, Phil., July 10, 1932 (18 inn)
Jimmie Foxx, Phil., June 8, 1933 #2
Bill Freehan, Det., Aug. 9, 1971
Nomar Garciaparra, Bos., May 10, 1999
Nomar Garciaparra, Bos., July 23(1g), 2002 #2
Lou Gehrig, NY, June 23, 1927
Lou Gehrig, NY, May 4, 1929 #2
Lou Gehrig, NY, May 22(2g), 1930 #3
Lou Gehrig, NY, June 3, 1932 #4
Troy Glaus, Ana., Sept. 15, 2002
Bill Glynn, Clev., July 5(1g), 1954
Jonny Gomes, TB, July 30, 2005 NL:1
Juan Gonzalez, Tex., June 7, 1992
Juan Gonzalez, Tex., Aug. 28, 1993 #2
Juan Gonzalez, Tex., Sept. 24, 1999 #3
Goose Goslin, Wash., June 19, 1925 (12 inn)
Goose Goslin, StL., Aug. 19, 1930 #2
Goose Goslin, StL., June 23, 1932 #3
Curtis Granderson, NY, June 19, 2012
Bobby Grich, Balt., June 18, 1974
Ken Griffey Jr., Sea., May 24, 1996
Ken Griffey Jr., Sea., Apr. 25, 1997 #2
Ronald Guzman, Tex., Aug. 10, 2018
Travis Hafner, Clev., July 20, 2004
Josh Hamilton, Tex., May 8, 2012
Ken Harrelson, Bos., June 14, 1968
Joe Hauser, Phil., Aug. 2, 1924
Dave Henderson, Oak., Aug. 3, 1991
George Hendrick, Clev., June 19, 1973
Larry Herndon, Det., May 18, 1982
Aaron Hicks, NY, July 1, 2018
Kyle Higashioka, NY, Sept. 16, 2020
Pinky Higgins, Phil., June 27, 1935
Pinky Higgins, Det., May 20, 1940 #2
Bobby Higginson, Det., June 30, 1997
Bobby Higginson, Det., June 24(2g), 2000 #2
Tony Horton, Clev., May 24(2g), 1970 (11 inn)
Willie Horton, Det., June 9, 1970
Willie Horton, Tex., May 15, 1977 #2
Torii Hunter, LA, June 13, 2009
Reggie Jackson, Oak., July 2, 1969
Reggie Jackson, Cal., Sept. 18, 1986 #2
Bo Jackson, KC, July 17, 1990
Brook Jacoby, Clev., July 3, 1987
Manny Jimenez, KC, July 4, 1964
Cliff Johnson, Clev., June 30, 1979
Dan Johnson, Chi., Oct. 3, 2012
Andruw Jones, Tex., July 8, 2009 NL:1
Wally Joyner, Cal., Oct. 3, 1987
Al Kaline, Det., Apr. 17, 1955
Charlie Keller, NY, July 28(1g), 1940
Ken Keltner, Clev., May 25, 1939
Max Kepler, Minn., Aug. 1, 2016
Max Kepler, Minn., June 6, 2019 #2
Harmon Killebrew, Minn., Sept. 21(1g), 1963
Jim King, Wash., June 8, 1964
Dave Kingman, Oak., Apr. 16, 1984 NL:4
Willie Kirkland, Clev., July 9(2g), 1961
Paul Konerko, Chi., July 7, 2009
Lee Lacy, Balt., June 8, 1986
Joe Lahoud, Bos., June 11, 1969

3 OR MORE HOME RUNS, GAME, A.L. (continued)
(4-HR Games in Boldface)

Carney Lansford, Cal., Sept. 1, 1979
Tony Lazzeri, NY, June 8, 1927 (11 inn)
Tony Lazzeri, NY, May 24, 1936 #2
Jim Lemon, Wash., Aug. 31, 1956
Don Leppert, Wash., Apr. 11, 1963
Adam Lind, Tor., Sept. 29, 2009
Evan Longoria, TB, Sept. 18, 2008
Evan Longoria, TB, Oct. 3, 2012 #2
Hector Lopez, KC, June 26, 1958 (12 inn)
Jose Lopez, Sea., Sept. 22, 2010
Fred Lynn, Bos., June 18, 1975
Manny Machado, Balt., Aug. 7, 2016
Manny Machado, Balt., Aug. 18, 2017 #2
Bill Madlock, Det., June 28, 1987 (11 inn)
Mickey Mantle, NY, May 13, 1955
Nick Markakis, Balt., Aug. 22, 2006
Tino Martinez, NY, Apr. 2, 1997
Edgar Martinez, Sea., July 6, 1996
Edgar Martinez, Sea., May 18, 1999 #2
J.D. Martinez, Det., June 21, 2015 NL:1
Victor Martinez, Clev., July 16, 2004
Victor Martinez, Det., June 16, 2016 #2
Charlie Maxwell, Det., May 3(2g), 1959
John Mayberry, KC, July 1, 1975
John Mayberry, KC, June 1, 1977 #2
Tom McCraw, Chi., May 24, 1967
Mark McGwire, Oak., June 27, 1987
Mark McGwire, Oak., June 11, 1995 #2 NL:3
Bill Melton, Chi., June 24(2g), 1969
Kevin Mench, Tex., June 30, 2005
Will Middlebrooks, Bos., Apr. 7, 2013
Kevin Millar, Bos., July 23, 2004
Randy Milligan, Balt., June 9, 1990
Johnny Mize, NY, Sept. 15, 1950 NL:5
Paul Molitor, Mil., May 12, 1982
Kendrys Morales, KC, Sept. 20, 2015
Kendrys Morales, Tor., Aug. 31, 2017 #2
Justin Morneau, Minn., July 6(2g), 2007
Bill Mueller, Bos., July 29, 2003
Pat Mullin, Det., June 26(2g), 1949
Bobby Murcer, NY, June 24(2g), 1970
Bobby Murcer, NY, July 13, 1973 #2
Eddie Murray, Balt., Aug. 29(2g), 1979
Eddie Murray, Balt., Sept. 14, 1980 (13 inn) #2
Eddie Murray, Balt., Aug. 26, 1985 #3
Trot Nixon, Bos., July 24, 1999
Ben Oglivie, Mil., July 8(1g), 1979
Ben Oglivie, Mil., June 20, 1982 #2
Ben Oglivie, Mil., May 14, 1983 (10 inn) #3
Tony Oliva, Minn., July 3, 1973
Al Oliver, Tex., May 23, 1979
Al Oliver, Tex., Aug. 17(2g), 1980 #2
Paul O'Neill, NY, Aug. 31, 1995
Larry Parrish, Tex., Apr. 29, 1985 NL:3
Freddie Patek, Cal., June 20, 1980
Steve Pearce, Bos., Aug. 2, 2018
Dustin Pedroia, Bos., June 24, 2010 (10 inn)
Carlos Pena, Det., May 19, 2003
Boog Powell, Balt., Aug. 10, 1963
Boog Powell, Balt., June 27, 1964 #2
Boog Powell, Balt., Aug. 15, 1966 (11 inn) #3
Jim Presley, Sea., Sept. 1, 1986
Carlos Quentin, Chi., May 24, 2011
Tim Raines, Chi., Apr. 18, 1994
Hanley Ramirez, Bos., July 20, 2016
Manny Ramirez, Clev., Sept. 15, 1998
Manny Ramirez, Clev., Aug. 25, 1999 #2
Josh Reddick, Oak., Aug. 9, 2013
Carl Reynolds, Chi., July 2(2g), 1930
Jim Rice, Bos., Aug. 29, 1977
Jim Rice, Bos., Aug. 29(2g), 1983 #2
Cal Ripken, Balt., May 28, 1996
Alex Rodriguez, Sea., Apr. 16, 2000
Alex Rodriguez, Tex., Aug. 17, 2002 #2
Alex Rodriguez, NY, Apr. 26, 2005 #3
Alex Rodriguez, NY, Aug. 14, 2010 #4
Alex Rodriguez, NY, July 25, 2015 #5
Ivan Rodriguez, Tex., Sept. 11, 1997
Eddie Rosario, Minn., June 13, 2017
Eddie Rosario, Minn., June 3, 2018 #2

Al Rosen, Clev., Apr. 29, 1952
Babe Ruth, NY, May 21(1g), 1930 NL:1
Gary Sanchez, NY, Apr. 7, 2019
Michael Saunders, Tor., June 17, 2016
Kyle Seager, Sea., Aug. 13, 2019
Pat Seerey, Clev., July 13, 1945
Pat Seerey, Chi., July 18(1g), 1948 (11 inn) #2
Pedro Severino, Balt., June 4, 2019
Al Simmons, Phil., July 15, 1932 (11 inn)
Cory Snyder, Clev., May 21, 1987 NL:1
Tony Solaita, KC, Sept. 7, 1975 (11 inn)
Moose Solters, StL., July 7, 1935
George Springer, Hou., Sept. 22, 2019
Mike Stanley, NY, Aug. 10(1g), 1995
Leroy Stanton, Cal., July 10, 1973 (10 inn)
Lee Stevens, Tex., Apr. 13, 1998
Darryl Strawberry, NY, Aug. 6, 1996 NL:1
Dale Sveum, Mil., July 17, 1987
Jim Tabor, Bos., July 4(2g), 1939
Danny Tartabull, KC, July 6, 1991
Mark Teixeira, Tex., July 13, 2006
Mark Teixeira, NY, May 8, 2010 #2 NL:1
Miguel Tejada, Oak., June 11, 1999
Miguel Tejada, Oak., June 30, 2001 #2
Frank Thomas, Chi., Sept. 15, 1996
Frank Thomas, Tor., Sept. 17, 2007 #2
Gorman Thomas, Sea., Apr. 11, 1985
Lee Thomas, LA, Sept. 5(2g), 1961
Jim Thome, Clev., July 22, 1994
Jim Thome, Clev., July 6, 2001 #2
Tom Tresh, NY, June 6(2g), 1965
Hal Trosky, Clev., May 30(2g), 1934
Hal Trosky, Clev., July 5(1g), 1937 #2
B.J. Upton, TB, Sept. 9, 2012
Danny Valencia, Oak., May 15, 2016
John Valentin, Bos., June 2, 1995 (10 inn)
Jose Valentin, Chi., July 30, 2003 NL:1
Jason Varitek, Bos., May 20, 2001
Mo Vaughn, Bos., Sept. 24, 1996
Mo Vaughn, Bos., May 30, 1997 #2
Otto Velez, Tor., May 4(1g), 1980 (10 inn)
Clyde Vollmer, Bos., July 26, 1951
Preston Ward, KC, Sept. 9, 1958
Claudell Washington, Chi., July 14, 1979 NL:1
Vernon Wells, Tor., May 30, 2006
Ernie Whitt, Tor., Sept. 14, 1987
Brad Wilkerson, Tex., July 3, 2007
Ken Williams, StL., Apr. 22, 1922
Matt Williams, Clev., Apr. 25, 1997
Ted Williams, Bos., July 14(1g), 1946
Ted Williams, Bos., May 8, 1957 #2
Ted Williams, Bos., June 13, 1957 #3
Dan Wilson, Sea., Apr. 11, 1996
Dave Winfield, Cal., Apr. 13, 1991
Chris Woodward, Tor., Aug. 7, 2002 (10 inn)
Carl Yastrzemski, Bos., May 19, 1976
Rudy York, Det., Sept. 1(1g), 1941
Dmitri Young, Det., Apr. 4, 2005
Ernie Young, Oak., May 10, 1996
Norm Zauchin, Bos., May 27, 1955
Gus Zernial, Chi., Oct. 1(2g), 1950

3 OR MORE HOME RUNS, GAME

(4-HR Games in Boldface)

NATIONAL LEAGUE

Hank Aaron, Mil., June 21, 1959
Joe Adcock, Mil., July 31, 1954
Edgardo Alfonzo, NY, Aug. 30, 1999
Dick Allen, Phil., Sept. 29, 1968
Moises Alou, Chi., July 4, 2003
Brian Anderson, Miami, Sept. 18(2g), 2020 (7 inn)
Cap Anson, Chi., Aug. 6, 1884
Aristides Aquino, Cin., Aug. 10, 2019
Nolan Arenado, Col., July 19, 2017
Jeff Bagwell, Hou., June 24, 1994
Jeff Bagwell, Hou., Apr. 21, 1999 #2
Jeff Bagwell, Hou., June 9, 1999 #3
Ed Bailey, Cin., June 24(1g), 1956
Ernie Banks, Chi., Aug. 4, 1955
Ernie Banks, Chi., Sept. 14(2g), 1957 #2
Ernie Banks, Chi., May 29, 1962 #3
Ernie Banks, Chi., June 9, 1963 #4
Jake Beckley, Cin., Sept. 26(1g), 1897
Gus Bell, Cin., July 21, 1955
Gus Bell, Cin., May 29, 1956 #2
Josh Bell, Pitt., July 1, 2019
Les Bell, Bos., June 2, 1928
Carlos Beltran, NY, May 12, 2011
Johnny Bench, Cin., July 26, 1970
Johnny Bench, Cin., May 9, 1973 #2
Johnny Bench, Cin., May 29, 1980 #3
Lance Berkman, Hou., Apr. 16, 2002
Mookie Betts, LA, Aug. 13, 2020 AL:5
Charlie Blackmon, Col., Aug. 12, 2016
Jeff Blauser, Atl., July 12, 1992 (10 inn)
Barry Bonds, SF, Aug. 2, 1994
Barry Bonds, SF, May 19, 2001 #2
Barry Bonds, SF, Sept. 9, 2001 (11 inn) #3
Barry Bonds, SF, Aug. 27, 2002 #4
Aaron Boone, Cin., Aug. 9, 2002
Aaron Boone, Cin., May 8, 2003 #2
Bret Boone, Cin., Sept. 20, 1998
Bret Boone, SD, June 23, 2000 (10 inn) #2
Russell Branyan, Cin., Aug. 4, 2002
Ryan Braun, Mil., Apr. 30, 2012
Ryan Braun, Mil., Apr. 8, 2014 #2
Dan Brouthers, Det., Sept. 10, 1886
Brant Brown, Chi., June 18, 1998
Tommy Brown, Brk., Sept. 18, 1950
Jay Bruce, Cin., Aug. 27, 2010
Kris Bryant, Chi., June 27, 2016
Kris Bryant, Chi., May 17, 2019 #2
Smoky Burgess, Cin., July 29, 1955
Jeromy Burnitz, Mil., May 10, 2001
Jeromy Burnitz, Mil., Sept. 25, 2001 #2
Johnny Callison, Phil., Sept. 27, 1964
Johnny Callison, Phil., June 6(2g), 1965 #2
Ken Caminiti, SD, July 12, 1998
Roy Campanella, Brk., Aug. 26, 1950
Robinson Cano, NY, July 23, 2019
Matt Carpenter, StL., July 20, 2018
Gary Carter, Mtl., Apr. 20, 1977
Gary Carter, NY, Sept. 3, 1985 #2
Rico Carty, Atl., May 31, 1970
Vinny Castilla, Col., June 5, 1999
Vinny Castilla, Hou., July 28(1g), 2001 #2
Orlando Cepeda, Atl., July 26(1g), 1970
Yoenis Cespedes, NY, Aug. 21, 2015
Yoenis Cespedes, NY, Apr. 11, 2017 #2
Hee Seop Choi, LA, June 12, 2005
Jeff Cirillo, Col., June 28, 2000
Roberto Clemente, Pitt., May 15, 1967 (10 inn)
Roberto Clemente, Pitt., Aug. 13, 1969 #2
Nate Colbert, SD, Aug. 1(2g), 1972
Darnell Coles, Pitt., Sept. 30(2g), 1987 AL:1
Roger Connor, NY, May 9, 1888
Walker Cooper, Cin., July 6, 1949
Eric Davis, Cin., Sept. 10, 1986
Eric Davis, Cin., May 3, 1987 #2
Glenn Davis, Hou., Sept. 10, 1987
Glenn Davis, Hou., June 1, 1990 (11 inn) #2
Ike Davis, NY, July 28, 2012
Andre Dawson, Mtl., Sept. 24, 1985
Andre Dawson, Chi., Aug. 1, 1987 #2
Paul DeJong, StL., July 24, 2019

Ed Delahanty, Phil., July 13, 1896
Don Demeter, LA, Apr. 21, 1959 (11 inn)
Don Demeter, Phil., Sept. 12, 1961 #2
Alex Dickerson, SF, Sept. 1, 2020
Derek Dietrich, Cin., May 28, 2019
Lucas Duda, NY, July 29, 2015
Adam Dunn, Wash., July 7, 2010
Erubiel Durazo, Ari., May 17, 2002 AL:1
Adam Duvall, Atl., Sept. 2, 2020
Adam Duvall, Atl., Sept. 9, 2020 #2
Damion Easley, Ari., June 3(2g), 2006
Bob Elliott, Bos., Sept. 24, 1949
Kevin Elster, LA, Apr. 11, 2000
Del Ennis, Phil., July 23, 1955
Morgan Ensberg, Hou., May 15, 2005
Bobby Estalella, Phil., Sept. 4, 1997
Andre Ethier, LA, June 26, 2009
Darrell Evans, SF, June 15, 1983
Prince Fielder, Mil., Sept. 27, 2011
Steve Finley, SD, May 19, 1997
Steve Finley, SD, June 23, 1997 #2
Steve Finley, Ari., Sept. 8, 1999 #3
Steve Finley, Ari., Apr. 28, 2004 #4
George Foster, Cin., July 14, 1977
Jack Fournier, Brk., July 13, 1926
Andres Galarraga, Col., June 25, 1995
Scooter Gennett, Cin., June 6, 2017
Jason Giambi, Col., May 19, 2011
Paul Goldschmidt, Ari., Aug. 3, 2017
Paul Goldschmidt, StL., Mar. 29, 2019 #2
Jonny Gomes, Cin., Aug. 13, 2009 AL:
Adrian Gonzalez, LA, Apr. 8, 2015
Adrian Gonzalez, LA, Aug. 22, 2016 #2
Carlos Gonzalez, Col., May 30, 2012
Carlos Gonzalez, Col., June 5, 2013 #2
Luis Gonzalez, Ari., June 8, 2001
Luis Gonzalez, Ari., May 10, 2004 #2
Yasmani Grandal, LA, July 8, 2016
Shawn Green, LA, Aug. 15, 2001
Shawn Green, LA, May 23, 2002 #2
Willie Greene, Cin., Sept. 24, 1996
Ken Griffey Sr., Cin., July 22, 1986 (11 inn)
Trent Grisham, SD, Aug. 22, 2020
Jeffrey Hammonds, Cin., May 19, 1999
Bryce Harper, Wash., May 6, 2015
George Harper, StL., Sept. 20(1g), 1928
Corey Hart, Mil., May 23, 2011
Von Hayes, Phil., Aug. 29, 1989
Chris Heisey, Cin., June 22(2g), 2011
Todd Helton, Col., May 1, 2000
Todd Helton, Col., May 29, 2003 #2
Butch Henline, Phil., Sept. 15, 1922
Babe Herman, Chi., July 20, 1933
Gene Hermanski, Brk., Aug. 5, 1948
Jim Hickman, NY, Sept. 3, 1965
Richard Hidalgo, Hou., Sept. 16, 2003
Aaron Hill, Mil., May 7, 2016 (10 inn)
Shea Hillenbrand, Ari., July 7, 2003
Gil Hodges, Brk., Aug. 31, 1950
Todd Hollandsworth, Col., Apr. 15, 2001 (10 inn)
Bob Horner, Atl., July 6, 1986
Rogers Hornsby, Chi., Apr. 24, 1931
Tyler Houston, Mil., July 9, 2000
Ryan Howard, Phil., Sept. 3(1g), 2006
Aubrey Huff, SF, June 2, 2011
Geoff Jenkins, Mil., Apr. 28, 2001
Geoff Jenkins, Mil., May 21, 2003 #2
Deron Johnson, Phil., July 11, 1971
Andruw Jones, Atl., Sept. 25, 2002 AL:1
Chipper Jones, Atl., June 4, 2006
Bill Joyce, Wash., Aug. 20, 1894
Alex Kampouris, Cin., May 9, 1937
George Kelly, NY, Sept. 17, 1923
George Kelly, NY, June 14, 1924 #2
Matt Kemp, Atl., Apr. 29, 2017
Ralph Kiner, Pitt., Aug. 16, 1947
Ralph Kiner, Pitt., Sept. 11(2g), 1947 #2
Ralph Kiner, Pitt., July 5(1g), 1948 #3
Ralph Kiner, Pitt., July 18, 1951 #4
Dave Kingman, NY, June 4, 1976
Dave Kingman, Chi., May 14, 1978 (15 inn) #2
Dave Kingman, Chi., May 17, 1979 (10 inn) #3
Dave Kingman, Chi., July 28, 1979 #4 AL:1
Chuck Klein, Phil., July 10, 1936 (10 inn)
Ted Kluszewski, Cin., July 1(1g), 1956 (10 inn)

3 OR MORE HOME RUNS, GAME, N.L. (continued)
(4-HR Games in Boldface)
Jason Kubel, Ari., July 21, 2012
Mike Lansing, Col., Sept. 22, 1998
Barry Larkin, Cin., June 28, 1991
Carlos Lee, Hou., Apr. 13, 2007
Hal Lee, Bos., July 6, 1934
Hank Leiber, Chi., July 4(1g), 1939
Mike Lieberthal, Phil., Aug. 10, 2002
Davey Lopes, LA, Aug. 20, 1974
Bobby Lowe, Bos., May 30(2g), 1894
Mike Lowell, Fla., Apr. 21, 2004 (12 inn)
Mike Lum, Atl., July 3(1g), 1970
Jack Manning, Phil., Oct. 9, 1884
Willard Marshall, NY, July 18, 1947
J.D. Martinez, Ari., Sept. 4, 2017 AL:1
Eddie Mathews, Bos., Sept. 27, 1952
Gary Matthews Sr., SF, Sept. 25, 1963
Lee May, Hou., June 21, 1973
Willie Mays, SF, Apr. 30, 1961
Willie Mays, SF, June 29(1g), 1961 (10 inn) #2
Willie Mays, SF, June 2, 1963 #3
Willie McCovey, SF, Sept. 22, 1963
Willie McCovey, SF, Apr. 22, 1964 #2
Willie McCovey, SF, Sept. 17, 1966 (10 inn) #3
Tom McCreery, Lou., July 12, 1897
Clyde McCullough, Chi., July 26(1g), 1942
Andrew McCutchen, Pitt., Aug. 1, 2009
Andrew McCutchen, Pitt., Apr. 26, 2016 #2
Andrew McCutchen, Pitt., July 30, 2017 #3
Casey McGehee, Mil., Aug. 3, 2011
Mark McGwire, StL., Apr. 14, 1998
Mark McGwire, StL., May 19, 1998 #2
Mark McGwire, StL., May 18, 2000 #3 AL:2
Roman Mejias, Pitt., May 4(1g), 1958
Kevin Mitchell, SF, May 25, 1990
George Mitterwald, Chi., Apr. 17, 1974
Johnny Mize, StL., July 13, 1938
Johnny Mize, StL., July 20(2g), 1938 #2
Johnny Mize, StL., May 13, 1940 (14 inn) #3
Johnny Mize, StL., Sept. 8(1g), 1940 #4
Johnny Mize, NY, Apr. 24, 1947 #5 AL:1
Rick Monday, Chi., May 16, 1972
Johnny Moore, Phil., July 22, 1936
Walt Moryn, Chi., May 30(2g), 1958
Don Mueller, NY, Sept. 1, 1951
Dale Murphy, Atl., May 18, 1979
Stan Musial, StL., May 2(1g), 1954
Stan Musial, StL., July 8, 1962 #2
Wil Myers, SD, July 7, 2018
Dioner Navarro, Chi., May 29, 2013
Phil Nevin, SD, Oct. 6, 2001
Bill Nicholson, Chi., July 23(1g), 1944
Kirk Nieuwenhuis, NY, July 12, 2015
Gene Oliver, Atl., July 30(2g), 1966
Jose Ortiz, Col., Aug. 17, 2001
Mel Ott, NY, Aug. 31(2g), 1930
Marcell Ozuna, Atl., Sept. 1, 2020
Andy Pafko, Chi., Aug. 2(2g), 1950
Jarrett Parker, SF, Sept. 26, 2015
Larry Parrish, Mtl., May 29, 1977
Larry Parrish, Mtl., July 30, 1978 #2
Larry Parrish, Mtl., Apr. 25, 1980 (11 inn) #3 AL:1
Jim Pendleton, Mil., Aug. 30(1g), 1953
Adolfo Phillips, Chi., June 11(2g), 1967
Mike Piazza, LA, June 29, 1996
A.J. Pollock, Ari., Apr. 30, 2018
A.J. Pollock, LA, Sept. 6, 2019 #2
Yasiel Puig, LA, Sept. 15, 2018
Albert Pujols, StL., July 20, 2004
Albert Pujols, StL., Apr. 16, 2006 #2
Albert Pujols, StL., Sept. 3, 2006 #3
Albert Pujols, StL., May 30, 2010 #4
Aramis Ramirez, Pitt., Apr. 8, 2001
Aramis Ramirez, Chi., July 30, 2004 #2
Aramis Ramirez, Chi., Sept. 16, 2004 #3
Aramis Ramirez, Chi., July 20, 2010 #4
Anthony Rendon, Wash., Apr. 30, 2017
Hunter Renfroe, SD, Sept. 20, 2017
Hunter Renfroe, SD, June 14, 2019 (12 inn) #2
Jose Reyes, NY, Aug. 15, 2006
Dusty Rhodes, NY, Aug. 26, 1953
Dusty Rhodes, NY, July 28, 1954 #2
Tuffy Rhodes, Chi., Apr. 4, 1994
Frank Robinson, Cin., Aug. 22, 1959

Bill Robinson, Pitt., June 5, 1976 (15 inn)
Pete Rose, Cin., Apr. 29, 1978
Cody Ross, Fla., Sept. 11, 2006
Babe Ruth, Bos., May 25, 1935 AL:1
Reggie Sanders, Cin., Aug. 15, 1995
Pablo Sandoval, SF, Sept. 4, 2013
Benito Santiago, Phil., Sept. 15, 1996
Hank Sauer, Chi., Aug. 28(1g), 1950
Hank Sauer, Chi., June 11, 1952 #2
Mike Schmidt, Phil., Apr. 17, 1976 (10 inn)
Mike Schmidt, Phil., July 7, 1979 #2
Mike Schmidt, Phil., June 14, 1987 #3
Corey Seager, LA, June 3, 2016
Corey Seager, LA, June 20, 2017 #2
Andy Seminick, Phil., June 2, 1949
Richie Sexson, Mil., Sept. 25, 2001
Richie Sexson, Mil., Apr. 25, 2003 #2
Art Shamsky, Cin., Aug. 12, 1966 (13 inn)
Frank Shugart, StL., May 10, 1894
Reggie Smith, StL., May 22, 1976
Duke Snider, Brk., May 30(2g), 1950
Duke Snider, Brk., June 1, 1955 #2
J.T. Snow, SF, Aug. 13, 2004
Cory Snyder, LA, Apr. 17, 1994 AL:1
Alfonso Soriano, Wash., Apr. 21, 2006
Alfonso Soriano, Chi., June 8, 2007 #2
Alfonso Soriano, Chi., Sept. 6, 2008 #3
Sammy Sosa, Chi., June 5, 1996
Sammy Sosa, Chi., June 15, 1998 #2
Sammy Sosa, Chi., Aug. 9, 2001 #3
Sammy Sosa, Chi., Aug. 22, 2001 #4
Sammy Sosa, Chi., Sept. 23, 2001 #5
Sammy Sosa, Chi., Aug. 10, 2002 #6
Willie Stargell, Pitt., June 24, 1965
Willie Stargell, Pitt., May 22, 1968 #2
Willie Stargell, Pitt., Apr. 10, 1971 (12 inn) #3
Willie Stargell, Pitt., Apr. 21, 1971 #4
Trevor Story, Col., Sept. 5, 2018
Darryl Strawberry, NY, Aug. 5, 1985 AL:1
Dick Stuart, Pitt., June 30(2g), 1960
Drew Stubbs, Cin., July 4, 2010
Eugenio Suarez, Cin., Sept. 5, 2020
Mark Teixeira, Atl., June 22, 2008 AL:2
Bill Terry, NY, Aug. 13(1g), 1932
Frank J. Thomas, Pitt., Aug. 16, 1958
Hank Thompson, NY, June 3, 1954
Bob Thurman, Cin., Aug. 18, 1956
Bob Tillman, Atl., July 30(1g), 1969
Jim Tobin, Bos., May 13, 1942
Jeff Treadway, Atl., May 26, 1990
Justin Turner, LA, May 7, 2019
Juan Uribe, StL., Sept. 9, 2013
Jose Valentin, Mil., Apr. 3, 1998 AL:1
Greg Vaughn, Cin., Sept. 7(2g), 1999
Christian Villanueva, SD, Apr. 3, 2018
Joey Votto, Cin., May 7, 2008
Joey Votto, Cin., May 13, 2012 #2
Joey Votto, Cin., June 9, 2015 #3
Larry Walker, Col., Apr. 5, 1997
Larry Walker, Col., Apr. 28, 1999 #2
Larry Walker, Col., June 25, 2004 (10 inn) #3
Tim Wallach, Mtl., May 4, 1987
Lee Walls, Chi., Apr. 24, 1958
Claudell Washington, NY, June 22, 1980 AL:1
George Watkins, StL., June 24(2g), 1931
Jayson Werth, Phil., May 16, 2008
Wes Westrum, NY, June 24, 1950
Bill White, StL., July 5, 1961
Mark Whiten, StL., Sept. 7(2g), 1993
Del Wilber, Phil., Aug. 27(2g), 1951
Billy Williams, Chi., Sept. 10, 1968
Cy Williams, Phil., May 11, 1923
Ned Williamson, Chi., May 30(2g), 1884
Hack Wilson, Chi., July 26, 1930
Jimmy Wynn, Hou., June 15, 1967
Jimmy Wynn, LA, May 11, 1974 #2
Mike Yastrzemski, SF, Aug. 16, 2019 (11 inn)
Christian Yelich, Mil., Apr. 15, 2019
Chris Young, Ari., Sept. 6, 2009
Ryan Zimmerman, Wash., May 29, 2013

GRAND SLAM HOME RUNS
Career Leaders
(Players active in 2020 in Boldface)

25	Alex Rodriguez
23	Lou Gehrig
21	Manny Ramirez
19	Eddie Murray
18	Willie McCovey
	Robin Ventura
17	Jimmie Foxx
	Carlos Lee
	Ted Williams
16	Hank Aaron
	Dave Kingman
	Babe Ruth
15	Ken Griffey Jr.
	Ryan Howard
	Albert Pujols
	Richie Sexson
14	Jason Giambi
	Gil Hodges
	Mark McGwire
	Mike Piazza

3,000 OR MORE HITS
(Players active in 2020 in Boldface)

4256	Pete Rose
4191	Ty Cobb
3771	Hank Aaron
3630	Stan Musial
3514	Tris Speaker
3465	Derek Jeter
3430	Honus Wagner
3419	Carl Yastrzemski
3319	Paul Molitor
3313	Eddie Collins
3283	Willie Mays
3255	Eddie Murray
3252	Nap Lajoie
3236	**Albert Pujols**
3184	Cal Ripken
3166	Adrian Beltre
3154	George Brett
3152	Paul Waner
3142	Robin Yount
3141	Tony Gwynn
3115	Alex Rodriguez
3110	Dave Winfield
3089	Ichiro Suzuki
3081	Cap Anson
3060	Craig Biggio
3055	Rickey Henderson
3053	Rod Carew
3023	Lou Brock
3020	Rafael Palmeiro
3010	Wade Boggs
3007	Al Kaline
3000	Roberto Clemente

HITTING STREAKS, 30 OR MORE GAMES, SEASON

AMERICAN LEAGUE:

G	Year	Player & Club
56	1941	Joe DiMaggio, NY
41	1922	George Sisler, StL.
40	1911	Ty Cobb, Det.
39	1987	Paul Molitor, Mil.
35	1917	Ty Cobb, Det.
34	1925	George Sisler, StL.
	1938	George McQuinn, StL.
	1949	Dom DiMaggio, Bos.
33	1907	Hal Chase, NY
	1933	Heinie Manush, Wash.
31	1906	Nap Lajoie, Clev.
	1924	Sam Rice, Wash.
	1980	Ken Landreaux, Minn.
30	1912	Tris Speaker, Bos.
	1934	Goose Goslin, Det.
	1976	Ron LeFlore, Det.
	1980	George Brett, KC
	1997	Sandy Alomar Jr., Clev.
	1997	Nomar Garciaparra, Bos.
	1998	Eric Davis, Balt.

NATIONAL LEAGUE:

G	Year	Player & Club
44	1897	Willie Keeler, Balt.
	1978	Pete Rose, Cin.
42	1894	Bill Dahlen, Chi.
37	1945	Tommy Holmes, Bos.
36	2005	Jimmy Rollins, Phil.
35	1895	Fred Clarke, Lou.
	2002	Luis Castillo, Fla.
	2006	Chase Utley, Phil.
34	1987	Benito Santiago, SD
33	1893	George Davis, NY
	1922	Rogers Hornsby, StL.
	2011	Dan Uggla, Atl.
31	1899	Ed Delahanty, Phil.
	1969	Willie Davis, LA
	1970	Rico Carty, Atl.
	1999	Vladimir Guerrero, Mtl.
30	1876	Cal McVey, Chi.
	1898	Elmer Smith, Cin.
	1950	Stan Musial, StL.
	1989	Jerome Walton, Chi.
	1999	Luis Gonzalez, Ari.
	2003	Albert Pujols, StL.
	2006	Willie Taveras, Hou.
	2007	Moises Alou, NY
	2009	Ryan Zimmerman, Wash.
	2011	Andre Ethier, LA
	2016	Freddie Freeman, Atl.

PITCHERS: GAMES WON, CONSECUTIVE, SEASON

19 Tim Keefe, NL:NY 1888
     Rube Marquard, NL:NY 1912
18 Hoss Radbourn, NL:Prov. 1884
17 Mickey Welch, NL:NY 1883
     John Luby, NL:Chi. 1890
     Roy Face, NL:Pitt. 1959
16 Jim McCormick, NL:Chi. 1886
     Smoky Joe Wood, AL:Bos. 1912
     Walter Johnson, AL:Wash. 1912
     Lefty Grove, AL:Phil. 1931
     Schoolboy Rowe, AL:Det. 1934
     Carl Hubbell, NL:NY 1936
     Ewell Blackwell, NL:Cin. 1947
     Jack Sanford, NL:SF 1962
     Roger Clemens, AL:NY 2001
     Gerrit Cole, AL:Hou. 2019
15 Scott Stratton, AA:Lou. 1890
     Dazzy Vance, NL:Brk. 1924
     General Crowder, AL:Wash. 1932
     Johnny Allen, AL:Clev. 1937
     Bob Gibson, NL:StL. 1968
     Dave McNally, AL:Balt. 1969
     Steve Carlton, NL:Phil. 1972
     Gaylord Perry, AL:Clev. 1974
     Roger Clemens, AL:Tor. 1998
     Roy Halladay, AL:Tor. 2003
14 Jocko Flynn, NL:Chi. 1886
     Joe McGinnity, NL:NY 1904
     Jim McCormick, UA:Cin. 1884
     Jack Chesbro, AL:NY 1904
     Ed Reulbach, NL:Chi. 1909
     Walter Johnson, AL:Wash. 1913
     Chief Bender, AL:Phil. 1914
     Lefty Grove, AL:Phil. 1928
     Whitey Ford, AL:NY 1961
     Steve Stone, AL:Balt. 1980
     Rick Sutcliffe, NL:Chi. 1984
     Dwight Gooden, NL:NY 1985
     Roger Clemens, AL:Bos. 1986
     John Smoltz, NL:Atl. 1996
13 Larry Corcoran, NL:Chi. 1880
     Charlie Buffinton, NL:Bos. 1884
     Cy Young, NL:Clev. 1892
     Frank Killen, NL:Pitt. 1893
     Amos Rusie, NL:NY 1894
     Frank Dwyer, NL:Cin. 1896
     Fred Klobedanz, NL:Bos. 1897
     Ed Lewis, NL:Bos. 1898
     Christy Mathewson, NL:NY 1909
     Deacon Phillippe, NL:Pitt. 1910
     Walter Johnson, AL:Wash. 1924
     Stan Coveleski, AL:Wash. 1925
     Burleigh Grimes, NL:NY 1927
     Wes Ferrell, AL:Clev. 1930
     Bobo Newsom, AL:Det. 1940
     Ellis Kinder, AL:Bos. 1949
     Brooks Lawrence, NL:Cin. 1956
     Phil Regan, NL:LA 1966
     Dock Ellis, NL:Pitt. 1971
     Dave McNally, AL:Balt. 1971
     Catfish Hunter, AL:Oak. 1973
     Ron Guidry, AL:NY 1978
     Lamarr Hoyt, AL:Chi. 1983
     Tom Glavine, NL:Atl. 1992
     Johan Santana, AL:Minn. 2004
     Chris Carpenter, NL:StL. 2005
     Stephen Strasburg, NL:Wash. 2016

PITCHERS: GAMES LOST, CONSECUTIVE, SEASON

19 Jack Nabors, AL:Phil. 1916
18 Cliff Curtis, NL:Bos. 1910
     Roger Craig, NL:NY 1963
16 Dory Dean, NL:Cin. 1876
     Jim Hughey, NL:Clev. 1899
     Craig Anderson, NL:NY 1962
     Mike Parrott, AL:Sea. 1980
     Shelby Miller, NL:Atl. 2015
15 Bob Groom, AL:Wash. 1909
14 Frank Gilmore, NL:Wash. 1887
     Frank Bates, NL:Clev. 1899
     Joe Harris, AL:Bos. 1906
     Jim Pastorius, NL:Brk. 1908
     Buster Brown, NL:Bos. 1911
     Howie Judson, AL:Chi. 1949
     Paul Calvert, AL:Wash. 1949
     Matt Keough, AL:Oak. 1979
     Anthony Young, NL:NY 1992
13 Sam Moffett, NL:Clev. 1884
     Guy Morton, AL:Clev. 1914
     Burleigh Grimes, NL:Pitt. 1917
     Roy Moore, AL:Phil. 1920
     Joe Oeschger, NL:Bos. 1922
     Dutch Henry, AL:Chi. 1930
     Ben Cantwell, NL:Bos. 1935
     Lum Harris, AL:Phil. 1943
     Dutch McCall, NL:Chi. 1948
     Terry Felton, AL:Minn. 1982
     Rick Honeycutt, NL:LA (11)-AL:Oak. (2) 1987
     Anthony Young, NL:NY 1993
     Jose Lima, NL:Hou. 2000
     Ricky Romero, AL:Tor. 2012
     Aaron Sanchez, AL:Tor. 2019
     Spencer Turnbull, AL:Det. 2019

WINNING TWO COMPLETE GAMES, ONE DAY

Joe McGinnity, (3) NL:NY Aug. 1, 8, 31, 1903
Grover Alexander, (2) NL:Phil. Sept. 23, 1916; Sept. 3, 1917
Mark Baldwin, (2) NL:Pitt. Sept. 12, 1891; May 30, 1892
Pud Galvin, (2) NL:Buff. July 12, 1879; July 4, 1882
Hi Bell, NL:StL. July 19, 1924
John Clarkson, NL:Bos. Sept. 12, 1889
Ray Collins, AL:Bos. Sept. 22, 1914
Cannonball Crane, PL:NY Sept. 27, 1890
Candy Cummings, NL:Hart. Sept. 9, 1876
Bert Cunningham, PL:Buff. Aug. 20, 1890
Dave Davenport, AL:StL. July 29, 1916
Al Demaree, NL:Phil. Sept. 20, 1916
Bill Doak, NL:StL. Sept. 18, 1917
Charlie Ferguson, NL:Phil. Oct. 9, 1886
Henry Gruber, PL:Clev. July 26, 1890
Guy Hecker, AA:Lou. July 4, 1884
Bill Hutchinson, NL:Chi. May 30, 1890
Tim Keefe, AA:NY July 4, 1883
Dutch Levsen, AL:Clev. Aug. 28, 1926
Carl Mays, AL:Bos. Aug. 30, 1918
Tony Mullane, AA:Cin. Sept. 20, 1888
George Mullin, AL:Det. Sept. 22, 1906
Frank Owen, AL:Chi. July 1, 1905
Pol Perritt, NL:NY Sept. 9, 1916
Hoss Radbourn, NL:Prov. May 30, 1884
Ed Reulbach, NL:Chi. Sept. 26, 1908
Amos Rusie, NL:NY Sept. 26, 1891
Doc Scanlon, NL:Brk. Oct. 3, 1905
Cy Seymour, NL:NY June 3, 1897
Urban Shocker, AL:StL. Sept. 6, 1924
Johnny Stuart, NL:StL. July 10, 1923
Ed Summers, AL:Det. Sept. 25, 1908
Fred Toney, NL:Cin. July 1, 1917
Ed Walsh, AL:Chi. Sept. 29, 1908
Monte Ward, NL:Prov. Aug. 8, 1878
Mule Watson, NL:Bos. Aug. 13, 1921
Mickey Welch, NL:Troy July 4, 1881
Jim Whitney, NL:Wash. Aug. 20, 1887
Cy Young, NL:Clev. Oct. 4, 1890

TWO OR MORE NO-HIT GAMES, LIFETIME

7 Nolan Ryan, AL:Cal. 1973(2)-75; NL:Hou.1981; AL:Tex. 90-91
4 Sandy Koufax, NL:LA 1962-65
3 Larry Corcoran, NL:Chi. 1880, 82, 84
   Bob Feller, AL:Clev. 1940, 46, 51
   Justin Verlander, AL:Det. 2007, 11; Hou. 19
   Cy Young, NL:Clev. 1897; AL:Bos. 1904, 08
2 Jake Arrieta, NL:Chi. 2015-16
   Al Atkinson, AA:Phil. 1884, 86
   Homer Bailey, NL:Cin. 2012-13
   Ted Breitenstein, AA:StL. 1891; NL:Cin. 1898
   Mark Buehrle, AL:Chi, 2007, 09
   Jim Bunning, AL:Det. 1958; NL:Phil. 1964
   Steve Busby, AL:KC 1973-74
   Carl Erskine, NL:Brk. 1952, 56
   Mike Fiers, AL:Hou. 2015; Oak. 19
   Bob Forsch, NL:StL. 1978, 83
   Pud Galvin, NL:Buff. 1880, 84
   Ken Holtzman, NL:Chi. 1969, 71
   Randy Johnson, AL:Sea. 1990; NL:Ari. 2004
   Addie Joss, AL:Clev. 1908, 10
   Dutch Leonard, AL:Bos. 1916, 18
   Tim Lincecum, NL:SF 2013-14
   Jim Maloney, NL:Cin. 1965, 69
   Christy Mathewson, NL:NY 1901, 05
   Hideo Nomo, NL:LA 1996; AL:Bos. 2001
   Allie Reynolds, AL:NY 1951(2)
   Max Scherzer, NL:Wash. 2015 (2)
   Frank Smith, AL:Chi. 1905, 08
   Warren Spahn, NL:Mil. 1960-61
   Bill Stoneman, NL:Mtl. 1969, 72
   Adonis Terry, AA:Brk. 1886, 88
   Virgil Trucks, AL:Det. 1952 (2)
   Johnny Vander Meer, NL:Cin. 1938 (2)
   Don Wilson, NL:Hou. 1967, 69

NO-HIT GAMES — INACTIVE LEAGUES

NINE OR MORE INNINGS

UNION ASSOCIATION (2)
1884
> Dick Burns, Cin. Aug. 26 (at KC) 3-1
> Ed Cushman, Mil. Sept. 28 (Wash.) 5-0

AMERICAN ASSOCIATION (15)
1882
> Tony Mullane, Lou. Sept. 11 (at Cin.) 2-0
> Guy Hecker, Lou. Sept. 19 (at Pitt.) 3-1

1884
> Al Atkinson, Phil. May 24 (Pitt.) 10-1
> Ed Morris, Colu. May 29 (at Pitt.) 5-0
> Frank Mountain, Colu. June 5 (at Wash.) 12-0
> Sam Kimber, Brk. Oct. 4 (Tol.) 0-0 (10 inn)

1886
> Al Atkinson, Phil. May 1 (NY) 3-2
> Adonis Terry, Brk. July 24 (StL.) 1-0
> Matt Kilroy, Balt. Oct. 6 (at Pitt.) 6-0

1888
> Adonis Terry, Brk. May 27 (Lou.) 4-0
> Henry Porter, KC June 6 (at Balt.) 4-0
> Ed Seward, Phil. July 26 (Cin.) 12-2
> Gus Weyhing, Phil. July 31 (KC) 4-0

1890
> Cannonball Titcomb, Roch. Sept. 15 (Syr.) 7-0

1891
> Ted Breitenstein, StL. Oct. 4(1g) (Lou.) 8-0
> **(First major-league start)**

FEDERAL LEAGUE (5)
1914
> Ed LaFitte, Brk. Sept. 19(1g) (KC) 6-2

1915
> Frank Allen, Pitt. Apr. 24 (StL.) 2-0
> Claude Hendrix, Chi. May 15 (Pitt.) 10-0
> Alex Main, KC Aug. 16 (Buff.) 5-0
> Dave Davenport, StL. Sept. 7(1g) (Chi.) 3-0

NO-HIT GAMES — AMERICAN LEAGUE

129 GAMES OF NINE OR MORE INNINGS
* Denotes Perfect Game

1902
Nixey Callahan, Chi. Sept. 20(1g) (Det.) 3-0
1904
*Cy Young, Bos. May 5 (Phil.) 3-0
Jesse Tannehill, Bos. Aug. 17 (at Chi.) 6-0
1905
Weldon Henley, Phil. July 22(1g) (at StL.) 6-0
Frank Smith, Chi. Sept. 6(2g) (at Det.) 15-0
Bill Dinneen, Bos. Sept. 27(1g) (Chi.) 2-0
1908
Cy Young, Bos. June 30 (at NY) 8-0
Bob Rhoads, Clev. Sept. 18 (Bos.) 2-1
Frank Smith, Chi. Sept. 20 (Phil.) 1-0
*Addie Joss, Clev. Oct. 2 (Chi.) 1-0
1910
Addie Joss, Clev. Apr. 20 (at Chi.) 1-0
Chief Bender, Phil. May 12 (Clev.) 4-0
1911
Smoky Joe Wood, Bos. July 29(1g) (StL.) 5-0
Ed Walsh, Chi. Aug. 27 (Bos.) 5-0
1912
George Mullin, Det. July 4(2g) (StL.) 7-0
Earl Hamilton, StL. Aug. 30 (at Det.) 5-1
1914
Joe Benz, Chi. May 31 (Clev.) 6-1
1916
Rube Foster, Bos. June 21 (NY) 2-0
Joe Bush, Phil. Aug. 26 (Clev.) 5-0
Dutch Leonard, Bos. Aug. 30 (StL.) 4-0
1917
Eddie Cicotte, Chi. Apr. 14 (at StL.) 11-0
George Mogridge, NY Apr. 24 (at Bos.) 2-1
Ernie Koob, StL. May 5 (Chi.) 1-0
Bob Groom, StL. May 6(2g) (Chi.) 3-0
Babe Ruth (0 inn) & Ernie Shore, (9 inn) Bos.
    June 23(1g) (Wash.) 4-0
1918
Dutch Leonard, Bos. June 3 (at Det.) 5-0
1919
Ray Caldwell, Clev. Sept. 10(1g) (at NY) 3-0
1920
Walter Johnson, Wash. July 1 (at Bos.) 1-0
1922
*Charlie Robertson, Chi. Apr. 30 (at Det.) 2-0
1923
Sam Jones, NY Sept. 4 (at Phil.) 2-0
Howard Ehmke, Bos. Sept. 7 (at Phil.) 4-0
1926
Ted Lyons, Chi. Aug. 21 (at Bos.) 6-0
1931
Wes Ferrell, Clev. Apr. 29 (StL.) 9-0
Bobby Burke, Wash. Aug. 8 (Bos.) 5-0
1935
Vern Kennedy, Chi. Aug. 31 (Clev.) 5-0
1937
Bill Dietrich, Chi. June 1 (StL.) 8-0
1938
Monte Pearson, NY Aug. 27(2g) (Clev.) 13-0
1940
Bob Feller, Clev. Apr. 16 (at Chi.) 1-0
(Opening Day)

1945
Dick Fowler, Phil. Sept. 9(2g) (StL.) 1-0
1946
Bob Feller, Clev. Apr. 30 (at NY) 1-0
1947
Don Black, Clev. July 10(1g) (Phil.) 3-0
Bill McCahan, Phil. Sept. 3 (Wash.) 3-0
1948
Bob Lemon, Clev. June 30 (at Det.) 2-0
1951
Bob Feller, Clev. July 1(1g) (Det.) 2-1
Allie Reynolds, NY July 12 (at Clev.) 1-0
Allie Reynolds, NY Sept. 28(1g) (Bos.) 8-0
1952
Virgil Trucks, Det. May 15 (Wash.) 1-0
Virgil Trucks, Det. Aug. 25 (at NY) 1-0
1953
Bobo Holloman, StL. May 6 (Phil.) 6-0
(First major-league start)
1956
Mel Parnell, Bos. July 14 (Chi.) 4-0
1957
Bob Keegan, Chi. Aug. 20(2g) (Wash.) 6-0
1958
Jim Bunning, Det. July 20(1g) (at Bos.) 3-0
Hoyt Wilhelm, Balt. Sept. 20 (NY) 1-0
1962
Bo Belinsky, LA May 5 (Balt.) 2-0
Earl Wilson, Bos. June 26 (LA) 2-0
Bill Monbouquette, Bos. Aug. 1(at Chi.) 1-0
Jack Kralick, Minn. Aug. 26 (KC) 1-0
1965
Dave Morehead, Bos. Sept. 16 (Clev.) 2-0
1966
Sonny Siebert, Clev. June 10 (Wash.) 2-0
1967
Steve Barber (8.2 inn) & Stu Miller (0.1 inn), Balt.
    Apr. 30(1g) (Det.) 1-2 lost
Dean Chance, Minn. Aug. 25(2g) (at Clev.) 2-1
Joe Horlen, Chi. Sept. 10(1g) (Det.) 6-0
1968
Tom Phoebus, Balt. Apr. 27 (Bos.) 6-0
*Catfish Hunter, Oak. May 8 (Minn.) 4-0
1969
Jim Palmer, Balt. Aug. 13 (Oak.) 8-0
1970
Clyde Wright, Cal. July 3 (Oak.) 4-0
Vida Blue, Oak. Sept. 21 (Minn.) 6-0
1973
Steve Busby, KC Apr. 27 (at Det.) 3-0
Nolan Ryan, Cal. May 15 (at KC) 3-0
Nolan Ryan, Cal. July 15 (at Det.) 6-0
Jim Bibby, Tex. July 30 (at Oak.) 6-0
1974
Steve Busby, KC June 19 (at Mil.) 2-0
Dick Bosman, Clev. July 19 (Oak.) 4-0
Nolan Ryan, Cal. Sept. 28 (Minn.) 4-0
1975
Nolan Ryan, Cal. June 1 (Balt.) 1-0
Vida Blue (5 inn), Glenn Abbott, (1 inn), Paul
    Lindblad (1 inn) & Rollie Fingers (2 inn), Oak.
    Sept. 28 (Cal.) 5-0

NO-HIT GAMES — AMERICAN LEAGUE

NINE OR MORE INNINGS   * *Denotes Perfect Game*
(continued)

1976
Blue Moon Odom (5 inn) & Francisco Barrios (4 inn), Chi. July 28 (at Oak.) 2-1

1977
Jim Colborn, KC May 14 (Tex.) 6-0
Dennis Eckersley, Clev. May 30 (Cal.) 1-0
Bert Blyleven, Tex. Sept. 22 (at Cal.) 6-0

1981
*Len Barker, Clev. May 15 (Tor.) 3-0

1983
Dave Righetti, NY July 4 (Bos.) 4-0
Mike Warren, Oak. Sept. 29 (Chi.) 3-0

1984
Jack Morris, Det. Apr. 7 (at Chi.) 4-0
*Mike Witt, Cal. Sept. 30 (at Tex.) 1-0

1986
Joe Cowley, Chi. Sept. 19 (at Cal.) 7-1

1987
Juan Nieves, Mil. Apr. 15 (at Balt.) 7-0

1990
Mark Langston (7 inn) & Mike Witt (2 inn), Cal. Apr. 11 (Sea.) 1-0
Randy Johnson, Sea. June 2 (Det.) 2-0
Nolan Ryan, Tex. June 11 (at Oak.) 5-0
Dave Stewart, Oak. June 29 (at Tor.) 5-0
Dave Stieb, Tor. Sept. 2 (at Clev.) 3-0

1991
Nolan Ryan, Tex. May 1 (Tor.) 3-0
Bob Milacki (6 inn), Mike Flanagan (1 inn), Mark Williamson (1 inn) & Gregg Olson (1 inn), Balt. July 13 (at Oak.) 2-0
Wilson Alvarez, Chi. Aug. 11 (at Balt.) 7-0
Bret Saberhagen, KC Aug. 26 (Chi.) 7-0

1993
Chris Bosio, Sea. Apr. 22 (Bos.) 7-0
Jim Abbott, NY Sept. 4 (Clev.) 4-0

1994
Scott Erickson, Minn. Apr. 27 (Mil.) 6-0
*Kenny Rogers, Tex. July 28 (Cal.) 4-0

1996
Dwight Gooden, NY May 14 (Sea.) 2-0

1998
*David Wells, NY May 17 (Minn.) 4-0

1999
*David Cone, NY July 18 (Mtl.) 6-0
Eric Milton, Minn. Sept. 11 (Ana.) 7-0

2001
Hideo Nomo, Bos. Apr. 4 (at Balt.) 3-0

2002
Derek Lowe, Bos. Apr. 27 (TB) 10-0

2007
Mark Buehrle, Chi. Apr. 18 (Tex.) 6-0
Justin Verlander, Det. June 12 (Mil.) 4-0
Clay Buchholz, Bos. Sept. 1 (Balt.) 10-0

2008
Jon Lester, Bos. May 19 (KC) 7-0

2009
*Mark Buehrle, Chi. July 23 (TB) 5-0

2010
*Dallas Braden, Oak. May 9 (TB) 4-0
Matt Garza, TB July 26 (Det.) 5-0

2011
Francisco Liriano, Minn. May 3 (at Chi.) 1-0
Justin Verlander, Det. May 7 (at Tor.) 9-0
Ervin Santana, LA July 27 (at Clev.) 3-1

2012
*Philip Humber, Chi. Apr. 21 (at Sea.) 4-0
Jered Weaver, LA May 2 (Minn.) 9-0
Kevin Millwood (6 inn), Charlie Furbush (0.2inn), Stephen Pryor (0.1 inn), Lucas Luetge (0.1 inn), Brandon League (0.2 inn) & Tom Wilhelmsen (1 inn), Sea. June 8 (NL:LA) 1-0
*Felix Hernandez, Sea. Aug. 15 (TB) 1-0

2015
Hisashi Iwakuma, Sea. Aug. 12 (Balt.) 3-0
Mike Fiers, Hou. Aug. 21 (NL:LA) 3-0

2018
Sean Manaea, Oak. Apr. 21 (Bos.) 3-0
James Paxton, Sea. May 8 (at Tor.) 5-0

2019
Mike Fiers, Oak. May 7 (NL:Cin.) 2-0
Taylor Cole (2 inn) & Felix Pena (7 inn), LA July 12 (Sea.) 13-0
Aaron Sanchez (6 inn), Will Harris (1 inn), Joe Biagini (1 inn) & Chris Devenski (1 inn), Hou. Aug. 3 (Sea.) 9-0
Justin Verlander, Hou. Sept. 1 (at Tor.) 2-0

2020
Lucas Giolito, Chi. Aug. 25 (NL:Pitt.) 4-0

NO-HIT GAMES – NATIONAL LEAGUE

152 GAMES OF NINE OR MORE INNINGS
* Denotes Perfect Game

1876
  George Bradley, StL. July 15 (Hart.) 2-0
1880
  *Lee Richmond, Wor. June 12 (Clev.) 1-0
  *Monte Ward, Prov. June 17 (Buff.) 5-0
  Larry Corcoran, Chi. Aug. 19 (Bos.) 6-0
  Pud Galvin, Buff. Aug. 20 (Wor.) 1-0
1882
  Larry Corcoran, Chi. Sept. 20 (Wor.) 5-0
1883
  Hoss Radbourn, Prov. July 25 (at Clev.) 8-0
  Hugh Daily, Clev. Sept. 13 (at Phil.) 1-0
1884
  Larry Corcoran, Chi. June 27 (Prov.) 6-0
  Pud Galvin, Buff. Aug. 4 (at Det.) 18-0
1885
  John Clarkson, Chi. July 27 (at Prov.) 4-0
  Charlie Ferguson, Phil. Aug. 29 (Prov.) 1-0
1891
  Tom Lovett, Brk. June 22 (NY) 4-0
  Amos Rusie, NY July 31 (Brk.) 6-0
1892
  Jack Stivetts, Bos. Aug. 6 (at Brk.) 11-0
  Ben Sanders, Lou. Aug. 22 (Balt.) 6-2
  Bumpus Jones, Cin. Oct. 15 (Pitt.) 7-1
    (First major league game)
1893
  Bill Hawke, Balt. Aug. 16 (at Wash.) 5-0
1897
  Cy Young, Clev. Sept. 18(1g) (Cin.) 6-0
1898
  Ted Breitenstein, Cin. Apr. 22 (Pitt.) 11-0
  Jim Hughes, Balt. Apr. 22 (Bos.) 8-0
  Red Donahue, Phil. July 8 (Bos.) 5-0
  Walter Thornton, Chi. Aug. 21(2g) (Brk.) 2-0
1899
  Deacon Phillippe, Lou. May 25 (NY) 7-0
  Vic Willis, Bos. Aug. 7 (Wash.) 7-1
1900
  Noodles Hahn, Cin. July 12 (Phil.) 4-0
1901
  Christy Mathewson, NY July 15 (at StL.) 5-0
1903
  Chick Fraser, Phil. Sept. 18(2g) (at Chi.) 10-0
1905
  Christy Mathewson, NY June 13 (at Chi.) 1-0
1906
  Johnny Lush, Phil. May 1 (at Brk.) 6-0
  Mal Eason, Brk. July 20 (at StL.) 2-0
1907
  Jeff Pfeffer, Bos. May 8 (Cin.) 6-0
  Nick Maddox, Pitt. Sept. 20 (Brk.) 2-1
1908
  Hooks Wiltse, NY July 4(1g) (10 inn) (Phil.) 1-0
  Nap Rucker, Brk. Sept. 5(2g) (Bos.) 6-0
1912
  Jeff Tesreau, NY Sept. 6(1g) (at Phil.) 3-0
1914
  George Davis, Bos. Sept. 9(2g) (Phil.) 7-0
1915
  Rube Marquard, NY Apr. 15 (Brk.) 2-0
  Jimmy Lavender, Chi. Aug. 31(1g) (at NY) 2-0
1916
  Tom Hughes, Bos. June 16 (Pitt.) 2-0
1917
  Fred Toney, Cin. May 2 (10 inn) (at Chi.) 1-0
1919
  Hod Eller, Cin. May 11 (StL.) 6-0
1922
  Jesse Barnes, NY May 7 (Phil.) 6-0
1924
  Jesse Haines, StL. July 17 (Bos.) 5-0

1925
  Dazzy Vance, Brk. Sept. 13(1g) (Phil.) 10-1
1929
  Carl Hubbell, NY May 8 (Pitt.) 11-0
1934
  Paul Dean, StL. Sept. 21(2g) (at Brk.) 3-0
1938
  Johnny Vander Meer, Cin. June 11 (Bos.) 3-0
  Johnny Vander Meer, Cin. June 15 (at Brk.) 6-0
    (consecutive appearances)
1940
  Tex Carleton, Brk. Apr. 30 (at Cin.) 3-0
1941
  Lon Warneke, StL. Aug. 30 (at Cin.) 2-0
1944
  Jim Tobin, Bos. Apr. 27 (Brk.) 2-0
  Clyde Shoun, Cin. May 15 (Bos.) 1-0
1946
  Ed Head, Brk. Apr. 23 (Bos.) 5-0
1947
  Ewell Blackwell, Cin. June 18 (Bos.) 6-0
1948
  Rex Barney, Brk. Sept. 9 (at NY) 2-0
1950
  Vern Bickford, Bos. Aug. 11 (Brk.) 7-0
1951
  Cliff Chambers, Pitt. May 6(2g) (at Bos.) 3-0
1952
  Carl Erskine, Brk. June 19 (Chi.) 5-0
1954
  Jim Wilson, Mil. June 12 (Phil.) 2-0
1955
  Sam Jones, Chi. May 12 (Pitt.) 4-0
1956
  Carl Erskine, Brk. May 12 (NY) 3-0
  Sal Maglie, Brk. Sept. 25 (Phil.) 5-0
1960
  Don Cardwell, Chi. May 15(2g) (StL.) 4-0
  Lew Burdette, Mil. Aug. 18 (Phil.) 1-0
  Warren Spahn, Mil. Sept. 16 (Phil.) 4-0
1961
  Warren Spahn, Mil. Apr. 28 (SF) 1-0
1962
  Sandy Koufax, LA June 30 (NY) 5-0
1963
  Sandy Koufax, LA May 11 (SF) 8-0
  Don Nottebart, Hou. May 17 (Phil.) 4-1
  Juan Marichal, SF June 15 (Hou.) 1-0
1964
  Ken Johnson, Hou. Apr. 23 (Cin.) 0-1 lost
  Sandy Koufax, LA June 4 (at Phil.) 3-0
  *Jim Bunning, Phil. June 21(1g) (at NY) 6-0
1965
  Jim Maloney, Cin. Aug. 19(1g) (10 inn) (at Chi.) 1-0
  *Sandy Koufax, LA Sept. 9 (Chi.) 1-0
1967
  Don Wilson, Hou. June 18 (Atl.) 2-0
1968
  George Culver, Cin. July 29(2g) (at Phil.) 6-1
  Gaylord Perry, SF Sept. 17 (StL.) 1-0
  Ray Washburn, StL. Sept. 18 (at SF) 2-0
1969
  Bill Stoneman, Mtl. Apr. 17 (at Phil.) 7-0
  Jim Maloney, Cin. Apr. 30 (Hou.) 10-0
  Don Wilson, Hou. May 1 (at Cin.) 4-0
  Ken Holtzman, Chi. Aug. 19 (Atl.) 3-0
  Bob Moose, Pitt. Sept. 20 (at NY) 4-0
1970
  Dock Ellis, Pitt. June 12(1g) (at SD) 2-0
  Bill Singer, LA July 20 (Phil.) 5-0
1971
  Ken Holtzman, Chi. June 3 (at Cin.) 1-0
  Rick Wise, Phil. June 23 (at Cin.) 4-0
  Bob Gibson, StL. Aug. 14 (at Pitt.) 11-0

NO-HIT GAMES — NATIONAL LEAGUE

NINE OR MORE INNINGS   ** Denotes Perfect Game*
(continued)

1972
Burt Hooton, Chi. Apr. 16 (Phil.) 4-0
Milt Pappas, Chi. Sept. 2 (SD) 8-0
Bill Stoneman, Mtl. Oct. 2(1g) (NY) 7-0
1973
Phil Niekro, Atl. Aug. 5 (SD) 9-0
1975
Ed Halicki, SF Aug. 24(2g) (NY) 6-0
1976
Larry Dierker, Hou. July 9 (Mtl.) 6-0
John Candelaria, Pitt. Aug. 9 (LA) 2-0
John Montefusco, SF Sept. 29 (at Atl.) 9-0
1978
Bob Forsch, StL. Apr. 16 (Phil.) 5-0
Tom Seaver, Cin. June 16 (StL.) 4-0
1979
Ken Forsch, Hou. Apr. 7 (Atl.) 6-0
1980
Jerry Reuss, LA June 27 (at SF) 8-0
1981
Charlie Lea, Mtl. May 10(2g) (SF) 4-0
Nolan Ryan, Hou. Sept. 26 (LA) 5-0
1983
Bob Forsch, StL. Sept. 26 (Mtl.) 3-0
1986
Mike Scott, Hou. Sept. 25 (SF) 2-0
1988
*Tom Browning, Cin. Sept. 16 (LA) 1-0
1990
Fernando Valenzuela, LA June 29 (StL.) 6-0
Terry Mulholland, Phil. Aug. 15 (SF) 6-0
1991
Tommy Greene, Phil. May 23 (at Mtl.) 2-0
*Dennis Martinez, Mtl. July 28 (at LA) 2-0
Kent Mercker (6 inn), Mark Wohlers (2 inn) &
   Alejandro Pena (1 inn) Atl. Sept. 11 (SD) 1-0
1992
Kevin Gross, LA Aug. 17 (SF) 2-0
1993
Darryl Kile, Hou. Sept. 8 (NY) 7-1
1994
Kent Mercker, Atl. Apr. 8 (at LA) 6-0
1995
Ramon Martinez, LA July 14 (Fla.) 7-0
1996
Al Leiter, Fla. May 11 (Col.) 11-0
Hideo Nomo, LA Sept. 17 (at Col.) 9-0
1997
Kevin Brown, Fla. June 10 (at SF) 9-0
Francisco Cordova (9 inn) & Ricardo Rincon (1 inn),
   Pitt. July 12 (10 inn) (Hou.) 3-0
1999
Jose Jimenez, StL. June 25 (at Ari.) 1-0
2001
A.J. Burnett, Fla. May 12 (at SD) 3-0
Bud Smith, StL. Sept. 3 (at SD) 4-0
2003
Kevin Millwood, Phil. Apr. 27 (SF) 1-0
Roy Oswalt (1 inn), Peter Munro (2.2 inn), Kirk
   Saarloos (1.1 inn), Brad Lidge (2 inn), Octavio
   Dotel (1 inn) & Billy Wagner (1 inn) Hou. June
   11 (at AL:NY) 8-0
2004
*Randy Johnson, Ari. May 18 (at Atl.) 2-0
2006
Anibal Sanchez, Fla. Sept. 6 (Ari.) 2-0
2008
Carlos Zambrano, Chi. Sept. 14 (vs. Hou. at Mil.) 5-0
2009
Jonathan Sanchez, SF July 10 (SD) 8-0

2010
Ubaldo Jimenez, Col. Apr. 17 (at Atl.) 4-0
*Roy Halladay, Phil. May 29 (at Fla.) 1-0
Edwin Jackson, Ari. June 25 (at AL:TB) 1-0
2012
Johan Santana, NY June 1 (StL.) 8-0
*Matt Cain, SF June 13 (Hou.) 10-0
Homer Bailey, Cin. Sept. 28 (at Pitt.) 1-0
2013
Homer Bailey, Cin. July 2 (SF) 3-0
Tim Lincecum, SF July 13 (at SD) 9-0
Henderson Alvarez, Mia. Sept. 29 (AL:Det.) 1-0
2014
Josh Beckett, LA May 25 (at Phil.) 6-0
Clayton Kershaw, LA June 18 (Col.) 8-0
Tim Lincecum, SF June 25 (SD) 4-0
Cole Hamels (6 inn), Jake Deikman (1 inn), Ken
   Giles (1 inn) & Jonathan Papelbon (1 inn), Phil.
   Sept. 1 (at Atl.) 7-0
Jordan Zimmermann, Wash. Sept. 28 (Mia.) 1-0
2015
Chris Heston, SF June 9 (at NY) 5-0
Max Scherzer, Wash. June 20 (Pitt.) 6-0
Cole Hamels, Phil. July 25 (at Chi.) 5-0
Jake Arrieta, Chi. Aug. 30 (at LA) 2-0
Max Scherzer, Wash. Oct. 3(2g) (at NY) 2-0
2016
Jake Arrieta, Chi. Apr. 21 (at Cin.) 16-0
2017
Edinson Volquez, Mia. June 3 (Ari.) 3-0
2018
Walker Buehler (6 inn), Tony Cingrani (1 inn), Yimi
   Garcia (1 inn) & Adam Liberatore (1 inn), LA May
   4 (at SD in Monterrey, Mexico) 4-0
2020
Alec Mills, Chi. Sept. 13 (at Mil.) 12-0

NO-HIT GAMES

Denotes Perfect Game

NO-HIT GAMES IN POSTSEASON

*Don Larsen, AL:NY Oct. 8, 1956 (NL:Brk.) 2-0
(World Series Game 5; perfect game)
Roy Halladay, NL:Phil. Oct. 6, 2010 (Cin.) 4-0
(NL Division Series Game 1)

REGULAR SEASON, FEWER THAN NINE INNINGS

retired every batter faced

EIGHT INNINGS

Charlie Gagus, UA:Wash. Aug. 21, 1884 (Wil.) 12-1
Charles King, PL:Chi. June 21, 1890 (Brk.) lost 0-1
Henry Gastright, AA:Colu. Oct. 12, 1890 (Tol.) 6-0
Fred Frankhouse, NL:Brk. Aug. 27, 1937 (Cin.) 5-0
(7.2 inn, rain)
Andy Hawkins, AL:NY July 1, 1990 (at Chi.) lost 0-4
Matt Young, AL:Bos. Apr. 12(1g), 1992 (at Clev.) lost 1-2
Jered Weaver (6 inn), Jose Arredondo (2 inn), AL:LA June
28, 2008 (at NL:LA) lost 0-1

SEVEN INNINGS

Ed Crane, NL:NY Sept. 27, 1888 (Wash.) 3-0
Matt Kilroy, AA:Balt. July 29(2g), 1889 (StL.) 0-0
George Nicol, AA:StL. Sept. 23, 1890 (Phil.) 21-2
(First major league game)
Elton Chamberlain, NL:Cin. Sept. 23(2g), 1893 (Bos.) 6-0
John Weimer, NL:Cin. Aug. 24(2g), 1906 (Brk.) 1-0
Grant McGlynn, NL:StL. Sept. 24(2g), 1906 (at Brk.) 1-1
*Ed Karger, NL:StL. Aug. 11(2g), 1907 (Bos.) 4-0
Len Cole, NL:Chi. July 31(2g), 1910 (at StL.) 4-0
Walter Johnson, AL:Wash. Aug. 25, 1924 (StL.) 2-0
Sam Jones, NL:SF Sept. 26, 1959 (at StL.) 4-0

SIX INNINGS

Larry McKeon, AA:Ind. May 6, 1884 (at Cin.) 0-0
Charlie Getzien, NL:Det. Oct. 1, 1884 (Phil.) 1-0
George Van Haltren, NL:Chi. June 21, 1888 (Pitt.) 1-0
Ed Stein, NL:Brk. June 2, 1894 (Chi.) 1-0
Al Leifield, NL:Pitt. Sept. 26(2g), 1906 (at Phil.) 8-0
John Lush, NL:StL. Aug. 6, 1908 (at Brk.) 2-0
Carl Cashion, AL:Wash. Aug. 20(2g), 1912 (Clev.) 2-0
Johnny Whitehead, AL:StL. Aug. 5(2g), 1940 (Det.) 4-0
Melido Perez, AL:Chi. July 12, 1990 (at NY) 8-0

FIVE INNINGS

Charlie Sweeney, (2 inn) & Henry Boyle (3 inn), UA:StL.
Oct. 5, 1884 (StP.) lost 0-1
Fred Shaw, NL:Prov. Oct. 7(1g), 1885 (at Buff.) 4-0
John Stivetts, NL:Bos. Oct. 15(2g), 1892 (at Wash.) 4-0
Red Ames, NL:NY Sept. 14(2g), 1903 (at StL.) 5-0
(First major league game)
Rube Waddell, AL:Phil. Aug. 15, 1905 (StL.) 2-0
Jim Dygert (3 inn) & Rube Waddell (2 inn), AL:Phil. Aug. 29,
1906 (Chi.) 4-3
Ed Walsh, AL:Chi. May 26, 1907 (NY) 8-0
Howie Camnitz, NL:Pitt. Aug. 23(2g), 1907 (at NY) 1-0
*Harry Vickers, AL:Phil. Oct. 5(2g), 1907 (at Wash.) 4-0
Jim Tobin, NL:Bos. June 22(2g), 1944 (Phil.) 7-0
Mike McCormick, NL:SF June 12, 1959 (at Phil.) 3-0
(allowed hit in 6th inning before game was rained out
and reverted to last full inning)
*Dean Chance, AL:Minn. Aug. 6, 1967 (Bos.) 2-0
*David Palmer, NL:Mtl. Apr. 21(2g), 1984 (at StL.) 4-0
Pascual Perez, NL:Mtl. Sept. 24, 1988 (at Phil.) 1-0
Devern Hansack, AL:Bos. Oct. 1, 2006 (Balt.) 9-0

NO HITS THROUGH NINE INNINGS, ALLOWED HIT IN EXTRA-INNING

Earl Moore, AL:Clev. (Chi.) May 9, 1901
(allowed hit in 10th, lost)
Bob Wicker, NL:Chi. (NY) June 11, 1904
(allowed hit in 10th, won in 12th)
Harry McIntire, NL:Brk. (Pitt.) Aug. 1, 1906
(allowed hit in 11th, lost in 13th)
Red Ames, NL:NY (Brk.) Apr. 15, 1909
(allowed hit in 10th, lost in 13th)
Tom Hughes, AL:NY (Clev.) Aug. 30(2g), 1910
(allowed hit in 10th, lost in 11th)
Jim Scott, AL:Chi. (at Wash.) May 14, 1914
(allowed hit in 10th, lost)
Hippo Vaughn, NL:Chi. (Cin.) May 2, 1917
(allowed hit in 10th, lost)
Bobo Newsom, AL:StL. (Bos.) Sept. 18, 1934
(allowed hit in 10th, lost)
Johnny Klippstein (7 inn), Hersh Freeman (1 inn) &
Joe Black (2.1 inns), NL:Cin. (at Mil.) May 26, 1956
(allowed hit in 10th, 2 hits in 11th, lost)
Harvey Haddix, NL:Pitt. (at Mil.) May 26, 1959
(12 innings perfect; allowed hit in 13th, lost)
Jim Maloney, NL:Cin. (NY) June 14, 1965
(allowed 2 hits in 11th, lost)
Mark Gardner, NL:Mtl. (at LA) July 26, 1991
(allowed 2 hits in 10th, lost)
Pedro Martinez, NL:Mtl. (at SD) June 3, 1995
(9 innings perfect, allowed hit in 10th, won)
Rich Hill, NL:LA (at Pitt.) Aug. 23, 2017
(allowed hit in 10th, lost)

BATTING AVERAGE

1900:	.381	Honus Wagner, NL:Pitt.
1901:	.422	Nap Lajoie, AL:Phil.
	.382	Jesse Burkett, NL:StL.
1902:	.376	Ed Delahanty, AL:Wash.
	.357	Ginger Beaumont, NL:Pitt.
1903:	.355	Honus Wagner, NL:Pitt. (2)
	.355	Nap Lajoie, AL:Clev. (2)
1904:	.381	Nap Lajoie, AL:Clev. (3)
	.349	Honus Wagner, NL:Pitt. (3)
1905:	.377	Cy Seymour, NL:Cin.
	.308	Elmer Flick, AL:Clev.
1906:	.358	George Stone, AL:StL.
	.339	Honus Wagner, NL:Pitt. (4)
1907:	.350	Ty Cobb, AL:Det.
	.350	Honus Wagner, NL:Pitt. (5)
1908:	.354	Honus Wagner, NL:Pitt. (6)
	.322	Ty Cobb, AL:Det. (2)
1909:	.376	Ty Cobb, AL:Det. (3)
	.339	Honus Wagner, NL:Pitt. (7)
1910:	.385	Ty Cobb, AL:Det. (4)
	.331	Sherry Magee, NL:Phil.
1911:	.419	Ty Cobb, AL:Det. (5)
	.333	Honus Wagner, NL:Pitt. (8)
1912:	.410	Ty Cobb, AL:Det. (6)
	.372	Heinie Zimmerman, NL:Chi.
1913:	.390	Ty Cobb, AL:Det. (7)
	.350	Jake Daubert, NL:Brk.
1914:	.368	Ty Cobb, AL:Det. (8)
	.329	Jake Daubert, NL:Brk. (2)
1915:	.369	Ty Cobb, AL:Det. (9)
	.320	Larry Doyle, NL:NY
1916:	.386	Tris Speaker, AL:Clev.
	.339	Hal Chase, NL:Cin.
1917:	.383	Ty Cobb, AL:Det. (10)
	.341	Edd Roush, NL:Cin.
1918:	.382	Ty Cobb, AL:Det. (11)
	.335	Zack Wheat, NL:Brk.
1919:	.384	Ty Cobb, AL:Det. (12)
	.321	Edd Roush, NL:Cin. (2)
1920:	.407	George Sisler, AL:StL.
	.370	Rogers Hornsby, NL:StL.
1921:	.397	Rogers Hornsby, NL:StL. (2)
	.394	Harry Heilmann, AL:Det.
1922:	.418	George Sisler, AL:StL. (2)
	.401	Rogers Hornsby, NL:StL. (3)
1923:	.402	Harry Heilmann, AL:Det. (2)
	.384	Rogers Hornsby, NL:StL. (4)
1924:	.424	Rogers Hornsby, NL:StL. (5)
	.378	Babe Ruth, AL:NY
1925:	.403	Rogers Hornsby, NL:StL. (6)
	.393	Harry Heilmann, AL:Det. (3)
1926:	.378	Heinie Manush, AL:Det.
	.353	Bubbles Hargrave, NL:Cin.
1927:	.398	Harry Heilmann, AL:Det. (4)
	.380	Paul Waner, NL:Pitt.
1928:	.387	Rogers Hornsby, NL:Bos. (7)
	.379	Goose Goslin, AL:Wash.
1929:	.398	Lefty O'Doul, NL:Phil.
	.369	Lew Fonseca, AL:Clev.
1930:	.401	Bill Terry, NL:NY
	.381	Al Simmons, AL:Phil.
1931:	.390	Al Simmons, AL:Phil. (2)
	.349	Chick Hafey, NL:StL.
1932:	.368	Lefty O'Doul, NL:Brk. (2)
	.367	Dale Alexander, AL:Det.-Bos.
1933:	.368	Chuck Klein, NL:Phil.
	.356	Jimmie Foxx, AL:Phil.
1934:	.363	Lou Gehrig, AL:NY
	.362	Paul Waner, NL:Pitt. (2)
1935:	.385	Arky Vaughan, NL:Pitt.
	.349	Buddy Myer, AL:Wash.
1936:	.388	Luke Appling, AL:Chi.
	.373	Paul Waner, NL:Pitt. (3)
1937:	.374	Joe Medwick, NL:StL.
	.371	Charlie Gehringer, AL:Det.
1938:	.349	Jimmie Foxx, AL:Bos. (2)
	.342	Ernie Lombardi, NL:Cin.
1939:	.381	Joe DiMaggio, AL:NY
	.350	Johnny Mize, NL:StL.
1940:	.355	Debs Garms, NL:Pitt.
	.352	Joe DiMaggio, AL:NY (2)
1941:	.406	Ted Williams, AL:Bos.
	.343	Pete Reiser, NL:Brk.
1942:	.356	Ted Williams, AL:Bos. (2)
	.330	Ernie Lombardi, NL:Bos. (2)
1943:	.357	Stan Musial, NL:StL.
	.328	Luke Appling, AL:Chi. (2)
1944:	.357	Dixie Walker, NL:Brk.
	.327	Lou Boudreau, AL:Clev.
1945:	.355	Phil Cavarretta, NL:Chi.
	.309	Snuffy Stirnweiss, AL:NY
1946:	.365	Stan Musial, NL:StL. (2)
	.353	Mickey Vernon, AL:Wash.
1947:	.363	Harry Walker, NL:StL.-Phil.
	.343	Ted Williams, AL:Bos. (3)
1948:	.376	Stan Musial, NL:StL. (3)
	.369	Ted Williams, AL:Bos. (4)
1949:	.343	George Kell, AL:Det.
	.342	Jackie Robinson, NL:Brk.
1950:	.354	Billy Goodman, AL:Bos.
	.346	Stan Musial, NL:StL. (4)
1951:	.355	Stan Musial, NL:StL. (5)
	.344	Ferris Fain, AL:Phil.
1952:	.336	Stan Musial, NL:StL. (6)
	.327	Ferris Fain, AL:Phil. (2)
1953:	.344	Carl Furillo, NL:Brk.
	.337	Mickey Vernon, AL:Wash. (2)
1954:	.345	Willie Mays, NL:NY
	.341	Bobby Avila, AL:Clev.
1955:	.340	Al Kaline, AL:Det.
	.338	Richie Ashburn, NL:Phil.
1956:	.353	Mickey Mantle, AL:NY
	.328	Hank Aaron, NL:Mil.
1957:	.388	Ted Williams, AL:Bos. (5)
	.351	Stan Musial, NL:StL. (7)
1958:	.350	Richie Ashburn, NL:Phil. (2)
	.328	Ted Williams, AL:Bos. (6)
1959:	.355	Hank Aaron, NL:Mil. (2)
	.353	Harvey Kuenn, AL:Det.
1960:	.325	Dick Groat, NL:Pitt.
	.320	Pete Runnels, AL:Bos.
1961:	.361	Norm Cash, AL:Det.
	.351	Roberto Clemente, NL:Pitt.
1962:	.346	Tommy Davis, NL:LA
	.326	Pete Runnels, AL:Bos. (2)
1963:	.326	Tommy Davis, NL:LA (2)
	.321	Carl Yastrzemski, AL:Bos.
1964:	.339	Roberto Clemente, NL:Pitt. (2)
	.323	Tony Oliva, AL:Minn.

BATTING AVERAGE (CONTINUED)

1965:	.329	Roberto Clemente, NL:Pitt. (3)
	.321	Tony Oliva, AL:Minn. (2)
1966:	.342	Matty Alou, NL:Pitt.
	.316	Frank Robinson, AL:Balt.
1967:	.357	Roberto Clemente, NL:Pitt. (4)
	.326	Carl Yastrzemski, AL:Bos. (2)
1968:	.335	Pete Rose, NL:Cin.
	.301	Carl Yastrzemski, AL:Bos. (3)
1969:	.348	Pete Rose, NL:Cin. (2)
	.332	Rod Carew, AL:Minn.
1970:	.366	Rico Carty, NL:Atl.
	.329	Alex Johnson, AL:Cal.
1971:	.363	Joe Torre, NL:StL.
	.337	Tony Oliva, AL:Minn. (3)
1972:	.333	Billy Williams, NL:Chi.
	.318	Rod Carew, AL:Minn. (2)
1973:	.350	Rod Carew, AL:Minn. (3)
	.338	Pete Rose, NL:Cin. (3)
1974:	.364	Rod Carew, AL:Minn. (4)
	.353	Ralph Garr, NL:Atl.
1975:	.359	Rod Carew, AL:Minn. (5)
	.354	Bill Madlock, NL:Chi.
1976:	.339	Bill Madlock, NL:Chi. (2)
	.333	George Brett, AL:KC
1977:	.388	Rod Carew, AL:Minn. (6)
	.338	Dave Parker, NL:Pitt.
1978:	.334	Dave Parker, NL:Pitt. (2)
	.333	Rod Carew, AL:Minn. (7)
1979:	.344	Keith Hernandez, NL:StL.
	.333	Fred Lynn, AL:Bos.
1980:	.390	George Brett, AL:KC (2)
	.324	Bill Buckner, NL:Chi.
1981:	.341	Bill Madlock, NL:Pitt. (3)
	.336	Carney Lansford, AL:Bos.
1982:	.332	Willie Wilson, AL:KC
	.331	Al Oliver, NL:Mtl.
1983:	.361	Wade Boggs, AL:Bos.
	.323	Bill Madlock, NL:Pitt. (4)
1984:	.351	Tony Gwynn, NL:SD
	.343	Don Mattingly, AL:NY
1985:	.368	Wade Boggs, AL:Bos. (2)
	.353	Willie McGee, NL:StL.
1986:	.357	Wade Boggs, AL:Bos. (3)
	.334	Tim Raines, NL:Mtl.
1987:	.370	Tony Gwynn, NL:SD (2)
	.363	Wade Boggs, AL:Bos. (4)
1988:	.366	Wade Boggs, AL:Bos. (5)
	.313	Tony Gwynn, NL:SD (3)
1989:	.339	Kirby Puckett, AL:Minn.
	.336	Tony Gwynn, NL:SD (4)
1990:	.335	Willie McGee, NL:StL. (2)
	.329	George Brett, AL:KC (3)
1991:	.341	Julio Franco, AL:Tex.
	.319	Terry Pendleton, NL:Atl.
1992:	.343	Edgar Martinez, AL:Sea.
	.330	Gary Sheffield, NL:SD
1993:	.370	Andres Galarraga, NL:Col.
	.363	John Olerud, AL:Tor.
1994:	.394	Tony Gwynn, NL:SD (5)
	.359	Paul O'Neill, AL:NY
1995:	.368	Tony Gwynn, NL:SD (6)
	.356	Edgar Martinez, AL:Sea. (2)
1996:	.358	Alex Rodriguez, AL:Sea.
	.353	Tony Gwynn, NL:SD (7)

1997:	.372	Tony Gwynn, NL:SD (8)
	.347	Frank Thomas, AL:Chi.
1998:	.363	Larry Walker, NL:Col.
	.339	Bernie Williams, AL:NY
1999:	.379	Larry Walker, NL:Col. (2)
	.357	Nomar Garciaparra, AL:Bos.
2000:	.372	Todd Helton, NL:Col.
	.372	Nomar Garciaparra, AL:Bos. (2)
2001:	.350	Larry Walker, NL:Col. (3)
	.350	Ichiro Suzuki, AL:Sea.
2002:	.370	Barry Bonds, NL:SF
	.349	Manny Ramirez, AL:Bos.
2003:	.359	Albert Pujols, NL:StL.
	.326	Bill Mueller, AL:Bos.
2004:	.372	Ichiro Suzuki, AL:Sea. (2)
	.362	Barry Bonds, NL:SF (2)
2005:	.335	Derrek Lee, NL:Chi.
	.331	Michael Young, AL:Tex.
2006:	.347	Joe Mauer, AL:Minn.
	.344	Freddy Sanchez, NL:Pitt.
2007:	.363	Magglio Ordonez, AL:Det.
	.340	Matt Holliday, NL:Col.
2008:	.364	Chipper Jones, NL:Atl.
	.328	Joe Mauer, AL:Minn. (2)
2009:	.365	Joe Mauer, AL:Minn. (3)
	.342	Hanley Ramirez, NL:Fla.
2010:	.359	Josh Hamilton, AL:Tex.
	.336	Carlos Gonzalez, NL:Col.
2011:	.344	Miguel Cabrera, AL:Det.
	.337	Jose Reyes, NL:NY
2012:	.336	Buster Posey, NL:SF
	.330	Miguel Cabrera, AL:Det. (2)
2013:	.348	Miguel Cabrera, AL:Det. (3)
	.331	Michael Cuddyer, NL:Col.
2014:	.341	Jose Altuve, AL:Hou.
	.319	Justin Morneau, NL:Col.
2015:	.338	Miguel Cabrera, AL:Det. (4)
	.333	Dee Gordon, NL:Mia.
2016:	.348	DJ LeMahieu, NL:Col.
	.338	Jose Altuve, AL:Hou. (2)
2017:	.346	Jose Altuve, AL:Hou. (3)
	.331	Charlie Blackmon, NL:Col.
2018:	.346	Mookie Betts, AL:Bos.
	.326	Christian Yelich, NL:Mil.
2019:	.335	Tim Anderson, AL:Chi.
	.329	Christian Yelich, NL:Mil. (2)
2020:	.364	DJ LeMahieu, AL:NY (NL 1)
	.351	Juan Soto, NL:Wash.

TOTAL BASES

Year	TB	Player
1900:	305	Elmer Flick, NL:Phil.
1901:	345	Nap Lajoie, AL:Phil.
	313	Jesse Burkett, NL:StL.
1902:	289	Piano Legs Hickman, AL:Bos.-Clev.
	256	Sam Crawford, NL:Cin.
1903:	281	Buck Freeman, AL:Bos.
	272	Ginger Beaumont, NL:Pitt.
1904:	304	Nap Lajoie, AL:Clev. (2)
	255	Honus Wagner, NL:Pitt.
1905:	325	Cy Seymour, NL:Cin.
	260	George Stone, AL:StL.
1906:	290	George Stone, AL:StL. (2)
	237	Honus Wagner, NL:Pitt. (2)
1907:	286	Ty Cobb, AL:Det.
	264	Honus Wagner, NL:Pitt. (3)
1908:	308	Honus Wagner, NL:Pitt. (4)
	276	Ty Cobb, AL:Det. (2)
1909:	296	Ty Cobb, AL:Det. (3)
	242	Honus Wagner, NL:Pitt. (5)
1910:	308	Nap Lajoie, AL:Clev. (3)
	263	Sherry Magee, NL:Phil.
1911:	367	Ty Cobb, AL:Det. (4)
	308	Frank Schulte, NL:Chi.
1912:	331	Joe Jackson, AL:Clev.
	318	Heinie Zimmerman, NL:Chi.
1913:	298	Gavvy Cravath, NL:Phil.
	298	Sam Crawford, AL:Det.
1914:	287	Tris Speaker, AL:Bos.
	277	Sherry Magee, NL:Phil. (2)
1915:	274	Ty Cobb, AL:Det. (5)
	266	Gavvy Cravath, NL:Phil. (2)
1916:	293	Joe Jackson, AL:Chi. (2)
	262	Zack Wheat, NL:Brk.
1917:	335	Ty Cobb, AL:Det. (6)
	253	Rogers Hornsby, NL:StL.
1918:	236	George Burns, AL:Phil.
	202	Charlie Hollocher, NL:Chi.
1919:	284	Babe Ruth, AL:Bos.
	223	Hy Myers, NL:Brk.
1920:	399	George Sisler, AL:StL.
	329	Rogers Hornsby, NL:StL. (2)
1921:	457	Babe Ruth, AL:NY (2)
	378	Rogers Hornsby, NL:StL. (3)
1922:	450	Rogers Hornsby, NL:StL. (4)
	366	Ken Williams, AL:StL.
1923:	399	Babe Ruth, AL:NY (3)
	311	Frankie Frisch, NL:NY
1924:	391	Babe Ruth, AL:NY (4)
	373	Rogers Hornsby, NL:StL. (5)
1925:	392	Al Simmons, AL:Phil.
	381	Rogers Hornsby, NL:StL. (6)
1926:	365	Babe Ruth, AL:NY (5)
	305	Jim Bottomley, NL:StL.
1927:	447	Lou Gehrig, AL:NY
	342	Paul Waner, NL:Pitt.
1928:	380	Babe Ruth, AL:NY (6)
	362	Jim Bottomley, NL:StL. (2)
1929:	409	Rogers Hornsby, NL:Chi. (7)
	374	Al Simmons, AL:Phil. (2)
1930:	445	Chuck Klein, NL:Phil.
	419	Lou Gehrig, AL:NY (2)
1931:	410	Lou Gehrig, AL:NY (3)
	347	Chuck Klein, NL:Phil. (2)
1932:	438	Jimmie Foxx, AL:Phil.
	420	Chuck Klein, NL:Phil. (3)
1933:	403	Jimmie Foxx, AL:Phil. (2)
	365	Chuck Klein, NL:Phil. (4)
1934:	409	Lou Gehrig, AL:NY (4)
	369	Ripper Collins, NL:StL.
1935:	389	Hank Greenberg, AL:Det.
	365	Joe Medwick, NL:StL.
1936:	405	Hal Trosky, AL:Clev.
	367	Joe Medwick, NL:StL. (2)
1937:	418	Joe DiMaggio, AL:NY
	406	Joe Medwick, NL:StL. (3)
1938:	398	Jimmie Foxx, AL:Bos. (3)
	326	Johnny Mize, NL:StL.
1939:	353	Johnny Mize, NL:StL. (2)
	344	Ted Williams, AL:Bos.
1940:	384	Hank Greenberg, AL:Det. (2)
	368	Johnny Mize, NL:StL. (3)
1941:	348	Joe DiMaggio, AL:NY (2)
	299	Pete Reiser, NL:Brk.
1942:	338	Ted Williams, AL:Bos. (2)
	292	Enos Slaughter, NL:StL.
1943:	347	Stan Musial, NL:StL.
	301	Rudy York, AL:Det.
1944:	317	Bill Nicholson, NL:Chi.
	297	Johnny Lindell, AL:NY
1945:	367	Tommy Holmes, NL:Bos.
	301	Snuffy Stirnweiss, AL:NY
1946:	366	Stan Musial, NL:StL. (2)
	343	Ted Williams, AL:Bos. (3)
1947:	361	Ralph Kiner, NL:Pitt.
	335	Ted Williams, AL:Bos. (4)
1948:	429	Stan Musial, NL:StL. (3)
	355	Joe DiMaggio, AL:NY (3)
1949:	382	Stan Musial, NL:StL. (4)
	368	Ted Williams, AL:Bos. (5)
1950:	343	Duke Snider, NL:Brk.
	326	Walt Dropo, AL:Bos.
1951:	355	Stan Musial, NL:StL. (5)
	295	Ted Williams, AL:Bos. (6)
1952:	311	Stan Musial, NL:StL. (6)
	297	Al Rosen, AL:Clev.
1953:	370	Duke Snider, NL:Brk. (2)
	367	Al Rosen, AL:Clev. (2)
1954:	378	Duke Snider, NL:Brk. (3)
	304	Minnie Minoso, AL:Chi.
1955:	382	Willie Mays, NL:NY
	321	Al Kaline, AL:Det.
1956:	376	Mickey Mantle, AL:NY
	340	Hank Aaron, NL:Mil.
1957:	369	Hank Aaron, NL:Mil. (2)
	331	Roy Sievers, AL:Wash.
1958:	379	Ernie Banks, NL:Chi.
	307	Mickey Mantle, AL:NY (2)
1959:	400	Hank Aaron, NL:Mil. (3)
	301	Rocky Colavito, AL:Clev.
1960:	334	Hank Aaron, NL:Mil. (4)
	294	Mickey Mantle, AL:NY (3)
1961:	366	Roger Maris, AL:NY
	358	Hank Aaron, NL:Mil. (5)
1962:	382	Willie Mays, NL:SF (2)
	309	Rocky Colavito, AL:Det. (2)
1963:	370	Hank Aaron, NL:Mil. (6)
	319	Dick Stuart, AL:Bos.
1964:	374	Tony Oliva, AL:Minn.
	352	Dick Allen, NL:Phil.
1965:	360	Willie Mays, NL:SF (3)
	308	Zoilo Versalles, AL:Minn.

TOTAL BASES (CONTINUED)

1966:	367	Frank Robinson, AL:Balt.
	355	Felipe Alou, NL:Atl.
1967:	360	Carl Yastrzemski, AL:Bos.
	344	Hank Aaron, NL:Atl. (7)
1968:	330	Frank Howard, AL:Wash.
	321	Billy Williams, NL:Chi.
1969:	340	Frank Howard, AL:Wash. (2)
	332	Hank Aaron, NL:Atl. (8)
1970:	373	Billy Williams, NL:Chi. (2)
	335	Carl Yastrzemski, AL:Bos. (2)
1971:	352	Joe Torre, NL:StL.
	302	Reggie Smith, AL:Bos.
1972:	348	Billy Williams, NL:Chi. (3)
	314	Bobby Murcer, AL:NY
1973:	341	Bobby Bonds, NL:SF
	295	Sal Bando, AL:Oak.
	295	Dave May, AL:Mil.
	295	George Scott, AL:Mil.
1974:	315	Johnny Bench, NL:Cin.
	287	Joe Rudi, AL:Oak.
1975:	322	Greg Luzinski, NL:Phil.
	318	George Scott, AL:Mil. (2)
1976:	306	Mike Schmidt, NL:Phil.
	298	George Brett, AL:KC
1977:	388	George Foster, NL:Cin.
	382	Jim Rice, AL:Bos.
1978:	406	Jim Rice, AL:Bos. (2)
	340	Dave Parker, NL:Pitt.
1979:	369	Jim Rice, AL:Bos. (3)
	333	Dave Winfield, NL:SD
1980:	342	Mike Schmidt, NL:Phil. (2)
	335	Cecil Cooper, AL:Mil.
1981:	228	Mike Schmidt, NL:Phil. (3)
	215	Dwight Evans, AL:Bos.
1982:	367	Robin Yount, AL:Mil.
	317	Al Oliver, NL:Mtl.
1983:	344	Jim Rice, AL:Bos. (4)
	341	Andre Dawson, NL:Mtl.
1984:	339	Tony Armas, AL:Bos.
	332	Dale Murphy, NL:Atl.
1985:	370	Don Mattingly, AL:NY
	350	Dave Parker, NL:Cin. (2)
1986:	388	Don Mattingly, AL:NY (2)
	304	Dave Parker, NL:Cin. (3)
1987:	369	George Bell, AL:Tor.
	353	Andre Dawson, NL:Chi. (2)
1988:	358	Kirby Puckett, AL:Minn.
	329	Andres Galarraga, NL:Mtl.
1989:	345	Kevin Mitchell, NL:SF
	344	Ruben Sierra, AL:Tex.
1990:	344	Ryne Sandberg, NL:Chi.
	339	Cecil Fielder, AL:Det.
1991:	368	Cal Ripken, AL:Balt.
	303	Will Clark, NL:SF
	303	Terry Pendleton, NL:Atl.
1992:	323	Gary Sheffield, NL:SD
	313	Kirby Puckett, AL:Minn. (2)
1993:	365	Barry Bonds, NL:SF
	359	Ken Griffey Jr., AL:Sea.
1994:	300	Jeff Bagwell, NL:Hou.
	294	Albert Belle, AL:Clev.
1995:	377	Albert Belle, AL:Clev. (2)
	359	Dante Bichette, NL:Col.

1996:	392	Ellis Burks, NL:Col.
	379	Alex Rodriguez, AL:Sea.
1997:	409	Larry Walker, NL:Col.
	393	Ken Griffey Jr., AL:Sea. (2)
1998:	416	Sammy Sosa, NL:Chi.
	399	Albert Belle, AL:Chi. (3)
1999:	397	Sammy Sosa, NL:Chi. (2)
	361	Shawn Green, AL:Tor.
2000:	405	Todd Helton, NL:Col.
	378	Carlos Delgado, AL:Tor.
2001:	425	Sammy Sosa, NL:Chi. (3)
	393	Alex Rodriguez, AL:Tex. (2)
2002:	389	Alex Rodriguez, AL:Tex. (3)
	364	Vladimir Guerrero, NL:Mtl.
2003:	394	Albert Pujols, NL:StL.
	373	Vernon Wells, AL:Tor.
2004:	389	Albert Pujols, NL:StL. (2)
	366	Vladimir Guerrero, AL:Ana. (NL 1)
2005:	393	Derrek Lee, NL:Chi.
	370	Mark Teixeira, AL:Tex.
2006:	383	Ryan Howard, NL:Phil.
	355	David Ortiz, AL:Bos.
2007:	386	Matt Holliday, NL:Col.
	376	Alex Rodriguez, AL:NY (4)
2008:	342	Albert Pujols, NL:StL. (3)
	331	Miguel Cabrera, AL:Det.
	331	Josh Hamilton, AL:Tex.
2009:	374	Albert Pujols, NL:StL. (4)
	344	Mark Teixeira, AL:NY (2)
2010:	351	Jose Bautista, AL:Tor.
	351	Carlos Gonzalez, NL:Col.
2011:	364	Jacoby Ellsbury, AL:Bos.
	353	Matt Kemp, NL:LA
2012:	377	Miguel Cabrera, AL:Det. (2)
	356	Ryan Braun, NL:Mil.
2013:	370	Chris Davis, AL:Balt.
	332	Paul Goldschmidt, NL:Ari.
2014:	338	Mike Trout, AL:LA
	299	Giancarlo Stanton, NL:Mia.
2015:	354	Nolan Arenado, NL:Col.
	352	Josh Donaldson, AL:Tor.
2016:	359	Mookie Betts, AL:Bos.
	352	Nolan Arenado, NL:Col. (2)
2017:	387	Charlie Blackmon, NL:Col.
	343	Jose Abreu, AL:Chi.
2018:	358	J.D. Martinez, AL:Bos.
	343	Christian Yelich, NL:Mil.
2019:	359	Rafael Devers, AL:Bos.
	351	Cody Bellinger, NL:LA
2020:	148	Jose Abreu, AL:Chi. (2)
	145	Marcell Ozuna, NL:Atl.

RUNS BATTED IN

1920:	136	Babe Ruth, AL:NY
	94	Rogers Hornsby, NL:StL.
	94	George Kelly, NL:NY
1921:	168	Babe Ruth, AL:NY (2)
	127	George Kelly, NL:NY (2)
1922:	154	Ken Williams, AL:StL.
	152	Rogers Hornsby, NL:StL. (2)
1923:	130	Babe Ruth, AL:NY (3)
	130	Tris Speaker, AL:Clev.
	125	Irish Meusel, NL:NY
1924:	136	George Kelly, NL:NY (3)
	129	Goose Goslin, AL:Wash.
1925:	143	Rogers Hornsby, NL:StL. (3)
	136	Bob Meusel, AL:NY
1926:	153	Babe Ruth, AL:NY (4)
	120	Jim Bottomley, NL:StL.
1927:	173	Lou Gehrig, AL:NY
	132	Paul Waner, NL:Pitt.
1928:	147	Lou Gehrig, AL:NY (2)
	136	Jim Bottomley, NL:StL. (2)
1929:	158	Hack Wilson, NL:Chi.
	157	Al Simmons, AL:Phil.
1930:	191	Hack Wilson, NL:Chi. (2)
	173	Lou Gehrig, AL:NY (3)
1931:	184	Lou Gehrig, AL:NY (4)
	121	Chuck Klein, NL:Phil.
1932:	169	Jimmie Foxx, AL:Phil.
	143	Don Hurst, NL:Phil.
1933:	163	Jimmie Foxx, AL:Phil. (2)
	120	Chuck Klein, NL:Phil. (2)
1934:	166	Lou Gehrig, AL:NY (5)
	135	Mel Ott, NL:NY
1935:	170	Hank Greenberg, AL:Det.
	130	Wally Berger, NL:Bos.
1936:	163	Hal Trosky, AL:Clev.
	138	Joe Medwick, NL:StL.
1937:	183	Hank Greenberg, AL:Det. (2)
	153	Joe Medwick, NL:StL. (2)
1938:	175	Jimmie Foxx, AL:Bos. (3)
	122	Joe Medwick, NL:StL. (3)
1939:	145	Ted Williams, AL:Bos.
	128	Frank McCormick, NL:Cin.
1940:	150	Hank Greenberg, AL:Det. (3)
	137	Johnny Mize, NL:StL.
1941:	125	Joe DiMaggio, AL:NY
	120	Dolph Camilli, NL:Brk.
1942:	137	Ted Williams, AL:Bos. (2)
	110	Johnny Mize, NL:NY (2)
1943:	128	Bill Nicholson, NL:Chi.
	118	Rudy York, AL:Det.
1944:	122	Bill Nicholson, NL:Chi. (2)
	108	Vern Stephens, AL:StL.
1945:	124	Dixie Walker, NL:Brk.
	111	Nick Etten, AL:NY
1946:	130	Enos Slaughter, NL:StL.
	127	Hank Greenberg, AL:Det. (4)
1947:	138	Johnny Mize, NL:NY (3)
	114	Ted Williams, AL:Bos. (3)
1948:	155	Joe DiMaggio, AL:NY (2)
	131	Stan Musial, NL:StL.
1949:	159	Ted Williams, AL:Bos. (4)
	159	Vern Stephens, AL:Bos. (2)
	127	Ralph Kiner, NL:Pitt.

1950:	144	Walt Dropo, AL:Bos.
	144	Vern Stephens, AL:Bos. (3)
	126	Del Ennis, NL:Phil.
1951:	129	Gus Zernial, AL:Chi.-Phil.
	122	Monte Irvin, NL:NY
1952:	121	Hank Sauer, NL:Chi.
	105	Al Rosen, AL:Clev.
1953:	145	Al Rosen, AL:Clev. (2)
	142	Roy Campanella, NL:Brk.
1954:	141	Ted Kluszewski, NL:Cin.
	126	Larry Doby, AL:Clev.
1955:	136	Duke Snider, NL:Brk.
	116	Ray Boone, AL:Det.
	116	Jackie Jensen, AL:Bos.
1956:	130	Mickey Mantle, AL:NY
	109	Stan Musial, NL:StL. (2)
1957:	132	Hank Aaron, NL:Mil.
	114	Roy Sievers, AL:Wash.
1958:	129	Ernie Banks, NL:Chi.
	122	Jackie Jensen, AL:Bos. (2)
1959:	143	Ernie Banks, NL:Chi. (2)
	112	Jackie Jensen, AL:Bos. (3)
1960:	126	Hank Aaron, NL:Mil. (2)
	112	Roger Maris, AL:NY
1961:	142	Orlando Cepeda, NL:SF
	141	Jim Gentile, AL:Balt.
	141	Roger Maris, AL:NY (2)
1962:	153	Tommy Davis, NL:LA
	126	Harmon Killebrew, AL:Minn.
1963:	130	Hank Aaron, NL:Mil. (3)
	118	Dick Stuart, AL:Bos.
1964:	119	Ken Boyer, NL:StL.
	118	Brooks Robinson, AL:Balt.
1965:	130	Deron Johnson, NL:Cin.
	108	Rocky Colavito, AL:Clev.
1966:	127	Hank Aaron, NL:Atl. (4)
	122	Frank Robinson, AL:Balt.
1967:	121	Carl Yastrzemski, AL:Bos.
	111	Orlando Cepeda, NL:StL. (2)
1968:	109	Ken Harrelson, AL:Bos.
	105	Willie McCovey, NL:SF
1969:	140	Harmon Killebrew, AL:Minn. (2)
	126	Willie McCovey, NL:SF (2)
1970:	148	Johnny Bench, NL:Cin.
	126	Frank Howard, AL:Wash.
1971:	137	Joe Torre, NL:StL.
	119	Harmon Killebrew, AL:Minn. (3)
1972:	125	Johnny Bench, NL:Cin. (2)
	113	Dick Allen, AL:Chi.
1973:	119	Willie Stargell, NL:Pitt.
	117	Reggie Jackson, AL:Oak
1974:	129	Johnny Bench, NL:Cin. (3)
	118	Jeff Burroughs, AL:Tex
1975:	120	Greg Luzinski, NL:Phil.
	109	George Scott, AL:Mil.
1976:	121	George Foster, NL:Cin.
	109	Lee May, AL:Balt.
1977:	149	George Foster, NL:Cin. (2)
	119	Larry Hisle, AL:Minn.
1978:	139	Jim Rice, AL:Bos.
	120	George Foster, NL:Cin. (3)
1979:	139	Don Baylor, AL:Cal.
	118	Dave Winfield, NL:SD
1980:	122	Cecil Cooper, AL:Mil.
	121	Mike Schmidt, NL:Phil.
1981:	91	Mike Schmidt, NL:Phil. (2)
	78	Eddie Murray, AL:Balt.

RUNS BATTED IN (CONTINUED)

1982:	133	Hal McRae, AL:KC
	109	Dale Murphy, NL:Atl.
	109	Al Oliver, NL:Mtl.
1983:	126	Cecil Cooper, AL:Mil. (2)
	126	Jim Rice, AL:Bos. (2)
	121	Dale Murphy, NL:Atl. (2)
1984:	123	Tony Armas, AL:Bos.
	106	Gary Carter, NL:Mtl.
	106	Mike Schmidt, NL:Phil. (3)
1985:	145	Don Mattingly, AL:NY
	125	Dave Parker, NL:Cin.
1986:	121	Joe Carter, AL:Clev.
	119	Mike Schmidt, NL:Phil. (4)
1987:	137	Andre Dawson, NL:Chi.
	134	George Bell, AL:Tor.
1988:	124	Jose Canseco, AL:Oak.
	109	Will Clark, NL:SF
1989:	125	Kevin Mitchell, NL:SF
	119	Ruben Sierra, AL:Tex.
1990:	132	Cecil Fielder, AL:Det.
	122	Matt Williams, NL:SF
1991:	133	Cecil Fielder, AL:Det. (2)
	117	Howard Johnson, NL:NY
1992:	124	Cecil Fielder, AL:Det. (3)
	109	Darren Daulton, NL:Phil.
1993:	129	Albert Belle, AL:Clev.
	123	Barry Bonds, NL:SF
1994:	116	Jeff Bagwell, NL:Hou.
	112	Kirby Puckett, AL:Minn.
1995:	128	Dante Bichette, NL:Col.
	126	Albert Belle, AL:Clev. (2)
	126	Mo Vaughn, AL:Bos.
1996:	150	Andres Galarraga, NL:Col.
	148	Albert Belle, AL:Clev. (3)
1997:	147	Ken Griffey Jr., AL:Sea.
	140	Andres Galarraga, NL:Col.
1998:	158	Sammy Sosa, NL:Chi.
	157	Juan Gonzalez, AL:Tex.
1999:	165	Manny Ramirez, AL:Clev.
	147	Mark McGwire, NL:StL.
2000:	147	Todd Helton, NL:Col.
	145	Edgar Martinez, AL:Sea.
2001:	160	Sammy Sosa, NL:Chi. (2)
	141	Bret Boone, AL:Sea.
2002:	142	Alex Rodriguez, AL:Tex.
	128	Lance Berkman, NL:Hou.
2003:	145	Carlos Delgado, AL:Tor.
	141	Preston Wilson, NL:Col.
2004:	150	Miguel Tejada, AL:Balt.
	131	Vinny Castilla, NL:Col.
2005:	148	David Ortiz, AL:Bos.
	128	Andruw Jones, NL:Atl.
2006:	149	Ryan Howard, NL:Phil.
	137	David Ortiz, AL:Bos. (2)
2007:	156	Alex Rodriguez, AL:NY (2)
	137	Matt Holliday, NL:Col.
2008:	146	Ryan Howard, NL:Phil. (2)
	130	Josh Hamilton, AL:Tex.
2009:	141	Prince Fielder, NL:Mil.
	141	Ryan Howard, NL:Phil. (3)
	122	Mark Teixeira, AL:NY
2010:	126	Miguel Cabrera, AL:Det.
	118	Albert Pujols, NL:StL.
2011:	126	Matt Kemp, NL:LA
	119	Curtis Granderson, AL:NY

2012:	139	Miguel Cabrera, AL:Det. (2)
	115	Chase Headley, NL:SD
2013:	138	Chris Davis, AL:Balt.
	125	Paul Goldschmidt, NL:Ari.
2014:	116	Adrian Gonzalez, NL:LA
	111	Mike Trout, AL:LA
2015:	130	Nolan Arenado, NL:Col.
	123	Josh Donaldson, AL:Tor.
2016:	133	Nolan Arenado, NL:Col. (2)
	127	Edwin Encarnacion, AL:Tor.
	127	David Ortiz, AL:Bos. (3)
2017:	132	Giancarlo Stanton, NL:Mia.
	119	Nelson Cruz, AL:Sea.
2018:	130	J.D. Martinez, AL:Bos.
	111	Javier Baez, NL:Chi.
2019:	126	Anthony Rendon, NL:Wash.
	123	Jose Abreu, AL:Chi.
2020:	60	Jose Abreu, AL:Chi. (2)
	56	Marcell Ozuna, NL:Atl.

RUNS SCORED

1900:	131	Roy Thomas, NL:Phil.
1901:	145	Nap Lajoie, AL:Phil.
	139	Jesse Burkett, NL:StL.
1902:	109	Dave Fultz, AL:Phil.
	109	Topsy Hartsel, AL:Phil.
	105	Honus Wagner, NL:Pitt.
1903:	137	Ginger Beaumont, NL:Pitt.
	107	Patsy Dougherty, AL:Bos.
1904:	113	Patsy Dougherty, AL:Bos.-NY (2)
	99	George Browne, NL:NY
1905:	124	Mike Donlin, NL:NY
	93	Harry Davis, AL:Phil.
1906:	104	Honus Wagner, NL:Pitt. (2)
	99	Elmer Flick, AL:Clev.
1907:	104	Spike Shannon, NL:NY
	103	Sam Crawford, AL:Det.
1908:	105	Matty McIntyre, AL:Det.
	101	Fred Tenney, NL:NY
1909:	126	Tommy Leach, NL:Pitt.
	115	Ty Cobb, AL:Det.
	115	Donie Bush, AL:Det.
1910:	110	Sherry Magee, NL:Phil.
	106	Ty Cobb, AL:Det. (2)
1911:	148	Ty Cobb, AL:Det. (3)
	121	Jimmy Sheckard, NL:Chi.
1912:	137	Eddie Collins, AL:Phil.
	120	Bob Bescher, NL:Cin.
1913:	125	Eddie Collins, AL:Phil. (2)
	99	Max Carey, NL:Pitt.
	99	Tommy Leach, NL:Chi. (2)
1914:	122	Eddie Collins, AL:Phil. (3)
	100	George Burns, NL:NY
1915:	144	Ty Cobb, AL:Det. (4)
	89	Gavvy Cravath, NL:Phil.
1916:	113	Ty Cobb, AL:Det. (5)
	105	George Burns, NL:NY (2)
1917:	112	Donie Bush, AL:Det. (2)
	103	George Burns, NL:NY (3)
1918:	86	Heinie Groh, NL:Cin.
	84	Ray Chapman, AL:Clev.
1919:	103	Babe Ruth, AL:Bos.
	86	George Burns, NL:NY (4)
1920:	158	Babe Ruth, AL:NY (2)
	115	George Burns, NL:NY (5)
1921:	177	Babe Ruth, AL:NY (3)
	131	Rogers Hornsby, NL:StL.
1922:	142	Rogers Hornsby, NL:StL. (2)
	134	George Sisler, AL:StL.
1923:	151	Babe Ruth, AL:NY (4)
	121	Ross Youngs, NL:NY
1924:	143	Babe Ruth, AL:NY (5)
	121	Frankie Frisch, NL:NY
	121	Rogers Hornsby, NL:StL. (3)
1925:	144	Kiki Cuyler, NL:Pitt.
	135	Johnny Mostil, AL:Chi.
1926:	139	Babe Ruth, AL:NY (6)
	113	Kiki Cuyler, NL:Pitt. (2)
1927:	158	Babe Ruth, AL:NY (7)
	133	Rogers Hornsby, NL:NY (4)
	133	Lloyd Waner, NL:Pitt.
1928:	163	Babe Ruth, AL:NY (8)
	142	Paul Waner, NL:Pitt.
1929:	156	Rogers Hornsby, NL:Chi. (5)
	131	Charlie Gehringer, AL:Det.

1930:	158	Chuck Klein, NL:Phil.
	152	Al Simmons, AL:Phil
1931:	163	Lou Gehrig, AL:NY
	121	Chuck Klein, NL:Phil. (2)
	121	Bill Terry, NL:NY
1932:	152	Chuck Klein, NL:Phil. (3)
	151	Jimmie Foxx, AL:Phil.
1933:	138	Lou Gehrig, AL:NY (2)
	122	Pepper Martin, NL:StL.
1934:	135	Charlie Gehringer, AL:Det. (2)
	122	Paul Waner, NL:Pitt. (2)
1935:	133	Augie Galan, NL:Chi.
	125	Lou Gehrig, AL:NY (3)
1936:	167	Lou Gehrig, AL:NY (4)
	122	Arky Vaughan, NL:Pitt.
1937:	150	Joe DiMaggio, AL:NY
	111	Joe Medwick, NL:StL.
1938:	144	Hank Greenberg, AL:Det.
	116	Mel Ott, NL:NY
1939:	139	Red Rolfe, AL:NY
	115	Bill Werber, NL:Cin.
1940:	134	Ted Williams, AL:Bos.
	113	Arky Vaughan, NL:Pitt. (2)
1941:	135	Ted Williams, AL:Bos. (2)
	117	Pete Reiser, NL:Brk.
1942:	141	Ted Williams, AL:Bos. (3)
	118	Mel Ott, NL:NY (2)
1943:	114	Arky Vaughan, NL:Brk. (3)
	102	George Case, AL:Wash.
1944:	125	Snuffy Stirnweiss, AL:NY
	116	Bill Nicholson, NL:Chi.
1945:	128	Eddie Stanky, NL:Brk.
	107	Snuffy Stirnweiss, AL:NY (2)
1946:	142	Ted Williams, AL:Bos. (4)
	124	Stan Musial, NL:StL.
1947:	137	Johnny Mize, NL:NY
	125	Ted Williams, AL:Bos. (5)
1948:	138	Tommy Henrich, AL:NY
	135	Stan Musial, NL:StL. (2)
1949:	150	Ted Williams, AL:Bos. (6)
	132	Pee Wee Reese, NL:Brk.
1950:	131	Dom DiMaggio, AL:Bos.
	120	Earl Torgeson, NL:Bos.
1951:	124	Ralph Kiner, NL:Pitt.
	124	Stan Musial, NL:StL. (3)
	113	Dom DiMaggio, AL:Bos. (2)
1952:	105	Solly Hemus, NL:StL.
	105	Stan Musial, NL:StL. (4)
	104	Larry Doby, AL:Clev.
1953:	132	Duke Snider, NL:Brk.
	115	Al Rosen, AL:Clev.
1954:	128	Mickey Mantle, AL:NY
	120	Stan Musial, NL:StL. (5)
	120	Duke Snider, NL:Brk. (2)
1955:	126	Duke Snider, NL:Brk. (3)
	123	Al Smith, AL:Clev.
1956:	132	Mickey Mantle, AL:NY (2)
	122	Frank Robinson, NL:Cin.
1957:	121	Mickey Mantle, AL:NY (3)
	118	Hank Aaron, NL:Mil.
1958:	127	Mickey Mantle, AL:NY (4)
	120	Willie Mays, NL:SF
	120	Ernie Banks, NL:Chi.
1959:	131	Vada Pinson, NL:Cin.
	115	Eddie Yost, AL:Det.
1960:	119	Mickey Mantle, AL:NY (5)
	112	Bill Bruton, NL:Mil.

RUNS SCORED (CONTINUED)

1961:	132	Roger Maris, AL:NY
	129	Willie Mays, NL:SF (2)
1962:	134	Frank Robinson, NL:Cin. (2)
	115	Albie Pearson, AL:LA
1963:	121	Hank Aaron, NL:Mil. (2)
	99	Bob Allison, AL:Minn.
1964:	125	Dick Allen, NL:Phil.
	109	Tony Oliva, AL:Minn.
1965:	126	Tommy Harper, NL:Cin.
	126	Zoilo Versalles, AL:Minn.
1966:	122	Felipe Alou, NL:Atl.
	122	Frank Robinson, AL:Balt.
1967:	113	Hank Aaron, NL:Atl. (3)
	113	Lou Brock, NL:StL.
	112	Carl Yastrzemski, AL:Bos.
1968:	98	Glenn Beckert, NL:Chi.
	95	Dick McAuliffe, AL:Det.
1969:	123	Reggie Jackson, AL:Oak.
	120	Bobby Bonds, NL:SF
	120	Pete Rose, NL:Cin.
1970:	137	Billy Williams, NL:Chi.
	125	Carl Yastrzemski, AL:Bos. (2)
1971:	126	Lou Brock, NL:StL. (2)
	99	Don Buford, AL:Balt.
1972:	122	Joe Morgan, NL:Cin.
	102	Bobby Murcer, AL:NY
1973:	131	Bobby Bonds, NL:SF (2)
	99	Reggie Jackson, AL:Oak. (2)
1974:	110	Pete Rose, NL:Cin. (2)
	93	Carl Yastrzemski, AL:Bos. (3)
1975:	112	Pete Rose, NL:Cin. (3)
	103	Fred Lynn, AL:Bos.
1976:	130	Pete Rose, NL:Cin. (4)
	104	Roy White, AL:NY
1977:	128	Rod Carew, AL:Minn.
	124	George Foster, NL:Cin.
1978:	126	Ron LeFlore, AL:Det.
	104	Ivan DeJesus, NL:Chi.
1979:	120	Don Baylor, AL:Cal.
	116	Keith Hernandez, NL:StL.
1980:	133	Willie Wilson, AL:KC
	111	Keith Hernandez, NL:StL. (2)
1981:	89	Rickey Henderson, AL:Oak.
	78	Mike Schmidt, NL:Phil.
1982:	136	Paul Molitor, AL:Mil.
	120	Lonnie Smith, NL:StL.
1983:	133	Tim Raines, NL:Mtl.
	121	Cal Ripken, AL:Balt.
1984:	121	Dwight Evans, AL:Bos.
	114	Ryne Sandberg, NL:Chi.
1985:	146	Rickey Henderson, AL:NY (2)
	118	Dale Murphy, NL:Atl.
1986:	130	Rickey Henderson, AL:NY (3)
	107	Tony Gwynn, NL:SD
	107	Von Hayes, NL:Phil.
1987:	123	Tim Raines, NL:Mtl. (2)
	114	Paul Molitor, AL:Mil. (2)
1988:	128	Wade Boggs, AL:Bos.
	109	Brett Butler, NL:SF
1989:	113	Wade Boggs, AL:Bos. (2)
	113	Rickey Henderson, AL:NY-Oak. (4)
	104	Will Clark, NL:SF
	104	Howard Johnson, NL:NY
	104	Ryne Sandberg, NL:Chi. (2)

1990:	119	Rickey Henderson, AL:Oak. (5)
	116	Ryne Sandberg, NL:Chi. (3)
1991:	133	Paul Molitor, AL:Mil. (3)
	112	Brett Butler, NL:LA (2)
1992:	114	Tony Phillips, AL:Det.
	109	Barry Bonds, NL:Pitt.
1993:	143	Len Dykstra, NL:Phil.
	124	Rafael Palmeiro, AL:Tex.
1994:	106	Frank Thomas, AL:Chi.
	104	Jeff Bagwell, NL:Hou.
1995:	123	Craig Biggio, NL:Hou.
	121	Albert Belle, AL:Clev.
	121	Edgar Martinez, AL:Sea.
1996:	142	Ellis Burks, NL:Col.
	141	Alex Rodriguez, AL:Sea
1997:	146	Craig Biggio, NL:Hou. (2)
	125	Ken Griffey Jr., AL:Sea.
1998:	134	Sammy Sosa, NL:Chi.
	127	Derek Jeter, AL:NY
1999:	143	Jeff Bagwell, NL:Hou. (2)
	138	Roberto Alomar, AL:Clev.
2000:	152	Jeff Bagwell, NL:Hou. (3)
	136	Johnny Damon, AL:KC
2001:	146	Sammy Sosa, NL:Chi. (2)
	133	Alex Rodriguez, AL:Tex. (2)
2002:	128	Alfonso Soriano, AL:NY
	122	Sammy Sosa, NL:Chi. (3)
2003:	137	Albert Pujols, NL:StL.
	124	Alex Rodriguez, AL:Tex. (3)
2004:	133	Albert Pujols, NL:StL. (2)
	124	Vladimir Guerrero, AL:Ana.
2005:	129	Albert Pujols, NL:StL. (3)
	124	Alex Rodriguez, AL:NY (4)
2006:	134	Grady Sizemore, AL:Clev.
	131	Chase Utley, NL:Phil.
2007:	143	Alex Rodriguez, AL:NY (5)
	139	Jimmy Rollins, NL:Phil.
2008:	125	Hanley Ramirez, NL:Fla.
	118	Dustin Pedroia, AL:Bos.
2009:	124	Albert Pujols, NL:StL. (4)
	115	Dustin Pedroia, AL:Bos. (2)
2010:	115	Albert Pujols, NL:StL. (5)
	113	Mark Teixeira, AL:NY
2011:	136	Curtis Granderson, AL:NY
	115	Matt Kemp, NL:LA
2012:	129	Mike Trout, AL:LA
	108	Ryan Braun, NL:Mil.
2013:	126	Matt Carpenter, NL:StL.
	109	Mike Trout, AL:LA (2)
2014:	115	Mike Trout, AL:LA (3)
	111	Anthony Rendon, NL:Wash.
2015:	122	Josh Donaldson, AL:Tor.
	118	Bryce Harper, NL:Wash.
2016:	123	Mike Trout, AL:LA (4)
	121	Kris Bryant, NL:Chi.
2017:	137	Charlie Blackmon, NL:Col.
	128	Aaron Judge, AL:NY
2018:	129	Mookie Betts, AL:Bos.
	129	Francisco Lindor, AL:Clev.
	119	Charlie Blackmon, NL:Col. (2)
2019:	135	Mookie Betts, AL:Bos. (2)
	127	Ronald Acuna, NL:Atl.
2020:	51	Freddie Freeman, NL:Atl.
	45	Tim Anderson, AL:Chi.
	45	Jose Ramirez, AL:Clev.

HITS

1900:	208	Willie Keeler, NL:Brk.
1901:	229	Nap Lajoie, AL:Phil.
	228	Jesse Burkett, NL:StL.
1902:	194	Ginger Beaumont, NL:Pitt.
	194	Piano Legs Hickman, AL:Bos.-Clev.
1903:	209	Ginger Beaumont, NL:Pitt. (2)
	195	Patsy Dougherty, AL:Bos.
1904:	211	Nap Lajoie, AL:Clev. (2)
	185	Ginger Beaumont, NL:Pitt. (3)
1905:	219	Cy Seymour, NL:Cin.
	187	George Stone, AL:StL.
1906:	214	Nap Lajoie, AL:Clev. (3)
	177	Harry Steinfeldt, NL:Chi.
1907:	212	Ty Cobb, AL:Det.
	187	Ginger Beaumont, NL:Bos. (4)
1908:	201	Honus Wagner, NL:Pitt.
	188	Ty Cobb, AL:Det. (2)
1909:	216	Ty Cobb, AL:Det. (3)
	172	Larry Doyle, NL:NY
1910:	227	Nap Lajoie, AL:Clev. (4)
	178	Bobby Byrne, NL:Pitt.
	178	Honus Wagner, NL:Pitt. (2)
1911:	248	Ty Cobb, AL:Det. (4)
	192	Doc Miller, NL:Bos.
1912:	227	Ty Cobb, AL:Det. (5)
	207	Heinie Zimmerman, NL:Chi.
1913:	197	Joe Jackson, AL:Clev.
	179	Gavvy Cravath, NL:Phil.
1914:	193	Tris Speaker, AL:Bos.
	171	Sherry Magee, NL:Phil.
1915:	208	Ty Cobb, AL:Det. (6)
	189	Larry Doyle, NL:NY (2)
1916:	211	Tris Speaker, AL:Clev. (2)
	184	Hal Chase, NL:Cin.
1917:	225	Ty Cobb, AL:Det. (7)
	182	Heinie Groh, NL:Cin.
1918:	178	George Burns, AL:Phil.
	161	Charlie Hollocher, NL:Chi.
1919:	191	Ty Cobb, AL:Det. (8)
	191	Bobby Veach, AL:Det.
	164	Ivy Olson, NL:Brk.
1920:	257	George Sisler, AL:StL.
	218	Rogers Hornsby, NL:StL.
1921:	237	Harry Heilmann, AL:Det.
	235	Rogers Hornsby, NL:StL. (2)
1922:	250	Rogers Hornsby, NL:StL. (3)
	246	George Sisler, AL:StL. (2)
1923:	223	Frankie Frisch, NL:NY
	222	Charlie Jamieson, AL:Clev.
1924:	227	Rogers Hornsby, NL:StL. (4)
	216	Sam Rice, AL:Wash.
1925:	253	Al Simmons, AL:Phil.
	227	Jim Bottomley, NL:StL.
1926:	216	George Burns, AL:Clev. (2)
	216	Sam Rice, AL:Wash. (2)
	201	Eddie Brown, NL:Bos.
1927:	237	Paul Waner, NL:Pitt.
	231	Earle Combs, AL:NY
1928:	241	Heinie Manush, AL:StL.
	231	Freddie Lindstrom, NL:NY
1929:	254	Lefty O'Doul, NL:Phil.
	215	Dale Alexander, AL:Det.
	215	Charlie Gehringer, AL:Det.
1930:	254	Bill Terry, NL:NY
	225	Johnny Hodapp, AL:Clev.

1931:	214	Lloyd Waner, NL:Pitt.
	211	Lou Gehrig, AL:NY
1932:	226	Chuck Klein, NL:Phil.
	216	Al Simmons, AL:Phil. (2)
1933:	223	Chuck Klein, NL:Phil. (2)
	221	Heinie Manush, AL:Wash. (2)
1934:	217	Paul Waner, NL:Pitt. (2)
	214	Charlie Gehringer, AL:Det. (2)
1935:	227	Billy Herman, NL:Chi.
	216	Joe Vosmik, AL:Clev.
1936:	232	Earl Averill, AL:Clev.
	223	Joe Medwick, NL:StL.
1937:	237	Joe Medwick, NL:StL. (2)
	218	Beau Bell, AL:StL.
1938:	209	Frank McCormick, NL:Cin.
	201	Joe Vosmik, AL:Bos. (2)
1939:	213	Red Rolfe, AL:NY
	209	Frank McCormick, NL:Cin. (2)
1940:	200	Doc Cramer, AL:Bos.
	200	Barney McCosky, AL:Det.
	200	Rip Radcliff, AL:StL.
	191	Stan Hack, NL:Chi.
	191	Frank McCormick, NL:Cin. (3)
1941:	218	Cecil Travis, AL:Wash.
	186	Stan Hack, NL:Chi. (2)
1942:	205	Johnny Pesky, AL:Bos.
	188	Enos Slaughter, NL:StL.
1943:	220	Stan Musial, NL:StL.
	200	Dick Wakefield, AL:Det.
1944:	205	Snuffy Stirnweiss, AL:NY
	197	Phil Cavarretta, NL:Chi.
	197	Stan Musial, NL:StL. (2)
1945:	224	Tommy Holmes, NL:Bos.
	195	Snuffy Stirnweiss, AL:NY (2)
1946:	228	Stan Musial, NL:StL. (3)
	208	Johnny Pesky, AL:Bos. (2)
1947:	207	Johnny Pesky, AL:Bos. (3)
	191	Tommy Holmes, NL:Bos. (2)
1948:	230	Stan Musial, NL:StL. (4)
	207	Bob Dillinger, AL:StL.
1949:	207	Stan Musial, NL:StL. (5)
	203	Dale Mitchell, AL:Clev.
1950:	218	George Kell, AL:Det.
	199	Duke Snider, NL:Brk.
1951:	221	Richie Ashburn, NL:Phil.
	191	George Kell, AL:Det. (2)
1952:	194	Stan Musial, NL:StL. (6)
	192	Nellie Fox, AL:Chi.
1953:	209	Harvey Kuenn, AL:Det.
	205	Richie Ashburn, NL:Phil. (2)
1954:	212	Don Mueller, NL:NY
	201	Nellie Fox, AL:Chi. (2)
	201	Harvey Kuenn, AL:Det. (2)
1955:	200	Al Kaline, AL:Det.
	192	Ted Kluszewski, NL:Cin.
1956:	200	Hank Aaron, NL:Mil.
	196	Harvey Kuenn, AL:Det. (3)
1957:	200	Red Schoendienst, NL:NY-Mil.
	196	Nellie Fox, AL:Chi. (3)
1958:	215	Richie Ashburn, NL:Phil. (3)
	187	Nellie Fox, AL:Chi. (4)
1959:	223	Hank Aaron, NL:Mil. (2)
	198	Harvey Kuenn, AL:Det. (4)
1960:	190	Willie Mays, NL:SF
	184	Minnie Minoso, AL:Chi.

HITS (CONTINUED)

1961:	208	Vada Pinson, NL:Cin.
	193	Norm Cash, AL:Det.
1962:	230	Tommy Davis, NL:LA
	209	Bobby Richardson, AL:NY
1963:	204	Vada Pinson, NL:Cin. (2)
	183	Carl Yastrzemski, AL:Bos.
1964:	217	Tony Oliva, AL:Minn.
	211	Roberto Clemente, NL:Pitt.
	211	Curt Flood, NL:StL.
1965:	209	Pete Rose, NL:Cin.
	185	Tony Oliva, AL:Minn. (2)
1966:	218	Felipe Alou, NL:Atl.
	191	Tony Oliva, AL:Minn. (3)
1967:	209	Roberto Clemente, NL:Pitt. (2)
	189	Carl Yastrzemski, AL:Bos. (2)
1968:	210	Felipe Alou, NL:Atl. (2)
	210	Pete Rose, NL:Cin. (2)
	177	Bert Campaneris, AL:Oak.
1969:	231	Matty Alou, NL:Pitt.
	197	Tony Oliva, AL:Minn. (4)
1970:	205	Pete Rose NL:Cin. (3)
	205	Billy Williams, NL:Chi.
	204	Tony Oliva, AL:Minn. (5)
1971:	230	Joe Torre, NL:StL.
	204	Cesar Tovar, AL:Minn.
1972:	198	Pete Rose, NL:Cin. (4)
	181	Joe Rudi, AL:Oak.
1973:	230	Pete Rose, NL:Cin. (5)
	203	Rod Carew, AL:Minn.
1974:	218	Rod Carew, AL:Minn. (2)
	214	Ralph Garr, NL:Atl.
1975:	213	Dave Cash, NL:Phil.
	195	George Brett, AL:KC
1976:	215	Pete Rose, NL:Cin. (6)
	215	George Brett, AL:KC (2)
1977:	239	Rod Carew, AL:Minn. (3)
	215	Dave Parker, NL:Pitt.
1978:	213	Jim Rice, AL:Bos.
	202	Steve Garvey, NL:LA
1979:	212	George Brett, AL:KC (3)
	211	Garry Templeton, NL:StL.
1980:	230	Willie Wilson, AL:KC
	200	Steve Garvey, NL:LA (2)
1981:	140	Pete Rose, NL:Phil. (7)
	135	Rickey Henderson, AL:Oak.
1982:	210	Robin Yount, AL:Mil.
	204	Al Oliver, NL:Mtl.
1983:	211	Cal Ripken, AL:Balt.
	189	Jose Cruz, NL:Hou.
	189	Andre Dawson, NL:Mtl.
1984:	213	Tony Gwynn, NL:SD
	207	Don Mattingly, AL:NY
1985:	240	Wade Boggs, AL:Bos.
	216	Willie McGee, NL:StL.
1986:	238	Don Mattingly AL:NY (2)
	211	Tony Gwynn, NL:SD (2)
1987:	218	Tony Gwynn, NL:SD (3)
	207	Kirby Puckett, AL:Minn.
	207	Kevin Seitzer, AL:KC
1988:	234	Kirby Puckett, AL:Minn. (2)
	184	Andres Galarraga, NL:Mtl.
1989:	215	Kirby Puckett, AL:Minn. (3)
	203	Tony Gwynn, NL:SD (4)
1990:	199	Willie McGee, NL:StL.-AL:Oak.
	192	Brett Butler, NL:SF
	192	Len Dykstra, NL:Phil.
	191	Rafael Palmeiro, AL:Tex.
1991:	216	Paul Molitor, AL:Mil.
	187	Terry Pendleton, NL:Atl.
1992:	210	Kirby Puckett, AL:Minn. (4)
	199	Terry Pendleton, NL:Atl. (2)
	199	Andy Van Slyke, NL:Pitt.
1993:	211	Paul Molitor, AL:Tor. (2)
	194	Len Dykstra, NL:Phil. (2)
1994:	165	Tony Gwynn, NL:SD (5)
	160	Kenny Lofton, AL:Clev.
1995:	197	Dante Bichette, NL:Col.
	197	Tony Gwynn, NL:SD (6)
	186	Lance Johnson, AL:Chi.
1996:	227	Lance Johnson, NL:NY (AL 1)
	225	Paul Molitor, AL:Minn. (3)
1997:	220	Tony Gwynn, NL:SD (7)
	209	Nomar Garciaparra, AL:Bos
1998:	219	Dante Bichette, NL:Col. (2)
	213	Alex Rodriguez, AL:Sea.
1999:	219	Derek Jeter, AL:NY
	206	Luis Gonzalez, NL:Ari.
2000:	240	Darin Erstad, AL:Ana.
	216	Todd Helton, NL:Col.
2001:	242	Ichiro Suzuki, AL:Sea.
	206	Rich Aurilia, NL:SF
2002:	209	Alfonso Soriano, AL:NY
	206	Vladimir Guerrero, NL:Mtl.
2003:	215	Vernon Wells, AL:Tor.
	212	Albert Pujols, NL:StL.
2004:	262	Ichiro Suzuki, AL:Sea. (2)
	221	Juan Pierre, NL:Fla.
2005:	221	Michael Young, AL:Tex.
	199	Derrek Lee, NL:Chi.
2006:	224	Ichiro Suzuki, AL:Sea. (3)
	204	Juan Pierre, NL:Chi. (2)
2007:	238	Ichiro Suzuki, AL:Sea. (4)
	216	Matt Holliday, NL:Col.
2008:	213	Dustin Pedroia, AL:Bos.
	213	Ichiro Suzuki, AL:Sea. (5)
	204	Jose Reyes, NL:NY
2009:	225	Ichiro Suzuki, AL:Sea. (6)
	203	Ryan Braun, NL:Mil.
2010:	214	Ichiro Suzuki, AL:Sea. (7)
	197	Carlos Gonzalez, NL:Col.
2011:	213	Adrian Gonzalez, AL:Bos.
	213	Michael Young, AL:Tex.
	207	Starlin Castro, NL:Chi.
2012:	216	Derek Jeter, AL:NY (2)
	194	Andrew McCutchen, NL:Pitt.
2013:	199	Adrian Beltre, AL:Tex.
	199	Matt Carpenter, NL:StL.
2014:	225	Jose Altuve, AL:Hou.
	184	Ben Revere, NL:Phil.
	184	Denard Span, NL:Wash.
2015:	205	Dee Gordon, NL:Mia.
	200	Jose Altuve, AL:Hou. (2)
2016:	216	Jose Altuve, AL:Hou. (3)
	203	Jean Segura, NL:Ari.
2017:	213	Charlie Blackmon, NL:Col.
	204	Jose Altuve, AL:Hou. (4)
2018:	192	Whit Merrifield, AL:KC
	191	Freddie Freeman, NL:Atl.
2019:	206	Whit Merrifield, AL:KC (2)
	189	Ozzie Albies, NL:Atl.
2020:	78	Trea Turner, NL:Wash.
	76	Jose Abreu, AL:Chi.

SINGLES

1900:	179	Willie Keeler, NL:Brk.
1901:	180	Jesse Burkett, NL:StL.
	155	Irv Waldron, AL:Mil.-Wash.
1902:	167	Ginger Beaumont, NL:Pitt.
	150	Fielder Jones, AL:Chi.
1903:	166	Ginger Beaumont, NL:Pitt. (2)
	160	Patsy Dougherty, AL:Bos.
1904:	162	Willie Keeler, AL:NY (NL 1)
	158	Ginger Beaumont, NL:Pitt. (3)
1905:	162	Mike Donlin, NL:NY
	151	Willie Keeler, AL:NY (AL 2; NL 1)
1906:	166	Willie Keeler, AL:NY (AL 3; NL 1)
	141	Miller Huggins, NL:Cin.
	141	Spike Shannon, NL:StL.-NY
1907:	163	Ty Cobb, AL:Det.
	150	Ginger Beaumont, NL:Bos. (4)
1908:	153	Mike Donlin, NL:NY (2)
	131	George Stone, AL:StL.
1909:	164	Ty Cobb, AL:Det. (2)
	147	Eddie Grant, NL:Phil.
1910:	162	Nap Lajoie, AL:Clev.
	134	Eddie Grant, NL:Phil. (2)
1911:	169	Ty Cobb, AL:Det. (3)
	146	Jake Daubert, NL:Brk.
	146	Doc Miller, NL:Bos.
1912:	167	Ty Cobb, AL:Det. (4)
	159	Bill Sweeney, NL:Bos.
1913:	152	Jake Daubert, NL:Brk. (2)
	145	Eddie Collins, AL:Phil.
1914:	160	Stuffy McInnis, AL:Phil.
	128	Beals Becker, NL:Phil.
1915:	161	Ty Cobb, AL:Det. (5)
	135	Larry Doyle, NL:NY
1916:	160	Tris Speaker, AL:Clev.
	142	Dave Robertson, NL:NY
1917:	151	Ty Cobb, AL:Det. (6)
	151	Clyde Milan, AL:Wash.
	141	Benny Kauff, NL:NY
	141	Edd Roush, NL:Cin.
1918:	141	George Burns, AL:Phil.
	130	Charlie Hollocher, NL:Chi.
1919:	144	Sam Rice, AL:Wash.
	140	Ivy Olson, NL:Brk.
1920:	171	George Sisler, AL:StL.
	170	Milt Stock, NL:StL.
1921:	179	Jack Tobin, AL:StL.
	161	Carson Bigbee, NL:Pitt.
1922:	178	George Sisler, AL:StL. (2)
	166	Carson Bigbee, NL:Pitt. (2)
1923:	172	Charlie Jamieson, AL:Clev.
	169	Frankie Frisch, NL:NY
1924:	168	Charlie Jamieson, AL:Clev. (2)
	149	Zack Wheat, NL:Brk.
1925:	182	Sam Rice, AL:Wash. (2)
	164	Milt Stock, NL:Brk. (2)
1926:	167	Sam Rice, AL:Wash. (3)
	160	Eddie Brown, NL:Bos.
1927:	198	Lloyd Waner, NL:Pitt.
	166	Earle Combs, AL:NY
1928:	180	Lloyd Waner, NL:Pitt. (2)
	161	Heinie Manush, AL:StL.
1929:	181	Lefty O'Doul, NL:Phil.
	181	Lloyd Waner, NL:Pitt. (3)
	151	Earle Combs, AL:NY (2)

1930:	177	Bill Terry, NL:NY
	158	Sam Rice, AL:Wash. (4)
1931:	172	Lloyd Waner, NL:Pitt. (4)
	142	Oscar Melillo, AL:StL.
	142	John Stone, AL:Det.
1932:	158	Lefty O'Doul, NL:Brk. (2)
	145	Heinie Manush, AL:Wash. (2)
1933:	167	Heinie Manush, AL:Wash. (3)
	162	Chick Fullis, NL:Phil.
1934:	169	Bill Terry, NL:NY (2)
	157	Doc Cramer, AL:Phil.
1935:	170	Doc Cramer, AL:Phil. (2)
	160	Woody Jensen, NL:Pitt.
1936:	161	Rip Radcliff, AL:Chi.
	160	Jo-Jo Moore, NL:NY
1937:	178	Paul Waner, NL:Pitt.
	162	Buddy Lewis, AL:Wash.
1938:	160	Frank McCormick, NL:Cin.
	158	Mel Almada, AL:Wash.-StL.
1939:	162	Buddy Hassett, NL:Bos.
	147	Doc Cramer, AL:Bos. (3)
1940:	160	Doc Cramer, AL:Bos. (4)
	141	Burgess Whitehead, NL:NY
1941:	153	Cecil Travis, AL:Wash.
	141	Stan Hack, NL:Chi.
1942:	165	Johnny Pesky, AL:Bos.
	127	Enos Slaughter, NL:StL.
1943:	172	Mickey Witek, NL:NY
	159	Doc Cramer, AL:Det. (5)
1944:	146	Snuffy Stirnweiss, AL:NY
	142	Phil Cavarretta, NL:Chi.
1945:	155	Stan Hack, NL:Chi. (2)
	139	Irv Hall, AL:Phil.
1946:	159	Johnny Pesky, AL:Bos. (2)
	142	Stan Musial, NL:StL.
1947:	172	Johnny Pesky, AL:Bos. (3)
	146	Tommy Holmes, NL:Bos.
1948:	162	Dale Mitchell, AL:Clev.
	150	Stan Rojek, NL:Pitt.
1949:	161	Dale Mitchell, AL:Clev. (2)
	160	Red Schoendienst, NL:StL.
1950:	150	Phil Rizzuto, AL:NY
	143	Eddie Waitkus, NL:Phil.
1951:	181	Richie Ashburn, NL:Phil.
	150	George Kell, AL:Det.
1952:	157	Nellie Fox, AL:Chi.
	145	Bobby Adams, NL:Cin.
1953:	169	Richie Ashburn, NL:Phil. (2)
	167	Harvey Kuenn, AL:Det.
1954:	167	Nellie Fox, AL:Chi. (2)
	165	Don Mueller, NL:NY
1955:	157	Nellie Fox, AL:Chi. (3)
	152	Don Mueller, NL:NY (2)
1956:	158	Nellie Fox, AL:Chi. (4)
	157	Johnny Temple, NL:Cin.
1957:	155	Nellie Fox, AL:Chi. (5)
	152	Richie Ashburn, NL:Phil. (3)
1958:	176	Richie Ashburn, NL:Phil. (4)
	160	Nellie Fox, AL:Chi. (6)
1959:	149	Nellie Fox, AL:Chi. (7)
	144	Don Blasingame, NL:StL.
1960:	154	Dick Groat, NL:Pitt.
	139	Nellie Fox, AL:Chi. (8)
1961:	150	Vada Pinson, NL:Cin.
	150	Maury Wills, NL:LA
	148	Bobby Richardson, AL:NY

SINGLES (CONTINUED)

1962:	179	Maury Wills, NL:LA (2)
	158	Bobby Richardson, AL:NY (2)
1963:	152	Curt Flood, NL:StL.
	139	Albie Pearson, AL:LA
1964:	178	Curt Flood, NL:StL. (2)
	148	Bobby Richardson, AL:NY (3)
1965:	165	Maury Wills, NL:LA (3)
	129	Don Buford, AL:Chi.
1966:	160	Sonny Jackson, NL:Hou.
	143	Luis Aparicio, AL:Balt.
1967:	162	Maury Wills, NL:Pitt. (4)
	140	Horace Clarke, AL:NY
1968:	160	Curt Flood, NL:StL. (3)
	139	Bert Campaneris, AL:Oak.
1969:	183	Matty Alou, NL:Pitt.
	147	Horace Clarke, AL:NY (2)
1970:	171	Matty Alou, NL:Pitt. (2)
	156	Alex Johnson, AL:Cal.
1971:	180	Ralph Garr, NL:Atl.
	171	Cesar Tovar, AL:Minn.
1972:	156	Lou Brock, NL:StL.
	143	Rod Carew, AL:Minn.
1973:	181	Pete Rose, NL:Cin.
	156	Rod Carew, AL:Minn. (2)
1974:	180	Rod Carew, AL:Minn. (3)
	167	Dave Cash, NL:Phil.
1975:	166	Dave Cash, NL:Phil. (2)
	151	Thurman Munson, AL:NY
1976:	164	Willie Montanez, NL:SF-Atl.
	160	George Brett, AL:KC
1977:	171	Rod Carew, AL:Minn. (4)
	155	Garry Templeton, NL:StL.
1978:	153	Larry Bowa, NL:Phil.
	153	Ron LeFlore, AL:Det.
1979:	159	Pete Rose, NL:Phil. (2)
	148	Willie Wilson, AL:KC
1980:	184	Willie Wilson, AL:KC (2)
	155	Gene Richards, NL:SD
1981:	117	Pete Rose, NL:Phil. (3)
	115	Willie Wilson, AL:KC (3)
1982:	157	Willie Wilson, AL:KC (4)
	147	Bill Buckner, NL:Chi.
1983:	160	Rafael Ramirez, NL:Atl.
	154	Wade Boggs, AL:Bos.
1984:	177	Tony Gwynn, NL:SD
	162	Wade Boggs, AL:Bos. (2)
1985:	187	Wade Boggs, AL:Bos. (3)
	162	Willie McGee, NL:StL.
1986:	161	Tony Fernandez, AL:Tor.
	157	Tony Gwynn, NL:SD (2)
	157	Steve Sax, NL:LA
1987:	162	Tony Gwynn, NL:SD (3)
	151	Kevin Seitzer, AL:KC
1988:	163	Kirby Puckett, AL:Minn.
	147	Steve Sax, NL:LA (2)
1989:	171	Steve Sax, AL:NY (NL 2)
	165	Tony Gwynn, NL:SD (4)
1990:	160	Brett Butler, NL:SF
	136	Rafael Palmeiro, AL:Tex.
1991:	162	Brett Butler, NL:LA (2)
	156	Julio Franco, AL:Tex.
1992:	152	Carlos Baerga, AL:Clev.
	143	Brett Butler, NL:LA (3)
1993:	149	Brett Butler, NL:LA (4)
	148	Kenny Lofton, AL:Clev.

1994:	117	Tony Gwynn, NL:SD (5)
	107	Kenny Lofton, AL:Clev. (2)
	107	Paul Molitor, AL:Tor.
1995:	154	Tony Gwynn, NL:SD (6)
	151	Otis Nixon, AL:Tex.
1996:	167	Paul Molitor, AL:Minn. (2)
	166	Lance Johnson, NL:NY
1997:	152	Tony Gwynn, NL:SD (7)
	142	Garret Anderson, AL:Ana.
	142	Derek Jeter, AL:NY
1998:	151	Derek Jeter, AL:NY (2)
	149	Tony Womack, NL:Pitt.
1999:	152	Randy Velarde, AL:Ana.-Oak.
	149	Doug Glanville, NL:Phil.
2000:	170	Darin Erstad, AL:Ana.
	158	Luis Castillo, NL:Fla.
2001:	192	Ichiro Suzuki, AL:Sea.
	163	Juan Pierre, NL:Col.
2002:	165	Ichiro Suzuki, AL:Sea. (2)
	160	Luis Castillo, NL:Fla. (2)
2003:	168	Juan Pierre, NL:Fla. (2)
	162	Ichiro Suzuki, AL:Sea. (3)
2004:	225	Ichiro Suzuki, AL:Sea. (4)
	184	Juan Pierre, NL:Fla. (3)
2005:	158	Ichiro Suzuki, AL:Sea. (5)
	152	Willy Taveras, NL:Hou.
2006:	186	Ichiro Suzuki, AL:Sea. (6)
	156	Juan Pierre, NL:Chi. (4)
2007:	203	Ichiro Suzuki, AL:Sea. (7)
	164	Juan Pierre, NL:LA (5)
2008:	180	Ichiro Suzuki, AL:Sea. (8)
	154	Ryan Theriot, NL:Chi.
2009:	179	Ichiro Suzuki, AL:Sea. (9)
	139	Ryan Theriot, NL:Chi. (2)
2010:	175	Ichiro Suzuki, AL:Sea. (10)
	139	Ryan Theriot, NL:Chi.-LA (3)
2011:	155	Juan Pierre, AL:Chi. (NL 5)
	155	Michael Young, AL:Tex.
	152	Starlin Casto, NL:Chi.
2012:	169	Derek Jeter, AL:NY (3)
	147	Marco Scutaro, NL:Col.-SF
2013:	143	Elvis Andrus, AL:Tex.
	140	Norichika Aoki, NL:Mil.
2014:	168	Jose Altuve, AL:Hou.
	162	Ben Revere, NL:Phil.
2015:	169	Dee Gordon, NL:Mia.
	151	Xander Bogaerts, AL:Bos.
2016:	149	Dustin Pedroia, AL:Bos.
	141	DJ LeMahieu, NL:Col.
2017:	170	Dee Gordon, NL:Mia. (2)
	137	Jose Altuve, AL:Hou. (2)
2018:	136	Jean Segura, AL:Sea.
	133	Jose Peraza, NL:Cin.
2019:	139	Whit Merrifield, AL:KC
	125	Amed Rosario, NL:NY
2020:	50	David Fletcher, AL:LA
	48	Charlie Blackmon, NL:Col.
	48	Raimel Tapia, NL:Col.

DOUBLES

1900:	45	Honus Wagner, NL:Pitt.
1901:	48	Nap Lajoie, AL:Phil.
	39	Jake Beckley, NL:Cin.
	39	Ed Delahanty, NL:Phil.
	39	Honus Wagner, NL:Pitt. (2)
1902:	43	Harry Davis, AL:Phil.
	43	Ed Delahanty, AL:Wash. (2)
	33	Honus Wagner, NL:Pitt. (3)
1903:	45	Socks Seybold, AL:Phil.
	32	Fred Clarke, NL:Pitt.
	32	Sam Mertes, NL:NY
	32	Harry Steinfeldt, NL:Cin.
1904:	50	Nap Lajoie, AL:Clev. (2)
	44	Honus Wagner, NL:Pitt. (4)
1905:	46	Harry Davis, AL:Phil. (2)
	40	Cy Seymour, NL:Cin.
1906:	50	Nap Lajoie, AL:Clev. (3)
	38	Honus Wagner, NL:Pitt. (5)
1907:	38	Honus Wagner, NL:Pitt. (6)
	35	Harry Davis, AL:Phil. (3)
1908:	39	Honus Wagner, NL:Pitt. (7)
	36	Ty Cobb, AL:Det.
1909:	39	Honus Wagner, NL:Pitt. (8)
	35	Sam Crawford, AL:Det.
1910:	53	Nap Lajoie, AL:Clev. (4)
	43	Bobby Byrne, NL:Pitt.
1911:	47	Ty Cobb, AL:Det. (2)
	38	Ed Konetchy, NL:StL.
1912:	53	Tris Speaker, AL:Bos.
	41	Heinie Zimmerman, NL:Chi.
1913:	40	Red Smith, NL:Brk.
	39	Joe Jackson, AL:Clev.
1914:	46	Tris Speaker, AL:Bos. (2)
	39	Sherry Magee, NL:Phil.
1915:	40	Larry Doyle, NL:NY
	40	Bobby Veach, AL:Det.
1916:	42	Bert Niehoff, NL:Phil.
	41	Jack Graney, AL:Clev.
1917:	44	Ty Cobb, AL:Det. (3)
	39	Heinie Groh, NL:Cin.
1918:	34	Tris Speaker, AL:Clev. (3)
	28	Heinie Groh, NL:Cin. (2)
1919:	45	Bobby Veach, AL:Det. (2)
	31	Ross Youngs, NL:NY
1920:	50	Tris Speaker, AL:Clev. (4)
	44	Rogers Hornsby, NL:StL.
1921:	52	Tris Speaker, AL:Clev. (5)
	44	Rogers Hornsby, NL:StL. (2)
1922:	48	Tris Speaker, AL:Clev. (6)
	46	Rogers Hornsby, NL:StL. (3)
1923:	59	Tris Speaker, AL:Clev. (7)
	41	Edd Roush, NL:Cin.
1924:	45	Harry Heilmann, AL:Det.
	45	Joe Sewell, AL:Clev.
	43	Rogers Hornsby, NL:StL. (4)
1925:	44	Jim Bottomley, NL:StL.
	44	Marty McManus, AL:StL.
1926:	64	George Burns, AL:Clev.
	40	Jim Bottomley, Jim NL:StL. (2)
1927:	52	Lou Gehrig, Lou AL:NY
	46	Riggs Stephenson, NL:Chi.
1928:	50	Paul Waner, NL:Pitt.
	47	Lou Gehrig, AL:NY (2)
	47	Heinie Manush, AL:StL.

1929:	52	Johnny Frederick, NL:Brk.
	45	Charlie Gehringer, AL:Det.
	45	Roy Johnson, AL:Det.
	45	Heinie Manush, AL:StL. (2)
1930:	59	Chuck Klein, NL:Phil.
	51	Johnny Hodapp, AL:Clev.
1931:	67	Earl Webb, AL:Bos.
	46	Sparky Adams, NL:StL.
1932:	63	Paul Waner, NL:Pitt. (2)
	47	Eric McNair, AL:Phil.
1933:	45	Joe Cronin, AL:Wash.
	44	Chuck Klein, NL:Phil. (2)
1934:	63	Hank Greenberg, AL:Det.
	42	Ethan Allen, NL:Phil.
	42	Kiki Cuyler, NL:Chi.
1935:	57	Billy Herman, NL:Chi.
	47	Joe Vosmik, AL:Clev.
1936:	64	Joe Medwick, NL:StL.
	60	Charlie Gehringer, AL:Det. (2)
1937:	56	Joe Medwick, NL:StL. (2)
	51	Beau Bell, AL:StL.
1938:	51	Joe Cronin, AL:Bos. (2)
	47	Joe Medwick, NL:StL. (3)
1939:	52	Enos Slaughter, NL:StL.
	46	Red Rolfe, AL:NY
1940:	50	Hank Greenberg, AL:Det. (2)
	44	Frank McCormick, NL:Cin.
1941:	45	Lou Boudreau, AL:Clev.
	39	Johnny Mize, NL:StL.
	39	Pete Reiser, NL:Brk.
1942:	40	Don Kolloway, AL:Chi.
	38	Marty Marion, NL:StL.
1943:	48	Stan Musial, NL:StL.
	38	Dick Wakefield, AL:Det.
1944:	51	Stan Musial, NL:StL. (2)
	45	Lou Boudreau, AL:Clev. (2)
1945:	47	Tommy Holmes, NL:Bos.
	35	Wally Moses, AL:Chi.
1946:	51	Mickey Vernon, AL:Wash.
	50	Stan Musial, NL:StL. (3)
1947:	45	Lou Boudreau, AL:Clev. (3)
	38	Eddie Miller, NL:Cin.
1948:	46	Stan Musial, NL:StL. (4)
	44	Ted Williams, AL:Bos.
1949:	41	Stan Musial, NL:StL. (5)
	39	Ted Williams, AL:Bos. (2)
1950:	56	George Kell, AL:Det.
	43	Red Schoendienst, NL:StL.
1951:	41	Alvin Dark, NL:NY
	36	George Kell, AL:Det. (2)
	36	Sam Mele, AL:Wash.
	36	Eddie Yost, AL:Wash.
1952:	43	Ferris Fain, AL:Phil.
	42	Stan Musial, NL:StL. (6)
1953:	53	Stan Musial, NL:StL. (7)
	43	Mickey Vernon, AL:Wash. (2)
1954:	41	Stan Musial, NL:StL. (8)
	33	Mickey Vernon, AL:Wash. (3)
1955:	38	Harvey Kuenn, AL:Det.
	37	Hank Aaron, NL:Mil.
	37	Johnny Logan, NL:Mil.
1956:	40	Jimmy Piersall, AL:Bos.
	34	Hank Aaron, NL:Mil. (2)
1957:	39	Don Hoak, NL:Cin.
	36	Billy Gardner, AL:Balt.
	36	Minnie Minoso, AL:Chi.
1958:	39	Harvey Kuenn, AL:Det. (2)
	38	Orlando Cepeda, NL:SF
1959:	47	Vada Pinson, NL:Cin.
	42	Harvey Kuenn, AL:Det. (3)
1960:	37	Vada Pinson, NL:Cin. (2)
	36	Tito Francona, AL:Clev.

DOUBLES (CONTINUED)

1961:	41	Al Kaline, AL:Det.
	39	Hank Aaron, NL:Mil. (3)
1962:	51	Frank Robinson, NL:Cin.
	45	Floyd Robinson, AL:Chi.
1963:	43	Dick Groat, NL:StL.
	40	Carl Yastrzemski, AL:Bos.
1964:	44	Lee Maye, NL:Mil.
	43	Tony Oliva, AL:Minn.
1965:	45	Zoilo Versalles, AL:Minn.
	45	Carl Yastrzemski, AL:Bos. (2)
	40	Hank Aaron, NL:Mil. (4)
1966:	40	Johnny Callison, NL:Phil.
	39	Carl Yastrzemski, AL:Bos. (3)
1967:	44	Rusty Staub, NL:Hou.
	34	Tony Oliva, AL:Minn. (2)
1968:	46	Lou Brock, NL:StL.
	37	Reggie Smith, AL:Bos.
1969:	41	Matty Alou, NL:Pitt.
	39	Tony Oliva, AL:Minn. (3)
1970:	47	Wes Parker, NL:LA
	36	Tony Oliva, AL:Minn. (4)
	36	Amos Otis, AL:KC
	36	Cesar Tovar, AL:Minn.
1971:	40	Cesar Cedeno, NL:Hou.
	33	Reggie Smith, AL:Bos. (2)
1972:	39	Cesar Cedeno, NL:Hou. (2)
	39	Willie Montanez, NL:Phil.
	33	Lou Piniella, AL:KC
1973:	43	Willie Stargell, NL:Pitt.
	32	Sal Bando, AL:Oak
	32	Pedro Garcia, AL:Mil.
1974:	45	Pete Rose, NL:Cin.
	39	Joe Rudi, AL:Oak.
1975:	47	Fred Lynn, AL:Bos.
	47	Pete Rose, NL:Cin. (2)
1976:	42	Pete Rose, NL:Cin. (3)
	40	Amos Otis, AL:KC (2)
1977:	54	Hal McRae, AL:KC
	44	Dave Parker, NL:Pitt.
1978:	51	Pete Rose, NL:Cin. (4)
	45	George Brett, AL:KC
1979:	48	Keith Hernandez, NL:StL.
	44	Cecil Cooper, AL:Mil.
	44	Chet Lemon, AL:Chi.
1980:	49	Robin Yount, AL:Mil.
	42	Pete Rose, NL:Phil. (5)
1981:	35	Bill Buckner, NL:Chi.
	35	Cecil Cooper, AL:Mil. (2)
1982:	46	Hal McRae, AL:KC (2)
	46	Robin Yount, AL:Mil. (2)
	43	Al Oliver, NL:Mtl.
1983:	47	Cal Ripken, AL:Balt.
	38	Bill Buckner, NL:Chi. (2)
	38	Al Oliver, NL:Mtl. (2)
	38	Johnny Ray, NL:Pitt.
1984:	44	Don Mattingly, AL:NY
	38	Tim Raines, NL:Mtl.
	38	Johnny Ray, NL:Pitt. (2)
1985:	48	Don Mattingly, AL:NY (2)
	42	Dave Parker, NL:Cin. (2)
1986:	53	Don Mattingly, AL:NY (3)
	46	Von Hayes, NL:Phil.
1987:	42	Tim Wallach, NL:Mtl.
	41	Paul Molitor, AL:Mil.
1988:	45	Wade Boggs, AL:Bos.
	42	Andres Galarraga, NL:Mtl.
1989:	51	Wade Boggs, AL:Bos. (2)
	42	Pedro Guerrero, NL:StL.
	42	Tim Wallach, NL:Mtl. (2)
1990:	45	George Brett, AL:KC (2)
	45	Jody Reed, AL:Bos.
	40	Gregg Jefferies, NL:NY

1991:	49	Rafael Palmeiro, AL:Tex.
	44	Bobby Bonilla, NL:Pitt.
1992:	46	Edgar Martinez, AL:Sea.
	46	Frank Thomas, AL:Chi.
	45	Andy Van Slyke, NL:Pitt.
1993:	54	John Olerud, AL:Tor.
	45	Charlie Hayes, NL:Col.
1994:	45	Chuck Knoblauch, AL:Minn.
	44	Craig Biggio, NL:Hou.
	44	Larry Walker, NL:Mtl.
1995:	52	Albert Belle, AL:Clev.
	52	Edgar Martinez, AL:Sea. (2)
	51	Mark Grace, NL:Chi.
1996:	54	Alex Rodriguez, AL:Sea.
	48	Jeff Bagwell, NL:Hou.
1997:	54	Mark Grudzielanek, NL:Mtl.
	47	John Valentin, AL:Bos.
1998:	51	Craig Biggio, NL:Hou. (2)
	50	Juan Gonzalez, AL:Tex.
1999:	56	Craig Biggio, NL:Hou. (3)
	45	Shawn Green, AL:Tor.
2000:	59	Todd Helton, NL:Col.
	57	Carlos Delgado, AL:Tor.
2001:	55	Lance Berkman, NL:Hou.
	47	Jason Giambi, AL:Oak.
2002:	56	Garret Anderson, AL:Ana.
	56	Nomar Garciaparra, AL:Bos.
	50	Bobby Abreu, NL:Phil.
2003:	51	Albert Pujols, NL:StL.
	49	Garret Anderson, AL:Ana. (2)
	49	Vernon Wells, AL:Tor.
2004:	53	Lyle Overbay, NL:Mil.
	50	Brian Roberts, AL:Balt.
2005:	50	Derrek Lee, NL:Chi.
	50	Miguel Tejada, AL:Balt.
2006:	53	Freddy Sanchez, NL:Pitt.
	53	Grady Sizemore, AL:Clev.
2007:	54	Magglio Ordonez, AL:Det.
	50	Matt Holliday, NL:Col.
2008:	54	Dustin Pedroia, AL:Bos.
	46	Lance Berkman, NL:Hou. (2)
	46	Nate McLouth, NL:Pitt.
2009:	56	Brian Roberts, AL:Balt. (2)
	46	Miguel Tejada, NL:Hou. (AL 1)
2010:	49	Adrian Beltre, AL:Bos.
	46	Jayson Werth, NL:Phil.
2011:	48	Miguel Cabrera, AL:Det.
	40	Joey Votto, NL:Cin.
2012:	51	Alex Gordon, AL:KC
	50	Aramis Ramirz, NL:Mil.
2013:	55	Matt Carpenter, NL:StL.
	51	Manny Machado, AL:Balt.
2014:	53	Jonathan Lucroy, NL:Mil.
	52	Miguel Cabrera, AL:Det. (2)
2015:	45	Michael Brantley, AL:Clev.
	44	Matt Carpenter, NL:StL. (2)
2016:	48	David Ortiz, AL:Bos.
	47	Daniel Murphy, NL:Wash.
2017:	56	Jose Ramirez, AL:Clev.
	43	Nolan Arenado, NL:Col.
	43	Daniel Murphy, NL:Wash. (2)
2018:	51	Alex Bregman, AL:Hou.
	44	Freddie Freeman, NL:Atl.
	44	Anthony Rendon, NL: Wash.
2019:	58	Nicholas Castellanos, AL:Det.-NL:Chi.
	54	Rafael Devers, AL:Bos.
	44	Anthony Rendon, NL:Wash. (2)
	44	Corey Seager, NL:LA
2020:	23	Freddie Freeman, NL:Atl. (2)
	20	Cesar Hernandez, AL:Clev.

TRIPLES

1900:	22	Honus Wagner, NL:Pitt.
1901:	21	Bill Keister, AL:Balt.
	21	Jimmy Williams, AL:Balt.
	19	Jimmy Sheckard, NL:Brk.
1902:	23	Sam Crawford, NL:Cin.
	21	Jimmy Williams, AL:Balt. (2)
1903:	25	Sam Crawford, AL:Det.
	19	Honus Wagner, NL:Pitt. (2)
1904:	19	Joe Cassidy, AL:Wash.
	19	Buck Freeman, AL:Bos.
	19	Chick Stahl, AL:Bos.
	18	Harry Lumley, NL:Brk.
1905:	21	Cy Seymour, NL:Cin.
	19	Elmer Flick, AL:Clev.
1906:	24	Elmer Flick, AL:Clev. (2)
	13	Fred Clarke, NL:Pitt.
	13	Frank Schulte, NL:Chi.
1907:	18	Elmer Flick, AL:Clev. (3)
	16	Whitey Alperman, NL:Brk.
	16	John Ganzel, NL:Cin.
1908:	20	Ty Cobb, AL:Det.
	19	Honus Wagner, NL:Pitt. (3)
1909:	19	Frank Baker, AL:Phil.
	17	Mike Mitchell, NL:Cin.
1910:	19	Sam Crawford, AL:Det. (2)
	19	Danny Murphy AL:Phil.
	18	Mike Mitchell, NL:Cin. (2)
1911:	25	Larry Doyle, NL:NY
	24	Ty Cobb, AL:Det. (2)
1912:	36	Owen Wilson, NL:Pitt.
	26	Joe Jackson, AL:Clev.
1913:	23	Sam Crawford, AL:Det. (3)
	21	Vic Saier, NL:Chi.
1914:	26	Sam Crawford, AL:Det. (4)
	17	Max Carey, NL:Pitt.
1915:	25	Tommy Long, NL:StL.
	19	Sam Crawford, AL:Det. (5)
1916:	21	Joe Jackson, AL:Chi. (2)
	16	Bill Hinchman, NL:Pitt.
1917:	24	Ty Cobb, AL:Det. (3)
	17	Rogers Hornsby, NL:StL.
1918:	15	Jake Daubert, NL:Brk.
	14	Ty Cobb, AL:Det. (4)
1919:	17	Bobby Veach, AL:Det.
	14	Hy Myers, NL:Brk.
	14	Billy Southworth, NL:Pitt.
1920:	22	Hy Myers, NL:Brk. (2)
	20	Joe Jackson, AL:Chi. (3)
1921:	18	George Sisler, AL:StL.
	18	Jack Tobin, AL:StL.
	18	Frankie Frisch, NL:NY
	18	Rogers Hornsby, NL:StL. (2)
	18	Ray Powell, NL:Bos.
1922:	22	Jake Daubert, NL:Cin. (2)
	18	George Sisler, AL:StL. (2)
1923:	19	Max Carey, NL:Pitt. (2)
	19	Pie Traynor, NL:Pitt.
	18	Goose Goslin, AL:Wash.
	18	Sam Rice, AL:Wash.
1924:	21	Edd Roush, NL:Cin.
	19	Wally Pipp, AL:NY
1925:	26	Kiki Cuyler, NL:Pitt.
	20	Goose Goslin, AL:Wash. (2)
1926:	22	Paul Waner, NL:Pitt.
	20	Lou Gehrig, AL:NY
1927:	23	Earle Combs, AL:NY
	18	Paul Waner, NL:Pitt. (2)
1928:	21	Earle Combs, AL:NY (2)
	20	Jim Bottomley, NL:StL.
1929:	20	Lloyd Waner, NL:Pitt.
	19	Charlie Gehringer, AL:Det.
1930:	23	Adam Comorosky, NL:Pitt.
	22	Earle Combs, AL:NY (3)
1931:	20	Bill Terry, NL:NY
	19	Roy Johnson, AL:Det.

1932:	19	Babe Herman, NL:Cin.
	18	Joe Cronin, AL:Wash.
1933:	19	Arky Vaughan, NL:Pitt.
	17	Heinie Manush, AL:Wash.
1934:	18	Joe Medwick, NL:StL.
	13	Ben Chapman, AL:NY
1935:	20	Joe Vosmik, AL:Clev.
	18	Ival Goodman, NL:Cin.
1936:	15	Earl Averill, AL:Clev.
	15	Joe DiMaggio, AL:NY
	15	Red Rolfe, AL:NY
	14	Ival Goodman, NL:Cin. (2)
1937:	17	Arky Vaughan, NL:Pitt. (2)
	16	Mike Kreevich, AL:Chi.
	16	Dixie Walker, AL:Chi.
1938:	18	Jeff Heath, AL:Clev.
	16	Johnny Mize, NL:StL.
1939:	18	Billy Herman, NL:Chi.
	16	Buddy Lewis, AL:Wash.
1940:	19	Barney McCosky, AL:Det.
	15	Arky Vaughan, NL:Pitt. (3)
1941:	20	Jeff Heath, AL:Clev. (2)
	17	Pete Reiser, NL:Brk.
1942:	17	Enos Slaughter, NL:StL.
	15	Stan Spence, AL:Wash.
1943:	20	Stan Musial, NL:StL.
	12	Johnny Lindell, AL:NY
	12	Wally Moses, AL:Chi.
1944:	19	Johnny Barrett, NL:Pitt.
	16	Johnny Lindell, AL:NY (2)
	16	Snuffy Stirnweiss, AL:NY
1945:	22	Snuffy Stirnweiss, AL:NY (2)
	13	Luis Olmo, NL:Brk.
1946:	20	Stan Musial, NL:StL. (2)
	16	Hank Edwards, AL:Clev.
1947:	16	Harry Walker, NL:StL.-Phil.
	13	Tommy Henrich, AL:NY
1948:	18	Stan Musial, NL:StL. (3)
	14	Tommy Henrich, AL:NY (2)
1949:	23	Dale Mitchell, AL:Clev.
	13	Stan Musial, NL:StL. (4)
	13	Enos Slaughter, NL:StL. (2)
1950:	14	Richie Ashburn, NL:Phil.
	11	Dom DiMaggio, AL:Bos.
	11	Bobby Doerr, AL:Bos.
	11	Hoot Evers, AL:Det.
1951:	14	Minnie Minoso, AL:Clev.-Chi.
	12	Gus Bell, NL:Pitt.
	12	Stan Musial, NL:StL. (5)
1952:	14	Bobby Thomson, NL:NY
	11	Bobby Avila, AL:Clev.
1953:	17	Jim Gilliam, NL:Brk.
	16	Jim Rivera, AL:Chi.
1954:	18	Minnie Minoso, AL:Chi. (2)
	13	Willie Mays, NL:NY
1955:	13	Dale Long, NL:Pitt.
	13	Willie Mays, NL:NY (2)
	11	Andy Carey, AL:NY
	11	Mickey Mantle, AL:NY
1956:	15	Bill Bruton, NL:Mil.
	11	Jackie Jensen, AL:Bos.
	11	Jim Lemon, AL:Wash.
	11	Minnie Minoso, AL:Chi. (3)
	11	Harry Simpson, AL:KC
1957:	20	Willie Mays, NL:NY (3)
	9	Hank Bauer, AL:NY
	9	Gil McDougald, AL:NY
	9	Harry Simpson, AL:KC-NY (2)
1958:	13	Richie Ashburn, NL:Phil. (2)
	10	Vic Power, AL:KC-Clev.
1959:	11	Wally Moon, NL:LA
	11	Charlie Neal, NL:LA
	9	Bob Allison, AL:Wash.
1960:	13	Bill Bruton, NL:Mil. (2)
	10	Nellie Fox, AL:Chi.
1961:	14	Jake Wood, AL:Det.
	12	George Altman, NL:Chi.

TRIPLES (CONTINUED)

1962:	15	Gino Cimoli, AL:KC
	10	Johnny Callison, NL:Phil.
	10	Willie Davis, NL:LA
	10	Bill Virdon, NL:Pitt.
	10	Maury Wills, NL:LA
1963:	14	Vade Pinson, NL:Cin.
	13	Zoilo Versalles, AL:Minn.
1964:	13	Dick Allen, NL:Phil.
	13	Ron Santo, NL:Chi.
	10	Rich Rollins, AL:Minn.
	10	Zoilo Versalles, AL:Minn. (2)
1965:	16	Johnny Callison, NL:Phil. (2)
	12	Bert Campaneris, AL:KC
	12	Zoilo Versalles, AL:Minn. (3)
1966:	13	Tim McCarver, NL:StL.
	11	Bobby Knoop, AL:Cal.
1967:	13	Vada Pinson, NL:Cin. (2)
	12	Paul Blair, AL:Balt.
1968:	14	Lou Brock, NL:StL.
	13	Jim Fregosi, AL:Cal.
1969:	12	Roberto Clemente, NL:Pitt.
	8	Del Unser, AL:Wash.
1970:	16	Willie Davis, NL:LA (2)
	13	Cesar Tovar, AL:Minn.
1971:	11	Roger Metzger, NL:Hou.
	11	Joe Morgan, NL:Hou.
	11	Freddie Patek, AL:KC
1972:	13	Larry Bowa, NL:Phil.
	9	Carton Fisk, AL:Bos.
	9	Joe Rudi, AL:Oak.
1973:	14	Roger Metzger, NL:Hou. (2)
	11	Al Bumbry, AL:Balt.
	11	Rod Carew, AL:Minn.
1974:	17	Ralph Garr, NL:Atl.
	11	Mickey Rivers, AL:Cal.
1975:	13	George Brett, AL:KC
	13	Mickey Rivers, AL:Cal. (2)
	11	Ralph Garr, NL:Atl. (2)
1976:	14	George Brett, AL:KC (2)
	12	Dave Cash, NL:Phil.
1977:	18	Garry Templeton, NL:StL.
	16	Rod Carew, AL:Minn. (2)
1978:	15	Jim Rice, AL:Bos.
	13	Garry Templeton, NL:StL. (2)
1979:	20	George Brett, AL:KC (3)
	19	Garry Templeton, NL:StL. (3)
1980:	15	Alfredo Griffin, AL:Tor.
	15	Willie Wilson, AL:KC
	13	Omar Moreno, NL:Pitt.
	13	Rodney Scott, NL:Mtl.
1981:	12	Craig Reynolds, NL:Hou.
	12	Gene Richards, NL:SD
	9	John Castino, AL:Minn.
1982:	15	Willie Wilson, AL:KC (2)
	10	Dickie Thon, NL:Hou.
1983:	13	Brett Butler, NL:Atl.
	10	Robin Yount, AL:Mil.
1984:	19	Juan Samuel, NL:Phil.
	19	Ryne Sandberg, NL:Chi.
	15	Dave Collins, AL:Tor.
	15	Lloyd Moseby, AL:Tor.
1985:	21	Willie Wilson, AL:KC (3)
	18	Willie McGee, NL:StL.
1986:	14	Brett Butler, AL:Clev. (NL 1)
	13	Mitch Webster, NL:Mtl.
1987:	15	Juan Samuel, NL:Phil. (2)
	15	Willie Wilson, AL:KC (4)
1988:	15	Andy Van Slyke, NL:Pitt.
	11	Harold Reynolds, AL:Sea.
	11	Willie Wilson, AL:KC (5)
	11	Robin Yount, AL:Mil. (2)
1989:	14	Ruben Sierra, AL:Tex.
	11	Robby Thompson, NL:SF
1990:	17	Tony Fernandez, AL:Tor.
	11	Mariano Duncan, NL:Cin.
1991:	15	Ray Lankford, NL:StL.
	13	Lance Johnson, AL:Chi.
	13	Paul Molitor, AL:Mil.

1992:	14	Deion Sanders, NL:Atl.
	12	Lance Johnson, AL:Chi. (2)
1993:	14	Lance Johnson, AL:Chi. (3)
	13	Steve Finley, NL:Hou.
1994:	14	Lance Johnson, AL:Chi. (4)
	9	Brett Butler, NL:LA (NL 2; AL 1)
	9	Darren Lewis, NL:SF
1995:	13	Kenny Lofton, AL:Clev.
	9	Brett Butler, NL:NY-LA (NL 3; AL 1)
	9	Eric Young, NL:Col.
1996:	21	Lance Johnson, NL:NY (AL 4)
	14	Chuck Knoblauch, AL:Minn.
1997:	14	Delino DeShields, NL:StL.
	11	Nomar Garciaparra, AL:Bos.
1998:	13	Jose Offerman, AL:KC
	12	David Dellucci, NL:Ari.
1999:	11	Bobby Abreu, NL:Phil.
	11	Neifi Perez, NL:Col.
	11	Jose Offerman, AL:Bos. (2)
2000:	20	Cristian Guzman, AL:Minn.
	14	Tony Womack, NL:Ari.
2001:	14	Cristian Guzman, AL:Minn. (2)
	12	Jimmy Rollins, NL:Phil.˙
2002:	11	Johnny Damon, AL:Bos.
	10	Jimmy Rollins, NL:Phil. (2)
2003:	14	Cristian Guzman, AL:Minn. (3)
	10	Steve Finley, Steve NL:Ari. (2)
	10	Rafael Furcal, Rafael NL:Atl.
2004:	19	Carl Crawford, AL:TB
	12	Juan Pierre, NL:Fla.
	12	Jimmy Rollins, NL:Phil. (3)
	12	Jack Wilson, NL:Pitt.
2005:	17	Jose Reyes, NL:NY
	15	Carl Crawford, AL:TB (2)
2006:	17	Jose Reyes, NL:NY (2)
	16	Carl Crawford, AL:TB (3)
2007:	23	Curtis Granderson, AL:Det.
	20	Jimmy Rollins, NL:Phil. (4)
2008:	19	Jose Reyes, NL:NY (3)
	13	Curtis Granderson, AL:Det. (2)
2009:	13	Shane Victorino, NL:Phil.
	10	Jacoby Ellsbury, AL:Bos.
	10	Denard Span, AL:Minn.
2010:	14	Dexter Fowler, NL:Col.
	13	Carl Crawford, AL:TB (4)
2011:	16	Jose Reyes, NL:NY (4)
	16	Shane Victorino, NL:Phil. (2)
	11	Peter Bourjos, AL:LA
	11	Austin Jackson, AL:Det.
2012:	15	Angel Pagan, NL:SF
	10	Austin Jackson, AL:Det. (2)
2013:	11	Denard Span, NL:Wash.
	10	Brett Gardner, AL:NY
2014:	12	Dee Gordon, NL:LA
	10	Michael Bourn, AL:Clev.
	10	Adam Eaton, AL:Chi.
2015:	15	Eddie Rosario, AL:Minn.
	10	David Peralta, NL:Ari.
2016:	11	Brandon Crawford, NL:SF
	11	Cesar Hernandez, NL:Phil.
	11	Chris Owings, NL:Ari.
	9	Adam Eaton, AL:Chi. (2)
2017:	14	Charlie Blackmon, NL:Col.
	10	Nicholas Castellanos, AL:Det.
2018:	12	Ketel Marte, NL:Ari.
	10	Yolmer Sanchez, AL:Chi.
	10	Mallex Smith, AL:TB
2019:	10	Hunter Dozier, AL:KC
	10	Whit Merrifield, AL:KC
	10	Adalberto Mondesi, AL:KC
	10	Eduardo Escobar, NL:Ari.
2020:	6	Kyle Tucker, AL:Hou.
	4	Trevor Story, NL:Col.
	4	Trea Turner, NL:Wash.
	4	Mike Yastrzemski, NL:SF

HOME RUNS

Year	HR	Player
1900:	12	Herman Long, NL:Bos.
1901:	16	Sam Crawford, NL:Cin.
	14	Nap Lajoie, AL:Phil.
1902:	16	Socks Seybold, AL:Phil.
	6	Tommy Leach, NL:Pitt.
1903:	13	Buck Freeman, AL:Bos.
	9	Jimmy Sheckard, NL:Brk.
1904:	10	Harry Davis, AL:Phil.
	9	Harry Lumley, NL:Brk.
1905:	9	Fred Odwell, NL:Cin.
	8	Harry Davis, AL:Phil. (2)
1906:	12	Harry Davis, AL:Phil. (3)
	12	Tim Jordan, NL:Brk.
1907:	10	Dave Brain, NL:Bos.
	8	Harry Davis, AL:Phil. (4)
1908:	12	Tim Jordan, NL:Brk. (2)
	7	Sam Crawford, AL:Det.
1909:	9	Ty Cobb, AL:Det.
	7	Red Murray, NL:NY
1910:	10	Fred Beck, NL:Bos.
	10	Frank Schulte, NL:Chi.
	10	Jake Stahl, AL:Bos.
1911:	21	Frank Schulte, NL:Chi. (2)
	11	Frank Baker, AL:Phil.
1912:	14	Heinie Zimmerman, NL:Chi.
	10	Frank Baker, AL:Phil. (2)
	10	Tris Speaker, AL:Bos.
1913:	19	Gavvy Cravath, NL:Phil.
	12	Frank Baker, AL:Phil. (3)
1914:	19	Gavvy Cravath, NL:Phil. (2)
	9	Frank Baker, AL:Phil. (4)
1915:	24	Gavvy Cravath, NL:Phil. (3)
	7	Braggo Roth, AL:Chi.-Clev.
1916:	12	Wally Pipp, AL:NY
	12	Dave Robertson, NL:NY
	12	Cy Williams, NL:Chi.
1917:	12	Gavvy Cravath, NL:Phil. (4)
	12	Dave Robertson, NL:NY (2)
	9	Wally Pipp, AL:NY (2)
1918:	11	Babe Ruth, AL:Bos.
	11	Tilly Walker, AL:Phil.
	8	Gavvy Cravath, NL:Phil. (5)
1919:	29	Babe Ruth, AL:Bos. (2)
	12	Gavvy Cravath, NL:Phil. (6)
1920:	54	Babe Ruth, AL:NY (3)
	15	Cy Williams, NL:Phil. (2)
1921:	59	Babe Ruth, AL:NY (4)
	23	George Kelly, NL:NY
1922:	42	Rogers Hornsby, NL:StL.
	39	Ken Williams, AL:StL.
1923:	41	Babe Ruth, AL:NY (5)
	41	Cy Williams, NL:Phil. (3)
1924:	46	Babe Ruth, AL:NY (6)
	27	Jack Fournier, NL:Brk.
1925:	39	Rogers Hornsby, NL:StL. (2)
	33	Bob Meusel, AL:NY
1926:	47	Babe Ruth, AL:NY (7)
	21	Hack Wilson, NL:Chi.
1927:	60	Babe Ruth, AL:NY (8)
	30	Cy Williams, NL:Phil. (4)
	30	Hack Wilson, NL:Chi. (2)
1928:	54	Babe Ruth, AL:NY (9)
	31	Jim Bottomley, NL:StL.
	31	Hack Wilson, NL:Chi. (3)
1929:	46	Babe Ruth, AL:NY (10)
	43	Chuck Klein, NL:Phil.
1930:	56	Hack Wilson, NL:Chi. (4)
	49	Babe Ruth, AL:NY (11)
1931:	46	Lou Gehrig, AL:NY
	46	Babe Ruth, AL:NY (12)
	31	Chuck Klein, NL:Phil. (2)
1932:	58	Jimmie Foxx, AL:Phil.
	38	Chuck Klein, NL:Phil. (3)
	38	Mel Ott, NL:NY
1933:	48	Jimmie Foxx, AL:Phil. (2)
	28	Chuck Klein, NL:Phil. (4)
1934:	49	Lou Gehrig, AL:NY (2)
	35	Ripper Collins, NL:StL.
	35	Mel Ott, NL:NY (2)
1935:	36	Jimmie Foxx, AL:Phil. (3)
	36	Hank Greenberg, AL:Det.
	34	Wally Berger, NL:Bos.
1936:	49	Lou Gehrig, AL:NY (3)
	33	Mel Ott, NL:NY (3)
1937:	46	Joe DiMaggio, AL:NY
	31	Joe Medwick, NL:StL.
	31	Mel Ott, NL:NY (4)
1938:	58	Hank Greenberg, AL:Det. (2)
	36	Mel Ott, NL:NY (5)
1939:	35	Jimmie Foxx, AL:Bos. (4)
	28	Johnny Mize, NL:StL.
1940:	43	Johnny Mize, NL:StL. (2)
	41	Hank Greenberg, AL:Det. (3)
1941:	37	Ted Williams, AL:Bos.
	34	Dolph Camilli, NL:Brk.
1942:	36	Ted Williams, AL:Bos. (2)
	30	Mel Ott, NL:NY (6)
1943:	34	Rudy York, AL:Det.
	29	Bill Nicholson, NL:Chi.
1944:	33	Bill Nicholson, NL:Chi. (2)
	22	Nick Etten, AL:NY
1945:	28	Tommy Holmes, NL:Bos.
	24	Vern Stephens, AL:StL.
1946:	44	Hank Greenberg, AL:Det. (4)
	23	Ralph Kiner, NL:Pitt.
1947:	51	Ralph Kiner, NL:Pitt. (2)
	51	Johnny Mize, NL:NY (3)
	32	Ted Williams, AL:Bos. (3)
1948:	40	Ralph Kiner, NL:Pitt. (3)
	40	Johnny Mize, NL:NY (4)
	39	Joe DiMaggio, AL:NY (2)
1949:	54	Ralph Kiner, NL:Pitt. (4)
	43	Ted Williams, AL:Bos. (4)
1950:	47	Ralph Kiner, NL:Pitt. (5)
	37	Al Rosen, AL:Clev.
1951:	42	Ralph Kiner, NL:Pitt. (6)
	33	Gus Zernial, AL:Chi.-Phil.
1952:	37	Ralph Kiner, NL:Pitt. (7)
	37	Hank Sauer, NL:Chi.
	32	Larry Doby, AL:Clev.
1953:	47	Eddie Mathews, NL:Mil.
	43	Al Rosen, AL:Clev. (2)
1954:	49	Ted Kluszewski, NL:Cin.
	32	Larry Doby, AL:Clev. (2)
1955:	51	Willie Mays, NL:NY
	37	Mickey Mantle, AL:NY
1956:	52	Mickey Mantle, AL:NY (2)
	43	Duke Snider, NL:Brk.
1957:	44	Hank Aaron, NL:Mil.
	42	Roy Sievers, AL:Wash.

HOME RUNS (CONTINUED)

1958:	47	Ernie Banks, NL:Chi.
	42	Mickey Mantle, AL:NY (3)
1959:	46	Eddie Mathews, NL:Mil. (2)
	42	Rocky Colavito, AL:Clev.
	42	Harmon Killebrew, AL:Wash.
1960:	41	Ernie Banks, NL:Chi. (2)
	40	Mickey Mantle, AL:NY (4)
1961:	61	Roger Maris, AL:NY
	46	Orlando Cepeda, NL:SF
1962:	49	Willie Mays, NL:SF (2)
	48	Harmon Killebrew, AL:Minn. (2)
1963:	45	Harmon Killebrew, AL:Minn. (3)
	44	Hank Aaron, NL:Mil. (2)
	44	Willie McCovey, NL:SF
1964:	49	Harmon Killebrew, AL:Minn. (4)
	47	Willie Mays, NL:SF (3)
1965:	52	Willie Mays, NL:SF (4)
	32	Tony Conigliaro, AL:Bos.
1966:	49	Frank Robinson, AL:Balt.
	44	Hank Aaron, NL:Atl. (3)
1967:	44	Harmon Killebrew, AL:Minn. (5)
	44	Carl Yastrzemski, AL:Bos.
	39	Hank Aaron, NL:Atl. (4)
1968:	44	Frank Howard, AL:Wash.
	36	Willie McCovey, NL:SF (2)
1969:	49	Harmon Killebrew, AL:Minn. (6)
	45	Willie McCovey, NL:SF (3)
1970:	45	Johnny Bench, NL:Cin.
	44	Frank Howard, AL:Wash. (2)
1971:	48	Willie Stargell, NL:Pitt.
	33	Bill Melton, AL:Chi.
1972:	40	Johnny Bench, NL:Cin. (2)
	37	Dick Allen, AL:Chi.
1973:	44	Willie Stargell, NL:Pitt. (2)
	32	Reggie Jackson, AL:Oak.
1974:	36	Mike Schmidt, NL:Phil.
	32	Dick Allen, AL:Chi. (2)
1975:	38	Mike Schmidt, NL:Phil. (2)
	36	Reggie Jackson, AL:Oak. (2)
	36	George Scott, AL:Mil.
1976:	38	Mike Schmidt, NL:Phil. (3)
	32	Graig Nettles, AL:NY
1977:	52	George Foster, NL:Cin.
	39	Jim Rice, AL:Bos.
1978:	46	Jim Rice, AL:Bos. (2)
	40	George Foster, NL:Cin. (2)
1979:	48	Dave Kingman, NL:Chi.
	45	Gorman Thomas, AL:Mil.
1980:	48	Mike Schmidt, NL:Phil. (4)
	41	Reggie Jackson, AL:NY (3)
	41	Ben Oglivie, AL:Mil.
1981:	31	Mike Schmidt, NL:Phil. (5)
	22	Tony Armas, AL:Oak.
	22	Dwight Evans, AL:Bos.
	22	Bobby Grich, AL:Cal.
	22	Eddie Murray, AL:Balt.
1982:	39	Reggie Jackson, AL:Cal. (4)
	39	Gorman Thomas, AL:Mil. (2)
	37	Dave Kingman, NL:NY (2)
1983:	40	Mike Schmidt, NL:Phil. (6)
	39	Jim Rice, AL:Bos. (3)
1984:	43	Tony Armas, AL:Bos. (2)
	36	Dale Murphy, NL:Atl.
	36	Mike Schmidt, NL:Phil. (7)
1985:	40	Darrell Evans, AL:Det.
	37	Dale Murphy, NL:Atl. (2)
1986:	40	Jesse Barfield, AL:Tor.
	37	Mike Schmidt, NL:Phil. (8)
1987:	49	Andre Dawson, NL:Chi.
	49	Mark McGwire, AL:Oak.

1988:	42	Jose Canseco, AL:Oak.
	39	Darryl Strawberry, NL:NY
1989:	47	Kevin Mitchell, NL:SF
	36	Fred McGriff, AL:Tor.
1990:	51	Cecil Fielder, AL:Det.
	40	Ryne Sandberg, NL:Chi.
1991:	44	Jose Canseco, AL:Oak. (2)
	44	Cecil Fielder, AL:Det. (2)
	38	Howard Johnson, NL:NY
1992:	43	Juan Gonzalez, AL:Tex.
	35	Fred McGriff, NL:SD (AL 1)
1993:	46	Barry Bonds, NL:SF
	46	Juan Gonzalez, AL:Tex. (2)
1994:	43	Matt Williams, NL:SF
	40	Ken Griffey Jr., AL:Sea.
1995:	50	Albert Belle, AL:Clev.
	40	Dante Bichette, NL:Col.
1996:	52	Mark McGwire, AL:Oak. (2)
	47	Andres Galarraga, NL:Col.
1997:	58	Mark McGwire, AL:Oak.-NL:StL. (ML 3)
	56	Ken Griffey Jr., AL:Sea. (2)
	49	Larry Walker, NL:Col.
1998:	70	Mark McGwire, NL:StL. (ML 4)
	56	Ken Griffey Jr., AL:Sea. (3)
1999:	65	Mark McGwire, NL:StL. (2, ML 5)
	48	Ken Griffey Jr., AL:Sea. (4)
2000:	50	Sammy Sosa, NL:Chi.
	47	Troy Glaus, AL:Ana.
2001:	73	Barry Bonds, NL:SF (2)
	52	Alex Rodriguez, AL:Tex.
2002:	57	Alex Rodriguez, AL:Tex. (2)
	49	Sammy Sosa, NL:Chi. (2)
2003:	47	Alex Rodriguez, AL:Tex. (3)
	47	Jim Thome, NL:Phil.
2004:	48	Adrian Beltre, NL:LA
	43	Manny Ramirez, AL:Bos.
2005:	51	Andruw Jones, NL:Atl.
	48	Alex Rodriguez, AL:NY (4)
2006:	58	Ryan Howard, NL:Phil.
	54	David Ortiz, AL:Bos.
2007:	54	Alex Rodriguez, AL:NY (5)
	50	Prince Fielder, NL:Mil.
2008:	48	Ryan Howard, NL:Phil. (2)
	37	Miguel Cabrera, AL:Det.
2009:	47	Albert Pujols, NL:StL.
	39	Carlos Pena, AL:TB
	39	Mark Teixeira, AL:NY
2010:	54	Jose Bautista, AL:Tor.
	42	Albert Pujols, NL:StL. (2)
2011:	43	Jose Bautista, AL:Tor. (2)
	39	Matt Kemp, NL:LA
2012:	44	Miguel Cabrera, AL:Det. (2)
	41	Ryan Braun, NL:Mil.
2013:	53	Chris Davis, AL:Balt.
	36	Pedro Alvarez, NL:Pitt.
	36	Paul Goldschmidt, NL:Ari.
2014:	40	Nelson Cruz, AL:Balt.
	37	Giancarlo Stanton, NL:Mia.
2015:	47	Chris Davis, AL:Balt. (2)
	42	Nolan Arenado, NL:Col.
	42	Bryce Harper, NL:Wash.
2016:	47	Mark Trumbo, AL:Balt.
	41	Nolan Arenado, Col. (2)
	41	Chris Carter, NL:Mil.
2017:	59	Giancarlo Stanton, NL:Mia. (2)
	52	Aaron Judge, AL:NY
2018:	48	Khris Davis, AL:Oak.
	38	Nolan Arenado, NL:Col. (3)
2019:	53	Pete Alonso, NL:NY
	48	Jorge Soler, AL:KC
2020:	22	Luke Voit, AL:NY
	18	Marcell Ozuna, NL:Atl.

WALKS

Year		
1910:	116	Miller Huggins, NL:StL.
1911:	148	Jimmy Sheckard, NL:Chi.
1912:	124	Jimmy Sheckard, NL:Chi. (2)
1913:	99	Burt Shotton, AL:StL.
	94	Bob Bescher, NL:Cin.
1914:	112	Donie Bush, AL:Det.
	105	Miller Huggins, NL:StL. (2)
1915:	119	Eddie Collins, AL:Chi.
	86	Gavvy Cravath, NL:Phil.
1916:	111	Burt Shotton, AL:StL. (2)
	84	Heinie Groh, NL:Cin.
1917:	94	Jack Graney, AL:Clev.
	75	George Burns, NL:NY
1918:	84	Ray Chapman, AL:Clev.
	62	Max Carey, NL:Pitt.
1919:	106	Jack Graney, AL:Clev. (2)
	82	George Burns, NL:NY (2)
1920:	150	Babe Ruth, AL:NY
	76	George Burns, NL:NY (3)
1921:	144	Babe Ruth, AL:NY (2)
	80	George Burns, NL:NY (4)
1922:	89	Whitey Witt, AL:NY
	80	Max Carey, NL:Pitt. (2)
1923:	170	Babe Ruth, AL:NY (3)
	101	George Burns, NL:Cin. (5)
1924:	142	Babe Ruth, AL:NY (4)
	91	Rogers Hornsby, NL:StL.
1925:	90	Max Bishop, AL:Phil.
	90	Willie Kamm, AL:Chi.
	86	Jack Fournier, NL:Brk.
1926:	144	Babe Ruth, AL:NY (5)
	69	Hack Wilson, NL:Chi.
1927:	137	Babe Ruth, AL:NY (6)
	86	Rogers Hornsby, NL:NY (2)
1928:	137	Babe Ruth, AL:NY (7)
	108	Rogers Hornsby, NL:Bos. (3)
1929:	129	Max Bishop, AL:Phil. (2)
	113	Mel Ott, NL:NY
1930:	136	Babe Ruth, AL:NY (8)
	105	Mel Ott, NL:NY (2)
	105	Hack Wilson, NL:Chi. (2)
1931:	128	Babe Ruth, AL:NY (9)
	80	Mel Ott, NL:NY (3)
1932:	130	Babe Ruth, AL:NY (10)
	100	Mel Ott, NL:NY (4)
1933:	115	Babe Ruth, AL:NY (11)
	75	Mel Ott, NL:NY (5)
1934:	111	Jimmie Foxx, AL:Phil.
	94	Arky Vaughan, NL:Pitt.
1935:	133	Lou Gehrig, AL:NY
	97	Arky Vaughan, NL:Pitt. (2)
1936:	130	Lou Gehrig, AL:NY (2)
	118	Arky Vaughan, NL:Pitt. (3)
1937:	127	Lou Gehrig, AL:NY (3)
	102	Mel Ott, NL:NY (6)
1938:	120	Mel Ott, NL:NY (7)
	119	Jimmie Foxx, AL:Bos. (2)
	119	Hank Greenberg, AL:Det.
1939:	110	Dolph Camilli, NL:Brk.
	110	Harlond Clift, AL:StL.
1940:	119	Elbie Fletcher, NL:Pitt.
	106	Charlie Keller, AL:NY
1941:	147	Ted Williams, AL:Bos.
	118	Elbie Fletcher, NL:Pitt. (2)

Year		
1942:	145	Ted Williams, AL:Bos. (2)
	109	Mel Ott, NL:NY (8)
1943:	106	Charlie Keller, AL:NY (2)
	103	Augie Galan, NL:Brk.
1944:	102	Augie Galan, NL:Brk. (2)
	97	Nick Etten, AL:NY
1945:	148	Eddie Stanky, NL:Brk.
	113	Roy Cullenbine, AL:Clev.-Det.
1946:	156	Ted Williams, AL:Bos. (3)
	137	Eddie Stanky, NL:Brk. (2)
1947:	161	Ted Williams, AL:Bos. (4)
	104	Hank Greenberg, NL:Pitt.
	104	Pee Wee Reese, NL:Brk.
1948:	133	Bob Elliott, NL:Bos.
	126	Ted Williams, AL:Bos. (5)
1949:	162	Ted Williams, AL:Bos. (6)
	117	Ralph Kiner, NL:Pitt.
1950:	145	Eddie Stanky, NL:NY (3)
	140	Eddie Yost, AL:Wash.
1951:	144	Ted Williams, AL:Bos. (7)
	137	Ralph Kiner, NL:Pitt. (2)
1952:	129	Eddie Yost, AL:Wash. (2)
	110	Ralph Kiner, NL:Pitt. (3)
1953:	123	Eddie Yost, AL:Wash. (3)
	105	Stan Musial, NL:StL.
1954:	136	Ted Williams, AL:Bos. (8)
	125	Richie Ashburn, NL:Phil.
1955:	113	Mickey Mantle, AL:NY
	109	Eddie Mathews, NL:Mil.
1956:	151	Eddie Yost, AL:Wash. (4)
	99	Duke Snider, NL:Brk.
1957:	146	Mickey Mantle, AL:NY (2)
	94	Richie Ashburn, NL:Phil. (2)
	94	Johnny Temple, NL:Cin.
1958:	129	Mickey Mantle, AL:NY (3)
	97	Richie Ashburn, NL:Phil. (3)
1959:	135	Eddie Yost, AL:Det. (5)
	96	Jim Gilliam, NL:LA
1960:	125	Eddie Yost, AL:Det. (6)
	116	Richie Ashburn, NL:Chi. (4)
1961:	126	Mickey Mantle, AL:NY (4)
	93	Eddie Mathews, NL:Mil. (2)
1962:	122	Mickey Mantle, AL:NY (5)
	101	Eddie Mathews, NL:Mil. (3)
1963:	124	Eddie Mathews, NL:Mil. (4)
	95	Carl Yastrzemski, AL:Bos.
1964:	106	Norm Siebern, AL:Balt.
	86	Ron Santo, NL:Chi.
1965:	97	Joe Morgan, NL:Hou.
	93	Rocky Colavito, AL:Clev.
1966:	103	Harmon Killebrew, AL:Minn.
	95	Ron Santo, NL:Chi. (2)
1967:	131	Harmon Killebrew, AL:Minn. (2)
	96	Ron Santo, NL:Chi. (3)
1968:	119	Carl Yastrzemski, AL:Bos. (2)
	96	Ron Santo, NL:Chi. (4)
1969:	148	Jimmy Wynn, NL:Hou.
	145	Harmon Killebrew, AL:Minn. (3)
1970:	137	Willie McCovey, NL:SF
	132	Frank Howard, AL:Wash.
1971:	114	Harmon Killebrew, AL:Minn. (4)
	112	Willie Mays, NL:SF
1972:	115	Joe Morgan, NL:Cin. (2)
	99	Dick Allen, AL:Chi.
	99	Roy White, AL:NY
1973:	124	Darrell Evans, NL:Atl.
	122	John Mayberry, AL:KC

WALKS (CONTINUED)

1974:	126	Darrell Evans, NL:Atl. (2)	2005:	119	Brian Giles, NL:SD
	110	Gene Tenace, AL:Oak.		108	Jason Giambi, AL:NY (4)
1975:	132	Joe Morgan, NL:Cin. (3)	2006:	124	Bobby Abreu, NL:Phil.-AL:NY
	119	John Mayberry, AL:KC (2)		119	David Ortiz, AL:Bos.
1976:	127	Jimmy Wynn, NL:Atl. (2)		115	Barry Bonds, NL:SF (11)
	97	Mike Hargrove, AL:Tex.	2007:	132	Barry Bonds, NL:SF (12)
1977:	125	Gene Tenace, NL:SD		111	David Ortiz, AL:Bos. (2)
	109	Toby Harrah, AL:Tex.	2008:	122	Adam Dunn, NL:Cin.-Ari.
1978:	117	Jeff Burroughs, NL:Atl.		111	Jack Cust, AL:Oak.
	107	Mike Hargrove, AL:Tex. (2)	2009:	119	Adrian Gonzalez, NL:SD
1979:	121	Darrell Porter, AL:KC		101	Chone Figgins, AL:LA
	120	Mike Schmidt, NL:Phil.	2010:	114	Prince Fielder, NL:Mil.
1980:	119	Willie Randolph, AL:NY		110	Daric Barton, AL:Oak.
	93	Dan Driessen, NL:Cin.	2011:	132	Jose Bautista, AL:Tor.
	93	Joe Morgan, NL:Hou. (4)		110	Joey Votto, NL:Cin.
1981:	85	Dwight Evans, AL:Bos.	2012:	105	Adam Dunn, AL:Chi. (NL 1)
	73	Mike Schmidt, NL:Phil. (2)		94	Dan Uggla, NL:Atl.
1982:	116	Rickey Henderson, AL:Oak.		94	Joey Votto, NL:Cin. (2)
	107	Mike Schmidt, NL:Phil. (3)	2013:	135	Joey Votto, NL:Cin. (3)
1983:	128	Mike Schmidt, NL:Phil. (4)		110	Mike Trout, AL:LA
	103	Rickey Henderson, AL:Oak. (2)	2014:	113	Carlos Santana, AL:Clev.
1984:	107	Eddie Murray, AL:Balt.		95	Matt Carpenter, NL:StL.
	103	Gary Matthews Sr., NL:Chi.	2015:	143	Joey Votto, NL:Cin. (4)
1985:	114	Dwight Evans, AL:Bos. (2)		110	Jose Bautista, AL:Tor. (2)
	90	Dale Murphy, NL:Atl.	2016:	116	Mike Trout, AL:LA (2)
1986:	105	Wade Boggs, AL:Bos.		110	Paul Goldschmidt, NL:Ari.
	94	Keith Hernandez, NL:NY	2017:	134	Joey Votto, NL:Cin. (5)
1987:	136	Jack Clark, NL:StL.		127	Aaron Judge, AL:NY
	106	Brian Downing, AL:Cal.	2018:	130	Bryce Harper, NL:Wash.
	106	Dwight Evans, AL:Bos. (3)		122	Mike Trout, AL:LA (3)
1988:	125	Wade Boggs, AL:Bos. (2)	2019:	119	Alex Bregman, AL:Hou.
	100	Will Clark, NL:SF		116	Rhys Hoskins, NL:Phil.
1989:	132	Jack Clark, NL:SD (2)	2020:	49	Bryce Harper, NL:Phil. (2)
	126	Rickey Henderson, AL:NY-Oak. (3)		47	Carlos Santana, AL:Clev. (2)
1990:	110	Mark McGwire, AL:Oak.			
	104	Jack Clark, NL:SD (3)			
1991:	138	Frank Thomas, AL:Chi.			
	108	Brett Butler, NL:LA			
1992:	127	Barry Bonds, NL:Pitt.			
	122	Mickey Tettleton, AL:Det.			
	122	Frank Thomas, AL:Chi. (2)			
1993:	132	Tony Phillips, AL:Det.			
	129	Len Dykstra, NL:Phil.			
1994:	109	Frank Thomas, AL:Chi. (3)			
	74	Barry Bonds, NL:SF (2)			
1995:	136	Frank Thomas, AL:Chi. (4)			
	120	Barry Bonds, NL:SF (3)			
1996:	151	Barry Bonds, NL:SF (4)			
	125	Tony Phillips, AL:Chi. (2)			
1997:	145	Barry Bonds, NL:SF (5)			
	120	Jim Thome, AL:Clev.			
1998:	162	Mark McGwire, NL:StL. (AL 1)			
	118	Rickey Henderson, AL:Oak. (4)			
1999:	149	Jeff Bagwell, NL:Hou.			
	127	Jim Thome, AL:Clev. (2)			
2000:	137	Jason Giambi, AL:Oak.			
	117	Barry Bonds, NL:SF (6)			
2001:	177	Barry Bonds, NL:SF (7)			
	129	Jason Giambi, AL:Oak. (2)			
2002:	198	Barry Bonds, NL:SF (8)			
	122	Jim Thome, AL:Clev. (3)			
2003:	148	Barry Bonds, NL:SF (9)			
	129	Jason Giambi, AL:NY (3)			
2004:	232	Barry Bonds, NL:SF (10)			
	95	Eric Chavez, AL:Oak.			

STRIKEOUTS

1910:	81	John Hummel, NL:Brk.
1911:	78	Bob Bescher, NL:Cin.
	78	Bob Coulson, NL:Brk.
1912:	91	Ed McDonald, NL:Bos.
1913:	114	Danny Moeller, AL:Wash.
	74	George Burns, NL:NY
1914:	120	Gus Williams, AL:StL.
	81	Fred Merkle, NL:NY
1915:	88	Doug Baird, NL:Pitt.
	83	Doc Lavan, AL:StL.
1916:	89	Gavvy Cravath, NL:Phil.
	82	Wally Pipp, AL:NY
1917:	78	Cy Williams, NL:Chi
	74	Braggo Roth, AL:Clev.
1918:	58	Babe Ruth, AL:Bos.
	49	Dode Paskert, NL:Chi.
	49	Ross Youngs, NL:NY
1919:	79	Ray Powell, NL:Bos.
	70	Red Shannon, AL:Phil.-Bos.
1920:	92	George Kelly, NL:NY
	84	Aaron Ward, AL:NY
1921:	88	Bob Meusel, AL:NY
	85	Ray Powell, NL:Bos. (2)
1922:	98	Jimmy Dykes, AL:Phil.
	93	Frank Parkinson, NL:Phil.
1923:	94	Babe Ruth, AL:NY (2)
	92	George Grantham, NL:Chi.
1924:	81	Babe Ruth, AL:NY (3)
	63	George Grantham, NL:Chi. (2)
1925:	77	Gabby Hartnett, NL:Chi.
	70	Marty McManus, AL:StL.
1926:	97	Tony Lazzeri, AL:NY
	77	Barney Friberg, NL:Phil.
1927:	89	Babe Ruth, AL:NY (4)
	70	Hack Wilson, NL:Chi.
1928:	94	Hack Wilson, NL:Chi. (2)
	88	Babe Ruth, AL:NY (5)
1929:	83	Hack Wilson, NL:Chi. (3)
	71	Lou Gehrig, AL:NY
1930:	84	Hack Wilson, NL:Chi. (4)
	66	Jimmie Foxx, AL:Phil.
	66	Ed Morgan, AL:Clev.
1931:	86	Nick Cullop, NL:Cin.
	86	Jim Levey, AL:StL.
1932:	104	Bruce Campbell, AL:Chi.-StL.
	85	Hack Wilson. NL:Brk. (5)
1933:	93	Jimmie Foxx, AL:Phil. (2)
	77	Wally Berger, NL:Bos.
1934:	100	Harlond Clift, AL:StL.
	94	Dolph Camilli, NL:Chi.-Phil.
1935:	113	Dolph Camilli, NL:Phil. (2)
	99	Jimmie Foxx, AL:Phil. (3)
1936:	119	Jimmie Foxx, AL:Bos. (4)
	96	Bill Brubaker, NL:Pitt.
1937:	111	Vince DiMaggio, NL:Bos.
	107	Frankie Crosetti, AL:NY
1938:	134	Vince DiMaggio, NL:Bos. (2)
	97	Frankie Crosetti, AL:NY (2)
1939:	107	Dolph Camilli, NL:Brk. (3)
	95	Hank Greenberg, AL:Det.
1940:	127	Chet Ross, NL:Bos.
	96	Sam Chapman, AL:Phil.
1941:	115	Dolph Camilli, NL:Brk. (4)
	103	Jimmie Foxx, AL:Bos. (5)

1942:	95	Joe Gordon, AL:NY
	87	Vince DiMaggio, NL:Pitt. (3)
1943:	127	Vince DiMaggio, NL:Pitt. (4)
	105	Chet Laabs, AL:StL.
1944:	99	Pat Seerey, AL:Clev.
	83	Vince DiMaggio, NL:Pitt. (5)
1945:	97	Pat Seerey, AL:Clev. (2)
	91	Vince DiMaggio, NL:Phil. (6)
1946:	109	Ralph Kiner, NL:Pitt.
	102	Charlie Keller, AL:NY
1947:	110	Eddie Joost, AL:Phil.
	83	Bill Nicholson, NL:Chi.
1948:	102	Pat Seerey, AL:Clev.-Chi. (3)
	86	Hank Sauer, NL:Cin.
1949:	92	Duke Snider, NL:Brk.
	91	Dick Kokos, AL:StL.
1950:	114	Roy Smalley, NL:Chi.
	110	Gus Zernial, AL:Chi.
1951:	101	Gus Zernial, AL:Chi.-Phil. (2)
	99	Gil Hodges, NL:Brk.
1952:	118	Eddie Mathews, NL:Bos.
	111	Larry Doby, AL:Clev.
	111	Mickey Mantle, AL:NY
1953:	125	Steve Bilko, NL:StL.
	121	Larry Doby, AL:Clev. (2)
1954:	107	Mickey Mantle. AL:NY (2)
	96	Duke Snider, NL:Brk. (2)
1955:	106	Norm Zauchin, AL:Bos.
	104	Wally Post, NL:Cin.
1956:	138	Jim Lemon, AL:Wash.
	124	Wally Post, NL:Cin. (2)
1957:	104	Duke Snider, NL:Brk. (3)
	94	Jim Lemon, AL:Wash. (2)
1958:	123	Mickey Mantle, AL:NY (3)
	95	Harry Anderson, NL:Phil.
1959:	126	Mickey Mantle, AL:NY (4)
	103	Wally Post, NL:Phil. (3)
1960:	136	Pancho Herrera, NL:Phil.
	124	Mickey Mantle, AL:NY (5)
1961:	141	Jake Wood, AL:Det.
	121	Dick Stuart, NL:Pitt.
1962:	142	Harmon Killebrew, AL:Minn.
	129	Ken Hubbs, NL:Chi.
1963:	175	Dave Nicholson, AL:Chi.
	136	Donn Clendenon, NL:Pitt.
1964:	143	Nelson Mathews, AL:KC
	138	Dick Allen, NL:Phil.
1965:	150	Dick Allen, NL:Phil. (2)
	122	Zoilo Versalles, AL:Minn.
1966:	152	George Scott, AL:Bos.
	143	Byron Browne, NL:Chi.
1967:	155	Frank Howard, AL:Wash.
	137	Jimmy Wynn, NL:Hou.
1968:	171	Reggie Jackson, AL:Oak.
	163	Donn Clendenon, NL:Pitt. (2)
1969:	187	Bobby Bonds, NL:SF
	142	Reggie Jackson, AL:Oak. (2)
1970:	189	Bobby Bonds, NL:SF (2)
	134	Reggie Jackson, AL:Oak. (3)
1971:	161	Reggie Jackson, AL:Oak. (4)
	154	Willie Stargell, NL:Pitt.
1972:	145	Bobby Darwin, AL:Minn.
	145	Lee May, NL:Hou.
1973:	148	Bobby Bonds, NL:SF (3)
	137	Bobby Darwin, AL:Minn. (2)
1974:	138	Mike Schmidt, NL:Phil.
	127	Bobby Darwin, AL:Minn. (3)

STRIKEOUTS (CONTINUED)

1975:	180	Mike Schmidt, NL:Phil. (2)
	155	Jeff Burroughs, AL:Tex.
1976:	149	Mike Schmidt, NL:Phil. (3)
	123	Jim Rice, AL:Bos.
1977:	162	Butch Hobson, AL:Bos.
	140	Greg Luzinski, :NL:Phil.
1978:	166	Gary Alexander, AL:Oak.-Clev.
	145	Dale Murphy, NL:Atl.
1979:	175	Gorman Thomas, AL:Mil.
	131	Dave Kingman, NL:Chi.
1980:	170	Gorman Thomas, AL:Mil. (2)
	133	Dale Murphy, NL:Atl. (2)
1981:	115	Tony Armas, AL:Oak.
	105	Dave Kingman, NL:NY (2)
1982:	156	Reggie Jackson, AL:Cal. (5)
	156	Dave Kingman, NL:NY (3)
1983:	150	Ron Kittle, AL:Chi.
	148	Mike Schmidt, NL:Phil. (4)
1984:	168	Juan Samuel, NL:Phil.
	156	Tony Armas, AL:Bos. (2)
1985:	166	Steve Balboni, AL:KC
	141	Dale Murphy, NL:Atl. (3)
	141	Juan Samuel, NL:Phil. (2)
1986:	185	Pete Incaviglia, AL:Tex
	142	Juan Samuel, NL:Phil. (3)
1987:	186	Rob Deer, AL:Mil.
	162	Juan Samuel, NL:Phil. (4)
1988:	153	Andres Galarraga, NL:Mtl.
	153	Rob Deer, AL:Mil. (2)
	153	Pete Incaviglia, AL:Tex. (2)
1989:	172	Bo Jackson, AL:KC
	158	Andres Galarraga, NL:Mtl. (2)
1990:	182	Cecil Fielder, AL:Det.
	169	Andres Galarraga, NL:Mtl. (3)
1991:	175	Rob Deer, AL:Det. (3)
	151	Delino DeShields, NL:Mtl.
1992:	154	Dean Palmer, AL:Tex.
	147	Ray Lankford, NL:StL.
1993:	169	Rob Deer, AL:Det.-Bos. (4)
	147	Cory Snyder, NL:LA
1994:	128	Travis Fryman, AL:Det.
	114	Reggie Sanders, NL:Cin.
1995:	150	Mo Vaughn, AL:Bos.
	146	Andres Galarraga, NL:Col. (4)
1996:	160	Henry Rodriguez, NL:Mtl.
	159	Jay Buhner, AL:Sea.
1997:	175	Jay Buhner, AL:Sea. (2)
	174	Sammy Sosa, NL:Chi.
1998:	171	Sammy Sosa, NL:Chi. (2)
	159	Jose Canseco, AL:Tor.
1999:	171	Sammy Sosa, NL:Chi. (3)
	171	Jim Thome, AL:Clev.
2000:	187	Preston Wilson, NL:Fla.
	181	Mo Vaughn, AL:Ana. (2)
2001:	185	Jose Hernandez, NL:Mil.
	185	Jim Thome, AL:Clev. (2)
2002:	188	Jose Hernandez, NL:Mil. (2)
	176	Mike Cameron, AL:Sea.
2003:	182	Jim Thome, NL:Phil. (AL 2)
	140	Jason Giambi, AL:NY
2004:	195	Adam Dunn, NL:Cin.
	177	Mark Bellhorn, AL:Bos.
2005:	168	Adam Dunn, NL:Cin. (2)
	167	Richie Sexson, AL:Sea.

2006:	194	Adam Dunn, NL:Cin. (3)
	174	Curtis Granderson, AL:Det.
2007:	199	Ryan Howard, NL:Phil.
	164	Jack Cust, AL:Oak.
2008:	204	Mark Reynolds, NL:Ari.
	197	Jack Cust, AL:Oak. (2)
2009:	223	Mark Reynolds, NL:Ari. (2)
	185	Jack Cust, AL:Oak. (3)
2010:	211	Mark Reynolds, NL:Ari. (3)
	170	Austin Jackson, AL:Det.
2011:	205	Drew Stubbs, NL:Cin.
	196	Mark Reynolds, AL:Balt. (NL 3)
2012:	222	Adam Dunn, AL:Chi. (NL 3)
	189	Danny Espinosa, NL:Wash.
2013:	212	Chris Carter, AL:Hou.
	186	Pedro Alvarez, NL:Pitt.
2014:	190	Ryan Howard, NL:Phil. (2)
	184	Mike Trout, AL:LA
2015:	208	Chris Davis, AL:Balt.
	199	Kris Bryant, NL:Chi.
2016:	219	Chris Davis, AL:Balt. (2)
	206	Chris Carter, NL:Mil. (AL 1)
2017:	208	Aaron Judge, AL:NY
	191	Trevor Story, NL:Col.
2018:	217	Yoan Moncada, AL:Chi.
	178	Chris Taylor, NL:LA
2019:	189	Eugenio Suarez, NL:Cin.
	178	Rougned Odor, AL:Tex.
	178	Jorge Soler, AL:KC
2020:	90	Miguel Sano, AL:Minn.
	85	Keston Hiura, NL:Mil.

STOLEN BASES

1900:	45	Patsy Donovan, NL:StL.
	45	George Van Haltren, NL:NY
1901:	52	Frank Isbell, AL:Chi.
	49	Honus Wagner, NL:Pitt.
1902:	47	Topsy Hartsel, AL:Phil.
	42	Honus Wagner, NL:Pitt. (2)
1903:	67	Frank Chance, NL:Chi.
	67	Jimmy Sheckard, NL:Brk.
	45	Harry Bay, AL:Clev.
1904:	53	Honus Wagner, NL:Pitt. (3)
	42	Elmer Flick, AL:Clev.
1905:	59	Art Devlin, NL:NY
	59	Billy Maloney, NL:Chi.
	46	Danny Hoffman, AL:Phil.
1906:	57	Frank Chance, NL:Chi. (2)
	40	Elmer Flick, AL:Clev. (2)
1907:	61	Honus Wagner, NL:Pitt. (4)
	54	Ty Cobb, AL:Det.
1908:	53	Honus Wagner, NL:Pitt. (5)
	47	Patsy Dougherty, AL:Chi.
1909:	78	Ty Cobb, AL:Det. (2)
	54	Bob Bescher, NL:Cin.
1910:	81	Eddie Collins, AL:Phil.
	70	Bob Bescher, NL:Cin. (2)
1911:	83	Ty Cobb, AL:Det. (3)
	81	Bob Bescher, NL:Cin. (3)
1912:	88	Clyde Milan, AL:Wash.
	67	Bob Bescher, NL:Cin. (4)
1913:	75	Clyde Milan, AL:Wash. (2)
	61	Max Carey, NL:Pitt.
1914:	74	Fritz Maisel, AL:NY
	62	George Burns, NL:NY
1915:	96	Ty Cobb, AL:Det. (4)
	36	Max Carey, NL:Pitt. (2)
1916:	68	Ty Cobb, AL:Det. (5)
	63	Max Carey, NL:Pitt. (3)
1917:	55	Ty Cobb, AL:Det. (6)
	46	Max Carey, NL:Pitt. (4)
1918:	58	Max Carey, NL:Pitt. (5)
	45	George Sisler, AL:StL.
1919:	40	George Burns, NL:NY (2)
	33	Eddie Collins, AL:Chi. (2)
1920:	63	Sam Rice, AL:Wash. (6)
	52	Max Carey, NL:Pitt. (6)
1921:	50	Frankie Frisch, NL:NY
	35	George Sisler, AL:StL. (2)
1922:	52	Max Carey, NL:Pitt. (7)
	51	George Sisler, AL:StL. (3)
1923:	51	Max Carey, NL:Pitt. (8)
	49	Eddie Collins, AL:Chi. (3)
1924:	49	Max Carey, NL:Pitt. (9)
	42	Eddie Collins, AL:Chi. (4)
1925:	46	Max Carey, NL:Pitt. (10)
	43	Johnny Mostil, AL:Chi.
1926:	35	Kiki Cuyler, NL:Pitt.
	35	Johnny Mostil, AL:Chi. (2)
1927:	48	Frankie Frisch, NL:StL. (2)
	27	George Sisler, AL:StL. (4)
1928:	37	Kiki Cuyler, NL:Chi. (2)
	30	Buddy Myer, AL:Bos.
1929:	43	Kiki Cuyler, NL:Chi. (3)
	28	Charlie Gehringer, AL:Det.
1930:	37	Kiki Cuyler, NL:Chi. (4)
	23	Marty McManus, AL:Det.

1931:	61	Ben Chapman, AL:NY
	28	Frankie Frisch, NL:StL. (3)
1932:	38	Ben Chapman, AL:NY (2)
	20	Chuck Klein, NL:Phil.
1933:	27	Ben Chapman, AL:NY (3)
	26	Pepper Martin, NL:StL.
1934:	40	Bill Werber, AL:Bos.
	23	Pepper Martin, NL:StL. (2)
1935:	29	Bill Werber, AL:Bos. (2)
	22	Augie Galan, NL:Chi.
1936:	37	Lyn Lary, AL:StL.
	23	Pepper Martin, NL:StL. (3)
1937:	35	Ben Chapman, AL:Wash.-Bos. (4)
	35	Bill Werber, AL:Phil. (3)
	23	Augie Galan, NL:Chi. (2)
1938:	27	Frankie Crosetti, AL:NY
	17	Stan Hack, NL:Chi.
1939:	51	George Case, AL:Wash.
	17	Stan Hack, NL:Chi. (2)
	17	Lee Handley, NL:Pitt.
1940:	35	George Case, AL:Wash. (2)
	22	Lonny Frey, NL:Cin.
1941:	33	George Case, AL:Wash. (3)
	18	Danny Murtaugh, NL:Phil.
1942:	44	George Case, AL:Wash. (4)
	20	Pete Reiser, NL:Brk.
1943:	61	George Case, AL:Wash. (5)
	20	Arky Vaughan, NL:Brk.
1944:	55	Snuffy Stirnweiss, AL:NY
	28	Johnny Barrett, NL:Pitt.
1945:	33	Snuffy Stirnweiss, AL:NY (2)
	26	Red Schoendienst, NL:StL.
1946:	34	Pete Reiser, NL:Brk. (2)
	28	George Case, AL:Clev. (6)
1947:	34	Bob Dillinger, AL:StL.
	29	Jackie Robinson, NL:Brk.
1948:	32	Richie Ashburn, NL:Phil.
	28	Bob Dillinger, AL:StL. (2)
1949:	37	Jackie Robinson, NL:Brk. (2)
	20	Bob Dillinger, AL:StL. (3)
1950:	35	Sam Jethroe, NL:Bos.
	15	Dom DiMaggio, AL:Bos.
1951:	35	Sam Jethroe, NL:Bos. (2)
	31	Minnie Minoso, AL:Clev.-Chi.
1952:	30	Pee Wee Reese, NL:Brk.
	22	Minnie Minoso, AL:Chi. (2)
1953:	26	Bill Bruton, NL:Mil.
	25	Minnie Minoso, AL:Chi. (3)
1954:	34	Bill Bruton, NL:Mil. (2)
	22	Jackie Jensen, AL:Bos.
1955:	25	Bill Bruton, NL:Mil. (3)
	25	Jim Rivera, AL:Chi.
1956:	40	Willie Mays, NL:NY
	21	Luis Aparicio, AL:Chi.
1957:	38	Willie Mays, NL:NY (2)
	28	Luis Aparicio, AL:Chi. (2)
1958:	31	Willie Mays, NL:SF (3)
	29	Luis Aparicio, AL:Chi. (3)
1959:	56	Luis Aparicio, AL:Chi. (4)
	27	Willie Mays, NL:SF (4)
1960:	51	Luis Aparicio, AL:Chi. (5)
	50	Maury Wills, NL:LA
1961:	53	Luis Aparicio, AL:Chi. (6)
	35	Maury Wills, NL:LA (2)
1962:	104	Maury Wills, NL:LA (3)
	31	Luis Aparicio, AL:Chi. (7)

STOLEN BASES (CONTINUED)

1963:	40	Luis Aparicio, AL:Balt. (8)
	40	Maury Wills, NL:LA (4)
1964:	57	Luis Aparicio, AL:Balt. (9)
	53	Maury Wills, NL:LA (5)
1965:	94	Maury Wills, NL:LA (6)
	51	Bert Campaneris, AL:KC
1966:	74	Lou Brock, NL:StL.
	52	Bert Campaneris, AL:KC (2)
1967:	55	Bert Campaneris, AL:KC (3)
	52	Lou Brock, NL:StL. (2)
1968:	62	Lou Brock, NL:StL. (3)
	62	Bert Campaneris, AL:Oak. (4)
1969:	73	Tommy Harper, AL:Sea.
	53	Lou Brock, NL:StL. (4)
1970:	57	Bobby Tolan, NL:Cin.
	42	Bert Campaneris, AL:Oak. (5)
1971:	64	Lou Brock, NL:StL. (5)
	52	Amos Otis, AL:KC
1972:	63	Lou Brock, NL:StL. (6)
	52	Bert Campaneris, AL:Oak. (6)
1973:	70	Lou Brock, NL:StL. (7)
	54	Tommy Harper, AL:Bos. (2)
1974:	118	Lou Brock, NL:StL. (8)
	54	Billy North, AL:Oak.
1975:	77	Davey Lopes, NL:LA
	70	Mickey Rivers, AL:Cal.
1976:	75	Billy North, AL:Oak. (2)
	63	Davey Lopes, NL:LA (2)
1977:	70	Frank Taveras, NL:Pitt.
	53	Freddie Patek, AL:KC
1978:	71	Omar Moreno, NL:Pitt.
	68	Ron LeFlore, AL:Det.
1979:	83	Willie Wilson, AL:KC
	77	Omar Moreno, NL:Pitt. (2)
1980:	100	Rickey Henderson, AL:Oak.
	97	Ron LeFlore, NL:Mtl.
1981:	71	Tim Raines, NL:Mtl.
	56	Rickey Henderson, AL:Oak. (2)
1982:	130	Rickey Henderson, AL:Oak. (3)
	78	Tim Raines, Tim NL:Mtl. (2)
1983:	108	Rickey Henderson, AL:Oak. (4)
	90	Tim Raines, NL:Mtl. (3)
1984:	75	Tim Raines, NL:Mtl. (4)
	66	Rickey Henderson, AL:Oak. (5)
1985:	110	Vince Coleman, NL:StL.
	80	Rickey Henderson, AL:NY (6)
1986:	107	Vince Coleman, NL:StL. (2)
	87	Rickey Henderson, AL:NY (7)
1987:	109	Vince Coleman, NL:StL. (3)
	60	Harold Reynolds, AL:Sea.
1988:	93	Rickey Henderson, AL:NY (8)
	81	Vince Coleman, NL:StL. (4)
1989:	77	Rickey Henderson, AL:NY-Oak. (9)
	65	Vince Coleman, NL:StL. (5)
1990:	77	Vince Coleman, NL:StL. (6)
	65	Rickey Henderson, AL:Oak. (10)
1991:	76	Marquis Grissom, NL:Mtl.
	58	Rickey Henderson, AL:Oak. (11)
1992:	78	Marquis Grissom, NL:Mtl. (2)
	66	Kenny Lofton, AL:Clev.
1993:	70	Kenny Lofton, AL:Clev. (2)
	58	Chuck Carr, NL:Fla.
1994:	60	Kenny Lofton, AL:Clev. (3)
	39	Craig Biggio, NL:Hou

1995:	56	Quilvio Veras, NL:Fla.
	54	Kenny Lofton, AL:Clev. (4)
1996:	75	Kenny Lofton, AL:Clev. (5)
	53	Eric Young, NL:Col.
1997:	74	Brian Hunter, AL:Det.
	60	Tony Womack, NL:Pitt.
1998:	66	Rickey Henderson, AL:Oak. (12)
	58	Tony Womack, NL:Pitt. (2)
1999:	72	Tony Womack, NL:Ari. (3)
	44	Brian Hunter, AL:Det.-Sea. (2)
2000:	62	Luis Castillo, NL:Fla.
	46	Johnny Damon, AL:KC
2001:	56	Ichiro Suzuki, AL:Sea.
	46	Juan Pierre, NL:Col.
	46	Jimmy Rollins, NL:Phil.
2002:	48	Luis Castillo, NL:Fla. (2)
	41	Alfonso Soriano, AL:NY
2003:	65	Juan Pierre, NL:Fla. (2)
	55	Carl Crawford, AL:TB
2004:	70	Scott Podsednik, NL:Mil.
	59	Carl Crawford, AL:TB (2)
2005:	62	Chone Figgins, AL:LA
	60	Jose Reyes, NL:NY
2006:	64	Jose Reyes, NL:NY (2)
	58	Carl Crawford, AL:TB (3)
2007:	78	Jose Reyes, NL:NY (3)
	50	Carl Crawford, AL:TB (4)
	50	Brian Roberts, AL:Balt.
2008:	68	Willie Taveras, NL:Col.
	50	Jacoby Ellsbury, AL:Bos.
2009:	70	Jacoby Ellsbury, AL:Bos. (2)
	61	Michael Bourn, NL:Hou.
2010:	68	Juan Pierre, AL:Chi. (NL 2)
	52	Michael Bourn, NL:Hou. (2)
2011:	61	Michael Bourn, NL:Hou.-Atl. (3)
	49	Coco Crisp, AL:Oak.
	49	Brett Gardner, AL:NY
2012:	49	Mike Trout, AL:LA
	44	Everth Cabrera, NL:SD
2013:	52	Jacoby Ellsbury, AL:Bos. (3)
	46	Eric Young Jr., NL:Col.-NY
2014:	64	Dee Gordon, NL:LA
	56	Jose Altuve, AL:Hou.
2015:	58	Dee Gordon, NL:Mia. (2)
	38	Jose Altuve, AL:Hou. (2)
2016:	62	Jonathan Villar, NL:Mil.
	43	Rajai Davis, AL:Clev.
2017:	60	Dee Gordon, NL:Mia. (3)
	34	Whit Merrifield, AL:KC
2018:	45	Whit Merrifield, AL:KC (2)
	43	Trea Turner, NL:Wash.
2019:	46	Mallex Smith, AL:Sea.
	37	Ronald Acuna, NL:Atl.
2020:	24	Adalberto Mondesi, AL:KC
	15	Trevor Story, NL:Col.

EARNED RUN AVERAGE

Year	ERA	Player
1912:	1.96	Jeff Tesreau, NL:NY
1913:	1.14	Walter Johnson, AL:Wash.
	2.06	Christy Mathewson, NL:NY
1914:	1.00	Dutch Leonard, AL:Bos.
	1.72	Bill Doak NL:StL.
1915:	1.22	Grover Alexander, NL:Phil.
	1.49	Smoky Joe Wood, AL:Bos.
1916:	1.55	Grover Alexander, NL:Phil. (2)
	1.75	Babe Ruth, AL:Bos.
1917:	1.54	Eddie Cicotte, AL:Chi.
	1.84	Grover Alexander, NL:Phil. (3)
1918:	1.27	Walter Johnson, AL:Wash. (2)
	1.74	Hippo Vaughn, NL:Chi.
1919:	1.48	Walter Johnson, AL:Wash. (3)
	1.72	Grover Alexander, NL:Chi. (4)
1920:	1.93	Grover Alexander, NL:Chi. (5)
	2.49	Stan Coveleski, AL:Clev.
1921:	2.47	Red Faber, AL:Chi.
	2.58	Bill Doak, NL:StL. (2)
1922:	2.81	Red Faber, AL:Chi. (2)
	3.00	Rosy Ryan, NL:NY
1923:	1.93	Dolf Luque, NL:Cin.
	2.76	Stan Coveleski, AL:Clev. (2)
1924:	2.16	Dazzy Vance, NL:Brk.
	2.72	Walter Johnson, AL:Wash. (4)
1925:	2.66	Dolf Luque, NL:Cin. (2)
	2.84	Stan Coveleski, AL:Wash. (3)
1926:	2.52	Lefty Grove, AL:Phil.
	2.61	Ray Kremer, NL:Pitt.
1927:	2.28	Wilcy Moore, AL:NY
	2.47	Ray Kremer, NL:Pitt. (2)
1928:	2.08	Dazzy Vance, NL:Brk. (2)
	2.53	Garland Braxton, AL:Wash.
1929:	2.85	Lefty Grove, AL:Phil. (2)
	3.08	Bill Walker, NL:NY
1930:	2.54	Lefty Grove, AL:Phil. (3)
	2.61	Dazzy Vance, NL:Brk. (3)
1931:	2.06	Lefty Grove, AL:Phil. (4)
	2.26	Bill Walker, NL:NY (2)
1932:	2.37	Lon Warneke, NL:Chi.
	2.84	Lefty Grove, AL:Phil. (5)
1933:	1.66	Carl Hubbell, NL:NY
	2.33	Monte Pearson, AL:Clev.
1934:	2.30	Carl Hubbell, NL:NY (2)
	2.33	Lefty Gomez, AL:NY
1935:	2.59	Cy Blanton, NL:Pitt.
	2.70	Lefty Grove, AL:Bos. (6)
1936:	2.31	Carl Hubbell, NL:NY (3)
	2.81	Lefty Grove, AL:Bos. (7)
1937:	2.33	Lefty Gomez, AL:NY (2)
	2.38	Jim Turner, NL:Bos.
1938:	2.66	Bill Lee, NL:Chi.
	3.07	Lefty Grove, AL:Bos. (8)
1939:	2.29	Bucky Walters, NL:Cin.
	2.54	Lefty Grove, AL:Bos. (9)
1940:	2.48	Bucky Walters, NL:Cin. (2)
	2.56	Bob Feller, AL:Clev.
1941:	2.20	Elmer Riddle, NL:Cin.
	2.37	Thornton Lee, AL:Chi.
1942:	1.77	Mort Cooper, NL:StL.
	2.10	Ted Lyons, AL:Chi.
1943:	1.64	Spud Chandler, AL:NY
	1.75	Howie Pollet, NL:StL.
1944:	2.12	Dizzy Trout, AL:Det.
	2.40	Bucky Walters, NL:Cin. (3)
1945:	1.81	Hal Newhouser, AL:Det.
	2.14	Hank Borowy, NL:Chi.
1946:	1.94	Hal Newhouser, AL:Det. (2)
	2.10	Howie Pollet, NL:StL. (2)
1947:	2.33	Warren Spahn, NL:Bos.
	2.46	Spud Chandler, AL:NY (2)
1948:	2.24	Harry Brecheen, NL:StL.
	2.47	Gene Bearden, AL:Clev.
1949:	2.50	Dave Koslo, NL:NY
	2.81	Mel Parnell, AL:Bos.
1950:	2.49	Jim Hearn, NL:StL.-NY
	3.20	Early Wynn, AL:Clev.
1951:	2.78	Saul Rogovin, AL:Det.-Chi.
	2.88	Chet Nichols, NL:Bos.
1952:	2.07	Allie Reynolds, AL:NY
	2.43	Hoyt Wilhelm, NL:NY
1953:	2.10	Warren Spahn, NL:Mil. (2)
	2.43	Ed Lopat, AL:NY
1954:	2.29	Johnny Antonelli, NL:NY
	2.64	Mike Garcia, AL:Clev.
1955:	1.97	Billy Pierce, AL:Chi.
	2.84	Bob Friend, NL:Pitt.
1956:	2.47	Whitey Ford, AL:NY
	2.71	Lew Burdette, NL:Mil.
1957:	2.45	Bobby Shantz, AL:NY
	2.66	Johnny Podres, NL:Brk.
1958:	2.01	Whitey Ford, AL:NY (2)
	2.47	Stu Miller, NL:SF
1959:	2.19	Hoyt Wilhelm, AL:Balt. (NL 1)
	2.82	Sam Jones, NL:SF
1960:	2.68	Frank Baumann, AL:Chi.
	2.70	Mike McCormick, NL:SF
1961:	2.40	Dick Donovan, AL:Wash.
	3.01	Warren Spahn, NL:Mil. (3)
1962:	2.21	Hank Aguirre, AL:Det.
	2.54	Sandy Koufax, NL:LA
1963:	1.88	Sandy Koufax, NL:LA (2)
	2.33	Gary Peters, AL:Chi.
1964:	1.65	Dean Chance, AL:LA
	1.74	Sandy Koufax, NL:LA (3)
1965:	2.04	Sandy Koufax, NL:LA (4)
	2.18	Sam McDowell, AL:Clev.
1966:	1.73	Sandy Koufax, NL:LA (5)
	1.98	Gary Peters, AL:Chi. (2)
1967:	1.87	Phil Niekro, NL:Atl.
	2.06	Joel Horlen, AL:Chi.
1968:	1.12	Bob Gibson, NL:StL.
	1.60	Luis Tiant, AL:Clev.
1969:	2.10	Juan Marichal, NL:SF
	2.19	Dick Bosman, AL:Wash.
1970:	2.56	Diego Segui, AL:Oak.
	2.81	Tom Seaver, NL:NY
1971:	1.76	Tom Seaver, NL:NY (2)
	1.82	Vida Blue, AL:Oak.
1972:	1.91	Luis Tiant, AL:Bos. (2)
	1.98	Steve Carlton, NL:Phil.
1973:	2.08	Tom Seaver, NL:NY (3)
	2.40	Jim Palmer, AL:Balt.
1974:	2.28	Buzz Capra, NL:Atl.
	2.49	Catfish Hunter, AL:Oak.
1975:	2.09	Jim Palmer, AL:Balt. (2)
	2.24	Randy Jones, NL:SD
1976:	2.34	Mark Fidrych, AL:Det.
	2.52	John Denny, NL:StL.
1977:	2.34	John Candelaria, NL:Pitt.
	2.54	Frank Tanana, AL:Cal.

EARNED RUN AVERAGE (CONTINUED)

1978:	1.74	Ron Guidry, AL:NY
	2.43	Craig Swan, NL:NY
1979:	2.71	J.R. Richard, NL:Hou.
	2.78	Ron Guidry, AL:NY (2)
1980:	2.21	Don Sutton, NL:LA
	2.47	Rudy May, AL:NY
1981:	1.69	Nolan Ryan, NL:Hou.
	2.32	Steve McCatty, AL:Oak.
1982:	2.40	Steve Rogers, NL:Mtl.
	2.96	Rick Sutcliffe, AL:Clev.
1983:	2.25	Atlee Hammaker, NL:SF
	2.42	Rick Honeycutt, AL:Tex.
1984:	2.48	Alejandro Pena, NL:LA
	2.79	Mike Boddicker, AL:Balt.
1985:	1.53	Dwight Gooden, NL:NY
	2.48	Dave Stieb, AL:Tor.
1986:	2.22	Mike Scott, NL:Hou.
	2.48	Roger Clemens, AL:Bos.
1987:	2.76	Jimmy Key, AL:Tor.
	2.76	Nolan Ryan, NL:Hou. (2)
1988:	2.18	Joe Magrane, NL:StL.
	2.45	Allan Anderson, AL:Minn.
1989:	2.16	Bret Saberhagen, AL:KC
	2.28	Scott Garrelts, NL:SF
1990:	1.93	Roger Clemens, AL:Bos. (2)
	2.21	Danny Darwin, NL:Hou.
1991:	2.39	Dennis Martinez, NL:Mtl.
	2.62	Roger Clemens, AL:Bos. (3)
1992:	2.08	Bill Swift, NL:SF
	2.41	Roger Clemens, AL:Bos. (4)
1993:	2.36	Greg Maddux, NL:Atl.
	2.56	Kevin Appier, AL:KC
1994:	1.56	Greg Maddux, NL:Atl. (2)
	2.65	Steve Ontiveros, AL:Oak.
1995:	1.63	Greg Maddux, NL:Atl. (3)
	2.48	Randy Johnson, AL:Sea.
1996:	1.89	Kevin Brown, NL:Fla.
	2.93	Juan Guzman, AL:Tor.
1997:	1.90	Pedro Martinez, NL:Mtl.
	2.05	Roger Clemens, AL:Tor. (5)
1998:	2.22	Greg Maddux, NL:Atl. (4)
	2.65	Roger Clemens, AL:Tor. (6)
1999:	2.07	Pedro Martinez, AL:Bos. (NL 1)
	2.48	Randy Johnson, NL:Ari. (AL 1)
2000:	1.74	Pedro Martinez, AL:Bos. (AL 2; NL 1)
	2.58	Kevin Brown, NL:LA(2)
2001:	2.49	Randy Johnson, NL:Ari. (AL 1; NL 2)
	3.05	Freddy Garcia, AL:Sea.
2002:	2.26	Pedro Martinez, AL:Bos. (AL 3; NL 1)
	2.32	Randy Johnson, NL:Ari. (AL 1; NL 3)
2003:	2.22	Pedro Martinez, AL:Bos. (AL 4; NL 1)
	2.34	Jason Schmidt, NL:SF
2004:	2.27	Jake Peavy, NL:SD
	2.61	Johan Santana, AL:Minn.
2005:	1.87	Roger Clemens, NL:Hou. (AL 6)
	2.86	Kevin Millwood, AL:Clev.
2006:	2.77	Johan Santana, AL:Minn. (2)
	2.98	Roy Oswalt NL:Hou.
2007:	2.54	Jake Peavy, NL:SD (2)
	3.01	John Lackey, AL:LA
2008:	2.53	Johan Santana, NL:NY (AL 2)
	2.54	Cliff Lee, AL:Clev.

2009:	2.16	Zack Greinke, AL:KC
	2.24	Chris Carpenter, NL:StL.
2010:	2.27	Felix Hernandez, AL:Sea.
	2.30	Josh Johnson, NL:Fla.
2011:	2.28	Clayton Kershaw, NL:LA
	2.40	Justin Verlander, AL:Det.
2012:	2.53	Clayton Kershaw, NL:LA (2)
	2.56	David Price, AL:TB
2013:	1.83	Clayton Kershaw, NL:LA (3)
	2.57	Anibal Sanchez, AL:Det.
2014:	1.77	Clayton Kershaw, NL:LA (4)
	2.14	Felix Hernandez, AL:Sea. (2)
2015:	1.66	Zack Greinke, NL:LA (AL 1)
	2.45	David Price, AL:Det.-Tor. (2)
2016:	2.13	Kyle Hendricks, NL:Chi.
	3.00	Aaron Sanchez, AL:Tor.
2017:	2.25	Corey Kluber, AL:Clev.
	2.31	Clayton Kershaw, NL:LA (5)
2018:	1.70	Jacob deGrom, NL:NY
	1.89	Blake Snell, AL:TB
2019:	2.32	Hyun-Jin Ryu, NL:LA
	2.50	Gerrit Cole, AL:Hou.
2020:	1.63	Shane Bieber, AL:Clev.
	1.73	Trevor Bauer, NL:Cin.

WINNING PERCENTAGE

Minimum: 15 decisions (except 2020: 6 decisions)

Year	Pct	W-L	Player
1900:	.778	28- 8	Joe McGinnity, NL:Brk.
1901:	.774	24- 7	Clark Griffith, AL:Chi.
	.737	14- 5	Sam Leever, NL:Pitt.
1902:	.824	28- 6	Jack Chesbro, NL:Pitt.
	.783	18- 5	Bill Bernhard, AL:Phil.-Clev.
1903:	.781	25- 7	Sam Leever, NL:Pitt. (2)
	.757	28- 9	Cy Young, AL:Bos.
1904:	.814	35- 8	Joe McGinnity, NL:NY (2)
	.774	41-12	Jack Chesbro, AL:NY
1905:	.800	20- 5	Sam Leever, NL:Pitt. (3)
	.730	27-10	Rube Waddell, AL:Phil.
1906:	.826	19- 4	Ed Reulbach, NL:Chi.
	.760	19- 6	Eddie Plank, AL:Phil.
1907:	.862	25- 4	Wild Bill Donovan, AL:Det.
	.810	17- 4	Ed Reulbach, NL:Chi. (2)
1908:	.774	24- 7	Ed Reulbach, NL:Chi. (3)
	.727	40-15	Ed Walsh, AL:Chi.
1909:	.806	25- 6	Howie Camnitz, NL:Pitt.
	.806	25- 6	Christy Mathewson, NL:NY
	.784	29- 8	George Mullin, AL:Det.
1910:	.875	14- 2	Deacon Phillippe, NL:Pitt.
	.821	23- 5	Chief Bender, AL:Phil.
1911:	.774	24- 7	Rube Marquard, NL:NY
	.773	17- 5	Chief Bender, AL:Phil. (2)
1912:	.872	34- 5	Smoky Joe Wood, AL:Bos.
	.727	24- 9	Claude Hendrix, NL:Pitt.
1913:	.837	36- 7	Walter Johnson, AL:Wash.
	.800	16- 4	Bert Humphries, NL:Chi.
1914:	.850	17- 3	Chief Bender, AL:Phil. (3)
	.788	26- 7	Bill James, NL:Bos.
1915:	.756	31-10	Grover Alexander, NL:Phil.
	.750	15- 5	Smoky Joe Wood, AL:Bos. (2)
1916:	.842	16- 3	Tom Hughes, NL:Bos.
	.684	13- 6	Nick Cullop, AL:NY
1917:	.778	14- 4	Ed Klepfer, AL:Clev.
	.750	21- 7	Ferdie Schupp, NL:NY
1918:	.762	16- 5	Sam Jones, AL:Bos.
	.741	20- 7	Claude Hendrix, NL:Pitt. (2)
1919:	.806	29- 7	Eddie Cicotte, AL:Chi.
	.760	19- 6	Dutch Ruether, NL:Cin.
1920:	.721	31-12	Jim Bagby, AL:Clev.
	.676	23-11	Burleigh Grimes, NL:Brk.
1921:	.750	27- 9	Carl Mays, AL:NY
	.737	14- 5	Babe Adams, NL:Pitt.
	.737	14- 5	Whitey Glazner, NL:Pitt.
1922:	.788	26- 7	Joe Bush, AL:NY
	.733	11- 4	Phil Douglas, NL:NY
1923:	.771	27- 8	Dolf Luque, NL:Cin.
	.760	19- 6	Herb Pennock, AL:NY
1924:	.842	16- 3	Emil Yde, NL:Pitt.
	.767	23- 7	Walter Johnson, AL:Wash. (2)
1925:	.800	20- 5	Stan Coveleski, AL:Wash.
	.714	15- 6	Bill Sherdel, NL:StL.
1926:	.769	20- 6	Ray Kremer, NL:Pitt.
	.711	27-11	George Uhle, AL:Clev.
1927:	.759	22- 7	Waite Hoyt, AL:NY
	.708	17- 7	Larry Benton, NL:Bos.-NY
1928:	.808	21- 5	General Crowder, AL:StL.
	.735	25- 9	Larry Benton, NL:NY (2)
1929:	.769	20- 6	Lefty Grove, AL:Phil.
	.760	19- 6	Charlie Root, NL:Chi.
1930:	.848	28- 5	Lefty Grove, AL:Phil. (2)
	.733	11- 4	Bud Teachout, NL:Chi.
1931:	.886	31- 4	Lefty Grove, AL:Phil. (3)
	.800	12- 3	Jesse Haines, NL:StL.
1932:	.810	17- 4	Johnny Allen, AL:NY
	.786	22- 6	Lon Warneke, NL:Chi.
1933:	.750	24- 8	Lefty Grove, AL:Phil. (4)
	.750	12- 4	Russ Van Atta, AL:NY
	.684	13- 6	Bud Tinning, NL:Chi.
1934:	.839	26- 5	Lefty Gomez, AL:NY
	.811	30- 7	Dizzy Dean, NL:StL.
1935:	.769	20- 6	Bill Lee, NL:Chi.
	.720	18- 7	Elden Auker, AL:Det.
1936:	.813	26- 6	Carl Hubbell, NL:NY
	.778	14- 4	Bump Hadley, AL:NY
1937:	.938	15- 1	Johnny Allen, AL:Clev. (2)
	.733	22- 8	Carl Hubbell, NL:NY (2)
1938:	.778	14- 4	Lefty Grove, AL:Bos. (5)
	.710	22- 9	Bill Lee, NL:Chi. (2)
1939:	.813	13- 3	Atley Donald, AL:NY
	.781	25- 7	Paul Derringer, NL:Cin.
1940:	.889	16- 2	Freddie Fitzsimmons, NL:Brk. (2)
	.842	16- 3	Schoolboy Rowe, AL:Det.
1941:	.826	19- 4	Elmer Riddle, NL:Cin.
	.750	15- 5	Lefty Gomez, AL:NY (2)
1942:	.813	13- 3	Howie Krist, NL:StL.
	.808	21- 5	Ernie Bonham, AL:NY
1943:	.833	20- 4	Spud Chandler, AL:NY
	.737	14- 5	Clyde Shoun, NL:Cin.
	.737	14- 5	Whitlow Wyatt, NL:Brk.
1944:	.810	17- 4	Ted Wilks, NL:StL.
	.783	18- 5	Tex Hughson, AL:Bos.
1945:	.789	15- 4	Harry Brecheen, NL:StL.
	.765	13- 4	Bob Muncrief, AL:StL.
1946:	.806	25- 6	Boo Ferriss, AL:Bos.
	.733	11- 4	Schoolboy Rowe, NL:Phil. (AL 1)
1947:	.808	21- 5	Larry Jansen, NL:NY
	.737	14- 5	Spec Shea, AL:NY
1948:	.813	13- 3	Rip Sewell, NL:Pitt.
	.783	18- 5	Jack Kramer, AL:Bos.
1949:	.793	23- 6	Ellis Kinder, AL:Bos.
	.722	13- 5	Ralph Branca, NL:Brk.
1950:	.818	18- 4	Sal Maglie, NL:NY
	.724	21- 8	Vic Raschi, AL:NY
1951:	.880	22- 3	Preacher Roe, NL:Brk.
	.733	22- 8	Bob Feller, AL:Clev.
	.733	11- 4	Morrie Martin, AL:Phil.
1952:	.833	15- 3	Hoyt Wilhelm, NL:NY
	.774	24- 7	Bobby Shantz, AL:Phil.
1953:	.800	16- 4	Ed Lopat, AL:NY
	.769	20- 6	Carl Erskine, NL:Brk.
1954:	.842	16- 3	Sandy Consuegra, AL:Chi.
	.750	21- 7	Johnny Antonelli, NL:NY
	.750	12- 4	Hoyt Wilhelm, NL:NY (2)
1955:	.800	20- 5	Don Newcombe, NL:Brk.
	.762	16- 5	Tommy Byrne, AL:NY
1956:	.794	27- 7	Don Newcombe, NL:Brk. (2)
	.760	19- 6	Whitey Ford, AL:NY
1957:	.727	16- 6	Dick Donovan, AL:Chi.
	.727	16- 6	Tom Sturdivant, AL:NY
	.720	18- 7	Bob Buhl, NL:Mil.
1958:	.750	21- 7	Bob Turley, AL:NY
	.667	22-11	Warren Spahn, NL:Mil.
	.667	20-10	Lew Burdette, NL:Mil.
1959:	.947	18- 1	Roy Face, NL:Pitt.
	.750	18- 6	Bob Shaw, AL:Chi.
1960:	.813	13- 3	Jim Coates, AL:NY
	.750	12- 4	Lindy McDaniel, NL:StL.

WINNING PERCENTAGE (CONTINUED)

Year	PCT	W-L	Player
1961:	.862	25-4	Whitey Ford, AL:NY (2)
	.783	18-5	Johnny Podres, NL:LA
1962	.821	23-5	Bob Purkey, NL:Cin.
	.733	11-4	Dave Wickersham, AL:KC
1963:	.842	16-3	Ron Perranoski, NL:LA
	.774	24-7	Whitey Ford, AL:NY (3)
1964:	.792	19-5	Wally Bunker, AL:Balt.
	.792	19-5	Sandy Koufax, NL:LA
1965:	.765	26-8	Sandy Koufax, NL:LA (2)
	.750	21-7	Mudcat Grant, AL:Minn.
1966:	.933	14-1	Phil Regan, NL:LA
	.706	12-5	Dave Boswell, AL:Minn.
1967:	.750	12-4	Jose Santiago, AL:Bos.
	.737	14-5	Nelson Briles NL:StL.
1968:	.838	31-6	Denny McLain, AL:Det.
	.750	18-6	Steve Blass, NL:Pitt.
1969:	.824	14-3	Bob Moose, NL:Pitt.
	.800	16-4	Jim Palmer, AL:Balt.
1970:	.824	14-3	Wayne Simpson, NL:Cin.
	.750	24-8	Mike Cuellar, AL:Balt.
1971:	.808	21-5	Dave McNally, AL:Balt.
	.733	11-4	Tug McGraw, NL:NY
1972:	.750	21-7	Catfish Hunter, AL:Oak.
	.750	15-5	Gary Nolan, NL:Cin.
1973:	.867	13-2	Roger Moret, AL:Bos.
	.800	12-3	George Stone, NL:NY
1974:	.813	13-3	Tommy John, NL:LA
	.733	11-4	Billy Champion, AL:Mil.
1975:	.824	14-3	Roger Moret, AL:Bos. (2)
	.813	13-3	Al Hrabosky, NL:StL.
1976:	.800	12-3	Rick Rhoden, NL:LA
	.773	17-5	Bill Campbell, AL:Minn.
1977:	.800	20-5	John Candelaria, NL:Pitt.
	.778	14-4	Don Gullett, AL:NY
1978:	.893	25-3	Ron Guidry, AL:NY
	.778	21-6	Gaylord Perry, NL:SD
1979:	.875	14-2	Ron Davis, AL:NY
	.750	12-4	Jim Bibby, NL:Pitt.
1980:	.781	25-7	Steve Stone, AL:Balt.
	.760	19-6	Jim Bibby, NL:Pitt. (2)
1981:	.875	14-2	Tom Seaver, NL:Cin.
	.778	14-4	Pete Vuckovich, AL:Mil.
1982:	.810	17-4	Phil Niekro, NL:Atl.
	.750	15-5	Jim Palmer, AL:Balt. (2)
	.750	18-6	Pete Vuckovich, AL:Mil. (2)
1983:	.813	13-3	Moose Haas, AL:Mil.
	.760	19-6	John Denny, NL:Phil.
1984:	.941	16-1	Rick Sutcliffe, NL:Chi.
	.739	17-6	Doyle Alexander, AL:Tor.
1985:	.864	19-3	Orel Hershiser, NL:LA
	.786	22-6	Ron Guidry, AL:NY (2)
1986:	.857	24-4	Roger Clemens, AL:Bos.
	.783	18-5	Bob Ojeda, NL:NY
1987:	.733	11-4	Dennis Martinez, NL:Mtl.
	.733	11-4	John Cerutti, AL:Tor.
	.733	11-4	Lee Guetterman, AL:Sea.
1988:	.870	20-3	David Cone, NL:NY
	.774	24-7	Frank Viola, AL:Minn.
1989:	.793	23-6	Bret Saberhagen, AL:KC
	.737	14-5	Sid Fernandez, NL:NY
	.737	14-5	Scott Garrelts, NL:SF
1990:	.818	27-6	Bob Welch, AL:Oak.
	.786	22-6	Doug Drabek, NL:Pitt.
1991:	.750	12-4	Joe Hesketh, AL:Bos.
	.714	20-8	John Smiley, NL:Pitt.
	.714	15-6	Jose Rijo, NL:Cin.
1992:	.783	18-5	Mike Mussina, AL:Balt.
	.762	16-5	Bob Tewksbury, NL:StL.
1993:	.824	14-3	Juan Guzman, AL:Tor.
	.818	18-4	Mark Portugal, NL:Hou.
1994:	.810	17-4	Jimmy Key, AL:NY
	.778	14-4	Bret Saberhagen, NL:NY (AL 1)
1995:	.905	19-2	Greg Maddux, NL:Atl.
	.900	18-2	Randy Johnson, AL:Sea.
1996:	.813	13-3	Jamie Moyer, AL:Bos.-Sea.
	.750	24-8	John Smoltz, NL:Atl.
1997:	.833	20-4	Randy Johnson, AL:Sea. (2)
	.826	19-4	Greg Maddux, NL:Atl. (2)
1998:	.850	17-3	John Smoltz, NL:Atl. (2)
	.818	18-4	David Wells, AL:NY
1999:	.852	23-4	Pedro Martinez, AL:Bos.
	.846	22-4	Mike Hampton, NL:Hou.
2000:	.769	20-6	Tim Hudson, AL:Oak.
	.731	19-7	Randy Johnson, NL:Ari. (AL 2)
2001:	.870	20-3	Roger Clemens, AL:NY (2)
	.824	14-3	Roy Oswalt, NL:Hou.
2002:	.833	20-4	Pedro Martinez, AL:Bos. (2)
	.828	24-5	Randy Johnson, NL:Ari. (AL 2; NL 2)
2003:	.800	12-3	Johan Santana, AL:Minn.
	.773	17-5	Jason Schmidt, NL:SF
2004:	.818	18-4	Roger Clemens, NL:Hou. (AL 2)
	.778	21-6	Curt Schilling, AL:Bos.
2005:	.813	13-3	Jorge Sosa, NL:Atl.
	.783	18-5	Cliff Lee, AL:Clev.
2006:	.800	12-3	Francisco Liriano, AL:Minn.
	.733	11-4	Chuck James, NL:Atl.
2007:	.800	16-4	Brad Penny, NL:LA
	.750	18-6	Justin Verlander, AL:Det.
2008:	.880	22-3	Cliff Lee, AL:Clev. (2)
	.783	18-5	Tim Lincecum, NL:SF
2009:	.810	17-4	Chris Carpenter, NL:StL.
	.792	19-5	Felix Hernandez, AL:Sea.
2010:	.765	13-4	Tommy Hunter, AL:Tex.
	.704	19-8	Ubaldo Jimenez, NL:Col.
2011:	.840	21-4	Ian Kennedy, NL:Ari.
	.828	24-5	Justin Verlander, AL:Det. (2)
2012:	.842	16-3	Kyle Lohse, NL:StL.
	.800	20-5	David Price, AL:TB
	.800	20-5	Jared Weaver, AL:LA
2013:	.875	21-3	Max Scherzer, AL:Det.
	.789	15-4	Zack Greinke, NL:LA
2014:	.875	21-3	Clayton Kershaw, NL:LA
	.800	16-4	Matt Shoemaker, AL:LA
2015:	.864	19-3	Zack Greinke, NL:LA (2)
	.824	14-3	Nathan Eovaldi, AL:NY
2016:	.882	15-2	Aaron Sanchez, AL:Tor.
	.792	19-5	Jon Lester, NL:Chi.
2017:	.867	13-2	Brad Peacock, AL:Hou.
	.842	16-3	Alex Wood, NL:LA
2018:	.833	15-3	Charlie Morton, AL:Hou.
	.818	18-4	Miles Mikolas, NL:StL.
2019:	.818	18-4	Domingo German, AL:NY
	.778	14-4	Walker Buehler, NL:LA
2020:	1.000	7-0	Max Fried, NL:Atl.
	.889	8-1	Shane Bieber, AL:Clev.

STRIKEOUTS

1900:	133	Rube Waddell, NL:Pitt.
1901:	239	Noodles Hahn, NL:Cin.
	158	Cy Young, AL:Bos.
1902:	225	Vic Willis, NL:Bos.
	210	Rube Waddell, AL:Phil.
1903:	302	Rube Waddell, AL:Phil. (2)
	267	Christy Mathewson, NL:NY
1904:	349	Rube Waddell, AL:Phil. (3)
	208	Christy Mathewson, NL:NY (2)
1905:	287	Rube Waddell, AL:Phil. (4)
	206	Christy Mathewson, NL:NY (3)
1906:	196	Rube Waddell, AL:Phil. (5)
	171	Fred Beebe, NL:Chi.-StL.
1907:	232	Rube Waddell, AL:Phil. (6)
	179	Christy Mathewson, NL:NY (4)
1908:	269	Ed Walsh, AL:Chi.
	259	Christy Mathewson, NL:NY (5)
1909:	205	Orval Overall, NL:Chi.
	177	Frank Smith, AL:Chi.
1910:	313	Walter Johnson, AL:Wash.
	190	Christy Mathewson, NL:NY (6)
1911:	255	Ed Walsh, AL:Chi. (2)
	238	Rube Marquard, NL:NY
1912:	303	Walter Johnson, AL:Wash. (2)
	195	Grover Alexander, NL:Phil.
1913:	244	Walter Johnson, AL:Wash. (3)
	168	Tom Seaton, NL:Phil.
1914:	225	Walter Johnson, AL:Wash. (4)
	214	Grover Alexander, NL:Phil. (2)
1915:	241	Grover Alexander, NL:Phil. (3)
	203	Walter Johnson, AL:Wash. (5)
1916:	228	Walter Johnson, AL:Wash. (6)
	169	Grover Alexander, NL:Phil. (4)
1917:	200	Grover Alexander, NL:Phil. (5)
	188	Walter Johnson, AL:Wash. (7)
1918:	163	Walter Johnson, AL:Wash. (8)
	148	Hippo Vaughn, NL:Chi.
1919:	147	Walter Johnson, AL:Wash. (9)
	141	Hippo Vaughn, NL:Chi. (2)
1920:	173	Grover Alexander, NL:Chi. (6)
	133	Stan Coveleski, AL:Clev.
1921:	144	Walter Johnson, AL:Wash. (10)
	136	Burleigh Grimes, NL:Brk.
1922:	149	Urban Shocker, AL:StL.
	135	Dazzy Vance, NL:Brk.
1923:	197	Dazzy Vance, NL:Brk. (2)
	132	Walter Johnson, AL:Wash. (11)
1924:	262	Dazzy Vance, NL:Brk. (3)
	159	Walter Johnson, AL:Wash. (12)
1925:	221	Dazzy Vance, NL:Brk. (4)
	116	Lefty Grove, AL:Phil.
1926:	197	Lefty Grove, AL:Phil. (2)
	140	Dazzy Vance, NL:Brk. (5)
1927:	184	Dazzy Vance, NL:Brk. (6)
	174	Lefty Grove, AL:Phil. (3)
1928:	200	Dazzy Vance, NL:Brk. (7)
	183	Lefty Grove, AL:Phil. (4)
1929:	170	Lefty Grove, AL:Phil. (5)
	166	Pat Malone, NL:Chi.
1930:	209	Lefty Grove, AL:Phil. (6)
	177	Bill Hallahan, NL:StL.
1931:	175	Lefty Grove, AL:Phil. (7)
	159	Bill Hallahan, NL:StL. (2)
1932:	191	Dizzy Dean, NL:StL.
	190	Red Ruffing, AL:NY

1933:	199	Dizzy Dean, NL:StL. (2)
	164	Lefty Gomez, AL:NY
1934:	195	Dizzy Dean, NL:StL. (3)
	158	Lefty Gomez, AL:NY (2)
1935:	190	Dizzy Dean, NL:StL. (4)
	163	Tommy Bridges, AL:Det.
1936:	238	Van Mungo, NL:Brk.
	175	Tommy Bridges, AL:Det. (2)
1937:	194	Lefty Gomez, AL:NY (3)
	159	Carl Hubbell, NL:NY
1938:	241	Bob Feller, AL:Clev.
	135	Clay Bryant, NL:Chi.
1939:	246	Bob Feller, AL:Clev. (2)
	139	Claude Passeau, NL:Phil.-Chi.
1940:	261	Bob Feller, AL:Clev. (3)
	137	Kirby Higbe, NL:Phil.
1941:	260	Bob Feller, AL:Clev. (4)
	202	Johnny Vander Meer, NL:Cin.
1942:	186	Johnny Vander Meer, NL:Cin. (2)
	113	Tex Hughson, AL:Bos.
	113	Bobo Newsom, AL:Wash.
1943:	174	Johnny Vander Meer, NL:Cin. (3)
	151	Allie Reynolds, AL:Clev.
1944:	187	Hal Newhouser, AL:Det.
	161	Bill Voiselle, NL:NY
1945:	212	Hal Newhouser, AL:Det. (2)
	148	Preacher Roe, NL:Pitt.
1946:	348	Bob Feller, AL:Clev. (5)
	135	Johnny Schmitz, NL:Chi.
1947:	196	Bob Feller, AL:Clev. (6)
	195	Ewell Blackwell, NL:Cin.
1948:	164	Bob Feller, AL:Clev. (7)
	149	Harry Brecheen, NL:StL.
1949:	153	Virgil Trucks, AL:Det.
	151	Warren Spahn, NL:Bos.
1950:	191	Warren Spahn, NL:Bos. (2)
	170	Bob Lemon, AL:Clev.
1951:	164	Don Newcombe, NL:Brk.
	164	Warren Spahn, NL:Bos. (3)
	164	Vic Raschi, AL:NY
1952:	183	Warren Spahn, NL:Bos. (4)
	160	Allie Reynolds AL:NY (2)
1953:	198	Robin Roberts, NL:Phil.
	186	Billy Pierce, AL:Chi.
1954:	185	Robin Roberts, NL:Phil. (2)
	185	Bob Turley, AL:Balt.
1955:	245	Herb Score, AL:Clev.
	198	Sam Jones, NL:Chi.
1956:	263	Herb Score, AL:Clev. (2)
	176	Sam Jones, NL:Chi. (2)
1957:	188	Jack Sanford, NL:Phil.
	184	Early Wynn, AL:Clev.
1958:	225	Sam Jones, NL:StL. (3)
	179	Early Wynn, AL:Chi. (2)
1959:	242	Don Drysdale, NL:LA
	201	Jim Bunning, AL:Det.
1960:	246	Don Drysdale, NL:LA (2)
	201	Jim Bunning, AL:Det. (2)
1961:	269	Sandy Koufax, NL:LA
	221	Camilo Pascual, AL:Minn.
1962:	232	Don Drysdale, NL:LA (3)
	206	Camilo Pascual, AL:Minn. (2)
1963:	306	Sandy Koufax, NL:LA (2)
	202	Camilo Pascual, AL:Minn. (3)
1964:	250	Bob Veale, NL:Pitt.
	217	Al Downing, AL:NY

STRIKEOUTS (CONTINUED)

1965:	382	Sandy Koufax, NL:LA (3)
	325	Sam McDowell, AL:Clev.
1966:	317	Sandy Koufax, NL:LA (4)
	225	Sam McDowell, AL:Clev. (2)
1967:	253	Jim Bunning, NL:Phil.
	246	Jim Lonborg, AL:Bos.
1968:	283	Sam McDowell, AL:Clev. (3)
	268	Bob Gibson, NL:StL.
1969:	279	Sam McDowell, AL:Clev. (4)
	273	Ferguson Jenkins, NL:Chi.
1970:	304	Sam McDowell, AL:Clev. (5)
	283	Tom Seaver, NL:NY
1971:	308	Mickey Lolich, AL:Det.
	289	Tom Seaver, NL:NY (2)
1972:	329	Nolan Ryan, AL:Cal.
	310	Steve Carlton, NL:Phil.
1973:	383	Nolan Ryan, AL:Cal. (2)
	251	Tom Seaver, NL:NY (3)
1974:	367	Nolan Ryan, AL:Cal. (3)
	240	Steve Carlton, NL:Phil. (2)
1975:	269	Frank Tanana, AL:Cal.
	243	Tom Seaver, NL:NY (4)
1976:	327	Nolan Ryan, AL:Cal. (4)
	235	Tom Seaver, NL:NY (5)
1977:	341	Nolan Ryan, AL:Cal. (5)
	262	Phil Niekro, NL:Atl.
1978:	303	J.R. Richard, NL:Hou.
	260	Nolan Ryan, AL:Cal. (6)
1979:	313	J.R. Richard, NL:Hou. (2)
	223	Nolan Ryan, AL:Cal. (7)
1980:	286	Steve Carlton, NL:Phil. (3)
	187	Len Barker, AL:Clev.
1981:	180	Fernando Valenzuela, NL:LA
	127	Len Barker, AL:Clev. (2)
1982:	286	Steve Carlton, NL:Phil. (4)
	209	Floyd Bannister, AL:Sea.
1983:	275	Steve Carlton, NL:Phil. (5)
	232	Jack Morris, AL:Det.
1984:	276	Dwight Gooden, NL:NY
	204	Mark Langston, AL:Sea.
1985:	268	Dwight Gooden, NL:NY (2)
	206	Bert Blyleven, AL:Clev.-Minn.
1986:	306	Mike Scott, NL:Hou.
	245	Mark Langston, AL:Sea. (2)
1987:	270	Nolan Ryan, NL:Hou. (AL 7)
	262	Mark Langston, AL:Sea. (3)
1988:	291	Roger Clemens, AL:Bos.
	228	Nolan Ryan, NL:Hou. (NL 2; AL 7)
1989:	301	Nolan Ryan, AL:Tex. (AL 8; NL 2)
	201	Jose DeLeon, NL:StL.
1990:	233	David Cone, NL:NY
	232	Nolan Ryan, AL:Tex. (AL 9; NL 2)
1991:	241	Roger Clemens, AL:Bos. (2)
	241	David Cone, NL:NY (2)
1992:	261	David Cone, NL:NY-AL:Tor. (ML 3)
	241	Randy Johnson, AL:Sea.
	215	John Smoltz, NL:Atl.
1993:	308	Randy Johnson, AL:Sea. (2)
	227	Jose Rijo, NL:Cin.
1994:	204	Randy Johnson, AL:Sea. (3)
	189	Andy Benes, NL:SD
1995:	294	Randy Johnson, AL:Sea. (4)
	236	Hideo Nomo, NL:LA
1996:	276	John Smoltz, NL:Atl. (2)
	257	Roger Clemens, AL:Bos. (3)

1997:	319	Curt Schilling, NL:Phil.
	292	Roger Clemens, AL:Tor. (4)
1998:	329	Randy Johnson, AL:Sea.-NL:Hou. (ML 4)
	300	Curt Schilling, NL:Phil. (2)
	271	Roger Clemens, AL:Tor. (5)
1999:	364	Randy Johnson, NL:Ari. (ML 5)
	313	Pedro Martinez, AL:Bos.
2000:	347	Randy Johnson, NL:Ari. (NL 2; ML 6)
	284	Pedro Martinez, AL:Bos. (2)
2001:	372	Randy Johnson, NL:Ari. (NL 3;ML 7)
	220	Hideo Nomo, AL:Bos. (NL 1)
2002:	334	Randy Johnson, NL:Ari. (NL 4; ML 8)
	239	Pedro Martinez, AL:Bos. (3)
2003:	266	Kerry Wood, NL:Chi.
	207	Esteban Loaiza, AL:Chi.
2004:	290	Randy Johnson, NL:Ari. (NL 5;ML 9)
	265	Johan Santana, AL:Minn.
2005:	238	Johan Santana, AL:Minn. (2)
	216	Jake Peavy, NL:SD
2006:	245	Johan Santana, AL:Minn. (3)
	216	Aaron Harang, NL:Cin.
2007:	240	Jake Peavy, NL:SD (2)
	239	Scott Kazmir, AL:TB
2008:	265	Tim Lincecum, NL:SF
	231	A.J. Burnett, AL:Tor.
2009:	269	Justin Verlander, AL:Det.
	261	Tim Lincecum, NL:SF (2)
2010:	233	Jered Weaver, AL:LA
	231	Tim Lincecum, NL:SF (3)
2011:	250	Justin Verlander, AL:Det. (2)
	248	Clayton Kershaw, NL:LA
2012:	239	Justin Verlander, AL:Det. (3)
	230	R.A. Dickey, NL:NY
2013:	277	Yu Darvish, AL:Tex.
	232	Clayton Kershaw, NL:LA (2)
2014:	271	David Price, AL:TB-Det.
	242	Johnny Cueto, NL:Cin.
	242	Stephen Strasburg, NL:Wash.
2015:	301	Clayton Kershaw, NL:LA (3)
	274	Chris Sale, AL:Chi.
2016:	284	Max Scherzer, NL:Wash.
	254	Justin Verlander, AL:Det. (4)
2017:	308	Chris Sale, AL:Bos. (2)
	268	Max Scherzer, NL:Wash. (2)
2018:	300	Max Scherzer, NL:Wash. (3)
	290	Justin Verlander, AL:Hou. (5)
2019:	326	Gerrit Cole, AL:Hou.
	255	Jacob deGrom, NL:NY
2020:	122	Shane Bieber, AL:Clev.
	104	Jacob deGrom, NL:NY (2)

MOST VALUABLE PLAYER
Baseball Writers Association of America *(Unanimous Selections Capitalized)*

AMERICAN LEAGUE	YEAR	NATIONAL LEAGUE
Lefty Grove, Phil. (p)	1931	Frankie Frisch, StL. (2b)
Jimmie Foxx, Phil. (1b)	1932	Chuck Klein, Phil. (of)
Jimmie Foxx, Phil. (1b)	1933	Carl Hubbell, NY (p)
Mickey Cochrane, Det. (c)	1934	Dizzy Dean, StL. (p)
HANK GREENBERG, Det. (1b)	1935	Gabby Hartnett, Chi. (c)
Lou Gehrig, NY (1b)	1936	CARL HUBBELL, NY (p)
Charlie Gehringer, Det. (2b)	1937	Joe Medwick, StL. (of)
Jimmie Foxx, Bos. (1b)	1938	Ernie Lombardi, Cin. (c)
Joe DiMaggio, NY (of)	1939	Bucky Walters, Cin. (p)
Hank Greenberg, Det. (of)	1940	Frank McCormick, Cin. (1b)
Joe DiMaggio, NY (of)	1941	Dolph Camilli, Brk. (1b)
Joe Gordon, NY (2b)	1942	Mort Cooper, StL. (p)
Spud Chandler, NY (p)	1943	Stan Musial, StL. (of)
Hal Newhouser, Det. (p)	1944	Marty Marion, StL. (ss)
Hal Newhouser, Det. (p)	1945	Phil Cavarretta, Chi. (1b)
Ted Williams, Bos. (of)	1946	Stan Musial, StL. (1b)
Joe DiMaggio, NY (of)	1947	Bob Elliott, Bos. (3b)
Lou Boudreau, Clev. (ss)	1948	Stan Musial, StL. (of)
Ted Williams, Bos. (of)	1949	Jackie Robinson, Brk. (2b)
Phil Rizzuto, NY (ss)	1950	Jim Konstanty, Phil. (p)
Yogi Berra, NY (c)	1951	Roy Campanella, Brk. (c)
Bobby Shantz, Phil. (p)	1952	Hank Sauer, Chi. (of)
AL ROSEN, Clev. (3b)	1953	Roy Campanella, Brk. (c)
Yogi Berra, NY (c)	1954	Willie Mays, NY (of)
Yogi Berra, NY (c)	1955	Roy Campanella, Brk. (c)
MICKEY MANTLE, NY (of)	1956	Don Newcombe, Brk. (p)
Mickey Mantle, NY (of)	1957	Hank Aaron, Mil. (of)
Jackie Jensen, Bos. (of)	1958	Ernie Banks, Chi. (ss)
Nellie Fox, Chi. (2b)	1959	Ernie Banks, Chi. (ss)
Roger Maris, NY (of)	1960	Dick Groat, Pitt. (ss)
Roger Maris, NY (of)	1961	Frank Robinson, Cin. (of)
Mickey Mantle, NY (of)	1962	Maury Wills, LA (ss)
Elston Howard, NY (c)	1963	Sandy Koufax, LA (p)
Brooks Robinson, Balt. (3b)	1964	Ken Boyer, StL. (3b)
Zoilo Versalles, Minn. (ss)	1965	Willie Mays, SF (of)
FRANK ROBINSON, Balt. (of)	1966	Roberto Clemente, Pitt. (of)
Carl Yastrzemski, Bos. (of)	1967	ORLANDO CEPEDA, StL. (1b)
DENNY McLAIN, Det. (p)	1968	Bob Gibson, StL. (p)
Harmon Killebrew, Minn. (3b)	1969	Willie McCovey, SF (1b)
Boog Powell, Balt. (1b)	1970	Johnny Bench, Cin. (c)
Vida Blue, Oak. (p)	1971	Joe Torre, StL. (3b)
Dick Allen, Chi. (1b)	1972	Johnny Bench, Cin. (c)
REGGIE JACKSON, Oak. (of)	1973	Pete Rose, Cin. (of)
Jeff Burroughs, Tex. (of)	1974	Steve Garvey, LA (1b)
Fred Lynn, Bos. (of)	1975	Joe Morgan, Cin. (2b)
Thurman Munson, NY (c)	1976	Joe Morgan, Cin. (2b)
Rod Carew, Minn. (1b)	1977	George Foster, Cin. (of)
Jim Rice, Bos. (of)	1978	Dave Parker, Pitt. (of)
Don Baylor, Cal. (of)	1979	Keith Hernandez, StL. (1b) (tied)
		Willie Stargell, Pitt. (1b) (tied)
George Brett, KC (3b)	1980	MIKE SCHMIDT, Phil. (3b)
Rollie Fingers, Mil. (p)	1981	Mike Schmidt, Phil. (3b)
Robin Yount, Mil. (ss)	1982	Dale Murphy, Atl. (of)
Cal Ripken, Balt. (ss)	1983	Dale Murphy, Atl. (of)
Willie Hernandez, Det. (p)	1984	Ryne Sandberg, Chi. (2b)
Don Mattingly, NY (1b)	1985	Willie McGee, StL. (of)
Roger Clemens, Bos. (p)	1986	Mike Schmidt, Phil. (3b)
George Bell, Tor. (of)	1987	Andre Dawson, Chi. (of)
JOSE CANSECO, Oak. (of)	1988	Kirk Gibson, LA (of)
Robin Yount, Mil. (of)	1989	Kevin Mitchell, SF (of)
Rickey Henderson, Oak. (of)	1990	Barry Bonds, Pitt. (of)
Cal Ripken, Balt. (ss)	1991	Terry Pendleton, Atl. (3b)
Dennis Eckersley, Oak. (p)	1992	Barry Bonds, Pitt. (of)
FRANK THOMAS, Chi. (1b)	1993	Barry Bonds, SF (of)
Frank Thomas, Chi. (1b)	1994	JEFF BAGWELL, Hou. (1b)
Mo Vaughn, Bos. (1b)	1995	Barry Larkin, Cin. (ss)
Juan Gonzalez, Tex. (of)	1996	KEN CAMINITI, SD (3b)
KEN GRIFFEY Jr., Sea. (of)	1997	Larry Walker, Col. (of)
Juan Gonzalez, Tex. (of)	1998	Sammy Sosa, Chi. (of)
Ivan Rodriguez, Tex. (c)	1999	Chipper Jones, Atl. (3b)
Jason Giambi, Oak. (1b)	2000	Jeff Kent, SF (2b)
Ichiro Suzuki, Sea. (of)	2001	Barry Bonds, SF (of)
Miguel Tejada, Oak. (ss)	2002	BARRY BONDS, SF (of)
Alex Rodriguez, Tex. (ss)	2003	Barry Bonds, SF (of)
Vladimir Guerrero, Ana. (of)	2004	Barry Bonds, SF (of)
Alex Rodriguez, NY (3b)	2005	Albert Pujols, StL. (1b)
Justin Morneau, Minn. (1b)	2006	Ryan Howard, Phil. (1b)
Alex Rodriguez, NY (3b)	2007	Jimmy Rollins, Phil. (ss)
Dustin Pedroia, Bos. (2b)	2008	Albert Pujols, StL. (1b)
Joe Mauer, Minn. (c)	2009	ALBERT PUJOLS, StL. (1b)
Josh Hamilton, Tex. (of)	2010	Joey Votto, Cin. (1b)
Justin Verlander, Det. (p)	2011	Ryan Braun, Mil. (of)
Miguel Cabrera, Det. (3b)	2012	Buster Posey, SF (c)
Miguel Cabrera, Det. (3b)	2013	Andrew McCutchen, Pitt. (of)
MIKE TROUT, LA (of)	2014	Clayton Kershaw, LA (p)
Josh Donaldson, Tor. (3b)	2015	BRYCE HARPER, Wash. (of)
Mike Trout, LA (of)	2016	Kris Bryant, Chi. (3b)
Jose Altuve, Hou. (2b)	2017	Giancarlo Stanton, Mia. (of)
Mookie Betts, Bos. (of)	2018	Christian Yelich, Mil. (of)
Mike Trout, LA (of)	2019	Cody Bellinger, LA (of)
Jose Abreu, Chi. (1b)	2020	Freddie Freeman, Atl. (1b)

CHALMERS AWARD

AMERICAN LEAGUE	YEAR
TY COBB, Det. (of)	1911
Tris Speaker, Bos. (of)	1912
Walter Johnson, Wash. (p)	1913
Eddie Collins, Phil. (2b)	1914

NATIONAL LEAGUE
Frank Schulte, Chi. (of)
Larry Doyle, NY (2b)
Jake Daubert, Brk. (1b)
Johnny Evers, Bos. (2b)

LEAGUE AWARD

AMERICAN LEAGUE	YEAR
George Sisler, StL. (1b)	1922
BABE RUTH, NY (of)	1923
Walter Johnson, Wash. (p)	1924
Roger Peckinpaugh, Wash. (ss)	1925
George Burns, Clev. (1b)	1926
Lou Gehrig, NY (1b)	1927
Mickey Cochrane, Phil. (c)	1928
No selection	1929

NATIONAL LEAGUE
No selection
No selection
Dazzy Vance, Brk. (p)
Roger Hornsby, StL. (2b)
Bob O'Farrell, StL. (c)
Paul Waner, Pitt. (of)
Jim Bottomley, StL. (1b)
Rogers Hornsby, Chi. (2b)

CY YOUNG AWARD

1956	Don Newcombe, NL:Brk.		1962	Don Drysdale, NL:LA
1957	Warren Spahn, NL:Mil.		1963	SANDY KOUFAX, NL:LA
1958	Bob Turley, AL:NY		1964	Dean Chance, AL:LA
1959	Early Wynn, AL:Chi.		1965	SANDY KOUFAX, NL:LA
1960	Vern Law, NL:Pitt.		1966	SANDY KOUFAX, NL:LA
1961	Whitey Ford, AL:NY			

AMERICAN LEAGUE	YEAR	NATIONAL LEAGUE
Jim Lonborg, Bos.	1967	Mike McCormick, SF
DENNY McLAIN, Det.	1968	BOB GIBSON, StL.
Mike Cuellar, Balt. (tied)	1969	Tom Seaver, NY
Denny McLain, Det.(tied)		
Jim Perry, Minn.	1970	Bob Gibson, StL.
Vida Blue, Oak.	1971	Ferguson Jenkins, Chi.
Gaylord Perry, Clev.	1972	STEVE CARLTON, Phil.
Jim Palmer, Balt.	1973	Tom Seaver, NY
Catfish Hunter, Oak.	1974	Mike Marshall, LA
Jim Palmer, Balt.	1975	Tom Seaver, NY
Jim Palmer, Balt.	1976	Randy Jones, SD
Sparky Lyle, NY	1977	Steve Carlton, Phil.
RON GUIDRY, NY	1978	Gaylord Perry, SD
Mike Flanagan, Balt.	1979	Bruce Sutter, Chi.
Steve Stone, Balt.	1980	Steve Carlton, Phil.
Rollie Fingers, Mil.	1981	Fernando Valenzuela, LA
Pete Vuckovich, Mil.	1982	Steve Carlton, Phil.
LaMarr Hoyt, Chi.	1983	John Denny, Phil.
Willie Hernandez, Det.	1984	RICK SUTCLIFFE, Chi.
Bret Saberhagen, KC	1985	DWIGHT GOODEN, NY
ROGER CLEMENS, Bos.	1986	Mike Scott, Hou.
Roger Clemens, Bos.	1987	Steve Bedrosian, Phil.
Frank Viola, Minn.	1988	OREL HERSHISER, LA
Bret Saberhagen, KC	1989	Mark Davis, SD
Bob Welch, Oak.	1990	Doug Drabek, Pitt.
Roger Clemens, Bos.	1991	Tom Glavine, Atl.
Dennis Eckersley, Oak.	1992	Greg Maddux, Chi.
Jack McDowell, Chi.	1993	Greg Maddux, Atl.
David Cone, KC	1994	GREG MADDUX, Atl.
Randy Johnson, Sea.	1995	GREG MADDUX, Atl.
Pat Hentgen, Tor.	1996	John Smoltz, Atl.
Roger Clemens, Tor.	1997	Pedro Martinez, Mtl.
ROGER CLEMENS, Tor.	1998	Tom Glavine, Atl.
PEDRO MARTINEZ, Bos.	1999	Randy Johnson, Ari.
PEDRO MARTINEZ, Bos.	2000	Randy Johnson, Ari.
Roger Clemens, NY	2001	Randy Johnson, Ari.
Barry Zito, Oak.	2002	RANDY JOHNSON, Ari.
Roy Halladay, Tor.	2003	Eric Gagne, LA
JOHAN SANTANA, Minn.	2004	Roger Clemens, Hou.
Bartolo Colon, LA	2005	Chris Carpenter, StL.
JOHAN SANTANA, Minn.	2006	Brandon Webb, Ari.
CC Sabathia, Clev.	2007	JAKE PEAVY, SD
Cliff Lee, Clev.	2008	Tim Lincecum, SF
Zack Greinke, KC	2009	Tim Lincecum, SF
Felix Hernandez, Sea.	2010	ROY HALLADAY, Phil.
JUSTIN VERLANDER, Det.	2011	Clayton Kershaw, LA
David Price, TB	2012	R.A. Dickey, NY
Max Scherzer, Det.	2013	Clayton Kershaw, LA
Corey Kluber, Clev.	2014	CLAYTON KERSHAW, LA
Dallas Keuchel, Hou.	2015	Jake Arrieta, Chi.
Rick Porcello, Bos.	2016	Max Scherzer, Wash.
Corey Kluber, Clev.	2017	Max Scherzer, Wash.
Blake Snell, TB	2018	Jacob deGrom, NY
Justin Verlander, Hou.	2019	Jacob deGrom, NY
SHANE BIEBER, Clev.	2020	Trevor Bauer, Cin.

ROOKIE OF THE YEAR AWARD
(Unanimous Selections Capitalized)

AMERICAN LEAGUE	YEAR	NATIONAL LEAGUE
One selection	1947	Jackie Robinson, Brk. (1b)
One selection	1948	Alvin Dark, Bos. (ss)
Roy Sievers, StL. (of)	1949	Don Newcombe, Brk. (p)
Walt Dropo, Bos. (1b)	1950	Sam Jethroe, Bos. (of)
Gil McDougald, NY (3b)	1951	Willie Mays, NY (of)
Harry Byrd, Phil. (p)	1952	Joe Black, Brk. (p)
Harvey Kuenn, Det. (ss)	1953	Jim Gilliam, Brk. (2b)
Bob Grim, NY (p)	1954	Wally Moon, StL. (of)
Herb Score, Clev. (p)	1955	Bill Virdon, StL. (of)
Luis Aparicio, Chi. (ss)	1956	FRANK ROBINSON, Cin. (of)
Tony Kubek, NY (of)	1957	Jack Sanford, Phil. (p)
Albie Pearson, Wash. (of)	1958	ORLANDO CEPEDA, SF (1b)
Bob Allison, Wash. (of)	1959	WILLIE McCOVEY, SF (1b)
Ron Hansen, Balt. (ss)	1960	Frank Howard, LA (of)
Don Schwall, Bos. (p)	1961	Billy Williams, Chi. (of)
Tom Tresh, NY (ss)	1962	Ken Hubbs, Chi. (2b)
Gary Peters, Chi. (p)	1963	Pete Rose, Cin. (2b)
Tony Oliva, Minn. (of)	1964	Dick Allen, Phil. (3b)
Curt Blefary, Balt. (of)	1965	Jim Lefebvre, LA (2b)
Tommie Agee, Chi. (of)	1966	Tommy Helms, Cin. (3b)
Rod Carew, Minn. (2b)	1967	Tom Seaver, NY (p)
Stan Bahnsen, NY (p)	1968	Johnny Bench, Cin. (c)
Lou Piniella, KC (of)	1969	Ted Sizemore, LA (2b)
Thurman Munson, NY (c)	1970	Carl Morton, Mtl. (p)
Chris Chambliss, Clev. (1b)	1971	Earl Williams, Atl. (c)
CARLTON FISK, Bos. (c)	1972	Jon Matlack, NY (p)
Al Bumbry, Balt. (of)	1973	Gary Matthews Sr., SF (of)
Mike Hargrove, Tex. (1b)	1974	Bake McBride, StL. (of)
Fred Lynn, Bos. (of)	1975	John Montefusco, SF (p)
Mark Fidrych, Det. (p)	1976	Butch Metzger, SD (p) (tied)
		Pat Zachry, Cin. (p)
Eddie Murray, Balt. (dh)	1977	Andre Dawson, Mtl. (of)
Lou Whitaker, Det. (2b)	1978	Bob Horner, Atl. (3b)
John Castino, Minn. (3b) (tied)	1979	Rick Sutcliffe, LA (p)
Alfredo Griffin, Tor. (ss)		
Joe Charboneau, Clev. (of)	1980	Steve Howe, LA (p)
Dave Righetti, NY (p)	1981	Fernando Valenzuela, LA (p)
Cal Ripken, Balt. (ss)	1982	Steve Sax, LA (2b)
Ron Kittle, Chi. (of)	1983	Darryl Strawberry, NY (of)
Alvin Davis, Sea. (1b)	1984	Dwight Gooden, NY (p)
Ozzie Guillen, Chi. (ss)	1985	VINCE COLEMAN, StL. (of)
Jose Canseco, Oak. (of)	1986	Todd Worrell, StL. (p)
MARK McGWIRE, Oak. (1b)	1987	BENITO SANTIAGO, SD (c)
Walt Weiss, Oak. (ss)	1988	Chris Sabo, Cin. (3b)
Gregg Olson, Balt. (p)	1989	Jerome Walton, Chi. (of)
SANDY ALOMAR Jr., Clev. (c)	1990	David Justice, Atl. (of)
Chuck Knoblauch, Minn. (2b)	1991	Jeff Bagwell, Hou. (1b)
Pat Listach, Mil. (ss)	1992	Eric Karros, LA (1b)
TIM SALMON, Cal. (of)	1993	MIKE PIAZZA, LA (c)
Bob Hamelin, KC (dh)	1994	RAUL MONDESI, LA (of)
Marty Cordova, Minn. (of)	1995	Hideo Nomo, LA (p)
DEREK JETER, NY (ss)	1996	Todd Hollandsworth, LA (of)
NOMAR GARCIAPARRA, Bos. (ss)	1997	SCOTT ROLEN, Phil. (3b)
Ben Grieve, Oak. (of)	1998	Kerry Wood, Chi. (p)
Carlos Beltran, KC (of)	1999	Scott Williamson, Cin. (p)
Kazuhiro Sasaki, Sea. (p)	2000	Rafael Furcal, Atl. (ss)
Ichiro Suzuki, Sea. (of)	2001	ALBERT PUJOLS, StL. (of)
Eric Hinske, Tor. (3b)	2002	Jason Jennings, Col. (p)
Angel Berroa, KC (ss)	2003	Dontrelle Willis, Fla. (p)
Bobby Crosby, Oak. (ss)	2004	Jason Bay, Pitt. (of)
Huston Street, Oak. (p)	2005	Ryan Howard, Phil. (1b)
Justin Verlander, Det. (p)	2006	Hanley Ramirez, Fla. (ss)
Dustin Pedroia, Bos. (2b)	2007	Ryan Braun, Mil. (3b)
EVAN LONGORIA, TB (3b)	2008	Geovany Soto, Chi. (c)
Andrew Bailey, Oak. (p)	2009	Chris Coghlan, Fla. (of)
Neftali Feliz, Tex. (p)	2010	Buster Posey, SF (c)
Jeremy Hellickson, TB (p)	2011	CRAIG KIMBREL, Atl. (p)
MIKE TROUT, LA (of)	2012	Bryce Harper, Wash. (of)
Wil Myers, TB (of)	2013	Jose Fernandez, Mia. (p)
JOSE ABREU, Chi. (1b)	2014	Jacob deGrom, NY (p)
Carlos Correa, Hou. (ss)	2015	KRIS BRYANT, Chi. (3b)
Michael Fulmer, Det. (p)	2016	Corey Seager, LA (ss)
AARON JUDGE, NY (of)	2017	CODY BELLINGER, LA (1b)
Shohei Ohtani, LA (dh-p)	2018	Ronald Acuna, Atl. (of)
YORDAN ALVAREZ, Hou. (dh)	2019	Pete Alonso, NY (1b)
KYLE LEWIS, Sea. (of)	2020	Devin Williams, NL:Mil. (p)

JOE DiMAGGIO, NEW YORK AL — 1941
56-GAME HITTING STREAK

Date		Opp	Club and Pitcher	AB	R	H	2B	3B	HR	RBI
May	15	Chi	Edgar Smith..	4	0	1	0	0	0	1
	16	Chi	Thornton Lee	4	2	2	0	1	1	1
	17	Chi	Johnny Rigney	3	1	1	0	0	0	0
	18	StL	Bob Harris (2)							
			Johnny Niggeling (1)	3	3	3	1	0	0	1
	19	StL	Denny Galehouse	3	0	1	1	0	0	0
	20	StL	Elden Auker	5	1	1	0	0	0	1
	21	Det	Schoolboy Rowe (1)							
			Al Benton (1)	5	0	2	0	0	0	1
	22	Det	Archie McKain	4	0	1	0	0	0	1
	23	Bos	Dick Newsome	5	0	1	0	0	0	2
	24	Bos	Earl Johnson	4	2	1	0	0	0	2
	25	Bos	Lefty Grove	4	0	1	0	0	0	0
	27	Wash	Ken Chase (1)							
			Red Anderson (2)							
			Alex Carrasquel (1)	5	3	4	0	0	1	3
	28n	Wash	Sid Hudson	4	1	1	0	1	0	0
	29	Wash	Steve Sundra	3	1	1	0	0	0	0
	30	Bos	Earl Johnson	2	1	1	0	0	0	0
	30	Bos	Mickey Harris	3	0	1	1	0	0	0
June	1	Clev	Al Milnar	4	1	1	0	0	0	0
	1	Clev	Mel Harder	4	0	1	0	0	0	0
	2	Clev	Bob Feller	4	2	2	1	0	0	0
	3	Det	Dizzy Trout	4	1	1	0	0	1	1
	5	Det	Hal Newhouser	5	1	1	0	1	0	1
	7	StL	Bob Muncrief (1)							
			Johnny Allen (1)							
			George Caster(1)	5	2	3	0	0	0	1
	8	StL	Elden Auker	4	3	2	0	0	2	4
	8	StL	George Caster (1)							
			Jack Kramer (1)	4	1	2	1	0	1	3
	10	Chi	Johnny Rigney	5	1	1	0	0	0	0
	12n	Chi	Thornton Lee	4	1	2	0	0	1	1
	14	Clev	Bob Feller	2	0	1	1	0	0	1
	15	Clev	Jim Bagby	3	1	1	0	0	1	1
	16	Clev	Al Milnar	5	0	1	1	0	0	0
	17	Chi	Johnny Rigney	4	1	1	0	0	0	0
	18	Chi	Thornton Lee	3	0	1	0	0	0	0
	19	Chi	Edgar Smith (1)							
			Buck Ross (2)	3	2	3	0	0	1	2
	20	Det	Bobo Newsom (2)							
			Archie McKain (2)	5	3	4	1	0	0	1
	21	Det	Dizzy Trout	4	0	1	0	0	0	1
	22	Det	Hal Newhouser (1)							
			Bobo Newsom (1)	5	1	2	1	0	1	2
	24	StL	Bob Muncrief	4	1	1	0	0	0	0
	25	StL	Denny Galehouse	4	1	1	0	0	1	3
	26	StL	Elden Auker	4	0	1	1	0	0	1
	27	Phil	Chubby Dean	3	1	2	0	0	1	2
	28	Phil	Johnny Babich (1)							
			Lum Harris(1)	5	1	2	1	0	0	0
	29	Wash	Dutch Leonard	4	1	1	1	0	0	0
	29	Wash	Red Anderson	5	1	1	0	0	0	1
July	1	Bos	Mickey Harris (1)							
			Mike Ryba (1)	4	0	2	0	0	0	1
	1	Bos	Jack Wilson	3	1	1	0	0	0	1
	2	Bos	Dick Newsome	5	1	1	0	0	1	3
	5	Phil	Phil Marchildon	4	2	1	0	0	1	2
	6	Phil	Johnny Babich (1)							
			Bump Hadley (3)	5	2	4	1	0	0	2
	6	Phil	Jack Knott	4	0	2	0	1	0	2
	10n	StL	Johnny Niggeling	2	0	1	0	0	0	0
	11	StL	Bob Harris (3)							
			Jack Kramer (1)	5	1	4	0	0	1	2
	12	StL	Elden Auker (1)							
			Bob Muncrief (1)	5	1	2	1	0	0	1
	13	Chi	Ted Lyons (2)							
			Jack Hallett (1)	4	2	3	0	0	0	0
	13	Chi	Thornton Lee	4	0	1	0	0	0	0
	14	Chi	Johnny Rigney	3	0	1	0	0	0	0
	15	Chi	Edgar Smith	4	1	2	1	0	0	2
	16	Clev	Al Milnar (2)							
			Joe Krakauskas (1)	4	3	3	1	0	0	0
	17n	Clev	Stopped in Cleveland (Al Smith and Jim Bagby)							

				PCT	AB	R	H	2B	3B	HR	RBI
			TOTALS	.408	223	56	91	16	4	15	55

ROGER MARIS, NEW YORK AL – 1961　　　61 HOME RUNS

HR	Team Game	Ind. Game	Date	Inn	Opponent	Pitcher
1	11	11	Apr. 26	5	at Detroit	Paul Foytack
2	17	17	May 3	7	at Minnesota	Pedro Ramos
3	20	20	May 6n	5	at Los Angeles	Eli Grba
4	29	29	May 17	8	Washington	Pete Burnside (L)
5	30	30	May 19n	1	at Cleveland	Jim Perry
6	31	31	May 20	3	at Cleveland	Gary Bell
7	32	32	May 21	1	Baltimore	Chuck Estrada
8	35	35	May 24	4	Boston	Gene Conley
9	38	38	May 28	2	Chicago	Cal McLish
10	40	40	May 30	6	at Boston	Gene Conley
11	40	40	May 30	8	at Boston	Mike Fornieles
12	41	41	May 31n	3	at Boston	Billy Muffett
13	43	43	June 2n	3	at Chicago	Cal McLish
14	44	44	June 3	8	at Chicago	Bob Shaw
15	45	45	June 4	3	at Chicago	Russ Kemmerer
16	48	48	June 6n	6	Minnesota	Ed Palmquist
17	49	49	June 7	3	Minnesota	Pedro Ramos
18	52	52	June 9n	7	Kansas City	Ray Herbert
19	55	55	June 11	3	Los Angeles	Eli Grba
20	55	55	June 11	7	Los Angeles	Johnny James
21	57	57	June 13n	6	at Cleveland	Jim Perry
22	58	58	June 14n	4	at Cleveland	Gary Bell
23	61	61	June 17n	4	at Detroit	Don Mossi (L)
24	62	62	June 18	8	at Detroit	Jerry Casale
25	63	63	June 19n	9	at Kansas City	Jim Archer (L)
26	64	64	June 20n	1	at Kansas City	Joe Nuxhall (L)
27	66	66	June 22n	2	at Kansas City	Norm Bass
28	74	74	July 1	9	Washington	Dave Sisler
29	75	75	July 2	3	Washington	Pete Burnside (L)
30	75	75	July 2	7	Washington	Johnny Klippstein
31	77	77	July 4	8	Detroit	Frank Lary
32	78	78	July 5	7	Cleveland	Frank Funk
33	82	82	July 9	7	Boston	Bill Monbouquette
34	84	84	July 13n	1	at Chicago	Early Wynn
35	86	86	July 15	3	at Chicago	Ray Herbert
36	92	92	July 21n	1	at Boston	Bill Monbouquette
37	95	95	July 25n	4	Chicago	Frank Baumann (L)
38	95	95	July 25n	8	Chicago	Don Larsen
39	96	96	July 25n	4	Chicago	Russ Kemmerer
40	96	96	July 25n	6	Chicago	Warren Hacker
41	106	105	Aug. 4n	1	Minnesota	Camilo Pascual
42	114	113	Aug. 11n	5	at Washington	Pete Burnside (L)
43	115	114	Aug. 12	4	at Washington	Dick Donovan
44	116	115	Aug. 13	4	at Washington	Bennie Daniels
45	117	116	Aug. 13	1	at Washington	Marty Kutyna
46	118	117	Aug. 15n	4	Chicago	Juan Pizarro (L)
47	119	118	Aug. 16	1	Chicago	Billy Pierce (L)
48	119	118	Aug. 16	3	Chicago	Billy Pierce (L)
49	123	122	Aug. 20	3	at Cleveland	Jim Perry
50	125	124	Aug. 22n	6	at Los Angeles	Ken McBride
51	129	128	Aug. 26	6	at Kansas City	Jerry Walker
52	135	134	Sept. 2	6	Detroit	Frank Lary
53	135	134	Sept. 2	8	Detroit	Hank Aguirre (L)
54	140	139	Sept. 6	4	Washington	Tom Cheney
55	141	140	Sept. 7n	3	Cleveland	Dick Stigman (L)
56	143	142	Sept. 9	7	Cleveland	Mudcat Grant
57	151	150	Sept. 16	3	at Detroit	Frank Lary
58	152	151	Sept. 17	12	at Detroit	Terry Fox
59	155	154	Sept. 20n	3	at Baltimore	Milt Pappas
60	159	158	Sept. 26n	3	Baltimore	Jack Fisher
61	163	161	Oct. 1	4	Boston	Tracy Stallard

Home–30　Road–31　　Off RHP–49　Off LHP–12　　Day-36　Night-25

BARRY BONDS, SAN FRANCISCO NL – 2001   73 HOME RUNS

HR	Team Game	Ind. Game	Date	Inn	Opponent	Pitcher
1	1	1	Apr. 2	5	San Diego	Woody Williams
2	9	8	Apr. 12	4	at San Diego	Adam Eaton
3	10	9	Apr. 13n	1	at Milwaukee	Jamey Wright
4	11	10	Apr. 14n	5	at Milwaukee	Jimmy Haynes
5	12	11	Apr. 15	8	at Milwaukee	David Weathers
6	13	12	Apr. 17n	8	Los Angeles	Terry Adams
7	14	13	Apr. 18n	7	Los Angeles	Chan Ho Park
8	16	15	Apr. 20n	4	Milwaukee	Jimmy Haynes
9	19	18	Apr. 24n	3	Cincinnati	Jim Brower
10	21	20	Apr. 26	8	Cincinnati	Scott Sullivan
11	24	22	Apr. 29	4	Chicago (NL)	Manny Aybar
12	26	24	May 2n	5	at Pittsburgh	Todd Ritchie
13	27	25	May 3n	1	at Pittsburgh	Jimmy Anderson (L)
14	28	26	May 4n	6	at Philadelphia	Bruce Chen (L)
15	35	32	May 11n	4	New York (NL)	Steve Trachsel
16	40	37	May 17n	3	at Florida	Chuck Smith
17	41	38	May 18n	8	at Atlanta	Mike Remlinger (L)
18	42	39	May 19n	3	at Atlanta	Odalis Perez (L)
19	42	39	May 19n	7	at Atlanta	Jose Cabrera
20	42	39	May 19n	8	at Atlanta	Jason Marquis
21	43	40	May 20	1	at Atlanta	John Burkett
22	43	40	May 20	7	at Atlanta	Mike Remlinger (L)
23	44	41	May 21n	4	at Arizona	Curt Schilling
24	45	42	May 22n	9	at Arizona	Russ Springer
25	47	44	May 24n	3	Colorado	John Thomson
26	50	46	May 27	1	Colorado	Denny Neagle (L)
27	53	49	May 30n	2	Arizona	Robert Ellis
28	53	49	May 30n	6	Arizona	Robert Ellis
29	54	50	June 1n	3	at Colorado	Shawn Chacon
30	57	53	June 4n	4	San Diego	Bobby J. Jones
31	58	54	June 5n	3	San Diego	Wascar Serrano
32	60	55	June 7	7	San Diego	Brian Lawrence
33	64	59	June 12n	1	Anaheim	Pat Rapp
34	66	61	June 14	6	Anaheim	Lou Pote
35	67	62	June 15n	1	Oakland	Mark Mulder (L)
36	67	62	June 15n	6	Oakland	Mark Mulder (L)
37	70	65	June 19n	5	at San Diego	Adam Eaton
38	71	66	June 20n	8	at San Diego	Rodney Myers
39	74	68	June 23n	1	at St. Louis	Darryl Kile
40	89	82	July 12n	1	at Seattle	Paul Abbott
41	95	88	July 18n	4	Colorado	Mike Hampton (L)
42	95	88	July 18n	5	Colorado	Mike Hampton (L)
43	103	96	July 26n	4	at Arizona	Curt Schilling
44	103	96	July 26n	5	at Arizona	Curt Schilling
45	104	97	July 27n	4	at Arizona	Brian Anderson (L)
46	108	101	Aug. 1n	1	Pittsburgh	Joe Beimel (L)
47	111	103	Aug. 4	6	Philadelphia	Nelson Figueroa
48	113	105	Aug. 7n	11	at Cincinnati	Danny Graves
49	115	107	Aug. 9n	3	at Cincinnati	Scott Winchester
50	117	108	Aug. 11	2	at Chicago (NL)	Joe Borowski
51	119	110	Aug. 14n	6	Florida	Ricky Bones
52	121	112	Aug. 16	4	Florida	A.J. Burnett
53	121	112	Aug. 16	8	Florida	Vic Darensbourg (L)
54	123	114	Aug. 18	8	Atlanta	Jason Marquis
55	127	118	Aug. 23n	9	at Montreal	Graeme Lloyd (L)
56	131	122	Aug. 27	5	at New York (NL)	Kevin Appier
57	135	126	Aug. 31n	8	Colorado	John Thomson
58	138	129	Sept. 3	4	Colorado	Jason Jennings
59	139	130	Sept. 4n	7	Arizona	Miguel Batista
60	141	132	Sept. 6	2	Arizona	Albie Lopez
61	144	135	Sept. 9	1	at Colorado	Scott Elarton
62	144	135	Sept. 9	5	at Colorado	Scott Elarton
63	144	135	Sept. 9	11	at Colorado	Todd Belitz (L)
64	147	138	Sept. 20	5	Houston	Wade Miller
65	150	141	Sept. 23	2	at San Diego	Jason Middlebrook
66	150	141	Sept. 23	4	at San Diego	Jason Middlebrook
67	151	142	Sept. 24n	7	at Los Angeles	James Baldwin
68	154	145	Sept. 28n	2	San Diego	Jason Middlebrook
69	155	146	Sept. 29	6	San Diego	Chuck McElroy (L)
70	159	150	Oct. 4n	9	at Houston	Wilfredo Rodriguez (L)
71	160	151	Oct. 5n	1	Los Angeles	Chan Ho Park
72	160	151	Oct. 5n	3	Los Angeles	Chan Ho Park
73	162	153	Oct. 7	1	Los Angeles	Dennis Springer

Home–37   Road–36   Off RHP–56   Off LHP–17   Day-26   Night-47

HALL OF FAME
EXECUTIVES, MANAGERS, UMPIRES, NEGRO LEAGUES

Walter Alston (1983)	Manager
Sparky Anderson (2000)	Manager
Al Barlick (1989)	Umpire
Ed Barrow (1953)	Manager-Executive
Cool Papa Bell (1974)	Negro League Player
Ray Brown (2006)	Negro League Player
Willard Brown (2006)	Negro League Player
Morgan Bulkeley (1937)	Executive
Alexander Cartwright (1938)	Executive
Henry Chadwick (1938)	Writer-Statistician
Happy Chandler (1982)	Commissioner
Oscar Charleston (1976)	Negro League Player
Nestor Chylak (1999)	Umpire
Charles Comiskey (1939)	Player-Executive
Jocko Conlan (1974)	Umpire
Tom Connolly (1953)	Umpire
Andy Cooper (2006)	Negro League Player
Bobby Cox (2014)	Manager
Candy Cummings (1939)	Pioneer Pitcher
Ray Dandridge (1987)	Negro League Player
Leon Day (1995)	Negro League Player
Martin Dihigo (1977)	Negro League Player
Barney Dreyfuss (2008)	Executive
Leo Durocher (1994)	Player-Manager
Billy Evans (1973)	Umpire-Executive
Bill Foster (1996)	Negro League Player
Rube Foster (1981)	Negro League Player
Ford Frick (1970)	Commissioner-Executive
Josh Gibson (1972)	Negro League Player
Warren Giles (1979)	Executive
Pat Gillick (2011)	Executive
Frank Grant (2006)	Pre-Negro League Player
Clark Griffith (1946)	Player-Manager-Executive
Ned Hanlon (1996)	Manager
Will Harridge (1972)	Executive
Bucky Harris (1975)	Player-Manager
Doug Harvey (2010)	Umpire
Whitey Herzog (2010)	Manager
Pete Hill (2006)	Pre-Negro League Player
Cal Hubbard (1976)	Umpire
Miller Huggins (1964)	Manager
William Hulbert (1995)	Executive
Monte Irvin (1973)	Negro League Player
Ban Johnson (1937)	Executive
Judy Johnson (1975)	Negro League Player
Bill Klem (1953)	Umpire
Bowie Kuhn (2008)	Commissioner
Kenesaw M. Landis (1944)	Commissioner
Tony LaRussa (2014)	Manager
Tommy Lasorda (1997)	Manager
Buck Leonard (1972)	Negro League Player
Pop Lloyd (1977)	Negro League Player
Al Lopez (1977)	Player-Manager
Connie Mack (1937)	Manager-Executive
Biz Mackey (2006)	Negro League Player
Larry MacPhail (1978)	Executive
Lee MacPhail (1998)	Executive
Effa Manley (2006)	Negro League Executive
Joe McCarthy (1957)	Manager
Bill McGowan (1992)	Umpire
John McGraw (1937)	Player-Manager
Bill McKechnie (1962)	Manager
Jose Mendez (2006)	Pre-Negro League Player
Marvin Miller (2020)	Players' Association Executive
Hank O'Day (2013)	Umpire
Walter O'Malley (2008)	Executive
Satchel Paige (1971)	Negro League Player
Alex Pompez (2006)	Negro League Executive
Cum Posey (2006)	Negro League Executive
Branch Rickey (1967)	Manager-Executive
Wilbert Robinson (1945)	Player-Manager
Joe Rogan (1998)	Negro League Player
Jacob Ruppert (2013)	Executive
Louis Santop (2006)	Pre-Negro League Player

HALL OF FAME
EXECUTIVES, MANAGERS, UMPIRES, NEGRO LEAGUES (continued)

John Schuerholz (2017)	Executive
Frank Selee (1999)	Manager
Bud Selig (2017)	Commissioner
Hilton Smith (2001)	Negro League Player
Billy Southworth (2008)	Manager
Al Spalding (1939)	Player-Executive
Turkey Stearns (2000)	Negro League Player
Casey Stengel (1966)	Player-Manager
Mule Suttles (2006)	Negro League Player
Ben Taylor (2006)	Pre-Negro League Player
Joe Torre (2014)	Manager
Cristobal Torriente (2006)	Negro League Player
Bill Veeck (1991)	Executive
Earl Weaver (1996)	Manager
George Weiss (1971)	Executive
Willie Wells (1997)	Negro League Player
Sol White (2006)	Pre-Negro League Executive
J.L. Wilkinson (2006)	Negro League Executive
Jud Wilson (2006)	Negro League Player
Dick Williams (2008)	Manager
Smokey Joe Williams (1999)	Negro League Player
George Wright (1937)	Player-Manager
Harry Wright (1953)	Manager
Tom Yawkey (1980)	Executive

HALL OF FAME PITCHERS
* *Special Committee Selection*
(Capitalized pitchers were elected in their first year of eligibility.)

	Inducted	Years	Years and Teams
Grover Alexander	1938	1911-1930	NL:Phil. 1911-17, 30; Chi. 18-26; StL. 26-29
*Chief Bender	1953	1903-1925	AL:Phil. 1903-14, 16-17; Chi. 25; FL:Balt. 15
Bert Blyleven	2011	1970-1992	AL:Minn. 1970-76, 85-88; Tex. 76-77; Clev. 81-85; Cal. 89-90, 92; NL:Pitt. 78-80
*Mordecai Brown	1949	1903-1916	NL:StL. 1903; Chi. 04-12, 16; Cin. 1913; FL:StL. 14; Brk. 14; Chi. 15
*Jim Bunning	1996	1955-1971	AL:Det. 1955-63; NL:Phil. 64-67, 70-71; Pitt. 68-69; LA 69
STEVE CARLTON	1994	1965-1988	NL:StL. 1965-71; Phil. 72-86; SF 86; AL:Chi. 86; Clev. 87; Minn. 87-88
*Jack Chesbro	1946	1899-1909	NL:Pitt. 1899-1902; AL:NY 03-09; Bos. 09
*John Clarkson	1963	1882-1894	NL:Wor. 1882; Chi. 84-87; Bos. 88-92; Clev. 92-94
*Stan Coveleski	1969	1912-1928	AL:Phil. 1912; Clev. 16-24; Wash. 25-27; NY 28
Dizzy Dean	1953	1930-1947	NL:StL. 1930, 32-37; Chi. 38-41; AL:StL. 47
Don Drysdale	1984	1956-1969	NL:Brk./LA 1956-69
DENNIS ECKERSLEY	2004	1975-1998	AL:Clev. 1975-77; Bos. 78-84, 98; Oak. 87-95; NL:Chi. 84-86; StL. 96-97
*Red Faber	1964	1914-1933	AL:Chi. 1914-33
BOB FELLER	1962	1936-1956	AL:Clev. 1936-41, 45-56
Rollie Fingers	1992	1968-1985	AL:Oak. 1968-76; Mil. 81-82, 84-85; NL:SD 77-80
Whitey Ford	1974	1950-1967	AL:NY 1950, 53-67
*Pud Galvin	1965	1879-1892	NL:Buff. 1879-85; Pitt. 87-89, 91-92; StL. 1892; AA:Pitt. 85-86; PL:Pitt. 90
TOM GLAVINE	2014	1987-2008	NL:Atl. 1987-2002, 08; NY 03-07
BOB GIBSON	1981	1959-1975	NL:StL. 1959-75
*Lefty Gomez	1972	1930-1943	AL:NY 1930-42; Wash. 43
Rich Gossage	2008	1972-1994	AL:Chi. 1972-76; NY 78-83, 89; Tex. 91; Oak. 92-93; Sea. 94; NL:Pitt. 97; SD 84-87; Chi. 88; SF 89
*Burleigh Grimes	1964	1916-1934	NL:Pitt. 1916-17, 28-29, 34; Brk. 18-26; NY 27; Bos. 30; StL. 30-31, 33-34; Chi. 32-33; AL:NY 34
Lefty Grove	1947	1925-1941	AL:Phil. 1925-33; Bos. 34-41
*Jesse Haines	1970	1918-1937	NL:Cin. 1918; StL. 20-37
ROY HALLADAY	2019	1998-2013	AL:Tor. 1998-2009; NL:Phil. 10-13
Trevor Hoffman	2018	1993-2010	NL:Fla. 1993; SD 93-2008; Mil. 09-10
*Waite Hoyt	1969	1918-1938	NL:NY 1918, 32; Brk. 32, 37-38; Pitt. 33-37; AL:Bos. 19-20; NY 21-30; Det. 30-31; Phil. 31
Carl Hubbell	1947	1928-1943	NL:NY 1928-43
Catfish Hunter	1987	1965-1979	AL:KC/Oak. 1965-74; NY 75-79
Ferguson Jenkins	1991	1965-1983	NL:Phil. 1965-66; Chi. 66-73, 82-83; AL:Tex. 74-75, 78-81; Bos. 76-77
RANDY JOHNSON	2015	1988-2009	NL:Mtl. 1988-89; Hou. 98; Ari. 99-2004, 07-08; SF 09; AL:Sea. 1989-98; NY 2005-06
WALTER JOHNSON	1936	1907-1927	AL:Wash. 1907-27
*Addie Joss	1978	1902-1910	AL:Clev. 1902-10
*Tim Keefe	1964	1880-1893	NL:Troy 1880-82; NY 85-89, 91; Phil. 1891-93; AA:NY 83-84; PL:NY 90
SANDY KOUFAX	1972	1955-1966	NL:Brk./LA 1955-66
Bob Lemon	1976	1941-1958	AL:Clev. 1941-42, 46-58
Ted Lyons	1955	1923-1946	AL:Chi. 1923-42, 46
GREG MADDUX	2014	1986-2008	NL:Chi. 1986-92, 2004-06; Atl. 1993-2003; LA 06, 08; SD 07-08
Juan Marichal	1983	1960-1975	NL:SF 1960-73; LA 75; AL:Bos. 74
*Rube Marquard	1971	1908-1925	NL:NY 1908-15; Brk. 15-20; Cin. 21; Bos. 22-25

HALL OF FAME PITCHERS (continued)

Special Committee Selection
(Capitalized pitchers were elected in their first year of eligibility.)

	Inducted	Years	Years and Teams
PEDRO MARTINEZ	2015	1992-2009	NL:LA 1992-93; Mtl. 94-97; NY 2005-08; Phil. 09; AL:Bos. 1998-2004
CHRISTY MATHEWSON	1936	1900-1916	NL:NY 1900-16; Cin. 16
*Joe McGinnity	1946	1899-1908	NL:Balt. 1899; Brk. 1900; NY 02-08; AL:Balt. 01-02
*Jack Morris	2018	1977-1994	AL:Det. 1977-90; Minn. 1991; Tor. 92-93; Clev. 94
Mike Mussina	2019	1991-2008	AL:Balt. 1991-2000; NY 01-08
*Hal Newhouser	1992	1939-1955	AL:Det. 1939-53; Clev. 54-55
*Kid Nichols	1949	1890-1906	NL:Bos. 1890-1901; StL. 04-05; Phil. 05-06
Phil Niekro	1997	1964-1987	NL:Mil./Atl. 1964-83, 87; AL:NY 84-85; Clev. 86-87; Tor. 87
JIM PALMER	1990	1965-1984	AL:Balt. 1965-67, 69-84
Herb Pennock	1948	1912-1934	AL:Phil. 1912-15; Bos. 15-17, 19-22, 34; NY 23-33
Gaylord Perry	1991	1962-1983	NL:SF 1962-71; SD 78-79; Atl. 81; AL:Clev. 72-75; Tex. 75-77, 80; NY 80; Sea. 82-83; KC 83
*Eddie Plank	1946	1901-1917	AL:Phil. 1901-14; StL. 16-17; FL:StL. 15
*Hoss Radbourn	1939	1880-1891	NL:Buff. 1880; Prov. 81-85; Bos. 86-89; Cin. 91; PL:Bos. 90
MARIANO RIVERA	2019	1995-2013	AL:NY 1995-2013
*Eppa Rixey	1963	1912-1933	NL:Phil. 1912-17, 19-20; Cin. 21-33
Robin Roberts	1976	1948-1966	NL:Phil. 1948-61; Hou. 65-66; Chi. 66; AL:Balt. 62-65
Red Ruffing	1967	1924-1947	AL:Bos. 1924-30; NY 30-42, 45-46; Chi. 47
*Amos Rusie	1977	1889-1901	NL:Ind. 1889; NY 1890-95, 97-98; Cin. 1901
NOLAN RYAN	1999	1966-1993	NL:NY 1966, 68-71; Hou. 80-88; AL:Cal. 72-79; Tex. 89-93
TOM SEAVER	1992	1967-1986	NL:NY 1967-77, 83; Cin. 77-82; AL:Chi. 84-86; Bos. 86
*Lee Smith	2019	1980-1997	NL:Chi. 1980-87; StL. 90-93; Cin. 96; Mtl. 97; AL:Bos. 88-90; NY 93; Balt. 94; Cal. 95-96
JOHN SMOLTZ	2015	1988-2009	NL:Atl. 1988-99, 2001-08, StL. 09; AL:Bos. 09
WARREN SPAHN	1973	1942-1965	NL:Bos./Mil. 1942; 46-64; NY 65; SF 65
Bruce Sutter	2006	1976-1988	NL:Chi. 1976-80; StL. 81-84; Atl. 85-86, 88
Don Sutton	1998	1966-1988	NL:LA 1966-80, 88; Hou. 81-82; AL:Mil. 82-84; Oak. 85; Cal. 85-87
Dazzy Vance	1955	1915-1935	NL:Pitt. 1915; Brk. 22-32, 35; StL. 33-34; Cin. 34; AL:NY 15, 18
*Rube Waddell	1946	1897-1910	NL:Lou. 1897, 99; Pitt. 1900-01; Chi. 01; AL:Phil. 02-07; StL. 08-10
*Ed Walsh	1946	1904-1917	AL:Chi. 1904-16; NL:Bos. 17
*Mickey Welch	1973	1880-1892	NL:Troy 1880-82; NY 83-92
Hoyt Wilhelm	1985	1952-1972	NL:NY 1952-56; StL. 57; Atl. 69-71; Chi. 70; LA 71-72; AL:Clev. 57-58; Balt. 58-62; Chi. 63-68; Cal. 69
*Vic Willis	1995	1898-1910	NL:Bos. 1898-1905; Pitt. 06-09; StL. 10
Early Wynn	1972	1939-1963	AL:Wash. 1939, 41-44, 46-48; Clev. 49-57, 63; Chi. 58-62
Cy Young	1937	1890-1911	NL:Clev. 1890-98; StL. 99-1900; Bos. 11; AL:Bos. 01-08; Clev. 09-11

HALL OF FAME BATTERS

Special Committee Selection
(Capitalized batters were elected in their first year of eligibility.)

	Inducted	Years	Years and Team(s)
HANK AARON	1982	1954-1976	NL:Mil./Atl. 1954-74; AL:Mil. 75-76
Roberto Alomar	2011	1988-2004	NL:SD 1988-90; NY 2002-03; Ari. 04; AL:Tor. 1991-95; Balt. 96-98; Clev. 99-2001; Chi. 03,04
*Cap Anson	1939	1876-1897	NL:Chi. 1876-97
Luis Aparicio	1984	1956-1973	AL:Chi. 1956-62, 68-70; Balt. 63-67; Bos. 71-73
Luke Appling	1964	1930-1950	AL:Chi. 1930-43, 45-50
*Richie Ashburn	1995	1948-1962	NL:Phil. 1948-59; Chi. 60-61; NY 62
*Earl Averill	1975	1929-1941	AL:Clev. 1929-39; Det. 39-40; NL:Bos. 41
Jeff Bagwell	2017	1991-2005	NL:Hou. 1991-2005
*Harold Baines	2019	1980-2001	AL:Chi. 1980-89, 96-97, 2000-01; Tex, 1989-90; Oak. 90-92; Balt. 93-95, 97-99, 2000; Clev. 1999
*Frank Baker	1955	1908-1922	AL:Phil. 1908-14; NY 16-19, 21-22
*Dave Bancroft	1971	1915-1930	NL:Phil. 1915-20; NY 20-23, 30; Bos. 24-27; Brk. 28-29
ERNIE BANKS	1977	1953-1971	NL:Chi. 1953-71
*Jake Beckley	1971	1888-1907	NL:Pitt. 1888-89, 91-96; NY 96-97; Cin. 97-1903; StL. 04-07; PL:Pitt. 1890
JOHNNY BENCH	1989	1967-1983	NL:Cin. 1967-83
Yogi Berra	1972	1946-1965	AL:NY 1946-63; NL:NY 65
Craig Biggio	2015	1988-2007	NL:Hou. 1988-2007
WADE BOGGS	2005	1982-1999	AL:Bos. 1982-92; NY 93-97; TB 98-99
*Jim Bottomley	1974	1922-1937	NL:StL. 1922-32; Cin. 33-35; AL:StL. 36-37
Lou Boudreau	1970	1938-1952	AL:Clev. 1938-50; Bos. 51-52
*Roger Bresnahan	1945	1897-1915	NL:Wash. 1897; Chi. 1900, 13-15; NY 02-08; StL. 09-12; AL:Balt. 01-02
GEORGE BRETT	1999	1973-1993	AL:KC 1973-93
LOU BROCK	1985	1961-1979	NL:Chi. 1961-64; StL. 64-79
*Dan Brouthers	1945	1879-1904	NL:Troy 1879-80; Buff. 81-85; Det. 86-88; Bos. 89; Brk. 92-93; Balt. 94-95; Lou. 95; Phil. 96; NY 1904; PL:Bos. 1890; AA:Bos. 91
*Jesse Burkett	1946	1890-1905	NL:NY 1890; Clev. 91-98; StL. 99-1901; AL:StL. 02-04; Bos. 05
Roy Campanella	1969	1948-1957	NL:Brk. 1948-57
ROD CAREW	1991	1967-1985	AL:Minn. 1967-78; Cal. 79-85
*Max Carey	1961	1910-1929	NL:Pitt. 1910-26; Brk. 26-29
Gary Carter	2003	1974-1992	NL:Mtl. 1974-84, 92; NY 85-89; SF 90; LA 91
*Orlando Cepeda	1999	1958-1974	NL:SF 1958-66; StL. 66-68; Atl. 69-72; AL:Oak. 72; Bos. 73; KC 74
*Frank Chance	1946	1898-1914	NL:Chi. 1898-1912; AL:NY 13-14
*Fred Clarke	1945	1894-1915	NL:Lou. 1894-99; Pitt. 1900-11, 13-15

HALL OF FAME BATTERS (continued)
*Special Committee Selection
(Capitalized batters were elected in their first year of eligibility.)

	Inducted	Years	Years and Team(s)
ROBERTO CLEMENTE	1973	1955-1972	NL:Pitt. 1955-72
TY COBB	1936	1905-1928 ·	AL:Det. 1905-26; Phil. 27-28
Mickey Cochrane	1947	1925-1937	AL:Phil. 1925-33; Det. 34-37
Eddie Collins	1939	1906-1930	AL:Phil. 1906-14, 27-30; Chi. 15-26
*Jimmy Collins	1945	1895-1908	NL:Lou. 1895; Bos. 95-1900; AL:Bos. 01-07; Phil. 07-08
*Earle Combs	1970	1924-1935	AL:NY 1924-35
*Roger Connor	1976	1880-1897	NL:Troy 1880-82; NY 83-89, 91, 93-94; Phil. 92; StL. 94-97; PL:NY 90
*Sam Crawford	1957	1899-1917	NL:Cin. 1899-1902; AL:Det. 03-17
Joe Cronin	1956	1926-1945	NL:Pitt. 1926-27; AL:Wash. 28-34; Bos. 35-45
*Kiki Cuyler	1968	1921-1938	NL:Pitt. 1921-27; Chi. 28-35; Cin. 35-37; Brk. 38
*George Davis	1998	1890-1909	NL:Clev. 1890-92; NY 93-1901, 03; AL:Chi. 02, 04-09
Andre Dawson	2010	1976-1996	NL:Mtl. 1976-86; Chi. 87-92; Fla. 95-96; AL:Bos. 93-94
*Ed Delahanty	1945	1888-1903	NL:Phil. 1888-89, 91-1901; PL:Clev. 1890; AL:Wash. 1902-03
Bill Dickey	1954	1928-1946	AL:NY 1928-43, 46
Joe DiMaggio	1955	1936-1951	AL:NY 1936-42, 46-51
*Larry Doby	1998	1947-1959	AL:Clev. 1947-55, 58; Chi. 56-57, 59; Det. 59
*Bobby Doerr	1986	1937-1951	AL:Bos. 1937-44, 46-51
*Hugh Duffy	1945	1888-1906	NL:Chi. 1888-89; Bos. 92-1900; Phil. 04-06; PL:Chi. 1890; AA:Bos. 91; AL:Mil. 1901
*Johnny Evers	1946	1902-1929	NL:Chi. 1902-13; Bos. 14-17, 29; Phil. 17; AL:Chi. 22
*Buck Ewing	1939	1880-1897	NL:Troy 1880-82; NY 83-89, 91-92; Clev. 95-97; PL:NY 90
*Rick Ferrell	1984	1929-1947	AL:StL. 1929-33, 41-43; Bos. 33-37; Wash. 37-41, 44-45, 47
Carlton Fisk	2000	1969-1993	AL:Bos. 1969, 71-80; Chi. 81-93
*Elmer Flick	1963	1898-1910	NL:Phil. 1898-1902; AL:Clev. 02-10
*Nellie Fox	1997	1947-1965	AL:Phil. 1947-49; Chi. 50-63; NL:Hou. 64-65
Jimmie Foxx	1951	1925-1945	AL:Phil. 1925-35; Bos. 36-42; NL:Chi. 42, 44; Phil. 45
Frankie Frisch	1947	1919-1937	NL:NY 1919-26; StL. 27-37
LOU GEHRIG	1939	1923-1939	AL:NY 1923-39
Charlie Gehringer	1949	1924-1942	AL:Det. 1924-42
*Joe Gordon	2009	1938-1950	AL:NY 1938-43, 46; Clev. 47-50
*Goose Goslin	1968	1921-1938	AL:Wash. 1921-30, 33, 38; StL. 30-32; Det. 34-37
Hank Greenberg	1956	1930-1947	AL:Det. 1930, 33-41, 45-46; NL:Pitt. 47
KEN GRIFFEY JR.	2016	1989-2010	AL:Sea. 1989-99, 2009-10; Chi. 08; NL:Cin. 2000-08
Vladimir Guerrero	2018	1996-2011	NL:Mtl. 1996-2003; AL:LA 05-09; Tex. 10; Balt. 11
TONY GWYNN	2007	1982-2001	NL:SD 1982-2001
*Chick Hafey	1971	1924-1937	NL:StL. 1924-31; Cin. 32-35, 37
*Billy Hamilton	1961	1888-1901	AA:KC 1888-89; NL:Phil. 90-95; Bos. 96-1901
Gabby Hartnett	1955	1922-1941	NL:Chi. 1922-40; NY 41
Harry Heilmann	1952	1914-1932	AL:Det. 1914, 16-29; NL:Cin. 30, 32
RICKEY HENDERSON	2009	1979-2003	AL:Oak. 1979-84, 89-93, 94-95, 98; NY 85-89; Tor. 93; Ana. 97; Sea. 2000; Bos. 02; NL:SD 1996-97, 01; NY 99-2000; LA 03
*Billy Herman	1975	1931-1947	NL:Chi. 1931-41; Brk. 41-43, 46; Bos. 46; Pitt. 47
*Harry Hooper	1971	1909-1925	AL:Bos. 1909-20; Chi. 21-25
Rogers Hornsby	1942	1915-1937	NL:StL. 1915-26, 33; NY 27; Bos. 28; Chi. 29-32; AL:StL. 33-37
REGGIE JACKSON	1993	1967-1987	AL:KC/Oak. 1967-75, 87; Balt. 76; NY 77-81; Cal. 82-86
*Travis Jackson	1982	1922-1936	NL:NY 1922-36
*Hughie Jennings	1945	1891-1918	AA:Lou. 1891; NL:Lou. 92-93; Balt. 93-99; Brk. 99-1900, 03; Phil. 01-02; AL:Det. 07, 09, 12, 18
DEREK JETER	2020	1995-2014	AL:NY 1995-2014
CHIPPER JONES	2018	1993-2012	NL: Atl. 1993, 95-2012
AL KALINE	1980	1953-1974	AL:Det. 1953-74
Willie Keeler	1939	1892-1910	NL:NY 1892-93, 1910; Brk. 1893, 99-1902; Balt. 1894-98; AL:NY 1903-09
*George Kell	1983	1943-1957	AL:Phil. 1943-46; Det. 46-52; Bos. 52-54; Chi. 54-56; Balt. 56-57
*Joe Kelley	1971	1891-1908	NL:Bos. 1891, 1908; Pitt. 1891-92; Balt. 92-98; Brk. 99-1901; Cin. 02-06; AL:Balt. 02
*George Kelly	1973	1915-1932	NL:NY 1915-17, 19-26; Pitt. 17; Cin. 27-30; Chi. 30; Brk. 32
*King Kelly	1945	1878-1893	NL:Cin. 1878-79; Chi. 80-86; Bos. 87-89, 91-92; NY 93; PL:Bos. 90; AA:Cin./Mil. 91; Bos. 91
Harmon Killebrew	1984	1954-1975	AL:Wash./Minn. 1954-74; KC 75
Ralph Kiner	1975	1946-1955	NL:Pitt. 1946-53; Chi. 53-54; AL:Clev. 55
*Chuck Klein	1980	1928-1944	NL:Phil. 1928-33, 36-44; Chi. 34-36; Pitt. 39
Nap Lajoie	1937	1896-1916	NL:Phil. 1896-1900; AL:Phil. 01-02, 15-16; Clev. 02-14
Barry Larkin	2012	1986-2004	NL:Cin. 1986-2004
*Tony Lazzeri	1991	1926-1939	AL:NY 1926-37; NL:Chi. 38; Brk. 39; NY 39
*Freddie Lindstrom	1976	1924-1936	NL:NY 1924-32; Pitt. 33-34; Chi. 35; Brk. 36
*Ernie Lombardi	1986	1931-1947	NL:Brk. 1931; Cin. 32-41; Bos. 42; NY 43-47
MICKEY MANTLE	1974	1951-1968	AL:NY 1951-68
*Heinie Manush	1964	1923-1939	AL:Det. 1923-27; StL. 28-30; Wash. 30-35; Bos. 36; NL:Brk. 37-38; Pitt. 38-39
Rabbit Maranville	1954	1912-1935	NL:Bos. 1912-20, 29-33, 35; Pitt. 21-24; Chi. 25; Brk. 26; StL. 27-28
Edgar Martinez	2019	1987-2004	AL:Sea. 1987-2004
Eddie Mathews	1978	1952-1968	NL:Bos./Mil./Atl. 1952-66; Hou. 67; AL:Det. 67-68
WILLIE MAYS	1979	1951-1973	NL:NY/SF 1951-52, 54-72; NY 72-73
*Bill Mazeroski	2001	1956-1972	NL:Pitt. 1956-72
*Tommy McCarthy	1946	1884-1896	UA:Bos. 1884; NL:Bos. 85; 92-95; Phil. 86-87; Brk. 96; AA:StL. 88-91
WILLIE McCOVEY	1986	1959-1980	NL:SF 1959-73, 77-80; SD 74-76; AL:Oak. 76

HALL OF FAME BATTERS (continued)

*Special Committee Selection
(Capitalized batters were elected in their first year of eligibility.)

	Inducted	Years	Years and Team(s)
*Bid McPhee	2000	1882-1899	AA:Cin. 1882-89; NL:Cin. 90-99
Joe Medwick	1968	1932-1948	NL:StL. 1932-40, 47-48; Brk. 40-43, 46; NY 43-45; Bos. 45
*Johnny Mize	1981	1936-1953	NL:StL. 1936-41; NY 42, 46-49; AL:NY 49-53
PAUL MOLITOR	2004	1978-1998	AL:Mil. 1978-92; Tor. 93-95; Minn. 96-98
JOE MORGAN	1990	1963-1984	NL:Hou. 1963-71, 80; Cin. 72-79; SF 81-82; Phil. 83; AL:Oak. 84
EDDIE MURRAY	2003	1977-1997	AL:Balt. 1977-88, 96; Clev. 94-96; Ana. 97; NL:LA 89-91, 97; NY 92-93
STAN MUSIAL	1969	1941-1963	NL:StL. 1941-44, 46-63
*Jim O'Rourke	1945	1876-1904	NL:Bos. 1876-78, 80; Prov. 79; Buff. 81-84; NY 85-89, 91-92, 1904; Wash. 1893; PL:NY 90
Mel Ott	1951	1926-1947	NL:NY 1926-47
Tony Perez	2000	1964-1986	NL:Cin. 1964-76, 84-86; Mtl. 77-79; Phil. 83; AL:Bos. 80-82
Mike Piazza	2016	1992-2007	NL:LA 1992-98; Fla. 98; NY 98-2005; SD 06; AL:Oak. 2007
KIRBY PUCKETT	2001	1984-1995	AL:Minn. 1984-95
Tim Raines	2017	1979-2002	NL:Mtl. 1979-90, 2001; Fla. 02; AL:Chi. 1991-95; NY 96-98; Balt. 2001
*Pee Wee Reese	1984	1940-1958	NL:Brk./LA 1940-42, 46-58
Jim Rice	2009	1974-1989	AL:Bos. 1974-89
*Sam Rice	1963	1915-1934	AL:Wash. 1915-33; Clev. 34
CAL RIPKEN	2007	1981-2001	AL:Balt. 1981-2001
*Phil Rizzuto	1994	1941-1956	AL:NY 1941-42, 46-56
BROOKS ROBINSON	1983	1955-1977	AL:Balt. 1955-77
FRANK ROBINSON	1982	1956-1976	NL:Cin. 1956-65; LA 72; AL:Balt. 66-71; Cal. 73-74; Clev. 74-76
JACKIE ROBINSON	1962	1947-1956	NL:Brk. 1947-56
IVAN RODRIGUEZ	2017	1991-2011	AL:Tex. 1991-2002, 09; Det. 04-08; NY 08; NL: Fla. 03; Hou. 09; Wash. 10-11
*Edd Roush	1962	1913-1931	AL:Chi. 1913; FL:Ind. 14; Nwk. 15; NL:NY 16, 27-29; Cin. 16-26, 31
BABE RUTH	1936	1914-1935	AL:Bos. 1914-19; NY 20-34; NL:Bos. 35
Ryne Sandberg	2005	1981-1997	NL:Phil. 1981; Chi. 82-94, 96-97
Ron Santo	2012	1960-1974	NL:Chi. 1960-73; AL:Chi. 74
*Ray Schalk	1955	1912-1929	AL:Chi. 1912-28; NL:NY 29
MIKE SCHMIDT	1995	1972-1989	NL:Phil. 1972-89
*Red Schoendienst	1989	1945-1963	NL:StL. 1945-56, 61-63; NY 56-57; Mil. 57-60
*Joe Sewell	1977	1920-1933	AL:Clev. 1920-30; NY 31-33
Al Simmons	1953	1924-1944	AL:Phil. 1924-32, 40-41, 44; Chi. 33-35; Det. 36; Wash. 37-38; Bos. 43; NL:Bos. 39; Cin. 39
*Ted Simmons	2020	1968-1988	NL:StL. 1968-80; Atl. 86-88; AL:Mil. 81-85
George Sisler	1939	1915-1930	AL:StL. 1915-22, 24-27; Wash. 28; NL:Bos. 28-30
*Enos Slaughter	1985	1938-1959	NL:StL. 1938-42, 46-53; Mil. 59; AL:NY 54-59; KC 55-56
OZZIE SMITH	2002	1978-1996	NL:SD 1978-81; StL. 82-96
Duke Snider	1980	1947-1964	NL:Brk./LA 1947-62; NY 63; SF 64
Tris Speaker	1937	1907-1928	AL:Bos. 1907-15; Clev. 16-26; Wash. 27; Phil. 28
WILLIE STARGELL	1988	1962-1982	NL:Pitt. 1962-82
Bill Terry	1954	1923-1936	NL:NY 1923-36
FRANK THOMAS	2014	1990-2008	AL:Chi. 1990-2005; Oak. 06, 08; Tor. 07-08
JIM THOME	2018	1991-2012	AL:Clev. 1991-2002, 11; Chi. 06-09; Minn. 10-11; Balt. 12; NL:Phil. 03-05, 12; LA 09
*Sam Thompson	1974	1885-1906	NL:Det. 1885-88; Phil. 89-98; AL:Det. 1906
*Joe Tinker	1946	1902-1916	NL:Chi. 1902-12, 16; Cin. 13; FL:Chi. 14-15
*Alan Trammell	2018	1977-1996	AL:Det. 1977-96
Pie Traynor	1948	1920-1937	NL:Pitt. 1920-35, 37
*Arky Vaughan	1985	1932-1948	NL:Pitt. 1932-41; Brk. 42-44, 47-48
HONUS WAGNER	1936	1897-1917	NL:Lou. 1897-99; Pitt. 1900-17
Larry Walker	2020	1989-2005	NL: Mtl. 1989-94; Col. 95-2004; StL. 04-05
*Bobby Wallace	1953	1894-1918	NL:Clev. 1894-98; StL. 99-1901, 17-18; AL:StL. 02-16
*Lloyd Waner	1967	1927-1945	NL:Pitt. 1927-41, 44-45; Bos. 41; Cin. 41; Phil. 42; Brk. 44
Paul Waner	1952	1926-1945	NL:Pitt. 1926-40; Brk. 41, 43-44; Bos. 41-42; AL:NY 44-45
*Monte Ward	1964	1878-1894	NL:Prov. 1878-82; NY 83-89, 93-94; Brk. 91-92; PL:Brk. 90
*Zack Wheat	1959	1909-1927	NL:Brk. 1909-26; AL:Phil. 27
*Deacon White	2013	1876-1890	NL:Chi. 1876; Bos. 77; Cin. 78-80; Buff. 81-85; Det. 86-88; Pitt. 89; PL:Buff. 90
Billy Williams	1987	1959-1976	NL:Chi. 1959-74; AL:Oak. 75-76
TED WILLIAMS	1966	1939-1960	AL:Bos. 1939-42, 46-60
*Hack Wilson	1979	1923-1934	NL:NY 1923-25; Chi. 26-31; Brk. 32-34; Phil. 34
DAVE WINFIELD	2001	1973-1995	NL:SD 1973-80; AL:NY 81-88, 90; Cal. 90-91; Tor. 92; Minn. 93-94; Clev. 95
CARL YASTRZEMSKI	1989	1961-1983	AL:Bos. 1961-83
*Ross Youngs	1972	1917-1926	NL:NY 1917-26
ROBIN YOUNT	1999	1974-1993	AL:Mil. 1974-93

BATTERS – 1,000 OR MORE GAMES · ACTIVE IN 2020

(OBA = On-Base Average)

XBH = Extra-Base Hits

PLAYER	YR	BA	SLG	OBA	G	AB	R	H	TB	XBH	1B	2B	3B	HR	RBI	BB	HBP	SO	SB	CS	GDP
Alonso, Yonder	10	.259	.404	.332	1072	3362	391	872	1357	283	589	181	2	100	426	366	16	648	22	8	94
Altuve, Jose	10	.311	.458	.361	1291	5177	766	1610	2373	469	1141	308	28	133	556	377	50	662	256	77	149
Andrus, Elvis	12	.274	.372	.330	1652	6366	893	1743	2370	427	1316	303	48	76	636	516	44	962	305	105	161
Arenado, Nolan	8	.293	.541	.349	1079	4118	649	1206	2227	524	682	262	27	235	760	362	22	684	16	15	121
Avila, Alex	12	.235	.394	.348	1018	2971	347	697	1171	258	439	146	8	104	388	509	17	1031	8	8	79
Belt, Brandon	10	.263	.453	.356	1135	3811	538	1003	1727	415	588	244	33	138	502	532	33	1021	43	19	41
Blackmon, Charlie	10	.304	.505	.360	1119	4313	744	1311	2180	465	846	239	48	178	553	317	74	801	131	55	45
Brantley, Michael	12	.297	.440	.354	1245	4800	655	1425	2112	438	987	303	21	114	640	419	31	573	123	32	116
Braun, Ryan	14	.296	.532	.358	1766	6622	1080	1963	3525	809	1154	408	49	352	1154	586	77	1363	216	60	179
Bruce, Jay	13	.245	.469	.314	1640	5930	836	1451	2780	661	790	311	32	318	948	595	28	1559	65	40	99
Cabrera, Asdrubal	14	.268	.426	.330	1713	6324	852	1693	2693	596	1097	380	28	188	827	554	65	1250	90	32	169
Cabrera, Miguel	18	.313	.540	.391	2457	9153	1457	2866	4942	1085	1781	581	17	487	1729	1159	64	1812	39	21	321
Cain, Lorenzo	11	.288	.413	.348	1050	3912	569	1128	1617	309	819	207	24	78	409	328	45	770	175	40	100
Calhoun, Kole	9	.248	.429	.323	1020	3737	565	927	1605	349	578	176	17	156	491	395	36	912	30	14	66
Cano, Robinson	16	.303	.492	.352	2234	8673	1257	2624	4263	938	1686	571	33	334	1302	616	85	1189	51	38	284
Carpenter, Matt	10	.266	.457	.371	1199	4196	734	1118	1918	469	649	290	27	152	555	664	59	995	25	17	35
Castro, Starlin	11	.280	.415	.319	1487	5836	674	1634	2421	475	1159	299	40	136	642	312	38	1047	89	51	171
Choo, Shin-Soo	16	.275	.447	.377	1652	6087	961	1671	2722	586	1085	339	29	218	782	868	152	1579	157	55	101
Crawford, Brandon	10	.250	.392	.317	1305	4402	509	1099	1727	378	721	234	38	106	564	413	41	984	32	30	96
Cruz, Nelson	16	.278	.529	.347	1742	6397	952	1777	3384	760	1017	330	13	417	1152	632	73	1625	76	32	147
Davis, Chris	13	.233	.459	.315	1418	4978	707	1160	2283	528	632	228	5	295	780	555	58	1852	19	11	62
Descalso, Daniel	10	.235	.362	.320	1080	2519	326	593	913	199	394	126	25	48	294	303	21	600	26	15	33
Desmond, Ian*	11	.263	.427	.315	1478	5442	724	1432	2326	495	937	277	37	181	711	387	43	1402	181	56	132
Donaldson, Josh	10	.272	.508	.369	1050	3922	666	1066	1993	465	601	228	12	225	656	575	46	909	38	8	94
Dozier, Brian	9	.244	.441	.325	1144	4316	664	1055	1904	444	611	231	21	192	561	488	47	973	105	36	89
Encarnacion, Edwin	16	.260	.496	.350	1960	7040	1099	1832	3494	804	1028	370	10	424	1261	903	105	1426	61	14	185
Fowler, Dexter	13	.259	.418	.358	1453	5020	814	1301	2099	462	839	253	82	127	516	739	51	1320	148	68	58
Frazier, Todd	10	.242	.448	.319	1231	4357	601	1056	1951	444	612	211	15	218	636	435	75	1079	73	38	94
Freeman, Freddie	11	.295	.509	.383	1406	5167	849	1524	2632	605	919	342	23	240	858	691	68	1205	45	21	115
Gardner, Brett	13	.259	.401	.343	1548	5350	896	1384	2144	433	951	235	69	129	539	639	64	1145	270	64	55
Goldschmidt, Paul	10	.293	.522	.392	1311	4763	837	1395	2487	574	821	305	20	249	828	770	35	1268	128	33	114
Gordon, Alex	14	.257	.410	.338	1753	6391	867	1643	2622	573	1070	357	26	190	749	684	121	1535	113	45	110
Harper, Bryce	9	.276	.513	.387	1142	4069	749	1122	2088	481	641	228	21	232	668	733	31	1055	98	36	81
Heyward, Jason	11	.261	.414	.345	1427	5067	731	1325	2096	435	890	249	36	150	601	606	49	1001	112	39	86

BATTERS – 1,000 OR MORE GAMES – ACTIVE IN 2020

(OBA = On-Base Average)

XBH = Extra-Base Hits

PLAYER	YR	BA	OBA	SLG	G	AB	R	H	TB	XBH	1B	2B	3B	HR	RBI	BB	HBP	SO	SB	CS	GDP
Hosmer, Eric	10	.278	.336	.435	1403	5366	714	1492	2332	468	1024	272	20	176	770	471	17	1047	71	26	137
Iannetta, Chris	14	.230	.345	.406	1197	3563	449	820	1446	333	487	181	11	141	502	576	69	1024	11	10	83
Jay, Jon	11	.283	.348	.373	1196	3824	530	1082	1428	247	835	185	25	37	340	285	110	714	55	33	90
Joyce, Matt	13	.244	.343	.428	1357	3663	531	893	1569	367	526	205	15	147	496	547	31	919	35	23	74
Kemp, Matt	15	.284	.337	.484	1750	6365	950	1808	3081	662	1146	338	37	287	1031	518	26	1641	184	63	184
Kendrick, Howie	15	.294	.337	.430	1622	5950	792	1747	2558	519	1228	354	38	127	724	349	61	1102	126	47	193
Kipnis, Jason	10	.260	.333	.416	1165	4404	607	1147	1833	410	737	260	24	126	545	467	39	951	136	33	76
LeMahieu, DJ	10	.305	.357	.430	1150	4242	651	1294	1825	326	968	206	35	85	478	342	19	688	83	41	130
Longoria, Evan	13	.266	.334	.473	1742	6576	916	1752	3108	722	1030	392	26	304	1043	645	69	1472	57	18	183
Lowrie, Jed*	12	.261	.335	.413	1118	3991	521	1043	1648	380	663	259	17	104	509	439	22	748	7	3	81
Lucroy, Jonathan	11	.274	.335	.416	1203	4121	481	1128	1716	348	780	216	24	108	545	366	34	658	30	9	136
Machado, Manny	9	.280	.337	.488	1142	4531	647	1268	2211	482	786	244	15	223	645	387	21	834	64	30	141
Markakis, Nick	15	.288	.357	.423	2154	8302	1119	2388	3513	725	1663	514	22	189	1046	891	51	1230	66	32	214
Marte, Starling	9	.287	.341	.450	1014	3875	591	1111	1745	363	748	206	43	114	447	208	120	853	249	79	74
Martinez, J.D.	10	.290	.354	.530	1122	4183	622	1213	2215	509	704	254	17	238	738	411	24	1129	25	11	129
Maybin, Cameron	14	.256	.324	.376	1153	3796	554	972	1429	279	693	173	34	72	354	365	24	909	186	55	87
McCutchen, Andrew	12	.285	.376	.478	1617	6038	974	1719	2887	634	1085	343	48	243	853	845	73	1286	191	77	98
Molina, Yadier	17	.281	.333	.404	2025	7115	713	2001	2876	548	1453	381	7	160	932	513	69	803	66	37	261
Moreland, Mitch	11	.252	.320	.448	1179	3842	499	968	1720	392	576	208	8	176	588	367	33	917	11	5	92
Moustakas, Mike	10	.251	.310	.442	1175	4273	501	1073	1890	431	642	235	6	190	588	334	49	752	19	10	101
Murphy, Daniel	12	.296	.341	.455	1452	5308	710	1572	2415	538	1034	371	29	138	735	364	25	709	68	25	124
Pedroia, Dustin	14	.299	.365	.439	1512	6031	922	1805	2649	549	1256	394	15	140	725	624	38	654	138	46	154
Pence, Hunter	14	.279	.334	.461	1707	6420	891	1791	2957	623	1168	324	55	244	942	520	26	1335	120	55	151
Posey, Buster*	11	.302	.370	.456	1258	4575	595	1380	2088	419	961	270	9	140	673	484	42	634	23	9	148
Pujols, Albert	20	.299	.377	.546	2862	10839	1843	3236	5923	1347	1889	669	16	662	2100	1331	108	1304	114	41	399
Reddick, Josh	12	.263	.322	.428	1251	4257	582	1118	1824	385	733	208	33	144	554	387	7	760	61	18	71
Rizzo, Anthony	10	.271	.372	.485	1265	4617	689	1249	2240	515	734	268	18	229	753	609	155	858	60	34	104
Rodriguez, Sean	13	.226	.301	.379	1103	2572	344	580	975	219	361	124	14	81	298	225	62	775	42	19	57
Sandoval, Pablo	13	.279	.331	.445	1311	4536	537	1266	2017	432	834	262	21	149	628	346	29	732	12	13	147
Santana, Carlos	11	.248	.366	.446	1495	5333	799	1325	2378	557	768	301	16	240	796	991	29	1056	46	18	138
Seager, Kyle	10	.256	.326	.443	1321	4958	632	1267	2194	500	767	280	13	207	706	474	59	959	52	26	100
Segura, Jean	9	.285	.327	.407	1099	4327	591	1232	1761	321	911	196	42	83	401	237	47	641	183	62	99
Simmons, Andrelton	9	.269	.317	.379	1060	3954	456	1064	1499	278	786	188	23	67	406	265	23	386	67	24	144
Smoak, Justin	11	.229	.322	.419	1286	4153	505	951	1739	394	557	196	2	196	570	552	25	1122	3	3	110

BATTERS – 1,000 OR MORE GAMES - ACTIVE IN 2020

(OBA = On-Base Average)

XBH = Extra-Base Hits

PLAYER	YR	BA	SLG	OBA	G	AB	R	H	TB	XBH	1B	2B	3B	HR	RBI	BB	HBP	SO	SB	CS	GDP
Stanton, Giancarlo	11	.268	.546	.359	1185	4329	698	1160	2364	569	591	246	11	312	796	584	46	1402	42	15	95
Gordon, Dee	10	.286	.360	.319	1002	3847	532	1100	1386	196	904	124	54	18	234	168	32	610	333	100	45
Suzuki, Kurt	14	.259	.392	.316	1513	5205	567	1347	2041	422	925	283	6	133	699	360	106	678	20	11	138
Trout, Mike	10	.304	.582	.418	1252	4539	944	1380	2642	610	770	260	48	302	798	838	84	1174	201	37	58
Turner, Justin	12	.292	.469	.369	1114	3521	504	1029	1653	367	662	234	9	124	495	351	93	583	35	10	92
Upton, Justin	14	.265	.474	.345	1739	6355	1009	1681	3015	682	999	337	38	307	959	740	74	1841	147	58	130
Votto, Joey	14	.304	.517	.419	1771	6274	1041	1908	3245	727	1181	412	20	295	966	1217	60	1354	79	29	151
Walker, Neil	12	.267	.426	.338	1306	4583	611	1224	1953	409	815	238	22	149	609	460	55	931	32	22	97
Wieters, Matt	12	.249	.409	.313	1167	3994	440	996	1634	341	655	190	5	146	550	368	21	847	9	4	102
Zimmerman, Ryan	15	.279	.475	.343	1689	6399	936	1784	3039	693	1091	401	22	270	1015	630	31	1307	43	16	203

PITCHERS – 100 OR MORE WINS – ACTIVE IN 2020

PLAYER	YR	ERA	W	L	PCT	G	GS	GF	SV	SHO	INN	H	AB	BFP	R	ER	HR	BB	HBP	SO	WP	BK
Bumgarner, Madison	12	3.20	120	96	.556	298	295	1	0	6	1887.2	1669	7085	7697	734	672	205	441	68	1824	25	7
Cole, Gerrit	8	3.19	101	55	.647	204	204	0	0	2	1268.0	1087	4700	5131	488	450	129	332	44	1430	47	5
Cueto, Johnny	13	3.41	128	90	.587	308	308	0	0	8	1919.2	1741	7194	7964	787	728	202	556	107	1612	34	16
Gonzalez, Gio	13	3.70	131	101	.565	344	328	4	0	2	1933.0	1744	7269	8242	857	795	171	815	50	1860	59	4
Greinke, Zack	17	3.37	208	126	.623	500	459	8	1	5	2939.0	2728	11124	12002	1181	1100	298	676	70	2689	89	6
Hamels, Cole	15	3.43	163	122	.572	423	422	0	0	7	2698.0	2424	10013	11115	1103	1027	310	767	100	2560	57	14
Happ, J.A.	14	3.98	123	92	.572	324	298	10	0	3	1741.1	1645	6628	7377	819	770	231	620	38	1539	43	5
Hernandez, Felix	15	3.42	169	136	.554	419	418	0	0	11	2729.2	2487	10264	11284	1157	1037	264	805	105	2524	156	7
Kershaw, Clayton	13	2.43	175	76	.697	357	354	1	0	15	2333.0	1756	8439	9179	690	631	181	585	34	2526	88	20
Leake, Mike	10	4.05	105	98	.517	301	296	2	0	2	1829.0	1940	7114	7693	905	824	238	403	68	1231	33	3
Lester, Jon	15	3.60	193	111	.635	424	423	0	0	4	2598.2	2451	9818	10860	1131	1040	269	837	87	2397	63	1
Lynn, Lance	9	3.57	104	71	.594	260	236	4	1	1	1426.2	1312	5384	6048	608	566	134	529	64	1415	46	0
Porcello, Rick	12	4.40	150	125	.545	355	351	2	0	3	2096.1	2270	8268	8912	1122	1025	260	489	84	1561	70	9
Price, David	12	3.31	150	80	.652	321	311	1	0	3	2029.2	1813	7654	8314	819	746	207	527	59	1981	39	5
Sale, Chris	10	3.03	109	73	.599	312	232	25	12	3	1629.2	1312	6024	6544	590	548	172	374	98	2007	38	1
Sanchez, Anibal	15	4.05	112	113	.498	350	327	9	0	7	1948.1	1905	7497	8315	953	877	225	653	56	1726	60	19
Scherzer, Max	13	3.21	175	93	.653	377	368	2	0	5	2357.1	1953	8741	9573	906	841	264	641	86	2784	71	7
Strasburg, Stephen	11	3.21	112	59	.655	242	242	0	0	2	1448.0	1200	5368	5864	568	517	144	379	51	1699	43	4
Verlander, Justin	16	3.33	226	129	.637	454	454	0	0	9	2988.0	2538	11155	12214	1192	1105	310	851	98	3013	87	19
Wainwright, Adam	15	3.38	167	98	.630	393	326	13	3	10	2169.1	2066	8200	9001	876	815	176	591	64	1830	41	3

CHAMPIONSHIP SERIES
Page

DIVISION SERIES
Page

WILD CARD GAMES / SERIES
Page

ALL-STAR GAME
Page